T0181696

Communications in Computer and Information Science 1516

More information about this series at https://link.springer.com/bookseries/7899

Teddy Mantoro · Minho Lee ·
Media Anugerah Ayu · Kok Wai Wong ·
Achmad Nizar Hidayanto (Eds.)

Neural
Information Processing

28th International Conference, ICONIP 2021
Sanur, Bali, Indonesia, December 8–12, 2021
Proceedings, Part V

 Springer

Editors
Teddy Mantoro ⓘ
Sampoerna University
Jakarta, Indonesia

Media Anugerah Ayu ⓘ
Sampoerna University
Jakarta, Indonesia

Achmad Nizar Hidayanto ⓘ
Universitas Indonesia
Depok, Indonesia

Minho Lee ⓘ
Kyungpook National University
Daegu, Korea (Republic of)

Kok Wai Wong ⓘ
Murdoch University
Murdoch, WA, Australia

ISSN 1865-0929   ISSN 1865-0937 (electronic)
Communications in Computer and Information Science
ISBN 978-3-030-92306-8   ISBN 978-3-030-92307-5 (eBook)
https://doi.org/10.1007/978-3-030-92307-5

This Springer imprint is published by the registered company Springer Nature Switzerland AG
The registered company address is: Gewerbestrasse 11, 6330 Cham, Switzerland

Preface

Welcome to the proceedings of the 28th International Conference on Neural Information Processing (ICONIP 2021) of the Asia-Pacific Neural Network Society (APNNS), held virtually from Indonesia during December 8–12, 2021.

The mission of the Asia-Pacific Neural Network Society is to promote active interactions among researchers, scientists, and industry professionals who are working in neural networks and related fields in the Asia-Pacific region. APNNS has Governing Board Members from 13 countries/regions – Australia, China, Hong Kong, India, Japan, Malaysia, New Zealand, Singapore, South Korea, Qatar, Taiwan, Thailand, and Turkey. The society's flagship annual conference is the International Conference of Neural Information Processing (ICONIP).

The ICONIP conference aims to provide a leading international forum for researchers, scientists, and industry professionals who are working in neuroscience, neural networks, deep learning, and related fields to share their new ideas, progress, and achievements. Due to the current COVID-19 pandemic, ICONIP 2021, which was planned to be held in Bali, Indonesia, was organized as a fully virtual conference.

The conference had four main themes, i.e., "Theory and Algorithms," "Cognitive Neurosciences," "Human Centred Computing," and "Applications." The proceedings consist of two CCIS volumes, which are organized in topical sections according to the four main themes mentioned previously, along with the topics covered in three special sessions. Another topic is from a workshop on Artificial Intelligence and Cyber Security which was held together with ICONIP 2021. Thus, in total, eight different topics were accommodated at the conference. The topics were also the names of the 15-minute presentation sessions at ICONIP 2021. The eight topics in the conference were: Theory and Algorithms; Cognitive Neurosciences; Human Centred Computing; Applications; Artificial Intelligence and Cybersecurity; Advances in Deep and Shallow Machine Learning Algorithms for Biomedical Data and Imaging; Reliable, Robust, and Secure Machine Learning Algorithms; and Theory and Applications of Natural Computing Paradigms.

Our great appreciation goes to the Program Committee members and the reviewers who devoted their time and effort to our rigorous peer-review process. Their insightful reviews and timely feedback ensured the high quality of the papers accepted for publication. Enormous thanks are addressed to the Organizing Committee who has done every effort to make this conference a successful one. Finally, thank you to all the authors of papers, presenters, and participants at the conference. Your support and engagement made it all worthwhile.

December 2021

Teddy Mantoro
Minho Lee
Media A. Ayu
Kok Wai Wong
Achmad Nizar Hidayanto

Proceedings Chairs

Adi Wibowo   Universitas Diponegoro, Indonesia
Sung Bae Cho   Yonsei University, South Korea

Publicity Chairs

Dwiza Riana   Universitas Nusa Mandiri, Indonesia
M. Tanveer   Indian Institute of Technology, Indore, India

Program Committee

Abdulrazak Alhababi   Universiti Malaysia Sarawak, Malaysia
Abhijit Adhikary   Australian National University, Australia
Achmad Nizar Hidayanto   University of Indonesia, Indonesia
Adamu Abubakar Ibrahim   International Islamic University Malaysia, Malaysia
Adi Wibowo   Diponegoro University, Indonesia
Adnan Mahmood   Macquarie University, Australia
Afiyati Amaluddin   Mercu Buana University, Indonesia
Ahmed Alharbi   RMIT University, Australia
Akeem Olowolayemo   International Islamic University Malaysia, Malaysia
Akira Hirose   University of Tokyo, Japan
Aleksandra Nowak   Jagiellonian University, Poland
Ali Haidar   University of New South Wales, Australia
Ali Mehrabi   Western Sydney University, Australia
Al-Jadir   Murdoch University, Australia
Ana Flavia Reis   Federal Technological University of Paraná, Brazil
Anaissi Ali   University of Sydney, Australia
Andrew Beng Jin Teoh   Yonsei University, South Korea
Andrew Chiou   Central Queensland University, Australia
Aneesh Chivukula   University of Technology Sydney, Australia
Aneesh Krishna   Curtin University, Australia
Anna Zhu   Wuhan University of Technology, China
Anto Satriyo Nugroho   Agency for Assessment and Application of
                                 Technology, Indonesia
Anupiya Nugaliyadde   Sri Lanka Institute of Information Technology,
                                 Sri Lanka
Anwesha Law   Indian Statistical Institute, India
Aprinaldi Mantau   Kyushu Institute of Technology, Japan
Ari Wibisono   Universitas Indonesia, Indonesia
Arief Ramadhan   Bina Nusantara University, Indonesia
Arit Thammano   King Mongkut's Institute of Technology Ladkrabang,
                                 Thailand
Arpit Garg   University of Adelaide, Australia
Aryal Sunil   Deakin University, Australia
Ashkan Farhangi   University of Central Florida, USA

Organization

Honorary Chairs

Jonathan Chan   King Mongkut's University of Technology Thonburi, Thailand
Lance Fung   Murdoch University, Australia

General Chairs

Teddy Mantoro   Sampoerna University, Indonesia
Minho Lee   Kyungpook National University, South Korea

Program Chairs

Media A. Ayu   Sampoerna University, Indonesia
Kok Wai Wong   Murdoch University, Australia
Achmad Nizar   Universitas Indonesia, Indonesia

Local Arrangements Chairs

Linawati   Universitas Udayana, Indonesia
W. G. Ariastina   Universitas Udayana, Indonesia

Finance Chairs

Kurnianingsih   Politeknik Negeri Semarang, Indonesia
Kazushi Ikeda   Nara Institute of Science and Technology, Japan

Special Sessions Chairs

Sunu Wibirama   Universitas Gadjah Mada, Indonesia
Paul Pang   Federation University Australia, Australia
Noor Akhmad Setiawan   Universitas Gadjah Mada, Indonesia

Tutorial Chairs

Suryono   Universitas Diponegoro, Indonesia
Muhammad Agni Catur Bhakti   Sampoerna University, Indonesia

Atul Negi	University of Hyderabad, India
Barawi Mohamad Hardyman	Universiti Malaysia Sarawak, Malaysia
Bayu Distiawan	Universitas Indonesia, Indonesia
Bharat Richhariya	IISc Bangalore, India
Bin Pan	Nankai University, China
Bingshu Wang	Northwestern Polytechnical University, Taicang, China
Bonaventure C. Molokwu	University of Windsor, Canada
Bo-Qun Ma	Ant Financial
Bunthit Watanapa	King Mongkut's University of Technology Thonburi, Thailand
Chang-Dong Wang	Sun Yat-sen University, China
Chattrakul Sombattheera	Mahasarakham University, Thailand
Chee Siong Teh	Universiti Malaysia Sarawak, Malaysia
Chen Wei Chén	Chongqing Jiaotong University, China
Chengwei Wu	Harbin Institute of Technology, China
Chern Hong Lim	Monash University, Australia
Chih-Chieh Hung	National Chung Hsing University, Taiwan
Chiranjibi Sitaula	Deakin University, Australia
Chi-Sing Leung	City University of Hong Kong, Hong Kong
Choo Jun Tan	Wawasan Open University, Malaysia
Christoph Bergmeir	Monash University, Australia
Christophe Guyeux	University of Franche-Comté, France
Chuan Chen	Sun Yat-sen University, China
Chuanqi Tan	BIT, China
Chu-Kiong Loo	University of Malaya, Malaysia
Chun Che Fung	Murdoch University, Australia
Colin Samplawski	University of Massachusetts Amherst, USA
Congbo Ma	University of Adelaide, Australia
Cuiyun Gao	Chinese University of Hong Kong, Hong Kong
Cutifa Safitri	Universiti Teknologi Malaysia, Malaysia
Daisuke Miyamoto	University of Tokyo, Japan
Dan Popescu	Politehnica University of Bucharest
David Bong	Universiti Malaysia Sarawak, Malaysia
David Iclanzan	Sapientia Hungarian Science University of Transylvania, Romania
Debasmit Das	IIT Roorkee, India
Dengya Zhu	Curtin University, Australia
Derwin Suhartono	Bina Nusantara University, Indonesia
Devi Fitrianah	Universitas Mercu Buana, Indonesia
Deyu Zhou	Southeast University, China
Dhimas Arief Dharmawan	Universitas Indonesia, Indonesia
Dianhui Wang	La Trobe University, Australia
Dini Handayani	Taylors University, Malaysia
Dipanjyoti Paul	Indian Institute of Technology, Patna, India
Dong Chen	Wuhan University, China

He Chen	Nankai University, China
He Huang	Soochow University, China
Hea Choon Ngo	Universiti Teknikal Malaysia Melaka, Malaysia
Heba El-Fiqi	UNSW Canberra, Australia
Heru Praptono	Bank Indonesia/Universitas Indonesia, Indonesia
Hideitsu Hino	Institute of Statistical Mathematics, Japan
Hidemasa Takao	University of Tokyo, Japan
Hiroaki Inoue	Kobe University, Japan
Hiroaki Kudo	Nagoya University, Japan
Hiromu Monai	Ochanomizu University, Japan
Hiroshi Sakamoto	Kyushu Institute of Technology, Japan
Hisashi Koga	University of Electro-Communications, Japan
Hiu-Hin Tam	City University of Hong Kong, Hong Kong
Hongbing Xia	Beijing Normal University, China
Hongtao Liu	Tianjin University, China
Hongtao Lu	Shanghai Jiao Tong University, China
Hua Zuo	University of Technology Sydney, Australia
Hualou Liang	Drexel University, USA
Huang Chaoran	University of New South Wales, Australia
Huang Shudong	Sichuan University, China
Huawen Liu	University of Texas at San Antonio, USA
Hui Xue	Southeast University, China
Hui Yan	Shanghai Jiao Tong University, China
Hyeyoung Park	Kyungpook National University, South Korea
Hyun-Chul Kim	Kyungpook National University, South Korea
Iksoo Shin	University of Science and Technology, South Korea
Indrabayu Indrabayu	Universitas Hasanuddin, Indonesia
Iqbal Gondal	RMIT University, Australia
Iuliana Georgescu	University of Bucharest, Romania
Iwan Syarif	PENS, Indonesia
J. Kokila	Indian Institute of Information Technology, Allahabad, India
J. Manuel Moreno	Universitat Politècnica de Catalunya, Spain
Jagdish C. Patra	Swinburne University of Technology, Australia
Jean-Francois Couchot	University of Franche-Comté, France
Jelita Asian	STKIP Surya, Indonesia
Jennifer C. Dela Cruz	Mapua University, Philippines
Jérémie Sublime	ISEP, France
Jiahuan Lei	Meituan, China
Jialiang Zhang	Alibaba, China
Jiaming Xu	Institute of Automation, Chinese Academy of Sciences
Jianbo Ning	University of Science and Technology Beijing, China
Jianyi Yang	Nankai University, China
Jiasen Wang	City University of Hong Kong, Hong Kong
Jiawei Fan	Australian National University, Australia
Jiawei Li	Tsinghua University, China

Jiaxin Li	Guangdong University of Technology, China
Jiaxuan Xie	Shanghai Jiao Tong University, China
Jichuan Zeng	Bytedance, China
Jie Shao	University of Science and Technology of China, China
Jie Zhang	Newcastle University, UK
Jiecong Lin	City University of Hong Kong, Hong Kong
Jin Hu	Chongqing Jiaotong University, China
Jin Kyu Kim	Facebook, USA
Jin Ren	Beijing University of Technology, China
Jin Shi	Nanjing University, China
Jinfu Yang	Beijing University of Technology, China
Jing Peng	South China Normal University, China
Jinghui Zhong	South China University of Technology, China
Jin-Tsong Jeng	National Formosa University, Taiwan
Jiri Sima	Institute of Computer Science, Czech Academy of Sciences, Czech Republic
Jo Plested	Australian National University, Australia
Joel Dabrowski	CSIRO, Australia
John Sum	National Chung Hsing University, China
Jolfaei Alireza	Federation University Australia, Australia
Jonathan Chan	King Mongkut's University of Technology Thonburi, Thailand
Jonathan Mojoo	Hiroshima University, Japan
Jose Alfredo Ferreira Costa	Federal University of Rio Grande do Norte, Brazil
Ju Lu	Shandong University, China
Jumana Abu-Khalaf	Edith Cowan University, Australia
Jun Li	Nanjing Normal University, China
Jun Shi	Guangzhou University, China
Junae Kim	DST Group, Australia
Junbin Gao	University of Sydney, Australia
Junjie Chen	Inner Mongolia Agricultural University, China
Junya Chen	Fudan University, China
Junyi Chen	City University of Hong Kong, Hong Kong
Junying Chen	South China University of Technology, China
Junyu Xuan	University of Technology, Sydney
Kah Ong Michael Goh	Multimedia University, Malaysia
Kaizhu Huang	Xi'an Jiaotong-Liverpool University, China
Kam Meng Goh	Tunku Abdul Rahman University College, Malaysia
Katsuhiro Honda	Osaka Prefecture University, Japan
Katsuyuki Hagiwara	Mie University, Japan
Kazushi Ikeda	Nara Institute of Science and Technology, Japan
Kazuteru Miyazaki	National Institution for Academic Degrees and Quality Enhancement of Higher Education, Japan
Kenji Doya	OIST, Japan
Kenji Watanabe	National Institute of Advanced Industrial Science and Technology, Japan

Kok Wai Wong	Murdoch University, Australia
Kitsuchart Pasupa	King Mongkut's Institute of Technology Ladkrabang, Thailand
Kittichai Lavangnananda	King Mongkut's University of Technology Thonburi, Thailand
Koutsakis Polychronis	Murdoch University, Australia
Kui Ding	Nanjing Normal University, China
Kun Zhang	Carnegie Mellon University, USA
Kuntpong Woraratpanya	King Mongkut's Institute of Technology Ladkrabang, Thailand
Kurnianingsih Kurnianingsih	Politeknik Negeri Semarang, Indonesia
Kusrini	Universitas AMIKOM Yogyakarta, Indonesia
Kyle Harrison	UNSW Canberra, Australia
Laga Hamid	Murdoch University, Australia
Lei Wang	Beihang University, China
Leonardo Franco	Universidad de Málaga, Spain
Li Guo	University of Macau, China
Li Yun	Nanjing University of Posts and Telecommunications, China
Libo Wang	Xiamen University of Technology, China
Lie Meng Pang	Southern University of Science and Technology, China
Liew Alan Wee-Chung	Griffith University, Australia
Lingzhi Hu	Beijing University of Technology, China
Linjing Liu	City University of Hong Kong, Hong Kong
Lisi Chen	Hong Kong Baptist University, Hong Kong
Long Cheng	Institute of Automation, Chinese Academy of Sciences, China
Lukman Hakim	Hiroshima University, Japan
M. Tanveer	Indian Institute of Technology, Indore, India
Ma Wanli	University of Canberra, Australia
Man Fai Leung	Hong Kong Metropolitan University, Hong Kong
Maram Mahmoud A. Monshi	Beijing Institute of Technology, China
Marcin Wozniak	Silesian University of Technology, Poland
Marco Anisetti	Università degli Studi di Milano, Italy
Maria Susan Anggreainy	Bina Nusantara University, Indonesia
Mark Abernethy	Murdoch University, Australia
Mark Elshaw	Coventry University, UK
Maruno Yuki	Kyoto Women's University, Japan
Masafumi Hagiwara	Keio University, Japan
Masataka Kawai	NRI SecureTechnologies, Ltd., Japan
Media Ayu	Sampoerna University, Indonesia
Mehdi Neshat	University of Adelaide, Australia
Meng Wang	Southeast University, China
Mengmeng Li	Zhengzhou University, China

Miaohua Zhang	Griffith University, Australia
Mingbo Zhao	Donghua University, China
Mingcong Deng	Tokyo University of Agriculture and Technology, Japan
Minghao Yang	Institute of Automation, Chinese Academy of Sciences, China
Minho Lee	Kyungpook National University, South Korea
Mofei Song	Southeast University, China
Mohammad Faizal Ahmad Fauzi	Multimedia University, Malaysia
Mohsen Marjani	Taylor's University, Malaysia
Mubasher Baig	National University of Computer and Emerging Sciences, Lahore, Pakistan
Muhammad Anwar Ma'Sum	Universitas Indonesia, Indonesia
Muhammad Asim Ali	Shaheed Zulfikar Ali Bhutto Institute of Science and Technology, Pakistan
Muhammad Fawad Akbar Khan	University of Engineering and Technology Peshawar, Pakistan
Muhammad Febrian Rachmadi	Universitas Indonesia, Indonesia
Muhammad Haris	Universitas Nusa Mandiri, Indonesia
Muhammad Haroon Shakeel	Lahore University of Management Sciences, Pakistan
Muhammad Hilman	Universitas Indonesia, Indonesia
Muhammad Ramzan	Saudi Electronic University, Saudi Arabia
Muideen Adegoke	City University of Hong Kong, Hong Kong
Mulin Chen	Northwestern Polytechnical University, China
Murtaza Taj	Lahore University of Management Sciences, Pakistan
Mutsumi Kimura	Ryukoku University, Japan
Naoki Masuyama	Osaka Prefecture University, Japan
Naoyuki Sato	Future University Hakodate, Japan
Nat Dilokthanakul	Vidyasirimedhi Institute of Science and Technology, Thailand
Nguyen Dang	University of Canberra, Australia
Nhi N. Y. Vo	University of Technology Sydney, Australia
Nick Nikzad	Griffith University, Australia
Ning Boda	Swinburne University of Technology, Australia
Nobuhiko Wagatsuma	Tokyo Denki University, Japan
Nobuhiko Yamaguchi	Saga University, Japan
Noor Akhmad Setiawan	Universitas Gadjah Mada, Indonesia
Norbert Jankowski	Nicolaus Copernicus University, Poland
Norikazu Takahashi	Okayama University, Japan
Noriyasu Homma	Tohoku University, Japan
Normaziah A. Aziz	International Islamic University Malaysia, Malaysia
Olarik Surinta	Mahasarakham University, Thailand

Olutomilayo Olayemi Petinrin	Kings University, Nigeria
Ooi Shih Yin	Multimedia University, Malaysia
Osamu Araki	Tokyo University of Science, Japan
Ozlem Faydasicok	Istanbul University, Turkey
Parisa Rastin	University of Lorraine, France
Paul S. Pang	Federation University Australia, Australia
Pedro Antonio Gutierrez	Universidad de Cordoba, Spain
Pengyu Sun	Microsoft
Piotr Duda	Institute of Computational Intelligence/Czestochowa University of Technology, Poland
Prabath Abeysekara	RMIT University, Australia
Pui Huang Leong	Tunku Abdul Rahman University College, Malaysia
Qian Li	Chinese Academy of Sciences, China
Qiang Xiao	Huazhong University of Science and Technology, China
Qiangfu Zhao	University of Aizu, Japan
Qianli Ma	South China University of Technology, China
Qing Xu	Tianjin University, China
Qing Zhang	Meituan, China
Qinglai Wei	Institute of Automation, Chinese Academy of Sciences, China
Qingrong Cheng	Fudan University, China
Qiufeng Wang	Xi'an Jiaotong-Liverpool University, China
Qiulei Dong	Institute of Automation, Chinese Academy of Sciences, China
Qiuye Wu	Guangdong University of Technology, China
Rafal Scherer	Częstochowa University of Technology, Poland
Rahmadya Handayanto	Universitas Islam 45 Bekasi, Indonesia
Rahmat Budiarto	Albaha University, Saudi Arabia
Raja Kumar	Taylor's University, Malaysia
Rammohan Mallipeddi	Kyungpook National University, South Korea
Rana Md Mashud	CSIRO, Australia
Rapeeporn Chamchong	Mahasarakham University, Thailand
Raphael Couturier	Université Bourgogne Franche-Comté, France
Ratchakoon Pruengkarn	Dhurakij Pundit University, Thailand
Reem Mohamed	Mansoura University, Egypt
Rhee Man Kil	Sungkyunkwan University, South Korea
Rim Haidar	University of Sydney, Australia
Rizal Fathoni Aji	Universitas Indonesia, Indonesia
Rukshima Dabare	Murdoch University, Australia
Ruting Cheng	University of Science and Technology Beijing, China
Ruxandra Liana Costea	Polytechnic University of Bucharest, Romania
Saaveethya Sivakumar	Curtin University Malaysia, Malaysia
Sabrina Fariza	Central Queensland University, Australia
Sahand Vahidnia	University of New South Wales, Australia

Saifur Rahaman	City University of Hong Kong, Hong Kong
Sajib Mistry	Curtin University, Australia
Sajib Saha	CSIRO, Australia
Sajid Anwar	Institute of Management Sciences Peshawar, Pakistan
Sakchai Muangsrinoon	Walailak University, Thailand
Salomon Michel	Université Bourgogne Franche-Comté, France
Sandeep Parameswaran	Myntra Designs Pvt. Ltd., India
Sangtae Ahn	Kyungpook National University, South Korea
Sang-Woo Ban	Dongguk University, South Korea
Sangwook Kim	Kobe University, Japan
Sanparith Marukatat	NECTEC, Thailand
Saptakatha Adak	Indian Institute of Technology, Madras, India
Seiichi Ozawa	Kobe University, Japan
Selvarajah Thuseethan	Sabaragamuwa University of Sri Lanka, Sri Lanka
Seong-Bae Park	Kyung Hee University, South Korea
Shan Zhong	Changshu Institute of Technology, China
Shankai Yan	National Institutes of Health, USA
Sheeraz Akram	University of Pittsburgh, USA
Shenglan Liu	Dalian University of Technology, China
Shenglin Zhao	Zhejiang University, China
Shing Chiang Tan	Multimedia University, Malaysia
Shixiong Zhang	Xidian University, China
Shreya Chawla	Australian National University, Australia
Shri Rai	Murdoch University, Australia
Shuchao Pang	Jilin University, China/Macquarie University, Australia
Shuichi Kurogi	Kyushu Institute of Technology, Japan
Siddharth Sachan	Australian National University, Australia
Sirui Li	Murdoch University, Australia
Sonali Agarwal	Indian Institute of Information Technology, Allahabad, India
Sonya Coleman	University of Ulster, UK
Stavros Ntalampiras	University of Milan, Italy
Su Lei	University of Science and Technology Beijing, China
Sung-Bae Cho	Yonsei University, South Korea
Sunu Wibirama	Universitas Gadjah Mada, Indonesia
Susumu Kuroyanagi	Nagoya Institute of Technology, Japan
Sutharshan Rajasegarar	Deakin University, Australia
Takako Hashimoto	Chiba University of Commerce, Japan
Takashi Omori	Tamagawa University, Japan
Tao Ban	National Institute of Information and Communications Technology, Japan
Tao Li	Peking University, China
Tao Xiang	Chongqing University, China
Teddy Mantoro	Sampoerna University, Indonesia
Tedjo Darmanto	STMIK AMIK Bandung, Indonesia
Teijiro Isokawa	University of Hyogo, Japan

Thanh Tam Nguyen	Leibniz University Hannover, Germany
Thanh Tung Khuat	University of Technology Sydney, Australia
Thaweesak Khongtuk	Rajamangala University of Technology Suvarnabhumi, Thailand
Tianlin Zhang	University of Chinese Academy of Sciences, China
Timothy McIntosh	Massey University, New Zealand
Toan Nguyen Thanh	Ho Chi Minh City University of Technology, Vietnam
Todsanai Chumwatana	Murdoch University, Australia
Tom Gedeon	Australian National University, Australia
Tomas Maul	University of Nottingham, Malaysia
Tomohiro Shibata	Kyushu Institute of Technology, Japan
Tomoyuki Kaneko	University of Tokyo, Japan
Toshiaki Omori	Kobe University, Japan
Toshiyuki Yamane	IBM, Japan
Uday Kiran	University of Tokyo, Japan
Udom Silparcha	King Mongkut's University of Technology Thonburi, Thailand
Umar Aditiawarman	Universitas Nusa Putra, Indonesia
Upeka Somaratne	Murdoch University, Australia
Usman Naseem	University of Sydney, Australia
Ven Jyn Kok	National University of Malaysia, Malaysia
Wachira Yangyuen	Rajamangala University of Technology Srivijaya, Thailand
Wai-Keung Fung	Robert Gordon University, UK
Wang Yaqing	Baidu Research, Hong Kong
Wang Yu-Kai	University of Technology Sydney, Australia
Wei Jin	Michigan State University, USA
Wei Yanling	TU Berlin, Germany
Weibin Wu	City University of Hong Kong, Hong Kong
Weifeng Liu	China University of Petroleum, China
Weijie Xiang	University of Science and Technology Beijing, China
Wei-Long Zheng	Massachusetts General Hospital, Harvard Medical School, USA
Weiqun Wang	Institute of Automation, Chinese Academy of Sciences, China
Wen Luo	Nanjing Normal University, China
Wen Yu	Cinvestav, Mexico
Weng Kin Lai	Tunku Abdul Rahman University College, Malaysia
Wenqiang Liu	Southwest Jiaotong University, China
Wentao Wang	Michigan State University, USA
Wenwei Gu	Chinese University of Hong Kong, Hong Kong
Wenxin Yu	Southwest University of Science and Technology, China
Widodo Budiharto	Bina Nusantara University, Indonesia
Wisnu Ananta Kusuma	Institut Pertanian Bogor, Indonesia
Worapat Paireekreng	Dhurakij Pundit University, Thailand

Contents – Part V

AI and Cybersecurity

Theory and Algorithms

Emoji-Based Co-Attention Network for Microblog Sentiment Analysis

Xiaowei Yuan[1,2], Jingyuan Hu[1], Xiaodan Zhang[1(✉)], Honglei Lv[1], and Hao Liu[1,2]

[1] Institute of Information Engineering, Chinese Academy of Sciences, Beijing, China
{yuanxiaowei,hujingyuan,zhangxiaodan,lvhonglei,liuhao}@iie.ac.cn
[2] School of Cyber Security, University of Chinese Academy of Sciences, Beijing, China

Abstract. Emojis are widely used in online social networks to express emotions, attitudes, and opinions. As emotional-oriented characters, emojis can be modeled as important features of emotions towards the recipient or subject for sentiment analysis. However, existing methods mainly take emojis as heuristic information that fails to resolve the problem of ambiguity noise. Recent researches have utilized emojis as an independent input to classify text sentiment but they ignore the emotional impact of the interaction between text and emojis. It results that the emotional semantics of emojis cannot be fully explored. In this paper, we propose an emoji-based co-attention network that learns the mutual emotional semantics between text and emojis on microblogs. Our model adopts the co-attention mechanism based on bidirectional long short-term memory incorporating the text and emojis, and integrates a squeeze-and-excitation block in a convolutional neural network classifier to increase its sensitivity to emotional semantic features. Experimental results show that the proposed method can significantly outperform several baselines for sentiment analysis on short texts of social media.

Keywords: Sentiment analysis · Emoji · Attention mechanism

1 Introduction

Nowadays, online social media such as Twitter, Facebook, and Weibo (the biggest Chinese microblog platform) have become the mainstream communication tools for the public, where people are inclined to express their emotions, attitudes, and opinions. Microblogs contain a vast amount of valuable emotional information and have become a hot research target for sentiment analysis [6,10]. Sentiment analysis has been a crucial component in many commercial applications such as recommendation systems, customer feedback classification, advertising strategy, and public opinion poll due to its effectiveness in constructing user portraits and analyzing their personality characteristics [14]. Recently, emojis have emerged as a popular way in social communication, and have a high frequency of occurrence in microblogs. Emojis are used to provide additional emotional information, change the tone, engage recipients or maintain relationships,

© Springer Nature Switzerland AG 2021
T. Mantoro et al. (Eds.): ICONIP 2021, CCIS 1516, pp. 3–11, 2021.
https://doi.org/10.1007/978-3-030-92307-5_1

etc. [1]. They can play an emotion-oriented role to express sentiment, which is analyzed statistically to be the most popular intention for using them [5].

Therefore, it is crucial to combine emojis with text to explore the emotional semantics for sentiment analysis tasks. The most common method is to utilize emojis as an important feature [15,20] or a natural annotation [2,3,12] to obtain better performance. However, existing work [2] show that using emojis directly as emotional tags will generate diverse noise because of the ambiguity of emoji labels, that is, the sentiments conveyed by the same emoji may vary according to the context. Many researchers also use emojis as an independent input to judge the emotional polarity of the entire text, without considering the impact of the interaction between emojis and plain text on sentiment analysis.Based on the above problems, we propose an Emoji-based Co-attention Network (ECN) to learn the mutual emotional semantics between text and emojis.

2   Related Work

As a significant branch of natural language processing (NLP), text sentiment analysis aims to mine and analyze the emotions, opinions, and attitudes of people from texts. In recent years, the rapid development of deep learning has played an important role in boosting the development of sentiment analysis researches. Socher et al. [17] applied Recursive Neural Network to text sentiment classification with the consideration of the syntactic structure information; Santos et al. [16] proposed Character to Sentence Convolutional Neural Network (CharSCNN) to analyze sentiment on the short text.

Emojis can be regarded as important semantic features about emotions towards the recipient or subject [18] for sentiment classification. For instance, Jiang et al. [7] combined structure features, sentence structure features, and emoji features in a SVM model to classify texts. This strategy fails to reflect the emotional impact of emojis on the text. Many studies also use emojis as heuristic information in social texts [2,3,12], where emojis serve for unsupervised learning in a large number of unlabeled data. Among existing research, the most similar work to our motivation is that Lou et al. [13] constructed an emoji-based Bi-LSTM model, which combined the attention mechanism to weigh the contribution of each word on the emotional polarity based on emoji. But this method only analyze the microblog data that contains a single emoji and cannot be generalized to process multiple types of emojis.

3   Model

In this paper, we propose a new neural network model called the Emoji-based Co-attention Network. Its architecture is illustrated in Fig. 1.

The model consists of three main components: *Text Feature Extractor*, *Co-attention Network*, and *SE-based CNN Classifier*. In the text feature extractor,

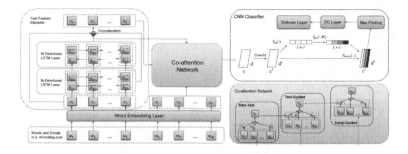

Fig. 1. The overview of the proposed ECN architecture

we build two stacked Bi-LSTM layers with skip-connection to obtain text features. Then we adopt a co-attention network to learn high-level emotional semantic features incorporating the text and emojis from their interaction. Finally, these features are fed into a CNN classifier integrated with a SE block to predict the probability distribution of sentiment labels of the microblog posts.

3.1 Text Feature Extractor

The plain text can be embedded into $X = [x_1, x_2, ..., x_L]$. Since the microblog emojis are converted into textual tags by Weibo API[1], the emojis can also be encoded into vectors by word embedding layer $E = [e_1, e_2, ..., e_N]$.

LSTM can overcome the problem of gradient vanishing and explosion with the capability to learn long-range dependencies in sequences. In order to capture both past and future information, the feature extractor adopts two stacked Bi-LSTM layers to learn the text representation bidirectionally. And we concatenate the hidden vectors from both directions to represent every single word as the output h_l of the layer. The second Bi-LSTM layer takes the output of the previous one as its input $H_1 = [h_{11}, h_{21}, .., h_{L1}]$, and computes unit stats of network in the same pattern before producing the output $H_2 = [h_{12}, h_{22}, .., h_{L2}]$.

3.2 Co-Attention Network

Intra-Text Attention Module. Through a skip-connection, the outputs of the below three layers (the embedding layer and the two Bi-LSTM layers) are concatenated as a whole vector, which will be sent into the text attention module as input. The l-th word in the input text can be denoted as $u_l = [x_l, h_{l1}, h_{l2}]$, where $x_l \in \mathbb{R}^d$, $h_{l1} \in \mathbb{R}^d$, and $h_{l2} \in \mathbb{R}^d$, d is the dimension of word feature. For the l-th word, the attention score is measured by

$$\alpha_l = \frac{\exp(W_\alpha u_l)}{\sum_{i=1}^{L} \exp(W_\alpha u_i)}, \tag{1}$$

---

[1] https://api.weibo.com/2/emotions.json.

where W_α is the weight matrix and $W_\alpha \in \mathbb{R}^{1 \times 3d}$. $\alpha_l \in \mathbb{R}^L$, which corresponds to the attention probability of each word. Using the attention scores as weights, the text can be represented as v_t, that aggregates the weights of individual words and transform the dimension to d through a fully connected layer.

Text-Guided Attention Module. In most cases, emoji occurrences in a post are related to the emotional semantics, but it depends on the contextual text that the different contribution of each emoji to predict the sentiment label. Therefore, we apply a text-guided attention module to decide crucial emoji by using the new text vector v_h to conduct the attention. We feed text feature v_t and emoji feature E through a fully connected network followed by a softmax function to obtain the attention distribution over the emojis in the post:

$$z_n = \tanh(W_E e_n + W_{v_t} v_t + b_1), \tag{2}$$

$$\beta_n = \frac{\exp(W_\beta z_n)}{\sum_{i=1}^{N} \exp(W_\beta z_i)}, \tag{3}$$

where $v_t \in \mathbb{R}^d$, $e_n \in \mathbb{R}^d$. W_E, W_{v_t} and W_β are weight matrices, and $W_E \in \mathbb{R}^{k \times d}$, $W_{v_t} \in \mathbb{R}^{k \times d}$, $W_\beta \in \mathbb{R}^{1 \times k}$, and b_1 is the bias. $\beta_n \in \mathbb{R}^N$ is corresponding to the attention probability of each emoji given text representation v_t. Based on β_n, the new emoji representation v_e can be generated by weighted sum.

Emoji-Guided Attention Module. The emoji-guided attention module joins text and emoji information together to measure the weight of each word that decides which words in the text should be attended to. We learn the emoji representation v_e from text-guided attention module, and higher-level text representation H_2 is obtained from the top Bi-LSTM layer. Similar to text-guided attention, we use these features to generate the attention distribution over the word embeddings and get a new text representation v_h that joins the semantics of text and emoji together.

3.3   SE-based CNN Classifier

After the text feature extractor and co-attention network, we obtain the text vector $v_t \in \mathbb{R}^d$, text-based emoji vector $v_e \in \mathbb{R}^d$ and emoji-based text vector $v_h \in \mathbb{R}^d$. We take these vectors as three-channel input $V \in \mathbb{R}^{d \times c}$ and transfer them into a CNN classifier to predict the probability distribution of sentiment labels of the microblog posts.

For the convolutional operation, we use $[w_1, w_2, ..., w_c]$ to represent the set of filter kernels that map the input $V \in \mathbb{R}^{d \times c}$ to a new feature map $U \in \mathbb{R}^{d' \times c'}$.

Since not all features contribute equally to predict the final sentiment label, we employ the SE block to measure the importance of each feature channel by modeling the correlation between channels and learning their weights [4]. Two parts are included in a SE block: *squeeze* (4) and *excitation* (5).

$$z_j = F_{sq}(u_j) = \frac{1}{d'}\sum_{i=1}^{d'} u_j(i), \tag{4}$$

$$\tilde{v}_j = F_{scale}(u_j, s_j) = s_j u_j = \sigma(W_2\delta(W_1 z_j))u_j, \tag{5}$$

where σ and δ denote the sigmoid and ReLU function respectively, weight matrices $W_1 \in \mathbb{R}^{\frac{C}{r}\times C}, W_2 \in \mathbb{R}^{C\times\frac{C}{r}}$, and F_{scale} represents to channel-wise multiplication.

4 Experiment

4.1 Dataset and Implementation Details

The labeled data used in our work are obtained from a public dataset[2] with positive and negative labels. We filter images, videos, and other URL links to eliminate noisy information. For stop word, we adopt the list from Harbin Institute of Technology's stop word database[3]. We use Python Chinese word segmentation module Jieba[4] to segment the sentences of the microblog posts and feed the segmentation results into the word embedding layer by pre-trained word vectors[5]. During the process, words and emojis are trained simultaneously since each emoji is transformed into Chinese characters by Weibo API.

Using a trained word2vec model, we trained our ECN method with 10 epochs and the performance achieved the highest value when the hidden units of bi-directional LSTM layers were set as 300 and dropout was applied at the rate of 0.5. We randomly split the emoji-rich posts into the training, validation and test sets in the proportion of 7:2:1 with balanced categories. We used the Adam algorithm [9] for optimization and initial learning rate was set to 10^{-3}. The whole framework was implemented in PyTorch[6].

4.2 Baselines and Performance Comparison

To evaluate the performance of ECN, we employ several representative classificational baseline methods (TextCNN [8], TextRCNN [11], Att-BiLSTM [21], TextGCN [19], EA-Bi-LSTM [13]) for sentiment analysis. In Table 1, ECN outperforms all four baseline methods. The results prove that our proposed method is more effective than the old methods that do not pay attention to the emojis. Looking more closely, the three shallow methods (TextCNN, TextRCNN, and Att-BLSTM) achieves an accuracy above 0.95. It is remarkable to find that ECN achieves an accuracy above 0.98 as it improves on the former methods by 1 to 2

---

[2] https://github.com/SophonPlus/ChineseNlpCorpus.
[3] https://github.com/goto456/stopwords.
[4] https://github.com/fxsjy/jieba.
[5] https://github.com/Embedding/Chinese-Word-Vectors.
[6] https://pytorch.org/docs/stable/nn.html.

percent approximately. A possible explanation for this might be that the architecture of ECN combines the Bi-LSTM and CNN, which could embed words into high-dimensional vectors and learn richer semantic representation for sentiment analysis incorporating emojis and text features. ECN also outperforms the EA-Bi-LSTM, the latest work on emojis, which demonstrates the effectiveness of our model. Comparing with other baseline models, the performance of TextGCN is worse than all other methods with an accuracy below 0.94. It might be explained that in text classification, GCN ignores the word features of sequence, which is of great importance for sentiment analysis.

Table 1. The Results of ECN and baseline methods

Models	P(%)	R(%)	F(%)	Acc(%)
TextCNN	96.66	95.63	96.55	96.24
TextRCNN	95.93	97.72	96.19	96.52
Att-BLSTM	97.19	99.20	97.59	97.09
TextGCN	94.02	93.86	93.94	93.72
EA-Bi-LSTM	96.73	98.29	98.04	97.53
ECN(our model)	**97.46**	**99.88**	**98.66**	**98.59**

[1] P represents the precision, R is the recall, and F is the F1-score

4.3 Model Analysis

The Power of Emojis. To further explore the influences of emojis in ECN, we conduct the subsequent experiments by removing the inputs of emojis or simplified architecture of ECN to evaluate the effectiveness of emojis. N-ECN detaches the emoji inputs. T-ECN removes the text-guided attention module of emoji representation learning. E-ECN removes the emoji-guided attention module of text representation learning.

Test accuracy of the modified model is illustrated in Table 2. We find that ECN significantly outperforms the N-ECN and T-ECN (the differences are statistically significant at the 22.02% and 11.57%), both of which only consider the text features before classification. That demonstrates the plain text does not contain rich emotional semantic information as emojis do occasionally in sentiment analysis. T-ECN outperforms the N-ECN by 10.45% in accuracy. This shows emoji-guided text representation learning can effectively improve the ability of the model to learn the emotional semantic. It also explains why our emoji-based method can achieve better accuracy compared to other baseline methods. The accuracy of E-ECN is also significantly higher than T-ECN by the 9.20% and slightly lower than the complete ECN model since E-ECN extracts sentiment information from text-guided emoji representation but fails to capture sentiment patterns of emoji-guided text representation.

Effectiveness of Co-Attention. To further explore the effect of co-attention mechanism in our proposed method, we compare the ECN model architecture to several attention-modified models. In RA1-ECN, we remove the intra-text attention module and take the output of last cell of the Bi-LSTM as the plain text representation v_t. In RA2-ECN, we replace the text-guided attention module with the average value of the emoji vectors $E = [e_1, e_2, ..., e_N]$ as the emoji representation v_e. In RA3-ECN, we replace the emoji-guided attention module with the average value of the text representation $H_2 = [h_{12}, h_{22}, .., h_{L2}]$ as the text representation v_h. In RSE-ECN, we remove the SE-Net module and concatenate the output of co-attention module(v_t, v_e, v_h) to a full-connected layer with a softmax function as a classifier.

The data of last two lines of the Table 2 show the improvements of SE-Net, which illustrates that this module can improve the accuracy. On the other hand, the difference between last two lines is slighter than the improvements of the whole ECN model compared with baselines. That indicates the co-attention module play the main role in our model.

Comparing the difference between these attention-simplified models in Table 2, it can be seen that the accuracy of the RA2-ECN has dropped the most. That model directly changes the attention mechanism of the emoji vector v_e to the average value of all emoji vectors, indicating that emojis take most of the weight for the emotional semantic analysis of the model. That means when the model cannot distinguish which emoji dominates the text emotion, the accuracy rate drops significantly. The slight difference of accuracy between the RA1-ECN and RA3-ECN model reveals that when the self-attention of the text is removed, the simplified v_t vector will further affect the representation of v_e as the emoji feature, and it results in the lower accuracy. While the RA3-ECN retains the first two representation of v_t and v_e features, only the last step of the text vector representation is replaced, it has the least impact on the model performance, indicating that the model can still make correct predictions from the v_e vector with a greater probability.

Table 2. Performance of ECN and its simplified versions

Models	P(%)	R(%)	F(%)	Acc(%)
N-ECN	75.79	77.03	76.04	76.57
T-ECN	95.08	77.65	85.49	87.02
E-ECN	95.85	**99.90**	97.83	97.82
RA1-ECN	95.02	96.18	95.04	95.57
RA2-ECN	93.06	94.18	94.08	94.22
RA3-ECN	97.32	98.59	97.92	97.92
RSE-ECN	96.80	99.03	97.89	98.25
ECN(our model)	**97.46**	99.88	**98.66**	**98.59**

5 Conclusion

We leverage emojis as important features to capture emotional patterns for sentiment analysis, and evaluate ECN with several representative baselines and our method achieves better performance with good interpretability.

Acknowledgement. The research is supported in part by the Strategic Priority Research Program of the Chinese Academy of Sciences, Grant No. XDC02060400.

References

1. Cramer, H., de Juan, P., Tetreault, J.: Sender-intended functions of emojis in us messaging. In: Proceeding of MobileHCI, pp. 504–509. ACM (2016)
2. Davidov, D., Tsur, O., Rappoport, A.: Enhanced sentiment learning using twitter hashtags and smileys. In: Proceeding of CICLing, pp. 241–249. ACL (2010)
3. Go, A., Bhayani, R., Huang, L.: Twitter sentiment classification using distant supervision. CS224150 (2009)
4. Hu, J., Shen, L., Albanie, S., Sun, G., Wu, E.: Squeeze-and-excitation networks. IEEE TPAMI **42**(8), 2011–2023 (2020)
5. Hu, T., Guo, H., Sun, H., Thi Nguyen, T.v., Luo, J.: Spice up your chat: the intentions and sentiment effects of using emoji. In: ICWSM, pp. 102–111 (2017)
6. Hu, X., Tang, J., Gao, H., Liu, H.: Unsupervised sentiment analysis with emotional signals. In: Proceeding of WWW, pp. 607–618. ACM (2013)
7. Jiang, F., Cui, A., Liu, Y., Zhang, M., Ma, S.: Every term has sentiment: learning from emoticon evidences for chinese microblog sentiment analysis. In: Zhou, G., Li, J., Zhao, D., Feng, Y. (eds.) NLPCC 2013. CCIS, vol. 400, pp. 224–235. Springer, Heidelberg (2013). https://doi.org/10.1007/978-3-642-41644-6_21
8. Kim, Y.: Convolutional neural networks for sentence classification. In: Proceedings of EMNLP, pp. 1746–1751. ACL (2014)
9. Kingma, D.P., Ba, J.: Adam: a method for stochastic optimization. In: The 3rd International Conference for Learning Representations (2014)
10. Korenek, P., Simko, M.: Sentiment analysis on microblog utilizing appraisal theory. In: World Wide Web, pp. 847–867 (2014)
11. Lai, S., Xu, L., Liu, K., Zhao, J.: Recurrent convolutional neural networks for text classification. In: Proceeding of AAAI, pp. 2267–2273 (2015)
12. Li, M., Ch'ng, E., Chong, A., See, S.: Multi-class twitter sentiment classification with emojis. Ind. Manag. Data Syst. **118** (2018)
13. Lou, Y., Zhang, Y., Li, F., Qian, T., Ji, D.: Emoji-based sentiment analysis using attention networks. In: Proceeding of TALLIP (2020)
14. Pang, B., Lee, L.: Opinion mining and sentiment analysis. Found. Trends Inf. Retr., 1–125 (2008)
15. Ptacek, T., Habernal, I., Hong, J.: Sarcasm detection on Czech and English twitter. In: Proceedings of COLING, pp. 213–223 (2014)
16. dos Santos, C., Gatti, M.: Deep convolutional neural networks for sentiment analysis of short texts. In: Proceeding of COLING, pp. 69–78. ACL (2014)
17. Socher, R., et al.: Recursive deep models for semantic compositionality over a sentiment treebank. In: EMNLP, pp. 1631–1642 (2013)
18. Walther, J.B., D'Addario, K.P.: The impacts of emoticons on message interpretation in computer-mediated communication. In: SSCR, pp. 324–347 (2001)

19. Yao, L., Mao, C., Luo, Y.: Graph convolutional networks for text classification. In: Proceedings of the AAAI Conference on Artificial Intelligence (2019)
20. Zhao, J., Dong, L., Wu, J., Xu, K.: Moodlens: an emoticon-based sentiment analysis system for Chinese tweets. In: Proceeding of KDD, pp. 1528–1531. ACM (2012)
21. Zhou, P., et al.: Attention-based bidirectional long short-term memory networks for relation classification. In: Proceedings of ACL, pp. 207–212. ACL (2016)

What Will You Tell Me About the Chart?
– Automated Description of Charts

Karolina Seweryn[1]([⊠]) [iD], Katarzyna Lorenc[1], Anna Wróblewska[1]([⊠]) [iD],
and Sylwia Sysko-Romańczuk[2] [iD]

[1] Faculty of Mathematics and Information Science,
Warsaw University of Technology, Warsaw, Poland
{karolina.seweryn,anna.wroblewska1}@pw.edu.pl
[2] Management Faculty, Warsaw University of Technology, Warsaw, Poland

Abstract. An automatic chart description is a very challenging task. There are many more relationships between objects in a chart compared to general computer vision problems. Furthermore, charts have a different specificity to natural-scene pictures, so commonly used methods do not perform well. To tackle these problems, we propose a process consisting of three sub-tasks: (1) chart classification, (2) detection of a chart's essential elements, and (3) generation of text description.

Due to the lack of plot datasets dedicated to the task of generating text, we prepared a new dataset – *ChaTa+* which contains real-made figures. Additionally, we have adjusted publicly available *FigureQA* and *PlotQA* datasets to our particular tasks and tested our method on them. We compared our results with those of the Adobe team [3], which we treated as a benchmark. Finally, we obtained comparable results of the models' performance, although we trained them on a more complex dataset (semi-synthetic *PlotQA*) and built a less resource-intensive infrastructure.

Keywords: Object detection · Text generation · Chart analysis

1 Introduction

Data charts are widely practised in our daily circumstances, e.g. in traditional media, such as statistical reports, newspapers, and many other sources. In general, a well-designed and developed data chart leads to an intuitive understanding of its underlying data. Hence, in recent years there has been growing interest in automated figure analysis, recognition and understanding [5–7,11,13,14].

One of our major contributions is assembling a refined dataset of real charts, which we call *ChaTa+*. Such a complex dataset has great potential for business

Research was funded by the Centre for Priority Research Area Artificial Intelligence and Robotics of Warsaw University of Technology within the Excellence Initiative: Research University (IDUB) programme (grant no 1820/27/Z01/POB2/2021).

use and inspires various research questions. This paper introduces a chart recognition and description process composed of three models : classifier, object detector, and text generator. These models form an integral framework; the architecture generates chart descriptions based on predictions of the previous model in the pipeline. Each sub-task in the pipeline was tested with various fine-tuned deep neural architecture. The analysis was carried out on three datasets: one real and two generated artificially. We compared our results to the study [3] on chart captioning, and we achieved similar results on the more complicated dataset (a semi-synthetic PlotQA compared with the synthetic FigureQA analysed by Adobe). Additionally, our study provides considerable insight into multifaceted chart analysis (three tasks). Finally, our results and datasets set a benchmark for automated figure analysis and understanding.

2 Datasets and Their Transformations

2.1 Analyzed Datasets

Unfortunately, obtaining big datasets required to build deep learning models is often associated with high costs. Simulated observations that faithfully represent reality could be used to reduce the amount of money spent on acquiring data. This approach was applied to some of the considered datasets (see Table 1). The datasets can be distinguished based on their origin:

- **synthetic data** – entirely artificially generated data; in the first step, values are generated and then visualised in the form of a figure (*FigureQA* [7]).
- **semi-synthetic data** – figures artificially generated from real data (*PlotQA* [11]). The dataset has been created by extracting data from online sources such as World Bank Open Data. Thus, *PlotQA* is composed of various statistics, e.g., about rainfall or coal production. The aesthetic parameters such as line style, font size, or legend position were selected randomly to provide the figures' variability. This way of generating charts makes them more similar to real data.
- **real data** – real figures and data; figures were collected from various sources, e.g. scientific articles. Our new dataset called *ChaTa+* (see Sect. 2.2) comprising figures from scientific articles was created at our university.

Table 1. The properties of the analysed datasets.

	FigureQA	PlotQA	ChaTa+
Real values	✗	✓	✓
Real plots	✗	✗	✓
Number of figures	140,000	224,377	1,640
Data	Synthetic	Semi-Synthetic	Real

All the datasets have annotations of chart types and bounding boxes of several plot elements, e.g., title, axes labels, legend. *FigureQA* and *PlotQA*, as their names suggest, additionally provide questions and answers related to charts. *ChaTa+* does not have such annotations (questions and answers) but contains chart captions and their textual descriptions. We conducted our analysis on subsets containing 4 chart types: lines, dot lines, vertical bar plots, and horizontal bar plots. To generate a chart description, we converted the questions from *PlotQA* into full sentence answers. Examples of transformations are in Table 2. Each chart description consisted of several generated utterances.

Table 2. Examples of questions and answers from *PlotQA* dataset that were converted into sentences.

Questions	Answers	Generated sentences
Are all the bars in the graph horizontal?	Yes	All bars in the graph are horizontal.
What is the title of the graph?	"Number of servers"	The title of the graph is "Number of servers".
How many legend labels are there?	4	There are 4 legend labels.

2.2   ChaTa+

In our experiments we used *ChaTa* dataset[1] (**Cha**rts and **Ta**bles annotation) consisting of figures and their annotations (Table 3). The charts come from scientific articles from *arXiv.org* and *WHO*.

Table 3. Left: the number of charts by type in *ChaTa* and *ChaTa+* datasets. Right: the number of annotated chart elements. H denotes horizontal, V-vertical.

Figure types	ChaTa	ChaTa+	Figure types	Figure elements	
Line plot	4,027	974	Line plot	Y axis	1,618
Dot plot	1,655	338	Dot-Line plot	X axis	1,567
Other plot	1,502	–	–	Chart description	1,407
H barplot	37	26	H barplot	Legend	853
V barplot	425	302	V barplot	X axis title	552
Box plot	360	–	–	Y axis title	265
Pie chart	11	–	–	Title	167
Sum	7,171	1,640		Reference in text	64

Each figure annotation includes information about the chart type and bounding boxes of essential elements such as title, axes, or a legend. Authors of publications often mention charts in two places: captions and paragraphs. Therefore,

---

[1] https://github.com/mini-pw/2019L-ProjektZespolowy.

ChaTa includes the acquisition of the text from both sources to obtain as much information about a chart as possible.

For the purpose of described tasks, a specific subset of observations, *ChaTa+* was separated from the main *ChaTa* dataset. It contains only selected chart types, and its annotations were validated by super annotators. Cases with complicated charts (e.g. figures containing several subfigures) were excluded and the dataset was limited to four types of chart. Moreover, in order to standardise the notation between the *FigureQA*, *PlotQA* and *ChaTa*, we chose only dot-line observations from the dot plots; the column plots were divided into vertical or horizontal arrangements.

3   Experiments

We defined our approach to chart recognition and description as the process of three machine learning tasks: (1) chart type classification, (2) object detection, and (3) textual chart description generation. All our models were trained on the training set *PlotQA*. In the object detection and text generation task, we used 50% of the training dataset due to limited computing capacity. The evaluation was carried out on separate test sets available in the described datasets. Considering real observations, the entire *ChaTa+* was considered the test set.

3.1   Chart Type Classification

We created four convolutional neural networks of varying depth. The shallowest one contains only two hidden layers constructed as a block of the ConvNet, ReLU activation function, and MaxPooling. Each subsequent architecture was enriched by one of the previously mentioned blocks. We have used a convolutional network with filter size (3,3), stride (1,1), and no padding. Max pooling size was (2,2). Each model had two dense layers with ReLU and softmax activation functions respectively, to obtain each class probability. In our experiments, the results of CNN were compared with *SVM* and *ResNet*. Throughout this paper the abbreviation L[N][CR] denotes the model with N convolution blocks, and CR indicates colour representation (RGB - Red Green Blue, G - Grayscale).

In order to choose the best classifier, we adapted the intuitive *TOPSIS* [2] method to our problem. The method is based on finding a solution that is the nearest to an ideal solution and as far as possible from the worst one, measured by Euclidean distance. We computed the TOPSIS ranking of nine metrics: accuracy, FNR, FPR, TNR, TPR, precision, recall, F1-score weighted, and F1-score average. It was hard to choose the best models because different models performed differently depending on the test datasets. We used *TOPSIS* with 9 measurements for each dataset, which gives 27 metrics in total. Additionally, we changed the uniform contribution of each dataset and used *TOPSIS* with the highest value of weight equal to $\frac{1}{2}$ for results on *ChaTa+*, $\frac{1}{3}$ for *PlotQA*, and $\frac{1}{6}$ for *FigureQA*. We assumed that the quality of models on real data is more relevant for the practical use case. The use of *TOPSIS* on 3 datasets with different

Table 4. Performance of chart type classifiers trained on *PlotQA*. *TOPSIS** included metric values for all datasets, so it was the same in dataset groups.

Test set	Model	Accuracy	F1-score	Precision	Recall	TOPSIS*
FigureQA	L3 G	**98.5**	**98.5**	**98.6**	**98.5**	2
	L5 G	90.3	89.9	92.7	90.3	1
	SVM G	87.9	87.1	90.7	87.9	3
	SVM RGB	76.9	72.7	82.3	76.9	5
	ResNet RGB	95.7	95.7	95.7	95.7	4
PlotQA	L3 G	**99.6**	**99.5**	**99.5**	**99.5**	2
	L5 G	99.4	99.2	99.2	99.2	1
	SVM G	99.3	98.9	98.9	98.9	3
	SVM RGB	**99.6**	**99.5**	**99.5**	**99.5**	5
	ResNet RGB	90.6	84.8	90.9	86.0	4
ChaTa+	L3 G	62.0	45.5	**50.6**	58.6	2
	L5 G	**67.6**	**49.5**	50.3	57.1	1
	SVM G	54.8	39.6	44.0	**60.7**	3
	SVM RGB	35.8	28.6	38.5	51.9	5
	ResNet RGB	48.7	40.6	42.3	52.8	4

weights was called *TOPSIS**. This approach revealed two outstanding models: *L3 G* and *L5 G*.

With the ranking, we examined the performance of models chosen in the previous step and compared them to *ResNet* and *SVM*. Three convolutional layers preprocessed input to the *SVM*. Afterwards, we chose the best classifier among the models abovementioned and investigated its behaviour. Table 4 shows that model *L5 G* achieved first place in *TOPSIS** ranking among all models, so this model is used in the following text generation task. Unexpectedly, *SVM* had the highest F1–score for test sets from the train test family (*PlotQA*). However, it had a problem with generalization and its performance on other datasets was not spectacular, especially on *ChaTa+*.

3.2   Detection of Chart Elements

This section investigates the problem of finding the location of 13 important regions in plots, e.g., legend and title . Models were trained on the *PlotQA* dataset and evaluated on *PlotQA* and *FigureQA* using COCO evaluation metrics.

We compared the *Faster R–CNN* model and *RetinaNet*. We used the *Faster R–CNN* [12] pretrained on the COCO dataset [10] with *ResNet50* [4] and the Feature Pyramid Network (FPN) [8] backbone. The second model was *RetinaNet* [9] pretrained on COCO. Table 5 shows that the value of the mean average precision (mAP) is higher for *Faster R–CNN* in comparison to *RetinaNet*. Moreover, average precision for each category is much worse for *RetinaNet* (see Fig. 1).

Table 5. Chart elements detector performance measured by mAP.

Model	Test set	mAP	mAP50	mAP75	mAPs	mAPm	mAPl
Faster R–CNN	FigureQA	**33.33**	**58.69**	**30.13**	19.51	**40.37**	**54.01**
	PlotQA	**80.45**	**89.07**	**86.71**	**66.62**	**83.35**	**93.48**
RetinaNet	FigureQA	29.32	56.17	23.40	**21.85**	35.11	47.83
	PlotQA	69.26	86.15	79.57	59.22	71.17	65.84

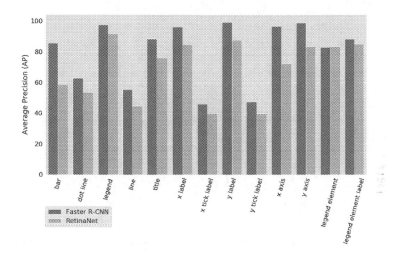

Fig. 1. Detector models performance per chart element category for *PlotQA*.

The metric mAPs (mAP for small regions) indicates that models had difficulty in finding small elements. The lowest AP values are for finding bounding boxes with 'x tick' and 'y tick' labels, which were one of the tiniest objects. The detector had difficulty finding the location of lines and dot lines. Due to the nature of the lines, there are many correct bounding boxes. However, the annotation was marked unambiguously; thus, the model predictions might differ from the annotation.

3.3   Generation of a Chart's Textual Description

In order to generate a chart description, we used two approaches: Encoder-Decoder and Table 2Text. Firstly, we built an encoder-decoder model with Bahdanau attention [1]. The InceptionV3 network transforms images, which are then passed through a single fully connected layer with the ReLU activation function. In the decoder part, a GRU network is used. Although the generator creates a relatively correct sentence structure, the descriptions are not compatible with the figures. The second model's construction is based on a structured knowledge base to avoid the difficulties encountered by the first model. The architecture can be divided into three parts (Fig. 2): (1) chart type classification, (2) detection of relevant objects and optical character recognition, (3) text generation.

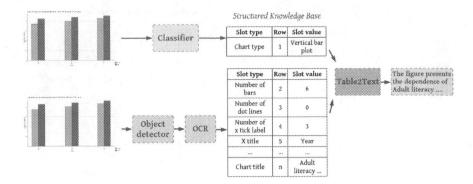

Fig. 2. Recognition and description process with the Table 2 Text model.

Table 6. Results of the generator on *PlotQA* test set.

Model	BLEU$_1$	BLEU$_2$	BLEU$_3$	BLEU$_4$	ROUGE-L
Endoder-Decoder	37	24.70	15.55	9.41	31.05
Table 2 Text	40	36.29	**32.59**	**29.05**	32.23
Adobe [3]	**40.4**	**36.7**	32.4	27.0	**48.9**

The text generator applies all the solutions proposed previously in this article. Initially, the input figure passed independently to two models. The first one was the classifier (*L5 G*), which prediction was converted to a single-row table with information about the chart type. The second model was the object detector (*Faster R-CNN*). Its output was additionally transformed to get a more elaborate table. Next, an OCR algorithm extracted text from the detected textual objects, such as the title or axis label. Then, the statistics on all found items were calculated to assemble relevant information captured by models. After that, the combination of both structures was transferred to the *Table 2Text*[2] model. The output from the model was a generated description of the input chart.

To sum up, the performance of the Table 2 Text model is higher than the Encoder-Decoder (see Table 6) and can be considered as a benchmark for generating chart descriptions.

4 Conclusions

The classifier trained on the semi-synthetic dataset *PlotQA* achieves high quality on the synthetic set *FigureQA*, but it often misclassifies real charts from the *ChaTa+* dataset. In the object detection task, the training *Faster-RCNN* model achieved satisfactory results (mAP 80.45). The text generator output constructs relatively correct sentence structures. The most common problems

---

[2] https://github.com/EagleW/Describing_a_Knowledge_Base.

relate to wrong text recognition by OCR or deviating the location of the bounding box determined by the detector. However, even more challenging for future research is generating descriptions that explain knowledge behind the charts and not only indicate the type, colors, and basic information. We believe that our process and prepared datasets[3] have a great potential for advancing future work. We consider our process as a benchmark for chart recognition and description modeling.

Acknowledgements. We would like to thank to Przemysław Biecek and Tomasz Stanisławek for their work on common idea for creating the *ChaTa* dataset of Charts and Tables along with annotations of their elements, and preliminary ideas of the system to annotate them, and we are grateful for many students from the Faculty of Mathematics and Information Science who contributed to the annotation tool and gathering the preliminary *ChaTa* dataset, which we modified further.

References

1. Bahdanau, D.: Neural machine translation by jointly learning to align and translate. In: ICLR (2015)
2. Behzadian, M., Otaghsara, S., Yazdani, M., Ignatius, J.: A state-of the-art survey of TOPSIS applications. Expert Syst. Appl. **39**, 13051–13069 (2012)
3. Chen, C., Zhang, R., et al.: Figure captioning with relation maps for reasoning. In: WACV (2020)
4. He, K., Zhang, X., Ren, S., Sun, J.: Deep residual learning for image recognition. In: CVPR (2015)
5. Jobin, K.V., Mondal, A., Jawahar, C.V.: Docfigure: a dataset for scientific document figure classification. In: ICDAR (2019)
6. Kafle, K., Price, B., Cohen, S., Kanan, C.: DVQA: understanding data visualizations via question answering. In: CVPR (2018)
7. Kahou, S.E., Michalski, V., Atkinson, A., Kadar, A., Trischler, A., Bengio, Y.: FigureQA: an annotated figure dataset for visual reasoning. In: ICLR (2018)
8. Lin, T.Y., Dollár, P., Girshick, R., He, K., Hariharan, B., Belongie, S.: Feature pyramid networks for object detection. In: CVPR (2017)
9. Lin, T.Y., Goyal, P., Girshick, R., He, K., Dollár, P.: Focal loss for dense object detection. In: ICCV (2017)
10. Lin, T.Y., et al.: Microsoft COCO: common objects in context. In: Fleet, D., Pajdla, T., Schiele, B., Tuytelaars, T. (eds.) ECCV 2014. LNCS, vol. 8693, pp. 740–755. Springer, Cham (2014). https://doi.org/10.1007/978-3-319-10602-1_48
11. Nitesh, M., Pritha, G., Mitesh, K., Pratyush, K.: PlotQA: reasoning over scientific plots. In: WACV (2020)
12. Ren, S., He, K., Girshick, R.B., Sun, J.: Faster R-CNN: towards real-time object detection with region proposal networks. In: NIPS (2015)
13. Savva, M., Kong, N., Chhajta, A., Fei-Fei, L., Agrawala, M., Heer, J.: ReVision: automated classification, analysis and redesign of chart images. In: ACM (2011)
14. Siegel, N., Horvitz, Z., Levin, R., Divvala, S., Farhadi, A.: FigureSeer: parsing result-figures in research papers. In: Leibe, B., Matas, J., Sebe, N., Welling, M. (eds.) ECCV 2016. LNCS, vol. 9911, pp. 664–680. Springer, Cham (2016). https://doi.org/10.1007/978-3-319-46478-7_41

---

[3] https://github.com/grant-TraDA.

Multi-Domain Adversarial Balancing for the Estimation of Individual Treatment Effect

Peifei Zhu[✉], Zisheng Li, and Masahiro Ogino

Hitachi, Ltd. Research and Development Group, Tokyo, Japan
{peifei.zhu.ww,zisheng.li.fj,masahiro.ogino.qk}@hitachi.com

Abstract. Estimating individual treatment effects (ITE) from observational data is an important topic in many fields. However, this task is challenging because data from observational studies has selection bias: the treatment assigned to an individual related to that individual's properties. In this paper, we proposed multi-domain adversarial balancing (MDAB), a method incorporates multi-domain adversarial learning with context-aware sample balancing to reduce the selection bias. It simultaneously learns confounder weights and sample weights through an adversarial learning architecture to generate a balanced representation. MDAB is empirically validated in public benchmark datasets, the results demonstrate that MDAB outperforms various state-of-the-art methods in both binary and multiple treatment settings.

1 Introduction

Estimating causal effects is an important topic in many domains. For example, analyzing which drug will have a better effect for a patient; evaluating which kind of job training will improve employment rates. These problems usually requires answering counterfactual questions [1] such as: "if this patient received another treatment, will this patient have lower blood sugar?" The gold standard for causal inference is Randomized Controlled Trial (RCT) which randomly assigns participants into different treatment groups. However, in many times it is expensive, impractical to implement, and might raise ethical problems. As a result, estimate causal effects from observational studies is significantly necessary. In this work, we focus on estimating the individual-level causal effect which is also known as Individual Treatment Effect (ITE).

Estimating ITE from observational data is challenging for two reasons: 1) We only obtain the factual outcomes (without counterfactual outcomes). For example, if a patient received a treatment, we could not obtain the results that the same patient received another treatment under the same situation. 2) Observational studies usually include selection bias. For example, richer patients might choose expensive treatments while poor patients prefer the cheap ones. Therefore, the sample distribution may differ significantly across different treatment

T. Mantoro et al. (Eds.): ICONIP 2021, CCIS 1516, pp. 20–27, 2021.
https://doi.org/10.1007/978-3-030-92307-5_3

groups. If we use standard supervised learning, the model might overfit to specific regions and thus could not generalize well to the entire distribution.

In this paper, we proposed multi-domain adversarial balancing (MDAB) to solve the problems in estimating ITE. MDAB incorporates multi-domain adversarial learning with context-aware sample balancing. It is applicable to any number of treatments. Our contributions are two-fold:

1. We propose the approach MDAB, which simultaneously learns confounder weights and sample weights through an adversarial learning architecture. MDAB regards multiple treatments as multiple domains and attempts to generate balanced distributions through multi-domain learning. Moreover, sample weights are calculated and combined to the factual loss which further reduce the selection bias.
2. MDAB is empirically validated in public observational datasets, the results demonstrate that it has a significant improvement compared to various state-of-the-art methods for both binary and multiple ITE estimations.

2   Related Work

Various methods have been proposed for estimating causal effect from observational data. A common method is re-weighting some instances to balance the control and treated distributions. A large proportion of re-weighting approaches is related to Inverse Propensity Weighting (IPW) [2]. Recently, many machine learning methods have been proposed. Balancing neural networks (BNN) [3] uses representation learning [4] to learn a balanced confounder distribution between the control and treatment groups. Counterfactual Regression Networks (CFR-NET) [5,6] further uses different discrepancy metrics to measure the imbalance across treatment groups. [7] identify disentangled representations of underlying factors and leverage this knowledge to reduce the negative impact of selection bias. While these methods reduce selection bias, they predominately focused on the basic setting with only binary treatments. This work focuses on handling selection bias for the ITE estimation with any number of treatments.

3   Methodology

3.1   Problem Settings and Assumptions

Problem Setting. Assume a dataset $\mathcal{D} = [x_i, t_i, y_i]_{i=1}^N$ has the following contents: for each instance, we have features (also known as confounders or covariates) $x_i \in \mathcal{X}$, a treatment $\mathcal{T} \to \mathbb{R}^k$ selected from a set of treatments $\mathcal{T}$, and an observed outcome $y_i \in \mathcal{Y}$ as a result of receiving treatment t_i. In our data, for each instance we only have the observed outcome of received treatment, the outcomes of other treatments cannot be observed (counterfactual outcomes). The set of treatments can be two (binary treatments) or more (multiple treatments). This paper focuses on estimating Individual Treatment Effect (ITE) for each instance. The target is to train a model f that can estimate both observed and counterfactual outcomes.

Assumptions. Our analysis relies on the strong ignorability assumption [8], as follows:

1. Unconfoundedness – Given confounders x, the assignment to treatment t is independent of outcome Y. Formally, $Y \perp t \,|\, x$. This assumption is also referred as no unobserved confounders and requires that all influences on both Y and t are measured.
2. Overlap – For each instance, there is nonzero probability of being assigned to any treatment. Formally, $0 < \Pr(t \,|\, x) < 1$, $\forall x \in \mathcal{X}$, $\forall t \in \mathcal{T}$.

3.2   Adversarial Confounder Balancing

In our method, we learn a representation $G_f : \mathcal{X} \to \mathbb{R}^l$ and a function G_y. The learned representation trades off two objectives: 1) reduce the prediction error of the observed outcomes (also known as factual loss), and 2) reduce the imbalance of the distributions between treatment groups. The first objective can be achieved by minimizing the "supervised loss" of the observed outcomes on a training set. To achieve the second objective, we proposed multi-domain adversarial balancing (MDAB).

Adversarial balancing has been used in causal inference. In the binary case of the ITE, the control and treated distributions can be regarded as the source and target domain [3]. We can learn a high-level representation where the treated and control distributions is as indistinguishable as possible. However, in multiple treatment cases, there are more than two distributions that need to be balanced. Multi-domain learning (MDL) learns a model of minimal risk from datasets drawn from multiple distinct underlying distributions. Based on this idea, we consider multiple treatments as multiple domains and attempts to generate balanced distributions through MDL.

The MDAB architecture is shown in Fig. 1. Let G_f be the feature extractor that learns a representation from observed variables, with parameter θ_f. Let G_y computes the potential outcomes of each treatment, with parameter θ_y. We use multi-head architecture for G_y. Each head is only trained on samples with respective treatment and only predicts one potential outcome. Let G_d with parameter θ_d be a domain discriminator which classifies the learned representations to the observed treatment, i.e., for an instance received a treatment t_i, we want to map the representation of this instance to class t_i. This is in contrast to standard GAN framework that we apply a multi-class cross-entropy loss of classifying in G_d. The prediction loss and the domain loss can be noted as

$$\mathcal{L}_y^i (\theta_f, \theta_y) = \| G_y (G_f (x_i; \theta_f); \theta_y) - y_i \|^2, \tag{1}$$

$$\mathcal{L}_d^i (\theta_f, \theta_d) = - \sum_k \log (G_d (G_f (x_i; \theta_f); \theta_d), t_i). \tag{2}$$

Model training contains two steps: 1) train G_d to maximize the probability of correctly classifying the treatment each instance received (multi-class classification), and 2) train G_f and G_y to minimize the accuracy of multi-class classification and the factual loss, that is

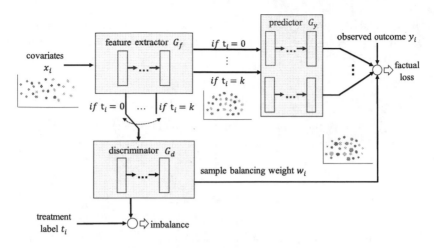

Fig. 1. The proposed MDAB architecture. Invariant representations can be obtained by the min-max game between G_f and G_d, and sample balancing weight is incorporated to further reduce the selection bias.

$$\mathcal{L}\left(\theta_f, \theta_y, \theta_d\right) - \frac{1}{N} \sum_{i=1}^{N} \left(\mathcal{L}_y^i\left(\theta_f, \theta_y\right) - \alpha \mathcal{L}_d^i\left(\theta_f, \theta_d\right)\right), \tag{3}$$

$$\hat{\theta}_d = \operatorname*{argmax}_{\theta_d} \mathcal{L}\left(\hat{\theta}_f, \hat{\theta}_y, \theta_d\right), \tag{4}$$

$$\left(\hat{\theta}_f, \hat{\theta}_y\right) = \operatorname*{argmin}_{\theta_f, \theta_y} \mathcal{L}\left(\theta_f, \theta_y, \hat{\theta}_d\right). \tag{5}$$

A saddle point $(\hat{\theta}_f, \hat{\theta}_y, \hat{\theta}_d)$ can be optimized by achieving an equilibrium between the prediction performance and the balance among treatment groups.

3.3 Context-Aware Sample Balancing

Adversarial confounder balancing uses re-weighting to determine the influence of a feature and thus enables to reduce certain selection bias. However, [6] pointed out that the learned representation cannot and should not remove all the selection bias, as the confounders not only contribute to choosing a treatment but also to determining the potential outcomes. Therefore, they incorporated a context-aware importance sampling weights into representation learning.

Borrow the idea from [6], our proposed method incorporates context-aware sample balancing to the multi-domain adversarial balancing framework. Our method has two major differences with [6] in calculating the importance weight: 1) instead of training an additional network, our method can directly use the output of G_d (the probability of assigning the observed t_i conditioned on the learned representation) to calculate the weight, 2) in contrast to [6] which can only be applied to binary treatment, our method is extended to address any number of treatments. The weight can be calculated by importance sampling and the output of G_d, formally

$$w_i(\theta_f, \theta_d) = 1 + \frac{\Pr(t_i)}{1 - \Pr(t_i)} \cdot \frac{1 - G_d\left(G_f\left(x_i; \theta_f\right); \theta_d\right)}{G_d\left(G_f\left(x_i; \theta_f\right); \theta_d\right)}, \tag{6}$$

where $\Pr(t_i)$ is the proportion of the instances using the treatment t_i.

Therefore, the objective function incorporating context-aware sample balancing becomes as the follows:

$$\mathcal{L}\left(\theta_f, \theta_y, \theta_d\right) = \frac{1}{N} \sum_{i=1}^{N} \left(w_i(\theta_f, \theta_d)\mathcal{L}_y^i\left(\theta_f, \theta_y\right) - \alpha \mathcal{L}_d^i\left(\theta_f, \theta_d\right)\right). \tag{7}$$

The updates of Eqs. (4–5) can be implemented using stochastic gradient descent. This leads to generate representations that are balanced among different treatment groups and also discriminative for prediction at the same time.

4   Experiment

4.1   Datasets

We use two semi-synthetic datasets (IHDP and News 4/8/16) and one real-world dataset (Jobs) to evaluate the performance of MDAB and compare to various state-of-the-art methods. Each dataset is randomly split into 63/27/10 train/validation/test set. We repeated experiments on IHDP 1000 times as previously used by [5], and repeated experiments on News 50 times as used by [17].

Infant Health and Development Program (IHDP): IHDP data [10] is from a randomized study that analyzes the influence of specialist visits to the childen's cognitive development. It consists data of 747 children with 25 confounders (features of the children and their mothers). The potential outcomes were simulated using the NPCI package [11].

Jobs: Jobs data [12] is composed of randomized data from the National Supported Work program and observational studies. The treatment is job training, and the outcomes are income and employment status after training. The dataset consists of 722 randomized samples and 2490 non-randomized samples, all with 8 covariates such as age, education and previous earnings.

News-2/4/8/16: The News dataset is composed of 5000 randomly sampled news based on the NY Times corpus [9]. The treatments (2/4/8/16) represent the number of news-viewing devices, such as PC, smartphone, television, etc. The outcome is the readers opinion of news articles viewing on certain devices.

4.2   Metrics and Settings

Metrics. We use two metrics to measure ITE for the semi-synthetic datasets. The expected Precision in Estimation of Heterogeneous Effect (PEHE) is defined in [3] for binary treatments. The error of the predict effect and the ground-truth effect is measured, that is

$$\epsilon_{PEHE}^{0,1} = \sqrt{\frac{1}{N} \sum_{i=1}^{N} \left(\widehat{\tau}_i - \tau_i \right)^2}, \tag{8}$$

where $\widehat{\tau}_i = \hat{y}_i^1 - \hat{y}_i^0$ is the predicted effect, $\tau_i = y_i^1 - y_i^0$ is the ground-truth effect, and N is the number of instances. For multiple treatments, we extend Equation (8) to calculate the average PEHE between every possible pair of treatments:

$$\epsilon_{mean-PEHE} = \frac{1}{\binom{k}{2}} \sum_{p=0}^{k-1} \sum_{q=0}^{p-1} \epsilon_{PEHE}^{p,q}, \tag{9}$$

where k is the number of available treatments.

For datasets collected from RCT (Jobs), policy risk defined as the average loss in value when treating according to the policy, is used to measure the performance of ITE estimation [5].

Models. We compare MDAB to various previous methods: Ordinary Least Squares with treatment as one feature (OLS-1), OLS with different regressors for different treatments (OLS-multi), k-nearest neighbor (k-NN) [13], Bayesian additive regression tree (BART) [10], random forests (RForest) [14], causal forests (CForest) [15], treatment-agnostic representation network (TARNET) [5], generative adversarial nets for inference of individualized treatment effect estimation (GANITE) [16], counterfactual regression with importance sampling weights (CFR-ISW) [6], disentangled representations for counterfactual regression (DR-CFR) [7], and dose response network (DRNet) [17].

Since methods such as TARNET and CFR-ISW cannot be directly applied to multiple treatments, we extend them to deal with the multiple treatments as the follows: one of the treatments is selected as a control treatment, and the remaining treatments create binary ITE estimation against the selected control treatment. Hyperparameters such as the number of hidden layers and batch size are chosen using Random Search [18]. We run each algorithm 10 times with new train/valid/test splits and calculate the average performances.

4.3   Experimental Results

We evaluate the performance of the listed models in settings of binary and multiple treatments. The results are shown in Table 1. For the IHDP dataset, MDAB achieves the best performance by a large margin (reduce $\epsilon_{PEHE}^{0,1}$ by 12% compared to the second-best method DR-CFR). For Jobs and News-2, MDAB reaches the second best in terms of R_{Pol} and $\epsilon_{PEHE}^{0,1}$. For the multiple treatment datasets (News-4/8/16), MDAB consistently outperforms all other methods in terms of $\epsilon_{mean-PEHE}$ (in many cases by large margin).

Table 1. Result represented in the form of "mean (standard deviation)". Bold shows the method that has the best performance. * indicates methods that MDAB shows a significant improvement over.

Methods	IHDP	Jobs	News-2	News-4	News-8	News-16
OLS-1	5.8 (.3)*	0.24 (.02)*	16.2 (.2)*	16.4 (.2)*	15.6 (.2)*	14.7 (.2)*
OLS-multi	2.5 (.1)*	0.24 (.02)*	12.9 (.2)*	13.7 (.1)*	14.3 (.2)*	12.9 (.1)*
k-NN	4.9 (.3)*	0.26 (.02)*	15.6 (.2)*	14.2(.2)*	15.2 (.2)*	14.1 (.2)*
BART	2.4 (.1)*	0.25 (.02)*	14.1 (.2)*	13.9 (.1)*	13.1 (.1)*	12.7 (.1)*
RForest	5.5 (.3)*	0.28 (.02)*	24.3 (.2)*	22.6 (.2)*	20.9 (.1)*	17.8 (.2)*
CForest	4.2 (.3)*	0.22 (.01)	25.1 (.1)*	23.2 (.2)*	21.8 (.1)*	17.9 (.2)*
TARNET	0.95 (.1)*	0.21 (.02)	15.5 (.1)*	16.2 (.1)*	14.3 (.1)*	14.3 (.1)*
GANITE	2.4 (.4)*	**0.15 (.01)**	13.7 (.1)*	15.1 (.1)*	13.9 (.1)*	13.5 (.1)*
CFR-ISW	0.77 (.1)*	0.20 (.01)	10.9 (.1)*	12.9 (.1)*	11.7 (.1)*	10.9 (.1)*
DR-CFR	0.65 (.4)*	0.22 (.01)	9.4 (.1)	12.2 (.1)*	12.0 (.1)*	11.5 (.1)*
DRNet	0.81 (.5)*	0.26 (.02)*	**8.2 (.1)**	11.6 (.1)	10.2 (.1)	10.4 (.1)*
MDAB	**0.57 (.1)**	0.18 (.01)	8.6 (.1)	**11.0 (.1)**	**9.6 (.1)**	**9.3 (.1)**

The reasons that MDAB performs better are two-fold: 1) unlike other methods that are designed for binary treatments and only be simply extend to multiple treatments by training pairs of the binary treatments, MDAB using multi-domain learning can be natural applied to multiple treatment and thus achieves better performance; 2) methods such as DR-CFR and DRNet focus on learning confounder weights to generate a balanced representation, while MDAB simultaneously learn confounder weights and sample weights to further reduce the selection bias. Therefore, MDAB significantly outperforms other methods.

4.4 Discussion

The experimental results provide various insights of the MDAB framework for ITE estimation. MDAB can not only be directly applied to any number of treatments but also outperforms previous methods in both binary and multiple treatment settings. A limitation is that MDAB can only be applied to ITE in the static setting currently. Extending MDAB to address the longitudinal setting would be an interesting topic.

4.5 Conclusion

In this paper we proposed a novel method MDAB for the ITE estimation. MDAB simultaneously learns confounder weights and sample weights through an adversarial learning architecture to reduce selection bias. We demonstrated that it outperforms many state-of-the-art methods on benchmark datasets and it is applicable to any number of treatments. Therefore, it has a potential to provide useful insights for observational studies for various domains, including healthcare, economics and education.

References

1. Rubin, D.B.: Causal inference using potential outcomes: design, modeling, decisions. J. Am. Stat. Assoc **100**(469), 322–331 (2005)
2. Austin, P.C.: An introduction to propensity score methods for reducing the effects of confounding in observational studies. Multivariate Behav. Res. **46**(3), 399–424 (2011)
3. Johansson, F., Shalit, U., Sontag, D.: Learning representations for counterfactual inference. In: International Conference on Machine Learning, pp. 3020–3029. PMLR (2016)
4. Bengio, Y., Courville, A., Vincent, P.: Representation learning: a review and new perspectives. IEEE Trans. Pattern Anal. Mach. Intell. **35**(8), 1798–1828 (2013)
5. Shalit, U., Johansson, F.D., Sontag, D.: Estimating individual treatment effect: generalization bounds and algorithms. In: International Conference on Machine Learning, pp. 3076–3085. PMLR (2017)
6. Hassanpour, N., Greiner, R.: Counterfactual regression with importance sampling weights. In: IJCAI, pp. 5880–5887 (2019)
7. Hassanpour, N., Greiner, R.: Learning disentangled representations for counterfactual regression. In: International Conference on Learning Representations (2019)
8. Rosenbaum, P.R., Rubin, D.B.: The central role of the propensity score in observational studies for causal effects. Biometrika **70**(1), 41–55 (1983)
9. Schwab, P., Linhardt, L., Karlen, W.: Perfect match: a simple method for learning representations for counterfactual inference with neural networks (2018). arXiv preprint arXiv:1810.00656
10. Hill, J.L.: Bayesian nonparametric modeling for causal inference. J. Comput. Graph. Stat. **20**(1), 217–240 (2011)
11. Dorie, V.: Non-parametrics for causal inference (2016)
12. LaLonde, R.J.: Evaluating the econometric evaluations of training programs with experimental data. Am. Econ. Rev. **76**, 604–620 (1986)
13. Crump, R.K., Hotz, V.J., Imbens, G.W., Mitnik, O.A.: Nonparametric tests for treatment effect heterogeneity. Rev. Econ. Stat. **90**(3), 389–405 (2008)
14. Breiman, L.: Random forests. Mach. Learn. **45**(1), 5–32 (2001)
15. Wager, S., Athey, S.: Estimation and inference of heterogeneous treatment effects using random forests. J. Am. Stat. Assoc **113**(523), 1228–1242 (2018)
16. Yoon, J., Jordon, J., Van Der Schaar, M.: Ganite: estimation of individualized treatment effects using generative adversarial nets. In: International Conference on Learning Representations (2018)
17. Schwab, P., Linhardt, L., Bauer, S., Buhmann, J.M., Karlen, W.: Learning counterfactual representations for estimating individual dose-response curves. In: Proceedings of the AAAI Conference on Artificial Intelligence, vol. 34, pp. 5612–5619 (2020)
18. Bergstra, J., Bengio, Y.: Random search for hyper-parameter optimization. J. Mach. Learn. Res. **13**(2), 281–305 (2012)

Exploring Self-training for Imbalanced Node Classification

Xin Juan[1], Meixin Peng[2], and Xin Wang[3(✉)]

[1] College of Software Engineering, Jilin University, Changchun 130012, China
[2] College of Computer Science and Technology, Jilin University,
Changchun 130012, China
[3] College of Artificial Intelligence, Jilin University, Changchun 130012, China
xinwang@jlu.edu.cn

Abstract. Graph Neural Networks (GNNs) have achieved tremendous success in various applications. However, datasets are usually imbalanced in many real-world scenarios. When trained on an imbalanced dataset, the performance of GNNs is distant from satisfactory for nodes of minority classes. Due to the small population, these minority nodes have less engagement in the objective function of training and the message-passing mechanism behind GNNs exacerbates this problem further. Hence, in this paper, we present a novel model-agnostic framework, named SET-GNN, which utilizes self-training to expand the labeled training set through using pseudo-labeled nodes for improving the performance of the semi-supervised learning based on GNNs for imbalanced node classification. Extensive experiments on various real-world datasets demonstrate SET-GNN is able to achieve state-of-the-art performance on solving the imbalanced node classification problem.

Keywords: Self-training · Pre-training · Imbalanced node classification · Graph Neural Networks

1 Introduction

Nowadays, graph-structured data can be found in a broad spectrum of application domains, such as social networks [8]. Different from image and text, graph-structured data with rich structures and inter dependencies can not be captured by Convolutional Nerual Networks (CNNs) on a regular grid and sequence. However, motivated by the achievements of CNNs in Computer Vision (CV), GNNs transfer convolutional operators to the graph domain and break the limitation that Deep Neural Networks are not applicable to graph-structured data. Graph Neural Networks, following a neighborhood aggregation scheme, are often trained in an end-to-end manner towards some specific tasks and achieve the competitive performance in various graph-based applications, such as node classification, link prediction and graph classification.

However, current GNNs and their variants ignore two important limitations. On the one hand, the impressive achievements of GNNs rely on a large amount of

© Springer Nature Switzerland AG 2021
T. Mantoro et al. (Eds.): ICONIP 2021, CCIS 1516, pp. 28–36, 2021.
https://doi.org/10.1007/978-3-030-92307-5_4

artificially annotated data, which is time-consuming and resource-costly. In the setting of semi-supervised learning, only the labeled nodes are actively involved during the training, while the rich information of unlabeled node are typically ignored. On the other hand, imbalanced data is ubiquitous in the real world, where large-scale datasets often exhibit long-tailed label distributions. For example, for the cora data set, the majority class with the most nodes accounted for 29% of the total nodes size, and the minority class with the smallest nodes accounted for 7% of the total nodes size. The above two limitations further hinder further hinders GNNs in making correct prediction. In order to solve the above limitations, a natural solution is to augment the labeled training set by obtaining more labels for unlabeled nodes, which can effectively alleviate the phenomenon of long-tailed label distributions. Recently, Self-training [3] is a well-known semi-supervised learning method, which has achieved fruitful progresses in various domains such as Computer Vision [7] and Natural Language Processing [4]. In the self-training setting, a base learner is firstly trained on labeled set. Then, the base learner is utilized to assign pseudo-labels for unlabeled data. Due to the impressive abilities of self-training, we assign pseudo-labels to unlabeled nodes for augmenting labeled training set.

Before utilizing self-training to resolve the aforementioned limitations, we first analysis the problems of self-training on the generated pseudo-labels noise. Since the labeled set is usually insufficient for learning, it is inevitable that the local classifier will misclassify a certain amount of unlabeled data. Thus, in preliminary training epochs, model will persistently learn wrong knowledge from these 'bad' samples and the mislabeled samples will keep on affecting the model in the following training epochs, resulting in irreparable impact. Therefore, it is obvious that identifying and removing the mislabeled samples in each iteration might help improve the generalization ability of the learned hypothesis. Specifically, in this paper, we aim to design an effective framework to solve the imbalanced node classification problem by employing self-training. In essence, we are facing with two challenges. First, how to design a strategy for alleviating the imbalanced node classification by utilizing self-training? Second, how to minimize the noise introduced by self-training?

In order to solve the aforementioned two challenges, we propose a novel model-agnostic framework, named SElf-Training Graph Neural Network (SET-GNN), which constructs a self-training learning task with concatenating the 'pseudo-labeled' data with the labeled training data and increases the contribution of minority nodes in the objective function to promote the propagation of minority nodes in the message passing process. By jointly optimizing the objective functions of node classification and self-training learning, the proposed framework is expected to improve the performance of GNNs on imbalanced node classification task. The main contributions can be summarized as follows:

- We investigate a novel problem of exploring the self-training learning for imbalanced node classification.

- We propose a model-agnostic approach for improving the performance on various GNNs, which can effectively augment the proportion of minority nodes in the labeled training set.
- Extensive experiments on real-world datasets demonstrate the effectiveness of our framework on imbalanced node classification and benefit various GNNs.

2   SET-GNN

In this section, we introduce our framework, SET-GNN, which integrates the shared GNN encoder, self-training module and loss construction. The architecture of SET-GNN is illustrated in Fig. 1.

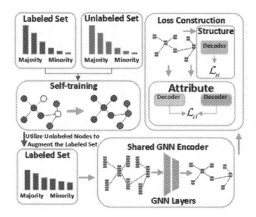

Fig. 1. Overall framework of the proposed SET-GNN. It consists of three main components: (1) The shared GNN encoder generates node representations of input graph, (2) self-training module assigns pseudo-labels to unlabeled nodes, and (3) Loss construction from structural and feature information.

2.1   Shared GNN Encoder

In our work, we take the GNN as the shared encoder, due to its effectiveness. The GCN induces the representation of the target node through message passing mechanism, which aggregates the feature information from neighboring nodes. Meanwhile, increasing the number of GCN layers can help the target node capture the feature information of higher-order neighbor nodes.

Formally, given a graph $\mathcal{G}$ and its adjacent matrix $\mathbf{A} \in \{0,1\}^{N \times N}$, The node representation is obtained by the following formulation:

$$\mathbf{Z} = \widetilde{\mathbf{L}}_{sym} \sigma \left(\widetilde{\mathbf{L}}_{sym} \mathbf{X} \mathbf{W}_0 \right) \mathbf{W}_1, \tag{1}$$

where $\mathbf{W}_0$ and $\mathbf{W}_1$ are weight matrices. $\mathbf{X} \in \mathbb{R}^{N \times d}$ denotes the feature matrix. d is the dimension of node features. σ represents the RELU activation function.

$\widetilde{\mathbf{L}}_{sym}$ is the normalisd symmetric adjacency matrix, which is defined as:

$$\widetilde{\mathbf{L}}_{sym} = \widetilde{\mathbf{D}}^{-\frac{1}{2}}\widetilde{\mathbf{A}}\widetilde{\mathbf{D}}^{-\frac{1}{2}},\tag{2}$$

where $\widetilde{\mathbf{D}}$ is the degree matrix of $\widetilde{\mathbf{A}}$, $\widetilde{\mathbf{A}} = \mathbf{A} + \mathbf{I}$. $\mathbf{I} \in \mathbb{R}^{N \times N}$ is the identity matrix.

2.2   Self-training for Assigning Pseudo-labels

In the setting of semi-supervised learning, since only very few labeled nodes in the graph, it further hinders GNNs in making correct prediction for node classification. One natural solution is to augment the training set, i.e., obtaining more labels for data samples. However, obtaining numerous annotation nodes is time-consuming and resource-costly. An alternative way is to employ self-training method, which assigns pseudo-labels to unlabeled nodes for enlarging the size of labeled training set. In this sense, we can improve the performance for both minority and majority nodes in the setting of imbalanced node classification. Specially, we exploit a popular self-training method, Label Propagation (LP) [11], to obtain additional supervision information for node classification.

LP applies the theory of Gaussian field and minimizes quadratic energy function to train the function f_{lp} for generating pseudo-labels. The energy function is defined as:

$$E(f_{lp}) = \frac{1}{2} \sum_{i,j} w_{i,j}(f_{lp}(\mathbf{v}_i) - f_{lp}(\mathbf{v}_j))^2,\tag{3}$$

where $w_{i,j}$ denotes the correlation coefficient between node v_i and node v_j. The process of obtaining pseudo-labels via LP can be formalized as:

$$P(\mathbf{Y}_u = c) = \sum_{j \in \mathcal{N}(u)} \frac{1}{D_u} P(\mathbf{Y}_j = c),\tag{4}$$

where $\mathcal{N}(u)$ denotes the set of the neighboring nodes of node u. The aforementioned limitation that the labeled training set is insufficient for learning in preliminary training epochs, which will introduce a great number of noise in the pseudo-labels assigned by the LP algorithm. Therefore, we utilize the condition that the output result of the neural network is consistent with the pseudo-label result assigned by LP algorithm to filter unlabeled nodes for augmenting the labeled training set. Meantime we construct auxiliary edges on minority nodes. Through the above method, we not only alleviate the problem of imbalanced class problem of the labeled training set, but also enhance the engagement of minority nodes in the message passing process.

2.3   Loss Construction

In imbalanced node classification, the training process is dominated by majority nodes since they have a much larger population than minority nodes. Hence, it is important to enhance the contribution of minority nodes and eliminate such bias. Discarding label information for training can effectively reduce the above intrinsic label bias. Thus, we construct two loss functions from structure and feature information.

From the structural perspective, we utilize the assumption of link prediction that the connected nodes tend to be similar, so the distance between the two nodes in the hidden space should be close. Specifically, we first randomly sample some edges from the graph and mask them. Then we try to recover the original graph structure by predicting whether there is an edge between a pair of nodes. The loss function for structure is defined as:

$$\mathcal{L}_{st} = \sum_{(v_i, v_j) \in \mathcal{V}} \mathcal{L}\left(g_\delta\left(z_i - z_j\right), e_{ij}\right), \tag{5}$$

where $\mathcal{L}(\cdot)$ is the loss function with cross-entropy, and g_δ denotes the decoder that maps the hidden embedding to one-dimensional space $\hat{e}_{ij}$. The e_{ij} is the real edge between v_i and v_j in graph. z_i and z_j are the hidden representations of node i and node j, respectively.

From the feature perspective, we utilize real-labels and pseudo-labels for prediction to construct the loss. Two different decoders are exploited for the real-labels prediction task and the pseudo-labels prediction task. Specifically, after obtaining node representations from shared GNN encoder, we feed them into two different decoders for node classification and get the predicted classes $\hat{\mathbf{Y}}_i$. The formulation of obtaining $\hat{\mathbf{Y}}_i$ can be defined as:

$$\hat{\mathbf{Y}} = \text{softmax}(\mathbf{v}) = \frac{exp(\mathbf{v})}{\sum_{i=1}^{|\mathbf{Y}|} exp(\mathbf{v}_i)}, \tag{6}$$

where $\mathbf{v}$ denotes the output result of the decoder and $|\mathbf{Y}|$ is the number of classes. Given a class label c for node u, the classifier module is optimized using cross-entropy loss as:

$$\mathcal{L}_{cl} = -\sum_{u \in V_L \cup V_U} \sum_c \mathbb{1}(\mathbf{Y}_u == c) \cdot \mathbf{Y}_u \cdot \ln \hat{\mathbf{Y}}_u, \tag{7}$$

where $\mathbb{1}(\cdot)$ is an indicator function. Then we combine the two loss function to get the overall objective function, which is defined as:

$$\mathcal{L} = \mathcal{L}_{cl} + \lambda * \mathcal{L}_{st}, \tag{8}$$

where λ is the hyper-parameter to balance the two aspects of training.

3   Experiments

In this section, we conduct experiments on three widely-used datasets to verify the effectiveness of the proposed framework.

3.1 Experimental Settings

Datasets. We evaluate our framework using three widely-used datasets: Cora, CiteSeer and PubMed. The statistics of each dataset are summarized in Table 1. Through observation, we can easily find that all the datasets are class imbalanced.

Table 1. Statistics of the datasets.

	Cora	Citeseer	PubMed
Nodes	2,708	3,327	19,717
Edges	5,429	4,732	44,338
Features	1,433	3,703	500
Classes	7	6	3
Imbalance-ratio	24%	38%	53%

Baselines. To verify the effectiveness of the proposed framework, we evaluate it using traditional imbalanced classification algorithm: Re-weight [9] and Over-sampling. We compare SET-GNN with network embedding and GNNs: DeepWalk [5] and GCN [2] . We also make the comparison with the variants of SMOTE: Embed-SMOTE [1] and GraphSMOTE [10].

Evaluation Metrics. We follow the common metrics for imbalanced classification to evaluate the performance, given by ACC, AUC and F-score.

Experimental Setting. We set the size of hidden embedding l as 128, the dropout rate as 0.5, the learning rate as 0.02 and β as 1. The hyper-parameter λ is searched in $\{0.01, 0.1, 1, 5, 10, 20, 50\}$. We randomly select half of the classes as the minority classes. Then we randomly sample 10 nodes from the minority classes and 20 nodes from the majority classes to form the training set.

Table 2. Comparison of different methods for imbalanced node classification.

Method	Cora			Citeseer			PubMed		
	ACC	AUC	F-Score	ACC	AUC	F-Score	ACC	AUC	F-Score
GCN	0.714	0.929	0.709	0.504	0.823	0.502	0.713	0.865	0.704
DeepWalk	0.672	0.809	0.651	0.369	0.337	0.621	0.657	0.742	0.562
Re-weight	0.697	0.928	0.684	0.567	0.861	0.52	0.739	0.898	0.737
Over-sampling	0.692	0.918	0.666	0.518	0.839	0.491	0.703	0.885	0.693
Embed-SMOTE	0.683	0.913	0.673	0.549	0.871	0.497	0.606	0.869	0.598
GraphSMOTE	0.736	0.934	0.727	0.549	0.836	0.548	0.745	0.907	0.744
SET-GNN	**0.765**	**0.952**	**0.758**	**0.663**	**0.878**	**0.628**	**0.759**	**0.918**	**0.748**

3.2 Imbalanced Classification Performance

The comparison results of our framework and the baselines on three datasets are shown in Table 2. SET-GNN shows significant improvements on imbalanced node classification, compared to Over-sampling and Re-weight, which are traditional imbalanced classification algorithm. Compared with over-sampling, SET-GNN achieves an improvement of 0.034, 0.039, 0.033 in AUC. Compared with the recent Graph-SMOTE, SET-GNN also obtains an improvement of 0.018, 0.042, 0.011 in AUC on Cora and Citeseer respectively. These results demonstrate the advantages of SET-GNN over others, in utilizing self-training for alleviating the impact of majority classes on node classification and enhancing the engagement of minority nodes.

3.3 Model-Agnostic Method for GNNs

In this subsection, we analyze the performance changes of the internal base model. We equip several state-of-the-art GNN models, i.e., GCN, GAT and SGC [6] with SET-GNN for illustrating the generality of our proposed framework. Comparison between SET-GNN and original GNN model is presented in Table 3. We can fine that SET-GNN adapts well to the three widely-used GNNs and improves them by a large margin on Cora, Citeseer and PubMed. For example, on Cora dataset, the performance that our SET-GNN achieves are 0.952, 0.942, 0.949 in AUC, which are 0.023, 0.021, 0.023 higher than the base model for Cora dataset, respectively. The results suggest that SET-GNN is a general framework that can be employed in various GNNs to boost their performance.

Table 3. Performance of SET-GNN and its internal base model.

Method	Cora		Citeseer		PubMed	
	ACC	AUC	ACC	AUC	ACC	AUC
GCN	0.714	0.929	0.504	0.823	0.713	0.865
SET-GNN$_{GCN}$	**0.765**	**0.952**	**0.663**	**0.878**	**0.759**	**0.918**
GAT	0.732	0.923	0.548	0.860	0.715	0.874
SET-GNN$_{GAT}$	**0.754**	**0.942**	**0.643**	**0.871**	**0.744**	**0.885**
SGC	0.711	0.926	0.543	0.874	0.706	0.871
SET-GNN$_{SGC}$	**0.768**	**0.949**	**0.652**	**0.893**	**0.752**	**0.924**

3.4 Parameter Analysis

In this subsection, we analyze the performance changes of the proposed framework w.r.t hyper-paremeters λ. The hyper-parameter λ is used to assess sensitivity to the SET-GNN by affecting the weight of $\mathcal{L}_{st}$. The experimental results are shown in Fig. 2, we make the following observations: (1) for Cora and Citeseer, the performance of SET-GNN steadily improves as λ increases from 0 to

1; and (2) the result supports that incorporating self-supervised link prediction can boost the performance of GNNs. However, as λ further increases, the performance reduces due to the over-fitting on the above task.

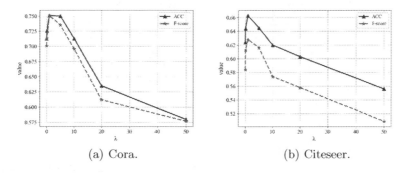

(a) Cora.   (b) Citeseer.

Fig. 2. Influence of γ on two datasets.

4   Conclusion

Graph neural networks can extract effective node representation by aggregating and transforming node features within the neighborhood. However, recent studies have shown that GNNs tend to classify the minority nodes into the majority classes when the training dataset is imbalanced. Therefore, we propose a novel framework called SET-GNN, which effectively enhances the engagement of the minority nodes by edge augmentation and overcomes the intrinsic label bias via self-supervised learning. Experimental results demonstrate that SET-GNN outperforms aforementioned baselines on a wide range of real-world datasets.

Acknowledgements. This work was supported by a grant from the National Natural Science Foundation of China under grants (No. 61872161 and No. 61976103), and the Nature Science Foundation of Jilin Province(No. 20200201297JC), and the Foundation of Development and Reform of Jilin Province(No. 2019C053-8), and the Foundation of Jilin Educational Committee (No. JJKH20191257KJ) and the Fundamental Research Funds for the Central Universities, JLU.

References

1. Ando, S., Huang, C.Y.: Deep over-sampling framework for classifying imbalanced data. In: Ceci, M., Hollmén, J., Todorovski, L., Vens, C., Džeroski, S. (eds.) ECML PKDD 2017. LNCS (LNAI), vol. 10534, pp. 770–785. Springer, Cham (2017). https://doi.org/10.1007/978-3-319-71249-9_46
2. Kipf, T.N., Welling, M.: Semi-supervised classification with graph convolutional networks (2016). arXiv preprint arXiv:1609.02907
3. Li, Q., Han, Z., Wu, X.M.: Deeper insights into graph convolutional networks for semi-supervised learning. In: Proceedings of the AAAI Conference on Artificial Intelligence, vol. 32 (2018)

4. Mukherjee, S., Awadallah, A.: Uncertainty-aware self-training for few-shot text classification. Adv. Neural Inf. Process. Syst. **33**, 1–14 (2020)
5. Perozzi, B., Al-Rfou, R., Skiena, S.: Deepwalk: online learning of social representations. In: Proceedings of the 20th ACM SIGKDD International Conference on Knowledge Discovery and Data Mining, pp. 701–710 (2014)
6. Wu, F., Souza, A., Zhang, T., Fifty, C., Yu, T., Weinberger, K.: Simplifying graph convolutional networks. In: International Conference on Machine Learning, pp. 6861–6871 (2019)
7. Xie, Q., Luong, M.T., Hovy, E., Le, Q.V.: Self-training with noisy student improves imagenet classification. In: Proceedings of the IEEE/CVF Conference on Computer Vision and Pattern Recognition, pp. 10687–10698 (2020)
8. Xu, J., et al.: Multivariate relations aggregation learning in social networks. In: Proceedings of the ACM/IEEE Joint Conference on Digital Libraries in 2020, pp. 77–86 (2020)
9. Yuan, B., Ma, X.: Sampling+ reweighting: boosting the performance of adaboost on imbalanced datasets. In: The 2012 International Joint Conference on Neural Networks (IJCNN), pp. 1–6. IEEE (2012)
10. Zhao, T., Zhang, X., Wang, S.: Tgraphsmote: imbalanced node classification on graphs with graph neural networks. In: Proceedings of the 14th International Conference on Web Search and Data Mining, pp. 600–608 (2021)
11. Zhu, X., Ghahramani, Z., Lafferty, J.D.: Semi-supervised learning using gaussian fields and harmonic functions. In: Proceedings of the 20th International conference on Machine learning (ICML-03), pp. 912–919 (2003)

Leveraging Multi-granularity Heterogeneous Graph for Chinese Electronic Medical Records Summarization

Rui Luo, Ye Wang, Shan Zhao, Tongqing Zhou, and Zhiping Cai[✉]

College of Computer, National University of Defense Technology, Changsha, China
{luorui19,wangye19,zhaoshan18,zhoutongqing,zpcai}@nudt.edu.cn

Abstract. With the advancement of digitalization in the medical field, electronic medical data has gradually gathered for the exploration of intelligent diagnosing. In particular, electronic medical record (EMR) summarization techniques can help doctors carry out diagnosis and treatment services more effectively, thus presenting substantial practical value. However, we point out there lacks investigation and dedicated designs for Chinese EMRs summarization. In this paper, by studying the characteristics of Chinese EMRs, we propose a novel summarization model MCMS by combining multi-granularity heterogeneous graphs and graph attention networks. The model can further capture potential information in Chinese EMRs by constructing a heterogeneous graph structure of words, basic chapter units, and sentences. We construct a Chinese EMR dataset and validate the proposed model on it. Experimental results show that our model outperforms the state-of-the-art summarization models.

Keywords: Applications · Chinese electronic medical record · Text summarization · Elementary discourse unit · Heterogeneous graphs

1 Introduction

By using text summarization technology to process a patient's medical record, a summarization of the medical record can be generated. This summarization provides doctors with a clear visualization of the patient's past medical history, which can effectively help them make a diagnosis. Unlike English summarization, Chinese grammar is more complex, and reading comprehension in Chinese is very dependent on contextualization [1,2]. In Chinese, there are also cases such as multiple meanings of words [13], so when dealing with medical texts, generative automatic summarization cannot guarantee the accuracy of the meaning of medical text summarization. Therefore, we consider the targeted optimization of extracted summarization, so that the extracted electronic medical record summarization can be better.

© Springer Nature Switzerland AG 2021
T. Mantoro et al. (Eds.): ICONIP 2021, CCIS 1516, pp. 37–45, 2021.
https://doi.org/10.1007/978-3-030-92307-5_5

We believe that the structure of Chinese EMRs can be better represented by introducing elementary discourse units (EDUs), which will effectively improve the quality of generated summarization. In chapter analysis, EDU is the smallest unit in a text. By combining chapter analysis with existing text summarization techniques, the ability to exist text summarization techniques to understand the underlying information of the input text can be improved.

In this paper, our main contribution is to propose a multi-granularity summarization extraction model MCMS optimized for Chinese EMRs. The model is capable of further capturing potential information in Chinese EHRs by constructing a multi-grained graph structure of words, EDUs and sentences. MCMS has good applicability to both single-document and multi-document summarization. When tested on raw hospital data, MCMS shows better results than other extractive models that do not use pre-trained models.

2   Related Work

In recent years' research work, graph neural networks (GNNs) have shown their unique advantages. By combining GNNs with text summarization techniques, the quality of generated summarization can be similarly effectively improved. Xu [12] proposed an extractive summarization model based on BERT coding by combining graph convolutional networks (GCN) [5] with discourse graphs. The model can generate information-rich summarization with little redundant information. In the text summarization, the sentences are generally used as the nodes of GNN. Wang et al. [11] combined heterogeneous graphs with GNN and proposed a HeterSumGraph (HSG) model for modeling the input text. They proposed that the HSG model can further mine the potential information in the input text by iteratively training the word nodes and sentence nodes. At the same time, the HSG model can mine the document-to-document relationships through word nodes. This makes the HSG model equally applicable to both single-document and multi-document summarization. The above research inspires our work.

In NLP, medical texts have always been a hot topic of interest for researchers. For this reason, many papers of related research are published every year. The same is valid for research related to medical text summarization. Dernoncourt et al. [3] proposed a sequential sentence classification model based on ANNs, mainly used to summarize medical texts. Seva et al. [8] designed a machine learning pipeline for medical text summarization to save clinical workers' time searching clinically relevant literature and identifying key sentences that are clinically relevant. Similarly, for the problem of automatic text summarization in medical conversation contexts, Song et al. [9] proposed a hierarchical coding annotation system based on neural memory networks. This system can annotate important information (questions and answers) based on the conversation between a doctor and a patient and generate a summarization based on the annotated results.

3   Methodology

This section refers to Wang's HSG model [11] and proposes a heterogeneous graph neural network model consisting of word nodes, EDU nodes, and sentence nodes based on the HSG model. The model architecture is shown in Fig. 1. The whole model is divided into three parts, the construction of the heterogeneous graph, the update of node weights, and the selection of sentences. In the first part, we mainly encode the word nodes, EDU nodes, and sentence nodes and construct the graph structure, as shown in Fig. 2. Subsequently, in the second part, we iteratively update all nodes using graph attention networks. In the third part, we classify the sentence nodes in the heterogeneous graph, extract the selected sentence nodes, and compose the summarization.

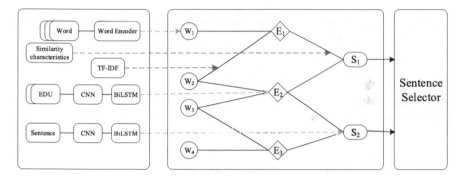

Fig. 1. The framework of MCMS. The left side is the encoding part, the middle is the heterogeneous graph part, and the right side is the sentence selection. The round nodes are word nodes, the diamond nodes are EDU nodes, and the oval nodes are sentence nodes. The yellow arrows indicate how the nodes are encoded, and the blue arrows indicate the feature information between the nodes. (Color figure online)

Suppose the document D consists of k sentences, i.e. $D = \{S_1, S_2, \cdots, S_k\}$, and a sentence contains m EDUs. We rate each sentence by a neural network and make a decision based on the rating. Our goal during training is to obtain an optimal sequence of sentences for the document D.

3.1   Construction of Heterogeneous Graphs

We use V to denote the set of nodes, E denote the edges between word nodes and EDU nodes, and E' denote the edges between EDU nodes and sentence nodes to construct an undirected anisotropic graph $G = \{V, E, E'\}$ by V, E and E'.

The node-set $V = V_w \bigcup V_e \bigcup V_s$, where $V_w = \{w_1, w_2, \cdots, w_n\}$, w_n denotes the nth word in the document, $V_e = \{d_1, d_2, \cdots, d_m\}$, d_m denotes the mth EDU in the document, and $V_s = \{s_1, s_2, \cdots, s_k\}$, s_k denotes the kth EDU in the document. E is a real-valued edge weight matrix, $e_{ij} \neq 0$, $i \in \{1, \cdots, n\}$, $j \in \{1, \cdots, m\}$. E' is a real-valued edge weight matrix, $e'_{jp} \neq 0$, $j \in \{1, \cdots, m\}$, $p \in \{1, \cdots, k\}$.

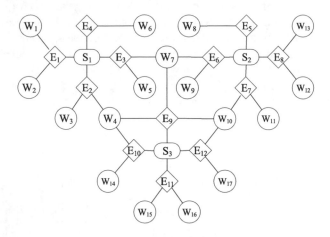

Fig. 2. Heterogeneous graph constructed from word nodes, EDU nodes, and sentence nodes. The length of the edges in the graph is independent of their feature information.

First, we use Glove to encode the vocabulary into word vectors. Meanwhile, we capture the local features of EDU and sentence by convolutional neural network CNN, and the global features of EDU by long and short-term memory network LSTM. The local features and global features are spliced as the encoding vectors of EDU nodes. The encoding vectors of sentence nodes are obtained in the same way as those of EDU nodes. To the joining edges of word nodes and EDU nodes, we add feature information computed by the TF-IDF method. This statistical method evaluates the importance of a word by counting the number of occurrences of the word in one document and the whole corpus, respectively. The more the word appears in a document, the more influential the word is. However, if the number of occurrences of the word in the corpus increases, the importance of the word decreases. Moreover, we add the feature information obtained by similarity calculation on the connecting edges of EDU nodes and sentence nodes. As shown in Fig. 2, there are only connecting edges between word nodes and EDU nodes and between EDU nodes and sentence nodes, and similar nodes are not connected in the whole heterogeneous graph.

3.2   Update of Node Weights

After the graph structure is built, given the node features of the graph as $V_w \cup V_e \cup V_s$, the edge features of the graph as $E \bigcup E'$. We need to update the semantic representation of the nodes in the graph. Here we perform message passing between nodes through graph attention network (GAT). We assume that h is the hidden state of the input node, $\mathbf{W}_a$ is the weight vector of the edge, $\mathbf{W}_q$ is the query vector, and $\mathbf{W}_k$ is the key vector. $\mathbf{e}_{ij}$ is the connected edge of word node and EDU node, and e'_{jh} is the connected edge of EDU node and sentence node. The specific settings of the GAT are as follows.

$$A_{ij} = LeakyReLU\left(\mathbf{W}_a\left[\mathbf{W}_q h_i; \mathbf{W}_k h_j; \mathbf{e}_{ij}\right]\right) \tag{1}$$

$$u_i = \sigma\left(\sum_{j\in i}\left(softmax_j A_{ij}\right)W_v h_j\right) + h_i \tag{2}$$

In Eqs. 1, $\mathbf{W}_a$, $\mathbf{W}_q$, $\mathbf{W}_k$ and $\mathbf{e}_{ij}$ are spliced together to calculate the Attention Score A_{ij}. A'_{jp} is calculated from $\mathbf{W}_a$, $\mathbf{W}_q$, $\mathbf{W}_k$ and $\mathbf{e}_{jp}$. All the matrices $\mathbf{W}$ are parameters that need to be trained for learning. To prevent the problem of gradient disappearance, we added a residual connection as shown in Eqs. 2. u_i is the output of the GAT layer. We integrate Eqs. 1 and Eqs. 2 into the function $gat(h_i, h_j, e_{ij})$. The inputs to this function are the hidden states of the two nodes and the connected edges.

We map the results of the GAT layer to a larger dimensional feature space through the FFN layer, then use ReLU to introduce nonlinearity for filtering, and finally recover back to the original dimensionality. With the computation of GAT and FFN layers, we can iteratively update between adjacent nodes. The following equation shows the process of updating from word nodes through EDU nodes and toward sentence nodes.

$$T^{t+1}_{w\to e} = GAT\left(K^t_e, K^t_w, K^t_w\right) \tag{3}$$

$$K^{t+1}_e = ReLU\left(FFN\left(T^{t+1}_{w\to e} + K^t_e\right)\right) \tag{4}$$

$$T^{t+1}_{e\to s} = GAT\left(K^t_s, K^{t+1}_e, K^{t+1}_e\right) \tag{5}$$

$$K^{t+1}_s = ReLU\left(FFN\left(T^{t+1}_{e\to s} + K^{t+1}_e\right)\right) \tag{6}$$

In Eqs. 3, $K^0_w = K^1_w = V_w$, $K^0_e = V_e$, $K^0_s = V_s$. K^t_s is used as the attention query, and both key and value are the same as K^t_e.

Taking Fig. 2 as an example, after the first-word node W_7 is initialized, we go through the GAT and FFN layers to update for its neighboring nodes. Then the update is further spread outward iteratively and passed until 3 sentences are reached. Throughout the update process, word nodes, EDU nodes, and sentence nodes update each other, while similar nodes are not connected, so there is no message passing between similar nodes.

Since we add the feature information of TF-IDF value and similarity to the graph, the important word nodes tend to aggregate the topic information in the document when performing iterative training. The EDU nodes with important word nodes will receive more attention from the model, and the probability of sentence nodes being selected as their parents will be greatly increased.

3.3   Selection of Sentences

After several rounds of iterative training, we obtained the final representation of all nodes. To generate the summarization, we need to select the sentences with high importance from the heterogeneous graph. When making predictions, the neural network outputs a probability distribution $\hat{\mathbf{y}} = \{\hat{y}_1, \cdots, \hat{y}_n\}$ that $\hat{y}_n$ represents the probability of the nth sentence being selected. This probability distribution will be used as the basis for sentence nodes to be selected as summaries. The model generates a summarization by selecting one sentence at a time until the number of selected sentences reaches a predefined summarization length. At this point, the selected sentences are stitched together in the order in which they were selected as the final summarization.

The Chinese electronic medical record summarization task is by nature a multi-document summarization. This is because we need to extract key information from many different types of EMRs to compose a summarization. In this paper, to facilitate data processing, we stitch multiple EMRs into one input document. This reduces the complexity of data pre-processing. However, the experiment can be completed without similar processing, but the data preprocessing effort will increase significantly.

In MCMS, all nodes are capable of being replaced by other semantic units. The combination of words, EDUs, and sentences can be replaced by the combination of words, sentences, and documents. Thus we can adapt different semantic units to different input data by combining different semantic units.

4   Experiment

We validate our model on the Chinese electronic medical record summarization task. The data used in our experiments are derived from real data from hospitals.

4.1   Data Set and Evaluation Indicators

We obtained over 10,000 hospital admissions from hospitals and selected patients who had only one complete hospitalization. Among the hospitalization information, there are different types of EMRs, such as admission records, ward records, surgery records, and discharge records. We selected the 'admission status' and 'hospitalization history' written by the doctor in the discharge summarization as the output of the training. Also, after careful study, we found that the hospitalization records contain many EMRs with invalid information and there are many EMRs with duplicate contents with other EMRs. For example, the contents recorded in the room visit records and consultation requests are particularly irrelevant compared to the contents of the summarization. The contents of the surgical application and the post-operative summarization were mostly duplicated, so we decided to remove similar EMRs from the training data after discussion. After filtering, all EMRs were stitched into one document as the training input. There are more than 4300 hospitalization records in the training set, 300 hospitalization records in the validation set, and 300 hospitalization records in the test set.

The judging metrics for this experiment are the rouge1, Rouge2, and RougeL values of the generated summarization.

4.2   Implementation Details

We get the embedding vector of the input words by GloVe. During initialization, we remove some of the words with low TF-IDF values. Each GAT layer is 8 heads with hidden size dh= 64, while the internal hidden size of the FFN layer is 512. during training, we use 16 batches and apply Adam optimizer with a learning rate of e-4. the maximum length of the input document is 50 sentences with no more than 20 sentences per EDUs, while the maximum length of each EDU is limited to 30 words. Training is stopped when the effective loss does not decrease for three consecutive iterations. The currently saved optimal model is used as the final model. Meanwhile, we limit the length of the output summarization to 15 sentences after counting the length of the output data in the dataset.

4.3   Experimental Results and Analysis

Table 1. Performance of our model and models of the same type on the Chinese EMR dataset.

Model	F1	F2	FL
LexRank [4]	22.2	11.2	17.6
TextRank [6]	27.5	12.5	21.9
PGN [7]	39.5	17.3	34.3
HSG [11]	42.5	28.2	35.6
MCMS	**47.7**	**30.6**	**39.1**
–Sent	46.7	19.7	30.6
–EDU	45.3	28.0	36.3

We performed training and testing on our constructed Chinese electronic medical record dataset, and the experimental results are shown in Table 1, where we evaluate the experimental results by F1, F2, and FL values. Due to the limitation of hardware facilities, we did not add pre-training work in MCMS, but this will be the direction of our future work. It is clear from the table that our model is ahead of the extractive summarization model without pre-training in all three evaluation metrics.

To verify the effectiveness of our graph structure with EDU nodes added, we also conducted ablation experiments, as shown in Table 1. There are two ablation experiments, one is to form a heterogeneous graph with word nodes and EDU nodes, and finally extract EDUs to form a summarization; the other is to form a heterogeneous graph with word nodes and EDU nodes, and finally extract sentences to form a summarization. The experimental results are shown in the table. After removing the heterogeneous graphs with multiple granularities, the performance of the model significantly decreases.

5   Conclusion

In this paper, we propose a multi-granularity-based Chinese electronic medical record summarization model MCMS. we construct a word-EDU-sentence three-layer graph structure by introducing EDUs and verify through experimental results that our model can better capture the underlying structure of the text. And our model can achieve better results on Chinese EMRs data compared with other models that also do not incorporate pre-training efforts. In the future, we will consider introducing pre-training models to further improve the effectiveness of text summarization.

Acknowledgments. This work is supported by the National Key Research and Development Program of China (2020YFC2003400).

References

1. Zhao, S., Hu, M., Cai, Z., Chen, H., Liu, F.: Dynamic modeling cross-and self-lattice attention network for Chinese ner. In: Proceedings of the AAAI Conference on Artificial Intelligence, vol. 35, pp. 14515–14523 (2021)
2. Zhao, S., Hu, M., Cai, Z., Liu, F.: Modeling dense cross-modal interactions for joint entity-relation extraction. In: IJCAI, pp. 4032–4038 (2020)
3. Dernoncourt, F., Lee, J.Y., Szolovits, P.: Neural networks for joint sentence classification in medical paper abstracts. In: EACL (2017)
4. Erkan, G., Radev, D.R.: Lexrank: graph-based lexical centrality as salience in text summarization. J. Artif. Intell. Res. **22**, 457–479 (2004)
5. Kipf, T., Welling, M.: Semi-supervised classification with graph convolutional networks (2017). ArXiv abs/1609.02907
6. Mihalcea, R., Tarau, P.: TextRank: bringing order into text. In: EMNLP, pp. 404–411 (2004)
7. See, A., Liu, P.J., Manning, C.D.: Get to the point: summarization with pointer-generator networks. In: ACL, pp. 1073–1083 (2017)
8. Ševa, J., Wackerbauer, M., Leser, U.: Identifying key sentences for precision oncology using semi-supervised learning. In: Proceedings of the BioNLP 2018 Workshop, pp. 35–46 (2018)
9. Song, Y., Tian, Y., Wang, N., Xia, F.: Summarizing medical conversations via identifying important utterances. In: COLING, pp. 717–729 (2020)
10. Wang, D., Liu, P., Zhong, M., Fu, J., Qiu, X., Huang, X.: Exploring domain shift in extractive text summarization (2019). ArXiv abs/1908.11664
11. Wang, D., Liu, P., Zheng, Y., Qiu, X., Huang, X.: Heterogeneous graph neural networks for extractive document summarization (2020). ArXiv abs/2004.12393

12. Xu, J., Durrett, G.: Neural extractive text summarization with syntactic compression. In: EMNLP/IJCNLP, pp. 3292–3303. ACL, Hong Kong (2019)
13. Zhao, S., Hu, M., Cai, Z., Zhang, Z., Zhou, T., Liu, F.: Enhancing chinese character representation with lattice-aligned attention. IEEE Trans. Neural Netw. Learn. Syst., 1–10 (2021). https://doi.org/10.1109/TNNLS.2021.3114378

Multi-objective Clustering: A Data-Driven Analysis of MOCLE, MOCK and Δ-MOCK

Adriano Kultzak[1], Cristina Y. Morimoto[1(✉)], Aurora Pozo[1], and Marcilio C. P. de Souto[2]

[1] Department of Informatics, Federal University of Paraná, Curitiba, Brazil
cristina.morimoto@ufpr.br, aurora@inf.ufpr.br
[2] LIFO, University of Orleans, Orleans, France
marcilio.desouto@univ-orleans.fr

Abstract. We present a data-driven analysis of MOCK, Δ-MOCK, and MOCLE. These are three closely related approaches that use multi-objective optimization for crisp clustering. More specifically, based on a collection of 12 datasets presenting different proprieties, we investigate the performance of MOCLE and MOCK compared to the recently proposed Δ-MOCK. Besides performing a quantitative analysis identifying which method presents a good/poor performance with respect to another, we also conduct a more detailed analysis on why such a behavior happened. Indeed, the results of our analysis provide useful insights into the strengths and weaknesses of the methods investigated.

Keywords: Clustering methods · Multi-objective clustering · Multi-objective optimization · Data mining

1 Introduction

Clustering is a type of unsupervised learning whose goal is to find the underlying structure, composed of clusters, present in the data [1]. Objects belonging to each cluster should share some relevant property regarding the data domain. Clustering techniques have been successfully applied in fields such as pattern analysis, data mining, image segmentation, as well as in other areas such as biology, medicine, and marketing [1]. Traditional clustering algorithms optimize only one clustering criterion and are often very effective for this purpose. However, in general, they fail for data under a different criterion. In practice, multiple criteria, considering different aspects of the quality (e.g., compactness and connectedness) of a clustering solution (partition), frequently represent conflicting goals for an optimization method [12]. This has motivated a great deal of work in which clustering is addressed as a multi-objective problem, relying on the simultaneous optimization of multiple clustering criteria [7,11,12,15,18].

In particular, in this paper, by means of data-driven analysis, we revisit two popular approaches that use multi-objective optimization for crisp clustering:

© Springer Nature Switzerland AG 2021
T. Mantoro et al. (Eds.): ICONIP 2021, CCIS 1516, pp. 46–54, 2021.
https://doi.org/10.1007/978-3-030-92307-5_6

MOCK [12] and MOCLE [7]. We will put these two algorithms into perspective with respect to the new MOCK's version, Δ-MOCK [11]. The purpose is to identify the strengths and weaknesses of these algorithms so as to point out directions for future research on the development of a high-quality multi-objective clustering algorithms. The remainder of this paper is organized as follows. Section 2 presents the main concepts concerning MOCK, Δ-MOCK, and MOCLE, pointing out their differences. Next, Sect. 3 describes the experimental design adopted. Then, in Sect. 4, we present the results of our experimental evaluation. Finally, Sect. 5 highlights our main findings and discusses future works.

2   Related Works and Background

As this paper focuses on a data-driven investigation of MOCLE, MOCK, and Δ-MOCK, it naturally shares similarities with other works [2,7–9,11]. However, different from these works, in this paper, besides performing quantitative analysis to compare the general performance of the algorithms, we will also conduct qualitative analysis to provide some insights on why such a behavior happened. Furthermore, it is important to point out that our analysis focuses on the ability of these methods to produce a set of solutions containing high-quality partitions. Thus, we will not be concerned with the model selection used to estimate the quality of the partitions and determines a set of potential solutions of such algorithms.

2.1   MOCK, Δ-MOCK and MOCLE

MOCK (Multi-Objective Clustering with automatic K-determination) is a well-known algorithm for multi-objective clustering. MOCK uses a graph-based encoding called locus-based adjacency representation [12]. The generation of the initial population consists of two phases: 1) Generation of Minimum Spanning Tree (MST) derived partitions, based on a measure called *degree of interestingness* (DI), 2) Generation of k-means derived partitions. MOCK relies on the multi-objective genetic algorithm PESA-II (Pareto envelope-based selection algorithm version II) [4], considering a standard uniform crossover and a neighborhood-biased mutation scheme (each object can only be linked to one of its L nearest neighbors) to optimize two complementary clustering criteria: overall deviation (*dev*) and connectivity (*con*) [12]. The *dev* can be defined according to (1), where π denotes a partition, $\mathbf{x}_i$ is an object belonging to cluster $\mathbf{c}_k$, $\boldsymbol{\mu}_k$ is the centroid of cluster $\mathbf{c}_k$, and $d(.,.)$ is the selected distance function.

$$dev(\pi) = \sum_{\mathbf{c}_k \in \pi} \sum_{\mathbf{x}_i \in \mathbf{c}_k} d(\mathbf{x}_i, \boldsymbol{\mu}_k), \qquad (1)$$

The *con* is computed according to (2), where n is the number of objects in the dataset, L is the parameter that determines the number of the nearest neighbors that contributes to the connectivity, a_{ij} is the jth nearest neighbor of object $\mathbf{x}_i$, and $\mathbf{c}_k$ is a cluster that belongs to a partition π. Depending on the value chosen for parameter L, different partitions could present the same optimal value for con [11]. As objective functions, both dev and con must be minimized [12].

$$con(\pi) = \sum_{i=1}^{n} \sum_{j=1}^{L} f(\mathbf{x}_i, a_{ij}), \text{where } f(\mathbf{x}_i, a_{ij}) = \begin{cases} \frac{1}{j}, \text{if } \nexists \mathbf{c}_k : \mathbf{x}_i, a_{ij} \in \mathbf{c}_k \\ 0, \text{otherwise} \end{cases} \quad (2)$$

Δ-MOCK was introduced by [11] to improve the scalability of MOCK [12]. For that, they introduced two alternative representations, the Δ-locus and the Δ-binary, to reduce the length of the genotype in the locus-based adjacency representation. These schemes are based on the original representation of MOCK; however, they can significantly reduce the length of the genotype by using the concepts of MST and DI according to the length of the encoding defined by a user-defined parameter (δ). Also, they proposed an alternative procedure based on the original first phase employed by MOCK, generating only MST-derived partitions. In terms of the optimization, Δ-MOCK replaces MOCK's PESA-II [4] with NSGA-II (Non-dominated Sorting Genetic Algorithm II) [5], and employed the intra-cluster variance (var) instead the dev as objective function. The var is computed according to (3), where π denotes a partition, n is the number of objects in the dataset, $\mathbf{x}_i$ is an object belonging to cluster $\mathbf{c}_k$, $\boldsymbol{\mu}_k$ is the centroid of the cluster $\mathbf{c}_k$, and $d(.,.)$ is the selected distance function. According to [11], although var and dev are conceptually similar, var was chosen because it facilitates the evaluation of a new candidate individual.

$$var(\pi) = \frac{1}{n} \sum_{\mathbf{c}_k \in \pi} \sum_{\mathbf{x}_i \in \mathbf{c}_k} d(\mathbf{x}_i, \boldsymbol{\mu}_k)^2 \quad (3)$$

MOCLE (Multi-Objective Clustering Ensemble) is an approach proposed in [7] that combines characteristics from both cluster ensemble techniques and multi-objective clustering methods. Like in cluster ensemble, starting with a diverse set of base partitions, MOCLE employs the multi-objective evolutionary algorithm to generate an approximation of the Pareto optimal set. It optimizes the same criteria as MOCK and uses a special crossover operator, which combines pairs of partitions using an ensemble method. No mutation is employed. The optimization process has been mainly performed by using NSGA-II [5] and the crossover operator by the Hybrid Bipartite Graph Formulation (HBGF) [10].

3   Experimental Design

We performed experiments with 12 datasets. Table 1 summarizes the main characteristics of them. D31, 20d_60c and ds2c2sc13 are synthetic datasets specially designed to contain several different properties [7,11]. For example, D31 contains 31 equal size and spread clusters that are slightly overlapping and distribute randomly in a 2-dimensional space; and ds2c2sc13 was designed to contain three different structures: E1, E2 and E3: E1 represents two well-separated clusters, in which E2 and E3 combine different types of clusters that could be hard to find

Table 1. Dataset characteristics: the number of objects n, the number of attributes d, and the number of *clusters* k^*

Type	Dataset	n	d	k^*
	D31	3100	2	31
	tevc_20_60_1	4395	20	60
Artificial	ds2c2sc13_E1	588	2	2
	ds2c2sc13_E2	588	2	5
	ds2c2sc13_E3	588	2	13

Type	Dataset	n	d	k^*
	Seeds	210	7	3
	Golub_E1	72	3571	2
	Leukemia_E2	327	271	7
Real	Libras	360	90	15
	OptDigits	5620	62	10
	Frogs_MFCC_E3	7195	22	10
	UKC1	29463	2	11

with techniques based only on connectedness or compactness. Concerning the real datasets, we also included datasets presenting different important characteristics: Golub_E1 and Leukemia_E2 [9] have a small number of objects, but a large number of attributes, typical of bioinformatics data; UKC1 have a very large number of objects. Libras, OptDigits and Frogs_MFCC_E3 were obtained from the UCI Machine Learning Repository (https://archive.ics.uci.edu/ml/datasets).

To execute MOCK and Δ-MOCK, we employed the same general settings as reported in [11,12]. Concerning the representation of the solutions for Δ-MOCK, in this paper, we used the Δ-locus scheme. We set δ based on one of the heuristics employed in [11], defined as a function of $\sim 5\sqrt{n}$, where n is the number of objects in the dataset. For the case of MOCLE, to generate the initial population, we used: k-means [14], the Ward linkage (WL) [17], the Shared Nearest Neighbor-based clustering (SNN) [6], and the Hierarchical Density-Based Spatial Clustering of Applications with Noise (HDBSCAN) [3]. Also, we applied the Euclidean distance as a distance function, $L=10$, and we adjusted the other parameters of such algorithms to produce partitions containing clusters in the range $\{2, 2k^*\}$, in the same way of the MOCK/Δ-MOCK's. Finally, as such algorithms are non-deterministic, we execute the experiments 30 times.

As the main indicator of clustering performance, in this work, we use the adjusted Rand index (ARI) [13]. This index measures the similarity between two partitions. Values of ARI close to 0 mean random partitions, and close to 1 indicates a perfect match between the partitions. Also, we use a non-parametric test to analyze the ARI results, the Kruskal-Wallis test with the Tukey-Kramer-Nemenyi post-hoc test [16] with 95% significance.

4   Results and Discussion

Table 2 presents the average and standard deviation for the ARI of best partitions, as well as for their number of clusters, found by MOCLE, MOCK, and Δ-MOCK over 30 executions. In this table, for each dataset, the average of the best ARI obtained is highlighted in boldface, and the average of the number of clusters is indicated in parenthesis. The highlighted values also represent

Table 2. ARI and the number of clusters of the best partition found by MOCLE, MOCK and Δ-MOCK—Average of 30 executions

Dataset	MOCLE	MOCK	Δ-MOCK
D31	**0.951** ±0.003 (31.3)	0.843 ±0.022 (46.7)	0.746 ±0.033 (30.0)
20d_60c	**0.942** ±0.000 (113.0)	0.794 ±0.025 (85.2)	0.900 ±0.020 (68.3)
ds2c2sc13_E1	**0.529** ±0.000 (4.0)	0.381 ±0.000 (5.0)	0.352 ±0.000 (6.0)
ds2c2sc13_E2	**1.000** ±0.000 (5.0)	**1.000** ±0.000 (5.0)	0.952 ±0.000 (6.0)
ds2c2sc13_E3	**1.000** ±0.000 (13.0)	0.873 ±0.005 (11.2)	0.872 ±0.000 (11.0)
Seeds	**0.729** ±0.004 (3.8)	0.710 ±0.008 (3.1)	0.667 ±0.041 (3.8)
Golub_E1	0.473 ±0.000 (3.0)	**0.803** ±0.096 (2.4)	0.541 ±0.025 (12.5)
Leukemia_E2	**0.787** ±0.000 (8.0)	0.782 ±0.013 (9.4)	0.771 ±0.002 (10.8)
Libras	0.345 ±0.000 (24.0)	**0.395** ±0.012 (15.0)	0.386 ±0.005 (14.9)
OptDigits	0.820 ±0.008 (11.0)	**0.893** ±0.013 (21.4)	0.834 ±0.002 (14.5)
Frogs_MFCC_E3	0.816 ±0.000 (6.0)	0.873 ±0.022 (15.9)	**0.905** ±0.006 (23.7)
UKC1	**1.000** ±0.000 (11.0)	0.998 ±0.002 (12.2)	0.996 ±0.001 (13.4)

the best result of each dataset considering the Kruskal-Wallis/Tukey-Kramer-Nemenyi test with a two-sided p-value adjustment. Furthermore, as the initial population of MOCLE is generated by k-means, WL, SNN, and HDBSCAN, the results of these algorithms are summarized in Table 3, in which * indicates the datasets where the SNN did not produce any partition with the number of clusters in the required range.

Table 3. ARI and the number of clusters of the best partition found by k-means, the WL, SNN and HDBSCAN

Dataset	k-means	WL	SNN	HDBSCAN
D31	**0.953** (31)	0.920 (31)	0.946 (32)	0.806 (31)
20d_60c	0.531 (115)	0.586 (109)	**0.942** (113)	0.303 (76)
ds2c2sc13_E1	**1.000** (2)	**1.000** (2)	0.684 (3)	**1.000** (2)
ds2c2sc13_E2	0.875 (5)	0.854 (8)	**1.000** (5)	**1.000** (5)
ds2c2sc13_E3	0.619 (18)	0.626 (20)	**1.000** (13)	**1.000** (13)
Seeds	0.717 (3)	**0.727** (4)	0.691 (3)	0.426 (3)
Golub_E1	**0.944** (2)	0.689 (2)	-0.013 (2)	0.444 (3)
Leukemia_E2	0.785 (8)	**0.787** (8)	0.522 (6)	0.503 (7)
Libras	0.322 (19)	**0.345** (24)	0.338 (27)	0.200 (13)
OptDigits	0.745 (11)	**0.814** (13)	0.600 (16)	0.655 (10)
Frogs_MFCC_E3	0.840 (5)	0.816 (6)	* (—)	**0.849** (21)
UKC1	0.991 (11)	**1.000** (11)	0.999 (13)	**1.000** (11)

Looking at Table 2, one can observe that, overall, across the different datasets, MOCLE, MOCK, and Δ-MOCK presented distinct results concerning the ARI. Indeed, according to the Kruskal-Wallis test, there is statistical evidence that for each dataset, one algorithm could be considered better in terms of ARI than the other; where based on the Tukey-Kramer-Nemenyi post-hoc test, we observed that MOCLE performed equal or better than MOCK and Δ-MOCK in all the artificial datasets and three real datasets (Seeds, Leukemia_E2 and UKC1); MOCK provided better results than MOCLE and Δ-MOCK in three real datasets: Golub_E1, Libras and OptDigits, and, it had a tied result with MOCLE regarding the artificial dataset ds2c2sc13_E2; while Δ-MOCK only stood out in the real dataset Frogs_MFCC_E3.

In order to understand why some methods performed poorly for certain datasets, we will perform an analysis based on both the characteristics (bias) of the methods and the properties of the datasets. This can give us some useful insights on strengths and weaknesses, mainly concerning MOCK and Δ-MOCK. For example, an analysis of the behavior of MOCK and Δ-MOCK for the dataset D31 sheds light on problems regarding the strategy to generate their initial population. D31 contains several compact globular (Gaussian) clusters that are slightly overlapping. Thus, one would expect that any algorithm that optimizes compactness such as k-means and WL method should be able to yield a partition with large ARI, as can be seen in Table 3. Indeed, MOCLE found, on average, high-quality partitions with ARI compatible with that returned by k-means (0.951 against 0.953). On the other hand, compared to MOCLE, on average, MOCK and Δ-MOCK yielded the best solutions with much smaller ARI (respectively, 0.843 and 0.746), being the performance of Δ-MOCK worse than that of MOCK. The main reason for the poor performance of Δ-MOCK on D31 could be in the procedure that it employs to create the initial population. Its initial population is created by removing *interesting* links from an MST built on the data. In the case of D31, as two clusters overlap, the density at the boundary of the clusters increases. As a consequence, objects in this region might have several nearest neighbors in common. This way, the links between objects in such regions would not be classified as *interesting* and, consequently, they would not be potential candidates to be removed and the clusters would remain merged.

Concerning ds2c2sc13, independently of the multi-objective clustering algorithm, our experimental results show that their structures present some challenges in what concerns the optimization of the objective functions, mainly the *con*. Depending on the value of the L used in the computation of the *con*, one can detect the two well-separated clusters in E1 but fail to identify the small clusters present in E3 and vice versa. Here, as in [11,12], we set L to 10. More specifically, for E1, MOCLE, MOCK, and Δ-MOCK could not find the two well-separated clusters presented in this structure. This happened for the true partition, π^*, was, in terms of the values of objective functions, dominated by other partitions whose values for the *con* was optimal as that of π^* ($con = 0$), but with smaller dev/var (these partitions had a larger number of clusters than π^*). This result contrasts to that in [7] in which with $L = 30$ (5% of the n) both MOCLE and MOCK found E1. For structure E2, like in [7], both MOCLE and MOCK found, in each of the 30 runs, a partition that corresponded to the ground truth π^*, that is, an ARI equals to 1. On the other hand, the best partition found by Δ-MOCK in each of the runs had an ARI equals to 0.952 and contained six clusters: one of the large globular clusters was split into two. In [7], with L set to 30, neither MOCK nor MOCLE found E3. In contrast, here, in all its runs, MOCLE found a partition corresponding to the true structure in E3 (ARI equals to 1). For the case of MOCK and Δ-MOCK, the most frequent best partition in 30 runs merged two pairs of close clusters. In summary, depending on the value of L and the underlying structure in the data, in terms of con, this could mean that several different solutions will have an optimal value ($con = 0$) and, as a consequence, the decision will be taken essentially based on the dev.

Turning our attention to the real datasets, in terms of poor performance according to the ARI, there is a case that stands out: the results of MOCLE and Δ-MOCK for Golub_E1 (respectively, 0.473 and 0.541) when compared to that of MOCK (0.803). In the case of MOCLE, in its initial population (see Table 3), there was a high-quality partition (ARI equals to 0.944) generated by k-means, yet such a partition was not kept in the set of final solution for it was dominated by one of the partitions generated by the SNN. For the case, Δ-MOCK versus MOCK, the good performance obtained with k-means for Golub_E1 could explain why MOCK performed much better than Δ-MOCK, as the MOCK initial population is built with not only MST-derived partitions like the Δ-MOCK, but also with partitions generated with k-means.

Regarding the number (size) of the clusters of the best partitions, according to the results presented in Table 2, for most datasets, MOCK, and Δ-MOCK generated partitions containing clusters having as few as five objects. For instance, for Golub_E1 the median best partition produced by Δ-MOCK presented more than one cluster containing a single object. Likewise, for OptDigits, both algorithms yielded median best partitions with some clusters having two objects. Indeed, the problem of partitions with outlier clusters was already present in the initial population. In other words, DI computed based on $L = 10$ nearest neighbors for most of the datasets analyzed was not effective in avoiding the isolation of outliers. Besides, as the con is also computed based on the L nearest neighbors, to a certain extent, this creates, during evolution, a bias towards solutions already present in the initial population.

5   Final Remarks

In this paper, we performed a data-driven analysis of three closely related multi-objective clustering algorithms: MOCLE, MOCK, and Δ-MOCK. We discussed some particularities regarding the application of each algorithm across 12 datasets. Furthermore, in order to understand this behavior, we made an analysis based on both the characteristics (bias) of the methods and the properties of the datasets. Such an analysis gave us useful insights on strengths and weaknesses, mainly concerning MOCK and Δ-MOCK. For example, we discussed how the initial population could influence the clustering performance in such multi-objective approaches. Also, we presented the limitation around the *con* as an objective function, considering its parameters setting.

One more interesting research direction is to investigate, for example, to what extent MOCLE can benefit from the use of base partitions generated by the initialization procedure employed by Δ-MOCK. Finally, an important issue not tackled in this paper concerns the model selection phase. The work in [2,18], for instance, presents promising approaches to address this question.

References

1. Aggarwal, C.C., Reddy, C.K.: Data Clustering: Algorithms and Applications, 1st edn. Chapman & Hall/CRC, Boca Raton (2013)
2. Antunes, V., Sakata, T.C., Faceli, K., de Souto, M.C.P.: Hybrid strategy for selecting compact set of clustering partitions. Appl. Soft Comput. **87**, 105971 (2020)
3. Campello, R.J.G.B., Moulavi, D., Sander, J.: Density-based clustering based on hierarchical density estimates. In: Pei, J., Tseng, V.S., Cao, L., Motoda, H., Xu, G. (eds.) PAKDD 2013. LNCS (LNAI), vol. 7819, pp. 160–172. Springer, Heidelberg (2013). https://doi.org/10.1007/978-3-642-37456-2_14
4. Corne, D.W., Jerram, N.R., Knowles, J.D., Oates, M.J.: PESA-II: region-based selection in evolutionary multiobjective optimization. In: Proceedings of the 3rd Annual Conference on Genetic and Evolutionary Computation, pp. 283–290. (2001)
5. Deb, K., Pratap, A., Agarwal, S., Meyarivan, T.: A fast and elitist multiobjective genetic algorithm: NSGA-II. IEEE Trans. Evol. Comput **6**(2), 182–197 (2002)
6. Ertoz, L., Steinbach, M., Kumar, V.: A new shared nearest neighbor clustering algorithm and its applications. In: Workshop on Clustering High Dimensional Data and its Applications, pp. 105–115 (2002)
7. Faceli, K., de Carvalho, A.C.P., de Souto, M.C.P.: Multi-objective clustering ensemble. Int. J. Hybrid Intell. Syst. **4**(3), 145–156 (2007)
8. Faceli, K., Sakata, T.C., de Souto, M.C.P., de Carvalho, A.C.P.: Partitions selection strategy for set of clustering solutions. Neurocomputing **73**(16–18), 2809–2819 (2010)
9. Faceli, K., de Souto, M.C.P., de Araújo, D.S., de Carvalho, A.C.: Multi-objective clustering ensemble for gene expression data analysis. Neurocomputing **72**(13–15), 2763–2774 (2009)
10. Fern, X.Z., Brodley, C.E.: Solving cluster ensemble problems by bipartite graph partitioning. In: Proceedings of the 21st International Conference on Machine Learning, p. 36. ACM (2004)
11. Garza-Fabre, M., Handl, J., Knowles, J.: An improved and more scalable evolutionary approach to multiobjective clustering. IEEE Trans. Evol. Comput. **22**(4), 515–535 (2018)
12. Handl, J., Knowles, J.: An evolutionary approach to multiobjective clustering. IEEE Trans. Evol. Comput. **11**(1), 56–76 (2007)
13. Hubert, L., Arabie, P.: Comparing partitions. J. Classif. **2**(1), 193–218 (1985)
14. MacQueen, J., et al.: Some methods for classification and analysis of multivariate observations. In: Proceedings of the 5th Berkeley Symposium on Mathematical Statistics and Probability, vol. 1, pp. 281–297 (1967)
15. Mukhopadhyay, A., Maulik, U., Bandyopadhyay, S.: A survey of multiobjective evolutionary clustering. ACM Comput. Surv. (CSUR) **47**(4), 61 (2015)

16. Pohlert, T., Pohlert, M.T.: Package PMCMR. R Package Vers. **1** (2018)
17. Ward, J.H., Jr.: Hierarchical grouping to optimize an objective function. J. Am. Stat. Assoc **58**(301), 236–244 (1963)
18. Zhu, S., Xu, L., Goodman, E.D.: Evolutionary multi-objective automatic clustering enhanced with quality metrics and ensemble strategy. Knowl. Based Syst. **188**, 105018 (2020)

Speech Dereverberation Based on Scale-Aware Mean Square Error Loss

Luya Qiang[1], Hao Shi[2], Meng Ge[1(✉)], Haoran Yin[1], Nan Li[1],
Longbiao Wang[1(✉)], Sheng Li[3], and Jianwu Dang[1,4]

[1] Tianjin Key Laboratory of Cognitive Computing and Application,
College of Intelligence and Computing, Tianjin University, Tianjin, China
{qiangluya,gemeng,longbiao_wang}@tju.edu.cn
[2] Graduate School of Informatics, Kyoto University, Sakyo-ku, Kyoto, Japan
[3] National Institute of Information and Communications Technology (NICT),
Kyoto, Japan
[4] Japan Advanced Institute of Science and Technology, Ishikawa, Japan

Abstract. Recently, deep learning-based speech dereverberation approaches have achieved remarkable performance by directly mapping the
input spectrogram to a target spectrogram or time-frequency mask.
However, these approaches are usually optimized under distance-related
objective functions—the mean square error (MSE). The traditional MSE
training criterion results in a strong inherent uniform variance statistical assumption on the target speech and noise during training, which
cannot be satisfied in real-world scenarios. To alleviate such an assumption mismatch problem, we propose a speech dereverberation solution
called Scale-aware Speech Dereverberation (SaSD) based on scaled-
MSE. Specifically, we modify the MSE with different scales for each
frequency band and progressively reduce the gap between the low- and
high-frequency ranges to make the error follow the assumption of MSE
assumption. Experiments demonstrated that SaSD achieved 1.0 SRMR
and 0.8 PESQ improvements over the mapping baseline system.

Keywords: Speech dereverberation · Scale-aware mean square error ·
Progressive learning · Deep learning

1 Introduction

In real-world environments, the sound reaching the ears comprises the clean
direct-path speech and its reflections from various surfaces, which drastically
reduce speech signal intelligibility [1]. To minimize the distortions in real-world
cases, speech dereverberation, as an important front-end signal processing module, is designed to remove the adverse effects of reverberation for the back-end
speech applications, such as speech recognition [3,8].

H. Shi—Joint first author.

© Springer Nature Switzerland AG 2021
T. Mantoro et al. (Eds.): ICONIP 2021, CCIS 1516, pp. 55–63, 2021.
https://doi.org/10.1007/978-3-030-92307-5_7

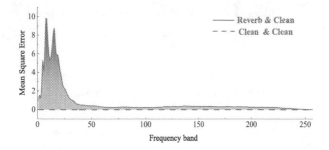

Fig. 1. The mean square error of the observed noisy speech and clean speech for all frequency bands on REVERB dataset.

Recently, some researchers have explored the use of deep neural networks for speech dereverberation, such as using spectral mapping methods [4,5]. The key strategy is to view the speech dereverberation as a regression problem, where the nonlinear regression function can be parametrized using deep neural networks. In recent years, there have been many models based on spectral mapping, such as DNN [18], CNN [20], RNN [21], GAN [22,24], CRNN [19], etc.

Generally, these spectral mapping approaches are optimized by a distance-related objective function, such as the mean square error (MSE) [13,14]. However, simple applying a distance-related objective function to dereverberation network training results in strong inherent assumptions on the statistics of the clean speech and noise [23]. For example, the MSE objective function assumes that the errors of all frequency bands have zero means and uniform variance [11]. Unfortunately, this assumption cannot be met in real-world scenarios because the target clean speech and noisy speech have a non-uniform spectral distribution as shown in Fig. 1. From it, we can observe that the error between the target clean speech and noisy speech in the approximately 1–50 frequency bands are much larger than that in higher frequency range. Such an assumption mismatch for the MSE has the problem of underestimating the error in the frequency range with lower power, leads to the training difficulty of speech dereverberation in the higher frequency range.

To address the above problem, we propose a speech dereverberation approach based on scaled-MSE loss function called Scale-aware Speech Dereverberation (SaSD). To make the error follow the statistical assumption of the MSE, we first modify the MSE loss function using different weights for frequency bands, where the low-frequency bands are given larger weights and the high-frequency bands are given smaller weights. Additionally, motivated by the idea of SNR-based progressive learning (PL) in the literature [6,7], we use the PL strategy to gradually reduce the gap between high- and low-frequency range. Thus, we can apply the MSE loss function with the help of the progressive learning approach to equally treat the error for each frequency. From the comparison of the loss curves, it can be observed that by using our method, the gap between high-frequency and low-frequency gradually decreases with the progress of the stage and significantly reduce the error between the predicted spectrogram and the target spectrogram. And from the experimental results, it is helpful to improve the speech dereverberation ability by using the method we proposed.

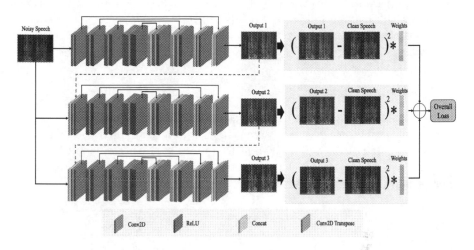

Fig. 2. The diagram of the SaSD. The whole system consists of three progressive stages. Each stage contains three FCN blocks and each block is a U-net structure, including four 2D convolution layers transposed convolution layers.

2 Spectral Mapping with MSE Loss

In real-world environments, the original source (direct sound) $s(t)$ is easily destroyed by convolutional noise $r(t)$ and additive background noise $b(t)$. Thus, the observed signal $y(t)$ can be written as follows:

$$y(t) = s(t) * r(t) + b(t) \tag{1}$$

Mapping-based methods aim to learn a nonlinear function $\mathcal{F}$ from the observed noisy speech $y(t)$ into the desired clean speech $s(t)$, as described by the following:

$$y(t) \xrightarrow{\mathcal{F}} s(t) \tag{2}$$

To learn $\mathcal{F}$, the neural network is trained to reconstruct the target speech spectrum $S(n, f)$ from the corresponding input noisy speech spectrum $Y(n, f)$ [15]. In traditional methods, the parameters of the model are determined by minimizing the mean square error (MSE) objective function as follows:

$$\mathcal{L}_{\mathrm{MSE}} = \frac{1}{N * F} \sum_{n=1}^{N} \sum_{f=1}^{F} ||\mathcal{F}(Y(n, f)) - S(n, f)||^2 \tag{3}$$

where N and F are the number of frames and frequency bands, respectively. The n and f are the corresponding index of the frame and frequency band.

3   Scale-Aware Speech Dereverberation Architecture

SaSD is a progressive mapping pipeline with multiple stages. We use a three-stage architecture in this work, as shown in Fig. 2. Different from the traditional MSE objective function, we use scaled-MSE for different frequency bands as the training criterion, and design three-stage progressive architecture to alleviate the assumptions in MSE loss.

3.1   Scaled-MSE Loss

Since the MSE objective function assumes that the mean error of all frequencies are zero and the variance are the same, this assumption cannot be met in the fact that the same distortion in different frequency bands has different effects on speech quality. Motivated by this, we firstly apply a scaled-MSE loss to reduce the error gap between low- and high-frequency bands, which is defined as:

$$\mathcal{L}_{\text{Scaled-MSE}}(w_f) = \frac{1}{N * F} \sum_{n=1}^{N} \sum_{f=1}^{F} w_f ||\mathcal{F}(Y(n,f)) - S(n,f)||^2 \qquad (4)$$

where w_f is the scale parameter of the f-th frequency band. Here, we use a linear function to define w_f, so the weight value will change as the frequency band changes. The formula is defined as follows:

$$w_f = 1 - \frac{1 - w_{min}}{F} * (f - 1) \qquad (5)$$

where w_{min} represents the minimum scale threshold hyperparameter. It is used to control the minimum weight of the high frequency band in the training process.

By applying scaled-MSE training criterion, the low-frequency bands are given large weights and the high-frequency bands are weighted with smaller scales. During the training stage, the dereverberaton network pays more attention to reducing the reconstruction error of low-frequency bands, rather than treating each frequency band equally.

3.2   Progressive Scaled-MSE Loss

Reducing the gap between high and low frequency bands is a complex learning process, and direct mapping optimization with scaled-MSE training criterion is hard to achieve the expected goal. Motivated by the progressive learning study in speech enhancement [6], we propose the progressive scaled-MSE loss to decompose the complicated non-linear mapping problem into a series of easier sub-problems. The key idea is to gradually reduce the reconstruction error between noisy and clean speech at low frequencies in a multi-stage manner, and finally apply the original MSE objective function to guide the dereverberation network. The progressive scaled-MSE loss is define as follow:

$$\mathcal{L}_{\text{Prog-MSE}} = \sum_{p=1}^{P} \alpha_p \mathcal{L}_{\text{Scaled-MSE}}(w_f^p)$$

$$= \frac{1}{NF} \sum_{p=1}^{P} \sum_{n=1}^{N} \sum_{f=1}^{F} \alpha_p w_f^p || \mathcal{F}(Y(n,f)) - S(n,f) ||^2 \qquad (6)$$

where P denotes the number of stages in the whole system, and α_p represents the weight coefficient of the p-th stage loss. The w_f^p is calculated from the parameter w_{min} at p-th stage using Eq. (5). In this study, we apply three-stage mapping architecture as shown in Fig. 2.

4   Experiments and Discussion

4.1   Dataset

The experiments were conducted on the REVERB challenge dataset [8]. The database contains simulated and real recordings, that have been sampled from different rooms with different reverberation levels and 20 dB SNR of background noise. The simulated data were generated by convolving the room impulse responses (RIRs) collected from rooms of three different sizes (small, medium, large) and two different microphone positions (near, far) by using single-channel microphones and clean speech utterances from WSJCAM0 [12]. The corpus was divided into training, validation and test sets. The training data included 7,861 simulated recordings, whereas the test data contained simulated and real recordings. The validation set used only the simulated data. All of the speech signals were sampled at 16 kHz.

4.2   Experimental Setup

For all models, the window length and hop size were 32 ms and 16 ms, and the FFT length was 512. All of the models were implemented on TensorFlow, and the weights of them were randomly initialized. The architecture of SaSD was divided into three stages with FCN blocks [16]; each block is a U-net structure [17] that mainly consists of four two-dimensional (2D) convolution layers and four 2D transposed convolution layers, where the numbers of filters for each convolution layer were 8, 16, 16, 32, 16, 16, 8 and 1. ReLU was used as the activation function, as shown in Fig. 2. The α_p of our proposed model for stages 1 and 2 is 0.1, and the α_p for stage 3 is 1. In the experiments, the perceptual evaluation of speech quality (PESQ) [9] and speech-to-reverberation modulation energy ratio (SRMR) [10] were used as the evaluation metrics. All approaches use noisy phase information to reconstruct the enhanced waveform. To choose the model for speech reverberation, several models were compared on the REVERB dataset, which are described as follows:

Traditional Methods: ①**Reverb**: reverberant spectrogram; ②**Mapping**: mapping system with one FCN block; ③**Naive Iteration**: mapping system with three naive iterative FCN blocks and use the final output to calculate the loss.

Proposed Methods (SaSD): the proposed system that consists of three progressive stages. During the training, the intermediate predicted spectrogram from previous stage is concatenated with the noisy spectrogram as input into the next stage. The overall loss is the sum of the loss value in each stage. According to the change of the weight value, it is divided into two cases as:

①*hard*: the proposed approach that divides the entire frequency domain into three equal parts, with each part adopting a fixed weight at each stage; in this experiment, $(1, 0.5, 0)$ and $(1, 0.75, 0.5)$ were used in stages 1 and 2, respectively. ②*linear* $(w_f^1$- w_f^2- $w_f^3)$: the approach in which the threshold of w_f for stages 1, 2, and 3 are w_f^1, w_f^2, and w_f^3, respectively. At each stage, as the frequency increases, the weight values of different frequencies linearly decrease from 1 to the threshold. In this experiment, we set a total of three sets of different weight thresholds to evaluate the performance of our proposed model.

Table 1. PESQ and SRMR in a comparative study on the REVERB dataset. In the table, w_{min} denotes the weight threshold of the high frequency band; *Mode* denotes the change in weight value; *hard* means each part adopting a fixed weight at each stage and *linear* means the weight values will linearly decrease from 1 to the threshold; *#1*, *#2*, *#3* denote the number of stages.

Model	Configurations				PESQ			SRMR					
	w_{min} (#stage)				Simulated			Simulated			Real		
	Mode	#1	#2	#3	Far	Near	Ave.	Far	Near	Ave.	Far	Near	Ave.
Reverb	–	–	–	–	2.15	2.59	2.37	3.43	3.94	3.68	3.19	3.17	3.18
Mapping	–	–	–	–	2.42	2.66	2.54	4.20	4.66	4.43	4.01	3.66	3.83
Naive iteration	–	–	–	–	2.42	2.74	2.58	4.25	4.70	4.47	3.86	3.55	3.71
SaSD	Hard	0	0.5	1	**2.46**	2.76	2.61	4.67	5.17	4.92	4.59	4.08	4.33
	Linear	0	0.5	1	2.43	2.70	2.57	**4.72**	5.14	**4.93**	**5.03**	**4.62**	**4.82**
	Linear	0.5	0.75	1	2.45	2.74	2.60	4.63	**5.19**	4.91	4.69	4.22	4.46
	Linear	1	1	1	**2.46**	**2.78**	**2.62**	4.32	4.89	4.60	4.15	3.70	3.93

4.3   Experimental Results and Discussion

We compared our SaSD with previous baseline systems on REVERB in terms of PESQ and SRMR in Table 1. Regardless of the evaluation index used, the experimental results showed that the highest scores were obtained by SaSD. Additionally, when the average frequency was divided into three parts with equal weights, a high PESQ measure was obtained. Furthermore, on simulated data,

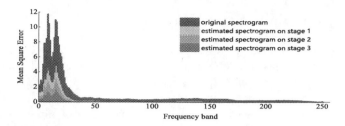

Fig. 3. Scaled mean square error loss values at each frequency range for different progressive stages.

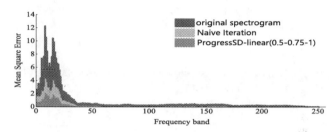

Fig. 4. Mean square error loss values at each frequency band for our SaASD and 3-mapping naive iteration system.

the naive iteration mapping model achieved better performance than the single mapping model in terms of both PESQ and SRMR. Conversely, the opposite was true for real data. This outcome may be due to the difference between the data distributions of the real and simulated datasets, and such a superimposed network may be more affected than a single network, thereby resulting in performance degradation on the real dataset. However, when the direct mapping of noisy speech to pure speech was decomposed into multiple stages as the frequency weight threshold increased, the model also achieved good performance. To verify the effectiveness of the progressive learning strategy, the mean square error for all frequency bands at each stage is shown in Fig. 3. It is observed from Fig. 3 that the gap between the high-frequency and low-frequency results gradually decreases with the progress of the stage. This fact shows that progressive learning with scaled loss can help the dereverberation network alleviate the assumption mismatch of MSE. In addition, we further verified the effectiveness with naive iteration scheme, as shown in Fig. 4. Compared with the results under the naive iteration scheme, we found that our ProgressSD approach can significantly reduce the deviation of the predicted spectrogram from the target spectrogram. This improvement is from the greater stability and better convergence of the dereverberation network trained under scaled-MSE.

5   Conclusion and Future Work

In this paper, we proposed a system featuring scaled-MSE and PL, which is called SaSD. We modified the MSE with different scales for each frequency band and progressively reduced the gap between the low- and high-frequency range that was used for speech dereverberation based on mapping; this was done in order to solve the problem of the nonuniform variance of different frequency bands that makes some regions in the spectrogram difficult to learn. The experimental results showed that the loss curve became more stable and showed better convergence with SaSD. It was also found that all the approaches of PL that used scaled-MSE exhibited improved performance, particularly with respect to SRMR and PESQ. In the future, we will replace our current network with a state-of-the-art network structure.

Acknowledgment. This work was supportedinpart by the National Natural Science Foundationof China under Grant 61771333.

References

1. Li, J., Deng, L., Gong, Y., Haeb-Umbach, R.: An overview of noise-robust automatic speech recognition. IEEE/ACM TASLP **22**, 745–777 (2014)
2. Zhang, Z., Wang, L., Kai, A., Yamada, T., Li, W., Iwahashi, M.: Deep neural network-based bottleneck feature and denoising autoencoder-based dereverberation for distant-talking speaker identification. EURASIP J. Audio Speech Music Process. **2015**, 1–13 (2015)
3. Nakatani, T., Yoshioka, T., Kinoshita, K., Miyoshi, M., Juang, B.-H.: Speech dereverberation based on variance-normalized delayed linear prediction. IEEE TASLP **18**, 1717–1731 (2010)
4. Févotte, C., Idier, J.: Algorithms for nonnegative matrix factorization with the β-divergence. Neural Comput. **23**(9), 2421–2456 (2011)
5. Han, K., Wang, Y., Wang, D., Woods, W.S., Merks, I., Zhang, T.: Learning spectral mapping for speech dereverberation and denoising. IEEE/ACM Trans. Audio Speech Lang. Process. **23**(6), 982–992 (2015)
6. Gao, T., Du, J., Dai, L.-R., Lee, C.-H.: Densely connected progressive learning for LSTM-based speech enhancement. In: Proceedings ICASSP. IEEE (2018)
7. Tang, X., Du, J., Chai, L., Wang, Y., Wang, Q., Lee, C.-H.: A LSTM-based joint progressive learning framework for simultaneous speech dereverberation and denoising. In: Proceedings APSIPA ASC. IEEE (2019)
8. Kinoshita, K., et al.: The reverb challenge: a common evaluation framework for dereverberation and recognition of reverberant speech. In: Proceedings WASPAA. IEEE (2013)
9. Rix, A.W., Beerends, J.G., Hollier, M.P., Hekstra, A.P.: Perceptual evaluation of speech quality (pesq)-a new method for speech quality assessment of telephone networks and codecs. In: Proceedings ICASSP, vol. 2. IEEE (2001)
10. Hu, Y., Loizou, P.C.: Evaluation of objective quality measures for speech enhancement. IEEE TASLP **16**(1), 229–238 (2007)
11. Takeuchi, D., Yatabe, K., Koizumi, Y., Oikawa, Y., Harada, N.: Data-driven design of perfect reconstruction filterbank for dnn-based sound source enhancement. In: Proceedings ICASSP. IEEE (2019)

12. Robinson, T., Fransen, J., Pye, D., Foote, J., Renals, S.: Wsjcamo: a british english speech corpus for large vocabulary continuous speech recognition. In: Proceedings ICASSP, vol. 1. IEEE (1995)
13. Martin, R.: Speech enhancement based on minimum mean-square error estimation and supergaussian priors. IEEE TASLP **13**(5), 845–856 (2005)
14. Erdogan, H., Hershey, J.R., Watanabe, S., Le Roux, J.: Phase-sensitive and recognition-boosted speech separation using deep recurrent neural networks. In: Proceedings ICASSP. IEEE (2015)
15. Avargel, Y., Cohen, I.: System identification in the short-time fourier transform domain with crossband filtering. IEEE TASLP **15**, 1305–1319 (2007)
16. Ronneberger, O., Fischer, P., Brox, T.: U-Net: convolutional networks for biomedical image segmentation. In: Navab, N., Hornegger, J., Wells, W.M., Frangi, A.F. (eds.) MICCAI 2015. LNCS, vol. 9351, pp. 234–241. Springer, Cham (2015). https://doi.org/10.1007/978-3-319-24574-4_28
17. Zhou, Z., Rahman Siddiquee, M.M., Tajbakhsh, N., Liang, J.: UNet++: a nested U-net architecture for medical image segmentation. In: Stoyanov, D., et al. (eds.) DLMIA/ML-CDS -2018. LNCS, vol. 11045, pp. 3–11. Springer, Cham (2018). https://doi.org/10.1007/978-3-030-00889-5_1
18. Xu, Y., Du, J., Dai, L.-R., Lee, C.-H.: An experimental study on speech enhancement based on deep neural networks. IEEE Signal Process. Lett. **21**, 65–68 (2013)
19. Tan, K., Wang, D.: Complex spectral mapping with a convolutional recurrent network for monaural speech enhancement. In: Proceedings ICASSP. IEEE (2019)
20. Park, S.R., Lee, J.: A fully convolutional neural network for speech enhancement (2016). arXiv preprint arXiv:1609.07132
21. Weninger, F., Watanabe, S., Tachioka, Y., Schuller, B.: Deep recurrent de-noising auto-encoder and blind de-reverberation for reverberated speech recognition. In: Proceedings ICASSP. IEEE (2014)
22. Wang, K., Zhang, J., Sun, S., Wang, Y., Xiang, F., Xie, L.: Investigating generative adversarial networks based speech dereverberation for robust speech recognition (2018). arXiv preprint arXiv:1803.10132
23. Fu, S.W., Yu, T., Lu, X., et al.: Raw waveform-based speech enhancement by fully convolutional networks. In: Proceedings APSIPA ASC. IEEE (2017)
24. Li, C., Wang, T., Xu, S., Xu, B.: Single-channel speech dereverberation via generative adversarial training (2018). arXiv preprint arXiv:1806.09325

A Novel Multi-source Domain Learning Approach to Unsupervised Deep Domain Adaptation

Rakesh Kumar Sanodiya[1](✉), Vishnu Vardhan Gottumukkala[1],
Lakshmi Deepthi Kurugundla[1], Pranav Reddy Dhansri[1],
Ravi Ranjan Prasad Karn[1], and Leehther Yao[2]

[1] Indian Institute of Information Technology, Sri City, Chittor, India
rakesh.s@iiits.in
[2] National Taipei University of Technology, Taipei 10608, Taiwan

Abstract. Even though it is anticipated that training and test data come from same distribution, but in many practical applications, they usually have different distributions, resulting in poor classification performance. To overcome this distribution difference, various Transfer Learning (TL) approaches such as Domain Adaptation (DA) have been proposed. Many existing DA approaches are capable of minimizing the distribution difference of single source and target domains, resulting in the transfer of useful information from only one source domain to the target domain. However, the useful information can also be transferred from multiple source domains to the target domain for further improving the performance. Therefore, in this paper, we proposed a novel Convolutional Neural Network (CNN) architecture that considers three (or more depending on a number of source domains) stream CNN networks and introduces domain confusion and discriminative losses, to learn a representation that is both semantically meaningful and domain invariant. Extensive experiments on different tasks of domain adaptation dataset such as PIE show that considering multiple sources can significantly boost the performance of deep domain adaptation model. As a result, our approach outperforms existing state-of-the-art methods in cross-domain recognition.

Keywords: Domain adaptation · Deep learning · Feature learning · Transfer learning · Classification

1 Introduction

In primitive supervised machine learning approaches, dataset deviation (or distribution difference) is a well-known problem for image classification. The deviation of the dataset may be caused by collecting data from different sources or environmental conditions to train and test the model [8]. Because of this deviation of the data, a model trained on the source domain with sufficient number

© Springer Nature Switzerland AG 2021
T. Mantoro et al. (Eds.): ICONIP 2021, CCIS 1516, pp. 64–72, 2021.
https://doi.org/10.1007/978-3-030-92307-5_8

of labeled data may not perform well when tested on the target domain with unlabeled data. To surmount this deviation between labelled specimens of the source domain data and unlabelled specimens of the target domain data, Domain Adaptation (DA) or Transfer Learning (TL) approaches have been proposed [2]. DA is an approach in which a classifier is learnt by training a model on a source domain with labeled samples and then using the learning to predict unlabeled samples of a target domain. More specifically, DA approaches learn a new representation of both domain samples where the deviation (or distribution difference) between the source and target domains is minimal so that the trained classifier can easily classify the target domain samples.

Feature-based adaptation, instance-based adaptation, and classifier-based adaptation are the most commonly used DA methods. The feature-based methods aim to learn a common feature space by minimizing the distribution gap between both domains. In instance-based adaptation methods, each sample of source domain is multiplied by some learned constant so that the sample draws much nearer to the target domain and minimizes the distribution difference between both domains. Since no label is available in the target domain in the unsupervised DA approaches, the classifier-based approach is not feasible. One of the main methods to lessen the distribution difference between the source domain and target domain is to learn the domain-invariant model from the data, which can bridge the gap between both domains in an isomorphic latent feature space. In this direction, previous works have achieved fruitful results, focusing on learning shallow features through distance metrics that jointly reduce domain differences. The DA methods which learn shallow features include Kernelized Unified Framework for Domain Adaptation (KUFDA) [4] etc. However, recent studies such as Joint Domain alignment and Discriminative feature learning (JDDA) [1] and Deep Domain Confusion (DDC) [8] have presented that deep neural networks can provide more transferable features for DA with breakthrough results for some DA datasets.

Inspired by the literature's newest grasp about the transferability of deep neural networks, we came up with a new CNN architecture, delineated in Fig. 1, which makes use of three CNN networks, two of them for two source domains and the third for the target domain. This architecture considers an adaptation layer along with a domain confusion loss based on CORrelation ALignment (CORAL) [7] to automatically learn a representation jointly trained to optimize for classification and domain invariance. Moreover, as the source domain is labeled, in the adaptation layer, we also preserve source domain discriminative information to ensure target domain samples are well aligned.

In this paper, we propose a novel multi-source domain learning approach for unsupervised deep domain adaptation, in which all layers corresponding to multi task-specific features are adapted in a layer-wise manner, hence benefiting from "deep adaptation".

2   Related Work

Recently, sizeable developments have happened in DA methods. Despite this fact, only a few that are paramount to our ongoing research have been addressed. One method among them is JDDA [1] which has abstracted domain discrepancy and achieved better accuracy compared to the other domain adaptation methods like Maximum Mean Discrepancy (MMD) [8], Correlation Alignment (CORAL) [7]. MMD is a approach of representing the distance between mean embeddings of source and target features. CORAL reduces the domain discrepancy by using co-variance of source and target features. In JDDA [1], shared weights are adopted which gives better training due to transfer learning. It makes use of two stream CNN architecture and the domain loss which is used for extracting the similar features from the source samples and the target samples by subtracting the co-variance of source features and target features. The other loss used is the discriminative loss in which samples in the same class should be very proximate to each other in the feature space and the samples from different classes should differ from each other by a huge margin. We summarize the circumscriptions of subsisting DA methods such as "MMD" [8] and "CORAL" [7] can only reduce the domain shift i.e. distance between source and target samples which is a major drawback and finally JDDA [1] came into existence which removed the domain shift. However, if the data set is small, the model cannot extract features accurately and which leads to misclassification. These methods inspired us to came up with an idea of multi source deep DA method where we proposed an approach of three stream CNN architecture with two source domains and one target domain.

3   Our Approach

3.1   Problem Definition

Let $\mathcal{X}^{s1} = \{(x_1^{s1}, y_1^{s1}), \ldots, (x_{ns1}^{s1}, y_{ns1}^{s1})\}$ denote the first source domain and their corresponding labels similarly, $\mathcal{X}^{s2} = \{(x_1^{s2}, y_1^{s2}), \ldots, (x_{ns2}^{s2}, y_{ns2}^{s2})\}$ denote the second source domain and their corresponding labels. $\mathcal{X}^{t} = \{(x_1^{t}, y_1^{t}), \ldots, (x_{n_t}^{t}, y_{n_t}^{t})\}$ denote the common target domain for both sources and their respective labels. Here $\mathcal{X}^{s1}, \mathcal{X}^{s2}$ and $\mathcal{X}^{t}$ shares the common feature space d dimension, And also $\mathcal{X}^{s1} \in \mathcal{R}^{d \times n_{s1}}, \mathcal{X}^{s2} \in \mathcal{R}^{d \times n_{s2}}$, and $\mathcal{X}^{t} \in \mathcal{R}^{d \times n_t}$ represent feature spaces of both sources and the target domains. Likewise, $\mathcal{Y}^{s1} \in \mathcal{R}^{1 \times n_{s1}}$, $\mathcal{Y}^{s2} \in \mathcal{R}^{1 \times n_{s2}}$ and $\mathcal{Y}^{t} \in \mathcal{R}^{1 \times n_t}$ represent the labels of the respective feature spaces for both the source and the target domains.

3.2   Proposed Loss Function

In this section, we will discuss our proposed approach loss function in more detail. In addition to the existing loss functions [1], we propose a new loss function with three stream CNN architecture where the weights (Θ) are shared. The three-stream CNN architecture is shown in Fig. 1. In this architecture, the first stream

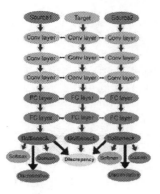

Fig. 1. Three stream CNN

handles the first source domain data, the second stream the target domain data, and the third stream the second source domain data. What strengthens our loss function, among other approaches, is to consider additional CNN layers, to have more source domain properties such as discriminative properties. As a result, we obtain more general and transferable features, which are inter-class separable and intra-class compact and are good for both domain alignment and final classification of the model.

Our proposed loss function for training the parameters (Θ) of our proposed 3-CNN network can be defined as follows:

$$\mathcal{L}(\Theta|\mathcal{X}^{s1}, \mathcal{X}^{s2}, \mathcal{Y}^{s1}, \mathcal{Y}^{s2}, \mathcal{X}^{t}) = \mathcal{L}_s + \lambda_1\mathcal{L}_{s1} + \lambda_2\mathcal{L}_{s2} + \lambda_3\mathcal{L}_d \tag{1}$$

$$\mathcal{L}_s = \frac{1}{ns1 + ns2} \sum_{i=1}^{ns1+ns2} c(\Theta|x_i, y_i) \tag{2}$$

$$\mathcal{L}_{s1} = CORAL(\mathcal{H}_{s1}, \mathcal{H}_t) \tag{3}$$

$$\mathcal{L}_{s2} = CORAL(\mathcal{H}_{s2}, \mathcal{H}_t) \tag{4}$$

$$\mathcal{L}_d = \mathcal{J}_d(\Theta|\mathcal{X}^{s1+s2}, \mathcal{Y}^{s1+s2}) \tag{5}$$

Here, $\mathcal{L}_s, \mathcal{L}_{s1}, \mathcal{L}_{s2}$, and $\mathcal{L}_d$ represent both source domain loss, domain discrepancy loss between first source domain and target domain, domain discrepancy loss between second source domain and target domain, and both source domain discriminative loss, respectively. λ_1, λ_2, and λ_3 are the trande-off parameters to balance the contribution of their respective losses. $c(\Theta|x_i, y_i)$ represents the standard classification loss with respect to the both source domain data.

$CORAL(\mathcal{H}_{s1}, \mathcal{H}_t)$ [6] represents the domain discrepancy loss between first source domain and target domain measured by the correlation alignment (CORAL). Similarly $CORAL(\mathcal{H}_{s2}, \mathcal{H}_t)$ represent the domain discrepancy loss between second source domain and target domain. Here $\mathcal{H}_{s1} \in \mathcal{R}^{b*L}$, $\mathcal{H}_{s2} \in \mathcal{R}^{b*L}$, and $\mathcal{H}_t \in \mathcal{R}^{b*L}$ denote the learned deep features in the bottleneck layer regard to the first source stream, second source stream, and target stream. b represents the batch size during the training time and L is then number of hidden neurons in the bottleneck layer. $\mathcal{J}_d(\Theta|\mathcal{X}^{s1+s2}, \mathcal{Y}^{s1+s2})$ [1] is the instance based discriminative loss.

3.3   Training

The proposed three stream CNN can be easily implemented via the mini-batch Stochastic Gradient Descent. For the three stream CNN architecture, the total loss is given as $\mathcal{L} = \mathcal{L}_s + \lambda_1 \mathcal{L}_{s1} + \lambda_2 \mathcal{L}_{s2} + \lambda_3 \mathcal{L}_d$ while the source loss $\mathcal{L}_s$ defined in (2) is defined by the conventional softmax classifier. Domain losses $\mathcal{L}_{s1}$ and $\mathcal{L}_{s1}$ defined in (3) and (4), and the discriminative loss defined in (5) are differentiable w.r.t. the inputs. Hence, the parameters Θ are updated by using the standard back propagation.

$$\Theta^{t+1} = \Theta^t - \eta \frac{\partial(\mathcal{L}_s + \lambda_1 \mathcal{L}_{s1} + \lambda_2 \mathcal{L}_{s2} + \lambda_3 \mathcal{L}_d)}{\partial x_i} \tag{6}$$

where η is the learning rate.

4   Experiments

Extensive tests are conducted in this section to demonstrate the efficiency, reliability, and robustness of the multi-source domain methodology as compared to the trailblazing primitive and DA approaches. Since unsupervised DA appears to be more pertinent to authentic-world challenges, we will primarily concentrate on testing unsupervised DA approaches. In this, we are going to assess the efficacy of our approach by comparing it with various deep DA methods on the PIE dataset [3]. This dataset consists of 68 output classes. The source code for three-stream CNN is relinquished online.

4.1   Setup

CMU-PIE [5] stands for CMU Pose, Illumination, and Expression (PIE) dataset. This dataset contains over 40,000 facial images divided into 68 groups with each image of 32×32 pixels. There are many different pose subsets, but we take five broadly used subsets: PIE29 (right pose), PIE27 (front pose), PIE09 (inverted pose), PIE07 (upward pose), and PIE05 (left pose) to compose cross-domain tasks. The images in different subsets differ significantly and have major distribution gaps. We can engender 30 cross-domain tasks utilizing three different subsets for two sources and one target. e.g., "PIE05, PIE09 $\longrightarrow$ PIE07", "PIE05,PIE07 $\longrightarrow$ PIE09",..., and "PIE29, PIE09 $\longrightarrow$ PIE27".

4.2 Comparing Approaches

We compared the performance of our proposed method with other existing deep DA approaches such as MMD [8], CORAL[7], JDDA [1], and concatenated model i.e. concatenation of two different source domains.

4.3 Implementation Details

For the assessments on the PIE dataset, we utilized the modified LeNet to assess the efficiency of our approach. We resized all images to 32× 32 pixels and eminently all the given images are grayscale. We performed six experiments for each target domain and a total of 30 combinations for all the transfer tasks and reported the results across them using different domain adaptation methods. For an unbiased comparison, all deep learning models above have the same architecture as our approach for the label prognosticator. All the methods have been executed in TensorFlow and trained with adam's optimizer. For each approach, we took a batch size of 480, and learning rate of 0.001 in each experiments.

Table 1. Classification accuracy of proposed and comparative approaches on the PIE dataset

S no	Sources, Target			Only S1 as Source					Only S2 as Source					Concatenation 3 CNN	
	S1	S2	T	S	D-CORAL S+C	DDC S+M	JDDA-I S+I+C	S+I+M	S	D-CORAL S+C	DDC S+M	JDDA-I S+I+C	S+I+M	JDDA-I S+I+C	Proposed S+I+C+C
1	07	09	05	27.64	32.01	34.89	35.86	35.89	44.12	43.36	45.5	49.3	48.97	60.78	**64.78**
2	27	29	05	74.67	79.78	77.89	85.67	86.78	44.21	49.76	51.45	54.78	59.98	84.56	**85.67**
3	05	27	07	37.32	43.95	40.89	49.78	41.23	67.4	82.5	78.89	83.57	78.123	85.89	**87.89**
4	09	29	07	35.76	42.84	35.78	45.21	36.54	41.25	40.97	42.56	45.6	43.12	57.67	**61.23**
5	05	27	09	44.53	52.3	49.78	53.45	49.97	76.45	87.45	84.57	88.125	80.078	90.76	**91.56**
6	05	29	09	44.53	52.3	49.78	53.45	49.97	45.75	51.12	51.56	53.76	49.7	81.12	**82.45**
7	07	29	09	31.23	37.8	35.67	44.78	34.45	45.75	51.12	51.56	53.76	49.7	66.56	**71.56**
8	07	09	27	53.45	59.38	57.89	61.2	56.76	71.56	71.14	70.23	79.4	69.36	91.23	**96.78**
9	07	29	27	53.45	59.38	57.89	61.2	56.76	62.25	64.75	65.6	68.7	63.87	88.9	**91.56**
10	09	29	27	71.56	71.14	70.23	79.4	69.36	62.25	64.75	65.6	68.7	63.87	91.45	**93.45**
11	05	27	29	33.54	39.79	41.27	45.67	44.57	64.5	74.3	70.89	77.89	72.08	84.56	**85.98**
12	07	09	29	28.37	32.91	33.89	35.67	28.45	45.78	50.2	45.78	51.2	46.9	60.51	**62.89**
Avg.				44.671	50.294	48.821	53.945	49.061	55.939	60.952	60.349	64.565	60.479	78.665	**81.317**

4.4 Results and Discussion

In this section, our proposed approach is compared to other deep DA methods to illustrate our approach's efficacy. When conducting the experiment, we kept the same parameter setting, architecture (LeNet), training and test data for our proposed method as well as other methods for calculating accuracy. In the first setting, only one source (S1) is considered for training the model and target domain (T) for testing. Further we make the setting with different losses or methods such as Setting "S": simply source domain (S1) is considered for training and target domain(T) for testing without any domain adaptation and discriminative losses, Setting "S+C":Setting "S" is extended by incorporating CORAL loss, Setting "S+M": "S" by incorporating MMD loss, Setting

"S+C+I": "S+C" by incorporating instance based discriminative loss [1], Setting "S+M+I": "S+M" by incorporating instance based discriminative loss. In the second experiment setting, only one source (S2) is used for training the model and the target domain (T) for testing. Similar to the first experiment setting, we setup the second experiment setting as well. In the third experiment setting "S + I + C", we first concatenate both source domains (S1 and S2), so only one CNN stream is considered for the source domain, and then the model is trained with classification, discriminative, and CORAL losses. In the fourth experiment setting "S+I+C+C" (our proposed method) where 3 -CNN streams are considered (two for source domains and third for target domain). The model is trained with classification, discriminative and two CORAL(one for S1 and another for S2 losses).

After experimenting with all the above discussed settings, the accuracy of our proposed model and other methods are reported in Table 1. The conclusion drawn from the experiments is that if we consider only one domain as the source domain (viz. S1) to train the model and test on the target domain without learning any domain invariant features, then, the average accuracy obtained for 12 tasks is 44.67% which is lesser than other deep DA methods. Among deep DA approaches, JDDA-I has better performance with 53.95% average accuracy.

Similarly, if we consider another source domain (i.e. S2) to train the model and test it on the target domain, the accuracy obtained is 60.95% which is also lower than other deep DA methods. Here also JDDA-I outperforms the other deep DA methods.

After combining both the source domains (i.e. S1 and S2) and then if we train the deep DA algorithm and test it on the target domain, the average accuracy obtained on 12 tasks is 78.65 which is 3.44% lesser than the proposed 3CNN architecture.

From the above discussion, it can be concluded that it is worth considering more than two CNN architectures, along with domain loss, discrimination and source losses, to improve the performance of the target domain. Moreover, it can also be concluded that the different domain discrepancy losses such as CORAL and MMD for different tasks work well to reduce the distribution difference between domains.

4.5   Feature Visualisation

To visualize how our proposed approach minimizes distribution gaps between the source domains and the target domain, we have randomly selected 5 classes samples out of 68 classes from each domain (i.e., source-1, source-2, and target domain) of the PIE face dataset. Using the t-SNE tool, we have projected high-dimensional data into 2-D space and plotted it in Fig. 2.

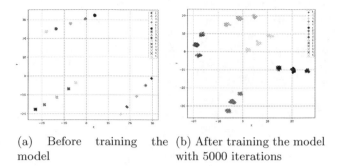

(a) Before training the model

(b) After training the model with 5000 iterations

Fig. 2. Feature visualization of a multi-source domain approach on a PIE dataset taking PIE07, PIE09 as the source tasks and PIE27 as the target task. Source1, source 2, and target domain samples are represented by (+), (.), and (x) symbols and different colors represent different classes.

5 Conclusion and Future Work

In this work, we have proposed a novel multi-source learning approach for unsupervised deep DA Problems. Unlike other deep DA approaches, we have considered a three-CNN architecture to transfer useful information from multiple source domains to the target domain. As our proposed framework is generalized, it can be easily extended to transfer information from more than two source domains to the target domain by only considering more CNN layers with domain losses. An extensive empirical evaluation on various tasks of the standard domain adaptation benchmark dataset demonstrates the efficacy of the proposed model against previous state-of-the-art deep domain adaptation approaches.

References

1. Chen, C., Chen, Z., Jiang, B., Jin, X.: Joint domain alignment and discriminative feature learning for unsupervised deep domain adaptation. In: Proceedings of the AAAI Conference on Artificial Intelligence, vol. 33, pp. 3296–3303 (2019)
2. Long, M., Cao, Y., Wang, J., Jordan, M.: Learning transferable features with deep adaptation networks. In: International Conference on Machine Learning, pp. 97–105. PMLR (2015)
3. Rasouli, A., Kotseruba, I., Kunic, T., Tsotsos, J.K.: Pie: a large-scale dataset and models for pedestrian intention estimation and trajectory prediction. In: International Conference on Computer Vision (ICCV) (2019)
4. Sanodiya, R.K., Mathew, J., Paul, B., Jose, B.A.: A kernelized unified framework for domain adaptation. IEEE Access **7**, 181381–181395 (2019)
5. Sim, T., Baker, S., Bsat, M.: The CMU pose, illumination, and expression (pie) database. In: Proceedings of Fifth IEEE International Conference on Automatic Face Gesture Recognition, pp. 53–58. IEEE (2002)
6. Sun, B., Feng, J., Saenko, K.: Return of frustratingly easy domain adaptation. In: Proceedings of the AAAI Conference on Artificial Intelligence, vol. 30 (2016)

7. Sun, Baochen, Saenko, Kate: Deep CORAL: correlation alignment for deep domain adaptation. In: Hua, Gang, Jégou, Hervé (eds.) ECCV 2016. LNCS, vol. 9915, pp. 443–450. Springer, Cham (2016). https://doi.org/10.1007/978-3-319-49409-8_35
8. Tzeng, E., Hoffman, J., Zhang, N., Saenko, K., Darrell, T.: Deep domain confusion: Maximizing for domain invariance (2014). arXiv preprint arXiv:1412.3474

More Than One-Hot: Chinese Macro Discourse Relation Recognition on Joint Relation Embedding

Junhao Zhou, Feng Jiang, Xiaomin Chu, Peifeng Li, and Qiaoming Zhu[✉]

School of Computer Science and Technology, Soochow University, Suzhou, China
{jhzhou0512,fjiang}@stu.suda.edu.cn,
{xmchu,pfli,qmzhu}@suda.edu.cn

Abstract. Discourse relation recognition is to identify the logical relations between discourse units (DUs). Previous work on discourse relation recognition only considered the loss of prediction and ground truth before back-propagation in the form of a one-hot vector, which cannot reflect the relation coherence. To remedy this deficiency, we propose a macro discourse relation recognition model based on the Joint Relation Embedding (JRE). This model contains two different relation embedding mechanisms, Relation Name Embedding (RNE) and Relation Translation Embedding (RTE), which can obtain relation encoding associated with semantic coherence. These two mechanisms are integrated through relation matching and joint learning. The experimental results on the Macro Chinese Discourse Treebank dataset show that our JRE outperforms baselines and effectively improves the performance of discourse relation recognition, especially those minority relations.

Keywords: Macro Chinese discourse relation · Relation recognition · Relation embedding

1 Introduction

In a coherent document, discourse units (DUs) are organized and hierarchically whole formed by a certain logical relation. Discourse analysis aims to analyze the structure of a document and the relations between DUs and can be divided into micro and macro levels. The latter studies focus on the discourse above the paragraph, explaining the structure and semantics at a higher level [1].

Chinese is more implicitly coherent because it is a paratactic language with fewer or no linguistic forms such as connectives. Moreover, the longer macro discourse unit and the larger and more complex information it contains bring a big challenge to macro discourse relation recognition [2]. Thus, relation recognition not only needs to dig out the semantic information of DUs, but also needs a deeper understanding and modeling of semantic coherence.

© Springer Nature Switzerland AG 2021
T. Mantoro et al. (Eds.): ICONIP 2021, CCIS 1516, pp. 73–80, 2021.
https://doi.org/10.1007/978-3-030-92307-5_9

The existing methods lacked the modeling of the discourse relation and only considered loss calculation in the form of a one-hot vector before the back-propagation. One-hot vector answers the most basic question, "which relation-ship can connect these two DUs", but it does not explain how the discourse relation acts the coherence between DUs.

In this paper, we propose a Joint Relation Embedding model (JRE) for modeling semantic coherence. First, we employ a Relation Name Embedding (RNE) to encode the representation of relation by explicitly inserting the names of the predefined relations as connectives. Then, we train a relation embedding matrix with a translation-based method in Relation Translation Embedding (RTE) to learn deep semantic coherence. Finally, we apply the relation matching and joint learning to mutually Combine RNE and RTE together, so as to enable them to share the representation and update parameters together. The experimental results on the Macro Chinese Discourse Treebank (MCDTB) [3] dataset show that our JRE outperforms the SOTA baselines and effectively improves the performance of discourse relation recognition, especially those minority relations.

2   Related Work

2.1   Corpus

In Chinese, most previous work evaluated their model on the Chinese Discourse Treebank (CDTB) [4], and Macro Chinese Discourse Treebank (MCDTB) [3]. On the macro level, MCDTB has annotated discourse topics, paragraph topics, discourse abstracts, discourse structure, and discourse relations. The newest MCDTB annotated 1200 articles and annotated paragraphs as elementary DUs. In terms of discourse relations, MCDTB contains 3 categories and further divided into 15 sub-categories.

2.2   Discourse Relation Recognition

Previous works devoted to better modeling of DUs and enhancing the semantic interaction between DUs. For example, Chen et al. [5] used gated relevance network to aggregate the semantic interactions between sentence pairs and aggregated semantic interaction information through the pooling layer. Guo et al. [6] mined associated word pairs from the preceding and following segments to establish clue pairs. Xu et al. [7] introduced three-layer attention neural network model to simulate human repeated reading for enhancing the representation of DUs. Liu et al. [8] proposes gated fusion and bilateral matching to enhance the representation of arguments with better contextual information. Xu et al. [9] proposed the topic tensor network to. He et al. [10] introduced the geometric structure information of argument-relation instances.

However, in macro Chinese discourse relation recognition. Zhou et al. [11] selected macro features of paragraphs and proposed a macro semantic representation method. Jiang et al. [12] proposed a method based on structure and topic gated semantic networks. The method hired joint learning with nuclearity in the meanwhile. Jiang et al. [13] hired BERT as relation recognition model in shift-reduce algorithm to construct discourse structure tree.

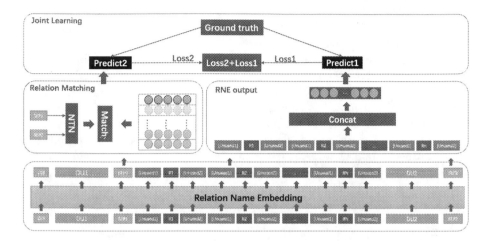

Fig. 1. The overall framework of Joint Label Embedding model

3   JRE Model

The specific structure of the model is shown in Fig. 1, which is entirely divided into the following three components:

1) Relation Name Embedding (RNE): We insert the names of the predefined relations as connectives into the input of the BERT-based encoder [14] to dynamically represent the discourse relation and units as well. So that we can turn the implicit connection into explicit connection.
2) Relation Translation Embedding (RTE): We project the discourse relations and DUs into a low-dimensional vector space. Hence, we can construct the trained embedding matrix of the discourse relation with translation-based [15] method. The embedding matrix saves the understanding of relation from a deeper perspective of semantic coherence.
3) Joint Embedding: With the object of mutually modeling, we use relation matching and joint learning to combine RNE and RTE.

3.1   RNE: Relation Name Embedding

Chinese is a paratactic language with fewer or no linguistic forms such as connectives between paragraphs. Therefore, the encoder's input is two DUs $DU1$ and $DU2$ and their relation set *Relation*, which becomes more in line with the

$DU1 + connectives + DU2$ form. This form is beneficial to learn the relative position of the discourse relation between the DUs, making the representation of the relation more consistent with the semantic coherence.

More specifically, we deploy a BERT-based encoder and insert the names of all predefined relations bordered by special tokens between the two units. The input form of RNE is shown in Fig. 1 like: "$[CLS]$ $DU1$ $[SEP1]$ $[unused1]$ $Relation_1$ $[unused2]$ $[unused1]$ $Relation_2$ $[unused2]$ ... $[unused1]$ $Relation_N$ $[unused2]$ $DU2$ $[SEP2]$". Where N is the number of relationships. We put each relationship's name between the special tokens $[unused1]$ and $[unused2]$ to locate the start and end boundary of the specific discourse relation in the input.

RNE uses $N \times [unused1]$ output $N \times h_{[unused1]} \in R^{N \times d}$ as the representation for each relation, d is the size of hidden layer in BERT, then we concatenate the dynamic representation of these N relations as the overall representation of all relations. Finally, we send it to the linear layer $l_1 = (WX + b_1)$, where $W \in R^{(N \times d) \times N}$, $b_1 \in R^N$. We find the index of the maximum probability through the $Argmax$ function and take the prediction $Predict1$ as RNE Results.

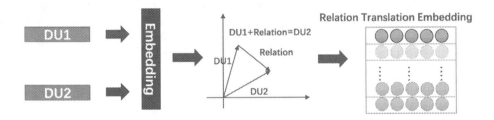

Fig. 2. Training process of Relation Translation Embedding

3.2   RTE: Relation Translation Embedding

We follow the work of TransE [15] in knowledge representation and projecting the DUs and the discourse relations into a low-dimensional space. In this space, every discourse unit and relation is expressed as a semantic vector. The discourse relation acts as a translation between two discourse unit vectors.

Specifically in Fig. 2, given the training triplet set, namely $(DU1, R, DU2)$ where $DU1$ and $DU2$ are the given DUs and R represents the corresponding relation, we first use the word-level encoder ELMO [16] to model the semantic features of $DU1$ and $DU2$. $DU1$ and $DU2$ are formalized as the word sequence $W = (w_1, w_2, w_3...w_n)$, where n is the total number of words in single DU, the word embedding of each word $E_{w_i} \in R^E$ is obtained through the encode where E is the dimension of ELMO encoder. We get the representation of the discourse unit through the average pooling as follows:

$$h_{DU} = \frac{1}{n} \sum_{i=1}^{n} E_{w_i} \qquad (1)$$

where E_{w_i} is the embedding vector of the ith word.

We set the translation formula as $DU1 + R \approx DU2$, which aims to make the relation embedding learn the deep semantic coherence, and reflect in the translation embedding. The loss function is as follows:

$$L = \sum_{(DU1,R,DU2)\in S} \sum_{(DU1,R',DU2)\in S'} [\gamma + D(DU1+R, DU2) - D(DU1+R', DU2)]_+$$

(2)

where γ is a margin hyper-parameter, $[]_+$ denotes the positive instances and $D()$ is the score function defined as follows:

$$D = \|h_{DU1} + h_r - h_{DU2}\|_2^2 \qquad (3)$$

where h_{DU1}, h_{DU2} denotes the representations of $DU1$ and $DU2$ respectively, and h_r denotes the embedding of specific relation. We construct the corrupted set of triples S' according to the formula as follows:

$$S' = \{(DU1, R', DU2)|R' \in M_R\} \qquad (4)$$

where M_R is the set of discourse relations, and we replace the relations in the triples with random relation in the set. We look for the relation embedding matrix and replace it with the vector of the corresponding relation.

Finally, we take the trained relation embedding matrix as the result of RTE.

3.3   Joint Embedding

We employ relation matching and joint learning mechanisms to enable them to interact with understanding and to jointly work.

More specifically, As shown in Fig. 1, we use encoder output of specific tokens $[SEP1]$, $[SEP2]$ ($S_1, S_2 \in R^d$) as the representation of $DU1$ and $DU2$ respectively. We hire a neural tensor network [17] to model the information interaction between tensors, defined as:

$$T(S_1, S_2) = f_N(S_1^T M^{[1:m]} S_2 + Q \begin{bmatrix} S_1 \\ S_2 \end{bmatrix} + b_2) \qquad (5)$$

where f_N is a single layer neural network with $ReLU$ as the activation function. $M^{[1:m]} \in R^{d \times d \times m}$ is sliced into $i = 1, 2, 3...m$ to simultaneously capture multiple linear interactions between vectors, then we calculate the product of $S_1^T M^{[1:m]} S_2$, where $Q \in R^{m \times 2d}$, bias $b_2 \in R^m$. To reduce the complexity of model parameters and calculation, we adopt tensor factorization [18], which uses two low rank matrices to approximate each tensor slice $M[i]$ as follows:

$$M^{[i]} = J^{[i]} U^{[i]} \qquad (6)$$

where $J^{[i]} \in R^{d \times r}$, $U^{[i]} \in R^{r \times d}$, $r \ll d$. Then we calculate the cosine similarity to match $T(S_1, S_2)$ with every relation embedding matrix in RTE, and select the relation with the highest similarity as the prediction $Predict2$.

We define the joint learning loss function as follows:

$$Joint\_loss = Loss1 + Loss2 \tag{7}$$

where $Loss1$ is the cross-entropy loss of $Predict1$ and the ground truth, and $Loss2$ is the cross entropy loss of $Predict2$ and the ground truth.

Finally, $Predict1$ is the final prediction of JRE during model inference.

4 Experimentation

4.1 Experimental Settings

We evaluate our mode JRE on MCDTB. We use Pytorch to implement JRE on 1080Ti GPU, with the learning rate of 2e−5, training epochs of 5, batch size of 4, and the Adam optimizer. In RNE, the BERT version is BERT base[1], the maximum length L of the discourse unit is set to 512, and the hidden size is d = 768. In RTE, the training batch size is 512, the number of training steps is 10000, the learning rate is 1e−4, margin hyper-parameter $\gamma = 1$, the size of word embedding and hidden layer is E = 1024. In Joint embedding, the number of tensor slices of NTN is m = 128, the parameter of tensor decomposition is r = 10.

4.2 Experimental Results

1) MSRN [11]: It introduces a representation of macro discourse semantics on word vectors and structure features to recognize macro discourse relation.
2) TTN [9]: It employs topic models and gated convolutional neural networks, which achieves excellent performance in the recognition of micro Chinese discourse relation recognition. We reproduce the model on MCDTB.
3) STGSN [12]: It uses a gated semantic network on structure and discourse topic. It is the SOTA model for Chinese macro discourse relation recognition.
4) BERT [14]: Since BERT has surpassed most previous models in the popular English corpus PDTB [19], it proves ability in macro Chinese discourse [13].

Table 1. Performance of JRE and baselines on MCDTB.

Model	Avg. P	Avg. R	Micro-F1	Macro-F1
MSRN	47.67	61.81	53.56	13.75
TTN	45.46	49.44	46.46	17.44
STGSN	53.97	58.67	55.65	15.24
BERT	62.31	63.85	62.83	28.13
JRE	**64.25**	**65.03**	**64.42**	**34.69**

---

[1] We borrow BERT code from Transformers url: https://github.com/huggingface/transformers.

As shown in Table 1, MSRN is limited because structure features are not enough for relation understanding. Despite TTN models both sentence-level and topic-level representations, gated convolutional network encoding cannot effectively capture the semantic information of the large granular DUs, which leads to a poor result. STGSN utilizes discourse structure features and topic gated semantic network, however, it cannot model semantic coherence, which also leads to poor results. Compared with the other three baselines, BERT achieves the higher performance on all metrics and improves the Micro-F1 and Macro-F1 by 7.18+ and 10.69+, respectively. This results verified the similar results in [19]. Compared with BERT, JRE gains improvements of 6.56 and 1.59 in Macro-F1 and Micro-F1 values respectively. This result proves that deeply modeling semantic coherence is beneficial to discourse relation recognition.

4.3 Analysis on RNE and RTE

The results of ablation experiments are shown in Table 2. First of all, by explicitly modeling the connection between DUs, Predict1 can directly bring a significant improvement compared to Predict2. It shows that RNE can saliently take advantage of explicit relation embedding. Moreover, we can find that embedding RNE and RTE together can achieve a significant improvement. It suggests that although RNE can turn an implicit connection into an explicit connection, the model can further achieve higher performance when we combine it with deeper semantic logic.

Table 2. Results of ablation experiments

Model	Micro-F1	Macro-F1
JRE	64.42	34.69
Predict1	63.59(−0.83)	33.13(−1.56)
Predict2	57.46(−6.96)	16.75(−17.94)

5   Conclusion

In this paper, we propose a Joint Relation Embedding (JRE) model consisting of Relation Name Embedding and Relation Translation Embedding to jointly model semantic coherence. We will focus on mining different representations for different relations and applying discourse relation embedding in other tasks.

Acknowledgments. The authors would like to thank the two anonymous reviewers for their comments on this paper. This research was supported by the National Natural Science Foundation of China (Nos. 61773276, 61836007 and 61772354), and the Priority Academic Program Development of Jiangsu Higher Education Institutions (PAPD).

References

1. Van Dijk, T.A.: Narrative macro-structures. PTL J. Descriptive Poetics Theory Literat. **1**, 547–568 (1976)
2. Chu, X., Jiang, F., Xu, S., Zhu, Q.: Building a macro chinese discourse treebank. In: LREC (2018)
3. Jiang, F., Xu, S., Chu, X., Li, P., Zhu, Q., Zhou, G.: Mcdtb: a macro-level chinese discourse treebank. In: COLING, pp. 3493–3504 (2018)
4. Li, Y., Feng, W., Sun, J., Kong, F., Zhou, G.: Building chinese discourse corpus with connective-driven dependency tree structure. In: EMNLP, pp. 2105–2114 (2014)
5. Chen, J., Zhang, Q., Liu, P., Qiu, X., Huang, X.-J.: Implicit discourse relation detection via a deep architecture with gated relevance network. In: ACL, pp. 1726–1735 (2016)
6. Guo, F., He, R., Jin, D., Dang, J., Wang, L., Li, X.: Implicit discourse relation recognition using neural tensor network with interactive attention and sparse learning. In: COLING, pp. 547–558 (2018)
7. Xu, S., Wang, T., Li, P., Zhu, Q.: Multi-layer attention network based chinese implicit discourse relation recognition. J. Chin. Inf. Process **33**(8), 12 (2019)
8. Liu, X., Ou, J., Song, Y., Jiang, X.: On the importance of word and sentence representation learning in implicit discourse relation classification arXiv (2020)
9. Xu, S., Li, P., Kong, F., Zhu, Q., Zhou, G.: Topic tensor network for implicit discourse relation recognition in chinese. In: ACL, pp. 608–618 (2019)
10. He, R., Wang, J., Guo, F., Han, Y.: Transs-driven joint learning architecture for implicit discourse relation recognition. In: ACL, 2020, pp. 139–148 (2020)
11. Zhou, Y., Chu, X., Zhu, Q., Jiang, F., Li, P.: Macro discourse relation classification based on macro semantics representation. J. Chin. Inf. Process **33**(3), 1–7 (2019)
12. F. Jiang, P. Li, and Q. Zhu, "Joint modeling of recognizing macro chinese discourse nuclearity and relation based on structure and topic gated semantic network," in NLPCC. Springer, 2019, pp. 276–286
13. Jiang, F., Chu, X., Li, P., Kong, F., Zhu, Q.: Chinese paragraph-level discourse parsing with global backward and local reverse reading. In: COLING, 2020, pp. 5749–5759 (2020)
14. Devlin, J., Chang, M.-W., Lee, K., Toutanova, K.: Bert: Pre-training of deep bidirectional transformers for language understanding. In: NAACL, pp. 4171–4186 (2019)
15. Bordes, A., Usunier, N., Garcia-Duran, A., Weston, J., Yakhnenko, O.: Translating embeddings for modeling multi-relational data. Adv. Neural Inf. Process. Syst. **26**, 2787–2795 (2013)
16. Peters, M., et al.: Deep contextualized word representations. In: NAACL (2018)
17. Socher, R., Chen, D., Manning, C.D., Ng, A.: Reasoning with neural tensor networks for knowledge base completion. Adv. Neural Inf. Process. Syst. **26**, 926–934 (2013)
18. Pei, W., Ge, T., Chang, B.: Max-margin tensor neural network for Chinese word segmentation. In: ACL, pp. 293–303 (2014)
19. Kim, N., Feng, S., Gunasekara, C., Lastras, L.: Implicit discourse relation classification: we need to talk about evaluation. In: ACL, pp. 5404–5414 (2020)

Abstracting Inter-instance Relations and Inter-label Correlation Simultaneously for Sparse Multi-label

Si-ming Lian and Jian-wei Liu[✉]

Department of Automation, College of Information Science and Engineering,
China University of Petroleum Beijing, Beijing, China
liujw@cup.edu.cn

Abstract. In this paper, both considering inter-instance relations and inter-label corre-lations simultaneously, a kernel Gaussian neural network sparse multi-label learning (GNN-SML) is proposed. More specifically, latent representation for sparse multi-label instance sets is constructed, both involving inter-instance and inter-label relations. The attacking problem is that instance features or label sets are too sparse to be extracted effectively hidden representation. Through both extracting inter-instance relations and inter-label correlations, it makes the learning latent representation more comprehensive, complete and accurate. At the same time, to grasp the uncertainty underlying in multi-label data, Gaussian process is introduced to denote the real underlying distribution of multi-label dataset. Additionally, this paper also incorporates self-attention mechanism to adjust its weight in the calculation of contributions of different features for the final prediction results. Finally, the effectiveness of the GNN-SML is validated on the sparse multi-label datasets.

Keywords: Sparse multi-label · Inter-instance relations · Inter-label correlations · Gaussian process

1 Introduction

Multi-label classification paradigm has been extensively applied in computer vision, speech recognition and recommendation system and so on. For multi-label classification task the most striking dissent over other classification tasks is that multi-label classification needs to find a one to many relationship, perhaps existing in instance and multi-label, there exist positive and negative correlations among labels, and the different similarity relationships among instances are also possible and common. Particularly, different features for each instance may also involve information on multiple labels, which is also possible to plays a pivot role in multi-label learning for other features. Needless to say, harvesting this sharing information in one instance to assist the learning of other instances with multi-label is feasible. Hence we attempt to create the kernelized layer in

© Springer Nature Switzerland AG 2021
T. Mantoro et al. (Eds.): ICONIP 2021, CCIS 1516, pp. 81–88, 2021.
https://doi.org/10.1007/978-3-030-92307-5_10

deep network and draw support from Gaussian kernel function to extract the similarity relation by figuring out the distance between instances in the kernel space.

Unfortunately, when we came true our envisagement, we encounter two Gordian knots: sparsity both for features and labels. To settle down this problem, we maybe have two means to deal with the sparsity issues. For the case of sparse features of instance, it usually tend to impede effectively extracting feature representation, instead of directly extracting the instance relations, we infer the instance relations by considering label correlation. On the other hand, in the case of the sparse label information, we can extract the multi-label relevant information with the help of the relationship between instance features. By this ways we bridge the gap and incompleteness both for sparse instance features and multi-labels, and by comprehensively fusing these multifaceted dependencies we envision that the derived feature representation by this way should reflect more complete and precise information underlying in multi-label data.

The introduction of the label correlations based on higher-order strategies is of great help to multi-label learning. For the sparse multi-label dataset, the introduced label correlations are inspired by the core idea of classifier chains [1], and the information of label correlations are helpful to transfer instance relations. However, for the sparse multi-label dataset, it may not be able to capture the complete label correlation by introducing the label information only, thus it needs to introduce the instance relations to deduce such correlation of the output space.

And besides, the diffusion function based on graph is benefit to transfer the instance relations, which keeps similar instances with similar label set. Recent researches for deep neural networks, most new proposed classification approaches including multi-label learning have renewed a strong interest in graph networks and manifolds [2–4]. Among successful graph approaches, the features in social network can be modeled as signals on the vertices of the graph in deep networks [5]. Other graph models also utilize the time-dependent signals as the vertices of the graph such as the sensor network [6]. In computer vision area, manifolds like Riemannian manifold are also leveraged to model classification task and endowed with the color texture on the surface [7,8]. Besides, some approaches unlock new applications on structured objects for which feature vectors are missing or too complex [9]. Specifically, feature information is divided into irrelevant and relevant part.

Inspired from above discussion, we propose a kernel Gaussian neural net-work sparse multi-label learning (GNN-SML). The GNN-SML starts from the simplest formulation in a simple deep forward network, with subsequently incorporating some feature transformation layers, e.g., the kernelized layer and diffusion mapping layer based on graph learning techniques.

The main contributions for this paper can be described as follows:

(1) The proposed GNN-SML approach incorporates the label information as the supervised item, and further gets the instances relations by means of the graph learning techniques, which takes advantage of the bidirectional

relations to fill the information which is essential for the sparse multi-label classification task.

(2) To better deduce the underlying distribution for multi label data and enhance the interpretability of the network, Gaussian process is added to neural network, which can get an intermediate hidden representation keeping topologic structure.

(3) We introduce attention vectors to balance the importance of different features. We fine-tune the weights of latent vectors for each component of label and fuse features for each type of label component through the alignment weights of attention mechanism, which are benefit to fill the missing information for sparse multi-label learning, which is essential to promote the performance of the model.

2   Problem Formulation

Assume that the instance set is $X := \left\{x_i \in R^{1 \times d}\right\}_{i=1}^{N}$. We divide X into train and test set $X_{tr} := \{x_1, x_2, \cdots, x_{N_r}\}$, $X_{te} := \{x_{N_r+1}, x_2, \cdots, x_N\}$, for X_{tr}, the corresponding training multi-label set is $Y_{tr} := \left\{y_i \in \{0,1\}^K\right\}_{i=1}^{N_r}$, and the testing instances set are unlabeled $N_s = N - N_r$ instances. Our aim is to deduce the label set of unlabeled testing instances with finding the sufficient information from training samples.

3   Framework for Sparse Multi-Label Learning

3.1   The Kernelized Layer

This subsection considers introducing the kernel layer, and we intend to utilize the kernel function to grasp the compact topology structure existing in hidden representation. Specifically, radial basis function (RBF) is used to build the kernelized layer. RBF generally defined as a similar monotonic function between any points, that is, when the point is far away from the other point, the value of the RBF is smaller. More precise, we have Eq. (1):

$$G(z_i, z_j) = E[m_i(z_i)m_j(z_j)] = \sigma_b^2 + \sigma_w^2 E_{z \sim GP(0,\sigma)}[z_i z_j] = \sigma_b^2 + \sigma_w^2 C(z_i z_j) \quad (1)$$

where σ_b^2 and σ_w^2 are bias and weight, assume that it is the i.i.d. samples. Note that, in the case of layer becoming the infinite width, for m_i, its probability law will be accurate Gaussian distributed, which is precise the definition of a Gaussian process. Thus we designate $m_i \sim GP(\mu, \sigma)$, i.e., a Gaussian process (GP) with the mean μ and covariance σ. The relationship between the kernel function outputs M_{te} and the testing intermediate outputs $z_i, i = N_r + 1, \cdots, N$ is as following:

$$
\begin{aligned}
&P(M_{te} \mid Z_{tr}, Y_{tr}, Z_{te}) \\
&= \int dM_{tr} P(M_{te} \mid Z_{tr}, M_{tr}, Z_{te}) P(M_{tr} \mid Z_{tr}, Y_{tr}) \\
&= \tfrac{1}{P(Y_{tr})} \int dM_{tr} P(M_{te}, M_{tr} \mid Z_{tr}, Z_{te}) P(Y_{tr} \mid M_{tr})
\end{aligned}
\quad (2)
$$

where M_{tr} and M_{te} denotes the training and testing probability respectively. And the $P(Y_{tr}|M_{tr})$ indicates the posterior probability corresponding to the estimated probability of training labels. As a matter of fact, the estimated results possibly are contaminated by the noise σ_ε. With this in mind, we assume that $M_{tr}, M_{te}|Z_{tr}, Z_{te} \sim N(0,\sigma)$ are governed by the multi-variate Gaussian distribution whose joint covariance matrix can be formulated as following:

$$\begin{pmatrix} y \\ f \end{pmatrix} \sim N\left(0, \begin{pmatrix} G_{\{Z_{tr},Y_{tr}\},\{Z_{tr},Y_{tr}\}}, G^{\mathrm{T}}_{Z_{te},\{Z_{tr},Y_{tr}\}} \\ G_{Z_{te},\{Z_{tr},Y_{tr}\}}, G_{Z_{te},Z_{te}} \end{pmatrix}\right) \tag{3}$$

where the Eq. (3) are refer to [11] and $G_{\{Z_{tr},Y_{tr}\},\{Z_{tr},Y_{tr}\}} \in R^{N_r \times N_r}$. The block structure is naturally divided by the training and test sets. The corresponding mean and variance for the true testing points' distribution $M_{te}|Z_{tr}, Y_{tr}, Z_{te} \sim N(\bar{\mu}, \bar{\sigma})$ are formulated as follows:

$$\begin{aligned} \bar{\mu} &= G_{Z_{te},\{Z_{tr},Y_{tr}\}}(G_{\{Z_{tr},Y_{tr}\},\{Z_{tr},Y_{tr}\}} + \sigma_\varepsilon^2 I)Y_{tr} \\ \bar{\sigma} &= G_{Z_{te},Z_{te}} - G_{Z_{te},\{Z_{tr},Y_{tr}\}}(G_{\{Z_{tr},Y_{tr}\},\{Z_{tr},Y_{tr}\}} + \sigma_\varepsilon^2 I)G^{\mathrm{T}}_{Z_{te},\{Z_{tr},Y_{tr}\}} \end{aligned} \tag{4}$$

where I is the identity matrix. Note that our RBF kernel function layer is utilized to acquire hidden kernel representation obeying the Gaussian distribution. Specifically, we first build K binary classifiers to obtain the special hidden representations for each component of multi-label. And then, these special hidden representations are recombined. Finally, the recombined hidden representations are further mapped by the Gaussian kernel functions, as shown in Eq. (3).

3.2   The Diffusion Mapping Layer

Roughly-speaking, the diffusion function can be built from the two different standpoints of the spatial-domain and frequency-domain. The pivot assumption is that the diffusion process obeys the diffusion equation [10], for our setup, the ker-nel layer's output M_{tr} is considered as the diffusion function, and then we introduce the following diffusion distance:

$$d_{ij} = G(m_i, m_j)^{N_r}_{i,j=1} \tag{5}$$

That is to say, the diffusion mapping method calculates the distance matrix by means of the latent matrix which is derived from the kernelized layer. Particularly, the distance matrix can be written as:

$$D = \begin{vmatrix} d_{11} & \cdots & d_{1Nr} \\ \vdots & \ddots & \vdots \\ d_{Nr1} & \cdots & d_{NrNr} \end{vmatrix} \tag{6}$$

where d_{ij} in matrix D denotes the similarity of latent features of the two points m_i and m_j from the kernelized layers. After deriving the distance matrix G from the ker-nelized layer, we need to impose the consistency constraints on the inter-instance relationships. First, through the symmetric matrix D with dimension

$Nr \times Nr$ and diagonal element is zero, where its elements are non-negative and represents the similarity degree between the i-th and the j-th element, the normalized symmetric matrix can be achieved by the following identities:

$$S = A^{-1/2}DA^{1/2}, A = diag(D_{1K}), \cdots , diag(D_{lK}) \tag{7}$$

where D denotes degree matrix and A refer to the all-ones vector. Assuming that we have the training label sets Y, and we can also obtain the estimating probability P of each class label, then the diffusion amounts for the estimating P can be written as:

$$P = (I - \alpha S)^{-1}Y_{tr} \tag{8}$$

The straightforward estimating probability matrix P by Eq. (8) is impractical for modest large n because computation cost for the inverse matrix is cubic increase with the dimension, which is intractable to calculate. We leverage the conjugate gradient to solve the linear equation:

$$(I - \alpha S)P = Y_{tr} \tag{9}$$

where $0 \leq \alpha < 1$ is a parameter and $P \in R^{Nr \times K}$. Finally, by solving the Eq. (9) we obtain the class label probability latent information $P_i = \{p_{i,1}, p_{i,2}, \cdots p_{i,K}\}$ for the training instance x_i, $i \in (1, \cdots , Nr)$.

3.3   The Self-attention Layer

In this subsection, the self-attention layer fires the integrated latent information P as well as the label probability vector to the output layer. Thus, suppose that all the weight scores are given to reconstruct the latent probability information, which can be written as:

$$\beta_{i,k} = \sum_{k=1}^{K} q_{i,k} \tanh(\sum_{j=1}^{K} V_{i,j} \times p_{i,k} + b_{i,k}) \tag{10}$$

$$\beta_{i,k} = \frac{\exp(\beta_{i,k})}{\sum_{k=1}^{K} \exp(\beta_{i,k})} \tag{11}$$

where $p_{i,k}$ is the special latent probability corresponding to $y_{i,k}$ derived from the previous diffusion method, and parameter $V_{i,j}$ denotes the alignment weight, which represents the importance of the j-th special features. Besides, other parameters $q_{i,k}$, and $b_{i,k}$ belong to the current label, not depend on the other label directly, also can be trained from the back propagation procedures of the deep neural network. Generally, the weight vectors are divided into the K parts with the predicted probability information.

4   The Objective Function

We construct the objective function for the kernel diffusion neural network for multi-label learning as follows:

$$
\begin{aligned}
J = \xi_1 \sum_{i=1}^{N_r} \sum_{k=1}^{K} \left\| y_i - \widehat{y}_i \right\|_2^2 + \xi_2 \sum_{i=1}^{N_r} \left| \sum_{k=1}^{K} \beta_{i,k} - K \right| \\
+ \xi_3 \sum_{i,j=1}^{N_r} w_{i,j} \left\| \frac{Z_i}{\sqrt{d_{ii}}} - \frac{Z_j}{\sqrt{d_{jj}}} \right\|^2 + \xi_4 \|\theta\|^2
\end{aligned}
\tag{12}
$$

The objective function can be divided into four parts, supervised item, attention weight constraint, diffusion constraint and regularization part. All the influencing factors which are related to GNN-SML model have been involved, our constraint and regularization term are built from these influencing factors, and the update of model parameters is affected by these constraints. And our thought is validated on the real-life datasets in experimental feasibility evaluation part.

5   Experiments

The six practical datasets from the different domains are used to verify that our thoughts. We first divide the datasets into the training and testing samples. The details of these datasets are shown in Table 1. In addition, the random state is set as 0, and we repeat the experiments 10 times to obtain the average value. Compare with the previous baseline approaches and state-of-the-art, we identified that the feasibility of GNN-SML framework according to the multi-label classification indexes. Besides, the mean error and standard deviation of the GNN-SML are given in Table 2.

Table 1. The characteristic of the datasets.

Dataset	Domain	N	D	K	Training and testing set	Density
Yeast	Biology	2417	103	14	1200/1216	0.046
Genbase	Biology	662	1186	27	300/362	0.303
Flags	Images	194	19	7	90/104	0.485
Scene	Image	2407	294	6	1200/1207	0.179
Emotions	Music	593	72	6	290/303	0.028
Medical	Text	978	1449	45	450/528	0.311

Table 2. Experimental results for different methods (Mean±Variance).

Methods	Accuracy (medical %)	Fscore (medical %)	Accuracy (emotion %)	Fscore (emotion %)
MLKNN	41.35±1.74	2.77±0.10	13.06±1.68	26.64±0.71
KISAR	54.62±50.0	5.57±0.52	51.68±27.4	37.19±5.85
BR	68.34 ±1.57	10.23±0.48	60.49±0.617	6.33±5.48
MANIAC	52.17±1.83	33.24 ±2.76	53.89±0.11	31.14±19.86
COINS	10.32±0.01	13.21±0.01	32.62±0.11	49.19±0.01
C2AE	83.39±0.19	78.70±0.06	46.70±4.46	61.00±3.81
MLCBMaD	41.06±0.18	43.14±0.00	56.30±0.77	33.14±1.66
GNN-SML	96.06 ±0.24	19.60±5.33	66.72±0.75	22.55±8.71

Methods	Accuracy (yeast %)	Fscore (yeast %)	Accuracy (scene %)	Fscore (scene %)
MLKNN	14.95±1.04	30.37±0.01	57.48±0.76	18.10±0.01
KISAR	44.81±29.8	38.45±7.89	31.59±0.35	17.25±0.98
BR	81.02±0.28	39.24±0.01	91.66±0.31	71.58±1.21
MANIAC	52.71±1.27	23.00±0.01	60.27±1.56	17.18±0.19
COINS	30.72±0.01	45.59±1.06	18.10±0.00	30.65±0.01
C2AE	46.91±0.59	40.22±0.96	53.51±6.51	64.79±4.39
MLCBMaD	57.00±0.01	34.00±0.01	47.27±0.17	54.06±1.78
GNN-SML	78.16±0.61	46.07±3.01	73.26±0.85	18.05±0.20

Methods	Accuracy (flags)	Fscore (flags)	Accuracy (genbase)	Fscore (genbase)
MLKNN	4.29±1.27	48.48±1.09	74.79±1.05	4.73±0.12
KISAR	51.59±22.8	40.09±27.6	51.54±22.7	41.03±26.4
BR	64.08+1.26	38.21±0.41	63.18±0.24	37.92±0.11
MANIAC	61.39±3.98	15.24±2.11	52.18±2.20	33.92±1.09
COINS	48.48±0.10	65.31±0.98	4.71±0.01	9.13±0.00
C2AE	52.07±1.67	47.41±2.77	67.68±12.5	48.83±4.57
MLCBMaD	55.54±1.10	54.84±0.98	84.09±0.50	83.03±0.14
GNN-SML	68.68±2.95	40.94±3.88	93.20±0.21	24.76±1.85

6   Conclusions and Future Work

In this paper, we not only consider the label correlation, but also interest in the instance relations. The multi-label learning with the plentiful relations, including label independence, partial label relations, and all label relations, is omnipresent in comparison with other classification tasks. The kernel function, which is the hub bridging low-dimensional and high-dimensional space, provides a means to encompass the feature representation by the inner product of high-dimensional space. Then, the kernel space is naturally compatible with the Gaussian process. Finally, by means of incorporating the attention mechanism, we make the learned feature representation for each label component to share with the ones for other label components, so that the learned feature representation has more complete information including in multi-label data. Furthermore, we verify the performance of the proposed GNN-SML on six real datasets, and obtain the following conclusions: (1) in view of different hypothesis: different feature representations are derived during the training process. By building different input matrix, we can deduce different label relations, which is benefit to boost the performance of unknown in-stance. (2) The Gaussian process is adopted to extract the instance information, which can distil the diversity instance information for different datasets. (3) The experimental comparison results confirm that the accuracies of GNN-SML is higher than that of most baseline methods on most data sets, which verifies the effectiveness of our GNN-SML.

GNN-SML connects the low-dimensional and high-dimensional space through the kernel function and uses the deep neural network as the framework. Further, in order to make up for the discarding of label correlation in the training process, we build different input matrix to make up for this deficiency and combine it with different data requirements. Finally, the experimental results show that our method is feasible. Further research may consider a semi-supervised approach, which would ideally modify the feature representation according to the target tasks.

Acknowledgement. This work was supported by the Science Foundation of China University of Petroleum, Beijing (No. 2462020YXZZ023).

References

1. Read, J., Pfahringer, B., Holmes, G., Frank, E.: Classifier chains for multi-label classification. In: Proceedings of the ECML PKDD 2009: Machine Learning and Knowledge Discovery in Databases, pp. 254–269 (2009)
2. Leordeanu, M.: Unsupervised Learning in Space and Time. ACVPR, Springer, Cham (2020). https://doi.org/10.1007/978-3-030-42128-1
3. Zhang, C.-Y., Hu, J., Yang, L., Chen, C.L.P., Yao, Z.: Graph de-convolutional networks. Inf. Sci. **518**, 330–340 (2020)
4. Kejani, M.T., Dornaika, F., Talebi, H.: Graph Convolution Networks with manifold regularization for semi-supervised learning. Neural Networks **127**, 160–167 (2020)
5. Zhou, J., Cui, G., Zhang, Z., Yang, C., Liu, Z., Sun, M.: Graph Neural Networks: A Review of Methods and Applications, CoRR abs/1812.08434 2018
6. Wang, Y., Yuan, Y., Ma, Y., Wang, G.: Time-dependent graphs: definitions, applications, and algorithms. Data Sci. Eng. **4**(4), 352–366 (2019)
7. Pennec, X., Fillard, P., Ayache, N.: A Riemannian framework for tensor computing. Int. J. Comput. Vis. **66**(1), 41–66 (2006)
8. Caseiro, R., Martins, P., Henriques, J.F., Batista, J.P.: A nonparametric Riemannian framework on tensor field with application to foreground segmentation. Pattern Recognit. **45**(11), 3997–4017 (2012)
9. Laforgue, P., Clémençon, S., d'Alché-Buc, F.: Autoencoding any data through kernel autoencoders. In: The 22nd International Conference on Artificial Intelligence and Statistics (AISTATS 2019), 1061–1069 (2019)
10. Xie, T., Wang, B., Kuo, C.C.J.: GraphHop, "An Enhanced Label Propagation Method for Node Classification," arXiv preprint arXiv:2101.02326 (2021)

L-DPSNet: Deep Photometric Stereo Network via Local Diffuse Reflectance Maxima

Kanghui Zeng[1], Chao Xu[1,2,3], Jing Hu[1,3(✉)], Yushi Li[2,4],
and Zhaopeng Meng[1,4]

[1] College of Intelligence and Computing, Tianjin University, Tianjin 300350, China
mavis_huhu@tju.edu.cn
[2] The Hong Kong Polytechnic University, Hung Hom, Hong Kong
[3] Higher Research Institute (Shenzhen), University of Electronic Science
and Technology of China, Shenzhen 518063, China
[4] Tianjin University of Traditional Chinese Medicine, Tianjin 300193, China

Abstract. Reconstructing surface normal from the reflectance observations of real objects is a challenging issue. Although recent works on photometric stereo exploit various reflectance-normal mapping models, none of them take both illumination and LDR maximum into account. In this paper, we combine a fusion learning network with LDR maxima to recover the normal of the underlying surface. Unlike traditional formalization, the initial normal estimated by solving the generalized bas-relief (GBR) ambiguity is employed to promote the performance of our learning framework. As an uncalibrated photometric stereo network, our method, called L-DPSNet, takes advantage of LDR-derived information in normal prediction. We present the qualitative and quantitative experiments implemented using synthetic and real data to demonstrate the effectiveness of the proposed model.

Keywords: Uncalibrated photometric stereo · Deep neural network · Diffuse reflectance maxima

1 Introduction

Photometric stereo is generally categorized into calibrated [1–3] and uncalibrated methods [4–8] depending on the lighting conditions. Uncalibrated photometric stereo can estimate surface normal when illumination conditions and reflectance knowledge are non-available, making it more flexible in practical applications.

Since deep neural networks have achieved impressive success in calibrated photometric stereo tasks, Chen et al. [9] proposed a deep uncalibrated photometric stereo network to predict surface normals by estimating the light direction and

Supported by the National Key R&D Program of China under Grant No. 2018YFB 1701700.

© Springer Nature Switzerland AG 2021
T. Mantoro et al. (Eds.): ICONIP 2021, CCIS 1516, pp. 89–97, 2021.
https://doi.org/10.1007/978-3-030-92307-5_11

intensity of the input image. This framework resolves GBR ambiguity [10] and significantly outperforms the traditional methods in normal prediction. Based on [9], Chen et al. [11] designed Guided Calibration Network (GCNet) that leverages object shape and shading information of the object to better estimate lighting.

Although these previous networks address the connection between lighting and normal estimation, there are still some deficiencies in them. LCNet [9] adopts two-stage network to estimate lighting information and surface normals. This work does not clarify how deep uncalibrated photometric stereo resolves GBR ambiguity and overlooks inter-image information. As an improvement of LCNet, GCNet employs shading clues to guide light estimation. However, this framework directly utilizes LCNet to extract lighting message, making it ineffective in exploiting clues.

To take advantage of clues information, we propose a fusion network that combines traditional methods with normal learning model. Importantly, we design a three-stage learning network to achieve accurate and efficient normal estimation. The first stage of L-DPSNet, denoted as Lighting Estimation Network (LENet), predicts the lighting directions and intensities from the input images. The second stage, named as Normal Estimation Network (NENet), takes the lighting information estimated by LENet and the input images as input to predict the lighting directions and intensities. The third stage-Fusion Estimation Network (FENet) computes the final surface normal. In summary, our contributions are:

- We discuss the similarities and differences between the traditional methods and the learning-based methods in solving the photometric stereo problem. We further analyze the effects of prior knowledge in the learning-based uncalibrated photometric stereo method.
- We propose a network architecture leveraging the local diffuse reflectance maxima clue to improve the surface normal estimation.
- We prove that the obtained model is capable to provide accurate results using both synthetic and real datasets.

2   Related Work

Traditional Methods. When the light source information is lacking, traditional methods generally assume a Lambertian reflection model. They uses matrix decomposition to constraint the Lambertian surface normal estimation to a 3×3 linear ambiguity [12]. In addition, surface integrability constraint is often employed for simplifying the linear ambiguity to a 3-parameter generalized bas-relief (GBR) ambiguity [10,13–16]. To resolve the GBR ambiguity, various approaches, such as inter-reflections [4], specularities [17], albedo priors [5,18], isotropic reflectance symmetry [6,19], special light source distributions [8], diffuse reflectance maxima [20], were proposed.

Learning Methods. Recently, the success of deep learning in calibrated photo-metric stereo [1–3,21,22] inspire researchers to introduce deep learning methods into the uncalibrated photometric stereo. Chen et al. [3] proposed UPS-FCN. The performance of UPS-FCN is competitive with PF14 [20] which is the best tradi-tional method. Chen et al. [9] introduced a deep uncalibrated photometric stereo network, to estimate the lighting and surface normal from the input image. This model outperforms the traditional methods in normal estimation. Furthermore, it solves the GBR ambiguity [10] involved in the traditional method. Based on LCNet, GCNet [11] uses shading clues to guide the network for better estimat-ing lighting feature, This improvement significantly promotes the performance of learning-based calibrated network in surface normal recovery.

3   Uncalibrated Photometric Stereo

3.1   Image Formation Model

We define the unit normal vector of the element at index p as $n_p \in \mathbb{S}^2$ for $p = 1, ..., P$, albedo coefficient α_p, where P is the total number of pixels in an image. We denote $l_q \in \mathbb{S}^2$ as the unit-normal corresponding to the q-th illumination direction and $e_q \in \mathbb{S}^2$ as the light intensity. Then, the intensity measured at a pixel index p with illumination q for the Lambertian case is:

$$i_{p,q} = \alpha_p \langle n_p, l_q \rangle e_q \qquad (1)$$

where $\langle \cdot, \cdot \rangle$ denotes inner product. Then, Eq. 1 is converted to the compact matrix form as:

$$I = \langle N, L \rangle \qquad (2)$$

where $\{I\}_{p,q} = i_{p,q}$.

3.2   GBR Ambiguity

According to [12], N and L can be obtained up to a linear ambiguity if the light matrix is unknown:

$$I = N^T G^{-1} G L \qquad (3)$$

where $G^{-1}G$ is the identity matrix. Then, following [10], we impose the integra-bility constraint to convert the ambiguities G to:

$$G = \begin{bmatrix} 1 & 0 & 0 \\ 0 & 1 & 0 \\ \mu & \nu & \lambda \end{bmatrix} \qquad (4)$$

where μ, ν, λ represent the set of GBR transformations, and $\lambda \neq 0$. After solving these parameters, we obtain the expression of G. Finally, the normal matrix is solved as: The normal matrix is solved as:

$$N = G^{-1}\tilde{N} \tag{5}$$

The traditional method introduces known clues, such as inter-reflection [4], specularities [17] and diffuse reflectance maxima [20], to resolve GBR ambiguity. Evaluation with DiLiGenT, PF14 outperforms other traditional methods.

By contrast, the existing deep learning methods generally use a great quantity of synthetic data to infer the relationship between the input image and the surface normal of the corresponding object. For instance, SDPS-Net [9] estimates surface normal using two steps. First, it learns the lighting. Then, this network employs the lighting information to estimate the surface normal. Based on SDPS, GCNet [11] leverages shading clues to guide the lighting estimation network and obtains better lighting estimation results.

4   Methodology

4.1   Motivation

The input data significantly impact the performance of learning models. GCNet uses the clue information of shading in normal inference, which noticeably improve the accuracy of surface normal estimation. Differently, we choose the feature that is more informative than shading to feed the network.

Surface Normal as Guidance. Taking SDPS as the benchmark, SDPS's network may not fully utilize representative information when using clues as the initial input. Moreover, using clues as SDPS's initial input would affect the information extracted by SDPS, resulting in more inferior results. Therefore, we add a new part, named FENet, to effectively make use of clues in normal estimation. In specific, we transform the clues to the normal map using traditional methods. Compared with GCNet, our framework reduces the difficulty of learning task and is more likely to obtain accurate normal vectors.

Surface Normal Obtained by PF14 as Guidance. We assume that the coarse normal extracted by traditional methods maintains representative information required by learning networks. In another word, pre-knowledge has the potential to help our learning model in estimating accurate normal vectors. Since the initial input plays an essential role in the performance of learning frameworks, we employ PF14 to provide the initial representation.

4.2   Network Architecture

As shown in Fig. 1(c), L-DPSNet consists of three components: LENet, NENet and FENet.

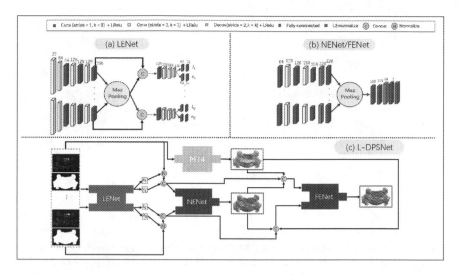

Fig. 1. Structure of (a) the LENet, (b) the NENet and the FENet, and (c) the entire L-DPSNet. Values in layers indicate the output channel number.

LENet. The architecture of LENet is similar to LCNet [9]. This network has fewer channels in the convolutional layers to reduce the model size (see Fig. 1(a)). Following LCNet, given Q images, the loss function of LENet is defined as:

$$L_{light} = \frac{1}{Q} \sum_q (L_{l_\alpha}^q + L_{l_\gamma}^q + L_\gamma^q) \qquad (6)$$

where $L_{l_\alpha}^q$, $L_{l_\gamma}^q$ and L_γ^q are the cross-entropy loss for light azimuth, elevation, and intensity classifications for the q-th input image.

NENet. The architecture of NENet is similar to PS-FCN [3] (see Fig. 1(b)). Then, the obtained normal is revised by the fusion network. Following PS-FCN, given the P number of pixels, the loss function of NENet is defined as:

$$L_{normal} = \frac{1}{p} \sum_p (1 - n_p^T \hat{n}_p) \qquad (7)$$

where n_p and $\hat{n}_p$ are the ground-truth and the predicted normal at pixel p respectively.

Specifically, NENet has six input channels (3 for the image, 3 for the lighting estimation obtained by LENet). In comparison, FENet has 12 (3 additional channels for the normal estimation obtained by NENet, 3 additional channels for the normal estimation obtained by PF14).

4.3 Training Detail

In our experiments, we use the publicly available synthetic Blobby and Sculpture Dataset [3]. First, we train LENet following GCNet's training procedure [11].

Second, we train NENet following SDPSNet's training procedure [9]. Third, we train FENet for 10 epochs, halving the learning rate every 2 epochs. The initial learning rate is 0.0005 for FENet.

5   Experimental Result

In this section, we evaluate our method on virtual datasets and real datasets. Mean Angular Error (MAE) is chosen to measure the surface normal [9].

5.1   Evaluation on Synthetic Data

Comparative Study. To verify the rationality of the proposed network, we conduct a comparative study, and the results are presented in Table 1. Experiments 0 & 1 & 4 verifies that the proposed method with fewer network parameters is competitive with the existing optimal uncalibrated photometric stereo network. In addition, we provide experiments 3 & 5 to illustrate the performance of FENet without PF14.

Table 1. Normal estimation results on the synthetic dataset. NENet' was trained in fewer channels. FENet' was trained with NENet results instead of traditional results as input.

ID	Method	Param	Bunny	Dragon
0	LCNet [9]+NENet	6.60M	4.06	5.59
1	GCNet [11]+NENet	6.86M	3.81	4.85
2	LENet+NENet'	2.88M	6.76	12.97
3	LENet+NENet	3.98M	3.93	5.04
4	LENet+NENet+FENet	6.18M	**3.78**	**4.77**
5	LENet+NENet+FENet'	6.18M	4.06	5.12

Results Under Different Light Distribution. To analyze the effect of different light distribution, L-DPSNet is evaluated under "Uniform", "Narrow" and "Upper" distributions. The results are summarized in Table 2. The comparison between experiments 0 & 1 & 2 and 0 & 3 & 4 verifies that FENet performs robustly when PF14 [20] shows stable performance. Experiments 2 & 3 verifies that the performance of L-DPSNet is worse than GCNet+NENet when the results for PF14 are not convincing.

Results Under Surfaces with SVBRDFs. To analyze the effect of SVBRDFs, we use two different material maps to generate a synthetic dataset with SVBRDF surface following Goldman et al. [23]. Table 3 shows that the performance of our method on the surface with SVBRDFs is worse than that of uniform BRDF, but it is still the better one.

Table 2. Normal estimation results on Dragon under three different lighting distributions.

ID	Model	Uniform	Narrow	Upper
0	PF14 [20]	27.299	29.465	34.548
1	LENet+NENet	5.068	7.498	8.234
2	L-DPSNet	4.787	7.035	8.453
3	GCNet [11]+NENet	4.796	6.962	**7.907**
4	GCNet+NENet+FENet	**4.629**	**6.656**	8.399

Table 3. Normal estimation results on Dragon rendered with SVBRDFs.

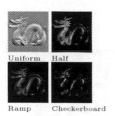

Uniform   Half

Ramp   Checkerboard

ID	Model	Uniform	Half	Ramp	Checkerboard
0	PF14 [20]	21.90	23.029	28.292	23.47
1	LENet+NENet	5.04	5.10	5.27	8.09
2	GCNet [11]+NENet	4.85	4.99	**5.03**	8.189
3	L-DPSNet	**4.77**	**4.88**	5.05	**7.60**

5.2 Evaluation on Real Data

To verify the proposed method's ability to handle non-Lambert objects in the real world, we evaluate it on the challenging DiLiGenT benchmark [24].

Evaluated on the DiLiGenT Benchmark. Table 4 compares the normal estimation of L-DPSNet with those of previous DiLiGenT methods. The results show that the average MAE of L-DPSNet is 9.13, which surpasses all methods except GCNet+NENet. Compared with SDPS, our method outperforms the results of SDPS with fewer parameters. In addition, the FENet part of our method can be effectively combined with GCNet+NENet to obtain an average MAE result that exceeds all uncalibrated photometric stereo methods.

Table 4. Results of L-DPSNet on the DiLiGenT benchmark.

ID	Model	Ball	Cat	Pot1	Bear	Pot2	Buddha	Goblet	Reading	Cow	Harvest	Avg.
0	AM07 [18]	7.27	31.45	18.37	16.81	49.16	32.81	46.54	53.65	54.72	61.70	37.25
1	SM10 [5]	8.9	19.84	16.68	11.98	50.68	15.54	48.79	26.93	22.73	73.86	29.60
2	WT13 [6]	4.39	36.55	9.39	6.24	14.52	13.19	20.57	58.96	19.75	55.51	23.91
3	LM13 [7]	22.43	25.01	32.82	15.44	20.57	25.76	29.16	48.16	22.53	34.45	27.63
4	PF14 [20]	5.87	9.02	9.63	9.20	15.97	15.45	30.79	26.18	19.58	33.69	17.54
5	SDPS-Net [9]	2.77	8.06	8.14	6.89	7.50	8.97	11.91	14.90	8.48	17.43	9.51
6	GCNet [11]+ NENet	2.48	7.87	7.21	5.55	7.05	**8.58**	9.62	14.92	7.81	16.22	8.73
7	L-DPSNet	2.67	**7.54**	7.78	6.59	**7.00**	8.72	11.62	**14.48**	8.18	16.74	9.13
8	GCNet+NENet+ FENet	**2.17**	7.71	6.75	5.31	6.54	8.80	**9.16**	14.00	7.15	16.09	8.37

Runtime. The runtimes of GCNet+NENet and L-DPSNet for processing an object from the DiLiGenT benchmark (96 images in total) are 6s and 7s, measured on a single k80 GPU. Although GCNet+NENet runs slightly faster, both methods are very fast.

6   Conclusions

This paper proposes a method to solve the normal estimation problem in deep uncalibrated photometric stereo. The experimental results on the synthetic and real datasets show that our method is significantly better than SDPS-Net in normal estimation. The fusion part of our method combined with GCNET+PS-FCN can achieve better results than GCNET+PS-FCN on the DiLiGenT dataset. In the future, we will explore better ways to enhance the performance of L-DPSNet under the "Upper" illumination distribution and the "Ramp" material maps.

Acknowledgments. This work was supported by the National Key R&D Program of China under Grant No. 2018YFB1701700.

References

1. Taniai, T., Maehara, T.: Neural photometric stereo reconstruction for general reflectance surfaces. CoRR abs/1802.10328 (2018), http://arxiv.org/abs/1802.10328

2. Ikehata, S.: Cnn-ps: Cnn-based photometric stereo for general non-convex surfaces. In: Proceedings of the European Conference on Computer Vision (ECCV), September 2018

3. Chen, G., Han, K., Wong, K.-Y.K.: PS-FCN: a flexible learning framework for photometric stereo. In: Ferrari, V., Hebert, M., Sminchisescu, C., Weiss, Y. (eds.) ECCV 2018. LNCS, vol. 11213, pp. 3–19. Springer, Cham (2018). https://doi.org/10.1007/978-3-030-01240-3_1

4. Chandraker, M.K., Kahl, F., Kriegman, D.J.: Reflections on the generalized bas-relief ambiguity. In: 2005 IEEE Computer Society Conference on Computer Vision and Pattern Recognition (CVPR 2005). vol. 1, pp. 788–795. IEEE (2005)

5. Shi, B., Matsushita, Y., Wei, Y., Xu, C., Tan, P.: Self-calibrating photometric stereo. In: 2010 IEEE Computer Society Conference on Computer Vision and Pattern Recognition, pp. 1118–1125. IEEE (2010)

6. Wu, Z., Tan, P.: Calibrating photometric stereo by holistic reflectance symmetry analysis. In: Proceedings of the IEEE Conference on Computer Vision and Pattern Recognition, pp. 1498–1505 (2013)

7. Lu, F., Matsushita, Y., Sato, I., Okabe, T., Sato, Y.: Uncalibrated photometric stereo for unknown isotropic reflectances. In: Proceedings of the IEEE Conference on Computer Vision and Pattern Recognition, pp. 1490–1497 (2013)

8. Zhou, Z., Tan, P.: Ring-light photometric stereo. In: Daniilidis, K., Maragos, P., Paragios, N. (eds.) ECCV 2010. LNCS, vol. 6312, pp. 265–279. Springer, Heidelberg (2010). https://doi.org/10.1007/978-3-642-15552-9_20

9. Chen, G., Han, K., Shi, B., Matsushita, Y., Wong, K.Y.K.: Self-calibrating deep photometric stereo networks. In: Proceedings of the IEEE/CVF Conference on Computer Vision and Pattern Recognition, pp. 8739–8747 (2019)

10. Belhumeur, P.N., Kriegman, D.J., Yuille, A.L.: The bas-relief ambiguity. Int. J. Comput. Vision **35**(1), 33–44 (1999)
11. Chen, G., Waechter, M., Shi, B., Wong, K.-Y.K., Matsushita, Y.: What is learned in deep uncalibrated photometric stereo? In: Vedaldi, A., Bischof, H., Brox, T., Frahm, J.-M. (eds.) ECCV 2020. LNCS, vol. 12359, pp. 745–762. Springer, Cham (2020). https://doi.org/10.1007/978-3-030-58568-6_44
12. Hayakawa, H.: Photometric stereo under a light source with arbitrary motion. JOSA A **11**(11), 3079–3089 (1994)
13. Ackermann, J., Goesele, M.: A survey of photometric stereo techniques. Found. Trends Comput. Graph. Vis. **9**(3–4), 149–254 (2015)
14. Epstein, R., Yuille, A.L., Belhumeur, P.N.: Learning object representations from lighting variations. In: Ponce, J., Zisserman, A., Hebert, M. (eds.) ORCV 1996. LNCS, vol. 1144, pp. 179–199. Springer, Heidelberg (1996). https://doi.org/10.1007/3-540-61750-7_29
15. Kriegman, D.J., Belhumeur, P.N.: What shadows reveal about object structure. JOSA A **18**(8), 1804–1813 (2001)
16. Yuille, A.L., Snow, D., Epstein, R., Belhumeur, P.N.: Determining generative models of objects under varying illumination: shape and albedo from multiple images using SVD and integrability. Int. J. Comput. Vision **35**(3), 203–222 (1999)
17. Drbohlav, O., Chaniler, M.: Can two specular pixels calibrate photometric stereo? In: Tenth IEEE International Conference on Computer Vision (ICCV'05) Volume 1. vol. 2, pp. 1850–1857. IEEE (2005)
18. Alldrin, N.G., Mallick, S.P., Kriegman, D.J.: Resolving the generalized bas-relief ambiguity by entropy minimization. In: 2007 IEEE Conference on Computer Vision and Pattern Recognition, pp. 1–7. IEEE (2007)
19. Tan, P., Mallick, S.P., Quan, L., Kriegman, D.J., Zickler, T.: Isotropy, reciprocity and the generalized bas-relief ambiguity. In: 2007 IEEE Conference on Computer Vision and Pattern Recognition, pp. 1–8. IEEE (2007)
20. Papadhimitri, T., Favaro, P.: A closed-form, consistent and robust solution to uncalibrated photometric stereo via local diffuse reflectance maxima. Int. J. Comput. Vision **107**(2), 139–154 (2014)
21. Li, J., Robles-Kelly, A., You, S., Matsushita, Y.: Learning to minify photometric stereo. In: Proceedings of the IEEE/CVF Conference on Computer Vision and Pattern Recognition, pp. 7568–7576 (2019)
22. Zheng, Q., Jia, Y., Shi, B., Jiang, X., Duan, L.Y., Kot, A.C.: Spline-net: sparse photometric stereo through lighting interpolation and normal estimation networks. In: Proceedings of the IEEE/CVF International Conference on Computer Vision, pp. 8549–8558 (2019)
23. Goldman, D.B., Curless, B., Hertzmann, A., Seitz, S.M.: Shape and spatially-varying brdfs from photometric stereo. IEEE Trans. Pattern Anal. Mach. Intell. **32**(6), 1060–1071 (2009)
24. Shi, B., Wu, Z., Mo, Z., Duan, D., Yeung, S.K., Tan, P.: A benchmark dataset and evaluation for non-lambertian and uncalibrated photometric stereo. In: Proceedings of the IEEE Conference on Computer Vision and Pattern Recognition, pp. 3707–3716 (2016)

Multi-scale Feature Fusion Network with Positional Normalization for Single Image Dehazing

Bin Hu$^{(\boxtimes)}$, Zhuangzhuang Yue, and Yuehua Li

School of Information Science and Technology, Nantong University,
Nantong 226019, Jiangsu, China
hubin@ntu.edu.cn

Abstract. In order to remove the haze from hazy images, we design an end-to-end trainable multi-scale feature fusion network with positional normalization named MSFFP-Net which does not rely on the physical atmosphere scattering model, and the backbone of the proposed network is a multi-scale network (MSNet). The MSNet uses a up-sampling and down-sampling block to connect different scales, so the information in the net can be exchanged efficiently. The basic convolution module of MSNet is a fusion-attention block named feature fusion group (FFG). The FFG fuses the channel attention in channel-wise and pixel attention in pixel-wise, and uses a positional normalization that normalizes exclusively across channels is used to learn more weight from important features. Lastly, the MSNet fuses the features from adjacent row stream and column stream to get the contributions from different scales. Experimental results in RESIDE dataset and real-word dataset indicate that the MSFFP-Net outperforms the state-of-the-art methods.

Keywords: Image dehazing · Multi-scale · Feature fusion

1 Introduction

As a low-level computer vision task, the goal of image dehazing is try to restore the clear image from the corrupted hazy image. In the last several years, lots of progress has been proposed to improve the problem. The atmosphere scattering model [1] is a most widely used model, and it proposed a simple model of the problem, which is:

$$I(z) = J(z)t(z) + A(1 - t(z)) \tag{1}$$

where $I(z)$ and $J(z)$ stand the hazy and clear image respectively, A represents the global atmospheric light intensity and $t(z)$ means the transmission map.

The formulation (1) can be re-written, so the clear scene radiance will be the output:

$$J(z) = \frac{1}{t(z)}I(z) - A\frac{1}{t(z)} + A \tag{2}$$

© Springer Nature Switzerland AG 2021
T. Mantoro et al. (Eds.): ICONIP 2021, CCIS 1516, pp. 98–105, 2021.
https://doi.org/10.1007/978-3-030-92307-5_12

From formulation (2), we can find that the clear image J(z) will be computed when A and $t(z)$ are estimated. However only hazy images are known normally, it is an ill-posed problem to restore the clear image from single hazy image.

In recent decades, lots of techniques have been proposed to solve image dehazing task. Most work is focus on the physical model such as the atmosphere scattering model [2,3]. With the rapid development of convolutional neural networks (CNNs), many CNN based methods are proposed [4,5]. With the massive data, the transmission map or the clear image can be directly regress from the network. Compared to traditional processes using hand-crafted features, CNN based methods achieve superior performance with robustness.

The main contribution of this work is a novel end-to-end network, named MSFFP-Net, for single image dehazing. The backbone of MSFFP-Net is a multi-scale grid network (MSNet), so the information can exchange across different scales to enhance the feature. The MSNet can estimate the model with fewer parameters from a low-dimensional statistical model via the training samples, and can approximate the high-dimensional model by parameterizing the neighborhood of the computed low-dimensional model repeatly. Each column of the MSNet has a bridge that connects adjacent scales by up-sampling and down-sampling blocks. And the MSNet fuses the features from adjacent row stream and column stream to get the information contributed by different scales. Furthermore, a feature fusion group, which fuses the channel attention in channel-wise and pixel attention in pixel-wise, as a basic module in the MSNet is used to learn more weight from important features. And the positional normalization (PONO) [6] that normalizes exclusively across channels adopt to train the network. The experiments will be shown that the MSFFP-Net achieves superior performance in comparison with the state-of-the-art methods.

2   Related Work

Early researchers mostly work on the physical atmospheric scattering model [2,3] to estimate $t(z)$ and A. DCP [2] discovers that in a clear image, there are low intensity at least one color channel which is defined as the dark channel prior (DCP). Since the DCP method is proposed, lots of DCP based methods are developed for improvements. However, the DCP method is often found to be unreliable when the objects in the scenes have a similar color to the atmospheric light.

With the fast development of CNN, most researchers now design various network to directly estimate $t(z)$ or clean image from large synthetic dehazing data-sets. DehazeNet [7] proposed a network to estimate $t(z)$ from the hazy image. MSCNN is proposed in [8] to generate a coarse-scale t(z) and then refine it gradually. The AOD-Net [9] proposes a novel end-to-end light-weight CNN to generate clean images directly first. The GridDehazeNet [10] chooses a multi-scale network as the backbone and proposes an end-to-end trainable CNN for single image dehazing. EPDN [11] designs an embedded generative adversarial network and an enhancing block to restore the image with more details. GFN

[12] also uses a multi-scale estimation with hand-selected pre-processing to solve image dehazing.

3   Proposed Method

We mainly detail the proposed MSFFP-Net in this section. The MSFFP-Net contains pre-processing, backbone and pre-processing three modules. The architecture of MSFFP-Net is depicted in Fig. 1. The pre-process module consists of a convolution layer and feature fusion group, symmetrically, the post-process consists of a feature fusion group and a convolution layer. The backbone is a multi-scale grid net.

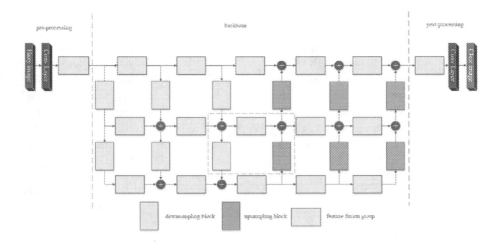

Fig. 1. The MSFFP-Net architecture

3.1   Multi-scale Grid Network

The MSNet is originally proposed for semantic segmentation, which has showed clear advantages in image restoration task. The MSNet we use in this paper has three rows and six columns. The basic module of MSNet is composed of down-sampling blocks, up-sampling block, feature fusion group (FFG), which is inspired by [13], as the dash block shows in Fig. 1.

Each row of the grid net consists of five FFGs which combines skip connection and feature fusion module, and the feature of each row have a different scale. Each column has a bridge that connects adjacent scales by up-sampling and down-sampling blocks. The size of the feature map is increased two times by the up-sampling operation, and the size is decreased two times via the down-sampling operation, and the two operations are both realized by a convolution layer. With the dense connections across different rows and columns by the two operations, and the information can exchange across the grid, so the bottleneck of information flows in network is circumvented by multi-scale grid network.

3.2   Feature Fusion Group

The FFG combines two attention mechanism: the channel and pixel attention. With the fusion attention structure, a rich contextual information by extracting the non-local feature and the local feature are provided. The architecture of FFG is depicted in Fig. 2(a), it consists of several basic fusion block (BF) and a shortcut connects the input feature and the output feature.

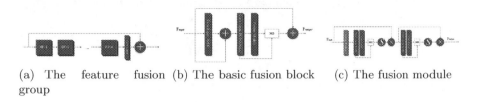

(a) The feature fusion group   (b) The basic fusion block   (c) The fusion module

Fig. 2. The feature fusion modules

The architecture of BF is depicted in Fig. 2(b), the second convolution layer adopts PONO with moment shortcut (MS) [6] to normalize the activation. A global residual learning connects the input feature and the output feature. With the local residual learning and global residual learning, the low-frequency regions from the input features can be learned by the skip connection.

The illustration of the fusion attention block is shown as Fig. 2(c), and the block can both non-local and local features, so the representational ability of CNN can be expanded.

(1) Channel attention module

In order to capture the non-local features, a channel attention module is proposed in [14] via modeling channel inter dependencies. Thus, we use that attention module to extract different weighted information from different channel features map.

Firstly, a global average pooling (GAP) is used to capture the channel-wise global spatial features.

$$g_c = H_p(F_c) = \frac{1}{H \times W} \sum_{i=1}^{H} \sum_{j=1}^{W} X_c(i,j) \tag{3}$$

where H_p means the GAP operation, $X_c(i,j)$ is the value of c-th channel of input X_c at position (i,j). And the dimension of the feature changes from $C \times H \times W$ to $C \times 1 \times 1$, C denotes the channels, and $H \times W$ is the size of feature map.

Then two convolution layers are applied, and the first convolution layers uses PONO to normalize the activation, then the feature from different channels are captured.

$$C_f = \sigma(Conv(\delta(Conv(g_c)))) \tag{4}$$

where σ stands for the sigmoid function, and δ is the ReLU function.

Finally, the weight of the channel F_c^* is computed by element-wise multiplying the input $F_i nput$ and C_f.

$$F_c^* = F_i nput \bigotimes C_f \tag{5}$$

(2) Pixel attention module

While on the different image pixels, the distribution of hazy image is variant. We use a pixel attention module to learn the spatially information from the hazy images adaptive.

The architecture of the attention module is depicted in Fig. 4, it consists of two convolution layers and sigmoid activation function, and the first convolution layers uses PONO to normalize the activation.

$$C_p = \sigma(Conv(\delta(Conv(F_c^*)))) \tag{6}$$

(3) Fusion module

We element-wise multiply F_c^* and C_p as the output of the fusion module finally.

3.3   Positional Normalization and Moment Shortcut

PONO is position dependent and reveal structural information at this particular layer of the deep net. It normalizes exclusively over the channels at all spatial positions, so it is translation, scaling, and rotation invariant. The PONO computes the mean μ and standard deviation θ in the layer. And the Moment Shorcut (MS) "fast-forword" the PONO information μ and θ.

4   Experiment Results

4.1   Data-Set and Training Settings

RESIDE [15] is a new synthetic benchmark proposed for image dehazing, and it contains images in both in-door and outdoor.

The size of images for training the network is resized to 240×240. The Adam optimizer is used for accelerated training, and smooth L_1 is used as the loss function. Each feature fusion group contains 5 basic fusion blocks in MSNet.

4.2   Results and Analysis

In this part, We compare MSFFP-Net with previous state-of-the-art image dehazing methods both quantitatively and qualitatively. The DCP is a prior-based method, and it is treated as a baseline. The other methods are CNN based. AS usual, we use peak signal to noise ratio (PSNR) and structure similarity (SSIM) to evaluate the results quantitatively. The quantitative comparison results are shown in Table 1.

Table 1. Quantitative comparison on SOTS

Method	Indoor		Outdoor	
	PSNR	SSIM	PSNR	SSIM
DCP	16.62	0.8179	19.13	0.8148
AOD-Net	19.06	0.8504	20.29	0.8765
GCANet	30.23	0.9800	–	–
GFN	22.30	0.8800	21.55	0.8444
DehazeNet	21.14	0.8472	22.46	0.8514
GridDehazeNet	32.16	0.9836	30.86	0.9819
Ours W/o PONO	35.56	0.9850	32.87	0.9832
Ours	36.61	0.9880	33.69	0.9852

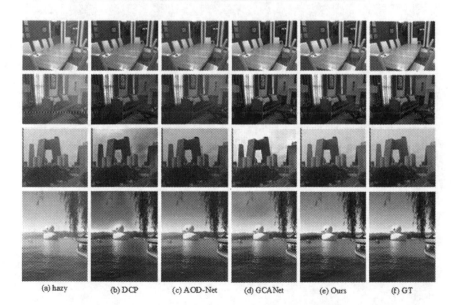

(a) hazy   (b) DCP   (c) AOD-Net   (d) GCANet   (e) Ours   (f) GT

Fig. 3. Qualitative comparisons on SOTS

From Table 1, it can be seen that the value of PSNR of our proposed MSFFP-Net is up to 36, which is a huge increase. Compared to the GriDehazeNet, we replace the residual dense block with feature fusion group, and use the PONO, the PSNR increased by 3.5% in Indoor dataset and 2.8% in Outdoor dataset. While not using PONO, the PSNR decreased both in Indoor and Outdoor dataset. In summary, our network outperforms in PSNR and SSIM.

Moreover, the comparison of the visual effect for qualitative comparisons on SOTS is depicted in Fig. 3. The upper two rows are indoor results, and the other two rows are outdoor results. The first column and the last column are the hazy input the ground-truth respectively, and the middle columns are dehazed results. We can observe that because of the underlying prior assumptions, the results of DCP lose the details and suffers from serious color distortion. AOD-Net is a simple network, so it cannot remove all the hazy regions such as the bridge region in row 4, and the brightness value of the output is lower than others. GCANet also suffers from serious color distortion, especially the blue sky area in row 4. The images recovered from our network are the best, especially, the restoration of sky images is much better.

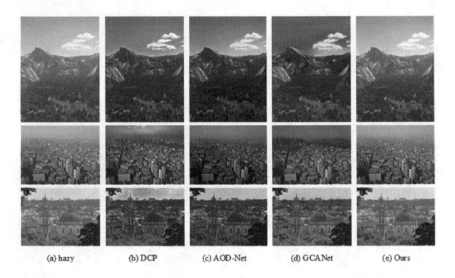

(a) hazy   (b) DCP   (c) AOD-Net   (d) GCANet   (e) Ours

Fig. 4. Qualitative comparisons on Real-world Dataset

We further give the qualitative comparisons on real-world dataset [16] in Fig. 4, and the results are similar to the synthetic dataset. We can observe that the results of our network are much better than other methods in image color and detail.

5   Conclusion

We propose an end-to-end trainable network for single image dehazing in this paper. The backbone of the proposed MSFFP-Net is a multi-scale grid network, and each row of the multi-scale grid network is consists of feature fusion group that combines the channel attention in channel-wise and pixel attention in pixel-wise. The results in RESIDE dataset and real-world dataset show that our network outperforms the state-of-the-arts and have a much better restoration results in image color and detail.

References

1. McCartney, E.J., Hall, F.: Optics of the atmosphere: scattering by molecules and particles. Phys. Today **24**, 76–77 (1976)
2. He, K.-M., Sun, J., Tang, X.: Single image haze removal using dark channel prior. In: CVPR, pp. 1956–1963. IEEE Press, New York (2009)
3. Ju, M., Gu, Z.-F., Zhang, D.-Y.: Single image haze removal based on the improved atmospheric scattering model. Neurocomputing **260**(18), 180–191 (2017)
4. Cai, B., Xu, X., Jia, K., et al.: DehazeNet: an end-to-end system for single image haze removal. IEEE Trans. Image Process. **25**(11), 5187–5198 (2016)
5. Kim, G., Ha, S., Kwon, J. : Adaptive patch based convolutional neural network for robust dehazing. In: ICIP, pp. 2845–2849. IEEE Press, New York (2018)
6. Li, B.-Y., Wu, F.-L., Kilian, Q., et al.: Positional normalization. In: NIPS, pp. 1620–1632. MIT press, Cambridge (2017)
7. Liu, Q., Gao, X., He, L., et al.: Single image dehazing with depth-aware non-local total variation regularization. IEEE Trans. Image Process. **27**(10), 5178–5191 (2018)
8. Ren, W., Liu, S., Zhang, H., Pan, J., Cao, X., Yang, M.-H.: Single image dehazing via multi-scale convolutional neural networks. In: Leibe, B., Matas, J., Sebe, N., Welling, M. (eds.) ECCV 2016. LNCS, vol. 9906, pp. 154–169. Springer, Cham (2016). https://doi.org/10.1007/978-3-319-46475-6_10
9. Li, B., Peng, X., Wang, Z., et al.: Aod-net: all-in-one dehazing network. In: CVPR, pp. 4770–4778, IEEE press, New York (2016)
10. Liu, X., Ma, Y., Shi, Z., et al.: GridDehazeNet: attention-based multi-scale network for image dehazing. In: ICCV, pp. 7313–7322. IEEE (2019)
11. Qu, Y., Chen, Y., Huang, J., Xie, Y.: Enhanced pix2pix dehazing network. In: ICCV, pp. 8160–8168. IEEE (2019)
12. Ren, W., et al.: Gated fusion network for single image dehazing. In: CVPR, pp. 3253–3261. IEEE (2018)
13. Qin, X., Wang, Z., Bai, Y., et al.: FFA-Net: feature fusion attention network for single image dehazing. In: AAAI, vol. 34(7), pp. 11908–11915. AAAI press, Palo Alto (2020)
14. Hu, J., Shen, L., Sun, G.: Squeeze-and-Excitation networks. In: CVPR, pp. 7132–7141. IEEE press, New York (2018)
15. Li, B., Ren, W., Fu, D., et al.: Benchmarking single-image dehazing and beyond. IEEE Trans. Image Process. **28**(1), 492–505 (2019)
16. Raanan, F.: Dehazing using color-lines. ACM Trans. Graph. **34**(1), 1–14 (2014)

Multitask Model for End-to-End Event Coreference Resolution

Congcheng Huang, Sheng Xu, Peifeng Li$^{(\boxtimes)}$, and Qiaoming Zhu

School of Computer Science and Technology, Soochow University, Jiangsu, China
{cchuangnlp,sxu}@stu.suda.edu.cn,
{pfli,qmzhu}@suda.edu.cn

Abstract. Event coreference resolution is an important task in natural language processing. An event coreference resolution system is often divided into two tasks: Event Detection and Event Coreference Resolution. The common pipelined approaches detect the events first and then complete the event coreference resolution. However, this kind of system will bring two problems: (1) it is difficult to make rational use of event subtype information; (2) errors generated by event detection will be propagated to the event coreference component, resulting in performance degradation. In view of the above shortcomings, we propose a multitask model, which combines event subtype re-detection task and event coreference resolution task. Our model not only updates and uses the event subtype information when computing the event coreference but also can suppress error propagation by a correction mechanism. Experimental results on KBP 2016 and KBP 2017 show that our proposed system outperforms the current state-of-the-art system.

Keywords: Event coreference resolution · Multitask model · Joint learning

1 Introduction

Event coreference resolution is an important task in natural language processing, which is of great significance to many downstream tasks, such as question answering [1] and information extraction [2]. The purpose of the within-document event coreference resolution task is to determine whether two event mentions in a document refer to the same real-world event, and link all event mentions which refer to a same event to an event chain. Take the following two event mentions as an example. The two event mentions are triggered by the words *arrested* and *seized* respectively, both refer to the same event "the attacker was arrested". Therefore, we consider they are coreferential.

S1: On Friday morning, in an unusually rapid response, the Mumbai police **arrested** one of the five attackers, and the police said they had identified the others.

© Springer Nature Switzerland AG 2021
T. Mantoro et al. (Eds.): ICONIP 2021, CCIS 1516, pp. 106–113, 2021.
https://doi.org/10.1007/978-3-030-92307-5_13

S2: "One of the five has been **seized** and he admitted he was there along with some others", Singh said at a news conference Friday afternoon.

The method of event coreference resolution has developed rapidly in recent years. Traditional feature-based methods directly rely on feature engineering [3–5]. However, these above works both rely on a lot of handcrafted features and rules, resulting in these methods being difficult to generalize. With the development of deep learning, recent works usually use various neural network models to solve the task of event coreference resolution [6–8].

Event detection is the upstream task of event coreference resolution, which aims to identify all the event mentions in the document and determine the event subtype for each event. The event trigger is the core of an event, so event detection is also called trigger detection.

Obviously, the information of event subtype is very important for the judgment of event coreference. If two event mentions are coreferential, their subtypes are always the same. Previous works tend to use the following two ways to take advantage of the event subtype information. The first is to extract event subtype features manually [9], and the second is to use the results of the event detection module directly [7]. However, neither of them can update the event subtype information while completing the event coreference resolution task. This will result in incomplete information and error propagation from the event subtype recognition, and these errors have no chance to be corrected.

Moreover, end-to-end event coreference resolution always faces the challenge of error propagation. Event coreference resolution is located downstream of the whole pipeline model, and its performance largely depends on its upstream event detection task. In many previous works, once the event detection errors occur, these errors will always exist in the system and affect the performance of the whole system. For example, if a mention is not an event but is incorrectly identified as an event, which generally occur in the event detection module, will lead to redundancy of event chains.

To address the above problems, we propose a multitask model. The contributions of our work are as follows: (1) We build a multitask model, which combines event subtype re-detection task and event coreference resolution task, in this way, we can update the event subtype information while completing event coreference resolution. (2) We propose an error correction mechanism, which can effectively suppress the error propagation and improve the performance of each task in the pipeline model. Experimental results on KBP 2016 and KBP 2017 show that our proposed system achieves state-of-art performance.

2   Method

Our system consists of three modules: event detection, event coreference resolution and an error correction mechanism. The whole system will be described in detail below.

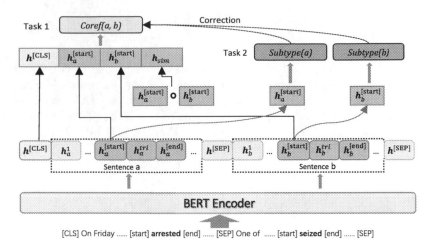

Fig. 1. Multitask model structure.

2.1 Event Detection

In this paper, we consider event detection as a sequence labeling task, which aims to assign each token a subtype. Formally, give the word sequence of a document $D = \{w_1, w_2, ..., w_n\}$, the model needs to determine whether each token w_i is a trigger to mention an event. If it is, w_i will be labeled as the event subtype, otherwise, w_i will be labeled as NULL.

Specifically, we first send the word sequence of the document into the pre-trained model SpanBERT to obtain the semantic representations. Then we feed these vectors into an inference layer to predict the event subtype of each token.

$$\boldsymbol{w}_1, \boldsymbol{w}_2, ..., \boldsymbol{w}_n = \text{SpanBERT}(w_1, w_2, ..., w_n)$$
$$s_i = \text{softmax}(\text{FFNN}(\boldsymbol{w}_i)) \tag{1}$$

where FFNN is a standard feed-forward neural network. For each word w_i, if its label $s_i \neq 0$, the word will be identified as a trigger and the sentence where w_i place will be extracted as the corresponding event mention text.

2.2 Multitask Model for Event Coreference Resolution

As shown in Fig. 1, we apply a pairwise multitask model to solve the problem of event coreference resolution. For all the event mentions obtained by the event detection module, we first pair all the event mentions in the same document and then compute whether each event pair is coreferential.

Formally, we use a pre-trained model (BERT, SpanBERT) to encode event pairs as a whole to capture the interactions between them. However, in many situations, a sentence will contain multiple events, therefore, it is difficult for the model to distinguish which is the target event we want to consider. To focus the model's attention on specific events, we add special tokens [start] and [end] around the trigger of key events. Considering that in the original pre-training task of BERT (or SpanBERT), [CLS] and [SEP] are two special tokens that play very important roles: the function of [SEP] is to separate two sentences, while [CLS] is used to capture the interactions between the two sentences. Be consistent with the pre-training task, we add [CLS] at the beginning of the sentence pairs and use [SEP] to connect the two sentences. Therefore, the input of the multitask model is:

$$S_{input} = \{[\text{CLS}], w_a^1, ..., [\text{start}], w_a^{tri}, [\text{end}]..., w_a^m, [\text{SEP}],$$
$$w_b^1, ..., [\text{start}], w_b^{tri}, [\text{end}]..., w_b^n, [\text{SEP}]\} \tag{2}$$

Task 1: Event Coreference Resolution. Token [start] is located before the event trigger to focus the attention of the model on the key event, therefore we consider that it can capture the rich content information of the event, which plays an important role in computing event coreference. And token [CLS] captures the interactions between the two sentences. Therefore, we choose $\boldsymbol{h}^{[\text{CLS}]}, \boldsymbol{h}_a^{[\text{start}]}, \boldsymbol{h}_b^{[\text{start}]}$ as the semantic features of each event mention pair to determine their coreference. Specifically, we simply apply a feed-forward neural network to calculate the coreference score for each pair of event mentions:

$$Core\ f(a, b) = \text{sigmoid}(\text{FFNN}_1([\boldsymbol{h}^{[\text{CLS}]}, \boldsymbol{h}_a^{[\text{start}]}, \boldsymbol{h}_b^{[\text{start}]}, \boldsymbol{h}_{sim}])) \tag{3}$$

where $\boldsymbol{h}_{sim} = \boldsymbol{h}_a^{[\text{start}]} \circ \boldsymbol{h}_b^{[\text{start}]}$ is the element-wise similarity of each mention pair, and $\circ$ denotes the element-wise multiplication.

Task 2: Event Subtype Re-Detection. Considering that the event subtype information is of great significance for event coreference resolution. To get better event subtype information when resolving event coreference, we add the auxiliary task of event subtype re-detection. We jointly learning these two tasks in a multitask framework sharing the same encoder layer, as shown in Fig. 1. Specifically, we choose $\boldsymbol{h}_a^{[\text{start}]}$ and $\boldsymbol{h}_b^{[\text{start}]}$ as the features of the two events, respectively. Then we feed them into another feed-forward neural network to determine the correspoonding event subtype, respectively.

$$Subtype(a) = \text{softmax}(\text{FFNN}_2(\boldsymbol{h}_a^{[\text{start}]}))$$
$$Subtype(b) = \text{softmax}(\text{FFNN}_2(\boldsymbol{h}_b^{[\text{start}]})) \tag{4}$$

The objective function of our multitask model consists of two parts: loss of the event coreference task $\mathcal{L}(\Theta)_{coref}$ and that of the event subtype re-detection task $\mathcal{L}(\Theta)_{subtype}$. We use Adam optimizer to minimize the objective function.

$$\mathcal{L}(\Theta) = \mathcal{L}(\Theta)_{coref} + \lambda\mathcal{L}(\Theta)_{subtype} \tag{5}$$

In this paper, we use the cross-entropy function as the loss function to optimize all the parameters of the model when completing these two tasks.

2.3   Error Correction Mechanism

Experience shows that a large number of non-event samples will be incorrectly identified as events in the event detection module. Such samples will generate many redundant event chains, leading to performance degradation.

To make our model master the ability to find out the non-event samples in the event mention pairs, we need to add negative samples to the training set. Specifically, we build a candidate set of trigger words, which is composed of all the triggers in the training set of KBP 2015. For each word in the candidate set, we find corresponding fake event mentions, that is, the word in these sentences does not play the role of the trigger (up to 5 sentences per word). We add these negative samples to the original training set, then train the multitask model in Fig. 1.

Define all events obtained by event detection module as set **E**. A sample i will be changed to non-event while it satisfies the following three conditions at the same time:

First of all, the coreference score of sample i with all other events in set **E** should be less than β, as shown in Eq. 6. Intuitively, if a sample is not an event, it should be non-coreferent with all other samples. In other words, if a sample is non-coreferent with all other samples, its probability of being event will be relatively low.

$$\forall j \in E \text{ and } j \neq i, \quad (Core\, f(i,j) < \beta) \; \wedge \; (Core\, f(j,i) < \beta) \tag{6}$$

Secondly, in the process of model inference, each sample will be inferred many times in different event pairs. We consider that the ratio of the times that a non-event sample i is determined as non-event to the total times that it appears should greater than γ, as shown in Eq. 7.

$$\frac{count(Subtype(i) = 0)}{count(Subtype(i) \in [0, 19])} >= \gamma \tag{7}$$

Finally, for all the sample i in an event pair is inferred to be non-event, the coreference score of this event pair should less than η, as shown in Eq. 8. This rule emphasizes the consistency of the model in the inference of two tasks.

$$\forall\, Subtype(i) = 0, \; Core\, f(i,j) < \eta \tag{8}$$

3   Experiments and Analysis

3.1   Experimental Setup

Following Lu [8], we use KBP 2015 [11] corpus as the training set. KBP 2015 contains 648 documents, of which 583 documents are used for model training and the remaining 65 documents for parameter tuning. We evaluate the model on KBP 2016 and KBP 2017, in which KBP 2016 contains 169 documents and KBP 2017 contains 167 documents.

We use four standard metrics to evaluate the performance of event coreference resolution, and use the official evaluation tools included in KBP 2017 corpus for calculation. The four metrics are MUC [12], B^3 [13], $CEAF_e$ [14] and BLANC [15]. To be consistent with previous studies [7,8], AVG-F is the unweighted average of F1 scores of the above four metrics, which is the most important metric to measure the performance of event coreference resolution.

We tune our parameters on the validation set. The parameters β, γ, η of the Error Correction Mechanism are set to $0.9, 0.6, 0.005$, respectively. The parameter λ in the loss function is 1.

3.2 Experimental Results

To exhibit the effectiveness of our model, we compare the performance of our model with two current state-of-the-art systems on KBP 2016 and KBP 2017, respectively. The experimental results are illustrated in Table 1.

Table 1. Event coreference resolution results on test sets.

KBP 2016					
System	MUC	B^3	$CEAF_e$	BLANC	AVG-F
Lu and Ng (2017)	27.4	40.9	39.0	25.0	33.1
Lu and Ng (2021) (SpanBERT-large)	**38.9**	52.6	51.9	35.0	44.6
Our system (SpanBERT-large)	38.3	**56.5**	**56.6**	**36.7**	**47.1**
KBP 2017					
System	MUC	B^3	$CEAF_e$	BLANC	AVG-F
Huang et al. (2019)	35.7	43.2	40.0	32.4	36.8
Lu and Ng (2021) (SpanBERT-large)	**42.8**	53.7	51.5	36.4	46.1
Our system (SpanBERT-large)	42.0	**55.7**	**56.3**	**36.5**	**47.6**

The results shows that our model outperforms the other baselines on most of the metrics, with large gains from 2.5 to 14.0 in the AVG-F on KBP 2016 and significant gains from 1.5 to 10.8 in the AVG-F on KBP 2017. Compared with the baselines, our multitask model not only captures the semantic interactions between event mentions representations encoded by SpanBERT, but also re-detects the event subtypes to correct the misidentified event mentions.

However, compared with Lu and Ng (2021), our multitask model has a slight performance degradation on the MUC metric, with a drop of 0.6 and 0.8 on KBP 2016 and KBP 2017, respectively. The reason behind this may be due to the fact that MUC only considers event chains whose length is greater than 2, and does not consider the influence of single chains. While our proposed model has a much stronger processing ability for single chains, therefore, it is more reasonable to observe the AVG-F.

Table 2. Ablation results on test sets.

System	MUC	B^3	$CEAF_e$	BLANC	AVG-F	Δ
KBP 2016						
Our system (SpanBERT-large)	**38.3**	**56.5**	**56.6**	**36.7**	**47.1**	
- Error Correction	38.1	55.8	55.2	36.0	46.3	−0.8
- Subtype Task	35.2	55.8	54.3	34.7	45.0	−2.1
KBP 2017						
Our system (SpanBERT-large)	**42.0**	**55.7**	**56.3**	**36.4**	**47.6**	
- Error Correction	41.5	54.8	54.9	35.7	46.7	−0.9
- Subtype Task	37.4	54.0	53.9	34.5	45.0	−2.6

3.3   Ablation Analysis

To further analyze the contribution of each part of our system to performance improvement, we conduct experiments on some variants of our multitask model with the results shown in Table 2.

Effectiveness of Error Correction Mechanism. As shown in Table 2, after removing the Error Correction Mechanism, the AVG-F value of the system has been decreased by 0.8 and 0.9 on KBP 2016 and KBP 2017, respectively, and the value of other metrics also has declined. In detail, on KBP 2016, 1492 non-events were incorrectly predicted as events. After correction, 453 (30.4%) non-events were corrected, with only 158 (5.6%) true events were wrongly changed to non-events. On KBP 2017, 1079 non-events were incorrectly predicted. After optimization, 352 (32.6%) non-events were corrected, and only 127 (4.5%) true events were changed to non-events.

Effectiveness of Multitask Model. As shown in Table 2, after removing Subtype Task, the AVG-F value of the system on KBP 2016 and KBP 2017 has been decreased by 2.1 and 2.6, respectively. The significance of our proposed multitask model is that we can update and get more comprehensive event subtype information through the event coreference resolution task.

4   Conclusion

In this paper, we propose a multitask model which combines event subtype re-detection and event coreference resolution. Meanwhile, we also build an error correction mechanism to correct the misidentified events. Evaluation on the KBP data set shows that we achieve a new state-of-art performance on the event coreference resolution task.

Considering that the pairwise model does not use the global information such as the document structure. In the future work, we will focus on how to introduce the global information into the event coreference resolution to further improve the performance.

Acknowledgments. The authors would like to thank the two anonymous reviewers for their comments on this paper. This research was supported by the National Natural Science Foundation of China (Nos. 61836007, 61772354 and 61773276.), and the Priority Academic Program Development of Jiangsu Higher Education Institutions (PAPD).

References

1. Weissenborn, D., Wiese, G., Seiffe, L.: Making neural qa as simple as possible butnotsimpler. In: Proceedings of the 21st Conference on Computational Natural Language Learning (CoNLL 2017), pp. 271–280 (2017)
2. Lin, Y., Ji, H., Huang, F., Wu, L.: A joint neural model for information extraction with global features. In: Proceedings of the ACL 2020, pp. 7999–8009 (2020)
3. Chen, Z., Ji, H., Haralick, R.: A pairwise event coreference model, feature impact and evaluation for event coreference resolution. In: Proceedings of the Workshop on Events in Emerging Text Types, pp. 17–22 (2009)
4. Liu, Z., Araki, J., Hovy, E. H., Mitamura, T.: Supervised within-document event coreference using information propagation. In: Proceedings of the LREC 2014, pp. 4539–4544 (2014)
5. Lu, J., Ng, V.: Joint learning for event coreference resolution. In: Proceedings of ACL 2017, pp. 90–101 (2017)
6. Choubey, P. K., Lee, A., Huang, R., Wang, L.: Discourse as a function of event: profiling discourse structure in news articles around the main event. In: Proceedings of ACL 2020, pp. 5374–5386 (2020)
7. Huang, Y. J., Lu, J., Kurohashi, S., Ng, V.: Improving event coreference resolution by learning argument compatibility from unlabeled data. In: Proceedings of NAACL 2019, pp. 785–795 (2019)
8. Lu, J., Ng, V.: Span-based event coreference resolution. In: Proceedings of the AAAI Conference on Artificial Intelligence, pp. 13489–13497 (2021)
9. Lu, J., Ng, V.: Event coreference resolution with non-local information. In: Proceedings of ACL-IJCNLP 2020, pp. 653–663 (2020)
10. Joshi, M., Chen, D., Liu, Y., et al.: SpanBERT: improving pre-training by representing and predicting spans. Trans. Assoc. Comput. Linguist. **8**, 64–77 (2020)
11. Mitamura, T., Liu, Z., Hovy, E.H.: Overview of tac kbp 2015 event nugget track. In: TAC (2015)
12. Vilain, M.B., Burger, J.D., Aberdeen, J.S., Connolly, D., Hirschman, L.: A model-theoretic coreference scoring scheme. In: Proceedings of the MUC 1995, Columbia, Maryland, USA, 6–8 November, 1995. DBLP (1995)
13. Bagga, A., Baldwin, B.: Algorithms for scoring coreference chains. In: Proceedings of the LREC 1998, pp. 563–566 (1998)
14. Luo, X.: On coreference resolution performance metrics. In: Proceedings of Human-Language Technology Conference and Conference on Empirical Methods in Natural Language Processing, pp. 25–32 (2005)
15. Recasens, M., Hovy, E.: BLANC: implementing the rand index for coreference evaluation. Natural language engineering, pp. 485–510 (2017)

Dependency Learning Graph Neural Network for Multivariate Forecasting

Arth Patel[1(✉)], Abishek Sriramulu[1], Christoph Bergmeir[1],
and Nicolas Fourrier[2]

[1] Monash University, Melbourne, Australia
{abishek.sriramulu,christoph.bergmeir}@monash.edu
[2] Léonard de Vinci Pôle Universitaire, Courbevoie, France

Abstract. Multivariate time series forecasting is an important topic in various disciplines. Many deep learning architectures have been proposed for accurate multivariate forecasting. However, most existing models fail to learn the dependencies between different time series. Lately, studies have shown that implementations of Graph Neural Networks in the field of Natural Language, Computer Vision, and Time Series have achieved exceptional performance. In this paper, we propose an attention-based Multivariate Dependency Learning Graph Neural Network, which aims to better learn the dependencies among variables of a multivariate dataset. The attention scores corresponding to each variable complement the construction process of the graph adjacency matrix to model the spatial dependencies. Our experiments on benchmark datasets show that the proposed architecture improves accuracy on different benchmark datasets compared with the state-of-the-art baseline models.

Keywords: Multivariate forecasting · Graph learning · Graph Neural Networks · Time series

1 Introduction

Forecasting multivariate time series is an important topic where multiple variables are observed at the same point in time, and there may be interdependency between them. For example, an increase in the sales of one product may cause a decrease in the sales of another product in retail datasets due to several reasons. Forecasting these time series is crucial as it helps businesses to develop profit bearing solutions.

Most of the existing time series forecasting methods do not assume dependencies between series, hence, they fail to explore the latent relationships among the input variables. Assumption of linear dependencies between series holds in traditional forecasting methods. However, the complexity for these models increases with an increase in the number of inputs. LSTNet [6] encodes the locality in the series using 1D convolutional layers, but the interdependencies between the

© Springer Nature Switzerland AG 2021
T. Mantoro et al. (Eds.): ICONIP 2021, CCIS 1516, pp. 114–123, 2021.
https://doi.org/10.1007/978-3-030-92307-5_14

series are not learned. IMV-LSTM [3] employs an attention-based Long-Short Term Memory (LSTM) to learn relationships in the data. However, it only performs well with small numbers of series. Attention mechanisms have been used to get accurate forecasts [3,4] by learning the relative importance of variables. However, most of these models fail to capture the non-linear relationships.

Graph Neural Network (GNN) has been successful in tackling many applications due to their local connectivity [11]. Multivariate time series datasets are represented in the graph form with each node representing one series and the edges representing dependencies among the series. However, most of the existing GNN models require a well-defined graph as input, which rarely exists. The only work in the literature that incorporates the learning of such a graph, to the best of our knowledge, is the work by Wu et al. [12], which we use as a starting point for our research. The performance of these models depend on the layer used for subset selection which is used for the construction of adjacency matrix.

We propose a Dependency Learning Graph Neural Network (DLGNN) model that uses the attention weights to enhance the process of construction and optimisation for a graph adjacency matrix that can be consumed by the graph convolution module to model the spatial dependencies among variables while the temporal convolution module models the temporal dependencies in the data.

2   Background

The high dimensionality of time series data and the existence of dependencies within the data makes multivariate forecasting challenging. Lately, neural networks have been proven to be successful multivariate models [6]. Lai et al. [6] proposed a model to forecast multivariate time series by employing a recurrent neural network (RNN) with skip connections. Sen et al. [8] introduced an approach to forecast high-dimensional time series data using a hybrid model that combines a temporal network, along with a global matrix factorisation. However, these models do not explore the underlying relationships among series.

In GNNs, a node's state depends on the states of the neighbouring nodes. To exploit spatial dependency, convolutional GNNs [5] have been introduced where information is passed between nodes. Graph convolutions are utilized to learn the spatial dependencies, on the other hand, temporal patterns are captured by using 1D convolution layers [13]. However, they are unable to work with multivariate time series that inherently possess relationships between series due to the lack of a predefined graph structure [12]. To overcome this, Wu et al. [12] introduced a graph learning layer that learns the adjacency matrix and captures dependencies.

For time series forecasting applications, Fan et al. [2] proposed a model that uses an attention mechanism to capture temporal patterns from univariate time series data. Lim et al. [7] proposed a temporal fusion transformer which uses self-attention layers to learn long-term dependencies. For multivariate time series forecasting, a dual self-attention neural network was presented by Huang et al. [4] that uses a self-attention mechanism to capture relationships between series.

However, in this model the attention weights' direction of correlation with the target is not taken into consideration.

3   Proposed Framework

We present a framework for multivariate time series forecasting. Let $Y_{i,t} \in \mathbb{R}$ be the value of a time series i at time t, and let T be the number of time steps in the training data and N be the number of time series. The ith time series is then defined by $Y_i = \{Y_{i,1}, Y_{i,2}, ...Y_{i,T}\}$. Our target is to predict the next values for the horizon of length H for all series. Hence, the predicted values are given by $\hat{Y}_i = \{\hat{Y}_{i,T+1}, \hat{Y}_{i,T+2}, ..., \hat{Y}_{i,T+H}\}$. Following [12], we mathematically define a graph as $G = (V, E)$ where V represents all nodes, and all edges are in the set E. The total number of nodes in the graph is equal to the total number of time series, N. Graphs can be defined as an adjacency matrix which is denoted as $A \in R^{N \times N}$ where $A[i,j] > 0$ if $(v_i, v_j) \in E$ and $A[i,j] = 0$ if $(v_i, v_j) \notin E$ [12].

3.1   Model Architecture

Figure 1 shows the model's conceptual diagram. Similar to Wu et al. [12] our model includes a graph learning layer, temporal convolution modules and graph convolution modules. The graph learning layer is responsible for building the adjacency matrix. Graph convolution module captures spatial relationships between nodes using this matrix. Temporal dependencies are learned by temporal convolution modules, which are placed alternating with graph convolution modules. In this architecture, skip connections are also employed from the temporal convolution layer's input to the output of the graph convolutions to avoid vanishing gradient problems. The outputs of temporal convolution layers are used by skip connections to avoid performance degradation of the network. Outputs from the skip connection layers get merged to compute the final output.

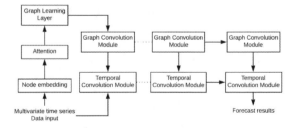

Fig. 1. DLGNN model conceptual architecture.

3.2   Graph Learning Layer

The graph learning layer is necessary for building the most accurate representation of the graph as the graph structure cannot be explicitly obtained from the data. This layer focuses on building the adjacency matrix such that hidden dependencies among different time series are captured. Following Wu et al. [12] we construct an adjacency matrix from a selected subset of node pairs. Improving the method to choose this neighbourhood subset selection of the node pairs can improve the model performance. We use an attention mechanism to improve this subset selection process which improves the accuracy.

Vaswani et al. [10] proposed an architecture based on an attention mechanism that calculates the attention weights based on a similarity metric. We use a similar idea to learn the graph structure. Each node of the graph is represented as an embedding and the goal is to learn the attention weights for spatial dependencies between nodes. These attention weights can be multiplied with the learned embedding to get a more accurate representation of the node. Hence, with the help of the attention mechanism, we improve the process of subset selection of nodes in constructing the graph adjacency matrix on the graph learning layer.

Spatial-temporal GNNs have proven to be effective to work on non-linear data having time dynamics [13]. In the light of these advancements, we use self-attention on spatial GNNs to learn the spatial dependencies. In this mechanism, for each embedding of the input series, a query vector Q, a key vector K, and a value vector V of the same size d_k are created [10]. We multiply the embedding by three weight matrices. Then, an attention score is calculated for each input series against all input variables. This score indicates the relative importance to be considered for predicting other variables. The dot product of the query vector and key vector is calculated to get this score for each series. All the scores are normalized using a softmax function. We follow the work of Vaswani et al. [10] for the implementation of multi-head attention. The final output from the attention module is considered to be a learned representation of each node embedding and it helps the model to better identify spatial dependencies between all nodes.

The use of multi-head attention provides considerable improvement because the model's capability to attend over multiple positions gets extended. We concatenate the outputs and pass the result through a feedforward layer which maps the concatenated output to a representation of size equal to that of a self-attention output. The graph learning algorithm can be mathematically represented as follows.

$$E_1 = \text{Multihead}(Q, K, V), \quad M_1 = tanh(E_1\theta_1), \quad M_2 = tanh(E_2\theta_2)$$

$$A = ReLU(tanh(\alpha(M_1M_2^T - M_2M_1^T))) \tag{1}$$

$$for \; i = 1, 2, ..., N$$
$$\text{idx} = argtopk(A[i, :]) \tag{2}$$
$$A[i, -\text{idx}] = 0, \tag{3}$$

Here, E_1 is the learned embedding generated from multihead attention, while E_2 is a randomly initialised embedding. E_2 will adjust based on how E_1 is learned. Furthermore, θ_1, θ_2 are model parameters [12]. Equation 1 creates the adjacency matrix A and the subtraction term helps the model to regularise better. Equations 2 and 3 make the graph sparse by selecting the top k neighbours.

3.3   Graph Convolution Module

The aim of this module is to use the information of the neighbourhood of a node to control relationships between nodes. We base our graph convolution module on the approach introduced by [1] where a mix-hop has been used for concatenating and propagating information from different hops. Two mix-hop propagation layers are used to handle the flow of information on dependent nodes in the graph convolution module [12]. Mix-hop propagation layers perform two steps: an information propagation step and an information selection step (Fig. 2).

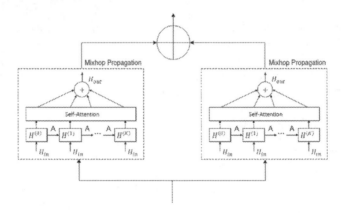

Fig. 2. Graph convolution module with self-attention

We introduce an attention mechanism for the information selection step to pick crucial information generated at each hop to benefit from deeper neighbourhood. The attention mechanism is a feedforward neural network, which consists of one layer with a weight vector.

3.4   Temporal Convolution Module

A temporal convolution module is used to learn temporal patterns in neighbouring series. A 1D convolution filter rolls over the input sequence of each time series to extract temporal features. In our model, multiple dilated convolutional filters are used, also known as dilated inception layer, which allows the model to manage short and long sequences [12].

Time series data often exhibits multiple temporal patterns. As the proportion with which each of these temporal patterns contribute to the forecast are unknown, we conjecture that an attention mechanism in the time dimension will also be beneficial.

We apply self-attention as described in Fig. 3. This way, we learn the importance of inputs from each filter that contribute to the improvements of forecasts. For $Y_i \in \mathbb{R}^T$ as a 1D input sequence, and filters as $f_{1\times2}, f_{1\times3}, f_{1\times6}$, and $f_{1\times7}$, the output of temporal attention is given as:

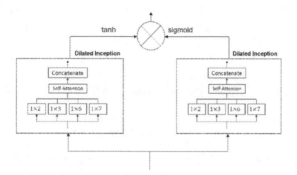

Fig. 3. Temporal convolution module with self-attention

$$Y_i = concat(\text{Attention}(Y_i \star f_{1\times2}, Y_i \star f_{1\times3}, Y_i \star f_{1\times6}, Y_i \star f_{1\times7})) \qquad (4)$$

where $Y_i \star f_{1\times k}$ denotes the dilated convolution.

4   Experiments and Results

We perform a validation study of our model (DLGNN) for single-step multivariate forecasting. Firstly, we make a comparison on performance of DLGNN with various methods on three benchmark datasets. We also calculate the loss metrics for all the models with different lengths of prediction horizons.

4.1   Dataset and Performance Metrics

We choose the same benchmark datasets that were used in Lai et al. [6] and Wu et al. [12], for ease of comparison. The solar energy[1] dataset consists of 137 series of length 52,560 recorded at 10 min interval. The electricity[2] dataset consists of 321 series of length 26,304 collected every 1 h. The traffic[3] dataset consists of 862 series of length 17,544 with data collected every hour.

---

[1] http://www.nrel.gov/grid/solar-power-data.html.
[2] https://archive.ics.uci.edu/ml/datasets/ElectricityLoadDiagrams20112014.
[3] http://pems.dot.ca.gov.

For all series, we use input windows of 168 data points and predict single step output at a time. As per Lai et al. [6], these datasets are divided into training set (60%), validation set (20%), and test set (20%) in a sequential manner. For performance evaluation, following Lai et al. [6], we use the evaluation metrics Root Relative Squared Error (RSE) and Correlation Coefficient (CORR).

4.2   Comparison with Baseline Methods

We compare our proposed model with the following existing baseline models: an auto-regressive linear model (**AR**), a composite model of a linear vector auto-regressive model and multilayer perceptron [14] (**VAR-MLP**), a model based on Gaussian Processes (**GP**), a model having convolution and recurrent layers [6] (**LSTNet**), an RNN model with attention mechanism [9] (**TPA-LSTM**), the state-of-the-art **MTGNN** model [12], and an MTGNN model which uses a pairwise Pearson correlation for its adjacency matrix (**MTGNN-Corr**).

4.3   Experimental Setup and Parameter Study

For training our DLGNN model, we use the Adam optimizer as it performs better where gradients are sparse. To prevent overfitting, we use $l2$ regularisation with a penalty of 1×10^{-4}. The size of node embedding is set to 50. For the attention mechanism in the graph learning layer, the number of heads is set to 4. We use 5 temporal convolution modules and 5 graph convolution modules. For training, we use the early stopping technique with maximum epochs set to 50 and patience value of 5. Following [12], the batch size is set to 4 for the solar energy and electricity datasets, while it is set to 20 for the traffic dataset.

The hyper-parameters considered in our study are: the size of node embedding, the number of neighbours k for the attention mechanism in the range of 10 to 50, the number of heads for the multi-head attention ranging from 2 to 8, and the number of graph convolution layers and temporal convolution layers in the range of 1 to 5. Based on the results on the validation set, these values are tuned empirically. From these experiments, we found that increasing the number of neighbours after some value degrades the performance of the model. We think this happens because less dependent nodes carry noise in the learning process which affects the model performance. Moreover, increasing the size of the head improved the performance, but after 4 heads, the results did not change.

4.4   Results

Table 1 shows the experimental results of the proposed DLGNN model along with the other baseline methods. We observe that our model outperforms the other baseline models in most of the cases.

In particular, for the solar energy dataset, we see a considerable improvement in the RSE metric by 7%, 7.6%, 7.7%, and 4% for the horizons of length 3, 6, 12, and 24, respectively. For the traffic dataset, we expected to achieve similar improvements. However, our experiments showed that as the number of nodes increases, it becomes more challenging to learn the dependencies for the attention mechanism. We observe that as the number of series in the dataset increases, the improvement in the results decreases. Hence, we see a slight degradation in the performance. To the best of our knowledge, no study has proved the effectiveness of attention mechanisms when the number of inputs is large.

4.5   Ablation Studies

We conduct an ablation study on DLGNN to understand the impact of fundamental components of the model which results in better forecasts on our proposed model. Experiments are conducted for following modifications in the model.

Table 1. Comparison of baseline methods for multivariate single-step forecasting

Dataset		Solar energy				Electricity				Traffic			
		Horizon				Horizon				Horizon			
Methods	Metric	3	6	12	24	3	6	12	24	3	6	12	24
AR	RSE	0.2435	0.3790	0.5911	0.8699	0.0995	0.1035	0.1050	0.1054	0.5911	0.6218	0.6252	0.6300
	CORR	0.9710	0.9263	0.8107	0.5314	0.8845	0.8632	0.8591	0.8595	0.7752	0.7568	0.7544	0.7519
VAR-MLP	RSE	0.1922	0.2679	0.4244	0.6841	0.1393	0.1620	0.1557	0.1274	0.5582	0.6579	0.6023	0.6146
	CORR	0.9829	0.9655	0.9058	0.7149	0.8708	0.8389	0.8192	0.8679	0.8245	0.7695	0.7929	0.7891
GP	RSE	0.2259	0.3286	0.5200	0.7973	0.1500	0.1907	0.1621	0.1273	0.6082	0.6772	0.6406	0.5995
	CORR	0.9751	0.9448	0.8518	0.5971	0.8670	0.8334	0.8394	0.8818	0.7831	0.7406	0.7671	0.7909
LSTNet	RSE	0.1843	0.2559	0.3254	0.4643	0.0864	0.0931	0.1007	0.1007	0.4777	0.4893	0.4950	0.4973
	CORR	0.9843	0.9690	0.9467	0.8870	0.9283	0.9135	0.9077	0.9119	0.8721	0.8690	0.8614	0.8588
TPA-LSTM	RSE	0.1803	0.2347	0.3234	0.4389	0.0823	0.0916	0.0964	0.1006	0.4487	0.4658	0.4641	0.4765
	CORR	0.9850	0.9742	0.9487	0.9081	0.9439	0.9337	0.9250	0.9133	0.8812	0.8717	0.8717	0.8629
MTGNN	RSE	0.1778	0.2348	0.3109	0.4270	0.0745	0.0878	0.0916	0.0953	**0.4162**	0.4754	**0.4461**	**0.4535**
	CORR	0.9852	0.9726	0.9509	0.9031	0.9474	0.9316	0.9278	0.9234	**0.896**	0.8667	**0.8794**	**0.8810**
MTGNN-Corr	RSE	0.1806	0.2378	0.3042	0.4173	0.0737	0.0841	0.0923	0.0971	0.4227	0.4378	0.4576	0.4579
	CORR	0.9848	0.9722	0.9534	0.9067	0.9475	0.9346	0.9263	0.9227	0.8937	0.8846	0.8746	0.8784
DLGNN	RSE	**0.1655**	**0.2171**	**0.2871**	**0.4099**	**0.0721**	**0.0809**	**0.0889**	**0.0931**	0.4201	**0.4326**	0.4509	0.4564
	CORR	**0.9874**	**0.9766**	**0.9553**	**0.9072**	**0.9486**	**0.9384**	**0.9288**	**0.9248**	0.8942	**0.8839**	0.8777	0.8794

1. w/o Spatial Attention: DLGNN without multi-head attention in the graph learning layer. The node embeddings are used without any explicit learning.

2. w/o Temporal Attention: DLGNN without self-attention for the dilated inception layer. The output of each filter is concatenated for the next layer.

3. w/o Temporal Inception: DLGNN with a dilated inception layer without inception component. Only one 1×7 filter is used for temporal convolution.

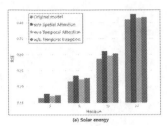
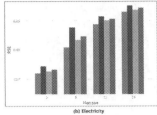

(a) Solar energy   (b) Electricity

Fig. 4. Results of the ablation study.

The results are shown in Fig. 4. We see that addition of spatial attention leads to a considerable improvement because the attention layers help the graph learning layer to improve the node subset selection. We note that using a single convolution filter of size 1×7 provides slightly worse results compared with the inception layer. Finally, the introduction of the temporal attention leads to a slight improvement in the RSE score due to attention weights for filters.

5   Conclusion

In this paper, we have introduced the DLGNN model which achieves state-of-the-art performance on two out of three benchmark datasets. It utilises a multi-head attention module in a graph learning layer, which has improved the neighbourhood selection. We have also incorporated a temporal self-attention mechanism to improve the temporal feature selection.

There are promising avenues for future research on this architecture. Firstly, for datasets with large numbers of series, clustering techniques can be used to create subsets, so the attention mechanism can be used on all such subsets. Moreover, the attention layers can be modified and reconstructed to understand their effectiveness, thereby improving the results. Thus, the method could be finally made scale invariant, though this is a challenging problem and opens a new direction of research on attention mechanisms.

References

1. Abu-El-Haija, S., et al.: Mixhop: higher-order graph convolutional architectures via sparsified neighborhood mixing. In: ICML. PMLR (2019)
2. Fan, C., et al.: Multi-horizon time series forecasting with temporal attention learning. In: Proceedings of the 25th ACM SIGKDD, pp. 2527–2535 (2019)
3. Guo, T., Lin, T., Antulov-Fantulin, N.: Exploring interpretable LSTM neural networks over multi-variable data **97**, 2494–2504 (2019)
4. Huang, S., Wang, D., Wu, X., Tang, A.: Dsanet: dual self-attention network for multivariate time series forecasting. In: ACM CIKM, pp. 2129–2132 (2019)
5. Klicpera, J., Bojchevski, A., Guunnemann, S.: Combining neural networks with personalized pagerank for classification on graphs. In: ICLR (2019)

6. Lai, G., Chang, W.C., Yang, Y., Liu, H.: Modeling long and short-term temporal patterns with deep neural networks. In: ACM SIGIR, pp. 95–104 (2018)
7. Lim, B., Arik, S.O., Loeff, N., Pfister, T.: Temporal fusion transformers for interpretable multi-horizon time series forecasting (2019)
8. Sen, R., Yu, H.F., Dhillon, I.S.: Think globally, act locally: a deep neural network approach to high-dimensional time series forecasting. In: NeurIPS 32 (2019)
9. Shih, S.Y., Sun, F.K., Lee, H.Y.: Temporal pattern attention for multivariate time series forecasting. 108(8–9), 1421–1441 (2019)
10. Vaswani, A., et al.: Attention is all you need. In: Advances in Neural Information Processing Systems 30, pp. 5998–6008. Curran Associates, Inc. (2017)
11. Wu, Z., Pan, S., Chen, F., Long, G., Zhang, C., Yu, P.S.: A comprehensive survey on graph neural networks. IEEE TNNLS, pp. 1–21 (2020)
12. Wu, Z., Pan, S., Long, G., Jiang, J., Chang, X., Zhang, C.: Connecting the dots: multivariate time series forecasting with graph neural networks. In: Proceedings of the 26th ACM SIGKDD (2020)
13. Yan, S., Xiong, Y., Lin, D.: Spatial temporal graph convolutional networks for skeleton-based action recognition. In: AAAI, pp. 7444–7452 (2018)
14. Zhang, G.P.: Time series forecasting using a hybrid arima and neural network model. Neurocomputing **50**, 159–175 (2003)

Research on Flame Detection Based on Anchor-Free Algorithm FCOS

Honggang Wang, Xing Wu[✉], Jingsheng Liu, and Jiangnan Li

College of Computer Science, Chongqing University, Chongqing, China
wuxing@cqu.edu.cn

Abstract. Currently, the deep learning anchor-based object detection algorithm has been widely used in flame detection. However, it relies too much on manual setting of anchor hyper-parameters and is insensitive to the change of object shape. Therefore, the improved anchor-free algorithm FCOS is introduced. Firstly, the Center-ness branch is replaced by the IoU prediction branch to make the bounding box location more accurate; then the random copy-pasting small objects and Mosaic data augmentation methods are used to improve the detection accuracy of small objects. The experimental results on the self-built dataset show that the AP and speed of FCOS are better than anchor-based algorithms. The use of IoU prediction branch can improve the location accuracy of the algorithm; the use of two data augmentation methods can further improve the AP of the algorithm for small objects by 9.6%.

Keywords: Flame detection · Anchor-free · IoU prediction · Small object augmentation

1 Introduction

As one of the most common natural disasters in human daily life, fire has strong destructive power and fast spread speed. It is of great significance to monitor the occurrence of fire timely and accurately. The traditional flame detection method based on sensor is not only slow in detection speed, but also only suitable for indoor and other fixed scenes. Another traditional method is to extract artificial features based on vision for flame detection. However, the artificial features designed based on prior knowledge often can not adapt to a variety of complex flame scenes, usually the generalization performance is poor, and the accuracy of flame detection is low.

In recent years, with the development of deep learning, more and more deep learning object detection algorithms are used for flame detection. Barmpoutis et al. [1] uses Faster R-CNN to extract network candidate bounding boxes, then analyzed the multidimensional texture features, and then uses SVM to classify these results. Huang Jie et al. [4] uses the color features of flame to guide the matching of positive samples with anchor boxes in Faster R-CNN. Park MJ et al. [9] uses Elastic Block to replace the convolution block in Darknet53, the

© Springer Nature Switzerland AG 2021
T. Mantoro et al. (Eds.): ICONIP 2021, CCIS 1516, pp. 124–131, 2021.
https://doi.org/10.1007/978-3-030-92307-5_15

backbone network of YOLOv3, and improves the detection accuracy of small objects. Li P et al. [6] comprehensively compares the performance of Faster R-CNN, R-CNN, YOLOv3, SSD and R-FCN in flame detection.

However, the above object detection algorithms are all anchor-based, which leads the following disadvantages:

(1) There are many hyper-parameters related to the anchors, which are difficult to adjust, including the size and aspect ratio of the anchor box.

(2) The fixed size and aspect ratio of the anchor box not only makes it difficult for the detector to detect objects beyond the range of the anchor box, but also limits the generalization performance of the detector.

In view of the above problems, we introduce an improved one-stage anchor-free algorithm FCOS to detect flame. Compared with the original FCOS [13] algorithm, firstly, the center-ness branch is replaced by the IoU prediction branch. In the prediction, the final confidence score of the prediction bounding box is the outcome of the classification score of the box and the IoU score, which is the output of the IoU prediction branch; Then, aiming at the problem of missing detection in the early stage of small flame, two data augmentation methods random copy-pasting small objects and Mosaic, are introduced to increase the number of small objects during model training and enrich the context information of small objects.

2 Improvements of FCOS Algorithm

2.1 IoU Prediction Branch

In this paper, the algorithm FCOS without anchor is adopted, and the FCOS algorithm is improved to achieve better results.

FCOS [13] innovatively proposes center-ness to suppress the weight of low-quality bounding boxes, but there are two problems in center-ness:

(1) The definition of center-ness is not directly related to the IoU between the prediction bounding box and the ground truth bounding box.

(2) When predicting, too small center-ness value may filter out some high-quality detection bounding boxes and reduce the recall of prediction bounding boxes.

In order to solve the above problems, we propose to directly output the IoU score of the prediction bounding boxes, and combine with the classification score to sort the prediction bounding boxes, so as to retain more high-quality prediction bounding boxes. In order to maintain the detection efficiency of the model, we directly use the IoU prediction branch to replace the original center-ness branch on the classification branch. The replaced detection sub-network is shown in Fig. 1.

The IoU prediction branch consists of only one 3×3 convolution layer and a sigmoid activation layer, therefore, it does not increase the amount of network parameters. Its output feature map size is $h \times W \times 1$, represents the IoU score

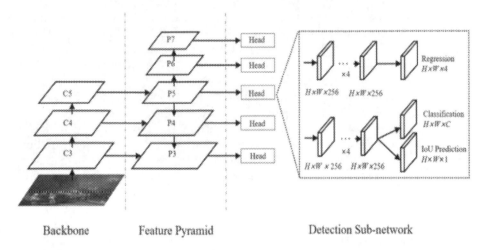

Fig. 1. Detection sub-network. The Center-ness branch in FCOS is replaced by our IOU prediction branch.

of the prediction bounding box and the ground truth bounding box. The IoU prediction branch uses binary cross-entropy as loss function.

$$L_{iou} = \frac{1}{N_{\text{pos}}} \sum_{x,y} I_{\left\{c_{x,y}^* > 0\right\}} BCE \left(IoU_{x,y}, IoU_{x,y}^*\right) \tag{1}$$

Where $IoU_{x,y}$ is the predicted IoU score, $IoU_{x,y}^x$ is the IoU of the regression branch output bounding box and the ground truth bounding box. We convert the $L_{center-ness}$ part of the loss function [7] of FCOS into L_{iou}, the total loss function of the model is calculated as follows.

$$L\left(\{p_{x,y}\}, \{t_{x,y}\}\right) = \frac{1}{N_{\text{pos}}} \sum_{x,y} L_{cls}\left(p_{x,y}, c_{x,y}^*\right) + \frac{1}{N_{pos}} \sum_{x,y} I_{\left\{c_{x,y}^* > 0\right\}} \left(L_{reg.}\left(t_{x,y}, t_{x,y}^*\right) + L_{iou}\right) \tag{2}$$

Where $p_{x,y}$ and $t_{x,y}$ respectively denotes the classification score and the prediction bounding box location predicted on the pixel (x, y), N_pos is the number of positive samples, $c_{x,y}^*$ is the classification target, $t_{x,y}^*$ is the coordinate of the labeled bounding box, $I_{c_{x,y}^* > 0}$ is the indicator function, when $c_{x,y}^* > 0 > 0$ it is 1, otherwise it is 0. $L_{cls}(p_{x,y}, c_{x,y}^*)$ is focal loss to solve the problem of imbalance between positive and negative samples. $L_{reg}(t_{x,y}, t_{x,y}^*)$ is IOU loss. Where a is used to adjust the weight of classification score and IoU score, and the value in this paper is 0.3.

2.2   Data Augmentation for Small Objects

Because of the small coverage area of small object, it is difficult for convolution neural network to extract its features. In fire detection, there are many small

---

Algorithm 1. Random copy-pasting small objects

Input: Input image and its labeled bounding box set B
Output: Augmented image and its labeled bounding box set B_{aug}
1: Initialize $B_{aug} = B$
2: **if** B has small objects **then**
3:    Randomly generate iteration number $n(n \leq 5)$
4:    **for** $t = 1, 2, \ldots, n$ **do**
5:        Select a small object bounding box randomly from B, and calculate the corner coordinates box_{ori} of the area 4 times around its center
6:        Randomly generate the location coordinates (x, y) and calculate the corner coordinates box_{aug} after box_{ori} moves to the location
7:        **if** $GIoU(B_{aug}, box_{aug}) < -0.5$ **then**
8:            Paste the pixel value of the area corresponding to box_{ori} to the (x, y) location
9:            Update $B_{aug} = B_{aug} + box_{aug}$

---

objects, which often represent the small flames in the early stage of fire, so the detection of small objects has more significance for fire prevention. Data augmentation is one of the important means to improve the accuracy of object detection, we introduces random copy-pasting small objects and Mosaic to improve the detection accuracy of small objects.

Random Copy-Pasting Small Objects. Random copy-pasting small objects by manually copying small objects to other locations in the image, greatly increasing the number of small objects during training, so that the model can more focus on small object learning [5]. The specific operation process of the algorithm in our experiments is shown in Algorithm 1.

The algorithm repeatedly randomly selects a small object bounding box from input image to copy to other locations. For obtaining the context information near the object, the region near the center of the object bounding box is actually copied 4 times. On the other hand, due to the ambiguity between two flame objects which are close to each other, it is necessary to ensure that the distances between the copied small object bounding boxes and the labeled object bounding boxes are far enough. Therefore, we adopt GIoU [12] to measure the distance between two boxes, that is, only when the GIoU value of the two boxes is less than -0.5, the box can be pasted.

Mosaic Data Augmentation. Mosaic is a new way of data augmentation [2], which stitches four images together according to randomly generated image positions in the original image. After the image is reduced according to the randomly generated position coordinates, new small objects may be generated, which increases the number of small objects and the probability of small objects in the training image. On the other hand, the combination of multiple images will also enrich the context information of these small objects, making the model suitable for small object detection in more scenes.

3   Experimental Results and Analysis

3.1   Dataset and Evaluation Protocol

The present public flame detection datasets such as bowfire [3] and Corsican fire [14], are not suitable for verifying the model effect due to the small number of images and insufficient scenes. Therefore, on the basis of the above two datasets, the images used in our experiment also contains a large number of images searched from Baidu, Google and other channels. The complete dataset includes images of forest fire, traffic accident, firewood pile, house fire, indoor fire, candle, torch and other scenes. The total number of images is 4513, which is divided into train set and test set according to the ratio of about 7:3. We follow the following principles when labeling:

(1) Try to reduce the background information, so as not to confuse the learning of background features and object features.

(2) In order to improve the learning ability of the model, we label as many small objects as possible.

We define the small object as the object whose length and width are less than $1/10$ of the image's length and width [9]. The statistics of the number of labeled bounding boxes in the dataset are shown in Table 1.

Table 1. Statistics of the number of labeled bounding box in dataset.

Dataset	Number of images	Number of small objects	Number of all objects
Train set	3159	1271	4518
Teat set	1354	597	1894

AP_{50} is the AP when the IoU threshold is 0.5. AP comprehensively considers the precision(P) and recall(R) under different confidence scores,

$$AP = \int_0^1 P(R)dR \tag{3}$$

AP_{50s} is defined as AP50 only considering small object detection. Since there is no specific measure to evaluate the location accuracy of the model in the field of flame detection, we adopt AP_{75} and $AP_{50\sim95}$ in COCO dataset to evaluate the location accuracy of the model. AP_{75} is the AP under the IoU threshold of 0.75, and $AP_{50\sim95}$ is the average AP under different IoU thresholds (0.5, 0.55, 0.60, 0.65,..., 0.95).

3.2   Ablation Experiment

This section is to verify the effectiveness of each improvement on FCOS. The experimental results on the test set are shown in Table 2.

Table 2. Influence of different methods on detection results. CN2IoU means the method of replacing center-ness branch with IoU prediction branch, CP means the method of random copy-pasting small objects, and Mos means the method of Mosaic. The first row indicates that no improvement is used on the original FCOS algorithm.

CN2IoU	CP	Mos	$AP_{50}\%$	$AP_{50s}\%$	$AP_{75}\%$	$AP_{50\sim95}\%$
			87.9	70.3	60.2	54.8
1			88.7	73.0	62.8	56.7
	1		89.2	74.9	62.0	55.8
		1	91.1	78.0	64.9	57.6
	1	1	91.4	79.8	65.4	58.1
1	1	1	91.8	79.9	67.1	60.2

(1) Compare the first row and the second row in Table 2, we can see that after using CN2IoU, $AP_{50\sim95}$ improves by 1.9%, AP_{50} by 0.8%, AP_{75} by 2.6%, which shows that the improved method CN2IoU has better effect on predicting high-quality bounding boxes.

(2) Compare the first row and the third row, we can see that the AP_{50s} can improve by 4.6% by using CP method.

(3) Compare the first and fourth rows, we can see that using Mos method can improve AP_{50s} by 7.7%.

(4) Compare the first row, the fifth row and the sixth row, we can see that the AP_{50s} can be further improved by 9.6% by using CP and Mos methods at the same time; after using CN2IoU, CP and Mos at the same time, $AP_{50\sim95}$ can improves by 2.1%, AP_{50} by 0.4% and AP_{75} by 1.7%. The above experimental results verify the effectiveness of CN2IoU for improving the location accuracy of the model, and CP and Mosaic for improving the accuracy of small object detection.

3.3   Comparision Experiment

Compare the detection accuracy and speed of the original FCOS algorithm, the improved FCOS algorithm, SSD [8], Faster [11], YOLOv3 [10] and RetinaNet [7] and other anchor-based algorithms. The comparison results are shown in Table 3.

Table 3. Comparison of detection results of different algorithms.

Model	AP	FPS
Faster R-CNN	86.3	6.8
SSD	86.0	24.4
YOLOv3	87.4	30.3
RetinaNet	87.7	27.0
FCOS	87.9	30.3
FCOS (ours)	91.8	30.3

(1) Compared with other anchor-based algorithms, AP_{50} of FCOS is 0.2% higher than that of the optimal algorithm (RetinaNet). From the comparison of P-R curves of different algorithms (as shown in Fig. 2), it can be seen that the precision and recall of FCOS under different IoU thresholds are also the highest. This shows that by using anchor-free detection paradigm, which reduces the dependence on manually setting anchor box hyper-parameters, can effectively improve the accuracy of flame detection. At the same time, the detection speed of FCOS is the fastest, reaching 30.3FPS (the same as YOLOv3), which can meet the needs of realtime detection. This is mainly because FCOS generates fewer detection bounding boxs than anchor-based algorithm, which reduces the amount of network computation.

(2) The improved FCOS algorithm can further improve AP_{50} of the original FCOS algorithm by 3.9%. Combined with the ablation experimental results, note that especially the object location accuracy and small object detection accuracy are improved, with no loss in detection speed. The P-R curve comparison shows that the improved FCOS algorithm is also significantly improved in the detection precision and recall.

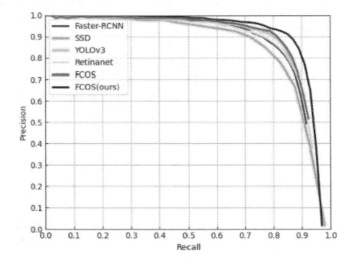

Fig. 2. Comparison of P-R curves of different algorithms

4 Conslusion

In this paper, FCOS is applied to flame detection for the first time. We use the IoU prediction branch to replace the original center-ness branch, and utilize the product of IoU score and classification score to sort the prediction bounding boxes and NMS; to increase the detection accuracy of small objects, random copy-pasting small objects and Mosaic data augmentation methods are adopted.

Experiments on the self-built dataset show that FCOS can achieve optimal accuracy and the fastest speed of flame detection compared with the anchor-based algorithms, and the improved FCOS algorithm can further improve the detection accuracy, especially the small object detection accuracy, and the object location accuracy is higher, which is suitable for all kinds of complex scenes that need realtime detection.

References

1. Barmpoutis, P., Dimitropoulos, K., Kaza, K., Grammalidis, N.: Fire detection from images using faster R-CNN and multidimensional texture analysis. In: ICASSP 2019–2019 IEEE International Conference on Acoustics, Speech and Signal Processing (ICASSP), pp. 8301–8305. IEEE (2019)
2. Bochkovskiy, A., Wang, C.Y., Liao, H.: Yolov4: optimal speed and accuracy of object detection (2020)
3. Chino, D.Y.T., Avalhais, L.P.S., Jr, J.F.R., Traina, A.J.M.: Bowfire: detection of fire in still images by integrating pixel color and texture analysis. In: 2015 28th SIBGRAPI Conference on Graphics, Patterns and Images, pp. 95–102 (2015)
4. Huang, J., et al.: Faster R-CNN based color-guided flame detection. J. Comput. Appl. **40**(5), 1470–1475 (2020)
5. Kisantal, M., Wojna, Z., Murawski, J., Naruniec, J., Cho, K.: Augmentation for small object detection. In: 9th International Conference on Advances in Computing and Information Technology (2019)
6. Li, P., Zhao, W.: Image fire detection algorithms based on convolutional neural networks. Case Stud. Thermal Eng. **19**, 100625 (2020)
7. Lin, T.Y., Goyal, P., Girshick, R., He, K., Dollár, P.: Focal loss for dense object detection. IEEE Trans. Pattern Anal. Mach. Intell. **PP**(99), 2999–3007 (2017)
8. Liu, W., et al.: SSD: single shot MultiBox detector. In: Leibe, B., Matas, J., Sebe, N., Welling, M. (eds.) ECCV 2016. LNCS, vol. 9905, pp. 21–37. Springer, Cham (2016). https://doi.org/10.1007/978-3-319-46448-0_2
9. Park, M., Ko, B.C.: Two-step real-time night-time fire detection in an urban environment using static elastic-yolov3 and temporal fire-tube. Sensors **20**(8), 2202 (2020)
10. Redmon, J., Farhadi, A.: Yolov3: an incremental improvement. arXiv e-prints (2018)
11. Ren, S., He, K., Girshick, R., Sun, J.: Faster R-CNN: towards real-time object detection with region proposal networks. IEEE Trans. Pattern Anal. Mach. Intell. **39**(6), 1137–1149 (2017)
12. Rezatofighi, H., Tsoi, N., Gwak, J.Y., Sadeghian, A., Reid, I., Savarese, S.: Generalized intersection over union: a metric and a loss for bounding box regression. In: IEEE/CVF Conference on Computer Vision & Pattern Recognition, pp. 658–666 (2019)
13. Tian, Z., Shen, C., Chen, H., He, T.: Fcos: fully convolutional one-stage object detection. In: 2019 IEEE/CVF International Conference on Computer Vision (ICCV), pp. 9627–9636 (2020)
14. Toulouse, T., Rossi, L., Campana, A., Celik, T., Akhloufi, M.A.: Computer vision for wildfire research: an evolving image dataset for processing and analysis. Fire Saf. J. **92**, 188–194 (2017)

Socializing in Interference: Quantum-Inspired Topic Model with Crystal-Like Structure Grid for Microblog Topic Detection

Tian Tian, Yuexian Hou$^{(\boxtimes)}$, Zan Li, Tingsan Pan, and Yingjie Gao

College of Intelligence and Computing, Tianjin University, Tianjin, China
{silber_tian,yxhou}@tju.edu.cn

Abstract. Capturing highly coherent topics from large-scale informal social media messages has always been a challenging task. Existing topic models fail to model the nonlinear dependence between text and structure, which is called the interference effect in quantum cognition. Therefore, we propose a Quantum-inspired Topic Model (QTM), which naturally admits a non-linear context composition. Specifically, based on the iterative-deepening random walks, we design a Crystal-like Structure Grid (CSG) to obtain the user structural features. Then, we propose a quantum density operator based network embedding. Such a density operator is essentially a nonlinear joint representation of the user structure and text information. The resulting user sequence embeddings are fed into the Neural Variational Inference (NVI) for topic detection. Extensive experimental results on three real-world microblog datasets demonstrate that QTM outperforms state-of-the-art models.

Keywords: Social media topic detection · Quantum-inspired Topic Model (QTM) · Neural Variational Inference (NVI)

1 Introduction

In social media such as Twitter and Sina Weibo, it is crucial, yet challenging, to extract topic semantics of such short and informal text, which may benefit downstream applications such as key phrase generation [2], short text classification [1] and recognition [3]. Essentially, the existing topic models only focus on text [4] or consider the text and structural relationship between users with simply concatenation [5,6]. Further, since the truncated user sequence is represented by the features of local adjacent nodes [7], the above methods only consider one certain

This work is funded in part by the National Key R&D Program of China (2017YFE0111900), the National Natural Science Foundation of China (61876129) and the European Unions Horizon 2020 research and innovation programme under the Marie Skodowska-Curie grant agreement No. 721321.

© Springer Nature Switzerland AG 2021
T. Mantoro et al. (Eds.): ICONIP 2021, CCIS 1516, pp. 132–140, 2021.
https://doi.org/10.1007/978-3-030-92307-5_16

topic community[1] for a user. Actually, the same user can participate in multiple intersecting communities. Moreover, there exists an acquiescent assumption that users are independent. But in fact, series of interactions between users make a subtle and enormous impact on their expression content or even interest preferences. This impact can be called the interference phenomenon of inter-individual cognition in quantum cognition.

Drawing inspiration from latest researches of quantum cognition, which shows that text representation [10] and human cognition [8,9] exhibit certain non-classical phenomena (e.g. The actual meaning of "ivory tower" cannot be derived from a linear combination of the meanings of "ivory" and "tower", but the quantum theoretical framework naturally allows for non-linear semantic composition with a complex vector word representation.), we propose a Quantum-inspired Topic Model (QTM) to formulate quantum-like phenomena in social activities and address the above problems. Notably, this is the first attempt to introduce quantum theory into the topic detection tasks and propose a theory-supported context[2] fusion approach.

2 Quantum Preliminaries

The mathematical framework of Quantum Theory is established on Hilbert Space, denoted as $\mathbb{H}^n$, which is our acquainted friend from linear algebra [15]. In line with previous studies on the quantum-inspired models [16,17], we restrict our problem to vector spaces over real numbers in $\mathbb{R}^n$. The standard Dirac Notation is often used, which denotes a unit vector that described the system state space is completely by its state vector. It expresses the state vector ψ as a ket $|\psi\rangle$ and its transpose ψ^T as a bra $\langle\psi|$, the inner product and the outer product of two vectors ϕ and ψ are denoted as $\langle\phi|\psi\rangle$ and $|\phi\rangle\langle\psi|$ respectively.

Density operator provides a much more convenient language for describing a quantum system. The mixture density operator $\rho = \sum_i p_i|\psi_i\rangle\langle\psi_i|$ can be defined as the weighted sum of a set of pure state $|\psi_i\rangle$ with probability p_i, where $|\psi_i\rangle\langle\psi_i|$ is the outer product of $|\psi_i\rangle$. ρ is a symmetric Hermitian matrix which is trace one $(\mathrm{tr}(\rho)=1)$ and positive semi-definite.

To infer the probabilistic properties of ρ, Gleason's theorem [23] is used to calculate the probability through projection measurement: $p_m(\rho) = \langle m|\rho|m\rangle = tr(\rho|m\rangle\langle m|)$. The measured probability $p_m(\rho)$ is a non-negative real-valued scalar, since both ρ and $|m\rangle\langle m|$ are Hermitian. The unitary trace property guarantees $\sum_{m\in M} p_m(\rho) = 1$ for M being a set of orthogonal basis states.

3 Quantum-Inspired Topic Model

3.1 Capturing User Structure Features

User Communication Network. Presume the network $G = (U, E, T)$, where U represents the collection of all users, $E \subset U \times U$ is the interaction set of

---

[1] Weibo topic community is a collection of users who are interested in a common topic.
[2] All information about the user, including text and structural features.

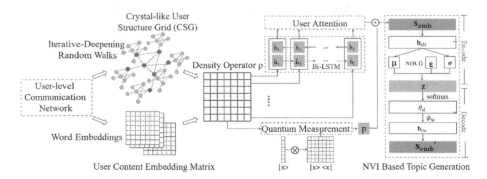

Fig. 1. Architecture of Quantum-inspired Topic Model. $\odot$ means that a sequence multiplies a number with each elements, $\otimes$ denotes a outer production to a vector.

reposting and commenting relationships between users. T is the set of users' text information, where words are represented as word embeddings. $t = (w_1, w_2, ..., w_n)$ is the text information of user v, where n is the number of words in t.

Crystal-Like User Structure Grid. We propose an iterative-deepening random walk method to acquire the Crystal-like user Structure Grid (CSG) as shown in Fig. 1. First, the classical random walk is carried out on the communication network G to obtain the user structure sequence $seq = (v_1, v_2, ..., v_l)$. Second, all nodes in the seq are taken as the starting nodes for random walks respectively. In details, we acquire the structure state sequence $s_i = (v_i, v_{i+1}, ..., v_{i+l})$ for the i-th user in the sequence seq, which means that the structural information of v_i is no longer represented by its own identity i, but by its local association structure sequence s_i. Finally, the CSG is obtained and denoted as $V^s = (s_1, s_2, ..., s_l)$. Moreover, the corresponding user text is represented as $V^t = (t_1, t_2, ..., t_l)$.

3.2   Network Embeddings

Quantum Density Operator Based Context Fusion. In order to use the mathematical formalism of quantum theory to model context characteristics, it is necessary to establish a Social Context Hilbert Space $\mathbb{H}^n$ to represent social networks. We assume that the user structure state is the particle state and the corresponding word embedding is the particle probability attribute. Then, we introduce the concept of quantum state vector to formulate this particle state, which is represented by a unit-length vector $|s_i'\rangle$ and achieved by normalizing the structure state sequence s_i as follows:

$$|s_i'\rangle = \frac{s_i}{\|s_i\|_2} \tag{1}$$

To obtain the composition of user's structure and text features, we formulate it as a quantum mixed system composed of the CSG $V^s = (s_1, s_2, ..., s_l)$ and the corresponding text word embeddings $V^t = (t_1, t_2, ..., t_l)$. The system is in a mixed state represented by a l-by-l density operator ρ on $\mathbb{H}^n$,

$$\rho = \sum_{i=0}^{l} p(i)|s_i'\rangle\langle s_i'| \tag{2}$$

where $p(i)$ is the probability of the state $|s_i'\rangle$. It indicates the contribution of the user v_i in seq to the overall Social Context Hilbert Space $\mathbb{H}^n$. To ensure the unit trace length of the density operator, the state probabilities represented by the user word embedding V^t are normalized to the probability values through the softmax operation: $p(i) = softmax(t_i)$. The density operator ρ can be regarded as a non-classical distribution of user's context features in the social communication network which encodes the interference effects among users.

Context Measurements. The density operator ρ, as a non-classical probability distribution, carries rich contextual information. To extract task-specific features from ρ, we build a set of measurement projectors $\{|x\rangle\langle x|\}$ and calculate the probability of the mixed system falling onto each projector as a high-level abstraction of context. The specific representation is as follows:

$$p = \langle x|\rho|x\rangle = tr(\rho|x\rangle\langle x|) \tag{3}$$

Encode Semantic Dependency. Due to the colloquialism and casualness of user expression in social situation, a Bi-directional LSTM layer is adopted to encode semantic dependencies for topic detection, where ρ_i means the i-th row of ρ. By concatenating (denote as $\oplus$) the corresponding hidden states, we acquire the user semantic embedding sequence $(h_1, h_2, ..., h_l) = (\overrightarrow{h_1} \oplus \overleftarrow{h_1}, \overrightarrow{h_2} \oplus \overleftarrow{h_2}, ..., \overrightarrow{h_l} \oplus \overleftarrow{h_l})$ and $\overrightarrow{h_i} = \overrightarrow{LSTM}(\rho_i, \overrightarrow{h_{i-1}})$, $\overleftarrow{h_i} = \overleftarrow{LSTM}(\rho_i, \overleftarrow{h_{i+1}})$. Moreover, we employ self-attention to learn the different contributions of users to the topic and to reduce the interference of noisy information. The importance coefficient sequence $(a_1, a_2, ..., a_l)$ can be represented as: $a_i = softmax(q_i^T \cdot tanh(W \cdot h_i + b))$.

Quantum Measurement Based User Sequence Embedding. We obtain the user sequence embedding s_{emb} by multiplying the measurement result p to supplement the original user context features lost in the training process: $s_{emb} = p \sum_{i=0}^{l} a_i h_i$. Then, we use negative sampling to reduce the cost of $P(v_j|v_i)$ and acquire the optimized objective function:

$$L_{emb} = - \sum_{v_j \in B_i} (log\, \sigma(h_j^T \cdot h_i) + \sum_{m=1}^{M} \mathbb{E}_{v_k \sim V}[log\, \sigma(-h_k^T \cdot h_i)]) \tag{4}$$

where $B_i = \{v_j|v_j \in seq, j \neq i\}$ are all the neighbors of user v_i in seq, $\sigma(x) = 1/(1 + exp(-x))$ and M is the size of negative samples and v_k is the noisy user sampled from the user set V.

3.3 Topic Generation

Neural Variational Inference (NVI) [19] estimates the results of the generative model with variational distribution parameterized by the neural networks. Inspired by the Neural Topic Model [20] and PCFTM [7], we feed the user sequence embedding s_{emb} into the Variational AutoEncoder (VAE) [13] to infer the document-topic distribution $\theta_d = (p(t_1|d), p(t_2|d), ..., p(t_K|d))$ and the topic-word distribution $\phi_w = (p(w|t_1), p(w|t_2), ..., p(w|t_K))$, where t_i is the i-th topic.

$$h_{dt} = ReLU(W^{dt}s_{emb} + b^{dt}) \tag{5}$$

$$\mu = W^\mu h_{dt} + b^\mu \qquad log\sigma^2 = W^\sigma h_{dt} + b^\sigma \tag{6}$$

By sampling $\varepsilon \sim N(0, I)$, the reparameterized latent semantic vector $z = \mu + \varepsilon \times \sigma$ is obtained and the document-topic distribution $\theta_d = softmax(z)$ is acquired.

We calculate the topic-word distribution ϕ_w as the parameter of the encoder network in VAE and the redefined user sequence embedding s'_{emb} is generated:

$$h_{tw} = softmax(\phi_w \times \theta_d^T) \tag{7}$$

$$s'_{emb} = ReLU(W^{tw}h_{tw} + b^{tw}) \tag{8}$$

The final objective function is defined as follows, where $g(z)$ is the prior gaussian distribution $N(0, I)$ and KL denotes the Kullback-Leibler divergence.

$$L_{gen} = KL(g(z) \| p(z|s_{emb})) - \mathbb{E}_{z \sim p(z|s_{emb})}[log\, p(s_{emb}|z)] \tag{9}$$

The ultimate aim is to minimize the following overall objective function: $L = (1 - \lambda)L_{emb} + \lambda L_{gen}$, where λ is the trade-off parameter to balance the loss of NVI-based topic generation L_{gen} and the loss of user sequence embedding L_{emb}. The parameter set is $\Theta = \{W^*, b^*\}$ is optimized by Adam algorithm [21].

4   Experiments

Based on the microblog corpus established by Li et al. [14], We obtained three datasets divided by month from May to July 2014 with a total of 596,318 posts. Note that Li et al. manually select 50 frequent hashtags as topics for each dataset.

All of our baselines use the original parameter settings reported in the paper. In QTM, in order to match the count of hashtags, we set K to 50. And then, we set K to 100, which is much larger than the real number of topics. For each topic, the consistence scores of the top $N = 10$, 15 and 20 words ranked by topic-word distribution ϕ_w are selected to evaluate the topic model. More specifically, we set the word embedding dimension to 200, the hidden dimension of Bi-LSTM to 300, the dimension of the recognition layer and the generation layer for VAE to 200 and 300. And we set the batch size to 64, learning rate to 1E-3, dropout probability to 0.4, the trade-off parameter λ to 0.9 The length of iterative-deepening random walks set to $l = 7$ for all the datasets.

Table 1. Coherence scores on three evaluation datasets. Higher is better. The best performed value is in bold.

Datasets	Model	K = 50			K = 100		
		N = 10	N = 15	N = 20	N = 10	N = 15	N = 20
May	LCTM [4]	−70.91	−165.37	−296.36	−58.65	−140.10	261.40
	LeadLDA [14]	−53.91	−138.53	−258.38	−58.15	−141.34	−261.65
	IATM [6]	−43.34	−112.64	−228.27	−47.32	−121.46	−219.96
	PCFTM [7]	−30.01	−70.21	−127.66	−31.10	−72.00	−130.24
	QTM (CSG)	−30.54	−71.21	−128.69	−30.01	−69.73	−126.07
	QTM (CSG+ρ)	−29.56	−68.78	−124.61	−29.96	−70.05	−127.00
	QTM	**−28.07**	**−66.87**	**−122.11**	**−29.58**	**−69.76**	**−126.66**
June	LCTM [4]	−91.72	−208.75	−367.76	−81.88	−181.57	−323.16
	LeadLDA [14]	−63.54	−150.18	−278.19	−72.07	−169.80	−309.40
	IATM [6]	−46.69	−113.09	−213.61	−59.11	−133.96	−225.48
	PCFTM [7]	−30.44	−71.16	−129.08	−31.03	−72.26	−131.07
	QTM (CSG)	−30.93	−70.59	−131.68	−30.67	−71.85	−129.91
	QTM (CSG+ρ)	−30.25	−70.63	−128.19	**−29.91**	**−69.93**	**−126.71**
	QTM	**−27.80**	**−66.58**	**−122.88**	−29.95	−70.49	−128.42
July	LCTM [4]	−72.78	−160.08	−275.58	−63.56	−137.36	−238.31
	LeadLDA [14]	−70.40	−157.83	−268.23	−59.75	−130.83	−226.62
	IATM [6]	−50.75	−119.48	−212.26	−46.80	−110.27	−204.35
	PCFTM [7]	−31.79	−75.23	−136.51	−32.36	−74.93	−134.73
	QTM (CSG)	−31.97	−74.62	−134.94	−32.47	−75.36	−135.47
	QTM (CSG+ρ)	−31.13	−72.86	−132.31	**−31.44**	**−73.09**	**−132.52**
	QTM	**−28.76**	**−68.46**	**−125.51**	−31.63	−74.05	−134.36

Including LCTM [4] as baselines to only consider text information, LeadLDA [14], IATM [6] and PCFTM [7] as baselines to consider both textual and structural information. The experimental results in Table 1 demonstrate the improvement of coherence over the aforementioned baselines on three datasets. Specially, to ensure the rigor and reliability of experimental data, the coherence results of QTM are obtained from the average of 10 experimental results. Especially, our proposed QTM performs best. It demonstrates the necessity of simultaneously considering textual and structural information in social media topic detection due to the potential quantum cognitive interference effect (i.e. the interaction among users will affect users' interest preferences and expression content). To intuitively understand the inferred topics, due to limited space, we select three best-performing models and list the top 10 words about the topic "MH17 Crash" shown in Table 2. In particular, in the first 10 words inferred by QTM, there are no words irrelevant to the topic. "Malaysia Airlines" and "crash", which are highly consistent with the topic of "MH17 crash", topped the list. However, the detail word "declare" which is weakly related to the topic is ranked fourth, which reduces the performance of QTM coherence scores.

5   Ablation Test

QTM (CSG). It uses the CSG obtained by iterative-deepening random walks and simply concatenates the structure and text information, but does not perform the quantum density operator based context fusion, nor does it add the quantum measurement component. As shown in Table 1, QTM (CSG) has similar coherence scores with PCFTM which employs classical random walks and extracts semantic information with CNN layer and Bi-LSTM layer. This manifests that the CSG extracts the effective user structure features and the performance of the iterative-deepening random walk is greatly improved compared with the classical random walk, and have similar improvement in terms of performance as a simple CNN.

Table 2. Top 10 words for the latent topic "MH17 Crash". Bold words are detailed information. Red words are related to other topics.

IATM	Malaysia Airlines, crash, ***support***, killed, Russia
	Malaysia, shoot down, Ukraine, Xiaomi, ***airliner***
PCFTM	Malaysia, crash, airplane, Ukraine, ***newest***
	killed, ***close down***, shoot down, aircrew, grief
QTM	Malaysia Airlines, crash, ***declare***, shoot down
	killed, aircrew, Ukraine, grief, Terrible, pray

QTM (CSG+ρ). It removes measurement results from QTM to verify the impact of measurement component on model performance. Compared with QTM (CSG), QTM (CSG+ρ) adopts the quantum density operator ρ to fuse context features. Experimental results further prove that this fusion is effective in acquiring the nonlinear correlation between text and structure. It is highlight that adding measurement can substantially improve the performance when K = 50, but the coherence scores on May do not fluctuate significantly when K = 100, and scores on June and July even drop slightly. This is consistent with the physical mechanism of quantum measurements, which extracts a low-dimensional representation of the real data state that each dataset is artificially limited to 50 topics.

6   Conclusions

To better model the non-linearity of social contexts and the quantum cognitive interference effects in social activities, we introduce the quantum mechanism modeling topic model and propose the Quantum-inspired Topic Model (QTM), which mainly includes three contributions. The cross-community user structure features are acquired by iterative-deepening random walks. The quantum density operator is used to fuse structure and text information seamlessly. The low-dimensional user context state is obtained by quantum measurement, which provides a novel approach for extracting dimensional reduction of large-scale unknown state datasets. The QTM shows promising performance in three real-world microblog datasets. Moreover, the quantum heuristic components defined in the Social Context Hilbert Space essentially conform to the corresponding physical mechanism, bringing benefits to the coherence of the induced topics in a comprehensive ablation study.

This work is the first step to apply the quantum framework to the topic model. We believe that it is an instructive and sustainable direction. In the future, we will further explore this work by considering quantum walks to eliminate the fluctuation caused by random walks and extract more stabilized and approximate structural features.

References

1. Zeng, J., Li, J., Song, Y., Gao, C., Lyu, M.R., King, I.: Topic memory networks for short text classification. In: EMNLP, pp. 3120–3131 (2018)
2. Wang, Y., Li, J., Chan, H.P., King, I., Lyu, M.R., Shi, S.: Topic-aware neural keyphrase generation for social media language. In: ACL, pp. 2516–2526 (2019)
3. Xu, S., Li, P., Kong, F., Zhu, Q., Zhou, G.: Topic tensor network for implicit discourse relation recognition in Chinese. In: ACL, pp. 608–618 (2019)
4. Hu, W., Tsujii, J.: A latent concept topic model for robust topic inference using word embeddings. In: ACL, pp. 380–386 (2016)
5. Chen, C., Ren, J.: Forum latent Dirichlet allocation for user interest discovery. Knowl.-Based Syst. **126**, 1–7 (2017)
6. He, R., Zhang, X., Jin, D., Wang, L., Dang, J., Li, X.: Interaction-aware topic model for microblog conversations through network embedding and user attention. In: COLING, pp. 1398–1409 (2018)
7. Liu, H., He, R., Wang, H., Wang, B.: Fusing parallel social contexts within flexible-order proximity for microblog topic detection. In: CIKM (2020). https://doi.org/10.1145/3340531.3412024
8. Aerts, D., Gabora, L., Sozzo, S.: Concepts and their dynamics: a quantum-theoretic modeling of human thought. Top. Cogn. Sci. **5**, 737–772 (2013). https://doi.org/10.1111/tops.12042
9. Lukasik, A.: Quantum models of cognition and decision. Int. J. Parallel Emergent Distrib. Syst. **33**, 1–10 (2018)
10. Wang, B., Li, Q., Melucci, M., Song, D.: Semantic Hilbert space for text representation learning, pp. 3293–3299 (2019)
11. Graves, A., Mohamed, A.-r., Hinton, G.: Speech recognition with deep recurrent neural networks. In: ICASSP 38 (2013). https://doi.org/10.1109/ICASSP.2013.6638947
12. Lin, Z., et al.: A structured self-attentive sentence embedding (2017)
13. Kingma, D.P., Welling, M.: Auto-encoding variational Bayes. In: ICLR (2014)
14. Li, J., Liao, M., Gao, W., He, Y., Wong, K.F.: Topic extraction from microblog posts using conversation structures. In: ACL, pp. 1731–1734 (2016)
15. Nielsen, M.A., Chuang, I.L.: Quantum computation and quantum information. Phys. Today **54**(2), 60 (2001)

16. Zhang, P., Niu, J., Su, Z., Wang, B., Ma, L., Song, D.: End-to-end quantum-like language models with application to question answering, pp. 5666–5673 (2018)
17. Jiang, Y., Zhang, P., Gao, H., Song, D.: A quantum interference inspired neural matching model for ad-hoc retrieval. In: SIGIR, pp. 19–28, July 2020. https://doi.org/10.1145/3397271.3401070
18. Fisher, R.: The use of multiple measurements in taxonomic problems. Ann. Eugenics **7**, 179–188 (1936)
19. Miao, Y., Grefenstette, E., Blunsom, P.: Discovering discrete latent topics with neural variational inference, pp. 2410–2419 (2017)
20. Srivastava, A., Sutton, C.: Autoencoding variational inference for topic models. In: ICLR (2017)
21. Kingma, D.P., Ba, J.: Adam: a method for stochastic optimization. In: ICLR (2014)
22. Mimno, D., Wallach, H., Talley, E., Leenders, M., McCallum, A.: Optimizing semantic coherence in topic models. In: EMNLP, pp. 262–272, July 2011
23. Gleason, A.: Measures on the closed subspaces of a Hilbert space. J. Math. Mech. (1975). https://doi.org/10.1512/iumj.1957.6.56050

Robust Trajectory Prediction of Multiple Interacting Pedestrians via Incremental Active Learning

Yi Xi[1], Dongchun Ren[1], Mingxia Li[2], Yuehai Chen[2], Mingyu Fan[3(✉)], and Huaxia Xia[1]

[1] Meituan, Beijing 100102, China
{xuyi14,rengdongchun,xiahuaxia}@meituan.com
[2] Xi'an Jiaotong University, Xi'an 710049, Shaanxi, China
{alicelmx,cyh0518}@stu.xjtu.edu.cn
[3] Wenzhou University, Wenzhou 325035, Zhejiang, China
fanmingyu@amss.ac.cn

Abstract. Pedestrian trajectory prediction is an important issue in many real applications, including autonomous driving, robot navigation, and intelligent monitoring. With rapid growing volume of pedestrian trajectory data, existing methods roughly learn pedestrian walking motion directly with increasing computation and time costs while neglecting checking the relative importance of the trajectory data. In order to address this issue, we propose a novel trajectory prediction model via incremental active learning, which is referred as "IAL-TP". In this method, we utilize a simple and effective strategy to evaluate the candidate data samples and then select the more valuable and representative samples. An active set is determined by our proposed strategy such that both noisy and redundant samples are not selected. The active learning strategy is implemented iteratively to improve the generalization ability of the model. Experimental results on benchmark public datasets demonstrate that our model is able to achieve better performance than state-of-the-art methods with only a small fraction of the training data.

Keywords: Trajectory prediction · Incremental active learning · Select strategy

1 Introduction

Future path prediction, which aims at forecasting the future trajectories of multiple agents in the next few seconds, has received a lot of attention in the multimedia community [27,32]. This is a fundamental problem in a variety of applications such as autonomous driving [7], long-tern object tracking [21], monitoring, robotics, etc. Recently, Recurrent Neural Network (RNN) and its variants, such as Long Short-Term Memory (LSTM) and Gated Recurrent Unit (GRU), have demonstrated promising performance in modeling the trajectory sequences [1,14].

Y. Xu and D. Ren are co-first authors. This work was done while Y. Xu was an intern in Meituan.

© Springer Nature Switzerland AG 2021
T. Mantoro et al. (Eds.): ICONIP 2021, CCIS 1516, pp. 141–150, 2021.
https://doi.org/10.1007/978-3-030-92307-5_17

Trajectory prediction is difficult because of its intrinsic properties: (1) The pedestrians walking in public often interact with each other and will change the walking paths to avoid collision or overtaking. (2) The pedestrians may follow several viable trajectories that could avoid collision, such as moving to the left, right, or stopping. Because of these properties, some trajectory prediction methods are proposed by modeling social interactions [1,11,23,35]. Some methods include additional surrounding semantics maps into their model such that the predicted trajectories will comply the restrictions in the maps [13,25,26]. Given the observed trajectories of agents in a scene, a pedestrian may take different trajectories depending on their latent goals. Because of future is uncertain, many researches focus on multiple future trajectory prediction [11,14,18]. Some recent works also proposed probabilistic multi-future trajectory prediction [23,28], which provide very useful quantity results. Moreover, some vision-based trajectory prediction methods apply raw camera data and LiDAR point cloud data directly for interaction modeling and trajectory prediction [12,22].

In practice, one can drive a car with a LiDAR [17] or use overhead surveillance cameras on open road to collect as many as possible trajectories of the road users. However, not all trajectory data are helpful in training a robust and accurate prediction model. Some observed trajectories are noisy because of the car movements in some scenes are relatively simple where the road users are moving at constant speeds. In this study, we propose a data efficient trajectory prediction active learning method through the selection of a compact less noisy and more informative training set from all the observed trajectory data. To the best of our knowledge, it is the first time considering the trajectory prediction problem from the perspective of trajectory samples. The main contributions of this study are summarized as follows.

- This study proposes a simple and efficient active learning strategy, which could remove noisy and redundant trajectory data for a compact and informative training set. The storage and computation costs at training stage are greatly reduced.
- Our proposed method could actively learn the streaming trajectory data incrementally and efficiently, which is the first work that consider the value of trajectory data in trajectory prediction task.
- Our proposed active prediction method is able to achieve better performance than the previous state-of-the-arts with much smaller training dataset on five public pedestrian trajectory datasets.

2   Related Work

With rapid development of deep learning, various methods have been proposed. Social-LSTM [1] is one of the earliest methods of applying Recurrent Neural Network for pedestrian prediction. In Social-LSTM, a pooling layer is designed for sharing human-human interaction features among pedestrians. Later work [4,19,30,34] followed this pattern, design different approaches for delivering information of human-human interactions. Instead of making only one determined trajectory of each pedestrian, Generative Adversarial Networks-based (GAN) methods [2,9,13,16,25,29] has been designed for multiple plausible trajectories prediction. Moreover, auto-encoder-based methods [5,20] have been developed for encoding important features of pedestrians and then making predictions with a decoder. Due to the big success of

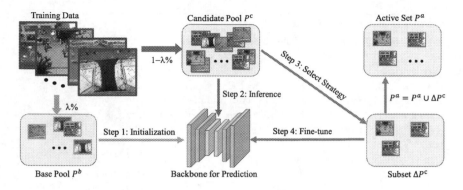

Fig. 1. The structure of our proposed IAL-TP model. At first, the model is initialized with samples from the base pool. At each iteration, a subset is selected out of the candidate pool based on the model inference and then added into the active set. Once the number of trajectory samples in active set meets the requirement, retrain the model with samples from the collected active set.

Transformer structure [29] in sequential processing [6]. Recent works [10,33] seek to utilize this structure for pedestrian trajectory prediction and achieve competitive performance. However, these methods roughly utilize all the available trajectory data to attempt to understand the movement pattern for future trajectory prediction. We argue that not all available data are useful or meaningful during training and blindly using such large amount of data could damage the performance of models, not to mention the expensive computation and time costs.

3   Model

In this section, we first give the problem definition and then detailed introduce our proposed model. The pipeline of our IAL-TP method is illustrated in Fig. 1.

3.1   Construct Two Pools

In real-world applications, trajectory data are easy to be collected automatically by sensors such as LiDAR and cameras. Previous methods save all the collected trajectories and then train their models on the collected data. However, the raw trajectory data are noisy and redundant and it is unnecessary to save and train all the collected data. Some collected trajectories fluctuate drastically with time and some trajectories are straight lines with constant speeds. The fluctuation trajectories are noisy and the straight trajectories with constant speeds are redundant and too easy for the prediction model. To address this issue, we begin with constructing two non-intersect pools, a base pool $\mathcal{P}^b$ only with a small amount of trajectory data for model initial learning, and a candidate pool $\mathcal{P}^c$ with the remaining trajectory data for incremental active learning. Following the above problem formulation, the whole training trajectory data is $\Gamma^{obs} = \{\Gamma_i^{obs} | \forall i \in \{1, 2, ..., N\}\}$, define the base pool $\mathcal{P}^b = \{\Gamma_j^{obs} | \forall j \in \mathcal{S}^b\}$, the candidate pool $\mathcal{P}^c = \{\Gamma_k^{obs} | \forall k \in \mathcal{S}^c\}$, where $\mathcal{S}^b$ and $\mathcal{S}^c$ are two disjoint subsets

Algorithm 1. Incremental Active Learning

Input: Untrained model M^0, whole trajectory data Γ_{obs}.
Input: Hyper-parameters: $\lambda\%$, $p\%$, learning rate, etc.
Output: Trained model M^a.
1: Construct base pool $\mathcal{P}^b$ and candidate pool $\mathcal{P}^c$ following the percentage $\lambda\%$.
2: Train an initial model M^b using the trajectory samples of base pool $\mathcal{P}^b$.
3: Define an active set $\mathcal{P}^a = \varnothing$. Define N^a is the number of trajectory samples of $\mathcal{P}^a$. Calculate the expected number $\hat{N}^a$ of trajectory samples with Equation 1.
4: **while** $N^a \leq \hat{N}^a$ **do**
5:     Infer all trajectory data in candidate pool $\mathcal{P}^c$ through model M^b.
6:     Select a subset $\Delta\mathcal{P}^c$ from $\mathcal{P}^c$ based on our incremental select strategy.
7:     Fine-tune model M^b with the subset $\Delta\mathcal{P}^c$.
8:     $\mathcal{P}^c \leftarrow \mathcal{P}^c - \Delta\mathcal{P}^c$, $\mathcal{P}^a \leftarrow \mathcal{P}^a \cup \Delta\mathcal{P}^c$.
9:     Update N^a.
10: **end while**
11: Train model M^0 with the active set $\mathcal{P}^a$ until convergence is realized.
12: **return** Trained model M^a.

---

and $\mathcal{S}^b \cup \mathcal{S}^a = \{1, 2, ..., N\}$. We randomly select $\lambda\%$ trajectory data from the whole training data as the base pool $\mathcal{P}^b$ and we set $\lambda = 5$ in our work.

3.2   Incremental Active Learning

Instead of learning from whole trajectory samples, we propose an active learning method to incrementally select partial "worthy" trajectory data from candidate pool merging in the active set $\mathcal{P}^a$, and then utilize these more valuable samples for model learning. Denote we expect to select $p\%$ trajectory samples from candidate pool, $\hat{N}^a$ is the expected number of trajectory samples of active set, which is defined as follow:

$$\hat{N}^a = p\% \times N \tag{1}$$

At each iteration, we infer all the trajectory samples from candidate pool $\mathcal{P}^c$ and rank these samples base on their inference errors, and choose the median ones as the subset $\Delta\mathcal{P}^c$. According to [3], the larger the error, the more noise the sample will have, the smaller the error is, the easier the sample can be learned. Therefore, our proposed select strategy is to select median trajectory samples merging in the active set. These median samples have less noise, and at the meantime, they are more representative than those with smaller error. In the experiments, we have explored different select strategies to shown the effectiveness of our proposed selection. Note that the subset will be removed from the candidate pool once selected. We iterate the above selection steps until the number of active set N^a equals to $\hat{N}^a$. The overall incremental active learning method is illustrated in Algorithm 1 followed with detailed explanation.

Beginning with the untrained model M^0, whole observed trajectories Γ_{obs}, and hyper-parameter $\lambda\%$, we firstly construct the base pool and candidate pool (line 1), and then train an initial model M^b with trajectory samples from base pool $\mathcal{P}^b$ (line 2). Before starting iteration, we define an empty active set $\mathcal{P}^a$, and calculate the number

Table 1. Experimental results of our proposed IAL-TP model with different $p\%$. We use four different $p\%$ to evaluate the influence of different numbers of trajectory samples that participate in the model training phase.

	Performance (ADE/FDE)					
	ETH	HOTEL	UNIV	ZARA1	ZARA2	Average
$p\% = 100\%$	**0.56/1.06**	0.52/0.91	**0.57/1.20**	**0.41**/0.90	**0.33/0.74**	0.48/0.96
$p\% = 50\%$	**0.56**/1.04	**0.42/0.89**	0.59/1.29	0.42/**0.89**	0.35/0.76	**0.46/0.95**
$p\% = 33\%$	0.69/1.20	0.52/1.04	0.63/1.33	0.46/1.00	0.40/0.86	0.54/1.09
$p\% = 25\%$	0.75/1.25	0.60/1.18	0.63/1.34	0.56/1.17	0.39/0.85	0.59/1.16

N^a of the trajectory samples in $\mathcal{P}^a$. Also, we calculate the expected number $\hat{N}^a$ of trajectory samples for final model learning (line3). At each iteration, we first inference all the samples of the candidate pool through model M^b and obtain the errors of these samples (line 5). Then, we select a batch of samples with median errors as the subset $\Delta\mathcal{P}^c$ from the candidate pool (line 6). Afterwards, the model M^b is fine-tuned with the subset $\Delta\mathcal{P}^c$ to ensure the model learn well on this subset, and thus avoid selecting similar samples at the next iteration (line 7). Finally, we update the $\mathcal{P}^c$, $\mathcal{P}^a$, and calculate the new number N^a in $\mathcal{P}^a$ (line 8, 9). When the number N^a equals to our expected $\hat{N}^a$, the iteration is finished, and we obtain an active set $\mathcal{P}^a$ within more valuable and representative trajectory samples. We retrain the model M^0 with the active set until convergence is realized to return the final model M^a.

3.3   Backbone for Prediction

In order to make accurate trajectory predictions, we utilize our previous state-of-the-art framework [31], which is able to extract global spatial-temporal feature representations of pedestrians for future trajectory prediction.

4   Experiments

We demonstrate the experimental results on two public datasets: ETH [24] and UCY [15]. We observe 8 frames and predict next 12 frames of trajectories.

4.1   Evaluation Metrics

Similar with other baselines, we use two evaluation metrics: Average Displacement Error (ADE) and Final Displacement Error (FDE).

4.2   Data Efficiency and Model Robustness

In our work, the most important hyper-parameter is the percentage $p\%$ denoting the number $\hat{N}^a$ of trajectory samples in the active set. The number $\hat{N}^a$ represents the number of trajectory samples that are learned by the model at the training phase. Note that

Table 2. Experimental results of baselines compared to our proposed model. Original Social-STGCNN model is a probabilistic model and we try our best to adapt it to a deterministic model.

Method	Performance (ADE/FDE)					
	ETH	HOTEL	UNIV	ZARA1	ZARA2	Average
Linear [1]	1.33/2.94	0.39/0.72	0.82/1.59	0.62/1.21	0.79/1.59	0.79/1.59
Social-LSTM [1]	1.09/2.35	0.79/1.76	0.67/1.40	0.47/1.00	0.56/1.17	0.72/1.54
Social-GAN [11]	1.13/2.21	1.01/2.18	0.60/1.28	**0.42**/0.91	0.52/1.11	0.74/1.54
TPNet [8]	1.00/2.01	**0.31/0.58**	0.55/**1.15**	0.46/0.99	**0.33/0.72**	0.71/1.08
TF-based [10]	1.03/2.10	0.36/0.71	**0.53**/1.32	0.44/1.00	0.34/0.76	0.54/1.17
Social-STGCNN*	0.98/2.10	0.54/1.10	0.57/1.20	0.46/1.00	0.37/0.78	0.58/1.24
IAL-TP (Ours)	**0.56/1.04**	0.42/0.89	0.59/1.29	**0.42/0.89**	0.35/0.76	**0.46/0.95**

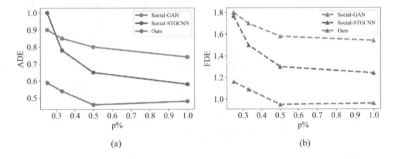

(a)   (b)

Fig. 2. Model performance versus part of the training trajectory samples. The x-axis shows the percentage of trajectory samples used. The y-axis shows the corresponding ADE/FDE error.

$p\% = 100\%$ means all trajectory samples are used in the candidate pool for model learning, which is the same with the existing baselines. Table 1 shows the performance of our proposed model with different $p\%$.

We can observe that when $p\% = 50\%$, namely using only half of the trajectory samples from the candidate pool, our proposed IAL-TP model achieves the best performance with the smallest error. It indicates that there are a lot of redundant trajectory samples in the datasets and it also validates the necessity of our proposed active learning idea. In specific, the ADE error on dataset ETH is the same with the result with $p\% = 100\%$, the ADE error on dataset HOTEL with $p\% = 50\%$ outperforms the result with $p\% = 100\%$ by 19.2%, which is a significant improvement. One possible reason is that the datasets ETH and HOTEL are relatively more crowded than other datasets [1]. It reflects that with more training data, active learning is more necessary and effective.

For comparison, Fig. 2 demonstrates the results of several existing methods with part of the training trajectory samples. Note that the original Social-GAN [11] and Social-STGCNN [23] are two probabilistic models, and we adapt them to deterministic models. We can observe that our model consistently outperforms the Social-GAN and Social-STGCNN models on both ADE and FDE metrics with shrinked training

Table 3. Experimental results (ADE/FDE) of our proposed IAL-TP model with three different strategies, "Max", "Median", and "Min".

Select strategy	Performance (ADE/FDE)
	Average
Max	0.52/1.06
Median	**0.46/0.95**
Min	0.54/1.11

trajectory data. In addition, with the same increase of $p\%$, our model has the least reduction on both ADE and FDE metrics, which validates the robustness of our proposed model. Note that without any specific indication, we set $p\% = 50\%$ in following sections.

4.3 Selection Strategy

In order to validate the effectiveness of our proposed "Median" selection strategy (introduced in Sect. 3.2), we design two others election strategies for comparison. One strategy is to select the samples with the largest error, which is referred as "Max", the other strategy is to select the samples with the smallest error, which is referred as "Min". Table 3 shows the results of three different select strategies. We can observe that the "Median" select strategy outperforms other strategies. This proves that samples with median inference errors are more representative. As discussed in Sect. 3.2, samples with larger error are more likely to have noise, which have negative influences on model learning. In addition, samples with smaller error are more likely to be too "easy" for model learning, namely these samples are less valuable. Thus our proposed "Median" select strategy is more appropriate while seeking the "worthy" trajectory samples.

4.4 Quantitative Analysis

Table 2 shows quantitative results of our proposed model and baseline. Overall, IAL-TP model outperforms all the baselines on the two metrics with only half of the training trajectory samples. The ADE metric improves by 14.8% compared to TF-based and the FDE metric improves by 12.0% compared to TPNet. In specific, the ADE error of our IAL-TP model on dataset ETH is 0.56, significantly improving by 42.8% compared to Social-STGCNN, the FDE error is 1.04, significantly improving by 48.3% compared to TPNet. It validates the necessity of our active learning idea in the pedestrian trajectory prediction problem. Additionally, it also validates the active set selected by our proposed strategy is a small but compact and representative training set.

5   Conclusion

In this paper, we propose a novel trajectory prediction model via incremental active learning (IAL-TP). In this model, we design a simple and effective method to iteratively select more valuable and representative trajectory samples for model learning, which can filter out noisy and redundant samples. This incremental active learning method greatly improves the generalization ability and the robustness of the model. Experimental results on five public datasets validate the effectiveness of our model. Additionally, it can achieve better performance than the state-of-the-art methods with only a small fraction of the whole training data.

Acknowledgments. This work was supported by the Beijing Nova Program under No. Z201100006820046, the National Natural Science Foundation of China under Grant No. 61772373, and the Beijing Science and Technology Project under Grant no. Z181100008918018.

References

1. Alahi, A., Goel, K., Ramanathan, V., Robicquet, A., Fei-Fei, L., Savarese, S.: Social LSTM: human trajectory prediction in crowded spaces. In: Proceedings of the IEEE Conference on Computer Vision and Pattern Recognition, pp. 961–971 (2016)
2. Amirian, J., Hayet, J.B., Pettré, J.: Social ways: learning multi-modal distributions of pedestrian trajectories with GANs. In: Proceedings of the IEEE Conference on Computer Vision and Pattern Recognition Workshops (2019)
3. Beygelzimer, A., Dasgupta, S., Langford, J.: Importance weighted active learning. In: Proceedings of the 26th Annual International Conference on Machine Learning, pp. 49–56 (2009)
4. Bisagno, N., Zhang, B., Conci, N.: Group LSTM: group trajectory prediction in crowded scenarios. In: Leal-Taixé, L., Roth, S. (eds.) ECCV 2018. LNCS, vol. 11131, pp. 213–225. Springer, Cham (2019). https://doi.org/10.1007/978-3-030-11015-4_18
5. Cheng, H., Liao, W., Tang, X., Yang, M.Y., Sester, M., Rosenhahn, B.: Exploring dynamic context for multi-path trajectory prediction. arXiv preprint arXiv:2010.16267 (2020)
6. Devlin, J., Chang, M.W., Lee, K., Toutanova, K.: BERT: pre-training of deep bidirectional transformers for language understanding (2018)
7. Djuric, N., et al.: Uncertainty-aware short-term motion prediction of traffic actors for autonomous driving. In: Proceedings of the IEEE Winter Conference on Applications of Computer Vision, pp. 2084–2093 (2020)
8. Fang, L., Jiang, Q., Shi, J., Zhou, B.: TPNet: trajectory proposal network for motion prediction. In: Proceedings of the IEEE Conference on Computer Vision and Pattern Recognition, pp. 6797–6806 (2020)
9. Fernando, T., Denman, S., Sridharan, S., Fookes, C.: GD-GAN: generative adversarial networks for trajectory prediction and group detection in crowds. In: Jawahar, C.V., Li, H., Mori, G., Schindler, K. (eds.) ACCV 2018. LNCS, vol. 11361, pp. 314–330. Springer, Cham (2019). https://doi.org/10.1007/978-3-030-20887-5_20
10. Giuliari, F., Hasan, I., Cristani, M., Galasso, F.: Transformer networks for trajectory forecasting. In: Proceedings of the International Conference on Pattern Recognition (2020)
11. Gupta, A., Johnson, J., Fei-Fei, L., Savarese, S., Alahi, A.: Social GAN: socially acceptable trajectories with generative adversarial networks. In: Proceedings of the IEEE Conference on Computer Vision and Pattern Recognition, pp. 2255–2264 (2018)
12. Hong, J., Sapp, B., Philbin, J.: Rules of the road: predicting driving behavior with a convolutional model of semantic interactions. In: Proceedings of the IEEE Conference on Computer Vision and Pattern Recognition, June 2019
13. Kosaraju, V., Sadeghian, A., Martín-Martín, R., Reid, I., Rezatofighi, H., Savarese, S.: Social-BiGAT: multimodal trajectory forecasting using bicycle-GAN and graph attention networks. In: Proceedings of the Advances in Neural Information Processing Systems, pp. 137–146 (2019)

14. Lee, N., Wongun, C., Paul, V., Choy, C.B., Torr, P.H.S., Manmohan, C.: DESIRE: distant future prediction in dynamic scenes with interacting agents. In: Proceedings of the IEEE Computer Vision and Pattern Recognition, pp. 2165–2174, July 2017
15. Lerner, A., Chrysanthou, Y., Lischinski, D.: Crowds by example. Comput. Graph. Forum **26**(3), 655–664 (2010)
16. Li, J., Ma, H., Tomizuka, M.: Conditional generative neural system for probabilistic trajectory prediction. arXiv preprint arXiv:1905.01631 (2019)
17. Li, Y., et al.: Deep learning for lidar point clouds in autonomous driving: a review. IEEE Trans. Neural Netw. Learn. Syst. **32**, 3412–3432 (2020)
18. Liang, J., Jiang, L., Murphy, K., Yu, T., Hauptmann, A.: The garden of forking paths: towards multi-future trajectory prediction. In: Proceedings of the IEEE Conference on Computer Vision and Pattern Recognition, pp. 10508–10518 (2020)
19. Liang, J., Jiang, L., Niebles, J.C., Hauptmann, A.G., Fei-Fei, L.: Peeking into the future: predicting future person activities and locations in videos. In: Proceedings of the IEEE Conference on Computer Vision and Pattern Recognition, pp. 5725–5734 (2019)
20. Mangalam, K., et al.: It is not the journey but the destination: endpoint conditioned trajectory prediction. In: Vedaldi, A., Bischof, H., Brox, T., Frahm, J.-M. (eds.) ECCV 2020. LNCS, vol. 12347, pp. 759–776. Springer, Cham (2020). https://doi.org/10.1007/978-3-030-58536-5_45
21. Mantini, P., Shah, S.K.: Multiple people tracking using contextual trajectory forecasting. In: IEEE Symposium on Technologies for Homeland Security, pp. 1–6 (2016)
22. Mayank, B., Alex, K., Abhijit, O.: ChauffeurNet: learning to drive by imitating the best and synthesizing the worst. In: Proceedings of Robotics: Science and Systems, June 2019
23. Mohamed, A., Qian, K., Elhoseiny, M., Claudel, C.: Social-STGCNN: a social spatio-temporal graph convolutional neural network for human trajectory prediction. In: Proceedings of the IEEE Conference on Computer Vision and Pattern Recognition, pp. 14424–14432 (2020)
24. Pellegrini, S., Ess, A., Schindler, K., Gool, L.J.V.: You'll never walk alone: modeling social behavior for multi-target tracking. In: IEEE International Conference on Computer Vision, pp. 261–268 (2009)
25. Sadeghian, A., Kosaraju, V., Sadeghian, A., Hirose, N., Rezatofighi, H., Savarese, S.: SoPhie: an attentive GAN for predicting paths compliant to social and physical constraints. In: Proceedings of the IEEE Conference on Computer Vision and Pattern Recognition, pp. 1349–1358 (2019)
26. Salzmann, T., Ivanovic, B., Chakravarty, P., Pavone, M.: Trajectron++: dynamically-feasible trajectory forecasting with heterogeneous data. In: Vedaldi, A., Bischof, H., Brox, T., Frahm, J.-M. (eds.) ECCV 2020. LNCS, vol. 12363, pp. 683–700. Springer, Cham (2020). https://doi.org/10.1007/978-3-030-58523-5_40
27. Sun, J., Jiang, Q., Lu, C.: Recursive social behavior graph for trajectory prediction. In: Proceedings of the IEEE Conference on Computer Vision and Pattern Recognition, pp. 660–669 (2020)
28. Tang, Y.C., Salakhutdinov, R.: Multiple futures prediction. In: Proceedings of the Advances in Neural Information Processing Systems (2019)
29. Vaswani, A., et al.: Attention is all you need. In: Proceedings of the Advances in Neural Information Processing Systems, pp. 5998–6008 (2017)
30. Vemula, A., Muelling, K., Oh, J.: Social attention: modeling attention in human crowds. In: Proceedings of the IEEE International Conference on Robotics and Automation, pp. 1–7 (2018)
31. Xu, Y., Ren, D., Li, M., Chen, Y., Fan, M., Xia, H.: Tra2Tra: trajectory-to-trajectory prediction with a global social spatial-temporal attentive neural network. IEEE Robot. Autom. Lett. **6**(2), 1574–1581 (2021)

32. Xu, Y., Yang, J., Du, S.: CF-LSTM: cascaded feature-based long short-term networks for predicting pedestrian trajectory. In: Proceedings of the AAAI Conference on Artificial Intelligence, pp. 12541–12548 (2020)
33. Yu, C., Ma, X., Ren, J., Zhao, H., Yi, S.: Spatio-temporal graph transformer networks for pedestrian trajectory prediction. arXiv preprint arXiv:2005.08514 (2020)
34. Zhang, P., Ouyang, W., Zhang, P., Xue, J., Zheng, N.: SR-LSTM: state refinement for LSTM towards pedestrian trajectory prediction. In: Proceedings of the IEEE Conference on Computer Vision and Pattern Recognition, pp. 12085–12094 (2019)
35. Zhu, Y., Qian, D., Ren, D., Xia, H.: StarNET: pedestrian trajectory prediction using deep neural network in star topology. arXiv preprint arXiv:1906.01797 (2019)

Dynamic Channel Pruning for Real-Time Object Detection Networks

Yibo Jin$^{(\boxtimes)}$, Ting Liu, Jinjie Chen, and Yuzhuo Fu

Shanghai Jiao Tong University, Shanghai 200240, China
{jinyibo,louisa_liu}@sjtu.edu.cn

Abstract. Real-time object detection is a highly practical technical means which has been the focus of research in recent years. While the high requirement of running memory and computing resources hinder the deployment on resource-limited devices. In this paper, we propose an effective method to dynamically enhance the sparsity on channel-level. To this end, we introduce dynamic sparsity coefficient (DSC) to balance model training and sparse training as well as adaptable sparsity regularization (TL_p) to reinforce sparsity. We monitor the saliency of channels to evaluate their significance for model performance during the sparse training process, according to which, we implement different sparsity strategy on channels. Aiming to maintain the representation ability of important parameters on a fine-grained level, we automatically discern insignificant channels and remove with channel pruning. We demonstrate our method on latest object detector YOLOv4 and lightweight model YOLOv4-Tiny. Compare with uncompressed model, our method can obtain 85.8% decrease of FLOPs, 88.9% declines of parameters with a moderate accuracy loss. Compared with other model compression methods, we achieves comparable results with fewer trainable parameters but better detection performance.

Keywords: Model compress · Sparse training · Object detection

1 Introduction

In recent years, credit to the widespread use of CNNs, many state-of-the-art works proceeded in vision-based tasks [8,12,15]. Object detection is a hot research topic in computer vision field. RetinaNet, YOLOv4 and EfficientDet [2,9,12] are the latest advancements of deep neural networks for target detection. However, these advanced detectors require a lot of running memory and computing resources to maintain high performance.

In this paper, we propose a network training scheme to address the challenge of deploying large CNNs on resource-limited devices. By impressing dynamic regularization on the scaling factors in batch normalization (BN) [7] layers, our

This research was supported by the National Natural Science Foundation of China under Project (Grant No. 61977045).

T. Mantoro et al. (Eds.): ICONIP 2021, CCIS 1516, pp. 151–158, 2021.
https://doi.org/10.1007/978-3-030-92307-5_18

method can remarkably identify insignificant channels. Based on this, we first propose to identify significant channels with a channel saliency evaluator. Then, we adaptively adjust the penalty coefficient imposed on each channel and dynamically modulate the form of regularization. With self-adaption strategy on sparse training, we implement dynamic channel pruning which yields a compact network with more representative weights without suffering from accuracy loss.

Following are the major contributions of this paper:

- We design an evaluation module to track and assess channel representation ability which can identify significant channels.
- We introduce a sparse training strategy with a group of sparsity coefficients which are modulated dynamically according to channel saliency information.
- We propose one improved format of sparsity regularization to enhance the concentration of parameter space and search optimal sparsity-induced penalty solution for networks.

2   Related Work

2.1   Regularization Constrains and Sparse Training

[4] proposed a method introducing sparsity by randomly deactivating channelwise connections before training and yield smaller models with moderate loss on accuracy. Sparse training can gather significant parameters and efficiently differentiate from subordinate ones, which make it convenient to prune unimportant weights. The network could get sparsified with regularization method to constrain the weights which is widely adopted. [10] constrained and pruned classification networks with L1 regularization. [1] obtained sparsified networks by introducing group lasso. TL1[11] is an improved regularization for introducing sparsity for image classification CNNs. [3] applied non-convex regularization to classification network to get pruned and sparse.

2.2   Dynamic Network Pruning

The network pruning is used to prune part of network structures, e.g., neurons, channels or layers and yield smaller networks. [6] identified unimportant areas in the feature map according to decision map generated with partial input channels. [5] proposed squeeze-excitation modules to find significant channels and neglect insignificant channels with low ability for classification. [13] trained the dynamic network to allocate sub-network for each input instance.

3   Preliminaries

3.1   Conventional Channel Pruning

The dataset with N samples as X, and Y denotes the corresponding labels. Weight parameters is given by $W_l \in \mathbb{R}^{c^l \times c^{l-1} \times k^l \times k^{l-1}}$ corresponding to l-th layer of convolution filters. The conventional channel pruning[10] is shown as:

$$\min_{\mathcal{W}} \sum_{i=1}^{N} \mathcal{L}_{task}(\mathbf{f}(x_i, \mathcal{W}), y_i) + \lambda \cdot \sum_{l=1}^{L} \|W_l\|_{2,1} \tag{1}$$

$\mathcal{W}$ denotes trainable weights of the network and the $\mathcal{L}_{task}$ denotes the basic loss for the task. $\| \cdot \|_{2,1}$ corresponds to the L_{21}-norm with convolution filters channel-level sparsified. The coefficient λ plays a role in balancing the two losses, and the larger the λ, the more compact network yielded but rising the risk of accuracy loss. It is a process of game between performance and sparsity ratio.

3.2 Characteristics of Regularization Constraints

L_1 and L_0 regularization have sparsity and proved mathematically where they can make the high-dimensional solution contain more zero-items. L_1 has been widely adopted to introduce sparsity, and one transformed L_1 regularization is proposed. In conclusion, L_1 and L_0 formulated in the form of:

$$L_p(x) : \|x\|_p = (\sum_{i=1}^{n} |x_i|^p)^{\frac{1}{p}} \tag{2}$$

Substitute $\alpha + 1$ with p and combine the formulation TL_1 [11] with L_p, we get:

$$TL_p(x) = \sum_{i=1}^{n} \frac{|x_i|^p}{p + (1-p)|x_i|^p} \tag{3}$$

4 Proposed Method

For a given CNN model with L layers, our approach can be formulated as:

$$\min_{\mathcal{W}} \sum_{i=1}^{N} \mathcal{L}_{task}(\mathbf{f}(x_i, \mathcal{W}), y_i) + \sum_{l=1}^{L} g(\prod_{c \in l} \mathbf{s}(\lambda_c)\gamma_c) \tag{4}$$

where $C = \{c_i\}_{i=1}^{l}$ denotes channels in l-th layer, and λ_c denotes sparsity coefficient for corresponding channel. $\mathbf{s}(\cdot)$ gives an adjusted value dynamically according to the evaluator, which measures the variation tendency of channel saliency and returns one score. $\mathbf{g}(\cdot)$ works as a penalty on the second sum-item and introduces sparsity with $L1$-norm which is widely adopted. In our experiment, we introduce TL_p to replace $L1$-norm.

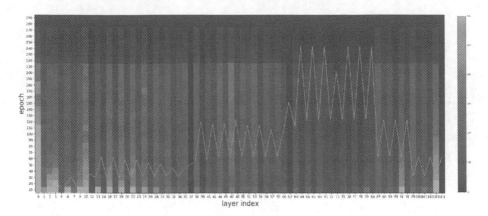

Fig. 1. Visualization of channel activity measured with scaling factors on layers of YOLOv3. Horizontal comparison corresponds to significance ranking (the brighter, the more significant) among channels while vertical comparison tells the sparse process of one single channel. The red line shows channel pruning percentage. (Color figure online)

4.1   Channel Saliency Evaluator

BN structure is widely used by modern CNNs to speed up training and convergence for networks. The input and output of BN layer is:

$$\hat{z} = \frac{z_{in} - \mu}{\sqrt{\sigma^2 + \epsilon}}; z_{out} = \gamma\hat{z} + \beta \tag{5}$$

where γ and β are trainable parameters after transformation, the value of γ fully determines the feature output capability.

We verified the necessity for evaluation whether channels differ in the representation ability based on γ. Some layers composed of channels with larger γ, and these channels are more likely to be retained after pruning operation (Fig. 1). We design an evaluation module to track and evaluate channel performance to guide coefficient adjustment:

$$\pi_i = \frac{e^{\gamma_i}}{\sum\limits_{l \in L} \sum\limits_{c \in l} e^{\gamma_c}} \tag{6}$$

4.2   Dynamic Sparsity Coefficient

We introduce simulated annealing (SA) [14] algorithm to do further processing on π_i which is based on the Monte Carlo method. It has asymptotic convergence and has been proven theoretically to converge to the global optimal solution. Therefore, we choose the SA algorithm to search for the best λ_i (Fig. 2).

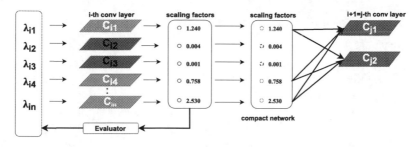

Fig. 2. We employ a group of sparsity coefficients to influence the scaling factors. An evaluator is designed to monitor channel significance ranking and feedback saliency information to update sparsity coefficients.

We use π_i from last iteration as the monitoring value of feedback system, and determine whether the amplitude of λ_i decreasing or increasing according to the bias of π_i between two iterations. Therefore, π_{prev} of previous iteration is used as the target function value corresponding to the prior solution λ_{prev}. When the target function value π_{new} is higher than the last one, the new solution λ_{new} would be directly accepted. Otherwise, λ_{new} would be adopted with a probability. Generally, we presuppose that when the fluctuation of π_i exceeds 0.5%, the new solution will be accepted with a probability of 50%. We get:

$$P_{Metropolis} = \frac{0.5\%}{k \cdot epoch_{total}} = 50\% \tag{7}$$

$$P_{accept} = exp(\frac{200ln2 \cdot (\pi_{new} - \pi_{prev}) \cdot epoch_{total}}{T}) \tag{8}$$

where T denotes to the current phase of training formulated as $\frac{epoch_{total}}{epoch_{current}+1}$.

The conventional SA algorithm adds random disturbances to the old solution λ_{init} and obtain new solution λ_{new}. Besides, we introduce a momentum to speedup the search process:

$$\lambda_{new} = \lambda_{init} + random(low = -bound, high = bound) + momentum \tag{9}$$

where *bound* represents the range of variation which is set twice over momentum.

To determine an appropriate value for momentum, we assume that with suitable momentum, new solution λ_i generated in each iteration could be accepted as the optimal solution for current target function. We get:

$$E(\lambda) = \lambda_{init} + momentum \cdot epoch_{total} \tag{10}$$

According to the experience of sparse training based on fixed form regularization constrains, λ with moderate accuracy drop yet maximum sparsity should be no greater than 0.008 where λ works as a global coefficient. We set $E(p) = 0.008$ and initialize λ_{init} with 0.003. The momentum finally can be calculated as $momentum = \frac{1}{200epoch_{total}}$

4.3   Adaptable Sparsity Regularization

In Eq. 3, when p moves towards 0^+, TL_p approaches L_0 while p impends over 1^-, TL_p approximates L_1. This allows us to look beyond traditional approaches of sparsity. There is the possibility to search optimal sparsity-induced penalty solution for certain model.

We apply SA algorithm to the dynamic adjustment of p to generate an adaptable regularization formulation for target model. Differently, we introduce the accuracy mAP as our target function for p. We work out initial value $momentum = \frac{1}{2epoch_{total}}$ and with a P_{accept}.

5   Experiments

We rigorously investigate our dynamic pruning method on object detection dataset VisDrone2019-Det [18] with YOLOv4 and YOLOv4-tiny. In order to restore network performance after sparse training and pruning operations, we fine-tuned compact models with similar conditions. BDD100k [16] is an automatic driving dataset which is used to compare our method with other works with similar size of parameters.

In our experiments, we prune the sparsified models with three global pruning ratio thresholds of 50%, 80% and 90%. Channel pruning decreases the FLOPs with 46.2%, 78.6%, 88.2%, reduces the trainable parameters by 66.7%, 93.5%, 97.8% on YOLOv4. Our method works well on lack-redundancy network YOLOv4-Tiny and achieves 30.7%, 48.8%, 69.8% reduce on FLOPs, together with 62.9%, 84.1%, 89.1% cost cutting on parameters (Table 2).

DSC performs better with a lower rate of pruning, while declines with high pruning ratio (80%). It can be interpreted that DSC relax constraints on significant channels during sparse training and the parameters cluster less tightly. Hence, with high percentage of pruning operation, some significant parameters are removed. DSC achieves better accuracy performance with permanent finely-trained channels (Table 1). In the meantime, sparsity with dynamic TL_p performs better with high pruning ratio(80%) and works well on reducing parameters to save memory size (Table 2).

Table 1. mAP of YOLOv4 and YOLOv4-Tiny after pruning and retraining.

With dynamic strategies, we got best results on several percentage of pruning ratio						
Model	DSC	TLp	50%	80%	90%	Unpruned
YOLOv4	✓	✓	22.94	**22.18**	20.31	23.34
		✓	**23.37**	22.15	**20.76**	
			22.63	21.77	19.26	
YOLOv4-Tiny	✓	✓	9.62	**8.07**	6.03	9.65
		✓	**9.89**	7.86	**6.06**	
			8.98	7.47	5.46	

Table 2. Parameters and FLOPs of pruned network on VisDrone2019-Det

Model	Prune%	TLp		DSC		DSC+TLp	
		Parameters	BFLOPs	Parameters	BFLOPs	Parameters	BFLOPs
YOLOv4 (608 * 608)	0%	64.36M	128.5	64.36M	128.5	64.36M	128.5
	50%	**21.4M**	69.167	21.5M	**69.119**	21.5M	70.091
	80%	**4.20M**	27.723	4.22M	**27.451**	4.20M	27.684
	90%	**1.44M**	15.119	1.45M	15.211	1.45M	**14.834**
YOLOv4-Tiny (416*416)	0%	6.056M	6.801	6.056M	6.801	6.056M	6.801
	50%	**2.246M**	4.711	2.39M	**4.262**	2.38M	4.703
	80%	**0.96M**	3.508	1.00M	**3.483**	0.99M	3.516
	90%	**0.66M**	**2.057**	0.67M	2.404	0.67M	2.127

We compare our method with light-weight object detection model YOLOv4-Tiny, state-of-the art efficient network EfficientDet and latest model pruning work SlimYOLOv3. To guarantee fairness, we set similar number of parameters and input size. On account of the higher benchmark consumption of YOLOv4, although we achieve a reduction of 78.5% on BFLOPs, it is inevitable to maintain a higher range. However, our combined strategy with 80% of channel pruned still obtains the best accuracy performance with minimal overhead on parameters (Table 3).

Table 3. Comparison with SlimYOLOv3, YOLOv4-Tiny, EfficientDet on BDD100K.

Networks	Parameters	BFLOPs	mAP
SlimYOLOv3 [17] (608)	8M	21.3	29.57
YOLOv4-Tiny [2] (608)	6.025M	14.761	21.03
EfficientDet-D1 [12] (640)	6.562M	**5.691**	32.1
YOLOv4+TLp+DSC80% pruned (608)	**4.201M**	27.677	**35.47**

6   Conclusion

We propose one dynamic channel pruning method to get more compact object detectors. We associate dynamic sparsity coefficients with channel scaling factors to balance detector training and sparse training, and introduce self-adapting regularization to optimize the sparsity process. Based on such approaches, we implement fine-grained mining the redundancy in the network on channel-level and enhance the sparse training process. We further demonstrate on YOLOv4 to achieve comparable detection accuracy with fewer parameters and faster speed as well less FLOPs. This provides an effective method for object detectors to deploy on embedded devices. For future research, we will explore more efficient dynamic regularization strategy for excavating the redundancy of networks.

References

1. Alvarez, J.M., Salzmann, M.: Learning the number of neurons in deep networks. arXiv preprint arXiv:1611.06321 (2016)
2. Bochkovskiy, A., Wang, C.Y., Liao, H.Y.M.: YOLOv4: optimal speed and accuracy of object detection. arXiv preprint arXiv:2004.10934 (2020)
3. Bui, K., Park, F., Zhang, S., Qi, Y., Xin, J., et al.: Nonconvex regularization for network slimming: compressing CNNs even more. In: Bebis, G. (ed.) ISVC 2020. LNCS, vol. 12509, pp. 39–53. Springer, Cham (2020). https://doi.org/10.1007/978-3-030-64556-4_4
4. Changpinyo, S., Sandler, M., Zhmoginov, A.: The power of sparsity in convolutional neural networks. arXiv preprint arXiv:1702.06257 (2017)
5. Gao, X., Zhao, Y., Dudziak, Ł., Mullins, R., Xu, C.z.: Dynamic channel pruning: feature boosting and suppression. arXiv preprint arXiv:1810.05331 (2018)
6. Hua, W., Zhou, Y., De Sa, C., Zhang, Z., Suh, G.E.: Channel gating neural networks. arXiv preprint arXiv:1805.12549 (2018)
7. Ioffe, S., Szegedy, C.: Batch normalization: accelerating deep network training by reducing internal covariate shift. In: International Conference on Machine Learning, pp. 448–456. PMLR (2015)
8. Jiang, L., Xu, M., Liu, T., Qiao, M., Wang, Z.: DeepVS: a deep learning based video saliency prediction approach. In: Ferrari, V., Hebert, M., Sminchisescu, C., Weiss, Y. (eds.) Computer Vision – ECCV 2018. LNCS, vol. 11218, pp. 625–642. Springer, Cham (2018). https://doi.org/10.1007/978-3-030-01264-9_37
9. Lin, T.Y., Goyal, P., Girshick, R., He, K., Dollár, P.: Focal loss for dense object detection. In: Proceedings of ICCV, pp. 2980–2988 (2017)
10. Liu, Z., Li, J., Shen, Z., Huang, G., Yan, S., Zhang, C.: Learning efficient convolutional networks through network slimming. In: Proceedings of ICCV, pp. 2736–2744 (2017)
11. Ma, R., Miao, J., Niu, L., Zhang, P.: Transformed l1 regularization for learning sparse deep neural networks. Neural Netw. **119**, 286–298 (2019)
12. Tan, M., Pang, R., Le, Q.V.: EfficientDet: scalable and efficient object detection. In: Proceedings of CVPR, pp. 10781–10790 (2020)
13. Tang, Y., Wang, Y., Xu, Y., Deng, Y., Xu, C., Tao, D., Xu, C.: Manifold regularized dynamic network pruning. In: Proceedings of CVPR, pp. 5018–5028 (2021)
14. Van Laarhoven, P.J., Aarts, E.H.: Simulated annealing. In: Simulated Annealing: Theory and Applications. MAIA, vol. 37, pp. 7–15. Springer (1987). https://doi.org/10.1007/978-94-015-7744-1_2
15. You, S., Huang, T., Yang, M., Wang, F., Qian, C., Zhang, C.: GreedyNAS: towards fast one-shot NAS with greedy Supernet. In: Proceedings of CVPR, pp. 1999–2008 (2020)
16. Yu, F., Xian, W., Chen, Y., Liu, F., Liao, M., Madhavan, V., Darrell, T.: BDD100K: a diverse driving video database with scalable annotation tooling. arXiv preprint arXiv:1805.04687 2(5), 6 (2018)
17. Zhang, P., Zhong, Y., Li, X.: SlimYOLOv3: narrower, faster and better for real-time UAV applications. In: Proceedings of ICCV Workshops (2019)
18. Zhu, P., et al.: VisDrone-VID2019: the vision meets drone object detection in video challenge results. In: Proceedings of ICCV Workshops (2019)

Know-GNN: An Explainable Knowledge-Guided Graph Neural Network for Fraud Detection

Yizhuo Rao[1], Xianya Mi[2(✉)], Chengyuan Duan[1], Xiaoguang Ren[2],
Jiajun Cheng[1(✉)], Yu Chen[1], Hongliang You[1], Qiang Gao[1], Zhixian Zeng[3],
and Xiao Wei[1]

[1] Military Science Information Research Center, Academy of Military Sciences,
Beijing, China
jiajun.chen@foxmail.com
[2] Artificial Intelligence Research Center, National Innovation Institute of Defense
Technology, Beijing, China
[3] The Sixty-Third Research Institute, National University of Defense Technology,
Nanjing, China

Abstract. Fraud is on the rise under modern e-commence scenarios, which will critically damage the market system. Thus, it is essential to detect fraudsters to prevent unpredictable risks. There are two challenges toward this problem. First, real world fraud detection usually lack of labeled samples. Second, recent ML-based detection method lack of interpretation. Knowledge may help with these problems. Hence, we propose a **Know**ledge-Guided **G**raph **N**eural **N**etwork, namely Know-GNN, which utilizes the expertise to roughly mark unlabeled data and uses an explainable semi-supervised method to train a fraud detector. We adopt Graph Functional Dependency (GFD) as a uniform expression of knowledge to mark unlabeled data and give explanations of the detection results. Experiments on banking transaction funds supervision data (BTFSD) demonstrate the effectiveness of our model. By utilizing only 13 GFD rules conducted by domain experts corresponding to BTFSD, the performance of our method yields about 14% improvement over the state-of-the-art methods, CARE-GNN. Moreover, the interpretable results can give interesting intuitions about the fraud detection tasks.

Keywords: Fraud detection · Explainable · Graph neural network · Knowledge-guided

1 Introduction

Fraud activities, such as credit card fraud [12], fake comment fraud [1] et al., are becoming common under e-commerce scenarios. These criminal activities will seriously damage the rights and interests of users and companies. Therefore, it is crucial to identify fraudulent behaviors and take every precaution to minimize the risk.

© Springer Nature Switzerland AG 2021
T. Mantoro et al. (Eds.): ICONIP 2021, CCIS 1516, pp. 159–167, 2021.
https://doi.org/10.1007/978-3-030-92307-5_19

Recently, graph-based methods have been widely used for fraud detection tasks. Gorka et al. [10] adopt graph database to discover frauds. Fan et al. [2] propose a semantic constraint on the graph, namely Graph Functional Dependency (GFD), to identify inconsistencies in graph data. Graph neural network (GNN) approaches have also been used to detect fraud behaviors automatically. Dou et al. [1] propose CARE-GNN, a GNN-based method, to discover the camouflage behaviors of fraudsters.

Graph has a natural ability to capture the intricate characteristics of many complex scenarios especially in modern e-commence situations such as transactions with variety of relation attributes (e.g. Fig. 2), or to find multi-hop transactions. However, GNN-based fraud detection still faces the following challenges: (1) **There are not enough labeled data for learning.** Very few of the data are labeled as fraud-related. And it is difficult for the GNN to obtain well generalization ability with skewed data. (2) **The GNN-based fraud detection model lacks interpretability.** The results of fraud detection often serve for financial risk control. It is required for financial regulators to have an interpretable model to provide a better knowledge of the predicted results.

To address these challenges above, we propose **Know**ledge-Guided **G**raph **N**eural **N**etwork, named *Know-GNN*. The basic idea of Know-GNN is that expertise can label unlabeled data automatically. Also, due to the integration of expert knowledge, the interpretability of the model is enhanced. In detail, we use Graph Functional Dependency (GFD) rules [5] to express expert knowledge and to roughly mark unlabeled data as noisy data. Figure 1 demonstrate the overall structure of Know-GNN. Before labeling, the *reliability* of GFD rules are initialized by marking labeled data. A training with noisy sample method, called *jointly-training*, is adopted to train GNN with both noisy data and labeled data cooperatively. Finally, we add an attention mechanism to the jointly-training network to decide the reliability vector of the detection results which indicates how much each GFD rule contributes to the fraud detection results.

We summarize our key contributions as follows:

- A novel knowledge-guided explainable GNN model, named Know-GNN, is proposed to utilize human knowledge to assist supervised GNN, which can obtain interpretable fraud detection results with just few labeled data and simple expertise.
- A learning with noisy label method, called *jointly-training*, is applied to GAT to train noisy data and labeled data comprehensively. The implementation with attention mechanism also enhanced model interpretability.
- Experimental results on fraud detection dataset BTFSD demonstrate that our approach yields about 14% better than the state-of-the-art fraud detection method CARE-GNN. Moreover, the interpretable results related to expertise also provide deep insights regarding the task.

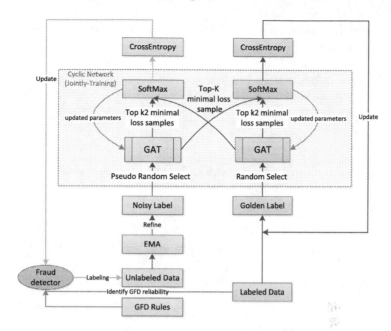

Fig. 1. Overall structure of Know-GNN. *Jointly-Training* is to train noisy labels with golden labels cooperatively. *Reliability vector* can make the results interpretable.

2 Methodology

In this section, we start from the overall architecture of Know-GNN. Afterward, we introduce how GFD rules label data with reliability. Finally, we show how Know-GNN trains and updates reliability.

2.1 Structure

The structure of the Know-GNN model is shown in Fig. 1. Original nodes are separated into two parts, one with supervised labels (called golden labels) is categorized as labeled data V_{lab}, while the other is categorized as unlabeled data V_{unlab}. Unlabeled data are labeled by these GFD rules with reliability vectors. Fraud data labeled by GFD rules are considered as noisy.

Before each training epoch of *Jointly-Training*, noisy data are sampled by pseudo-random method into noisy labels N_{data}. Golden data are randomly selected in the same size from V_{data} to golden labels G_{data}. These two datasets will be used for training noisy network f and golden network g independently. After the neighbors are aggregated by GAT [11] at each training batch, the top-K small-loss data out of this batch are selected to be fed into its peer network as the useful knowledge for updating parameters. Each network also retains the top-K2 small-loss data of itself to renew the parameters. The proportion of data from its own and peer network is controlled by minimal loss node selection rate σ_{se}.

After each training epoch, the noisy network f will be used for re-labeling the unlabeled data and renewing or marking its reliability vector for the next round of training. The reliability vector can provide interpretability to the model. The noisy network f is the final binary explainable fraud detector of the model.

2.2 Labeling Unlabeled Data

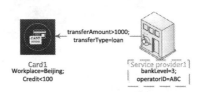

Fig. 2. An example of 2-bounded GFD rules. The red dotted boxes represent the fraudulent nodes identified by the GFD rules. (Color figure online)

We use GFD rules to represent expertise.

Graph Functional Dependency (GFD). A graph functional dependency is denoted as $Q[\bar{x}](X \rightarrow Y)$, where $Q[\bar{x}]$ is a graph pattern and X and Y are two sets of literals of $\bar{x}$ [3]. For instance, a GFD rule shown in Fig. 2 to identify an abnormal card is denoted as $Q[\bar{x}](X \rightarrow Y)$. Where $Q[\bar{x}]$ is shown in Fig. 2, $X = \{F_a(Card) = (Workplace =' Beijing'; Credit < 100); F_a(e) = (transferAmount > 1000; transferType =' loan')\}$, $Y = \{F_a(SP) = (bankLevel = 3; operatorID = ABC; isFraud = True)\}$. This expression denotes that if a transaction can match graph pattern $Q[\bar{x}]$ and GFD constraint X, then Service Provider (SP) with $bankLevel = 3$ and $operatorID = ABC$ is fraud.

We introduce *Reliability* to indicate the applicability of GFD for the current task.

Reliability. RE is to identify the noise level of the data which can be renewed by the noisy network f. v_{RE} is the reliability vector of a fraud instance which includes RE of all GFD rules that can identify it, while other GFDs are set to 0. The reliability of noisy data is the same with the smallest number in v_{RE}. The reliability vector of the golden data is calculated the same as noisy data thus the reliability RE of golden data is set to 1.

The initial RE of GFD rules are calculated by using GFD rules to label golden data and use the F1-score as the initial RE of GFDs. The lower bound of RE is set to 0.8.

2.3   Know-GNN

We adopt GAT [11] as the basic method of our algorithm. The eigenvector h_i of a node i is its feature vector $\bar{h}_i$ in concat with its reliability vector v_{RE}. Neighbor aggregate is constructed in the same way as graph attention network.

$$h_i = \sigma(\frac{1}{K} \sum_{k=1}^{K} \sum_{j \in N_i} \alpha_{ij}^k W^k h_j) \tag{1}$$

The loss of Know-GNN is represented by cross entropy. Golden network g is a classical GAT. And we modify the cross entropy loss with reliability to accommodate the label uncertainty for Noisy network f.

$$\mathcal{L}_f = \frac{1}{N} \sum_{j \in N_{data}} \{-[log(RE_j) + log(p_j)] \tag{2}$$

We add $log(RE)$ to the cross entropy, indicating that the higher the reliability is, the smaller the penalty is. In addition, the reliability vector v_{RE} and reliability RE is updated as below:

$$v_{RE}^i = \frac{1}{K} \sum_{k=1}^{K} \sum_{j \in N_i} \alpha_{ij}^k v_{RE}^j \tag{3}$$

The reliability RE is updated by the smallest non-zero value in the reliability vector v_{RE}.

3   Experiments

3.1   Experimental Setup

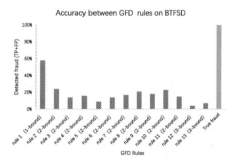

Fig. 3. Accuracy among different GFD Rules. Rules are sorted by their complexities.

Datasets. We use a real world dataset, i.e. 2017 **B**anking **T**ransaction **F**unds **S**upervision **D**ata (BTFSD), from our cooperator, which contains 92k nodes and 10.7m edges, and its fraud rate is 13.2%.

GFD Rules Analysis. GFD rules are made by the domain experts who are guided by the *Guidelines on anti-money laundering work of financial companies* whitepaper. These GFD rules contain 11-bounded GFD rule, 10 2-bounded GFD rules, and 2 3-bounded GFD rules. We verify these GFD rules by detecting frauds in BTFSD. The accuracy is shown in Fig. 3.

Baselines. To verify the ability of Know-GNN in detecting fraudsters, we compare it with various GNN baselines under the semi-supervised learning setting. We select GCN [9] and GAT [11] to represent general GNN models. We choose CARE-GNN [1] as the state-of-the-art GNN-based fraud detector. We also implement several variants of Know-GNN: Know-noRule, Know-Single, Know-Co, and Know-noRE. The detailed information is shown as follows.

- **GCN**: GCN learns node's embedding by assembling its own embedding and the neighbors'.
- **GAT**: It is an improved version of the GCN method, which uses the attention mechanism to aggregate the neighborhoods.
- **CARE-GNN**: CARE-GNN is also a state-of-the-art GNN model for detecting fraudsters, which utilizes a label-aware similarity measure and a similarity-aware neighbor selector using reinforcement learning.
- **Know-noRule**: It doesn't use GFD rules to assist which means the unlabeled data are randomly marked as fraud.
- **Know-Single**: It learns noisy network f. With this implementation, the reliability of golden data is set to 1. Then those golden data are mixed with noisy data for sampling.
- **Know-noRE**: It removes the reliability of each noisy label data.

Implementation Details. Since all datasets are fully labeled, we divide the datasets into two parts by a specific ratio and remove the labels of the noisy part, i.e. 100%, 50%, 10% of total fraud in golden data. Non-fraudulent data are used to supplement those data with removed labels, to keep the ratio of unlabeled data as 5% in the total data. The ratio is called *golden label rate* which represents the ratio of labeled nodes assigned to golden labeled set to all labeled data. This setting mimics the problem of sparse labels in the real world. For example, a 10% Golden label rate indicates that only 10% of the sample information is manually filtered, and the other 90% information is hidden in the unlabeled.

Before training, we adopt node2vec [6] to generate original features for each node. We randomly initialize parameters and optimize the model with Adam [8]. The learning parameters is set the same as Co-teaching [7] and GAT [11].

3.2   Performance Evaluation

Overall Evaluation. From Table 1, we find out that our method and its variants perform better than the baselines. Traditional GNN methods GCN and GAT only aggregate the characteristics of nodes themselves and their neighbor structures, and the performance of these methods is much worse than that of CARE-GNN and our method. Our method outperforms CARE-GNN by about 14%. That is because Know-GNN utilizes the domain expertise of humans expressed by GFD rules to acquire extensive knowledge, which includes more condensed information than the graph itself.

Table 1. Fraud detection performance (%) on BTFSD under different percentage of Golden labels.

DATASETS	METRIC	GOLDEN LABEL RATE%	GCN	GAT	CARE-GNN	Know-noRule	Know-Single	Know-noRE	Know-GNN
BTFSD	AUC	100%	53.72	59.03	70.28	67.38	**82.71**	77.33	77.37
		50%	51.21	56.91	69.15	69.02	81.59	81.89	**82.14**
		10%	50.19	53.44	64.28	62.47	78.27	80.35	**80.98**
	Recall	100%	54.37	56.08	54.71	**74.63**	69.62	72.56	73.05
		50%	52.03	54.50	58.69	56.52	73.24	77.68	**78.23**
		10%	50.03	50.76	60.38	52.60	69.35	76.89	**77.19**

Golden Label Rate. Results in Table 1 exhibit that under each golden label rate, the proposed method and its variants always achieve better performance than the baselines. It demonstrates the validity of combining human knowledge with supervised information. Moreover, our proposed method is particularly good at dealing with a low golden label rate compared to other methods, which has strong practicability in various application scenarios.

Interpretability. Since we use an attention mechanism to aggregate neighbors' representations, the value of the attention term can be seen as the importance of the neighbors. The reliability v_{RE} is calculated by its neighbors using Eq. 3. Figure 4 shows the interpretable results of a fraud node in Fig. 2. It can be observed that the GFD rule that marks it (rule 2) contributes the most, and the second contribution, 1-bounded GFD rule (rule 1), indicates abnormal behavior on the node's own attribute. The other two GFD rules (rule 4 and 5) belong to their nearest fraud type. The experimental results show that the main fraud reason for the node in Fig. 2 is rule 2, also its own attribute has the abnormal behavior shown by rule 1. Finally, this type of fraud may result in or from fraud marked by rule 4 and 5. In summary, the result can be interpreted as that when a card with credit less than 100 is cooperated with a bank with a banklevel greater than 3, it is more likely to commit fraud.

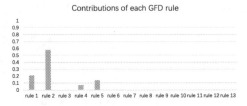

Fig. 4. Contribution of GFDs on one of the detection result.

Know-GNN Variants. It can be observed from the last four columns of Table 1 that compared with those Know-GNN implementations with the assistance of GFD rules, the performance of Know-noRule is far lower than them. It suggests that expert knowledge could indeed assist the training of GNN. In addition, Know-noRule performs better than traditional baselines, which demonstrates that Jointly-Training can handle noisy data.

With the ascend of golden label rate, Know-GNN does not perform as well as the reduced implementation Know-Single, since in the Jointly-Training process, noisy network f contains too few useful positive data, and the knowledge learned only through parameter transfer of its peer network golden network g is not enough to help train a good GNN. While in the Know-Single structure, as the proportion of useful data increases, the single training model can learn a better network.

The implementation of reliability does not bring much improvement to the model performance, but it can still provide fraud researchers with an explainable result.

4   Conclusion

In this paper, a knowledge-guided graph neural network is proposed for detecting fraudsters. Human knowledge is used to tackle the problem of labeled data scarcity as well as add interpretability to the model. We use GFD rules as expertise to label unlabeled data. *Reliability* and reliability vector is used to identify the noise level and demonstrate the detection reason. Additionally, an ingenious model, *Jointly-Training*, is designed to train a classifier from labeled data and noisy data cooperatively. Experiments with real-world financial fraud datasets and their corresponding GFDs demonstrate the effectiveness of our model. A feasible idea for further research is to use methods of automatic knowledge mining on knowledge graphs, such as GFD mining [3] and GAR [4], to mine domain knowledge automatically to assist Know-GNN.

References

1. Dou, Y., Liu, Z., Sun, L., Deng, Y., Peng, H., Yu, P.S.: Enhancing graph neural network-based fraud detectors against Camouflaged Fraudsters. In: International Conference on Information and Knowledge Management, Proceedings, pp. 315–324 (2020)
2. Fan, W.: Dependencies for graphs: challenges and opportunities. J. Data Inf. Qual. **11**(2), 1–10 (2019)
3. Fan, W., Hu, C., Liu, X., Lu, P.: Discovering graph functional dependencies. ACM Trans. Database Syst. **45**(3), 1–42 (2020)
4. Fan, W., Jin, R., Liu, M., Lu, P., Tian, C., Zhou, J.: Capturing associations in graphs. Proc. VLDB Endow. **13**(11), 1863–1876 (2020)
5. Fan, W., Lu, P.: Dependencies for graphs. ACM Trans. Database Syst. **44**(2), 1–56 (2019)
6. Grover, A., Leskovec, J.: node2vec: scalable feature learning for networks. In: Proceedings of the 22nd ACM SIGKDD International Conference on Knowledge Discovery and Data Mining (2016)
7. Han, B., et al.: Co-teaching: Robust training of deep neural networks with extremely noisy labels. arXiv (NeurIPS), pp. 1–11 (2018)
8. Kingma, D., Ba, J.: Adam: a method for stochastic optimization. Computer Science (2014)
9. Kipf, T.N., Welling, M.: Semi-supervised classification with graph convolutional networks. In: International Conference on Learning Representations (ICLR) (2017)
10. Sadowksi, G., Rathle, P.: Fraud detection: Discovering connections with graph databases. [EB/OL] (2014)
11. Velickovic, P., Cucurull, G., Casanova, A., Romero, A., Lio, P., Bengio, Y.: Graph attention networks. In: International Conference on Learning Representations (2018)
12. Zheng, W., Yan, L., Gou, C., Wang, F.Y.: Federated meta-learning for fraudulent credit card detection. In: IJCAI International Joint Conference on Artificial Intelligence 2021, pp. 4654–4660 (2020)

A Pointer-Generator Based Abstractive Summarization Model with Knowledge Distillation

Tao Dong, Shimin Shan, Yu Liu$^{(\boxtimes)}$, Yue Qian, and Anqi Ma

School of Software, Dalian University of Technology, Dalian 116620, China
dongtao2019@mail.dlut.edu.cn, {ssm,yuliu,tsien}@dlut.edu.cn,
maanqi@mail.dlut.edu.cn

Abstract. The use of large-scale pre-trained models for text summarization has attracted increasing attention in the computer science community. However, pre-training models with millions of parameters and long training time cause difficulty to deployment. Furthermore, pre-training models focus on understanding language but ignore reproduction of factual details when generating text. In this paper, we propose a method for text summarization that applies knowledge distillation to a pre-trained model called the teacher model. We build a novel sequence-to-sequence model as the student model to learn from the teacher model's knowledge for imitation. Specifically, we propose a variant of the pointer-generator network, which integrates multi-head attention mechanism, coverage mechanism and copy mechanism. We apply the variant to our student model to solve the word repetition and out-of-vocabulary words problem, so that improving the quality of generation. With experiments on Gigaword and Weibo datasets, our model achieves better performance and costs less time beyond the baseline models.

Keywords: Natural language processing · Abstractive summarization · Knowledge distillation · Pointer-generator

1 Introduction

Text summarization generation is an important task in the field of natural language processing (NLP), and the target is to condense long documents into short summaries which still contain the key point of the original. In general, there are two categories of summarization methods: extractive and abstractive. Extractive summarization selects the original words from the input text, while abstractive summarization may create new words as human-written summaries do.

As the typical model for processing time series, recurrent neural network (RNN) and its variants have obtained significant achievements on text summarization task [2,10–12]. Due to the high parallelism of Transformer [16], pre-training models [4] based on Transformer have shown superiority over RNN on many NLP tasks, including text abstractive summarization [13,17] in recent

© Springer Nature Switzerland AG 2021
T. Mantoro et al. (Eds.): ICONIP 2021, CCIS 1516, pp. 168–177, 2021.
https://doi.org/10.1007/978-3-030-92307-5_20

years. However, pre-trained models entail complex calculation with billions of parameters, which costs much training time. Consequently, it is hard to deploy pre-trained models in the industrial environment. Furthermore, pre-training models focus on understanding language but ignore the reproduction of factual details when generating text, so the models tend to generate repetitive words and out-of-vocabulary (OOV) words.

In this paper, we propose a novel approach to distill knowledge [3,7] learned in the pre-trained model for tackling the above challenges. We fine-tune a pre-trained model PoDA [17] on small labeled corpora and name this large-scale model as the teacher model. Next, we apply the knowledge distillation method to extract knowledge from the teacher network for generating the sequences of word probability. We build a sequence-to-sequence (Seq2Seq) [14] model (which is treated as student model) with the multi-head attention mechanism [1] to learn from the teacher model's knowledge for imitation. Lastly, we propose a variant that integrates the coverage mechanism [15] and copy mechanism [5]. The attention mechanism tends to repeat high-frequency words in the input text, while the coverage mechanism attempts to inhibit the attention of high-frequency words and improve the attention of low-frequency words moderately. So the coverage mechanism can balance the attention of all words and solve the repetition problem. As for handling OOV words, the copy mechanism allows the decoder to copy the words from the input sentences besides choosing words from the vocabulary. Lastly, we apply the variant to the student model for solving the word repetition and OOV words problem. With experiments on Gigaword [11] and Weibo[1] summary datasets, our model achieves better performance and costs less time beyond the baseline models.

Precisely, our work makes these contributions: (1) We build a novel Seq2Seq-based abstractive summarization model as the student model to learn from the teacher model's output for imitation. (2) We use the multi-head attention mechanism and average pooling layer to enhance the connection between encoder and decoder. (3) We apply the coverage mechanism for avoiding word repetition in the output. (4) We handle OOV words by the copy mechanism for helping our model generate text better.

2   Related Work

2.1   Abstractive Summarization

The studies on abstractive summarization based on neural network have achieved prominent progress. Summarization aims to condense longer input text into shorter output text. Therefore, abstractive summarization task can use Seq2Seq [14] as the backbone architecture. ABS+ [11] first applied Seq2Seq with attention mechanism to abstractive summarization and realized significant achievements.

---

[1] The Weibo dataset is available at https://drive.google.com/file/d/1ihnpHuVU1u HAUiaC4EpHjX3gRKp9ZW8h/view.

PGNet [12] is a milestone in abstractive summarization, which integrated attention mechanism, coverage mechanism [15] and copy mechanism [5] in the vanilla Seq2Seq model, so PGNet can avoid word repetition and handle OOV words.

As the successful application of pre-training models such as BERT [4] in many NLP tasks, researchers also begin to pre-train Transformer in summarization task. MASS [13] randomly masked the sentence in the encoder, and predicted the fragment from the unmasked part in the decoder. PoDA [17] utilized denoising auto encoder tasks to corrupt text in the encoder, and denoising the noise-corrupted text in the decoder. Moreover, PoDA also added a pointer-generator layer [12] for improving the generation performance.

2.2 Knowledge Distillation

Hinton et al. [7] creatively put forward the idea of knowledge distillation. They defined the knowledge of a model as the ability to transform the input into the output. Knowledge distillation can transfer the knowledge from a larger teacher model to a smaller student model, which not only make the model easy to deploy but also ensure the effectiveness of the model.

Many existing works have adopted knowledge distillation methods on text generation task and achieved significant improvements. Trm+Bert [3] proposed conditional masked language modeling approach to fine-tune BERT (teacher) so that helping Seq2Seq model (student) learn the bidirectional nature. MiniLM [18] introduced the scaled dot-product in the last Transformer layer of the teacher model, and applied the teacher assistant to bridge the scale gap between the teacher model and student model.

3 Model

The student model learns some prior information and knowledge from the teacher model PoDA through knowledge distillation, so that it can understand the language information from the teacher model. For generating summaries better, we construct a novel Seq2Seq model [14] with multi-head attention mechanism, coverage mechanism and copy mechanism. The architecture of our approach is depicted in Fig. 1, and each component of the model is explained as follows.

3.1 Teacher Model

We choose PoDA [17] as our teacher model that is based on Transformer. For handling OOV words, PoDA adds a pointer-generator layer [12] with the copy mechanism behind the decoder. PoDA has been pre-trained on large-scale unlabeled corpora, so we fine-tune it on labeled datasets of text summarization.

At last, we can get the output of the teacher model, i.e. the generated summaries to the input sentences. The information contained in the output can be regarded as the knowledge that will be transferred to the student model.

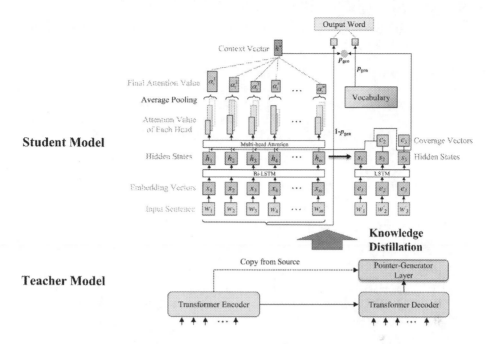

Fig. 1. The architecture of the proposed abstractive summarization model

3.2 Student Model

In the encoder, we take the input sentence as word sequence $\{w_1, w_2, \ldots, w_m\}$. And then, we map the word sequence into word vectors $\{x_1, x_2, \ldots, x_m\}$. After a bidirectional LSTM [6] layer, the encoder generates a hidden state matrix $H_{enc} = [h_1, h_2, \ldots, h_m]$, which will participate in the attention calculation. Besides, h_m will be regarded as the beginning hidden state vector of the decoder.

At time step t of the decoder, we can get the coverage vector c_t, which is the sum of attention vectors α over all previous time steps:

$$c_t = \sum\nolimits_{j=0}^{t-1} \alpha_j = c_{t-1} + \alpha_{t-1} \tag{1}$$

Here c_t represents the degree of coverage that the previous words have generated according to the attention mechanism.

For the kth head of multi-head attention ($1 <= k <= K$, where K is the number of the heads), we can get the attention vector $\alpha_t^{[k]}$ as follows:

$$\overline{\alpha}_t^{i[k]} = v^{[k]^T} \cdot \tanh(W_{attn}^{[k]} \cdot concat(h_i, s_t, c_{t-1}^i) + b_{attn}^{[k]}) \tag{2}$$

$$\alpha_t^{i[k]} = softmax(\overline{\alpha}_t^{i[k]}) \tag{3}$$

Where h_i is the hidden state vector in the encoder at time step i, s_t is the hidden state vector in the decoder at time step t, $W_{attn}^{[k]}$ is the weight matrix, $b_{attn}^{[k]}$ and $v^{[k]}$ are the parameter vectors.

Next, we apply an average pooling layer to get the final attention vector α_t:

$$\alpha_t = \frac{1}{K}\sum_{j=1}^{K}\alpha_t{}^{[j]} \tag{4}$$

Intuitively, α_t^i in α_t denotes how much connection between s_t and h_i.

With a weighted sum of H_{enc} by α_t, we can get the context vector h_t^*. Then we concatenate s_t, h_t^* and the embedding vector e_t of the decoder at time step t, and then apply a LSTM layer to get the next hidden state vector s_{t+1}:

$$h^* = H_{enc}{}^T\alpha_t \tag{5}$$

$$s_{t+1} = LSTM(W_{LSTM} \cdot concat(s_t, h_t^*, e_t) + b_{LSTM}) \tag{6}$$

Where W_{LSTM} is the weight matrix, and b_{LSTM} is the bias vector.

Then we apply the copy mechanism to get the probability p_{gen}, which depicts the probability of generating word from the vocabulary:

$$p_{gen} = \sigma(W_{gen} \cdot concat(s_t, h_t^*, e_t) + b_{gen}) \tag{7}$$

Where W_{gen} is the weight matrix, b_{gen} is the bias vector and σ is the sigmoid activation function. Finally, we can calculate the probability of the output word $p(w_t)$ and the loss function of the student model:

$$p(w_t) = p_{gen}P_{vocab}(w_t) + (1 - p_{gen})\sum_{i:w_i=w_t}\alpha_t^i \tag{8}$$

$$loss = \sum_{t=1}^{n}(-\log p(w_t) + \sum_{i=1}^{m}min\{\alpha_t^i, c_t^i\}) \tag{9}$$

Where $P_{vocab}(w_t)$ is the sampling probability for word w_t over the vocabulary.

4   Experiment

4.1   Setup

We do our experiments on GTX 1080Ti GPU. The hyper-parameter settings of the teacher model are consistent with PoDA [17]. As for the student model, the dimension of word embedding is 128, and the dimension of the hidden state vector of LSTM is 256. We set 8 heads in the multi-head attention mechanism. We choose Adagrad optimizer to train the model, and the learning rate is 0.15 with an initial accumulator value of 0.1. The maximum gradient norm is 2.

4.2   Dataset

We use two summarization datasets: Gigaword [11] and Weibo. Each example in Gigaword consists of one sentence with an average length of 31.3 words and one short headline with an average length of 8.3 words. The second dataset Weibo comes from news published by mainstream Chinese media Sina Weibo. On average, each news in Weibo dataset has about 191.3 words, and each summary has about 29.1 words. The number of training, validation and test set of Weibo is 600,000, 70,000 and 9,898 respectively.

4.3   Evaluation

We use the Rouge [9] metric to evaluate our model and baselines. Rouge is one of the most popular metrics used in text summarization, which can evaluate the similarity between the candidate summary and the reference summary. We report experiment results in terms of ROUGE-1, ROUGE-2 and ROUGE-L.

4.4   Results on Gigaword

We use ABS+ [11], PGNet [12], CGU [10], FTSum [2], PoDA [17], Trm+Bert [3], IAS [8], SAGCopy [19] and Zheng's model [20] as the baseline for Gigaword dataset. CGU uses convolutional gating units to perform global encoding for reducing the probability of repetition. FTSum adopts information extraction and dependency parse to avoid fake facts in a summary. IAS applies reinforcement learning to learn human reading strategies. SAGCopy calculates the centrality score for each source word and incorporates the score into the copy mechanism. Zheng's model uses entities in the source text as the guidance to generate summaries.

As shown in Table 1, our model outperforms all baselines on Rouge-1 and Rouge-L metrics, which demonstrates the effectiveness of our model on enhancing the readability and correctness of the output text. ABS+, PGNet, CGU, FTSum, Re^{3}Sum are all traditional neural networks, so they perform worse than other models. Our teacher model PoDA utilizes pre-training method, which is more advanced than the traditional methods. Trm+Bert also uses knowledge distillation, but it has no summarization-specific design such as copy mechanism we use. Although IAS adopts reinforcement learning, the performance is not satisfactory. Lastly, both SAGCopy and Zheng's model obtain competitive results. However, we also find that our model performs worse than several models on Rouge-2 metric. The reason may be that the information transferred from the teacher model pay more attention to words rather than bigram phrases.

Table 1. Rouge scores results on Gigaword dataset

	Rouge-1	Rouge-2	Rouge-L
ABS+	29.76	11.88	26.96
PGNet	35.98	15.99	33.33
CGU	36.30	18.00	33.80
FTSum	37.27	17.65	34.24
PoDA (Teacher model)	38.29	19.06	34.53
Trm+Bert Teacher	37.57	18.59	34.82
IAS	33.27	15.26	30.92
SAGCopy	38.84	**20.39**	36.27
Zheng's model	40.03	17.93	36.74
Our model	**42.00**	16.80	**38.65**

4.5   Results on Weibo

Limited by the lack of available open source code, we choose PGNet [12], CGU [10], PoDA [17] as the baselines for Weibo dataset. As Table 2 shows, our model can get the best performance on Rouge-1 and Rouge-L metrics, which is similar to the result for Gigaword dataset. The experiment results prove that our model can also be suitable for other languages. Regrettably, the results on Rouge-2 is still slightly worse than the teacher model PoDA, which proves that the information transferred from the teacher model focuses on words once again.

Table 2. Rouge Scores results on Weibo dataset

	Rouge-1	Rouge-2	Rouge-L
PGNet	22.53	15.34	21.23
CGU	27.58	16.25	25.74
PoDA (Teacher model)	30.50	**17.09**	27.30
Our model	**30.74**	17.05	**27.83**

4.6   Ablation Experiment

The major novelty of our student model is that it integrates the multi-head attention mechanism, coverage mechanism and copy mechanism for abstractive summarization. In order to show the effectiveness of the three mechanisms, we set the ablation experiment to validate the performance of the variants by removing each mechanism from our complete student model. Table 3 demonstrates that each mechanism is important for the student model, and the combination of the three mechanisms can make the model perform the best achievement.

Table 3. Ablation experiment results on Gigaword and Weibo datasets

		Rouge-1	Rouge-2	Rouge-L
Gigaword	One-head attention	38.18	16.46	35.25
	Without coverage	37.90	16.17	33.44
	Without copy	34.70	16.15	30.52
	Our model	**42.00**	**16.80**	**38.65**
Weibo	One-head attention	28.64	16.50	26.06
	Without coverage	28.32	16.59	25.29
	Without copy	27.00	16.00	24.37
	Our model	**30.74**	**17.05**	**27.83**

5   Discussion

5.1   Model Training Time Analysis

One of the advantages of knowledge distillation is that the training time is significantly reduced. For Gigaword dataset, we set batch size to 64. We fine-tune the teacher model for 45 epochs, and each epoch costs 9,187 s. However, we train the student model for 35 epochs, and each epoch only costs 4,577 s. For Weibo dataset, we set batch size to 32. We fine-tune the teacher model for 40 epochs, and each epoch costs 3,970.8 s. However, we train the student model for 35 epochs and each epoch only costs 1,068.75 s.

5.2   Linguistic Quality Analysis

In Table 4, we show two examples from Gigaword dataset generated by the teacher model PoDA and our model.

In the first example, our model deletes the useless information "one of the most prosperous in the caribbean", which is just the introduction of the country Trinidad and Tobago. Meanwhile, our model successfully maintains the name of the country "trinidad and tobago" but PoDA misses "tobago". Furthermore, our model emphasizes "parliamentary elections" rather than "elections" or "poll".

In the second example, our model successfully deletes the unimportant information "after a reformed communist won the first round of voting". Besides, our model highlights the meaning of "presidential run-off" compared with the output of PoDA. Furthermore, our model deletes "main" in "poland's main opposition

Table 4. Examples of generated summaries from Gigaword Dataset

Source	Turnout was heavy for parliamentary elections monday in trinidad and tobago after a month of intensive campaigning throughout the country, one of the most prosperous in the caribbean
Target	Trinidad and tobago poll draws heavy turnout by john babb
PoDA	Turnout heavy for trinidad elections
Our model	Turnout heavy for trinidad and tobago parliamentary elections
Source	Poland 's main opposition party tuesday endorsed president lech walesa in an upcoming presidential run-off election after a reformed communist won the first round of voting
Target	Walesa receives opposition boost
PoDA	Poland 's main opposition party endorses walesa
Our model	polish opposition party endorses walesa in presidential run-off

party", which is as same as the target. As a result, our model can continue to learn from PoDA, retain the key information and make the output more concise.

6   Conclusion

In this work, we propose a method that applies knowledge distillation to a pre-trained model called teacher model for text summarization. We build a novel Seq2Seq model as the student model to learn from the knowledge produced by teacher model for imitation. Specifically, we apply the multi-head attention mechanism, coverage mechanism and copy mechanism to the student model for solving word repetition and OOV words problem. Experiment results show that our model outperforms state-of-the-art models in terms of Rouge metrics, and we also prove the effectiveness of three mechanisms. Furthermore, the training cost and the quality of candidate summaries demonstrate that our model has better generation performance than baselines. For future work, we will explore new modules for improving the performance of the summarization model.

References

1. Bahdanau, D., Cho, K., Bengio, Y.: Neural machine translation by jointly learning to align and translate. In: ICLR (2015)
2. Cao, Z., Wei, F., Li, W., Li, S.: Faithful to the original: fact aware neural abstractive summarization. In: AAAI 2018, pp. 4784–4791 (2018)
3. Chen, Y., Gan, Z., Cheng, Y., Liu, J., Liu, J.: Distilling knowledge learned in BERT for text generation. In: ACL 2020, pp. 7893–7905 (2020)
4. Devlin, J., Chang, M., Lee, K., Toutanova, K.: BERT: pre-training of deep bidirectional transformers for language understanding. In: NAACL-HLT 2019, Volume 1 (Long and Short Papers), pp. 4171–4186 (2019)
5. Gu, J., Lu, Z., Li, H., Li, V.O.K.: Incorporating copying mechanism in sequence-to-sequence learning. In: ACL 2016, Volume 1: Long Papers (2016)
6. Hochreiter, S., Schmidhuber, J.: Long short-term memory. Neural Comput. **9**, 1735–1780 (1997). https://doi.org/10.1162/neco.1997.9.8.1735
7. Hinton, G.E., Vinyals, O., Dean, J.: Distilling the knowledge in a neural network. arXiv preprint arXiv: 1503.02531 (2015)
8. Li, J., Zhang, C., Chen, X., Cao, Y., Jia, R.: Improving abstractive summarization with iterative representation. In: IJCNN 2020, pp. 1–8 (2020)
9. Lin, C., Rey, M.: ROUGE: A Package for Automatic Evaluation of Summaries (2001)
10. Lin, J., Sun, X., Ma, S., Su, Q.: Global encoding for abstractive summarization. In: ACL 2018, Volume 2: Short Papers, pp. 163–169 (2018)
11. Rush, A., Chopra, S., Weston, J.: A neural attention model for abstractive sentence summarization. In: EMNLP 2015, pp. 379–389 (2015)
12. See, A., Liu, P.J., Manning, C.D.: Get to the point: summarization with pointer generator networks. In: ACL 2017, vol. 1, pp. 1073–1083 (2017)
13. Song, K., Tan, X., Qin, T., Lu, J., Liu, T.Y.: MASS: masked sequence to sequence pre-training for language generation. In: ICML 2019, pp. 5926–5936 (2019)

14. Sutskever, I., Vinyals, O., Le, Q.V.: Sequence to sequence learning with neural networks. In: NIPS 2014, pp. 3104–3112 (2014)
15. Tu, Z., Lu, Z., Liu, Y., Liu, X., Li, H.: Modeling coverage for neural machine translation. In: ACL 2016, vol. 1 (2016)
16. Vaswani, A., et al.: Attention is all you need. In: NIPS 2017, pp. 5998–6008 (2017)
17. Wang, L., Zhao, W., Jia, R., Li, S., Liu, J.: Denoising based sequence-to-sequence pretraining for text generation. In: EMNLP-IJCNLP 2019, pp. 4001–4013 (2019)
18. Wang, W., et al.: MiniLM: deep self-attention distillation for task-agnostic compression of pre-trained transformers. In: NeurIPS (2020)
19. Xu, S., Li, H., Yuan, P., Wu, Y., He, X., Zhou, B.: Self-attention guided copy mechanism for abstractive summarization. In: ACL 2020, pp. 1355–1362 (2020)
20. Zheng, C., Cai, Y., Zhang, G., Li, Q.: Controllable abstractive sentence summarization with guiding entities. In: COLING 2020, pp. 5668–5678 (2020)

FiLMing Multimodal Sarcasm Detection with Attention

Sundesh Gupta[1], Aditya Shah[1], Miten Shah[1], Laribok Syiemlieh[2], and Chandresh Maurya[1(✉)]

[1] Indian Institute of Technology Indore, Indore, India
{cse180001057,cse180001049,chanderesh}@iiti.ac.in
[2] NIT Meghalaya, Shillong, India

Abstract. Sarcasm detection identifies natural language expressions whose intended meaning is different from what is implied by its surface meaning. Today, social media has given rise to an abundant amount of multimodal data where users express their opinions through text and images. Our paper aims to leverage multimodal data to improve the performance of the existing systems for sarcasm detection. We propose a novel architecture that uses the RoBERTa model with a co-attention to incorporate context incongruity between input text and image attributes. Further, we integrate feature-wise affine transformation (FiLM) by conditioning the input image through FiLMed ResNet blocks with the textual features to capture the multimodal information. The output from both the models and CLS token from RoBERTa is concatenated for the final prediction. Our results demonstrate that our proposed model outperforms the existing state-of-the-art methods by **6.14% F1 score** on the public Twitter multimodal sarcasm detection dataset (Our code+data is available at https://tinyurl.com/kp2ruj7c).

Keywords: Machine learning · Sarcasm detection · Multimodal learning

1 Introduction

According to wiki, *sarcasm is a sharp, bitter, or cutting expression or remark; a bitter gibe or taunt.* Thus, sarcasm is defined as a sharp remark whose intended meaning is different from what it looks like. Sarcasm does not necessarily involve irony, but more often than not, sarcasm is used as an ironic remark[1]. Sarcasm detection is an important task in many natural language understanding tasks such as opinion mining, dialogue systems, customer support, online harassment detection, to name a few.

A plethora of works automatically detects sarcasm in unimodal data, using either text or images. One of the examples of sarcasm in multimodal data is presented in Fig. 1. Detecting sarcasm in multimodal data can be arduous as

---

[1] www.thefreedictionary.com.

© Springer Nature Switzerland AG 2021
T. Mantoro et al. (Eds.): ICONIP 2021, CCIS 1516, pp. 178–186, 2021.
https://doi.org/10.1007/978-3-030-92307-5_21

compared to unimodal data simply because what the text says is irreconcilable to the image, for example, in Fig. 1(a), the text says "lovely, clean, pleasant train home" whereas the associated image implies the opposite. Similarly, in Fig. 1(b), the textual description and image semantics are alluding to opposite meanings. Such a phenomena is called *incongruity* [4,11] and has been leveraged to tackle multimodal sarcasm detection [13,15].

 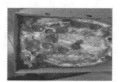

(a) lovely, clean, pleasant train home   (b) well that looks appetising #ubereats

Fig. 1. Examples from the Twitter data showing text modality alone is insufficient for sarcasm detection.

Following previous multimodal sarcasm detection approaches, we propose a deep learning-based architecture. We compute the incongruity in two ways. Firstly, the image attribute is extracted using ResNet [3], and the co-attention matrix is calculated. This operation captures the *intra-modality incongruity* between the text and image attribute. Secondly, the *inter-modality incongruity* is computed between the text and image features. The two incongruity representations are fused together and used for identifying sarcasm. Concretely, we make the following contributions:

(1) A novel deep learning-based architecture is proposed that captures the inter-modality incongruity between the image and text.
(2) Empirical demonstration shows that we are able to boost the F1 score by 6.14% of the current SOTA on the benchmark Twitter dataset.

2   Related Works

One of the first works to utilize multimodal data for sarcasm detection is [13] which presents two approaches. The first one exploits visual semantics and concatenates the semantic features with the textual features. The second method adopts a pretrained network on ImageNet for multimodal sarcastic posts. CNN is used to encode cognitive features for feature representation in [8]. The work in [1] extracts visual features and attributes from images using ResNet and builds a hierarchical fusion model to detect sarcasm. Along the same lines, the recurrent network model in [12] proposes the idea of a gating mechanism to leak information from one modality to the other. The authors of [15] use pre-trained BERT and ResNet models to encode text and image data and merge them using a gate called a bridge along with a 2D-Intra-Attention layer.

The multimodal work that closely matches with our work is [9] which proposes a BERT-based architecture for modeling intra- and inter-modality incongruity. Self-attention is used to model inter-modality incongruity, whereas co-attention is used to model intra-modality incongruity. Contrary to this work, we model inter-modality incongruity between the *text* and *visual attributes* in **two ways**. The first uses visual attributes and text, and the latter uses visual features and text. We further integrate feature-wise linear transformation [10] to compute FiLM parameters using the text data and inject the FiLM layers (see [10] for more details) in between the ResNet layers. The FiLMed ResNet outputs the visual features, which acts like the inter-modality incongruity. More details are given in the next section.

3 Methodology

3.1 Proposed Model

We propose a novel multimodal architecture using RoBERTa [6] for detecting sarcasm. Figure 2 gives an overview of the model.

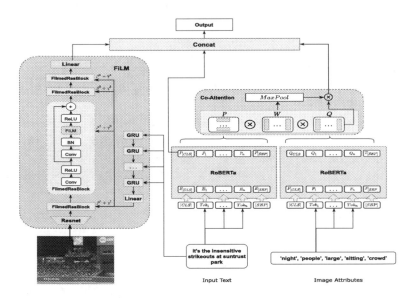

Fig. 2. Overview of our proposed model

Image, Text and Image Attribute Representation: We consider text as a sequence of words $E = \{[CLS], E_1, E_2, \ldots, E_n, [SEP]\}$, where $E_i \in \mathbb{R}^d$, n denotes maximum length of the input text, and d is the embedding size. For extracting features $P \in \mathbb{R}^{N \times d}$, we consider the output of the first encoder layer of RoBERTa as the representation of the text. Here, N depicts the length of set E and d is the hidden size of RoBERTa. Similarly, for the representation of image attributes, we have $F = \{[CLS], F_1, F_2, \ldots, F_m, [SEP]\}$ and its features will be represented by $Q \in \mathbb{R}^{M \times d}$ where M is the length of set F.

Inter-modal Incongruity Between Visual and Text Representation: We capture the image information based on the textual features. Inspired by the work of [10], we apply the feature-wise affine transformation (FiLM) on the image by conditioning it on the input text. Further, we use GRU network [2] to process the text. The final layer of the GRU network outputs FiLM parameters (γ_i^n, β_i^n) for n^{th} FiLMed residual block. The γ_i and β_i are the output of the functions g and h, which are learned by the FiLM for the input x_i as $\gamma_{i,c} = g_c(x_i)$, $\beta_{i,c} = h_c(x_i)$; where g, h are arbitrary functions.

In our experiment, we use 4 FiLMed residual blocks with a linear layer attached on top which outputs the final output $Q_{film} \in R^{1024}$. Mathematically, the parameters γ and β perform the feature-wise affine transformation on the image feature maps extracted by ResNet as: $FiLM(F_{i,c}) = \gamma_{i,c} * F_{i,c} + \beta_{i,c}$ where $F_{i,c}$ corresponds to the ith input's c^{th} image feature map.

Intra-modal Incongruity Between Visual Attributes and Text Representation: To model the contradiction between the input-text and image attribute, we use a co-attention mechanism motivated by [7]. The output of the RoBERTa model through input text and high-level image representation, i.e., image attributes is used for co-attention. Formally, we first calculate the affinity matrix C using bi-linear transformation W to capture the interaction between the input text and the image attributes as: $C = tanh(PWQ^T)$, where $P \in R^{N \times d}$ represent input-text features, $Q \in R^{M \times d}$ represent image attribute features, $W \in R^{d \times d}$ is a learnable parameter. The attention weight $\alpha \in R^M$ is then calculated using 2D max-pooling operation over affinity matrix C. Intuitively, α calculates the attention weights over each word in the text as: $\alpha = MaxPool(C)$. Finally, the image attribute attention matrix captures the contradiction between text and image features as: $Q_{att} = \alpha Q$

Final Fusion: We take the $Q_{film} \in \mathbb{R}^{1024}$ output from the FiLM and Q_{att} from co-attention mechanism as mentioned above. Along with this, we also use the $[CLS] \in R^d$ token from input-text feature representation of RoBERTa, and concatenated them to form the fusion vector as: $H_{fusion} = concat(Q_{film}, [CLS], Q_{att})$; where $H_{fusion} \in R^{1024+2 \times d}$. We pass this fusion vector through a fully connected layer followed by the sigmoid function for the classification.

4   Experiments

4.1   The Dataset

We use the publicly available multimodal Twitter dataset collected by [1]. The total number of tweets is 24635 and there is no data imbalance. The dataset is divided by [1] into the training set, validation set, and test set in the ratio 80%:10%:10%. The dataset is preprocessed to separate words, emoticons, and hashtags with the NLTK toolkit. We present results on only one dataset consisting of text and image combined with image attribute since this is the only dataset where *image attributes have been manually verified.*

4.2   Baselines

We use the following baselines for comparison: (a) **ResNet**: An image only model [3] which is fine-tuned on the same Twitter multimodal dataset, (b) **CNN**: A popular text only CNN [5] model which performs well on text classification problems, (c) **Multi-dimensional Intra-Attention Recurrent Network (MIARN)** [14]: proposed a novel architecture for text-only sarcasm detection by using 2D-attention mechanism, (d) **Hierarchical Fusion Model (HFM)** proposed by [1], it takes text, image, and attribute feature as modalities. Features of the modalities are then reconstructed and fused for prediction, (e) **Res-bert** [9] implements Res-bert as a model to concatenate the output of image features from ResNet and text features from BERT, (f) **Intra and Inter-modality Incongruity (IIMI-MMSD)** [9] proposes a BERT-based model with self-attention and co-attention mechanism to capture inter and intra-modality incongruity, respectively, and (g) **Bridge-RoBERTa** [15] uses pre-trained RoBERTa and ResNet, to connect their vector spaces through a Bridge Layer along with 2D-Intra-Attention layer which capture incongruity.

4.3   Experimental Settings and Hyper-Parameters

We use pre-trained RoBERTa-base [6] with 12 layers, and pre-trained ResNet-50 [3]. For text and image attributes, we use output of the first layer of RoBERTa encoder. The model is run on NVIDIA Tesla V100-PCIE GPU. We take Adam optimizer and set the learning rate for FiLMed network as $3e{-}4$, for RoBERTa as $1e{-}6$, and $1e{-}4$ for co-attention layer. The batch size of 32 is used for training. We add weight decay of $1e{-}2$ and gradient clipping set to 1.0. The maximum length of tokenised text is 360 and we take the standard dropout rate of 0.1. The model is fine-tuned for 15 epochs.

4.4   Results and Discussion

Table 1 shows the comparison of our proposed model with other baseline models. Our model outperforms the current state-of-the-art model [15] on all the four metrics viz. F1-score, Precision, Recall, and Accuracy. Specifically, our model gives an improvement of 6.14% on F1-score and 5.15% on accuracy over the current SOTA thus verifying the effectiveness of our model.

We can also verify from Table 1 that treating images or text independently does not perform well on the sarcasm detection problem. Intuitively, image-only models perform worse than text-only models as an image alone does not contain sufficient information to identify underlying sarcasm. Our proposed model

Table 1. Comparison of baselines with our proposed model

Modality	Method	F1-score	Precision	Recall	Accuracy
Image	ResNet [3]	0.6513	0.5441	0.7080	0.6476
Text	CNN [5]	0.7532	0.7429	0.7639	0.8003
	MIARN [14]	0.7736	0.7967	0.7518	0.8248
Image + Text	HFM [1]	0.8018	0.7657	0.8415	0.8344
	Res-Bert [9]	0.8157	0.7887	0.8446	0.8480
	IIMI-MMSD [9]	0.8292	0.8087	0.8508	0.8605
	Bridge-RoBERTa [15]	0.8605	0.8295	0.8939	0.8851
	Our Method	**0.9219**	**0.9056**	**0.9387**	**0.9366**

achieves better results than other multimodal approaches as it can capture the contradiction between the text and images in two stages: First, using FiLM, we get a representation of the image conditioned on the input text, thereby extracting image features that are incongruous to the text features. FiLM layers enable the GRU network over the input text to impact the neural network computation (ResNet in our case), thereby allowing our model to capture inter modality incongruity. Second, the co-attention mechanism enables the image attributes to attend to each word in the input text. This helps us get a representation of high-level image features conditioned on the text. Motivated by the approach in [15], using the output of $[CLS]$ token from RoBERTa for the final concatenation layer helps the proposed model to identify the underlying sarcasm. Thus, conditioning the image and image attributes on input text using FiLM and co-attention respectively are effective for sarcasm detection.

4.5 Model Analysis

To understand the visual significance of our model, we plot image attention representations. Figure 3 illustrates that our model can attend to regions of image that are incongruous to text. Since final predictions are made using the features of these highlighted areas, it gives an overall boost to the model performance. Moreover, we can verify from Fig. 3(a) and 3(b) that our model is able to attend to text like "pack of almonds" and "stupid people" without the need to explicitly use noisy Optical Character Recognition (OCR).

(a) thanks god i have such a wonderful   (b) yup lol.
reseal in my pack of almonds

Fig. 3. Examples from the Twitter data showing attention visualization of sarcastic tweets.

4.6 Ablation Study

To evaluate the effectiveness of each component in our network, we conduct a detailed ablation study on the proposed architecture. Firstly, we remove the FiLM network which is represented as w/o FiLM. Secondly, co-attention between the visual attribute and the text is clipped, and the model is called w/o co-attention. Further, the importance of the [CLS] token during the fusion is denoted by w/o cls. We experiment our approach with two other models namely BERT and ELECTRA. The resultant networks are called FiLM-Bert and FiLM-Electra. The ablation results are shown in Table 2.

Table 2. Results of ablation studies. The 'w/o' means removal of the component.

Ablation	F1-score	Precision	Recall	Accuracy
w/o FiLM	0.6217	0.5667	0.6890	0.6660
w/o co-attention	0.7607	0.7360	0.7871	0.8029
w/o cls	0.7638	0.7225	0.8104	0.8003
FiLM-Electra	0.7683	0.7178	0.8265	0.8013
FiLM-Bert	0.7727	0.7131	0.8439	0.8026
Our Method	**0.9219**	**0.9056**	**0.9387**	**0.9366**

We can see that the removal of FiLM (w/o FiLM) significantly hampers the model's performance. Next, we eliminate the co-attention module (w/o co-attention) and concatenate the output from FiLM and RoBERTa. This decreases the model performance which implies that capturing incongruity between image and textual features through co-attention is important for sarcasm detection. Further, output from the [CLS] token positively contributes to the model. When we try our network with the BERT and ELECTRA model (FiLM-Bert and FiLM-Electra), then we observe sharp decline in the performance. This shows that RoBERTa is better at harnessing textual features. From the above results, we can conclude that FiLM network fused with RoBERTa and attention mechanism helps to capture incongruity between image and text modality, thereby effectively learning the underlying sarcasm.

5   Conclusion and Future Work

The present work tackles the problem of sarcasm detection through capturing inter-modality incongruity. The proposed architecture handles the inter-modality incongruity in two ways: the first uses the co-attention, and the second is via FiLM network. Comparison with baselines on Twitter benchmark datasets reveals that the proposed architecture can better capture the contradiction present between the image and text modality. The ablation study highlights the importance of FiLM and co-attention layer between the image, image attribute embeddings and the text embeddings. Comparison with several baselines on benchmark dataset shows the effectiveness and superiority of our model.

References

1. Cai, Y., Cai, H., Wan, X.: Multi-modal sarcasm detection in Twitter with hierarchical fusion model. In: Proceedings of the 57th Annual Meeting of the Association for Computational Linguistics, pp. 2506–2515 (2019)
2. Chung, J., Gülçehre, Ç., Cho, K., Bengio, Y.: Empirical evaluation of gated recurrent neural networks on sequence modeling. CoRR abs/1412.3555 (2014). http://arxiv.org/abs/1412.3555
3. He, K., Zhang, X., Ren, S., Sun, J.: Deep residual learning for image recognition. In: Proceedings of the IEEE Conference on Computer Vision and Pattern Recognition, pp. 770–778 (2016)
4. Joshi, A., Sharma, V., Bhattacharyya, P.: Harnessing context incongruity for sarcasm detection. In: Proceedings of the 53rd Annual Meeting of the Association for Computational Linguistics and the 7th International Joint Conference on Natural Language Processing (Volume 2: Short Papers), pp. 757–762 (2015)
5. Kim, Y.: Convolutional neural networks for sentence classification. CoRR abs/1408.5882 (2014). http://arxiv.org/abs/1408.5882
6. Liu, Y., et al.: RoBERTa: a robustly optimized BERT pretraining approach. arXiv preprint arXiv:1907.11692 (2019)
7. Lu, J., Yang, J., Batra, D., Parikh, D.: Hierarchical question-image co-attention for visual question answering. In: Proceedings of the 30th International Conference on Neural Information Processing Systems, NIPS 2016, pp. 289–297. Curran Associates Inc., Red Hook (2016)
8. Mishra, A., Dey, K., Bhattacharyya, P.: Learning cognitive features from gaze data for sentiment and sarcasm classification using convolutional neural network. In: Proceedings of the 55th Annual Meeting of the Association for Computational Linguistics (Volume 1: Long Papers), pp. 377–387 (2017)
9. Pan, H., Lin, Z., Fu, P., Qi, Y., Wang, W.: Modeling intra and inter-modality incongruity for multi-modal sarcasm detection. In: Proceedings of the 2020 Conference on Empirical Methods in Natural Language Processing: Findings, pp. 1383–1392 (2020)
10. Perez, E., Strub, F., De Vries, H., Dumoulin, V., Courville, A.: FiLM: visual reasoning with a general conditioning layer. In: Proceedings of the AAAI Conference on Artificial Intelligence, vol. 32 (2018)
11. Riloff, E., Qadir, A., Surve, P., De Silva, L., Gilbert, N., Huang, R.: Sarcasm as contrast between a positive sentiment and negative situation. In: Proceedings of the 2013 Conference on Empirical Methods in Natural Language Processing, pp. 704–714 (2013)

12. Sangwan, S., Akhtar, M.S., Behera, P., Ekbal, A.: I didn't mean what i wrote! Exploring multimodality for sarcasm detection. In: 2020 International Joint Conference on Neural Networks (IJCNN), pp. 1–8. IEEE (2020)

13. Schifanella, R., de Juan, P., Tetreault, J., Cao, L.: Detecting sarcasm in multimodal social platforms. In: Proceedings of the 24th ACM International Conference on Multimedia, pp. 1136–1145 (2016)

14. Tay, Y., Luu, A.T., Hui, S.C., Su, J.: Reasoning with sarcasm by reading in-between. In: Proceedings of the 56th Annual Meeting of the Association for Computational Linguistics (Volume 1: Long Papers), pp. 1010–1020. Association for Computational Linguistics, Melbourne, July 2018. https://doi.org/10.18653/v1/P18-1093. https://www.aclweb.org/anthology/P18-1093

15. Wang, X., Sun, X., Yang, T., Wang, H.: Building a bridge: a method for image-text sarcasm detection without pretraining on image-text data. In: Proceedings of the First International Workshop on Natural Language Processing Beyond Text, pp. 19–29 (2020)

Implicit Neural Network for Implicit Data Regression Problems

Zhibin Miao[1], Jinghui Zhong[1(✉)], Peng Yang[2], Shibin Wang[3], and Dong Liu[3,4]

[1] School of Computer Science and Engineering, South China University
of Technology, Guangzhou, China
jinghuizhong@scut.edu.cn
[2] Guangdong Provincial Key Laboratory of Brain-Inspired Intelligent Computation,
Department of Computer Science and Engineering, Southern University of Science
and Technology, Shenzhen, China
[3] College of Computer and Information Engineering, Henan Normal University,
Xinxiang, China
[4] Key Laboratory of Artificial Intelligence and Personalized Learning in Education
of Henan Province, Xinxiang, China

Abstract. Artificial neural network (ANN) is one of the most common methods for data regression. However, existing ANN based methods focus on fitting data with explicit relationships, where the output y can be explicitly expressed by the inputs x in the form of $y = f(x)$. In contrast, implicit relationships (i.e., $f(x, y) = 0$) are more expressive in that they can concisely present complex closed surfaces and mathematical functions with multiple outputs. However, so far, little effort has been made on applying ANN to fit data with implicit relationships of variables. In this paper, for the first time, we propose an implicit neural network (INN) for implicit data regression. In this framework, an evolutionary implicit neural network (EINN) module is proposed, which is trained by the regression data to capture the implicit relationships among variables. Then, an explicit-implicit cooperate (EIC) mechanism is proposed based on the EINN component to train an explicit ANN model to predict the outputs of new unseen inputs. The proposed framework is tested on eight benchmark problems and the experimental results have demonstrated the efficacy of the proposed method.

Keywords: Neural network · Data regression · Implicit data
regression · Evolutionary algorithm

1 Introduction

Data regression is a common application task which aims to construct a model to fit a given dataset, which is used to determine the relationships between the inputs (or features) and the outputs, and to predict outputs of new unseen inputs. Besides, by abstracting the information processing of brain neural network, ANN composes different networks according to the connection modes. Because of its

© Springer Nature Switzerland AG 2021
T. Mantoro et al. (Eds.): ICONIP 2021, CCIS 1516, pp. 187–195, 2021.
https://doi.org/10.1007/978-3-030-92307-5_22

strong nonlinear function approximation, ANN has become one of the most common methods for data regression applications [1–3,5,8].

However, existing neural networks for data regression are all focused on fitting data with explicit relationship, i.e., the outputs y can be expressed by inputs x in the form of $y = f(x)$. In contrast, implicit relationship does not distinguish the dependent variables from the independent variables, and takes all the features as inputs so as to construct more complex mathematical models in the form of $f(x_D, y) = 0$. The implicit relationships are more loose in form and are more flexible to describe the relationships among variables. However, little research effort has been made on applying ANN to fit data with implicit relationships of variables. The main reason is that it is difficult to guarantee the effectiveness of the implicit ANN regression model. If the data contain implicit relationships, there can be many-to-many mapping among the variables, that is, the same input variables may correspond to multiple different outputs. These contradictory data seriously affect the convergence of a gradient method for training the ANN. Besides, since the implicit equation is always equal to zero, the model constructed usually are meaningless (e.g., $x^0 + x - x - 1 = 0$). These problems make it difficult to apply ANN to fit data with implicit relationships.

Keeping the above in mind, in this article, an evolutionary implicit neural network (EINN) is proposed to capture the implicit relationship of variables hidden inside the regression data. The implicit ANN takes all features of the training data as inputs, and the Comprehensive Learning Fitness Evaluation Mechanism (CL-FEM) [4] is employed to verify this model. Further more, in order to predict the outputs of new unseen inputs, an explicit-implicit cooperate (EIC) mechanism is proposed based on the EINN to train an explicit ANN model. Experiment results on eight data regression problems have shown that, the proposed EINN is effective to capture the implicit relationships of variables and the explicit ANN trained by the proposed framework can better fit the regression data.

2   Implicit Relationship Discovery Problems

Implicit equations adopt all data features as input and the output is equivalent to zero, as expressed by:

$$f(x, y, ...) = 0 \tag{1}$$

where x, y, and others are variables of the dataset. Compared with the explicit equations, the implicit relationships have fewer formal constraints and better expressiveness, which are usually used to concisely define continuous closed geometric surfaces and the many-to-many relationship between variables. Nevertheless, a major challenge of the implicit equation discovery is the effectiveness of the found implicit model cannot be guaranteed. Because the implicit equation is always equal to zero, this identity property might easily make it converge to some meaningless equations (e.g., $sin^2(x) + cos^2(x) - 1 = 0$).

To overcome the above issue, Schmidt and Lipson proposed a Derivative-based Evaluation Mechanism (DBEM) [7], which verifies the effectiveness of a given implicit equation model by fitting partial derivatives derived from the data points to the implicit derivatives of this equation. By comparing the partial derivatives of the candidate implicit equations at each data point with the derivatives obtained from the training data, it can avoid finding invalid equations to some extent. Another recently proposed method is the CL-FEM [4,10]. To verify that the candidate implicit model is only valid in the given data space, CL-FEM compares the model output value obtained from the original data set with the output values on the generated stochastic datasets for each dimension. Only when all dimensions contribute to the equation formula, the implicit equation model is effective. Compared to DBEM, CL-FEM is suitable for both dense and sparse datasets, and it requires less calculation overhead.

3   Proposed Implicit Neural Network Framework

This section will describe the general framework of the proposed implicit neural network (INN) for implicit data regression problems. It is mainly composed of two modules: a) the evolutionary implicit neural network (EINN) module, and b) the explicit-implicit cooperate (EIC) module. First, the EINN model is trained to find out the implicit relationship between variables, where the CL-FEM [4] is adopted to help evolutionary algorithm tune the parameters of the network. In the EIC module, an explicit ANN (named EIC-NN) is trained based on the well-trained EINN and differential evolution (DE). The trained EINN model is used to evaluate the fitness of a given EIC-NN, and the DE is used to tune the parameters of the EIC-NN.

3.1   The Evolutionary Implicit Neural Network Module

Figure 1 illustrates the general structure of the proposed EINN module. The implicit ANN model takes all features (i.e., $(x_1, x_2, ..., y)$) of the training data as inputs, and the results calculated by this model will be compared with zero for error analysis. The CL-FEM verifies model effectiveness by using the disturbed data to test if this model can uniquely identify points in the dataset and exclude other irrelevant points. Since traditional gradient descent cannot effectively work on data with implicit relationships, DE [9] is adopted as the optimizer of the EINN model. Next, we will introduce the specific operations in detail.

Optimizer Selection and DE Operations. The EINN module aims to find the implicit relationship between the input variables. However, since the data may contain many-to-many mapping among variables, this will result in multiple gradients on a data point. In addition, the existence of some piecewise functions in the implicit relationship makes the gradient at the disconnection point nonexistent. What is worse, the loss function is the mean square error compared with zero, which leads to the gradient descent method falling into local optimum quickly. These drawbacks make the traditional gradient descent optimization method no longer suitable for tuning the network parameters.

To address the above issue, the widely used DE algorithm with CL-FEM is adopted as the optimizer of the EINN model. In DE, each individual in the population is encoded as a linear vector of the parameters of the EINN model, including the connection weights and biases between each layer. Then, the mutation, crossover, and selection operations are performed repeatedly to evolve the individuals until reaching a termination condition.

Fitness Evaluation and CL-FEM. For the EINN regression, its fitness evaluation function is to minimize the average difference between the calculated value and zero. The fitness value can be obtained simply by calculating the following mean-squares-error:

$$\mathbf{MSE} = \frac{1}{N} \sum_{i=1}^{N} (O_i - 0)^2 \tag{2}$$

where O_i is the output value calculated by the neural network on the ith input data.

To avoid searching for meaningless equation relationships, the CL-FEM is adopted to the fitness assessment process, which uses the stochastic data information outside the range of the training data space to verify the neural network model. During evaluating the given model with CL-FEM, first, a stochastic

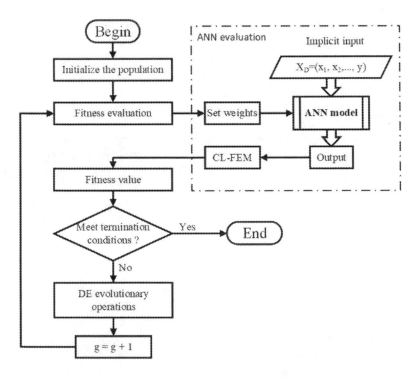

Fig. 1. The general structure of the proposed EINN training and verification module.

dataset is generated for each dimension of the implicit input. Therefore, there are total D stochastic datasets. The stochastic dataset D_k of the kth dimension is produced from the original data:

$$d_{ij}^k = \begin{cases} rand(L_k, U_k), & j = k \\ x_{ij}, & \text{otherwise} \end{cases} \quad i = 1, 2, ..., N \quad j = 1, 2, ..., D \quad (3)$$

where N is the sample number of the input dataset, D is the dimension number, L_k and U_k are the upper bound and the lower bound of the kth dimension respectively.

Then, the results calculated from the input dataset and stochastic datasets with the given EINN model are used to form a set consisting $(D+1)$ result vectors $\{S, S^1, S^2, ..., S^D\}$. S is the result vector obtained from the input dataset with the candidate EINN model and the others are gained from the D stochastic datasets. Next, the candidate EINN model is estimated by calculating the difference between S and S^k:

$$m_k = \frac{1}{N} \sum_{i=1}^{N} (S_i - S_i^k)^2, \quad k = 1, 2, ..., D \quad (4)$$

Since the ith variable value of the S and S^k are different, their results should be different if the ith dimension contributes to the implicit model output. In CL-FEM, the tolerance degree is set to be 10^{-4}. If all the calculated differences m_k are greater than the tolerance degree, the final fitness value of the given model is set to be its MSE, otherwise, it is set to be a huge constant value (e.g., 10^6) which means this model is invalid.

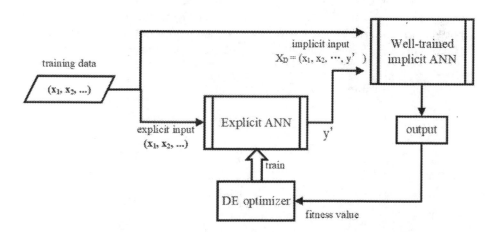

Fig. 2. The general structure of the proposed EIC framework.

3.2   The Explicit-Implicit Co-operate Module

When a well-trained EINN regression model is obtained, it then can be used to assist the training of explicit NN model (EIC-NN) to predict outputs of new unseen inputs. Figure 2 illustrates the general procedure of training the EIC-NN based on a well-trained EINN. In this module, the trained EINN model plays the role of fitness evaluation calculation. Its implicit input data includes the explicit input variables (i.e., $(x_1, x_2, ...)$) of the training set and the output value (y') calculated by the EIC-NN model. After that, the output calculated by the well-trained EINN model is used as the fitness value of the candidate EIC-NN model. Through the EIC module, the interaction information of the features obtained from the EINN can be utilized to train the EIC-NN model.

4   Experiments and Analysis

4.1   Experiment Setting

In the experimental study, eight benchmark problems are used to test the proposed method, as listed in Table 1. We first compared the proposed EINN with the normal explicit backpropagation neural network (eBPNN) and explicit differential evolution neural network (eDENN), which utilizes DE to tune parameters of the neural network. Our purpose is to check whether the proposed EINN can work better than the existing explicit ANN to fit data with implicit relationships. Each algorithm is performed independently for 20 times on each problem. Besides, the maximum training epochs of the ANN with backpropagation is set to 1000 times; the maximum generation of the ANN with DE is set to 1000.

In the experiment, all ANN models are set as a fully connected neural network with three hidden layers, which are implemented based on keras [6], and the loss functions are MSE. For DE, the population size is 30 and the length of individual vector is equal to the number of parameters of the neural network. The mutation factor F and the crossover factor CR are set to be 0.5 and 0.8, respectively.

Table 1. Eight benchmark problems for testing.

Problem	Category	Target function to generate the dataset	Data set
F_1	Circle	$x^2 + y^2 - 1 = 0$	$x \in U[-1, 1, 1000]$
F_2	Circle	$(x-1)^2 + (y-1)^2 - 1 = 0$	$x \in U[0, 2, 1000]$
F_3	Elliptic	$y^2 - x^3 + x - 1 = 0$	$x \in U[-1.5, 3, 1000]$
F_4	Elliptic	$x^3 + x - y^2 - 1.5 = 0$	$x \in U[0.5, 5, 1000]$
F_5	Hyperbola	$x^2 - y^2 - 1 = 0$	$|x| \in U[1, 3, 1000]$
F_6	Parabolic	$y^2 - 2x - 3 = 0$	$x \in U[0, 1.5, 1000]$
F_7	Sphere	$x^2 + y^2 + z^2 - 1 = 0$	$x \in U[-1, 1, 1000]$
F_8	Sphere	$(x-2)^2 + (y-2)^2 + (z-2)^2 - 4 = 0$	$x \in U[0, 4, 1000]$

$U[a, b, c]$ represents c uniform random samples from a to b.

4.2   Results and Analysis

Table 2 summarizes the average MSE obtained by these three algorithms. It can be observed from the table that, compared with the traditional explicit ANN model, the proposed EINN has obvious advantages in fitting data with implicit relationships. Among these eight benchmark problems, EINN achieved the best fitting errors. In addition, these test problems all have many-to-many relationship mapping between variables. The contradiction between these data makes the explicit neural network unable to converge under sufficient training epochs or evolutionary generations. In contrast, EINN converges on all test problems, which proves the effectiveness of the proposed EINN.

Table 2. Comparsion of MSE results of eBPNN, eDENN and EINN.

Algorithm	F_1	F_2	F_3	F_4	F_5	F_6	F_7	F_8
eBPNN	0.6427	0.6598	4.8800	40.9501	3.2939	4.4271	0.3195	1.2538
eDENN	0.6434	0.6587	4.7371	40.8808	3.3086	4.4182	0.3254	1.3098
EINN	3.05e−06	6.05e−06	0	0	4.650e−06	1.825e−05	3.8e−06	1.56e−05

For implicit relationships similar to the case of many-to-many mapping among variables or multi-dimensional closed surfaces, the traditional MSE evaluation can no longer be an appropriate measure metric. Therefore, we use scatter plots as another metric. To intuitively show the fitting situation, we draw a scatter diagram of the data predicted by the EIC-NN, and compare it with the training data to analyze the fitting distribution.

Figure 3 lists some scatter diagram examples of the prediction output of eDENN, eBPNN and EIC-NN obtained in training on different test problems. Among them, the black scattered points in the figure represent the original training data. On the whole, the fitting accuracy of the EIC-NN is significantly higher than that of other simple explicit regression ANN models. Because there is a common situation in the training data that one independent variable corresponds to multiple dependent variables, this makes it impossible for eDENN and eBPNN to take into account multiple convergence trends at the same time, and finally can only search for a compromise position. As shown in Fig. 3(a) (c) (d) (e) (f), most of the predicted values of eDENN and eBPNN are distributed between the target models and cannot converge at all. It can be seen from the figure that these test problems mainly have two data distribution curves. The proposed EIC-NN can fit some of the local distributions well (Fig. 3(a) (c) (e)), and even in some examples, it can perfectly fit one of the complete data curve (e.g., Fig. 3(f)). With the aid of a well-trained EINN model, the distribution of the predicted value of the EIC-NN is obviously more consistent with the data distribution of the target model. On the other hand, under the guidance of MSE metric, eBPNN and eDENN tends to be a compromise optimization, and can not guide the fitting of many-to-many mapping relationship in implicit regression.

194   Z. Miao et al.

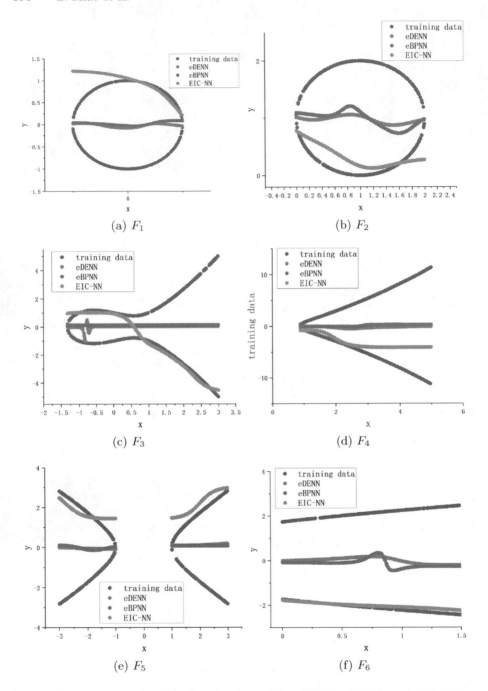

Fig. 3. The scatter plots of predicted values of the eBPNN, eDENN and EIC-NN on
(a) F_1, (b) F_2, (c) F_3, (d) F_4, (e) F_5, (f) F_6.

5   Conclusion

In this paper, an implicit neural network framework is proposed for implicit data regression problems. The key idea is to construct an implicit ANN model with the CL-FEM verification, and then employ it to assist the evolution of explicit ANN model. The experimental results show that the INN framework is efficient to train an implicit network which can capture the implicit relationships of the variables. In future work, the proposed INN framework will be applied to some practical industrial applications to further test its feasibility.

Acknowledgments. This work is supported by the National Natural Science Foundation of China (Grant No. 62076098), the Program for Guangdong Introducing Innovative and Entrepreneurial Teams (Grant No.: 2017ZT07X183), the Guangdong Provincial Key Laboratory (Grant No. 2020B121201001), and the Stable Support Plan Program of Shenzhen Natural Science Fund (Grant No. 20200925154942002).

References

1. Abiodun, O.I., Jantan, A., Omolara, A.E., Dada, K.V., Mohamed, N.A., Arshad, H.: State-of-the-art in artificial neural network applications: a survey. Heliyon **4**(11), e00938 (2018)
2. Sateesh Babu, G., Zhao, P., Li, X.-L.: Deep convolutional neural network based regression approach for estimation of remaining useful life. In: Navathe, S.B., Wu, W., Shekhar, S., Du, X., Wang, X.S., Xiong, H. (eds.) DASFAA 2016. LNCS, vol. 9642, pp. 214–228. Springer, Cham (2016). https://doi.org/10.1007/978-3-319-32025-0_14
3. Besseris, G.J.: Taguchi-generalized regression neural network micro-screening for physical and sensory characteristics of bread. Heliyon **4**(3), e00551 (2018)
4. Chen, Y., Zhong, J., Tan, M.: Comprehensive learning gene expression programming for automatic implicit equation discovery. In: Shi, Y., et al. (eds.) ICCS 2018. LNCS, vol. 10860, pp. 114–128. Springer, Cham (2018). https://doi.org/10.1007/978-3-319-93698-7_9
5. Li, H.z., Guo, S., Li, C.j., Sun, J.q.: A hybrid annual power load forecasting model based on generalized regression neural network with fruit fly optimization algorithm. Knowl.-Based Syst. **37**, 378–387 (2013)
6. O'Malley, T., et al.: Keras tuner (2019). https://github.com/keras-team/keras-tuner
7. Schmidt, M., Lipson, H.: Symbolic regression of implicit equations. In: Riolo, R., O'Reilly, U.M., McConaghy, T. (eds.) Genetic Programming Theory and Practice VII. GEVO, pp. 73–85. Springer, Boston (2010). https://doi.org/10.1007/978-1-4419-1626-6_5
8. Shi, B., Bai, X., Liu, W., Wang, J.: Deep regression for face alignment. arXiv preprint arXiv:1409.5230 (2014)
9. Storn, R., Price, K.: Differential evolution-a simple and efficient heuristic for global optimization over continuous spaces. J. Global Optim. **11**(4), 341–359 (1997)
10. Zhong, J., Yang, J., Chen, Y., Liu, W.L., Feng, L.: Mining implicit equations from data using gene expression programming. IEEE Trans. Emerg. Top. Comput. (2021). https://doi.org/10.1109/TETC.2021.3068651

Missing Glow Phenomenon: Learning Disentangled Representation of Missing Data

Marcin Sendera(✉) ⓘ, Łukasz Struski ⓘ, and Przemysław Spurek ⓘ

Faculty of Mathematics and Computer Science, Jagiellonian University,
Kraków, Poland
{marcin.sendera,Przemyslaw.Spurek}@ii.uj.edu.pl,
lukasz.struski@uj.edu.pl

Abstract. Learning from incomplete data has been recognized as one of the fundamental challenges in deep learning. There are many more or less complicated methods for processing missing data by neural networks in the literature. In this paper, we show that flow-based generative models can work directly on images with missing data to produce full images without missing parts. We name this behavior Missing Glow Phenomenon. We present experiments that document such behaviors and propose theoretical justification of such phenomena.

Keywords: Generative models · Normalizing flows · Glow · Disentanglement · Missing data

1 Introduction

Missing data is a widespread problem in real-life machine learning challenges [5]. A typical strategy for working with incomplete inputs relies on filling absent attributes based on observable ones [14], which is the mean imputation. Another possible solution is to replace the typical neuron's response in the first hidden layer by its expected value [20]. All of the existing methods use a more or less complicated mechanism to solve the above problems. In generative models [22, 23], we have the same problem. To produce full images without missing parts, we have to use an analogical solution like the classification task.

This paper shows that flow-based generative models like Glow [8] can work directly on images with missing data to produce full images without missing parts.
We name this behavior Missing Glow Phenomenon.

The above phenomenon is obtained by producing a disentangled representation in latent space. During the training procedure, the model simultaneously creates representations of objects with missing parts and full images. The above factors are independent, and therefore we can sample from two separated areas

T. Mantoro et al. (Eds.): ICONIP 2021, CCIS 1516, pp. 196–204, 2021.
https://doi.org/10.1007/978-3-030-92307-5_23

of latent space to produce full images and items with missing parts. The behavior is presented in Fig. 1. We use the original Glow model with sampling temperature $t = 0.7$, for which we should expect to appear about 60% of full images as shown in Table 1.

Fig. 1. Missing Glow Phenomenon. Glow was trained on a missing dataset and then sampled with temperature $t = 0.7$ (standard temperature for Glow), which gives about 60% of the full images.

The proposed approach's main advantage is the ability to train a neural network on datasets containing incomplete samples to produce a generative model on full images (the model does not see any full images during training). This approach distinguishes it from recent models like denoising autoencoder [22] or modified generative adversarial network [23], which require complete data as an input of the network in training.

In the paper, we show experiments that describe Missing Glow Phenomenon (see Sect. 3) and present the theoretical explanation of such behaviors (see Sect. 4).

2   Related Works

There is a rich literature on handling missing values [11]. Theoretical guarantees of estimation strategies or imputation methods rely on assumptions regarding the missing-data mechanism, i.e., the cause of the lack of data. There are three mechanisms for the formation of missing data. Missing Completely At Random (MCAR) if the probability of being missing is the same for all observations. Missing At Random (MAR) if the probability of being missing only depends on observed values, and the last Missing Not At Random (MNAR) if the unavailability of the data depends on both observed and unobserved data such as its value itself.

A classical approach to estimating parameters with missing values consists of maximizing the observed likelihood, using, for instance, an Expectation - Maximization algorithm [3]. One of its main drawbacks is to rely on strong parametric assumptions for the distributions of the covariates. Another popular strategy to fix the missing values issue is predicting the missing values based on observable ones, e.g., mean or k-NN imputation. One can also train separate models, e.g., neural networks [18], extreme learning machines (ELM) [21], k-nearest neighbors [1].

In [17], the appropriateness of ignoring the missing process when approach likelihood-based or Bayesian inference was introduced and formalized. Under certain assumptions on the missing mechanism, we can build a probabilistic model of incomplete data, which is subsequently fed into a particular learning model [19].

A body of research on deep frameworks that can learn from partially observed data has emerged in recent years. Initial work focused on extensions of generative models such as Variational Auto Encoders (VAEs) [9] and Generative Adversarial Networks (GANs) [6]. In [24] used generative adversarial net (GAN) to fill in absent attributes with realistic values. In [7] was proposed the supervised imputation, which learns a replacement value for each missing attribute jointly with the remaining network parameters. This group also includes models such as the Missing Data Importance-Weighted Autoencoder (MIWAE) [13] and the Generative Adversarial Imputation Network (GAIN) [25]. More recently, the state-of-the-art benchmark on learning from incomplete data has been pushed by bidirectional generative frameworks, which leverage the ability to map back and forth between the data space and the latent space. Two such examples include the Monte-Carlo Flow model (MCFlow) [16] and the Partial Bidirectional GAN (PBiGAN) [10].

Fig. 2. Reconstructed images for 20×20 missing dataset. Parameter α is a scaling factor of original images' representations in a latent space. For $\alpha = 1.0$, we have an original missing image.

3   Experiments

3.1   Missing Dataset

For the purpose of the experiments, we construct a special dataset with missings, based on a CelebA - a large-scale dataset with more than 200K celebrities' images annotated with about 40 attributes [12]. We resize each of the images into 64×64 pixels size and impute a grey square box, which is a missing part of an image, as shown in Fig. 1 (left image). The missing squares are placed at the beginning of the training, and their locations come from the uniform distribution. Thus, the model always sees each of the original images with the square in the same position. We used different sizes of missing squares in the following experiments - from 2×2 up to 20×20 pixels. Note that the small missing square (e.g. 2×2 or 4×4) could be seen as an attribute by a model. Whereas images with the missing squares larger than 20×20 are, in fact, too corrupted to recreate.

3.2   Glow Model Architecture

Normalizing Flows. Across many areas of research in the field of deep learning, generative models are perhaps one of the most popular. However, besides the well-known Generative Adversarial Networks (GAN) [6] and Variational Autoencoders (VAE) [9], there is another group of generative models becoming popular - Normalizing Flows (NF) [15]. The main idea standing for Normalizing Flows is to transform a simple prior distribution $P(Z)$ (e.g., Gaussian one) defined on the latent space Z into a complex one in the original space, represented by data distribution X. It could be done by stacking together the series of n invertible mappings: $f_1, \ldots, f_n : Z \to X$. The probability distribution of the final target variable is obtained by flowing through the following chain of transformations:

$$x = F(z) = f_n \circ f_{n-1} \circ \cdots \circ f_1(z).$$

Moreover, for Normalizing Flows models, the log-probability density of the output variable is given by the change of variables formula:

$$\log P(x) = \log P(z) - \sum_{k=1}^{n} \log \left| \det \frac{\partial f_k}{\partial z_{k-1}} \right|,$$

where the usage of inverse flow with its form:

$$z = f_1^{-1} \circ f_2^{-1} \circ \cdots \circ f_n^{-1}(x),$$

allows for computing z from x.

In the general framework of Normalizing Flows, the main challenge is to design intermediate layers f_i in such a way to assure that both inverse map and the Jacobian are easily computable. In the case of *continuous* data x, the Continuous Normalizing Flows [2] are the extensions of the described *discrete* approach. In this setting, we allow the mappings to be defined by a solution to a differential equation $\frac{\partial z(t)}{\partial t} = f(z(t), t)$, and f could be a neural network of unrestricted architecture. The most fundamental advantage of the discrete and continuous Normalizing Flows is that we are not restricted to any specific class of functions, e.g., Gaussian densities. Moreover, unlike GANs and VAEs, the Normalizing Flows models learn the original data distribution explicitly and are able to describe densities of high dimensional images [8].

Glow Model. In order to process the missing dataset properly, we use a powerful flow-based model - Glow [8], where invertible 1×1 convolutions assure invertibility. Glow is known for its competitive results among other Normalizing Flow models, e.g., RealNVP [4], on describing the densities of high dimensional image data.

The Glow model consists of a series of flow steps. However, each of its flow steps could be divided into the following three substeps:

1. **Activation normalization (actnorm)**, for performing an affine transformation of the activations using a scale and bias parameter per channel;
2. **Invertible 1×1 convolution**, which is a generalization of a permutation operation;
3. **Affine coupling layer**, designed in the same way as in RealNVP [4].

For all of our experiments, we use the same standard Glow architecture with the following hyperparameters: 4 blocks, 32 flows in each block, 5 bits, and 3 input channels.

3.3   Imputing Missings

We learned a Glow model on a specific missing dataset for each of the missing squares' sizes. In our setting, we use batch size 16 and 200k iterations. After training, we process the data follow the procedure: (1) take image x from missing dataset; (2) create its latent representation z with Glow by the embedding: $z = \Phi(x)$, where $\Phi : \mathbb{R}^N \to \mathbb{R}^N$; (3) move along the vector z in a latent space by multiplying it by the parameter α. For $\alpha \in (0.0, 1.0]$ create a vector $z' = \alpha z$; (4) reconstruct imputed image x' by the operation $x' = \Phi^{-1}(z')$, which is the same as $x' = \Phi^{-1}(\alpha z)$ for $\alpha \in (0.0, 1.0]$.

Fig. 3. Images sampled from Glow with the temperatures $t = 0.5$, $t = 0.6$, and $t = 0.7$ (from top to bottom) - in these regions of the latent space, Glow put good faces with a small number of missing squares.

We present the partial results for the missing dataset with 20×20 missing boxes in Fig. 2. Glow model was trained for 200k iterations, and we reconstruct the images by multiplying latent representations by parameter $\alpha \in \{0.1, 0.2, \ldots, 1.0\}$. However, for parameter α in range $(0.5, 0.7)$, the reconstruction is actually an original image with an imputed missing part.

3.4   Sampling from a Latent Representation

All the previously introduced experiments were initial parts for sampling images from Glow's latent space with a specific temperature t.

We observe various behaviors in different parts of latent space. As shown in Fig. 3, the images sampled with a temperature $t \in (0.5, 0.7)$ are characterized by faces similar to the original ones with a relatively small number of missing squares. On the other hand, Glow samples fuzzy images, full of missing regions, when taking the temperatures $t \geq 1.0$ (Fig. 4).

Fig. 4. Exemplary images sampled with the temperatures $t = 1.0$ (top image) and $t = 1.2$ (bottom image). We observe that images in this region are fuzzy and with a large number of missing boxes.

4   Theoretical Studies

In this section, we are going to explain the Missing Glow Phenomenon showed in the experiments. Firstly, we introduce the theoretical justification, and then, we provide its ablation study.

4.1   Theoretical Explanation

Let us recall that to sample from temperature t, we sample z in the latent and return $\Phi^{-1}(tz)$.

For intuition, consider the case when the data comes from the normal distribution $N(0, \Sigma)$, and then the flow can be chosen to be a linear function. Then by sampling from temperature t, we sample, in fact, from the normal density $N(0, t^2 \Sigma)$. Consequently, for t going to zero, we sample from the data with covariance converging to zero, while increasing t leads to the covariance increase. Moreover, if $\mathbb{X} \sim N(0, \Sigma)$, then to sample from the temperature $t = \sqrt{l}$, we can sample $X_1, \ldots, X_l$ independently and return $X_1 + \ldots + X_l$. The last follows from the fact that the covariance of the sum of independent random variables is the sum of their covariances.

Table 1. Distribution of the number of missing squares when sampling with a specific temperature. We provide both empirical and theoretical expected values $\mathbb{E}$.

Temperature t	0.1	0.2	0.3	0.4	0.5	0.6	0.7	0.8	0.9	1.0	1.1	1.2	1.3	1.4	1.5
Frequency(%)															
0 squares	100	100	100	98	92	70	64	56	50	42	30	30	24	22	22
1 square	0	0	0	2	8	26	30	34	38	44	54	44	46	46	44
2 squares	0	0	0	0	0	4	6	10	12	10	10	18	22	24	24
3 squares	0	0	0	0	0	0	0	0	0	4	4	4	4	4	6
4 squares	0	0	0	0	0	0	0	0	0	0	2	4	4	4	4
Number of missing squares in the reconstruction image															
Empirical $\mathbb{E}$	0.00	0.00	0.00	0.02	0.08	0.34	0.42	0.54	0.62	0.76	0.94	1.08	1.18	1.22	1.26
Theoretical $\mathbb{E}$	0.01	0.04	0.09	0.16	0.25	0.36	0.49	0.64	0.81	1.00	1.21	1.44	1.69	1.96	2.25

So let us now continue our discussion in the case when the data is an independent sum of two Gaussian variables. Assume that the random vector $\mathbb{X}$ generating the data can be decomposed into the sum of independent Gaussian random vectors: $\mathbb{X} = \mathbb{V} + \mathbb{W}$. Then sampling from $\mathbb{X}$ with temperature t is equivalent to sampling from $\mathbb{V}$ and $\mathbb{W}$ with temperature t.

Let us now try to interpret the above in the case of our experiment. Then $\mathbb{X}$ denotes the random vector, which selects an image and then changes color to gray at the randomly chosen square of size $K \times K$. Thus we can interpret our model as the independent composition of two operations:

- $\mathbb{V}$: sampling a random image from our original dataset,
- $\mathbb{W}$: changing the color of the randomly chosen square of size $K \times K$ to gray.

Then sampling from $\mathbb{V}$ with temperature $t = \sqrt{2}$ is easy, as we simply sample two images, add their latent representations, and process back to input space.

However, a crucial role is played by the operation $\mathbb{W}$. By applying the above reasoning informally, we obtain that for covariance $t\mathrm{Cov}\mathbb{W}$, where $t = \sqrt{l}$, we obtain t^2 times randomly covering by squares of $K \times K$. Extrapolating this formula for all t, we obtain the theoretical value for the expected number of squares

$$\mathbb{E}(\text{number of missing squares} \mid \text{random sample from temperature } t) = t^2.$$

For verification, we compare this with the values obtained in the experiments.

4.2   Ablation Study

Moreover, we provide an ablation study for the expected number of missing squares when sampling with a set temperature t and compare the results to the theoretical results. We sampled a set of 50 images for each of the temperatures and manually calculated the number of missing squares. Then, we calculated empirical expected values

$$\mathbb{E}(\text{number of missing squares} \mid \text{random sample from temperature } t)$$

and compared them to the theoretical ones.

As shown in Table 1, the empirical expected number of missing squares is much different from theoretical numbers. The reason for these dissimilarities is the fact that Glow models are weak and imperfect learners. Moreover, we suppose that Glow's restriction on the rigid representation could cause such differences. However, we noticed similar expected numbers of missing squares for the sampling temperature $t = 0.7$, which is the original Glow model [8], which suggests that for such t, Glow fulfills its theoretical properties.

5   Conclusion

In this paper, we show that flow-based generative models like Glow [8] can be trained on images with missing data and produce full images without missing parts. The above phenomenon is obtained by producing a disentangled representation in latent space. During the training procedure, the model simultaneously creates representations of objects with missing parts and full images. The above factors are independent, and therefore we can sample from two separated areas of latent to produce full images and items with missing parts.

References

1. Batista, G.E., Monard, M.C., et al.: A study of k-nearest neighbour as an imputation method. In: HIS, vol. 87, pp. 251–260 (2002)
2. Chen, R.T., Rubanova, Y., Bettencourt, J., Duvenaud, D.: Neural ordinary differential equations. arXiv preprint arXiv:1806.07366 (2018)
3. Dempster, A.P., Laird, N.M., Rubin, D.B.: Maximum likelihood from incomplete data via the EM algorithm. J. Roy. Stat. Soc. Ser. B (Methodol.) **39**(1), 1–22 (1977)
4. Dinh, L., Sohl-Dickstein, J., Bengio, S.: Density estimation using real NVP. arXiv preprint arXiv:1605.08803 (2016)
5. Goodfellow, I., Bengio, Y., Courville, A., Bengio, Y.: Deep Learning, vol. 1. MIT Press (2016)
6. Goodfellow, I.J., et al.: Generative adversarial networks. arXiv preprint arXiv:1406.2661 (2014)
7. Gupta, M., et al.: Monotonic calibrated interpolated look-up tables. J. Mach. Learn. Res. **17**(1), 3790–3836 (2016)
8. Kingma, D.P., Dhariwal, P.: Glow: generative flow with invertible 1×1 convolutions. arXiv preprint arXiv:1807.03039 (2018)
9. Kingma, D.P., Welling, M.: Auto-encoding variational Bayes. arXiv preprint arXiv:1312.6114 (2013)
10. Li, S.C.X., Marlin, B.: Learning from irregularly-sampled time series: a missing data perspective. In: International Conference on Machine Learning, pp. 5937–5946. PMLR (2020)
11. Little, R.J., Rubin, D.B.: Statistical Analysis with Missing Data, vol. 793. Wiley, Hoboken (2019)
12. Liu, Z., Luo, P., Wang, X., Tang, X.: Deep learning face attributes in the wild. In: Proceedings of the IEEE International Conference on Computer Vision, pp. 3730–3738 (2015)

13. Mattei, P.A., Frellsen, J.: MIWAE: deep generative modelling and imputation of incomplete data sets. In: International Conference on Machine Learning, pp. 4413–4423. PMLR (2019)
14. McKnight, P.E., McKnight, K.M., Sidani, S., Figueredo, A.J.: Missing Data: A Gentle Introduction. Guilford Press (2007)
15. Rezende, D., Mohamed, S.: Variational inference with normalizing flows. In: International Conference on Machine Learning, pp. 1530–1538. PMLR (2015)
16. Richardson, T.W., Wu, W., Lin, L., Xu, B., Bernal, E.A.: MCFlow: Monte Carlo flow models for data imputation. In: Proceedings of the IEEE/CVF Conference on Computer Vision and Pattern Recognition, pp. 14205–14214 (2020)
17. Rubin, D.B.: Inference and missing data. Biometrika **63**(3), 581–592 (1976)
18. Sharpe, P.K., Solly, R.: Dealing with missing values in neural network-based diagnostic systems. Neural Comput. Appl. **3**(2), 73–77 (1995)
19. Śmieja, M., Struski, Ł, Tabor, J., Marzec, M.: Generalized RBF kernel for incomplete data. Knowl. Based Syst. **173**, 150–162 (2019)
20. Smieja, M., Struski, Ł., Tabor, J., Zieliński, B., Spurek, P.: Processing of missing data by neural networks. In: Proceedings of the 32nd International Conference on Neural Information Processing Systems, pp. 2724–2734 (2018)
21. Sovilj, D., et al.: Extreme learning machine for missing data using multiple imputations. Neurocomputing **174**, 220–231 (2016)
22. Xie, J., Xu, L., Chen, E.: Image denoising and inpainting with deep neural networks. Adv. Neural. Inf. Process. Syst. **25**, 341–349 (2012)
23. Yeh, R.A., Chen, C., Yian Lim, T., Schwing, A.G., Hasegawa-Johnson, M., Do, M.N.: Semantic image inpainting with deep generative models. In: Proceedings of the IEEE Conference on Computer Vision and Pattern Recognition, pp. 5485–5493 (2017)
24. Yoon, J., Jordon, J., Schaar, M.: GAIN: missing data imputation using generative adversarial nets. In: International Conference on Machine Learning, pp. 5689–5698. PMLR (2018)
25. Zhang, Y., Zheng, Z., Hu, R.: Super resolution using segmentation-prior self-attention generative adversarial network. arXiv preprint arXiv:2003.03489 (2020)

A Novel Deep Reinforcement Learning Framework for Stock Portfolio Optimization

Shaobo Hu[1], Hongying Zheng[2], and Jianyong Chen[1(✉)]

[1] College of Computer Science and Software Engineering, Shenzhen University,
Shenzhen 518060, Guangdong, China
jychen@szu.edu.cn
[2] Sino-German Robotics School, Shenzhen Institute of Technology Information,
Shenzhen 518060, Guangdong, China

Abstract. Deep reinforcement learning (DRL) is a recently concerned research field for stock portfolio optimization. The existing solutions face various challenge. In this paper, we propose a DRL framework to the stock portfolio optimization problem, which mainly includes the following three contributions: 1) We propose an Over-fitting Prevention Objective Function (OPOF) to avoid over-fitting in the training process. 2) An algorithm called Batch-Forward Recurrent Reinforcement Learning (BFRRL) is proposed to improve the stability of the training process. 3) A neural network called Multi Times Scale Transformer (MTS-Trans) is proposed to enhance stock series local feature extraction ability in multiple time scales. Compared with the current SOTA algorithm, our approach improves returns by 63% in the Chinese stock market and 138% in the U.S. stock market, while the strategy's risk is also reduced.

Keywords: Deep reinforcement learning · Portfolio optimization · Stock price

1 Introduction

The study of portfolio optimization is important to investors, who can regroup and diversify their investments according to their target returns and their risk tolerance level [5,9]. Traditional portfolio optimization is mainly based on analytical methods which performance in practice is not as good as deep learning. Researchers have proposed many deep neural networks for stock market prediction. Temporal Convolution Network (TCN) [1] is a kind of neural network that mainly uses dilated causal convolution to process time series, it can process long series data very fast, and it can alleviate gradient disappearance and gradient explosion. The TCN based Stock2Vec model proposed by Wang et al. [14], the performance of the model significantly exceeds LSTM and ordinary convolutional neural networks. Transformer is proposed in 2017 [13]. By using the attention

© Springer Nature Switzerland AG 2021
T. Mantoro et al. (Eds.): ICONIP 2021, CCIS 1516, pp. 205–212, 2021.
https://doi.org/10.1007/978-3-030-92307-5_24

mechanism, Transformer is considered to learn dynamic global context information in long-span sequences, which has been widely used in natural language processing and computer vision. In 2020, Lim et al. [8] proposed a multi-variable time series prediction network combining LSTM and attention mechanism, which uses LSTM to process the local features of the sequence and attention mechanism to process the global features, and achieves better results in multiple time series tasks. However, there are two defects in using the deep learning method for Portfolio Optimization: 1) It may fall into local optimal solution. 2) It is independent of transaction path and thus can not optimize the transaction cost. Deep reinforcement learning can solve the above problems because it models the whole transaction process as a Markov decision process. In the continuous trading with the market, the policy neural network gradually learns each time step's optimal (or near-optimal) decision. DQN [10] algorithm was first applied in portfolio optimization by Jin et al. [4] in 2016. However, it only supports discrete action space which is not flexible enough. Therefore, many researchers proposes various Actor-Critic Category algorithms (e.g., DDPG [6,7,16] and SAC [2]) to support continuous action space. However, in practice, it is found that the Actor-Critic algorithms are poor in training stability [7]. There is also a reinforcement learning method using only one actor model – Recurrent Reinforcement Learning (RRL) [11]. This method has both continuous action space and stable training. In 2017, Jiang et al. proposed Online Stochastic Batch Learning (OSBL) [3] with better performance than both CNN and LSTM. In 2020, Relation-Aware Transformer (RAT) is proposed which also uses OSBL for neural network training [17]. It is the first algorithm to use Transformer for portfolio optimization.

In this paper, we continue to study the deep reinforcement learning algorithm for portfolio optimization with only one actor model and propose the following contributions: 1) To avoid over-fitting, we add a penalty term to the original objective function to control the degree of investment diversification. 2) To solve the problem of instability and local optimization, we propose a new training algorithm called BFRRL. 3) To enhance the ability of the transformer to extract local features of stock price series data, we propose an MTS-Trans neural network which can effectively extract local features of stock price data at different time scales.

2   Method

The framework proposed in this paper is shown in Fig. 1. At the beginning of the training, we sample the historical stock price and the corresponding future stock price from the training set. Then, MTS-Trans neural network receives historical stock price and outputs trading strategy. And then, OPOF scores the historical performance of the trading strategy according to the future stock price. Finally, we update the MTS-Trans by back-propagation to maximize the OPOF. After many updates, the output strategy of MTS-Trans is closer and closer to the optimal strategy until it finally converges.

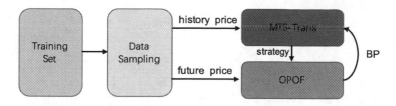

Fig. 1. The framework.

OPOF is defined as follows:

$$R_n = \log\left(\mu_n y_n \cdot w_n - I_n - 1\right) - \lambda \max_i w_{i,n} \tag{1}$$

R_n is the reward on the nth day. $\log\left(\mu_n y_n \cdot w_n - I_n - 1\right)$ is the logarithmic return on day n after taking into account transaction costs and short sale interest. μ_n is the transaction remainder factor, representing the proportion of total assets left over due to transaction costs. y_n is the price relative sequence, representing the increase in closing price over the next trading period. I_n is the interest generated on the nth day due to the leased stock. $-\lambda \max_i w_{i,n}$ is the penalty term we use to control investment diversification, which is negatively correlated with the maximum daily investment target weight. λ is the hyperparameter used to control the level of penalty.

This section introduces the training algorithm of our strategy of BFRRL. Comparing with the previous training method, there are three significant improvements: 1) In the data sampling stage, we design a batch dimension, and each training will extract B consecutive T-day training data, which brings two benefits: A. Due to multiple batch dimensions, the algorithm can avoid the gradient noise and be more stable. B. Concurrency and speed of the algorithm can be improved by adding a batch dimension. 2) The algorithm can reduce the transaction cost and short selling interest. Moreover, gradient truncation is used in the back-propagation stage to avoid slow calculation speed of the neural network and disappearance of gradient explosion/gradient. 3) We use Gaussian noise to generate a random initial portfolio weight vector, which improves diversity of the trading paths and generalisation of the algorithm.

The training process of BFRRL is shown in the Fig. 2. The red line indicates the back-propagation path.

The formula of random initialization of portfolio weight is as follows:

$$
\begin{aligned}
z_1 &\sim \mathcal{N}\left(\mu, \sigma^2\right) \\
z_2 &\sim \mathcal{N}\left(\mu, \sigma^2\right) \\
w_0 = 2 * \operatorname{softmax}\left(z_1\right) &- \operatorname{softmax}\left(z_2\right)
\end{aligned} \tag{2}
$$

w_0 is the initial portfolio weight vector. The sum of the vector is 1. The value range of each element is $[-1, 2]$ (negative number means short-selling).

The architecture of MTS-Trans is shown in Fig. 3, which mainly includes four parts: 1) Concatenate Temporal Convolution Network (CTCN). CTCN is

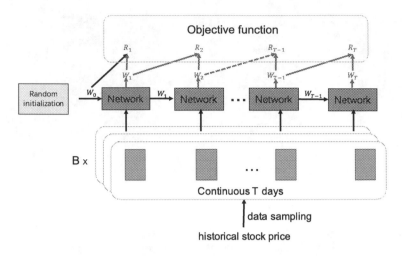

Fig. 2. Batch-Forward recurrent reinforcement learning.

used to generate local features of multiple time scales. 2) Encoder. Mainly based on attention mechanism, processes dynamic global context information in stock price series. 3) Decoder. It summarizes the current market situation according to the encoder's output and short-term historical stock price. 4) Decision making. According to the current market status (outputs by the decoder) and the previous trading day's portfolio weight, output the current transaction's target portfolio weight.

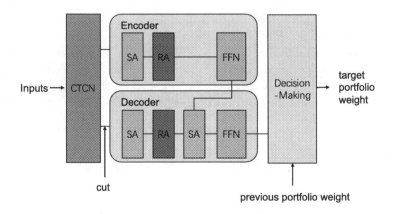

Fig. 3. MTS-Trans architecture.

The structure of CTCN is shown in Fig. 4, which is composed of multiple CTCN-Blocks in series. In order to reduce the performance impact of the neural network due to too many layers, we add skip-connection to each Block. Moreover, due to the noise of stock data is very large, we add a Layer-Norm layer before the activation layer to normalize the feature dimension, making the neural network more stable in training. The output of each Block contains local features of a specific time scale. After concatenated and linear combination, the final outputs contains local features of multiple time scales.

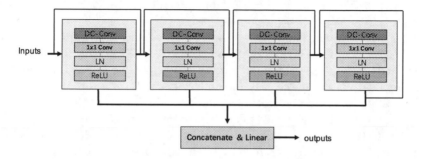

Fig. 4. The detail of CTCN.

The internal structure of encoder and decoder is similar. SA (Self-Attention) uses the attention mechanism to deal with the global dynamic context in time dimension. RA (Relation-aware-Attention) was proposed by RAT [17] which uses the attention mechanism to extract the relationship between different stocks. FFN refers to Feed-Forward Network [13].

The decision-making module follows the structure of RAT.

3   Experimental Setup

In order to verify the generalization of the algorithm in different markets, we select 8 stocks in Shanghai Stock Exchange 50 and 64 stocks in NASDAQ 100. We use the flat fake price-movement method [3] to filling the missing data. The detailed statistical information of the dataset is in Table 1:

Table 1. The detailed statistical information of the dataset.

	Number of stock	Training data	Testing data
SSE50	8	2000-03 to 2016-01	2016-01 to 2019-12
NASDAQ100	64	2000-02 to 2015-12	2015-12 to 2019-12

Each day, we use a fixed-length S historical stock price series (including opening price, highest price, lowest price and closing price) as the input data of each trading day. The ratio of the training set to test set is 8:2.

In order to maintain a stable distribution of the input data in different historical periods, we processed the daily input data. We used the normalized method proposed by Jiang et al. [3]. The main approach is to divide the daily historical stock price tensor by the last day's closing price.

Similar to RAT [17], this paper mainly uses the following three evaluating indicators to evaluate the trading strategy, i.e., APV (Accumulative Portfolio Value), SR (Sharp Ratio) and CR (Calmar Ratio). Details of their definitions can be found in [17].

During training, the daily input data contains 32 days of historical stock price data. There are four identical CTCN blocks in the MTS-Trans. The number of dilated causal Conv model's input and output channels is 30, the number of 1×1 Conv output channels is 10. In the encoder and decoder, two headers are used for attention, and the feature space of each header is 12. The length of the history stock price sequence taken by the decoder is 5. The learning rate is set to 5e−6. In the data-sampling phase, 20 consecutive 10 days were selected for training (b = 20, t = 10) each time. Each experiment is conducted ten times according to different random seeds. The model is trained 25000 times in each experiment, and the final experimental results are taken as the average of ten experiments. All experiments in this paper are run on a single NVIDIA Tesla V100 GPU.

4   Results

Our experiment uses the RAT as the control group (group A). In order to fully compare the impact of each improvement on the algorithm, we set up another four experimental groups, of which three experimental groups are each improvement applied separately (group B, C, D), and one experimental group is of three improvements all applied (group E).

Table 2. Backtest results on SSE50.

	OPOF	BFRRL	MTS-Trans	APV	SR	CR
A	✗	✗	✗	18.37	0.1011	52.63
B	✓	✗	✗	21.88	0.1075	60.42
C	✗	✓	✗	23.14	0.1054	66.56
D	✗	✗	✓	25.86	0.1032	70.78
E	✓	✓	✓	**29.96**	**0.1127**	**70.32**

Tables 2 and 3 show the backtest results for the SSE50 and NASDAQ100 datasets, respectively. It can be seen that experimental groups B, C, and D exceed experimental group A in all evaluation metrics, which indicates that each of our improvements can improve the performance of the algorithm. According to the results of the comparison between experimental group E and experimental

Table 3. Backtest results on NASDAQ100.

	OPOF	BFRRL	MTS-Trans	APV	SR	CR
A	✗	✗	✗	4.53	0.0511	8.02
B	✓	✗	✗	9.88	0.0731	19.96
C	✗	✓	✗	5.97	0.0594	10.97
D	✗	✗	✓	5.03	0.0608	11.28
E	✓	✓	✓	**10.78**	**0.0758**	**22.06**

group A, our method ended up with 63% higher returns than RAT, 11.4% higher Sharpe ratio and 33.6% higher Calmar ratio than RAT. In NASDAQ100, our method achieves a final return 138% higher than RAT, a Sharpe ratio 48.6% higher than RAT, and a Calmar ratio 175% higher than RAT. The experimental results show that our method yields a higher return and a lower risk trading strategy. Moreover, comparing the experimental results of experimental groups B, C, D and E, we can find that the algorithm performance is improved the most when the three improvements are applied simultaneously. Figure 5 shows the change of portfolio value during the backtest, with the horizontal coordinate being the trading days and the vertical coordinate being the current portfolio value.

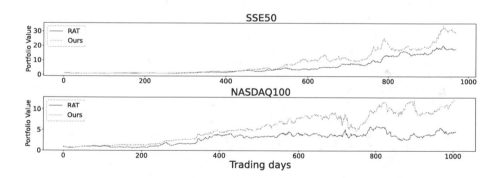

Fig. 5. Change of portfolio value in backtest.

5   Conclusion

This paper proposes a novel solution to the stock portfolio optimization problem, which improves the existing algorithm in three aspects: objective function, training method and neural network model. First of all, we propose the over-fitting prevention objective function, which can effectively prevent the over-fitting phenomenon in the training process. Then, we propose a Batch-Forward Recurrent

Reinforcement Learning algorithm, which improves the concurrency and stability of the algorith. Finally, we propose MTS-trans neural network model. Comparing with the RAT model, the simulations of our approach greatly improve the returns and reduces the risk at the same time.

Acknowledgements. This work was supported in part by the National Nature Science Foundation of China under Grant U2013201 and in part by the Pearl River Talent Plan of Guangdong Province under Grant 2019ZT08X603.

References

1. Bai, S., Kolter, J.Z., Koltun, V.: An empirical evaluation of generic convolutional and recurrent networks for sequence modeling. arXiv preprint arXiv:1803.01271 (2018)
2. Bakshaev, A.: Market-making with reinforcement-learning (SAC). arXiv preprint arXiv:2008.12275 (2020)
3. Jiang, Z., Xu, D., Liang, J.: A deep reinforcement learning framework for the financial portfolio management problem. arXiv preprint arXiv:1706.10059 (2017)
4. Jin, O., El-Saawy, H.: Portfolio management using reinforcement learning. Stanford University (2016)
5. Kelly Jr., J.L.: A new interpretation of information rate. In: The Kelly Capital Growth Investment Criterion: Theory and Practice, pp. 25–34. World Scientific (2011)
6. Li, X., Li, Y., Zhan, Y., Liu, X.Y.: Optimistic bull or pessimistic bear: adaptive deep reinforcement learning for stock portfolio allocation. arXiv preprint arXiv:1907.01503 (2019)
7. Liang, Z., Chen, H., Zhu, J., Jiang, K., Li, Y.: Adversarial deep reinforcement learning in portfolio management. arXiv preprint arXiv:1808.09940 (2018)
8. Lim, B., Arık, S.Ö., Loeff, N., Pfister, T.: Temporal fusion transformers for interpretable multi-horizon time series forecasting. Int. J. Forecast. **37**, 1748–1764 (2021)
9. Markowitz, H.: Portfolio selection. J. Financ. **7**(1), 77–91 (1952)
10. Mnih, V., et al.: Human-level control through deep reinforcement learning. Nature **518**(7540), 529–533 (2015)
11. Moody, J., Wu, L., Liao, Y., Saffell, M.: Performance functions and reinforcement learning for trading systems and portfolios. J. Forecast. **17**(5–6), 441–470 (1998)
12. Mozer, M.C.: A focused back-propagation algorithm for temporal pattern recognition. Complex Syst. **3**(4), 349–381 (1989)
13. Vaswani, A., et al.: Attention is all you need. arXiv preprint arXiv:1706.03762 (2017)
14. Wang, X., Wang, Y., Weng, B., Vinel, A.: Stock2Vec: a hybrid deep learning framework for stock market prediction with representation learning and temporal convolutional network. arXiv preprint arXiv:2010.01197 (2020)
15. Williams, R.J., Zipser, D.: A learning algorithm for continually running fully recurrent neural networks. Neural Comput. **1**(2), 270–280 (1989)
16. Xiong, Z., Liu, X.Y., Zhong, S., Yang, H., Walid, A.: Practical deep reinforcement learning approach for stock trading. arXiv preprint arXiv:1811.07522 (2018)
17. Xu, K., Zhang, Y., Ye, D., Zhao, P., Tan, M.: Relation-aware transformer for portfolio policy learning. In: IJCAI (2020)

Simultaneous Progressive Filtering-Based Monaural Speech Enhancement

Haoran Yin[1], Hao Shi[2], Longbiao Wang[1(✉)], Luya Qiang[1], Sheng Li[3],
Meng Ge[1], Gaoyan Zhang[1(✉)], and Jianwu Dang[1,4]

[1] Tianjin Key Laboratory of Cognitive Computing and Application,
College of Intelligence and Computing, Tianjin University, Tianjin, China
{haoran_yin,longbiao_wang,gaoyan_zhang}@tju.edu.cn
[2] Graduate School of Informatics, Kyoto University, Sakyo-ku, Kyoto, Japan
[3] National Institute of Information and Communications Technology, Kyoto, Japan
[4] Japan Advanced Institute of Science and Technology, Ishikawa, Japan

Abstract. Speech enhancement (SE) benefits from multi-stage stacking. However, this will introduce a lot of new parameters to the neural network. In this paper, we propose a simultaneous progressive filtering-based monaural SE model. Mapping-based and masking-based SE systems are simultaneously obtained with multi-target learning (MTL). Different from other MTL systems, our proposed model addresses different enhancement needs. The mapping-based SE system aims to recover speech signals from noisy features. While the masking-based SE system serves as a post-filtering to further reduce the noise that still exists after the mapping-based SE system. With the high signal-to-noise ratio inputs, noise reduction of the masking-based SE system is obvious with little speech signal loss. These two stages share one neural network which controls the parameters of the entire system with little or no increase. In addition, our approach is easy to integrate with existing methods and improve their performance significantly and stably. The experiments on Valentini-Botinhao data set show our proposed model achieves 0.12 PESQ improvement compared with direct mapping-based and masking-based SE systems both in single-target and multi-target learning.

Keywords: Speech enhancement · Multi-target learning · Simultaneous progressive filtering · Deep learning

1 Introduction

Speech is the main mode of communication of human beings and has a wide range of applications. However, the unavoidable inclusion of a high level of undesirable noise in real scenes considerably reduces the intelligibility and quality of speech and seriously deteriorates performance in speech applications [1]. Speech enhancement (SE) is the major front-processing method for recovering clean

---

H. Shi—Joint first author.

© Springer Nature Switzerland AG 2021
T. Mantoro et al. (Eds.): ICONIP 2021, CCIS 1516, pp. 213–221, 2021.
https://doi.org/10.1007/978-3-030-92307-5_25

speech from noisy speech and an indispensable technique in speech field. Therefore, many researchers are exploring more effective SE systems [2,3].

Deep learning-based methods get an enormous improvement over traditional
methods [4–7], especially in unsteady-state noisy environments [8]. Mapping and
masking are two commonly used learning targets of deep learning-based SE
system. Mapping methods [8–10] use the nonlinear mapping ability of neural
networks to recover clean speech features from noisy features. However, limited
by the capabilities of current DNN models, mapping-enhanced features contain
residual noise. Masking methods [11–13] first learn a mask, and the estimated
mask is multiplied with noisy features to reconstruct enhanced features. As a
ratio mask is used to extract a speech signal from a noisy speech signal during
masking, some speech signals may be lost [13]. Furthermore, some researchers
have observed complementarity between mapping and masking targets in SE
tasks [14,15]. Multi-stage approaches [16,17] outperform single-stage approaches
by completing more than one task during different stages. However, multi-stage
approaches commonly require more parameters and thus, more training time
and computing resources. Although multi-target learning (MTL) with mapping
and masking targets perform well with the complementarities between mapping-
based and masking-based system, it is still hard to further use these two outputs.

In this paper, we propose a simultaneous progressive filtering-based monaural
SE approach to eliminate the shortcomings of the above mentioned approaches.
We get mapping-based and masking-based systems simultaneously with MTL.
First, we use the mapping-based SE system to enhance the original noisy features. The mapping-based SE system keeps the speech information well but there
are still some noise residue. Then we use the masking-based SE system to do the
post-filtering. Difference from previous work, masking-based SE system recover
the output of the mapping-based SE system. Although some masking-based SE
systems lead to the loss of speech signal, the masking-based SE system with
high signal-to-noise ratio inputs has obvious noise reduction and little speech
signal loss. As mapping and masking share a common hidden layer, complementary information is available for both processes. Furthermore, the number
of parameters of our entire system are not increased at all or only by a small
number.

The rest of this paper is organized as follows. Section 2 presents conventional SE methods. Our proposed method is discussed in Sect. 3. Section 4 shows
detailed experiments and results. Section 5 draws conclusions.

2   Conventional SE Methods

The mean squared error (MSE) is a widely used loss function in SE systems. The
MSE loss function of **direct mapping (DM)** method is represented as follows:

$$\mathcal{L}_{DM} = \frac{1}{TF} \sum |||\widetilde{X}_{DM}| - |X|||_F^2 \tag{1}$$

$\mathcal{L}_{DM}$ is the loss for the DM approach. $|\widetilde{X}_{DM}|$ and $|X|$ denote the mapping-
estimated spectrogram and the reference clean spectrogram respectively.

Signal approximation (SA) is an effective masking technique. SA trains a ratio mask [11] to approximate the spectrogram of clean speech using the product of the estimated mask and the noisy spectrogram, where the MSE loss function for the SA method is represented as follows:

$$\mathcal{L}_{SA} = \frac{1}{TF} \sum ||\widetilde{M} \odot |Y| - |X|||_F^2 = \frac{1}{TF} \sum |||\widetilde{X}_{SA}| - |X|||_F^2 \qquad (2)$$

where $|Y|$ denotes the noisy speech spectrogram and $|\widetilde{X}_{SA}|$ denotes the masking-enhanced spectrogram. $\odot$ denotes point-wise matrix multiplication. $\mathcal{L}_{SA}$ denotes the loss for the SA approach and $\widetilde{M}$ denotes the estimated mask.

The principle of **multi-target learning (MTL)** is to learn different targets in one model. Complementary learning targets result in enhanced performance of all outputs. Therefore, MTL can be used to tarin mapping and masking targets. The MTL loss function is represented as follows:

$$\mathcal{L}_{MTL} = \alpha \mathcal{L}_{DM} + (1 - \alpha)\mathcal{L}_{SA} \qquad (3)$$

$\mathcal{L}_{MTL}$ is the loss for the MTL method. α is the weight coefficient of the two MSE target items. The MTL-based SE flowchart is shown in Fig. 1(a).

3   Simultaneous Progressive Filtering

Simultaneous progressive filtering (SPF) contains two modules: mapping-based pre-filtering and masking-based post-filtering modules. The mapping-based pre-filtering module aims to recover speech signal from noisy features and obtain the high SNR pre-enhanced spectrogram. While the masking-based post-filtering module further reduces the noise that still exists in the pre-enhanced spectrogram. With the high SNR inputs, noise reduction of the masking-based post-filtering module is obvious with little speech signal loss.

3.1   Mapping-Based Pre-filtering Module

The pre-filtering module maps the noisy magnitude spectrogram to the pre-enhanced spectrogram to preserve the clean speech signals and increase the SNR of the spectrogram. We use a mapping target to train this module. The loss function of the pre-filtering module is calculated in the same way as $\mathcal{L}_{DM}$. However, we use a different symbol, $\mathcal{L}_{pre}$, to represent the loss function of this module, which is given as follows:

$$\mathcal{L}_{pre} = \frac{1}{TF} \sum |||\widetilde{X}_{pre}| - |X|||_F^2 \qquad (4)$$

where $\mathcal{L}_{pre}$ is the loss of the pre-filtering module. $|\widetilde{X}_{pre}|$ is the enhanced spectrogram of the pre-filtering module.

3.2   Masking-Based Post-filtering Module

The post-filtering module reduces the residual noise of pre-filtering enhanced spectrogram and is trained using the masking target. The use of masking targets may result in the loss of clean speech signals but greatly reduces noise. As using the pre-filtering enhanced spectrogram as the input to the post-filtering module considerably increases the SNR over that of the original noisy spectrogram, the masking target that we used dose not cause serious speech distortion and enhances performance. The loss function of this module $\mathcal{L}_{post}$ is given as follows:

$$\mathcal{L}_{post} = \frac{1}{TF} \sum || \widetilde{M} \odot |\tilde{X}_{pre}| - |X| ||_F^2 = \frac{1}{TF} \sum |||\tilde{X}_{post}| - |X| ||_F^2 \quad (5)$$

where $\widetilde{M}$ is the estimated mask of the post-filtering module. $|\tilde{X}_{post}|$ is the output spectrogram of the post-filtering module and the final enhanced spectrogram.

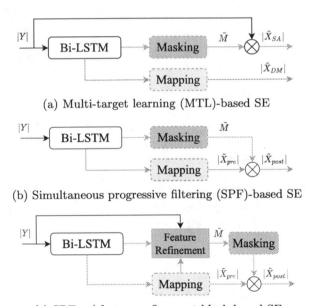

(a) Multi-target learning (MTL)-based SE

(b) Simultaneous progressive filtering (SPF)-based SE

(c) SPF w/ feature refinement block-based SE

Fig. 1. Multi-target learning (MTL)-based and our proposed SE flowcharts: (a) MTL-based SE have $|\tilde{X}_{SA}|$ and $|\tilde{X}_{DM}|$ two outputs. (b) SPF-based SE simply uses MTL to achieve simultaneous progressive filtering without introducing new parameter. (c) SPF w/ feature refinement block-based SE adding a feature refinement block to the post-filtering module, the input of the block contains three components in this configuration. The green part in the flowcharts denotes masking-based module and the blue part denotes mapping-based module (Color figure online).

3.3   Simultaneous Progressive Filtering System

The loss function of the entire SPF system $\mathcal{L}_{SPF}$ is given as follows:

$$\mathcal{L}_{SPF} = \beta \mathcal{L}_{pre} + (1 - \beta) \mathcal{L}_{post} \tag{6}$$

We compress the pre-filtering and post-filtering modules in one bidirectional long short-term memory (Bi-LSTM) neural network and utilize the complementarity features through sharing the Bi-LSTM layers to the pre-filtering and post-filtering modules. Therefore, the Bi-LSTM output layer contains information common to both the pre-filtering and post-filtering modules. Thus, we simply use MTL to run the pre-filtering module and post-filtering modules simultaneously and do not introduce any new parameters into the SPF system. Moreover, our system fully utilizes the complementarity between the mapping and masking targets and use the masking method to filter the mapping-enhanced spectrogram again. The flowchart of SPF is shown in Fig. 1(b).

3.4   Feature Refinement Block

We design a feature refinement block to refine the shared information and supplement speech information that may be lost in the pre-filtering module. The block consists of a concatenation part and a hidden layer. The task of concatenation part is to concatenate the 2 or 3 inputs as the input of hidden layer.

Based on the SPF system, we add a feature refinement block into the post-filtering module to estimate a better mask. We explore 3 configurations of SPF with feature refinement block. In the first configuration, the input of the hidden layer only contains the hidden output of the shared Bi-LSTM. In the second configuration, the input of the hidden layer is the concatenation of the hidden outputs of the shared Bi-LSTM and the pre-filtering enhanced spectrogram $|\widetilde{X}_{pre}|$. In the third configuration, we concatenate the hidden output of the shared Bi-LSTM, the noisy spectrogram $|Y|$, and the pre-filtering enhanced spectrogram $|\widetilde{X}_{pre}|$ as the input of the hidden layer. The SPF with feature refinement block system are trained in the same way as the SPF system. But the addition of the hidden layer in the block introduces several new parameters into the SPF with feature refinement block system. The flowchart of SPF with feature refinement block in the third configuration is shown in Fig. 1(c).

4   Experiments

We conduct experiments using the Valentini-Botinhao data set [18]. Some of the noise in the data set is obtained from the Demand database [19] and the speech database is obtained from the Voice Banking Corpus [20]. We adopt the validation set to control the learning rate (initialized as 0.001), which is decreased by 50% in the absence of improvement between two consecutive epochs. All speech signals are sampled at 16 kHz. The Hamming window is used for framing, where the frame size is set to 512 with a 50% overlap. We use the magnitude spectrogram as the input and output features.

We implement our model using TensorFlow. All the baseline models use Bi-LSTM, where the Bi-LSTM model contains a 257-dimensional input layer and two hidden layers with 1024 nodes each. A 257-dimensional output layers are used for each of the mapping or masking targets for the single-target mapping or masking methods. Two 257-dimensional output layers are used simultaneously for both the mapping and masking outputs in the multi-target learning method. For our SPF approach, SPF has the same structure as the multi-target learning method. For SPF with feature refinement block, we add a fully connected hidden layer with 512 nodes after the Bi-LSTM layers. The input of the feature refinement block has three components: the hidden outputs of the shared Bi-LSTM, the noisy spectrogram, and the pre-filtering enhanced spectrogram. We simply concatenate the three components to form the input. The parameters of our models are randomly initialized.

We evaluate the performance of SPF and baseline methods, by using the CSIG, CBAK and COVL [21] to measure the speech intelligibility and use the PESQ [22] to measure the speech quality.

Table 1. Results obtained using **baseline** and **our proposed methods**. The "Input of Post-filtering Config" part displays the configurations of the input of the masking-based post-filtering module, all the inputs are concatenated as the input of the post-filtering module in the feature refinement block if there are more than 1 input.

	Models	Input of post-filtering Config			Metrics			
		Output of Bi-LSTM	Output of pre-filtering	Noisy spectrogram	CSIG	CBAK	COVL	PESQ
Noisy	–	–	–	–	3.345	2.442	2.631	1.970
Baseline	STL-DM	–	–	–	3.849	2.547	3.226	2.604
	STL-SA	–	–	–	3.650	2.488	3.072	2.513
	MTL-DM	–	–	–	3.820	2.538	3.205	2.594
	MTL-SA	–	–	–	3.785	2.551	3.202	2.631
Ours	SPF	✓	✗	✗	3.556	2.601	3.138	2.721
	SPF w/	✓	✗	✗	3.874	2.610	3.301	2.729
	Feature	✓	✓	✗	3.860	2.603	3.288	2.717
	Refinement	✓	✓	✓	3.841	2.632	3.297	2.752

4.1 The Effect of Multi-target Learning

The upper half part of Table 1 lists the CSIG, CBAK, COVL, and PESQ performance obtained using different baseline systems with the test data sets. "Noisy" denotes the performance for untreated noisy speech. "STL-DM" and "STL-SA" denote the two single-target learning methods used for mapping and masking, as shown in Eq. (1) and Eq. (2), respectively. "MTL-DM" and "MTL-SA" denote the two outputs of the MTL method, as shown in Eq. (3). The hyperparameter α is set to 0.5 for the MTL. Using MTL improves the SE performance, e.g., The PESQ of "MTL-SA" is 0.118 higher than that of "STL-SA". However, using MTL causes a slight drop in the performance for some systems, e.g., the performance of "MTL-DM" was slightly lower than that of "STL-DM".

4.2   The Performance of Proposed Methods

The bottom half part of Table 1 shows the results obtained using our SPF methods. "SPF" is described in Sect. 3.3, and the corresponding β was set to 0.2. The 3 configurations of "SPF with feature refinement block" are described in Sect. 3.4, and the corresponding β values were set to 0.9, 0.8 and 0.3, respectively. All of proposed methods considerably outperformed the conventional SE methods. Even without the feature refinement block, the PESQ of "SPF" was 0.09 higher than the best performance obtained using the baseline methods. These results shows that our simultaneous progressive filtering approach can be used to produce an enhancement system with superior performance and without introducing any new parameters. The main reason for the enhanced performance is that designing our mask for the mapping-enhanced spectrogram instead of the original spectrogram fully utilizes the complementarity of the two targets.

The β of "SPF" was set to 0.2. Thus, the masking-based pre-filtering module is more important than the mapping-based post-filtering module in "SPF". Unlike "STL-SA" and "MTL-SA", masking is used to recover a high-SNR spectrogram instead of a noisy spectrogram using "SPF". Thus, the masking method lowers the information loss for high-SNR spectrograms. However, for "SPF with feature refinement block", the focus of the network gradually shifts from the pre-filtering module to the post-filtering module as more information is added to the hidden layer. Compared with the baseline methods, "SPF with feature refinement block" not only exhibited a PESQ improvement of more than 0.12 but also showed improved performance in the other three indicators. These results provide strong evidence that our proposed method can recover speech signals and remove residual noise more effectively than existing methods.

5   Conclusions and Future Work

In this paper, we proposed a simultaneous progressive filtering-based monaural speech enhancement approach. Two filtering modules were used: a mapping-based pre-filtering module and a masking-based post-filtering module. The pre-filtering module obtained a mapping-enhanced spectrogram from a noisy spectrogram to preserve clean speech signals and obtain a high-SNR spectrogram. The post-filtering module reduced the residual noise of the enhanced spectrogram obtained using the pre-filtering module. Our proposed simultaneous progressive filtering method exhibited a high SE performance; e.g., "SPF with feature refinement block" had a PESQ improvement of more than 0.12. As the post-filtering module filters the high-SNR spectrogram instead of the original noisy spectrogram, masking reduced the information loss and enhanced performance. As a multi-target learning strategy was used to develop these two modules, the number of the parameters of our proposed system was not increased or only by a small number. In addition, our SPF strategy can be easily integrated with many existing methods. In the future, we will apply this system to other speech processing tasks such as ASR.

Acknowledgment. This work was supported by the National Key R&D Program of China (Grant NO. 2018YFB1305200), the National Natural Science Foundation of China (Grant NO. 61771333) and the Tianjin Municipal Science and Technology Project (Grant NO. 18ZXZNGX00330).

References

1. Li, J., Deng, L., Gong, Y., Haeb-Umbach, R.: An overview of noise-robust automatic speech recognition. TASLP **22**(4), 745–777 (2014)
2. Wang, Y., Narayanan, A., Wang, D.: On training targets for supervised speech separation. TASLP **22**(12), 1849–1858 (2014)
3. Xia, B., Bao, C.: Wiener filtering based speech enhancement with weighted denoising auto-encoder and noise classification. Speech Commun. **60**, 13–29 (2014)
4. Scalart, P., et al.: Speech enhancement based on a priori signal to noise estimation. In: ICASSP, vol. 2, pp. 629–632. IEEE (1996)
5. Boll, S.: Suppression of acoustic noise in speech using spectral subtraction. TASSP **27**(2), 113–120 (1979)
6. Deng, F., Bao, F., Bao, C.-C.: Speech enhancement using generalized weighted β-order spectral amplitude estimator. Speech Commun. **59**, 55–68 (2014)
7. Vihari, S., Murthy, A.S., Soni, P., Naik, D.: Comparison of speech enhancement algorithms. Procedia Comput. Sci. **89**, 666–676 (2016)
8. Wang, D., Chen, J.: Supervised speech separation based on deep learning: an overview. TASLP **26**(10), 1702–1726 (2018)
9. Xu, Y., Du, J., Dai, L.-R., Lee, C.-H.: An experimental study on speech enhancement based on deep neural networks. IEEE Sig. Process. Lett. **21**(1), 65–68 (2013)
10. Xu, Y., Du, J., Dai, L.-R., Lee, C.-H.: A regression approach to speech enhancement based on deep neural networks. TASLP **23**(1), 7–19 (2014)
11. Srinivasan, S., Roman, N., Wang, D.: Binary and ratio time-frequency masks for robust speech recognition. Speech Commun. **48**, 1486–1501 (2006)
12. Narayanan, A., Wang, D.: Ideal ratio mask estimation using deep neural networks for robust speech recognition. In: ICASSP, pp. 7092–7096. IEEE (2013)
13. Williamson, D.S., Wang, Y., Wang, D.: Complex ratio masking for monaural speech separation. TASLP **24**(3), 483–492 (2015)
14. Shi, H., Wang, L., Ge, M., Li, S., Dang, J.: Spectrograms fusion with minimum difference masks estimation for monaural speech dereverberation. In: ICASSP, pp. 7544–7548. IEEE (2020)
15. Sun, L., Du, J., Dai, L.-R., Lee, C.-H.: Multiple-target deep learning for LSTM-RNN based speech enhancement. In: HSCMA, pp. 136–140. IEEE (2017)
16. Hao, X., et al.: Masking and inpainting: a two-stage speech enhancement approach for low snr and non-stationary noise. In: ICASSP, pp. 6959–6963. IEEE (2020)
17. Jin, Y.G., Lee, C.M., Cho, K., Kim, N.S.: A data-driven residual gain approach for two-stage speech enhancement. In: ICASSP, pp. 4752–4755. IEEE (2011)
18. Botinhao, C.V., Wang, X., Takaki, S., Yamagishi, J.: Speech enhancement for a noise-robust text-to-speech synthesis system using deep recurrent neural networks. In: Interspeech 2016, pp. 352–356 (2016)

19. Thiemann, J., Ito, N., Vincent, E.: The diverse environments multi-channel acoustic noise database (demand): a database of multichannel environmental noise recordings, vol. 19, no. 1, p. 035081 (2013)
20. Veaux, C., Yamagishi, J., King, S.: The voice bank corpus: Design, collection and data analysis of a large regional accent speech database. In: O-COCOSDA/CASLRE, pp. 1–4. IEEE (2013)
21. Hu, Y., Loizou, P.C.: Evaluation of objective quality measures for speech enhancement. TASLP **16**(1), 229–238 (2007)
22. ITU-T Recommendation: Perceptual evaluation of speech quality (PESQ): an objective method for end-to-end speech quality assessment of narrow-band telephone networks and speech codecs. ITU-T Recommendation P.862 (2001)

Using a Two-Stage GAN to Learn Image Degradation for Image Super-Resolution

Jiarui Cheng[1], Ning Jiang[1(✉)], Jialiang Tang[1], Xin Deng[1], Wenxin Yu[1],
and Peng Zhang[2]

[1] School of Computer Science and Technology,
Southwest University of Science and Technology, Mianyang 621000, Sichuan, China
jiangning@swust.edu.cn
[2] School of Science, Southwest University of Science and Technology,
Mianyang 621000, Sichuan, China

Abstract. Recent super-resolution (SR) methods based on generative adversarial networks (GANs) almost assume that the degradation process is known. Most of these works are to use bicubic or bilinear down-sampling to obtain low-resolution (LR) images, but for real-world images, these methods often can not recover the details well. Thus affecting the performance. In this paper, we propose to first build a self-attention gradient degradation GAN, then build a self-attention gradient super-resolution GAN to alleviate the above problem. Specifically, first of all, we learn the down-sampling process by self-attention gradient degradation GAN to approximate the real-world degradation of high-resolution (HR) images, and use unpaired HR and LR images in the training process. Then, we get the LR images by self-attention gradient degradation GAN, and send them into the self-attention gradient super-resolution GAN together with the corresponding original HR images to get the SR images. The experimental results show that our method is superior to other state-of-the-art methods in terms of FID and we get competitive results on PSNR. It also potentially means that our method can be used for other categories of images.

Keywords: Generative adversarial network (GAN) · Image degradation · Image super-resolution

1 Introduction

At present, mainly includes image SR methods [2,5,6,11] use bilinear or bicubic down-sampling to artificially generate LR images as the input of SR task, and achieve good results. However, the application of these methods to real-world image SR task may often be unsatisfactory, because the degradation process of bilinear and bicubic down-sampling is different from that of real-world images. Another important point is that in reality, paired images are often difficult to obtain. In addition, we all know that GAN can restore the reality of the image,

T. Mantoro et al. (Eds.): ICONIP 2021, CCIS 1516, pp. 222–230, 2021.
https://doi.org/10.1007/978-3-030-92307-5_26

but the process of training GAN is relatively difficult, and the SR image restord by GAN-based methods [2,5,11,13] also has some geometric distortions and shortcomings in some details. In [7], gradient maps is utilized to alleviate the distortion caused by GAN-based SR methods, because gradient maps can provide more structure priors for SR tasks and preserve the structural appearance of images in GAN-based SR methods. But it has not been applied to real-world images to prove its effectiveness. With the development of deep learning, most of the existing super-resolution methods are based on convolutional neural networks(CNNs). However, they did not study a more common SR situation, that is, real-world LR data without corresponding HR data.

Up to now, the super-resolution method based on generative adversarial network (GAN) has also been developed and achieved great progress. Ledig et al. [5] proposed SRGAN, which used perceptual loss and adversarial loss for the first time to complete the SR task and achieved great SR results. Wang et al. [11] further improved the network architecture and perceptual loss to enhance the super-resolution generative adversarial networks(ESRGAN). Because cycle-consistent adversarial networks(CycleGAN) [13] introduced cyclic consistency. CinCGAN [12] an unsupervised model, was proposed to capture LR images of real images and utilize unpaired HR and LR images. [1,8] adopted two processes to construct two networks to solve the super-resolution task, respectively and maintain the consistency of the cycle. However, above methods mostly do not consider the degradation process of the real-world image. The paired HR and LR images are almost unavailable in reality, so it will bring a lot of trouble to the training process. Therefore, how to learn the degradation process of real-world images and obtain real-world HR and LR image pairs is still an attractive direction in the super-resolution task. In this paper, we also want to improve the performance of GAN-based SR methods through the proposed method by us.

To solve the above problems, we propose a two-stage generative adversarial networks composed of the degradation network and the super-resolution network to learn the degradation and super-resolution tasks of real-world images, respectively. The degradation network proposed in this paper can be trained without paired images. After training, the generated LR images can be the input of super-resolution network training under a paired image setting to obtain super-resolution images. We call the two networks: self-attention gradient degradation generative adversarial network (SAGD-GAN) and self-attention gradient super-resolution generative adversarial network (SAGSR-GAN) respectively.

2 Method

2.1 Overview

The proposed architecture consists of two parts: a self-attention gradient degradation generative adversarial network (referred to as SAGD-GAN) and a self-attention gradient super-resolution generative adversarial network (referred to as SAGSR-GAN). We also mosaic the noise vector z with the HR image, in order to

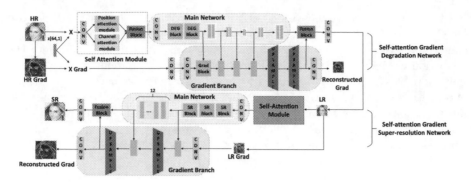

Fig. 1. This is our overall framework. The details of self-attention module are shown in Fig. 2.

hope that the degradation network can produce better and more diverse realistic LR images.

The overall architecture is end-to-end trainable and is shown in Fig. 1. The detailed description of SAGD-GAN and SAGSR-GAN is in Sect. 2.2 and 2.3, respectively.

2.2   Self-attention Gradient Degradation Network

The network consists of three parts, a self-attention module, a main network and a gradient branch.

Main Network. The main network (see Fig. 1) is based on GAN architecture. The generator part is similar to the one used in [1], except that the number of convolution channels in the first layer is changed to facilitate the connection with the following self-attention module, and the fusion module is added at the end to fuse the main network with the features extracted by the gradient branch.

The generator network adopts encoder-decoder structure and contains 12 DEG blocks(residual blocks without batch normalization layers), one group for every two blocks, a total of 6 groups. In the first four groups, each group has a pooling layer to reduce the resolution by a total of four times, while in the last two groups, each group uses a pixel shuffle layer to double the resolution. At the same time, we also incorporate the DEG blocks of the first four groups into gradient branch to enhance the performance of gradient branch. The architecture of discriminator is based on [9], using six residual blocks (without batch normalization layers), followed by a full connection layer.

Self-attention Module. Following [3], we introduce position attention module and channel attention module. Position attention module (see Fig. 2(a)) can capture the spatial dependence between any two positions of the feature map. Specifically, as shown in Fig. 2(a), for the local feature O ($C \times H \times W$) of the network output, we use three convolution layers to get three feature maps of P, Q and R. Then, P, Q and R are reshaped to $S_1 \in \mathbb{R}^{C \times N}$ respectively, where

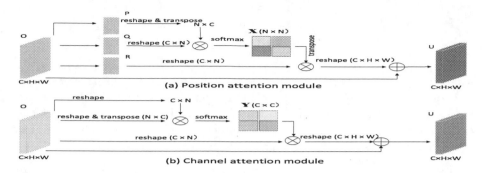

Fig. 2. The details of position attention module (a) and channel attention module (b), where $\otimes$ represents matrix multiplication and $\oplus$ represents element sum.

$N = H \times W$, and the transpose of P is multiplied by Q, and then the position attention map X (N, N) is obtained by softmax. Then, the transpose of X is multiplied by R matrix, and the result is reshaped to $S_2 \in \mathbb{R}^{C \times H \times W}$, multiplied by a scale factor, and then the original features O is added to get the final output map U.

Channel attention module (see Fig. 2(b)) can capture the interdependence between any two channels and update the value of a channel by using the weighted sum of all channels. Specifically, as shown in Fig. 2(b). O is reshaped to $S_1 \in \mathbb{R}^{C \times N}$, and then O is matrix multiplied with the transpose of O. After softmax, the channel attention map Y $(C \times C)$ is obtained, and then multiplied by O $(C \times N)$. The output reshaped to $S_2 \in \mathbb{R}^{C \times H \times W}$ is multiplied by the scale factor and added with the original features O to obtain the final output map U.

Finally, we transform the output of the two attention modules through a convolution layer, sum the elements to complete the feature fusion, using dropout to make it less dependent on some local features, and then send them to the main network.

Gradient Branch. Inspired by [7], we design a gradient branch (see Fig. 1) for main network to estimate the translation of gradient maps from HR mode to LR mode. The gradient map is obtained by calculating the difference between adjacent pixels (The gradient map is extracted according to the method in [7].).

As shown in Fig. 1, there are four Grad blocks in the gradient branch, and here we also use the residual structure. The gradient branch contains the intermediate layer representation of multiple main network, which can bring rich structural information for the recovery of gradient maps and improve the performance of gradient branch. After obtaining LR gradient map by gradient branch, the obtained gradient features are fed back to the main network to fuse the features and guide the reconstruction process of LR image.

Loss Function. The discriminator is trained by GAN loss, and the generator is trained by the combination of L_1 loss, GAN loss, perceptual loss and gradient loss. The overall objective loss is shown in Sect. 2.4.

Pixel loss. We use L_1 loss to accelerate convergence:

$$l_{pix} = \mathbb{E} \left\| I_g - I_r \right\|_1. \tag{1}$$

where $I_g = I_{LR'} = G(I_{HR}, z)$, $I_r = I_{LR}$ in Self-attention Gradient Degradation Network, while $I_g = I_{SR} = G(I_{LR'})$, $I_r = I_{HR}$ in Self-attention Gradient Super-resolution Network. z is the noise vector. I_{LR}, I_{HR}, $I_{LR'}$ and I_{SR} are LR image, HR image, generated LR image and generated SR image, respectively. Note that the above variables also apply to the following loss functions.

GAN Loss. For each network, we construct a discriminator D to distinguish the real image from the corresponding generated image, and a generator G to try to fool D respectively as follows:

$$l_{Dis} = -\mathbb{E} \left[log \left(1 - D \left(I_g \right) \right) \right] - \mathbb{E} \left[log D \left(I_r \right) \right], \tag{2}$$

$$l_{adv} = -\mathbb{E} \left[log D \left(I_g \right) \right]. \tag{3}$$

So we use l_{Dis} to train discriminator D.

Perceptual loss. The features containing semantic information are extracted from the pre trained VGG network [10]. Therefore, following [11], for each network the Euclidean distance between the features of original images and generated images is minimized in terms of perception loss:

$$l_{per} = \mathbb{E} \left\| \phi_{i,j} \left(I_g \right) - \phi_{i,j} \left(I_r \right) \right\|_1. \tag{4}$$

Where $\phi_{i,j} \left(\cdot \right)$ is the output of the j-th convolution layer before the i-th max-pooling layer of the VGG model. Here we set $i = 5$ and $j = 4$, respectively.

Gradient loss. We describe the gradient loss by minimizing the distance between the gradient extracted from the original image and the corresponding generated image. As follows:

$$l_{grad} = \mathbb{E} \left\| M \left(I_g \right) - M \left(I_r \right) \right\|_1. \tag{5}$$

Where $M(\cdot)$ is the operation of extracting image gradient.

2.3   Self-attention Gradient Super-Resolution Network

The network also consists of three parts, a self-attention module, a main network and a gradient branch.

Main Network. Our main network (see Fig. 1) is also based on GAN architecture. The generator part has 15 SR blocks(residual blocks without batch normalization layers) and is divided into two groups, one group of 3 blocks and the other group of 12 blocks. Each group has an upsampling layer, and the resolution is doubled by bicubic upsampling. Similarly, we also add two groups of SR blocks in the main network to the gradient branch to improve its performance. The discriminator, like the one used in degradation networks.

Fig. 3. Qualitative results on test set from Widerface. Compared with the method of Bulat et al. [1], our method also produces good results and is superior to other methods.

Self-attention Module. It is very similar to the self-attention module used in degradation networks, but we increase the number of channels to obtain more image features, which is helpful for SR image reconstruction.

Gradient Branch. Similarly, the gradient branch (see Fig. 1) for main network to estimate the translation of gradient maps from LR mode to SR mode. Here, gradient branch produces an approximate gradient map for SR images. And the gradient branch architecture is consistent with the gradient branch architecture in degradation networks. We use two Grad blocks with residual structure. After the SR gradient image is obtained by gradient branch, the gradient features are fed back to the main network for feature fusion to guide the SR image reconstruction.

Loss Function. This is very similar to the loss in degradation network. The difference between degradation network and super-resolution network is mainly in the training set. Here, we train super-resolution network with paired data sets (e.g. HR images I_{HR} and corresponding degraded images $I_{LR'}$.).

2.4 Overall Objective

We utilize l_{Dis} to optimize each discriminator. For each network discriminator, the overall objective is:

$$l_D = l_{Dis}. \tag{6}$$

For each network generator, we utilize the combination of L_1 loss, GAN loss, perceptual loss and gradient loss to optimize. The overall objective is:

Table 1. The performance comparison of FID is on real-world test set (3000 images from LR training set), and PSNR is on LS3D-W (The input LR image is obtained by bilinear down-sampling). The best results are highlighted.

Method	FID	PSNR
	Test set	LS3D-W
SRGAN [5]	104.80	23.19
CycleGAN [13]	19.01	16.10
Wavelet-SRNet [4]	149.46	**23.98**
FSRNet [2]	157.29	19.45
Bulat et al. [1]	14.89	19.30
Ours	**13.09**	20.02

$$l_G = \alpha l_{pix} + \beta l_{adv} + \gamma l_{per} + \delta l_{grad}. \tag{7}$$

α, β, γ and δ denote trade-off parameters. And we set $\alpha = 1$, $\beta = 0.005$, $\gamma = 0.1$ and $\delta = 0.01$, respectively.

3 Experiment

3.1 Datasets and Evaluation Metrics

We evaluate the SR performance of our proposed SR network method. Since we use [1] as the baseline, we follow [1] to create our training sets and test set.

We utilize a randomly selected subset of 60,000 faces from Celeb-A, the whole AFLW, a subset of LS3D-W, and a subset of VGGFace2 as HR training sets, a total of 182866 facial images. And all HR training sets are cropped to 64 × 64. Widerdace contains faces affected by various degradation and noise types. We selected more than 50000 images from Widerface as the real-world LR training set, and selected 3000 of them as the test set. The LR datasets is all 16 × 16 pixels. We use the Fréchet Inception Distance (FID) score and peak signal to noise ratio (PSNR) as the evaluation metrics.

3.2 Comparison with State-of-the-Arts Methods

In this section, we follow the configuration of [1] to complete this experiment since we take [1] as the baseline. We compare the FID performance of five state-of-the-art methods on test set and LS3D-W respectively, including SRGAN [5], CycleGAN [13], Wavelet-SRNet [4], FSRNet [2] and Bulat et al. [1]. Among them, the method of [1] is very similar to ours, which also adopts two-stage model. For completeness, we also compare the results of PSNR on 1000 images form LS3D-W dataset. The performance comparison of each method is shown in Table 1.

Our qualitative results can be seen in Fig. 3. In terms of FID, our method is superior to other methods, while competitive results were obtained by ours on LS3D-W in terms of PSNR.

4 Conclusion

In this paper, we propose a two-stage GAN to complete the real-world face super-resolution task: first, we utilize the self-attention gradient degradation network to learn the real-world degradation of HR images through unpaired high- and low-resolution images, then utilize paired of LR images obtained by the degradation network with corresponding original HR images as the input to train the self-attention gradient super-resolution network to complete the SR images. In each network, the self-attention module can capture the context dependence well and make the image restoration more texture details. Moreover, gradient branch and gradient loss can alleviate the image distortion based on GAN-methods, keeping the appearance of the image structure. The quantitative results on the test set and LS3D-W also show that the proposed method achieves the task of real-world face image degradation and super-resolution. In the future, we hope our method can be applied to other categories of images.

Acknowledgements. This work was supported in part by the Sichuan Science and Technology Program under Grant 2020YFS0307, Mianyang Science and Technology Program 2020YFZJ016, SWUST Doctoral Foundation under Grant 19zx7102, 21zx7114.

References

1. Bulat, A., Yang, J., Tzimiropoulos, G.: To learn image super-resolution, use a GAN to learn how to do image degradation first. In: Ferrari, V., Hebert, M., Sminchisescu, C., Weiss, Y. (eds.) ECCV 2018. LNCS, vol. 11210, pp. 187–202. Springer, Cham (2018). https://doi.org/10.1007/978-3-030-01231-1_12
2. Chen, Y., Tai, Y., Liu, X., Shen, C., Yang, J.: FSRNet: end-to-end learning face super-resolution with facial priors. In: CVPR (2018)
3. Fu, J., et al.: Dual attention network for scene segmentation. In: CVPR (2019)
4. Huang, H., He, R., Sun, Z., Tan, T.: Wavelet-SRNet: a wavelet-based CNN for multi-scale face super resolution. In: ICCV (2017)
5. Ledig, C., et al.: Photo-realistic single image super-resolution using a generative adversarial network. In: CVPR (2017)
6. Lim, B., Son, S., Kim, H., Nah, S., Lee, K.M.: Enhanced deep residual networks for single image super-resolution. In: CVPRW (2017)
7. Ma, C., Rao, Y., Cheng, Y., Chen, C., Lu, J., Zhou, J.: Structure-preserving super resolution with gradient guidance. In: CVPR (2020)
8. Maeda, S.: Unpaired image super-resolution using pseudo-supervision. In: CVPR (2020)
9. Miyato, T., Kataoka, T., Koyama, M., Yoshida, Y.: Spectral normalization for generative adversarial networks. In: ICLR (2018)
10. Simonyan, K., Zisserman, A.: Very deep convolutional networks for large-scale image recognition. In: ICLR (2015)
11. Wang, X., et al.: ESRGAN: enhanced super-resolution generative adversarial networks. In: Leal-Taixé, L., Roth, S. (eds.) ECCV 2018. LNCS, vol. 11133, pp. 63–79. Springer, Cham (2019). https://doi.org/10.1007/978-3-030-11021-5_5

12. Yuan, Y., Liu, S., Zhang, J., Zhang, Y., Dong, C., Lin, L.: Unsupervised image super-resolution using cycle-in-cycle generative adversarial networks. In: CVPR (2018)
13. Zhu, J., Park, T., Isola, P., Efros, A.A.: Unpaired image-to-image translation using cycle-consistent adversarial networks. In: ICCV (2017)

Deep Learning Based Placement Acceleration for 3D-ICs

Wenxin Yu[1], Xin Cheng[1(✉)], Zhiqiang Zhang[2], and Jun Gong[3]

[1] Southwest University of Science and Technology, Mianyang, China
[2] Hosei University, Tokyo, Japan
[3] Beijing Institute of Technology, Beijing, China

Abstract. Placement plays an essential role in the very-large-scale integrated (VLSI) circuits physical design automation. But, it is a time-consuming step in the VLSI design stages. In this paper, we proposes algorithm for three-dimension integrated circuits (3D-ICs), which accelerate graphics processing unit placement based on deep learning (DL). First, we compare the electrostatic system with the placement instance. Later, we transformed the 3D placement problem into a neural network training problem for acceleration. In particular, we use the deep learning toolkit PyTorch to implement the 3D placement algorithm and design special 3D wirelength and density computations in C++/CUDA. The results show that our algorithm is effective. Compared with the state-of-the-art 3D algorithm ePlace-3D, our algorithm can achieve an average **3.96×** speedup on the IBM-PLACE benchmarks.

Keywords: Placement · Physical design · Deep learning

1 Introduction

Placement is a fundamental, critical step in physical design automation [3,10]. Placement solution performance has obviously influence on the overall design quality of results. As placement has many cells and macros, It is usually a very complicated and time-consuming stage. Besides, as the complexity of integrated circuits increases, 3D IC technology has emerged as one of the most promising solutions for overcoming the challenges. 3D placement is more time-consuming than two-dimension (2D) placement. Therefore, A fast and high-quality 3D placement algorithm is urgently needed.

Most of the current work is based on partitioning, using CPU multi-threading for parallelization for 2D placement acceleration. As the number of threads increases, the placement acceleration can only increase by up to 5× with quality degradation of 2–6% [4,6,9]. The authors [1] explored GPU acceleration for analytical placement. Their placement algorithm got an average of 15% speedup with less than 1% quality degradation by parallelizing the nonlinear placement

---

W. Yu and X. Cheng—Contributed equally to this work.

T. Mantoro et al. (Eds.): ICONIP 2021, CCIS 1516, pp. 231–238, 2021.
https://doi.org/10.1007/978-3-030-92307-5_27

part. The paper [5] computed wirelength gradient computation and area accumulation based on GPU acceleration techniques, but they do not have a complete GPU-accelerated placement framework. Another paper [7] proposed a GPU-accelerated placement framework DREAMPlace, and got a fast and efficient placement solution, but it failed to achieve 3D placement. The above works are only for 2D placement acceleration. Currently, 3D placement is the focus of research. As far as we know, there is no algorithm research on 3D placement acceleration based on deep learning.

In this work, we proposed a novel and fast 3D placement algorithm based on deep learning (DL). It was exploit with the PyTorch and transformed the 3D placement problem into a training problem of convolutional neural network for acceleration. Our placement algorithm is based on the leading analytical 3D placement algorithm ePlace-3D, but we further enhance the performance of 3D-IC placement and shorten the runtime. Our contribution is as follows:

- We transform a nonlinear placement problem into a problem of training neural networks, and develop a novel, GPU-acceleration 3D placement algorithm with deep learning toolkit PyTorch.
- We realize efficient 3D wirelength and density computation with CUDA.
- Our 3D-IC placer outperforms the state-of-the-art (SOTA) algorithms ePlace-3D 10% shorter wirelength, while run 3.96× faster on average of all the ten IBM-PLACE benchmarks.

The rest of this paper is concluded as follows. The background knowledge is introduced in Sect. 2. The summary of our algorithm is description in Sect. 3 and we discusses the customized kernel for 3D wirelength and density computation. Experimental results are shown in Sect. 4, and conclusions are provided in Sect. 5.

2   Preliminary

In this section, we discuss the basic methods of ePlace-3D. We then discuss the analogy between 3D placement problem and training a neural network.

2.1   The Details Algorithm of ePlace-3D

In physical design filed, a SOTA 3D-IC placer ePlace-3D [8] models every placement objects as positive charge and the placement instance as a electrostatic system. Research [2] shows that the modeling error is upper bounded by $\varepsilon_w A(e) \leq \frac{\gamma \Delta x}{1+exp\Delta x/n}$.

$$WA_e = \frac{\sum_{i\in e} x_i e^{\frac{x_i}{\gamma}}}{\sum_{i\in e} e^{\frac{x_i}{\gamma}}} - \frac{\sum_{i\in e} x_i e^{-\frac{x_i}{\gamma}}}{\sum_{i\in e} e^{-\frac{x_i}{\gamma}}} \tag{1}$$

where γ is to control the accuracy and smoothness of the approximation to half-perimeter wirelength (HPWL). The smaller γ can obtain a more accurate approximate HPWL, but it will reduce the smoothness. The smoothing parameter γ cannot be set arbitrarily small due to the computation precision constraint.

Its density function eDensity-3D is quite different from other analytical placers. To convert the entire placement instance object to a positively charged cuboid, we modeling instance objects such as standard cells, macros, and fillers. Then, we force all the objects away from the high-density region by the electric repulsive. After solving a 3D Poisson's, to obtain the resolution value of the electric potential and field distribution equation, they utilize the spectral-based algorithm.

$$
\begin{cases}
\Delta \cdot \Delta\Phi(x, y, z) = -\rho(x, y, z), \\
\hat{n} \cdot \Delta\Phi(x, y, z) = 0, (x, y, z) \in R \\
\iiint\limits_{R} \Phi(x, y, z) = \iiint\limits_{R} \rho(x, y, z) = 0
\end{cases}
\tag{2}
$$

Here $\hat{n}$ is the outer unit normal of the placement cube R. ∂R is the boundary and consists of orthogonal rectangular planes to enclose the placement cuboid. Other numerical solutions can be computed as follows,

$$
a_{j,k,l} = \frac{1}{n^3} \sum_{x,y,z} \rho(x, y, z) \cos(w_j x) \cos(w_k y) \cos(w_l z)),
\tag{3}
$$

$$
\rho(x, y, z) = \sum_{j,k,l} a_{j,k,l} \cos(w_j x) \cos(w_k y) \cos(w_l z)),
\tag{4}
$$

$$
\Phi(x, y, z) = \sum_{j,k,l} \frac{a_{j,k,l}}{w_j^2 + w_k^2 + w_l^2} \cos(w_j x) \cos(w_k y) \cos(w_l z).
\tag{5}
$$

$$
\begin{cases}
E_x(x, y, z) = \sum_{j,k,l} \frac{a_{j,k,l} w_j}{w_j^2 + w_k^2 + w_l^2} \sin(w_j x) \cos(w_k y) \cos(w_l z), \\
E_x(x, y, z) = \sum_{j,k,l} \frac{a_{j,k,l} w_k}{w_j^2 + w_k^2 + w_l^2} \cos(w_j x) \sin(w_k y) \cos(w_l z), \\
E_x(x, y, z) = \sum_{j,k,l} \frac{a_{j,k,l} w_l}{w_j^2 + w_k^2 + w_l^2} \cos(w_j x) \cos(w_k y) \sin(w_l z).
\end{cases}
\tag{6}
$$

where $a_{j,k,l}$ denotes the 3D coefficients of the density frequency, $\rho(x, y, z)$ is the spatial density, $\Phi(x, y, z)$ denotes the electric potential, and $E_x(x, y, z)$, $E_y(x, y, z)$, $E_z(x, y, z)$ represent the electric field (EF) at the $x, y, and\ z$ coordinates. For each bin, at the condition of the electric field defined, calculate each cell's density gradient in the system as the overall force adopt by the cell.

2.2   3D Analytical Placement Parallel to NN

The 3D analytical placement problem is essentially to solve a nonlinear optimization problem, and its core is similar to the training of the neural networks. Therefore, we analyze the two issues by analogy. Specifically, we compare the wirelength to the error estimate and the density to the regularization term. In the training of NN, the instance for each data that has label y_i and feature vector x_i are input to the NN, and the NN is trained to output the real label $\phi(x_i; w)$ as much as possible. The aim of NN's training is to minimize the total objective loss of the weights w in the NN, and the expectation includes the mean classification errors of all data. In the 3D placement analogy with neural network training, we merge the cell positions (x, y, z) into w. Each instance is instead by zero label and a network with the feature e_i. Then, NN calculates the spend of wirelength $WL(e_i; w)$. Use the error loss function $f(\hat{y}, y) = |\hat{y} - y|$ (absolute), the minimization of the prediction error becomes $\sum_i^n WL(e_i; w)$. The density cost $D(w)$ corresponds to the regularization term $R(w)$.

3   Our Proposed 3D Placement Algorithm

Our total algorithm step is shown in Fig. 1. Our algorithm mainly consists of 5 parts. They are the initial placement, 3D global placement (GP-3D), 2D global placement (GP-2D), legalization, and detailed placement. Our focus is mainly on the 3D global placement. We will mainly introduce the implementation of 3D placement acceleration based on deep learning.

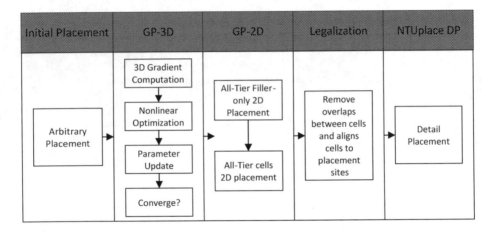

Fig. 1. The flowchart of our 3D placement framework.

3.1   3D Wirelength Computation

Equation (7) defined Direct implementation of WA wirelength may result in numerical overflow, so we convert $e^{\frac{x_i}{\gamma}}$ to $e^{\frac{x_i - \max_{j \in e} x_j}{\gamma}}$, and $e^{-\frac{x_i}{\gamma}}$ to $e^{-\frac{x_i - \max_{j \in e} x_j}{\gamma}}$ in Eq. (7) (an equivalent transformation). And for a pin location, we can calculate the WA wirelength's gradient as,

$$\frac{\partial WL_e}{\partial x_i} = \frac{(1 + \frac{x_i}{\gamma})b_e^+ - \frac{1}{\gamma}c_e^+}{(b_e^+)^2} \cdot a_i^+ - \frac{(1 - \frac{x_i}{\gamma})b_e^- + \frac{1}{\gamma}c_e^-}{(b_e^-)^2} \cdot a_i^-. \tag{7}$$

Then, the possibility of pin-level parallelization is taken into consideration as follows. The computation can be completed in four steps: 1) compute $x^\pm$; 2) compute and store $a^\pm$; 3) compute and store $b^\pm$, $c^\pm$; 4) compute WL_e in forward or $\frac{\partial WL_e}{\partial x_i}$ in backward. For simple description, We integrate the CUDA functions together. It is noted that it should be separate in implementation. Moreover, even all the calculations for an array have various $\pm$ signs such as x^+ and x^-, we wrote them together. And in the implementation, we separated these calculations into various CUDA streams. In the method, total of 6 kernels are needed. The $x^\pm$ kernel requires atomic maximum and minimum operations, and the $b^\pm$, $c^\pm$ kernels require atomic addition. At the tail of the propagation function, we use summation reduction to calculate the overall wirelength cost, which is provided by the deep learning toolkit.

3.2 3D Density Computation

For 3D density computation. The calculations include mainly four parts: 1) calculate density map; 2) calculate $a(i, j, k)$ 3) ϕ in front or E in backward; 4) D in front or $\frac{\partial D}{\partial x_i}$ in last. For step2 and step3, which are used as bulk computation parts, because the DCT/IDCT is necessary for potential and field computation.

DCT/IDCT for Electric Potential and Field

$$DCT(x_n)_k = \sum_{n=0}^{N-1} x_n \cos(\frac{\pi}{N}(n + \frac{1}{2})k), \tag{8}$$

$$IDCT(x_n)_k = \frac{1}{2}x_0 + \sum_{n=1}^{N-1} x_n \cos(\frac{\pi}{N}(k + \frac{1}{2})), \tag{9}$$

where $k = 0, 1, \ldots, N - 1$. For the infer of IDXST, we written the function as,

$$IDXST(x_n)_k = \sum_{n=0}^{N-1} x_n \sin(\frac{\pi}{N}n(k + \frac{1}{2})) = (-1)^k IDCT(x_{N-n})_k. \tag{10}$$

x_N in equation is 0. Then, the electric field and potential is able to calculate utilize DCT/IDCT, IDXST routines according to an $M \times M$ density map ρ.

$$a_{u,v} = DCT(DCT(\rho)^T)^T, \tag{11}$$

$$\psi_{DCT} = IDCT(IDCT(\frac{a_{u,v}}{w_u^2 + w_v^2})^T)^T, \tag{12}$$

$$\xi_{DSCT}^X = IDXST(IDCT(\frac{a_{u,v}w_u}{w_u^2 + w_v^2})^T)^T, \tag{13}$$

$$\xi_{DSCT}^Y = IDCT(IDXST(\frac{a_{u,v}w_v}{w_u^2 + w_v^2})^T)^T, \tag{14}$$

where $(\cdot)^T$ represents the transposition of matrix. The 2D DCT/IDCT is first calculated by implementation 1D DCT/IDCT to columns, then implement same operateration for rows. It is obvious that through proper transformations, all breaks of calculations decline to the 1D DCT/IDCT kernels. So, it's important to the ability that uses the optimized DCT/IDCT kernels.

Specifically, we leverage Fourier transform (FFT) to compute DCT. Since the fast optimized Fourier transform can easily obtain by deep learning tools. For example, Torch utilize the implementation using $2N$-point FFT. We choose the N-point FFT implementation and demonstrate better efficiency in the experiments. For real sequences, since the symmetry of FFT, we take advantage of one-sided real FFT/IFFT to reduce almost half of the sequence. DCT/IDCT can be obtained by an N-point real FFT/IFFT through secondary processing kernels like multiplication and linear-time recording.

4   Experiments

In this section, we describe our experimental setups and results. We implement our 3D-IC placement algorithm in Python with PyTorch for optimizers and API, and C++/CUDA for low-level operators. We perform experiments on a server of Linux system, use a 24-core Intel Xeon E5-2680 v3 @ 2.50 GHz and one 2080Ti GPU. Our implementation has no benchmark-specific code or tuning. Experiments are performed on IBM-PLACE benchmarks. For the IBM-PLACE benchmarks, all benchmarks are collected from realistic IC design, there are not any macros or blockages. In detail, We use the same transformation of benchmarks that by ePlace-3D. We compare the performance of our method with the SOTA 3D-IC placement ePlace-3D.

4.1   Results on IBM-PLACE Benchmark Suite

Table 1 shows the HPWL in $\times 10^7$ and runtime in seconds on IBM-PLACE benchmarks. According to the same solution (with 0.17 difference), our method can achieve acceleration on all benchmarks. For the mean value of total of ten circuits, our 3D placement framework outperforms ePlace-3D with $3.96\times$ shorter runtime. In particular, we shortened the runtime by more than $4\times$ with $0.18\times$ quality degradation in IBM13 benchmark. The experiment proves that our method is fast and efficient. ePlace-3D is a mixed-size 3D placement algorithm, and our 3D placement framework can only handle simple benchmarks, but we just use the simple mode of ePlace-3D for our experiments. Therefore, Our experimental comparison is fair relative to the experimental results. As the wirelength increases, we analyze the reason is that our preconditions in the 3D placement framework are different from ePlace-3D. Theoretically, preconditioning improves the convergence rate instead of solution performance. But, as placement has a property of highly nonlinear, non-convex, and ill-conditioned problem, the Hessian matrix with updated condition number would renew the direction for search the nonlinear solver to follow. So, preconditioning can given the following research a new view, it is respectable for its a surprising quality enhancement.

Table 1. HPWL (e7) and runtime (seconds) on the IBM-PLACE benchmark suite.

Categories			ePlace-3D		Our method	
Benchmarks	#Cells	#Nets	HPWL	Runtime	HPWL	Runtime
IBM01	12K	12K	0.25	34.80	0.30	**11.60**
IBM03	22K	22K	0.56	79.80	0.81	**22.90**
IBM04	27K	26K	0.74	112.81	1.01	**25.35**
IBM06	32K	33K	0.92	178.81	1.23	**40.67**
IBM07	45K	44K	1.50	232.22	1.95	**50.60**
IBM08	51K	48K	1.54	285.34	2.01	**70.38**
IBM09	52K	50K	1.40	337.81	1.73	**80.91**
IBM13	82K	84K	2.67	519.21	3.22	**110.56**
IBM15	158K	161K	6.39	2415.00	8.20	**642.37**
IBM18	210K	201K	9.47	3784.21	10.17	**1240.47**
Ratio	–	–	0.83	3.96	1.0	1.0

5 Conclusion

To solve the problem of 3D placement, we propose a 3D-IC placement algorithm take advantage of the speed up of the GPU. Based on the analogy between the 3D analytical placement problem and a neural network training problem, we implement the algorithm in and C++/CUDA and PyTorch, which is powerful and meaningful to accelerate ePlace-3D without little quality degradation. On average, of all the IBM-PLACE benchmarks, compared to the original SOTA 3D placer ePlace-3D, our 3D placement algorithm is able to obtain about **3.96×** acceleration for the global placement with little quality degradation. In addition, our placement framework is highly extensible to comprise an algorithm/solvers. Based on the 3D placement framework, we plan to accelerate the mixed-size 3D placement algorithm, which has a more complicated design process and more numerical operations. We think our work will open a new direction for 3D-ICs placement.

Acknowledgements. This work was supported in part by the Sichuan Science and Technology Program under Grant 2020YFS0307, Mianyang Science and Technology Program 2020YFZJ016, SWUST Doctoral Foundation under Grant 19zx7102.

References

1. Cong, J., Zou, Y.: Parallel multi-level analytical global placement on graphics processing units. In: 2009 IEEE/ACM International Conference on Computer-Aided Design-Digest of Technical Papers, pp. 681–688. IEEE (2009)
2. Hsu, M.K., Balabanov, V., Chang, Y.W.: TSV-aware analytical placement for 3-D IC designs based on a novel weighted-average wirelength model. IEEE Trans. Comput. Aided Des. Integr. Circ. Syst. **32**(4), 497–509 (2013)

3. Kahng, A.B.: Advancing placement. In: Proceedings of the 2021 International Symposium on Physical Design, pp. 15–22 (2021)
4. Li, W., Li, M., Wang, J., Pan, D.Z.: UTPlaceF 3.0: a parallelization framework for modern FPGA global placement. In: 2017 IEEE/ACM International Conference on Computer-Aided Design (ICCAD), pp. 922–928. IEEE (2017)
5. Lin, C.X., Wong, M.D.: Accelerate analytical placement with GPU: a generic approach. In: 2018 Design, Automation & Test in Europe Conference & Exhibition (DATE), pp. 1345–1350. IEEE (2018)
6. Lin, T., Chu, C., Wu, G.: POLAR 3.0: an ultrafast global placement engine. In: 2015 IEEE/ACM International Conference on Computer-Aided Design (ICCAD), pp. 520–527. IEEE (2015)
7. Lin, Y., et al.: DREAMPlace: deep learning toolkit-enabled GPU acceleration for modern VLSI placement. IEEE Trans. Comput. Aided Des. Integr. Circ. Syst. **40**(4), 748–761 (2020)
8. Lu, J., Zhuang, H., Kang, I., Chen, P., Cheng, C.K.: ePlace-3D: Electrostatics based placement for 3D-ICs. In: Proceedings of the 2016 on International Symposium on Physical Design, pp. 11–18 (2016)
9. Ludwin, A., Betz, V., Padalia, K.: High-quality, deterministic parallel placement for FPGAs on commodity hardware. In: Proceedings of the 16th International ACM/SIGDA Symposium on Field Programmable Gate Arrays, pp. 14–23 (2008)
10. Markov, I.L., Hu, J., Kim, M.C.: Progress and challenges in VLSI placement research. Proc. IEEE **103**(11), 1985–2003 (2015)

Self-supervised Continual Learning for Object Recognition in Image Sequences

Ruiqi Dai[1,3(✉)], Mathieu Lefort[2,3(✉)], Frédéric Armetta[2,3(✉)],
Mathieu Guillermin[4(✉)], and Stefan Duffner[1,3(✉)]

[1] INSA Lyon, Université de Lyon, Lyon, France
ruiqi.dai@insa-lyon.fr, stefan.duffner@liris.cnrs.fr
[2] Université Claude Bernard Lyon 1, Université de Lyon, Lyon, France
{mathieu.lefort,frederic.armetta}@univ-lyon1.fr
[3] LIRIS, CNRS, UMR5205, Villeurbanne Cedex, France
[4] Université Catholique de Lyon, Lyon, France
mguillermin@univ-catholyon.fr

Abstract. The autonomous learning of different objects in images, with a continual and unsupervised context, relies on detecting unknown objects and recognizing known ones based on the learned visual representation. Novelty detection is challenging because of the internal representation drifts of known objects not been seen for a long time. Most existing approaches either perform *offline* unsupervised learning on a large dataset, or continual *supervised* learning. Nevertheless, very few existing approaches propose unsupervised continual learning for object recognition. In this paper, we propose a new neural network-based approach for continually learning representations of objects from image sequences, that is able to autonomously detect novel objects and to recognize previously learned ones during training. It is based on a statistical test, performed on internal representations, adapted to counterbalance the concept drift, without storing any image. Experimental results show that our approach outperforms the state of the art on MNIST and Fashion-MNIST datasets. In particular, our approach avoids to over-segment the distribution of clusters, which artificially increases traditional indicators such as clustering accuracy.

1 Introduction

For an agent, it is very challenging to autonomously and continuously learn and make use of object representations of its open environment. The system has to detect novelty and introduce a new concept or class if necessary while maintaining the already acquired knowledge. This is part of the more general problem of finding a meaningful and robust representation under the stability-plasticity dilemma. Recently, unsupervised visual representation learning methods based on deep neural networks have been proposed [2,11]. But learning these models online with a continuous stream of images is not straightforward due to the

© Springer Nature Switzerland AG 2021
T. Mantoro et al. (Eds.): ICONIP 2021, CCIS 1516, pp. 239–247, 2021.
https://doi.org/10.1007/978-3-030-92307-5_28

nature of stochastic gradient descent optimization and the fact that most of them rely on an i.i.d. data assumption which is not valid in open environments.

The literature on continual learning with neural networks [3,17,20] partially responds to this issue by applying strategies alleviating catastrophic forgetting, such as experience replay [3,20], which either retain a memory of real images or generate new ones. In addition, *novelty detection* is an important aspect in unsupervised continual learning. However, in current representation learning approaches based on generative deep neural networks, the problem of correctly re-identifying reappearing objects or detecting unknown categories is not explicitly addressed. In fact, most existing algorithms rely on the observation likelihood, the loss function or a separate classifier [3], but these methods have some serious drawbacks with continuously evolving models and are difficult to calibrate [6]. As a consequence, they tend to keep expanding ignoring the true number of categories. Moreover, more advanced techniques [7,14] operate on statistical estimates of sample distributions, but in general they can only be applied *offline*.

In this paper, we target autonomous agent systems and propose a deep neural network model performing continual learning for visual object recognition. In this setting, the objects are learned in sequential order and are presented class by class, yet can reappear later. Our model is a modified version of a recently proposed Variational Auto-Encoder (VAE) model for continual unsupervised learning [3]. The main contribution of this paper is a new method to detect new object classes and recognize old ones in an image stream based on a statistical hypothesis test on the distributions of internal representation vectors. Our algorithm does not store any previous processed image, it only relies on the first two moments of the distributions that are estimated on-line during training.

2   Related Work

Novelty Detection. Detecting novelty, anomalies or outliers in a data sample distribution has been studied for several decades [9,19]. Some of the works consider the problem as one-class classification problem, i. e. only modelling the nominal class, or by creating a single artificial class, but their performances suffer when the number of categories increases[6]. In classification applications, one usual approach is to infer abnormality from the output scores of the classifier. However, samples from unknown classes may produce high confidence values by strongly activating one of the known classes [6,14]. For example, in neural networks, the softmax function indicates the confidence in the classification, but the interpretation as a true probability estimate is questionable [8]. Multi-class novelty detection can be formulated as "open-set recognition" [6], i.e. examples of unknown classes are explicitly handled by the model and rejected. For neural networks, for instance, models based on the calibration (of softmax) have been proposed such as ODIN [15] or G-OpenMax [5]. Also, removing the softmax normalisation may improve the discrimination between inliers and outliers [16]. A more probabilistic approach consists in using the likelihood ratio between inliers and a background distribution for outlier detection [21,23]. Other methods compute the uncertainty of model predictions using ensembles of deep models [13].

Despite these advances, two major challenges with generative neural networks remain: it may be difficult to disentangle known from unknown classes [6,18], and most methods operate offline, which either requires all the feature vectors extracted for known classes or explicitly train a separate mapping function that is independent from the learnt representation [1].

Continual Learning with Neural Networks. Various methods have been proposed to alleviate catastrophic forgetting, such as *regularization strategies* [12,25] that try to conserve weights w.r.t. their relevance to already learned classes. Other strategies include *structural approaches* [17,22] that dynamically expand network structures for new tasks, or *experience replay* [20] with either partial storage of real training examples or generated examples for learned categories [3]. However, these approaches are usually applied to supervised settings.

Among the unsupervised approaches, the Self-Taught Associative Memory (STAM) architecture [24] uses a specific hierarchical feature representation based on image patch exemplars of different sizes obtained from clustering, which may limit its scalability. SOINN [4] proposed a model with Self-Organizing Incremental Neural Network based on a distance metric to incrementally learn the topology of input data. Our model is based on the Continual Unsupervised Representation Learning (CURL) model [3] that will be presented in Sect. 3.

3   Representation Learning Algorithm and model

Our model is an extension of [3], a type of Variational Auto-Encoder (VAE) with a Gaussian Mixture Model (GMM), adapted to a class-incremental learning setting. More formally, it estimates the probability $p(x, y, z) = p(y)p(z|y)p(x|z)$ of the input x, the label y and the latent code z, using variational inference, and approximates the posterior $p(y, z|x)$ with $q(y, z|x) = q(y|x)q(z|x, y)$, where $q(y|x)$ is the output of a dense layer followed by softmax determining the component posterior given an input x, and $q(z|x, y)$ is the distribution of z encoded by the component-wise encoder. Instead of a single multivariate Gaussian as in classical VAE, CURL uses several components modelled as dense neural layers that output the different means and variances, and that are dynamically added during training when a certain number of outliers are detected. A modified ELBO (Evidence Lower Bound) objective is optimized during learning: $E(x) =$

$$\sum_{k=1}^{K} q(y=k|x) \Big[\underbrace{\log p(x|\widetilde{z}^{(k)})}_{\substack{\text{component-wise} \\ \text{reconstruction}}} - \underbrace{\mathrm{KL}(q(z|x, y=k)||p(z|y=k))}_{\substack{\text{Kullback-Leibler divergence} \\ \text{regularization on z}}} \Big] - \underbrace{\mathrm{KL}(q(y|x)||p(y))}_{\substack{\text{categorical} \\ \text{regularization}}}$$

$$(1)$$

with $\widetilde{z}^{(k)} \sim q(z|x, y = k)$ being the sampled latent code, $p(z|y = k)$ and $p(y)$ being the prior distributions (normal and uniform respectively). By maximizing Eq. 1, the model maximizes the data likelihood via reconstruction (first term), and regularises the model such that z tends to be normally distributed (second term) and samples are evenly distributed over components (third term).

During training, the model alleviates catastrophic forgetting by following the *mixture generative replay* strategy, mixing real examples of the current category with generated images of past categories. To detect outliers, the model uses the ELBO loss (Eq. 1) as an indicator of learning quality, modelling the likelihood of an example belonging to a learned category. For more details, refer to [3].

The authors also introduced a supervised form of the ELBO loss that replaces the unsupervised ELBO objective (Eq. 1) when used in a supervised setting (in this case the component y to update is not determined by the internal classifier $q(y|x)$ but selected by y_m): $E_{sup}(x) =$

$$\log q(y = y_m|x) + \log p(x|\bar{z}^{y_m}, y = y_m) - KL(q(z|x, y = y_m)||p(z|y = y_m)) \quad (2)$$

In our model the labels y_m are a self-supervision signal generated automatically based on a statistical hypothesis test - a two-sample t^2 Hotelling test that we adapted (cf. Sect. 4.1) - performed on the internal representation of the model.

4 Proposed Approach

4.1 Continual Detection and Recognition of Objects

In our model, one object category is supposed to be modelled by a *single* component, contrary to CURL that uses a GMM model allowing multiple components per category. As the latent variable z for each category tends to follow a multivariate normal distribution, because of the KL regularisation term during training, to decide if the current observation batch corresponds to a given class, we perform a two-sample Hotelling t^2 test [10], which is a statistical test for multivariate normal distributions. To this end, we compute the t^2 statistics:

$$t^2 = \frac{n_y * n_b}{n_y + n_b}(\bar{z}_y - \bar{z}_b)^T \widehat{\Sigma}^{-1}(\bar{z}_y - \bar{z}_b) , \quad (3)$$

with $\widehat{\Sigma}$ being the pooled covariance matrix determined by

$$\widehat{\Sigma} = \frac{(n_y - 1)\widehat{\Sigma}_{y_{sh}} + (n_b - 1)\widehat{\Sigma}_b}{n_y + n_b - 2} , \quad (4)$$

$\bar{z}_y$ and $\Sigma_{y_{sh}}$ the sample mean and covariance matrix of latent variable z corresponding to an object category y, $\bar{z}_b$ and Σ_b the sample mean and covariance matrix of the input batch and n_y, n_b the sample sizes of the two distributions respectively. The t^2 distribution follows the F distribution up to a factor, where d is the dimension of z:

$$\frac{n_y + n_b - d - 1}{(n_y + n_b - 2)d}t^2 \sim F(d, n_y + n_b - 1 - d) \quad (5)$$

Our null hypothesis H_0 is that the two means μ_y, μ_b of object class y and input batch b are equal, and we reject it if the left hand side of Eq. 5 is below a critical value related to a given p-value threshold. In practice, we compute the p-values for the tests between the current batch and each trained object category, and we select the class with the highest p-value if it is above the defined threshold. Otherwise, it is considered belonging to a new object category.

4.2   Online Parameter Estimation

In our continual learning setting, the embedding in the latent space of the VAE gradually evolves. To compute the mean and covariance of previous objects without storing past images, we approximate them by running averages. However, these approximated covariance matrices slightly underestimate the actual variance. This may lead to too large values in the t^2 statistics (Eq. 3) and eventually to very small p-values for known classes. To alleviate this problem, we apply a shrinkage operation to the running covariance matrices such that the diagonal entries are more homogeneous and the difference between eigenvalues is reduced.

$$\bar{z}_y(t) = (1 - \alpha)\bar{z}_y(t-1) + \alpha z_y(t) \,, \tag{6}$$

$$\widehat{\Sigma}_y(t) = (1 - \alpha)\widehat{\Sigma}_y(t-1) + \alpha(z_y(t) - \bar{z}_y(t))^T(z_y(t) - \bar{z}_y(t)) \,. \tag{7}$$

$$\widehat{\Sigma}_{y_{sh}}(t) = (1 - \gamma)\widehat{\Sigma}_y + \gamma * \frac{\mathrm{tr}(\widehat{\Sigma}_y)}{d}I \,, \tag{8}$$

where $z_y(t)$ is the embedding of class y, $\alpha \in (0,1)$ a small update factor, $\gamma > 0$ is the shrinkage coefficient and I the identity matrix. The equations are applied for the current class with real observations and for all the other classes with synthetic examples from generative replay. Finally, we do the Hotelling t^2 test (Eq. 4) using $\bar{z}_y$ and $\widehat{\Sigma}_{y_{sh}}$.

5   Experiments

5.1   Protocol

We evaluated our proposed approach on MNIST and Fashion-MNIST, each including 10 classes, a total of 60000 images of size 28×28 for training and 10000 images for test. The VAE architecture we used is the same as the one of CURL, i. e. a 4-layer MLP {1200, 600, 300, 150} as encoder and a two-layer MLP {500, 500} as decoder, with a 32-dimensional latent space. The learning rate is set to 10^{-3} with an Adam optimizer. The size of the outlier buffer is 100 for CURL, 200 for our model and for "CURL with HT" (as the test is performed on batches, we slightly increase the buffer to contain 2 batches and avoid potential fluctuations). The batch size is 100, thus $n_b = 100$ and n_y is empirically set to 20.

Our protocol consists of two consecutive sequences. In the first one, we present half of the training examples class by class in a random order to test the ability of the model to detect new classes. In the second one, we present the second half of the training data still class by class, in the same order as in the first sequence, to test the recognition performance of the model. We compared our approach with CURL [3], SOINN [4] and CURL combined with Hotelling t-squared test as an ablation study.

Table 1. Comparison with the state of the art on MNIST (mean of 3 runs ±SD).

Model	AMI	ARI	# Components	Accuracy
CURL [3]	0.518 ± 0.013	0.156 ± 0.02	126.6 ± 17.74	1.0 ± 0.0
CURL with HT	0.6 ± 0.04	0.41 ± 0.025	22.6 ± 1.69	0.87 ± 0.04
SOINN [4]	0.367 ± 0.002	0.013 ± 0.008	1507 ± 11.34	1.0 ± 0.0
Ours	$\mathbf{0.778 \pm 0.012}$	$\mathbf{0.769 \pm 0.02}$	$\mathbf{11 \pm 1.41}$	$\mathbf{1.0 \pm 0.0}$

Table 2. Comparison with the state of the art on Fashion-MNIST (mean of 3 runs ± SD).

Model	AMI	ARI	# Components	Accuracy
CURL [3]	0.429 ± 0.004	0.1006 ± 0.0111	170.0 ± 0.0	0.993 ± 0.004
CURL with HT	0.473 ± 0.0054	0.25 ± 0.008	31.3 ± 6.34	0.857 ± 0.03
SOINN [4]	0.342 ± 0.0016	0.016 ± 0.0003	1009 ± 17.518	$\mathbf{1.0 \pm 0.0}$
Ours	$\mathbf{0.57 \pm 0.02}$	$\mathbf{0.395 \pm 0.03}$	$\mathbf{13.33 \pm 0.94}$	0.798 ± 0.002

5.2   Results

To evaluate the quality of the learned clustering, we compute different standard metrics on the two test sets: accuracy (the label of each component is obtained by post labelling via majority vote), the Adjusted Mutual Information (AMI) and the Adjusted Random Index (ARI) measuring the correspondence of the learned clustering w.r.t. the Ground Truth. Our model considers that all examples of a batch belong to the category, while the other tested models evaluate each example individually. For a fair comparison, the other models are also evaluated batch by batch via majority vote of prediction amongst the batch.

On the MNIST dataset (Table 1), our model performs better than all other models for all indicators. In particular, the number of components is much closer to the real number of categories, thus greatly improving the AMI and ARI score, while not impacting the accuracy which remains at 100%. It is interesting to note that the application of the Hotelling test on CURL, decreases significantly the number of learned components. However, this does allow the model to reach the AMI and ARI score of our model and induces a drop in accuracy performance. This validates the need of using the supervised ELBO loss in our model.

On the Fashion-MNIST dataset (Table 2), the trend for AMI and ARI are similar to the ones observed on MNIST. However, here, this is obtained at the cost of a drop in accuracy. This may be explained as the Fashion-MNIST dataset is harder and by the fact that having a higher number of clusters facilitates a high accuracy (as the chance of mixing different classes in one component is reduced). However, for an autonomous agent, we prefer to have a smaller number of clusters as less examples can be required to label them.

In Fig. 1 we illustrate the evolution of model performance during training on Fashion-MNIST on the *detection accuracy*, i. e. the binary classification of "known" and "unknown" classes, and the *clustering accuracy* of the classes that have been learned by the agent, i. e. known classes (except for those considered by error as unknown). We can observe that each new class is detected at the right time and that the model is not subject to catastrophic forgetting.

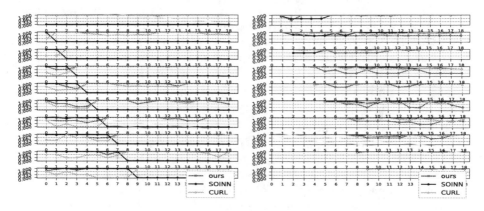

Fig. 1. The evolution of detection (left) and clustering accuracy (right) on Fashion-MNIST during training. The rows represent the 10 classes in the learned order.

6   Conclusion

In this paper, we proposed a self-supervised continual object representation learning algorithm extending the CURL model [3]. Our contribution lies in combining the model with a statistical hypothesis test allowing to detect unknown categories and to recognize previously learned categories, and in this way, to self-supervise the learning process without storing any previous examples. Compared to the state of the art, our model demonstrates its capacity to recognize learned objects in an online scenario while avoiding creating and reallocating new components for learned categories. Thus the model becomes more effective in automatically detecting the number of categories. Our proposal permits to moderate the amount of over-segmentation and achieves better performance in terms of standard clustering metrics AMI and ARI compared to the state-of-the-art algorithms CURL and SOINN [4] but may have lower accuracy due to fewer component creation. The introduced statistical test allows to detect properly the novel classes and recognize learned categories. In the future, we will evaluate our approach on more realistic scenarios for autonomous agents with video streams of more complex objects in difficult and varying environments. The balance to be found between the quantity of over segmentation and accuracy can be of primary interest in this context as well.

References

1. Bodesheim, P., Freytag, A., Rodner, E., Kemmler, M., Denzler, J.: Kernel null space methods for novelty detection. In: CVPR (2013)
2. Chen, T., Kornblith, S., Norouzi, M., Hinton, G.: A simple framework for contrastive learning of visual representations. In: ICML, pp. 1597–1607 (2020)
3. Rao, D., Visin, F., Rusu, A., Pascanu, R., Teh, Y.W., Hadsell, R.: Continual unsupervised representation learning. In: NeurIPS (2019)
4. Furao, S., Hasegawa, O.: An incremental network for on-line unsupervised classification and topology learning. Neural Netw. **19**(1), 90–106 (2006)
5. Ge, Z., Demyanov, S., Chen, Z., Garnavi, R.: Generative OpenMax for multi-class open set classification. In: BMVC (2017)
6. Geng, C., Huang, S.-J., Chen, S.: Recent advances in open set recognition: a survey. IEEE Trans. Pattern Anal. Mach. Intell. **43**, 3614–3631 (2020)
7. Hendrycks, D., Gimpel, K.: A baseline for detecting misclassified and out-of- distribution examples in neural networks. In: ICLR (2017)
8. Hess, S., Duivesteijn, W., Mocanu, D.: Softmax-based classification is k-means clustering: Formal proof, consequences for adversarial attacks, and improvement through centroid based tailoring. CoRR, abs/2001.01987 (2020)
9. Hodge, V., Austin, J.: A survey of outlier detection methodologies. Artif. Intell. Rev. **22**, 85–126 (2004)
10. Hotelling, H.: The generalization of student's ratio. Ann. Math. Stat. **2**(3), 360–378 (1931)
11. Kingma, D.P., Welling, M.: Auto-encoding variational Bayes. In: International Conference on Learning Representations (2014)
12. Kirkpatrick, J., et al.: Overcoming catastrophic forgetting in neural networks. Proc. Natl. Acad. Sci. **114**(13), 3521–3526 (2017)
13. Lakshminarayanan, B., Pritzel, A., Blundell, C.: Simple and scalable predictive uncertainty estimation using deep ensembles. In: NeurIPS, pp. 6402–6413 (2017)
14. Lee, K., Lee, K., Lee, H., Shin, J.: A simple unified framework for detecting out-of-distribution samples and adversarial attacks. In: NeurIPS (2018)
15. Liang, S., Li, Y., Srikant, R.: Enhancing the reliability of out-of-distribution image detection in neural networks. In: ICLR (2018)
16. Liu, W., Wang, X., Owens, J.D., Li, Y.: Energy-based out-of-distribution detection. In: Advances in Neural Information Processing Systems (2020)
17. Lopez-Paz, D., Ranzato, M.: Gradient episodic memory for continual learning. In: Advances in Neural Information Processing Systems, pp. 6467–6476 (2017)
18. Nalisnick, E., Matsukawa, A., Teh, Y.W., Gorur, D., Lakshminarayanan, B.: Do deep generative models know what they don't know? In: ICLR (2019)
19. Pimentel, M.A.F., Clifton, D.A., Clifton, L., Tarassenko, L.: A review of novelty detection. Sig. Process. **99**, 215–249 (2014)
20. Rebuffi, S., Kolesnikov, A., Sperl, G., Lampert, C.: iCaRL: incremental classifier and representation learning. In: CVPR, pp. 2001–2010 (2017)

21. Ren, J., et al.: Likelihood ratios for out-of-distribution detection. In: Advances in Neural Information Processing Systems (2019)
22. Rusu, A., et al.: Progressive neural networks. arXiv preprint arXiv:1606.04671 (2016)
23. Serrà, J., Alvarez, D., Gómez, V., Slizovskaia, O., Núñez, J.F., Luque, J.: Input complexity and out-of-distribution detection with likelihood-based generative models. In: International Conference on Learning Representations (2020)
24. Smith, J., Taylor, C., Baer, S., Dovrolis, C.: Unsupervised progressive learning and the STAM architecture. In: IJCAI (2021)
25. Zenke, F., Poole, B., Ganguli, S.: Continual learning through synaptic intelligence. In: International Conference on Machine Learning, pp. 3987–3995 (2017)

Towards Scalable Simulation of Federated Learning

Tomasz Kołodziej and Paweł Rościszewski[(✉)]

Department of Computer Architecture, Faculty of Electronics, Telecommunications
and Informatics, Gdańsk University of Technology, Gdańsk, Poland
pawel.rosciszewski@pg.edu.pl

Abstract. Federated learning (FL) allows to train models on decentralized data while maintaining data privacy, which unlocks the availability of large and diverse datasets for many practical applications. The ongoing development of aggregation algorithms, distribution architectures and software implementations aims for enabling federated setups employing thousands of distributed devices, selected from millions. Since the availability of such computing infrastructure is a big barrier to experimenting with new approaches, we claim that efficient simulation of FL is necessary and propose the PaSSiFLora library for simulating FL clients in a cluster environment. In PaSSiFLora, the training algorithm is actually performed on real data, but each cluster node can simulate multiple FL clients. Because uniform random selection of clients results in poor simulation performance due to load imbalance, we propose to use uniform random selection of MultiClients. Each MultiClient runs on a single cluster node and in each training iteration is responsible for simulating several clients, selected from a set of local clients. Our experimental results based on the FEMNIST dataset show that PaSSiFLora is capable of simulating 1536 clients and has a good scalability on 48 cluster nodes, which reduces the average iteration time to 13.57 s, from 330.61 s in the case of one cluster node. The MultiClient architecture allows to improve the average performance by up to 75% while it does not cause significant differences in model accuracy during the training. Additionally, correctness of the training is verified against existing FL frameworks: LEAF and TFF.

Keywords: Federated learning · Simulation · HPC

1 Introduction

In *deep learning*, it is empirically predictable how model accuracy improves as the training dataset increases [6]. Availability of data is crucial, not only in terms of dataset size, but also in terms of data diversity. For example, empirical results from multi-institutional collaborations in medical applications clearly indicate that sharing data between institutions allows to train models of significantly higher generalizability [12]. Yet, due to privacy sensitivity or large data quantity,

© Springer Nature Switzerland AG 2021
T. Mantoro et al. (Eds.): ICONIP 2021, CCIS 1516, pp. 248–256, 2021.
https://doi.org/10.1007/978-3-030-92307-5_29

it is often not possible to keep the whole dataset in a datacenter. This is where we can benefit from *federated learning* (FL) [10], a new approach in machine learning allowing for collaboration of machines that possess their own data and resources to train a shared model without exchanging the data itself.

Federated Learning was first presented as "loose federation of participating devices (to which we refer as clients) which are coordinated by a central server" [10]. Clients are autonomous devices capable of gathering, storing and processing data. Those devices can cooperate in a synchronous manner, performing local training and contributing the results to improve the shared model, stored and distributed by the server. FL is divided into iterations, each consisting of client selection, model and training program broadcast, client computation, update aggregation and model update. Each of these steps can be fine-tuned to better solve the learning task, hence the need for efficient way of simulating, that would facilitate further research and prototyping.

A recent review of FL applications [9] classifies them into three categories: *applications in mobile devices applications in industrial engineering*, and *applications in health care*. One of the first practical FL applications were improving virtual keyboard search suggestion quality [13] and further smartphone-related improvements deployed at Google. Production system design proposed in [1] aims for FL workloads scaling up to tens of thousands of participants selected from hundreds of millions of mobile devices. The proposed FL protocol consists of iterations called *rounds*, each divided into three phases: *selection* of participants from the available devices, *configuration* of the FL plan for the selected devices and *reporting* along with aggregating or abandoning the model updates. Apart from such a scalable system design, implementing FL in large scale requires advancements in aggregation algorithms, because efficiency of the basic *federated averaging* is limited to hundreds of devices in each round. Since model convergence depends on multiple factors, simulation solutions are needed for empirical testing of new approaches without the need to employ thousands of target mobile devices.

In practice, models trained in the FL paradigm would be fed with datasets acquired by millions of distributed devices, each drawing from a potentially different statistical distribution. Effectively, the datasets would be significantly larger than the traditional ones that could be stored and processed in a datacenter. This means that experimenting with FL approaches requires different benchmark datasets than in the case of centralized setups [2]. Although standard datasets such as MNIST or CIFAR-10 are still being used, they are not realistic for the federated scenario, while many of the more realistic ones are proprietary [2]. It is a common approach to derive realistic datasets from publicly available data using statistically adequate partitioning of existing datasets, automatic data generation or clever preprocessing. For example, the Sentiment140 dataset consists of short posts from a social network automatically annotated based on contained emoticons. A selection of open-source datasets is proposed within LEAF [2], a FL benchmarking framework that, apart from the datasets,

contributes certain reference implementations and metrics that facilitate reproducible experimentation.

Recently, main challenges in FL include high communication cost [8], statistical and structural heterogeneity and preserving privacy in FL applications by
defending against re-identification, dataset reconstruction and tracing attacks.
Solutions include secure implementations, data anonymization, data encryption, decentralized storage and secure multi-party computation. There is a need
for efficient and reliable simulation environments that would allow for testing
new approaches in all the aforementioned development fields. The remainder of
this paper is organized as follows. In Sect. 2 we provide an overview of existing approaches to FL simulation. In Sect. 3.1 we propose PaSSiFLora (Parallel
Scalable Simulation of Federated Learning)[1], a MPI-based Python library that
allows for scalable simulation of FL training on clusters. Additionally, it introduces the MultiClient architecture, described in Sect. 3.2, which eliminates load
imbalance, while preserving approximately correct training results. Experimental results are reported and discussed in Sect. 4, while conclusions and future
work are described in Sect. 5.

2   Simulation of Federated Learning

Since FL is targeted for distributed hardware environments with heterogeneous
computing devices, latencies, data resources and reliability levels, it is difficult,
if not impossible to perform repeatable end reliable experiments on the target
hardware environments. Thus, evaluating new FL approaches (e.g. communication optimizations or privacy protection) requires a simulation environment that
would run in a more accessible hardware setup and produce reliable experimental results in terms of quality metrics for the federated model, training performance and convergence. All of these targets rely heavily on training data and
the trained model, so such simulations should actually execute the local training
steps, but communication should be modeled with regard to the aforementioned
target hardware heterogeneity.

PrivacyFL [11] is a FL simulator that focuses on modeling privacy mechanisms such as differential privacy [4] and differentially private federated logistic
regression [7]. This allows to evaluate the model accuracy, total training time,
approximate convergence bounds and influence of real-time dropouts depending
on configuration of encryption, local and global noise, dropout tolerance, client
latencies and dataset options. In particular, the reported experimental results
based on the KDDCup99 dataset show how increasing the number of clients from
10 through 50 up to 100, as well as increasing the privacy leakage threshold from
0.01 through 0.1 to 1 improves the federated model accuracy. The results show
also how the simulator can be used to select the optimal strategy for each client
in the case of imbalanced client datasets and different privacy requirements.
The proposed case study illustrates a situation when it is beneficial for all three
clients to collaborate using their required privacy constraints, even though one

---

[1] https://github.com/TomKolo/passiflora.

of the clients has significantly higher privacy requirements. Further results show a case where FL can be beneficial in a serverless setting and a case where different client latencies are considered by the simulator in calculating the time to receive the federated weights. Although PrivacyFL is characterized as scalable, no scalability results are reported in the paper. The framework utilizes a scalable agent-based architecture with communication via messages between the agents, however the communication is implemented as invocation of methods between the agent objects in Python, which does not support distributed simulations.

Dedicated simulation approaches can be used for specific applications. For example, the FL approach to browser history suggestions in Firefox [5] is presented as the first non-simulation application outside of Google. Since learning is performed in an actually private environment, the authors had no access to target data, so the system had to be developed without knowing the data characteristics. Because of that, Rprop optimization algorithm has been chosen, that dynamically adapts learning rates for individual weights. Although it is a practical deployment, simulations were used to evaluate optimization approaches.

The existing FL frameworks aimed for training in real federated setups can be also successfully used for experimentation. The aforementioned LEAF benchmarking framework supports experiment reproducibility by providing a set of datasets, metrics and reference implementations, however it does not focus on scalability of the experiments. The most straight-forward, but also the least efficient way of performing FL is to compute each of clients updates sequentially, on a single machine. This is the way the LEAF implementation, as well as TensorFlow Federated (TFF)[2] work. It allows for no distribution and even though it puts very little limitations on training's parameters (e.g. number of clients participating in iteration) it does not support large-scale experimentation due to long execution time. We argue that both implementation and conceptual advancements are needed, focusing on reproducible FL simulations at scale.

3   Scalable FL Simulation with PaSSiFLora

3.1   Implementation

In PaSSiFLora simulations, the client-server model underlying the FL scheme is imitated by a MPI-based architecture with server responsible for orchestration and clients performing actual model training on local data subsets. Such approach allows to utilize cluster resources in order to increase the simulation performance. The communication scheme has been implemented in Python using the mpi4py MPI wrapper and consists of initialization phase and multiple training iterations.

In the initialization phase, client processes are registered and model weights are distributed across them. Because large target datasets could not be stored on one node, there is an option to distribute the data via MPI. Alternatively,

---

[2] https://www.tensorflow.org/federated.

data can be read from local hard drives. The library comes with a set of scripts for downloading, partitioning and distribution of data using the SCP protocol.

The training iterations consist of distributing the weights, performing local training using the TensorFlow library and sending the weight updates for *averaging* and model update on the server side.

Both clients and server are Python programs, distributed among the available computational nodes, that take certain FL parameters as arguments. The client requires standard training parameters such as *minibatch size, optimizer, learning rate* and *number of epochs*, while parameters for the server are FL-related and include: *number of clients participating in each iteration, client selection method, percentage of discarded client updates (dropout)* and *type of model update averaging*.

3.2 The MultiClient Architecture

While FL aims for selecting thousands from millions of available clients, the typical cluster environment comes with dozens of nodes. Because of that, in each round of PaSSiFLora simulation, each node should be able to simulate multiple clients. In the basic architecture depicted in Fig. 1a, a set of Clients is selected by the server in a random uniform manner for each round. This setup is similar to the birthday paradox: in a set of randomly chosen clients, the probability that some pair of them will be simulated by the same cluster node causes significant load imbalance between the cluster nodes.

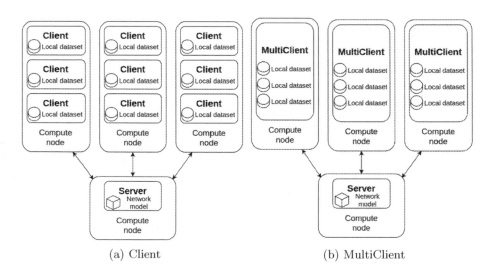

(a) Client   (b) MultiClient

Fig. 1. The Client and MultiClient architectures

To prevent this imbalance, we propose a combination of sequential and parallel approach, depicted by Fig. 1b where each computational node possesses a set of client datasets and performs the training sequentially, acting on behalf of multiple clients in each iteration. The Server assigns a number of clients to be simulated on each node and the specific clients are selected in a random uniform manner by each MultiClient. This allows for equal distribution of computations, preventing overloading some nodes while potentially the rest of them remain idle. In order for this approach to work, due to limitations of training data storage, only a subset of clients can be simulated by a MultiClient. This limitation might influence the resultant model accuracy and make the proposed approach infeasible, so the significance of this influence should be examined empirically.

4   Experimental Results

In this Section we provide and discuss results for a set of experiments involving federated training of a 2D convolutional model for classification of written digits and characters from the FEMNIST (Federated Extended MNIST[3]) dataset. The aim of these experiments is to empirically evaluate the proposed simulation library. The experiments were performed on computing nodes equipped with 8-core Intel Xeon CPUs, running GNU/Linux OS. The scalability and Multi-Client experiments described in Sects. 4.2 and 4.3 were performed on a 49-node cluster (48 clients and 1 coordinating server) on a big (50%) subset of the FEMNIST dataset. In the experiments for comparison against different frameworks (Sect. 4.1), a smaller subset (5%) of FEMNIST was used. For all experiments, the required data was distributed across the appropriate nodes beforehand. The training parameters used for the individual experiments are outlined in Table 1.

Table 1. Training parameter configurations

Parameter	Sect. 4.1	Sect. 4.2	Sect. 4.3
FL parameters			
Training iterations	1000	–	2000
Clients per iteration	3	48	48–432
Weight update method	Mean, weighted by the local dataset size		
Local training parameters			
Epochs	100	10	
Batch size	10	64	
Training algorithm	SGD	Adadelta	
Loss function	Sparse categorical crossentropy		
Learning rate	0.005	–	

---

[3] https://leaf.cmu.edu/.

4.1 Verification Against Existing Libraries

A comparison of average iteration times (averaged from 1000 iterations), achieved test accuracies (averaged from 3 runs) and loss function values (averaged from 3 runs) is presented in Table 2 for LEAF, TFF 0.17.0 and PaSSiFLora (running on a single node and running on three nodes). The achieved model accuracies and loss function values are similar, which shows the correctness of PaSSiFLora.

Table 2. Comparison of PaSSiFLora against chosen existing libraries

Metric	LEAF	TFF	PaSSiFLora (1 node)	PaSSiFLora (3 nodes)
Avg. iteration time	162.01 s	91.19 s	202.64 s	79.68 s
Test accuracy	78.9%	77.08%	77.76%	77.34%
Loss function value	1.121	1.42	1.17	1.13

In the single-node setup, TFF has the best performance. This is probably caused by an optimized low-level implementation of model weight exchange mechanism. Also, the single-node performance of PaSSiFLora is around 25% worse than LEAF, which is probably caused by communication overheads introduced by the distributed implementation of PaSSiFLora, which has to distribute copies of the locally stored model. On the other hand, the distributed implementation allows for parallel execution on multiple nodes and the results show that three nodes are sufficient to achieve the best training performance.

4.2 Scalability Results

Average iteration execution times depending on the number of nodes used in the cluster are presented in Fig. 2. The results show good scalability of the proposed implementation, where the execution time of 330.61 s for one node has been successfully reduced to 13.57 s using 48 nodes.

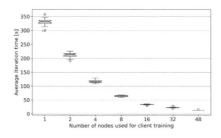

Fig. 2. Scalability of the proposed PaSSiFLora library

4.3   MultiClient Performance and Convergence

The proposed MultiClient architecture described in Sect. 3.2 is compared to the basic Client architecture in terms of computational performance in Fig. 3a and in terms of trained model convergence in Fig. 3b. In all cases, 48 cluster nodes were used for the training and 1 node was used as the coordinating server.

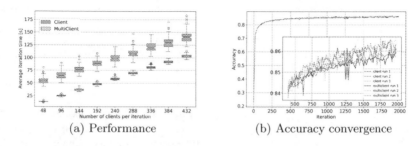

(a) Performance   (b) Accuracy convergence

Fig. 3. Client vs MultiClient comparison

The results show that in average, the MultiClient architecture allows to significantly improve the training performance. In the case of one client selected per computing node, the average iteration time is reduced from 54.84 s to 13.54 s, while in the case of 9 clients per node, it is reduced from 141.75 s to 103.21 s. Additionally, the results reveal large iteration time discrepancies in the basic Client architecture, that is prevented by the MultiClient solution. At the same time, the results show that the differences in model's convergence and overall accuracy between Client and MultiClient solutions are not very significant, though noticeable (average accuracy difference of 0.235% points).

5   Conclusions and Future Work

In this paper, we have pointed out the need for scalable simulations of *Federated Learning* and proposed PaSSiFLora, a Python library that allows for scalable FL simulation on clusters. Additionally, we have proposed the MultiClient architecture that significantly improves scalability of the simulations, while preserving reasonable training accuracy. Unlike many of the SOTA applications, FL does not necessarily involve big models, so legacy clusters with CPUs seem to be feasible for such simulations, instead of high performance workstations with GPUs.

In the future, PaSSiFLora should be extended by additional simulation parameters, such as performance, power consumption and reliability modeling [3]. Also, performance within a single node should be profiled and optimized.

References

1. Bonawitz, K., et al.: Towards federated learning at scale: system design. arXiv:1902.01046 [cs, stat] (February 2019). http://arxiv.org/abs/1902.01046

2. Caldas, S., et al.: LEAF: a benchmark for federated settings. arXiv:1812.01097 [cs, stat] (December 2019). http://arxiv.org/abs/1812.01097

3. Czarnul, P., et al.: MERPSYS: an environment for simulation of parallel application execution on large scale HPC systems. Simula. Model. Pract. Theor. **77**(C), 124–140 (2017). https://doi.org/10.1016/j.simpat.2017.05.009

4. Dwork, C., McSherry, F., Nissim, K., Smith, A.: Calibrating noise to sensitivity in private data analysis. In: Halevi, S., Rabin, T. (eds.) TCC 2006. LNCS, vol. 3876, pp. 265–284. Springer, Heidelberg (2006). https://doi.org/10.1007/11681878_14

5. Hartmann, F., Suh, S., Komarzewski, A., Smith, T.D., Segall, I.: Federated learning for ranking browser history suggestions. arXiv:1911.11807 [cs, stat] (November 2019)

6. Hestness, J., et al.: Deep learning scaling is predictable, empirically. arXiv preprint arXiv:1712.00409 (2017)

7. Jayaraman, B., Wang, L., Evans, D., Gu, Q.: Distributed learning without distress: privacy-preserving empirical risk minimization. In: Proceedings of the 32nd International Conference on Neural Information Processing Systems, NIPS 2018, Montréal, Canada, pp. 6346–6357. Curran Associates Inc., Red Hook (2018)

8. Konecný, J., McMahan, H.B., Yu, F.X., Richtárik, P., Suresh, A.T., Bacon, D.: Federated learning: strategies for improving communication efficiency. CoRR abs/1610.05492 (2016). http://arxiv.org/abs/1610.05492

9. Li, L., Fan, Y., Tse, M., Lin, K.Y.: A review of applications in federated learning. Comput. Ind. Eng. **149**, 106854 (2020). https://doi.org/10.1016/j.cie.2020.106854. http://www.sciencedirect.com/science/article/pii/S0360835220305532

10. McMahan, H.B., Moore, E., Ramage, D., Hampson, S.: Communication-efficient learning of deep networks from decentralized data. arXiv preprint arXiv:1602.05629 (2016)

11. Mugunthan, V., Peraire-Bueno, A., Kagal, L.: PrivacyFL: a simulator for privacy-preserving and secure federated learning. In: Proceedings of the 29th ACM International Conference on Information & Knowledge Management, pp. 3085–3092. Association for Computing Machinery, New York (October 2020). https://doi.org/10.1145/3340531.3412771

12. Sheller, M.J., et al.: Federated learning in medicine: facilitating multi-institutional collaborations without sharing patient data. Sci. Rep. **10**(1), 12598 (2020). https://doi.org/10.1038/s41598-020-69250-1. https://www.nature.com/articles/s41598-020-69250-1

13. Yang, T., et al.: Applied federated learning: improving Google keyboard query suggestions. arXiv:1812.02903 [cs, stat] (December 2018)

DYME: A Dynamic Metric for Dialog Modeling Learned from Human Conversations

Florian von Unold[1,2] , Monika Wintergerst[1(✉)] , Lenz Belzner[3], and Georg Groh[1]

[1] Department of Informatics, Technical University of Munich, Boltzmannstr. 3, 85748 Garching, Germany
{florian.von-unold,monika.wintergerst}@tum.de
[2] MaibornWolff GmbH, Theresienhoehe 13, 80338 Munich, Germany
[3] Faculty of Electrical Engineering and Information Technology, Technische Hochschule Ingolstadt, Esplanade 10, 85049 Ingolstadt, Germany

Abstract. With increasing capabilities of dialog generation methods, modeling human conversation characteristics to steer the dialog generation towards natural, human-like interactions has garnered research interest. So far, dialogs have mostly been modeled with developer-defined, static metrics. This work shows that metrics change within individual conversations and differ between conversations, illustrating the need for flexible metrics to model human dialogs. We propose DYME, a DYnamic MEtric for dialog modeling learned from human conversational data with a neural-network-based approach. DYME outperforms a moving average baseline in predicting the metrics for the next utterance of a given conversation by about 20%, demonstrating the ability of this new approach to model dynamic human communication characteristics.

Keywords: Dialog modeling · Conversational metrics · Dialog systems · Natural language processing

1 Introduction and Related Work

State-of-the-art methods for written, open-domain dialog generation, for example [1] and [19], can produce syntactically correct and often semantically suitable responses. However, they tend to lack mechanisms to include human preferences in the generation process. One of the main challenges is expressing criteria of "good" human dialog in models that can then be used to optimize dialog systems. Even when such criteria are defined, they usually represent only individual aspects of what makes a good dialog.

There has been previous research on communication characteristics in dialogs and their progression within conversations. Chaves and Gerosa [4] derive social

---

F. von Unold and M. Wintergerst—Contributed equally

© Springer Nature Switzerland AG 2021
T. Mantoro et al. (Eds.): ICONIP 2021, CCIS 1516, pp. 257–264, 2021.
https://doi.org/10.1007/978-3-030-92307-5_30

characteristics for chatbots to improve human-machine interaction, such as *conscientiousness* and *emotional intelligence*. Ghosal et al. [8] conduct a comprehensive investigation on the utterance-level view of written dialog and the importance of context. They examine which labels follow each other in a conversation. However, their investigation is limited to discrete human labels already present in the data. Sharma et al. [16] label a conversational dataset with an empathy classification model [17]. Their dataset only contains post-response pairs, whereas our proposed approach considers multi-turn dialogs.

When human communication characteristics have been identified, they can be modeled as computable metrics. These can then be used to define reward functions for optimizing dialog systems. Jaques et al. [9] design several intrinsic reward functions, such as eliciting positive sentiment or laughter from users, to improve a dialog model's conversational ability through *Reinforcement Learning (RL)*. Other RL-based approaches use dialog acts to steer the conversation [20], or a combination of the metrics *coherence, informativity*, and *ease of answering* [10]. Saleh et al. [15] demonstrate that a dialog model can be optimized for asking more questions by providing a positive reward for generated utterances with question words and question marks. As optimizing for single metrics may lead to a worse overall conversation quality [9], Saleh et al. [15] define a composite reward function based on multiple metrics, where fixed coefficients place different weights on the different rewards.

Overall, we can see that previous research on modeling dialogs through metrics applies static, developer-defined rules that every utterance in a dialog should adhere to. However, a conversational partner should not always act the same but react to the given dialog history. We hence propose a flexible, data-driven dialog metric predictor to model dynamic communication characteristics.

This work investigates the hypothesis that metrics in human dialogs are dynamic and that static, developer-defined metric models might not cover such dynamic behavior. An analysis of written conversations shows that metrics in human dialogs are indeed dynamic. Thus, a neural-network-based approach to learning metrics' dynamics within human conversations is developed. The model is called *DYME - a DYnamic MEtric for dialog modeling*. Experiments show that DYME outperforms a moving average baseline by about 20% in predicting the metrics of a dialog's continuation given the dialog's context[1].

2   Metric Dynamics in Human Dialogs

This section presents the metrics used in our experiments and our findings regarding their dynamic changes throughout human dialogs.

Most metrics used in our work are adapted versions of the reward functions in [15]. In contrast to the original reward functions, which act over the whole conversation to return a certain reward, a metric computes a real-valued number for a single utterance. It does not judge or interpret the outcome a priori.

---

[1] Code and models on GitHub: https://github.com/florianvonunold/DYME.

- *Utterance length* is the count of words in the given utterance.
- *Self repetition* is the count of distinct words in the given utterance that occur also in any of the previous utterances of the current speaker.
- *Utterance repetition* is the count of distinct words in the given utterance that occur also in the previous utterance.
- *Word repetition* is the count of words that occur multiple times within the given utterance, i.e., the count of word duplicates.
- *Question* indicates whether the given utterance contains both a question word and a question mark.
- *Deepmoji sentiment pos/neg* is the positive/negative value of the given utterance's sentiment, provided by the Deepmoji model [7]. The Deepmoji model originally generates outputs in the range $[-1,+1]$. Since our experiments require ratio-scale variables, the sentiment is split into the positive and the negative part to obtain two variables in ratio-scale.
- *Deepmoji coherence, Infersent coherence, USE similarity*, and *Word2Vec coherence* are the cosine similarities between the Deepmoji [7], Infersent [5], Universal Sentence Encoder [3], and Word2Vec [13] embeddings of the given utterance and the previous utterance, respectively.
- *Conversation repetition* is the count of distinct words in the given utterance that have already been used in the whole conversation so far. This metric is an extension to the adapted metrics from [15] and measures how often conversation partners reuse words from the whole dialog history.

In addition to the adapted reward function metrics above, three empathy-based metrics are implemented. Each of these metrics is an instance of the RoBERTa-based bi-encoder model for identifying empathy by Sharma et al. [17]:

- *Emotional reaction level* indicates whether the given utterance expresses emotion in response to the previous utterance.
- *Interpretation level* indicates whether the utterance communicates an understanding of feelings and experiences in response to the previous one.
- *Exploration level* indicates whether the given utterance explores feelings and experiences not stated in the previous utterance.

All three models are trained from scratch using the default parameters and the Reddit dataset provided by Sharma et al. [17]. The models predict the correct labels similarly well as originally reported in [17].

Two open-domain, human-written, two-speaker, multi-turn dialog datasets, DailyDialog [11] and EmpatheticDialogues [14], are used in this work. The dialogs in each dataset are grouped per dialog length to investigate differences between dialogs of different lengths. Length groups with less than 100 dialogs are discarded to ensure a meaningful amount of samples per group.

The utterances in each dialog in both datasets are labeled with the metrics introduced above. Then, the *Coefficient of Variation (CV)* [2] is applied to quantify the variability of metrics within the dialogs. The CV divides the metric's standard deviation by the metric's mean. It has several attractive characteristics for the investigation of metric variability. First, the CV is dimensionless, enabling comparisons of variables of different scales [2]. Secondly, it yields the variability in units of the mean. The CV is only meaningful if the data is on a ratio scale [2], which is valid for all used metrics.

We use $CV_{l,m}$ to denote the CV for a group of dialogs of length l and a given metric m. It divides the average intra-dialog standard deviation of metric m over all dialogs of length l by the average intra-dialog metric mean for all dialogs of length l. In both datasets, $CV_{l,m}$ amounts to at least 1.0 for the majority of the metrics and across most dialog lengths. This shows that the metric values are variable within the dialogs in both datasets.

We further consider that metrics may be independent of the dialog's length but dependent on the position of the utterance in the dialog. The CV per dialog position, $CV_{p,m}$, is derived similarly to $CV_{l,m}$. It divides the standard deviation of metric m, computed at position p, by the metric mean of all utterances at p. Figure 1 shows a heatmap of $CV_{p,m}$ for all positions and all metrics in Daily-Dialog. Larger values have darker colors. An undefined $CV_{p,m}$, shown by blank cells, occurs at early positions for metrics that refer to previous utterances.

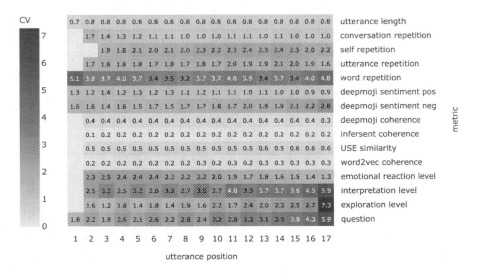

Fig. 1. Heatmap of $CV_{p,m}$, the average variability of metric m across all utterances at position p, for all utterance positions and all metrics in the dialogs in DailyDialog

Figure 1 shows that for *question*, positions with high variability are followed by positions with lower variability, and vice versa. Further, the CVs for *question* and *exploration level* seem to correlate. This was also observed in a qualitative analysis of sample dialogs. The circulatory behavior between these two metrics and the metric *interpretation level* can be interpreted as a transfer of information between speakers, as explained by the concept of bi-turn dialog flow [11]. All these behaviors were also observed in the EmpatheticDialogues dataset, indicating that they are not merely characteristics of this specific dataset.

3   DYME - a DYnamic MEtric for Dialog Modeling

This section presents an approach to learn the metrics' dynamics from human dialogs, combining them into a single dynamic metric, coined DYME.

DYME is a regression head on top of a pre-trained BERT model [6] with frozen layers. The input consists of three major elements: the textual context, the metric context, and the prediction position q. For the textual context, the raw texts of all utterances $u_1, ..., u_q$ in the dialog until prediction position q are concatenated into a single sequence of characters and passed to a pre-trained BERT model [18], which creates an embedding. For the metric context, the values of all utterance metrics for each utterance position up to and including the prediction position q are concatenated into another vector. The metric context vector must always have the same size due to the fixed layer sizes in the regression head. Hence, for predictions at earlier positions, the missing metric values for the remaining positions are filled with -1, referred to as *filling values*.

The textual context, the metric context, and the prediction position q are finally concatenated into a single vector. This vector is passed to the regression head, consisting of a fully connected dense layer, an application of the *rectified linear unit function (ReLu)*, a dropout layer, and an output projection layer that returns the predicted metric values for position $q + 1$.

The labeled DailyDialog and EmpatheticDialogues datasets are used for supervised training with a split of 80/10/10 for training, validation, and testing, respectively. A training sample is generated from a dialog using all positions up to the last utterance position as the input and the final utterance position as the prediction target. Only one sample is generated per dialog in the datasets. Earlier experiments showed that generating multiple samples from a single dialog may introduce a leak of information from seen to unseen samples. Furthermore, only dialogs with a maximum length of eight are used. Dialogs shorter than eight utterances are present in both datasets, meaning the model can be trained and tested on a more diverse set of samples. In total, this generates roughly 33,000 samples, which are shuffled randomly. Except for the filling values, the metrics are normalized to the range [0, 1] using min-max normalization. The learning objective is to minimize the *Mean Squared Error (MSE)* loss between the predicted and the true metric values. DYME is trained for five epochs with a batch size of 16 samples, using the AdamW optimizer [12] with a learning rate of 0.0005. The learning rate is linearly decreased to 0 over the whole training procedure.

DYME is compared to a simple baseline model that uses the per-metric average of the given metric context as prediction of the metrics at the next utterance position, and does not use the textual context. It is used to investigate whether DYME's context-dependent modeling is beneficial for the metric prediction. If each metric were static within a dialog, the moving average baseline would predict the correct metric value at any given utterance position.

On the test set, the baseline makes an average prediction error across all positions and all metrics of roughly 23%, whereas DYME only makes a prediction error of roughly 18%. More precisely, the *Root Mean Square Error (RMSE)* of the baseline is 0.2326, and the RMSE of DYME is 0.1845, representing 4.81% points absolute improvement or 20.68% relative improvement of DYME over the baseline. Table 1 shows the prediction errors for each metric, averaged across all utterance positions. Overall it shows that DYME improves over the baseline across almost all metrics except *utterance length*. The improvement is more notable for the more complex metrics, such as the coherence and empathy metrics. For the word-count-based repetition metrics, it is less striking.

Table 1. Average RMSE for each metric in descending order of the improvement of DYME over the baseline (the reported value for a metric m describes the model's average prediction error across all positions when predicting the value of metric m)

Metric	DYME	Baseline	Absolute improvement	Relative improvement (%)
Word2Vec coherence	0.1237	0.2575	0.1338	51,96
Infersent coherence	0.1086	0.2232	0.1146	51,34
Deepmoji coherence	0.2114	0.2879	0.0765	26,57
Question	0.2121	0.2804	0.0683	24,36
USE similarity	0.1552	0.2002	0.0450	22,48
Exploration level	0.3048	0.3599	0.0551	15,31
Emotional reaction level	0.2621	0.3059	0.0438	14,32
Interpretation level	0.3370	0.3791	0.0421	11,11
Word repetition	0.0600	0.0671	0.0071	10,58
Conversation repetition	0.0781	0.0854	0.0073	8,55
Deepmoji sentiment	0.1568	0.1700	0.0041	7,76
Self repetition	0.1068	0.1149	0.0081	7,05
Utterance repetition	0.0954	0.1020	0.0066	6,47
Utterance length	0.1039	0.0954	−0.0085	−8,91

4   Discussion and Conclusion

The analysis of two different datasets shows that there are measurable metric dynamics in human dialogs, revealing the need for dynamic dialog modeling.

DYME's performance is not perfect with an average prediction error of roughly 18%. We observe that DYME outperforms the baseline on all metrics except *utterance length*. This could be due to the rather low variability of the metric, which makes the moving average baseline a good predictor of it.

It must be noted that most experiments were only performed once using a particular subset of training and validation data, and should be repeated multiple times using different data folds to ensure more robust results.

One may argue that BERT embeddings already implicitly entail metric information, and that explicitly labeling dialogs with metrics might therefore be redundant. However, dialogs generated by current methods have weaknesses like repetitiveness or lack of semantic coherence. Current research attempts to remedy these weaknesses through human-defined metrics or specific reward functions. This indicates that BERT embeddings either do not contain the desired metric information or that current dialog generation methods cannot use this information properly yet. DYME continues this line of research by explicitly learning the dynamic of previously defined metrics in human dialogs. Moreover, predicting human-defined metrics at any given position in a dialog could allow for an interpretation of why a dialog model generates a particular utterance.

Our approach depends on a set of developer-defined metrics. However, it is not intended to learn a universal metric encompassing all aspects of human dialog. It is merely demonstrated that metrics in human dialogs are dynamic and that such dynamic behavior can be learned from human dialog data. In that regard, DYME can and should be extended with new metrics as required.

Our results encourage further research. Fine-tuning pre-trained dialog models using the deviation from DYME's predicted metrics as negative reward signal could show whether this approach generates dialog utterances that reflect human communication characteristics. This approach can be applied to any RL fine-tuning method and any dialog model architecture.

References

1. Bao, S., et al.: PLATO-2: Towards building an open-domain chatbot via curriculum learning. arXiv preprint arXiv:2006.16779 (2020)
2. Brown, C.E.: Coefficient of variation. In: Applied Multivariate Statistics in Geohydrology and Related Sciences, pp. 155–157. Springer (1998). https://doi.org/10.1007/978-3-642-80328-4_13
3. Cer, D., et al.: Universal sentence encoder. arXiv preprint arXiv:1803.11175 (2018)
4. Chaves, A.P., Gerosa, M.A.: How should my chatbot interact? A survey on social characteristics in human-chatbot interaction design. Int. J. Hum.-Comput. Interact. **37**(8), 729–758 (2021)
5. Conneau, A., Kiela, D., Schwenk, H., Barrault, L., Bordes, A.: Supervised learning of universal sentence representations from natural language inference data. In: Proceedings of the 2017 Conference on Empirical Methods in Natural Language Processing, pp. 670–680. Association for Computational Linguistics, Copenhagen, Denmark, September 2017. https://doi.org/10.18653/v1/D17-1070
6. Devlin, J., Chang, M.W., Lee, K., Toutanova, K.: BERT: Pre-training of deep bidirectional transformers for language understanding. In: Proceedings of the 2019 Conference of the North American Chapter of the Association for Computational Linguistics: Human Language Technologies, Volume 1 (Long and Short Papers), pp. 4171–4186 (2019)
7. Felbo, B., Mislove, A., Søgaard, A., Rahwan, I., Lehmann, S.: Using millions of emoji occurrences to learn any-domain representations for detecting sentiment, emotion and sarcasm. In: Conference on Empirical Methods in Natural Language Processing (EMNLP) (2017)

8. Ghosal, D., Majumder, N., Mihalcea, R., Poria, S.: Utterance-level dialogue understanding: an empirical study. arXiv preprint arXiv:2009.13902 (2020)

9. Jaques, N., et al.: Way off-policy batch deep reinforcement learning of implicit human preferences in dialog. arXiv preprint arXiv:1907.00456 (2019)

10. Li, J., Monroe, W., Ritter, A., Jurafsky, D., Galley, M., Gao, J.: Deep reinforcement learning for dialogue generation. In: Proceedings of the 2016 Conference on Empirical Methods in Natural Language Processing, pp. 1192–1202. Association for Computational Linguistics, Austin, Texas, November 2016. https://doi.org/10.18653/v1/D16-1127

11. Li, Y., Su, H., Shen, X., Li, W., Cao, Z., Niu, S.: DailyDialog: A manually labelled multi-turn dialogue dataset. In: Proceedings of the Eighth International Joint Conference on Natural Language Processing (Volume 1: Long Papers), pp. 986–995 (2017)

12. Loshchilov, I., Hutter, F.: Decoupled weight decay regularization. arXiv preprint arXiv:1711.05101 (2017)

13. Mikolov, T., Chen, K., Corrado, G., Dean, J.: Efficient estimation of word representations in vector space. arXiv preprint arXiv:1301.3781 (2013)

14. Rashkin, H., Smith, E.M., Li, M., Boureau, Y.L.: Towards empathetic open-domain conversation models: A new benchmark and dataset. In: Proceedings of the 57th Annual Meeting of the Association for Computational Linguistics, pp. 5370–5381 (2019)

15. Saleh, A., Jaques, N., Ghandeharioun, A., Shen, J., Picard, R.: Hierarchical reinforcement learning for open-domain dialog. In: Proceedings of the AAAI Conference on Artificial Intelligence, vol. 34, pp. 8741–8748 (2020)

16. Sharma, A., Lin, I.W., Miner, A.S., Atkins, D.C., Althoff, T.: Towards facilitating empathic conversations in online mental health support: A reinforcement learning approach. In: Proceedings of the Web Conference 2021, pp. 194–205 (2021)

17. Sharma, A., Miner, A., Atkins, D., Althoff, T.: A computational approach to understanding empathy expressed in text-based mental health support. In: Proceedings of the 2020 Conference on Empirical Methods in Natural Language Processing (EMNLP), pp. 5263–5276 (2020)

18. Wolf, T., et al.: Transformers: State-of-the-art natural language processing. In: Proceedings of the 2020 Conference on Empirical Methods in Natural Language Processing: System Demonstrations, pp. 38–45. Association for Computational Linguistics, Online, October 2020

19. Xiao, D., et al.: ERNIE-GEN: An enhanced multi-flow pre-training and fine-tuning framework for natural language generation. arXiv preprint arXiv:2001.11314 (2020)

20. Xu, C., Wu, W., Wu, Y.: Towards explainable and controllable open domain dialogue generation with dialogue acts. arXiv preprint arXiv:1807.07255 (2018)

Auto-Encoder Based Model for High-Dimensional Imbalanced Industrial Data

Chao Zhang[1,2] and Sthitie Bom[1(✉)]

[1] Seagate Technology, Bloomington, MN 55435, USA
sthitie.e.bom@seagate.com
[2] University of Chicago, Chicago, IL 60637, USA
chaozhang@uchicago.edu

Abstract. With the proliferation of IoT devices, the distributed control systems are now capturing and processing more sensors at higher frequency than ever before. These new data, due to their volume and novelty, cannot be effectively consumed without the help of data-driven techniques. Deep learning is emerging as a promising technique to analyze these data, particularly in soft sensor modeling. The strong representational capabilities on complex data and the flexibility it offers from an architectural perspective make it an active topic of applied research in industrial settings. However, the successful applications of deep learning in soft sensing are still not widely integrated in factory control systems, because most of the research on soft sensing do not have access to large scale industrial data which are varied, noisy and incomplete. The results published in most research papers are therefore not easily reproduced when applied to the variety of data in industrial settings. Here we provide manufacturing data sets that are much larger and more complex than public open soft sensor data. Moreover, the data sets are from Seagate factories on active service with only necessary anonymization, so that they reflect the complex and noisy nature of real-world data. We introduce a variance weighted multi-headed quality-driven auto-encoder classification model that fits well into the high-dimensional and highly imbalanced data. Besides the use of weighting or sampling methods to handle the highly imbalanced data, the model also simultaneously predicts multiple outputs by exploiting output-supervised representation learning and multi-task weighting.

Keywords: Auto-encoder · Big data · Deep learning · Process control · Multi-task learning · Soft sensing · Wafer production

1 Introduction

Data-driven soft sensing models in the past few years have generated active research and investment due to their efficient handling of complex data relationships and reduced reliance on first principles. They offer reliable and economical

Supported by Seagate Technology.

© Springer Nature Switzerland AG 2021
T. Mantoro et al. (Eds.): ICONIP 2021, CCIS 1516, pp. 265–273, 2021.
https://doi.org/10.1007/978-3-030-92307-5_31

alternatives to rule-based, first principles-driven expensive measuring sensors, thereby enabling effective feedback, and control strategies for process monitoring [12].

A variety of deep learning techniques have been proposed over the last years in soft sensor application, including stacked auto-encoders [2–6], gated units [13], and flavors of recurrent [15] and convolutional neural nets [7]. The interest is motivated by promising empirical results of these deep learning techniques, which show improved representation ability, ability to exploit the unlabeled data to improve performance, and potential for non-linear feature extraction.

While the body of research around soft sensing has been non-trivial and has contributed well to the increased research interest in data-driven soft sensing, we still see a gap between laboratory outcomes and industrial deployments of these soft sensors [8].

One of the reasons for this gap is the lack of real-world data that these models can sufficiently be exercised upon. For example, most of the soft sensors related work cited in this article, use datasets such as the benchmark TE (Tennessee Eastman) and the Debutanizer column. These have relatively low volume and dimensions (number of samples up to 30K and dimensions up to 52). A real distributed control system in an industrial plant, on the other hand, monitors thousands of operations generating tens of thousands of sensors from hundreds of equipment capturing millions of observations per day. Additionally, there are inherent data imbalance problem that none of these studies capture and address. From a practical implementation perspective, we believe that there is also a need to have an architecture that can not only learn the interaction of all these sensors within a tool but also be able to simultaneously predict operations down the manufacturing line, so proactive process monitoring and controls can be established.

This paper proposes a scalable soft sensor application that is motivated by the above-mentioned current gap in the variety of process data for research and the speed of deployment and generalizability for broad coverage in industrial process control. We propose a variance weighted multi-headed classification model that simultaneously predicts multiple outputs by exploiting output-supervised representation learning and multi-task weighting.

Our contributions are:

1. A generalized imbalance-weighted algorithm that uses sensor data captured from the process tools to predict multiple outcomes measured by multiple measurement tools
2. Open release of the preprocessed real-world data to advance further research in soft sensing using a diverse family of semiconductor process manufacturing tools.

In the following sections of this paper, we describe the proposed variance weighted multi-headed classification model and present a case study on wafer manufacturing data from Seagate to show the performance of the proposed model.

2 Methodology

2.1 Variance-Weighted Multi-headed Quality-Driven Auto-Encoder

While existing auto-encoder based models have shown good performance on public data sets, their work does not consider the imbalance in the class labels, and may be prohibitive in environments where there are a large amount of process and output quality variables. To address these practical limitations, we propose a variance weighted multi-headed quality-driven auto-encoder (VWMHQAE) classification architecture which learns and predicts multiple quality-relevant features simultaneously. This is a combined method that predicts all measurement steps within the same model, thus much more efficient and scalable than individual methods.

We simplified the soft sensing problem into a classification problem because our main objective is to predict whether a wafer passes measurements. This is considered to be easier to interpret compared to a numerical output. At a mathematical level, a classification model is no different from regression except that the loss function is cross-entropy instead of mean-square-error.

In a Seagate manufacturing line at any given processing step, there are a number of sensors being captured which can be used to monitor and analyze multiple quality attributes of that process. Typically, these quality measurements are performed across multiple steps. To mimic this process, we designed a model with multiple heads, with each head denoting a measurement step. At each measurement step, specific properties of the wafer are measured to determine whether the properties pass the specification, which corresponds to a binary classification problem. As shown in Fig. 1, several binary classification units are put together, to form a combined model to predict all the measurement steps at the same time.

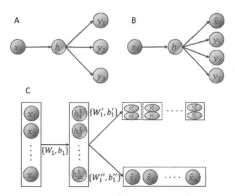

Fig. 1. A) Illustration of multi-headed model. B) learning the reconstruction and target variable in the same time. C) multi-headed auto-encoder model

To calculate the loss functions for all the binary classifications together, we added a weight to each class for each head to handle the imbalance from the source data. The loss function for the entire classification problem is as Eq. 1.

$$J_y(W,b) = \frac{1}{N} \sum_{j}^{N_h} \sum_{i}^{n_j} [-y_{ij}^0 log(\hat{y}_{ij}^0) * w_j^0 - y_{ij}^1 log(\hat{y}_{ij}^1) * w_j^1] \tag{1}$$

N is the number of data points, N_h is the number of heads, n_j is the number of data points for the jth head, W, b are the model weights and bias, and w_j^0, w_j^1 are the class weights for negative and positive cases for the jth head. The class weights are calculated as Eq. 2, with t indicating the negative and positive labels.

$$w_i^t = \frac{N}{2N_h * n_j^t} \tag{2}$$

Note that the J_y in Eq. 1 is not yet the final loss function for our model. To learn a representation of the input data and the features relating to the target variables in the same time, an auto-encoder based architecture is used. This requires the objective function to be modified to include loss functions for both input reconstruction and target prediction. In our case, the reconstruction loss is an MSE loss for the input variables J_x, and the target prediction loss is J_y as Eq. 1. Figure 1B illustrates the workflow for the two loss functions, in which the target prediction loss is shown as multiple heads. Figure 1C shows the details on the multi-headed binary classification model.

However, to combine J_x and J_y, it is not acceptable to simply add them up because they have different scales. [10] proposed a method to minimize multi-task loss functions in the same time. The authors showed that maximizing a multi-task likelihood is equivalent to minimizing a combination of individual task losses with variance dependent weights, with an assumption of homoscedastic uncertainty for each task. They achieved better performance with the multi-task weightings than individual tasks trained separately. Applying their method to our model, we have the loss function as Eq. 3, with σ_1 and σ_2 standing for trainable variance parameters for J_x and J_y:

$$J = \frac{1}{2\sigma_1^2} J_x + \frac{1}{\sigma_2^2} J_y + log\sigma_1 + log\sigma_2 \tag{3}$$

We used the manufacturing data from Seagate, specifically sensor data captured during the wafer processing steps within one family of deposition tools. This data has hundreds of dimensions. To make the model powerful enough to deal with the complicated data sets, a stacked version of the variance weighted multi-headed auto-encoder based classifier is developed.

The stacked model also added a multi-headed classifier to auto-encoder, making it able to learn a representation that captures the features that are most relevant to characterizing and predicting a series of key wafer quality-control measurements. Given that the dimension of the heads is much smaller than the features, this model only adds negligible complexity to auto-encoder thus trains as fast as traditional auto-encoders.

2.2   Model Implementation

Given a high dimensional input, a stacked encoder-decoder structure is used to reduce the dimension gradually. While the input data dimension is 632, and output dimension is 16, we chose four layers of the stacked encoder-decoder structure, with the layers as [400, 200, 100, 50] so that in each iteration the dimension is effectively reduced and not too much information is lost.

To further illustrate the effectiveness of the multi-heading mechanism, Fig. 2 shows the comparison of the multi-headed model with the single-head model taking the heads as input categorical variables instead. In the original data, the feature indicating which measurement is done on that wafer is a column that has no difference with any other categorical variables. To what we know, researchers have been taking this kind of variables as categorical variables in the input. However, we found that the measurement feature can not only be a categorical variable in input data, but also be an output head given that the distinct values are not too many (8 in this data set). As shown in Fig. 2, it turns out that taking the measurement variable as output heads not only improves the interpretability, but also helps the model converges much faster and with less fluctuations in the loss function as in Eq. 3. Noted that the loss values went to negative because of the variance weighting in the formula, and the absolute values in Fig. 2 may not linearly reflect the accuracy of the model. However, it's shown that the multi-headed mechanism accelerates the convergence and leads to a lower value of the loss function.

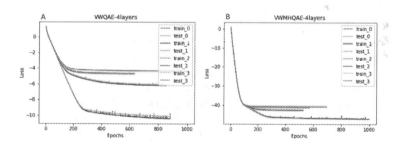

Fig. 2. Comparison for the multi-headed model with a model taking the heads as categorical feature. A) Variance-weighted quality-driven auto-encoder model, treating measurement feature as input categorical variable, B) Variance-weighted multi-headed quality-driven auto-encoder model, treating measurement feature as output heads.

In the experiments, we used a four-layer stacked model to learn on a data set with 632 dimensions which has about 0.2 million data points. We used an Adam optimizer with learning rate as 1e−3, batch size as 512, and an early-stopping with minimum delta as 1e−5. There are 8 different measurement steps, leading to 16 heads in the model. The dimensions of the four hidden layers are (400, 200, 100, 50). Comparing with a regular auto-encoder model with the same layers, our VWMHQAE model only has 1.7% more parameters. The complexity of our model is almost the same as a stacked auto-encoder. With a training data of 0.16 million and dimension 632, the training for a four-layer VWMHQAE model takes about 30 min on a NVIDIA Tesla V100 SXM2 GPU.

3   Data Description

The main purpose of this work is to find a generalized and computationally feasible soft sensing technique that can be applied to a diverse family of equipment. The model also needs to perform well in class imbalance and be able to simultaneously learn to predict output of multiple measurement steps that are critical to ensure the quality of a particular point.

For the purpose of this work, one year's worth of process variables (sensor) data was used, with the corresponding measurement (quality) variables. The sampling rate of the sensors is mostly per second. The measurement data is collected as a wafer is physically measured which could range from minutes to hours. The data is published at https://github.com/Seagate/softsensing_data.

The process tool used in this work is a vacuum tool that deposits thin film. Processes on this tool include both etc.hing and deposition steps. Materials are sputtered from the target deposits on the substrate to create a film.

The tool family considered in this study comprises 14 physical deposition equipment. Each equipment has 130 sensors installed which are captured at a frequency of about every second.

As is expected from most real-world data, the sensor data used here are highly imbalanced. Data imbalance in this study is considered from two perspectives. First, there is class imbalance, which is the ratio of positive versus negative classes. Second, we refer to the difference in scale or unit between the mean squared and the cross-entropy losses used in the combined loss function as imbalance in the task. The class imbalance biases the learning towards the majority class due to its increased prior probability. The task imbalance, or the difference in units of the combined loss function used in the two tasks of the proposed model can result in imbalanced weights for the different losses, biasing the learning towards the higher weighted loss and also possibly causing the lower weighted loss to suffer from vanishing gradients.

4   Results and Discussion

Both the data level and algorithm level techniques were tested to address the class imbalance in this work. First, synthetic minority over-sampling technique (SMOTE) was utilized since it is a widely accepted benchmark for learning from imbalanced data [1]. This method utilizes the oversampling approach to rebalance the original training set. Instead of applying a simple replication of the minority class instances, it introduces synthetic examples which are created by interpolation between several minority class instances within a defined neighborhood.

For soft sensor modeling, however, algorithm-level approaches were shown to be more effective. The loss function was adjusted to take weights into consideration in order to reduce bias towards the negative class, as in Eq. 1. The introduction of the weights in the loss function allows the minority samples to contribute more to the loss. The successful use of class weight was also demonstrated by Wang et al. [14].

For evaluation and comparison purposes, we consider true positive rate(recall) to be a more useful metric because the cost of false negative is much higher than the cost of false positive in this case. We tested the proposed architecture using several data imbalance techniques to determine what best suits the data. Both SMOTE and Weighted Class techniques were tested on models which included logistic regression (LR), neural network (NN) with three fully connected layers, VWMHQAE+LR/NN (LR/NN using quality-based latent variables) and Stacked VWMHQAE+LR/NN. The results showed that algorithm-based approach, in this case, weighted class outperforms SMOTE in most cases. Therefore, the subsequent experiments use class weights to handle class imbalance.

Additionally, two different approaches were used in order to handle the different scales in the combined loss of the models. In the first approach, we use a naïve weighted sum of losses to combine the reconstruction loss and the binary cross entropy loss. The second approach sees the two loss functions as a multi-task learning problem and uses a variance based weighting mechanism as proposed by [10].

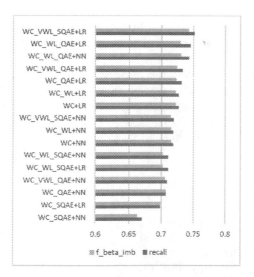

Fig. 3. Average output performance for variations of the VWMHQAE model. The abbreviations are: AE: auto-encoder, Q: short for 'VWMHQ', S: stacked (with hidden layers [400,200,100,50]), WC: weighted class, WL: weighted loss, VWL: variance weighted loss, LR: linear regression classifier, NN: fully connected neural net classifier (with hidden layers [100,50])

As Fig. 3 shows, auto-encoder based models consistently perform better than models without pre-trained auto-encoder. The highest performing model across all outputs is a weighted class and variance weighted stacked quality-driven auto-encoder with a logistic regression classifier (recall = 0.75), followed very closely by naively weighted quality-driven auto-encoder model (recall = 0.74). F_beta_imb is the F_beta score with β equals to the imbalance ratio. F_beta_imb is showing the same conclusion as recall.

5   Conclusion and Future Work

In this work, we present an efficient multi-headed auto-encoder based architecture that learns to simultaneously classify multiple outcomes by exploiting the feature representation guided by quality relevant features. We consider this to be an important contribution to the operationalization of soft sensor modeling in a manufacturing environment with complex non-linear interactions among thousands of complex operations. The capability of using sensors to characterize impact on the outcome of multiple steps in a feed forward manner allows us to be more proactive about the potential issues that may arise, and at the same time enables skipping of certain measurement steps, thereby saving tool capacity and improving time to ship window.

We used several techniques to address the challenge of class imbalance and the imbalance in the scale of the different loss function and concluded with an optimal model suited for this dataset. This architecture can also be trivially generalized to regression models or multi-class classification models.

Future work can extend the architecture to consider the contribution at each layer of the stacked auto-encoder for an ensemble model. Convolutional network can also be applied on the raw time-series sensor data to exploit the locality and stationarity features in the data. We also believe that the generality of this architecture can further be improved by exercising these soft sensing models on a diverse set of equipment with their own function specific sensors. In the meantime, we make available the manufacturing and sensing data sets from Seagate Technology, with the hope that it enables the research community to develop more scalable and applicable AI techniques.

References

1. Fernández, A., Garcia, S., Herrera, F., Chawla, N.V.: Smote for learning from imbalanced data: progress and challenges, marking the 15-year anniversary. J. Artif. Intell. Res. **61**, 863–905 (2018)
2. Erhan, D., Courville, A., Bengio, Y., Vincent, P.: Why does unsupervised pre-training help deep learning? In: Proceedings of the Thirteenth International Conference on Artificial Intelligence and Statistics, pp. 201–208. JMLR Workshop and Conference Proceedings (2010)
3. Yuan, X., Huang, B., Wang, Y., Yang, C., Gui, W.: Deep learning-based feature representation and its application for soft sensor modeling with variable-wise weighted SAE. IEEE Trans. Industr. Inf. **14**(7), 3235–3243 (2018)

4. Yuan, X., Zhou, J., Huang, B., Wang, Y., Yang, C., Gui, W.: Hierarchical quality-relevant feature representation for soft sensor modeling: a novel deep learning strategy. IEEE Trans. Industr. Inf. **16**(6), 3721–3730 (2019)

5. Han, K., Wang, Y., Zhang, C., Li, C., Xu, C.: Autoencoder inspired unsupervised feature selection. In: 2018 IEEE International Conference on Acoustics, Speech and Signal Processing (ICASSP), pp. 2941–2945. IEEE (2018)

6. Sagheer, A., Kotb, M.: Unsupervised pre-training of a deep LSTM-based stacked autoencoder for multivariate time series forecasting problems. Sci. Rep. **9**(1), 1–16 (2019)

7. Yuan, X., Qi, S., Shardt, Y.A., Wang, Y., Yang, C., Gui, W.: Soft sensor model for dynamic processes based on multichannel convolutional neural network. Chemom. Intell. Lab. Syst. **203**, 104050 (2020)

8. Jiang, Y., Yin, S., Dong, J., Kaynak, O.: A review on soft sensors for monitoring, control and optimization of industrial processes. IEEE Sens. J. **21**(11), 12868–12881 (2021)

9. Johnson, J.M., Khoshgoftaar, T.M.: Survey on deep learning with class imbalance. J. Big Data **6**(1), 1–54 (2019). https://doi.org/10.1186/s40537-019-0192-5

10. Kendall, A., Gal, Y., Cipolla, R.: Multi-task learning using uncertainty to weigh losses for scene geometry and semantics. In: Proceedings of the IEEE Conference on Computer Vision and Pattern Recognition, pp. 7482–7491 (2018)

11. Krawczyk, B.: Learning from imbalanced data: open challenges and future directions. Prog. Artif. Intell. **5**(4), 221–232 (2016). https://doi.org/10.1007/s13748-016-0094-0

12. Erpek, T., O'Shea, T.J., Sagduyu, Y.E., Shi, Y., Clancy, T.C.: Deep learning for wireless communications. In: Pedrycz, W., Chen, S.-M. (eds.) Development and Analysis of Deep Learning Architectures. SCI, vol. 867, pp. 223–266. Springer, Cham (2020). https://doi.org/10.1007/978-3-030-31764-5_9

13. Sun, Q., Ge, Z.: Deep learning for industrial KPI prediction: when ensemble learning meets semi-supervised data. IEEE Trans. Industr. Inf. **17**(1), 260–269 (2020)

14. Wang, S., Liu, W., Wu, J., Cao, L., Meng, Q., Kennedy, P.J.: Training deep neural networks on imbalanced data sets. In: 2016 International Joint Conference on Neural Networks (IJCNN), pp. 4368–4374. IEEE (2016)

15. Huang, C.J., Kuo, P.H.: A deep CNN-LSTM model for particulate matter (PM2.5) forecasting in smart cities. Sensors **18**(7), 2220 (2018)

ST-NAS: Efficient Optimization of Joint Neural Architecture and Hyperparameter

Jinhang Cai[1], Yimin Ou[1], Xiu Li[1,2(✉)], and Haoqian Wang[1,2(✉)]

[1] Tsinghua University, Beijing, China
{caijh19,oym19}@mails.tsinghua.edu.cn
[2] Tsinghua Shenzhen International Graduate School, Tsinghua University,
Shenzhen 518055, People's Republic of China
{li.xiu,wangyizhai}@sz.tsinghua.edu.cn

Abstract. Deep learning models often require intensive efforts in neural architecture search and hyperparameter optimization. Conventional hyperparameter optimization methods are inefficient because they refer to multi-trial: different configurations are undertaken in parallel to find the best one. In this paper, we propose ST-NAS, an efficient optimization framework of joint neural architecture and hyperparameter. ST-NAS generalizes the efficient weight sharing strategy from architecture search to hyperparameter optimization. Hence, ST-NAS can jointly optimize both architecture and hyperparameter in a single training phrase. Fundamentally, we design a new module, ST-layer, based on STN, then further extend it to ST-super-net. With the ST-layer, each sub-model's hyperparameter configurations can simultaneously update using the shared weight while training. Thus, with these designs, ST-NAS can efficiently couple with its architecture searching and hyperparameter schedulers. Extensive experiments show ST-NAS can collaborate well with three different NAS algorithms and consistently improves performance across search spaces, datasets, and tasks.

Keywords: Deep learning · Neural network search · Hyperparameter optimization · Hypernetwork

1 Introduction

Optimizing hyperparameters and architectures have a significant effect on neural network models. Few researchers have considered the joint optimization of neural architectures and hyperparameters so far. However, most of them focus on small datasets and small search space [4,17] or require evaluating thousands of architecture and hyperparameter pairs [9,19,22,24]. AutoHAS [5] can also joint search for both hyperparameters and architectures in a single model. However, each model is only coupled with its own best hyperparameters, which is fixed, and now some studies [11,16] and applications (e.g. learning rate schedule) have shown that a hyperparameter schedule can achieve better performance (We also demonstrate it in this paper).

J. Cai and Y. Ou—contributed equally.

© Springer Nature Switzerland AG 2021
T. Mantoro et al. (Eds.): ICONIP 2021, CCIS 1516, pp. 274–281, 2021.
https://doi.org/10.1007/978-3-030-92307-5_32

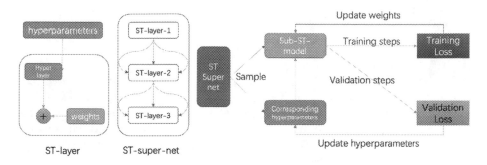

Fig. 1. The overview of ST-NAS framework. ST-layer views the hyperparameters as input and constructs the ST-super-net. The arrows from ST-layer-i to ST-layer-i+1 are operators (i.e. 1 * 1 convolution and 3 * 3 convolution) in search space and not necessarily three. During the search, sub-ST-model and its corresponding hyperparameters are sampled from ST-super-net. The weights of model are updated at training steps using training loss and validation loss is calculated to update the hyperparameters during validation steps

To efficiently optimize the joint neural architecture and hyperparameter, we propose ST-NAS. An overview of the framework is shown as Fig. 1. At first, we use ST-layer, which accepts an additional vector of hyperparameters as input, to conduct the super-net, which is called ST-super-net. In ST-super-net, because the hyperparameters are introduced into the calculation graph and can be updated during training, hyperparameters will also enjoy the efficiency of the weight-sharing strategy as the weights. Specifically, at each training step, ST-NAS optimizes the sub-model sampled by existing super-net sampling methods (e.g. SPOS [10], NAO [15], GNAS [6]) with a combination of its corresponding hyperparameters and the shared weights of ST-super-net are also used to update the hyperparameters of the sampled sub-model at the validation steps. We summarize our contributions below:

1. **Sharing the architectures and hyperparameters simultaneously**: We propose ST-layer and ST-super-net that jointly share not necessarily three and the weights of architectures.
2. **Joint efficient architecture search and hyperparameter optimization**: The optimized hyperparameters schedulers are produced during training the ST-super-net, which perform better than the fixed hyperparameters. Furthermore, the high-performance architectures are generated by conducting the evolutionary search to use the ST-super-net. The joint search (ST-NAS) cost is the ST-super-net training time and evolutionary search time, which is reduced by order of magnitude than the multi-trial algorithms like random search and Bayesian optimization.
3. **Generalizable ST-super-net**: ST-super-net applies to most super-net-based NAS algorithms. In experiments, ST-NAS show improvements on different NAS search spaces and datasets based on different existing super-net sampling algorithms, such as 0.93% accuracy gain on DARTS search space using SPOS [10].

2   Related Work

2.1   Neural Architecture Search (NAS)

NAS refers to the task of automatically learning neural network architectures from data [8]. The efficiency of NAS algorithms has been improved by weight sharing [18], and super-net training in weight-sharing NAS has remained virtually unchanged since its first appearance in [12]. Even if NAS avoids the manual optimization of architecture design, they still need to tune the hyperparameter configurations after a good architecture is discovered.

2.2   Hyperparameter Optimization (HPO)

Grid search is the most fundamental model-free hyperparameter optimization approach. [1] proposed random search based on grid search. Commonly, HPO is treated as a black-box optimization. Bayesian Optimization (BO) [2,20] is a popular framework for global optimization of expensive black-box functions and has shown great success in HPO [21]. Population-Based Training (PBT) [11] considers schedules for hyperparameter configurations.

2.3   Joint NAS + HPO

Few researchers so far have considered the joint optimization of architectures and hyperparameter configurations. [4,17] used the random-forest-based black-box BO method SMAC to jointly optimize both architectures and hyperparameter configurations (e.g. number of filters, number of layers/blocks, and conditional layer hyperparameters that are only active if a layer exists). However, they focus on small datasets and small search space. FBNet-V3 [3] learns an acquisition function to predict the performance for the pair of hyperparameter and architecture. They require evaluating thousands of pairs to optimize this function and thus cost much more computational resources. AutoHAS [5] extended NAS methods using one-shot models to also consider hyperparameters. As it generalizes weight sharing techniques from architectures to hyperparameters, AutoHAS could search for both hyperparameters and architectures efficiently. However, it also needs to optimize an RL controller, which is not very efficient and does not decouple the shared weights and the RL controller well to reduce the computation cost.

3   Method

3.1   ST-Layer

Lorraine and Duvenaud [14] locally model the best-response function with a hypernetwork. Self-Tuning Network(STN) [16] extend this approach by constructing a structured hypernetwork for each layer in neural networks in order to scale well with the number of hyperparameters. They parameterize the best-response function as:

$$\hat{W}_\phi(\lambda) = W_{elem} + (V\lambda) \odot_{row} W_{hyper},$$
$$\hat{b}_\phi(\lambda) = b_{elem} + (C\lambda) \odot b_{hyper} \tag{1}$$

where $W_{elem} \in R^{D_{out} \times D_{in}}$ and $b \in R^{D_{out}}$ is the weight matrix and bias of a layer of a neural network. The best response for the given layer is approximated as an affine transformation of the hyperparameters λ. $\odot$ indicates element-wise multiplication and $\odot_{row}$ indicates row-wise rescaling. This architecture computes the usual elementary weight/bias, plus an additional weight/bias, which has scaled a linear transformation of the hyperparameters.

Based on Eq. (1), we propose ST-layer as shown in Fig. 1. ST-layer accepts an additional vector of hyperparameters as input and then hyperparameters are introduced into the calculation graph, so that the gradient of hyperparameters can be easily computed to update the hyperparameters. Because the hyperparameters are adapted online, computational effort expended to fit the best-response function around previous hyperparameters is not wasted.

3.2   ST-Super-Net

The weight sharing technique proposed by [13,18]. The main idea is to train a super-net, where each candidate in the architecture space is its sub-model. Using a super-net can avoid training millions of candidates from scratch. ST-NAS extends its scope from architecture search to both architecture and hyperparameter search. We not only share the weights of super-net with each architecture but also share this super model across hyperparameters.

Specifically, we design super-net based on ST-layer to generate ST-super-net as shown in Fig. 1. When we train the ST-super-net with different super-net-based NAS algorithms, the hyperparameters of each architecture are also optimized online and can enjoy the efficiency of the weight-sharing strategy.

3.3   Training ST-Super-Net

We now describe the complete ST-super-net training algorithm. Let L_{train} and L_{val} denote training and validation losses which are functions of the hyperparameters λ and parameters w. The full algorithm is given in Algorithm 1. ST-layer and ST-super-net can be used for different super-net-based NAS algorithms. In training steps, architecture is sampled by the NAS algorithm, and the weights of architecture are updated using gradient descent. In validation phrase, the hyperparameters are optimized based on the approximated best-response function.

When the ST-super-net is converged, we will get the schedulers of the hyperparameters and a predictor which can inference the accuracy on validation datasets of each sub-model in the ST-super-net using the shared weights.

Algorithm 1: ST-super-net Training and Using Algorithm

Initialize: model parameters w, hyperparameters λ, ST-super-net S, neural architecture sample algorithm NAS, training steps T_{train} and validation steps T_{val}, training losses L_{train} and validation losses L_{val}, learning rates $\{\alpha_i\}_{i=1}^{2}$;

1   **Training ST-super-net**

2   **while** *not converged* **do**

3   **for** $t = 1, \ldots, T_{train}$ **do**

4         $w = NAS(S); \; \epsilon \sim p(\epsilon | \sigma)$

5         $w \leftarrow w - \alpha_1 \frac{\partial}{\partial w} L_{train}(\lambda + \epsilon, w, \theta)$

6   **end**

7   **for** $t = 1, \ldots, T_{valid}$ **do**

8         $w = NAS(S)$

9         $\lambda \leftarrow \lambda - \alpha_2 \frac{\partial}{\partial \lambda} L_{val}(\lambda, w, \theta)$

10   **end**

11 **end**

---

4   Experiments

4.1   Results on Different NAS Benchmarks with Different Sampling Algorithms

We select single-path one-shot (SPOS) as a representative unbiased architecture sampling algorithm. We use SPOS to train the super-net, followed by an evolutionary search to select the best models based on the super-net performance [10]. Among the learning-based architecture sampling methods, we select neural architecture optimization (NAO) [15], which trains an explicit auto-encoder-based performance predictor. Finally, for differentiable architecture search, we select the gradient-based search using a differentiable architecture sampler (GNAS) [6].

Since the inception of NAS, CIFAR-10 and CIFAR-100 have acted as the primary datasets to benchmark NAS performance. We utilize two search spaces, NASBench-101 [23] and NASBench-201 [7], for which the stand-alone performance of many architectures is known.

As shown in Table 1, on NASBench-101, STN improves the ranking correlation KdT from 0.134 to 0.220 for SPOS, and from 0.245 to 0.371 for NAO. The best architecture discovered on this search space, thanks to our method, ranks 7102th, which corresponds to the top 2% of architectures. Furthermore, on NASBench-201, STN consistently improves the ranking correlation (KdT) and best accuracy across both datasets. Moreover, such an improvement only increases the cost by less than one time.

4.2   Results on ImageNet and COCO

To further demonstrate the efficiency and generality of our ST-NAS, we also perform experiments on ImageNet classification and COCO detection. We use

Table 1. Results on NASBench-101 and NASBench-201. ST-SPOS, ST-NAO, and ST-GNAS denote ST-super-net trained with SPOS, NAO and GNAS. The KdT at the end of the training, the best rank, and the best accuracy are reported. Each method was run three times.

Search Space	Dataset	Method	KdT	Best Rank	Best Acc	Cost (hours)
NASBench-101	CIFAR-10	SPOS	0.134	38953	92.82	11.89
		ST-SPOS	0.220	26399	**93.13**	22.59
		NAO	0.245	131969	91.60	15.46
		ST-NAO	0.371	7102	**93.38**	29.37
NASBench-201	CIFAR-10	SPOS	0.52	3383	92.30	6.26
		ST-SPOS	0.67	2585	**92.52**	11.89
		NAO	0.40	649	93.35	3.51
		ST-NAO	0.58	137	**93.80**	6.67
		GNAS	0.44	463	93.48	14.42
		ST-GNAS	0.61	143	**93.79**	27.40
NASBench-201	CIFAR-100	SPOS	0.56	3217	68.33	6.30
		ST-SPOS	0.70	2381	**68.92**	11.97
		NAO	0.42	506	70.42	3.54
		ST-NAO	0.61	101	**71.51**	6.73
		GNAS	0.42	473	70.48	14.46
		ST-GNAS	0.59	134	**71.23**	27.47

the popular DARTS search space, which provides 120 architectures trained for 50 epochs. We follow the setup of [13] and use stochastic gradient descent with a cosine learning rate scheduler. We tune the weight decay of each model in the search space by STN and use a label smoothing coefficient of 0.1 for all models. As shown in Table 2, the models found by ST-super-net can achieve better performance.

Table 2. Results on ImageNet. The best model was generated by evolutionary search using ST-super-net and trained with the schedulers found during the ST-super-net training.

Method	KdT	Params	Best-Top-1 (50/250)	Cost (hours)
SPOS	0.18	4.579M	67.88/73.69	7.29
ST-SPOS	0.22	4.688M	**68.71/74.62**	16.77
NAO	0.23	4.675M	68.21/73.71	9.13
ST-NAO	0.26	4.383M	**69.41/74.82**	21.00
GNAS	0.22	5.076M	67.26/74.03	8.39
ST-GNAS	0.24	5.077M	**68.41/74.99**	19.30

We show the detailed COCO detection results in Table 3. With similar or higher mAP, our ST-NAS reduces the FLOPs and number of parameters compared to EfficientNet and FBNet backbones.

Table 3. Object detection results of Faster RCNN with different backbones on COCO

Method	Params(M)	FLOPs(G)	mAP
EfficientNetB0	8.0	3.6	30.2
FBNetV3-A	5.3	2.9	30.5
ST-NAS	4.7	2.6	30.7
EfficientNetB1	13.3	5.6	32.2
FBNetV3-E	10.6	5.3	33.0
ST-NAS	10.1	4.9	33.5

5 Conclusion

This paper proposed an automated and unified framework ST-NAS, which can efficiently search for both hyperparameters and architectures. ST-NAS provides a novel perspective of AutoML algorithms by generalizing the weight sharing technique from architecture search to both architecture and hyperparameter optimization. Our strategy applies to most NAS algorithms. After training and using the ST-super-net, our experiments have shown that it consistently improves both the ranking correlation between the super-net and stand-alone performance as well as the final performance across three different search algorithms and three different tasks.

Acknowledgments. This research was partly supported by the National Natural Science Foundation of China (Grant No. 41876098), the National Key R & D Program of China (Grant No. 2020AAA0108303), and Shenzhen Science and Technology Project (Grant No. JCYJ20200109143041798).

References

1. Bergstra, J., Bengio, Y.: Random search for hyper-parameter optimization. J. Mach. Learn. Res. **13**(2) (2012)
2. Brochu, E., Cora, V.M., De Freitas, N.: A tutorial on Bayesian optimization of expensive cost functions, with application to active user modeling and hierarchical reinforcement learning. arXiv preprint arXiv:1012.2599 (2010)
3. Dai, X., et al.: FBNetV3: joint architecture-recipe search using neural acquisition function. arXiv e-prints pp. arXiv-2006 (2020)
4. Domhan, T., Springenberg, J.T., Hutter, F.: Speeding up automatic hyperparameter optimization of deep neural networks by extrapolation of learning curves. In: Twenty-Fourth International Joint Conference on Artificial Intelligence (2015)
5. Dong, X., Tan, M., Yu, A.W., Peng, D., Gabrys, B., Le, Q.V.: AutoHAS: differentiable hyper-parameter and architecture search. arXiv preprint arXiv:2006.03656 (2020)
6. Dong, X., Yang, Y.: Searching for a robust neural architecture in four GPU hours. In: Proceedings of the IEEE/CVF Conference on Computer Vision and Pattern Recognition, pp. 1761–1770 (2019)

7. Dong, X., Yang, Y.: NAS-bench-201: extending the scope of reproducible neural architecture search. arXiv preprint arXiv:2001.00326 (2020)
8. Elsken, T., Metzen, J.H., Hutter, F., et al.: Neural architecture search: a survey. J. Mach. Learn. Res. **20**(55), 1–21 (2019)
9. Falkner, S., Klein, A., Hutter, F.: BOHB: robust and efficient hyperparameter optimization at scale. In: International Conference on Machine Learning, pp. 1437–1446. PMLR (2018)
10. Guo, Z., et al.: Single path one-shot neural architecture search with uniform sampling. In: Vedaldi, A., Bischof, H., Brox, T., Frahm, J.-M. (eds.) ECCV 2020. LNCS, vol. 12361, pp. 544–560. Springer, Cham (2020). https://doi.org/10.1007/978-3-030-58517-4_32
11. Jaderberg, M., et al.: Population based training of neural networks. arXiv preprint arXiv:1711.09846 (2017)
12. Li, L., Talwalkar, A.: Random search and reproducibility for neural architecture search. In: Uncertainty in Artificial Intelligence, pp. 367–377. PMLR (2020)
13. Liu, H., Simonyan, K., Yang, Y.: DARTS: differentiable architecture search. arXiv preprint arXiv:1806.09055 (2018)
14. Lorraine, J., Duvenaud, D.: Stochastic hyperparameter optimization through hypernetworks. CoRR abs/1802.09419 (2018). arXiv:1802.09419
15. Luo, R., Tian, F., Qin, T., Chen, E., Liu, T.Y.: Neural architecture optimization. arXiv preprint arXiv:1808.07233 (2018)
16. MacKay, M., Vicol, P., Lorraine, J., Duvenaud, D., Grosse, R.: Self-tuning networks: bilevel optimization of hyperparameters using structured best-response functions. arXiv preprint arXiv:1903.03088 (2019)
17. Mendoza, H., Klein, A., Feurer, M., Springenberg, J.T., Hutter, F.: Towards automatically-tuned neural networks. In: Workshop on Automatic Machine Learning, pp. 58–65. PMLR (2016)
18. Pham, H., Guan, M., Zoph, B., Le, Q., Dean, J.: Efficient neural architecture search via parameters sharing. In: International Conference on Machine Learning, pp. 4095–4104. PMLR (2018)
19. Runge, F., Stoll, D., Falkner, S., Hutter, F.: Learning to design RNA. arXiv preprint arXiv:1812.11951 (2018)
20. Shahriari, B., Swersky, K., Wang, Z., Adams, R.P., De Freitas, N.: Taking the human out of the loop: a review of Bayesian optimization. Proc. IEEE **104**(1), 148–175 (2015)
21. Snoek, J., Swersky, K., Zemel, R., Adams, R.: Input warping for Bayesian optimization of non-stationary functions. In: International Conference on Machine Learning, pp. 1674–1682. PMLR (2014)
22. Zela, A., Klein, A., Falkner, S., Hutter, F.: Towards automated deep learning: efficient joint neural architecture and hyperparameter search. arXiv preprint arXiv:1807.06906 (2018)
23. Zela, A., Siems, J., Hutter, F.: NAS-Bench-1Shot1: benchmarking and dissecting one-shot neural architecture search. arXiv preprint arXiv:2001.10422 (2020)
24. Zimmer, L., Lindauer, M., Hutter, F.: Auto-Pytorch: multi-fidelity meta learning for efficient and robust AutoDL. IEEE Trans. Patt. Anal. Mach. Intell. (2021)

Early Rumor Detection with Prior Information on Social Media

Zhengliang Luo, Tiening Sun, Xiaoxu Zhu$^{(\boxtimes)}$, Zhong Qian, and Peifeng Li

School of Computer Science and Technology, Soochow University, Suzhou, China
{zlluo,tnsun}@stu.suda.edu.cn, {xiaoxzhu,qianzhong,pfli}@suda.edu.cn

Abstract. With the rapid development of social media on the Internet, many would-be rogues use social media to spread rumors, and rumor detection is born out of this. Rumors on social media change in real time. The earlier we can discover the truth of the event, the more effective it is to curb rumors spreading. This paper studies automatic event-level rumor detection in social media, which is a series of posts that appear in chronological order after an event published. The difficulty of early rumor detection is the available information is limited. Therefore, we take the prior events as auxiliary information and use the fusion of prior events and current event to judge rumors. The model can learn representations of events in the early stage more accurately and realize early rumor detection. Our method can effectively achieve good performance with lack of information in the early stage of social media. Experiments on three benchmark datasets show the proposed method has better advantages.

Keywords: Social media · Rumor detection · Prior events

1 Introduction

Rumor is defined as an unverified statement, which may be unintentionally created or deliberately fabricated [1]. A rumor event is a collection of original posts and following posts (such as comments or retweets) on social media. The rumor detection task is a text classification problem, with the purpose of deciding whether an event is a rumor or not. As described by Veyseh [2], rumors contain four categories, i.e., non-rumor, true-rumor, false-rumor, and unverified.

Ma et al. [4] organized the event source posts and its response posts into a tree structure, and each post is represented as a node. They used recursive neural network to simulate the transmission of information in the propagation tree. Similar to Ma, Kumar et al. [5] proposed several variations of branching and tree LSTM. However, their methods did not consider the the lack of recursive neural networks, and the information a user can obtain is not limited to his propagation link, but to the entire structure. Early in the spread of rumors, the available information is rare, and only have one source post and a few comment posts. Fortunately, we found that some different events discuss the same topic. We give an example in Fig. 1. To overcome the limitations of existing methods,

© Springer Nature Switzerland AG 2021
T. Mantoro et al. (Eds.): ICONIP 2021, CCIS 1516, pp. 282–289, 2021.
https://doi.org/10.1007/978-3-030-92307-5_33

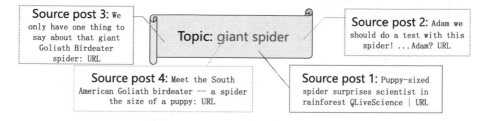

Fig. 1. An example that different events discuss the same topic.

we propose an early rumor detection method based on the prior events of relevant topics. We calculate the cosine similarity of all source posts. Then we judge the release time to get priors. When the rumor category of a certain event judges, the event and the prior events are allowed to enter a same BERT model, and we integrate the output of BERT by Multi-head Attention. Finally, the fused representation is used to judge rumor category. The main contributions of this paper are:

- We present the first work to calculate the similarity of the source post, and use the events on similar topics to perform early rumor detection.
- We use prior events of related topics for rumor detection, and carry out a series of experiments on three real world datasets.
- The experiment results prove that our model could improve the performance, and the prior information is effective for early rumor detection.

2   Method

2.1   Task Statement

We defind each of event as a collection of n related posts $E = \{m_1, m_2, ..., m_n\}$, where m_1 is original message of this event at t_1 timing, referring to in this article as the source post, and each of m_i is the i-th response post at time t_i after m_1 appears. Thus, after sorting all the posts chronologically, we get a set of events in time series $E = \{(m_1|t_1), (m_2|t_2), ..., (m_n|t_n)\}$. The goal of rumor detection is to predict the category tag y of the event E. So, we define $D = \{E_1, E_2, ..., E_{|D|}\}$ for the dataset, where $|D|$ is the total number of dataset events.

2.2   Event Classification

In this paper, we calculate text similarity to judge whether any two events E_i and E_j in dataset discuss the same topic, and the formula of cosine similarity is:

$$similar_{E_i, E_j} = \frac{\left|vec_{E_i} \cdot vec_{E_j}\right|}{\sqrt{\left|vec_{E_i}\right| * \left|vec_{E_j}\right|}} \tag{1}$$

where vec_{E_i} and vec_{E_j} are source post sentence vectors of event E_i and E_j.

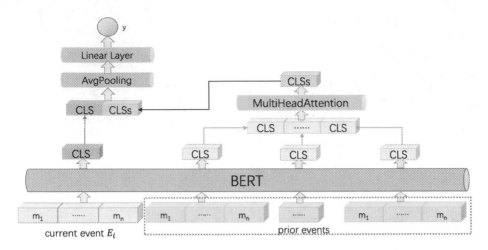

Fig. 2. The model proposed in this paper.

Referring to the method of calculating text similarity in Peirsman [7], the vector representation of the sentence can be obtained by averaging all word vectors in the sentence, and then the similarity is calculated using the cosine similarity formula Eq. (1). Next, we formulate a rule. If this rule is satisfied, E_j can be identified as one of priori of E_i, and we record the event Id of E_j. The rules show as follows:

1) The similarity is greater than the threshold (the threshold of Weibo dataset is 0.95, and the threshold of Twitter15/16 is 0.9);
2) The source post of E_j event appears earlier than the source post of E_i event.

For the word vectors of events E_i and E_j, we adopt BERT to train the model, and get word embeddings for source posts. The BERT word vector model will not use in the prediction section that follows.

2.3   Prior Information

In the previous subsection, we obtained the Id prior event, which defined as prior information. Next, we query events by Id, and then get source tweets and comments about prior events. The model proposed in this paper shows in Fig. 2.

We mark the priori of the event E_i as the set $pres = \{p_1, p_2, ..., p_7\}$. Note that we take a maximum of 7 relevant priors (if it has). Each of p_i in the $pres$ set connects to BERT network respectively, and the formula shows as follow:

$$out_{p_i} = BERT(p_i) \tag{2}$$

where $out_{p_i} \in \mathbb{R}^{N_L \times d}$, d is the dimension of hidden states in BERT, and N_L is the sentence length of p_i. The CLS set of each out_{p_i} is denoted as $cls\_set = \{cls_1, cls_2, ..., cls_7\}$, then we use CONCAT to splice the cls_set set. The result of CONCAT is $pres_{cls}$, where $pres_{cls} \in \mathbb{R}^{n \times d}$, and n is the number of priori. Then we get the weight of each CLS by using Multi-head Attention(MHA) on $pres_{cls}$, the formula shows as follow:

$$Z = MHA(pres_{cls}, pres_{cls}, pres_{cls}) \tag{3}$$

where $Z \in \mathbb{R}^{n \times d}$, which is equal to $pres_{cls}$. Finally, we take position 0 of Z as the final representation of the prior set $pres$, marked as Z_0.

2.4   Merged with Prior Information

For our proposed model, the prior events and the event E_i share parameters of BERT, so E_i connects to the same BERT model as above.

$$out_{E_i} = BERT(E_i) \tag{4}$$

where $out_{E_i} \in \mathbb{R}^{N_L \times d}$, d is the dimension of hidden states, and N_L is the sentence length of p_i. Similarly, we only use the CLS of out_{E_i} as the representation. We denote as cls_{E_i}. Then, we concatenate cls_{E_i} and Z_0 (previous subsection), and we denote the result of CONCAT as E_c. Next, E_c passes through an average pooling layer to obtain a fused representation. Finally, the output of average pooling is used to perform rumor prediction through the Linear Layer and SoftMax.

$$p = SoftMax(ReLU(\omega \cdot AvgPool(E_c) + b)) \tag{5}$$

where ω and b is learnable parameters, and p is the predict result of E_i.

3   Experiments

In this section, we introduce the datasets, data processing methods, experimental methods and experimental results we use.

3.1   Experimental Setup

To verify the effectiveness of our proposed method, we conducte experiments on Twitter15/16 and Weibo dataset, which are three real world datasets.

For the Twitter15/16, we adopt the same processing method as that adopted by Khoo et al. [8], with 5 fold cross-validation. Since the Twitter event may have been deleted, we only get 90% of the Twitter15/16 that was originally published. The Twitter15/16 datasets are labeled in four categories: 1) non-rumor; 2) true-rumor; 3) false-rumor; 4) unverified, and we show the data statistics in Table 1.

Weibo dataset was published by Ma et al. [3]. For Weibo dataset, events are marked as rumor and non-rumor. The statistics of Weibo show in Table 2.

Table 1. Statistics of Twitter15/16.

Dataset	Event counts	Non-rumor	True-rumor	False-rumor	Unverified
Twitter15	1306	363	325	311	307
Twitter16	678	194	180	149	155

Table 2. Statistics of Weibo.

Dataset	Event counts	Rumor	Non-rumor
Weibo	4664	2351	2313

3.2   Baseline Models

We compare the proposed model with other rumor detection models. The main evaluation indicators are accuracy rate and F1 value. The categories of these datasets distribute equally, so the focus is on accuracy rate. We use the same experimental settings for the experiments on Twitter15/16 and Weibo datasets. Our model compares with the following baseline rumor detection models.

Models for comparison of Twitter15/16 datasets:

- **BU-RvNN and TD-RvNN** are tree-based recursive neural network models proposed by Ma et al. [4].
- **HiAN** is the model of Dong et al. [9], which considers both users and emotional information at word level and tweet level.
- **PPC** a fake news propagation path classification detection model combining recurrent network and convolutional network [6].

Models for comparison of Weibo dataset:

- **PPC** a fake news propagation path classification detection model combining recurrent network and convolutional network [6].
- **NM-DPS** a dynamic propagation structure is used to increase rumor detection in social media [11].

For the Twitter15/16 datasets, we compare with BU-RvNN, TD-RvNN, HiAN and PPC. While for the Weibo dataset, we compare with PPC and NM-DPS since two RvNN and HiAN only reported their results on the Twitter15/16 datasets. Table 3 shows the results among different models on the three datasets.

3.3   Result and Analysis

It can be see from Table 3, the performance of the model we proposed is higher than that of the baseline model in Twitter15 and Weibo datasets.

For Twitter15, the accuracy of our model is 1.8 higher than HiAN, and 1.2 higher than PPC. For Twitter16, the proposed model is 3.28 higher than HiAN, but 0.8 lower than PPC model. Since the number of events in the Twitter16

Table 3. Performance on three datasets.

(a) Performance on Twitter15/16. (NR: non-rumor; TR: true-rumor; FR: false-rumor; UR: unverified-rumor)

Dataset	Model	Accuracy	NR(F1)	TR(F1)	FR(F1)	UR(F1)
Twitter15	BU-RvNN	70.8	69.5	75.9	72.8	65.3
	TD-RvNN	72.3	68.2	82.1	75.8	65.4
	HiAN	83.6	84.2	88.1	83.3	78.8
	PPC	84.2	81.1	81.8	**87.5**	**79**
	Ours	**85.4**	**93.7**	85.1	82	77.6
Twitter16	BU-RvNN	71.8	72.3	77.9	71.2	65.9
	TD-RvNN	73.7	66.2	83.5	74.3	65.9
	HiAN	82.2	80.6	90.9	77.6	78.2
	PPC	**86.3**	82.0	84.3	**89.8**	**83.7**
	Ours	85.5	**90.3**	**91.9**	75.7	79.6

(b) Performance on Weibo.

Dataset	Model	Accuracy	Non-Rumor(F1)	Rumor(F1)
Weibo	PPC	92.1	92.3	91.8
	NM-DPS	94.3	94.5	93.8
	Ours	**96.6**	**96.6**	**96.6**

dataset is small, the effect of the pre-training model on small datasets may not be as good as that on large datasets. In the future, the datas are bound to become larger, so the model in this paper still adapts to the trend. For the Weibo dataset, our model is also superior to the baseline model. The accuracy was 4.4 and 2.2 higher than PPC and NM-DPS, respectively.

The experimental results show that the proposed method is superior to the existing baseline model. Among the two propagation tree-based approaches, TD-RvNN and BU-RvNN models are tree-structured and utilize representation learning following propagation structure. However, these tree-based methods will lose too much information in the propagation of recursive neural networks, because of recursive networks will selectively forget past information.

As for PPC and HiAN methods of deep neural network, these models can learn the internal features of text, and use users' characteristics and emotional information to assist rumor detection. However, the user characteristics and emotional information are less influential than the prior information. Because user emotion is subjective, and has a negative impact on rumor detection. Besides, user characteristics are difficult to extract, and often noisy, these factors have side effects on the neural network. And prior information is more objective and stable than them. Similarly, for Weibo dataset, the baseline model only considers the user information and transmission information, without considering these information will be selectively forgotten in model learning.

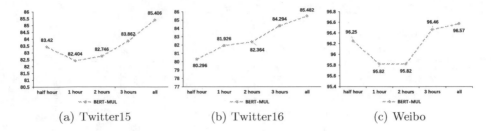

(a) Twitter15   (b) Twitter16   (c) Weibo

Fig. 3. Early rumor detection curve on three datasets. The time period is incrementally divided into half an hour, one hour, two hours, three hours and the whole time.

Table 4. Experiment on prior number. (NR: non-rumor; TR: true-rumor; FR: false-rumor; UR: unverified-rumor)

Dataset	Count	Accuracy	NR(F1)	TR(F1)	FR(F1)	UR(F1)
Twitter15 (Multi-head)	3	83.00	92.97	82.17	77.49	77.00
	5	83.86	92.70	82.21	80.55	76.44
	7	**85.41**	**93.67**	**85.13**	**81.97**	**77.56**

3.4 Early Rumor Detection

To evaluate the performance of our proposed model in early rumor detection, we set comparative experiments at different time points. We divide the time into half an hour, an hour, two hours, three hours and the whole time. And the posts within each time period are obtained respectively. Specific early detection results illustrate in Fig. 3. The figure shows the model we proposed can achieve better performance in the early stage of rumor detection, which indicates the effectiveness of adding prior information in the early stage. Since some noise in comment posts affects the judgment, the curve decreases in first two hours.

3.5 Number of Prior Events

In this paper, we only use seven prior events to assist the event E_i in rumor detection. We also conduct a comparative test on the Twitter15 dataset for the number of prior events. The results show in Table 4. As can be seen from the results, the effect of 7 priors performs best at all. Therefore, the more priors, the better the effect of the experiment will be. Because more priors can extract more useful information of event E_i, they are effective for rumor detection.

4   Conclusion and Future Work

We propose a new early rumor detection model, which uses the prior information to classify rumor types. After getting the prior information by cosine similarity, we use the multi-head attention mechanism to obtain the centralized representation of the prior information, and then we use the prior information to assist rumor detection. Experimental results on three datasets show the model we proposed is superior to existing methods in rumor detection. Because our model use prior information, it can obtain good performance in the early stage of rumor detection. In the future we will also consider shifting from rumor detection of events to rumor detection of topics.

Acknowledgments. The authors would like to thank the three anonymous reviewers for their comments on this paper. This research was supported by the National Natural Science Foundation of China (No. 61836007, 62006167 and 61772354.), and the Priority Academic Program Development of Jiangsu Higher Education Institutions (PAPD).

References

1. DiFonzo, N., Bordia, P.: Rumor Psychology: Social and Organizational Approaches. American Psychological Association (2007)
2. Veyseh, A.P.B., Thai, M.T., Nguyen, T.H., Dou, D.: Rumor detection in social networks via deep contextual modeling. In: Proceedings of the 2019 IEEE/ACM International Conference on Advances in Social Networks Analysis and Mining, pp. 113–120 (2019)
3. Ma, J., Gao, W., Mitra, P., Kwon, S., Jansen, B.J., Wong, K.F., Cha, M.: Detecting rumors from microblogs with recurrent neural networks (2016)
4. Ma, J., Gao, W., Wong, K.F.: Rumor Detection on Twitter with Tree-Structured Recursive Neural Networks. Association for Computational Linguistics (2018)
5. Kumar, S., Carley, K.M.: Tree LSTMs with convolution units to predict stance and rumor veracity in social media conversations. In: Proceedings of the 57th Annual Meeting of the Association for Computational Linguistics, pp. 5047–5058 (2019)
6. Liu, Y., Wu, Y.F.B.: Early detection of fake news on social media through propagation path classification with recurrent and convolutional networks. In: Thirty-Second AAAI Conference on Artificial Intelligence (2018)
7. Peirsman, Y.: Comparing sentence similarity methods. http://nlp.town/blog/sentence-similarity
8. Khoo, L.M.S., Chieu, H.L., Qian, Z., Jiang, J.: Interpretable rumor detection in microblogs by attending to user interactions. In: Proceedings of the AAAI Conference on Artificial Intelligence, vol. 34, pp. 8783–8790 (2020)
9. Dong, S., Qian, Z., Li, P., Zhu, X., Zhu, Q.: Rumor detection on hierarchical attention network with user and sentiment information. In: Zhu, X., Zhang, M., Hong, Yu., He, R. (eds.) NLPCC 2020. LNCS (LNAI), vol. 12431, pp. 366–377. Springer, Cham (2020). https://doi.org/10.1007/978-3-030-60457-8_30
10. Li, Q., Zhang, Q., Si, L., Liu, Y.: Rumor detection on social media: datasets, methods and opportunities. ArXiv arXiv:1911.07199 (2019)
11. Wang, S., Kong, Q., Wang, Y., Wang, L.: Enhancing rumor detection in social media using dynamic propagation structures. 2019 IEEE International Conference on Intelligence and Security Informatics (ISI), pp. 41–46 (2019)
12. Lin, X., Liao, X., Xu, T., Pian, W., Wong, K.F.: Rumor detection with hierarchical recurrent convolutional neural network. In: NLPCC (2019)
13. Liu, X., Nourbakhsh, A., Li, Q., Fang, R., Shah, S.: Real-time rumor debunking on Twitter. In: Proceedings of the 24th ACM International on Conference on Information and Knowledge Management (2015)

Multi-modal Code Summarization Fusing Local API Dependency Graph and AST

Xuejian Gao, Xue Jiang, Qiong Wu, Xiao Wang, Chen Lyu[✉], and Lei Lyu

School of Information Science and Engineering, Shandong Normal University,
Jinan, China
lvchen@sdnu.edu.cn

Abstract. Automatically obtaining descriptions of the functions of code snippets in natural language, i.e., code summarization, is an important issue in software engineering. In recent years, abstract syntax tree (AST)-based code summarization models for modelling syntactic structures have continued to emerge. In addition to syntactics, the semantics of the code are gradually gaining attention. In this paper, we propose a code summarization approach that incorporates local-ADG and AST, called GTsum. In particular, we introduce a novel local-ADG-based approach that can effectively filter out irrelevant semantics in the modelling of the semantic structure of code. GTsum learns semantics and syntactics in the local-ADG and AST through graph convolutional networks (GCNs) and then fuses them using Transformer. We evaluate our model on two Java language datasets with several metrics. The results demonstrate that our model achieves state-of-the-art performance compared to the existing models.

Keywords: Code summarization · Local API dependency graph · Abstract syntax tree · Graph convolutional network

1 Introduction

Code summarization aims to automatically generate concise and accurate functional descriptions for code snippets, which not only reduces software development and maintenance costs, but also helps program developers with program comprehension.

Research in recent years has shown that abstract syntax trees (ASTs) can effectively represent code syntax information. There is a significant amount of current work applying ASTs to code summarization tasks. For example, Tree2Seq [1], DeepCom [2], etc. Those work demonstrates the ability of ASTs to effectively characterize code syntactic structures. However, existing code summarization models lack a deep exploration of the semantic structure of the code. To remedy this regret, we proposed the ADG-Seq2Seq method to model the representation of API call relations in our previous work [3] and proposed global-ADG to model all APIs' call dependencies the codebase, which effectively enhances the

© Springer Nature Switzerland AG 2021
T. Mantoro et al. (Eds.): ICONIP 2021, CCIS 1516, pp. 290–297, 2021.
https://doi.org/10.1007/978-3-030-92307-5_34

representation of the semantic structure of the code. Global-ADG features API dependencies within and between all code snippets in the codebase. However, the code summarization task requires understanding the internal semantics of a single code snippet to generate appropriate annotations.

To this end, we propose a code semantic representation based on the local API call dependency graph (Local-ADG). Unlike global-ADG, local-ADG ignores API dependencies between code snippets and only portrays the API call dependencies contained in a single code snippet. In this way, irrelevant dependency information from outside the current code snippet can be blocked out while preserving the call constraints and call order between its internal APIs. Figure 1 shows the difference between global-ADG and local-ADG.

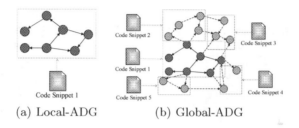

(a) Local-ADG   (b) Global-ADG

Fig. 1. Global-ADG and Local-ADG comparison results.

In this paper, we propose a multi-modal code summarization method fusing local-ADG and AST, called GTsum. Specifically, we first model the code snippet as an AST and a local-ADG. Then, we obtain local-ADG embedding and AST embedding using graph convolutional network (GCN), respectively. Finally, we input the semantic embedding and syntactic embedding into Transformer to complete the multi-modal fusion and subsequent generation of code summaries.

The main contributions of this paper are as follows:

- We propose a semantic structure model of the code: local-ADG, which focuses on generating API dependencies for each code snippet to enhance code semantic structure representation.
- We propose a novel multi-modal code summarization method: GTsum. This method can effectively learn and fuse both semantic and syntactic modalities of the codes expressed by the local-ADG and AST and provide a more comprehensive and accurate characterization of the code structure.

2   Related Work

The core idea of automatic code summarization is the joint modelling of code and natural language, and the difficulty lies in the "structural gap" problem. Specifically, unlike serialized natural languages, code has structural complexity.

It contains program syntax information and a large number of API call relationships, parameter reference, program framework information, etc.

Deep neural networks have shown state-of-the-art performance in feature extraction and abstraction. For example, CODE-NN [4] models code using LSTM and attention mechanisms. The Graph2Seq model [5] performs graph modelling for SQL languages and uses graph networks for learning. Hu et al. [6] proposed TL-CodeSum to exploit the API information in the code; the model serially encodes and learns the APIs, which improves the model's ability to characterize the semantics of the code.

3   Approach

In this paper, we propose a new multi-modal code summarization method, GTsum, as shown in Fig. 2. The method is divided into three submodules: 1) Multi-modal code representation. 2) Code embedding. 3) Fusion mechanism.

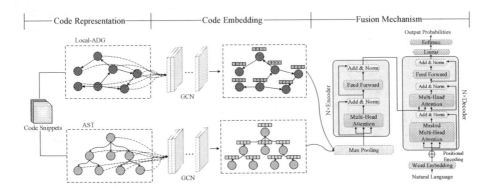

Fig. 2. Overall framework of our approach.

3.1   Multi-modal Code Representation

The representation of the code in different modalities captures more comprehensive information about the code. We use local-ADG to extract code semantic knowledge and AST to capture code syntactic knowledge.

Local-ADG Code Representation. Local-ADG is a graph model that represents the dependencies of API calls inside the target code snippet. Figure 3 shows an illustrative example of Local-ADG. For example: method "$getWorkingCopyManager()$" corresponds to node "m_2", which has an input type "A" and an output type "B". Node "m_2" can be invoked and perform its function after input "A" is become available, while input type "A" is provided by node "m_1". Therefore, there is an edge from "m_1" to "m_2" with the weight "A." For a more detailed construction process, please see Lyu et al. [3].

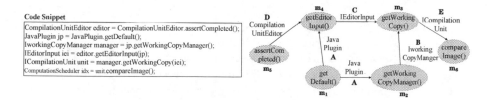

Fig. 3. Example of Local-ADG.

AST Code Representation. AST refers to the tree structure to express the code syntax structure information. A structured representation of the syntax of code snippets can improve the accuracy of code summarization models. Thus, in this paper, we use an AST to express the syntactic structure of code snippets.

3.2   Code Embedding

A GCN generalizes convolution operators to graph data and plays a vital role in capturing structural dependencies. We embed local-ADG and AST with GCNs to obtain more information about the code structure.

Local-ADG Code Embedding

We use Flair[1] to vectorize each node of the local-ADG to construct the initialization vector matrix of the local-ADG: $S^{(0)} = \{S_1^{(0)}, S_2^{(0)}, ..., S_V^{(0)}\}$ where V is the number of nodes contained in the local-ADG. We input the adjacency matrix A_{V*V} of the local-ADG into the GCN for node information embedding to generate the local-ADG embedding.

$$S^{(l+1)} = \delta(D_\sim^{-\frac{1}{2}} \cdot A_\sim \cdot D_\sim^{-\frac{1}{2}} \cdot S^{(l)} \cdot W^{(l)}) \tag{1}$$

Where $S^{(l)}$ represents the node embedding vector matrix at the l layer, and each row in the matrix represents the local-ADG node vector representation after GCN embedding at the l layer, denoted $S^{(l)} = \{S_1^{(l)}, S_2^{(l)}, ..., S_V^{(l)}\}$, δ is the activation function, $A_\sim$ denotes the sum of the adjacency matrix A and the unit matrix E, i.e., $A_\sim = A + E$, $D_\sim$ denotes the degree matrix of $A_\sim$, $S^{(0)}$ is the initial vector representation, and $W^{(l)}$ is the weight of the GCN embedding at the l layer.

AST Code Embedding

Similar to the local-ADG embedding, we represent the initialized vector matrix of the AST as $H^{(0)} = \{H_1^{(0)}, H_2^{(0)}, ..., H_R^{(0)}\}$ and use GCN to obtain the embedding $H^{(l+1)}$ of the AST according to Eq. 1.

---

[1] https://github.com/flairNLP/flair.

3.3　Fusion Mechanism

We propose the following fusion mechanism to explore the fusion of information from different perspectives of code snippets in depth. First, we act on the local-ADG embedding vector and the AST embedding vector by the $topk\_nodes()$ operation, and then integrate them into a single representation using the cascade operation. The equation is as follows:

$$x = W[topk\_nodes(H^{(l+1)}||topk\_nodes(S^{(l+1)})] \tag{2}$$

Where $H^{(l+1)}$ and $S^{(l+1)}$ denote the AST embedding and local-ADG embedding, respectively. $topk\_nodes$ selects the first k vectors in the matrix. For example, $H^{(l+1)}$ contains 100 feature vectors, each containing 512 elements. $topk\_nodes$ selects the top k largest elements of each of these vectors to form a vector matrix of $(k, 512)$ dimensions. W is the parameter matrice.

Note that, the use of the $topk\_nodes()$ operation aims to keep the dimensionality of the local-ADG embedding vector consistent with that of the AST embedding vector. $topk\_nodes()$ act on the vector elements, and in this paper, we take the minimum number of nodes of local-ADG and AST as the K value.

We input x into Transformer for fusion and use its multi-head self-attention mechanism for weight assignment. Finally, the fused representation vector is fed into the decoder to be trained together with the target summary.

The encoder of Transformer consists of N blocks, and each block contains two parts: the multi-head self-attention mechanism and the feed-forward network. In addition, residual connection and normalization are added after each part.

$$A^n = LayerNorm(\tilde{A} + FFN(\tilde{A})) \tag{3}$$

$$\tilde{A} = LayerNorm(A^{n-1} + MultiAttn(A^{n-1}, A^{n-1}, A^{n-1})) \tag{4}$$

$$FFN(\tilde{A}) = max(0, \tilde{A}W_1 + b_1)W_2 + b_2 \tag{5}$$

where A^{n-1} is the output of the previous encoder block, the FFN contains two fully connected layers, W_1, W_2, b_1, and b_2 are the weights and biases of the FFN, and $MultiAttn$ denotes the multi-head attention mechanism, which contains multiple self-attention heads, and is calculated as follows.

$$MultiAttn(Q, K, V) = Concat(head_1, ..., head_h)W^O \tag{6}$$

$$head_i = Attention(QW_i^Q, KW_i^K, VW_i^V) \tag{7}$$

$$Attention(\tilde{Q}, \tilde{K}, \tilde{V}) = softmax(\frac{\tilde{Q}\tilde{K}^T}{\sqrt{d_k}}\tilde{V}) \tag{8}$$

where Q, K, and V are from the previous block A^{n-1}. i is the number of self-attention heads; $\sqrt{d_k}$ is the square root of a head dimension; W^O, W^Q, W^K, and W^V are learnable parameter matrices.

The construction of the decoder is basically the same as that of the encoder. The decoder's input is the natural language encoding g and the output vector of the encoder, and the output is the probability distribution of the output words corresponding to position j. In addition, the Q of the self-attention mechanism is a linear transformation of the output from the previous position, and K and V are linear transformations of the output vector from the encoder.

Before inputting the natural language encoding g, Transformer first adds the positional code to g to determine the input order. The equation as follows:

$$PE_{(pos,2i)} = \sin(pos/10000^{2i/d_{model}}) \tag{9}$$

$$PE_{(pos,2i+1)} = \cos(pos/10000^{2i/d_{model}}) \tag{10}$$

where pos is the position index; i.e. if the length of x is L, then $pos = 0, 1, 2, ..., L-1$. d_{model} is the vector dimension, if $d_{model} = 512$, $2i$ represents an even dimension, and $2i+1$ represents an odd dimension; i.e., ($2i \leq d_{model}, 2i+1 \leq d_{model}$).

4 Experiments

We evaluate our model using two Java language datasets and several metrics and compare it with several existing baselines.

4.1 Datasets

We use two publicly available Java datasets, CA-Java [8] and MTG [9], for code summarization experiments. We conduct data cleaning on the CA-Java and MTG datasets. We remove low-quality $< code, summary >$ pairs. We conduct a partition of the CA-Java and MTG datasets, where 80% was used for training, 10% for validation, and 10% for testing. Table 1 shows the detailed statistical information of CA-Java and MTG datasets.

Table 1. Statistics for code snippets and comments in our datasets.

	CA-Java	MTG
Train	26352	11969
Dev	3294	664
Test	3294	664
Avg. tokens in code	99.94	70.92
Avg. words in comment	22.56	50.00

4.2   Experimental Setup

In the training process, the maximum number of nodes for the AST and the local-ADG is set to 400. In addition, the number of encoder and decoder layers $N = 6$ for the Transformer, $h = 8$ for the self-attention header. GTsum utilizes two layers of GCNs with a fixed hidden state of 256 dimensions. The word embedding dimension is 256-dimensional. We use a stochastic gradient descent strategy with $p_{drop} = 0.1$. The training batch size is set to $\{2048, 4096, 8129\}$, the number of epochs is set to 100, and the learning rate is set to 0.001. GTsum utilizes Glorot initialization to randomly initialize all parameters and uses the Adam optimizer to optimize our experiments.

4.3   Metrics

We use BLEU [10], METEOR [11], and ROUGE [12] to assess the validity of the experiment.

4.4   Experiments and Analysis

Table 2. Code summarization results comparison with baselines.

Method	CA-Java			MTG		
	BLEU	METEOR	ROUGE-N	BLEU	METEOR	ROUGE-N
CODE-NN [4]	25.66	16.59	26.08	24.52	17.65	25.39
Funcome [13]	35.59	20.33	32.44	34.99	20.91	31.61
DeepCom [2]	31.84	15.44	29.67	31.41	16.03	29.83
Graph2Seq [5]	28.42	17.86	28.12	28.25	16.94	27.68
TL-Codesum [6]	33.68	18.96	30.19	34.22	19.47	30.85
HAN-based [7]	37.15	21.54	34.83	36.99	22.77	33.93
GTsum	**38.11**	**23.14**	**36.17**	**38.49**	**24.31**	**36.55**

Table 2 shows the results of the experimental comparison of GTsum with different baselines. The HAN-based approach performs best of all baselines. For the MTG dataset, Since the data volume of MTG is smaller than that of the CA-Java dataset, the performance of baseline in MTG is slightly lower than that of the CA-Java dataset overall. Combining the results on both datasets, it is clear that GTsum achieves the best performance in all evaluation metrics. The reason is that GTsum effectively circles the API dependencies closely related to code snippets based on the local-ADG, which shields the traditional ADG from containing external noise and thus can more accurately characterize the code features of a single snippet. In summary, GTsum has an advantage in the code summarization task.

5   Conclusion

This paper proposes a new code summarization method called GTsum, for generating natural language descriptions of code snippets; innovatively, this method uses local-ADG semantic structure model and jointly with AST to fuse code representations of different modalities using transformers. We conducted code summarization experiments on two Java datasets and showed that GTsum outperforms the existing approaches.

Acknowledgments. This work is financially supported by the National Natural Science Foundation of China (61602286, 61976127) and the Special Project on Innovative Methods (2020IM020100).

References

1. Chen, M., Wan, X.: Neural comment generation for source code with auxiliary code classification task. In: Asia-Pacific Software Engineering Conference, APSEC, pp. 522–529 (2019)
2. Hu, X., Li, G., Xia, X., Lo, D., Jin, Z.: Deep code comment generation. In: 2018 IEEE/ACM 26th International Conference on Program Comprehension (ICPC), pp. 200–210 (2018)
3. Lyu, C., Wang, R., Zhang, H., Zhang, H., Hu, S.: Embedding API dependency graph for neural code generation. Empir. Softw. Eng. **26**(4), 1–51 (2021)
4. Iyer, S., Konstas, I., Cheung, A., Zettlemoyer, L.: Summarizing source code using a neural attention model. In: Association for Computational Linguistics, pp. 2073–2083 (2016)
5. Xu, K., Wu, L., Wang, Z., Feng, Y., Sheinin, V.: Sql-to-text generation with graph-to-sequence model. In: Association for Computational Linguistics (2014)
6. Hu, X., Li, G., Xia, X., Lo, D., Lu, S., Jin, Z.: Summarizing source code with transferred api knowledge. In: International Joint Conference on Artificial Intelligence (IJCAI), pp. 802–810 (2018)
7. Wang, W., et al.: Reinforcement-learning-guided source code summarization via hierarchical attention. IEEE Trans. Softw. Eng. (2020)
8. Allamanis, M., Peng, H., Sutton, C.: A convolutional attention network for extreme summarization of source code. In: International Conference on Machine Learning (ICML), vol. 48, pp. 2091–2100 (2016)
9. Ling, W., et al.: Latent predictor networks for code generation (2016)
10. Papineni, K., Roukos, S., Ward, T., Zhu, W.J.: Bleu: a method for automatic evaluation of machine translation. In: Association for Computational Linguistics, pp. 311–318 (2002)
11. Banerjeee, S., Lavie, A.: METEOR: an automatic metric for MT evaluation with improved correlation with human judgments. In: Association for Computational Linguistics, pp. 65–72 (2005)
12. Lin, C.Y.: Rouge: a package for automatic evaluation of summaries. In: Text Summarization Branches, pp. 74–81 (2004)
13. LeClair, A., Jiang, S., McMillan, C.: A neural model for generating natural language summaries of program subroutines. In: International Conference on Software Engineering (ICSE), pp. 795–806 (2019)

Code Representation Based on Hybrid Graph Modelling

Qiong Wu[1], Xue Jiang[1], Zhuoran Zheng[2], Xuejian Gao[1], Chen Lyu[1(✉)], and Lei Lyu[1]

[1] School of Information Science and Engineering, Shandong Normal University, Jinan, China
lvchen@sdnu.edu.cn
[2] School of Computer Science and Engineering, Nanjing University of Science and Technology, Nanjing, China

Abstract. Several sequence- or abstract syntax tree (AST)-based models have been proposed for modelling lexical-level and syntactic-level information of source code. However, an effective method of learning code semantic information is still lacking. Thus, we propose a novel code representation method based on hybrid graph modelling, called HGCR. HGCR is a code information extraction model. Specifically, in HGCR, two novel graphs, the Structure Graph (SG) and the Execution Data Flow Graph (EDFG), are first extracted from AST to model the syntactic structural and semantic information of source code, respectively. Then, two improved graph neural networks are applied to learn the graphs to obtain an effective code representation. We demonstrate the effectiveness of our model on two common code understanding tasks: code classification and code clone detection. Empirically, our model outperforms state-of-the-art models.

Keywords: Source code representation · Supervised contrastive learning · Code classification · Graph neural network · Code clone detection

1 Introduction

Deep learning models have been used to solve many tasks in software engineering (SE). Early studies of code representation [1,3] relied on approaches similar to natural language processing (NLP), in which source code was treated as a sequence of tokens. However, these approaches will lose considerable information. Richer code representations have been proposed now. Based on the existing work, we have summarized the following points that need to be addressed.

(1) Noise reduction. Current studies rely on abstract syntax tree (AST) to learn code representation. However, when the code snippets have the same semantics, the nodes representing the variables still differ in the extracted ASTs, because they are set subjectively. **(2) Effective modelling.** Empirically, AST

ⓒ Springer Nature Switzerland AG 2021
T. Mantoro et al. (Eds.): ICONIP 2021, CCIS 1516, pp. 298–306, 2021.
https://doi.org/10.1007/978-3-030-92307-5_35

contains rich syntactic structural information in source code but less semantic information. Therefore, several graphs reflecting semantic information have been proposed, such as control flow graphs (CFG) [9] and data flow graphs (DFG) [2,7], but they still have shortcomings. CFG does not contain fine-grained information within code blocks. Moreover, CFG is more challenging to obtain than AST. DFG reflects only the data flow of local variables but not the global data flow reflected in the code execution. **(3) Effective Learning.** Previous works [7,9] have used GNNs to extract information from graphs by making use of features from nodes while ignoring features from edges. In addition, the classical GNNs are insensitive to the node position, but in some structures such as AST, the node position has important implications. For example, the nodes of a multi-layer cyclic nested structure in codes will be located at different levels.

In this paper, we propose a novel code representation method based on hybrid graph modelling and supervised contrastive learning, called HGCR. The pipeline consists of the following steps.

First, to reduce the influence of noise, we replace the nodes representing variable names in traditional AST with the corresponding variable types. **Second,** structure graph (SG) and execution data flow graph (EDFG) are then constructed based on the AST nodes and the edges formed by the different construction rules, which contain syntactic structural information and the semantic information of its data flow in source code, respectively. **Third,** we propose two improved GNNs to learn these two graphs. We modify the graph convolutional network (GCN) [6] to T-GCN for SG learning, which incorporates position coding and edge features. We use an enhanced graph attention network(GAT) [11], called E-GAT, to learn EDFG, which can aggregate nodes and edge features using an attention mechanism. After that, we introduce a gating mechanism to fuse the two representations of each node. Moreover, we fuse all node features to obtain a representation of the input code snippet.

The main contributions of our approach are as follows:

- We propose a noise reduction method for nodes in AST and a novel graph representation in which SG and EDFG are used to model the syntactic structure and semantics, respectively, of source code more comprehensively.
- We propose T-GCN to fully learn the syntactic structural information of SG by adding node position encoding and considering edge features. Meanwhile, we propose E-GAT, which also considers edge features and aggregates the semantic information of the data flow in EDFG by an attention mechanism.

2   Related Work

Inspired by previous work [6,11], researchers have applied GNNs in the field of SE. Hua et al. [4] used GCN to build the CFG reflecting the high-level control flow information of source code. Wang et al. [12] applied GGNN and GMN to learn AST with different types of edges, where GGNN learns a single graph and GMN jointly learns a pair of graphs. Wang et al. [13] modelled flattened AST that preserve the sequential and cyclic structures of programs and then used AST graph attention blocks to learn the representation of the program.

3   Approach

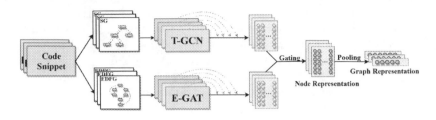

Fig. 1. The architecture of HGCR.

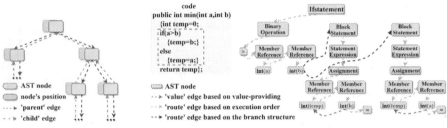

(a) The architecture of SG.

(b) An example of EDFG (corresponding to the code snippet in the green rectangle). The variable name before the replacement is marked in red font.

Fig. 2. Building graphs from abstract syntax tree. SG (left) and EDFG (right).

The architecture of HGCR is shown in Fig. 1. We first parse a code snippet into an AST and reduce its noise. Then, SG and EDFG are extracted from AST. We obtain node representations using the multi-layer T-GCN and E-GAT, respectively. Subsequently, we use a gating mechanism to obtain hybrid node representations. Finally, we use sum pooling to generate a vector representation that represents the features of the code snippet.

3.1   Building Graphs from Abstract Syntax Tree

Firstly, we reduce the noise in AST by replacing the nodes representing variable names with variable types. For example, when using a variable of type *int* in a program, some people name it *number* and some people name it *a*. In the AST, we will consistently represent it as *int*.

Then, the SG and EDFG are extracted from AST. Suppose we have a graph $G = (V, E, X, Y)$, V denotes the set of nodes, and E denotes the set of edges. X^S and Y^S denote the node feature set and the edge feature set, respectively. The nodes of EDFG are the same as those of SG, which are nodes in AST. But they have different rules for edge building.

Structure Graph. To learn the syntactic structural information contained in source code, we construct corresponding SG (as shown in Fig. 2(a)). The SG's backbone is AST. We add a directed edge tagged 'parent' and a directed edge tagged 'child' between each pair of parent and child nodes. For each $v_i \in V$ and $e_{ij} \in E$, we use the vectors $h_{c,i}^{(0)}$ and $m_{c,ij}$ to denote the feature of the i-th node and the edge feature between the i-th node and the j-th node respectively.

Execution Data Flow Graph. To obtain more information about source code semantics, we create EDFG (as shown in Fig. 2(b)). We add a directed edge tagged 'route' between the nodes based on the order of code execution, which represents the global data flow. If the execution of the code contains a branch structure, it is reflected as a branch structure in EDFG. We also add a directed edge tagged 'value' between each node representing a variable and the node that provides its value, which represents the local data flow. Note that a branch structure generally appears as an *ifstatement*, while a *switchstatement* appears less frequently (see Table 1 in Sect. 5). Therefore, *switchstatement* is not considered in our approach. The vectors $h_{a,i}^{(0)}$ and $m_{a,ij}$ denote the features of the i-th node and the edge features between the i-th node and the j-th node in EDFG, respectively.

3.2   Graph Representation Learning

Previous GNNs have used the node features and edge relations in graphs for code representation learning. In this paper, we use two improved GNNs to learn SG and EDFG, using edge features in addition to node features and edge relations.

T-GCN. GCN is an excellent model for learning arbitrarily structured graphs. As mentioned above, since the core skeleton of SG is a tree, the hierarchical position of the nodes is crucial, which the graph-based structure is insensitive to. Therefore, we propose an improved T-GCN to remedy this deficiency. First, we calculate the position encoding, $h_{(i,p)}^{(0)} \in \mathbb{R}^F$, of each node in SG, which is proposed by Vaswani et al. [10] to make use of the order of the sequence.

$$h_{i,p}^{(0)}(pos, 2d) = sin(\frac{pos}{10000^{2d/F}})$$
$$h_{i,p}^{(0)}(pos, 2d+1) = cos(\frac{pos}{10000^{2d/F}}) \tag{1}$$

where pos denotes the hierarchical position of the node, and d is the dimension. F is the dimensionality of position encoding. Then, we concatenate (denoted by the symbol $||$) the word embedding $h_{i,w}^{(0)}$ and the position encoding $h_{i,p}^{(0)}$ into a vector and feed it into a single-layer linear network to obtain the vector representation of node i in SG, $h_{c,i}^{(0)}$.

$$h_{c,i}^{(0)} = W^{(fu)}[h_{i,w}^{(0)}||h_{i,p}^{(0)}] \tag{2}$$

where $W^{(fu)} \in \mathbb{R}^F$ balances the composition of the resulting node representation in terms of position encoding and word embedding.

302   Q. Wu et al.

In our model, we aggregate not only the features of the neighboring nodes of each node but also the features of the edges. We first sum the features $h_{c,j}^{(l)}$ of the j-th node with the feature $m_{c,ij}$ of the edge connecting nodes i and j and then perform the convolution operation. We implement T-GCN based on the Deep Graph Library[1] (DGL). The calculation is shown in the following equation:

$$h_{c,i}^{(l+1)} = \sigma(b^{(l)} + \sum_{j \in N_{(i)}} \frac{1}{c_{ij}}(h_{c,j}^{(l)} + m_{c,ij})W_c^{(l)}) \tag{3}$$

where $h_{c,i}^{(l)}$ is the feature vector of the i-th node, with l denoting l-th rounds of aggregation the GNN; $W_c^{(l)}$ is a learnable weight matrix; $b^{(l)}$ is a bias vector; $N_{(i)}$ is the set of neighbours of node i and $|N_{(i)}|$ is its cardinality; $c_{ij} = \sqrt{|N_{(j)}|}\sqrt{|N_{(i)}|}$; and σ is an activation function.

E-GAT. GAT enables (implicitly) specifying different weights to different nodes in a neighborhood via an attention mechanism. In our model, we use the above property of GAT to aggregate global and local data flow information in EDFG and improve it so that it can take into account the features of the edges. We refer to the improved GAT as E-GAT. First, a shared attentional mechanism $b : \mathbb{R}^{F'} \times \mathbb{R}^{F'} \to \mathbb{R}$ computes attention coefficients. We use $p_{ij}^{(l)}$ to indicate the importance of node j's features to the node i.

$$p_{ij}^{(l)} = b(W_a^{(l)}h_{a,i}^{(l)}, W_a^{(l)}h_{a,j}^{(l)}), j \in N_{(i)} \tag{4}$$

where $W_a^{(l)} \in \mathbb{R}^{F' \times F}$ is a shared linear transformation weight matrix applied to each node; b is a single-layer feedforward neural network. We normalize them across all choices of j using the softmax function:

$$\alpha_{ij}^{(l)} = \frac{exp(p_{ij}^{(l)})}{\sum_{j \in N_{(i)}} exp(p_{ij}^{(l)})} \tag{5}$$

We use the normalized attention coefficients to aggregate the summation of the node features and edge features. Then, the vector representation of the i-th node is obtained by applying a multi-head attention mechanism:

$$h_{a,i}^{(l+1)} = \mathop{\|}_{k=1}^{K} \sigma(\sum_{j \in N_{(i)}} \alpha_{ij}^k W^k(h_{a,j}^{(l)} + m_{a,ij})) \tag{6}$$

where $W^k \in \mathbb{R}^{(FK) \times F}$ is the weight matrix, K denotes the times of independent execution of the attention mechanism, and $\|$ represents concatenation.

After the learning of SG and EDFG, we can obtain a syntactic structural representation and a semantic representation of each node. Then, we fuse them using the gating mechanism proposed by Sun et al. [8]. Finally, we deal with the embedding vectors of all nodes via sum pooling to obtain the representation of the code snippet, denoted as r.

---

[1] https://www.dgl.ai/.

4   Applications

In this section, we present the application of the model to downstream tasks. **1) Code classification.** The code classification task is to classify the functionality of code snippets. When training, we use the cross-entropy loss as loss function. **2) Code clone detection.** This task is as follows: given two code snippets and then decide whether this clone pair is a true clone pair. Typically, there are five types of code clones: Type-1 (T1), Type-2 (T2), strong T3 (ST3), moderate T3 (MT3), and weak T3/T4 (WT3/T4), where each type is more difficult to detect than the previous one. In our work, we use the mean squared error as the loss function.

5   Experiment

In this section, we evaluate the performance of our model on two tasks. The datasets we use are widely used for code understanding tasks and the statistics of these datasets are shown in Table 1.

Table 1. Basic information statistics of the datasets.

	Code classification	Code clone detection	
Dataset	OJ	GCJ	BCB
Language	C	Java	Java
Total number of if branch	182510	5184	144459
Total number of switch branch	1243	22	1624
Average code lines	35.4	61.2	27.1
MAX code lines	1302	644	1818
Average SG edges	189.5	396.9	205.6
MAX SG edges	7027	2608	15217
Average EDFG edges	245.0	441.3	222.8
MAX EDFG edges	8917	2846	16207

5.1   Experiment Setting

We use pycparser[2] and javalang[3] tool to parse the C codes and Java codes to get the corresponding AST respectively. For each obtained AST, we use the skip-gram model in word2vec to encode the tokens in the dataset. Specifically, we set the initial encoding dimensionality to 128, the batch size to 64, the epoch size to 100, and the ratio of the sizes of the training, validation, and test sets to 8:1:1. We use the Adam optimizer [5] with a learning rate of 0.0001 for training.

---

[2] https://github.com/eliben/pycparser.
[3] https://github.com/c2nes/javalang.

5.2 Metrics

For the code classification task, we use the accuracy matrix to evaluate the effectiveness of each model. And for the code clone detection task, we use precision (P), recall (R) and F1 score (F1) as our evaluation metrics.

5.3 Results

(1) The code classification task. The experimental results are shown in Table 2. The results show that HGCR has achieved better accuracy than the other baselines. Specifically, Tree-LSTM, TBCNN, and ASTNN methods are all based on the tree structure. We observe that the graph-based approach, GGNN, is less effective in practice than tree-based approaches. This may be because the tree-based approaches make full use of the special tree structure of AST, whereas GGNN treats AST as an ordinary graph structure.

Table 2. OJ dataset classification experiment results.

Methods	Test accuracy
Tree-LSTM	88.2
TBCNN	94.0
ASTNN	98.2
GGNN	79.5
HGCR	**99.3**

Table 3. GCJ clone detection experiment results

Metric	ASTNN	FA-AST	FCCA	HGCR
P	95.4	96.3	96.7	**98.7**
R	87.2	85.5	89.8	**94.2**
F1	91.1	90.6	93.1	**96.4**

Table 4. BCB clone detection experiment results.

Type	ASTNN			FA-AST			FCCA			HGCR		
	P	R	F1	P	R	F1	P	R	F1	P	R	F1
T-1	100	100	100	100	100	100	100	100	100	100	100	100
T-2	100	100	99.9	100	100	100	100	100	100	100	100	100
ST-3	99.9	94.2	97.0	100	99.6	99.8	100	99.8	99.9	100	100	100
MT-3	99.5	91.7	95.4	98.7	96.5	97.6	98.7	95.9	97.3	99.9	97.2	98.5
T-4	99.8	88.3	93.7	97.7	90.5	94.0	98.2	92.3	95.2	99.5	95.6	97.5
ALL	**99.8**	88.4	93.8	97.7	90.6	94.0	98.2	92.4	95.2	**99.5**	**95.6**	**97.5**

(2) The code clone detection task. As seen from Table 3, the experimental F1 scores of all models on the GCJ dataset are slightly worse than those on the BCB datasets. We speculate that the reason for this is the long code snippets in the GCJ dataset. As seen from Table 4, the results show that FA-AST and FCCA perform better than ASTNN. This is because they mine the semantic information from source code. The results show that HGCR achieves F1 scores that are higher than the other baselines.

6   Conclusion

In this work, we propose a novel code representation model based on hybrid graph modelling called HGCR. HGCR comprehensively captures both the syntactic structural and semantic information of source code. We evaluate our model on three datasets (OJ, GCJ, and BCB) for two common code understanding tasks. The results show that our model is effective in code understanding.

Acknowledgement. This work is financially supported by the National Natural Science Foundation of China (61602286, 61976127) and the Special Project on Innovative Methods (2020IM020100).

References

1. Allamanis, M., Peng, H., Sutton, C.: A convolutional attention network for extreme summarization of source code. In: ICML (2016)
2. Gu, W., et al.: CRaDLe: deep code retrieval based on semantic dependency learning. Neural Netw. **141**, 385–394 (2021)
3. Hindle, A., Barr, E.T., Gabel, M., Su, Z., Devanbu, P.: On the naturalness of software. Commun. ACM **59**, 122–131 (2016)
4. Hua, W., Sui, Y., Wan, Y., Liu, G., Xu, G.: FCCA: hybrid code representation for functional clone detection using attention networks. IEEE Trans. Reliabil. **70**, 304–318 (2020)
5. Kingma, D.P., Ba, J.: Adam: A method for stochastic optimization. In: ICLR (2014)

6. Kipf, T.N., Welling, M.: Semi-supervised classification with graph convolutional networks. In: ICLR (2017)
7. Mehrotra, N., Agarwal, N., Gupta, P., Anand, S., Lo, D., Purandare, R.: Modeling functional similarity in source code with graph-based Siamese networks. arXiv preprint arXiv:2011.11228 (2020)
8. Sun, Z., Zhu, Q., Xiong, Y., Sun, Y., Mou, L., Zhang, L.: TreeGen: a tree-based transformer architecture for code generation. In: AAAI (2020)
9. Tufano, M., Watson, C., Bavota, G., Di Penta, M., White, M., Poshyvanyk, D.: Deep learning similarities from different representations of source code. In: MSR (2018)
10. Vaswani, A., et al.: Attention is all you need. In: NeurIPS (2017)
11. Veličković, P., Cucurull, G., Casanova, A., Romero, A., Lio, P., Bengio, Y.: Graph attention networks. In: ICLR (2018)
12. Wang, W., Li, G., Ma, B., Xia, X., Jin, Z.: Detecting code clones with graph neural network and flow-augmented abstract syntax tree. In: SANER (2020)
13. Wang, Y., Li, H.: Code completion by modeling flattened abstract syntax trees as graphs. arXiv preprint arXiv:2103.09499 (2021)

Deep Neural Network Architecture for Low-Dimensional Embedding and Classification of Cosmic Ray Images Obtained from CMOS Cameras

Tomasz Hachaj[ID], Marcin Piekarczyk[✉][ID], and Łukasz Bibrzycki[ID]

Institute of Computer Science, Pedagogical University of Krakow, Podchorążych 2, 30-084, Kraków, Poland
{tomasz.hachaj,marcin.piekarczyk,lukasz.bibrzycki}@up.krakow.pl

Abstract. In this paper we propose and evaluate several deep neural network (DNN) architectures that are capable to generate low-dimensional embedding of cosmic ray images obtained from CMOS cameras. All images have been acquired by the CREDO distributed cosmic ray observatory infrastructure. The embedding we obtained can also be used to classify those images using a threshold schema that models an uncertainty of class assignment. The proposed method has also a potential to be a filtering mechanism in order to search data set for images that satisfy certain criteria. The training and validation of the model has been performed on the labelled subset of the CREDO data set that contains 2350 images. We also performed an embedding and classification for the first time on a large subset of CREDO data containing 3.5 million unlabelled images. To the best of our knowledge, this is the most comprehensive study of this scale, published with CREDO imaging data. Both the CREDO data set and the source codes of our method can be downloaded in order to reproduce the results. We also make available for download the data set embedding and classification results.

Keywords: Cosmic rays · CNN · Image classification · Image embedding · Uncertainty modelling · CMOS detectors · Smartphones

1 Introduction

Cosmic Ray Extremely distributed Observatory (CREDO) is a citizen science project aimed at the worldwide detection of cosmic rays with CMOS cameras of smartphones [1,5]. There are several other initiatives of this type on the scientific market, like DECO [9,12] or CRAYFIS [2,11]. Unambiguous association between the particle types and track properties is not straightforward. Therefore here we focus on providing an abstract signal representation based exclusively on its morphological properties.

Convolutional neural networks (CNNs) have emerged as one of the most efficient methods for image-based pattern recognition [3,6] and in many applications they outperform more classical approaches based on manual definition

© Springer Nature Switzerland AG 2021
T. Mantoro et al. (Eds.): ICONIP 2021, CCIS 1516, pp. 307–316, 2021.
https://doi.org/10.1007/978-3-030-92307-5_36

of shape representations. In this context, the transfer learning approach is one of the most useful techniques for adapting pre-trained CNN architectures to specific image types [7,10]. With the help of transfer learning, it is possible to train an effective deep neural network (DNN) architecture with a limited number of training samples, since it is possible to reuse previously trained layers that generate an effective feature vector representation. The methodology presented in this paper is inspired by previous research in the DECO [12] and CREDO [8] projects that utilizes DNN to classify cosmic ray images and our previous CREDO project paper [4] in which the threshold schema for uncertain class assignment has been introduced. There are several important differences and improvements between research presented in this paper and those already published. First, we focused on creating a method that is embedding-oriented rather than classification-oriented. By the application of data set augmentation we have eliminated the necessity of image preprocessing that was very time demanding operation in already published solutions. We have also proposed simplified DNN architectures which are capable to operate with high frequency and are capable to process data sets that contain millions of images. Also the scale of the experiment and amount of data that we analyzed are many times higher than in previously published papers. For example in [12] the data set contained about 45 000 images, in [4,8] 2350 images whereas this paper evaluates nearly 3.5 million images. Due to this fact the results presented in this paper are pioneering in the field of application of DNN in the process of embedding and classification of cosmic ray images acquired by smartphone cameras on such large, global scale. The proposed method has also a potential to be a filtering mechanism in order to search a data set for images that satisfy certain criteria. Both the CREDO data set[1] and the source codes[2] of our method can be downloaded in order to reproduce the results.

2   Materials and Methods

2.1   Problem Formulation

We have two goals: to generate low-dimensional embedding method, that can meaningfully describe the similarity of each image obtained from CMOS camera to some abstract (ideal) description of certain class and to utilize that embedding to assign class labels to each image. In order to prepare the image deep learning based embedding, we have utilized an approach similar to one that was introduced in [4]. Our training data set is composed of images that were labelled by annotators who assigned each image to at most one class from the following group: spots, tracks, wiggles (which we here call worms) and artefacts. This description defines a four-dimensional vector y, each coordinate of which

---

[1] Link to CREDO data set https://user.credo.science/user-interface/download/images/.
[2] Link to source codes and results https://github.com/browarsoftware/credo_dnn_rays_embedding/.

equals to the number of votes that was assigned to a given class by annotators. For example vector [0,1,2,3] informs us that 0 annotators have voted for spots class, one annotator has voted for tracks class, two annotators have voted for worms and three annotators have voted for artefacts. There have been at least 6 different annotators, because it is possible that someone has skipped voting. In the next step we normalize each y_i by dividing it by the number N_i, which is the number of annotators who have taken part in labelling certain images, including those, who have skipped assigning y_i to one of four classes. After this operation we have an image data set labelled with four-dimensional vectors with each coordinate assuming a value from the $[0-1]$ interval. When a certain coordinate of a vector equals 1, it means that all annotators have assigned an image to the same class. If a certain coordinate of a vector equals 0, that means, that no one have assigned an image to respective class. In all other cases we have an uncertain voting. The role of the embedding generated by our networks is to model that uncertainty by approximation of annotators' voting. The embedding defined in such a way allows us to approximate the similarity of certain image to the "ideal" description of a certain class. The embedding can be formally defined as a function f, that maps a 24-bit RGB images to four dimensional vectors. Because in the case of CREDO data set, those images have resolution 60x60 we can define our embedding f using the following equation:

$$f : \{0, 1, \cdots 255\}^{3 \times 60 \times 60} \rightarrow [0, 1]^4 \tag{1}$$

In order to classify an image, we can apply the threshold scheme originally proposed in [4], which assigns an image to a certain class provided that embedding coordinate that represents certain class has a maximal value among coordinates of the vector y_i and that coordinate value is above certain threshold $t \in [0, 1)$:

$$C(v_i, t) = \begin{cases} C(v_i) \ if \ max(v_i) \geq t \\ NA \ \ \ \ if \ max(v_i) < t \end{cases} \tag{2}$$

where NA denotes the lack of assignment, because it is below threshold, and $C(v_i)$ is class id which has the highest coordinate value in embedding vector:

$$C(v_i) = max_{id} v_i \tag{3}$$

2.2   Network Architectures

We have proposed and evaluated several DNN architectures that were capable to generate an embedding that satisfies Eq. 1. The layouts of these architectures are presented in Fig. 1. The four architectures considered in this study were split in two groups according to their training strategy. The well-known VGG16 architecture was pre-trained on the ImageNet dataset with the only last two dense layers trained from scratch with labeled data set. On the other hand, the $V1$, $V2$ and $V3$ models were trained entirely from scratch. These approaches differ from the training strategies discussed in [4] where the transfer learning strategy was used exclusively. Application of DNN with convolutional layers has

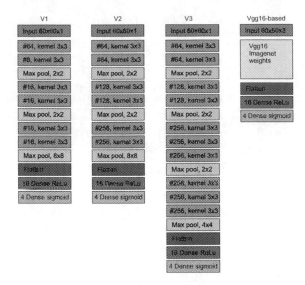

Fig. 1. DNN architectures considered to obtain image embedding.

allowed for elimination of any additional image preprocessing of input CMOS images (see [4]). This fact highly speeds up the whole proposed solution allowing a high-frequency prediction of input images.

2.3 Training and Inference on CREDO Images

The training data set consisted of 2350 CREDO images labelled by five annotators. After the data set labelling, 527 images have been assigned to the spot class, 360 to the track class, 305 to the worm class, and 1158 to the artefact class. The labelled credo data set has been used to train the DNN architectures introduced in Sect. 2.2. These architectures included morphological image analysis and classification. Then, these models have been applied to the whole CREDO data set that contains over 3.4 million unlabelled images. Results that we present in the following chapter are the first attempt of such comprehensive analysis of CREDO images.

3   Results

We have minimized the mean squared error loss function using Adam optimizer. Because our training labelled data set is relatively small, we have configured additional data set augmentation by adding rotation in range ±20°, horizontal and vertical shift in range ±20% and also a horizontal flip. We have performed a 10-fold cross validation by splitting labelled data set into training (90% of data) and validation (10% of data) subsets. Obtained results have been averaged and

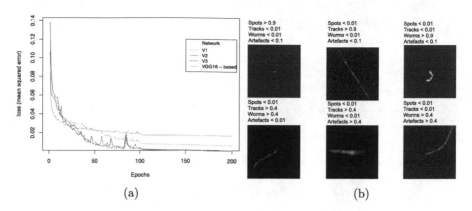

Fig. 2. Results of method evaluation. Loss function (a). Images that meet a search criterion (filtering) on image embedding (b).

are presented in the form average ± standard deviation. In Fig. 2a we present the process of minimizing of loss function during network training.

In Tables 1, 2, 3 and 4 we present classification results in the form of confusion matrices of all proposed networks calculated according to method described by Eq. 3. As can be seen, the highest recognition rate has been obtained for VGG16-based solution. The accuracy of approximation is calculated as $(1 - mse) \cdot 100\%$ averaged over 10-fold validation on all networks and equals: for V1 88.60% ± 1.51%, for V2 89.41% ± 2.09%, for V3 90.48% ± 1.37%, for VGG16-based 90.52% ± 0.72%. The averaged classification time measured in images per second equals: for V1 136.24 ± 1.30 ips, for V2 127.55 ± 1.11 ips, for V3 117.05 ± 1.45 ips, for VGG16-based 95.51 ± 1.26 ips.

Table 1. Confusion matrix for V1 classification. Results are given in percentages.

	Spots	Tracks	Worms	Artefacts
Spots	80.27 ±5.25	8.39 ± 4.90	9.19 ±3.86	2.15 ± 1.80
Tracks	7.42 ± 3.80	68.40 ± 7.11	23.21 ± 6.32	0.99 ± 1.58
Worms	4.10 ± 3.08	34.17 ± 5.47	57.55 ± 8.87	4.18 ± 3.76
Artefacts	1.62 ± 1.45	0.09 ± 0.28	0.46 ± 0.66	97.83 ± 1.86

As can be seen, the best accuracy results have also been obtained for VGG16-based architecture. Due to the fact that the processing time measured in ips is fast enough for our needs, we decided to utilize VGG16-based architecture for further evaluation as being the most reliable. In the next step of evaluation we have studied to what extent the data is filtered-out by applying the threshold schema from Eq. 2, depending on the value of t. Those calculations for VGG16-based architecture are shown in Tables 5, 6 and 7. As can be seen, we have also

Table 2. Confusion matrix for V2 classification. Results are given in percentages.

	Spots	Tracks	Worms	Artefacts
Spots	84.08 ± 7.00	06.14 ± 5.61	7.64 ± 3.48	2.14 ± 2.18
Tracks	4.27 ± 3.02	72.45 ± 7.23	23.04 ± 5.84	0.24 ± 0.77
Worms	5.51 ± 4.41	30.43 ± 9.24	62.39 ± 9.56	1.66 ± 2.28
Artefacts	1.27 ± 1.37	0.18 ± 0.39	0.54 ± 0.63	98.01 ± 2.03

Table 3. Confusion matrix for V3 classification. Results in the table are in percentages.

	Spots	Tracks	Worms	Artefacts
Spots	85.31 ±4.62	03.78 ± 2.85	07.84 ± 3.95	3.07 ± 2.55
Tracks	6.32 ±3.54	71.21 ± 6.73	21.54 ± 5.70	0.93 ± 1.50
Worms	6.86 ±4.84	27.47 ± 6.35	63.31 ± 7.38	2.37 ± 3.90
Artefacts	1.34 ±1.41	0.36 ± 0.64	0.46 ± 0.65	97.84 ± 1.99

estimated, using labelled data, the trade-off between accuracy of classification (certainty) and the number of images that are filtered-out from the data set. We are aware of the limitations of this approach when applied to an unlabeled data set. Still it enables us to flexibly adjust the level of certainty of class assignment.

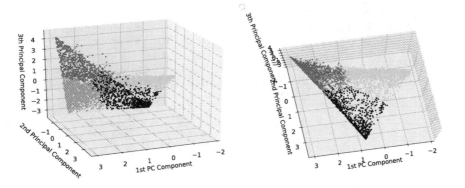

Fig. 3. Three-dimensional Principal Components Analysis (PCA) projection of random 10 000 CREDO data set images embedding. Data is color-coded according to classes calculated with Eq. 3. (Color figure online)

The last part of our study was to perform an embedding and classification of the whole CREDO data set. For this purpose we have utilized one of the VGG16-based DNNs which was validated in the previous step. The results generated by VGG16-based network on the whole CREDO data set are presented in Table 8. We have also estimated the number of objects that belong to the certain class

Table 4. Confusion matrix for VGG16-based classification. Results in the table are in percentages.

	Spots	Tracks	Worms	Artefacts
Spots	86.20 ± 5.66	02.94 ± 2.41	07.82 ± 4.82	3.05 ± 2.15
Tracks	7.96 ± 5.26	77.49 ± 7.46	12.84 ± 6.75	1.70 ± 1.50
Worms	3.92 ± 3.00	21.99 ± 5.99	64.20 ± 8.52	9.90 ± 5.90
Artefacts	1.36 ± 1.43	0.27 ± 0.43	1.18 ± 0.98	97.20 ± 2.11

Table 5. Confusion matrix (in percentages) for the VGG16-based classification with the threshold set to 0.5. For this threshold ratios of images assigned to particular classes are: Spots (82.99 ± 4.76)%; Tracks (80.65 ± 8.01)%; Worms (77.76 ± 6.18)%; Artefacts (98.65 ± 1.27)%. The rest of the data has not been classified.

	Spots	Tracks	Worms	Artefacts
Spots	96.31 ± 1.77	0.66 ± 1.07	0.95 ± 1.72	2.08 ± 1.37
Tracks	3.77 ± 3.93	85.38 ± 8.07	10.19 ± 6.95	0.66 ± 1.38
Worms	1.43 ± 1.89	19.94 ± 9.29	69.01 ± 10.87	9.63 ± 5.86
Artefacts	0.93 ± 0.99	0.18 ± 0.38	0.73 ± 0.59	98.16 ± 1.10

using approach defined by Eqs. (2) and (3) with various threshold values. In Fig. 3 we have visualized the three-dimensional projection of embedding of random 10 000 images from CREDO data set generated by our approach. In order to better represent the spatial correspondence of points we have created two plots that differ in the angle of axis towards observer. The percentage of variance explained by 1st PC is 51.58%, by the 2nd PC is 32.45% and by the third is 15.96%. Because those three dimensions explain about 99.99% of data set variance it seems that Fig. 3 presents spatial correspondence of images embedding in reliable way. The points that represent embedding in those two figures have been additionally color-coded according to classes calculated by Eq. (3). Color codes are: red - spots, green - tracks, blue - worms and, black - artefacts.

Table 6. Confusion matrix (in percentages) for the VGG16-based classification with the threshold set to 0.75. For this threshold ratios of images assigned to particular classes are: Spots (58.21 ± 5.01)%; Tracks (34.99 ± 6.81)%; Worms (34.64 ± 6.80)%; Artefacts (95.49 ± 1.92)%. The rest of the data has not been classified.

	Spots	Tracks	Worms	Artefacts
Spots	99.68 ± 1.02	0.00 ± 0.00	0.00 ± 0.00	0.32 ± 1.02
Tracks	3.89 ± 6.03	94.87 ± 7.08	1.24 ± 2.65	0.00 ± 0.00
Worms	0.00 ± 0.00	12.28 ± 11.47	75.39 ± 14.39	12.34 ± 11.60
Artefacts	0.09 ± 0.29	0.00 ± 0.00	0.18 ± 0.38	99.73 ± 0.44

Table 7. Confusion matrix (in percentages) for the VGG16-based classification with the threshold set to 0.85. For this threshold ratios of images assigned to particular classes are: Spots $(39.49 \pm 6.23)\%$; Tracks $(15.19 \pm 6.11)\%$; Worms $(19.41 \pm 7.01)\%$; Artefacts $(94.07 \pm 2.60)\%$. The rest of the data has not been classified.

	Spots	Tracks	Worms	Artefacts
Spots	100.00 ± 0.00	0.00 ± 0.00	0.00 ± 0.00	0.00 ± 0.00
Tracks	1.43 ± 4.52	98.57 ± 4.52	0.00 ± 0.00	0.00 ± 0.00
Worms	0.00 ± 0.00	7.43 ± 13.55	81.59 ± 21.68	10.98 ± 12.48
Artefacts	0.00 ± 0.00	0.00 ± 0.00	0.18 ± 0.38	99.82 ± 0.38

4   Discussion

The training of each proposed network architecture has nicely converged and the stable solution has been obtained. Although the smallest value of loss function has been obtained for V3 network (see Fig. 2a) the best accuracy and classification results have been obtained for VGG16-based solution. It is probably caused by the fact that our labelled training data set is relatively small and the networks that are learning their convolution layers from scratch are not able to create all necessary filters. On the other hand, the large pretrained architecture has these filters already set. The difference in V3 and VGG16-based network accuracy is very small (0.04%), however it affects the classification results presented in Table 3 and 4. VGG16-based network can do much better distinguishing between classes Tracks and Worms that are most similar to each other. Thanks to the GPU-based implementation of DNN architectures, the VGG16-based solution operates relatively fast even though it has a large number of weights. Results presented in Tables 5, 6 and 7 show nicely a trade-off between classification accuracy and the number of images that are filtered off the data set due to low certainty in the threshold scheme defined by Eq. 2. We can also observe this fact in the whole CREDO data set classification results in Table 8. For example when $t = 0.85$ 52.65% of images have not been assigned to any class. Statistics presented in Table 8 correspond to embedding projection presented in Fig. 3. As can be seen, there are not many objects that are assigned to two or more classes with a similar probability. It can be clearly observed because the median value for each coordinate of embedding is relatively small which corresponds to a fairly even distribution of classes. This fact is especially visible in Fig. 3 where the interior of triangle-shaped region is relatively empty. The last interesting application of our proposed approach is utilizing embedding as the filtering mechanism in order to search data set for images that satisfy certain criteria (see Fig. 2b).

The evaluation results obtained from the DNN-based architectures applied for the classification and low-dimensional embedding of cosmic ray images proved to be reliable and promising tool for exploring data that are stored in constantly growing CREDO data set. Besides proven accuracy, proposed methods are also fast enough to deal with data sets containing millions of images. We believe that

Table 8. Statistical analysis of embedding and classification results generated by VGG16 on the whole CREDO data set, where NA indicates the number of images not assigned to any class, #Objects means number of objects that have been classified to certain class using 3 or 2 using certain threshold.

	Spots	Tracks	Worms	Artefacts	NA
Min	0.00	0.00	0.00	0.00	–
1st quantile	0.00	0.00	0.00	0.06	–
Median	0.15	0.05	0.03	0.28	–
Mean	0.33	0.12	0.09	0.46	–
3rd quantile	0.74	0.14	0.10	0.98	–
Max	0.99	1.00	1.00	1.00	–
#Objects	1348835	296499	205026	1581239	0
#Objects t = 0.50	1202677	181429	117155	1492668	437670 (12.75%)
#Objects t = 0.75	826958	50010	28339	1265787	1260505 (36.73%)
#Objects t = 0.85	482545	18740	12237	1111301	1806776 (52.65%)

the DNN embedding we have created can also be used to search the CREDO dataset for images matching the specified image pattern.

References

1. Bibrzycki, Ł, et al.: Towards a global cosmic ray sensor network: CREDO detectoras the first open-source mobile application enabling detection of penetrating radiation. Symmetry **12**(11), 1802 (2020). https://doi.org/10.3390/sym121118
2. Borisyak, M., et al.: Muon trigger for mobile phones. J. Phys. Conf. Seri. **898**, 032048. IOP Publishing (2017)
3. Gao, M., et al.: RGB-D-based object recognition using multimodal convolutional neural networks: a survey. IEEE Access **7**, 43110–43136 (2019)
4. Hachaj, T., et al.: Recognition of cosmic ray images obtained from CMOS sensors used in mobile phones by approximation of uncertain class assignment with deep convolutional neural network. Sensors **21**(6) (2021). https://doi.org/10.3390/s21061963
5. Homola, P., et al.: Cosmic-ray extremely distributed observatory. Symmetry **12**(11)(2020). https://doi.org/10.3390/sym12111835
6. Jiao, L., et al.: A survey of deep learning-based object detection. IEEE Access **7**, 128837–128868 (2019)
7. Krishna, S.T., Kalluri, H.K.: Deep learning and transfer learning approaches for image classification. Int. J. Recent Technol. Eng. (IJRTE) **7**(5S4), 427–432 (2019)
8. Piekarczyk, M., et al.: CNN-based classifier as an offline trigger for the CREDO experiment. Sensors **21**(14), 4804 (2021). https://doi.org/10.3390/s21144804
9. Vandenbroucke, J., et al.: Measurement of cosmic-ray muons with the distributed electronic cosmic-ray observatory, a network of smartphones. J. Instrum. **11**(04), P04019 (2016)

10. Wang, S., et al.: Class-specific reconstruction transfer learning for visual recognition across domains. IEEE Trans. Image Process. **29**, 2424–2438 (2019)
11. Whiteson, D., et al.: Searching for ultra-high energy cosmic rays with smartphones. Astropart. Phys. **79**, 1–9 (2016)
12. Winter, M., et al.: Particle identification in camera image sensors using computer vision. Astropart. Phys. **104**, 42–53 (2019). https://doi.org/10.1016/j.astropartphys.2018.08.009

RepoMedUNM: A New Dataset for Feature Extraction and Training of Deep Learning Network for Classification of Pap Smear Images

Dwiza Riana(✉)[iD], Sri Hadianti[iD], Sri Rahayu[iD], Frieyadie[iD],
Muhamad Hasan[iD], Izni Nur Karimah[iD], and Rafly Pratama[iD]

Universitas Nusa Mandiri, East Jakarta, Indonesia
`dwiza@nusamandiri.ac.id`

Abstract. Morphological changes in the cell structure in Pap Smear images are the basis for classification in pathology. Identification of this classification is a challenge because of the complexity of Pap Smear images caused by changes in cell morphology. This procedure is very important because it provides basic information for detecting cancerous or precancerous lesions. To help advance research in this area, we present the RepoMedUNM Pap smear image database consisting of non-ThinPrep (nTP) Pap test images and ThinPrep (TP) Pap test images. It is common for research groups to have their image datasets. This need is driven by the fact that established datasets are not publicly accessible. The purpose of this study is to present the RepoMedUNM dataset analysis performed for texture feature cells on new images consisting of four classes, normal, L-Sil, H-Sil, and Koilocyt with K-means segmentation. Evaluation of model classification using reuse pretrained network method. Convolutional Neural Network (CNN) implements the pre-trained CNN VGG16, VGG19, and ResNet50 models for the classification of three groups namely TP, nTP and all datasets. The results of feature cells and classification can be used as a reference for the evaluation of future classification techniques.

Keywords: Pap smear images · ThinPrep · Cervical cell classification · Cell image database · K-Means · Convolutional Neural Network

1 Introduction

Some aspects of digital image processing in Pap smear images are identification of cell objects, image enhancement, artifact limitation, object segmentation, depiction of overlapping cells, elimination of inflammatory cells, etc. All of these are performed so that the interpretation of Pap Smear images can be done automatically. This study is an interesting field in cytological image analysis. Many

T. Mantoro et al. (Eds.): ICONIP 2021, CCIS 1516, pp. 317–325, 2021.
https://doi.org/10.1007/978-3-030-92307-5_37

attempts have been made to automatically detect areas of interest in the image as well as various techniques used such as feature and image base [1], nucleus and inflamantory cell [2], feature Interpretation [3], image base [4], width of cytoplasm [5]. This was done as an effort to tackle cervical cancer which was statistically reported as the fourth most common cancer-causing death [6]. The annual death toll is 311,000 women, of which 85% of these deaths occur in low- and middle-income countries [6].

Researchers observed the characteristics of Pap Smear images as the basis for an appropriate diagnosis in cytomorphological classification to detect cancerous or precancerous lesions. To the best of our knowledge, currently, the single-cell dataset available is Herlev [7] and SiPakMed [1] which are generally accessible in a limited number of Herlev as many as 917 images [7] and a fairly large data of SiPakMed as many as 4049 images [1]. The dataset that we introduce is different because it consists of a dataset of clustered cells that is generally available. So far, several image data collections have been made by several researchers privately to evaluate the performance of their methods. The weakness of this private dataset is that it is difficult to compare with different classification techniques because it only applies to data sets.

Repository Medical Image Processing of UNM (RepoMedUNM) contains the novel image which is publicly available that we introduce in this paper. RepoMe-dUNM consists of 6,168 clustered cell images from TP and nTP Pap test processes. Slides have been classified by pathologists into fourth different classes. It is specifically divided into the first group of TP Pap test which consists of three categories, namely normal cells, intermediate and sometimes in metaplastic (koilocyt cells), and benign cells pre-cancerous lesions called high grade squamous intraepithelial lesions (H -Sil). The second group of nTP Pap tests which consists of two categories, namely normal cells, and mild or moderate abnormal cells are called Low-grade Squamous Intraepithelial Lesion (L-Sil). In our image database, the texture features of each class were calculated to show the differences in these features in the two TP and nTP groups which as far as our observations have not been carried out by other studies. In general, the available datasets only come from one type of Pap test. In the end, we also provided evaluation results using several classification models based on image features. To the best of our knowledge, this study presented a classification without segmentation for grouped images or complete slides without manual cropping into single cells using CNN with a very large number of images. Previous research used a limited number of 966 images [1], and 917 images [7] while we presented a total of 6,168 images with a partially different CNN model classification evaluation. In addition, we use the reuse pretrained network for the new images with transfer learning in a deep learning application that has not been used by other researchers in the realm of cervical cancer research. Structure of the paper follows Sect. 2 and 3 discusses the RepoMedUNM dataset and evaluation, Sect. 4 is the experiment result, and Sect. 5 is the conclusion.

2 RepoMed UNM Dataset

The RepoMedUNM database consists of 6,168 Pap smear cell images. Images were obtained through an OLYMPUS CX33RTFS2 optical microscope and an X52-107BN microscope with a Logitech camera.The quantitative description of the dataset for each class there are 3083 nTP normal, 818 L-shil and for TP normal there are 1513, koilocyt 434 and H-shil 410 images. The total of images are 6168 images. From the datasets we have collected, detailed information and differences can be seen in Table 1. Only two data sets are publicly available [1], [7]. RepoMedUNM is our dataset available for public access. Researchers can access this dataset at link [8] by citing this paper. Our different datasets have more slides and smear images.

Table 1. Dataset Pap smear images available.

No	Data	Slide	Image	Image size	Cells	No	Datasets	Slide	Image	Image size	Cells
1	[7]	NA	NA	NA	1499	4	[2]	NA	222	NA	488
2	[9]	20	NA	640 × 480	479	5	[4]	NA	917	NA	917
3	[10]	NA	966	NA	4049	6	RepoMedUNM	24	6168	1600 × 1200	NA

3 Evaluation on RepoMedUNM

3.1 Evaluation on RepoMedUNM Dataset with Feature Textures

In the identification and evaluation of Pap smear cell features, six texture features from the Gray Level Co-Occurrence Matrix (GLCM) were used which consist of metric features, eccentricity, contrast, correlation, energy, and homogeneity [12]. The RGB Pap smear image is converted into an L*a*b image [11]. K-means segmentation classifies Pap smear images based on the proximity of the color to the image. These six features are commonly used for Pap smear image cell identification. The texture feature extraction is carried out in stages as shown in Fig. 1. The results of the feature extraction process stages can be seen in Fig. 2.

Fig. 1. RepoMedUNM dataset feature extraction steps

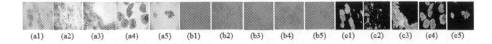

Fig. 2. The samples of image RGB (a1–a5), L*A*B (b1–b5), segmentation (c1–c5)

3.2 Evaluation on RepomedUNM Database by Implementing Pre-trained CNN Models

We have tested several classification models of CNN in the RepoMedUNM Database to evaluate the performance of the classification models on the differences in various cell types in the TP Pap test groups, nTP Pap test groups, and the combined data. Furthermore, we have used a reused pre-trained network [5,15,16]. We used transfer learning to retrain CNN to classify a new set of images. The network takes an image of RepoMedUNM as input and then outputs a label for the object in the image together with the probabilities for each of the object categories in 5 classes. Transfer learning is used in deep learning such as VGG16 [13,14], VGG19 [1], and RessNet50 [4] which have been used and resulted in a good classification of Pap smear images [1]. Figure 3 shows the overall stages of this classification evaluation process.

The process of loading the trained network is performed on the new image. In this experiment 6168 new Pap smear images were stored in the database. We divided the training dataset into 80% and 20% for validation. Next load the trained GoogLeNet network [17].

Detailed information about the network layer can be obtained by displaying an interactive visualization of the network architecture using analyze Network. The image input layer is the first element of the layers property of the network. In this experiment, a layer that requires an input image of 224 × 224 × 3 is used, where 3 is the number of color channels.

Replace final layers is done to retrain the network that has been trained in classifying new images. This is done by replacing these two layers with new layers that match the database. Image feature extraction is carried out by the network convolution layer used by the last layer. This can be studied and the final classification layer to classify the input image. The network requires an input image of 224 × 224 × 3, but the size of the image in the image data storage

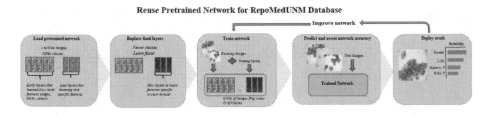

Fig. 3. Reuse pretrained network for RepoMedUNM database. (c1–c5)

is different. Use advanced image data storage to automatically resize training images. Decide what to do with the exercise image and other magnifications: the mirrored exercise image is randomly moved up to 30 pixels along the vertical axis, and increased up to 10% in the horizontal and vertical directions. An increased amount of data helps prevent organizations from overfitting and stores accurate details in training drawings. To automatically adjust the size of the verified image without further enlarging the data, use the enlarged image data store without specifying additional pre-processing steps. Set training parameters. Set InitialLearnRate to a low value to slow down unfrozen transport layer training. In the previous step, you added the appropriate last shift's learning rate factor to accelerate learning of the new last shift. The combination of learning speed settings results in fast learning in new levels, slower learning in intermediate levels, and no learning in previous frozen levels. Determine the number of training periods. When doing portable learning, there is no need to practice many times. The epoch is a complete learning cycle for the entire training data set. Specify the mini-batch size and verification date. Verification accuracy rate is calculated once every epoch. Use training data to train the network. By default, trainNetwork uses the GPU when available. This requires Parallel Computing Toolbox™ and a compatible GPU device. For information about supported devices, see Parallel Computing Toolbox (GPU) support provided by version. TrainNetwork uses CPU. Use the name-value pair training options in the Execution Environment parameter to specify runtime. Because the data set is small, learning is fast.

The initial contribution of the VGG model is to decompose layers with small granularity by introducing a convolutional structure, thereby improving the performance of visual classification tasks. Teramoto and Shuno analyzed the hierarchical folding structure in the VGG model for repeatable visual classification tasks, such as the continuity of the primary visual cortex [17]. ResNet50 is the third network used in our dataset classification test. RasNet50 is famous for the concept of solving the problem of decreasing accuracy as the network depth increases. ResNet50 is able to classify 1,000 objects in 1 iteration. 50 layers of RasNet have a fairly reliable classification capability [4].

4   Experiment Result

We have extracted the texture features presented in our database which can be seen in Fig. 4. The average value of the 6 texture features has also been presented in Fig. 4. Due to the presence of normal cells in TP and nTP, it can be seen that the difference is quite striking in contrast features. The mean value of contrast features in the TP group was higher. This supports the knowledge that indeed TP results produce more segregated cells, less clustering, and a minimum number of inflammatory cells and other artifacts. The texture features in our dataset can then be used as a source to do various things, especially those related to image analysis. It can even be an alternative to study differences between classes to detect cervical cancer early.

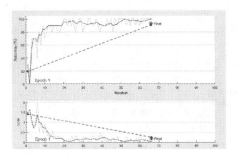

Fig. 4. RepoMedUNM's features   **Fig. 5.** ResNet50 of TP's curve

We also tested the classification model that we stored in our database where the classification results of the 3 applied models can be seen in Table 2. Of the three classification models applied to the three dataset groups, the results show that the ResNet50 classification model has the highest accuracy value compared to the other two models. ResNet50 excels for all groups of TP datasets by 98,83% and nTP data by 95,38%. We conducted experiments for all data on RasNet50 by classifying them into 4 classes, namely Normal, Koulocyt, L-Sil and H-Sil. The normal class is a combination of the nTP and TP normal classes. The combination of these classes was decided based on information from the evaluation of texture features which showed that there were no significant differences between the two normal classes and that the cell cytology was the same, only differing in contrasting features.

Accuracy of all data is 97,52%. Also, in Fig. 6 we present confusion matrices for all the employed classifiers. From the overall results, it can be seen that there are still difficulties in classifying all classes that contain completely normal and abnormal cells. This opens up opportunities for evaluation of other classification models.

The classification model used produces optimum classification and is neither overfitting nor underfitting. It can be seen that all of the accuracy value is lower than the accuracy training value. This is also supported by the graphical display in Fig. 5 for the TP data by ResNet50.

In determining the number of epochs to be trained in the evaluation of this classification, we carried out several conditions. When the transfer learning process does not practice for many epochs. Epoch remains a full training cycle across our entire training dataset.

We also specify a mini-batch size of $56 \times 56 \times 256$ and validation data. Furthermore, the process of calculating the validation accuracy once per epoch as the example in Fig. 5 shows a curve with a validation accuracy value of 93,21.

Table 2. RepomedUnm classification's evaluation results

CNN Model	Pap Test	Images	Class	% accuracy	% val accuracy	% loss	%val loss
VGG16	TP/nTP	2357/3901	3/2	96,61/91,34	93,84/86,61	0,00/0,17	0,23/0,31
VGG19	TP/nTP	2357/3901	3/2	90,08/77,07	88,53/77,03	0,07/1,54	0,40/1,93
ResNet50	TP/nTP/ All	2357/3901 /6168	3/2/4	98,83/95,38 /97,52	93,21/91,60 /92,86	0,03/0,15 /0,06	0,19/0,21 /0,24

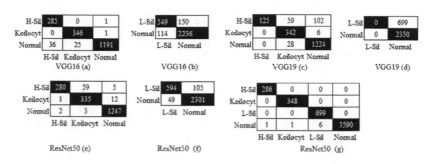

Fig. 6. Confusion matrics (a–b)TP/nTP, (c–d)TP/nTP, (e–g)TP/nTP/All

5   Conclusion

The RepoMedUNM cell image database introduced in this paper is publicly available [8]. This dataset was obtained from Pap smear slides with two Pap test methods, namely TP and nTP which contain grouped cell images. There are two groups of images divided into four categories of normal cells, intermediate and superficial abnormal cells and sometimes in metaplastic (koilocytic cells), mild or moderate abnormal cells (L-Sil), and benign cells pre-cancerous lesions (HSIL). Each Pap smear slide is identified by a pathologist. Six texture features, image lab, and image segmentation are provided for a limited number of five classes in our dataset. The purpose of implementing the CNN classification model in this experiment is as an initial reference for the evaluation of various techniques in the future for the classification of TP and nTP Pap smear cell images. In the future, the RepoMedUNM database can become public data that provides data for the cell image analysis community to research because this dataset provides new and competitive challenges for researchers in their fields.

Acknowledgments. The authors would like to thank the Directorate General of Higher Education, Ministry of Education, Culture, Research, and Technology Republik Indonesia for supporting this research through the national competitive applied research grant 2021.

References

1. Plissiti, M.E., Dimitrakopoulos, P., Sfikas, G., Nikou, C., Krikoni, O., Charchanti, A.: SIPAKMED: a new dataset for feature and image based classification of normal and pathological cervical cells in Pap smear images. In: 2018 25th IEEE International Conference on Image Processing (ICIP), pp. 3144–3148. IEEE, October 2018
2. Riana, D., Plissiti, M.E., Nikou, C., Widyantoro, D.H., Mengko, T.L.R., Kalsoem, O.: Inflammatory cell extraction and nuclei detection in Pap smear images. Int. J. E-Health Med. Commun. (IJEHMC) **6**(2), 27–43 (2015)
3. Kiran G.V.K., Reddy, G.M.: Automatic classification of whole slide pap smear images using CNN With PCA based feature interpretation. In: Proceedings of the IEEE/CVF Conference on Computer Vision and Pattern Recognition Workshops (2019)
4. Khamparia, A., Gupta, D., de Albuquerque, V.H.C., Sangaiah, A.K., Jhaveri, R.H.: Internet of health things-driven deep learning system for detection and classification of cervical cells using transfer learning. J. Supercomput. **76**(11), 8590–8608 (2020). https://doi.org/10.1007/s11227-020-03159-4
5. Chen, Y.F., et al.: Semi-automatic segmentation and classification of pap smear cells. IEEE J. Biomed. Heal. Informat. **18**, 94–108 (2014). https://doi.org/10.1109/JBHI.2013.2250984
6. Human Papillomavirus (HPV) and Cervical Cancer. Accessed July 2021. https://www.who.int/news-room/fact-sheets/detail/human-papillomavirus-(hpv)-and-cervical-cancer
7. Jantzen, J., Norup, J., Dounias, G., Bjerregaard, B.: Pap-smear benchmark data for pattern classification. In: Proceedings of Nature inspired Smart Information Systems (NiSIS), pp. 1–9 (2005)
8. Riana, D., et al.: Repository Medical Imaging Citra Pap Smear. http://repomed.nusamandiri.ac.id/ (2021)
9. Walker, R.F., Jackway, P., Lovell, B., Longstaff, I.D.: Classification of Cevical cell nuclei using morphological segmentation and textural feature extraction. In: Proceedings of ANZIIS 1994-Australian New Zealnd Intelligent Information Systems Conference, pp. 297–301 (1994)
10. Sulaiman, S.N., Isa, N.A.M., Yusoff, I.A., Othman, N.H.: Overlapping cells separation method for cervical cell images. In: Proceedings of the 2010 10th International Conference on Intelligence System Design and Applications ISDA-10 1218–1222 (2010). https://doi.org/10.1109/ISDA.2010.5687020
11. Merlina, N., Noersasongko, E., Nurtantio, P., Soeleman, M.A., Riana, D., Hadianti, S.: Detecting the width of pap smear cytoplasm image based on GLCM feature. In: Smart Trends in Computing and Communications: Proceedings of SmartCom 2020, pp. 231–239. Springer, Singapore (2021). https://doi.org/10.1007/978-981-15-5224-3_22
12. Riana, D., Rahayu, S., Hasan, M.: Comparison of segmentation and identification of Swietenia Mahagoni wood defects with augmentation images. Heliyon, e07417 (2021)
13. Liu, Z., et al.: Improved kiwifruit detection using pre-trained VGG16 with RGB and NIR information fusion. IEEE Access **8**, 2327–2336 (2020). https://doi.org/10.1109/ACCESS.2019.2962513
14. Hridayami, P., Putra, I.K.G.D., Wibawa, K.S.: Fish species recognition using VGG16 deep convolutional neural network. J. Comput. Sci. Eng. **13**(3), 124–130 (2019). https://doi.org/10.5626/JCSE.2019.13.3.124

15. Train Deep Learning Network to Classify New Images. Accessed 12 July 2021. Available: https://www.mathworks.com/help/deeplearning/ug/train-deep-learning-network-to-classify-new-images.html
16. BVLC GoogLeNet Model. Accessed 12 July 2021. Available: https://github.com/BVLC/caffe/tree/master/models/bvlc_googlenet
17. Lan, K., Wang, D.T., Fong, S., Liu, L.S., Wong, K.K., Dey, N.: A survey of data mining and deep learning in bioinformatics. J. Med. Syst. **42**(8), 139 (2018)

Consistent Knowledge Distillation Based on Siamese Networks

Jialiang Tang[1], Xiaoyan Yang[1], Xin Cheng[1], Ning Jiang[1(✉)], Wenxin Yu[1], and Peng Zhang[2]

[1] School of Computer Science and Technology, Southwest University of Science and Technology, Mianyang, China
jiangning@swust.edu.cn
[2] School of Science, Southwest University of Science and Technology, Mianyang, China

Abstract. In model compression, knowledge distillation is most used technique that uses a large teacher network to transfer knowledge to a small student network to improve student network performance. However, most knowledge distillation algorithms only focus on exploring informative knowledge for transferring but ignore the consistency between the teacher network and the student network. In this paper, we propose a new knowledge distillation framework (SNKD) to calculate the consistency of the teacher network and the student network based on the siamese networks. The teacher network and student network features are input into the siamese networks to calculate the discrepancies between them based on the contrastive learning loss. Through minimizing the contrastive learning loss, the student network is promoted to consistent with the teacher network and obtain a ability close to the teacher. We have verify the efficiency of the SNKD by experiment on popular datasets. All SNKD trained student network models have reached ability similar or even better than teacher networks.

Keywords: Knowledge distillation · Model compression · Siamese networks · Contrastive learning · Convolutional neural networks

1 Introduction

Convolutional neural networks (CNNs) are widely used in computer vision tasks. In general, a large neural network can achieve better performance than a small neural network. But these large-scale neural networks with superior performance often with huge calculations and parameters. For example, the advanced ResNet152 [4] includes 58.16 million (M) parameters, which processes a 32×32 sized RGB image cost about 3.74 Giga (G) floating point operations (FLOPs) calculations. These memory and calculate consumption burdens are prohibitive for resource-limited artificial intelligence (AI) devices, for example smartphones and automobiles. This problem limits the CNNs to application in real life.

© Springer Nature Switzerland AG 2021
T. Mantoro et al. (Eds.): ICONIP 2021, CCIS 1516, pp. 326–333, 2021.
https://doi.org/10.1007/978-3-030-92307-5_38

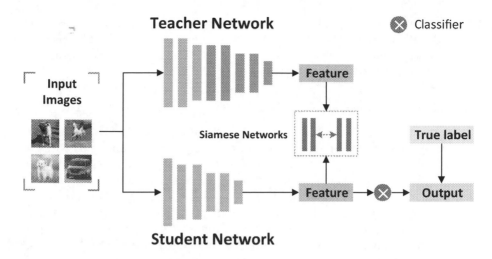

Fig. 1. The diagram of the SNKD, include a teacher network, student network, and siamese networks in SNKD.

In this paper, we proposes a new knowledge distillation, which combine the siamese networks (abbreviated as SNKD) to improve the consistency of the teacher network and the student network. The ability of the teacher is superior. If the student is consistent with the teacher, the student may also achieve excellent performance. The siamese networks [2,9] consist of two weight shared neural networks with identical structures. During the training of SNKD, the features of the teacher and the student are input into the siamese networks together. The two neural networks in the siamese networks are first mapped the input features as two representations in the new feature space. Then the consistency of the two representations is determined by the siamese networks based on the contrastive loss. And the consistency of the teacher and the student is promoted by minimizing the contrastive loss. In the end, the student achieves a performance similar to or even beyond the teacher.

2   Related Work

2.1   Knowledge Distillation

Knowledge distillation is a widely researched model compression method. Hinton et al. [6] systematically interpret the knowledge distillation, used a large teacher network to train the small student network, them uses a temperature parameter to the softmax layer to control the soften degree of the soft-targets. FitNets [13] proposes to use the feature maps of middle layer of the teacher as the knowledge and successfully trained a deeper student network. Similarity-preserving knowledge distillation (SPKD) [15] proposes that semantically similar inputs tend to output similar activations in a trained network and guides the student network to produce activations similar to the teacher network. Correlation congruence knowledge distillation (CCKD) [12] extracts the correlation of sample based on Taylor series expansion, which transfers not only the instance-level information but also the correlation between instances.

2.2   Siamese Networks

The siamese networks were first proposed in [2] for check the provided signature whether is same as the reserved one. Nair [9] adjust the siamese networks to implement face verification, two faces are first input to the siamese networks, and then output same or different. Hoffer et al. [7] propose the three-class conjoined triplet networks whose outputs contain one positive example and two negative examples. The triplet networks is aimed to reduce the distance between the same categories and enlarge the distance between different categories. In this paper, we also use the siamese networks to promote the consistency of the outputs of the teacher network and the student network.

3   Approch

In this section, we will introduce how to implement our SNKD. The total structure of our SNKD is display at Fig. 1. Specifically, SNKD consists of a large teacher network, a small student network, siamese networks.

3.1   Siamese Networks for Knowledge Distillation

In this paper, the siamese networks are used to calculate the consistency of the output features of the teacher network and student network. The performance of the teacher network is significant superior than the small student network. For the same purpose, if the output features of the student and teacher are consistent, the student network can achieve a similar performance to the teacher network. We define the features before the classification layer of the teacher network and the student network as $F_t = \{f_t^1, f_t^2, \cdots, f_t^n\}$ and $F_s = \{f_s^1, f_s^2, \cdots, f_s^n\}$, n means the batchsize. To simulate the training settings of the siamese networks, we set the features obtained by the teacher network and the student network processing the same picture as the paired feature and the paired label is '0'. In detail, for n features F_t obtained by the teacher network and n features F_s obtained by the student network, we select the first $n/2$ features of F_t and F_s as the paired feature maps F_p, and the paired label is set as '0'. And we select the first $n/2$ feature maps in F_t and the last $n/2$ feature maps in F_s to compose the unpaired feature maps F_{up}, and the unpaired label is set as '1'. The final feature sets are $F = [F_p, F_{up}]$. Each item in F contains two feature map f_1 and f_2, and the correspondence label Y. Based on the final feature sets F, the distance can be calculated as follows:

$$dist = \sqrt{\sum_{i=1}^{n} \left(f_1^i - f_2^i\right)^2} \tag{1}$$

And the Siamese loss is also calculated as:

$$\mathcal{L}_{sia}\left(Y, f_1, f_2\right) = \tfrac{1}{2} \cdot (1 - Y)\left(dist\right)^2 + \tfrac{1}{2} \cdot Y \left\{\max\left(0, m - dist\right)\right\}^2 \qquad (2)$$

By minimizing the contrastive loss $\mathcal{L}_{sia}$, the distance between paired features is minimized while the distance between unpaired features is maximized. It means the student network features are more consistent with the teacher network's features, and the student network can get similar performance to the teacher network.

In the conventional training of the CNNs, the CNNs are trained by the image and real labels. In our proposed SNKD, we also use the ground-truth labels to train the student network to classify more accurately. The classification results of the student network $Y_s = \left\{y_s^1, y_s^2, \cdots, y_s^n\right\}$ are calculated the cross-entropy loss with the ground-truth labels $L = \left\{l^1, l^2, \cdots, l^n\right\}$ as:

$$\mathcal{L}_{label} = \frac{1}{n} \sum_{i=1}^{n} \mathcal{H}_{cross}\left(y_s^i, l^i\right) \qquad (3)$$

The $\mathcal{H}_{cross}$ is the Cross-Entropy loss to calculate the difference between two input.

3.2 Total Objective Function

By combining above proposed loss functions, the total objective function of SNKD can be defined as:

$$\mathcal{L}_{Total} = \alpha \cdot \mathcal{L}_{label} + \beta \cdot \mathcal{L}_{sia} \qquad (4)$$

The α and β are the hyperparameters, which are used to balance the two loss functions in the total objective function.

4 Experiment

In this section, we demonstrate the effectiveness of SNKD through extensive experiments. We select ResNet-family networks [4], VGGNet-family networks [14], WideResNet-family networks [19] to experiment on CIFAR [8], STL10 [3] and SVHN [10] datasets. We first conduct experiments on all benchmark datasets to verification the efficiency of SNKD. Then we compare SNKD with other knowledge distillation algorithms to demonstrate that SNKD can achieve state-of-the-art (SOTA) performance.

4.1 Experiments on a Benchmark Datasets

In this section, we choose popular convolutional neural networks ResNet, VGGNet, and WideResNet as experimental models. These neural networks are

Table 1. Results of selected CNNs on the various benchmark datasets. The WRS denotes the abbreviation of WideResNet. M and G represent million and Giga, respectively.

Model	Algorithm	Parameters	FLOPs	CIFAR10	CIFAR100	STL10	SVHN
Teacher	VGGNet16	~14.72M	~0.31G	93.56%	73.31%	85.38%	95.59%
Student	VGGNet13	~9.41M	~0.23G	94.42%	76.32%	86.92%	95.76%
Teacher	ResNet34	~21.28M	~1.16G	94.85%	77.34%	89.25%	95.53%
Student	ResNet18	~11.17M	~0.56G	95.32%	78.33%	89.71%	95.86%
Teacher	WRS40_2	~2.25M	~0.36G	93.99%	73.84%	85.26%	95.55%
Student	WRS28_2	~1.47M	~0.24G	94.79%	74.23%	85.79%	95.75%

widely used in computer vision tasks. In detail, when ResNet is selected as the experimental model, ResNet34 with 34 convolutional layers and ResNet18 with 18 convolutional layers are used as the teacher and student. For VGGNet, the 16 layers VGGNet16 is the teacher, and the 13 layers VGGNet13 is the student. If WideResNet is selected as the experimental model, WideResNet40_2 is used as the teacher and WideResNet28_2 (WRS28_2) is used as the student. These selected convolutional neural networks experiment on CIFAR, STL10, SVHN datasets. The experimental settings are described in Sect. 4.

The classification data of the SNKD trained student on the experimental data are exhibit in Table 1. For experiments performed on VGGNet. Since VGGNet is simply a stack of several convolutional blocks, its parameters are not efficiently utilized, which means that VGGNet has a large performance improvement potential. Therefore, on all benchmark datasets, the student network VGGNet13 achieved obviously superior performance than the teacher VGGNet16. The student network achieved the performance of 94.42%, 76.32%, 86.92%, 95.76% on the CIFAR10, CIFAR100, STL10, SVHN datasets, and the accuracy of the student network was 0.86%, 3.01%, 1.54%, 0.17% higher than the teacher, respectively.

ResNet uses residual connections to improve the network structure, and its network structure and performance are better than VGGNet. The number of computation and parameter of the ResNet18 are 11.17M and 0.56G floating-point operations (FLOPs), respectively, which are half of that of the ResNet34. But the student network ResNet18 still achieved higher accuracy than the teacher ResNet34. The SNKD trained ResNet18 achieved 95.32%, 78.33%, 89.71%, 95.86% accuracy on the CIFAR10, CIFAR100, STL10, SVHN datasets, and the accuracy of the ResNet18 was 0.37%, 0.99%, 0.46%, 0.33% higher than the accuracy of the ResNet34, respectively.

WideResNet is an improvement of ResNet, which has fewer parameters and computations than the ResNet. The teacher network WideResNet40_2 has only about 2.25M parameters and 0.36G FLOPs computations, and the student network WideResNet28_2 has only about 1.47M parameters and 0.24G FLOPs computations. A more optimized network structure means that the parameters in the network are used very efficiently and the performance improvement poten-

Table 2. The classification results of student network obtained by our SNKD to compare with various knowledge distillation algorithms. Accuracy$^+$ means the accuracy improved of the student.

Methos	Parameters	Calculations	CIFAR10		CIFAR100	
			Accuracy	Accuracy$^+$	Accuracy	Accuracy$^+$
Teacher	~20.04M	~0.40G	93.31%	\	73.26%	\
Standard BP	~9.41M	~0.23G	93.05%	\	73.03%	\
FitNets [13]	~9.41M	~0.23G	93.28%	0.23%	73.16%	0.13%
PMAT [18]	~9.41M	~0.23G	93.64%	0.59%	74.28%	1.25%
KDGAN [17]	~9.41M	~0.23G	93.88%	0.83%	75.69%	2.66%
RKD [11]	~9.41M	~0.23G	93.97%	0.92%	75.94%	2.91%
AB [5]	~9.41M	~0.23G	93.99%	0.94%	76.03%	3.00%
AFDS [16]	~9.41M	~0.23G	94.01%	0.96%	75.97%	2.94%
SPKD [15]	~9.41M	~0.23G	94.02%	0.97%	76.06%	3.03%
CCKD [12]	~9.41M	~0.23G	94.11%	1.06%	76.10%	3.07%
MDKD (ours)	~9.41M	~0.23G	**94.42%**	**1.37%**	**76.32%**	**3.29%**

tial of the network is much small. But, WideResNet28_2 trained by SNKD also achieves better performance than the teacher WideResNet40_2 on the experimental datasets. The student network WideResNet28_2 achieved 94.79%, 74.23%, 85.79%, 95.75% accuracy on the CIFAR10, CIFAR100, STL10, SVHN, which are 0.80%, 0.39%, 0.53%, 0.20% higher than the larger WideResNet40_2, respectively.

These experiments prove that SNKD can be widely used to improve the accuracy of small CNNs. And SNKD works better on datasets (CIFAR100) with more categories and datasets (STL10) with fewer labeled images.

4.2 Experiments Compare to Other Methods

SNKD can achieve the SOTA performance and significantly outperforms existing knowledge distillation methods. To further demonstrate the effectiveness of our proposed SNKD, we compare the student network trained by SNKD with student networks trained by advanced methods (from 2015 to 2020). We selected the CIFAR10 and the CIFAR100 as training datasets, using VGGNet19 as the teacher network and VGGNet13 as the student network. The teacher network VGGNet16 has about 20.04M parameters, 0.40G calculations, which is about twice that of the student network (9.41M parameters and 0.23G calculations). The student networks are trained by knowledge distillation (KD) [6], FitNets [13], paying more attention (PMAT) [18], KDGAN [17], relational knowledge distillation (RKD) [11], activation boundaries (AB) [5], attentive feature distillation and selection (AFDS) [16], similarity-preserving knowledge distillation (SPKD) [15], correlation congruence knowledge distillation (CCKD) [12] and our proposed SNKD, respectively. The experimental setups of all selected algorithms are the same as those elaborated in Sect. 4.

The experimental results of the student trained by our SNKD and the student got by compared model compression approches are shown in Table 2. First, student networks trained by KD methods all obtained better results than those thar trained by standard backpropagation (BP). This results demonstrated that these KD methods are more effective in improving the ability of small CNNs. It is surprising that SNKD trained the student (VGGNet13) achieves significantly higher accuracy than selected knowledge distillation algorithms, with 94.42% accuracy on the CIFAR10 dataset and 76.32% accuracy on the CIFAR100 dataset. Compared to the original student trained, the SNKD trained VGGNet13's accuracy increased by 1.37% and 3.29% on the CIFAR10 and CIFAR100. For early knowledge distillation of KD and FitNets, other algorithms have trained the student network to achieve a performance beyond the teacher network and the student trained by our SNKD achieves the best performance. Compared with CCKD, which has the highest accuracy among in the selected compared algorithms, the capacity of the SNKD trained student is higher than CCKD on CIFAR10 and CIFAR100 by 0.31% and 0.22%, respectively. Compared to the teacher network VGGNet16, which contains more parameters and calculations than student network VGGNet13, the SNKD trained student is still 0.61% and 2.81% higher than the teacher on the CIFAR10 dataset and the CIFAR100 dataset. These results show the SNKD is more effective than other knowledge distillation algorithms, and the SNKD can achieve SOTA performance.

5   Conclusion

In general, existing CNNs are over-parameterized. These CNNs require great parameters and calculations to train on the dataset to obtain satisfactory ability. This paper, we proposes siamese networks knowledge distillation called SNKD to compress the CNNs. SNKD can measure and promote the consistency between the features of the teacher network and the student network based on contrastive learning loss. Experiments on various benchmark datasets demonstrate that our proposed SNKD can effectively facilitate the consistency of the large teacher and small student, thus enhancing the student network to obtain a ability similar or superior to the large teacher.

Acknowledgement. This work was supported by the Mianyang Science and Technology Program 2020YFZJ016, SWUST Doctoral Foundation under Grant 19zx7102, 21zx7114, Sichuan Science and Technology Program under Grant 2020YFS0307.

References

1. Bertinetto, L., Valmadre, J., Henriques, J.F., Vedaldi, A., Torr, P.H.S.: Fully-convolutional siamese networks for object tracking. In: Hua, G., Jégou, H. (eds.) ECCV 2016. LNCS, vol. 9914, pp. 850–865. Springer, Cham (2016). https://doi.org/10.1007/978-3-319-48881-3_56

2. Bromley, J., Guyon, I., LeCun, Y., Säckinger, E., Shah, R.: Signature verification using a siamese time delay neural network. Adv. Neural Inf. Process. Syst. **6**, 737–744 (1993)

3. Coates, A., Ng, A., Lee, H.: An analysis of single-layer networks in unsupervised feature learning. In: Proceedings of the Fourteenth International Conference on Artificial Intelligence and Statistics, pp. 215–223. JMLR Workshop and Conference Proceedings (2011)

4. He, K., Zhang, X., Ren, S., Jian, S.: Deep residual learning for image recognition. In: 2016 IEEE Conference on Computer Vision and Pattern Recognition (CVPR) (2016)

5. Heo, B., Lee, M., Yun, S., Choi, J.Y.: Knowledge transfer via distillation of activation boundaries formed by hidden neurons. In: Proceedings of the AAAI Conference on Artificial Intelligence, vol. 33, pp. 3779–3787 (2019)

6. Hinton, G., Vinyals, O., Dean, J.: Distilling the knowledge in a neural network. Comput. Sci. **14**(7), 38–39 (2015)

7. Hoffer, E., Ailon, N.: Deep metric learning using triplet network. In: Feragen, A., Pelillo, M., Loog, M. (eds.) SIMBAD 2015. LNCS, vol. 9370, pp. 84–92. Springer, Cham (2015). https://doi.org/10.1007/978-3-319-24261-3_7

8. Krizhevsky, A., Hinton, G., et al.: Learning multiple layers of features from tiny images (2009)

9. Nair, V., Hinton, G.E.: Rectified linear units improve restricted boltzmann machines. In: ICML (2010)

10. Netzer, Y., Wang, T., Coates, A., Bissacco, A., Wu, B., Ng, A.Y.: Reading digits in natural images with unsupervised feature learning (2011)

11. Park, W., Kim, D., Lu, Y., Cho, M.: Relational knowledge distillation. In: Proceedings of the IEEE/CVF Conference on Computer Vision and Pattern Recognition, pp. 3967–3976 (2019)

12. Peng, B., et al.: Correlation congruence for knowledge distillation (2019)

13. Romero, A., Ballas, N., Kahou, S.E., Chassang, A., Gatta, C., Bengio, Y.: Fitnets: hints for thin deep nets. Comput. Sci. (2014)

14. Simonyan, K., Zisserman, A.: Very deep convolutional networks for large-scale image recognition. arXiv preprint arXiv:1409.1556 (2014)

15. Tung, F., Mori, G.: Similarity-preserving knowledge distillation. In: Proceedings of the IEEE/CVF International Conference on Computer Vision, pp. 1365–1374 (2019)

16. Wang, K., Gao, X., Zhao, Y., Li, X., Dou, D., Xu, C.Z.: Pay attention to features, transfer learn faster CNNs. In: International Conference on Learning Representations (2019)

17. Xu, Z., Hsu, Y.C., Huang, J.: Training shallow and thin networks for acceleration via knowledge distillation with conditional adversarial networks (2017)

18. Zagoruyko, S., Komodakis, N.: Paying more attention to attention: Improving the performance of convolutional neural networks via attention transfer. arXiv preprint arXiv:1612.03928 (2016)

19. Zagoruyko, S., Komodakis, N.: Wide residual networks. arXiv preprint arXiv:1605.07146 (2016)

Graph Convolutional Network Based on Higher-Order Neighborhood Aggregation

Gang-Feng Ma[1], Xu-Hua Yang[1(✉)], Lei Ye[1], Yu-Jiao Huang[2], and Peng Jiang[3]

[1] College of Computer Science and Technology, Zhejiang University of Technology,
Hangzhou 310023, People's Republic of China
{gf_ma,xhyang,yelei}@zjut.edu.cn

[2] Zhijiang College, Zhejiang University of Technology,
Hangzhou 310023, People's Republic of China
huangyujiao@zjut.edu.cn

[3] Department of Science and Technology Cooperation, Westlake University,
Hangzhou 310023, People's Republic of China
Jiangpeng77@westlake.edu.cn

Abstract. The graph neural network can use the network topology, the attributes and labels of nodes to mine the potential relationships on network. In paper, we propose a graph convolutional network based on higher-order Neighborhood Aggregation. First, an improved graph convolutional module is proposed, which can more flexibly aggregate higher-order neighborhood information in convolution kernel. It alleviates the over-smooth problem caused by high-order aggregation to a certain extent. Then, we propose two different neighborhood aggregation models. The first model trains multiple embeddings independently for the network and obtains the final embedding through connection, that is, focuses on processing the overall information of the neighborhood. The other is analogous to the three-dimensional convolutional neural network on image. It concatenates features in each layer which pays more attention to processing the hierarchical information of the neighborhood. Our algorithm is a general network model enhancement algorithm which is suitable for different network architectures. Experiments on 6 real network datasets show that our algorithm has good results in node classification, link prediction, etc.

Keywords: GCN · Higher-order Neighborhood Aggregation · End-to-end learning · Node classification · Link precision

1 Introduction

The network is an important manifestation of complex systems in real world. However, the data in network is often high-dimensional and sparse, which makes it difficult to directly processed. Network embedding uses dense low-dimensional

T. Mantoro et al. (Eds.): ICONIP 2021, CCIS 1516, pp. 334–342, 2021.
https://doi.org/10.1007/978-3-030-92307-5_39

vectors to represent the nodes and edges in network, which can greatly extract key information and filter redundant information. As one of the most important methods of network embedding, graph convolutional network has received widespread attention because it can improve the accuracy while reducing the complexity of the model.

GCN [4] makes a good uniformity of spectral method and spatial method, and achieves the convolution operation on non-Euclidean networks. GAE/VGAE [5] adds the auto-encoder and Gaussian distribution to restrict the embedding vectors. DGI [13] introduces contrast learning into graph neural networks. SGC [15] removes the non-linear activation function between layers, and FastGCN [2] reduces the number of nodes per training through node sampling. GAT [12] introduces an attention mechanism to obtain the importance of neighbor nodes through neural network.

Graph convolutional network actually continuously stacks node features through the adjacency of the nodes. When graph convolutional network deepens, the node features will be constantly close to each other, which will eventually make the nodes difficult to distinguish. This is called over-smooth [4] which makes it unable to obtain higher-order neighborhood information. In this paper, we propose the solution called graph convolutional network based on higher-order Neighborhood Aggregation. It contains two network models. The first model of multi-channel convolution learns multiple independent embeddings, and obtains the final embedding through accumulation. It only deals with the overall embedding relationship of the neighborhood. The second model of multi-core convolution uses three-dimensional convolution to find the relationship between network embedding of each layer, that focus on hierarchical information of the neighborhood. Both methods use neural network training to captures higher-order neighborhood information in each single neural network layer that effectively avoids multi-layer stacking and alleviates over-smooth.

The rest of paper is organized as follows. Section 2 is related work, Sect. 3 describes the method proposed in paper in detail, Sect. 4 uses experiments to prove the superiority of our method, and Sect. 5 gives the conclusion.

2   Related Work

Graph convolutional network includes two methods, one is spectral method and the other is spatial method. Spectral method is analogous to Fourier transform, which uses the eigenvectors of the regularized laplacian as the basis of the Fourier transform. It uses the inverse Fourier transform to avoid explicit calculation of the convolution kernel, and successfully implements the convolution operation on graph. ChebNet [3] use polynomials to approximate the convolution kernel. GCN [4] uses the first-order ChebNet and adds a renormalization technique to avoid gradient disappearance/explosion. GWNN [16] uses wavelet transform instead of Fourier transform. Spatial method is to learn the node embedding of the network from the perspective of network topology, which can explain the graph convolutional network more intuitively. FastGCN [2] reduces the number of parameters for each training through importance sampling. IGCN [6] uses the continuous multiplication result of GCN convolution kernel with a fixed number of layers as the IGCN convolution kernel. GAT [12] uses the attention mechanism to calculate the attention between current node and neighbor node.

3   Graph Convolutional Network Based on Higher-Order Neighborhood Aggregation

We propose two models based on higher-order neighborhood aggregation. They can both capture the hidden information of a given order through a more flexible convolution kernel and the combination of different orders.

3.1   Problem Description

Let $G = (V, E)$ denote an undirected graph, where $V = \{v_1, v_2, ..., v_N\}$, $N = |V|$ is the number of nodes, and E is edge set. $H = \{h^{(0)}, h^{(1)}, ..., h^{(l)}\}$ contains all the features of input, hidden and output layer, where $X = h^{(0)}$ is the initial feature of nodes, l is the number of neural network layers. $A = [a_{ij}] \in R^{N \times N}$ is the adjacency matrix, $D = diag(d_1, d_2, ..., d_N)$ is the degree matrix, where $d_i = \sum_j a_{ij}$. The convolution kernel of GCN is $\overline{A} = \widetilde{D}^{-1/2} \widetilde{A} \widetilde{D}^{-1/2}$, where $\widetilde{A} = A + I$, $\widetilde{D} = D + I$. And the filter coefficient of GCN is $g = 1 - \widetilde{\lambda}$ [15], where $\widetilde{\lambda} \in [0, 2)$ is the eigenvalue of symmetric regular Laplacian matrix of $\widetilde{A}$.

3.2   Algorithm Framework of HNA-GCN

Different from most graph convolutional network models, we think that different convolution kernels can work together in same neural network. Based on this assumption, we propose the general representation method of HNA-GCN:

$$y = softmax\left(\overline{A}^{K_2} relu\left(\overline{A}^{K_1} XW^{(1)}\right) W^{(2)}\right) \tag{1}$$

where K_1 and K_2 are two hyper-parameters. We can get the filter coefficient of the first layer as $g = \left(1 - \widetilde{\lambda}\right)^{K_1}$, while the second as $g = \left(1 - \widetilde{\lambda}\right)^{K_2}$. The multiplication of low-pass filter is still low-pass filter [15]. From the perspective of spectral, the low-pass filter can better ensure the similarity between adjacent nodesr. From the perspective of spatial, the algorithm can adjust the amount of high-order neighborhood information obtained by each layer. We define the hyperparameter $K_{ne} = K_1 + K_2$, and then traverse all possible combinations of K_1 and K_2 to further reduce the number of hyperparameters. Next, we will elaborate two models in detail.

M-Channel Model. This model use different channels to handle combinations of different order neighbourhoods, in which each individual channel is a graph convolutional network with modified convolution kernel. Limiting $K_1 \geq K_2$ to reduce the number of combinations, M-Channel can be expressed as.

$$\sum_{i=\lceil K_{ne}/2 \rceil}^{K_{ne}-1} \overline{A}^{K_{ne}-i} relu\left(\overline{A}^i XW^{(1)}\right) W^{(2)} \tag{2}$$

where i is a positive integer, $\lceil K \rceil$ means rounding up K. No matter which channel it is, the model always captures the neighborhood information of K_{ne}-th order of node. The model is shown in Fig. 1.

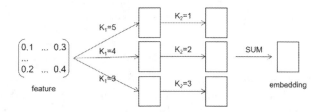

Fig. 1. M-Channel model: Taking $K_{ne} = 6$ as an example, each channel finally aggregates 6th-order neighborhood information

M-Core Model. This model is analogous to the three-dimensional convolution in CNN, which connects different channels to form a new convolution kernel. The model will more comprehensively consider all neighborhood information from second-order to K_{ne}-th order. In order to balance the amount of information captured by the two-layer network, we limit $K_1 + K_2 \leq K_{ne}$ and $K_1 \leq (K_{ne} + 1)/2$ for $\forall K_1$ and $\forall K_2$. We use $conv_k(X_i) = \overline{A}^K X_i W$ to represent the convolution operation of feature X in the i-th channel. Then, the graph convolution operation of the single convolution kernel in second layer can be expressed as:

$$\overline{H}_j^{(2)} = \sum_{i \in K_1} conv_j(H_i^{(1)}) \tag{3}$$

where $j \in K_2$, $H_i^{(1)}$ is the output feature of the i-th channel in first layer. The final output of the second layer can be expressed as

$$H^{(2)} = Avg_{j \in K_2}\left(\overline{H}_j^{(2)}\right) \tag{4}$$

where Avg is average operation. The model is shown in Fig. 2. From the perspective of two-dimensional convolution, M-Core is equivalent to enumerating all possible combinations of K_1 and K_2.

3.3   Time Complexity Analysis

Our algorithm provides a flexible idea to build graph convolutional networks which can well capture higher-order neighborhood information of nodes and

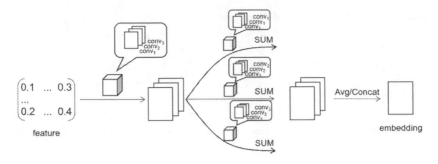

Fig. 2. M-Core model: Analogy to CNN and do three-dimensional convolution operations on features. Take $K_{ne} = 6$ as an example, the value of K_1 and K_2 can both be 1,2,3

adjust the amount of information for different network structures. Taking two neural network layers as an example, the time complexity of GCN is $\mathbf{O}(2|E|d)$, while Multi-Channel is $\mathbf{O}(K_{ne}|E|d)$, Multi-Core is $\mathbf{O}(K_{ne}^2|E|d)$, where d is the dimension of nodes and $K_{ne} \ll |E|$. Therefore, the time complexity of the two models is consistent with GCN, which is $\mathbf{O}(|E|)$.

4   Experiments

4.1   Experimental Setup

Table 1. Datasets

Datasets	#Nodes	#Edges	#Classes	#Train/Dev/Test node
Cora	2,708	5,429	7	140/300/1000
Citeseer	3,327	4,732	6	120/500/1000
PubMed	19,717	44,338	3	60/500/1000
Ego-facebook	2,888	2,981	/	/
Fb-pages-food	620	2,102	/	/
Opsahl-powergrid	4,941	6,594	/	/

We evaluate our method on three attributes citation network datasets - Cora, Citeseer, PubMed [10] and three attributeless network datasets - ego-facebook [7], fb-pages-food [9], opsahl-powergrid [14]. Data statistics are in Table 1. In link prediction, our models are compared with GAE/VGAE [5] and IGCN [6]. In experiments without prior features, we also add Deepwalk [8], Grarep [1], LINE [11] as the comparison algorithms. In node classification, we use ChebNet [3], GCN [4], SGC [15], FastGCN [2], IGCN [6], GAT [12] and DGI [13] as the comparative experiment. We use Adam to do gradient descent, and set initial learning rate as 0.01. We use two layer neural network, where the dimention of hidden layer is 32 and the dimention of embedding layer is 16. In Grarep, we use fourth order neighborhood information. We set the random seed to 0 and $K_{ne} = 6$. In addition, in link prediction experiment, we randomly hide 5% of the edges as the verification set, and hide 10% of the edges as the test set.

4.2   Link Prediction

Table 2. Link prediction results of datasets with features

Method	Cora		Citeseer		PubMed	
	AUC	AP	AUC	AP	AUC	AP
GAE	90.89	91.74	89.49	90.68	95.97	96.11
VGAE	91.24	**92.58**	86.88	89.07	94.48	94.73
IGCN(GAE)	89.89	91.52	87.98	89.55	95.82	96.02
IGCN(VGAE)	91.22	92.67	89.30	91.10	92.98	93.51
M-Channel(GAE)	90.85	91.63	89.48	90.70	**96.21**	**96.56**
M-Channel(VGAE)	**91.40**	92.55	88.96	90.91	92.67	93.29
M-Core(GAE)	**91.37**	**92.77**	89.87	**91.12**	96.17	96.41
M-Core(VGAE)	90.35	91.37	**90.90**	**92.61**	91.12	91.76

Table 3. Link prediction results of datasets without features

Method	Ego-facebook		Fb-pages-food		Opsahl-powergrid	
	AUC	AP	AUC	AP	AUC	AP
Deepwalk	18.88	49.16	71.56	73.01	71.36	74.58
Grarep	20.37	48.20	56.28	53.50	69.89	71.38
LINE	16.15	47.45	73.72	77.65	61.82	66.77
GAE	25.72	45.84	88.37	91.32	69.57	74.79
VGAE	38.58	58.54	86.86	90.80	70.22	75.15
IGCN(GAE)	19.90	39.41	89.38	**92.06**	71.32	77.63
IGCN(VGAE)	35.58	58.67	88.42	91.12	70.47	76.26
M-Channel(GAE)	14.61	38.91	88.49	91.41	**73.95**	**79.13**
M-Channel(VGAE)	**44.74**	**64.76**	90.15	**92.61**	71.53	77.50
M-Core(GAE)	10.72	36.20	87.07	90.63	72.96	**77.87**
M-Core(VGAE)	**42.85**	**63.31**	89.53	91.28	**73.34**	77.70

The purpose of link prediction is to predict the edges in network through the representations generated by the model. We use AUC and AP [5] to evaluate the model. The AUC indicator calculates the probability that the predicted positive sample value is greater than the negative sample value. The AP indicator calculates the average accuracy of predictions under different recall rates. We multiply the final result by 100 for a clear representation. Table 2 shows the experimental results of datasets with features, and Table 3 is the experimental results of datasets without features.

Experiments show that our algorithm obtains better AUC results on all experimental datasets, and better AP results on most experimental datasets.

4.3   Node Classification

The purpose of node classification is to predict the labels of unsampled nodes. We use Accuracy [4] as an evaluation index for node classification. Accuracy describes the proportion of correctly classified nodes to the total predicted nodes. Similarly, we multiply the final result by 100 for a clear representation. The experiment results are shown in Table 4.

Table 4. Node classification accuracy

Method	Cora	Citeseer	PubMed
ChebNet	78.8	70.2	75.8
GCN	81.6 ± 0.2	70.8 ± 0.4	79.2 ± 0.4
SGC	81.0 ± 0.2	70.2 ± 0.1	78.9 ± 0.2
FastGCN	73.0 ± 0.3	62.3 ± 0.9	72.0 ± 0.3
DGI	82.5 ± 0.5	72.2 ± 0.4	77.3 ± 0.5
IGCN	82.9 ± 0.8	70.8 ± 0.1	80.0 ± 0.3
GAT	83.5 ± 0.3	**72.8 ± 0.3**	79.0 ± 0.0
M-Channel	**84.1 ± 0.4**	71.2 ± 0.6	**80.9 ± 0.0**
M-Core	83.0 ± 0.4	71.1 ± 0.2	80.3 ± 0.4

Experiments show that the M-Channel model obtains better node classification accuracy in Cora and Pubmed while the performance is not optimal in Citeseer. The reason we analysis may be that our method highly aggregates neighborhood information. In the case of fewer training samples, the problem of missing part of the information in the Citeseer has emerged.

5   Conclusion

We propose two general graph convolution methods. The first model enumerates all possible combinations of specified order, which focuses on overall information. The second model is analogous to CNN and performs a three-dimensional convolution on network, which pays attention to the hierarchical information. Experimental results show that our methods achieve good results in unsupervised link prediction and semi-supervised node classification tasks. In future work, we will further explore the influence of different order neighborhoods on network, and consider introducing the attention mechanism to evaluate the importance of different combinations.

Acknowledgments. This work was supported by the National Natural Science Foundation of China under Grant 61773348.

References

1. Cao, S., Lu, W., Xu, Q.: Grarep: learning graph representations with global structural information. In: Proceedings of the 24th ACM International on Conference on Information and Knowledge Management, pp. 891–900 (2015)
2. Chen, J., Ma, T., Xiao, C.: Fastgcn: fast learning with graph convolutional networks via importance sampling. In: Proceedings of the 6th International Conference on Learning Representations (2018)
3. Hammond, D.K., Vandergheynst, P., Gribonval, R.: Wavelets on graphs via spectral graph theory. Appl. Comput. Harmonic Anal. **30**(2), 129–150 (2011)
4. Kipf, T.N., Welling, M.: Semi-supervised classification with graph convolutional networks. In: Proceedings of the 5th International Conference on Learning Representations (2017)
5. Kipf, T.N., Welling, M.: Variational graph auto-encoders. arXiv preprint arXiv:1611.07308 (2016)
6. Li, Q., Wu X, M., Liu, H., et al.: Label efficient semi-supervised learning via graph filtering. In: Proceedings of the IEEE/CVF Conference on Computer Vision and Pattern Recognition, pp. 9582–9591 (2019)
7. McAuley, J.J., Leskovec, J.: Learning to discover social circles in ego networks. In: Conference and Workshop on Neural Information Processing Systems, pp. 548–556 (2012)
8. Perozzi, B., Al-Rfou, R., Skiena, S.: Deepwalk: online learning of social representations. In: Proceedings of the 20th ACM SIGKDD International Conference on Knowledge Discovery and Data Mining, pp. 701–710 (2014)
9. Rossi, R., Ahmed, N.: The network data repository with interactive graph analytics and visualization. In: Proceedings of the AAAI Conference on Artificial Intelligence, vol. 29, no. 1 (2015)
10. Sen, P., Namata, G., Bilgic, M., et al.: Collective classification in network data. AI Mag. **29**(3), 93–93 (2008)
11. Tang, J., Qu, M., Wang, M., et al.: Line: large-scale information network embedding. In: Proceedings of the 24th International Conference on World Wide Web, pp. 1067–1077 (2015)

12. Veličković, P., Cucurull, G., Casanova, A., et al.: Graph attention networks. In: Proceedings of the 6th International Conference on Learning Representations (2018)
13. Velickovic, P., Fedus, W., Hamilton W, L., et al.: Deep graph infomax. In: Proceedings of the 7th International Conference on Learning Representations (2019)
14. Watts D.J., Strogatz S.H.: Collective dynamics of 'small-world' networks. Nature **393**(6684), 440–442 (1998)
15. Wu, F., Souza, A., Zhang, T., et al.: Simplifying graph convolutional networks. In: International conference on machine learning, PMLR, pp. 6861–6871 (2019)
16. Xu, B., Shen, H., Cao, Q., et al.: Graph convolutional networks using heat kernel for semi- supervised learning. In: Proceedings of the 28th International Joint Conference on Artificial Intelligence, pp. 1928–1934 (2019)

Continuous-Time Stochastic Differential Networks for Irregular Time Series Modeling

Yingru Liu[1]($\boxtimes$)(iD), Yucheng Xing[1], Xuewen Yang[1], Xin Wang[1], Jing Shi[2], Di Jin[3], Zhaoyue Chen[1], and Jacqueline Wu[4]

[1] Stony Brook University, Stony Brook, NY 11794, USA
[2] University of Rochester, Rochester, NY 14627, USA
[3] Amazon Alexa AI, Sunnyvale, CA 94089, USA
[4] Ward Melville High School, East Setauket, NY 11733, USA

Abstract. Learning continuous-time stochastic dynamics is a fundamental and essential problem in modeling irregular time series, whose observations are irregular and sparse in both time and dimension. For a given system whose latent states and observed data are multivariate, it is generally impossible to derive a precise continuous-time stochastic process to describe the system behaviors. To solve the above problem, we apply Variational Bayesian method and propose a flexible continuous-time stochastic recurrent neural network named *Variational Stochastic Differential Networks (VSDN)*, which embeds the complicated dynamics of the irregular time series by neural Stochastic Differential Equations (SDE). VSDNs capture the stochastic dependency among latent states and observations by deep neural networks. We also incorporate two differential Evidence Lower Bounds to efficiently train the models. Through comprehensive experiments, we show that VSDNs outperform state-of-the-art continuous-time deep learning models and achieve remarkable performance on prediction and interpolation tasks for irregular time series.

Keywords: Neural Stochastic Differential Equations · Stochastic recurrent neural network · Irregular time series

1 Introduction and Related Works

Many real-world systems experience complicated stochastic dynamics over a continuous time period. The challenges on modeling the stochastic dynamics mainly come from two sources. First, the underlying state transitions of many systems are often uncertain, as they are placed in unpredictable environment with their states continuously affected by unknown disturbances. Second, the monitoring data collected may be sparse and at irregular intervals as a result of the sampling strategy or data corruption. The irregular data sequence loses a large amount of information and system behaviors hidden behind the intervals of the observed

© Springer Nature Switzerland AG 2021
T. Mantoro et al. (Eds.): ICONIP 2021, CCIS 1516, pp. 343–351, 2021.
https://doi.org/10.1007/978-3-030-92307-5_40

data. In order to accurately model and analyze dynamics of these systems, it is important to reliably and efficiently represent the continuous-time stochastic process based on the discrete-time observations.

In this paper, we propose a new continuous-time stochastic recurrent network called **Variational Stochastic Differential Network (VSDN)** that incorporates SDEs into recurrent neural model to effectively model the continuous-time stochastic dynamics based only on sparse or irregular observations. Taking advantage of the capacity of deep neural networks, VSDN has higher flexibility and generalizability in modeling the nonlinear stochastic dependency from multivariate observations.

The rest of this paper is organized as follows. In Sect. 2, we first present the continuous-time variants of VAE loss, and then derive a continuous-time IWAE loss to train continuous-time state-space models with deep neural networks. In Sect. 3, we propose the deep learning structures of VSDN. Comprehensive experiments are presented in Sect. 4 and conclusion is given in Sect. 5.

2   Continuous-Time Variational Bayes

In this section, we first introduce the basic notations and formulate our problem. We then define the continuous-time variants of the Variational Auto-Encoding (VAE) and Importance-Weighted Auto-Encoding (IWAE) lower bounds to enable the efficient training of our models.

2.1   Basic Notations and Problem Formulation

Throughout this paper, we define $X_t \in \mathbb{R}^{d_1}$ as the continuous-time latent state at time t and $Y_n \in \mathbb{R}^{d_2}$ as the n_{th} discrete-time observed data at time t_n. d_1 and d_2 are the dimensions of the latent state and observation respectively. $X_{<t}$ is the continuous trajectory before time t and $X_{\leq t}$ is the trajectory up to time t. $Y_{n_1:n_2}$ is the sequence of data points from t_{n_1} to t_{n_2}. $\mathcal{Y}_t = \{Y_n | t_n < t\}$ is the historical observations before t and $\mathbb{Y}_t = \{Y_n | t_n \geq t\}$ is the current and future observations. For simplicity, we also assume that the initial value of the latent state is constant. The results in this paper can be easily extended to the situation that the initial states are also random variables. Given K data sequences $\{y_{1:n_i}^{(i)}\}, i = 1, \cdots, K$, the target of our study is to learn an accurate continuous-time generative model $\mathcal{G}$ that maximizes the log-likelihood:

$$\mathcal{G} = \arg\max_{\mathcal{G}} \frac{1}{K} \sum_{i=1}^{K} \log P_{\mathcal{G}}(y_{1:n_i}^{(i)}). \tag{1}$$

For multivariate sequential data, there exists a complicated nonlinear relationship between the observed data and the unobservable latent state, which can be either the physical state of a dynamic system or the low-dimensional manifold of data. In our study, the latent state evolves in the continuous time domain and generates the observation through some transformation.

2.2   Continuous-Time Variational Inference

In order to capture the underlying stochastic process from irregular data, we design the generative model as a neural continuous-time state-space model, which consists of a latent Stochastic Differential Equation (SDE) and a conditional distribution of the observation. The latent SDE describes the stochastic process of the latent states and the conditional distribution depicts the probabilistic dependency of the current data with the latent states and historical observations:

$$dX_t = H_{\mathcal{G}}(X_t, \mathcal{Y}_t; t)dt + R_{\mathcal{G}}(\mathcal{Y}_t; t)dW_t, \tag{2}$$

$$P_{\mathcal{G}}(Y_n|Y_{1:n-1}, X_{t_n}) = \Phi(Y_n|f(Y_{1:n-1}, X_{t_n})), \tag{3}$$

where $H_{\mathcal{G}}$ and $R_{\mathcal{G}}$ are the drift and diffusion functions of the latent SDE. W_t denotes the Wiener process, which is also called standard Brownian motion. To integrate the information of the observed data, $H_{\mathcal{G}}$ is the function of the current state X_t and the historical observations $\mathcal{Y}_t$. However, $R_{\mathcal{G}}$ only uses the historical data as input. It is not beneficial to include X_t as the input of the diffusion function, as it will inject more noise terms into gradients of the network parameters. $\Phi(\cdot)$ is a parametric family of distributions over the data and $f(\cdot)$ is the function to compute the parameters of Φ. With the advance of deep learning methods, we parameterize $H_{\mathcal{G}}$, $R_{\mathcal{G}}$ and $f(\cdot)$ by deep neural networks.

Continuous-Time Auto-Encoding Variational Bayes: The exact log-likelihood of the generative model is given as

$$\log P_{\mathcal{G}}(y_{1:n}) = \log \int P_{\mathcal{G}}(X_{\leq t_n}) \prod_{i=1}^{n} P_{\mathcal{G}}(y_i|y_{1:n-1}, X_{t_i})dX_{\leq t_n} \tag{4}$$

which does not have the closed-form solution in general. Therefore, $\mathcal{G}$ can not be directly trained by maximizing log-likelihood. To overcome this difficulty, an inference model $\mathcal{Q}$ is introduced to depict the stochastic dependency of the latent state on observed data. Similar to the generative model, $\mathcal{Q}$ consists of a posterior SDE:

$$dX_t = H_{\mathcal{Q}}(X_t, \mathcal{Y}_t, \mathbb{Y}_t; t)dt + R_{\mathcal{G}}(\mathcal{Y}_t; t)dW_t, \tag{5}$$

where $H_{\mathcal{Q}}$ is the posterior drift function. Different from $H_{\mathcal{G}}$, $H_{\mathcal{Q}}$ also uses the future observation $\mathbb{Y}_t$ as the input and therefore the inference model $\mathcal{Q}$ induces the posterior distribution $P_{\mathcal{Q}}(X_{\leq t_n}|y_{1:n})$.

Based on Auto-Encoding Variational Bayes [10], it is straightforward to introduce a continuous-time variant of the VAE lower bound of the log-likelihood:

$$\mathcal{L}_{VAE}(y_{1:n}) = -\beta KL(P_{\mathcal{Q}}||P_{\mathcal{G}}) + \sum_{i=1}^{n} \mathbb{E}_{P_{\mathcal{Q}}(X_{t_i})} \log P_{\mathcal{G}}(y_i|y_{1:n-1}, X_{t_i}), \tag{6}$$

$$KL(P_{\mathcal{Q}}||P_{\mathcal{G}}) = \frac{1}{2} \int_0^{t_n} \mathbb{E}_{P_{\mathcal{Q}}(X_t)} \Big((H_{\mathcal{Q}} - H_{\mathcal{G}})^T [R_{\mathcal{G}} R_{\mathcal{G}}^T]^{-1} (H_{\mathcal{Q}} - H_{\mathcal{G}})\Big)dt. \tag{7}$$

where $P_{\mathcal{G}}(X_{\leq t_n})$ and $P_{\mathcal{Q}}(X_{\leq t_n})$ are the probability density of the latent states induced by the prior SDE Eq. (2) and the posterior SDE Eq. (5). $KL(\cdot||\cdot)$ denotes the KL divergence between two distributions and β is a hyper-parameter to weight the effect of the KL terms. In this paper, we fix β as 1.0 and $\mathcal{L}_{VAE}$ is the original VAE objective [10]. In β-VAE [3,8], it is shown that a larger β can encourage the model to learn more efficient and disentangled representation from the data. Eq. (5) is restricted to having the same diffusion function as Eq. (2). A feasible $\mathcal{L}_{VAE}$ can not be defined to train VSDN without this restriction, as the KL divergence of two SDEs with different diffusions will be infinite [1].

The VAE objective has been widely used for discrete-time stochastic recurrent modals, such as LFADS [16] and VRNN [5]. The major difference between these models and our work is that we incorporate a continuous-time latent state into our model while the latent states of the discrete-time models evolve only at distinct and separate time slots.

Continuous-Time Importance Weighted Variational Bayes: $\mathcal{L}_{VAE}(y_{1:n})$ equals the exact log-likelihood when $P_{\mathcal{Q}}(X_{\leq t_n})$ of the inference model is identical to the exact posterior distribution induced by the generative model. The errors of the inference model can result in the looseness of the VAE loss for the model training. Under the framework of Importance-Weighted Auto-Encoder (IWAE) [2,6], we can define a tighter evidence lower bound:

$$\widetilde{\mathcal{L}}_{IWAE}^{K}(y_{1:n}) = \mathbb{E}_{x_{\leq t_n}^1, \cdots, x_{\leq t_n}^K \sim P_{\mathcal{Q}}(x_{\leq t_n})} \left(\log \frac{1}{K} \sum_{k=1}^{K} w_k \prod_{i=1}^{n} P_{\mathcal{G}}(y_i|y_{1:n-1}, X_{t_i}) \right),$$
(8)

where the importance weights satisfy the following SDE:

$$d \log w_k = d \log \frac{P_{\mathcal{G}}(x_{\leq t_n}^k)}{P_{\mathcal{Q}}(x_{\leq t_n}^k)} = -\frac{1}{2}(H_{\mathcal{Q}} - H_{\mathcal{G}})^T [R_{\mathcal{G}} R_{\mathcal{G}}^T]^{-1}$$
$$\times (H_{\mathcal{Q}} - H_{\mathcal{G}})dt - (H_{\mathcal{Q}} - H_{\mathcal{G}})^T [R_{\mathcal{G}}]^{-1} dW_t.$$
(9)

Given the variational auto-encoding lower bound $\mathcal{L}_{VAE}(\cdot)$ and the importance weighted auto-encoding lower bound $\mathcal{L}_{IWAE}^{K}(\cdot)$ for the continuous-time generative model, the tightness of the lower bounds are given by the following inequality:

$$\log P_{\mathcal{G}}(y_{1:n}) \geq \widetilde{\mathcal{L}}_{IWAE}^{K+1}(\cdot) \geq \widetilde{\mathcal{L}}_{IWAE}^{K}(\cdot) \geq \mathcal{L}_{VAE}(\cdot),$$
(10)

for any positive integer K. Consequently, $\widetilde{\mathcal{L}}_{IWAE}^{K}(\cdot)$ is infinite if the diffusions of Eq. (2) and Eq. (5) are different. In our implementation, we notice that the training of our models by $\widetilde{\mathcal{L}}_{IWAE}^{K}$ is not stable, possibly due to the drawbacks of importance sampling and the Signal-To-Noise problem [14]. To alleviate the problem, we train our model by a convex combination of the VAE and IWAE losses:

$$\mathcal{L}_{IWAE}^{K}(y_{1:n}) = (1-\alpha)\mathcal{L}_{VAE}(y_{1:n}) + \alpha \widetilde{\mathcal{L}}_{IWAE}^{K}(y_{1:n}), \quad \alpha \in (0,1).$$
(11)

With the use of reparameterization [10], both $\mathcal{L}_{VAE}(y_{1:n})$ and $\mathcal{L}_{IWAE}^K(y_{1:n})$ are differentiable with respect to the parameters of the generative and inference models. Therefore, they can be applied to train continuous-time stochastic models with deep learning components.

3   Variational Stochastic Differential Networks

We propose a new continuous-time stochastic recurrent network called **Variational Stochastic Differential Network (VSDN)** (Fig. 1). VSDN introduces the latent state to capture the underlying unobservable factors that generate the observed data, and incorporates efficient deep learning structures to compute the components in the generative model Eq. (2)–(3) and inference model Eq. (5).

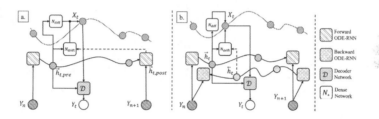

Fig. 1. Model architectures of (a) VSDN-F (filtering); (b) VSDN-S (smoothing).

Generative Model $\mathcal{G}$: Inside the generative model, the latent SDE Eq. (2) depicts the dynamics of the latent state trajectory controlled by the historical observations $\mathcal{Y}_t$. Both the drift and diffusion functions have the dependency on $\mathcal{Y}_t$. Therefore, we first apply a forward ODE-RNN [15] to embed the information of historical data into the hidden feature $\overrightarrow{h}_{t,pre}$. Two feed-forward networks are defined to compute drift and diffusion respectively. The decoder network further computes the parameters of the conditional distribution in Eq. (3) by the concatenation of the latent state and forward feature:

$$H_{\mathcal{G}} = N_{drift}([X_t, \overrightarrow{h}_{t,pre} = \text{ODE-RNN}_1(\mathcal{Y}_t; t)]),$$

$$R_{\mathcal{G}} = \exp(N_{diff}(\overrightarrow{h}_{t,pre})), \; P_{\mathcal{G}}(Y_t|\mathcal{Y}_t, X_t) = \Phi(Y_n|f = \mathcal{D}([X_t, \overrightarrow{h}_{t,pre}])). \quad (12)$$

Inference Model $\mathcal{Q}$: We propose two types of inference models in VSDN: a filtering model, and a smoothing model. $\mathcal{L}_{VAE}(y_{1:n})$ and $\mathcal{L}_{IWAE}^K(y_{1:n})$ equal the exact log-likelihood when $P_{\mathcal{Q}}(X_{\leq t_n})$ is identical to the exact posterior distribution $P_{\mathcal{G}}(X_{\leq t_n}|y_{1:n})$. The inference model must process the the whole data sequence to compute $H_{\mathcal{Q}}$ at a time. According to d-separation, the latent state X_t is dependent on both the historical data $\mathcal{Y}_t$ and future observations $\mathbb{Y}_t$. Therefore, we first define $\mathcal{Q}$ as a smoothing model by introducing a backward ODE-RNN to embed the information of the future observations into a hidden feature $\overleftarrow{h}_t$. The drift function is computed as:

$$H_{\mathcal{Q}} = N_{drift}([X_t, \overrightarrow{h}_{t,pre} + \overleftarrow{h}_t]), \quad \overleftarrow{h}_t = \text{ODE-RNN}_2(\mathbb{Y}_t; t)]). \tag{13}$$

In real-world applications, it is sometimes possible to have promising performance in inference without processing the future observations. Besides, the future measurements are intractable in online systems. Therefore, we also design a filtering inference model that infers the latent state from the historical and current data. The drift of the filtering model is given as:

$$H_{\mathcal{Q}} = \begin{cases} N_{drift}([X_t, \overrightarrow{h}_{t,pre} + \overrightarrow{h}_{t,post}]) & \text{if } \exists y_t \text{ at } t \\ H_{\mathcal{G}} & \text{otherwise} \end{cases} \tag{14}$$

where $\overrightarrow{h}_{t,post}$ is the post-observation updated feature of the forward ODE-RNN [15]. The filtering model does not have to include a backward RNN to process the future observations and thus its running speed is faster.

The whole architectures of VSDN with filtering $\mathcal{Q}$ (VSDN-F) and smoothing $\mathcal{Q}$ (VSDN-S) are shown in Fig. 1 (a) - (b). The inference model and the generative model share the drift network. This strategy can force the ODE-RNNs to embed more information into the hidden features and reduce the model complexity.

4   Experiments

In this section, we conduct comprehensive experiments to validate the performance of our models and demonstrate its advantages in real-world applications. We compare the performance of VSDN with state-of-the-art continuous-time recurrent neural networks (i.e. ODE-RNN [15] and GRU-ODE [7]), LatentODE [4] and LatentSDE [11].

We evaluate the performance of different models on the prediction and interpolation problems for human motion capturing. For a given sequence of data points sampled at irregular time intervals, the prediction task is defined to estimate the next observed data in the time axis, and the interpolation task is defined to recover the missing parts of the whole data trajectory. In both prediction and interpolation tasks, only the generative models of VSDNs are evaluated. The experiments are conducted on the following datasets - **Human3.6M** [9]: We apply the same data pre-processing as [13]; **CMU MoCap**[1]: We follow the data pre-processing in [12].

After data pre-processing, we randomly remove half of the frames in the data sequence as missing data. To quantify the model performance, we consider two evaluation metrics: one is the negative log-likelihood (NLL) per frame; the other is the frame-level mean square error (MSE) between the ground-true and estimated values. The model performance is shown in Tables 1 and 2.

---

[1] http://mocap.cs.cmu.edu/.

Table 1. Model performance on Human3.6M dataset

	Prediction		Interpolation	
	NLL	MSE	NLL	MSE
LatentODE	-45.34 ± 0.85	1.6421 ± 0.041	-45.31 ± 0.85	1.6477 ± 0.041
LatentSDE	-63.01 ± 1.26	0.8278 ± 0.059	-62.93 ± 1.28	0.8311 ± 0.060
GRU-ODE	-93.70 ± 2.34	0.3201 ± 0.062	-93.71 ± 2.34	0.3207 ± 0.062
ODE-RNN	-93.78 ± 1.48	0.2981 ± 0.075	-93.78 ± 1.48	0.2984 ± 0.076
VSDN-F (VAE)	-122.64 ± 2.79	0.2373 ± 0.064	-122.62 ± 2.79	0.2367 ± 0.064
VSDN-S (VAE)	-126.93 ± 3.35	0.2374 ± 0.086	-126.88 ± 3.35	0.2368 ± 0.086
VSDN-F (IWAE)	-125.55 ± 6.64	$\mathbf{0.1751 \pm 0.092}$	-125.51 ± 6.62	$\mathbf{0.1746 \pm 0.092}$
VSDN-S (IWAE)	$\mathbf{-127.12 \pm 5.19}$	0.1797 ± 0.073	$\mathbf{-127.08 \pm 5.17}$	0.1790 ± 0.073

Table 2. Model performance on MoCap dataset

	Prediction		Interpolation	
	NLL	MSE	NLL	MSE
LatentODE	14.99 ± 1.64	49.51 ± 0.38	14.91 ± 1.81	49.88 ± 0.39
LatentSDE	-59.83 ± 2.13	30.11 ± 0.28	-60.13 ± 2.59	30.43 ± 0.31
GRU-ODE	-51.83 ± 0.48	32.77 ± 0.11	-51.91 ± 0.49	33.17 ± 0.12
ODE-RNN	-51.75 ± 1.16	31.81 ± 0.21	-51.82 ± 1.18	33.22 ± 0.21
VSDN-F (VAE)	-110.71 ± 3.92	20.64 ± 0.39	-111.40 ± 3.88	20.95 ± 0.39
VSDN-S (VAE)	-114.31 ± 4.44	$\mathbf{19.05 \pm 0.59}$	-114.97 ± 4.40	$\mathbf{19.35 \pm 0.59}$
VSDN-F (IWAE)	-109.84 ± 5.32	20.47 ± 0.53	-110.54 ± 5.33	20.76 ± 0.53
VSDN-S (IWAE)	$\mathbf{-114.57 \pm 2.58}$	19.84 ± 0.18	$\mathbf{-115.24 \pm 2.50}$	20.12 ± 0.18

VSDN incorporates SDE to model the stochastic dynamics, and also applies a recurrent structure to embed the information of the irregular time series into the whole latent state trajectory. With these advances, VSDN outperforms the baseline models in both the prediction and interpolation tasks. VSDN has much smaller negative log-likelihood, which indicates that it can better model the underlying stochastic process of the data. Furthermore, VSDN trained by IWAE losses has similar and sometimes better performance than those with VAE losses. As the latent state in the inference model has stochastic dependency on the future observations, VSDN-S using the smoothing model has slightly lower NLL and is a better choice than VSDN-F using filtering model.

5   Conclusions

In this paper, we propose a continuous-time stochastic recurrent neural network called VSDN to learn the continuous-time stochastic dynamics from irregular data sequence. We provide two variants, one is VSDN-F whose inference model is a filtering model, and the other is VSDN-S with smoothing inference model. The continuous-time variants of the VAE and IWAE losses are incorporated to efficiently train our model. We demonstrate the effectiveness of VSDN through evaluations on different datasets and tasks, and our results show that VSDN can achieve much better performance than state-of-the-art continuous-time deep learning models. In the future work, we will investigate along several potential directions: First, we will apply our models to higher dimensional and more complicated data, such as videos, which are more challenging to model yet, especially under the premise of increasing demand for producing videos in high resolution and frame-per-second (FPS); Second, as stochastic differential equations are the base of many significant control methodologies, we will try to further extend the capacity of our models such that they can be used in precise control scenarios.

Acknowledgments. This work has been supported by NSF OIA 2040599, NSF OIA 2134840 and DOE 38456.

References

1. Archambeau, C., Opper, M., Shen, Y., Cornford, D., Shawe-taylor, J.S.: Variational inference for diffusion processes. In: Advances in Neural Information Processing Systems 20 (2008)
2. Burda, Y., Grosse, R., Salakhutdinov, R.: Importance weighted autoencoders. ArXiv arXiv:1509.00519 (2016)
3. Burgess, C.P., et al.: Understanding disentangling in β-VAE (2018)
4. Chen, T.Q., Rubanova, Y., Bettencourt, J., Duvenaud, D.K.: Neural ordinary differential equations. In: Advances in Neural Information Processing Systems vol. 31, pp. 6571–6583 (2018)
5. Chung, J., Kastner, K., Dinh, L., Goel, K., Courville, A.C., Bengio, Y.: A recurrent latent variable model for sequential data. In: Advances in Neural Information Processing Systems, vol. 28, pp. 2980–2988 (2015)
6. Cremer, C., Morris, Q., Duvenaud, D.: Reinterpreting importance-weighted autoencoders. In: International Conference on Learning Representations (ICLR) - Workshop Track (2017)
7. De Brouwer, E., Simm, J., Arany, A., Moreau, Y.: GRU-ODE-Bayes: continuous modeling of sporadically-observed time series. In: Advances in Neural Information Processing Systems, vol. 32, pp. 7379–7390 (2019)
8. Higgins, I., et al.: β-VAE: Learning basic visual concepts with a constrained variational framework. In: International Conference on Learning Representations (ICLR) (2017)
9. Ionescu, C., Papava, D., Olaru, V., Sminchisescu, C.: Human3.6m: large scale datasets and predictive methods for 3d human sensing in natural environments. IEEE Trans. Pattern Anal. Mach. Intell. **36**(7), 1325–1339 (2014)
10. Kingma, D.P., Welling, M.: Auto-encoding variational bayes. In: International Conference on Learning Representations (ICLR) (2014)
11. Li, X., Wong, T.K.L., Chen, R.T.Q., Duvenaud, D.: Scalable gradients for stochastic differential equations. In: 23rd International Conference on Artificial Intelligence and Statistics, pp. 3870–3882 (August 2020)
12. Liu, Y., Xie, D., Wang, X.: Generalized boltzmann machine with deep neural structure. In: The 22nd International Conference on Artificial Intelligence and Statistics (AISTATS), vol. 89, pp. 926–934 (April 2019)

13. Martinez, J., Hossain, R., Romero, J., Little, J.J.: A simple yet effective baseline for 3d human pose estimation. In: IEEE/CVF International Conference on Computer Vision (ICCV) (2017)
14. Rainforth, T., et al.: Tighter variational bounds are not necessarily better. In: Proceedings of the 35th International Conference on Machine Learning, pp. 4274–4282 (2018)
15. Rubanova, Y., Chen, T.Q., Duvenaud, D.K.: Latent ordinary differential equations for irregularly-sampled time series. In: Advances in Neural Information Processing Systems, vol. 32, pp. 5321–5331 (2019)
16. Sussillo, D., Józefowicz, R., Abbott, L.F., Pandarinath, C.: LFADS - latent factor analysis via dynamical systems. ArXiv arXiv:1608.06315 (2016)

An Adaptive Logarithm Quantization Method for DNN Compression

Yuan Wang[1], Zhaoliang He[2], Chen Tang[3], Zhi Wang[3(✉)], and Wenwu Zhu[2(✉)]

[1] Tsinghua-Berkeley Shenzhen Institute, Tsinghua University, Shenzhen, China
wangyuan19@mails.tsinghua.edu.cn
[2] Department of Computer Science and Technology, Tsinghua University,
Beijing, China
hezl19@mails.tsinghua.edu.cn, wwzhu@tsinghua.edu.cn
[3] Shenzhen International Graduate School, Tsinghua University, Shenzhen, China
tc20@mails.tsinghua.edu.cn, wangzhi@sz.tsinghua.edu.cn

Abstract. The size and complexity of Neural Network models grow rapidly in recent years, which makes the inference of these models require more computational and memory resources. To reduce the required resources, quantization is one of the promising methods. Logarithm quantization can both reduce the model size and the computational complexity because the time-consuming multiplication operation can be replaced with the addition operation in logarithm domain. However, the previous logarithm quantization methods use a fixed logarithm base. Therefore, they cannot adapt according to the distribution of data and bit-width budgets, which causes performance degradation. To address such a problem, we propose an adaptive quantization method to optimize the quantization function. Our method first finds an optimized weight quantization function by minimizing the quantization loss of the model's weight data under a given bit-width budget. Then we use a zero-shot way to find an optimized quantization function for activation data. Finding the optimized parameters is time-consuming. We propose a heuristic algorithm to solve the optimization problem fast. Compared to the previous logarithm quantization methods, our method can achieve up to 72.53% higher Top-1 accuracy under the same bit-width constraint.

Keywords: Neural network · Logarithm quantization · Optimization · Zero-shot model compression

1 Introduction

Nowadays, we witness a prosperous development of Neural Network (NN), especially deep Neural Network (DNN) technology. The DNN models show great performance in varieties of tasks, such as image classification and object detection. To obtain better inference performance, the number of layers of DNN models becomes larger and the structures become more complex [6]. Training and deploying these large and complex DNN models require a huge amount of

© Springer Nature Switzerland AG 2021
T. Mantoro et al. (Eds.): ICONIP 2021, CCIS 1516, pp. 352–359, 2021.
https://doi.org/10.1007/978-3-030-92307-5_41

resources [4]. However, in reality, we sometimes need to deploy the models in a cheaper and resource-limited edge device, such as a mobile device [14]. Thus, the deployment of these models arises the problem of how to compress the existed models to satisfy the resource constraints on the edge devices while preserving the good performance of the original DNN models and keeping the inference procedure within an acceptable time limit. The main resources that influence the inference time are memory bandwidth and the amount of available computational resources [13].

To address such a problem, one promising method is to quantize the weight or activation data of DNN models to lower bit-width representation. After quantization, both the memory and the computational resource requirement will be reduced. However, the quantization procedure may result in the DNN models' performance degradation compared to the original ones [3].

To address this, many quantization technologies are proposed. The quantization methods can be classified into two categories based on whether retraining is required [10] or not. One is quantization-aware training method. The other one is post-training quantization. Another classification bases on the quantization function. The quantization function can be linear or non-linear [5]. Among the non-linear quantization functions, the logarithm quantization function is a promising one because the time-consuming multiplication operation can be replaced with a more efficient addition operation in the logarithm domain [9].

However, the traditional logarithm quantization method uses a fixed base quantization function, which cannot adapt to different models and bit-width constraints [1,12]. As shown in Fig. 1, the original float point data (the blue part, representing the density) are quantized to several quantization values (the red part, representing the occurrence frequency) by a quantization function.

Comparing Fig. 1(a) and Fig. 1(b), the quantization values remain the same for the larger data when the quantization bit width changes.

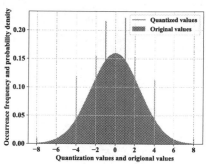

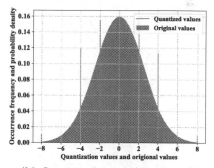

(a) Quantization result using 3 bits.   (b) Quantization result using 4 bits.

Fig. 1. Quantization results of a fixed base quantization function under different bit-width constraints.

Therefore, we propose a quantization scheme to address the above problems. Our method adds a new degree of freedom by automatically and adaptively selecting FSR and the base of the logarithm quantization function to preserve the performance of the DNN models better. In particular, our contributions are as follows.

– The logarithm quantization is analyzed. How the different factors influence the logarithm quantization results is shown.
– We propose an adaptive logarithm quantization scheme that can adjust the quantization function according to the distribution of DNN models' parameters, the distribution of activation data and bit-width constraints.
– We design a fast heuristic searching algorithm to find the parameters of the quantization function.
– A more efficient quantization method for activation data is designed.

2   Methodology

2.1   Loss Function

In most previous post-training quantization works, the loss function is designed as follows: $J = \|w - Q(w)\|_2^2$. The w is the original data, and the $Q(\cdot)$ is the quantization function that quantizes the w to a lower bit width representation w_q. The w can be the weight data or activation data in a DNN model. We need to find the best quantization function $Q(\cdot)$ to reduce the quantization loss.

2.2   Logarithm Quantization

For the basic logarithm quantization method, the quantization function is as follows:

$$\text{LogQuant}(x, \text{bitwidth}, \text{FSR}) = s \cdot 2^{\tilde{x}} \tag{1}$$

$$\tilde{x} = \text{Clip}(\text{Round}(\log_2 x), \text{FSR} - 2^{\text{bitwidth}-1}, \text{FSR}) \tag{2}$$

$$\text{Clip}(x, \min, \max) = \begin{cases} \min + 1 & x \le \min \\ \max & x \ge \max \\ x & \text{otherwise} \end{cases} \tag{3}$$

where bitwidth means how many bits are used to represent the quantized data, FSR stands for full scale range, and s stands for the sign of x.

As shown in Fig. 2, when we change the base of logarithm function to a smaller one $\sqrt{2}$ and compare with Fig. 1(b), the quantization results are more suitable for the bit-width constraint.

To find the best quantization function for different models and bit widths, we proposed a quantization algorithm that adaptively chooses the base of the logarithm quantization function to minimize the quantization loss. The quantization function is revised as:

$$\text{LogQuant}(x, \text{bitwidth}, \text{FSR}, b) = s \cdot b^{\tilde{x}} \tag{4}$$

$$\tilde{x} = \text{Clip}(\text{Round}(\log_b x), \text{FSR} - 2^{\text{bitwidth}-1}, \text{FSR}) \qquad (5)$$

Such revision influences the representation range of the quantization function. When the bit width remains the same and the maximum quantization value $m = b^{FSR}$ remains the same value by adjusting FSR, the quantization range R can be calculated as $R = m(1 - \frac{1}{b^{2^{\text{bitwidth}-1}}})$. We can figure out that a smaller base provides denser quantization results, but the quantization range is narrow. Both the density and the quantization range influence the quantization error.

2.3   Analysis Using Random Data

The weight data of a DNN model follow nearly normal distribution with zero mean [6]. For models that use Batch Normalization (BN) layers, the BN layers make the activation data nearly normally distributed with zero means [8]. That helps us make use of a set of standard normal distribution and change the scaling factor to simulate the different data distributions. However, such scaling operation introduces a scaling factor σ to the original data.

Assuming a set of original data ϕ follows a zero-mean normal distribution as $\phi \sim \mathcal{N}(0, \sigma^2)$, we can transform ϕ to a standard normal distribution as follows: $\frac{\phi}{\sigma} \sim \mathcal{N}(0, 1)$. The converse transform can be done as follows: $\sigma\varphi \sim \mathcal{N}(0, \sigma^2)$, where data φ follows standard normal distribution as $\varphi \sim \mathcal{N}(0, 1)$.

Given a set of random data, the loss function is not derivable in many points. As shown in Fig. 3, the quantization loss for one data has several sudden changes when the base changes. For different quantization data values, the sudden changes occur at different quantization base points. In addition, the number of the weights data is large. That means the sudden change will appear almost everywhere and the derivation of loss function will frequently disappear when the base changes. That also makes it very time-consuming to apply a grid search approach.

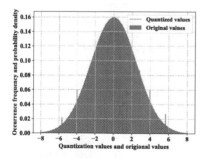

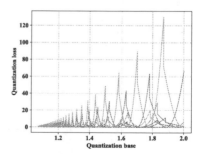

Fig. 2. Quantization results using 4 bits and a fixed logarithm function with a lower base.

Fig. 3. Quantization loss for eight random values when quantization base changes.

To test the influence of the scaling factor, we simulate how the quantization loss changes along with the scaling factor changing. The results are shown in Fig. 4.

We can see that the quantization errors seesaw around a mean value while the scaling factor changes. However, compared to the influence of the base of the quantization function, the scaling factor makes an ignorable contribution to the quantization procedure. The scaling step helps us find the FSR for the quantization function.

To better understand the relationship between the quantization loss and the quantization base, we apply the change of base formula: $\log_b x = \frac{\log_2 x}{\log_2 b} = c \cdot \log_2 x, c = \frac{1}{\log_2 b}$. We call c the revised quantization base. The quantization function can be rewritten as:

$$\text{LogQuant}(x, \text{bitwidth}, c, M) = s \cdot M \cdot 2^{\frac{\tilde{x}}{c}} \tag{6}$$

$$\tilde{x} = \text{Clip}(\text{Round}(c \cdot \log_2 \frac{x}{M}), -2^{\text{bitwidth}-1}, 0) \tag{7}$$

Then the relativity between quantization loss and revised quantization base c is shown in Fig. 5.

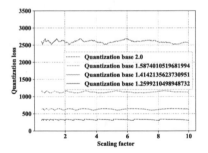
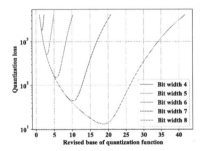

Fig. 4. Quantization loss for the data set $\varphi \sim \mathcal{N}(0,1)$ with different scaling factors and quantization bases.

Fig. 5. Quantization loss for the data set $\varphi \sim \mathcal{N}(0,1)$ when the revised quantization base changes.

The minimal quantization loss is the global minimum of the function.

According to the results above, we assume that the quantization loss is a nearly "cup" like function of the parameter c. Therefore, we propose a heuristic algorithm to find the best quantization base for the quantization function.

Step 1: scaling the data a using the maximum absolute value M of data. Choose a stop threshold th.

Step 2: random choose an initial revised base c for the quantization function (6) and an initial step length l.

Step 3: set the base of quantization function to $c-l$, c, and $c+l$. Then we get three different quantization function $Q_1(\cdot)$, $Q_2(\cdot)$ and $Q_3(\cdot)$. Quantize the data using these three quantization functions and compute the quantization losses.

Step 4: compare three losses and find the quantization function of the lowest and the second lowest quantization loss. According to different results, select a new initial revised base. Repeat step3 and step4 until the end condition.

2.4 Quantization for Activation Data

We adopt the method from reference [2] to generate a batch of representative data x^r. Then the data x^r is input into the original model. For activation data of each layer, we get a batch of representative results. We can therefore apply our optimization algorithm to the results to find the optimized quantization function.

3 Evaluation

3.1 Effectiveness of the Searching Method

We use Intel E5-2650 CPU to run our algorithm and record the time that different searching methods use. The result shows that the searching time of our algorithm is significantly shorter than the grid search method.

Table 1. Time consumption comparison between the proposed algorithm and grid search method on two generated data sets that follow standard normal distribution.

Dataset size	Method	Grid search number									
		100	200	300	400	500	600	700	800	900	1000
10000	Proposed	0.103	0.105	0.103	0.104	0.226	0.233	0.102	0.104	0.101	0.232
	Grid search	1.20	2.34	3.42	4.66	5.71	6.96	8.02	9.34	10.4	11.7
10000000	Proposed	7.85	7.87	7.85	8.10	7.86	7.85	7.87	23.4	24.5	23.5
	Grid search	113	226	339	457	568	679	799	996	1190	1336

3.2 Accuracy Results

We select three CNN models (ResNet18/50 [7], InceptionV3 [11]) to test our method due to that CNN is one kind of the most common DNN model. These models are all pretrained on the ImageNet data set. We apply our quantization method to both weight data and activation data.

The results of different bit-width representations of activation data and weight data for ResNet18/50 and InceptionV3 are shown in Fig. 6 and Fig. 7. We compare the accuracy results of our quantization method with those of the basic quantization method using a fixed base quantization function as described in [9] combining with the method in [2].

From the results, we can see that our method provides a better accuracy result in most of the cases. Especially when the bit width goes up, our method can benefit a lot compared to the fixed base method. When the quantization bit

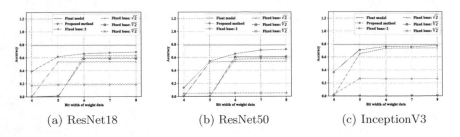

(a) ResNet18   (b) ResNet50   (c) InceptionV3

Fig. 6. Top-1 accuracy of different models under different quantization bit-width conditions for weight data when the activation data are quantized using 4 bits.

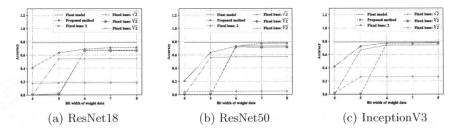

(a) ResNet18   (b) ResNet50   (c) InceptionV3

Fig. 7. Top-1 accuracy of different models under different quantization bit-width conditions for weight data when the activation data are quantized using 8 bits.

widths for weight data and activation data are both 8, our method shows almost no performance degradation. The fixed base method is only suitable for some cases of bit-width constraints and models. However, our method can find a better quantization function adaptively according to different bit-width constraints and models.

4   Conclusion

In this paper, we propose a new post-training logarithm quantization method. We design an algorithm to find the best quantization parameters faster rather than use the cumbersome grid search method. We test the effectiveness of our searching method and conclude that our searching method can significantly reduce the searching time. Then we test our quantization method by both quantizing the weight data and activation data. The results show that our method can adaptively find a better logarithm quantization function for different bit-width constraints and models. Our method can quantize the CNN models with lower quantization loss and less performance degradation.

Acknowledgements. This work is supported in part by NSFC (Grant No. 61872215), and Shenzhen Science and Technology Program (Grant No. RCYX20200714114 523079).

References

1. Cai, J., Takemoto, M., Nakajo, H.: A deep look into logarithmic quantization of model parameters in neural networks. In: Proceedings of the 10th International Conference on Advances in Information Technology, IAIT 2018, Association for Computing Machinery, New York (2018)
2. Cai, Y., Yao, Z., Dong, Z., Gholami, A., Mahoney, M.W., Keutzer, K.: ZeroQ: a novel zero shot quantization framework. In: Proceedings of the IEEE/CVF Conference on Computer Vision and Pattern Recognition (CVPR) (June 2020)
3. Chen, Y., et al.: T-DLA: An open-source deep learning accelerator for ternarized DNN models on embedded FPGA. In: 2019 IEEE Computer Society Annual Symposium on VLSI (ISVLSI), pp. 13–18 (2019)
4. Deng, L., Li, G., Han, S., Shi, L., Xie, Y.: Model compression and hardware acceleration for neural networks: a comprehensive survey. Proc. IEEE **108**(4), 485–532 (2020)
5. Gong, C., Chen, Y., Lu, Y., Li, T., Hao, C., Chen, D.: VecQ: minimal loss DNN model compression with vectorized weight quantization. IEEE Trans. Comput. 70(5), 696–710 (2021). https://doi.org/10.1109/TC.2020.2995593
6. Gong, C., Li, et al.: μL2Q: An ultra-low loss quantization method for DNN compression. In: 2019 International Joint Conference on Neural Networks (IJCNN), pp. 1–8 (2019)
7. He, K., Zhang, X., Ren, S., Sun, J.: Deep residual learning for image recognition. In: Proceedings of the IEEE Conference on Computer Vision and Pattern Recognition (CVPR) (June 2016)
8. Ioffe, S., Szegedy, C.: Batch normalization: Accelerating deep network training by reducing internal covariate shift. ArXiv arXiv:1502.03167 (2015)
9. Miyashita, D., Lee, E.G., Murmann, B.: Convolutional neural networks using logarithmic data representation. ArXiv arXiv:1603.01025 (2016)
10. Nogami, W., Ikegami, T., O'uchi, S., Takano, R., Kudoh, T.: Optimizing weight value quantization for CNN inference. In: 2019 International Joint Conference on Neural Networks (IJCNN), pp. 1–8 (2019)
11. Szegedy, C., Vanhoucke, V., Ioffe, S., Shlens, J., Wojna, Z.: Rethinking the inception architecture for computer vision. In: Proceedings of the IEEE Conference on Computer Vision and Pattern Recognition (CVPR) (June 2016)
12. Vogel, S., Liang, M., Guntoro, A., Stechele, W., Ascheid, G.: Efficient hardware acceleration of CNNs using logarithmic data representation with arbitrary logbase. In: Proceedings of the International Conference on Computer-Aided Design, ICCAD 2018, Association for Computing Machinery, New York (2018)
13. Wang, E., et al.: Deep neural network approximation for custom hardware: Where we've been, where we're going. ACM Comput. Surv. **52**(2), 1–39 (2019)
14. Wang, K., Liu, Z., Lin, Y., Lin, J., Han, S.: HAQ: hardware-aware automated quantization with mixed precision. In: 2019 IEEE/CVF Conference on Computer Vision and Pattern Recognition (CVPR), pp. 8604–8612 (2019)

A REINFORCEd Variational Autoencoder Topic Model

Amit Kumar[1,2(✉)], Nazanin Esmaili[1], and Massimo Piccardi[1]

[1] University of Technology Sydney, Broadway, Sydney, NSW 2007, Australia
{nazanin.esmaili,massimo.piccardi}@uts.edu.au
[2] Food Agility CRC Ltd, 81 Broadway, Ultimo 2007, Australia

Abstract. Topic modeling is an unsupervised natural language processing approach for automatically extracting the main topics from a large collection of documents, and simultaneously assigning the individual documents to the extracted topics. While many algorithms for topic modelling have been proposed in the literature, to date there has been little use of the popular reinforcement learning framework for this task. For this reason, in this paper we leverage two pillars of reinforcement learning – the policy gradient theorem and the REINFORCE algorithm – to define a novel loss function for training topic models. In the paper, the loss function is applied to a state-of-the-art topic model based on a variational autoencoder. Experimental results on two social media datasets have shown that the proposed approach has been able to outperform the original variational autoencoder and other baselines in terms of evaluation measures such as model perplexity and topic coherence.

Keywords: Topic models · Deep neural networks · Variational autoencoders · Reinforcement learning · REINFORCE

1 Introduction and Related Work

The continued growth of digital data sources, and especially social media, has led to an unprecedented rise in the volume of available text documents. This presents a major challenge for the systematic analysis of their contents, together with their management and organisation. While until the recent past these tasks could be undertaken based on human annotation, nowadays there is a compelling need for computational tools that can automatically extract topics and patterns from document collections and organise them accordingly.

In recent years, topic models have emerged as a powerful, unsupervised tool for identifying useful structure in such vast amounts of unstructured text data. In technical terms, a topic model is an algorithm that can efficiently discover the main topics of a potentially large corpus of documents, and assign the individual

Supported by funding from Food Agility CRC Ltd, funded under the Commonwealth Government CRC Program. The CRC Program supports industry-led collaborations between industry, researchers and the community.

documents to the topics. A "topic" is commonly intended as a characteristic probability distribution over the words of a vocabulary. For example, a topic like "computers" can be described by a probability distribution where words such as "motherboard," "CPU", "monitor," "mouse" and the like have the highest probabilities. In turn, individual documents can be assigned to multiple topics in specific proportions. Topic models have proved useful for the analysis of a variety of data, from scientific publications to user posts on social media [1].

Many topic models have been proposed over the years, primarily based on techniques such as non-negative matrix factorization and variational inference. Latent semantic indexing (LSI) is generally regarded as the first "proper" topic model [4]. However, the most widespread topic model is likely the latent Dirichlet allocation (LDA) [2]. LDA's basic components are: 1) the word distributions of each topic, and 2) the topic proportions of each document. Since both are modeled as multinomial distributions, LDA conveniently uses an eponymous Dirichlet distribution as their prior. The conjugacy between the multinomial and the Dirichlet makes it easy to derive the posteriors and support inference (more details are provided in the following section). In addition, many LDA derivatives have been proposed over time, including, among others, sparse [3], sequential [5], and hierarchical [12] versions.

Recently, neural topic models have started to appear in the literature, joining the benefits of traditional models such as LDA with those of *deep generative models* [6,7,13,15,18]. Some neural topic models have made use of generative adversarial networks (GANs) [6,7] and convolutional neural networks (CNNs) [18]. However, the most effective neural topic models seem to be those based on *variational autoencoders* (VAEs) [13,15]. Miao et al. in [13]. have proposed a VAE based neural topic model using the logistic normal distribution and the stick-breaking construction to infer the topic proportions. More recently, Srivastava and Sutton in [15] have proposed a neural topic model integrating LDA with a variational autoencoder, establishing state-of-the-art performance on all the tested datasets.

Despite the many available models, to date topic modeling has made limited use of the popular *reinforcement learning* framework [16]. Reinforcement learning offers the potential to leverage both differentiable and non-differentiable "rewards" to guide the extraction of the topics. An example of topic modeling with reinforcement learning has been presented in [8], leveraging word-reweighting rewards to encourage within-topic coherence and between-topic separation. However, we are not aware of any model that has used reinforcement learning to learn an effective *policy* over the topics. For this reason, in this paper we propose a topic model that uses the policy gradient theorem and the REINFORCE algorithm [17] to improve learning of an effective topic model. Experiments performed over two challenging datasets (20 Newsgroups and Amazon Fine Food Reviews, both collected from social media) have shown that the proposed approach has achieved a better performance than all the compared approaches in terms of topic coherence and model perplexity in a large majority of cases.

2   Topic Modeling with Variational Autoencoders

In recent years, deep generative models have gained widespread adoption in
the deep learning community, thanks to their effective integration of features of
generative models, Bayesian inference and deep neural networks. In particular,
variational autoencoders (VAEs) have proven specially effective at learning representations for latent variables [10], making them appealing for topic modeling.

A VAE is basically a generalized version of an autoencoder, which is a neural network subdivided into an encoder and a decoder. The encoder takes in
input a multidimensional measurement, and produces a latent representation in
output. In turn, the decoder takes in input the latent representation and produces a "reconstruction" of the original measurement. In the case of a VAE,
the reconstruction is simply meant as the probability of the measurement in
the parametrized decoder. When VAEs are used for topic modeling, the measurement in input is a document representation, w (typically, a bag-of-words or
a TF-IDF vector), while the latent variable is its topic vector, θ. In turn, the
likelihood of the document representation, w, can be obtained by marginalizing
the topic vector, θ, as in:

$$p(w|\alpha,\beta) = \int_\theta p(w,\theta|\alpha,\beta)d\theta \tag{1}$$

where α is the parameter of the prior probability over the topics, β is the matrix
of the word distributions for all the topics, and $p(w,\theta|\alpha,\beta)$ is the joint probability
of the document representation and the topic vector.

The training of a VAE aims to maximize (1) over the given document col-
lection. However, this is typically impossible to perform directly. Therefore, the
VAE sets to maximize a tractable lower bound (the evidence lower bound, or
ELBO) [10]:

$$\mathcal{L}(w|\alpha,\beta) = \mathbb{E}_{q(\theta|w)}\big[\log p(w|\theta,\beta)\big] - D_{\mathrm{KL}}(q(\theta|w)\|p(\theta|\alpha)) \tag{2}$$

Hereafter, we briefly describe the meaning of the terms in (2); further details
can be found in [10]. Term $q(\theta|w)$ (the "encoder") estimates the probability of
the topic vector for the given document. Term $\log p(w|\theta,\beta)$ (the "decoder") is the
log-probability of the document given its topic vector and the word distributions;
its expectation over $q(\theta|w)$, $\mathbb{E}_{q(\theta|w)}\big[\log p(w|\theta,\beta)\big]$, is the "reconstruction term".
Finally, term $p(\theta|\alpha)$ is a trainable prior over the topic vectors. During training,
(2) trades off increasing the reconstruction term against reducing the Kullback-
Leibler divergence (D_{KL}) between the encoder and the prior.

To facilitate the reparametrization of the encoder and the prior, Srivastava
and Sutton in [15] have proposed replacing the usual Dirichlet distribution with a
logistic normal distribution. Samples of a logistic normal distribution, $\mathcal{LN}(\mu,\Sigma)$,
can be conveniently obtained by applying the softmax operator to samples of
a Gaussian distribution of equal parameters, $\mathcal{N}(\mu,\Sigma)$. In turn, the Gaussian
distribution can be reparametrized with the common inverse transform approach.
Srivastava and Sutton's model, called *AVITM* (from autoencoding variational

inference for topic models), models the prior as $p(\theta|\alpha) = \mathcal{LN}(\theta|\mu(\alpha), \Sigma(\alpha))$, where $\mu(\alpha)$ and $\Sigma(\alpha)$ are closed-form expressions for the mean and the variance obtained with a Laplace approximation [9]. In turn, the encoder is modeled as $q(\theta|w) = \mathcal{LN}(\theta|\mu(w, \phi_1), \Sigma(w, \phi_2))$, where ϕ_1 and ϕ_2 are the parameters of two feed-forward neural networks that infer, respectively, the mean and covariance of the encoder. Finally, the decoder is given by:

$$p(w|\theta, \beta) = \text{Mult}(w \,|\, \text{softmax}(\beta)\,\theta) \tag{3}$$

where Mult() denotes the multinomial distribution, and the word distributions are parametrized as logits rather than probabilities to bypass the simplex constraint during gradient descent. A second version of the decoder, inspired by products-of-experts and nicknamed *ProdLDA*, first computes the product, and then the softmax:

$$p(w|\theta, \beta) = \text{Mult}(w \,|\, \text{softmax}(\beta\theta)). \tag{4}$$

3   The Proposed Approach: A VAE Topic Model with REINFORCE

Reinforcement learning has become increasingly popular in recent years thanks to its ability to train models beyond conventional maximum-likelihood approaches. The main advantages of reinforcement learning are its ability to minimize non-differentiable training objectives and its use of sampling, which permits a certain degree of *exploration* in the parameter space. In the case of our model, the loss function in (2) is an expectation over θ, the topic vector for the document, and should therefore not depend on it. However, since the expectation is empirical and based on typically only one sample per document, some dependence on θ persists, and we emphasize it by noting the loss as $\mathcal{L}(\theta)$ in the following. To improve the estimate of the encoder distribution, $q(\theta|w)$, we choose to minimize the *predictive risk*:

$$\mathcal{R} = \mathbb{E}_{q(\theta|w)}\big[\mathcal{L}(\theta)\big] = \int_\theta \mathcal{L}(\theta)q(\theta|w)d\theta \tag{5}$$

which is the expectation of the loss function, $\mathcal{L}(\theta)$, over the probability of variable θ, the document's topic vector. In order to minimize (5), training will attempt to assign high probability to values of θ that cause low values of the loss, and the vice versa, thus promoting an effective encoder. The minimization of (5) can be performed using the policy gradient theorem [17], which ignores the indirect dependence of the loss on the model's parameters and only differentiates the probability distribution in its own parameters, ϕ:

$$\frac{\partial}{\partial \phi}\mathcal{R} = \int_\theta \mathcal{L}(\theta)\frac{\partial}{\partial \phi}q(\theta|w)d\theta$$

$$= \int_\theta \mathcal{L}(\theta)\frac{\partial}{\partial \phi}\log q(\theta|w)q(\theta|w)d\theta \qquad (6)$$

$$= \mathbb{E}_{q(\theta|w)}\Big[\mathcal{L}(\theta)\frac{\partial}{\partial \phi}\log q(\theta|w)\Big]$$

As common in practice, we compute the resulting expectation empirically from a single sample:

$$\frac{\partial}{\partial \phi}\mathcal{R} \approx \mathcal{L}(\theta)\frac{\partial}{\partial \phi}\log q(\theta|w), \quad \theta \sim q(\theta|w) \qquad (7)$$

The above estimator of the gradient of the predictive risk is the popular REINFORCE, a fundamental approach of reinforcement learning which has been applied successfully in many fields [17]. However, the REINFORCE estimator typically suffers from high variance, often affecting the stability of training. This issue can be mollified by subtracting a baseline, b, from the loss (an approach known as REINFORCE *with baseline*):

$$\frac{\partial}{\partial \phi}\mathcal{R} \approx \big(\mathcal{L}(\theta) - b\big)\frac{\partial}{\partial \phi}\log q(\theta|w), \theta \sim q(\theta|w) \qquad (8)$$

With this modification, a training iteration will decrease $q(\theta|w)$ only if the loss, $\mathcal{L}(\theta)$, is greater than b (i.e., a remarkably bad value). Otherwise, it will increase it or leave it unchanged. In addition, from the gradient estimator we can derive an expression for a loss that can be automatically differentiated by common autodiff tools[1].:

$$\mathcal{L}_{REINF} = \big(\mathcal{L}(\theta) - b\big)_{nograd}\log q(\theta|w) \qquad (9)$$

where subscript *nograd* prevents differentiating the subscripted term.

The VAE loss (2) and the REINFORCE loss (9) can also be conveniently mixed, to explore trade-offs between the two. We therefore define the overall loss as:

$$\mathcal{L}_{overall} = \mathcal{L}(w|\alpha, \beta) + \epsilon\,\mathcal{L}_{REINF} \qquad (10)$$

4   Experiments and Results

The experiments have been carried out over two probing datasets, *20 Newsgroups* (a benchmark for the field) and *Amazon Fine Food Reviews*. The 20 Newsgroups dataset comprises $18,846$ documents from news shared on social media, while Amazon Fine Food Reviews consists of $568,454$ user-posted food reviews. These datasets are very challenging because of their great variety of topics and their

---

[1] http://www.autodiff.org/, https://www.tensorflow.org/guide/autodiff.

utmost diversity of authors. As models, we have compared the proposed approach against two strong baselines (LDA and LSI) and the state-of-the-art topic
model of Srivastava and Sutton, in its two versions AVITM and ProdLDA. For
this reason, we present the results for the corresponding versions of our model,
AVITM-REINF and ProdLDA-REINF. As hyperparameters, for those shared
with the model of Srivastava and Sutton we have used the same values. For
the loss balance parameter, ϵ, we have carried out a preliminary evaluation and
chosen $\epsilon = 10^{-15}$ since the scale of $\mathcal{L}_{REINF}$ is much larger. To set the baseline,
b, we have first trained the models without the REINFORCE loss and recorded
the value of their loss at convergence, noted as l; then, we have set b in the range
$[l, l \pm 25, l \pm 50]$, using only the training set for the selection. As a number of
topics to explore, we have used the oft-used values of 20 and 50. For performance
evaluation, we have adopted two popular measures, the *perplexity* and the *topic
coherence*. The perplexity measures how poorly the model fits a given set of data
(NB: lower values are better); to assess the models' ability to generalize, we have
measured it over the test sets. The topic coherence measures the internal "coherence" of the extracted topics (NB: higher values are better). Since coherence can
be quantified in different ways, we report both the *normalized pointwise mutual
information* (`coher-NMPI`) [11] and the C_V *coherence* (`coher-Cv`) [14]. Unlike
the perplexity, the coherence is computed over the training set itself to ensure
that all of the topics' M most-frequent words are present in the set. In all the
experiments, M has been set to 10. Given the significantly different nature of
the perplexity and the topic coherence, some disagreement in their ranking of
the models is to be expected.

4.1   Results

Tables 1 and 2 show the experimental results for the 20 Newsgroups dataset for
20 and 50 topics, respectively. Due to the different architecture and amount of
degrees of freedom, the perplexity values for LDA cannot be directly compared to
those of the autoencoder models; for this reason, we display them in italics. At its
turn, LSI is not a probabilistic model and the perplexity values are not defined.
When compared to the variational autoencoder approaches in terms of coherence, both LDA and LSI have reported significantly worse results and cannot
be considered competitive. AVITM has achieved better perplexity values than
ProdLDA, but ProdLDA has achieved higher coherence values in most cases,
so there is no clear winner between them. However, both our proposed variants
have been able to gain improvements over AVITM and ProdLDA, respectively:
compared to AVITM, AVITM-REINF has achieved better perplexity and coherence in the case of 20 topics, and coherence in the case of 50 topics; compared
to ProdLDA, ProdLDA-REINF has achieved better perplexity as well as coherence in the case of 20 topics, and coherence in the case of 50 topics. Overall,
AVITM-REINF has achieved the best perplexity of all compared models, and
ProdLDA-REINF the best coherence.

Tables 3 and 4 show the results for the Amazon Fine Food Reviews dataset
with 20 and 50 topics, respectively. Again, LDA and LSI have reported significantly lower coherence values than all the autoencoder models and cannot

Table 1. Results on the 20 Newsgroups dataset with 20 topics.

Metrics	LDA	LSI	AVITM	ProdLDA	AVITM-REINF	ProdLDA-REINF
Perplexity	*1480.3*	—	1140.2	1173.3	**1137.8**	1167.8
Coher-NPMI	-0.033	-0.053	0.094	0.141	0.131	**0.153**
Coher-Cv	0.309	0.371	0.671	0.779	0.734	**0.786**

Table 2. Results on the 20 Newsgroups dataset with 50 topics.

Metrics	LDA	LSI	AVITM	ProdLDA	AVITM-REINF	ProdLDA-REINF
Perplexity	*2389.6*	—	1133.1	1159.9	**1132.1**	1162.8
Coher-NPMI	-2.346	-0.062	0.117	0.111	0.115	**0.141**
Coher-Cv	-0.053	0.294	0.704	0.751	0.699	**0.763**

Table 3. Results on the Amazon Fine Food Reviews dataset with 20 topics.

Metrics	LDA	LSI	AVITM	ProdLDA	AVITM-REINF	ProdLDA-REINF
Perplexity	*1480.3*	—	**1000.9**	1099.7	1137.8	1091.4
Coher-NPMI	0.047	0.004	**0.144**	0.066	0.131	0.105
Coher-Cv	0.493	0.395	0.707	0.651	**0.734**	0.676

Table 4. Results on the Amazon Fine Food Reviews dataset with 50 topics.

Metrics	LDA	LSI	AVITM	ProdLDA	AVITM-REINF	ProdLDA-REINF
Perplexity	*2697.3*	—	1008.6	1012.5	**1008.3**	1009.0
Coher-NPMI	0.033	−0.008	0.144	−0.048	**0.155**	0.036
Coher-Cv	0.470	0.359	0.682	0.430	**0.699**	0.588

be regarded as competitive. For this dataset, AVITM has neatly outperformed ProdLDA in both perplexity and coherence. At its turn, our proposed AVITM-REINF has outperformed AVITM in 4 out of 6 measures across 20 and 50 topics, and should be deemed as the best performing model for this dataset. In addition, ProdLDA-REINF has improved in all measures compared to the original ProdLDA. Overall, we can conclude that our REINFORCE-based models have led to marked improvements over both datasets.

As further analysis, we have explored the sensitivity of the topic coherence to the value of the baseline, b, using the test set to simultaneously probe generalization. To this aim, Fig. 1 plots the values of the C_V coherence for ProdLDA-REINF (20 Newsgroups, 50 topics) over the range of the baseline values. The coherence value for ProdLDA is also displayed for comparison. In this experiment, the loss at convergence without REINFORCE has been $l = 630$, and the best coherence value over the training set has been obtained for $b = l - 25 = 605$. Figure 1 shows that this has also been the best value for the test set, showing excellent generalization. In addition, ProdLDA-REINF has achieved better coherence values than ProdLDA for all values of the baseline.

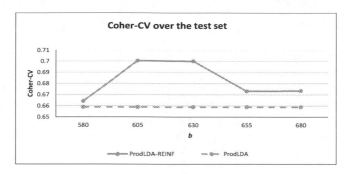

Fig. 1. Comparison of `coher-CV` on the test data for ProdLDA and ProdLDA-REINF (20 Newsgroups, 50 topics) by varying the baseline, b.

Finally, for a qualitative analysis of the results, Table 5 displays a few examples of topics extracted from the 20 Newsgroups dataset. The first topic extracted by LDA is clearly meaningful, but the other two (highlighted in red) seem incoherent. The third topic extracted by AVITM also seems, at least, uninformative. Conversely, all the examples of topics extracted by AVITM-REINF seem consistent and properly descriptive.

Table 5. Topics discovered from the 20 Newsgroups dataset (50 topics). Seemingly incoherent topics are highlighted in red.

LDA:

Monitor keyboard event appl mac usa ibm adapt use multi

date paper star robert confer divis surface mean june present

know say dont week white go your think year that

AVITM:

Car bike ride honda bmw gear motorcycle rear dod ford

Game team baseball player pitcher braves hitter score pitch fan

sea newspaper mountain april ii times angeles york francisco cambridge

---

AVITM-REINF:

Windows microsoft memory setup mode modem nt port video vga

Clinton congress economic government bush country administration economy american billion

Laboratory nasa shuttle lab space engineering flight institute solar spacecraft

---

5   Conclusion

This paper has presented a novel training loss function for VAE topic models based on the reinforcement learning framework. In the proposed approach, we leverage the predictive risk and the REINFORCE algorithm to learn an effective policy over the topic vectors. The experimental results over two social media datasets have shown that the proposed approach has been able to attain a strong performance as measured by perplexity and topic coherence, with improvements of up to 2.4 percentage points in NPMI coherence and 2.7 percentage points in C_V coherence compared to the runner-up. In addition, the model has given evidence of good generalization over new documents. In the near future, we plan to explore other architectures for the implementation of the model's neural networks, possibly including transformers and document embeddings.

References

1. Blei, D.M.: Probabilistic topic models. Commun. ACM **55**(4), 77–84 (2012)
2. Blei, D.M., Ng, A.Y., Jordan, M.I.: Latent Dirichlet allocation. J. Mach. Learn. Res. **3**, 993–1022 (2003)
3. Cheng, X., Yan, X., Lan, Y., Guo, J.: BTM: topic modeling over short texts. IEEE Trans. Knowl. Data Eng. **26**(12), 2928–2941 (2014)
4. Deerwester, S.C., Dumais, S.T., Landauer, T.K., Furnas, G.W., Harshman, R.A.: Indexing by latent semantic analysis. J. Am. Soc. Inf. Sci. **41**(6), 391–407 (1990)
5. Du, L., Buntine, W., Jin, H., Chen, C.: Sequential latent Dirichlet allocation. Knowl. Inf. Syst. **31**, 475–503 (2012)
6. Glover, J.: Modeling documents with generative adversarial networks. In: NIPS 2016 Workshop on Adversarial Training, pp. 1–7 (2016)
7. Grover, A., Dhar, M., Ermon, S.: Flow-GAN: combining maximum likelihood and adversarial learning in generative models. In: The Thirty-Second AAAI Conference on Artificial Intelligence, (AAAI-18), pp. 3069–3076. AAAI Press (2018)
8. Gui, L., Leng, J., Pergola, G., Zhou, Y., Xu, R., He, Y.: Neural topic model with reinforcement learning. In: Inui, K., Jiang, J., Ng, V., Wan, X. (eds.) The 2019 Conference on Empirical Methods in Natural Language Processing and the 9th International Joint Conference on Natural Language Processing (EMNLP-IJCNLP), pp. 3476–3481. Association for Computational Linguistics (2019)
9. Hennig, P., Stern, D.H., Herbrich, R., Graepel, T.: Kernel topic models. In: The Fifteenth International Conference on Artificial Intelligence and Statistics, AISTATS 2012. JMLR Proceedings, vol. 22, pp. 511–519 (2012)
10. Kingma, D.P., Welling, M.: Auto-encoding variational bayes. In: The 2nd International Conference on Learning Representations (ICLR 2014), pp. 1–14 (2014)
11. Lau, J.H., Newman, D., Baldwin, T.: Machine reading tea leaves: automatically evaluating topic coherence and topic model quality. In: The 14th Conference of the European Chapter of the Association for Computational Linguistics (EACL 2014), pp. 530–539 (2014)
12. Li, W., Yin, J., Chen, H.: Supervised topic modeling using hierarchical Dirichlet process-based inverse regression: Experiments on e-commerce applications. IEEE Trans. Knowl. Data Eng. **30**(6), 1192–1205 (2018)

13. Miao, Y., Grefenstette, E., Blunsom, P.: Discovering discrete latent topics with neural variational inference. In: The 34th International Conference on Machine Learning (ICML 2017), pp. 2410–2419 (2017)
14. Röder, M., Both, A., Hinneburg, A.: Exploring the space of topic coherence measures. In: The Eighth ACM International Conference on Web Search and Data Mining (WSDM 2015), pp. 399–408 (2015)
15. Srivastava, A., Sutton, C.A.: Autoencoding variational inference for topic models. In: The 5th International Conference on Learning Representations, (ICLR 2017), pp. 1–12 (2017)
16. Sutton, R.S., Barto, A.G.: Reinforcement Learning: An Introduction. 2nd edn, MIT Press, Cambridge (2018)
17. Williams, R.J.: Simple statistical gradient-following algorithms for connectionist reinforcement learning. Mach. Learn. **8**, 229–256 (1992)
18. Zhang, Y., Xu, B., Zhao, T.: Convolutional multi-head self-attention on memory for aspect sentiment classification. IEEE/CAA J. Automatica Sinica **7**, 1038–1044 (2020)

LFMAC: Low-Frequency Multi-Agent Communication

Cong Cong[1,2(✉)], Chuxiong Sun[1,2], Ruiping Liu[3], Rui Wang[1], and Xiaohui Hu[1]

[1] Institute of Software, Chinese Academy of Sciences, Beijing 100190, China
{congcong2020,chuxiong2016,wangrui,hxh}@iscas.ac.cn
[2] University of Chinese Academy of Sciences, Beijing 100049, China
[3] School of Computer Science and Technology, Beijing Institute of Technology,
Beijing 100081, China

Abstract. An essential challenge of cooperative multi-agent reinforcement learning lies in boosting the efficiency of communication. However, the full communication mechanism adopted by existing methods would generate large communication costs. Furthermore, the redundant messages might even degrade the collaboration performance. We believe that it is not necessary to share the similar information from continuous observations. Hence we propose a Low-Frequency Multi-Agent Communication (LFMAC) method, which enables agents to learn when to communicate (for both sending and receiving messages) and how to act in a multi-task manner. Concretely, we learn a behavioral policy and a communicational policy for each agent through a multi-head actor network. Then we implement a gating mechanism to cut unnecessary messages, and a communication-skipping trick to reduce communication frequency. In addition, we evaluate LFMAC in a variety of scenarios from StarCraft II micromanagement tasks. The results demonstrate that LFMAC can achieve efficient communication under lower communication costs.

Keywords: Multi-agent reinforcement learning · Cooperation ·
Low-frequency communication

1 Introduction

Recently, a wide range of real-world scenarios require collaborative control of multiple agents, such as autonomous vehicle planning, network packet delivery and sensor networks [1–3]. These scenarios are typically modeled as Cooperative Multi-Agent Reinforcement Learning (Coop-MARL) problems, in which communication could be critical for improving the performance of cooperation.

However, the traditional predefined communication protocols [4,5] are not flexible. The assumption that agents should keep in touch with each other all the

X. Hu—Supported by National Key Research and Development Program of China (2019YFB1405100), National Natural Science Foundation of China (61802380 61802016).

T. Mantoro et al. (Eds.): ICONIP 2021, CCIS 1516, pp. 370–378, 2021.
https://doi.org/10.1007/978-3-030-92307-5_43

time [6–8] would result in huge communication and computation costs. There-fore, ATOC [9] and TarMAC [10] utilize attention mechanisms to weaken the information sharing among agents, but still assume continuous communication over time. In addition, most of the above methods decide whether to use messages after they are delivered, which would cause congestion.

In this work, we aim to improve the efficiency and reduce the cost of communication. We adopt the paradigm of *centralized training with decentralized execution* (CTDE), which can alleviate the non-scalability and non-stationarity problems of MARL simultaneously. We assume that the adjacent observations are similar. Hence, it is enough to communicate every $k(k \geq 1)$ time steps. To this end, we propose a novel Low-Frequency Multi-Agent Communication (LFMAC) framework with a gating mechanism and a communication-skipping trick. Specifically, the method learns a behavioral policy and a low-frequency communicational policy for each agent through a multi-head actor network. It can be seen as a multi-task learning method. Furthermore, the communicational policy specifies the timing of communication and controls the process of sending and receiving messages, so some useless communication can be skipped automatically. In addition, we use a shared channel to integrate information to reduce communication costs and assist decision-making processes.

Finally, we compare LFMAC against multiple benchmark methods in the testbed of StarCraft II micromanagement environment. Experimental results demonstrate that our method can achieve efficient communication under lower communication costs.

2 Related Work

Fully Coop-MARL problems can be formulated as Decentralized Partially Observable Markov Decision Processes (Dec-POMDPs) [11]. A variety of methods can be utilized to solve these problems. The simplest approach is to train independent agents [12], but it doesn't work well in practice [13]. Then the QMIX [14] based on the idea of *value function decomposition* are proposed, which assumes that the individual Q-value functions and the joint Q-value function conform to a monotonicity relationship.

CommNet [6] and BiCNet [7] make their communication channel differentiable by employing continuous communication, but they expose all the local information of all agents and have low scalability. IC3Net [8] uses gating mechanisms to control when to send messages. ATOC [9] controls message sending through an attention mechanism and integrates information through a bi-directional LSTM unit. Similarly, TarMAC [10] uses an attention mechanism to determine both what messages to send and whom to address them. However, the above methods assume continuous communication between agents, which would result in huge communication and computation costs.

Moreover, SchedNet [15] establishes an explicit communication scheduling module. NDQ [16] focuses more on efficient pruning of messages. Gated-ACML [17] attempts to use explicit gating signals to control interactions.

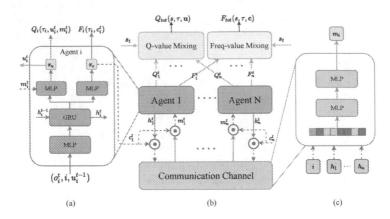

Fig. 1. An overview of LFMAC. (a) Agent network structure. It learns a behavioral policy and a communicational policy. (b) The overall LFMAC framework. Agent i controls the process of sending and receiving messages according to the gating signal c_i, and feeds its individual Q-value and F-value to their respective mixing networks. (c) Shared communication channel structure.

3   Method

In this section, we introduce our LFMAC model. As shown in Fig. 1, LFMAC consists of a tow-head actor network, a Q-value mixing network, a F-value mixing network, and a shared communication channel. Furthermore, it implements a gating mechanism and a communication-skipping trick.

Fistly, assuming that agent i communicates l_i time steps in one episode, and its life length is L_i, then the average frequency $freq_{avg}$ of multi-agent communication can be defined as [18]:

$$freq_{avg} = \frac{1}{|N|} \sum_{i=1}^{|N|} freq_i = \frac{1}{|N|} \sum_{i=1}^{|N|} \frac{l_i}{L_i} \tag{1}$$

Since the survival time of each agent is uncertain, it's infeasible to calculate the average frequency of communication during training. We can achieve the purpose of reducing communication frequency by a communication-skipping trick.

3.1   Multi-task Learning Agents

Multi-task learning uses a shared upstream network to train multiple tasks in parallel to obtain a more generalizable representation. In this paper, LFMAC learns a behavioral policy and a communicational policy for each actor through a two-head DRQN network [19] (see Fig. 1(a)).

At each time step, agent i uses a GRU unit (parameterized by θ_g) to encode its action-observation history:

$$h_i^t = GRU(e(o_i^t, i, u_i^{t-1}), h_i^{t-1}; \theta_g), \tag{2}$$

where o_i, u_i denote the observation and the action of agent i respectively, and h_i denotes the hidden feature of the GRU unit.

Then, an action-value head (parameterized by θ_u, and outputs the Q-value for behavioral policy) estimates the local Q-value function $Q_i(\tau_i, u_i^t, mask(m_i); \theta_g, \theta_u)$ based on the hidden feature h_i^t and received messages m_i (if it has). Meanwhile, the other communication-value head (parameterized by θ_c, and outputs the F-value for communicational policy) estimates a local F-value function $F_i(\tau_i, c_i^t; \theta_g, \theta_c)$.

Note that the communication signal is also a kind of action. The joint F-value function and individual F-value functions naturally satisfy the monotonicity relationship. Similar to QMIX [14], we design a mixing network for each part.

3.2 Communication-Skipping

It is not necessary to share the similar information from continuous observations. Therefore, the communicational policy needs to skip some useless time steps. In LFMAC, the communication-value head uses a periodic decision-making method. To be specific, the parameters of the Q-value network are updated every 1 time step, while the parameters of the F-value network are updated every D time steps and keep fixed during the following D time steps. This mechanism makes the communication discontinuous, thus redundant information could be skipped. Furthermore, the GRU unit is guided by two tasks, so the learned model will be more robust.

3.3 Communication Through a Shared Channel

We use a shared communication channel to integrate messages. Note that for point-to-point communication, a control matrix of $|N| \times |N|$ with a complexity of $O(|N|^2)$ is required. We use the paradigm of broadcast to reduce this complexity to $O(|N|)$. Specifically, for agent i, the received messages are encoded as $m_i = enc(i, h_1 \cdot c_1, ..., h_n \cdot c_n; \theta_e)$ by a two-layer MLP (see Fig. 1(c)).

The message is controlled by a gating signal c_i, which is generated by the communicational policy. Benefiting from the discontinuous communication, the channel is activated only when the gate is open, otherwise it will be frozen, which further reduces calculation costs.

3.4 Centralized Training

The CTDE based framework allows us to add additional global state information during end-to-end training. Therefore, we design centralized mixing networks for Q-value function and F-value function respectively,

$$
\begin{aligned}
Q_{tot} &= Q[Q_1, \ldots, Q_n, s; \theta_{mix_q}], \\
F_{tot} &= F\left[F_1(\tau_1, c_1; \theta_g, \theta_c), ..., F_n(\tau_n, c_n; \theta_g, \theta_c), s; \theta_{mix_f}\right]
\end{aligned}
\tag{3}
$$

where $Q_i \triangleq Q_i(\tau_i, u_i, mask(m_i); \theta_g, \theta_u);$ $\theta_g, \theta_u, \theta_c, \theta_{mix_q}, \theta_{mix_f}$ denote the parameters of the GRU unit, the action selector, the communication action selector, the Q-value mixing network, and the F-value mixing network for each agent respectively.

Finally, we use the *TD loss* to train the LFMAC networks like DQN [20]. For the Q-value function, LFMAC is trained to minimize the MSE loss:

$$\mathcal{L}(\theta_g, \theta_u, \theta_{mix_q}) = \sum_{i=1}^{b} \left[(Q_{tot}(s, \tau, \mathbf{u}; \theta_g, \theta_u, \theta_{mix_q}) - y_i^{tot})^2 \right],$$

$$y^{tot} = r + \gamma max_{u'} Q_{tot}(s', \tau', \mathbf{u}'; \theta_g^-, \theta_u^-, \theta_{mix_q}^-) \tag{4}$$

where b is the batch size of transitions sampled from the replay buffer; and $\theta_g^-, \theta_u^-, \theta_{mix_q}^-$ are the parameters of target networks.

For the F-value function, in order to reduce the communication frequency, we add an additional penalty term as follows:

$$\mathcal{L}(\theta_g, \theta_c, \theta_{mix_f}) = \sum_{i=1}^{b} \left[(F_{tot}(s, \tau, \mathbf{c}; \theta_g, \theta_c, \theta_{mix_f}) - z_i^{tot})^2 + \beta \frac{l_i}{L_i} \right],$$

$$z^{tot} = r + \gamma max_{c'} F_{tot}(s', \tau', \mathbf{c}'; \theta_g^-, \theta_c^-, \theta_{mix_f}^-) \tag{5}$$

where β is a communication penalty factor; l_i / L_i is the communication frequency of agent i; θ_c^- and $\theta_{mix_f}^-$ are the parameters of target networks. The parameters of F-value network are updated every D time steps.

4 Experiments

In this section, we compare the performance of our LFMAC with three baselines in six challenging scenarios from StarCraft II micromanagement tasks.

4.1 Experimental Setup

Environments. Recently, StarCraft Multi-Agent Challenge (SMAC) [21] environment has become a popular decentralized training benchmark for Coop-MARL. It includes a variety of challenging StarCraft II micromanagement scenarios. Table 1 illustrates several hard or super-hard scenarios we used. In these scenarios, each agent needs to decide how to act (move, attack, stop and no-action) based on its local observation within a limited sight range, to defeat the powerful built-in enemy AI. The observation of each agent is a vector composed of relative position, distance, unit type, HP, and other attributes.

In the selected scenarios, influences of different difficulty levels and different agent attributes are taken into account. We adopt the following procedure to estimate each method's performance: for each method, we pause the training every 2000 episodes and run 20 independent testing episodes, and then calculate the average winning rate of ally agents as the intermediate test result.

Table 1. The selected SMAC challenges.

Name	Ally units	Enemy units	Type	Difficulty
5m_vs_6m	5	6	Homogeneous	Hard
2c_vs_64zg	2	64	Homogeneous	Hard
bane_vs_bane	24	24	Heterogeneous	Hard
so_many_banelings	7	32	Homogeneous	Super hard
corridor	6	24	Homogeneous	Super hard
MMM2	10	12	Heterogeneous	Super hard

Baselines. We compared the performance of LFMAC with the following baselines:

- **QMIX.** QMIX is a value decomposition method without communication and performs well in many benchmarks. We use it as a fundamental non-communicating baseline under the CTED architecture.
- **QMIX with Full Communication (QMIX+FC).** We implement a full communication version of QMIX. QMIX+FC is used to compare the impacts of different communication frequencies, and at the same time analyze the negative effects of redundant messages.
- **QMIX+TarMAC.** TarMAC is a communicational MARL method with an attention mechanism. It achieves the state-of-the-art performance in several simple multi-agent communication tasks. TarMAC can be trained more efficiently by combining it with the QMIX architecture [10, 14].

As shown in Sect. 3, our LFMAC model pays more attention to how to reduce redundant information and communication costs through low-frequency communication. We implement this model based on QMIX architecture.

Ablations. We perform ablation experiments to investigate the influence of different communication frequencies. We select three illustrative scenarios that have a normal number (5 to 10) of agents. Then we test the average winning rate of the model under different inference interval D. The parameter D represents a continuous time-step interval, during which agents decide to communicate or not according to the communicational policy. The larger the parameter D is, the sparser the communicational actions will be, that is, the lower the communication frequency will be.

4.2   Main Results

Figure 2 manifests the learning curves of our method ($D = 5$) and baselines. In the selected six scenarios, our method generates the best result. In comparison, the performance of TarMAC is second only to ours, while QMIX has an

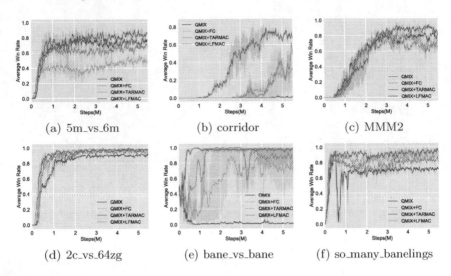

Fig. 2. Learning curves of our method ($D = 5$) and baselines in scenarios that vary in difficulty and agent attributes.

unstable performance: in relatively simple scenarios, QMIX can achieve the same performance as TarMAC, but it performs poorly in arduous tasks.

Specifically, Fig. 2(a), 2(b), 2(d) and 2(e) show the performance of the methods under different difficulties. LFMAC performs much better than methods with non-communication (QMIX) or full-communication (FC). The winning rate of QMIX in super-hard *corridor* scenario is consistently less than 2%. TarMAC is also a continuous communication method, and its performance is even inferior to QMIX in the less formidable scenarios (*5m_vs_6m*), which confirms the negative effects of redundant information. The results show that our low-frequency communication method can improve the effectiveness of cooperation.

We compare the performance in scenarios with different types (Fig. 2(a), 2(b) and 2(c)) or different number (Fig. 2(d), 2(e) and 2(f)) of agents, and the results demonstrate that our method is more robust than the others. It suggests that, for homogeneous multiple agents, sharing messages with each other brings more useful information and thus improving the performance; while for heterogeneous multiple agents, blind communication brings redundant information, which is harmful to the decision-making process.

4.3 Ablation Results

Figure 3 shows the stability of our method under different communication frequencies. To be specific, at a medium frequency ($D = 5$), the method can generally achieve a better performance; a higher communication frequency ($D = 3$) results in a slightly lower performance, indicating that redundant information has a negative impact; sparse communication ($D = 10$) would also make performance worse. The results verify the effectiveness of the communication-skipping technique.

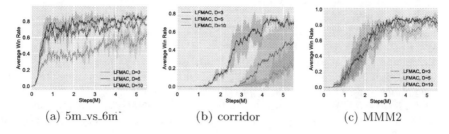

Fig. 3. Learning curves of ablation experiments. The hyperparameter D represents a continuous time-step interval, during which agents decide to communicate all the time or not according to the communicational policy.

In addition, in Fig. 3(a) and 3(b), the performances of different communication frequencies differ greatly in homogeneous multi-agent scenarios. This instability demonstrates the significance of appropriate communication. Figure 3(c) shows that the winning rates of the different approaches are similar in the heterogeneous multi-agent scenario. It suggests that appropriate communication frequency might be more crucial to homogeneous multi-agent tasks.

5   Conclusions

In this work, we propose LFMAC, a novel low-frequency communication method for fully cooperative multi-agent reinforcement learning. We learn a behavioral policy and a communicational policy for each agent through a multi-task learning manner. Furthermore, we adopt a gating mechanism to reduce redundant information and a communication-skipping trick to reduce communication costs.

We evaluate LFMAC in a variety of scenarios from StarCraft II micromanagement environment. The results demonstrate that LFMAC can reduce redundant information using appropriate low communication frequencies. Meanwhile, LFMAC can achieve competitive performances in scenarios with different difficulty levels and agent attributes.

References

1. Cao, Y., Yu, W., Ren, W., Chen, G.: An overview of recent progress in the study of distributed multi-agent coordination. IEEE Trans. Ind. Inf. **9**(1), 427–438 (2012)
2. Ye, D., Zhang, M., Yang, Y.: A multi-agent framework for packet routing in wireless sensor networks. Sensors **15**(5), 10026–10047 (2015)
3. Zhang, C., Lesser, V.: Coordinated multi-agent reinforcement learning in networked distributed pomdps. In: Proceedings of the AAAI Conference on Artificial Intelligence, vol. 25 (2011)
4. Lope, J.D.: Coordination of communication in robot teams by reinforcement learning. Robot. Auton. Syst. **61**(7), 661–666 (2013)

5. Melo, F.S., Spaan, M.T.J., Witwicki, S.J.: QUERYPOMDP: POMDP-based communication in multiagent systems. In: Cossentino, M., Kaisers, M., Tuyls, K., Weiss, G. (eds.) EUMAS 2011. LNCS (LNAI), vol. 7541, pp. 189–204. Springer, Heidelberg (2012). https://doi.org/10.1007/978-3-642-34799-3_13
6. Sukhbaatar, S., Szlam, A., Fergus, R.: Learning multiagent communication with backpropagation (2016). arXiv preprint arXiv:1605.07736
7. Peng, P., et al.: Multiagent bidirectionally-coordinated nets: Emergence of human-level coordination in learning to play starcraft combat games (2017). arXiv preprint arXiv:1703.10069
8. Singh, A., Jain, T., Sukhbaatar, S.: Learning when to communicate at scale in multiagent cooperative and competitive tasks (2018). arXiv preprint arXiv:1812.09755
9. Jiang, J., Lu, Z.: Learning attentional communication for multi-agent cooperation (2018). arXiv preprint arXiv:1805.07733
10. Das, A., et al.: Tarmac: Targeted multi-agent communication. In: International Conference on Machine Learning, pp. 1538–1546. PMLR (2019)
11. Oliehoek, F.A., Amato, C.: A Concise Introduction to Decentralized POMDPs. Springer, Heidelberg (2016). https://doi.org/10.1007/978-3-319-28929-8
12. Tan, M.: Multi-agent reinforcement learning: independent vs. cooperative agents. In: Proceedings of the Tenth International Conference on Machine Learning, pp. 330–337 (1993)
13. Matignon, L., Laurent, G.J., Le Fort-Piat, N.: Independent reinforcement learners in cooperative Markov games: a survey regarding coordination problems. Knowl. Eng. Rev. **27**(1), 1–31 (2012)
14. Rashid, T., Samvelyan, M., Schroeder, C., Farquhar, G., Foerster, J., Whiteson, S.: Qmix: monotonic value function factorisation for deep multi-agent reinforcement learning. In: International Conference on Machine Learning, pp. 4295–4304. PMLR (2018)
15. Kim, D., et al.: Learning to schedule communication in multi-agent reinforcement learning (2019). arXiv preprint arXiv:1902.01554
16. Wang, T., Wang, J., Zheng, C., Zhang, C.: Learning nearly decomposable value functions via communication minimization (2019). arXiv preprint arXiv:1910.05366
17. Mao, H., Zhang, Z., Xiao, Z., Gong, Z., Ni, Y.: Learning agent communication under limited bandwidth by message pruning. In: Proceedings of the AAAI Conference on Artificial Intelligence, vol. 34, pp. 5142–5149 (2020)
18. Mood, A., Graybill, F., Boes, D.: Introduction to the Theory of Statistics, 3rd ed. (1974)
19. Hausknecht, M., Stone, P.: Deep recurrent q-learning for partially observable mdps (2015). arXiv preprint arXiv:1507.06527
20. Mnih, V., et al.: Human-level control through deep reinforcement learning. Nature **518**(7540), 529–533 (2015)
21. Samvelyan, M., et al.: The starcraft multi-agent challenge (2019). arXiv preprint arXiv:1902.04043

A Better Multiway Attention Framework for Fine-Tuning

Kaifeng Hao$^{(\boxtimes)}$, Jianfeng Li, Cuiqin Hou, and Pengyu Li

Ping An Technology (Shenzhen) Co., Ltd, Shenzhen, China
{HAOKAIFENG551,LIJIANFENG777,HOUCUIQIN042,LIPENGYU448}@piangan.com.cn

Abstract. Powerful pre-training models have been paid widespread attention. However, little attention has been devoted to solve downstream natural language understanding (NLU) tasks in fine-tuning stage. In this paper, we propose a novel architecture named multiway attention framework (MA) in fine-tuning stage. Which utilizes a concatenated feature of the first and the last BERT-style model (e.g., BERT, ALBERT) layers, and a mean-pooling feature of the last BERT-style model layer as input. Then it applies four various attention mechanisms on the input features to learn a sentence embedding in phrase-level and semantic-level. Moreover, it aggregates the output of multiway attention, and sends this result to self-attention to learn the best combination scheme of multiway attention for target task. Experimental results on GLUE, SQuAD and RACE benchmark datasets show that our approach can obtain significant performance improvement.

Keywords: Fine-tuning · Sentences representation · Multiway attention

1 Introduction

The "Pre-training and fine-tuning" manner has led to a series of breakthroughs in natural language understanding (NLU) tasks. Powerful pre-training models like BERT [1], XLNet [2], RoBERTa [3], ALBERT [4] have established state-of-the-art (SOTA) on lots of benchmark NLU tasks, which has attracted widespread attention to pre-training models. However, it is also valuable to explore how to solve downstream NLU tasks in fine-tuning stage effectively. Most current models per-form fine-tuning in a straightforward manner like multi-layer perceptron (MLP). Thence, we summarize two significant issues in current fine-tuning stage: richer input features need to be learned and the model architecture is too simple to fully learn the sentence feature. To address these problems, we present a novel multi-way attention framework (MA) involved two strategies as follows:

We transform the input features based on previous researches. Sentence-Bert [5] have demonstrated that mean-pooling of context embeddings from the last

---

Supported by Ping An Technology (Shenzhen) Co., Ltd.

T. Mantoro et al. (Eds.): ICONIP 2021, CCIS 1516, pp. 379–386, 2021.
https://doi.org/10.1007/978-3-030-92307-5_44

BERT layer is consistently better than the [CLS] in siamese network. Thence, we utilize a mean-pooling feature of the last pre-training model layer as one of the model input. Moreover, Jawahar [6] have proposed that BERT encodes semantic-level information in top layers and phrase-level information in bottom layers. According to this result, we utilize a concatenated feature of the first and the last pre-training model layers as another model input for a better sentence representation in phrase-level and semantic-level.

In order to sufficiently learn the pre-training model output layer features, we introduce the attention mechanism [7] which applies on current models widely. Specifically, Tan [8] present a multiway attention network to enhance the performance of matching sentence pairs. However, the model encoder is weak in feature extraction, and the post-processing of multiway attention ignores another sentence information. Moreover, the model cannot handle single-sentence input. Therefore, we extend this model and propose a multiway attention framework: It incorporates pre-training BERT-style model (e.g., BERT, ALBERT) as its shared text encoding layers. Then, we utilize multiway attention and self-attention to learn a better sentence representation in phrase-level and semantic-level. In gen-eral, this framework can construct rich input features from the pre-training model output layer and guide the model to better exploit the sufficient information on the input features. Our contributions of this work are as follows:

- We utilize a mean-pooling feature and a concatenated feature as input of downstream tasks to obtain richer input features.
- We propose a framework based on multiway attention to learn a better sentence embedding in phrase-level and semantic-level. We also utilize self-attention based on multiway attention to learn the best combination scheme of multiway attention for target task.
- We conduct experiments on benchmark corpus: GLUE[9], SQuAD[10] and RACE[11]. Experimental results show that our multiway attention networks obtain universal performance improvement.

2   Related Works

Recent studies enhance the fine-tuning stage from data and architecture, Liu [12] present a Multi-Task Deep Neural Network (MT-DNN) in fine-tuning stage, which learn universal sentence representations across multiple NLU tasks like ERNIE2.0 [13]; Sun [14]conduct series experiments to explore different fine-tuning methods of BERT to provide a general solution for text classification in fine-tuning; Xu [15] propose a curriculum learning approach which is similar to human learning procedure to improve model performance; Nicole [16] propose a novel topic-informed BERT-based architecture named tBERT for pairwise semantic similarity detection. They demonstrate that the addition of topics to BERT helps particularly with resolving domain-specific cases. Our approach belongs to modify architecture, unlike tBERT, we utilize multiway attention in fine-tuning stage.

3   Our Approach

We show the framework In Fig. 1 which consists of four parts. First, we obtain
contextual sentence representation from pre-training model output layer. Then
we gain a mean-pooling feature from the last pre-training model layer, a concatenate feature from the first and the last pre-training model layers as input.
Subsequently, we employ four attention functions to get multidimensional sentence representation from model input. Next, we apply self-attention mechanism
based on the concatenate features of multiway attention result. Finally, we use
mean-pooling to get the result representation and feed it into an MLP for the
final decision.

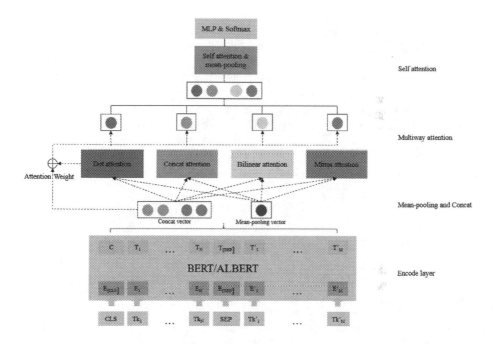

Fig. 1. The framework of BertCA network.

3.1   Encode Layer

We first convert the single sentence or sentence pair to their word-level embeddings and contextual representation by BERT model. We obtain the final hidden
states h_t from the input sequence of N tokens w_t:

$$h_t = BERT(w_t) \tag{1}$$

3.2   Mean-Pooling and Concatenate

We prepare two features for the next multiple attention, the first feature p obtains from the mean-pooling of the last pre-training model layer and the second one q_t aggregates the first and the last pre-training model layers:

$$p = mean - pooling(h_t) \tag{2}$$

$$q_t = [h_1, h_{12}] \tag{3}$$

3.3   Multiway Attention

We design four various attention functions to get multidimensional sentence representation in the architecture, named dot [17], concat [17], bilinear [18] and minus attention. Therefore, we can match each position t of q_t and p using four attention functions:

$$q_t^x = f_x(h^p, h_t^q, W_x) \tag{4}$$

where h^p is the representation of p, h_t^q is the representation of q_t at position t, and q_t^x is the result of attention functions f_x based on the matrix W_x, where $x = (d,c,b,m)$, which represents the dot, concat, bilinear and minus attention, respectively.

Dot Attention:

$$d_t^j = v_d^T tanh(W_d^1(h_j^q \odot h_t^p)) \tag{5}$$

Concat Attention:

$$c_t^j = v_c^T tanh(W_c^1 h_j^q + W_c^2 h_t^p) \tag{6}$$

Bilinear Attention:

$$b_t^j = (h_j^q)^T W_b h_t^p \tag{7}$$

Minus Attention:

$$n_t^j = v_m^T tanh(W_m^1(h_j^q + h_t^p)) \tag{8}$$

$$\alpha_t^i = \frac{exp(g_t^i)}{\sum_{j=1}^N exp(g_t^j)}(g_t^j \in d_t^j, c_t^j, b_t^j, n_t^j) \tag{9}$$

$$q_t^g = \sum_{i=1}^N \alpha_t^i h_i^q (q_t^g \in q_t^d, q_t^c, q_t^b, q_t^m) \tag{10}$$

3.4 Self-attention and MLP

We concatenate the results of multiple attention. Further, the self-attention is used for the aggregative intermediate. Then we get the final sentence representation by mean-pooling. We employ a single layer network as the MLP, we send the final feature to MLP and Softmax for getting the predict result.

$$q_t^r = concat(q_t^d, q_t^c, q_t^b, q_t^m) \tag{11}$$

$$q_t^e = Self - attention(q_t^r) \tag{12}$$

$$u = mean - pooling(q_t^e) \tag{13}$$

$$r = MLP(u) \tag{14}$$

where q_t^r is the aggregative intermediate, q_t^e is the result of self-attention, u is the mean- pooling of q_t^e and r is the result label.

4 Experiments

4.1 Dataset

We run experiments on three NLU benchmarks: GLUE, SQuAD and RACE.

GLUE. It is the standard benchmark providing collections of datasets for NLU tasks.

SQuAD. It is a reading comprehension dataset which collects crowdsourced question-answer pairs from Wikipedia, the task is to predict the answer text span in the passage.

RACE. It is an English reading comprehension dataset of Chinese middle school. It has a larger scale than SQuAD and pays more attention to natural language inference.

We use BERT-style model as our pre-trained language model to demonstrate the effectiveness of our approach, the training was conducted on two NVIDIA Tesla V100 GPUs with a batch size of 32(batch size of 16 on SQuAD and RACE) and learning rate of 2e–5, All training epochs are 3. The initialization method of the parameters is Xavier.

4.2 Result on GLUE

The comparison results of BERT-base [1], BERT (stacking) [19], SesameBERT [20], PPBERT-base [21], ALBERT-base [4] and our model have shown in Table 1. Our multiway attention networks have a proportion of 0.9 % and 0.5 % than BERT-base and ALBERT-base on GLUE test dataset, respectively.

4.3 Result on SQuAD and RACE

The comparison results have shown in Table 2. Our multiway attention networks have a proportion of 0.3 % and 0.4 % than BERT-base and ALBERT-based on

Table 1. The result of our model on GLUE

Model	CoLA	SST2	MRPC	STSB	QQP	MNLI(m/mm)	QNLI	RTE	Average
BERT–base	52.1	92.6	88.9	85.8	71.1	84.1/83.4	90.5	66.4	79.4
BERT(stacking)	**56.2**	93.9	88.2	84.2	70.4	84.4/**84.2**	90.1	67.0	79.8
SesameBERT	52.7	**94.2**	88.9	85.5	70.8	83.7/83.6	91.0	67.6	79.8
PPBERT-base	52.8	93.0	88.6	**87.7**	**71.5**	**84.7**/83.6	**91.1**	67.0	80.0
BERT + MA	54.5	93.2	**89.9**	86.2	71.0	84.0/83.6	**91.1**	**69.5**	**80.3**
ALBERT–base	**57.1**	92.6	89.5	88.4	70.9	83.7/82.5	91.1	70.6	80.7
ALBERT + MA	**57.1**	**93.7**	**90.2**	**88.5**	71.0	**84.0**/83.4	**91.8**	**71.3**	**81.2**

SQuADv1.1 dev dataset, respectively; our model also has a proportion of 0.4 % and 0.5 % than BERT-base and ALBERT-base on SQuADv2.0 dev dataset, respectively; outperforming the ALBERT-base performance by 3.9 % on RACE test dataset.

Table 2. Result on SQuAD and RACE

Model	SQuADv1.1(F1)	SQuADv2.0(F1)	RACE(F1)
BERT–base	88.5	76.9	
BERT+ MA	88.8	77.3	
ALBERT–base	89.9	81.3	66.8
ALBERT+ MA	**90.2**	**81.8**	**70.7**

4.4   Ablation Tests

Effects of Sufficient Input Features. In order to explore a sufficient feature from pre-training model, we propose several methods to replace the [CLS] and conduct series of experiments on benchmark corpus. We utilize a series combination manners on [CLS], the mean-pooling feature of the last pre-training model layer $mean_{12}$ and concatenate feature of the first and the last pre-training model layers $[h_1, h_{12}]$ mentioned above, respectively. According to the result analysis, we find that the attention based on $mean_{12}$ and $[h_1, h_{12}]$ obtains significant performance improvement. Experimental results justify the significance of sufficient input features, which have shown in Table 3.

Effects of Multiway Attention. To certificate the necessity of multiway attention, we conduct ablation tests on two datasets by using single attention based on p and q_t respectively. The result has been shown in Table 4, experimental results show that the multiway attention network performs significant improvement than single attention, which proves that the multiway attention plays a vital role in whole framework.

Table 3. Result on SQuAD and RACE

Model	MRPC	RTE
[CLS]	88.9	66.4
$mean_{12}$	88.3	66.2
$[h_1,h_{12}]$	89.1	68.9
Attention([CLS],$mean_{12}$)	88.8	65.6
Attention([CLS],$[h_1,h_{12}]$)	89.2	69.1
Self-attention([$mean_{12}$, h_1,h_{12}])	88.9	68.0
Attention($mean_{12}$,$[h_1,h_{12}]$)	**89.4**	**69.3**

Table 4. Result on SQuAD and RACE

Model	MRPC	RTE
BERT-base	88.9	66.4
Dot attention	89.3	68.2
Concatenate attention	89.1	68.1
Bilinear attention, $mean_{12}$)	89.0	68.6
Minus attention	89.0	66.4
BERT+ MA	**88.9**	**69.5**

5   Conclusion

In this paper we propose a framework based on multiway attention and self-attention, which can help learn a suitable sentence representation for target task. Experimental results on GLUE, SQuAD and RACE benchmark corpus show that MA can indeed improve pre-training model performance. These also validate our ideas and show that our approach is universal and robust.

References

1. Devlin, J., Chang, M.W., Lee, K., Toutanova, K.: Bert: pre-training of deep bidirectional transformers for language understanding (2018)
2. Yang, Z., Dai, Z., et al.: XLNet: generalized autoregressive pretraining for language understanding. In: NeurIPS (2019)
3. Liu, Y., Ott, M., et al.: Roberta: a robustly optimized BERT pretraining approach (2019). arXiv preprint arXiv:1907.11692
4. Lan, Z., Chen, M., et al.: Albert: a lite bert for self-supervised learning of language representations (2019)
5. Reimers, N., Gurevych, I.: Sentence-BERT: sentence embeddings using Siamese BERT-networks. In: EMNLP-IJCNLP, pp. 2982–3992 (2019)
6. Jawahar, G., Sagot, B., Seddah, D.: What does BERT learn about the structure of language? In: ACL, pp. 3651–3657 (2019)

7. Vaswani, A., Shazeer, N., et al.: Attention is all you need. In: Advances in Neural Information Processing Systems, pp. 5998–6008 (2017)
8. Tan, C., Wei, F., et al.: Multiway attention networks for modeling sentence pairs. In: IJCAI, pp. 4411–4417 (2018)
9. Wang, A., Singh, A., et al.: Glue: a multi-task benchmark and analysis platform for natural language understanding (2018). arXiv preprint arXiv:1804.07461
10. Rajpurkar, P., Jia, R., Liang, P.: Know what you don't know: unanswerable questions for SQuAD. In: ACL, pp. 784–789 (2018)
11. Lai, G., Xie, Q., et al.: RACE: large-scale reading comprehension dataset from examinations. In: EMNLP, pp. 785–794 (2017)
12. Liu, X., He, P., Chen, W., Gao, J.: Multi-task deep neural networks for natural language understanding. In: ACL (2019)
13. Sun, Y., Wang, S., Li, Y.K., Feng, S.: ERNIE 2.0: a continual pre-training framework for language understanding. AAAI **34**(05), 8968–8975 (2019)
14. Sun, C., Qiu, X., Xu, Y., Huang, X.: How to fine-tune BERT for text classification? In: Sun, M., Huang, X., Ji, H., Liu, Z., Liu, Y. (eds.) CCL 2019. LNCS (LNAI), vol. 11856, pp. 194–206. Springer, Cham (2019). https://doi.org/10.1007/978-3-030-32381-3_16
15. Xu, H., Zhang, L., et al.: Curriculum learning for natural language understanding. In: ACL, pp. 6095–6104 (2020)
16. Peinelt, N., Nguyen, D., Liakata, M.: tBERT: topic models and BERT joining forces for semantic similarity detection. In: ACL, pp. 7047–7055 (2020)
17. Luong, T., Pham, H., Manning, C.D.: Effective approaches to attention-based neural machine translation. In: EMNLP, pp. 1412–1421 (2015)
18. Kim, J.-H., Jun, J., Zhang, B.T.: Bilinear attention networks. In: NIPS (2018)
19. Gong, L., He, D., et al.: Efficient training of BERT by progressively stacking, pp. 2337–2346 (2019)
20. Ta-Chun, S., Cheng, H.-C.: Attention for anywhere. DSAA, SesameBERT (2020)
21. Arase, Y., Tsujii, J.: Transfer fine-tuning of BERT with phrasal paraphrases. Comput. Speech Lang. **66**, 101164 (2021)

Task-Driven Super Resolution: Object Detection in Low-Resolution Images

Muhammad Haris[1]([envelope]), Greg Shakhnarovich[2], and Norimichi Ukita[3]

[1] Universitas Nusa Mandiri, Jakarta, Indonesia
muhammad.uhs@nusamandiri.ac.id
[2] Toyota Technological Institute at Chicago, Chicago, USA
greg@ttic.edu
[3] Toyota Technological Institute, Nagoya, Japan
ukita@toyota-ti.ac.jp

Abstract. We consider how image super-resolution (SR) can contribute to an object detection task in low-resolution images. Intuitively, SR gives a positive impact on the object detection task. While several previous works demonstrated that this intuition is correct, SR and detector are optimized independently in these works. This paper analyze a framework to train a deep neural network where the SR sub-network explicitly incorporates a detection loss in its training objective, via a tradeoff with a traditional detection loss. This end-to-end training procedure allows us to train SR preprocessing for any differentiable detector. We demonstrate extensive experiments that show our task-driven SR consistently and significantly improves the accuracy of an object detector on low-resolution images from COCO and PASCAL VOC data set for a variety of conditions and scaling factors.

Keywords: Super-resolution · Object detection · End-to-end learning · Task network · Machine perception · Joint optimization

1 Introduction

Image Super-Resolution (SR) belongs to image restoration and enhancement (e.g., denoising and deblurring) algorithms, widely studied in computer vision and graphics. In both communities, the goal is to reconstruct an image from a degenerated version as accurately as possible. The quality of the reconstructed image is evaluated by pixel-based quantitative metrics such as PSNR (peak signal-to-noise ratio) and SSIM (structure similarity) [15]. Recently-proposed perceptual quality ([2, 14]) can also be employed for evaluation as well as for optimizing the reconstruction model. Relationships between the pixel-based and perceptual quality metrics have been investigated in the literature ([4, 9]) in order to harmonize these two kinds of metrics. Ultimately, the goal of SR is still to restore an image as well as possible in accordance with criteria in human visual perception.

Main work has been done during postdoctoral at TTI Japan.

© Springer Nature Switzerland AG 2021
T. Mantoro et al. (Eds.): ICONIP 2021, CCIS 1516, pp. 387–395, 2021.
https://doi.org/10.1007/978-3-030-92307-5_45

(a) HR   (b) LR   (c) Bicubic SR   (d) SR (no task) (e) TDSR (proposed)
                                PSNR: 21.26   PSNR: 22.02   PSNR: 21.54

Fig. 1. Scale sensitivity in object detection and the effectiveness of our proposed method (i.e., end-to-end learning in accordance with the mutual improvement of SR and object detection tasks). Images shown in the top row show (a) an original high resolution image, (b) its low-resolution image (here 1/8-size, padded with black), (c) SR image obtained by bicubic interpolation, (d) SR image obtained by the SR model optimized with no regard to detection, and (e) SR image obtained by our proposed task-driven SR method, using the same model as in (d). For each of the reconstructed HR images, we also report PSNR w.r.t. the original. Despite ostensibly lower PSNR, the TDSR result recovers the correct detection results with high scores, in this case even suppressing a false detection present in the original HR input.

We propose to bridge this isolation by explicitly incorporating the objective of the downstream task (such as object detection) into training of an SR module. Figure 1 illustrates the effect of our proposed, task-driven approach to SR. Our proposal (e) generated from a low-resolution (LR) image (b) can successfully bring recognition accuracy close to the score of their original high-resolution (HR) image (a).

Our approach is motivated by two observations. (1) SR is ill-posed. Many possible HR images when downsampled produce the same LR image. We expect that the additional cue given by the downstream task objective such as detection may help guide the SR solution. (2) Human perception and machine perception differ. It is known that big differences are observed between human and machine perceptions, in particular, with highly-complex deep networks. Thus, if our goal is to super-resolve an image in part for machine perception, we believe it is prudent to explicitly "cater" to the machine perception when learning SR.

The main contributions of this paper are:

- An approach to SR that uses the power of end-to-end training in deep learning to combine low-level and high-level vision objectives, leading to what we call *Task-Driven Super Resolution* (TDSR). As a means of increasing robustness of SR methods for computer vision tasks, this approach provides results substantially better than other SR methods, and is potentially applicable to a broad range of low-level image processing tools and high-level tasks.
- A simple yet effective view of SR, explicitly acknowledging the generative or semantic aspects of SR in high scaling factors, which we hope will encourage additional work in the community to help further reduce the gap between low-level and high-level vision.
- Extensive experiments to handle more difficult scenarios where the image are afflicted by additional sources of corruption such as blur and noise.

2   Related Work

2.1   Image Super Resolution

A huge variety of image SR techniques have been proposed; see survey papers ([13, 16]) for more details.

Like other vision problems, SR has benefited from recent advances in deep convolutional neural networks (DCNNs). One of most notable work is DBPN-SR ([5]). It shares the SR features at different scales by iterative forward and backward projections and enables the networks to preserve the HR components by learning various up- and down-sampling operators while generating deeper features. While deep features provided by DCNNs allow us to preserve clear high-frequency photo-realistic textures, it is difficult to completely eliminate blur artifacts. This problem has been addressed by introduction of novel objectives, such as perceptual similarity ([2, 7]) and adversarial losses ([3, 17]). Finally, the two ideas can be combined, incorporating perceptual similarity into generative adversarial networks (GANs) in SRGAN ([10]). In contrast to prior work, we explicitly incorporate the objective of a well defined, discriminative task (such as detection) into the SR framework.

2.2   Detection of Small Objects

One of the remaining problems in computer vision, such as object detection and scene parsing, is to detect small objects. This issue has been investigated by ([6, 8]). Most of these methods proposed context-aware network by re-scaling the input to several resolutions then training the networks at each resolution or proposing a mechanism to select the pooling field size to preserve the small details. Here we consider an alternative: transform the LR images into HR images using SR. So that, instead of designing more LR friendly detector, we can try to make LR images "look like HR image", for which we have plenty of examples, in the hope that the existing detector "used to HR" will then be able to detect objects. In other words, rather than improve the detector, we pre-process the input to make it more amenable to the detector as is.

3   Task Driven Super-Resolution

Our method relies on two building blocks: an SR network S and a task network D as shown in Fig. 2. The SR network maps an LR image x^l to an HR image x^h producing an SR image $x^{sr} = S(x^l; \theta_{SR})$, where θ_{SR} denotes all the parameters of the SR network. The task network takes an image x^{sr} and outputs a (possibly structured) prediction $\widehat{y} = D(x^{sr}; \theta_D)$. We refer to these predictors as "networks" because they are likely to be deep neural networks. However our approach does not presume anything about S and D beyond differentiability for training the whole network with an end-to-end learning scheme.

We assume that the task network D has been trained and its parameters θ_D remain fixed throughout training (and will, for brevity, be omitted from notation).

Our method is applicable to any task network. It can be used for a variety of tasks, for example, depth estimation or semantic segmentation. However, in this paper, we

$$L_{rec}(x^h, x^{sr}) \qquad\qquad L_{task}(y, \widehat{y}(x^{sr}))$$

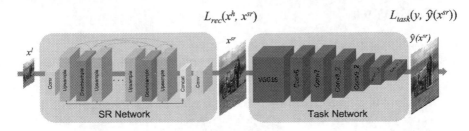

Fig. 2. Network Architecture. Here, we use DBPN ([5]) as an SR network and SSD ([11]) as a task network concatenate to perform end-to-end training.

restrict our attention to the object detection task, in which $\widehat{y}$ consists of a set of scored bounding boxes for given object classes.

3.1 Component Networks

We use the recently proposed Deep Back-Projection Networks (DBPN) [5] as the SR component. The DBPN achieve state of the art or competitive results on standard SR benchmarks, when trained with the MSE reconstruction loss

$$L_{rec}\left(x^h, x^{sr}\right) = \frac{1}{N}\sum_{i=1}^{N}(x_i^h - x_i^{sr})^2 \qquad (1)$$

where i ranges of the N pixel indices in the HR image x^h.

As the detector, we use the Single Shot MultiBox Detector (SSD) [11]. The SSD detector works with a set of default bounding boxes, covering a range of positions, scales and aspect ratios; each box is scored for presence of an object from every class. Given the ground truth for an image x^h, B is the number of matched default boxes to the ground truth boxes y. These matched boxes form the predicted detections $\widehat{y}(x^{sr})$. The task (detection) loss of SSD is combined of confidence loss and localization loss:

$$L_{task}(y, \widehat{y}(x^{sr})) = \frac{1}{B}\left[L_{conf}(y, \widehat{y}(x^{sr})) + \lambda L_{loc}(y, \widehat{y}(x^{sr}))\right] \qquad (2)$$

The confidence loss L_{conf} penalizes incorrect class predictions for the matched boxes. The localization loss L_{loc} penalizes displacement of boxes vs. the ground truth, using smooth L_1 distance. Both losses in (2) are differentiable with respect to their inputs.

Importantly, every default bounding box in SSD is associated with a set of cells in feature maps (activation layers) computed by a convolutional neural network. As a result, since the loss in (2) decomposes over boxes, it is a differentiable function of the network activations and thus a function of the pixels in the input image, allowing us to incorporate this task loss in the TDSR objective described below.

3.2 Task Driven Training

Normally, learning-based SR systems are trained using some sort of reconstruction loss L_{rec}, such as mean (over pixels) squared error (MSE) between x^h and x^{sr}. In contrast, the detector is trained with L_{task} intended to improve the measure of its accuracy, typically measured as the average precision (AP) for one class, and the mean AP (mAP) over classes for the entire data set.

Let x^h be the image with detection ground truth labels y, and x^l is a downscaled image by a fixed factor. We propose the compound loss, which on the example (x^h, y) is given by

$$
\begin{aligned}
L(x^h, y; \theta_{SR}) = & \alpha L_{rec}\left(x^h, S(x^l; \theta_{SR})\right) + \\
& \beta L_{task}\left(y, D(S(x^l; \theta_{SR}); \theta_D)\right)
\end{aligned}
\tag{3}
$$

where α and β are weights determining relative strength of the reconstruction loss and the detection loss. Under the assumption that both S and D are differentiable, we can use the chain rule, and compute the gradient of L_{task} with respect to its input, the super-resolved x^l. Then this per-pixel gradient is combined with the per-pixel gradient of the reconstruction loss L_{rec}. The SR parameters θ_{SR} are then updated using standard back-propagation from this combined gradient:

$$
\begin{aligned}
& \alpha \frac{\partial}{\partial \theta_{SR}} L_{rec}\left(x^h, S(x^l; \theta_{SR})\right) + \\
& \beta \frac{\partial L_{task}\left(y, D(S(x^l); \theta_D)\right)}{\partial S(x^l)} \frac{\partial S(x^l)}{\partial \theta_{SR}}
\end{aligned}
\tag{4}
$$

4 Experimental Results

4.1 Implementation Details

Base networks. DBPN ([5]) constructs mutually-connected up- and down-sampling layers each of which represents different types of image degradation and HR components. The stack of up- and down- projection units creates an efficient way to iteratively minimize the reconstruction error, to reconstruct a huge variety of SR features, and to enable large scaling factors such as 8× enlargement. We used the setting recommended by the authors: "a 8×8 convolutional layer with four striding and two padding" and "a 12×12 convolutional layer with eight striding and two padding" are used for 4× and 8× SRs, respectively, in order to construct a projection unit. Here, we use D-DBPN which is one of DBPN variants. For object detection, we use SSD300 where the input size is 300×300 pixels. The network uses VGG16 through conv5_3 layer, then uses conv4_3, conv7 (fc7), conv8_2, conv9_2, conv10_2, and conv11_2 as feature maps to predict the location and confidence score of each detected object. The code for both networks are publicly accessible in the internet.

Datasets. We initialized all experiments with DBPN model pretrained on the DIV2K data set ([1]), made available by the authors of ([5]). We used SSD network pretrained on PASCAL VOC0712 trainval and MSCOCO train2017. When fine-tuning DBPN in our experiments, with or without task-driven objective, we reused PASCAL VOC0712 trainval and MSCOCO train2017, with data augmentation. The augmentation consists of photometric distortion, scaling, flipping, random cropping that are recommended to train SSD. Test images on VOC2007 test and MSCOCO val2017

Table 1. VOC2007 `test` detection results on 4× and 8×.

Scale	Method	n-iter : w_{td}	PSNR	AP	aero	bike	bird	boat	bottle	bus	car	cat	chair	cow	table	dog	horse	bike	person	plant	sheep	sofa	train	tv
	HR	-	-	75.8	79.3	85.4	74.1	68.9	46.6	83.7	85.5	86.1	59.1	81.3	77.1	83.5	85.2	82.9	77.6	46.7	73.8	79.9	84.8	73.8
	LR	-	-	41.7	48.9	46.8	33.5	31.9	10.7	57.7	48.6	55.9	18.5	31.7	50.1	50.2	61.3	54.2	45.0	18.5	32.8	52.3	33.4	
	Bicubic	-	25.30	41.3	50.9	43.9	37.3	22.0	14.5	53.2	53.9	55.8	18.8	35.6	37.9	52.1	56.9	53.5	49.5	18.7	40.3	51.1	41.8	38.5
	SRGAN	-	23.51	44.6	62.2	45.0	37.0	29.3	15.9	63.0	56.7	44.6	26.5	40.4	46.4	47.9	59.2	52.1	53.1	18.1	40.5	56.9	48.6	47.9
4×	DBPN	-	22.87	41.9	61.3	41.5	34.4	25.4	16.1	57.7	55.1	43.4	28.9	35.6	44.2	40.7	52.4	47.3	50.0	15.6	32.5	59.1	47.0	50.2
	SR-FT	100k : 0	26.65	52.6	59.5	61.7	44.3	33.5	26.5	65.6	63.8	61.2	36.2	45.1	55.5	55.7	67.6	64.3	59.4	21.8	45.3	65.8	58.6	60.2
	SR-FT+	100k : 1 : 0+200k : 1 : 0	26.72	53.6	59.6	62.9	45.0	34.8	28.3	67.3	64.6	60.7	36.7	45.5	57.5	56.4	68.0	67.0	60.0	22.1	47.9	68.0	59.1	60.7
	TDSR	100k : 1 : 0+200k : 1 : 0.01	24.06	62.2	70.6	70.1	55.9	49.4	29.8	71.4	71.1	74.4	41.3	62.6	66.4	69.8	76.1	71.7	67.7	32.8	59.9	71.8	70.9	62.0
	LR	-	-	16.6	23.8	17.6	12.2	11.3	9.09	24.6	26.1	23.5	6.27	14.3	13.7	20.1	20.5	23.5	20.6	9.53	10.3	16.2	15.0	12.9
	Bicubic	-	21.85	11.2	13.6	9.80	10.9	1.71	9.09	12.3	18.9	22.7	9.09	7.41	9.91	18.8	10.8	16.9	16.1	2.42	9.09	5.67	2.60	16.1
	SRGAN	-	18.72	13.4	27.2	10.1	12.3	9.96	6.13	15.8	15.6	15.6	9.39	9.89	8.16	18.6	11.7	13.0	20.5	9.44	10.8	17.1	6.59	19.9
8×	DBPN	-	17.50	10.6	25.0	9.09	10.8	9.54	0.80	16.3	14.7	13.6	3.45	9.09	7.56	12.2	9.09	9.49	13.52	1.96	9.09	16.1	4.55	16.69
	SR-FT	100k : 0	22.77	22.0	32.0	19.3	18.0	10.7	9.60	34.9	34.6	26.4	13.0	14.5	25.1	27.0	22.2	26.9	31.0	9.46	10.9	26.7	18.1	30.3
	SR-FT+	100k : 1 : 0+200k : 1 : 0	22.82	22.9	32.3	24.1	19.7	11.4	9.74	34.8	34.6	27.7	13.3	14.5	24.5	26.7	23.3	28.8	31.9	9.58	11.3	30.1	18.4	30.8
	TDSR	100k : 1 : 0+200k : 1 : 0.01	22.26	37.5	49.3	40.9	30.9	25.9	11.4	51.6	47.8	45.6	15.2	31.5	44.1	41.9	50.3	45.6	47.6	14.4	30.6	46.3	40.3	39.6

Table 2. Results on MSCOCO `val2017`. The bracket values is for (4× : 8×) respectively.

	HR	LR	Bicubic	DBPN	SRGAN	SR-FT	SR-FT+	TDSR
AP@[IoU = 0.50 : 0.95 l area= all]	24.2	(8.2 : 1.9)	(8.1 : 2.0)	(1.2 : 0.1)	(0.6 : 0.1)	(13.7 : 4.4)	(14.1 : 4.8)	(16.7 : 9.8)
AP@[IoU = 0.50 l area= all]	42.2	(15.5 : 4.1)	(14.9 : 3.7)	(2.3 : 0.2)	(1.2 : 0.1)	(24.8 : 8.1)	(25.4 : 8.8)	(30.2 : 18.8)
AP@[IoU = 0.75 l area= all]	24.6	(7.9 : 1.7)	(7.8 : 1.9)	(1.1 : 0.0)	(0.6 : 0.0)	(13.7 : 4.3)	(14.0 : 4.7)	(16.7 : 9.2)
AP@[IoU = 0.50 : 0.95 l area= small]	7.2	(0.2 : 0.0)	(0.9 : 0.1)	(0.1 : 0.0)	(0.1 : 0.0)	(2.0 : 0.3)	(2.2 : 0.3)	(2.7 : 0.7)
AP@[IoU = 0.50 : 0.95 l area= medium]	26.7	(3.8 : 0.4)	(6.5 : 1.2)	(0.9 : 0.0)	(0.4 : 0.1)	(12.8 : 3.3)	(13.2 : 3.6)	(15.8 : 6.7)
AP@[IoU = 0.50 : 0.95 l area= large]	39.4	(19.9 : 4.7)	(17.6 : 5.2)	(2.7 : 0.1)	(1.5 : 0.1)	(27.2 : 11.0)	(28.0 : 11.4)	(31.0 : 20.8)

were used for testing in all experiments. The input of DBPN was a LR image that was obtained by bicubic downscaling the original (HR, 300×300) image from the data set with a particular scaling factor (i.e., $1/4$ or $1/8$ in our experiments, corresponding to 4× and 8× SR).

Training Setting. We used a batch size of 6. The learning rate was initialized to $1e - 4$ for all layers and decreased by a factor of 10 after 2×10^5 iterations for training runs consisting of 300,000 iterations. For optimization, we used Adam with momentum set to 0.9. All experiments were conducted using PyTorch 0.3.1 on NVIDIA TITAN X GPUs.

4.2 Performance on VOC and COCO Dataset

Table 1 shows detailed results per class for comparing our TDSR method to other SR approaches trained on VOC0712 `trainval` and evaluated on VOC2007 `test`, including the baseline bicubic SR, and a recently proposed state-of-the-art SR method (SRGAN [10]). Comparison to SRGAN is particularly interesting since it uses a different kind of objective (adversarial/perceptual) which may be assumed to be better suited for task-driven SR. Note that all the other SR models were just pretrained, and not fine-tuned on Pascal. We also compared results obtained directly from LR images (padded with black to fit to the pretrained SSD300 detector). It is shown that SR-FT+ successfully to have highest PSNR. However, TDSR overpowered other methods for all classes and boosted the performance of LR images.

We see that reduction in resolution has a drastic effect on the AP of the detector, dropping it from 75.8 to 41.7 for 4× and 16.6 for 8× as shown in Table 1. This is presumably due to both the actual loss of information, and the limitations of the detector architecture which may miss small bounding boxes. The performance is not significantly improved by non-task-driven SR methods, which in some cases actually harm it further! However, our proposed TDSR approach obtains significantly better results for both scaling factors, and recovers a significant fraction of the detection accuracy lost in LR.

In accordance with VOC results, the results trained on COCO dataset is also shown the effectiveness of TDSR. Table 2 shows detailed result on COCO eval2017. TDSR is successfully to increase the accuracy of LR images roughly by 100% and 500% for $4\times$ and $8\times$, respectively and outperform other methods. TDSR consistently has better performance than SR-FT+ for most of the classes especially on $8\times$.

4.3   Qualitative Analysis

Figures. 3, 4, and 5 show examples of our results compared with those of other methods. The results for SRGAN ([10]) and SR-FT+ sometimes confuse the detector and recognize it as different object classes, again indicating that optimizing L_{rec} and high PSNR do not necessarily correlate with the accuracy. Meanwhile, unique pattern that produced by our proposed optimization helps the detector to recognize the objects better. Note that the TDSR does produce, in many images, artifacts somewhat reminiscent of those in DeepDream ([12]), but those are mild, and are offset by a drastically increased detection accuracy.

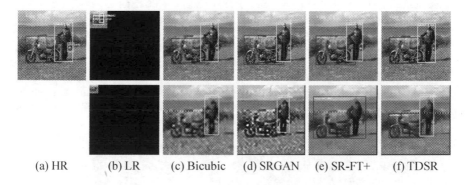

(a) HR   (b) LR   (c) Bicubic   (d) SRGAN   (e) SR-FT+   (f) TDSR

Fig. 3. Sample results for $4\times$ (upper row) and $8\times$ (lower row).

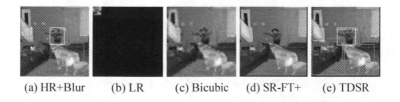

(a) HR+Blur   (b) LR   (c) Bicubic   (d) SR-FT+   (e) TDSR

Fig. 4. Sample results on blur images for $8\times$ (lower row).

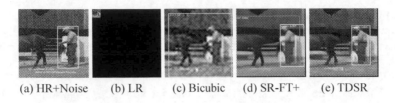

(a) HR+Noise   (b) LR   (c) Bicubic   (d) SR-FT+   (e) TDSR

Fig. 5. Sample results on noise images for $4\times$ (upper row).

5   Conclusions

We have proposed a simple yet effective objective for training SR: a compound loss that caters to the downstream semantic task, and not just to the pixel-wise image reconstruction task as traditionally done. Our results, which consistently exceed alternative SR methods in all conditions, indicate that modern end-to-end training enables joint optimization of tasks what has traditionally been separated into low-level vision (super-resolution) and high-level vision (object detection).

References

1. Agustsson, E., Timofte, R.: Ntire 2017 challenge on single image super-resolution: dataset and study. In The IEEE Conference on Computer Vision and Pattern Recognition (CVPR) Workshops (July 2017)
2. Dosovitskiy, A., Brox, T.: Generating images with perceptual similarity metrics based on deep networks. In: Advances in Neural Information Processing Systems, pp. 658–666 (2016)
3. Goodfellow, I., et al.: Generative adversarial nets. In: Advances in Neural Information Processing Systems, pp. 2672–2680 (2014)
4. Hanhart, P., Korshunov, P., Ebrahimi, T.: Benchmarking of quality metrics on ultra-high definition video sequences. In: 2013 18th International Conference on Digital Signal Processing (DSP), pp. 1–8. IEEE (2013)
5. Haris, M., Shakhnarovich, G., Ukita, N. Deep back-projection networks for super-resolution. In: IEEE Conference on Computer Vision and Pattern Recognition (2018)
6. Hu, P., Ramanan, D.: Finding tiny faces. In: 2017 IEEE Conference on Computer Vision and Pattern Recognition (CVPR), pp. 1522–1530. IEEE (2017)
7. Johnson, J., Alahi, A., Fei-Fei, L.: Perceptual losses for real-time style transfer and super-resolution. In: Leibe, B., Matas, J., Sebe, N., Welling, M. (eds.) ECCV 2016. LNCS, vol. 9906, pp. 694–711. Springer, Cham (2016). https://doi.org/10.1007/978-3-319-46475-6_43
8. Kong, S., Fowlkes, C.: Recurrent scene parsing with perspective understanding in the loop. In: Proceedings of 2018 IEEE Conference on Computer Vision and Pattern Recognition (CVPR) (2018)
9. Kundu, D., Evans, B.L.: Full-reference visual quality assessment for synthetic images: a subjective study. In: 2015 IEEE International Conference on Image Processing (ICIP), pp. 2374–2378. IEEE (2015)
10. Ledig, C., et al. Photo-realistic single image super-resolution using a generative adversarial network. In: IEEE Conference on Computer Vision and Pattern Recognition (CVPR) (July 2017)

11. Liu, W., et al.: SSD: single shot multibox detector. In: Leibe, B., Matas, J., Sebe, N., Welling, M. (eds.) ECCV 2016. LNCS, vol. 9905, pp. 21–37. Springer, Cham (2016). https://doi.org/10.1007/978-3-319-46448-0_2
12. Mordvintsev, A., Tyka, M., Olah, C.: Inceptionism: Going deeper into neural networks. https://research.googleblog.com/2015/06/inceptionism-going-deeper-into-neural.html (June 2015)
13. Nasrollahi, K., Moeslund, T.B.: Super-resolution: a comprehensive survey. Mach. Vis. Appl. **25**(6), 1423–1468 (2014). https://doi.org/10.1007/s00138-014-0623-4
14. Sajjadi, M.S., Schölkopf, B., Hirsch, M.: Enhancenet: single image super-resolution through automated texture synthesis. In: 2017 IEEE International Conference on Computer Vision (ICCV), pp. 4501–4510. IEEE (2017)
15. Wang, Z., Bovik, A.C., Sheikh, H.R., Simoncelli, E.P.: Image quality assessment: from error visibility to structural similarity. IEEE Trans. Image Process. **13**(4), 600–612 (2004)
16. Yang, C.-Y., Ma, C., Yang, M.-H.: Single-image super-resolution: a benchmark. In: Fleet, D., Pajdla, T., Schiele, B., Tuytelaars, T. (eds.) ECCV 2014. LNCS, vol. 8692, pp. 372–386. Springer, Cham (2014). https://doi.org/10.1007/978-3-319-10593-2_25
17. Yu, X., Porikli, F.: Ultra-resolving face images by discriminative generative networks. In: Leibe, B., Matas, J., Sebe, N., Welling, M. (eds.) ECCV 2016. LNCS, vol. 9909, pp. 318–333. Springer, Cham (2016). https://doi.org/10.1007/978-3-319-46454-1_20

Knowledge-Based Multiple Lightweight Attribute Networks for Zero-Shot Learning

Zehuan Zhang[1], Qiang Liu[1(✉)], and Difei Guo[2]

[1] Tianjin Key Laboratory of Imaging and Sensing Microelectronics Technology, School of Mictoelectronics, Tianjin University, Tianjin, China
qiangliu@tju.edu.cn
[2] Tianjin Communication & Broadcasting Group Co., Ltd., Tianjin, China

Abstract. Zero-shot learning aims to recognize unseen objects. From the start of zero-shot learning research, attributes have played an important role. However, previous attribute-based methods do not fully exploit attributes and their relationships. In order to overcome these drawbacks, we propose a new framework. This framework consists of the convolutional neural network, fully connected networks and the attribute knowledge graph to make classification. This framework incorporates knowledge and is suitable for incremental learning. Also, the framework treats different attributes unequally according to their relationships, which further improves the recognition accuracy. Experiments show that this framework has achieved the comparable accuracy on the AWA2 dataset. At the same time, trainable parameters are reduced by about 100 times compared to previous attribute-based methods.

Keywords: Knowledge graph · Zero-shot learning · Attribute

1 Introduction

Recently, zero-shot learning (ZSL) [1] has developed rapidly. The aim of the zero-shot learning algorithm is to recognize classes that are not included in the training set, i.e., the unseen classes. The pioneer work [2] of zero-shot learning makes use of the attributes to infer the labels of unseen classes. Attributes refer to descriptions of certain characteristic of objects, such as shape, color and size. The attribute-based zero-shot learning methods have good interpretability and are appropriate for the domain-specific applications. The early works use attributes independently without considering the relationships among attributes. Also, contributions of the attributes are different, but the early works fail to use attributes discriminately. As a result, the use of attributes is insufficient and accuracy of the early works is low. Most recently, the work [5] proposes that

© Springer Nature Switzerland AG 2021
T. Mantoro et al. (Eds.): ICONIP 2021, CCIS 1516, pp. 396–404, 2021.
https://doi.org/10.1007/978-3-030-92307-5_46

different attributes should be used differently. Following that, work [4,6,7] incorporate the attention mechanism to make zero-shot learning models focus on local parts of images. These works have achieved accuracy improvement, but usually design monolithic models with millions of trainable parameters to incorporate attribute information. Therefore, further exploration of exploiting attributes and reducing trainable parameters is needed.

Inspired by the thinking process [3] of the human brain, we incorporate knowledge into our framework. The framework consists of three parts: feature extraction network, attributes recognition networks and the attribute knowledge graph. The feature extraction network is a convolutional neural network (CNN). The attribute recognition networks are a set of fully connected (FC) networks, each recognizing an attribute. The attribute knowledge graph, representing knowledge, contains the attributes of different classes. During the recognition process, the CNN extracts the features of the input image, then the attribute recognition networks detect the attributes from the features, and finally the attribute knowledge graph is searched to find the class with the most similar attributes. In addition, different attributes are of different importance to different classes, so different attributes are paid attention differently. In this way, deficiencies in the previous attribute-based methods works are overcome and the accuracy of ZSL is further improved. Also, since we use separate attribute networks in our model, the complexity is greatly reduced.

Our work makes the following contributions:

(1) We propose a framework combining convolutional network for feature extraction, a number of small fully connected networks for attribute recognition and knowledge graph to recognize unseen classes. The framework reduces the complexity and training cost of ZSL, and is suitable for incremental learning scenarios.
(2) We propose attribute selection approach to pay more attention on key attributes to improve recognition accuracy.
(3) We evaluate the framework on the AWA2 [1] dataset and compare with the existing approaches. The results show that the framework achieves high accuracy with trainable parameters reduced significantly.

2   Proposed Approach

The proposed framework is comprised of three parts: the convolutional neural network, fully connected networks and the attribute knowledge graph. The structure of the proposed framework is shown in Fig. 1.

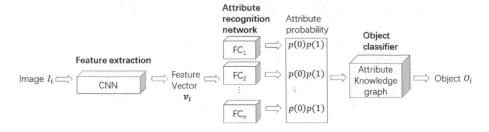

Fig. 1. The structure of the proposed framework

2.1 CNN Feature Extraction

Convolutional neural networks (CNNs) have led to impressive performance on visual recognition tasks. Image features can be extracted by a pre-trained convolutional neural network such as ResNet [14]. In addition, global average pooling (GAP) is proposed by [13], which not only prevents overfitting during training but also reduces the dimensionality of high-dimensional features. Therefore, we use the CNN and the GAP layer to convert images to one-dimensional vectors, which represent the most distinctive features.

In real applications, the pre-trained CNN may be fine-tuned to adapt to specific datasets. We use $CNN(\cdot)$ to denote the convolutional layers, I to denote the input samples, $f_{GAP}(\cdot)$ to denote the global average-pooling operations and V to denote the feature vectors. Then we obtain

$$V = f_{GAP}(CNN(I)) \tag{1}$$

2.2 Attribute Recognition Network

The attribute recognition network detects an attribute from the extracted feature vector. In order to simplify the learning of the attribute recognition network, we use multiple small networks to recognize different attributes. Each attribute is recognized by the corresponding neural network. The number of the networks is the same as the number of attributes. As shown in Fig. 1, each attribute recognition network is a fully connected network, the input of the network is the feature vector, and there are 2 output neurons. The two outputs are transformed to probabilities using the softmax function denoted as $softmax(\cdot)$. The probabilities are represented by $p(1)$ and $p(0)$, which indicate the probabilities of having the attribute and not having, respectively.

The fully connected network has a simple structure, thus greatly reducing training costs. At the same time, such a simple classification model may not perfectly capture all attributes, and the recognition accuracy of some attributes may be low. As will be seen later, the knowledge contained in the knowledge graph can compensate for the low accuracy of attribute recognition.

2.3   Attribute Knowledge Graph

Knowledge graph, represented by a graph data structure, describes things and their relations, in which nodes represent things and edges represent relationships between things. There are also attribute relations in the knowledge graph.

As for zero-shot datasets with attributes labels, such as AWA2 [1], the attribute knowledge graph can be constructed using the classes and their attribute labels. The nodes consist of classes and attributes. The relationship between nodes indicates whether the class contains attributes. The attribute knowledge graph can be shown in the form of bipartite graph. In the bipartite graph, there are two sets of nodes. One set of nodes include classes and the other set of nodes include attributes. There are no edges between two nodes in one set. The edge between two sets indicates that the class contains the corresponding attribute. For example, in Fig. 2, class Cow has three attributes: Patches, Spots and Tail.

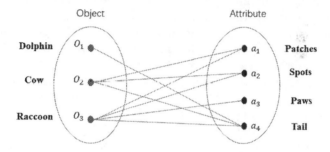

Fig. 2. Toy attribute knowledge graph

2.4   Training and Inference Process

During the training process, all images are transformed by the adopted CNN to one-dimensional feature vectors. When training a certain attribute, images containing the same attribute have the same binary labels. We use $FC_j(\cdot)$ to denote each fully connected layer and use cross-entropy function, denoted as $CE(\cdot, \cdot)$, as the loss function. All classes have binary attribute labels so that the attribute label representation of the i-th class is $a^i = (a_1^i, ..., a_j^i, ..., a_M^i)$. a_j^i is a boolean value and M is the number of attributes. V_i denotes the feature vector of the i-th class. The training loss is the following:

$$Loss = CE(softmax(FC_j(V_i)), a_j^i) \tag{2}$$

In our work, each attribute recognition network is trained separately. When adding new attributes, only the new attribute networks needs to be trained and other networks can be retained, which means that the proposed framework is suitable for incremental learning scenarios.

During the inference process, the feature vectors extracted by CNNs are used as inputs of the trained attribute recognition networks to recognize attributes. With attribute probabilities (i.e. $p(1)$ and $p(0)$) of each image and attribute knowledge of each class in the knowledge graph, we can calculate the sum of the probabilities. If there is an edge between a class node and an attribute node, the probability value $p(1)$ is added; otherwise, the probability value $p(0)$ is added. For each image, the class corresponding to the maximum value is the result as shown in (3), where U is the number of unseen classes.

$$class = \arg\max_{i=1,...U} \sum_{j=1}^{M} p(a_j^i) \tag{3}$$

3　Selective Use of Attributes

Different attributes show different importance to different classes. In other words, different classes may have different key attributes. These key attributes are critical to recognize the classes. In addition, different attributes also show different recognition difficulties. Therefore, the attributes should be treated differently.

The proposed approach selectively uses attributes considering two factors. The first factor is the recognition accuracy of attributes. Some attributes have high recognition accuracy, which is conducive to classification. The recognition accuracy of some attributes may be low, or even lower than the level of random probability. These attributes will have a negative impact on the recognition results. Therefore, our framework is made to focus on attributes with high recognition accuracy.

The second factor is the information amount (IA) of attributes. This factor indicates how important the attribute is to classes for recognition. We use r_i to represent the ratio of classes containing the i-th attribute. r_i can be calculated according to the attribute bipartite graph:

$$r_i = \frac{\#edges\,of\,the\,attribute\,node\,i}{\#number\,of\,class\,nodes} \tag{4}$$

IA can be calculated as entropy:

$$IA_i = -r_i log(r_i) - (1 - r_i)log(1 - r_i) \tag{5}$$

A small entropy value indicates that only a few classes have this attribute, so the contribution of this attribute to classification is significant. For example, a model learns the "stripe" attribute in the training process. Through attribute knowledge graph, we also know that only the "raccoon" class in the test set contains the "stripe" attribute. Therefore, to recognize the "raccoon" class, it is reasonable to pay more attention on the "stripe" attribute. When the image is recognized as containing the "stripe" attribute, it can be classified as "raccoon".

In order to optimize the object recognition accuracy, the attribute network with low recognition accuracy is ignored. Removing these low-accuracy attributes has a two-sided effect. On the one hand, removing low-precision attributes will help improve the overall object recognition accuracy, because the negative effects of attribute misjudgment are removed. On the other hand, removing the attributes also loses the information that these attributes help distinguish the unseen classes. This impact will degrade the overall object recognition accuracy. So this is a trade-off.

Overall, attributes with high recognition accuracy and attributes with low information entropy are helpful for object recognition. Paying more attention to such attributes can improve the overall object recognition accuracy. We select the key attributes with high accuracy and small IA values, and assign a weight greater than 1, denoted as w. This is a hyperparameter in the proposed framework. If the value of w is too small, it is not enough to highlight the key attributes. If the value of w is too large, it will cause the model to pay too much attention to the key attributes and ignore the roles of other attributes.

4 Experiments and Results

The experiments are conducted on the widely used ZSL benchmark AWA2 [1] dataset which contains 37322 images of 50 animal classes with 85 attributes.

We adopt ResNet101 [14] pretrained on ImageNet [15] as the backbone and jointly fine-tune the entire model in an end to end fashion to improve the image representation. We use SGD optimizer [16] and set momentum 0.9. The learning rate is initialized as 10^{-3} and decreased every 10 epochs by a factor of 0.1. We use Xeon CPU E5-2630 v4 (2.20GHz) to conduct experiments.

4.1 Zero-Shot Learning Results

We evaluate the proposal approach following conventional ZSL setting [1]. We use the average recognition accuracy of unseen classes to evaluate the performance as stated in [1].

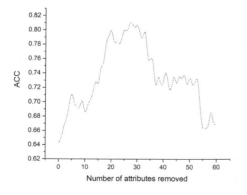

Fig. 3. Influence of attributes removal on object recognition accuracy

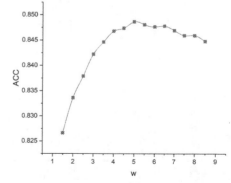

Fig. 4. Influence of attribute weights on object recognition accuracy

The results are shown in Table 1. We compare our approach with attribute-based models and cross-modal embedding models.

The proposed approach is implemented in three versions. We call them as the "naive version", "selective version" and "selective and attention version".

Firstly, we implement the approach without differentiating attributes, denoted as "ours_naive" in Table 1. Each attribute is used equally. The object recognition accuracy is 64.2%.

Secondly, we sequentially remove attributes with low attribute recognition accuracy and observe the changes in object recognition accuracy of the test set. The object accuracy varies as shown in Fig. 3. The accuracy increases initially and decreases finally, which shows that removing attributes has a two-sided effect as mentioned in Sect. 3. The best accuracy can reach 80.9%. We denote this version as "ours_select". This result also means if the recognition accuracy of all attributes is high, then the overall accuracy can be improved.

Thirdly, the key attributes, which have high attribute recognition accuracy and low information entropy, are assigned with the same weight. The value of the weight determines the impact of key attributes on the object recognition accuracy. As shown in Fig. 4, we set the value of weight w incrementally. The object recognition accuracy shows a trend of increasing initially and then decreasing. The object recognition accuracy increases first because when the model pays more attention to the key attributes, the object accuracy of the model will

Table 1. Comparison of accuracy and trainable parameters

Methods	Accuracy(%)	Trainable Parameters(Millions)
DAP [2]	58.7	–
IAP [2]	46.9	–
CONSE [4]	67.9	–
SSE [19]	67.5	–
LATEM [18]	68.7	–
ALE [10]	80.3	–
DEVISE [8]	68.6	–
SJE [11]	69.5	–
ESZSL [12]	75.6	–
SYNC [17]	71.2	–
SAE [9]	80.7	–
SGMA [4]	83.5	80.89
AREN [6]	86.7	61.73
LFGAA+Hybrid [7]	84.3	42.51
ours_naive	64.2	0.35
ours_select	80.9	0.35
ours_select_attention	84.9	0.35

increase. However, as the weight is further increased, the model excessively magnifies the importance of key attributes and ignores other attributes, leading to reduced object recognition accuracy. When the weight w is set as 5.0, the accuracy reaches 84.9%. We denote this version as "ours_select_attention".

Table 1 shows the accuracy and model size (the number of trainable parameters) of three versions of our approach and some existing approaches for ZSL. Among the three versions, the third version achieves the best accuracy. Compared to the existing approaches, our approach achieves the comparable accuracy, but significantly reduces the model size by two orders of magnitudes. Our approach uses a lightweight network architecture to achieve comparable accuracy with the help of knowledge.

5   Conclusion

In this work, we design a ZSL framework that combines feature extraction, attribute recognition and attribute knowledge graph. We use multiple lightweight networks to recognize attributes and make classification using attributes and their relationships contained in the attribute knowledge graph. Our framework achieves comparable accuracy and greatly reduces the neural network model size.

Acknowledgment. This work was supported in part by the National Natural Science Foundation of China under Grant 61974102.

References

1. Xian, Y., Lampert, C.H., Schiele, B., Akata, Z.: Zero-shot learning - a comprehensive evaluation of the good, the bad and the ugly. IEEE Trans. Pattern Anal. Mach. Intell. **41**(9), 2251–2265 (2019)
2. Lampert, C.H., Nickisch, H., Harmeling, S.: Attribute-based classification for zero-shot visual object categorization. IEEE Trans. Pattern Anal. Mach. Intell. **36**(3), 453–465 (2014)
3. Zeithamova, D., Schlichting, M.L., Preston, A.R.: The hippocampus and inferential reasoning: building memories to navigate future decisions. Front. Human Neurosci. **6**(70), 1–14 (2012)
4. Zhu, Y., Xie, J., Tang, Z., et al.: Semantic-guided multi-attention localization for zero-shot learning. arXiv preprint arXiv:1903.00502 (2019)
5. Guo, Y., Ding, G., Han, J., et al.: Zero-shot learning with attribute selection. In: AAAI, pp. 6870–6877 (2018)
6. Xie, G.S., Liu, L., Jin, X., et al.: Attentive region embedding network for zero-shot learning. In: CVPR, pp. 9384–9393 (2019)
7. Liu, Y., Guo, J., Cai, D., et al.: Attribute attention for semantic disambiguation in zero-shot learning. In: CVPR, pp. 6698–6707 (2019)
8. Frome, A., Corrado, G., Shlens, J., et al.: Devise: A deep visual-semantic embedding model. In: NIPS, pp. 2121–2129 (2013)
9. Kodirov, E., Xiang, T., Gong, S.: Semantic autoencoder for zero-shot learning. In: CVPR, pp. 3174–3183 (2017)

10. Akata Z, Perronnin F, Harchaoui Z., et al.: Label-embedding for attribute-based classification. In CVPR, pp. 819–826 (2013)
11. Akata, Z., Reed, S., Walter, D., et al.: Evaluation of output embeddings for fine-grained image classification. In CVPR, pp. 2927–2936 (2015)
12. Romera-Paredes, B., Torr, P.: An embarrassingly simple approach to zero-shot learning. In PMLR, pp. 2152–2161 (2015)
13. Lin, M., Chen, Q., Yan, S.: Network in network. arXiv preprint arXiv:1312.4400 (2013)
14. Kaiming, H., Xiangyu, Z., Shaoqing, R., Jian, S.: Deep residual learning for image recognition. In: CVPR, pp. 770–778 (2016)
15. Deng, J., Dong, W., Socher, R., et al.: Imagenet: a large-scale hierarchical image database. In: CVPR, pp. 248–255 (2009)
16. Bottou, L.: Large-scale machine learning with stochastic gradient descent. In: COMPSTAT 2010, pp. 177–186 (2009)
17. Changpinyo, S., Chao, W.L., Gong, B., et al.: Synthesized classifiers for zero-shot learning. In: CVPR, pp. 5327–5336 (2016)
18. Xian, Y., Akata, Z., Sharma, G., et al.: Latent embeddings for zero-shot classification. In: CVPR, pp. 69–77 (2016)
19. Zhang, Z., Saligrama, V.: Zero-shot learning via semantic similarity embedding. In: CVPR, pp. 4166–4174 (2015)

Detecting Anomaly Features in Facial Expression Recognition

Zhu Liu[1,2], Tingsong Ma[1], Yuanlun Xie[1], Hengxin Zhang[1], Jian Wang[1],
and Wenhong Tian[1,2(✉)]

[1] School of Information and Software Engineering, University of Electronic Science
and Technology of China, Chengdu, China
{leo.z.liu,201811090811,201911090911,hengxincheung,
201921090217}@std.uestc.edu.cn, tian_wenhong@uestc.edu.cn
[2] Yangtze Delta Region Institute (Huzhou), University of Electronic Science
and Technology of China, Huzhou 313001, China

Abstract. In facial expression recognition task, humans and machines
may give very different result on the same facial expression image. To
solve this problem, this paper analyzes the reason that causes this phenomenon. Our research find that expression features of anomaly samples
often deviate from standard expression features, which makes the recognition results different from that of human's. In order to detect anomaly
of facial expression, we propose Emo-Encoder Network (EEN), which
consists of three modules: feature extractor, classifier and anomaly detector. Feature extractor is used to extract facial expression features. Based
on extracted features, we can get classification results by classifier and
anomaly degree by anomaly detector, where classification results denotes
what kind of expression is, while anomaly degree displays how likely is
this expression anomaly. To demonstrate our idea, we build a mixed
dataset consisting of images collected from the Internet as well as the
RAFDB dataset, and we relabel them with anomaly labels. Through our
experiments, our model achieve anomaly detection accuracy of **87.09%**
on the mixed dataset. We find that expressions with high classification
confidence cannot be directly adopted as the final results, unless the
results is at high confidence and low anomaly degree.

Keywords: Facial expression recognition · Anomaly features ·
Emo-encoder network · Machine understanding

1 Introduction

Facial expression recognition (FER) technology has become a major research
direction in the field of computer vision. A large amount of researchers has proposed advanced models on FER, however, the judgments of many expressions

This research is partially supported by National Key Research and Development Program of China with ID 2018AAA0103203.

T. Mantoro et al. (Eds.): ICONIP 2021, CCIS 1516, pp. 405–413, 2021.
https://doi.org/10.1007/978-3-030-92307-5_47

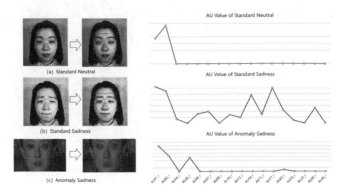

Fig. 1. Action Units (AU) features' comparison between standard pictures and anomaly pictures. The AU features are extracted by OpenFace [1], and features of standard neutral expression and anomaly sadness expression are highly similar.

models in the wild are still controversial. The problem reflects that machine and humans are inconsistent on FER. However machine judgment sometimes is also very reasonable. For example, in Fig. 1, human can easily distinguish standard neutral and anomaly sadness, but machine give them the same prediction due to similar features. Those anomaly expressions like Fig. 1 affect the unified standard of human and machine judgement, and have a serious impact on machine understanding. In this paper, we define the anomaly expression as the expression with similar features of another expression. And we use anomaly degree to tell how much a facial expression features deviates from the typical expression. According to the previous observation, we notice that the pure expression recognition technology has limited ability to discriminate anomaly expressions.

To solve the above-mentioned human-machine divergence problem on FER, we design Emo-Encoder network (EEN) to detect anomaly expressions. EEN consists of 3 modules, feature extractor, classifier and anomaly detector.

In general, the main contributions of this paper are presented as follows:

(1) An EEN method is proposed to determine whether an expression images have anomaly feature distribution or not.
(2) This paper, for the first time, establishes an anomaly facial expression dataset to verify facial expressions' anomaly degree. According to action units (AU) extracted by the Facial Action Coding System (FACS) [3], we can analyse which image is deviated from standard expression, then relabel images with anomaly labels. The anomaly degree of a given facial expression is defined as the degree of the features of given expression deviating from the standard features.
(3) The EEN detection method is verified. EEN achieves anomaly detection accuracy of 87.09% on our collected dataset.

2   Related Work

The features of anomaly expression reflect an anomaly data distribution. For example, the normal neutral expressions and the anomaly sad expressions in Fig. 1

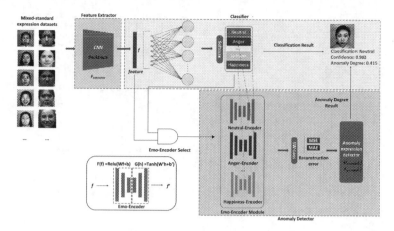

Fig. 2. The pipeline of Emo-Encoder network. Emo-Encoder consists of three module: feature extractor, classifier, anomaly detector.

have extremely similar data distributions. Some scholars view such a situation as the consequence of high inter-class similarity and high intra-class variance. Some work has been carried out in this direction. Wen et al. [9] propose center loss for face recognition. Cai et al. [2] propose a novel island loss to enhance the discriminative power of deeply learned features. Some scholars also believe that noisy labels cause this recognition error problem. Veit et al. [8] propose multi-task network to clean noisy annotations and classify images. This paper focuses on anomaly expression recognition from the level of features distribution of expression images.

3   Emo-Encoder Network

Our main goal is to recognize anomaly facial expressions images, this work proposes a simple yet efficient network framework EEN (Emo-Encoder Network). In this section, we first introduce the overview of EEN, and then explain our method in details. Emo-Encoder Network consists of three module: feature extractor, classifier and anomaly detector (as shown in Fig. 2). Firstly, a batch of face images is fed into the CNN model for extracting features. Secondly, the output features from the CNN backbone will be classified. Thirdly, the facial feature is also fed into Emo-Encoder module for reconstructing error, and the result of reconstruction error is calculated by MSE and MAE. The EEN network will calculate the anomaly degree of the facial expression image through the anomaly detector module by using the reconstruction error.

3.1   Emotion Classifier and Feature Extractor

The first step of EEN is to train an expression classifier with CNN. In order to obtain standard facial features and reduce the noise influence of the facial expression datasets, this paper only uses the expression datasets in the laboratory environment to train the classifier. In this way, the expression classifier will

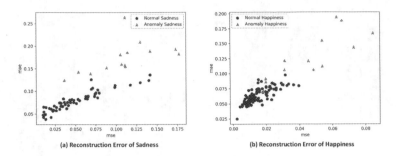

Fig. 3. A comparison chart of the reconstruction error of expression features. The red triangles represent anomaly data and the blue dots represent normal data. (a) is a comparison of reconstruction errors of sadness expressions, and (b) is a reconstruction error of happiness expressions.

have high accuracy and good feature performance. The second step of EEN is to build an expression feature extractor. With reference to feature-based transfer learning, we freeze the parameters of the last fully-connected (FC) layer and previous layers of CNN classifier as a feature extractor for facial expression. Let $\mathbf{X} = [\mathbf{x}_1, \mathbf{x}_2, \ldots, \mathbf{x}_N] \in R^{D \times N}$ denote the facial features with D dimension of N images for network input. Classifier and feature extractor can be formulated as:

$$C_{out} = softmax(F_{extractor}(\mathbf{W}_a^\top \mathbf{x}_i)), \tag{1}$$

Where C_{out} is result of facial expression classifier, $\mathbf{W}_a$ represents the trained parameters in the CNN backbone, and $F_{extractor}$ represents the feature extractor.

3.2   Anomaly Detector Module

The Emo-Encoder module is the most important part of anomaly detector. Emo-Encoder is constructed by under-complete AutoEncoder, and each Emo-Encoder matches corresponding facial expression category. EEN is not a end-to-end model. So in order to build Emo-Encoder module, we firstly train feature extractor, then train seven Emo-Encoders to learn feature distribution of seven standard expression features from feature extractor.

$F = [f_1, f_2, ..., f_n]$ is facial expression features with n dimension extracted by $F_{extractor}$, The encoder encodes f from high-dimension into a low-dimensional hidden representation $h = [h_1, h_2, ..., h_m]$ by a function $E(.)$

$$h = E(f) = Relu(Wf + b) \qquad f' = G(h) = Tanh(W'h + b') \tag{2}$$

where the encoder is parameterized by weight matrix W and a bias vector b. f' represents a reconstruction mapped by hidden representation h through function $G(.)$, weight matrix W' and bias vector b' are combined into parameters of the decoder.

Anomaly detector module can compute the anomaly degree of expression features by reconstruction error, and learn the overall distribution of pure expression features. The main way of reconstruction error is using Mean Absolute Error

Table 1. Metrics comparison of different traditional CNNs on facial expression database.

CNN	JAFFE			CK+			JAFFE & CK+		
	acc	F1	mAP	acc	F1	mAP	acc	F1	mAP
MobileNetV2	98.94	99.26	99.13	99.75	99.75	99.69	99.42	99.23	99.41
MobileNet	97.64	98.94	99.26	-	-	-	99.21	99.14	99.52
VGG19	-	-	-	96.26	97.21	95.23	98.40	99.20	99.35
ResNet50	-	-	-	-	-	-	99.32	99.14	99.30

(MAE) and mean square error (MSE) function. MAE and MSE functions are used as error functions in the model. MAE and MSE function are given by:

$$E_{MAE}(f) = \frac{1}{n}\sum_{i=0}^{n}|f_i - f_i'| \qquad E_{MSE}(f) = \frac{1}{n}\sum_{i=0}^{n}(f_i - f_i')^2 \qquad (3)$$

When training the Emo-Encoder module, the switch-loss is used as its loss function to ensure that the reconstruction error has reached the state of convergence. The loss function switch-loss will be changed in training phase. With the training progress going on, the loss function E_{MSE} will be switched to E_{MAE} when the loss value exceeds a threshold σ.

Finally, the anomaly degree of the entire feature is calculated by the anomaly degree formula. Let $F_{AE} = [f_1, f_2, ..., f_n]$ represent each facial feature of facial expression dataset, which can be obtained through the feature extractor.

$$MAE_{avg} = \frac{1}{n}\sum_{i=1}^{n}E_{MAE}(f_i) \qquad MSE_{avg} = \frac{1}{n}\sum_{i=1}^{n}E_{MSE}(f_i) \qquad (4)$$

MAE_{avg} and MSE_{avg} is the mean anomaly degree of dataset, represents standard facial expression features. In prediction, anomaly degree of a facial expression can be formulated as:

$$\mathcal{D}_{anomaly}(x) = \alpha\frac{E_{MAE}(x)}{MAE_{avg}} + \beta\frac{E_{MSE}(x)}{MSE_{avg}} \qquad (5)$$

$$F_{anomaly}(x) = \begin{cases} 1, & \text{if } \mathcal{D}_{anomaly}(x) > \delta_d \\ 0, & \text{otherwise} \end{cases} \qquad (6)$$

α and β are hyperparameters for $\mathcal{D}_{anomaly}(x)$, whose default values are both set to 0.5. $\mathcal{D}_{anomaly}(x)$ represents the degree of features deviating. δ_d is a threshold for judging anomaly, which default value is 1.0. $F_{anomaly}(x)$ is a function that determines whether the input is anomaly, 1 and 0 denote anomaly and normal, respectively.

4   Experiments

In this section, we first introduce our datasets. Subsequently, we compare the results of the expression classifiers among different CNNs, and then search the

Table 2. Comparison of the results using different parameter settings in test datasets. Those hyperparameters are explained in formula 5 and 6. More parameters have been set, only better one is shown in the table.

Dataset	α	β	δ_d	Acc
AffectNet	0.5	0.5	1.0	56.41
AffectNet	0.5	0.5	1.1	43.59
AffectNet	0.3	0.7	1.0	84.61
Mixed-dataset	0.5	0.5	1.0	**87.09**
Mixed-dataset	0.3	0.7	1.3	70.96

best CNN backbone to implement the Emo-Encoder module. Finally, we evaluate the detection performance and show the performance of this EEN.

4.1   Datasets

Dataset for Classifier: Both CK+ [5] and JAFFE [6] datasets come from datasets in a constrained lab environment, with complete facial expressions and no occlusion issues. In order to obtain pure facial features and improve the generalization ability of the model, we obtain new training set for classifier to train by merging CK+ and JAFFE, new test set is created by the same way.

Test Set for EEN: In order to obtain a anomaly expression test set, this paper collects actual images from the Internet. RAF-DB [4] is used as a supplement. Because images of RAF-DB contain composite expressions, have more anomaly features, and has annotation based on FACS. Mixed-dataset has a total of 251 images, in which anomaly images accounts for 12%, this satisfies that the proportion of anomaly data is small in overall data. To further verify our results, we also re-annotated the data from AffectNet [7] and selected 180 high-confidence images, including 21% anomaly images. According to degree of features extracted by FACS deviating from standard features, anomaly degree labels are marked.

4.2   Classifier and EEN Verification

Table 1 has shown comparisons of different CNN backbones, we can observe that MobileNetV2 shows the best accuracy performance with less parameters.

After verifying the above-mentioned CNNs, we use MobileNetV2 to implement EEN. First, we train an expression classifier, then freeze the parameters of model as an expression feature extractor. Next, we use the CK+ and JAFFE data to train the Emo-Encoder module with the features output from the extractor. Then, seven separate Emo-Encoders are adopted for seven different expressions, respectively, where seven different MSE_{avg} and MAE_{avg} are calculated to represent the degree of each standard expressions anomaly degree in a laboratory environment. In prediction, we classify test set with classifier, and then use the

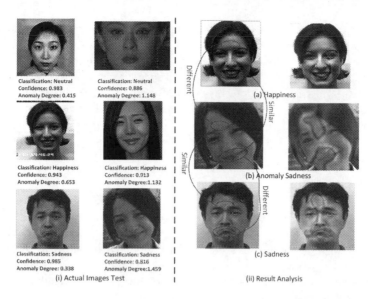

Fig. 4. Actual images test and result analysis. (i) is actual images test. Text marked with green is normal facial expression (column 1), and text marked with red is facial expression with anomaly feature distribution (column 2). Confidence refers to the output of the softmax layer after the image is evaluated by classifier model. (ii) is result analysis. Column 3 shows facial action units' status in standard and anomaly facial expression. Column 4 shows feature's heatmap in standard and anomaly facial expression.

input and output of Emo-Encoder to calculate the E_{MSE} and E_{MAE} with formula 3. Finally we calculate the anomaly degree according to the formula 5. Through experimental calculations, the average MSE_{avg} of various expressions is 0.068, and the MAE_{avg} is 0.091, which represent average standard facial features anomaly degree. Some test results are shown in Table 2.

It can be seen from Fig. 3 that there is a significant gap between normal expressions and anomaly expressions. Therefore, after reconstructing error by the Emo-Encoder module, MAE and MSE of anomaly facial features are far from that of the standard features. So, we reconstruct error with Emo-Encoder module, then calculate the anomaly degree of the facial expression image, by using which the model is able to distinguish the anomaly image.

From the results of Fig. 4(i) Actual Images Test, we can know that, when a result is in the case of high confidence and low anomaly degree, this result should be adopted, but not just high confidence. In Fig. 4(ii) Result Analysis, we analyse some reasons for facial expression anomaly degree. For the facial action units, anomaly expressions contain several standard expressions features. For example, anomaly sadness in (b) contains frowning and mouth-lifting, but mouth-lifting in (b) is similar to that of happiness in (a), and frowning is similar to that of sadness in (c). For the heat map, the main peaks of (b) are concentrated between the eyebrows and mouth, the peaks of (a) are concentrated on the mouth and nose, and the peaks of (c) are concentrated on the eyebrows. The focus area of the heat map in (b) overlaps (a) and (c). From the overall view of facial action units and heat maps, anomaly expressions and normal expressions have great similarities, but there are also obvious differences. When α and β in formula 5 are set to 0.5, and the judgment threshold of anomaly degree σ_d in formula 6 is set to 1.0, the anomaly degree judgment result of mixed dataset can achieve an accuracy of **87.09%**. Some parameters settings are shown in Table 2.

5   Conclusion

This paper proposes Emo-Encoder network (EEN) to detect expression images with anomaly feature distribution. First, we use facial expression datasets in the lab to train classifier. Then, we freeze model's parameters to get feature extractor. Following, we design a anomaly detector with Emo-Encoder module, and calculate the anomaly degree of facial expression images. Then, we carry some experiments on test actual images in the wild to verify results. This paper believes that the decision-making and judgment of artificial intelligence have limitations, and the results need a anomaly degree detector module to judge. It should be adopted when the result is at high confidence and low anomaly degree. In the future, we will use more datasets to improve and verify our method, and apply our achievement to improve FER performance, or other fields.

References

1. Baltrusaitis, T., Zadeh, A., Lim, Y.C., Morency, L.P.: Openface 2.0: facial behavior analysis toolkit. In: 2018 13th IEEE International Conference on Automatic Face and Gesture Recognition, FG 2018, pp. 59–66. IEEE (2018)
2. Cai, J., Meng, Z., Khan, A.S., Li, Z., O'Reilly, J., Tong, Y.: Island loss for learning discriminative features in facial expression recognition. In: 2018 13th IEEE International Conference on Automatic Face and Gesture Recognition, FG 2018, pp. 302–309. IEEE (2018). https://doi.org/10.1109/fg.2018.00051
3. Friesen, E., Ekman, P.: Facial action coding system: a technique for the measurement of facial movement. Palo Alto **3**(2), 5 (1978)
4. Li, S., Deng, W., Du, J.: Reliable crowdsourcing and deep locality-preserving learning for expression recognition in the wild. In: Proceedings of the IEEE Conference on Computer Vision And Pattern Recognition, pp. 2852–2861 (2017)
5. Lucey, P., Cohn, J.F., Kanade, T., Saragih, J., Ambadar, Z., Matthews, I.: The extended Cohn-Kanade dataset (CK+): a complete dataset for action unit and emotion-specified expression. In: 2010 IEEE Computer Society Conference on Computer Vision and Pattern Recognition-Workshops, pp. 94–101 (2010)
6. Lyons, M., Kamachi, M., Gyoba, J.: Japanese female facial expression (JAFFEE) database (2017). https://doi.org/10.21090/ijaerd.0105116
7. Mollahosseini, A., Hasani, B., Mahoor, M.H.: AffectNet: a database for facial expression, valence, and arousal computing in the wild. IEEE Trans. Affect. Comput. **10**(1), 18–31 (2017). https://doi.org/10.1109/taffc.2017.2740923

8. Veit, A., Alldrin, N., Chechik, G., Krasin, I., Gupta, A., Belongie, S.: Learning from noisy large-scale datasets with minimal supervision. In: Proceedings of the IEEE Conference on Computer Vision and Pattern Recognition, pp. 839–847 (2017)
9. Wen, Y., Zhang, K., Li, Z., Qiao, Yu.: A discriminative feature learning approach for deep face recognition. In: Leibe, B., Matas, J., Sebe, N., Welling, M. (eds.) ECCV 2016, Part VII. LNCS, vol. 9911, pp. 499–515. Springer, Cham (2016). https://doi.org/10.1007/978-3-319-46478-7_31

A Heterogeneous Collaborative Filtering Model for Social Recommendation

Wenzhuo Huang, Xuntian Yan, Zhen Yan, and Jinkui Xie[✉]

School of Computer Science and Technology, East China Normal University,
Shanghai, China
{elop,Tino,51205901033}@stu.ecnu.edu.cn, jkxie@cs.ecnu.edu.cn

Abstract. With the rapid development of social networks, many social recommender algorithms based on graph neural networks have been proposed to improve the performance of recommender systems. However, there are two problems with these models. First, many methods fail to consider the heterogeneity between social interaction and user-item interaction. Second, when modeling item representation, they fail to consider high-order neighbor information in the social graph. In order to address the above problems, in this paper, we propose a Heterogeneous Social Collaborative Filtering model based on graph convolutional network (HSCF), which extracts the high-order collaborative signals of nodes in the social space and interaction space, respectively, so that the heterogeneity of node representation can be fully considered. Moreover, when modeling item embedding, we consider the high-order social neighbors' information to enhancing item representation. Comprehensive experiments on two real-world datasets show that our proposed model outperforms the state-of-the-art baselines.

Keywords: Social network · Recommender system · Graph convolutional network · Collaborative filtering

1 Introduction

In social recommendation, there are two kinds of interaction data: user-user social relationship and user-item interaction. As shown in Fig. 1, user-user and user-item interactions can be treated as graph-structured data. Therefore, graph neural networks (GNNs), especially graph convolutional networks (GCNs) as powerful graph learning methods, have been widely applied in social recommendations [3,13,14]. In GNNs, the representation of a node is calculated by recursively extracting the embedding of its neighbor nodes.

However, there are two problems with these methods. First, these approaches fail to consider the heterogeneity between user-user and user-item interaction. User-user interactions represent social relationships, while user-item interaction represent user's preferences for items. Second, they do not take the user's social relationship into account when modeling the embedding of items. As shown in Fig. 1, each item is not only influenced by users that interact with it but also by

© Springer Nature Switzerland AG 2021
T. Mantoro et al. (Eds.): ICONIP 2021, CCIS 1516, pp. 414–421, 2021.
https://doi.org/10.1007/978-3-030-92307-5_48

Fig. 1. An illustration of user-item and user-user interaction

high-order social neighbors of the users. For example, although i_4 is not directly connected to u_2, i_4 may be affected by u_2 because there are two paths $u_2 - u_4 - i_4$ and $u_2 - u_5 - i_4$. Therefore, u_2 is also useful for modeling the embedding of i_4 to ensure that user's high-order social neighbors are used for item embedding learning.

In order to address the above problems, we propose a Heterogeneous Social Collaborative Filtering model (HSCF) to extract high-order collaborative signals in the social space and the interaction space by GCNs, respectively. Specifically, for each user or item, his information is obtained from two parts: social space aggregation and interaction space aggregation. Social space aggregation extracts high-order neighbor information in the social graph, and interaction space aggregation extracts high-order neighbor information in the user-item interaction graph. So our main contributions in this paper can be summarized as follows:

- We propose an HSCF model to extract high-order collaborative signals hidden in social and user-item interaction graph, respectively. In this way, the heterogeneity between user-user and user-item interaction can fully considered.
- We highlight the importance of high-order social neighbors for item embedding learning. When modeling item embedding, we not only aggregate information of the users that interact with it but also extract high order social neighbors' information of these users.

2   Related Work

Collaborative filtering (CF) [8,11] algorithms assume that users with similar characteristics may prefer similar items. By treating user-item interaction as a bipartite graph, Many algorithms [2,5,12] applies a graph convolutional network on the bipartite graph to modeling user and item embeddings.

However, most users only have a little interaction data, and CF suffers from data sparsity issues [1]. So many social recommendation algorithms have been proposed [3,4,6,9,13,14]. GraphRec [3] adopts a graph neural network to model user embedding from user-item interaction and user-user relationship and then unifies them as the user's final representation. However, it only considers the node's first-order neighbors. DiffNet [14] adopts a graph convolutional network to extract user's high-order collaborative information in the social graph.

DiffNet++ [13] extracts the high-order information from social network and interaction graph in a unified model for user embedding learning.

3   The Proposed Framework

3.1   Problem Formulation

let $U = \{1, 2, \ldots, n\}$ and $I = \{1, 2, \ldots, m\}$ denote the sets of users and of items, respectively. Let $R \in \mathbb{R}^{n \times m}$ denotes the user-item interaction matrix. The social matrix can be represented as $S \in \mathbb{R}^{n \times n}$. In the social matrix S, where $s_{ij} = 1$ indicates user u_i trusts u_j in the social network and $s_{ij} = 0$ otherwise. In the user-item interaction matrix R, where $r_{ij} = 1$ denotes u_i is interested in item v_j, otherwise $r_{ij} = 0$. Besides, users are associated with rich auxiliary information (e.g., user profile), we adopt attribute matrix $X \in \mathbb{R}^{n \times d1}$ to denote it. Also, item attribute matrix can be denoted as $Y \in \mathbb{R}^{m \times d2}$. So we can summarize the problems studied in this article as follows:

> **Input:** the user-item interaction R, user social matrix S, user attribute matrix X and item attribute matrix Y.
> **Output:** $\hat{R} = f(R, S, X, Y)$, where $\hat{R}$ represents users' predicted preferences to items.

3.2   The Architecture of the Model

The main framework of our proposed model is shown in Fig. 2. The model mainly consists of four parts. We describe each part in detail as follows.

Embedding Layer. We randomly initialize $P \in \mathbb{R}^{n \times d}$ and $Q \in \mathbb{R}^{m \times d}$ to represent the free embeddings of users and items, d is embedding size. Given the IDs of user u or item i, embedding layer outputs latent vector p_u or q_i.

Fusion Layer. For each user u, by feeding free embedding p_u and her associated attribute vector x_u, the fusion layer outputs her initial embedding representation e_u^0.

$$e_u^0 = g(W_1 \times [p_u, x_u]) \tag{1}$$

where $g(x)$ is an activation function, W_1 is a transformation matrix, and $[p_u, x_u]$ is the concatenation operation. Similarly, for each item i, the initial embedding representation e_i^0 is modeled as:

$$e_i^0 = g(W_2 \times [q_i, y_i]) \tag{2}$$

Diffusion Layer. By feeding the initial embedding e_u^0 of user u and the initial embedding e_i^0 of item i into diffusion layer, the diffusion layer takes advantage of GCN to aggregate high-order neighbor information in the social and interaction graph, respectively. The initial embedding $e_u^{S,0}$ ($e_u^{I,0}$) of user u in the social space (interaction space) is set to e_u^0. Similarly, the initial embedding $e_i^{S,0}$ ($e_i^{I,0}$)

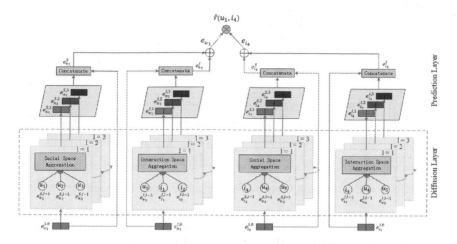

Fig. 2. The overall architecture of our proposed model

of item i in the social space (interaction space) is also set to e_i^0. For each user u or item i, his information is obtained from two parts: social space aggregation and interaction space aggregation.

Social Space Aggregation: For each user u, given her embedding $e_u^{S,l}$ after l-th layer convolution in social space, the (l+1)-th layer embedding of user u in social space is modeled as:

$$e_u^{S,l+1} = w_3 e_u^0 + w_4 \sum_{v \in S_u} \frac{1}{\sqrt{|S_u||S_v|}} (e_v^{S,l} + e_v^{S,l} \odot e_u^{S,l}) \tag{3}$$

where S_u and S_v denote the set of user u's social neighbors and user v's social neighbors, respectively. w_3 and w_4 denote the aggregation weight. $\odot$ denotes the element-wise multiplication. For item node, it only exists in the user-item interaction graph. In order to extract its high-order collaborative signals in the social graph, we aggregate the high-order social neighbor information of the users that interact with it. Specifically, for each item i, given its embedding $e_i^{S,l}$ after l-th layer convolution in social space and the l-th layer embedding $e_u^{S,l}$ of users that interact with the item i in social space, the (l+1)-th layer embedding of item i in social space is modeled as:

$$e_i^{S,l+1} = w_3 e_i^0 + w_4 \sum_{u \in N_i} \frac{1}{\sqrt{|N_u||N_i|}} (e_u^{S,l} + e_u^{S,l} \odot e_i^{S,l}) \tag{4}$$

where N_u represents the user u's neighbor set in the interaction graph, N_i denotes item i's neighbor set in the interaction graph, $e_i^{S,l}$ denotes l-th layer embedding of item i in social space.

Interaction Space Aggregation: In order to extract the high-order collaborative signals of nodes in interaction graph, for each user u, given her embedding $e_u^{I,l}$

Table 1. Dataset statistics

Statistics	Yelp	Flickr
#users	17237	8358
#items	38342	82120
#ratings	204448	314809
#trusts	143765	187273
#rating density (%)	0.031	0.046
#trust density (%)	0.048	0.268

after l-th layer convolution in interaction space and the l-th layer embedding $e_i^{I,l}$ of items that are interacted with user u in interaction space, the (l+1)-th layer embedding of user u in interaction space is modeled as:

$$e_u^{I,l+1} = w_3 e_u^0 + w_4 \sum_{i \in N_u} \frac{1}{\sqrt{|N_u||N_i|}} (e_i^{I,l} + e_i^{I,l} \odot e_u^{I,l}) \qquad (5)$$

For each item i, given its embedding $e_i^{I,l}$ after l-th layer convolution in interaction space and the l-th layer embedding $e_u^{I,l}$ of users that interact with item i in interaction space, the (l+1)-th layer embedding of item i in interaction space is modeled as:

$$e_i^{I,l+1} = w_3 e_i^0 + w_4 \sum_{u \in N_i} \frac{1}{\sqrt{|N_u||N_i|}} (e_u^{I,l} + e_u^{I,l} \odot e_i^{I,l}) \qquad (6)$$

Prediction Layer. For each user u, after propagating with l layers, her embedding in social space is represented as: $e_u^S = [e_u^{S,0}||e_u^{S,1}||...||e_u^{S,l}]$ that concatenates her embedding in social space at each layer. Similarly, her embedding in interaction space is denoted as: $e_u^I = [e_u^{I,0}||e_u^{I,1}||...||e_u^{I,l}]$. The final representation of user u is denoted as: $e_u = e_u^S + e_u^I$. Similarly, the final representation of item i can be denoted as: $e_i = e_i^S + e_i^I$, where $e_i^S = [e_i^{S,0}||e_i^{S,1}||...||e_i^{S,l}]$ and $e_i^I = [e_i^{I,0}||e_i^{I,1}||...||e_i^{I,l}]$. The predicted rating of user u to item i is modeled as: $\hat{r}_{ui} = e_u^T e_i$.

3.3   Model Training

Like diffnet++, we also adopt a ranking based loss function [10] to training:

$$L = \min_\theta \sum_{(u,i) \in R^+ \cup (u,j) \in R^-} - \ln \sigma(\hat{r}_{ui} - \hat{r}_{uj}) + \lambda ||\Theta||^2 \qquad (7)$$

where $\sigma(x)$ is an activation function, λ is the trade-off parameter to avoid model overfitting. R^+ represents positive sample data (observed user-item interactions) and R^- represents negative sample data (sampled from unobserved user-item interactions). θ represent all parameters used in the method.

Table 2. Performance comparison

Dataset	Method	HR@N			NDCG@N		
		N = 5	N = 10	N = 15	N = 5	N = 10	N = 15
Yelp	TrustSVD	0.1906	0.2915	0.3693	0.1385	0.1738	0.1983
	GraphRec	0.1915	0.2912	0.3623	0.1279	0.1812	0.1956
	DiffNet	0.2276	0.3461	0.4217	0.1679	0.2118	0.2307
	DiffNet++	0.2503	0.3694	0.4493	0.1841	0.2263	0.2497
	HSCF	**0.2737**	**0.3984**	**0.4818**	**0.2035**	**0.2484**	**0.2735**
Flickr	TrustSVD	0.1072	0.1427	0.1741	0.0970	0.1085	0.1200
	GraphRec	0.0931	0.1231	0.1482	0.0784	0.0930	0.0992
	DiffNet	0.1210	0.1641	0.1952	0.1142	0.1273	0.1384
	DiffNet++	0.1412	0.1832	0.2203	0.1269	0.1420	0.1544
	HSCF	**0.1592**	**0.2063**	**0.2494**	**0.1426**	**0.1594**	**0.1736**

4 Experiments

4.1 Experimental Settings

Datasets. We evaluate the performance of our method on Yelp and Flickr datasets provided in DiffNet [14]. These two datasets have been introduced in detail in DiffNet. The statistics of the two datasets are shown in Table 1.

Baselines. We compare with the following baseline algorithms to fully show the performance of our proposed model:

- **TrustSVD** [4]. Based on the SVD++ [7], TrustSVD further integrates explicit and implicit effect of social neighbors.
- **GraphRec** [3]. GraphRec adopts a graph neural network to unify user's representations learned from interaction graph and social graphs as the final user's representation.
- **DiffNet** [14]. In order to learn the user's latent embedding, DiffNet designs a graph convolutional network to extract user's high-order information from user's social relationship and enhances user embedding by considering the influence of items that are interacted with her.
- **DiffNet++** [13]. DiffNet++ extracts the high-order information hidden from social and interaction graph in a unified model for user embedding learning.

Evaluation Metrics. We adopt Hit Ratio (HR) and Normalized Discounted Cumulative Gain (NDCG) commonly used in ranking prediction tasks to evaluate the effect of models. These two evaluation metrics are defined as follows:

$$HR = \frac{hits}{N}, NDCG = \frac{DCG}{IDCG} \tag{8}$$

Implementation Details. To train our model, we randomly split 80% of datasets as the training set, 10% as the validation set, and the remaining 10% as the test set. All activation functions are sigmoid functions. For each positive sample, we randomly select four negative samples from the unobserved data for training. In order to reduce the calculation time, We randomly select 1000 unrated items as negative samples and then mix them with the positive data in test set to evaluate the performance. Through our experiment, we set the embedding size d to 64, the trade-off parameter λ to 0.01, and the convolution layers l to 3. w_3 and w_4 are set to 0.5. The learning rate is set to 0.0005. The parameters of all baseline algorithms are adjusted to achieve the best results.

4.2   Performance Comparison

We compared the proposed method with other algorithms on two datasets. The experimental results are shown in Table 2. According to the result, we have the following observations:

- Compared with GraphRec and DiffNet, our model performs better. GraphRec only models the user embedding from the user's first-order neighbors, ignoring the high-order relationship between nodes. DiffNet only models user's high-order social information in social networks, ignoring the user's latent collaborative interest hidden in interaction graph. Therefore, it is necessary to consider the high-order information of users in both the social graph and the interaction graph.
- Compared with DiffNet++, our model improves NDCG@10 by 9.77% and 12.25% on Yelp and Flickr datasets, respectively. This is because our model considers the heterogeneity between user-user interaction and user-item interaction when modeling user embedding. Moreover, when modeling item embedding, we also aggregate the high-order social neighbors' information of the users that interact with it.

5   Conclusion

In order to consider the heterogeneity of user-user interaction and user-item interaction, we propose a Heterogeneous Social Collaborative Filtering model based on graph convolutional network (HSCF) that learns the embedding of users and items in social subspace and interaction subspace, respectively. In particular, when learning the embedding of an item, we propose to extract collaborative information of the high-order social neighbors of users interacting with it in the social subspace. Experimental results show that our HSCF model outperforms state-of-the-art methods on two real-world datasets.

In many fields, users and items are associated with rich auxiliary information. Therefore, we plan to consider more side information to further enhance performance in the future.

References

1. Adomavicius, G., Tuzhilin, A.: Toward the next generation of recommender systems: a survey of the state-of-the-art and possible extensions. IEEE Trans. Knowl. Data Eng. **17**, 734–749 (2005)
2. Berg, R.V.D., Kipf, T.N., Welling, M.: Graph convolutional matrix completion (2017). arXiv preprint arXiv:1706.02263
3. Fan, W., et al.: Graph neural networks for social recommendation. In: The World Wide Web Conference, WWW 2019, San Francisco, CA, USA, 13–17 May , 2019. pp. 417–426. ACM (2019)
4. Guo, G., Zhang, J., Yorke-Smith, N.: TrustSVD: collaborative filtering with both the explicit and implicit influence of user trust and of item ratings. In: Proceedings of the Twenty-Ninth AAAI Conference on Artificial Intelligence, pp. 123–129. AAAI Press (2015)
5. He, X., Deng, K., Wang, X., Li, Y., Zhang, Y., Wang, M.: LightGCN: simplifying and powering graph convolution network for recommendation. In: Proceedings of the 43rd ACM International conference on research and development in Information Retrieval, SIGIR, pp. 639–648. ACM (2020)
6. Jamali, M., Ester, M.: A matrix factorization technique with trust propagation for recommendation in social networks. In: Proceedings of the 2010 ACM Conference on Recommender Systems, RecSys, pp. 135–142. ACM (2010)
7. Koren, Y.: Factorization meets the neighborhood: a multifaceted collaborative filtering model. In: Proceedings of the 14th ACM International Conference on Knowledge Discovery and Data Mining, pp. 426–434. ACM (2008)
8. Koren, Y., Bell, R.M., Volinsky, C.: Matrix factorization techniques for recommender systems. Computer **42**, 30–37 (2009)
9. Ma, H., Yang, H., Lyu, M.R., King, I.: SoRec: social recommendation using probabilistic matrix factorization. In: Proceedings of the 17th ACM Conference on Information and Knowledge Management, CIKM, pp. 931–940. ACM (2008)
10. Rendle, S., Freudenthaler, C., Gantner, Z., Schmidt-Thieme, L.: BPR: Bayesian personalized ranking from implicit feedback. In: Bilmes, J.A., Ng, A.Y. (eds.) UAI 2009, Proceedings of the Twenty-Fifth Conference on Uncertainty in Artificial Intelligence, pp. 452–461. AUAI Press (2009)
11. Sarwar, B.M., Karypis, G., Konstan, J.A., Riedl, J.: Item-based collaborative filtering recommendation algorithms. In: Proceedings of the Tenth International World Wide Web Conference, WWW, pp. 285–295. ACM (2001)
12. Wang, X., He, X., Wang, M., Feng, F., Chua, T.: Neural graph collaborative filtering. In: Proceedings of the 42nd ACM International Conference on Research and Development in Information Retrieval, SIGIR, pp. 165–174. ACM (2019)
13. Wu, L., Li, J., Sun, P., Hong, R., Ge, Y., Wang, M.: DiffNet++: a neural influence and interest diffusion network for social recommendation. IEEE Trans. Knowl. Data Eng. (2020). https://doi.org/10.1109/TKDE.2020.3048414
14. Wu, L., Sun, P., Fu, Y., Hong, R., Wang, X., Wang, M.: A neural influence diffusion model for social recommendation. In: Proceedings of the 42nd ACM International Conference on Research and Development in Information Retrieval, SIGIR, pp. 235–244. ACM (2019)

Combining Pretrained and Graph Models for Text Classification

Kaifeng Hao[✉], Jianfeng Li, Cuiqin Hou, Xuexuan Wang, and Pengyu Li

Ping An Technology (Shenzhen) Co., Ltd., Shenzhen, China
{HAOKAIFENG551,LIJIANFENG777,HOUCUIQINO42,WANGXUEXUAN445,
LIPENGYU448}@piangan.com.cn

Abstract. Large-scale pretrained models have led to a series of break-throughs in Text classification. However, Lack of global structure information limits the performance of pertrained models. In this paper, we propose a novel network named BertCA, which employs Bert, Graph Convolutional Networks (GCN) and Graph Attention Networks (GAT) to handle the task of text classification simultaneously. It aims to learn a rich sentence representation involved semantic representation, global structure information and neighborhood nodes features. In this way, we are able to leverage the complementary strengths of pretrained models and graph models. Experimental results on R8, R52, Ohsumed and MR benchmark datasets show that our model obtains significant performance improvement and achieves the state-of-the-art results in four benchmark datasets.

Keywords: Pertrained models · Graph models · Semantic representation · Global structure information

1 Introduction

Text classification is a basic task in natural language processing (NLP). Multiple deep learning models have been applied to text classification tasks, such as Convolutional Neural Networks [1] (CNN); Recurrent Neural Networks [2] (RNN) and Long Short-Term Memory [3] (LSTM). Recently, the pretrained models (e.g., Bert, GPT-2 and GPT-3) have led to a series of breakthroughs in NLP tasks and obtain state-of-the-art (SOTA) results. Although the pretrained model can obtain contextual sentence representation, it could not process the long text input well and lack global structure information. To addressing this problem, we introduce the Graph Neural Networks (GNN) in this paper.

Recently, GNN has attracted widespread attention. It is effective in NLP tasks which require massive relations and can preserve global structure information in graph embeddings. Graph Convolutional Networks [4] (GCN) can capture high order structure information by combining GNN and CNN. Graph Attention Networks [5] (GAT) introduce the attention mechanism to compute the

Supported by Ping An Technology (Shenzhen) Co., Ltd.

T. Mantoro et al. (Eds.): ICONIP 2021, CCIS 1516, pp. 422–429, 2021.
https://doi.org/10.1007/978-3-030-92307-5_49

hidden representations of each node in the graph by attending over its neighborhood. Thence GCN and GAT can enhance the structure information in different dimensions. However, GCN-style models (such as TextGCN [6]) use one-hot representation to initialize word and document nodes features, This manner will make node features lack semantic level information. Lin [7] proposes BertGCN to solve this problem. This network uses the hidden layer embeddings of Bert [8] as initial nodes features, However, as the increasing of hidden layers, there is still a problem of over-smooth. In GAT model, neighborhood nodes can enhance the center node embedding, This will increase the divergence between nodes and non-adjacent nodes and address the over-smooth. Therefore, we employ Bert, GCN and GAT to handle the task of text classification simultaneously. In this way, we are able to leverage the complementary strengths of pretrained models and graph models.

In this paper, we propose a novel network named BertCA, which employs GCN to learn global structure information based on the hidden layer embeddings of Bert, and computes the hidden representation of each node through GAT for avoiding over-smooth. The result of GAT is treated as a significant weight contained structure information, which is combined with [CLS] embeddings for the final decision. Our work is summarized as follows:

- We propose BertCA, a novel model which combines the powers of pre-trained models and graph networks for text classification.
- The experimental results show that BertCA achieves the state-of-the-art results in several text classification tasks.

2   Related Works

Pretrained Models. Recently researchers have discovered the advantages of combining pretrained models (PTMs) learned on large-scale datasets with downstream models for text classification tasks. Early PTMs focused on learning context-free word embeddings, such as GloVe [9], which aims to obtain global vectors for word representation, GloVe has push lots of models to SOTA on similarity tasks and named entity recognition. Then ELMo [10], which pretrain on a large text corpus and learn functions of the internal states of a deep bidirectional language model. ELMo significantly improve the state of the art across six challenging NLP problems and take a significant step toward context-aware word embeddings.

With the emergence of the Transformer [11], GPT [12] and Bert have brought text classification tasks into a new era. These models focus on modifying the Transformer decoder and encoder, respectively. Later, XLNet [13] learns contextual feature by maximizing the expected likelihood over all permutations of the factorization order and employs transformer-XL to overcome the length limitations of BERT. RoBerta [14] finds that Bert is significantly undertrained and robustly optimizes the training procedure of Bert based on random mask and massive amount corpus. ALBert [15] presents factorized embedding parameterization and cross-layer parameter sharing for reducing the number of parameters and increasing the training speed of Bert. In a word, powerful pretrained models have greatly promoted the development of NLP.

Graph Models. Models mentioned above already have outstanding performance in processing text classification tasks. However, these models lack ability of learning global structure information. GCN can capture the relationship between graph nodes, this structured graph networks also provide a new perspective for others NLP tasks.

TextGCN is a successful example, which addresses the text classification problem by learning the document-word relationship in the text graph based on word co-occurrence. However, the word and document nodes in graph are initialized with straightforward manner like one-hot representations. Different with TextGCN, The nodes of BertGCN are initialized with the output vector of Bert hidden layer. It combines the advantages of both PTMs and GCN, and achieve SOTA results in this manner. Although several GCN models give outstanding performance, the model has unnecessary complexity and redundant computation. SGC [16] reduces the complexity by converting the nonlinear into linear transformation which not only matches GCN in performance, but it is also faster. Our work is inspired by the work of BertGCN, unlike BertGCN, we employ both GCN and GAT models in the same network.

3   Our Approach

We show the network framework in Fig. 1. Our network employ Bert-style model (e.g., Bert, RoBerta) to initialize the nodes features in text graph, which are used as input of GCN. Then the output of GCN is treated as input for GAT, and the document representations will be iteratively updated based on GCN and GAT, respectively. The outputs of GAT will be sent to softmax function and make a hadamard product with the [CLS] feature of Bert-style models. Finally we add this feature with initial [CLS] feature like Resnet [17], and send the final sentence representation to classifier for predictions. In this manner, we obtain a sentence representation with semantic-level and global structure information which content high order neighborhood nodes information.

3.1   Bulid Graph

We construct a text graph containing word and document nodes following TextGCN. We define word-document edges by the term frequency-inverse document frequency (TF-IDF), and construct word-word edges based on positive point-wise mutual information (PPMI). The weight of an edge between two nodes i and j is defined as:

$$A_{i,j} = TextGCN(i,j) \tag{1}$$

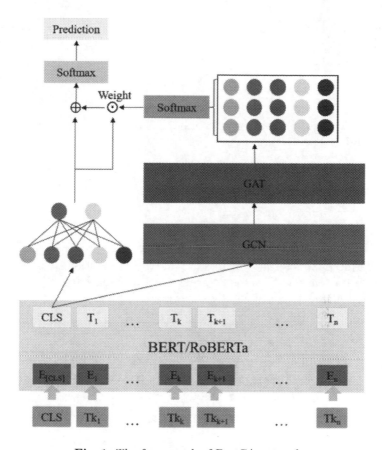

Fig. 1. The framework of BertCA network.

3.2   Bert Layer

We first apply the Bert model to convert the input sentence to word-level embeddings and contextual representation. We obtain the final hidden states h_t from the input sequence of N tokens w_t, and the first [CLS] token is sent to multi-layer perceptron (MLP) for getting the processed feature f_{cls}:

$$h_{cls}, h_i = BERT(w_i) \tag{2}$$
$$f_{cls} = MLP(h_{cls}) \tag{3}$$

3.3   GCN Layer

We replace the node feature with the f_{cls} and feed it into GCN model. The output feature matrix of the i-th GCN layer L^1 is computed as:

$$L^i = \sigma(\overline{A}L^{i-1}W^i) \tag{4}$$

Where σ is the activation function, $\overline{A}$ is the normalized adjacency matrix and W^i is the weight matrix. $L^0 = f_{cls}$ is the initial input of the graph network and we utilize one layer GCN in our network.

3.4 GAT Layer

We feed the output of GCN layer as the input of GAT model. The output feature matrix is updated as:

$$\alpha_{i,j} = \frac{exp(LeakyReLU(\alpha^T W h_i \| W h_j))}{\sum_{k \in N_i} exp(LeakyReLU(\alpha^T W h_i \| W h_j))} \tag{5}$$

$$h_i' = \sigma(\frac{1}{K} \sum_{k=1}^{K} \sum_{j \in N_i} \alpha_{i,j}^k W^k h_j) \tag{6}$$

Where α is the parameter matrix, σ is the activation function, K is the number of multi-head attention, N_i is the adjacent node of node i and W is the weight matrix. We apply one layer GAT in our network.

3.5 Output Layer

We employ softmax function to normalize the output of GAT. Then we make a hadamard product with the f_{cls} and the normalize matrix. Finally we add this feature with f_{cls} to get the final decision:

$$W_g = softmax(GAT(GCN(f_{cls}, A))) \tag{7}$$
$$R = f_{cls} * W_g + f_{cls} \tag{8}$$

4 Experiments

4.1 Dataset

Our experiments employ four benchmark datasets: R8, R52, Ohsumed and Movie Review (MR). The scale and metrics of datasets are detailed in Table 1:

R8. It is a text classification data set containing 8 kinds of labels. Which source is the finance news and it is part of the benchmark dataset ApteMod.

R52. It is a text classification data set containing 52 kinds of labels. Which source is the finance news and it is other part of the benchmark dataset Apte-Mod.

Ohsumed. The OHSUMED dataset contains the titles and abstracts of 270 medical journals during the five years from 1987 to 1991. Which consists of 8 fields.

MR. It is a movie review classification data set containing two types of labels, and the difference between these movie reviews is obvious.

Table 1. An example of three line table

Dataset	Docs	Training	Test	Words	Nodes	Classes	Average length
R8	7674	5485	2189	7688	15362	8	66
R52	9100	6532	2568	8892	17992	52	70
Ohsumed	7400	3357	4043	14157	21557	23	136
MR	10662	7108	3554	18764	29426	2	20

We use BERT and RoBERTa as our pretrained models, and employ GCN and GAT as the graph models. First, we complete fine-tune stage on dataset based on single pretrained model, and then use it to initialize the Bert parameters in BertCA, finally we train the whole network on the target dataset. The training was conducted on two NVIDIA Tesla V100 GPUs with a batch size of 32. The learning rete of pretrained models is 2e−5 in single model fine-tune stage, the learning rete of pretrained models and graph models is 2e−6 and 1e−3 in training BertCA stage, respectively.

4.2 Results

Table 2. An example of three line table

Model	R8	R52	Ohsumed	MR
TextGCN	97.1	93.6	68.4	76.7
SGC	97.2	94.0	68.5	75.9
Bert	97.8	96.4	70.5	85.7
BertGCN	98.1	96.6	72.8	86.0
BertCA	**98.5**	**97.0**	**73.2**	**87.4**
RoBerta	97.8	96.2	70.7	89.4
RoBertaGCN	98.2	96.1	72.8	89.7
RoBertaCA	**98.3**	**96.7**	**73.0**	**89.9**

The comparison results of TextGCN, SGC, Bert, RoBerta, BertGCN, RoBertaGCN and our model are detailed in Table 2. The results show that our BertCA networks obtain universal performance improvement and achieve SOTA results on text classification benchmark corpus. The main reason is that our network leverages the complementary strengths of Bert, GCN and GAT. Especially, our method has the most obvious improvement in short text corpus like MR. This is because of the additional feature obtained from GAT. Which enhance the center node embedding and prevent over-smooth. On the contrary, the long text corpus like Ohsumed and R52 have slight improvement. That may because that the long text have adequate information than short text, and the additional feature is not required.

In this way, the [CLS] feature can obtain global structured information from GCN and neighborhood nodes information from GAT, respectively. Therefore, the final sentence representation can successfully satisfy the needs of semantic or structural information in various tasks.

5   Conclusion

In this paper, we propose a novel network named BertCA, which can help learn a rich sentence representation involved semantic representation, global structured information and neighborhood nodes features. Experimental results on four benchmark datasets show that our network obtains significant performance improvements and achieve SOTA results, especially on short text corpus. In the future, we look forward to learning the global structured information and neighborhood features in one model simultaneously, and constructing the weight edges between nodes in a semantic level, and it also worth exploring other short text NLU tasks based on BertCA.

References

1. Krizhevsky, A., Sutskever, I., Hinton, G.: ImageNet classification with deep convolutional neural networks. Adv. Neural Inf. Process. Syst. **25**(2), 1097–1105 (2012)
2. Zaremba, W., Sutskever, I., Vinyals, O.: Recurrent neural network regularization. Eprint Arxiv (2014)
3. Hochreiter, S., Schmidhuber, J.: Long short-term memory. Neural Comput. **9**(8), 1735–1780 (1997)
4. ThoKipf, M.N., Welling, M.: Semisupervised classification with graph convolutional networks. arXiv preprint arXiv:1609.02907 (2016)
5. Velickovic, P., Cucurull, G., Casanova, A., Romero, A., Lio, P., Bengio, Y.: Graph attention networks. arXiv preprint arXiv:1710.10903 (2017)
6. Yao, L., Mao, C., Luo, Y.: Graph convolutional networks for text classification. In: Proceedings of the AAAI Conference on Artificial Intelligence, vol. 33, pp. 7370–7377 (2019)
7. Lin, Y., Meng, Y., Sun, X., et al.: BertGCN: transductive text classification by combining GCN and BERT. In: Proceedings of the 59th Annual Meeting of the Association for Computational Linguistics (2021)
8. Devlin, J., Chang, M.W., Lee, K., Toutanova, K.: BERT: pre-training of deep bidirectional transformers for language understanding (2018)
9. Pennington, J., Socher, R., Manning, C.D.: GloVe: global vectors for word representation. In: EMNLP (2014)
10. Peters, M.E.: Deep contextualized word representations. In: NAACL-HLT (2018)
11. Vaswani, A., et al.: Attention is all you need. In: NeurIPS (2017)
12. Radford, A., Narasimhan, K., Salimans, T., Sutskever, I.: Improving language understanding by generative pre-training (2018)
13. Yang, Z., Dai, Z., Yang, Y., Carbonell, J., Salakhutdinov, R., Le, Q.V.: Generalized autoregressive pretraining for language understanding. In: NeurIPS, XLNet (2019)

14. Liu, Y., et al.: RoBERTa: A robustly optimized BERT pretraining approach. arXiv preprint arXiv:1907.11692 (2019)
15. Lan, Z., Chen, M., Goodman, S., Gimpel, K., Sharma, P., Soricut, R.: ALBERT: a lite BERT for self-supervised learning of language representations (2019)
16. Wu, F., Zhang, T., de Souza, A.H., Jr., Fifty, C., Yu, T., Weinberger, K.Q.: Simplifying graph convolutional networks. arXiv preprint arXiv:1902.07153 (2019)
17. He, K., Zhang, X., Ren, S., Sun, J.: Deep residual learning for image recognition. IEEE (2016)

FedPrune: Personalized and Communication-Efficient Federated Learning on Non-IID Data

Yang Liu[1], Yi Zhao[1(✉)], Guangmeng Zhou[1], and Ke Xu[1,2,3]

[1] Department of Computer Science and Technology, Tsinghua University, Beijing, China
{liuyang19,zgm19}@mails.tsinghua.edu.cn, {zhao_yi,xuke}@tsinghua.edu.cn
[2] Beijing National Research Center for Information Science and Technology (BNRist), Beijing, China
[3] Peng Cheng Laboratory (PCL), Shenzhen, China

Abstract. Federated learning (FL) has been widely deployed in edge computing scenarios. However, FL-related technologies are still facing severe challenges while evolving rapidly. Among them, statistical heterogeneity (i.e., non-IID) seriously hinders the wide deployment of FL. In our work, we propose a new framework for communication-efficient and personalized federated learning, namely *FedPrune*. More specifically, under the newly proposed FL framework, each client trains a converged model locally to obtain critical parameters and substructure that guide the pruning of the network participating FL. FedPrune is able to achieve high accuracy while greatly reducing communication overhead. Moreover, each client learns a personalized model in FedPrune. Experimental results has demonstrated that FedPrune achieves the best accuracy in image recognition task with varying degrees of reduced communication costs compared to the three baseline methods.

Keywords: Federated learning · Private preserving · Network pruning

1 Introduction

Federated learning (FL) [7,11] is a new machine learning paradigm that is already widely used in personal devices and financial enterprises. FL has been widely accepted as an artificial intelligence (AI) application that protects the data privacy of users [16]. While FL promises better privacy and efficiency, there are still two major challenges [8] in FL. The first one is the significant communication overhead, which has hampered the development of federated learning. In fact, the federated network is likely to be composed of many clients and the communication in the network is very frequent and more time consuming compared to local computing. The second challenge is the statistical heterogeneity, meaning that the distribution of data across clients is non-IID (non-identically independently distributed). The data at the client side may be very different

© Springer Nature Switzerland AG 2021
T. Mantoro et al. (Eds.): ICONIP 2021, CCIS 1516, pp. 430–437, 2021.
https://doi.org/10.1007/978-3-030-92307-5_50

in size and type. In this work, we focus on both challenges and thus propose a framework that can jointly take on them.

In our work, we propose a new framework for communication-efficient and personalized federated learning, namely *FedPrune*. Specifically, each client trains a converged model locally to obtain critical parameters and substructure that guide the pruning of the network participating federated learning. Clients with large differences in data distribution do not interfere with each other, while clients with similar data distribution can enhance each other. Finally, a personalized model will be learned at each client. We show that FedPrune is able to achieve high accuracy while greatly reducing communication overhead. Moreover, it only requires negligible computational and storage costs. We conduct experiments on the MNIST, CIFAR-10 and CIFAR-100 datasets and compared FedPrune with FedAvg [11], FedProx [9] and LG-FedAvg [10]. The experimental results show that FedPrune is significantly better than the compared methods in terms of accuracy and communication cost on non-IID data.

2   Related Work

AI has been integrated into many fields, such as mobile social networks [15] and smart cities [17]. To further protect user privacy, academia and industry propose to use federated learning [8,11] to achieve intelligence. However, Zhao et al. [18] shows that non-IID data distribution may significantly reduce the prediction accuracy of FL. FedProx [9] solves this problem by adding regularization terms to the local optimization so that the local model does not change too much compared to the global model. Model personalization is a worthwhile approach to tackle statistical heterogeneity. Jiang et al. [6] introduce the MAML [3] algorithm in the field of meta learning into federated learning to realize the personalization of models on each client. Vahidian et al. [13] obtain personalized models by structured pruning and unstructured pruning, but introduce hyperparameters that are very dependent on the network structure, making it difficult to tune and deploy in practice.

How to reduce the communication overhead of federated learning is another problem that puzzles researchers. Previous work [1,5,7,12] reduces the size of the model transferred between the client and the server through data compression techniques such as sketching, sparsification and quantization. Wang et al. [14] dynamically tunes the frequency of updating the model according to the available communication resources.

3   Design of FedPrune

We denote N clients by $\mathcal{C} = \{C_1, ..., C_N\}$. We denote w_g as the weights of the global model, and w_k $(k = 1, ..., N)$ as the local model weights on each client C_k. We let $\{w_{ij,k}\}$ denote the weights of the connections between pairs of neurons $n_{i,k}$ and $n_{j,k}$ in the model w_k. We denote $\Omega_{ij,k}$ as the importance value for each parameter $\{w_{ij,k}\}$. We use the superscript t, e.g., w_i^t, to indicate the weights learned in round t. Each client C_k learns a local mask $m_k \in \{0,1\}^{w_k}$, which indicates whether the weights are pruned or not. In a local mask, a value of 0 means that the corresponding weight is pruned, and 1 means vice versa.

3.1 Estimating Parameter Importance

According to *the lottery ticket hypothesis* [4], there always exists the optimal sub-network, also called the winning ticket, that can achieve similar performance as the original network. That is, if the sub-networks of each client participate in federated learning, they can not only achieve the performance of the original model, but also avoid the interference of the model parameters of other clients.

In this work, we adapt the MAS [2] algorithm, which measures the importance of parameters, to the federated learning scenario. Each client trains a model locally using local data before participating in federated learning. The model is considered to have learned an approximation F to the true function $\bar{F}$ when it reaches a local optimum. We characterize the importance of a parameter in the network in terms of the sensitivity of the function F to that parameter. When the input is x_d, the output of the function is $F(x_d; w)$. Applying a small perturbation $\delta = \{\delta_{ij}\}$ to the parameters $w = \{w_{ij}\}$, the output of the function can be approximated by:

$$F(x_d; w + \delta) - F(x_d; w) \approx \sum_{i,j} g_{ij}(x_d)\delta_{ij} \tag{1}$$

where $g_{ij}(x_d) = \frac{\partial(F(x_d;w))}{\partial w_{ij}}$ is the gradient of the function F with respect to the parameter w_{ij} at the data point x_d. δ_{ij} is the small perturbation applied to the parameter w_{ij}. Assuming that δ_{ij} is a constant, we can use the magnitude of the gradient g_{ij} to characterize the importance of the parameter. We accumulate the gradients obtained from all the input data and sum up to obtain the importance weight Ω_{ij} for parameter w_{ij}:

$$\Omega_{ij} = \frac{1}{N_{dp}} \sum_{d=1}^{N_{dp}} \|g_{ij}(x_d)\| \tag{2}$$

where N_{dp} is the number of input data points.

3.2 Training Process of FedPrune

The details of FedPrune are described in Algorithm 1. Typically, the training process of FedPrune is as follows:

Prior to training for federated learning, the server initializes the global model w_g^0 and sends that model to each client. Once the global model is received, each client trains the local model w_k' as a way to obtain the masks needed to prune the models involved in federated learning. Specifically, we can obtain the importance of the parameters by the approach introduced in Sect. 3.1. Given a target pruning

---

Algorithm 1: Training of FedPrune. K is the random sampling rate, $\mathcal{B}$ is the set of local mini-batches, η is the learning rate, and $l(\cdot)$ is the loss function.

---

1 **Server executes: // Run on the server**
2 initialize the global model w_g^0;
3 ClientGetMask(w_g^0); // executed in parallel
4 **for** *each round* $t = 1$ **to** T **do**
5 $\quad$ $k \leftarrow \max(N \times K, 1)$;
6 $\quad$ $\mathcal{S}_t \leftarrow \{C_1, ..., C_k\}$;
7 $\quad$ **for** *each client* $k \in S_t$ ***in parallel*** **do**
8 $\quad\quad$ $\mid$ $w_k^{t+1} \leftarrow$ ClientUpdate(w_g^t);
9 $\quad$ **end**
10 $\quad$ $w_g^{t+1} \leftarrow$ aggregate subnetworks of clients, w_k^{t+1}, and average the intersection of them;
11 **end**

12 **ClientGetMask(w_g^0): // Run on client** k
13 Train the local model $w_k^{'}$ for E_l epochs based on w_g^0;
14 Compute $\{\Omega_{ij,k}\}$ by Eq.(2);
15 m_k, the mask for w_k, is obtained based on $\{\Omega_{ij,k}\}$ and target pruning rate p;

16 **ClientUpdate(w_g^t): // Run on client** k
17 $w_k^t \leftarrow w_g^t \odot m_k$;
18 $\mathcal{B} \leftarrow$ split local training data into batches;
19 **for** *each local epoch from 1 to E* **do**
20 $\quad$ **for** *batch* $b \in \mathcal{B}$ **do**
21 $\quad\quad$ $\mid$ $w_k^{t+1} \leftarrow w_k^t - \eta \nabla_{w_k^t} l(w_k^t; b) \odot m_k$;
22 $\quad$ **end**
23 **end**
24 return w_k^{t+1} to server;

---

ratio p, a binary mask of the same size as the model is derived. The process of client training a local model to obtain a mask is asynchronous to the whole process of federated learning, and clients who have already obtained a mask can start federated training earlier.

Given the round t, the server samples a random set of clients $\mathcal{S}$ and distributes a global model to each of them. Note that C_k trains $w_g^t \odot m_k$, the global model w_g^t pruned by the mask m_k, as the initial model for this round, instead of training the global model directly. Then C_k performs training for E epochs with the local data, and then uploads the updated w_k^{t+1} to the server.

At the end of the round, the server performs aggregation on all received local models (i.e., w_k^{t+1}). Different from FedAvg, we only take the average on the intersection of unpruned parameters for each client, just like the **By-unit** approach described in Zhou et al. [19]. This aggregation method allows networks with different structures that imply large differences in data distribution not to interfere with each other. Meanwhile, this approach enables networks with similar structures to further enhance each other.

4   Experiments

4.1   Experimental Setup

We conduct an empirical study of FedPrune and compare it with classical FL algorithms i.e. FedAvg [11], FedProx [9] and LG-FedAvg [10]. Our experimental studies are conducted over three datasets, MNIST, CIFAR-10 and CIFAR-100.

To evaluate each method in terms of statistical heterogeneity, we divide the data in the same way as in McMahan et al. [11]. The architecture we used for MNIST is a CNN with two 5×5 convolution layers, a fully connected layer with 50 units, and a final softmax output layer. We add ReLU activation functions to all layers except the last one. For CIFAR-10 and CIFAR-100 datasets we use LeNet-5 architecture. In all experiments, we have 100 clients, each with local batch size 10 and local epoch 5. In addition, we use an SGD optimizer with learning rate and momentum of 0.01 and 0.5, respectively. For FedPrune, we set the number of epochs for the local model $E_l = 50$. For FedProx, we show the experimental results at the coefficient of the regularization term $\mu = 0.01$.

We compare FedPrune with three methods, i.e., FedAvg, FedProx and LG-FedAvg. FedAvg is a classical federated learning method. FedProx improves on FedAvg by adding a regularisation term called *proximal term*. In LG-FedAvg, each client learns a compact local representations and all clients learn a global model together. We use the classification accuracy of the test data on each client to evaluate the performance of personalization and report the average accuracy of all clients. We use the number of parameters of the model to measure the communication overhead.

4.2   Results and Analysis

We compare the results of our proposed algorithms against several baselines, as shown in Table 1.

Accuracy: We show the accuracy of the model after pruning 30%, 50% and 70% of the parameters in Table 1. As can be seen from the table, the variation of accuracy with the pruning rate is not drastic and the accuracy always maintains at a high level. Even with 70% of the parameters pruned, the accuracy of the FedPrune algorithm is still much higher than that of other methods. This result illustrates that more parameters of the model do not mean better performance.

Overhead: As seen in Table 1, FedPrune achieves communication efficiency with a small loss of accuracy. In the experiments on FedPrune, the client needs to train a local model for 50 epochs as a way to get the critical parameters and substructure, which seems to impose some computational overhead on the client. However, the computational overhead of this part is only 10% or less compared

Table 1. Comparing the classification accuracy and communication overhead of Fed-Prune against several baselines.

Dataset	Method	Acc	% Pruned param	Communication cost
MNIST	FedAvg	98.75%	0	1.75 GB
	FedProx	98.75%	0	1.75 GB
	LG-FedAvg	98.20%	0	1.71 GB
	FedPrune	**99.39%**	30%	**1.23 GB**
	FedPrune	**99.49%**	50%	**0.88 GB**
	FedPrune	**99.39%**	70%	**0.53 GB**
CIFAR-10	FedAvg	49.21%	0	4.96 GB
	FedProx	50.21%	0	4.96 GB
	LG-FedAvg	76.28%	0	4.54 GB
	FedPrune	**80.68%**	30%	**3.47 GB**
	FedPrune	**81.02%**	50%	**2.48 GB**
	FedPrune	**79.63%**	70%	**1.49 GB**
CIFAR-100	FedAvg	14.91%	0	5.57 GB
	FedProx	13.13%	0	5.57 GB
	LG-FedAvg	47.60%	0	5.17 GB
	FedPrune	**84.91%**	30%	**3.90 GB**
	FedPrune	**83.95%**	50%	**2.79 GB**
	FedPrune	**81.98%**	70%	**1.67 GB**

to the whole federated learning process. For the vast majority of edge devices, it is acceptable. Theoretically, the storage overhead of FedPrune is small. We need only 1 bit to encode the mask per parameter. For example, in our experiments, the network size of LeNet-5 for CIFAR-100 is 0.28 MB. The overhead of adding a mask to this network is about 8.7 KB. A parameter is typically represented by 4 bytes, and adding a mask results in an additional storage overhead of 1/32 of the initial model size, which is ideal for edge computing devices with small storage space. Note that it is not necessary for the local model and the model participating in federated learning to exist simultaneously.

Sensitivity Evaluation: We will study the variation of accuracy with target pruning ratio p. Figure 1 plots the average test accuracy over all clients versus various pruning percentages. At the beginning, the accuracy of the model keep improving as the number of parameters being pruned increases. As we expect, in federated learning, too many parameters are not beneficial for model training, but lead to mutual interference among clients. As the number of parameters being pruned continues to increase, the accuracy of the model begins to slowly decrease. This is because the critical parameters are also pruned and the optimal substructure is corrupted. Surprisingly, however, even at very high pruning ratio, the accuracy does not drop dramatically and remains even higher than baselines. From the figure we can see that for CIFAR-10, the accuracy of the classification can still reach 73.94% and 64.75% when the pruning ratio is 95% and 99%, respectively. For CIFAR-100, the accuracy reaches 76.01% and 68.67% at the same pruning ratio, respectively. This result sufficiently illustrates that our method does find the critical parameters and optimal substructure, which guarantee a good performance even when the model is extremely compressed.

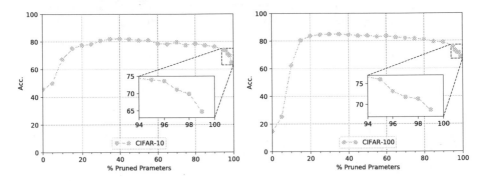

Fig. 1. Average test accuracy of FedPrune over all clients for the CIFAR-10 (left) and CIFAR-100 (right) datasets.

5   Conclusion

In this work, we propose a federated learning framework, FedPrune, that maintains a high level of accuracy while greatly reducing communication overhead. Moreover, the framework is easy to implement and has limited computational and storage overhead, making it suitable for deployment in mobile and edge computing devices. In addition, FedPrune has only one more hyperparameter than FedAvg, target pruning ratio p, making it easy to tune and deploy to production environments.

References

1. Alistarh, D., Grubic, D., Li, J., Tomioka, R., Vojnovic, M.: QSGD: Communication-efficient SGD via gradient quantization and encoding, pp. 1709–1720 (2017)
2. Aljundi, R., Babiloni, F., Elhoseiny, M., Rohrbach, M., Tuytelaars, T.: Memory aware synapses: learning what (not) to forget. In: Ferrari, V., Hebert, M., Sminchisescu, C., Weiss, Y. (eds.) ECCV 2018, Part III. LNCS, vol. 11207, pp. 144–161. Springer, Cham (2018). https://doi.org/10.1007/978-3-030-01219-9_9
3. Finn, C., Abbeel, P., Levine, S.: Model-agnostic meta-learning for fast adaptation of deep networks. In: Precup, D., Teh, Y.W. (eds.) Proceedings of the 34th International Conference on Machine Learning. Proceedings of Machine Learning Research, vol. 70, pp. 1126–1135. PMLR, 06–11 August 2017. http://proceedings.mlr.press/v70/finn17a.html

4. Frankle, J., Carbin, M.: The lottery ticket hypothesis: finding sparse, trainable neural networks. In: International Conference on Learning Representations (2019). https://openreview.net/forum?id=rJl-b3RcF7

5. Ivkin, N., Rothchild, D., Ullah, E., Braverman, V., Stoica, I., Arora, R.: Communication-efficient distributed SGD with sketching. In: Proceedings of NeurIPS, pp. 1–23 (2019)

6. Jiang, Y., Konečný, J., Rush, K., Kannan, S.: Improving Federated Learning Personalization via Model Agnostic Meta Learning. CoRR abs/1909.12488 (2019). http://arxiv.org/abs/1909.12488

7. Konečný, J., McMahan, H.B., Yu, F.X., Richtárik, P., Suresh, A.T., Bacon, D.: Federated learning: strategies for improving communication efficiency. In: Proceedings of NeurIPS Workshop (2016)

8. Li, T., Sahu, A.K., Talwalkar, A., Smith, V.: Federated learning: challenges, methods, and future directions. IEEE Signal Process. Mag. **37**(3), 50–60 (2020)

9. Li, T., Sahu, A.K., Zaheer, M., Sanjabi, M., Talwalkar, A., Smith, V.: Federated optimization in heterogeneous networks. In: Proceedings of MLSys (2018)

10. Liang, P.P., Liu, T., Ziyin, L., Salakhutdinov, R., Morency, L.P.: Think locally, act globally: Federated learning with local and global representations. arXiv preprint arXiv:2001.01523 (2020)

11. McMahan, B., Moore, E., Ramage, D., Hampson, S., y Arcas, B.A.: Communication-efficient learning of deep networks from decentralized data. In: Proceedings of AISTATS, pp. 1273–1282 (2017)

12. Reisizadeh, A., Mokhtari, A., Hassani, H., Jadbabaie, A., Pedarsani, R.: FedPAQ: a communication-efficient federated learning method with periodic averaging and quantization. In: Proceedings of AISTATS, pp. 2021–2031 (2020)

13. Vahidian, S., Morafah, M., Lin, B.: Personalized Federated Learning by Structured and Unstructured Pruning under Data Heterogeneity. CoRR abs/2105.00562 (2021), https://arxiv.org/abs/2105.00562

14. Wang, S., et al.: Adaptive federated learning in resource constrained edge computing systems. IEEE J. Sel. Areas Commun. (JSAC) **37**(6), 1205–1221 (2019)

15. Zhao, Y., et al.: TDFI: two-stage deep learning framework for friendship inference via multi-source information. In: IEEE INFOCOM 2019 - IEEE Conference on Computer Communications, pp. 1981–1989 (2019). https://doi.org/10.1109/INFOCOM.2019.8737458

16. Zhao, Y., Xu, K., Wang, H., Li, B., Jia, R.: Stability-based analysis and defense against backdoor attacks on edge computing services. IEEE Netw. **35**(1), 163–169 (2021). https://doi.org/10.1109/MNET.011.2000265

17. Zhao, Y., Xu, K., Wang, H., Li, B., Qiao, M., Shi, H.: MEC-enabled hierarchical emotion recognition and perturbation-aware defense in smart cities. IEEE IoT J. 1 (2021). https://doi.org/10.1109/JIOT.2021.3079304

18. Zhao, Y., Li, M., Lai, L., Suda, N., Civin, D., Chandra, V.: Federated learning with non-iid data. arXiv preprint arXiv:1806.00582 (2018)

19. Zhou, G., Xu, K., Li, Q., Liu, Y., Zhao, Y.: AdaptCL: Efficient Collaborative Learning with Dynamic and Adaptive Pruning. CoRR abs/2106.14126 (2021), https://arxiv.org/abs/2106.14126

Depth Privileged Object Detection with Depth-Enhanced DCN

Yan Liu, Zhijie Zhang, and Liqing Zhang$^{(\boxtimes)}$

MoE Key Lab of Artificial Intelligence, Department of Computer Science
and Engineering, Shanghai Jiao Tong University, Shanghai 201100, China
{loseover,zzj506506}@sjtu.edu.cn, zhang-lq@cs.sjtu.edu.cn

Abstract. Deep learning has achieved excellent performance in object
detection but remains challenging due to the poor illumination, object
occlusion, *etc.* Some works have attempted to leverage the additional
depth images to assist for the RGB object detection since the depth
images can provide complementary information for RGB images. However, owing to the less prevalence of depth sensors, depth images are
not always available in general scenarios. In this paper, we focus on the
depth privileged object detection (DPOD), in which the depth images
are privileged and only available in the training stage. Specifically,
we propose a novel depth-enhanced deformable convolutional network
(DEDCN) to adapt to the depth input and transfer the knowledge in
depth information to RGB information using learned offsets and derived
modulations. Furthermore, we design a three-branch network equipped
with DCNv2/DEDCN to fulfill the offset and modulation hallucination.
Extensive experiments on NYUDv2 and SUN RGB-D demonstrate that
our method outperforms the state-of-the-art approaches for DPOD.

Keywords: Object detection · Knowledge transfer · Learning using
privileged information

1 Introduction

With the ubiquitous application of convolutional neural networks (CNN) and
the development of modern detectors, object detection has achieved dramatical
advances in recent years. However, the large variations, *i.e.*, the poor illumination, the object occlusion, and the confusing object appearance, cause performance degradation in the RGB object detection.

To tackle the limitations in RGB object detection, many works ([7,8,16])
involve depth images into the training and testing stages (*i.e.*, RGB-D object
detection), since the depth images can provide complementary and color-
insensitive information for RGB images, which can benefit the detector in some
color-confusing scenes. However, RGB-D object detection requires depth data
both in training and testing stages, which is not always available in a general scenario since the less prevalence of the depth capturing devices. As a consequence,

© Springer Nature Switzerland AG 2021
T. Mantoro et al. (Eds.): ICONIP 2021, CCIS 1516, pp. 438–446, 2021.
https://doi.org/10.1007/978-3-030-92307-5_51

the detectors should work well with only RGB images as input. Therefore, we focus on the depth privileged setting, in which the depth data is the privileged information [5,14] and only available in the training stage.

The key to exploiting the privileged information (*i.e.*, depth) is how to transfer the knowledge in depth to RGB information. *e.g.*, Hoffman *et al.* [6] transfer the depth feature learned by a pretrained network which takes in the depth images as input, while ROCK [10] utilizes the intermediate feature to predict auxiliary depth representation with the privileged depth information as the supervision. The latest work of DPOD [17] transfers the depth deformation learned by deformable convolutional network (DCN) [3], which inspires our work. Nevertheless, we transfer not only the deformation (*i.e.*, offsets), but also the modulations with DCNv2 [18]. Besides, considering the distribution gap between depth images and RGB images, we propose the depth-enhanced DCN (DEDCN), which is more adaptive to the depth images than DCN. In specific, we conjecture that the pixels near the center of the convolutional kernel with a similar depth as the center should be assigned higher weights compared with those with distinct depth. Therefore we replace the modulation in DCNv2 with depth locality [2], which is inversely proportional to the depth difference between the current pixel and the convolutional kernel center.

Following [6,17], we build our network with three branches, *i.e.*, RGB branch (R-branch), hallucination branch (H-branch), and depth branch (D-branch). Each branch is a complete detector, which consists of a backbone, an FPN, and several detection heads. And to fulfill the depth knowledge transfer, we replace some standard convolutional layers in D-branch (*resp.*, R-branch and H-branch) with DEDCN (*resp.*, DCNv2) to learn the offsets and modulations of depth (*resp.*, RGB) images.

Comprehensive experiments are conducted on two datasets: NYUDv2 [11] and SUN RGB-D [12]. The results demonstrate that our proposed approach with DEDCN can significantly boost the performance of DPOD. Our contribution can be summarized as follows:

- As far as we know, we are the first to transfer the offsets and modulations from depth modality to RGB modality.
- We propose the depth-enhanced DCN, which can adapt to the depth images.
- Our method outperforms all state-of-the-art methods for DPOD on two datasets.

2   Methodology

2.1   Depth-Enhanced DCN

Dai *et al.* [3] argue that the standard convolution with fixed spatial sampling locations can limit the transformation modeling capability of CNNs and propose the deformable convolution, which augments the standard convolution with learned offsets.

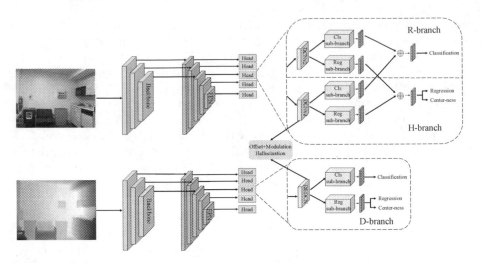

Fig. 1. Illustration of our framework. The pre-trained D-branch provides the offsets and modulations as guidance. H-branch is enforced to mimic the offsets and modulations offered by D-branch. The outputs of the R-branch and H-branch are concatenated for the final classification and regression. In the training stage, the D-branch is frozen. In the testing stage, only R-branch and H-branch are used.

For standard convolutional kernel with K sampling locations, we denote the convolutional weight and pre-specified offset for the k-th sampling location as w_k and p_k, respectively. For instance, given a 3×3 convolutional kernel, $K = 9$ and $p_k \in \{(-1, -1), (-1, 0), \ldots, (1, 1)\}$. The standard convolution can be formulated as

$$y(i) = \sum_{k=1}^{K} w_k \cdot x(i + p_k), \tag{1}$$

where $x(i)$ and $y(i)$ are the value at position i on the input feature map x and output feature map y, respectively.

Then, deformable convolution augments each pre-specified sampling location with a 2D offset $\Delta p_{i,k}$ to shift the sampling location to the region of interest. Besides, modulated deformable convolution [18] applies a scalar $\Delta m_{i,k}$ as the modulation to suppress redundant context, which can be formulated as

$$y(i) = \sum_{k=1}^{K} w_k \cdot x(i + p_k + \Delta p_{i,k}) \cdot \Delta m_{i,k}. \tag{2}$$

Note that the offset $\Delta p_{i,k}$ may not be an integer coordinate, thus $x(i + p_k + \Delta p_{i,k})$ is computed via bilinear interpolation. The offsets and modulations are all learned through a separate convolutional layer, which is applied over the same input feature map x. This convolutional layer outputs a field of $3K$ channels, where the first $2K$ channels correspond to the 2D offsets $\{\Delta p_{i,k}\}_{k=1}^{K}$ and the last K channels are further fed to a sigmoid layer to produce the modulate scalars

$\{\Delta m_{i,k}\}_{k=1}^{K}$. The field has the same spatial resolution as the output feature map of the current convolutional layer and produces offsets/modulations for the convolutional kernel at each spatial location i.

However, the modulated deformable convolution is proposed for improving the standard convolution on RGB images. We can not tell the offsets and modulations learned from depth images are better than the ones learned from RGB images since the distribution gap of depth and RGB images. Intuitively, the region of one object in depth images should have similar depth, but the neighboring regions in similar color in RGB images may contain several objects. Therefore, we follow [2] and design a depth-enhanced deformable convolution (DEDC) to address the issue. Specifically, We replace the modulation $\Delta m_{i,k}$ with the depth locality $\Delta l_{i,k}$, which is inversely proportional to the depth difference between the current pixel and the convolutional kernel center:

$$\Delta l_{i,k} = exp\{-(\frac{d_{i+p_k+\Delta p_{i,k}} - d_i}{\sigma})^2\}, \tag{3}$$

in which $d_{i+p_k+\Delta p_{i,k}}$ and d_i are the depth value at position $i+p_k+\Delta p_{i,k}$ and i of depth image d, respectively. And σ is a hyper-parameters and set as 40 via cross-validation. Similarly, $d_{i+p_k+\Delta p_{i,k}}$ is computed by bilinear interpolation. Finally, DEDC can be formulated as

$$y(i) = \sum_{k=1}^{K} w_k \cdot x(i + p_k + \Delta p_{i,k}) \cdot \Delta l_{i,k}. \tag{4}$$

In this way, DEDC can adapt to the depth images and learn the offsets in a depth-aware manner.

2.2   Network Architecture

As depicted in Fig. 1, we adopt the framework in [6,17] and construct our framework with three branches: RGB branch (R-branch), hallucination branch (H-branch), and depth branch (D-branch), all equipped with DCNv2/DEDCN. R-branch and H-branch take RGB images as input, while D-branch takes depth images as input. Each branch is built upon FCOS [13] and comprised of a backbone, an FPN, and several detection heads. Specifically, the R-branch and H-branch share the same backbone and FPN but have different detection heads. Each detection head consists of two sub-branches, i.e., a classification sub-branch and a regression sub-branch. Follow [17], the two sub-branches in D-branch (resp., R-branch and H-branch) share the first M convolutional layers which are replaced by depth-enhanced deformable convolutional layers (resp., modulated deformable convolutional layers), referred to as DEDCN (resp., DCNv2). Therefore, each detection head can learn the offsets and modulations with DEDCN or DCNv2. To integrate the feature outputs by R-branch and H-branch, for the detection heads taking in the same scale input feature map, we concatenate the classification (resp., regression) sub-branch output features in two branches.

The fused features are then used for the final classification (*resp.*, regression) after channel reduction.

In the training stage, the D-branch is first pre-trained and frozen when the R-branch and H-branch are trained to provide the stable guidance for H-branch. In the testing stage, only the R-branch and H-branch are used owing to the lack of depth images.

2.3   Offset Hallucination

To hallucinate the offsets in depth images, we encourage the learned offsets in H-branch match those in D-branch with the loss:

$$L_o = \sum_{s=1}^{S} \sum_{m=1}^{M} \sum_{i=1}^{h_s \times w_s} \sum_{k=1}^{K} \|\Delta p_{s,m,i,k}^{H} - \Delta p_{s,m,i,k}^{D}\|_2^2, \tag{5}$$

in which S and M are the number of the scales of FPN and the number of DEDCN/DCNv2, respectively, $h_s \times w_s$ is the size of the feature map of the s-th scale, $\Delta p_{s,m,i,k}^{H}$ (*resp.*, $\Delta p_{s,m,i,k}^{D}$) denotes the offset for the k-th sampling location at position i in the feature map output by m-th DCNv2 (*resp.*, DEDCN) of the s-th scale in H-branch (*resp.*, D-branch).

2.4   Modulation Hallucination

In addition to hallucinating offsets, we also force the modulations learned by H-branch to mimic the ones computed by D-branch with the loss:

$$L_m = L_o = \sum_{s=1}^{S} \sum_{m=1}^{M} \sum_{i=1}^{h_s \times w_s} \sum_{k=1}^{K} \|\Delta m_{s,m,i,k}^{H} - \Delta l_{s,m,i,k}\|_2^2, \tag{6}$$

in which $\Delta m_{s,m,i,k}^{H}$ is the corresponding modulation of $\Delta p_{s,m,i,k}^{H}$, and $\Delta l_{s,m,i,k}$ denotes the depth locality for the k-th sampling location at position i in the feature map output by m-th DEDCN of the s-th in D-branch.

2.5   The Full Objective Function

Integrating all the losses for the joint training of R-branch and H-branch, We formulate the full objective function as

$$L_{full} = L_d + \lambda_1 L_o + \lambda_2 L_m, \tag{7}$$

where L_d is the loss of FCOS, *i.e.*, the loss for classification and regression in detection heads, λ_1 and λ_2 are the trade-off parameters and set as 0.1 and 0.01 via cross-validation, respectively.

Table 1. Ablation Studies on different components of our method. 'Offset' and 'Modulation' denote the offset hallucination and modulation hallucination, respectively.

	Offset	Modulation	DEDCN	mAP(%)
1				44.32
2	✓		✓	47.11
3		✓	✓	46.12
4	✓	✓		47.23
5	✓	✓	✓	47.91

Table 2. Comparison with the state-of-the-arts on NYUDv2 and SUN RGB-D. The best results are denoted in boldface.

Method	mAP(%)	
	NYUDv2	SUN RGB-D
FCOS	42.73	52.94
Hoffman et al. [6]	45.22	55.35
ROCK [10]	44.89	55.14
Cao et al. [1]	44.96	55.27
Zhang et al. [17]	46.88	56.84
Ours	**47.91**	**59.07**

3 Experiment

3.1 Datasets

In this paper, we evaluate our method on two datasets: NYUDv2 [11] and SUN RGB-D [12]. NYUDv2 contains 1449 pairs of RGB and depth images, which are split into 795 training images and 654 test images. SUN RGB-D contains 5285 paired RGB-D images for training and 5050 paired ones for testing.

Following [6,17], for both datasets, we evaluate our method on the 19 most common categories: bathtub, bed, bookshelf, box, chair, counter, desk, door, dresser, garbage bin, lamp, monitor, nightstand, pillow, sink, sofa, table, television, and toilet.

3.2 Implementation Details

Our proposed framework is built upon FCOS [13] with ResNeXt-101 [15] pre-trained on ImageNet [4] as the backbone. We train our model using the SGD optimizer. The learning rate is initialized to 1×10^{-3} and reduced to 1×10^{-4}. The weight decay and momentum are set to 1×10^{-4} and 0.9, respectively. The random seed is set to 123. Following [17], we set the number of DCNv2/DEDCN as 2 and apply them to the detection heads. All experiments are conducted on two 24 GB TITAN RTX. We adopt mean average precision (mAP) as the evaluation metric.

3.3 Ablation Study

To explore the validity of each component of our method, we conduct ablation studies on NYUDv2. The results are summarized in Table 1. Note that row 1 is the plain RGB detector for comparison.

Study on Offset Hallucination. To validate the effectiveness of the offset hallucination, we add L_o to L_d and report the result in row 2. By comparing row 2 with row 1, we can see that incorporate the offset hallucination to the plain detector can dramatically increase the performance, *i.e.*, 47.11% *v.s.* 44.32%.

Study on Modulation Hallucination. In addition to offset hallucination, we also apply the only modulation hallucination to the plain detector by adding L_m to L_d. Compared with row 1, the performance gain of row 3, *i.e.*, 46.12% *v.s.* 44.32%, indicates that hallucinating modulations generated from depth can benefit DPOD.

Study on DEDCN. Instead of DEDCN, the network can also learn the offsets and modulations with DCNv2. To explore the better depth adaptability of DEDCN, we replace the DEDCN in D-branch with DCNv2. The results in row 5 and row 4, *i.e.*, 47.91% *v.s.* 47.23%, verify that our proposed DEDCN is more adaptive to depth images and the learned offsets and generated modulations from DEDCN can provide more complementary information.

3.4   Comparison with State-of-the-Arts

We compare our method with the state-of-the-art approaches on NYUDv2 and SUN RGB-D, including [1,6,10], and [17]. For a fair comparison, we use FCOS with ResNeXt pretrained on ImageNet for all baselines. And for the baselines using the same initial detection network and backbone as ours, we directly copy their results.

The results are summarized in Table 2, from which we can see that our method achieves the best results in both datasets. And compared with the strongest baseline, *i.e.*, Zhang *et al.* [17], our method significantly outperforms it.

3.5   Visualization

To better explore the effectiveness of hallucinating offsets and modulations, we visualize the learned offsets and modulations in three branches in Fig. 2.

As we can see, the offsets and modulations in RGB images tend to be color-oriented, while those in depth images tend to be depth-oriented and also geometry-oriented owing to the similar depth of different pixels in one single object. For instance, for the bed of the third row of Fig. 2, the offsets in R-branch are almost all focused on the white quilt, whereas the ones in D-branch can cover most of the bed. And also, the modulations in R-branch are almost the same in the similar color region, while the ones in D-branch vary as the depth changes. After hallucination, the offsets and modulations in H-branch are similar to the ones in D-branch and can complement the RGB ones. *e.g.*, some of the offsets in R-branch of the second row of Fig. 2 are outside the bounding box, but the ones in H-branch are similar to the ones in D-branch and bound by the door's contour.

In summary, the D-branch can provide guidance for the H-branch with the offsets and modulations. Therefore the depth information can be hallucinated and complement the RGB information, which leads to the performance gain even without depth images in the testing stage.

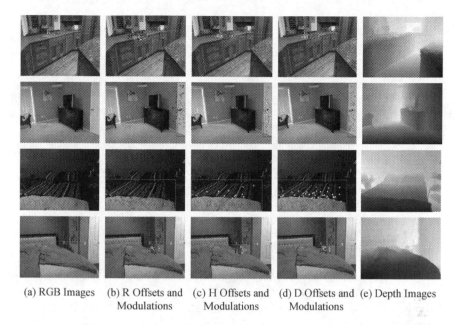

(a) RGB Images   (b) R Offsets and   (c) H Offsets and   (d) D Offsets and (e) Depth Images
                    Modulations   Modulations   Modulations

Fig. 2. Visualization of the offsets and modulations in three branches. From (a) to (e): RGB images, offsets and modulations in R-branch, H-branch, D-branch, and normalized depth images, respectively. The red squares represent the 81 (9×9 for 2 DCNv2/DEDCN) sampling locations, with grayscale indicating the modulations. The blue square is the center of the ground-truth bounding box (green). (Color figure online)

4   Conclusion

In this paper, we have designed a novel depth-enhanced deformable convolutional network (DEDCN), which can be adaptive to the depth images. Furthermore, we have investigated depth privileged object detection (DPOD) with DEDCN by hallucinating the depth offsets and depth modulations using RGB images. Extensive experiments have proved the effectiveness of our proposed method.

Acknowledgements. The work was supported by the NSF of China (Grant No. 62076162), the Shanghai Municipal Science and Technology Major Project (Grant No. 2021SHZDZX0102), and the Shanghai Municipal Science and Technology Key Project (Grant No. 20511100300).

References

1. Cao, Y., Shen, C., Shen, H.T.: Exploiting depth from single monocular images for object detection and semantic segmentation. IEEE Trans. Image Process. **26**(2), 836–846 (2016)

2. Chen, Y., Mensink, T., Gavves, E.: 3D neighborhood convolution: learning depth-aware features for RGB-D and RGB semantic segmentation. In: 2019 International Conference on 3D Vision (3DV), pp. 173–182. IEEE (2019)

3. Dai, J., et al.: Deformable convolutional networks. In: Proceedings of the IEEE International Conference on Computer Vision, pp. 764–773 (2017)

4. Deng, J., Dong, W., Socher, R., Li, L.J., Li, K., Fei-Fei, L.: ImageNet: a large-scale hierarchical image database. In: 2009 IEEE Conference on Computer Vision and Pattern Recognition, pp. 248–255. IEEE (2009)

5. Gu, Z., Niu, L., Zhao, H., Zhang, L.: Hard pixel mining for depth privileged semantic segmentation. IEEE Trans. Multimed. **23**, 3738–3751 (2020)

6. Hoffman, J., Gupta, S., Darrell, T.: Learning with side information through modality hallucination. In: Proceedings of the IEEE Conference on Computer Vision and Pattern Recognition, pp. 826–834 (2016)

7. Hoffman, J., Gupta, S., Leong, J., Guadarrama, S., Darrell, T.: Cross-modal adaptation for RGB-D detection. In: 2016 IEEE International Conference on Robotics and Automation (ICRA), pp. 5032–5039. IEEE (2016)

8. Kim, J., Koh, J., Kim, Y., Choi, J., Hwang, Y., Choi, J.W.: Robust deep multimodal learning based on gated information fusion network. In: Jawahar, C.V., Li, H., Mori, G., Schindler, K. (eds.) ACCV 2018, Part IV. LNCS, vol. 11364, pp. 90–106. Springer, Cham (2019). https://doi.org/10.1007/978-3-030-20870-7_6

9. Lai, K., Bo, L., Ren, X., Fox, D.: A large-scale hierarchical multi-view RGB-D object dataset. In: 2011 IEEE International Conference on Robotics and Automation, pp. 1817–1824. IEEE (2011)

10. Mordan, T., Thome, N., Henaff, G., Cord, M.: Revisiting multi-task learning with rock: a deep residual auxiliary block for visual detection. In: 32nd Conference on Neural Information Processing Systems (NeurIPS) (2018)

11. Silberman, N., Hoiem, D., Kohli, P., Fergus, R.: Indoor segmentation and support inference from RGBD images. In: Fitzgibbon, A., Lazebnik, S., Perona, P., Sato, Y., Schmid, C. (eds.) ECCV 2012, Part V. LNCS, vol. 7576, pp. 746–760. Springer, Heidelberg (2012). https://doi.org/10.1007/978-3-642-33715-4_54

12. Song, S., Lichtenberg, S.P., Xiao, J.: Sun RGB-D: a RGB-D scene understanding benchmark suite. In: Proceedings of the IEEE Conference on Computer Vision and Pattern Recognition, pp. 567–576 (2015)

13. Tian, Z., Shen, C., Chen, H., He, T.: FCOS: fully convolutional one-stage object detection. In: Proceedings of the IEEE/CVF International Conference on Computer Vision, pp. 9627–9636 (2019)

14. Vapnik, V., Vashist, A.: A new learning paradigm: learning using privileged information. Neural Netw. **22**(5–6), 544–557 (2009)

15. Xie, S., Girshick, R., Dollár, P., Tu, Z., He, K.: Aggregated residual transformations for deep neural networks. In: Proceedings of the IEEE Conference on Computer Vision and Pattern Recognition, pp. 1492–1500 (2017)

16. Xu, X., Li, Y., Wu, G., Luo, J.: Multi-modal deep feature learning for RGB-D object detection. Pattern Recognit. **72**, 300–313 (2017)

17. Zhang, Z., Liu, Y., Chen, J., Niu, L., Zhang, L.: Depth privileged object detection in indoor scenes via deformation hallucination. In: Proceedings of the AAAI Conference on Artificial Intelligence, vol. 35, pp. 3456–3464 (2021)

18. Zhu, X., Hu, H., Lin, S., Dai, J.: Deformable convnets v2: more deformable, better results. In: Proceedings of the IEEE/CVF Conference on Computer Vision and Pattern Recognition, pp. 9308–9316 (2019)

CSMOTE: Contrastive Synthetic Minority Oversampling for Imbalanced Time Series Classification

Pin Liu[1,2], Xiaohui Guo[2(✉)], Rui Wang[1,2], Pengpeng Chen[1], Tianyu Wo[1,2], and Xudong Liu[1,2]

[1] State key Lab of Software Development Environment, Beihang University, Beijing, China
{liupin,guoxh,wangrui,chenpp,woty,liuxd}@act.buaa.edu.cn
[2] Hangzhou Innovation Institute, Beihang University, Hangzhou, China

Abstract. The class imbalanced classification is pervasive in real-world applications for a long time, such as image, tabular, textual, and video data analysis. The imbalance issue of time series data attracts especial attention recently, with the development of the Industrial Internet. The Oversampling method is one of the most popular techniques, which usually heuristically re-establishes the balance of the dataset, i.e., interpolation or adversarial generative technology for minority class instances augmentation. However, the high dimensional and temporal dependence characteristics pose great challenge to time series minority oversampling. To this end, this paper proposes a Contrastive Synthetic Minority Oversampling (CSMOTE) for imbalanced time series classification. Specifically, we assume that the minority class example is composed of its peculiar private information and common information shared with majority classes. According to the variational Bayes technology, we encode this information into two separated Gaussian latent spaces. The minority class synthetic instances are generated from the combination of private and common representation draws from the two latent spaces. We evaluate CSMOTE's performance on five real-world benchmark datasets, and it outperforms other oversampling baselines in most of the cases.

Keywords: Time series · Synthetic oversampling · Class imbalance · Classification · Contrastive learning

1 Introduction

The data imbalance problem is long-standing [4] and especially severe in current IoT time series analysis scenarios [10], e.g., disease screening [6], fraud or intrusion detection, and prognostics and health management of industrial equipment [9]. Simply feeding the imbalance samples to models, results in biases toward the majority class, meanwhile the minority class has a negligible or very lesser recall. But, it is the performance of the minority class that is most important in safety and healthy critical applications.

© Springer Nature Switzerland AG 2021
T. Mantoro et al. (Eds.): ICONIP 2021, CCIS 1516, pp. 447–455, 2021.
https://doi.org/10.1007/978-3-030-92307-5_52

Resampling is one of the most commonly preferred strategies struggling with data imbalance. Besides vanilla oversampling duplicating examples in the minority class, synthesizing virtual minority examples from the existing examples is a prevalent and promising approach, also known as synthetic oversampling [3]. But the sample interpolation based minority class synthesis method is hard to be applied directly to imbalanced time series classification. From our experimental observation, imbalanced time series datasets tend to manifest a prominent characteristic that the minority and majority classes share some *common* information to a large extent. The minority class samples usually superimpose some extra *private* information onto their shared one. For example, certain anomalous signals always reside in the normal ones. This naturally arises in the physical generation process of time series, e.g., the fraud behavior being concealed behind ordinary intersection, the disease's physiological index subtly differing from healthy individuals' in some local time intervals.

From this perspective, we abstract these two kinds of shared and private information of time series into two probabilistic latent variables, and propose a contrastive synthetic oversampling method for imbalanced time series called CSMOTE. Resorting to variational auto-encoding framework, the minority class samples are encoded into two disentangled Gaussian distributed latent spaces, one of which is shared with majority class. The majority class samples are encoded into the shared latent space only. In the decoding phase, we reconstruct the minority class samples from the shared and private latent vectors concatenated representation and the majority class examples from shared information only. To mitigate the imbalanced problem, we augment the minority class synthetic instances via the above generative process, i.e., oversampling the minority class. The two probabilistic encoders use multi-layer 1D-CNN networks to extract high dimensional and temporal dependence characteristics of time series, and the decoder restores the series via 1D deconvolution networks.

The remainder of this paper is organized as follows. Section 2 summarizes the related work for class imbalanced problems and synthetic oversampling methods. We detail the proposed method CSMOTE in Sect. 3. Section 4 presents the experimental setup and demonstrates the experimental results. We conclude this paper and discuss the future work in Sect. 5.

2 Related Work

A representative seminal oversampling approach SMOTE [3], generates minority instances by interpolation between the positive instances that lie together in feature space. Adaptively shifts the decision boundary to focus on those samples difficult to learn, ADASYN [5] rebalances the data via minority class distribution characterizing the learning difficultly. They however concentrate on the minority class' characteristics, but overlook the majority, which may therefore negatively impact imbalance learnability. SWIM [8] utilizes the majority distributional information to guide the synthetic minority oversampling in majority class' low density regions. By preserving the main covariance structure of time

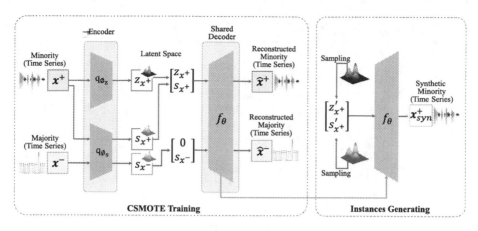

Fig. 1. CSMOTE's architecture

series data, SPO [1] intelligently synthesizes minority time series data in the void data space without being too closely mingled with existing minority samples.

Deep generative models [2], like VAE and GAN, produce realistic-looking data including time series, and naturally serve as minority oversampling and instances augmentation module. But VAE's single-mode Gaussian assumption and GAN's boundary distortion [7], facing the formidable extremely skewed real data distribution, limit the imbalance mitigation performance.

3   Method

In this section, we present a variational Bayes auto-encoding generative process for imbalanced two class time series data. A probabilistic time series decoder is learned and could be used to augment the minority class. This is an unified method suitable for imbalanced binary classification and supervised anomaly detection on time series.

Model Architecture. From the observation that minority sample enriches unique private variation to common information shared with majority, we assume some random process, involving two isotropic multivariate Gaussian latent variables s, $z \sim \mathcal{N}(0, I)$ for common and private implicate information respectively, generates the imbalanced two class time series data, $D = D^+ \cup D^-$ and $|D^+| \ll |D^-|$. Figure 1 shows the entire CSMOTE's architecture.

The generative process could be treated as two branches. For an observed minority sample $x^+ \in D^+$, $z_{x^+} \sim \mathcal{N}(0, I)$, $s_{x^+} \sim \mathcal{N}(0, I)$, $x^+ \sim p(x|<z_{x^+}, s_{x^+}>)$, but a majority sample $x^- \in D^-$, $s_{x^-} \sim \mathcal{N}(0, I)$, $x^- \sim p(x|<0, s_{x^-}>)$, where $p(x|<z, s>)$ are also from Gaussian distribution family, and $<\cdot, \cdot>$ denotes concatenation operation. Obviously, the marginal likelihood $P(X) = \int p(Z)p(S)p_\Theta(X|<Z, S>)dZdS$ and true posterior $p_\Theta(<Z, S>|X)$ are intractable. Here the capital letters are compact vectorization expressions.

Algorithm 1: CSMOTE Training

Input: D^+, D^-, K, q_{ϕ_z}, q_{ϕ_s}, f_θ, $p(z)$, $p(s)$

1 Randomly initialize ϕ_z, ϕ_s and θ, and do following iteration until converges. **for**
   $i = 1, \cdots, K$ **do**

2   Encode: $\mu_{z_i}^+, \sigma_{z_i}^+ \leftarrow q_{\phi_z}(x_i^+)$; $\mu_{s_i}^+, \sigma_{s_i}^+ \leftarrow q_{\phi_s}(x_i^+)$; $\mu_{s_i}^-, \sigma_{s_i}^- \leftarrow q_{\phi_s}(x_i^-)$;

3   Sampling: $z_i^+ \leftarrow \mu_{z_i}^+ + \epsilon \odot \sigma_{z_i}^+, \epsilon \sim \mathcal{N}(0, I)$;
       $s_i^+ \leftarrow \mu_{s_i}^+ + \epsilon_z \odot \sigma_{s_i}^+, \epsilon_z \sim \mathcal{N}(0, I)$; $s_i^- \leftarrow \mu_{s_i}^- + \epsilon_s \odot \sigma_{s_i}^-, \epsilon_s \sim \mathcal{N}(0, I)$;

4   Concatenate: $h_i^+ \leftarrow\ <z_i^+, s_i^+>$; $h_i^- \leftarrow\ <0, s_i^->$;

5   Decode: $x_i^+ \leftarrow f_\theta(h_i^+)$; $x_i^- \leftarrow f_\theta(h_i^-)$;

6   Compute loss for D^+: $\mathcal{L}^+ = \mathbb{E}_{q_{\phi_z}(z)q_{\phi_s}(s)}[f_\theta(x_i^+ \mid h_i^+)] - KL(q_{\phi_z}(z \mid x_i^+)\|p(z)) - KL(q_{\phi_s}(s \mid x_i^+)\|p(s))$;

7   Compute loss for D^-: $\mathcal{L}^- = \mathbb{E}_{q_{\phi_s}(s)}[f_\theta(x_i^- \mid h_i^-)] - KL(q_{\phi_s}(s \mid x_i^-)\|p(s))$;

8   Combine final loss: $\mathcal{L}(\phi_z, \phi_s, \theta) = \mathcal{L}^+ + \mathcal{L}^-$;

9   Back-propagate the gradients.

10 **end**

Output: trained encoders q_{ϕ_z}, q_{ϕ_s} and decoder f_θ

Therefore we introduce a recognition model $q_\Phi(<Z, S>|X)$ and turn to neural networks to approximate the posteriors. Namely, the private information posterior $q_{\phi_z}(z|x)$ is reparametrized by $z = \mu(x) + \sigma(x) \odot \epsilon$ and $\epsilon \sim \mathcal{N}(0, I)$ as an encoder, the posterior $q_{\phi_s}(s|x)$ is the same. The probabilistic decoder $p(x|<z, s>)$ is represented by $\hat{x} = f_\theta(<z, s>)$ or $f_\theta(\hat{x}|z, s)$.

For minority class dataset D^+, we can derive the expected likelihood lower bound as an optimization objective

$$\mathcal{L}^+ = \mathbb{E}_{q_{\phi_z}(z)q_{\phi_s}(s)}[f_\theta(x^+ \mid z, s)] - KL(q_{\phi_z}(z \mid x^+)\|p(z)) - KL(q_{\phi_s}(s \mid x^+)\|p(s))$$

For majority class dataset D^-, the optimization objective is as follows

$$\mathcal{L}^- = \mathbb{E}_{q_{\phi_s}(s)}[f_\theta(x^- \mid 0, s)] - KL(q_{\phi_s}(s \mid x^-)\|p(s))$$

Given two weights γ_1 and γ_2, $\mathcal{L}$ is the ultimately optimization objective. Algorithm 1 shows the entire training process of CSMOTE.

$$\mathcal{L} = \gamma_1 * (\mathbb{E}_{q_{\phi_z}(z)q_{\phi_s}(s)}[f_\theta(x^+ \mid z, s)] + \mathbb{E}_{q_{\phi_s}(s)}[f_\theta(x^- \mid 0, s)])$$
$$- \gamma_2 * (KL(q_{\phi_z}(z \mid x^+)\|p(z)) + KL(q_{\phi_s}(s \mid x^+)\|p(s)) + KL(q_{\phi_s}(s \mid x^-)\|p(s)))$$

Encoder and Decoder. To capture the time series' high dimensional and temporal dependence characteristics, we construct encoder via 3 layers 1D convolution network with 32 filters for each layer. The decoder network is composed by 2 1D deconvolution layers with 32 filters for each, and 1 1D deconvolution layer with 1 filer. All the kernel sizes are set to 3.

Oversampling and Classification. After CSMOTE's training process converges, the parameters of q_{ϕ_z}, q_{ϕ_s} and f_θ are inferred. Since this work's focus is

Table 1. Summary of the imbalanced time series datasets

Datasets	Length	Training data		Testing data	
		Min/Maj	IR	Min/Maj	IR
Wafer	152	97/903	9.3	665/5499	8.27
ECG200	96	31/69	2.23	36/64	1.78
FordA	500	184/1846	10	68/681	10
FreezerRegular	301	8/75	9.37	140/1425	10.18
Drive251	1600	22/224	10	22/224	10

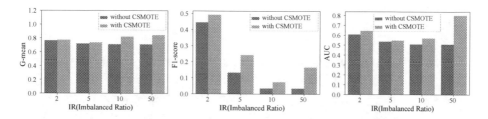

Fig. 2. Imbalance classification performance with and without CSMOTE.

rebalancing the datasets, we use the trained decoder f_θ to generate the synthetic minority samples. First, we sample the Gaussian latent variables $z \sim \mathcal{N}(0, I)$, $s \sim \mathcal{N}(0, I)$, and concatenate them together. Then, we map the minority latent vector to the observed sample space, i.e., $x_{syn}^+ = f_\theta(<z, s>)$. We use SVM to classify both the balanced and imbalanced datasets, as previous studies [1] has shown that widely used 1NN and 1NN-DTW time series classifier have worse performance than SVM with respect to F1-score and G-mean metrics.

4   Experimental Study

In this section, we first demonstrate the CSMOTE's imbalance mitigation effects via data pre/post-augmentation comparison visualization, and then assess its imbalanced time series classification performance. All the codes are publicly available[1], and the experimental setups are as follows.

Datasets. We use five real-world benchmark time series datasets from UCR 2018 and CWRU. Table 1 statistically summarizes the properties of these five datasets, therein *IR* is imbalanced ratio (#majority class samples/#minority class samples). Each dataset we used contains only two classes. The original Wafer and ECG200 are imbalanced datasets. It is worth noting that FordA, FreezerRegular and Drive251 are balance datasets originally, and we downsample arbitrary one class of each to validate our method. All of these datasets are rebalanced through oversampling finally.

---

[1] https://github.com/liupin-source/csmote.

Table 2. Imbalanced time series classification performance. Bold numbers indicate the best, and underlined numbers is the second. Standard deviations are shown in parenthesis.

Datasets	Methods					
	Base	ROS	SMOTE	ADASYN	VAE	CSMOTE
F1-score						
Wafer	0.3408	0.6841	0.6840	0.7631	<u>0.7735</u>	**0.7883(0.01)**
ECG200	0.6667	0.6667	0.6769	0.7000	**0.7778**	0.7187(0.02)
FordA	0.0000	<u>0.1823</u>	0.1814	0.1821	0.1685	**0.3222(0.02)**
FreezerRegular	0.1206	0.3241	0.2567	<u>0.4589</u>	0.3882	**0.5946(0.02)**
Drive251	0.0351	0.0582	0.0422	0.0689	<u>0.0748</u>	**0.0832(0.01)**
G-mean						
Wafer	0.7482	0.6860	0.6849	0.7631	<u>0.7618</u>	**0.7763(0.01)**
ECG200	0.7659	0.7495	0.7804	0.7292	**0.8204**	0.8046(0.03)
FordA	NaN	<u>0.3181</u>	0.3171	0.3120	0.2969	**0.6995(0.02)**
FreezerRegular	0.4719	0.4408	0.3827	<u>0.5695</u>	0.4969	**0.7609(0.04)**
Drive251	0.7103	<u>0.7932</u>	0.7598	0.7135	0.7102	**0.8446(0.02)**
AUC						
Wafer	0.6028	0.6860	0.6849	0.7496	<u>0.7574</u>	**0.7674(0.01)**
ECG200	0.7431	0.7413	0.7509	0.7595	**0.7971**	0.7803(0.02)
FordA	0.5000	0.5511	0.5496	0.5511	<u>0.5203</u>	**0.5864(0.01)**
FreezerRegular	0.5270	0.7577	0.6838	<u>0.7875</u>	**0.7891**	0.7000(0.02)
Drive251	0.5089	<u>0.7053</u>	0.6339	0.5178	0.5334	**0.7991(0.03)**

Metrics. Evaluating imbalanced classification is tricky, and we use two threshold metrics, F1-score = $(2 \times \text{Recall} \times \text{Precision})/(\text{Recall} + \text{Precision})$, G-mean = $\sqrt{\text{Sensitivity} \times \text{Specificity}}$, and a ranking metric, ROC-AUC, i.e., the area under the receiver operating characteristics curve (AUC). They are all popular and useful for classification with a skewed class distribution, e.g., the number of examples in minority class is extreme small in our case.

Baselines. We adopt the following oversampling methods as baselines for comparison with our CSMOTE. Two probabilistic samplers for minority class augmentation, random oversampling (ROS) and VAE based deep generator. Two vicinal samples interpolation based synthetic oversamples, synthetic minority oversampling (SMOTE), adaptive weighted synthetic sampler (ADASYN). The hyperparameters of SMOTE and ADASYN are set to the default value of k_neighbors = 5. The hyperparameters of VAE and CSMOTE are finetuned. The number of nodes in the latent layer is 4. CSMOTE's training process has the same problem of posterior collapse as VAE. In order to reduce the impact of this problem, we add corresponding weights to the regularization term and reconstruction term of $\mathcal{L}$. Specifically, γ_1 and γ_2 are set to 2e−5 and 1, respectively.

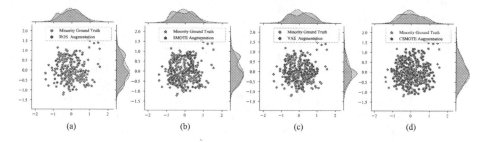

Fig. 3. PCA plots of original minority class instances and minority class synthetic instances generated by four oversampling methods in dataset Drive251. ROS (a), SMOTE (b), VAE (c) and CSMOTE (d).

4.1   Imbalance Mitigation Effects

First, we build datasets with different imbalanced ratios on Drive251 to verify whether CSMOTE can mitigate the imbalanced effects. Each imbalanced ratio dataset contains two classification experiments. One is to classify the imbalanced dataset and the other is to classify the balanced dataset with CSMOTE synthetic instances supplemented. Figure 2 records the binary classification metrics F1-score, G-mean and AUC with/without CSMOTE.

It shows that the three metrics without CSMOTE all decrease as the imbalanced ratio increases, which also verifies the negative impact of the imbalanced problem on classification performance. In addition, comparing these metrics of with/without CSMOTE in each ratio, we can know that classification performance after with CSMOTE is improved under each imbalanced ratio. Moreover, as the ratio increases, the performance improvement becomes more obvious, which also verifies that CSMOTE is more suitable for solving classification problems with a high imbalanced ratio.

4.2   Classification Performance

Table 2 reports average F1-score, G-mean, and AUC for the best performing classifier obtained over the various datasets by our method CSMOTE, ROS, SMOTE, ADASYN, VAE, and Base (classifier which is performed on originally imbalanced datasets). Results demonstrate that CSMOTE achieves the best performance because it got the largest G-mean in 4 of the 5 datasets. The F1-score and AUC results obtained the maximum value on more than 3 datasets. The second-best performance method is VAE, and its three metrics have also obtained the largest and second-ranked in multiple datasets.

It is important to emphasize that the F1-score and G-mean of our method CSMOTE on FordA, FreezerRegular and Drive251 have been significantly improved. This is attributed to the large imbalanced ratios of these four datasets. CSMOTE relies on the majority class with rich information to assist the generation of the minority class synthetic instances. Moreover, all of these metrics include the evaluation of minority class samples, so that excellent minority class synthetic instances can help improve these two metrics.

In order to more intuitively understand why CSMOTE performs best. We constructed data visualization experiments for qualitative analysis. Figure 3 shows the PCA plots for the original minority class training dataset and the minority class synthetic instances obtained by ROS, SMOTE, VAE, and CSMOTE on Drive251. Moreover, PCA plots also draw the marginal probability density distribution in the directions of two principal components. It can be clearly seen from Fig. 3(d) that the data space formed by the samples generated by CSMOTE almost restores the minority ground truth data space. Moreover, their marginal probability density distributions in the directions of two principal components are relatively close to the original minority class dataset. On the contrary, the data space of the samples generated by the other three methods is quite different from the minority ground truth data space. This is also the fundamental reason why the performance of classification using these samples cannot reach the performance on the original balanced dataset.

5   Conclusions

This paper proposes a contrastive synthetic oversampling method in order to overcome the limitations of existing oversampling methods on time series. It has empirically compared CSMOTE with existing oversampling methods based on three evaluation metrics F1-score, G-mean and AUC on 5 real-world benchmark time series datasets. The experimental results demonstrate that CSMOTE significantly improved the classification performance of imbalanced time series and achieved the highest average value on 4 datasets. In future, we will continue to explore the solution of oversampling methods for extreme and absolute class imbalanced time series and generalizing this work to multi-class long tailed data.

Acknowledgments. This work is supported by the National Key Research and Development Program (2018YFB1306000).

References

1. Cao, H., et al.: SPO: structure preserving oversampling for imbalanced time series classification. In: ICDM, pp. 1008–1013. IEEE (2011)
2. Fajardo, V.A., et al.: On oversampling imbalanced data with deep conditional generative models. Expert Syst. Appl. **169**, 114463 (2021)
3. Fernández, A., et al.: Smote for learning from imbalanced data: progress and challenges, marking the 15-year anniversary. JAIR **61**, 863–905 (2018)
4. He, H., Garcia, E.A.: Learning from imbalanced data. Trans. Knowl. Data Eng. **21**(9), 1263–1284 (2009)
5. He, H., et al.: ADASYN: adaptive synthetic sampling approach for imbalanced learning. In: IJCNN, pp. 1322–1328. IEEE (2008)
6. Miri Rostami, S., et al.: Extracting predictor variables to construct breast cancer survivability model with class imbalance problem. J. AI Data Min. **6**(2), 263–276 (2018)

7. Santurkar, S., Schmidt, L., Madry, A.: A classification-based study of covariate shift in GAN distributions. In: ICML, pp. 4480–4489. PMLR (2018)
8. Sharma, S., et al.: Synthetic oversampling with the majority class: a new perspective on handling extreme imbalance. In: ICDM, pp. 447–456. IEEE (2018)
9. Wang, S., et al.: Resampling-based ensemble methods for online class imbalance learning. IEEE Trans. Knowl. Data Eng. **27**(5), 1356–1368 (2014)
10. Wen, Q., et al.: Time series data augmentation for deep learning: a survey. In: IJCAI, pp. 4653–4660 (2021)

CCAD: A Collective Contextual Anomaly Detection Framework for KPI Data Stream

Ganghui Hu[1,2], Jing Wang[1,2,3(✉)] (iD), Yunxiao Liu[1,2,3], Wang Ke[1], and Youfang Lin[1,2,3,4] (iD)

[1] School of Computer and Information Technology, Beijing Jiaotong University, Beijing, China
{ganghuihu,wj,lyxiao,KeWang,yflin}@bjtu.edu.cn
[2] Beijing Key Laboratory of Traffic Data Analysis and Mining, Beijing, China
[3] CAAC Key Laboratory of Intelligent Passenger Service of Civil Aviation, Beijing, China
[4] Key Laboratory of Transport Industry of Big Data Appalication Technologies for Comprehensive Transport, Beijing, China

Abstract. KPI (Key Performance Indicator) anomaly detection is critical for Internet companies to safeguard the availability and stability of services. Many online anomaly detection algorithms have been proposed in recent years. However, they are mainly designed to detect point anomalies, which fail to identify collective or contextual anomalies very well. Thus in this paper, we propose a framework of Collective Contextual Anomaly Detection (CCAD) for KPI data stream. Via Pearson correlation coefficient-based method to adapt to KPI stream, our framework addresses the limitation of time series discords algorithm and achieves a huge improvement in the accuracy for KPI stream. Moreover, instead of using a static threshold, we employ SPOT to generate an automatic threshold to determine anomalies. Extensive experimental results and analysis on multiple public KPIs show the competitive performance of CCAD and the significance of collective contextual anomalies.

Keywords: Collective contextual · Anomaly detection · Concept drift · Data stream

1 Introduction

With the rapid development of internet-based services, large internet companies usually need to closely monitor various KPIs [4,8,10] of their services in real-time. However, it is not easy to provide anomaly detection services on online platforms due to the following three key challenges: **Huge amounts of KPIs.** In large internet companies, there are thousands to millions of KPIs are generated every minute. It is difficult to extract features for training complex anomaly detection models, and it is not practical to provide a large number of labels, which makes

© Springer Nature Switzerland AG 2021
T. Mantoro et al. (Eds.): ICONIP 2021, CCIS 1516, pp. 456–463, 2021.
https://doi.org/10.1007/978-3-030-92307-5_53

supervised models [2,6] insufficient in the industrial scenario. **Timely response.** Online KPI stream anomaly detection requires the model to respond within a limited time. Hence the models with high time complexity are not suitable in an online scenario. Even they are good at accuracy. **Diverse types of anomalies.** According to [2], there are three different types of anomalies: point, contextual and collective. As shown in Fig. 1, point anomalies refer to the occurrence of a value that is considered anomalous compared to the rest of the data. Contextual anomalies take contextual or periodic patterns into account to identify anomalies. Collective anomalies refer to the situation in which a set of related data instances is anomalous compared to the rest of the data. As shown in Fig. 1, there is an essential type of anomaly in KPIs, which loses its inherent periodic pattern, and when it appears, it's a series of anomalies that persist over time. Considering the types of anomalies mentioned above, in the following paper, We call this type of anomaly in KPIs collective contextual anomaly.

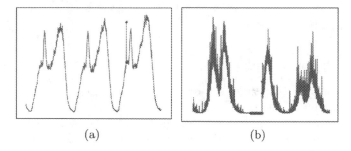

(a)   (b)

Fig. 1. Examples of point anomalies and collective contextual anomalies in KPIs. Anomalies are marked by red dots. (Color figure online)

Existing KPI anomaly detection methods [4,8,10] can detect point anomalies but fail to identify collective contextual anomalies altogether to our best knowledge. Therefore, we proposed a new, simple and effective Collective Contextual Anomaly Detection framework(CCAD) for KPI data stream.

The contributions of this paper can be summarized as follows: (1) To our best knowledge, our work identifies the significance of collective contextual anomaly in KPIs for the first time and propose a simple and effective collective contextual anomaly detection framework for KPI data stream; (2) We use periodic patterns as a breakthrough point, and design a Pearson correlation coefficient based method to overcome limitations of time series discords [5], which is robust to concept drifts [7] in KPI Stream; (3) We evaluate our framework on multiple public datasets. The experiment results show that our framework can effectively detect collective contextual anomalies and outperforms other baselines.

2   Preliminaries

KPI is a kind of time series data and can be denoted as $X = [x_1, x_2, ..., x_n]$, where x_i is the metric value at time index i for $i \in 1, 2, ..., n$, and n is the length of X, and $X_{i,j} = [x_i, x_{i+1}, ..., x_j]$ represents a subsequence from time index i to j. **KPI Anomalies** refer to a subset of data points in a KPI that do not conform to a well-defined notion of normal behavior. Unexpected patterns (i.e., anomalies) in KPIs usually indicate potential failures of the relevant devices or services. Based on the above definitions, **KPI anomaly detection** can be defined as finding all anomalies for a given KPI. Furthermore, online KPI anomaly detection can be formulated as follows: for a KPI $X = [x_1, x_2, ..., x_n]$, given historical observations $[x_{t-T+1}, ..., x_t]$, the task is to determine the label at time t , denoted by $y_t \in \{0, 1\}$, where 1 indicates an anomaly.

3   Framework

Our proposed CCAD framework consists of four components: data preprocessing, baseline extraction, KPI discords finding, and automatic thresholding. This section will introduce these modules one by one and finally summarize the overall streaming detection framework.

3.1   Data Preprocessing

It is common for KPIs to suffer from missing values due to some reasons, such as server downtime or network crashes. The widely used linear interpolation is suitable for short-missing segments but not for long-missing segments. Thus, based on the length of the missing segment, our filling strategy can be divided into two cases: (1) if the length of missing points is less than 5, it is filled with linear interpolation; (2) otherwise, we use the values of the same time slot from the previous period to fill the missing segment.

3.2   Baseline Extraction

Noises have a significant impact on changing the shapes of KPI curves and mislead shape-based similarity. Thus we need a simple and fast method to remove those noises, and then a baseline (including normal patterns that indicate its expected behavior) can be extracted to be used to find KPI discords. Exponentially Weighted Moving Average (EWMA) [3] is a suitable method to separate KPI into two parts: baseline and residuals.

3.3   KPI Discords Finding

The original time series discords algorithm [5] only works for batch mode and assumes that the same type of anomaly occurs only once in the time series, which is unsuitable for detecting collective contextual anomalies in KPI data stream. Thus, we consider several modifications to propose a KPI discords finding algorithm including four steps, namely candidate subsequence reduction, shape-based distance measure, concept drift adaptation, and MOM-based automatic thresholding. We describe four steps in detail in the following.

Candidate Subsequence Reduction. In original time series discords algorithm [5], it needs to scan along the time series to examine each subsequence,
which is impractical for KPI data stream generated continuously. However, based
on the periodic pattern, we do not need to example each subsequence, only examine the same time slots in different periods in the base sample set. Specifically,
suppose the base sample set $P = \{P_1, P_2, \cdots, P_N\}$ consists of the first N normal periods in KPI, $P_i = X_{(i-1)l+1,il}$ represents the i-th period in KPI and the
period length is l. For point $x_t, t > Nl, (t = Nl + m, Nl + 2m, ...)$, suppose it
is the T-th $(0 \leq T < l)$ point of the k-th periods in KPI, we define its discord
distance S_t based on its historical observations $X_{t-m+1,t}$ as follow:

$$S_t = \min(Dist(P_i, x_t)), i = 1, \cdots, N \qquad (1)$$
$$= \min(Dist(X_{(i-1)l+T-m+1,(i-1)l+T}, X_{t-m+1,t})) \qquad (2)$$

where $X_{(i-1)l+T-m+1,(i-1)l+T}$ denotes the same time slot of $X_{t-m+1,t}$ in the i-th
normal period of set P; m denotes the number of historical observations used,
and we set $S_{t-j} = S_t, j = 1, m - 1$; $Dist$ is a distance measure, the selection of
specific distance measure will be described in the next section.

Shape-Based Distance Measure. In the literature, many time series distance
measures have been proposed. L_p-norms [11] are a group of widely-used distance
measures due to their efficiency and simplicity, but they are sensitive to noises,
phase shifts and amplitude differences. Dynamic Time Warping (DTW) [9] is
distinguished for its robustness against phase shifts, scaling distortion, and other
shape variations. Even though its computational complexity is $O(n^2)$, in our
discords distance, the subsequence length is less than 20. Thus DTW [9] is a
suitable distance measure in our algorithm.

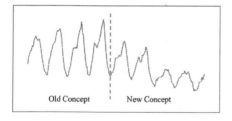

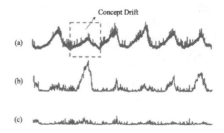

Fig. 2. A concept drift in KPI stream.

Fig. 3. (a) The raw time series; (b) and
(c) are the discord scores without/with
PCCs-based adaptation.

Concept Drift Adaptation. As mentioned above, our framework uses the first
N normal periods in KPI as a base sample set to start up KPI discords finding. It works well in simple situations, however, finding KPI discords in stream
mode consists of additional challenges due to data stream evolving, especially

the problem of concept drift [7], which shown in Fig. 2. Inspired by an important insight in [7] that the relationship between new concepts and old concepts can be almost perfectly fitted by linear regression, we propose a Pearson correlation coefficient (PCCs) based method robust to concept drift. Specifically, we assume $U = X_{(u-l)l+1,ul}$ is the u-th period, $V = X_{(v-1)l+1,vl}$ is the v-th period. Then PCCs between the two periods can be calculated as follows:

$$PCCs(u,v) = \frac{\sum_{i=1}^{l} \left(U_i - \bar{U}\right)\left(V_i - \bar{V}\right)}{\sqrt{\sum_{i=1}^{l} \left(U_i - \bar{U}\right)^2}\sqrt{\sum_{i=1}^{l} \left(V_i - \bar{V}\right)^2}} \tag{3}$$

where $PCCs(u,v)$ denotes the PCCs between U and V; l denotes the period length; $\bar{V}$ and $\bar{U}$ denotes the mean of U and V respectively.

When a period has just ended, it will be determined by the PCCs-based method whether it is used to update the base sample set. The whole PCCs-based approach is summarized in Algorithm 1. Through this method, our framework can update the base sample set timely and use the latest base-sample set to calculate KPI discords distance in the data stream. Considering collective contextual anomalies lose their periodic pattern, PCCs between them and base samples will be very low. Therefore this method will not add collective contextual anomalies to the sample set.

Algorithm 1: PCCsAdapation(PCCsAd)

Input: the uth period $U = X_{(u-1)l+1,ul}$,   7 **end**
      base sample set P: $P_i = X_{(i-1)l+1,il}$,   8 $MeanRatio =$
      $i = 1, \cdots, N$, threshold of PCCs $(mean(U) - MaxMean)/(MaxMean)$
      th_{PCCs} and threshold of mean ratio   9 **if** $MaxPCCs > th_{PCCs}$ *and*
      th_m $MeanRatio > th_m$ **then**
1   $MaxPCCs = 0, MaxMean = 0$ 10 | Add U to base sample set P
2   **for** $i = 1$ *to* N **do**   11 **end**
3 | **if** $PCCs(U, P_i) > MaxPCCs$ **then**
4 | | $MaxPCCs = PCCs(U, P_i)$
5 | | $MaxMean = mean(P_i)$
6 | **end**

3.4 MOM-Based Automatic Thresholding

After KPI discords finding, we can apply a simple static threshold to detect anomalies. However, such a strategy is too simple to obtain satisfactory results and deal with complex situations. Inspired by FluxEV [4], we adopt the SPOT [10] algorithm for selecting a threshold dynamically, and Method of Moments (MOM) [4] is used to replace MLE to speed up SPOT further.

3.5 Overall Streaming Detection

Algorithm 2 shows our streaming anomaly detection framework. First, we need $a = s + Nl$ points to start the baseline extraction and KPI discords finding. After that, extra w points are used to initialize SPOT [10]. From the $(a + w + 1)$-th point, we can carry out anomaly detection in a streaming way.

Algorithm 2: Stream Detection in CCAD

Input: input data $X = [x_1, ..., x_n]$;
window sizes s, m, base sample
set size N; period l, threshold of
PCCs th_{PCCs}, threshold of mean
ratio th_m; risk q, point num to
initialize SPOT $w(l|w)$.

Output: detection result $R_j \in \{0, 1\}$

1   $a = s + Nl$;

2   $P = \{P_1, P_2, \cdots, P_N\}, P_i = B_{s+(i-1)*l+1, s+il}$; // after Baseline Extraction

3   $init([P_{a+1,...,a+w}], q)$ // init SPOT

4   **for** $j >= a + w + 1$ **do**

5     $b_j = \text{EWMA}(X_{j-s, j-1})$;

6   **if** $m \mid (j - a - w)$ **then**

7   **for** $i = 1$ *to* N **do**

8         $S_j = \min(Dist(P_i, b_j))$;

9   **end**

10       $S_{j-k} = S_j$

11       $R_{j-k} \leftarrow SPOT(S_{j-k}, q), k = 0, \cdots, m - 1$;

12   **end**

13   **if** $l \mid (j - s)$ **then**

14       $PCCsAd(U, P, th_{PCCs}, th_m)$;

15   **end**

16   **end**

---

4   Experiments

4.1   Datasets

The datasets used are collected from KPI dataset [1]. KPI dataset is provided by AIOps Challenge [1]. It contains KPI curves with anomaly labels collected from many large-scale Internet companies. In this paper, five KPIs that contain collective contextual anomalies are chosen for experiments. Each KPI has three record values: timestamp, value, and label (0/1). The first 20% of each KPI is used as the training set, and the last 80% is used to test the performance of our model.

Table 1. Statistics of datasets, CC Anomalies denotes collective contextual anomalies and it accounts for the vast majority of total anomalies.

Dataset	Total	Missing	Anomalies	CC anomalies
$\mathcal{A}$	213859	2141/0.99%	16113/7.53%	14694/6.87%
$\mathcal{B}$	239251	24339/9.23%	9491/3.97%	9209/3.85%
$\mathcal{C}$	239513	24077/9.1%	9677/4.04%	9281/3.87%
$\mathcal{D}$	240047	23543/8.9%	11508/4.79%	8022/3.34%
$\mathcal{E}$	292230	6823/2.3%	3303/1.13%	2091/0.72%

4.2   Baselines and Metrics

We compare our framework with four state-of-the-art algorithms include FluxEV [4], SR [8], SPOT and DSPOT [10]. As a standard evaluation metric, F1-score has been widely used in the anomaly detection field. Thus, we use F1-score to evaluate our model's overall performance and report the corresponding precision and recall.

Table 2. Overall performance

	Metrics	SPOT	DSPOT	SR	FluxEV	CCAD
$\mathcal{A}$	P	0.09	0.12	0.21	0.11	0.57
	R	0.16	0.42	0.05	0.04	0.61
	F1	0.11	0.18	0.08	0.06	**0.59**
$\mathcal{B}$	P	0.22	0.28	0.08	0.07	0.51
	R	0.97	0.94	0.02	0.03	0.83
	F1	0.37	0.43	0.04	0.04	**0.63**
$\mathcal{C}$	P	0.24	0.38	0.36	0.15	0.38
	R	0.88	0.36	0.03	0.02	0.97
	F1	0.38	0.37	0.06	0.03	**0.54**
$\mathcal{D}$	P	0.69	0.38	0.76	0.38	0.81
	R	0.74	0.77	0.19	0.14	0.75
	F1	0.71	0.51	0.31	0.2	**0.78**
$\mathcal{E}$	P	0.1	0.23	0.46	0.03	0.35
	R	0.62	0.4	0.15	0.15	0.48
	F1	0.17	0.29	0.22	0.05	**0.41**

Table 3. Effects of PCCs-based adaptation method

Method	$w/oPCCs$	$CCAD$
$\mathcal{A}$	0.46	**0.59**
$\mathcal{B}$	0.23	**0.63**
$\mathcal{C}$	0.1	**0.54**
$\mathcal{D}$	0.74	**0.78**
$\mathcal{E}$	0.09	**0.41**

4.3   Overall Performance

Set Up. For CCAD, we set the hyper-parameters empirically. In baseline extraction, window size s is set as 10, smoothing factor α is set as 0.5. In KPI discords finding, the initial size N of the base sample set is set as 10, the number of historical observations used m is set as 10. In PCCs-based adaptation method, the threshold of mean ratio th_m is set as 0.1, and the threshold of PCCs th_{PCCs} is set between 0.7 and 0.95 for five datasets. In automatic thresholding, risk coefficient q is set as 4.5×10^{-3}. For other baseline models, recommended configurations from original papers or codes published by the authors are adopted.

Result. The overall experimental results are shown in Table 2. CCAD outperforms other methods on all five KPIs. Specifically, FluxEV [4] uses EWMA [3] to focus on fluctuations in data. However, it does not consider the periodic pattern in data, which causes it fails to detect collective contextual anomalies. SR [8] assumes that anomaly points are usually salient in the visual perspective. However, this assumption is not suitable for the collective contextual anomaly. And SPOT and DSPOT [10] are only sensitive to the extreme values in the entire data distribution. By contrast, CCAD utilizes the characteristics of the collective contextual anomaly in KPI and achieves huge improvement.

4.4   Impact of PCCs-Based Adaptation

In this section, we investigate the effectiveness of PCCs-based adaptation. The results are shown in Table 3. We notice that the PCCs-based adaptation method improves performance significantly. Figure 3 visually shows the effect of PCCs-based adaptation. If we do not use PCCs-based adaptation in places where concept drift occurs, it is likely to mislead the threshold discriminator and produce false positives.

5 Conclusion

In this paper, we proposed CCAD, a simple and effective collective contextual anomaly detection framework for KPI data stream. We take the periodic pattern as a breakthrough point and design a KPI discords finding method to overcome the limitations of the original time series discords algorithm.

References

1. Aiops challenge, final dataset. http://iops.ai/dataset_detail/?id=10
2. Braei, M., Wagner, S.: Anomaly detection in univariate time-series: a survey on the state-of-the-art. arXiv preprint arXiv:2004.00433 (2020)
3. Hunter, J.S.: The exponentially weighted moving average. J. Qual. Technol. **18**(4), 203–210 (1986)
4. Li, J., Di, S., Shen, Y., Chen, L.: FluxEV: a fast and effective unsupervised framework for time-series anomaly detection. In: Proceedings of the 14th ACM International Conference on Web Search and Data Mining, pp. 824–832 (2021)
5. Lin, J., Keogh, E., Fu, A., Van Herle, H.: Approximations to magic: finding unusual medical time series. In: 18th IEEE Symposium on Computer-Based Medical Systems (CBMS 2005), pp. 329–334. IEEE (2005)
6. Liu, D., et al.: Opprentice: towards practical and automatic anomaly detection through machine learning. In: Proceedings of the 2015 Internet Measurement Conference, pp. 211–224 (2015)
7. Ma, M., Zhang, S., Pei, D., Huang, X., Dai, H.: Robust and rapid adaption for concept drift in software system anomaly detection. In: 2018 IEEE 29th International Symposium on Software Reliability Engineering (ISSRE), pp. 13–24. IEEE (2018)
8. Ren, H., et al.: Time-series anomaly detection service at Microsoft. In: Proceedings of the 25th ACM SIGKDD International Conference on Knowledge Discovery & Data Mining, pp. 3009–3017 (2019)
9. Sakoe, H., Chiba, S.: Dynamic programming algorithm optimization for spoken word recognition. IEEE Trans. Acoust. Speech Signal Process. **26**(1), 43–49 (1978)
10. Siffer, A., Fouque, P.A., Termier, A., Largouet, C.: Anomaly detection in streams with extreme value theory. In: Proceedings of the 23rd ACM SIGKDD International Conference on Knowledge Discovery and Data Mining, pp. 1067–1075 (2017)
11. Yi, B.K., Faloutsos, C.: Fast time sequence indexing for arbitrary LP norms (2000)

Scale Semantic Flow Preserving Across Image Pyramid

Zhili Lin, Guanglu Song, and Biao Leng[(⊠)]

Beihang University, Beijing, China
{lin,guanglusong,lengbiao}@buaa.edu.cn

Abstract. Image pyramid based face detector is powerful yet time consuming when cooperated with convolutional neural network, and thus hard to satisfy the computational requirement in real-world applications. In this paper, we proposed a novel method using Semantic Preserving Feature Pyramid ($SPFP$) to eliminate the computational gap between image pyramid and feature pyramid based detectors. Since a feature tensor of an image can be upsampled or downsampled by Reversible Scale Semantic Flow Preserving (RS^2FP) network, we do not need to feed images with all scales but a middle scale into the network. Extensive experiments demonstrate that the proposed algorithm can accelerate image pyramid by about 5× to 7× on widely used face detection benchmarks while maintaining the comparable performance.

Keywords: Face detection · Scale attention · Semantic preserving

1 Introduction

As the basis of other tasks such as face alignment, face recognition and tracking, face detection task has received extensive attention as the Convolutional Neural Network (CNN) went on [5,9,22]. However, the limited computational budget in real-world applications deeply limits the scale of the detector backbone and the receptive field is not big enough to support the detector to handle large scale targets [8]. Feature pyramid mechanism is very effective for tiny face detection with large scale variance [7], the scale semantic information in different levels is comfortable for detecting the corresponding scales [17]. The single-shot multi-scale detector can achieve better performance because the sufficient parameters provide the strong support for the ability of handling large scale variance. It's worth thinking about that arguably, multi-shot single-scale detector based on image pyramid can perform better with insufficient parameters [3], because it only need to focus on a certain scale range of faces. The image pyramid is used to assist the single-scale multi-shot detector by computing feature maps multiple times for multi-scale face detection.

However, the computational cost caused by image pyramid is huge. Considering the problems mentioned above, we propose a Landmark-Guided Scale Attention Network (LGSAN) to predict the potential scales more efficient. LGSAN is

© Springer Nature Switzerland AG 2021
T. Mantoro et al. (Eds.): ICONIP 2021, CCIS 1516, pp. 464–471, 2021.
https://doi.org/10.1007/978-3-030-92307-5_54

a very tiny network with feature pyramid mechanism which is more friendly to large scale variations. Furthermore, we proposed a novel Reversible Scale Semantic Flow Preserving network (RS^2FP) which contains Scale Semantic Flow Up unit (S^2FU) and Scale Semantic Recurrently Flow Down unit (S^2RFD). All of the components can be incorporated into a unified CNN framework and trained end-to-end. Experiments show that our approach can largely accelerates face detection based on image pyramid and achieves the comparable results.

To sum up, our contributions in this work are as follows:

(1) We propose LGSAN to predict the potential scales in an image with feature pyramid mechanism which is very lightweight but achieve excellent performance.

(2) We prove that the scale semantic information between different scale images in image pyramid can be transferred reversible, not only from large scale to small, but vice versa.

(3) We devise RS^2FP. Given a feature map with an arbitrary scale, both of the high-level feature map generated by S^2FU for detecting $2^{-n}\times$ scale target and the rest feature maps for detecting larger scale target can be generated by S^2RFD, which fully leverages efficiency and accuracy.

Extensive experiments show that our proposed algorithm can largely accelerate image-pyramid-based face detector by about $5\times$ to $7\times$ on widely used face detection benchmarks.

2 Related Work

The emergence of CNN drives the great development of face detection, many effective backbone networks which make great improvement in classification tasks have been applied to detection [5]. To give CNN the scale-invariant ability, image pyramid is a reasonable way to realize this [3]. Image pyramid is a multi-scale representation of an image, such that the face detection can own the scale-invariant ability, in other words, detecting large and small faces using images with different scale [15]. Arguably, the image-pyramid based single-scale detector can achieve higher performance when the amount of parameters is close to single-shot multi-scale detector [14,25]. Despite its satisfactory performance, the huge computational time makes it less acceptable than another one in real-world applications. In order to better alleviate this problem, researchers tried to predict face scale straightforwardly by a shallow CNN [8], the maximum feature map is computed and other small scale feature maps can be computed by it via the RSA unit [12]. However, it can only transfer the scale semantic information from large scale to smaller scale and using a large size image is still a huge amount of computation.

3 Proposed Method

In this section, we propose LGSAN for predicting the potential scale in an image and the invalid layers are ignored in image pyramid for decreasing the detecting operation on invalid feature maps. Furthermore, RS^2FP is proposed for reversible scale semantic transform, it can greatly accelerate the image-pyramid based face detector without performance loss.

3.1 Landmark Guided Scale Attention Network

The biggest bottleneck in image pyramid is that we need to densely sample layers to ensure the single-scale detector can capture all the targets with different scales. Aimless sampling brings huge time-consuming and to better alleviate this problem, we design LGSAN with only 800K parameters. The input of LGSAN is an image I with size 224×224 and the output is a vector S_i with a length of 60 where each pixel value represents the existing probability of the corresponding scale target. We can get this 224×224 image from an arbitrary size image by image resizing and border interpolating. Given an image I with long edge $L_{max} = 224$ and its ground truth $B_i = (x_l t, y_l t, x_r d, y_r d)$ where means top left coordinate and lower right coordinate, the mapping between scale index in S_i and the B_i can be formulated as:

$$x(t) = \sqrt{((y_{rd}(t) - y_{lt}(t)) \cdot (x_{rd}(t) - x_{lt}(t)))} \tag{1}$$

$$k(t) = 10 \cdot \left(\log_2 \left(\frac{x(t)}{L_{\max}} \times 2048 \right) - 5 \right) \tag{2}$$

$$S_i(k(t)) = 1 \tag{3}$$

where $t \in [0, T)$ means the number of bounding boxes in B_i. So the face scale between $x(t) \in (32, 1024]$ can be decoded into the vector S_i.

The training loss of S_i are sigmoid cross entropy loss:

$$L = -\frac{1}{N} \sum_{n=1}^{N} [p_n \log(\hat{p}_n) + (1 - p_n) \log(1 - \hat{p}_n)] \tag{4}$$

where p_n means the computed label and $\hat{p}_n$ means the output of LGSAN. In the stage of inference, we can compute the potential face scale in an image according to the predicted S_i and the specific layers in image pyramid will be selected to make sure all of the faces can drop in the detection range.

3.2 Reversible Scale Semantic Flow Network

Figure 1 depicts the details of RS^2FP and the backbone is based on ResNet. Numbers in green boxes mean the L2 loss between ground truth and the transferred scale semantic feature map and middle scale means the half size of the max image scale in image pyramid. In stage of inference, given a middle image $I_{1/2}$, the corresponding feature maps $\mathcal{F}_{\text{res } 2a\_1/2}$ and $\mathcal{F}_{\text{res } 2b\_1/2}$ can be generated by f_{res}. The scale semantic information $\hat{\mathcal{F}}_{\text{res } 3a\_1}$ corresponding to I_1 can be transferred by S^2FU using $\mathcal{F}_{\text{res } 2a\_1/2}$. Other scale semantic information $\hat{\mathcal{F}}_{\text{res } 2b\_1/2^n}$ can be recurrently transferred by S^2RFD using $\mathcal{F}_{\text{res } 2b\_1/2}$.

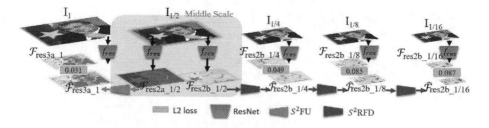

Fig. 1. The details of RS^2FP.

Let $f_{res}(\cdot)$ represent the outputs of ResNet, the corresponding feature maps of I_1 can be formulated as:

$$\mathcal{F}_{res-\frac{1}{2^n}} = f_{res}(\frac{I_1}{2^n}) \tag{5}$$

Both of the S^2FU and S^2RFD are some convolution operations with Batch Normalize and the total stride is 2. Let $M \in [1, N]$ represent the middle scale and we define the operations of S^2FU and S^2RFD as:

$$\hat{\mathcal{F}}_{res\,3a-\frac{1}{2^{n-1}}} = S^2FU\left(\mathcal{F}_{res2a\,-2^n} \mid w_U\right), n = M$$

$$\hat{\mathcal{F}}_{res2b-\frac{1}{2^{n+1}}} = \begin{cases} S^2RFD(\mathcal{F}_{res2b-\frac{1}{2^n}} \mid w_D), n = M \\ S^2RFD(\hat{\mathcal{F}}_{res2b-\frac{1}{2^n}} \mid w_D), n > M \end{cases} \tag{6}$$

where w_U and w_D mean the parameters in S^2FU and S^2RFD, respectively. In the training stage, the L2 Loss is used by RS^2FP and is defined as:

$$\mathcal{L} = \frac{1}{2N} \sum_{n=1}^{N} \| \mathcal{F} - \hat{\mathcal{F}} \|^2 \tag{7}$$

where N is the number of pixels in F.

We can observe from both the L2 loss and scale semantic transferred feature maps in each scale level that S^2RFD is capable of approximating the feature maps not only transformed from large scale to small scale, but vice versa.

4   Experiments

AFW with 205 images [26], FDDB with 2845 images [4], MALF with 5250 images [18] and WIDER FACE with 32303 images [19] are used to evaluate our algorithm. The structure of our model is a shallow version of the ResNet101 from conv1 to res3b3 with ~6M parameters. The base detector is a single-scale face detector with detection range from 32 to 64 and the single anchor is assigned. Inference time is tested on GTX1080.

4.1   Performance of LGSAN

As a lightweight CNN structure, we evaluate the performance of LGSAN using the same protocol. Figure 2 demonstrates the performance and the comparison with S^2AP [12], RSA [26], SAFD [2]. It can be seen clearly that our method has outperformed other methods with a standard gap. We use AP(Average Precision) as evaluation criteria to measure our proposed method, AP means the ratio of total predicted scale number to total ground truth number.

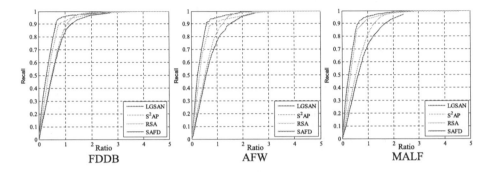

Fig. 2. Comparison of LGSAN with other straightforward scale predictors.

4.2   Ablation Study on Face Detection Benchmarks

In this section, we perform serial well-designed ablation study on AFW, FDDB, MALF and WIDER FACE to prove the effectiveness of LGSAN and RS^2FP in detail. We use RPN $+RS^2FP$+LGSAN to compare with ICC-CNN [24], Unit-Box [23], Faceness [20], Conv3d [6], Faster-RCNN [13], SFD [25], RSA [12], RetinaFace [1], Face R-CNN [16], HR [3], Two-stage CNN [19], Scale-Face [21], Multitask Cascade CNN [24], LDCF+ [11] and SSH [10] as shown in Fig. 3.

Table 1. The details of performance on AFW, FDDB, MALF and WIDER FACE hard validation set.

Component	Res-101	$+RS^2FP$	+LGSAN	$+RS^2FP$+LGSAN
AP@AFW	99.96%	99.95%	**99.97%**	99.96%
Inference time (ms)	122.6	55.6	25.6	**16.7**
AP@FDDB	91.59%	92.02%	92.17%	**92.52%**
Inference time (ms)	114.6	56.0	35.9	**22.1**
AP@MALF	89.07%	88.92%	89.16%	**89.17%**
Inference time (ms)	112.2	51.3	36.8	**22.9**
AP@WIDER	85.29%	85.24%	**85.29%**	85.28%
Inference time (ms)	141.2	62.1	42.5	**24.8**

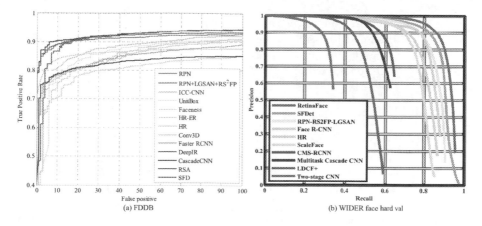

(a) FDDB

(b) WIDER face hard val

Fig. 3. Performance of our proposed lightweight pipeline on FDDB and WIDER FACE hard validation set.

On AFW, our algorithm achieves 99.96%AP. On FDDB, Fig. 4 shows LGSAN can help depose some false positives via ignoring some invalid layers in image pyramid, and finally achieve 92.52%AP which is higher than baseline detector. On MALF, our algorithm obtains 89.17%AP. On WIDER FACE hard validation set, which is more challenging than other benchmarks, our lightweight pipeline still obtains comparable 85.28%AP. Our algorithm can accelerate the base detector by $\sim7.3\times$, $\sim5.2\times$, $\sim4.9\times$ and $\sim5.7\times$ on FDDB, AFW, MALF and WIDER FACE respectively as shown in Table 1.

The details of performance and inference speed proved that our proposed lightweight pipeline can accelerate the face detector based on image pyramid by about $5\times$ to $7\times$ while maintaining the comparable performance.

Fig. 4. Visualization in various cases from FDDB dataset. The first line is the result of base detector and the second line is the result of our proposed pipeline. The red boxes are false positives deposed by LGSAN. (Color figure online)

We would like to emphasize that the novelty of our proposed method is that the well-designed LGSAN can predict potential scales and devise creative RS^2FP to generate feature map directly, which greatly reduces the computation of face detection pipeline without the loss of accuracy.

5   Conclusion

In this paper, we propose RS^2FP to perform fast face detection in a scale semantic flow manner. We proved that scale semantic information can be transferred not only from large scale with sufficient information to smaller scale but also from small scale with insufficient information to larger scale. Furthermore, we design a very lightweight but excellent performance LGSAN which utilizes the landmark information and feature pyramid mechanism jointly. Our whole algorithm can accelerate the face detector based on image pyramid by about 5× to 7× on widely used face detection benchmarks while maintaining the comparable performance.

Acknowledgement. This work is supported by the National Key R&D Program of China (No. 2019YFB2102400).

References

1. Deng, J., Guo, J., Ververas, E., Kotsia, I., Zafeiriou, S.: RetinaFace: single-shot multi-level face localisation in the wild. In: Proceedings of the IEEE/CVF Conference on Computer Vision and Pattern Recognition, pp. 5203–5212 (2020)
2. Hao, Z., Liu, Y., Qin, H., Yan, J., Li, X., Hu, X.: Scale-aware face detection. In: Proceedings of the IEEE Conference on Computer Vision and Pattern Recognition, pp. 6186–6195 (2017)
3. Hu, P., Ramanan, D.: Finding tiny faces. In: Proceedings of the IEEE Conference on Computer Vision and Pattern Recognition, pp. 951–959 (2017)
4. Jain, V., Learned-Miller, E.: FDDB: a benchmark for face detection in unconstrained settings. Tech. rep., UMass Amherst technical report (2010)
5. Kumar, A., et al.: Luvli face alignment: estimating landmarks' location, uncertainty, and visibility likelihood. In: Proceedings of the IEEE/CVF Conference on Computer Vision and Pattern Recognition, pp. 8236–8246 (2020)
6. Li, Y., Sun, B., Wu, T., Wang, Y.: Face detection with end-to-end integration of a ConvNet and a 3D model. In: Leibe, B., Matas, J., Sebe, N., Welling, M. (eds.) ECCV 2016, Part III. LNCS, vol. 9907, pp. 420–436. Springer, Cham (2016). https://doi.org/10.1007/978-3-319-46487-9_26
7. Lin, T.Y., Dollár, P., Girshick, R., He, K., Hariharan, B., Belongie, S.: Feature pyramid networks for object detection. In: Proceedings of the IEEE Conference on Computer Vision and Pattern Recognition, pp. 2117–2125 (2017)
8. Liu, Y., Li, H., Yan, J., Wei, F., Wang, X., Tang, X.: Recurrent scale approximation for object detection in CNN. In: Proceedings of the IEEE International Conference on Computer Vision, pp. 571–579 (2017)
9. Liu, Y., Wei, F., Shao, J., Sheng, L., Yan, J., Wang, X.: Exploring disentangled feature representation beyond face identification. In: Proceedings of the IEEE Conference on Computer Vision and Pattern Recognition, pp. 2080–2089 (2018)

10. Najibi, M., Samangouei, P., Chellappa, R., Davis, L.S.: SSH: single stage headless face detector. In: ICCV (2017)
11. Ohn-Bar, E., Trivedi, M.M.: Multi-scale volumes for deep object detection and localization. Pattern Recognit. **61**, 557–572 (2017)
12. Song, G., Liu, Y., Jiang, M., Wang, Y., Yan, J., Leng, B.: Beyond trade-off: accelerate FCN-based face detector with higher accuracy. In: Proceedings of the IEEE Conference on Computer Vision and Pattern Recognition, pp. 7756–7764 (2018)
13. Sun, X., Wu, P., Hoi, S.C.: Face detection using deep learning: an improved faster RCNN approach. Neurocomputing **299**, 42–50 (2018)
14. Tang, X., Du, D.K., He, Z., Liu, J.: PyramidBox: a context-assisted single shot face detector. In: Ferrari, V., Hebert, M., Sminchisescu, C., Weiss, Y. (eds.) ECCV 2018, Part IX. LNCS, vol. 11213, pp. 812–828. Springer, Cham (2018). https://doi.org/10.1007/978-3-030-01240-3_49
15. Viola, P., Jones, M.J.: Robust real-time face detection. Int. J. Comput. Vis. **57**(2), 137–154 (2004)
16. Wang, H., Li, Z., Ji, X., Wang, Y.: Face R-CNN. arXiv preprint arXiv:1706.01061 (2017)
17. Wang, J., Yuan, Y., Yu, G.: Face attention network: an effective face detector for the occluded faces. arXiv preprint arXiv:1711.07246 (2017)
18. Yang, B., Yan, J., Lei, Z., Li, S.Z.: Fine-grained evaluation on face detection in the wild. In: 2015 11th IEEE International Conference and Workshops on Automatic Face and Gesture Recognition (FG), vol. 1, pp. 1–7. IEEE (2015)
19. Yang, S., Luo, P., Loy, C.C., Tang, X.: Wider face: a face detection benchmark. In: Proceedings of the IEEE Conference on Computer Vision and Pattern Recognition, pp. 5525–5533 (2016)
20. Yang, S., Luo, P., Loy, C.C., Tang, X.: Faceness-net: face detection through deep facial part responses. IEEE Trans. Pattern Anal. Mach. Intell. **40**(8), 1845–1859 (2018)
21. Yang, S., Xiong, Y., Loy, C.C., Tang, X.: Face detection through scale-friendly deep convolutional networks. arXiv preprint arXiv:1706.02863 (2017)
22. Yoon, J.S., Shiratori, T., Yu, S.I., Park, H.S.: Self-supervised adaptation of high-fidelity face models for monocular performance tracking. In: Proceedings of the IEEE/CVF Conference on Computer Vision and Pattern Recognition, pp. 4601–4609 (2019)
23. Yu, J., Jiang, Y., Wang, Z., Cao, Z., Huang, T.: Unitbox: an advanced object detection network. In: Proceedings of the 24th ACM International Conference on Multimedia, pp. 516–520 (2016)
24. Zhang, K., Zhang, Z., Wang, H., Li, Z., Qiao, Y., Liu, W.: Detecting faces using inside cascaded contextual CNN. In: Proceedings of the IEEE International Conference on Computer Vision, pp. 3171–3179 (2017)
25. Zhang, S., Zhu, X., Lei, Z., Shi, H., Wang, X., Li, S.Z.: S3FD: single shot scale-invariant face detector. In: Proceedings of the IEEE International Conference on Computer Vision, pp. 192–201 (2017)
26. Zhu, X., Ramanan, D.: Face detection, pose estimation, and landmark localization in the wild. In: 2012 IEEE Conference on Computer Vision and Pattern Recognition, pp. 2879–2886. IEEE (2012)

Causality Extraction Based on Dependency Syntactic and Relative Attention

Chuan He[1,2,3] and Rong Yan[1,2,3]([⊠])

[1] College of Computer Science, Inner Mongolia University, Hohhot 010021, China
csyanr@imu.edu.cn
[2] National and Local Joint Engineering Research Center of Intelligent Information Processing Technology for Mongolian, Hohhot 010021, China
[3] Inner Mongolia Key Laboratory of Mongolian Information Processing Technology, Hohhot 010021, China

Abstract. Mining causal relation in text is a complex and critical natural language understanding task. Recently, many efforts focus on extracting causal event pairs in text by exploiting sequence labeling. However, few studies give the uniform definition of the annotation scheme and the labeling boundary of causal events. To address these issues, this paper proposes a novel causal event labeling scheme based on dependency syntactic, which can express the complete semantics of causal relation, as well as delineate the causal event boundaries explicitly. In addition, combined with the relative attention and dependency syntactic, we construct a causal event extraction model named DGLSTM-GRAT-CRF. Experimental results indicate that our model achieves better performance compared with state-of-the-art causality extraction models. Besides, we attempt to explore the influence of various additional features on causal extraction.

Keywords: Causality extraction · Sequence labeling · Dependency syntactic · Attention mechanism

1 Introduction

Causality extraction plays a vital role in many natural language processing tasks, such as event prediction [11]. Many studies have combined with text classification [3] and sequence labeling [15] for causal extraction. Among them, using sequence labeling to obtain causal pairs can be better applied to the construction of causal relation network and other upper-level causal mining tasks. In this paper, we focus on causality extraction through sequence labeling in our research.

Most existing causal event labeling schemes merely focus on short noun phrases [7], which cannot express the complete causal semantics. In this paper, we attempt to leverage the dependency for enabling causal pairs to remedy

© Springer Nature Switzerland AG 2021
T. Mantoro et al. (Eds.): ICONIP 2021, CCIS 1516, pp. 472–479, 2021.
https://doi.org/10.1007/978-3-030-92307-5_55

the incompleteness for expressing clear causality semantics, and delineate causal event labeling boundaries more distinctly.

Recently, Jie et al. [4] proposed a dependency-guided model that exploited inter-word dependency relations for sequence labeling. Inspired by their work, we propose a novel network, namely Graph Relative Attention Network (GRAT), which improved by means of a relative attention [16] and was in conjunction with the dependency syntactic. Based on these, we construct a causal extraction model named DGLSTM-GRAT-CRF, which has an ability to capture long-range dependencies and can identify causal events accurately.

2 Related Work

The ambiguity and diversity of natural language make text causality extraction more challenge. Most existing work use machine learning for causal relation extraction, including causal text classification and causal sequence labeling.

Recently, much efforts focused on sentence-level causal text classification. Li et al. [6] proposed a knowledge-oriented convolutional neural network for causal text classification, which consisted of a knowledge-oriented channel and a data-oriented channel. Feng et al. [3] applied generative adversarial networks to causal pair extraction. Through adversarial training, the basic extraction model could learn highly discriminative causal features from the causality enhancement model. However, these research mainly focused on detect whether a sentence contained casual relation, and did not extract causal pairs.

Causal sequence labeling is used to extract causal event pairs from texts. Li et al. [7] exploited Flair [1] and attention mechanism to improve the performance of causal extraction model. Once an event represented both the cause of one causal pair and the result of another in a sentence, these two causal pairs were called 'chain causality', and this labeling scheme use '*Emb*' to label such events. Xu et al. [15] proposed a BiLSTM-CRF-SGAT causality extraction model based on graph attention networks [14]. They also proposed a causal core word labeling scheme, which only chose the core word (one word) of the causal event for tagging. These labeling schemes above only focused on tagging short noun phrases or core word, which in some cases was ambiguous and could not express the causal semantics clearly.

3 Methods

3.1 Causal Sequence Labeling Scheme

Based on the existing causal sequence labeling schemes and the semantic integrity of causal events, we propose a causal event annotation method based on dependency syntactic.

In general, the causal event boundary can be delimitated by the inter-word dependency relations. Figure 1 shows an example of dependency tree for causality sentence. In this example, 'crisis' and 'restructuring' are the core words for

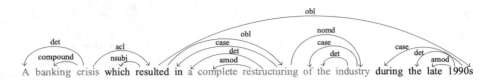

Fig. 1. Example of dependency tree for causality sentence.

causal and effect events respectively, 'restructuring' points to 'industry' and is connected with the preposition 'of' in its dependency tree. Then in the component 'the late 1990's' that follows 'industry' through the preposition 'during', the parent node of '1990's' is 'resulted'. Therefore, the ending boundary of the effect event should be 'industry', and the causal pair extracted from this example is 'a banking crisis → a complete restructuring of industry'.

In this paper, we use the '*BIOES*' [12] format to label the causal event boundaries and use '*C*' (Cause), '*E*' (Effect) and '*Emb*' (Embedded Causality) to indicate the causal semantics of events.

3.2 DGLSTM-GRAT-CRF Model

Figure 2 shows the architecture of DGLSTM-GRAT-CRF model. As given the sequence embedding of a sentence, the model can capture contextual information through BiLSTM layer and GRAT layer. Afterwards, the output of GRAT and BiLSTM are residual-connected and fed to the next BiLSTM layer or CRF layer. Finally, it predicts a corresponding label sequence, in which related cause and effect events are tagged. In order to accurately extract the causal events based on dependency, we regard the GRAT layer as the interaction function of dependency-guided LSTM [4].

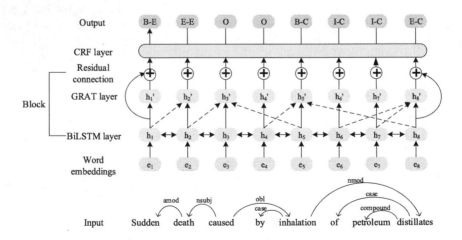

Fig. 2. The architecture of DGLSTM-GRAT-CRF model.

GRAT interacts the information of each node by pointing to the inter-word dependencies in the dependency tree, as well as calculates attention score based on the neighboring nodes. It integrates all child nodes information of the parent node to generate new features to the next layer. First, for the BiLSTM hidden layer's output $h = [h_1, h_2, \cdots, h_n] \in \mathbb{R}^{n \times d_h}$, the attention score of each token can be calculated by Eq. (1)–(4):

$$Q, K, V = hW_q, hW_k, hW_v \tag{1}$$

$$R_{t-j} = [\cdots sin(\frac{t-j}{10000^{2i/d_k}})cos(\frac{t-j}{10000^{2i/d_k}}) \cdots]^T \tag{2}$$

$$e_{tj} = Q_t K_j^T + Q_t R_{t-j}^T + \mu K_j^T + v R_{t-j}^T \tag{3}$$

$$\alpha_{tj} = softmax(e_{tj}) = \frac{exp(e_{tj})}{\sum_{j=1}^n A_{tj} exp(e_{tj})} \tag{4}$$

where the relative position encoding of t-th token and j-th token is calculated by R_{t-j} in Eq. (2), which can distinguish the direction and distance between tokens. In Eq. (3), e_{tj} represents the importance of the j-th token to the t-th token. We use A as an $n \times n$ dependency graph, and compute e_{tj} by the softmax to obtain attention coefficient α_{tj}. Inspired by Zhang et al. [17], we perform similar graph convolution operation with attention coefficients on the reinforcement features V of all neighboring tokens for t-th token in the dependency graph through Eq. (5):

$$h_t' = ||_{k=1}^K (\sum_{j=1}^n A_{tj} \alpha_{tj}^k W_1^k V_j + \sum_{j=1}^n I_{tj} W_2^k V_j) \tag{5}$$

Since the nodes do not have edges connected to themselves, so it is necessary to add a self-loop to each node, and I is the same unit matrix as the structure of A. We believe that the information should be propagated along the edges in different ways, so different weight matrices W_1 and W_2 are used to learn the propagation of dependency edges and self-loop respectively. In addition, we find that it is beneficial to the model by using multi-head attention [13]. Several independent attention mechanisms are transformed to obtain different feature representations, and then these individual features are concatenated together.

4   Experiments

4.1   Datasets

- **SemEval** is a widely used dataset for relation extraction. We obtain 1,325 causal sentences containing the label 'Cause-Effect' and randomly select 1,150 as non-causal sentences.
- **ADE** is a corpus for research of drug-effect and drug-dosage relations, which is a popular dataset in causal relation. Finally, we obtain 2,800 causal sentences and 2,800 randomly selected non-causal sentences to form the dataset.

In the experiments, we use Stanford CoreNLP [8] to perform dependency parsing on sentences and manually review the results of automatic annotation, then label the data according to the causal labeling scheme proposed in Sect. 3.1. We randomly selected 80% as train set and 20% as test set, respectively.

4.2 Experimental Settings

In the experiments, we perform the grid search and 5-fold cross validation on train set to find the optimal hyper-parameters. We use 100-dimensional GloVe [9] word embedding in all models. The hidden size of all networks (i.e., BiLSTM, GRAT) is set to 200. We use the dropout of 0.3 to regularize our model in the general layers and 8 heads in the GRAT layers. All models are optimized by Adam [5] with 16 batch size and $1e-3$ learning rate.

4.3 Comparison Criterion

In the experiments, we employ causal pair and causal event as the comparison criterion respectively. Causal pair evaluation is used to evaluate the ability of the model to correctly extract causal event pairs by using causal pairs as the unit of assessment. We use precision, recall and $F1$-score as evaluation metrics, and $Tag2Triplet$ [7] is used to extract the causal pairs based on the causal tags in sentences. Causal event evaluation assess the ability of the model to correctly classify event types and to extract complete events. The extracted causal events are judged according to individual events as cause, effect or 'Emb'.

4.4 Baselines

In the experiments, we perform six baselines to verify the effectiveness of our proposed model, where the latter three methods utilize dependency graph.

- **BiLSTM-CRF**: It is a popular sequence labeling method that consists of a BiLSTM encoder and a CRF classifier.
- **BiLSTM-ATT-CRF**: It is an improvement of the BiLSTM+Self-ATT model, which is added a CRF layer after the attention layer.
- **BiLSTM-RAT-CRF**: The relative attention [16] is used to replace the self attention in the BiLSTM-ATT-CRF model.
- **DGLSTM-CRF(MLP)** [4]: The interaction function is added between two BiLSTM layers. We use its best MLP interaction function for comparison.
- **BiLSTM-CRF-SGAT(dir)** [15]: Adding GAT [14] to the BiLSTM-CRF, we use its best result with three-block stacking model of directed graph.
- **BiLSTM-GCN-CRF**: Replace the GAT layer in BiLSTM-CRF-SGAT using graph convolutional networks [17].

Table 1. Results for causal pair extraction.

Model	SemEval			ADE		
	P (%)	R (%)	F (%)	P (%)	R (%)	F (%)
BiLSTM-CRF-1	73.20	67.20	70.07	75.77	69.36	72.42
BiLSTM-CRF-3	74.73	70.48	72.54	73.91	72.55	73.22
BiLSTM-ATT-CRF-3	75.90	72.21	74.01	76.82	71.08	73.84
BiLSTM-RAT-CRF-3	74.66	75.17	74.91	75.35	73.04	74.18
BiLSTM-GCN-CRF-3	76.98	77.68	77.33	75.21	75.12	75.17
BiLSTM-CRF+S-GAT(dir)-3	77.60	78.13	77.86	75.93	75.00	75.46
DGLSTM-CRF(MLP)-2	**79.85**	76.49	78.13	77.52	74.18	75.81
DGLSTM-GRAT-CRF-3	79.59	**78.86**	**79.22**	**77.75**	**75.22**	**76.46**

Table 2. Result for causal event extraction.

Model	SemEval				ADE			
	All-F	C-F	E-F	Emb-F	All-F	C-F	E-F	Emb-F
BiLSTM-CRF-1	81.58	82.71	81.21	22.22	80.83	82.43	79.40	81.90
BiLSTM-CRF-3	82.92	81.60	85.15	22.22	81.01	82.59	79.88	80.24
BiLSTM-ATT-CRF-3	83.81	84.50	84.54	14.29	82.03	83.15	81.11	80.77
BiLSTM-RAT-CRF-3	84.94	84.25	86.65	20.00	82.11	84.18	80.74	79.19
BiLSTM-GCN-CRF-3	85.77	87.22	85.04	36.36	82.81	83.68	82.08	82.00
BiLSTM-CRF+SGAT(dir)-3	85.94	87.73	85.33	35.29	82.82	83.57	82.48	81.43
DGLSTM-CRF(MLP)-2	86.03	86.60	86.61	37.50	83.21	83.44	**83.11**	83.81
DGLSTM-GRAT-CRF-3	**87.24**	**87.79**	**87.67**	**47.06**	**83.66**	**85.74**	81.35	**89.72**

4.5 Results and Analysis

In the experiments, we compare baselines on stacking several blocks to find the optimal experimental results, where the number marked after the model indicates the number of stacked blocks.

Table 1 gives the results of causal pair extraction for both datasets respectively. As shown in Table 1, we can see that our DGLSTM-GRAT-CRF model achieves the best performance. Furthermore, the following conclusions can also be drawn: (1) adding attention mechanism can improve the causal pair extraction performance, and relative attention is better than self attention in causal sequence labeling task. (2) event boundary can be more clearly delineated with the help of dependency graph, and DGLSTM-CRF(MLP) fused graph features is slightly better than using GAT and GCN in causal extraction task.

Table 2 gives the results of causal event extraction. As shown in Table 2, we can see that our proposed DGLSTM-GRAT-CRF model has a distinct advantages than the comparison model in most of metrics, indicating that our model has a strong ability to correctly classify event types and extract complete events. However, 'Emb' events used to represent 'chain causality' are poorly extracted in SemEval. We analysis the reason is that insufficient informative features for

Table 3. Result for causal pair extraction after adding additional feature. (**dep**: dependency label embedding)

Model	Additional feature	SemEval			ADE		
		P (%)	R (%)	F (%)	P (%)	R (%)	F (%)
DGLSTM-GRAT-CRF-3	Original	79.59	78.86	79.22	77.75	75.22	76.46
	+20d dep	**83.18**	81.14	82.15	**78.68**	76.54	77.60
	+50d dep	82.75	**81.86**	**82.30**	78.34	**77.11**	**77.72**
	+Flair	84.67	**85.60**	85.13	79.34	78.15	78.74
	+BERT	84.68	84.01	84.34	78.74	80.02	79.37
	+ELMO	**87.35**	84.97	**86.14**	**79.75**	**80.86**	**80.30**

the model to learn due to the small number of 'Emb' events in SemEval. But it is not the same scene in ADE.

4.6   Additional Feature Experiments

Besides, we explore the effectiveness with adding additional features on causal pair extraction. Table 3 shows the comparison after adding additional features.

In the experiments, we concatenate word representation with the 20-dimensional and 50-dimensional dependency label embedding respectively, to confirm that certain dependency label have relationships with causal events. From the first line of Table 3, the model performs better when adding dependency label embedding especially with 50-dimensional.

Furthermore, we compare the performance of model after adding contextualized word representation, including Flair [1], BERT [2] and ELMO [10]. As shown in Table 3 (line 2), we can see that using the contextualized word representation can largely improve the performance of the model. Among them, adding ELMO achieves the best results. In addition, we also find that the model combined with BERT is more effective than adding Flair for ADE, but reversely for SemEval. It concludes that BERT can work better than Flair in medical domain.

5   Conclusion

In this paper, we propose a novel causal event labeling scheme based on dependency syntactic, which not only enables causal pairs to express complete causality semantics, but also clearly delineates causal event annotation boundaries. Furthermore, combining dependency graph, relative attention and dependency-guided LSTM framework, we propose a causality extraction model. Experimental results show that the effectiveness of our proposed model for the causality extraction task. In the next, we will explore causality in other domains and develop into implicit causality and cross-sentence causality extraction methods.

Acknowledgements. This research is supported by the National Natural Science Foundation of China (Grant No. 61866029).

References

1. Akbik, A., Blythe, D., Vollgraf, R.: Contextual string embeddings for sequence labeling. In: Proceedings of the 27th International Conference on Computational Linguistics, Santa Fe, New Mexico, USA, pp. 1638–1649. ACL (2018)
2. Devlin, J., Chang, M., Lee, K., Toutanova, K.: BERT: pre-training of deep bidirectional transformers for language understanding. In: Proceedings of the 2019 Conference of the North American Chapter of the Association for Computational Linguistics, Minneapolis, Minnesota, pp. 4171–4186. ACL (2019)
3. Feng, C., Qi, K., Shi, G., Huang, H.: Causality extraction with GAN. Acta Automatica Sinica **44**(5), 811–818 (2018)
4. Jie, Z., Lu, W.: Dependency-guided LSTM-CRF for named entity recognition. In: Proceedings of the 2019 Conference on Empirical Methods in Natural Language Processing and the 9th International Joint Conference on Natural Language Processing, Hong Kong, China, pp. 3862–3872. ACL (2019)
5. Kingma, D.P., Ba, J.: Adam: a method for stochastic optimization. In: Proceedings of the International Conference on Learning Representations (2015)
6. Li, P., Mao, K.: Knowledge-oriented convolutional neural network for causal relation extraction from natural language texts. Expert Syst. Appl. **115**, 512–523 (2019)
7. Li, Z., Li, Q., Zou, X., Ren, J.: Causality extraction based on self-attentive BiLSTM-CRF with transferred embeddings. Neurocomputing **423**, 207–219 (2021)
8. Manning, C., Surdeanu, M., Bauer, J., Finkel, J., Bethard, S., McClosky, D.: The Stanford CoreNLP natural language processing toolkit. In: Proceedings of the 52nd Annual Meeting of the Association for Computational Linguistics: System Demonstrations, Baltimore, Maryland, pp. 55–60. ACL (2014)
9. Pennington, J., Socher, R., Manning, C.: GloVe: global vectors for word representation. In: Proceedings of the 2014 Conference on Empirical Methods in Natural Language Processing, Doha, Qatar, pp. 1532–1543. ACL (2014)
10. Peters, M., Neumann, M., Iyyer, M., Gardner, M., Clark, C.: Deep contextualized word representations. In: Proceedings of the 2018 Conference of the North American Chapter of the Association for Computational Linguistics: Human Language Technologies, pp. 2227–2237. ACL (2018)
11. Radinsky, K., Davidovich, S., Markovitch, S.: Learning causality for news events prediction. In: Proceedings of the 21st International Conference on World Wide Web, New York, pp. 909–918. ACM (2012)
12. Ramshaw, L., Marcus, M.: Text chunking using transformation-based learning. In: Proceedings of the Third Workshop on Very Large Corpora, pp. 82–94. ACL (1995)
13. Vaswani, A., et al.: Attention is all you need. arXiv e-prints 1706.03762 (2017)
14. Velickovic, P., Cucurull, G., Casanova, A., Romero, A., Lió, P., Bengio, Y.: Graph attention networks. arXiv e-prints 1710.10903 (2017)
15. Xu, J., Zuo, W., Liang, S.: Causal relation extraction based on graph attention networks. J. Comput. Res. Dev. **57**(1), 159–174 (2020)
16. Yan, H., Deng, B., Li, X., Qiu, X.: TENER: adapting transformer encoder for named entity recognition. arXiv e-prints 1911.04474 (2019)
17. Zhang, Y., Qi, P., Manning, C.D.: Graph convolution over pruned dependency trees improves relation extraction. In: Proceedings of the 2018 Conference on Empirical Methods in Natural Language Processing, pp. 2205–2215 (2018)

Fed-FiS: a Novel Information-Theoretic Federated Feature Selection for Learning Stability

Sourasekhar Banerjee$^{(\boxtimes)}$ (ID), Erik Elmroth$^{(\boxtimes)}$ (ID), and Monowar Bhuyan$^{(\boxtimes)}$ (ID)

Department of Computing Science, Umeå University, 901 87 Umeå, Sweden
{sourasb,elmroth,monowar}@cs.umu.se

Abstract. In the era of big data and federated learning, traditional feature selection methods show unacceptable performance for handling heterogeneity when deployed in federated environments. We propose Fed-FiS, an information-theoretic federated feature selection approach to overcome the problem occur due to heterogeneity. Fed-FiS estimates feature-feature mutual information (FFMI) and feature-class mutual information (FCMI) to generate a local feature subset in each user device. Based on federated values across features and classes obtained from each device, the central server ranks each feature and generates a global dominant feature subset. We show that our approach can find stable features subset collaboratively from all local devices. Extensive experiments based on multiple benchmark iid (independent and identically distributed) and non-iid datasets demonstrate that Fed-FiS significantly improves overall performance in comparison to the state-of-the-art methods. This is the first work on feature selection in a federated learning system to the best of our knowledge.

Keywords: Federated learning · Feature selection · Mutual information · Classification · Statistical heterogeneity

1 Introduction

Feature subset selection is a crucial task in data mining, knowledge discovery, pattern recognition, and machine learning to construct cost-effective models for multiple applications. Information-theoretic measures have been widely used and established paradigm for feature selection. Specifically, mutual information-based feature selection (MIFS) empowers identifying relevant features subset by removing redundant and irrelevant features without impacting classifiers reachable performance. In general, feature selection techniques are classified into four categories [1] such as filter, wrapper, embedded, and hybrid. Traditional MIFS approaches [2,3] are designed for centralized systems where data stored in the server. Having terabytes of user generated data and bringing them to the central server for constructing a model increases communication cost and also violate users privacy. Hence, the primary solution is to learn the model

This work was partially supported by the Wallenberg AI, Autonomous Systems and Software Program (WASP) funded by Knut and Alice Wallenberg Foundation.

© Springer Nature Switzerland AG 2021
T. Mantoro et al. (Eds.): ICONIP 2021, CCIS 1516, pp. 480–487, 2021.
https://doi.org/10.1007/978-3-030-92307-5_56

at the edge of the network using federated machine learning. Performing feature selection without relocating data to a centralized server is challenging because data present in local devices suffer from statistical heterogeneity. Real-world data combines iid and non-iid data and massively distributed across multiple devices. Moreover, local devices are low-end with limited resources, e.g., computation power. In such scenarios, traditional machine learning (ML) methods face difficulty in handling terabytes of data with statistical heterogeneity. Therefore, feature selection is essential and paramount to process such data and uncover useful knowledge for developing low-cost models. Feature selection is worthwhile for federated learning from many aspects, including (1) finding the common features set from the local device's data; hence, federated machine learning algorithms could learn efficiently, (2) dimensionality reduction leads to lowering the computational cost and the model size. The proposed work covered these aspects and introduced a federated feature selection method using mutual information.

Classical feature selection methods are widely developed for centralized systems to solve computational problems that occur due to higher dimensionality [2–4]. Also, federated feature selection is different from the distributed feature selection [5–7] being presence of heterogeneity. We propose a novel information-theoretic federated feature selection approach (Fed-FiS) for identifying relevant features subset from the federated dataset to learn ML models with stability. A federated dataset can be horizontal or iid where all devices have complete information of the features and classes and hybrid or non-iid where all devices don't have full details of the features and classes. But every device must have a features subset that is common in every device. Our major contributions are as follows.

① Fed-FiS introduces a local feature subset selection method by using mutual information and clustering.
② We develop a score function based on FFMI (minimize redundancy) and FCMI (maximize relevance) for global feature subset selection.
③ Fed-FiS finds a most relevant features subset from all devices where data is distributed in horizontal or iid manner and in hybrid or non-iid manner.
④ We evaluate Fed-FiS with multiple benchmark datasets and achieved cost-effective model performance in both iid and non-iid data partitions.

2   Problem Statement

Consider a federated learning system consists of q local devices ($\forall_{i=1}^{q} Cl_i$) and a server. We assume that $q \geq 2$, if $q = 1$, then it is considered as a centralized system having full information of the dataset. Suppose the dataset $D = \mathbb{R}^{m \times n+1}$ contains the features set $F = \{f_1, f_2, \ldots, f_n\}$, where $f_k \in \mathbb{R}^{n \times 1}$ is the kth feature and n is the total number of features, and class $C \in \{0, 1\}^{m \times |F|}$ where m is the number of data samples. D is distributed across q devices such that $\forall_i^q Cl_i$ contains the features set $F_{Cl_i} = \{f_1^{Cl_i}, f_2^{Cl_i}, \ldots, f_{|F_{Cl_i}|}^{Cl_i}\}$, where $f_k^{Cl_i}$ is the kth feature of the ith device, Cl_i. $| F_{Cl_i} |$ is the number of features present in Cl_i and $| F_{Cl_i} | \leq n$. Class $C^{Cl_i} \in \{0, 1\}^{m^{Cl_i} \times |F_{Cl_i}|}$, where m^{Cl_i} is number of data samples in the ith device and $m^{Cl_i} \leq m$. The data distribution creates statistical heterogeneity, i.e., each device (Cl_i) doesn't have complete information on the entire dataset. Our objective is to uncover λ strongly relevant features subset (F_λ'') that are present in every device. Hence, $accuracy(\psi(< F_\lambda'', C^{Cl_i} >)) \geq \delta$ and obtain stable global model performance. Here, $\psi(< F_\lambda'', C^{Cl_i} >)$ is the trained model on λ features at local device (Cl_i) and δ is the threshold for model accuracy.

3   Fed-FiS: the Proposed Approach

Fed-FiS is a mutual information-based federated feature selection approach that selects subset of strongly relevant features without relocating raw data from local devices to the server (see Fig. 1 for proposed framework). Fed-FiS has two parts, local features selection and global features selection. Initially, local devices independently produce the local features subset, and later, the server generates global features subset. The proposed approach is described as follows.

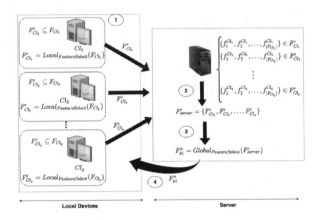

Fig. 1. Fed-FiS: the proposed framework.

3.1   Local Feature Selection

Fed-FiS employs MI to measure the amount of uncertainty in a feature variable with respect to a target variable. Algorithm 1 first computes aFFMI and FCMI scores of all features (steps 2 to 4). $F_{Cl_i}^{aFFMI}$ and $F_{Cl_i}^{FCMI}$ are two 1d vector that contains aFFMI and FCMI scores of all features at local device, Cl_i (steps 5 and 6). The aFFMI score close to zero indicates low redundancy and FCMI score near to one means high relevance of a feature. Here, our objective is to find the features that have low redundancy or high relevance. Based on the aFFMI and FCMI scores, we compute CLUSTER($F_{Cl_i}^{aFFMI}$) and CLUSTER($F_{Cl_i}^{FCMI}$) (steps 7 and 8) using the procedure CLUSTER (step 11 to 24) to generate feature clusters with lower aFFMI scores and higher FCMI scores. Suppose clustering on aFFMI scores produce β_1 clusters, and similarly clustering on FCMI scores generate β_2 clusters then the objective function can be defined as follows, $F_{Cl_i}^{aFFMI} = \arg\min_{\forall i \in \beta_1} centroid\ (cluster_i)$ and

$F'_{Cl_i}{}^{FCMI} = \arg\max_{\forall i \in \beta_2} centroid(cluster_i)$, where $centroid(cluster_i)$ returns the centroid value of the ith cluster, and $|\ cluster_i\ |$ is the cardinality of $cluster_i$. Union of the output of steps 7 and 8 produces the final local features subset $F'_{Cl_i} \subseteq F_{Cl_i}$ (steps 9). Figure 2 illustrates how MI and clustering help to obtain strongly relevant local features subset in i^{th} local device, Cl_i.

Algorithm 1. Fed-FiS (Local feature selection)

Input: $F_{Cl_i} = \{f_1^{Cl_i}, f_2^{Cl_i}, \ldots, f_{|F_{Cl_i}|}^{Cl_i}\}$ is the original feature set with $|F_{Cl_i}|$ dimension and class C^{Cl_i} for the ith local device Cl_i

Output: F'_{Cl_i} is the local features subset from the ith local device Cl_i

1: **procedure** $LocalFeatureSelect(< F_{Cl_i}, C^{Cl_i} >)$
2:     **for** $f_k^{Cl_i} \in F_{Cl_i}$ **do**
3:         $f_k^{aFFMI} = aFFMI(f_k^{Cl_i}) = \frac{1}{|F_{Cl_i}|-1} \sum_{j=1, f_j^{Cl_i} \in F_{Cl_i} \setminus f_k^{Cl_i}}^{|F_{Cl_i}|-1} FFMI(f_k^{Cl_i}, f_j^{Cl_i})$. $\triangleright$ return averaged FFMI score of f_k
4:         $f_k^{FCMI} = FCMI(f_k^{Cl_i}, C^{Cl_i}) \triangleq \sum_{f_k^{Cl_i}, C^{Cl_i}} Pr(f_k^{Cl_i}, C^{Cl_i}) log \frac{Pr(f_k^{Cl_i}, C^{Cl_i})}{Pr(f_k^{Cl_i})Pr(C^{Cl_i})}$. $\triangleright$ return FCMI score of f_k
5:         $F_{Cl_i}^{aFFMI} = \{f_k^{aFFMI} |\forall_{k=1}^d f_k^{aFFMI} \in [0,1]\}$ $\triangleright$ vector of aFFMI scores of all features at Cl_i
6:         $F_{Cl_i}^{FCMI} = \{f_k^{FCMI} |\forall_{k=1}^d f_k^{FCMI} \in [0,1]\}$ $\triangleright$ vector of FCMI scores of all features at Cl_i
7:         $F'_{Cl_i}{}_{aFFMI} = CLUSTER(F_{Cl_i}^{aFFMI})$ $\triangleright$ return cluster of features with low aFFMI scores
8:         $F'_{Cl_i}{}_{FCMI} = CLUSTER(F_{Cl_i}^{FCMI})$ $\triangleright$ return cluster of features with high FCMI scores
9:         $F'_{Cl_i} = F'_{Cl_i}{}_{FCMI} \bigcup F'_{Cl_i}{}_{aFFMI}$ $\triangleright$ union of features with high FCMI and low aFFMI scores
10:     **return** F'_{Cl_i} $\triangleright$ $F'_{Cl_i} \subseteq F_{Cl_i}$
11: **procedure** $CLUSTER(F_{Cl_i}^x)$ $\triangleright$ x is either aFFMI or FCMI
12:     initialize μ random cluster centroid.
13:     **repeat**
14:         $\forall_{k=1}^{|F_{Cl_i}^x|} f_k \in F_{Cl_i}^x$
15:         minimum $\leftarrow 0$
16:         cluster_member $\leftarrow 0$
17:         $\forall_{c=1}^{\mu} centroid\ c \in \mu$
18:         dist $\leftarrow$ Distance(f_k, c)
19:         **if** dist $<$ minimum **then**
20:             minimum $\leftarrow$ dist
21:             cluster_member $\leftarrow$ c
22:             recalculate centroid(c)
23:     **until** converge
24:     **return** $F'_{Cl_i}{}^x$. $\triangleright$ it returns cluster of features with lowest centroid while clustering aFFMI scores and highest centroid while clustering FCMI scores.

3.2 Global Feature Selection

The steps for global feature selection is given in Algorithm 2. Where each local device (Cl_i) sends triplets of locally selected features $(\tau_k^{Cl_i} =< f_k^{Cl_i}, f_{k_{FCMI}}^{Cl_i}, f_{k_{aFFMI}}^{Cl_i} >)$ to the server for computing the global scores. The triplet vector F'_{Cl_i} of the ith device Cl_i is defined as: $F'_{Cl_i} = \{\tau_1^{Cl_i}, \tau_2^{Cl_i}, \ldots, \tau_k^{Cl_i}\}$. Server receives feature triplets from q local devices (step 2). A single feature f_k can be shared by multiple local devices. F_{server} may

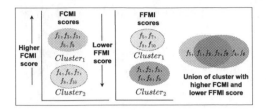

Fig. 2. Illustration of the local feature selection.

have multiple similar features with different aFFMI and FCMI scores. Server averages aFFMI and FCMI scores of the similar features, respectively (step 3). Server generates the unique features set F'_{server} (step 4). We propose a score function to globally rank each features and produce strongly relevant features subset.

Algorithm 2. Fed-FiS (Global feature selection)

Input: $F_{Server} = \{F'_{Cl_1}, F'_{Cl_2} \cdots F'_{Cl_q}\}$ ▷ collection of feature triplets from q local devices
Output: F''_k ▷ global feature subset

1: **procedure** $Global_{FeatureSelect}(F_{Server})$
2:     server obtained $F_{server} = \{F'_{Cl_i}|\forall_{i=1}^q, F'_{Cl_i} \in Cl_i\}$.
3:     obtain global feature triplet by performing average over aFFMI and FCMI scores individually.
4:     obtain $\{F'_{server}|\forall f_k \in F'_{server}\ are\ unique\}$
5:     compute $S(f_k), \forall f_k \in F'_{server}$ using $S(f_k) = f_{k_{FCMI}} - \frac{1}{(|F'_{server}|-1)} \times f_{k_{aFFMI}}$, where $|F'_{server}| > 1$ and $S(f_k) \in [1,-1]$

6:     $\forall_{i=1}^q Cl_i$ send $< S(f_k), f_k >$ to all Cl_i iff $f_k \in F'_{server}$ and $f_k \in F'_{Cl_i}$
7:     $\forall_{i=1}^q Cl_i$, each Cl_i selects a feature subset $F''_{Cl_i} \subseteq F'_{server}$, where $accuracy(\psi(< F''_{Cl_i}, C^{Cl_i} >)) \geq \delta$ ▷ δ is an accuracy
       threshold and send F''_{Cl_i} to server.
8:     server applies $\bigcap_{i=1}^q F''_{Cl_i} = F''_\lambda$ to generate global feature subset F''_λ of size λ
9:     return F''_λ to all local devices.

3.2.1 Global Score Function

Server computes the score of each feature present in F'_{server} to rank features based on FCMI and aFFMI scores (Step 5). $S(f_k) = 1$ iff $f_{k_{FCMI}} = 1$ and $f_{k_{aFFMI}} = 0$, similarly $S(f_k) = -1$ iff $f_{k_{FCMI}} = 0$, $f_{k_{aFFMI}} = 1$ and $|F'_{server}| = 2$. The server ranks each feature based on the descending order of the global scores and sends the feature score vector $< S(f_k), f_k >$ to all local devices iff the device originally contains this feature (step 6). $\forall_{i=1}^q Cl_i$, each Cl_i selects a feature subset F''_{Cl_i} from the F'_{server}, where $accuracy(\psi(< F''_{Cl_i}, C^{Cl_i} >)) \geq \delta$ (step 7). Here, $\psi(< F''_{Cl_i}, C^{Cl_i} >)$ is a learning model, and δ is the benchmark accuracy collected for comparing with state-of-the-art methods. Server collects dominant features set from each local devices and perform intersection $(\bigcap_{i=1}^q F''_{Cl_i} = F''_\lambda)$ and produce global features subset F''_λ (step 8) of size λ. Finally, server distributes optimal features subset to all local devices (step 9) for learning.

4 Evaluation

In this section, we were carried out exhaustive experiments to validate the performance of Fed-FiS using simulated environment with multiple benchmark datasets, considering numerous number of local devices. We used the NSL-KDD99 [8], and the anonymized credit card transactions (ACC)[1] datasets for our experiments. We divide both datasets into horizontal (iid) and hybrid (non-iid) manner across five local devices. We carried out the analysis of the results in three parts: (1) cluster analysis at each local device for local features subset selection, (2) global features subset selection at server, and (3) performance of selected features with multiple learning models.

4.1 Cluster Analysis and Local Features Subset Selection

We employ the k-means clustering to group the estimated aFFMI and FCMI scores obtain from each feature in NSL-KDD99 dataset distributed among five devices. The primary task is to identify lowest redundant and strongly relevant features subset. Each cluster verifies with silhouette coefficient (SC) to ensure obtaining quality and optimal clusters. From Fig. 3(a), we observed that the cluster size two makes maximum averaged SC for all devices. Similarly, cluster size three provides maximum average SC observed from Fig. 3(b). Hence, we consider the cluster size 3 for aFFMI and 2 for FCMI for our experiments. From Fig. 3(c), we select cluster 2 that has maximum centroid value (centroid -2). Similarly, from Fig. 3(d), we select cluster 1 with minimum centroid value (centroid -1). Union among these two selected clusters produce the local feature subset for the ith device Cl_i. The local feature subset of device Cl_1 has 30 features. Now, we are able to exclude 11 irrelevant features. For other datasets, we followed the similar approach to obtain the strongly relevant and optimal features set.

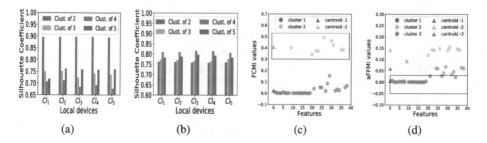

(a)	(b)	(c)	(d)

Fig. 3. Cluster analysis for local feature selection on horizontal or iid distribution of NSL-KDD99 dataset among five local devices. (a) FCMI cluster analysis, (b) aFFMI cluster analysis, (c) Clusters of features with respect to the FCMI scores for device Cl_1, (d) Clusters of features with respect to the aFFMI scores for device Cl_1.

[1] Worldline and the ULBML Group. Anonymized credit card transactions labeled as fraudulentor genuine. https://www.kaggle.com/mlg-ulb/creditcardfraud, 2020.

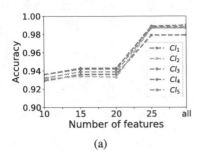
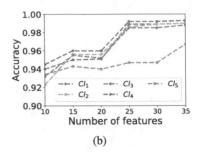

(a)   (b)

Fig. 4. Global feature selection using single-objective optimization for NSL-KDD99 dataset. (a) Feature subset for iid dataset at five local devices, (b) Feature subset for non-iid dataset at five local devices.

4.2 Global Features Subset Selection

We learned the KNN model at each local device keeping $\delta = 97\%$. All local devices reach the threshold (see Fig. 4(a)) using the top 23 features for NSL-KDD99 iid dataset.Similarly for the NSL-KDD99 non-iid dataset, local devices C1 to C4 crossed the threshold for the top 23 features, and C5 has crossed the threshold with top 35 features (see Fig. 4(b)). The intersection among these features generates the global relevant features subset of size 8.

4.3 Steady Learning Ability

We trained the federated forest model on both iid and non-iid division of NSL-KDD99 and the ACC datasets across 5 local devices. We compare the feature's subset size and the model's performance in Table 1 among Fed-FiS, MI-based baseline feature selection method[2] (state-of-the-art), and without using feature selection (without FS). In the baseline method, we computed MI of all features that are present in different devices and then does the intersection among them to obtain feature subset for learning.

On NSL-KDD99 and ACC iid dataset, Fed-FiS selects global features subset of sizes 23 and 10, respectively, and achieves 99.3% and 99.83% accuracy, respectively. In contrast, without choosing any features, the federated forest achieves 99.5% and 99.96% accuracy, respectively. The state-of-the-art method generates subsets of sizes 23 and 6, respectively and produces accuracy of 99.24% and 99.3%, respectively. The performance of proposed method is almost equivalent with minimum number of relevant features set in compare to the state-of-the-art and without FS.

For both NSL-KDD99 and ACC non-iid dataset, Fed-FiS selects a global feature subset of 9 and achieves 89.33% and 99.83% accuracy, respectively. The state-of-the-art method selects features subset of size 7 and 10, respectively and obtain 92.75% and 99.83% accuracy, respectively. Without FS, i.e., only selecting common features of five devices, it achieves 54.07% and 99.81% accuracy, respectively. For the non-iid

---

[2] https://scikit-learn.org/stable/modules/generated/sklearn.feature_selection.mutual_info_classif.html.

Table 1. Performance of Fed-FiS with without feature selection and baseline models across Federated Forest

Datasets	Fed-FiS		Without FS		Classical MI-based FS	
	Optimal feature subset	Accuracy (%)	Feature set	Accuracy (%)	Feature subset	Accuracy (%)
NSL-KDD99 iid	23	99.3	41	99.5	23	99.24
NSL-KDD99 non-iid	9	89.33	15	54.07	7	92.75
ACC iid	10	99.95	29	99.96	6	99.3
ACC non-iid	9	99.83	14	99.81	10	99.83

scenario, the algorithm also depends on the common features set of each local device. If all devices share features more extensively, then the feature selection yields stability in learning.

5   Conclusion and Future Work

In this paper, we propose Fed-FiS, a mutual information-based federated feature selection method to select strongly relevant features subset for stable and low-cost federated learning. We used local feature selection on every local device using clustering of aFFMI and FCMI scores to select feature subset in federated settings. The server produces the global rank of each feature and generates a global feature subset. Fed-FiS achieved expected model performance with lower number of features set, verified with federated forest algorithm. The extension of this work for anomaly detection in edge clouds is underway.

References

1. Manikandan, G., Abirami, S.: Feature selection is important: state-of-the-art methods and application domains of feature selection on high-dimensional data. In: Kumar, R., Paiva, S. (eds.) Applications in Ubiquitous Computing. EICC, pp. 177–196. Springer, Cham (2021). https://doi.org/10.1007/978-3-030-35280-6_9
2. Hoque, N., et al.: MIFS-ND: a mutual information-based feature selection method. Expert Syst. Appl. **41**(14), 6371–6385 (2014)
3. Liu, G., et al.: Feature selection method based on mutual information and support vector machine. Int. J. Pattern Recogn. Artif. Intell. **35**, 2150021 (2021)
4. Zheng, L., et al.: Feature grouping and selection: a graph-based approach. Inf. Sci. **546**, 1256–1272 (2021)
5. Gui, Y.: ADAGES: adaptive aggregation with stability for distributed feature selection. In: Proceedings of the ACM-IMS on Foundations of Data Science Conference, pp. 3–12 (2020)
6. Soheili, M., et al.: DQPFS: distributed quadratic programming based feature selection for big data. J. Parallel Distrib. Comput. **138**, 1–14 (2020)
7. Morán-Fernández, L., et al.: Centralized vs. distributed feature selection methods based on data complexity measures. Knowl.-Based Syst. **117**, 27–45 (2017)
8. Tavallaee, M., et al.: A detailed analysis of the KDD CUP 99 data set. In: IEEE Symposium on Computational Intelligence for Security and Defense Applications, pp. 1–6 (2009)

Model Compression for a Plasticity Neural Network in a Maze Exploration Scenario

Baolun Yu[1(✉)], Wanrong Huang[2], Long Lan[1], and Yuhua Tang[1]

[1] Institute for Quantum Information and HPCL, College of Computer, National University of Defense Technology, Changsha, China
{yubaolun,long.lan,yhtang62}@nudt.edu.cn
[2] Artificial Intelligence Research Center, National Innovation Institute of Defense Technology, Changsha, China
huangwanrong12@nudt.edu.cn

Abstract. Plastic neural networks provide a new type of biological heuristic method for "meta-learning" or "learning to learn", opening a new door for research on lifelong learning and fast memory of artificial intelligence. They can combine typical neural networks with the famous Hebb's rule in biological neurology, and uses Hebbian trace to express the connection strength between neurons. However, redundancy exists in previously designed plastic neural networks since not all neurons have strong connections. In this paper, we first time propose a model compression strategy for an RNN-based plastic neural network in a maze exploration scenario. With a reinforcement learning process, the network is trained and the hidden neurons have different variation trends. As convergent hidden neurons are conceptually able to memory some invariant feature of the maze, connections of nonconvergent hidden neurons are skillfully pruned. We successfully realize our approach and achieve plastic neural network compression in experiments. While ensuring the performance of the algorithm, the compression rate reaches 3.8 and the speedup rate is about 4.1 in theory and up to 16.

Keywords: Plastic neural networks · Meta-learning · Lifelong learning · Hebb's rule · Network compression

1 Introduction

Differentiable Plasticity [1,2] provides a new biological heuristic method, which can be used to solve the classical problem of "meta-learning" or "learning to learn". Compared with traditional networks, plastic networks can store information in plastic connections, which endows the traditional network with the ability of long-term learning. Facing the unseen environmental state, plastic network can adapt to the environment and find solutions [3]. In plastic neural network, Hebbian traces indicates the strength of connection between neurons,

T. Mantoro et al. (Eds.): ICONIP 2021, CCIS 1516, pp. 488–497, 2021.
https://doi.org/10.1007/978-3-030-92307-5_57

a formal expression of Hebb's rule [4]. In actual tasks, not all neurons have a strong connection and some of the connections may be redundant.

Therefore, this work studies the compression method of plastic neural network aiming at the redundancy in plastic neural network. Through the Hebbian traces, we observe that some neurons maintain stable strong connections, and they determine whether the agent can reach the reward point quickly. Based on these findings, we implement our compression strategy for the plastic neural network in maze exploration scene and clips the connections according to the numerical variation trend of Hebbian traces and hidden layer neurons. To the best of our knowledge, our proposed compression method is the first one for the plastic neural network in the case of maze exploration.

The remaining parts of this work are organized as follows. Section 2 describes the mainstream compression methods and evaluation criteria for traditional neural networks. In Sect. 3, we discuss the principle of plastic neural network, and propose the evaluation method of redundant information and compression strategy. Section 4 shows our experimental results, and successfully realizes the compression and acceleration of plastic neural network. In Sect. 5, we summarize our work and look forward to the future research directions.

2   Related Work

Lightweight devices have relatively small requirements for storage space and computing power. However, the current models are getting bigger and bigger, and there are significant redundancies in the models [5]. Model compression can reduce model complexity and unnecessary computational overhead.

Compression methods for deep neural networks can be divided into four categories [6]: parameter pruning and quantization, low rank factorization, transferred/compact convolution filters and knowledge distillation. The main idea of parameter pruning and quantization is to find redundant parameters in the network and eliminate them [7,8]. [8] uses the channel pruning method to generate a small and compact model to compress the CNN. Low-rank factorization is to represent the dense full-rank matrix as the combination of several low-rank matrices, and the low-rank matrix can be decomposed into the product of small-scale matrices to achieve the purpose of simplification [9,10]. [9] use redundancy to construct low-rank filters or tensors. Transferred/compact convolution filter is designed to reduce parameter space and save computation and memory by designing a special structure of convolution filter [11,12]. Knowledge distillation adopts transfer learning, which trains another simple network (Student Model) by using the output of pre-trained complex model (Teacher Model) as supervision signal [13,14]. [13] leverages weight quantization and distillation of larger networks (teachers) into compressed networks (students).

In addition, compression rate and speedup rate are commonly used as standards to measure compression quality [6]. Suppose p is the number of parameters in original model M and the number of parameters in compressed model M^* is p^*, then the compression rate $\alpha(M, M^*)$ of M^* on M is:

$$\alpha\left(M, M^{*}\right)=\frac{p}{p^{*}} \tag{1}$$

Another measure is called space saving rate, which is defined in [15] as:

$$\beta\left(M, M^{*}\right)=\frac{p-p^{*}}{p^{*}} \tag{2}$$

If M has a run time of t and M^{*} has a run time of t^{*}, the speedup rate is:

$$\delta\left(M, M^{*}\right)=\frac{t}{t^{*}} \tag{3}$$

3   Methods

3.1   Principles of Plasticity Neural Network

Compared with non-plastic neural networks, plastic neural networks add some plastic weights to the original weights, as shown in Eq. (4),

$$x_{j}(t)=\sigma\left\{\sum_{i \in \text { inputs }}\left[w_{i, j} x_{i}(t-1)+\alpha_{i, j} \operatorname{Hebb}_{i, j}(t) x_{i}(t-1)\right]\right\} \tag{4}$$

$$\operatorname{Hebb}_{i, j}(t+1)=\eta x_{i}(t-1) x_{j}(t)+(1-\eta) \operatorname{Hebb}_{i, j}(t) \tag{5}$$

where $x_{j}(t)$ represents the output of neuron j at time t. The fixed connection weight between neurons i and j is $w_{i, j}$, which is updated by gradient descent. Hebbian trace (Eq. (5)) is the plasticity weight, which is a formal expression of synaptic plasticity. α is the plasticity coefficient, which determines the relative importance of plastic weights.

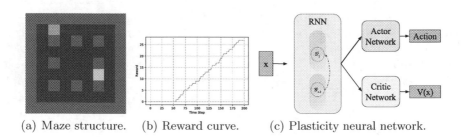

(a) Maze structure.   (b) Reward curve.   (c) Plasticity neural network.

Fig. 1. Maze exploration task. (Color figure online)

Maze exploration is a typical problem in reinforcement learning. In the maze exploration problem, it is found that plastic neural network has better performance [1]. In an episode, the maze structure (Fig. 1(a)) and the position of the reward point remain unchanged. Every time agent (green) reaches the reward point (yellow), it will be randomly placed in another empty position. Figure 1(b) is the reward curve. The plastic network is shown in Fig. 1(c). Only the connections between hidden layer neurons use plastic connections (blue dashed line).

3.2   Deep Neural Network Compression Methods

The existing deep neural network compression methods are optimized for the convolutional layer and the fully connected layer. The most commonly used network pruning method is the optimal brain damage, which is based on the Hessian matrix of the loss function to calculate the contribution of each parameter. But RNN is not suitable for calculating Hessian matrix. Low rank factorization and the transferred/compact convolution filters are both replacements for the convolution kernel, so they are not applicable. The main idea of knowledge distillation uses supervised learning to learn the mapping relationship between input and output, so it is not suitable for processing reinforcement learning tasks.

In view of these limitations of deep neural network compression methods, we need to find new methods to compress plastic networks. Therefore, for the plastic neural network, we start from its principle, study the characteristics of the network, try to find the redundant information in it, and then compress the network.

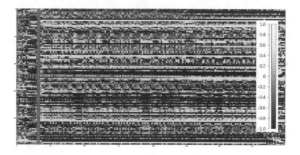

Fig. 2. States of hidden layer neurons in an episode.

3.3   Redundant Information Evaluation

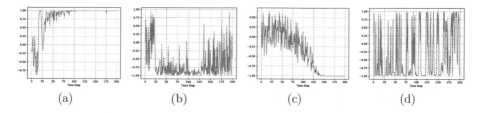

|(a)|(b)|(c)|(d)|

Fig. 3. Hidden layer state curves: (a) Complete convergence. (b) Approximate convergence. (c) Partial convergence. (d) Nonconvergence.

The hidden layer states are shown in Fig. 2. Each column is the state vector of the hidden layer at the corresponding time. Note that there is a red line added in the figure. The hidden layer states before it are rather chaotic, and the values of some neurons are more stable after the red line. It's no coincidence that the agent reached the reward point for the first time around the red line. The network quickly adjusts the neuron state to remember the position of the reward point when it gets the positive reward. In Fig. 2, those neurons that maintain a stable state are likely responsible for memorizing location information.

Figure 3 draws the change curve of each neuron within an episode. We roughly divide them into 4 categories according to the change curve of neurons: complete convergence (Fig. 3(a)), approximate convergence (Fig. 3(b)), partial convergence (Fig. 3(c)), nonconvergent neurons (Fig. 3(d)).

Table 1. Statistics of neurons.

Type	Quantity
Complete convergence	18
Approximate convergence	8
Partial convergence	9
Nonconvergence	65

Table 1 shows the number of various types of hidden neurons in the network when a specific reward point is given. It should be pointed out that the amount of neurons of each type is slightly different when given different reward points.

3.4   Compression Strategy

Invariant features should be memorized in the maze exploration problem. Most of the hidden layer neurons are nonconvergent and can not reflect the invariant features. Therefore, it is better to find the neurons that remember the position of the reward point from a small number of useful neurons, and then crop the rest.

In order to verify whether the selected neurons are useful, we only kept the selected group of neurons, cut off the others and their related connections (Compressed Network), and then observed whether the network can complete the task (lines 1–12 in Algorithm 1). In the maze exploration task, we used the cumulative reward as the evaluation criterion.

Algorithm 1. Compression Strategy for Plastic Neural Network

Data: Initialize the result set NN ={Complete convergence}, A ={All Neurons}, C ={Neurons removed}, AC ={Approximate convergence}, PC ={Partial convergence}, RN ={Redundant Neurons}, Performance degradation threshold: θ, Performance of original network: P, Performance of pruning network: P^*.

Result: Necessary Neurons set: NN.
1: $C = A - NN$
2: Test the cumulative reward of the pruning network P^*.
3: **while** $(P - P^*)/P \geq \theta$ **do**

4:      **if** $AC \neq \emptyset$ **then**
5:          $AC = AC - \{N_a\}, N_a \in AC$
6:          $NN = NN \cup \{N_a\}$
7:      **else if** $PC \neq \emptyset$ **then**
8:          $PC = PC - \{N_p\}, N_p \in PC$
9:          $NN = NN \cup \{N_p\}$
10:     **end if**
11:     Test the cumulative reward of the pruning network P^*.
12: **end while**
13: $C = NN$
14: Test the cumulative reward of the pruning network P^*.
15: **if** $(P - P^*)/P \geq \theta$ **then**
16:     $RN = A - NN$
17: **end if**

In turn, it is necessary to verify that the deleted neurons and their connections are redundant. We kept this part of the neurons, on the contrary, cut down the useful neurons selected above (Redundant Network). Then tested the performance of the network (lines 13–17 in Algorithm 1).

In an episode, since the position of the reward point is unchanged, the hidden layer neurons with convergence characteristics are all used as candidate neurons. Complete convergent neurons are the first to be considered. If these neurons are not enough, we need to add some from the approximately convergent neurons and partially converged neurons.

4   Results

4.1   Experiment Setting

In this paper, the same network setting as in [1] is adopted. Based on RNN, the connections in the hidden layer are changed to plastic connections, while the input layer and output layer still use non-plastic connections. The network input includes a environment vector, action vector, and reward value. The redundant neurons and connections found by the compression algorithm are cut down.

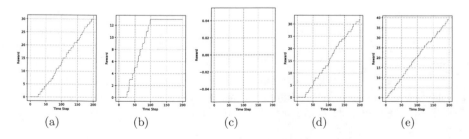

(a)   (b)   (c)   (d)   (e)

Fig. 4. Reward curves: (a) Normal Network. (b) Remove convergent neurons as step 100. (c) Remove convergent neurons at step 0. (d) Remove nonconvergent neurons at step 100. (e) Remove nonconvergent neurons at step 0.

4.2 Compression

In order to verify the conjecture that these convergent hidden neurons record the location information of reward points. Using the compression strategy we proposed, we trim these convergent hidden neurons and their connections, and then observed the changes in the reward value of the network.

The result is shown in Fig. 4. When the cutting operation is performed at 100 steps, it is difficult for the agent to reach the reward point again (Fig. 4(b)). And if nonconvergent neurons are removed (Fig. 4(d)), there is no change in the reward value curve.

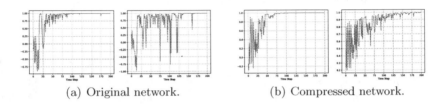

(a) Original network.   (b) Compressed network.

Fig. 5. The hidden state of original and compressed network.

Figure 5 shows the state of the hidden layer in the original network and the compressed network. Completely convergent neurons are still in a state of rapid convergence in the compression network. Approximate convergent neurons becomes more stable. However, if only redundant neurons are retained, all neurons will become chaotic except some partially convergent neurons.

Table 2. Statistics of the number of parameters and floating-point multiplications.

		Input layer	Hidden layer	Hebbian traces	Output layer	Total
Original network	Param	1800	20200	10000	505	32505
	FMUL	1700	20000	20000	500	42200
Compressed network	Param	1800	4120	2000	505	8425
	FMUL	1700	4000	4000	500	10200

On the basis of guaranteeing the network performance, we cut down redundant neurons and connections, and successfully realized plastic neural network compression.

In the plastic network model that we use, about 20% of the hidden neurons are useful on average. We have made statistics on the number of parameters and floating-point multiplications in the original and compressed network, as shown in Table 2.

According to the above formula (Eq. (1) and (2)), the compression rate is about 3.8, and the space saving rate is about 2.8. In other words, about 74% of the parameters in the network are redundant.

4.3   Speedup Rate

The most time-consuming and more frequent operation in the network is floating-point multiplication. If the number of floating-point multiplications is used to approximately replace the network running time, the theoretically calculated speedup is about 4.1 (Eq. (3)).

The speedup is affected by factors such as the implementation of the algorithm, hardware resources, and data volume. Therefore, in order to more truly reflect the acceleration effect brought by compression, we used different implementation methods to measure the acceleration rate under different hardware resources and data volumes. Figure 6 shows the average time required for network testing and speedup rate under different batch sizes.

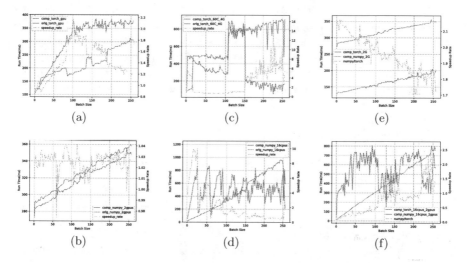

Fig. 6. Speedup rate of compressed network: (a) PyTorch models on GPU. (b) NumPy models on GPU. (c) PyTorch models on CPU. (d) NumPy models on CPU. (e) PyTorch and NumPy compressed models on GPU. (f) PyTorch and NumPy compressed models on CPU.

Figure 6(a) is the curve of network implemented by PyTorch, running on the GPU. When the batch size is greater than 25, a good speedup rate can always be maintained, and the highest is around 2.2. When the network implemented using NumPy runs on the GPU, there is no obvious acceleration effect (Fig. 6(b)). If running on the CPU, when the batch size is less than 100, using NumPy can get a speed increase of up to 10 times (Fig. 6(d)), when the batch size is greater than 150, using PyTorch can increase the speed up to 16 times (Fig. 6(c)). When running a compressed network on the GPU, the network implemented using PyTorch is faster (Fig. 6(e)). If we run a compressed network on the CPU, NumPy is faster when the batch size is less than 220, and PyTorch is more advantageous when the batch size is larger (Fig. 6(f)).

Our theoretical speedup rate is 4.1, however, the maximum measured value can reach 16. In reality, PyTorch/NumPy's optimization of computational graphs, GPU acceleration, data volume and other factors will further enlarge or reduce the speed increase brought by reducing the number of operations.

5   Discussion and Conclusion

In this paper, we studied the compression of plastic neural networks. Firstly, we understood some basic principles of plastic neural network through experiments. On this basis, we proposed a reliable redundancy evaluation method, and found out the redundant plastic connections and neurons in the network. Then, using our evaluation method, we proposed a compression strategy of plastic neural network for the first time in maze exploration situation. Finally, the performance stability of our compression strategy was verified by experiments, and high compression rate and speedup rate were obtained, which also proves that our evaluation method for redundant information is correct again.

We will always pay attention to the application and optimization of the plastic network compression algorithm on its complex model in the future.

References

1. Miconi, T., Stanley, K., Clune, J.: Differentiable plasticity: training plastic neural networks with backpropagation. In: International Conference on Machine Learning, pp. 3559–3568. PMLR (2018)
2. Miconi, T., Rawal, A., Clune, J., Stanley, K.O.: Backpropamine: training self-modifying neural networks with differentiable neuromodulated plasticity. arXiv preprint arXiv:2002.10585 (2020)
3. Najarro, E., Risi, S.: Meta-learning through Hebbian plasticity in random networks. arXiv preprint arXiv:2007.02686 (2020)
4. Hebb, D.O.: The Organization of Behavior; A Neuropsycholocigal Theory, vol. 62, p. 78 (1949). A Wiley Book in Clinical Psychology
5. Denil, M., Shakibi, B., Dinh, L., Ranzato, M., De Freitas, N.: Predicting parameters in deep learning. arXiv preprint arXiv:1306.0543 (2013)
6. Cheng, Y., Wang, D., Zhou, P., Zhang, T.: A survey of model compression and acceleration for deep neural networks. arXiv preprint arXiv:1710.09282 (2017)
7. Mao, H., et al.: Exploring the regularity of sparse structure in convolutional neural networks. arXiv preprint arXiv:1705.08922 (2017)
8. Liu, Z., Li, J., Shen, Z., Huang, G., Yan, S., Zhang, C.: Learning efficient convolutional networks through network slimming. In: Proceedings of the IEEE International Conference on Computer Vision, pp. 2736–2744 (2017)
9. Denton, E., Zaremba, W., Bruna, J., LeCun, Y., Fergus, R.: Exploiting linear structure within convolutional networks for efficient evaluation. arXiv preprint arXiv:1404.0736 (2014)
10. Tulloch, A., Jia, Y.: High performance ultra-low-precision convolutions on mobile devices. arXiv preprint arXiv:1712.02427 (2017)
11. Howard, A.G., et al.: MobileNets: efficient convolutional neural networks for mobile vision applications. arXiv preprint arXiv:1704.04861 (2017)

12. Zhang, X., Zhou, X., Lin, M., Sun, J.: ShuffleNet: an extremely efficient convolutional neural network for mobile devices. In: Proceedings of the IEEE Conference on Computer Vision and Pattern Recognition, pp. 6848–6856 (2018)
13. Polino, A., Pascanu, R., Alistarh, D.: Model compression via distillation and quantization. arXiv preprint arXiv:1802.05668 (2018)
14. Anil, R., Pereyra, G., Passos, A., Ormandi, R., Dahl, G.E., Hinton, G.E.: Large scale distributed neural network training through online distillation. arXiv preprint arXiv:1804.03235 (2018)
15. Moczulski, M., Denil, M., Appleyard, J., de Freitas, N.: ACDC: a structured efficient linear layer. arXiv preprint arXiv:1511.05946 (2015)

NSF-Based Mixture of Gaussian Processes and Its Variational EM Algorithm

Xiangyang Guo, Daqing Wu, Tao Hong, and Jinwen Ma[✉]

Department of Information and Computational Sciences, School of Mathematical Sciences and LMAM, Peking University, Beijing 100871, China
{guoxy,wudq,paul.ht}@pku.edu.cn, jwma@math.pku.edu.cn

Abstract. Mixture of Gaussian processes (MGP) is a powerful model for dealing with data with multi-modality. However, input distributions of Gaussian process (GP) components of an MGP are designed to be Gaussians, which cannot model complex distributions that frequently appear in datasets. It has been proven that neural spline flow (NSF) models can transform a simple base distribution into any complex target distribution through the change of variables formula. In this paper, we propose an NSF-based mixture model of Gaussian processes (NMGP), which extends the conventional MGP by using distributions modeled by NSFs for the input variables instead of Gaussians. In addition, a variational EM algorithm is established to estimate the parameters of an NMGP. It is demonstrated by the experimental results that our proposed NMGP models outperform classic MGPs.

Keywords: Mixture of Gaussian processes · Neural spline flows · EM algorithm · Variational inference

1 Introduction

Gaussian process (GP) has proven to be an effective tool for a wide variety of applications in machine learning, such as modeling the inverse dynamics of a robot arm [1]. Unfortunately, GPs fail to handle multimodal datasets and, given N training samples, training a GP suffers from an expensive time complexity scaling as $O(N^3)$. To overcome these two limitations, Tresp [2] proposed the mixture of Gaussian processes (MGP), in which more than one GP is combined through a gating network. The gating network of an MGP is set to be a Gaussian mixture model (GMM) [2–5], in which each Gaussian determines the input distribution of a GP component. However, Gaussians cannot model complex distributions which frequently appear in datasets. Therefore, Yuan et al. [6] suggested replacing the Gaussians with GMMs. Although GMMs can alleviate the problem, we must determine the number of Gaussians in each GMM in advance. Inappropriate numbers may lead to bad predictive accuracy. In addition, Li et al.

© Springer Nature Switzerland AG 2021
T. Mantoro et al. (Eds.): ICONIP 2021, CCIS 1516, pp. 498–505, 2021.
https://doi.org/10.1007/978-3-030-92307-5_58

[7] proposed using Student's t-distributions as the input distributions to deal with multimodal data with overlaps between different modalities. Both GMMs and Student's t-distributions are parametric, which are not flexible enough to model a complex distribution.

One of the most important tasks in machine learning and statistics is to model an unknown probability distribution given samples drawn from that distribution, and normalizing flow models, proposed by Tabak et al. [8] and Tabak et al. [9], are widely applied to this problem [10]. Normalizing flow is an invertible differentiable function, which can transform a simple base distribution, e.g. $\mathcal{N}(\mathbf{0}, \mathbf{I})$, into any complex distribution through the change of variables formula.

In this paper, we propose a neural-spline-flow-based mixture model of Gaussian processes (NMGP), where the neural spline flows (NSF), to be introduced in Sect. 3, are a kind of normalizing flows. In an NMGP model, the input distributions are designed to be distributions generated via NSFs instead of Gaussians. A variational EM algorithm is developed to train our proposed NMGP models, and experimental results show that NMGPs not only produce smaller errors compared to the conventional MGPs but also explore the true input distributions.

The remainder of this paper is organized as follows. We briefly introduce GP and MGP models in Sect. 2. Section 3 describes the construction of NMGPs. The variational EM algorithm is described in Sect. 4. Then, we present the experimental results in Sect. 5 and Sect. 6 concludes this paper.

2   GP and MGP Models

First, a short description of GP models is given. A GP, expressed as $\{f(\mathbf{x})|\mathbf{x} \in \mathbb{X}\}$, is a collection of random variables, any finite number of which follow a multivariate Gaussian distribution [1], and it is completely specified by its mean function $m(\mathbf{x})$ and covariance function $c(\mathbf{x}, \mathbf{x}')$, where $m(\mathbf{x}) = \mathbb{E}[f(\mathbf{x})]$ and $c(\mathbf{x}, \mathbf{x}') = \mathbb{E}[(f(\mathbf{x}) - m(\mathbf{x}))(f(\mathbf{x}') - m(\mathbf{x}'))]$. In practice, we usually use a noisy GP, $\{y(\mathbf{x})|\mathbf{x} \in \mathbb{X}\}$, obtained by adding i.i.d. Gaussian noise to each $f(\mathbf{x})$, i.e. $y(\mathbf{x}) = f(\mathbf{x}) + \epsilon(\mathbf{x})$ with $\epsilon(\mathbf{x}) \sim \mathcal{N}(0, r^{-1})$, where r^{-1} denotes the noise level. We write a noisy GP as $y \sim \mathcal{GP}(m(\mathbf{x}), c(\mathbf{x}, \mathbf{x}') + r^{-1}\delta(\mathbf{x}, \mathbf{x}'))$, where $\delta(\mathbf{x}, \mathbf{x}')$ is the Kronecker delta function.

In this paper, we set $m(\mathbf{x})$ to be zero for simplicity and use the squared-exponential covariance function, defined as $c(\mathbf{x}, \mathbf{x}'|\boldsymbol{\sigma}) = \sigma_0^2 \exp\{-1/2 \sum_{i=1}^{d}(x_i - x_i')^2/\sigma_i^2\}$, where $\sigma_i > 0$ and d is the dimensionality of $\mathbf{x}$. In such a setting, given a training set $\mathcal{D} = \{(\mathbf{x}_n, y_n)\}_{n=1}^{N}$ from a GP, we have

$$\mathbf{y}|\mathbf{X} \sim \mathcal{N}(\mathbf{0}, \mathbf{C} + r^{-1}\mathbf{I}_N), \tag{1}$$

where $\mathbf{C}(m, n) = c(\mathbf{x}_m, \mathbf{x}_n|\boldsymbol{\sigma})$.

Next, we briefly introduce MGP models. Here, suppose that $\mathcal{D}$ is drawn from an MGP composed of K GP components. We introduce an indicator variable τ_n for each sample $(\mathbf{x}_n, y_n)$. The generative process of $\mathcal{D}$ is given by:

$$p(\tau_n = k) = \pi_k, \quad \mathbf{x}_n|\tau_n = k \sim \mathcal{N}(\boldsymbol{\mu}_k, \boldsymbol{\Sigma}_k), \tag{2}$$

and

$$y_n|\tau_n = k \sim \mathcal{GP}(0, c(\mathbf{x}, \mathbf{x}'|\boldsymbol{\sigma}_k) + r_k^{-1}\delta(\mathbf{x}, \mathbf{x}')). \tag{3}$$

3   NSF-Based Mixture of Gaussian Processes

Let $\mathbf{z} \sim \mathcal{N}(\mathbf{0}, \mathbf{I}_d)$ be the base variable and $\mathbf{x}$ the target variable following the distribution we want to model. Suppose that $h(x|\boldsymbol{\theta})$ is a monotonic rational-quadratic spline [11] parameterized by $\boldsymbol{\theta}$, whose inverse and derivative are easily computed. Then a one-layer NSF[1] $\mathbf{z} = \mathbf{h}(\mathbf{x})$ is given by $z_1 = h(x_1|\boldsymbol{\theta}_1)$ and $z_i = h(x_i|\boldsymbol{\theta}_i(\mathbf{x}_{1:i-1})), i = 2, \ldots, d$, where $\boldsymbol{\theta}_i(\mathbf{x}_{1:i-1}), i = 2, \ldots, d$, are neural networks taking $\mathbf{x}_{1:i-1}$ as inputs [12]. The inverse, $\mathbf{x} = \mathbf{h}^{-1}(\mathbf{z})$, is $x_1 = h^{-1}(z_1|\boldsymbol{\theta}_1)$ and $x_i = h^{-1}(z_i|\boldsymbol{\theta}_i(\mathbf{x}_{1:i-1})), i = 2, \ldots, d$. Recursively, a J-layer NSF is defined as $\mathbf{z} = \boldsymbol{\varphi}(\mathbf{x}) = \mathbf{h}_J(\mathbf{h}_{J-1}(\ldots \mathbf{h}_1(\mathbf{x}) \ldots))$. It is obtained that $p_{\mathbf{x}}(\mathbf{x}) = p_{\mathbf{z}}(\boldsymbol{\varphi}(\mathbf{x})) \prod_{j=1}^{J} |\det(\partial \mathbf{x}_j / \partial \mathbf{x}_{j-1})|$, where $\mathbf{x}_j = \mathbf{h}_j(\mathbf{h}_{j-1}(\ldots \mathbf{h}_1(\mathbf{x}) \ldots))$, $j = 1, \ldots, J$, $\mathbf{x}_J = \mathbf{z}$, and $\mathbf{x}_0 = \mathbf{x}$. Computing the determinants is cheap because the Jacobians are lower triangular. Therefore, we can easily calculate the likelihood of $\mathbf{x}$.

In an NMGP, a base variable $\mathbf{z}_k$, subject to $\mathcal{N}(\mathbf{0}, \mathbf{I}_d)$, and an NSF $\boldsymbol{\varphi}_k(\mathbf{x}|\boldsymbol{\omega}_k)$, where $\boldsymbol{\omega}_k$ denotes the parameters, are introduced for kth GP. Then, to build an NMGP, we only need to replace the $\mathcal{N}(\boldsymbol{\mu}_k, \boldsymbol{\Sigma}_k)$ in Eq. (2) with the probability distribution of $\mathbf{x} = \boldsymbol{\varphi}_k^{-1}(\mathbf{z}_k|\boldsymbol{\omega}_k)$, i.e. $p(\mathbf{x}|\boldsymbol{\omega}_k) = p_{\mathbf{z}_k}(\boldsymbol{\varphi}_k(\mathbf{x}|\boldsymbol{\omega}_k))|\det(\partial \boldsymbol{\varphi}_k(\mathbf{x}|\boldsymbol{\omega}_k)/\partial \mathbf{x})|$.

4   Variational EM Algorithm

4.1   E-Step

Similar to the variational EM algorithm for MGP models, the linear GP model [6,13–15], an approximation of the standard GP, is used to eliminate the dependency between the outputs $y_n, n = 1, \ldots, N$. To construct a linear GP, we need to choose M ($\ll N$) samples from $\mathcal{D}$ to form a support set $\mathcal{D}'$. Let $\boldsymbol{\lambda}$ follow $\mathcal{N}(\mathbf{0}, \mathbf{C}_{MM}^{-1})$, where $\mathbf{C}_{MM}$ is the $M \times M$ covariance matrix consisting of covariance functions between samples in $\mathcal{D}'$. Then we assume that $y_n|\boldsymbol{\lambda} \sim \mathcal{N}(c(\mathbf{x}_n, \mathcal{D}')\boldsymbol{\lambda}, r^{-1})$. It follows that $\mathbf{y} \sim \mathcal{N}(\mathbf{0}, \mathbf{C}_{NM}\mathbf{C}_{MM}^{-1}\mathbf{C}_{NM}^T + r^{-1}\mathbf{I}_N)$, where $\mathbf{C}_{NM}$ is composed of covariance functions between samples in $\mathcal{D}$ and $\mathcal{D}'$. That is identical to the likelihood of a sparse Gaussian process obtained via the subset of regressors (SoR) method [16], which shows the rationality of linear models. The most important advantage of linear models is that, given $\boldsymbol{\lambda}$, $y_n, n = 1, 2, \ldots, N$, are independent.

In order to develop a variational EM algorithm for NMGPs, we pick K support sets $\mathcal{D}_k, k = 1, 2, \ldots, K$, and introduce corresponding variables $\boldsymbol{\lambda}_k, k = 1, 2, \ldots, K$. Then, K linear GPs are built to take the place of K standard GPs. We give $\boldsymbol{\pi}$ a Dirichlet prior $\text{Dir}(\boldsymbol{\alpha})$ and r_k a Gamma prior $\Gamma(a, b)$. The graphical model representation for the proposed model is shown in Fig. 1.

For simplicity, we denote all the latent variables as $\boldsymbol{\Gamma} = \{\pi_k, \boldsymbol{\lambda}_k, r_k, \tau_n | k = 1, 2, \ldots, K, n = 1, 2, \ldots, N\}$. In the framework of linear models, the complete data log-likelihood is given by

---

[1] In this paper, only autoregressive transforms are utilized.

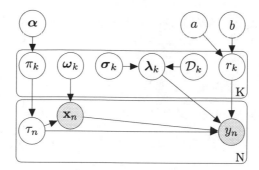

Fig. 1. The graphical model representation for the proposed model.

$$
\ln p(\boldsymbol{\Gamma}, \mathbf{X}, \mathbf{y}) = \ln p(\boldsymbol{\pi}) + \sum_{k=1}^{K} (\ln p(\boldsymbol{\lambda}_k) + \ln p(r_k)) + \sum_{n=1}^{N} \ln p(\tau_n | \boldsymbol{\pi})
$$
$$
+ \sum_{n=1}^{N} (\ln p(\mathbf{x}_n | \tau_n) + \ln p(y_n | \tau_n, \mathbf{x}_n, \boldsymbol{\lambda}_{\tau_n}, r_{\tau_n})). \tag{4}
$$

According to variational inference based on mean field theory, we choose a variational posterior distribution of the form

$$
q(\boldsymbol{\Gamma}) - q(\boldsymbol{\pi}) \prod_{k=1}^{K} \{q(\boldsymbol{\lambda}_k) q(r_k)\} \prod_{n=1}^{N} q(\tau_n) \tag{5}
$$

to approximate the true one in the E-step. Formulas used to calculate the above variational factors iteratively are standard [15] and thus omitted here.

4.2 M-Step

In an NMGP, the whole parameters, their current values, and the current variational posterior are denoted as $\boldsymbol{\Theta}$, $\boldsymbol{\Theta}_t$, and $q_t(\boldsymbol{\Gamma})$, respectively. The true Q-function, $Q(\boldsymbol{\Theta} | \boldsymbol{\Theta}_t) = \mathbb{E}_{p(\boldsymbol{\Gamma} | \mathbf{X}, \mathbf{y}, \boldsymbol{\Theta}_t)} \ln p(\boldsymbol{\Gamma}, \mathbf{X}, \mathbf{y} | \boldsymbol{\Theta})$, cannot be computed analytically. Therefore, we use $\hat{Q}(\boldsymbol{\Theta} | \boldsymbol{\Theta}_t) = \mathbb{E}_{q_t(\boldsymbol{\Gamma})} \ln p(\boldsymbol{\Gamma}, \mathbf{X}, \mathbf{y} | \boldsymbol{\Theta})$ as its approximation. We maximize $\hat{Q}(\boldsymbol{\Theta} | \boldsymbol{\Theta}_t)$ w.r.t. $\boldsymbol{\Theta}$ through gradient ascent methods. The deep learning framework PyTorch is utilized so there is no need to calculate the gradient manually.

4.3 Updating Support Sets

The first step of the variational EM algorithm is to determine K support sets randomly, and then a certain number, denoted as S, of E-steps and M-steps are performed. After that, to improve the result, the K support sets are updated according to certain criteria, and E-steps and M-steps are conducted again. We repeat the process T times determined in advance.

Fixing the parameters and variational posteriors of $\mathbf{\Gamma}\backslash\{\boldsymbol{\lambda}_k\}_{k=1}^{K}$, it is reasonable to assume that the best $\mathcal{D}_k$ maximizes the value of $q(\boldsymbol{\lambda}_k)$ at the mean [6,13–15]. That is equivalent to maximizing

$$|\mathbf{T}_k| = |\mathbf{C}_k + \mathbb{E}_q r_k \sum_{n=1}^{N} q_{nk} c_k(\mathbf{x}_n) c_k(\mathbf{x}_n)^T|, \tag{6}$$

where $\mathbf{C}_k$ is the covariance matrix composed of covariance functions between data points in $\mathcal{D}_k$ and $c_k(\mathbf{x}_n)$ is the column vector consisting of covariance functions between $\mathbf{x}_n$ and training samples in $\mathcal{D}_k$. $|\mathbf{T}_k|$ can be thought of as a function of $\mathcal{D}_k$.

Finding the best $\mathcal{D}_k$ from $\binom{N}{M}$ candidates is an NP problem. Therefore, a greedy algorithm [6,13–15] is employed to find a suboptimal solution.

4.4 Predictive Distribution

Assume that $\mathbf{x}^*$ is a new input and y^* represents its predictive output. We need to calculate the distribution $p(y^*|\mathbf{x}^*, \mathcal{D}) = \int p(y^*|\mathbf{x}^*, \mathbf{\Gamma}) p(\mathbf{\Gamma}|\mathcal{D}) d\mathbf{\Gamma}$. Similar to the calculation of Q-function, we can replace $p(\mathbf{\Gamma}|\mathcal{D})$ with the variational posterior $q(\mathbf{\Gamma})$ obtained in the last E-step. Thus, we have

$$p(y^*|\mathbf{x}^*, \mathcal{D}) \approx \int p(y^*|\mathbf{x}^*, \mathbf{\Gamma}) q(\mathbf{\Gamma}) d\mathbf{\Gamma} \approx p(y^*|\mathbf{x}^*, \mathbb{E}_q \mathbf{\Gamma})$$

$$= \sum_k \frac{\mathbb{E}_q \pi_k p(\mathbf{x}^*|\boldsymbol{\omega}_k)}{\sum_i \mathbb{E}_q \pi_i p(\mathbf{x}^*|\boldsymbol{\omega}_i)} \mathcal{N}(c_k(\mathbf{x}^*)^T \mathbb{E}_q(\boldsymbol{\lambda}_k), (\mathbb{E}_q r_k)^{-1}), \tag{7}$$

which is the weighted sum of K independent Gaussian distributions.

5 Experiments

In this section, experiments on three datasets are presented. In all experiments, $\boldsymbol{\alpha}$, a and b are set to be $(1, 1, \dots, 1)^T$, 0.01 and 0.0001, respectively [6]. In addition, we set $T = 10$ and $S = 10$. We use the root mean squared error (RMSE) to measure the prediction accuracy. Let $\{(\mathbf{x}_i, y_i)\}_{i=1}^{I}$ be a test set and $\{\hat{y}_i\}_{i=1}^{I}$ the set of predictive values, the RMSE is defined as

$$\text{RMSE} = \sqrt{\frac{1}{I} \sum_{i=1}^{I} (y_i - \hat{y}_i)^2}. \tag{8}$$

It is demonstrated by the results to be discussed that our proposed NMGP models outperform the conventional MGP models.

5.1 Synthetic Dataset

This synthetic dataset, shown in Fig. 2, is drawn from the following three functions:

$$f_0(x) = -2.5 \sin(2\pi x/12.5), \quad x \sim 0.5\mathcal{N}(-12.5, 1.2^2) + 0.5\mathcal{N}(-7.5, 1.5^2),$$

$$f_1(x) = 6 \sin(2\pi x/10), \quad x \sim 0.5\mathcal{N}(-2.5, 1.5^2) + 0.5\mathcal{N}(2.5, 1.5^2), \tag{9}$$

$$f_2(x) = -4.5 \sin(2\pi x/15), \quad x \sim 0.5\mathcal{N}(7.5, 1.5^2) + 0.5\mathcal{N}(12.5, 1.2^2).$$

The training set contains 300 points, in which points from three functions account for 30%, 40%, and 30%, respectively. The test set consists of 300 points evenly distributed in $[-15, 15]$. Gaussian noise, following $\mathcal{N}(0, 0.3^2)$, is added to all samples in this dataset.

We employ an NMGP consisting of three GP components to model the dataset and set $M = 30$ and $Q = 30$. The predictive curve, pointwise standard deviations, and three learned input distributions, similar to the true ones, are plotted in Fig. 2. The RMSEs of our NMGP and baseline models are shown in Table 1. The result demonstrates that our proposed NMGP not only caused smaller error but also produced more proper approximations of the true input distributions.

Table 1. RMSEs on three datasets

	Synthetic dataset	Coal gas dataset	Motorcycle dataset
MGP (MCMC EM) [5]	0.5411	0.6011	24.2000
TMGP (Hard-cut EM) [7]	0.5322	0.5939	23.8888
TMGP (Variational EM) [15]	0.5245	0.5854	21.6147
Our NMGP	**0.5139**	**0.5799**	**21.5936**

5.2 Coal Gas Dataset

The proposed NMGP model was also applied to a coal gas dataset [7,15], where the training set consists of 200 samples and the test set consists of 113 samples. Here, we set $K = 4$, $M = 20$ and $Q = 20$ following Guo et al. [15]. We display the dataset and the predictions in Fig. 2, and the RMSEs in Table 1.

5.3 Motorcycle Dataset

Finally, we employed the NMGP model to fit the motorcycle dataset [5,15] composed of 133 samples. The whole dataset is used to train the model and compute the RMSEs. Figure 2 shows the dataset and the result of our proposed model, and the RMSEs are presented in Table 1.

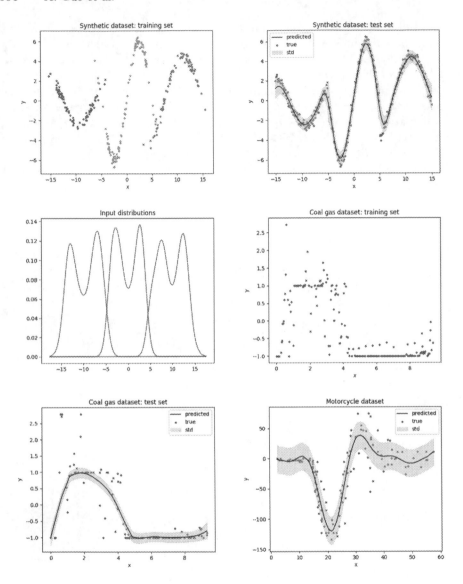

Fig. 2. Three datasets

6   Conclusion

We have proposed an NSF-based mixture model of Gaussian processes and developed a variational EM algorithm for training this model. NMGPs model input distributions using NSF models instead of Gaussians. It is demonstrated by the experimental results on three datasets that our proposed NMGP models outperform MGPs. However, the variational EM algorithm cannot be applied to large datasets since the calculation of the variational posterior involves the sum of N terms. Thus, an algorithm with lower computational complexity should be developed in the future, e.g. hard-cut EM algorithm.

Acknowledgment. This work is supported by the National Key R & D Program of China (2018AAA0100205).

References

1. Rasmussen, C.E., Williams, C.K.I.: Gaussian Processes for Machine Learning. MIT Press, Cambridge (2006)
2. Tresp, V.: Mixtures of Gaussian processes. In: Advances in Neural Information Processing Systems, vol. 13, pp. 654–660 (2001)
3. Yang, Y., Ma, J.: An efficient EM approach to parameter learning of the mixture of Gaussian processes. In: Liu, D., Zhang, H., Polycarpou, M., Alippi, C., He, H. (eds.) ISNN 2011, Part II. LNCS, vol. 6676, pp. 165–174. Springer, Heidelberg (2011). https://doi.org/10.1007/978-3-642-21090-7_20
4. Chen, Z., Ma, J., Zhou, Y.: A precise hard-cut EM algorithm for mixtures of Gaussian processes. In: Huang, D.-S., Jo, K.-H., Wang, L. (eds.) ICIC 2014. LNCS (LNAI), vol. 8589, pp. 68–75. Springer, Cham (2014). https://doi.org/10.1007/978-3-319-09339-0_7
5. Wu, D., Chen, Z., Ma, J.: An MCMC based EM algorithm for mixtures of Gaussian processes. In: Hu, X., Xia, Y., Zhang, Y., Zhao, D. (eds.) ISNN 2015. LNCS, vol. 9377, pp. 327–334. Springer, Cham (2015). https://doi.org/10.1007/978-3-319-25393-0_36
6. Yuan, C., Neubauer, C.: Variational mixture of Gaussian process experts. In: Advances in Neural Information Processing Systems, vol. 21, pp. 1897–1904 (2009)
7. Li, X., Li, T., Ma, J.: The unν-hardcut EM algorithm for non-central student-t mixtures of Gaussian processes. In: 15th IEEE International Conference on Signal Processing (ICSP), pp. 289–294 (2020)
8. Tabak, E.G., Vanden-Eijnden, E.: Density estimation by dual ascent of the log-likelihood. Commun. Math. Sci. **8**(1), 217–233 (2010)
9. Tabak, E.G., Turner, C.V.: A family of nonparametric density estimation algorithms. Commun. Pure Appl. Math. **66**(2), 145–164 (2013)
10. Kobyzev, I., Prince, S.J.D., Brubaker, M.A.: Normalizing flows: an introduction and review of current methods. IEEE Trans. Pattern Anal. Mach. Intell. **43**, 3964–3979 (2020)
11. Gregory, J., Delbourgo, R.: Piecewise rational quadratic interpolation to monotonic data. IMA J. Numer. Anal. **2**(2), 123–130 (1982)
12. Durkan, C., Bekasov, A., Murray, I., Papamakarios, G.: Neural spline flows. In: Advances in Neural Information Processing Systems, vol. 32 (2019)
13. Sun, S., Xu, X.: Variational inference for infinite mixtures of Gaussian processes with applications to traffic flow prediction. IEEE Trans. Intell. Transp. Syst. **12**(2), 466–475 (2011)
14. Luo, C., Sun, S.: Variational mixtures of Gaussian processes for classification. In: Proceedings of the 26th International Joint Conference on Artificial Intelligence, vol. 26, pp. 4603–4609 (2017)
15. Guo, X., Li, X., Ma, J.: Variational EM algorithm for Student-t mixtures of Gaussian processes. In: International Conference on Intelligent Computing (2021)
16. Smola, A.J., Bartlett, P.: Sparse greedy Gaussian process regression. In: Advances in Neural Information Proceeding System, vol. 13, pp. 619–625 (2001)

A Novel Adaptive PID Optimizer of Deep Neural Networks

Weishan Tang, Yixin Zhao, Wenjing Xie, and Wei Huang[✉]

School of Computer and Information Science, Southwest University,
Chongqing, China
weihuang@swu.edu.cn

Abstract. Proportional integral derivative (PID) optimizers have shown superiority in alleviating the oscillation problem suffered by stochastic gradient descent with momentum (SGD-M). To restrain high-frequency noises caused by minibatch data, the existing PID optimizers utilized the filtered gradient difference as D term, which slows the response and may influence convergence performance. In this paper, a new adaptive PID optimizer is proposed without using any filter. The optimizer combines present gradient (P), momentum item (I), and improved gradient difference term (D). The improved D term is obtained by imposing an adaptive saturation function on gradient difference, which can suppress oscillation and high-frequency noises. Furthermore, that function has an adaptive magnitude related to PI term, well balancing the contributions of PI and D terms. As a result, the proposed adaptive PID optimizer can reduce the oscillation phenomena, and achieves up to 32% acceleration with competitive accuracy, which is demonstrated by experiments on three commonly used benchmark datasets with different scales.

Keywords: Deep neural networks · SGD-M · PID optimizer

1 Introduction

Deep neural network (DNN) is one of the most popular and powerful tools for solving computer science problems [1], such as image recognition [2], objection detection [3], speech recognition [4]. However, it is very difficult to train a DNN with massive parameters, which requires an efficient optimizer to constantly update these parameters till reaching optimal point. To reach global optimum more easily, SGD-M [5] considers both present and past gradients, which always suffers from oscillation/overshoot problem, slowing the convergence speed and degrading the model performance.

In the literature, two promising approaches were developed to alleviate the overshoot phenomenon of SGD-M [6–9]. Firstly, the works [6,7] combined SGD-M optimizer (PI term) with the gradient difference (D term) to design a PID-based optimization algorithm, and additionally imposed a standard low-pass

© Springer Nature Switzerland AG 2021
T. Mantoro et al. (Eds.): ICONIP 2021, CCIS 1516, pp. 506–513, 2021.
https://doi.org/10.1007/978-3-030-92307-5_59

filter on D term to avoid enlarging high-frequency noises. Following this idea, Shi et al. added an individual P term and exploited a new filter on D term, providing a complete PID optimizer [8]. It can be found that the low-pass filter in [6,7] took the first order difference equation with a slow response and a low sensitivity, and the filter in [8] did not output the actual value of gradient difference, leading to error. Secondly, the work [9] employed integral-separated PI method without D term, and only got a low accuracy since past gradients were discarded under some condition. The above analyses show that it is very desirable to develop a new optimization method to suppress overshoot phenomenon and simultaneously achieve a satisfactory performance.

In this paper, a new adaptive PID optimizer is proposed to guarantee high accuracy and low overshoot in the training process of DNN. Among the PID optimizer, P and I terms respectively correspond to the current gradient and the weighted sum of past gradients, ensuring a high accuracy at the cost of overshoot. Besides, an adaptive saturated D term is designed to reduce overshoot without decreasing accuracy. The magnitude of D term is proportional to the absolute value of the PI term. This adaptive saturated D term design has three advantages: alleviates the overshoot problem, reduces the interference of high-frequency noises, and renders the ratio of D term to PI term tunable so that the contributions of D and PI terms can be well balanced. Experiments are implemented on three datasets: MNIST, CIFAR10, and CIFAR100. Detailed comparisons and analysis are conducted among four optimizers: SGD-M, the existing two PID optimizers, and the new optimizer. Final results show that the new optimizer has the best performance.

The contributions of this paper can be summarized as follows. (1) The new optimizer has an individual P term and the adaptive D term without using a low-pass filter. It realizes a more stable training process, a quicker response, and therefore a faster convergence. (2) This optimizer adopts the adaptive D term without filter and achieves a higher accuracy.

The rest of this paper is organized as follows. Section 2 presents similarities between feedback control and DNN optimization, and Sect. 3 briefly reviews related works. Section 4 provides the design of optimizer. Experimental results and detailed analysis are shown in Sect. 5. Section 6 concludes this paper.

2   Similarities Between Feedback Control and DNN Optimization

A feedback control system is a dynamic system, and can be described by $z_{t+1} = f(z_t, u_t), \xi_t = h(z_t)$, where $z_t \in R^n$ is state vector, $u_t \in R^p$ and $\xi_t \in R^q$ are control input and system output respectively, and $f(z_t, u_t)$ and $h(z_t)$ are functions. The system uses sensor device to measure ξ_t, then utilizes error-feedback controller to compute the control signal $u_t(e_t)$, where $e_t = d_t - \xi_t$ is error and d_t is desired value. With the calculated control signal, the system automatically changes itself to achieve $\xi_t \to d_t$.

DNN optimization is also a dynamic system, and can be written as $\theta_{t+1} = \gamma(\theta_t, O_t)$, $\hat{y}_t = g(x, \theta_t)$, where θ_t denotes weight parameter, O_t and $\hat{y}_t$ represent optimizer and DNN output respectively, and $\gamma(\theta_t, O_t)$ and $g(x, \theta_t)$ are functions with x as input. Based on the loss function $L_t(\hat{y}_t, y)$ that represents the gap between $\hat{y}_t$ and actual output y, DNN optimization system computes the gradient value $\frac{\partial L_t}{\partial \theta_t}$ and propagates the gradient backwards to optimizer, then exploits gradient-dependent optimizer to determine the update value O_t. With this update value, the optimization system updates θ_t to minimize L_t and hence ensures $\hat{y}_t$ get close to y_t, making the trained DNN accurately map the relation from input to output.

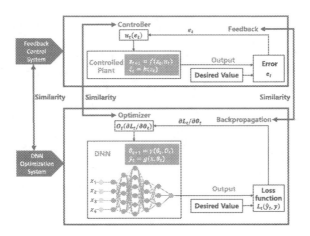

Fig. 1. Similarities between DNN optimization and feedback control.

DNN optimization is highly similar to feedback control, see Fig. 1. Firstly, they are both dynamic systems with similar objectives of steering outputs tend to desired values. Secondly, they take backpropagation or feedback to establish automatic update mechanisms. Thirdly, they both use adjuster (i.e., optimizer and controller) to change themselves to achieve objectives.

3   Related Works

The first PID optimizer [6,7] is

$$v_{t+1} = \alpha v_t + r g_t,$$
$$u_{t+1} = \alpha u_t + (1 - \alpha)(g_t - g_{t-1}),$$
$$\theta_{t+1} = \theta_t - v_{t+1} - K_d u_{t+1},$$

which is equivalent to the PID-type update rule: $\theta_{t+1} = \theta_t - r g_t - r \sum_{j=0}^{t-1} \alpha^{t-j} g_j - K_d \sum_{j=0}^{t} \alpha^{t-j}(1 - \alpha)(g_t - g_{t-1})$ in case of $u_0 = 0$ and $v_0 = 0$. Here, θ_t is weight,

g_t is gradient, $g_t - g_{t-1}$ is gradient difference, $\alpha \in (0,1)$ is factor, r and K_d are learning rate and gain parameter respectively.

The second PID optimizer [8] is

$$v_{t+1} = \alpha v_t + g_t,$$

$$\omega_{t+1} = \begin{cases} \frac{g_t - g_{t-1}}{|g_t - g_{t-1}| + \varepsilon} \eta \, |g_t|, & \text{if } |g_t - g_{t-1}| > \eta \, |g_t| \\ g_t - g_{t-1}, & \text{if } |g_t - g_{t-1}| \leq \eta \, |g_t| \end{cases}$$

$$u_{t+1} = \beta u_t + \omega_{t+1},$$

$$\theta_{t+1} = \theta_t - K_p g_t - K_i v_{t+1} - K_d u_{t+1},$$

which, under $u_0 = 0$ and $v_0 = 0$, can be transformed into PID form: $\theta_{t+1} = \theta_t - K_p g_t - K_i \sum_{j=0}^{t} \alpha^{t-j} g_j - K_d \sum_{j=0}^{t} \beta^{t-j} \omega_j$. Here, (K_p, K_i, K_d) are gain coefficients, η and β are coefficients, $\beta \in (0,1)$ is a scale factor similar to α.

4   Adaptive PID Optimizer for DNN

In this section, a new adaptive PID optimizer is proposed in three steps.

Step 1: Standard PID Optimizer
To construct a new PID optimizer, let us begin with the standard PID optimizer:

$$\begin{cases} v_{t+1} = \alpha v_t + g_t, \\ \Delta g_t = g_t - g_{t-1}, \\ \theta_{t+1} = \theta_t - K_p g_t - K_i v_{t+1} - K_d \Delta g_t, \end{cases} \tag{1}$$

whose final form is $\theta_{t+1} = \theta_t - K_p g_t - K_i \sum_{j=0}^{t} \alpha^{t-j} g_j - K_d \Delta g_t$.

The output of standard PID optimizer will encounter sharp oscillation, since Δg_t can amplify high-frequency noises and become very large sometimes. So, we make an effort to improve the D term in what follows.

Step 2: PID Optimizer with Saturated D Term
To avoid big D term, a saturation function is imposed on D term to limit the magnitude of D term. The above standard PID optimizer is improved as

$$\begin{cases} v_{t+1} = \alpha v_t + g_t, \\ \Delta g_t = g_t - g_{t-1}, \\ \theta_{t+1} = \theta_t - K_p g_t - K_i v_{t+1} - K_d \, \text{sat} \, (\Delta g_t), \end{cases} \tag{2}$$

where sat $(\cdot)$ is saturation function and defined as:

$$\text{sat} \, (\Delta g_t) = \begin{cases} 1, & \text{if } \Delta g_t \geq \varepsilon; \\ \frac{\Delta g_t}{\varepsilon}, & \text{if } |\Delta g_t| < \varepsilon; \\ -1, & \text{if } \Delta g_t \leq -\varepsilon. \end{cases} \tag{3}$$

In (3), $\varepsilon > 0$ is a tunable factor. The improved D term meets $K_d \, |\text{sat} \, (\Delta g_t)| \leq K_d$, which prevents large value, and reduces the inference of high-frequency noises. Nevertheless, it is difficult to choose an appropriate magnitude K_d to guarantee optimizer achieve a satisfactory performance. To overcome this difficulty, this D term is modified to has an adaptive magnitude in the next step.

Step 3: PID Optimizer with Adaptive Saturated D Term

PID optimizer uses the sum of P, I and D terms to decide the update value. Adjusting (K_p, K_i, K_d) means balancing the contributions of P, I and D terms to the overall update. Motivated by this fact, we plan to adaptively regulate the magnitude of D term according to the sum of P and I terms.

Based on the above idea, the optimizer (2) is modified as

$$\begin{cases} v_{t+1} = \alpha v_t + g_t, \\ \Delta g_t = g_t - g_{t-1}, \\ \theta_{t+1} = \theta_t - K_p g_t - K_i v_{t+1} - K_d \text{adsat}\left(\Delta g_t\right), \end{cases} \tag{4}$$

where the adaptive saturation function adsat $(\cdot)$ is defined as:

$$\text{adsat}\left(\Delta g_t\right) = \begin{cases} A_{\text{PI},t} & \text{if } \Delta g_t \geq \varepsilon A_{\text{PI},t}; \\ \frac{\Delta g_t}{\varepsilon}, & \text{if } |\Delta g_t| < \varepsilon A_{\text{PI},t}; \\ -A_{\text{PI},t}, & \text{if } \Delta g_t \leq \varepsilon A_{\text{PI},t}, \end{cases} \tag{5}$$
$$A_{\text{PI},t} = |K_p g_t + K_i v_{t+1}|.$$

In (5), $A_{\text{PI},t}$ is the absolute of sum of P and I terms. The D term now satisfies

$$K_d \left|\text{adsat}\left(\Delta g_t\right)\right| \leq K_d |K_p g_t + K_i v_{t+1}|.$$

This shows that the magnitude of D term is proportional to the effect of P and I terms, and the ratio of D term to PI term is not bigger than K_d, well balancing the contributions of P, I and D terms.

Novelties of our optimizer (4) can be summarized as the following three points. Firstly, PID structure is adopted to restrain the overshoot phenomenon. Secondly, D term takes the saturation function of Δg_t, reducing the interference of high-frequency noises. Compared with filtered D terms in [6–8], our saturated D term obtains a quicker response and a higher sensitivity. Thirdly, the adaptive magnitude of D term is designed to be relevant to PI term, overcoming the difficulty of choosing constant magnitude. Besides, this adaptive magnitude is beneficial for balancing the contributions of D and PI terms to overall update, achieving satisfactory performance.

5   Experiments

5.1   Datasets

Experiments are implemented on three datasets: **MNIST, CIFAR10 and CIFAR100. MNIST** is a handwritten digit (0–9) dataset, which contains 60,000 training images and 10,000 testing images [10]. These images are 28×28 pixels with only one channel. **CIFAR10** dataset involves 50,000 training images and 10,000 testing images, which are 32×32 color images in 10 different classes, with 6,000 images per class [11]. **CIFAR100** dataset consists of 100 classes with 600 images for each class, and these 600 images in each class have 500 training samples and 100 testing ones [11].

5.2 Experiments on MNIST

A three-layer Multilayer perceptron (MLP) was trained on MNIST, then experimental results were provided to demonstrate the effectiveness of the proposed PID optimizer. The MLP was established by using ReLu activation function, hidden layer with 1000 hidden nodes, and output layer with softmax function. Batch size, epoch and learning rate were set as 128, 20 and 0.01 respectively. K_p, K_i, K_d, ε were selected as 20, 10, 10 and 0.01 respectively. Experimental results were depicted in Fig. 2, where FPID and SPID respectively denote the first and the second PID optimizers in Sect. 3. The following results can be concluded from Fig. 2. First of all, SGD-M, FPID and our PID optimizer have better training performances than SPID, because the filtered D term in SPID does not reflect the real value of Δg_t, affecting the performance. Secondly, FPID and our PID optimizer perform better than SGD-M, due to the added D term. This confirms that D term can reduce the overshoot phenomenon, yielding a faster training speed. Finally, compared with others, our optimizer achieves a quicker convergence of training process and a higher accuracy. This is mainly because our PID optimizer takes the adaptive saturated D term, which not only restrains the overshoot phenomenon and the inference of high-frequency noises, but also has a quick response, a high sensitivity and a good balance with PI term.

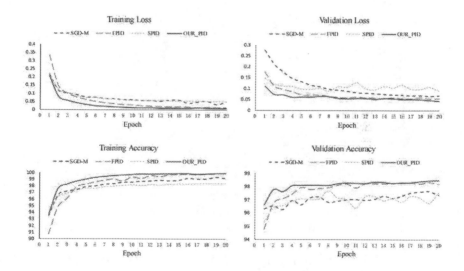

Fig. 2. Trajectories of loss and accuracy of MLP for various optimizers on MINST.

5.3 Results on CIFAR Datasets

To further check the generality capability, SGD-M, FPID, SPID and our optimizers are utilized to train four deeper network models on larger CIFAR datasets.

The four models are ResNet [2], DenseNet [12], PreActResNet [13], and WRN [14]. Batch size, epoch and learning rate were set as 128, 200 and 0.1. The decreasing schedule is set as 50% and 75% of training epochs. Detailed experimental data is listed in Table 1.

The following results can be concluded by analyzing Table 1. Firstly, the results on CIFAR10 are identical to those on CIFAR100. Secondly, the training performance by SPID is actually degraded to some extent. With D term to alleviate overshoot phenomenon, FPID and our optimizer require less epochs to reach the best accuracy. Finally, among these four optimizers, our optimizer gets the smallest test error through the least epochs, i.e., achieves the best performance with a high accuracy and a fast convergence rate. More specifically, the training convergence rate is increased by average of 20% and up to 32%, compared with other optimizers. This verifies that our method is able to suppress overshoot to accelerate the optimization process without destroying accuracy. These results are shown the same as those on MNIST regardless of deeper networks and larger datasets. In conclusion, the good generalization capability of our PID optimizer is demonstrated by the previous results.

Table 1. Comparisons between our optimizer and other optimizers on CIFAR datasets.

Model	Depth-k	Params (M)	CIFAR10	Epochs	CIFAR100	Epochs
-	-	-	SGD-M/FPID/ SPID/OUR_PID	SGD-M/FPID/ SPID/OUR_PID	SGD-M/FPID/ SPID/OUR_PID	SGD-M/FPID/ SPID/OUR_PID
Resnet [2]	20	0.27M	8.2/8.16/8.84/**7.48**	169/161/146/**126**	33.45/32.15/35.76/**31.02**	112/**103**/**103**/106
	32	0.46M	8.19/7.12/8.5/**6.92**	187/**139**/154/141	29.74/31.42/34.52/**29.63**	121/118/104/**102**
	44	0.66M	6.67/6.45/8.16/**6.32**	193/189/197/**153**	30.79/29.49/34.09/**27.71**	109/158/134/**105**
	56	0.85M	6.59/6.45/7.41/**6.19**	184/177/165/**164**	30.05/28.80/33.55/**26.34**	113/170/124/**111**
Densenet [12]	100-12	0.8M	5.08/6.31/8.21/**5.01**	180/142/147/**135**	29.52/28.38/35.46/**24.20**	108/132/111/**107**
	190-40	25.6M	3.8/5.39/6.04/4.5	164/165/171/**161**	23.21/20.15/28.73/**18.92**	168/195/186/**157**
PreactResnet [13]	18	11.17M	7.35/6.36/8.51/**6.24**	134/193/148/**107**	24.85/24.60/25.55/**23.95**	177/199/190/**166**
	34	21.28M	6.17/6.13/9.4/**5.76**	134/130/157/**124**	26.39/**24.80**/28.08/25.23	172/**167**/168/185
	50	23.51M	5.85/5.28/5.73/**5.15**	171/198/194/**169**	24.02/23.14/24.33/**22.61**	188/156/197/**147**
WRN [14]	16-8	11M	5.35/4.80/6.36/**4.71**	175/175/183/**137**	23.85/23.20/25.30/**22.06**	192/197/176/**159**

6   Conclusion

In this paper, a novel adaptive PID optimizer is proposed for solving the overshoot/oscillation problem of SGD-M. The proposed optimizer adopts PID structure and adaptive saturated D term. Different from the previous filtered D terms, the adaptive saturated D term is for the first time designed by assigning an adaptive magnitude for D term, in which the magnitude is dependent on the absolute value of PI term. Owing to this novel form, the adaptive D term enjoys three advantages: (1) has a quick response and a high sensitivity with respect to gradient difference; (2) removes some high-frequency noises and alleviates the overshoot phenomenon (yielding fast convergence); (3) helps to balance the contributions of P, I and D terms. These advantages facilitate the proposed optimizer achieve a satisfactory performance, which is demonstrated by experiments on datasets with different scales. Future research includes more comparisons with other complex algorithms and the extension of PID optimizer to other networks.

References

1. LeCun, Y., Bengio, Y., Hinton, G.: Deep learning. Nature **521**(7553), 436–444 (2015)
2. He, K., Zhang, X., Ren, S., Sun, J.: Deep residual learning for image recognition. In: Proceedings of the IEEE Conference on Computer Vision and Pattern Recognition, pp. 770–778 (2016)
3. Redmon, J., Farhadi, A.: Yolo9000: better, faster, stronger. In: Proceedings of the IEEE Conference on Computer Vision and Pattern Recognition, pp. 7263–7271 (2017)
4. Hinton, G., et al.: Deep neural networks for acoustic modeling in speech recognition: the shared views of four research groups. IEEE Sig. Process. Mag. **29**(6), 82–97 (2012)
5. Qian, N.: On the momentum term in gradient descent learning algorithms. Neural Netw. **12**(1), 145–151 (1999)
6. An, W., Wang, H., Sun, Q., Xu, J., Dai, Q., Zhang, L.: A PID controller approach for stochastic optimization of deep networks. In: Proceedings of the IEEE Conference on Computer Vision and Pattern Recognition, pp. 8522–8531 (2018)
7. Wang, H., Luo, Y., An, W., Sun, Q., Jun, X., Zhang, L.: PID controller-based stochastic optimization acceleration for deep neural networks. IEEE Trans. Neural Netw. Learn. Syst. **31**(12), 5079–5091 (2020)
8. Shi, L., Zhang, Y., Wang, W., Cheng, J., Lu, H.: Rethinking the PID optimizer for stochastic optimization of deep networks. In: 2020 IEEE International Conference on Multimedia and Expo (ICME), pp. 1–6. IEEE (2020)
9. Wang, D., Ji, M., Wang, Y., Wang, H., Fang, L.: SPI-optimizer: an integral-separated PI controller for stochastic optimization. In: 2019 IEEE International Conference on Image Processing (ICIP), pp. 2129–2133. IEEE (2019)
10. LeCun, Y., Bottou, L., Bengio, Y., Haffner, P.: Gradient-based learning applied to document recognition. Proc. IEEE **86**(11), 2278–2324 (1998)
11. Krizhevsky, A., Hinton, G., et al.: Learning multiple layers of features from tiny images (2009)
12. Huang, G., Liu, Z., Van Der Maaten, L., Weinberger, K.Q.: Densely connected convolutional networks. In: Proceedings of the IEEE Conference on Computer Vision and Pattern Recognition, pp. 4700–4708 (2017)
13. He, K., Zhang, X., Ren, S., Sun, J.: Identity mappings in deep residual networks. In: Leibe, B., Matas, J., Sebe, N., Welling, M. (eds.) ECCV 2016. LNCS, vol. 9908, pp. 630–645. Springer, Cham (2016). https://doi.org/10.1007/978-3-319-46493-0_38
14. Zagoruyko, S., Komodakis, N.: Wide residual networks. arXiv preprint arXiv:1605.07146 (2016)

What Pushes Self-supervised Image Representations Away?

Bartosz Zieliński[(✉)] and Michał Górszczak

Faculty of Mathematics and Computer Science, Jagiellonian University,
Łojasiewicza 6, 30-428 Krakow, Poland
bartosz.zielinski@uj.edu.pl

Abstract. Self-supervised models provide on par or superior results to their fully supervised competitors, yet it is unclear what information about images they contain. As a result, a visual probing framework was recently introduced to probe image representations for interesting visual features. While visual probing provides information about semantic knowledge, complexity, and consistency, it does not directly and exhaustively explain which visual features push self-supervised image representations away and which are neutral. In this paper, we fill this gap by proving a method that removes particular visual features from the image and analyzes how such a distortion influences the representation. Our key findings emphasize that discrepancies in features like lines and forms push self-supervised representations away more than brightness, color, shape, and especially texture changes. Our work is complementary to visual probing and provides more direct explanations of the mechanisms behind the contrastive loss.

Keywords: Explainability · Self-supervised representation · Computer vision · Deep learning

1 Introduction

Recently introduced self-supervised representation learning obtains encouraging results on multiple visual tasks [7,9,11,16]. Despite various modifications, these methods generally involve certain forms of Siamese networks [6] and the mechanism of contrastive learning. More specifically, they define the inputs as two augmentations of one image and maximize the similarity subject to different conditions. While self-supervised representations obtained this way can obtain accuracy similar to their supervised counterparts [9], it is unclear what visual features are important for contrastive loss and which are peripheral.

Supported by grant no POIR.04.04.00-00-14DE/18-00 carried out within the Team-Net program of the Foundation for Polish Science co-financed by the European Union under the European Regional Development Fund and Priority Research Area Digiworld under the program Excellence Initiative – Research University at the Jagiellonian University in Kraków.

Motivated by this observation, the Visual Probing (VP) framework was recently introduced [3,14] to explain the self-supervised models by leveraging probing tasks employed previously in natural language processing. For this purpose, it provides a mapping between visual and textual modalities that constructs a visual taxonomy. While VP shows that leveraging the relationship between language and vision serves as an effective and intuitive tool for explaining self-supervised models, it does not directly and exhaustively explain which visual features push self-supervised image representations away and which are neutral.

In this paper, we fill this gap by proving a distortion-based analysis built on the cognitive visual systematic defined in [14] with features like brightness, color, textures, lines, shape, and form. We distort the image by removing a superpixel corresponding to a specified feature and analyze how such distortion influences the representation. The results we obtain provide us with insights into the mechanism of contrastive loss, *e.g.* we discover that lines and forms have the highest impact on the distance between two representations, while the texture is generally negligible. Moreover, we observe that the rarest visual features have the highest impact on this distance. From this perspective, our analysis of the self-supervised representations is complementary to existing explainability methods.

2   Related Works

Our work corresponds to two research areas: self-supervised learning and explainable artificial intelligence. We briefly cover the latest achievements in these two topics in the following paragraphs.

Self-supervised Image Representations. Recently published self-supervised methods usually base on contrastive loss [10], which aims to discriminate between positive and negative pairs, *i.e.* two differently modified versions of the same image and two different images from the same dataset. It is used, *e.g.* in MoCo v1 [11], SimCLR v2 [16], BYOL [9], and SwAV [7]. Our paper provides a method for analyzing what pushes pair of self-supervised image representations of the image pair away.

Explainable Artificial Intelligence. eXplainable Artificial Intelligence (XAI) aggregates methods that allow human users to comprehend the output of machine learning algorithms [8]. One type of such method is saliency map [1]. Another common approach is perturbation-based interpretability, which applies changes to either data [5] or features [15] and observes the influence of such distortions on the output. Moreover, some methods verify the relevance of network hidden layers [2] or focus on understanding the function of hidden layers [4]. More recent methods are inspired by the human brain and how it explains its visual judgments by pointing to prototypical features that an object possesses [17]. Finally, recently introduced visual probing analyzes the information stored in self-supervised image representations using probing tasks employed from NLP.

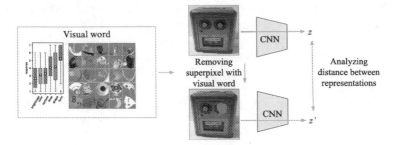

Fig. 1. Our distortion-based analysis examines how important a considered visual word is for the distance between self-supervised image representations. For this purpose, we generate representations for an original image and its modification without a superpixel assigned to this visual word. Since the visual words correspond to visual features, the distance between those representations provides information on how important the particular visual features are for the representation.

Our work is complementary to visual probing and provides more direct explanations of the mechanisms behind the contrastive loss.

3   Method

In this section, we provide a method that explains which visual features push a pair of self-supervised image representations away and which are neutral. For this purpose, we first introduce visual words and describe them with six visual features from the Marr's computational theory of vision [13]. Such visual words are then assigned to superpixels of an image using three steps: segmentation into superpixels, their encoding, and assignment to the nearest visual words in the activation space. Finally, we distort the image by removing a superpixel with specific visual words and analyze how such distortion influences the representation. Since visual words correspond to particular features, we can conduct an in-depth analysis of the self-supervised representations.

Generating Visual Words. In order to obtain the visual words, we use the approach proposed in [3]. It is based on the ACE algorithm [8] that uses TCAV methodology [12] and generates high-level concepts important for prediction and easily understandable by humans. ACE returns separate concepts for each class. Hence, to obtain a reliable dictionary with visual words shared between classes, all concepts for all classes are passed to the k-means algorithm to obtain 50 clusters considered as visual words.

Cognitive Vision Systematic. To obtain the meaning of the visual words, we apply cognitive visual systematic defined in [14]. It adapts Marr's computational theory of vision [13] and consists of six visual features: intensity (brightness), color, texture, lines, shape, and form (examples are depicted in the second column of Table 1).

Distortion-Based Analysis. To determine which visual word, and consequently visual feature, is crucial for self-supervised image representation, we conduct the procedure presented in Fig. 1 separately for each visual word. It first examines the dataset to obtain images with at least one superpixel assigned to the considered visual word (see the upper image from Fig. 1). Each of the collected images is then modified to contain the mean image value in the region of such superpixel (see the bottom image from Fig. 1). Then, both original and modified images are passed through a self-supervised model (CNN) to obtain image representations (z and z'). Finally, the distance between z and z' is calculated with Euclidean distance. If repeated for sufficiently many images, reliable statistics on this distance can be obtained and used to conduct our analysis.

4 Experimental Setup

We use procedure and hyperparameters from [3] to obtain visual words. Moreover, we examine four self-supervised methods: MoCo v1 [11], SimCLR v2 [16], BYOL [9], and SwAV [7]. For all of them, we use publicly available models trained on ImageNet[1]. To assign a superpixel to a visual word, we first pass it through the GoogLeNet to generate a representation from the *mixed4c* layer (similarly to generating visual words) and then we use a two-stage assignment, like in [3].

The distortion statistics for each visual word are based on 100 images containing at least one superpixel of resolution 50 assigned to this visual word. However, to guarantee that the superpixel does not correspond to more than one visual word, the proportion of distance to the closest and the second closest visual word has to be smaller than 0.9. In the modified version of the image, the superpixel region is filled with the mean color of the training images. Finally, the mean distance between the original and modified image representations is calculated over all 100 images normalized using min-max standarization.

5 Results and Discussion

According to our experiments, discrepancies in lines and forms are more crucial for self-supervised representations than changes in brightness, color, shape, or texture. Moreover, the rarer the features, the larger influence they have on the representation. In the following, we analyze those aspects in greater detail.

There are Significant Differences Between Representation Changes Among Different Visual Features. As presented in Fig. 2, changes in different visual words impact the self-supervised image representation differently. The largest impact is obtained for complex visual word (*e.g.* number 37 or 26), corresponding to

---

[1] We use the following implementations of self-supervised methods: https://github. com/{google-research/simclr, yaox12/BYOL-PyTorch, facebookresearch/swav, facebookresearch/moco}. We use ResNet-50 (1x) variant for each self-supervised method.

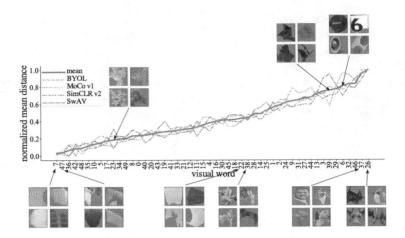

Fig. 2. Mean change in image representation after extracting superpixel with a particular visual word, sorted in ascending order. The visual words with the lowest (number 7 and 47), medium (number 22 and 38), and highest (number 37 and 26) values are depicted below the plot. Moreover, three visual words with the highest variance between the considered self-supervised methods are provided above the plot.

human and dog body parts. At the same time, simple visual words (*e.g.* number 7 and 47) usually relate to the background and are insignificant for the representation. Between them, there are visual words (*e.g.* number 22 and 38) with medium complexity.

Since 20 out of 50 visual words are assigned to six visual features, they can be further analyzed to investigate the influence of the increased level of the particular features on the representation. As a result, interesting patterns are obtained for texture, lines, and form, as shown in Fig. 3. One can observe that together with the increased level of lines and forms in visual word, its removal from the image increases the distance between the original and modified image. At the same time, we observe the opposite situation in the case of texture. We support these observations by computing the Pearson correlation between the increased level of visual feature and change in image representation (see Table 1). The correlation coefficients for texture, lines, and form are -0.6053, 0.5812, and 0.7081, respectively. Our observations are in line with the results of visual probing [14], which indicate that self-supervised image representations are lines- and form-biased.

Changes Caused by the Visual Features Vary Unnoticeably Across the Considered Self-Supervised Methods. While there are significant changes in representations after extracting different visual words from the image, their variance across considered self-supervised methods is unnoticeable. There are only a few visual words with higher variance (*e.g.* number 23, 39, and 6 presented above the plot of Fig. 2) without explicitly visible patterns. However, the closer look on Fig. 2 reveals that MoCo v1, in contrast to SimCLR v2, works significantly worse than

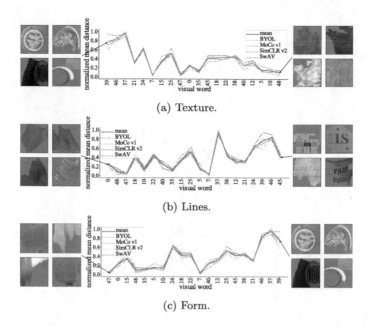

(a) Texture.

(b) Lines.

(c) Form.

Fig. 3. Mean change in image representation after extracting superpixel with a particular visual word, sorted by the increased level of a specified visual feature, like texture (a), lines (b), and form (c). One can observe the positive correlation for lines and form and the negative correlation for textures. Notice that the visual words with the lowest and highest levels of a particular visual feature are presented on the left and right sides of a plot.

the remaining methods for the less complex visual words but wins in the case of the more complicated.

Removing the Rarest Visual Features Reflects in More Significant Representation Changes. Finally, we analyze the frequency of the visual words by taking the percentage of all training superpixels assigned to this word. We then use the same order as in Fig. 2 and plot this frequency in Fig. 4. We observe that the rarest, more complex visual words (*e.g.* number 13, 39, and 37) are best represented by self-supervised methods. Moreover, the most common superpixels correspond to simple, uniform visual words (*e.g.* number 42, 8, and 11). We provide the correlation coefficients in Table 1.

Table 1. Visualisation of the features from Marr's computational theory of vision together with the Pearson correlation between an increased level of a specified visual feature and mean change caused by extracting visual words (column "mean dist.") or its frequency (column "frequency"). One can observe that in the case of lines and forms, mean change grows together with the increasing level of the feature, even though both of them are very rare (negative correlation coefficient).

visual features from Marr's theory	mean dist.	frequency
brightness	-0.1125	**0.5802**
color	-0.0810	**0.5140**
texture	**-0.6053**	0.6823
lines	0.5812	-0.7254
shape	-0.0185	0.0105
form	**0.7081**	**-0.6129**

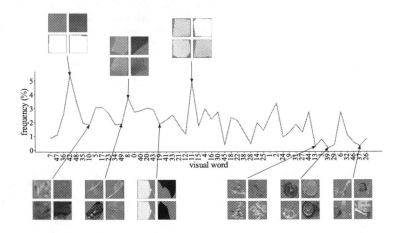

Fig. 4. Frequency of the visual words sorted by the mean change in image representation. One can observe that frequency drops with increasing change (Pearson correlation equals −0.507). Moreover, the most frequent visual words (above the plot) correspond to the background, while these crucial and less frequent (below the plot) correspond to more complex foreground structures.

6   Conclusions

In this work, we introduce a novel distortion-based analysis that investigates the information stored in self-supervised image representations. It removes particular visual features from the image to analyze how such a distortion influences the representation. For this purpose, we build on the visual taxonomy and cognitive visual systematic defined by visual probing. However, in contrast to visual probing, we introduce a direct explanation of the mechanisms behind the contrastive loss.

The results of the provided experiments confirm the applicability of our method in understanding self-supervised representations. We verify that the representation is biased toward specific visual features and compared this behavior through the considered self-supervised methods. Consequently, we provide insight that can be used in the future to build a more reliable and effective representation based on contrastive loss.

References

1. Adebayo, J., Gilmer J., Muelly, M., Goodfellow, I., Hardt, M., Kim, B.: Sanity checks for saliency maps. In: NeurIPS (2018)
2. Alain, G., Bengio, Y.: Understanding intermediate layers using linear classifier probes. In: ICLR Workshop (2016)
3. Basaj, D., et al.: Explaining self-supervised image representations with visual probing. In: ICJAI (2021)
4. Bau, D., Zhou, B., Khosla, A., Oliva, A., Torralba, A.: Network dissection: quantifying interpretability of deep visual representations. CoRR (2017)
5. Bernard, J., Hutter, M., Ritter, C., Lehmann, M., Sedlmair, M., Zeppelzauer, M: Visual analysis of degree-of-interest functions to support selection strategies for instance labeling. In: EuroVA (2019)
6. Bromley, J., Guyon, I., LeCun, Y., Säckinger, E., Shah, R.: Signature verification using a "Siamese" time delay neural network. In: NeurIPS (1993)
7. Caron, M., Misra, I., Mairal, J., Goyal, P., Bojanowski, P., Joulin, A.: Unsupervised learning of visual features by contrasting cluster assignments. arXiv (2020)
8. Ghorbani, G., Wexler, J., Zou, J., Kim, B.: Towards automatic concept-based explanations. In: NeurIPS (2019)
9. Grill, J.-B. et al.: Bootstrap your own latent: a new approach to self-supervised learning. arXiv (2020)
10. Hadsell, R., Chopra, S., LeCun, Y.: Dimensionality reduction by learning an invariant mapping. In: CVPR (2006)
11. He, K., Fan, H., Wu, Y., Xie, S., Girshick, R.: Momentum contrast for unsupervised visual representation learning. In: CVPR (2020)
12. Kim, B., et al.: Interpretability beyond feature attribution: quantitative testing with concept activation vectors (TCAV). In: ICML (2018)
13. Marr, D.: Vision: A Computational Investigation into the Human Representation and Processing of Visual Information. Henry Holt and Co., Inc. (1982)
14. Oleszkiewicz, W., et al.: Visual probing: cognitive framework for explaining self-supervised image representations. arXiv (2020)
15. Ribeiro, M.T., Singh, S., Guestrin, C.: Why should i trust you?: explaining the predictions of any classifier. CoRR (2016)
16. Chen, T., Kornblith, S., Swersky, K., Norouzi, M., Hinton, G.: Big self-supervised models are strong semi-supervised learners. In: NeurIPS 2020 (2020)
17. Chen, C., Li, O., Barnett, A., Su, J., Rudin, C.: This looks like that: deep learning for interpretable image recognition. In: NeurIPS 2020 (2020)

Single-Image Super-Resolution Reconstruction Based on the Differences of Neighboring Pixels

Huipeng Zheng[1], Lukman Hakim[1], Takio Kurita[2(✉)], and Junichi Miyao[2]

[1] Department of Information Engineering, Hiroshima University, 1-4-1 Kagamiyama, Higashi-Hiroshima 739-8527, Japan
{m191504,lukman-hakim}@hiroshima-u.ac.jp
[2] Graduate School of Advanced Science and Engineering, Hiroshima University, 1-4-1 Kagamiyama, Higashi-Hiroshima-shi, Hiroshima 739-8527, Japan
{tkurita,miyao}@hiroshima-u.ac.jp

Abstract. The deep learning technique was used to increase the performance of single image super-resolution (SISR). However, most existing CNN-based SISR approaches primarily focus on establishing deeper or larger networks to extract more significant high-level features. Usually, the pixel-level loss between the target high-resolution image and the estimated image is used, but the neighbor relations between pixels in the image are seldom used. On the other hand, according to observations, a pixel's neighbor relationship contains rich information about the spatial structure, local context, and structural knowledge. Based on this fact, in this paper, we utilize pixel's neighbor relationships in a different perspective, and we propose the differences of neighboring pixels to regularize the CNN by constructing a graph from the estimated image and the ground-truth image. The proposed method outperforms the state-of-the-art methods in terms of quantitative and qualitative evaluation of the benchmark datasets.

Keywords: Super-resolution · Convolutional neural networks · Deep learning

1 Introduction

Single-Image Super-Resolution (SISR) is a technique to reconstruct a high-resolution (HR) image from a low-resolution (LR) image. The challenges problem in the super-resolution task is the ill-pose problem. Many SISR techniques have been developed to address this challenge, including interpolation-based [1,2], reconstruction-based [3], and deep learning-based methods [4].

Even though CNN-based SISR has significantly improved learning-based approaches bringing good performances, existing SR models based on CNN still

Supported by organization x.

have several drawbacks. Most SISR techniques based on CNN are primarily concerned with constructing deeper or larger networks to acquire more meaningful high-level features. Usually, we use the pixel-level loss between the target high-resolution image and the estimated image and neglect the neighbor relations between pixels.

Basically, natural images have a strong pixel neighbor relationship. It means that a pixel has a strong correlation with its neighbors, but a low correlation with or is largely independent of pixels further away [11]. In addition, the neighboring relationship of a pixel also contains rich information about the spatial structure, local context, and structural knowledge [7]. Based on this fact, the authors proposed to introduce the pixel neighbor relationships as a regularizer in the loss function of CNN and applied for Anime-like Images Super-Resolution and Fundus Image Segmentation [5]. The regularizer is named Graph Laplacian Regularization based on the Differences of Neighboring Pixels (GLRDN). The GLRDN is essentially deriving from the graph theory approach. The graph is constructed from the estimated image and the ground-truth image. The graphs use the pixel as a node and the edge represented by the "differences" of a neighboring pixel. The basic idea is that the differences between the neighboring pixels in the estimated images should be close to the differences in the ground-truth image.

This study propose the GLRDN for general single image super-resolution and show the effectiveness of the proposed approach by introducing the GLRDN to the state-of-the-art SISR methods (EDSR [6] and RCAN [12]). The proposed GLRDN can combine with the existing CNN-based SISR methods as a regularizer by simply adding the GLRDN term into their loss functions. We can easily improve the quality of the estimated super-resolution image of the existing SISR methods.

The contribution of this paper can summarize as follow: (1) Proposed GLRDN to capture the relationship between neighboring pixels for general single image super-resolution; (2) Analyzed the baseline architecture with and without our regularizer; (3) Explored our proposed methods with state-of-the-art methods in single image super-resolution.

The structure of this paper is as follows. In Sect. 2, we presented some related methods with our work. In Sect. 3, we explain the proposed method. The results and experiments are detailed in Sect. 4. Finally, Sect. 5 is presented the conclusion of this study.

2   Related Work

2.1   Graph Laplacian Regularization Based on the Differences of Neighboring Pixels

The GLRDN was proposed by Hakim et al. [5]. This regularizer uses the graph theory approach to capture the relationship of the difference between pixels. Assume that we have two images, estimated image y and target image t. Then $G = (V, E)$ constructed be a graph where $V = \{i | i = 1, \ldots, N\}$ is the set of the pixel indices with N pixels and the $E = \{(i, j) | i, j \in V\}$ is the neighboring relations between the pixels. Furthermore, the differences of neighboring pixels of two images s_G are given as

$$
\begin{aligned}
S_G(\boldsymbol{t}, \boldsymbol{y}) &= \sum_{(i,j)\in E} \{(t_i - t_j) - (y_i - y_j)\}^2 \\
&= \sum_{(i,j)\in E} (\Delta t_{ij} - \Delta y_{ij})^2 \\
&= (\Delta \boldsymbol{t} - \Delta \boldsymbol{y})^T (\Delta \boldsymbol{t} - \Delta \boldsymbol{y}) \\
&= (B\boldsymbol{t} - B\boldsymbol{y})^T (B\boldsymbol{t} - B\boldsymbol{y}) \\
&= (\boldsymbol{t} - \boldsymbol{y})^T B^T B(\boldsymbol{t} - \boldsymbol{y}) \\
&= (\boldsymbol{t} - \boldsymbol{y})^T L(\boldsymbol{t} - \boldsymbol{y})
\end{aligned}
\tag{1}
$$

where B is incident matrix and L is the Laplacian matrix that is defined from the identity matrix.

3   Method

This study aims to capture neighboring pixel's relationships from the reconstructed image estimated from the LR image and the HR images and minimize the differences of the adjacent pixels differences. As a result, the loss is defined as the squared errors of the differences between the predicted image and HR images. In the following sections, we will go through the specifics of the proposed approach.

3.1   Estimation of the Differences Neighboring Pixels

Let us consider the set of training samples $X = \{(\boldsymbol{x}_m, \boldsymbol{t}_m)|m = 1, ..., M\}$ where $\boldsymbol{x}_m$ is a mth input image and $\boldsymbol{t}_m$ is the mth target image. M is define as the total of images in training samples. The network is trained to predict the output HR image $\boldsymbol{y}_m$ from the mth input LR image $\boldsymbol{x}_m$.

The GLRDN is defined as the graph, which is pixels as nodes and sum of the squared differences of the differences of neighboring pixels between the target image $\boldsymbol{t}_m$ and the estimated images $\boldsymbol{y}_m$ as edges. Then the GLRDN is given as

$$
S_G = \sum_{m=1}^{M} S_G(\boldsymbol{t}_m, \boldsymbol{y}_m) = \sum_{m=1}^{M} (\boldsymbol{t}_m - \boldsymbol{y}_m)^T L(\boldsymbol{t}_m - \boldsymbol{y}_m)
\tag{2}
$$

This measure S_G becomes small if the neighboring relations of the pixels in the estimated output images are similar to those of the target images.

3.2   CNN-Based Super-Resolution with GLRDN

We can apply the proposed GLRDN to any existing CNN-based Super-Resolution algorithms by simply adding the GLRDN term in the loss function

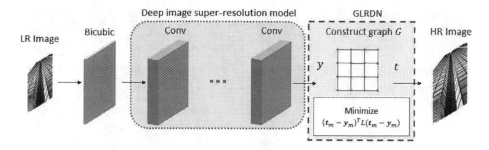

Fig. 1. Illustration of the proposed method on CNN-based Super-Resolution

for the training. The proposed method is illustrated in Fig. 1. The CNN-based Super-Resolution is trained to estimate the HR image as y for a given LR input image x. The first convolutional layer retrieves a series of feature maps. The second layer non-linearly transfers these feature maps to high-resolution patch representations. To construct the final high-resolution image, the last layer integrates the estimates within a spatial neighborhood.

In the Super-resolution task, using the Sum Squared Error (SSE) as the objective function is common. The Sum Squared Error is given by

$$E_{sse} = \sum_{m=1}^{M} (\boldsymbol{t}_m - \boldsymbol{y}_m)^2 \tag{3}$$

For the training of the parameters of the network, we combine the SSE loss with the regularization term as

$$Q_{sr} = E_{sse} + \lambda S_G \tag{4}$$

where λ is a parameter to adjust the regularization. The network learning process is more robust by adding the term regularization because it considers the relationship between pixels rather than just comparing pixels with pixels.

4 Experiments

4.1 Experimental Setting

We adopt the EDSR and RCAN as our baseline models due to their great performance on image super-resolution tasks. In all these settings, we compare the performance with and without our regularizer. We set 300 epochs and batch size to 16. We set the learning rate to 10^{-4} and divided at every 2×10^5 minibatch.

Our experiments are performed under the ×2, ×3, ×4 scale factor. During training, we use the RGB input patches with the size of 48 × 48 in each batch. Augmentation technique also used on the training images by rotating 90°, 180°, 270°, and flipped randomly. This experiments implemented on DIV2K [13], Set5 [14], Set14 [15], B100 [10], Urban100 [9], and Manga109 [8] datasets. We asses the improvement of our method using PSNR and SSIM measurements.

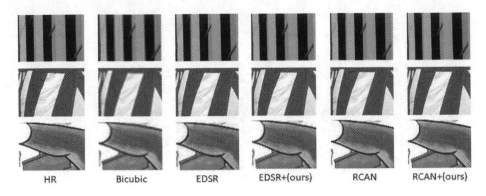

HR   Bicubic   EDSR   EDSR+(ours)   RCAN   RCAN+(ours)

Fig. 2. Visual comparison of our proposed methods on Urban100, B100, and Manga109 datasets.

Table 1. Ablation study on Set5, Set14, and B100 datasets.

Method	λ	Set5		Set14		B100	
		PSNR	SSIM	PSNR	SSIM	PSNR	SSIM
Bicubic	-	28.42	0.8104	26.00	0.7027	25.96	0.6675
EDSR	0	30.89	0.8683	27.66	0.7515	27.12	0.7159
EDSR+ours	0.1	31.69	0.8851	28.15	0.7655	27.49	0.7279
EDSR+ours	1	**31.75**	**0.8863**	**28.19**	**0.7663**	**27.52**	**0.7643**
EDSR+ours	5	31.74	0.8857	28.18	0.7653	**27.52**	0.7262
EDSR+ours	10	31.75	0.8855	28.18	0.7641	**27.52**	0.7252
EDSR+ours	100	31.65	0.8840	28.12	0.7620	27.49	0.7230

Table 2. Ablation study on Urban100 and Manga109 datasets.

Method	λ	Urban100		Manga109	
		PSNR	SSIM	PSNR	SSIM
Bicubic	-	23.14	0.6577	24.89	0.7866
EDSR	0	25.12	0.7445	29.68	0.8999
EDSR+ours	0.1	25.83	0.7749	30.84	0.9061
EDSR+ours	1	25.92	0.7749	**30.95**	**0.9084**
EDSR+ours	5	**25.95**	**0.7767**	30.91	0.9072
EDSR+ours	10	**25.95**	0.7762	30.86	0.9062
EDSR+ours	100	25.92	0.7736	30.84	0.9042

5   Result and Discussion

Ablation Study. In this part, the ablation study presented the effect of the proposed regularizer. We combined EDSR with our regularizer by setting different λ. We started with a simple EDSR model by setting the number of layers $B = 12$ and the number of feature channels $F = 64$ with a scaling factor of 1. We compared the PSNR/SSIM result on the different testing datasets by setting the scale factor as 4. Table 1 showing the ablation study on Set5, Set14, and B100 datasets, and Table 2 showing the ablation study on Urban100 and Manga109 datasets. The best results are highlighted in bold. As shown in Table 1 and Table 2, the best parameter λ in Eq. 4 is 1 which highest PSNR and SSIM on Set5, Set14, B100, and Manga109 datasets. Meanwhile, we found that

Table 3. Performance of our proposed method compared with the state of the art method.

Method	Scale	Set5		Set14		B100		Urban100		Manga109	
		PSNR	SSIM	PSNR	SSIM	PSNR	SSIM	PSNR	SSIM	PSNR	SSIM
Bicubic	×2	33.66	0.9299	30.24	0.8688	29.56	0.8431	26.88	0.8403	30.80	0.9339
SRCNN	×2	36.66	0.9542	32.45	0.9067	31.36	0.8879	29.50	0.8946	35.60	0.9663
FSRCNN	×2	37.05	0.9560	32.66	0.9090	31.53	0.8920	29.88	0.9020	36.67	0.9710
VDSR	×2	37.53	0.9590	33.05	0.9130	31.90	0.8960	30.77	0.9140	37.22	0.9750
LapSRN	×2	37.52	0.9591	33.08	0.9130	31.08	0.8950	30.41	0.9101	37.27	0.9740
MemNet	×2	37.78	0.9597	33.28	0.9142	32.08	0.8978	31.31	0.9195	37.72	0.9740
EDSR	×2	38.07	0.9606	33.65	0.9167	32.20	0.9004	31.88	0.9214	38.22	0.9763
SRMDNF	×2	37.79	0.9601	33.32	0.9159	32.05	0.8985	31.33	0.9204	38.07	0.9761
D DBPN	×2	38.09	0.9600	33.85	0.9190	32.27	0.9006	32.55	0.9324	38.89	0.9775
RDN	×2	38.24	0.9614	34.01	0.9212	32.34	0.9017	32.89	0.9353	39.18	0.9780
RCAN	×2	38.25	0.9608	34.08	0.9213	32.38	0.9020	33.29	0.9363	39.22	0.9778
EDSR+(ours)	×2	38.17	0.9610	33.74	0.9182	32.25	0.9000	31.96	0.9248	38.57	0.9764
RCAN+(ours)	×2	**38.31**	**0.9612**	**34.20**	**0.9222**	**32.39**	**0.9022**	**33.30**	**0.9369**	**39.27**	**0.9781**
Bicubic	×3	30.39	0.8682	27.55	0.7742	27.21	0.7385	24.46	0.7349	26.95	0.8556
SRCNN	×3	32.75	0.9090	29.30	0.8215	28.41	0.7863	26.24	0.7989	30.48	0.9117
FSRCNN	×3	33.18	0.9140	29.37	0.8240	28.53	0.7910	26.43	0.8080	31.10	0.9210
VDSR	×3	33.67	0.9210	29.78	0.8320	28.83	0.7990	27.14	0.8290	32.01	0.9340
LapSRN	×3	33.82	0.9227	29.87	0.8320	28.82	0.7980	27.07	0.8280	32.21	0.9350
MemNet	×3	34.09	0.9248	30.00	0.8350	28.96	0.8001	27.56	0.8376	32.51	0.9369
EDSR	×3	34.26	0.9252	30.08	0.8418	29.20	0.8106	28.48	0.8638	33.20	0.9415
SRMDNF	×3	34.12	0.9254	30.04	0.8382	28.97	0.8025	27.57	0.8398	33.00	0.9403
RDN	×3	34.71	0.9296	30.57	0.8468	29.26	0.8093	28.80	0.8653	34.13	0.9484
RCAN	×3	34.79	0.9255	30.39	0.8374	29.40	0.8158	29.24	0.8804	33.99	0.9469
EDSR+(ours)	×3	34.41	0.9253	30.18	0.8443	29.27	0.8141	28.49	0.8672	33.76	0.9416
RCAN+(ours)	×3	**34.85**	**0.9259**	**30.50**	**0.8392**	**29.41**	**0.8186**	**29.25**	**0.8838**	**34.15**	**0.9484**
Bicubic	×4	28.42	0.8104	26.00	0.7027	25.96	0.6675	23.14	0.6577	24.89	0.7866
SRCNN	×4	30.48	0.8628	27.50	0.7513	26.90	0.7101	24.52	0.7221	27.58	0.8555
FSRCNN	×4	30.72	0.8660	27.61	0.7550	26.98	0.7150	24.62	0.7280	27.90	0.8610
VDSR	×4	31.35	0.8830	28.02	0.7680	27.29	0.7260	25.18	0.7540	28.83	0.8870
LapSRN	×4	31.54	0.8850	28.19	0.7720	27.32	0.7270	25.21	0.7560	29.09	0.8900
MemNet	×4	31.74	0.8893	28.26	0.7723	27.40	0.7281	25.50	0.7630	29.42	0.8942
EDSR	×4	32.04	0.8926	28.43	0.7755	27.70	0.7351	26.45	0.7908	30.25	0.9028
SRMDNF	×4	31.96	0.8925	28.35	0.7787	27.49	0.7337	25.68	0.7731	30.09	0.9024
D-DBPN	×4	32.47	0.8980	28.82	0.7860	27.72	0.7400	26.38	0.7946	30.91	0.9137
RDN	×4	32.47	0.8990	28.81	0.7871	27.72	0.7419	26.61	0.8028	31.00	0.9151
RCAN	×4	32.78	0.8988	28.68	0.7832	27.85	0.7418	27.07	0.8121	31.02	0.9157
EDSR+(ours)	×4	32.21	0.8934	28.51	0.7768	27.75	0.7369	26.52	0.7937	30.53	0.9057
RCAN+(ours)	×4	**32.90**	**0.8992**	**28.79**	**0.7849**	**27.86**	**0.7423**	**27.13**	**0.8139**	**31.10**	**0.9163**

$\lambda = 5$ is the best on Urban100 datasets. We obtained these values by performing parameter experiments in the ranges 0 to 100, $\lambda = 0$ means we use only EDSR as a baseline without a regularizer. Along with increasing lambda, the stronger the influence of the relationship between pixels in the learning process. Compared to baseline, our approach achieved an improvement of PSNR and SSIM scores over all datasets.

Comparation with State-of-the-Art. To know the advantages of our proposed regularizer, we combine our regularizer with EDSR and RCAN and then compare the result with state-of-the-art CNN-based SR methods. Table 3 summarizes all of the quantitative data for the various scaling factors. The best results are highlighted in bold. Compared to competing approaches, joining RCAN and our methods achieve the best results across all datasets and scaling factors. The qualitative result of our approach is shown in Fig. 2. To know the differences in detail, we zoomed in on a portion of the image area. Figure 2 showing our approach demonstrated more realistic visual results compared to other methods on Urban100, B100, and Manga109 datasets. It means the proposed regularizer succeeds in reconstructing the details of the HR image generate from the LR image compared over baseline methods.

6 Conclusion

This paper shows that the differences in pixels neighbor relationships can establish the network more robust on super-resolution tasks. Our method employs the adjacent pixels differences as a regularizer with existing CNN-based SISR methods to ensure that the differences between pixels in the estimated image are close to different pixels in the ground truth images. The experimental findings on five datasets demonstrate that our method outperforms the baseline CNN without regularization. Our proposed method generates more detailed visual results and improved PSNR/SSIM scores compared to other state-of-the-art methods. Future work will implement the differences in pixel neighbor relationships as a regularizer on different computer vision tasks.

Acknowledgments. This work was partly supported by JSPS KAKENHI Grant Number 21K12049.

References

1. Zhou, F., Yang, W., Liao, Q.: Interpolation-based image super-resolution using multisurface fitting. IEEE Trans. Image Process. **21**(7), 3312–3318 (2012)
2. Anbarjafari, G., Demirel, H.: Image super resolution based on interpolation of wavelet domain high frequency subbands and the spatial domain input image. ETRI J. **32**(3), 390–394 (2010)
3. Zhang, K., Gao, X., Tao, D., Li, X.: Single image superresolution with non-local means and steering kernel regression. TIP **21**(11), 4544–4556 (2012)

4. Dong, C., Loy, C.C., He, K., Tang, X.: Learning a deep convolutional network for image super-resolution. In: Fleet, D., Pajdla, T., Schiele, B., Tuytelaars, T. (eds.) ECCV 2014. LNCS, vol. 8692, pp. 184–199. Springer, Cham (2014). https://doi.org/10.1007/978-3-319-10593-2_13

5. Hakim, L., Zheng, H., Kurita, T.: Improvement for Single Image Super-resolution and Image Segmentation by Graph Laplacian Regularizer based on Differences of Neighboring Pixels. Manuscript submitted for publication (2021)

6. Lim, B., Son, S., Kim, H., Nah, S., Mu Lee, K.: Enhanced deep residual networks for single image super-resolution. In: Proceedings of the IEEE Conference on Computer Vision and Pattern Recognition Workshops, pp. 136–144 (2017)

7. Zhou, W., Wang, Y., Chu, J., Yang, J., Bai, X., Xu, Y.: Affinity space adaptation for semantic segmentation across domains. IEEE Trans. Image Process. **30**, 2549–2561 (2020)

8. Matsui, Y., et al.: Sketch-based manga retrieval using Manga109 dataset. Multimedia Tools Appl. **76**(20), 21811–21838 (2016). https://doi.org/10.1007/s11042-016-4020-z

9. Huang, J.B., Singh, A., Ahuja, N.: Single image super-resolution from transformed self-exemplars. In: Proceedings of the IEEE Conference on Computer Vision and Pattern Recognition, pp. 5197–5206 (2015)

10. Martin, D., Fowlkes, C., Tal, D., Malik, J.: A database of human segmented natural images and its application to evaluating segmentation algorithms and measuring ecological statistics. In: Proceedings Eighth IEEE International Conference on Computer Vision. ICCV 2001, vol. 2, pp. 416–423. IEEE, July 2001

11. Zhang, Z., Wang, X., Jung, C.: DCSR: dilated convolutions for single image super-resolution. IEEE Trans. Image Process. **28**(4), 1625–1635 (2018)

12. Zhang, Y., Li, K., Li, K., Wang, L., Zhong, B., Fu, Y.: Image super-resolution using very deep residual channel attention networks. In: Proceedings of the European Conference on Computer Vision (ECCV), pp. 286–301 (2018)

13. Agustsson, E., Timofte, R.: Ntire 2017 challenge on single image super-resolution: dataset and study. In: Proceedings of the IEEE Conference on Computer Vision and Pattern Recognition Workshops, pp. 126–135 (2017)

14. Bevilacqua, M., Roumy, A., Guillemot, C., Alberi-Morel, M.L.: Low-complexity single-image super-resolution based on nonnegative neighbor embedding (2012)

15. Zeyde, R., Elad, M., Protter, M., et al.: On single image scale-up using sparse-representations. In: Boissonnat, J.-D. (ed.) Curves and Surfaces 2010. LNCS, vol. 6920, pp. 711–730. Springer, Heidelberg (2012). https://doi.org/10.1007/978-3-642-27413-8_47

Learning Attacker's Bounded Rationality Model in Security Games

Adam Żychowski⬤ and Jacek Mańdziuk$^{(\boxtimes)}$⬤

Faculty of Mathematics and Information Science, Warsaw University of Technology,
Koszykowa 75, 00-662 Warsaw, Poland
{a.zychowski,j.mandziuk}@mini.pw.edu.pl

Abstract. The paper proposes a novel neuroevolutionary method
(NESG) for calculating leader's payoff in Stackelberg Security Games.
The heart of NESG is strategy evaluation neural network (SENN). SENN
is able to effectively evaluate leader's strategies against an opponent who
may potentially not behave in a perfectly rational way due to certain
cognitive biases or limitations. SENN is trained on historical data and
does not require any direct prior knowledge regarding the follower's target preferences, payoff distribution or bounded rationality model. NESG
was tested on a set of 90 benchmark games inspired by real-world cybersecurity scenario known as deep packet inspections. Experimental results
show an advantage of applying NESG over the existing state-of-the-art
methods when playing against not perfectly rational opponents. The
method provides high quality solutions with superior computation time
scalability. Due to generic and knowledge-free construction of NESG, the
method may be applied to various real-life security scenarios.

Keywords: Bounded rationality · Security games · Cybersecurity

1 Introduction

One of the salient application domains of Computational Intelligence is security
management (surveillance, guards patrolling, anti-poaching operations, cybersecurity, etc.) in which Security Games (SG) [15] are one of the most popular models of attacker-defender scenarios. SGs follow the idea of Stackelberg games [10]
and involve two players: the *leader* and the *follower*. SG consists of two phases.
First, the leader commits to a certain strategy. Next, the follower, based on the
leader's decision, chooses their strategy. This sequence of decisions establishes
information asymmetry (favouring the follower) and mimics real-world scenarios
in which the attacker (follower) can observe the defender's (leader's) strategy
(e.g. patrol schedules) and plan their attack accordingly.

The goal of SG is to find a pair of players' strategies that form the so-
called Stackelberg Equilibrium (StE) [10]. For the leader, *mixed strategies* are
considered which are probability distributions of various deterministic strategies
(a.k.a *pure strategies*). Consequently, the follower despite knowing the mixed

© Springer Nature Switzerland AG 2021
T. Mantoro et al. (Eds.): ICONIP 2021, CCIS 1516, pp. 530–539, 2021.
https://doi.org/10.1007/978-3-030-92307-5_62

leader's strategy does not know which realization of this strategy (which pure strategy) would actually be played by the leader - he/she is only aware of the probability distribution of them. SG solutions have been deployed in various practical domains. Please consult a survey paper [15] for details.

Bounded Rationality. One of the fundamental assumptions in SGs is that the attacker chooses an optimal response strategy. However, in real-life cases, which involve humans (e.g. terrorists, thieves, poachers, hackers), this assumption may not hold, due to limitation of the players' senses, his/her cognitive biases [5], partial knowledge about the problem, or imprecisely defined goals [13]. This deviation from optimal response selection is known as *bounded rationality* (BR) behaviour [14]. Hence in practice, playing the StE strategy by the leader may be non-optimal. **Considering human BR biases by the leader when selecting their strategy can potentially improve their expected results.** There are several BR models proposed in the literature, e.g.: Anchoring Theory (AT) [16], Prospect Theory (PT) [6], Quantal Response (QR) [11], or Framing Effect (FE) [5]. While each of them is justified by psychological experiments and emphasizes different aspect of human behaviour, there is no consensus on which of them reflects the human BR bias most closely.

The vast majority of BR papers in SG domain incorporates a particular BR model into single-step SG by modifying the fully-rational behavioral model which assumes possessing prior knowledge about which BR model best fits a given adversarial behaviour. **In this paper, we approach the problem in a novel way by learning the actual behavioral model of the attacker based on observing his/her past performance.**

Motivation and Contribution. In real-world SG scenarios the role of the follower is performed by a human whose action selection process may be non-optimal due to certain BR biases. At the same time, the defenders (playing the role of the leader) usually have little or no knowledge about their adversaries (e.g. terrorists, poachers, smugglers, hackers) and have no clue about which BR model would best reflect their behaviour. Furthermore, in SG literature it is usually assumed that exact opponent's payoffs are known to both players, which is infeasible in real-world scenarios.

Due to the above reasons there is a strong need to apply generic SG solutions, that abstract from precise assumptions about the follower's BR model and his/her preferences, and are capable of inferring them from available data (e.g. analysis of the follower's past behaviour). From the leader's perspective, such a system should be able to **learn** the relations between utilities and follower's decisions. Such a system is proposed in the paper.

The main contribution of the paper can be summarized as follows: **(1)** To our knowledge, this paper presents the first successful neural network application to the leader's strategy estimation in SGs (SENN). **(2)** SENN is further extended to an end-to-end neuroevolutionary system (NESG) for finding high quality leader's strategies in SGs. **(3)** NESG does not use any assumption about the follower's BR model or knowledge about his/her payoff distribution. **(4)** Experimental results in the cybersecurity domain outperform those of state-of-the-art methods in terms of both computation time and quality of results.

2 Problem Definition

We consider m step games with two players: the leader (L) and the follower (F). There is a predefined set of n targets $T = \{t_1, t_2, \ldots, t_n\}$. Each target $t \in T$ is associated with 4 payoffs: U_t^j, $j \in \{L+, L-, F+, F-\}$ representing the leader's reward (U_t^{L+}), their penalty (U_t^{L-}), the follower's reward (U_t^{F+}) and their penalty (U_t^{F-}).

The leader possesses k units. Leader's *pure strategy* σ^L is units allocation over targets in m time steps. Units allocation can be different in different time steps - they can be reallocated between the steps. Formally $\sigma^L = \{a_{us}\}$, where $a_{us} \in T$ is a target allocated for unit u in time step s, $u \in \{1, \ldots, k\}, s \in \{1, \ldots, m\}$.

Let's denote a set of all pure strategies of the leader by Σ^L. Then, a *mixed strategy* π^L is a probability distribution over Σ^L: $\pi^L = \{(\sigma_i^L, p_i)\}$, where p_i is the probability of playing strategy $\sigma_i^L \in \Sigma^L$.

Target t coverage in step s (denoted by $c_s(t)$) for mixed strategy π^L is the probability of the event that at least one unit is allocated to t in step s playing strategy π^L: $c_s(t) = \sum_{\sigma_i^L \in \pi^L} p_i : \underset{a_{us} \in \sigma_i^L}{\exists} a_{us} = t$.

Follower's strategy σ^F is choosing one of the targets from T. Let's denote this target by x. The players' payoffs are computed as follows:

- If in any time step leader's unit is allocated to x, the follower is *caught* and players receive U_x^{L+} and U_x^{F-}, respectively.
- If in no time step leader's unit is allocated to x, the follower's attack is successful and players receive U_x^{L-} and U_x^{F+}, respectively.

Therefore, expected leader's and follower's payoffs $(U^L$ and $U^F)$ equal
$$U^L = P_x U_x^{L-} + (1 - P_x)U_x^{L+} \quad \text{and} \quad U^F = P_x U_x^{F+} + (1 - P_x)U_x^{F-},$$
where $P_x = \prod_{s=1,\ldots,m} 1 - c_s(x)$ is probability of successful attack on target x.

The game model employs Stackelberg Game principles which means that first the leader commits to their strategy π^L and then the follower, being aware of π^L, determines his/her strategy.

3 Cybersecurity Scenario

Let us consider cybersecurity domain as a use case scenario (cf. Fig. 1). One of the methods of preventing attacks on computer networks is *deep packet inspections* [4] which relies on periodical selection of a subset of packets in a computer network for analysis. This problem can be formulated as SG in which the detection system plays the role of the leader and the attacker (e.g. hacker, intruder system) plays the role of the follower. Network computers (hosts) are targets. The detection system chooses a subset of hosts and inspects packets sent to them for some fixed time. Then, the next subset of hosts is checked (next time step in SG definition). If malicious packets go through undetected the attack is successful and the intruder controls the infected host. Packet inspections cause unwanted latency and the defender has to decide where to inspect network traffic in order to maximize the probability of a successful malicious packet detection. While the defender has no knowledge about potential invaders, historical data or simulations can be used to approximate their preferences or capabilities.

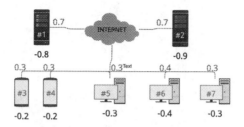

Fig. 1. Sample network with 7 hosts. The numbers below hosts are leader's penalties in case of successful attack, the numbers above connections are probabilities of protecting given nodes in sample defender's strategy. See the extended version of this paper [19] for further details.

4   State-of-the-Art Approaches

There are two main types of SGs solution methods: exact and approximate. Exact approaches base on Mixed-Integer Linear Programming (MILP) [12], where SG is formulated as an optimization problem with linear constraints and the strategies are computed using specially optimized software engine. The main disadvantage of MILP methods is exponential time and memory scalability. The most efficient methods from this group are BC2015 [1] and C2016 [2] which transform the game to equivalent form with substantially smaller MILP representation, what enables effective solving of bigger games.

Approximate methods offer a viable alternative and calculate close-to-optimal results much faster and for larger games, which are beyond capabilities of exact methods. CBK2018 [3] is an example of a time-optimized MILP algorithm. O2UCT [8] utilizes UCB method [9] – a variant of Monte Carlo Tree Search – and combines sampling the follower's strategy space with calculating the respective best leader's strategy. EASG [17,18] maintains a population of candidate leader's strategies and applies specifically designed mutation and crossover operators. Besides the above general methods, there are also heuristic approaches devoted to particular SG formulations. e.g. [7].

5   Proposed Solution

In this paper we improve EASG framework by replacing the most time-consuming part of the algorithm, solutions evaluation procedure, with a strategy evaluation neural network (SENN), to assess strategies from the current population. Figure 2 presents an overview of the proposed system. The multilayer perceptron SENN is first trained on historical data and then used to evaluate individuals in each generation.

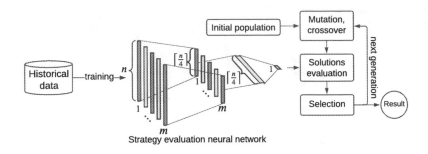

Fig. 2. System overview with SENN component.

Strategy Evaluation Neural Network. SENN is used to evaluate a given leader's strategy. Instead of exact calculation of the leader's payoff by finding an optimal follower's response (which is time-consuming and requires knowledge about the follower's preferences, or bounded rationality model) SENN approximates this value, taking the leader's mixed strategy as input. The strategy is encoded in the following way. Each input node is feed with target coverage $c_s(t)$, i.e. a probability that at least one leader's unit is allocated to the target t in time step s. Hence, the number of input neurons equals nm. Neurons' outputs from the first layer are grouped by time step number - for each time step $\lceil \frac{n}{4} \rceil$ neurons are created - and then signals from all time steps are combined in the second hidden layer with $\lceil \frac{n}{4} \rceil$ neurons. A single output neuron returns the result.

NESG. SENN described in the previous section is incorporated into the EASG algorithm [18] leading to NESG (NeuroEvolutionary for Security Games) method. NESG follows the general EASG protocol for solution finding. Each individual represents a possible solution, i.e. a mixed strategy of the leader. Initially, a population of individuals is generated, each of them representing a randomly selected pure strategy, i.e. leader's units are assigned to randomly chosen targets. Then, the following procedure is repeated until the limit for generation number is reached. A subset of individuals is randomly selected and divided into pairs. To each pair a crossover operator is applied that combines two strategies into one mixed strategy with halved probabilities. Then, a mutation is applied to a randomly selected subset of the population. The mutation changes one pure strategy (in a mixed strategy represented by a mutated individual) by randomly changing the allocation of an arbitrary subset of leader's units. Afterward, the population is evaluated, i.e. for each individual the expected leader's payoff (assuming the strategy encoded by this individual is played) is calculated. Finally, the selection procedure picks individuals based on their evaluation and promotes them to the next generation. Please consult [18] for the details.

EASG evaluation procedure iteratively checks all follower's strategies and selects the one with the highest follower's payoff [18]. The approach becomes infeasible for large games due to high number of strategies that need to be evaluated. In this paper the EASG evaluation procedure is replaced by SENN estimation of the expected leader's payoff.

6 Experimental Setup

Benchmark Games. We tested NESG method on 90 randomly generated game instances which reflect real-world cybersecurity scenario described in Sect. 3. Five games were created for each number of time steps $m \in \{1, 2, 4\}$ and targets $n = 2^i$, $i \in \{2, \ldots, 7\}$. Payoffs U_t^{L-} and U_t^{F-} were real numbers drawn independently from interval $(-1; 0)$, while U_t^{L+} and U_t^{F+} were sampled from $(0; 1)$. The number of leader's units was drawn from interval $[\lfloor \frac{n}{4m} \rfloor; \lceil \frac{3n}{4m} \rceil]$ (independently for each game instance), i.e. at least $\frac{1}{4}$ and at most $\frac{3}{4}$ of the targets could be effectively protected.

We followed EASG parameterization recommended in [18] with no additional parameter tuning: population size = 100, number of generations = 1000, mutation rate = 0.5, crossover rate = 0.8, selection in the form of a binary tournament with selection pressure = 0.9 and elite size = 2.

Please recall that SENN is a multilayer perceptron with mn, $m \lceil \frac{n}{4} \rceil$, $\lceil \frac{n}{4} \rceil$ and 1 units in subsequent layers. SENN was trained with backpropagation with minibatch and Adam optimization. Hyperbolic tangent activation was used in the output node. Due to space limits we skip a discussion on SENN training data generation and SENN efficacy. A respective discussion is presented in [19].

We considered three most popular BR models: Anchoring theory (AT) [16], Quantal response (QR) [11], and Prospect theory (PT) [6]. These BR models are further discussed in [19]. The following bias parameter values were assumed in BR models - AT: $\delta = 0.5$, QR: $\lambda = 0.8$, PT: $\gamma = 0.64, \theta = 2.25, \alpha = \beta = 0.88$.

7 Experimental Results

Payoffs Comparison. In order to evaluate the practical efficacy of NESG, the method was compared with the following 5 methods: **C2016** - generates optimal (exact) solutions without considering follower's BR, **EASG** - original EASG formulation (generates approximate solution with no BR model employed), **EASG_BR** where BR $\in$ {AT, QR, PT} - EASG method incorporating the respective BR model, i.e. the follower's response in the evaluation procedure is calculated assuming a given BR model.

For C2016 and EASG, first the leader's strategy was generated (without considering the follower's BR bias) and then the associated payoff was calculated under the assumption that the follower would actually not respond optimally but would follow a particular BR model. Please note that it is not possible to incorporate BR models directly into MILP solutions (e.g. C2016) since BR models

Table 1. Average payoffs comparison for 1, 2 and 4 time steps games.

1 step	Anchoring theory				Quantal response				Prospect theory			
Targets	C2016	EASG	EASG_AT	NESG	C2016	EASG	EASG_QR	NESG	C2016	EASG	EASG_PT	NESG
4	−0.470	−0.472	−0.468	−0.469	−0.406	−0.408	−0.404	−0.405	−0.419	−0.420	−0.417	−0.418
8	−0.456	−0.457	−0.440	−0.440	−0.418	−0.422	−0.386	−0.388	−0.422	−0.423	−0.407	−0.407
16	−0.387	−0.391	−0.371	−0.371	−0.377	−0.378	−0.336	−0.338	−0.329	−0.335	−0.315	−0.318
32	−0.411	−0.412	−0.393	−0.397	−0.428	−0.429	−0.390	−0.394	−0.397	−0.404	−0.367	−0.370
64	−0.579	−0.586	−0.567	−0.568	−0.582	−0.584	−0.536	−0.537	−0.560	−0.564	−0.483	−0.486
128	−0.397	−0.405	−0.369	−0.372	−0.578	−0.578	−0.526	−0.529	−0.462	−0.463	−0.345	−0.347
2 steps	**Anchoring theory**				**Quantal response**				**Prospect theory**			
Targets	C2016	EASG	EASG_AT	NESG	C2016	EASG	EASG_QR	NESG	C2016	EASG	EASG_PT	NESG
4	−0.566	−0.566	−0.563	−0.564	−0.540	−0.541	−0.534	−0.535	−0.548	−0.549	−0.547	−0.547
8	−0.568	−0.572	−0.553	−0.555	−0.526	−0.528	−0.510	−0.512	−0.556	−0.556	−0.517	−0.518
16	−0.327	−0.331	−0.314	−0.317	−0.326	−0.331	−0.301	−0.302	−0.326	−0.331	−0.291	−0.294
32	−0.499	−0.500	−0.475	−0.479	−0.487	−0.487	−0.435	−0.435	−0.501	−0.502	−0.454	−0.457
64	−0.457	−0.463	−0.427	−0.427	−0.421	−0.424	−0.403	−0.408	−0.466	−0.471	−0.407	−0.410
128	−0.607	−0.614	−0.563	−0.567	−0.601	−0.604	−0.540	−0.544	−0.593	−0.595	−0.566	−0.571
4 steps	**Anchoring theory**				**Quantal response**				**Prospect theory**			
Targets	C2016	EASG	EASG_AT	NESG	C2016	EASG	EASG_QR	NESG	C2016	EASG	EASG_PT	NESG
4	−0.479	−0.481	−0.478	−0.479	−0.487	−0.489	−0.485	−0.486	−0.511	−0.512	−0.508	−0.510
8	−0.497	−0.500	−0.466	−0.467	−0.509	−0.513	−0.455	−0.456	−0.517	−0.519	−0.496	−0.499
16	−0.545	−0.547	−0.525	−0.525	−0.531	−0.534	−0.502	−0.503	−0.570	−0.574	−0.535	−0.538
32	−0.478	−0.484	−0.460	−0.464	−0.500	−0.505	−0.468	−0.470	−0.525	−0.531	−0.492	−0.496
64	−0.563	−0.568	−0.547	−0.551	−0.587	−0.593	−0.553	−0.555	−0.600	−0.600	−0.561	−0.563
128	−0.531	−0.536	−0.493	−0.497	−0.545	−0.549	−0.503	−0.505	−0.553	−0.555	−0.512	−0.512

introduce *nonlinear* modifications to payoffs or probabilities whose implementation in MILP would require using non-linear constraints.

Table 1 presents the average leader's payoffs for games with 1, 2 and 4 time steps. In all cases, NESG yielded better results than methods not considering (any) BR model (C2016 and EASG). The NESG advantage grows with the increasing number of targets. It can be concluded that when playing against not perfectly rational follower, it is better to use approximate NESG algorithm than playing the optimal strategy (generated by C2016) though without BR consideration.

For a given BR $\in$ {AT, QR, PT}, the difference between EASG_BR and NESG lays only in the population evaluation procedure. EASG_BR computes the *exact* follower's response which precisely employs a given BR model and then, based on that response, calculates the leader's payoff. NESG uses a neural network to *estimate* the BR model of the follower. Since EASG_BR *knows* the exact BR model and directly implements the BR function it should be treated as an *oracle* model, whereas NESG is considered as its *realistic* approximation relying on the past data in the network training process. Hence, NESG results presented in the tables are slightly worse than those of EASG_BR. Please note, however, that in a real-world scenario the leader, when calculating their strategy, *is not aware* of the opponent's BR model. What is more the actual BR model of the follower may differ from any of the 3 models considered in our experiments.

In such a case, using a particular EASG_BR implementation would become inefficient contrary to model-free NESG learning approach.

Time Scalability. Figure 3 shows time scalability of the proposed algorithm vs. other methods described in the previous section. Two variants of NESG computation time are presented: with and without SENN training time, although typically the training procedure is performed once in a separate preprocessing stage and its time requirements do not affect the network inference process.

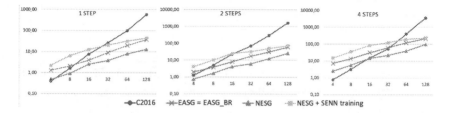

Fig. 3. Comparison of NESG time scalability vs state-of-the-art methods.

It can be concluded from the figure that C2016 (MILP based) scales visibly worse than evolutionary methods. Its computation time groves exponentially with respect to the number of targets. EASG, EASG_BR and NESG scale much better in time and similar to each other. All 3 curves are roughly parallel and linear with respect to the number of targets. Computation times of EASG and EASG_BR are the same because the difference between the methods lays only in the evaluation procedure. In EASG_BR instead of getting the follower's payoff directly, the BR model is imposed whose calculation is of meaningless cost. NESG computation time advantage over EASG and EASG_BR stems from different ways of leader's strategy calculation. EASG/EASG_BR need to (1) iterate over all follower's strategies in order to find the best one and (2) compute the respective leader's payoff, which is time-consuming especially when the follower's strategy space is large. NESG gets an approximated leader's payoff directly from the neural network output.

8   Conclusions

This paper proposes a novel method for calculating leader's payoff in Stackelberg Security Games that uses strategy evaluation neural network (SENN). SENN is trained on historical data (results of previous games) with no explicit knowledge about the follower's payoff distribution or BR model, which well reflects real-world SG settings. In this paper, SENN is incorporated into evolutionary algorithm method (EASG), leading to an end-to-end SG solution (NESG), however, due to its generic nature, SENN can also be combined with other SG solution methods. Experimental results on 90 benchmark games proven NESG efficacy and good time scalability. The method provides high quality result with low computation cost.

The main advantages of NESG are learning capabilities and knowledge-free nature. Most of existing algorithms require full information about the attacker's payoff distribution, which is often impossible in practical security management scenarios where the knowledge about the attackers is limited. Furthermore, current methods typically assume perfect rationality of the attacker, which may not be the case in practice due to certain cognitive biases, wrong perception or imperfect information about the problem. NESG does not assume perfect rationality of the attacker and infers his/her *cognitive decision model/BR model* through the learning process.

Acknowledgments. The project was funded by POB Research Centre Cybersecurity and Data Science of Warsaw University of Technology within the Excellence Initiative Program - Research University (ID-UB).

References

1. Bošanský, B., Čermak, J.: Sequence-form algorithm for computing Stackelberg equilibria in extensive-form games. In: AAAI 2015, pp. 805–811 (2015)
2. Cermak, J., Bosansky, B., Durkota, K., Lisy, V., Kiekintveld, C.: Using correlated strategies for computing Stackelberg equilibria in extensive-form games. In: AAAI 2016, pp. 439–445 (2016)
3. Černý, J., Boỳanskỳ, B., Kiekintveld, C.: Incremental strategy generation for Stackelberg equilibria in extensive-form games. In: Proceedings of the 2018 ACM Conference on Economics and Computation, pp. 151–168. ACM (2018)
4. El-Maghraby, R.T., Abd Elazim, N.M., Bahaa-Eldin, A.M.: A survey on deep packet inspection. In: ICCES 2017, pp. 188–197 (2017)
5. Kahneman, D.: Thinking, Fast and Slow. Macmillan (2011)
6. Kahneman, D., Tversky, A.: Prospect theory: an analysis of decision under risk. In: Handbook of the Fundamentals of Financial Decision Making: Part I, pp. 99–127. World Scientific (2013)
7. Karwowski, J., Mańdziuk, J., Żychowski, A., Grajek, F., An, B.: A memetic approach for sequential security games on a plane with moving targets. In: AAAI 2019, pp. 970–977 (2019)
8. Karwowski, J., Mańdziuk, J.: Double-oracle sampling method for Stackelberg equilibrium approximation in general-sum extensive-form games. In: AAAI 2020, pp. 2054–2061 (2020)
9. Kocsis, L., Szepesvári, C.: Bandit based Monte-Carlo planning. In: Fürnkranz, J., Scheffer, T., Spiliopoulou, M. (eds.) ECML 2006. LNCS (LNAI), vol. 4212, pp. 282–293. Springer, Heidelberg (2006). https://doi.org/10.1007/11871842_29
10. Leitmann, G.: On generalized Stackelberg strategies. J. Optim. Theory Appl. **26**(4), 637–643 (1978)
11. McKelvey, R.D., Palfrey, T.R.: Quantal response equilibria for normal form games. Games Econ. Behav. **10**(1), 6–38 (1995)
12. Paruchuri, P., Pearce, J.P., Marecki, J., Tambe, M., Ordonez, F., Kraus, S.: Playing games for security: an efficient exact algorithm for solving Bayesian Stackelberg games. In: AAMAS 2008, pp. 895–902 (2008)

13. Rubinstein, A.: Modeling Bounded Rationality. MIT Press (1998)
14. Simon, H.A.: Models of Man: Social and Rational. Wiley, New York (1957)
15. Sinha, A., Fang, F., An, B., Kiekintveld, C., Tambe, M.: Stackelberg security games: looking beyond a decade of success. In: IJCAI 2018, pp. 5494–5501 (2018)
16. Tversky, A., Kahneman, D.: Judgment under uncertainty: heuristics and biases. Science 185(4157), 1124–1131 (1974)
17. Żychowski, A., Mańdziuk, J.: A generic metaheuristic approach to sequential security games. In: AAMAS 2020, pp. 2089–2091 (2020)
18. Żychowski, A., Mańdziuk, J.: Evolution of strategies in sequential security games. In: AAMAS 2021, pp. 1434–1442 (2021)
19. Żychowski, A., Mańdziuk, J.: Learning attacker's bounded rationality model in security games. arXiv:2109.13036 (2021)

Learning Attentive Cooperation in Multi-agent Reinforcement Learning with Graph Convolutional Network

Yuqi Zhu[1], Yuntao Liu[1,2], Xinhai Xu[1(✉)], and Yuan Li[1]

[1] Academy of Military Science, Beijing, China
{xuxinhai,yuan.li}@nudt.edu.cn
[2] National University of Defense Technology, Changsha, Hunan, China

Abstract. Cooperative multi-agent reinforcement learning (MARL) is a key tool for addressing many real-world problems and is becoming a growing concern due to communication constraints during execution and partial observation. In prior works, the popular paradigm of centralized training with decentralized execution (CTDE) is used to mitigate this problem. However, the intensity of the cooperative relationship is not paid too much attention. In this paper, we propose an Attentive Cooperative MARL framework based on the Neighborhood Graph Convolutional Network (AttCoop-Q) to help agents communicate with each other and generate cooperative features for attentive cooperative policy learning. AttCoop-Q consists of the neighborhood graph convolutional network (NGCN) module and the attentive cooperation policy learning module. NGCN encodes the current situation, constructs a neighboring agent graph and uses the architecture of Neighborhood Graph Convolutional Network (GCN) to extracts cooperative features. The attentive cooperation policy learning module generates weight vectors using cooperative features to generate adapted Q-values which are further used to learn the total Q value. Experimental results on challenging multi-agent Star-Craft benchmark tasks show that our proposed method greatly boosts the performance compared with other popular MARL approaches.

Keywords: Multi-agent reinforcement learning · Graph Convolutional Network · Multi-agent cooperation

1 Introduction

The cooperative multi-agent reinforcement learning (MARL) problem has received broad attention in recent years and has achieved great success in many real-world tasks. The goal of MARL problems is to make agents in the system learn coordinated policies to achieve higher rewards from the environment [3]. One intuitive method to tackle this problem is regarding the multi-agent

---

Y. Zhu and Y. Liu—Equal contribution.

© Springer Nature Switzerland AG 2021
T. Mantoro et al. (Eds.): ICONIP 2021, CCIS 1516, pp. 540–548, 2021.
https://doi.org/10.1007/978-3-030-92307-5_63

system as a whole environment and applying the single-agent learning method. However, this method encounters two challenges of scalability and partial observability. The joint state-action space grows exponentially as the number of agents increases. The partial observability and communication constraints of the environment require each agent to make individual decisions based on local action-observation histories [2].

To mitigate this issue, a MARL training paradigm of *centralized training with decentralized execution* (CTDE) has been developed rapidly. In CTDE, the policy of each agent is trained based on global information from the environment in a centralized way and executed only based on the agent's local histories in a decentralized way. However, CTDE mechanisms are lack of cooperation modeling which is only contained in the centralized training procedure.

The graph approach is an option for learning the cooperation information in MARL tasks which proposes graphs for communication among agents and embedding graph models into the training process [1,4]. The nodes in graph models represent agents, while communication and cooperation between agents are contained in the edges. Wang, W. [10] proposes an approach that constructs a global graph that connects all agents with edges. This approach can capture all possible cooperation information and helps to learn higher-level cooperation. However, the training efficiency of this approach is low and noises contained in the cooperation information may cause training collapse.

In this work, we propose a novel multi-agent attentive cooperation approach based on the neighborhood graph convolutional networks (GCN) to effectively capture the useful cooperation information among agents and combine our approach with the CTDE framework to improve the training efficiency. Our approach, Attentive Cooperative Neighborhood Graph Convolutional Network (AttCoop-Q), combines the architecture of GCN with QMIX [6] to generate attentive cooperative policies for agents to solve the cooperative MARL problem. First, our approach constructs an agent graph modeling the cooperative information between neighboring agents and utilizes the GCN model to extract cooperative features. Then, we design the attentive cooperative policy learning mechanism. It consists of a weight encoder, an attentive cooperative Q-values generator and a mixing network. The weight encoder takes the cooperative features as inputs and outputs the weight vector for the attentive cooperative Q-values generator to generate adapted Q-values. The mixing network finally mixes up these Q-values for attentive cooperative policy learning. Empirical results on challenging MARL benchmark SMAC show that our proposed method greatly boosts the performance compared with other popular MARL approaches.

2 Background

2.1 Dec-POMDP

A fully cooperative multi-agent sequential decision-making task can be described as a decentralised partially observable Markov decision process (Dec-POMDP). A Dec-POMDP is defined by a tuple $\mathcal{G} = \langle \mathcal{N}, \mathcal{S}, \mathcal{A}, \mathcal{P}, \Omega, \mathcal{O}, r, \gamma \rangle$, where $\mathcal{N} =$

$1, 2, \ldots, n$ is a finite set of agents and $s \in \mathcal{S}$ is a finite set of global states. At each time step, every agent $i \in \mathcal{N}$ chooses an action $a_i \in \mathcal{A} = \langle \mathcal{A}^{(1)}, \ldots, \mathcal{A}^{|\mathcal{A}|} \rangle$ on a global state s, which forms a joint action $\mathbf{a} = [a_i]_{i=1}^n \in \mathbf{A} = \mathcal{A}^n$. It results in a joint reward $r(s, a)$ and a transition to the next global state $s' \sim \mathcal{P}(\cdot|s, \mathbf{a})$. $\gamma \in [0, 1)$ is a discount factor. We consider a partially observable setting, where each agent i receives an individual partial observation $o_i \in \Omega$ according to the observation probability function $O(o_i|s, a_i)$. Each agent i has an observation-action history $\tau_i \in \mathcal{T} = (\Omega \times \mathcal{A})^*$ and constructs its individual policy $\pi_i(a|\tau_i)$ to jointly maximize team performance.

2.2   Value-Based Deep Multi-agent Reinforcement Learning

Value-based Deep MARL approaches have been developed in a quick manner. Algorithms such as VDN [9], QMIX [6], QTRAN [8] based on the CTDE mechanisms have achieved great performance on many challenging MARL tasks. VDN computes Q-value Q_i based only on individual observations and actions and then adds them to the total Q-value Q_{tot} for centralized training: $Q_{tot}^{VDN}(\boldsymbol{\tau}, \boldsymbol{a}) = \sum_{i=1}^n Q_i(\tau_i, a_i)$. Strict assumption between the Q_{tot} and Q_i and abscent of global state information are both limitations of VDN. QMIX is proposed to alleviate the limitations of VDN by employing a mixing network which estimates Q_{tot} as a complex non-linear combination of $Q_i(\tau_i, a_i)$. QMIX also enforces a monotonicity constraint: $\frac{\partial Q_{tot}}{\partial Q_i} \geq 0$, which allows computationally tractable maximization of the joint action-value in off-policy learning. Compared with VDN and QMIX, QTRAN guarantees optimal decentralization inheriting the additive assumption and improves the representation of agents' observations. Unfortunately, such multi-agent algorithms ignore cooperative information modeling, which plays a vital role in cooperative MARL tasks.

2.3   Graph Convolutional Network

Graph Convolutional Network (GCN) introduces convolutions on graphs. Each GCN layer applies message passing to compute a node representation, where each node aggregates feature vectors of neighboring nodes. Formally, a GCN model consists of K-layers and the k-th layer is implemented as Eq. 1

$$X^{(k)} = ReLU(AX^{(k-1)}W^{(k)}) \tag{1}$$

where A is the adjacency matrix of the graph. $X^{(k)} \in \mathbb{R}^{N \times d_k}$ is the hidden feature matrix at layer k. $X^{(0)} \in \mathbb{R}^{N \times d}$ is the input observation vector. The parameter matrix of layer k is represented as $W^{(k)} \in \mathbb{R}^{d_k \times d_k}$. In the GCN model, features are often fed into an activation function before they are forwarded to the next layer. In this paper, the cooperation feature is modeled by the GCN. The graph is undirected which is represented by $G = (V, E)$. V is the vertex set and each vertex $v_i \in V$ represents an agent entry in the environment. Each edge e_{ij} in the edge set E connects two agents $\{a_i, a_j\}$, which reflects the cooperation relation between agent a_i and agent a_j. For the GCN model, each agent can communicate with others by passing their local observations, which improves the performance of MARL methods.

3   Methods

In this section, we propose an attentive cooperative MARL framework (AttCoop-Q). Figure 1 shows the whole framework. We first introduce the overall architecture, then describe two crucial components, namely the neighborhood graph convolutional (NGCN) and the attentive cooperation policy learning mechanism.

3.1   Overall Architecture

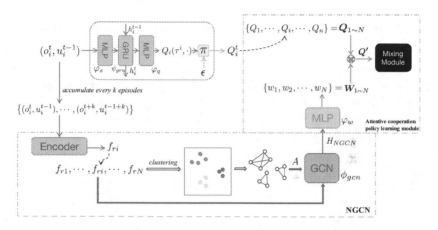

Fig. 1. Overall architecture of AttCoop-Q. AttCoop-Q consists of the NGCN module and the attentive cooperation policy learning module.

Our framework consists of the local utility agent network, the NGCN and the attentive cooperation policy learning module. The local utility agent network includes a local observation encoder and a local action generator. The local state encoder is a Multilayer Perception φ_s (MLP). The local observation o_i^t and latest selected action u_i^{t-1} of agent i is encoded to a local feature $f_i^t = \varphi_s(o_i^t, u_i^{t-1})$ by φ_s. The local action generator contains a Gated Recurrent Unit ψ_{gru} (GRU) and a Q-value network φ_q. The GRU takes the agent's local feature f_i^t as input, and outputs the hidden feature $h_i^t = \psi_{gru}(f_i^t, h_i^{t-1})$. Then h_i^t is passed through the Q-value network to generate the local Q-value $Q_i^t = \varphi_q(h_i^t)$ of agent i. Next, we introduce the adaptive mixing network which mixes up local Q-values of all agents to generate the joint Q-value for total loss objective computation. The adaptive mixing network in our framework is an attentive cooperation-based mixing network, which involves a NGCN ϕ_{gcn}, an attentive cooperation policy learning module φ_w and a mixing network. Inputs of the NGCN model ϕ_{gcn} contain the neighborhood graph adjacent matrix A, and the local agent observation o_i^t. Then NGCN outputs feature g_i^t with attentive cooperative information. The attentive cooperation policy learning module φ_w uses attentive cooperative features g_i^t extracted from the NGCN model to generate weight w_i^t for the attentive cooperation-based mixing network. The mixing network's architecture is similar to that in QMIX. The introduction of the attentive cooperative policy learning mechanism allows learning of more sophisticated total Q functions as well as facilitates agents for better action selection. Exchanging information between agents can provide more accurate weights for the individual Q-values mixing up. Moreover, our framework is under the CTDE paradigm. During training, the action is chosen with the ϵ-greedy policy [11] and then mixed up in the mixing network. During execution, there is no mixing network and each agent selects its action based on its local observation.

3.2   Determining Neighborhood Graph Convolutional Network

In this subsection, we elaborate in more detail the design of our NGCN which enables cooperation and communication between agents.

How to construct the agent graph based on the neighbor relationships is the key to the NGCN model, because only neighboring agents cooperate and communicate effectively with each other, if nodes that represent non-neighboring agents are connected, it may disturb the training. To this end, we design a neighborhood agent graph that revealing neighboring agents and connecting them. The neighboring agents are classified by cluster methods during training. Every k episode, we collect agents' local observation and actions which are accumulated and encoded into each agent's latent representation f_r. With f_r, we use cluster methods to divide agents into n_c clusters where n_c is a hyper-parameter. Agents that are clustered into the same cluster are considered neighbors. The K-means clustering method is used in this paper, but it can be extended to other clustering methods depending on the scenario. Once we get the clustering result, the neighborhood agent graph is defined by connecting agents in the same cluster. Formally, we can compute the adjacency matrix A of NGCN by:

$$A_{ij} = \begin{cases} 1, C[i] = C[j]. \\ 0, C[i] \neq C[j]. \end{cases} \tag{2}$$

where C is the clustering result vector of agents and $C[i]$ represents the cluster that agent i is belonging to. Inspired by the idea of self-looping [5], we add the identity matrix I to keep the feature of the agent itself.

After obtaining the adjacency matrix, we describe the architecture of the NGCN model ϕ_{gcn}^j. Here, $j \in \{1, \cdots, m\}$ represents the number of layers in the NGCN model, m is the total number of layers contained in the NGCN. Each NGCN layer ϕ_{gcn}^j takes the output feature H_{NGCN}^{j-1} of the previous layer as input and outputs a vector H_{NGCN}^j. Formally, each layer computes:

$$H_{NGCN}^j = \sigma(C_i(A + I)H_{NGCN}^{j-1}W) \tag{3}$$

where $C_i(\cdot)$ indicates the clip function for the adjacency matrix, W is the parameters of each layer of the NGCN model and σ is the non-linear activation function

ReLU. Particularly, the first NGCN layer's input H_{NGCN}^0 is the connection of latent representations of all agents:

$$H_{NGCN}^0 = \{f_{r1}, f_{r2}, \cdots, f_{rN}\} \tag{4}$$

The NGCN model uses feature exchange to achieve communication between neighboring agents and outputs high quality features H_{NGCN} for subsequent training of attentive cooperation policy learning.

3.3   Learning Attentive Cooperative Policies

Once the cooperative features extracted from the NGCN model are obtained, they can be combined with a weight encoder φ_w to generate proper weights for attentive cooperative policy learning. Formally, weights are computed by:

$$\boldsymbol{W}_{1\sim N} = \varphi_w(H_{NGCN}) \tag{5}$$

where $\boldsymbol{W}_{1\sim N} = \{w_1, w_2, \cdots, w_N\}$ is the weight vector and its i-th element w_i represents the Q-value weight of the i-th agent. The weight vector $\boldsymbol{W}_{1\sim N}$ is further combined with the individual Q-values for attentive cooperative policy learning. We get attentive cooperative Q-values $\boldsymbol{Q}' = \{Q_1', Q_2', \cdots, Q_n'\}$ of all agents by multiplying the weight vector $\boldsymbol{W}_{1\sim N}$ and Q-values $\boldsymbol{Q}_{1\sim N} = \{Q_1, Q_2, \cdots, Q_n\}$, which is shown in Eq. 6:

$$\boldsymbol{Q}' = \boldsymbol{W}_{1\sim N} \circ \boldsymbol{Q}_{1\sim N} \tag{6}$$

where $\boldsymbol{Q}_{1\sim N}$ is the individual Q-values of all agents and $\circ$ represents the element-wise multiplication between two vectors. Notice that the weight w_i of the agent i is encoded based on the cooperative information. Therefore, Q_i' represents the new Q-value after adjusting Q_i based on the cooperation between neighbors with which the agent can effectively achieve better performance.

Attentive cooperative Q-value $\boldsymbol{Q}'$ are fed into a mixing network ϕ_{mix} to compute the global action-value Q_{total} which is used to compute the TD loss. The architecture of the mixing network is similar to that proposed by QMIX which contains a hyper-net to generate networks' parameters ϕ_{mix} conditioned on the global state. Formally, the learning objective of our method is defined as:

$$\mathcal{L}(\Theta) = \mathcal{L}_{TD}(\Theta) = [r + \gamma max_{\mathbf{a}'} Q_{total}(s', \mathbf{a}'; \Theta^-) - Q_{total}(s, \mathbf{a}; \Theta)]^2 \tag{7}$$

where $\Theta = (\varphi_{obs}, \varphi_w, \phi_{gcn}, \psi_{gru}, \varphi_q, \phi_{mix})$, α_e is the scaling factor of feature estimator and Θ^- are parameters of the target network.

4   Experiments

4.1   Settings

We choose the StarCraft Multi-Agent Challenge (SMAC) environment [7] to evaluate the performance of AttCoop-Q. In SMAC, each agent controls an army

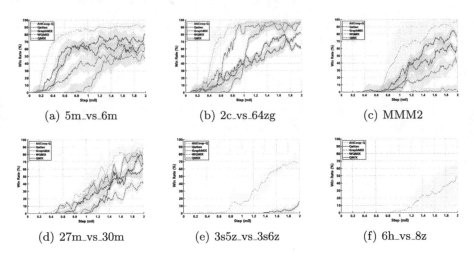

(a) 5m_vs_6m   (b) 2c_vs_64zg   (c) MMM2

(d) 27m_vs_30m   (e) 3s5z_vs_3s6z   (f) 6h_vs_8z

Fig. 2. Different visual confusion label trees based on different parameters τ.

unit and selects actions from follows: move 4 directions, attack one enemy, stop
and the null action. The observation contains information of allies and enemies
on sight such as positions, unit types and health. Enemy units are controlled
by handcrafted AI provided by SMAC. We keep the settings of training and
evaluation episodes and other hyper-parameters the same as QMIX in the SMAC
environment. To reduce the effect of randomness, all experiments are conducted
based on 5 different random seeds. We use two hard scenarios and four super
hard scenarios to evaluate the performance of AttCoop-Q.

4.2   Main Results

In this subsection, we compare AttCoop-Q with several state-of-the-art MARL
methods based on attentive policies and QMIX. Figure 2 shows the median test
win rate of different algorithms across all aforementioned scenarios. We first validate our method on two hard scenarios. *5m_vs_6m* is an asymmetric scenario
in which 5 allied agents fight against 6 enemy units and it requires precise controlling to win. The performance of AttCoop-Q in Fig. 2(a) is higher than those
of other methods and the convergence speed is also the fastest. The reason is
that attentive cooperative policies learned by AttCoop-Q are suitable for precise
controlling in this scenario. In *2c_vs_64zg*, although the number of enemies is
much larger than allies, AttCoop-Q manages to learn the winning strategy to
kite enemies and outperforms other methods in Fig. 2(b).

Next, we test the performance of AttCoop-Q on super hard scenarios. *MMM2*
is a complex scenario because different units in this scenario have different functions, i.e., attacking or healing. AttCoop-Q learns an effective strategy that
heading units to absorb enemies' firing and then retreating and healing them for
a sustained fight. Figure 2(c) shows that AttCoop-Q achieves great performance
improvement compared with Qatten, WQMIX and GraphMIX. *27m_vs_30m* is

a more difficult asymmetric scenario compared to *5m_vs_6m* because the gap between the units number of allies and enemies becomes bigger. The result in Fig. 2(d) shows that the performance of AttCoop-Q is the highest. Compared with other methods, ally units are deployed to the accurate position in the AttCoop-Q method and cooperate with each other to win the game based on the learned attentive cooperative policies. *3s5z_vs_3s6z* includes 8 allied agents and 9 enemy units which makes it an asymmetric and heterogeneous scenario. Only AttCoop-Q and Qatten can learn effective strategies, while the way Q values are weighted in Qatten limits its performance and AttCoop-Q achieves better performance. Results in Fig. 2(f) demonstrate that *6h_vs_8z* is a very challenging scenario because all existing methods cannot learn any strategy to win. In contrast, AttCoop-Q achieves a nearly 50% win rate after 2 million training steps.

4.3 Ablation Study

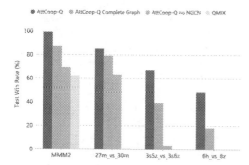

Fig. 3. Ablation study.

In this subsection, we perform ablation experiments to investigate the influence of two components in our method: (A) the neighboring agents revealing mechanism in the NGCN model; (B) the NGCN model itself. To test the effect of component A, we replace the neighborhood agent graph with a complete graph which allows all agents to communicate with each other as the input of the GCN model. To test the effect of component B, we remove the NGCN model and feed observations and actions into the weight encoder to generate the weight vector directly. Results on four super hard scenarios from the benchmark are shown in Fig. 3. It is interesting to see that AttCoop-Q with neighboring agent graph outperforms that with the complete graph in all scenarios. The reason is that the complete agent graph contains too much cooperative information which may make harm to the attentive cooperative policy learning. We can find that the performance of AttCoop-Q without the NGCN model is close to the baseline method, which is lower than other methods on all scenarios. This demonstrates that the NGCN model plays a crucial role in attentive cooperative policy learning. In summary, with the NGCN model and the neighboring agents revealing mechanism, AttCoop-Q achieves a new state-of-the-art on the SMAC benchmark.

5   Conclusion

This paper proposes AttCoop-Q, a novel multi-agent RL framework that combines attentive cooperative information between agents with the Q-learning method to facilitates large-scale agent cooperation. The neighboring agents revealing mechanism can construct a neighboring agent graph and the NGCN model uses it to abstract attentive cooperative feature. Attentive cooperative features generated by the NGCN model are then used by the attentive cooperative policy learning mechanism. Experimental results show that AttCoop-Q obtains the best performance on decentralized unit micromanagement tasks in StarCraft II over other state-of-the-art MARL methods.

Acknowledgments. This work is supported in part by the National Natural Science Foundation of China under Grant 61902425.

References

1. Agarwal, A., Kumar, S., Sycara, K.: Learning transferable cooperative behavior in multi-agent teams. arXiv preprint arXiv:1906.01202 (2019)
2. Foerster, J., Farquhar, G., Afouras, T., Nardelli, N., Whiteson, S.: Counterfactual multi-agent policy gradients. In: Proceedings of the AAAI Conference on Artificial Intelligence, vol. 32 (2018)
3. Gupta, J.K., Egorov, M., Kochenderfer, M.: Cooperative multi-agent control using deep reinforcement learning. In: Sukthankar, G., Rodriguez-Aguilar, J.A. (eds.) AAMAS 2017. LNCS (LNAI), vol. 10642, pp. 66–83. Springer, Cham (2017). https://doi.org/10.1007/978-3-319-71682-4_5
4. Jiang, J., Dun, C., Huang, T., Lu, Z.: Graph convolutional reinforcement learning. In: International Conference on Learning Representations (2019)
5. Kipf, T.N., Welling, M.: Semi-supervised classification with graph convolutional networks. arXiv preprint arXiv:1609.02907 (2016)
6. Rashid, T., Samvelyan, M., De Witt, C.S., Farquhar, G., Foerster, J., Whiteson, S.: QMIX: monotonic value function factorisation for deep multi-agent reinforcement learning. arXiv preprint arXiv:1803.11485 (2018)
7. Samvelyan, M., et al.: The StarCraft multi-agent challenge. arXiv preprint arXiv:1902.04043 (2019)
8. Son, K., Kim, D., Kang, W.J., Hostallero, D.E., Yi, Y.: QTRAN: learning to factorize with transformation for cooperative multi-agent reinforcement learning. arXiv preprint arXiv:1905.05408 (2019)
9. Sunehag, P., et al.: Value-decomposition networks for cooperative multi-agent learning based on team reward. In: AAMAS, pp. 2085–2087 (2018)
10. Wang, W., et al.: From few to more: large-scale dynamic multiagent curriculum learning. In: AAAI, pp. 7293–7300 (2020)
11. Wunder, M., Littman, M.L., Babes, M.: Classes of multiagent Q-learning dynamics with epsilon-greedy exploration. In: ICML (2010)

Average Mean Functions Based EM Algorithm for Mixtures of Gaussian Processes

Tao Li[1], Xiao Luo[2], and Jinwen Ma[1(✉)]

[1] Department of Information and Computational Sciences, School of Mathematical Sciences and LMAM, Peking University, Beijing 100871, China
jwma@math.pku.edu.cn
[2] Department of Probability and Statistics, School of Mathematical Sciences and LMAM, Peking University, Beijing 100871, China

Abstract. The mixture of Gaussian process functional regressions (mix-GPFR) utilizes a linear combination of certain B-spline functions to fit the mean functions of Gaussian processes. Although mix-GPFR makes the mean functions active in the mixture of Gaussian processes, there are two limitations: (1). This linear combination approximation introduces many parameters and thus a heavy cost of computation is paid for learning these mean functions. (2). It is implicitly assumed that the mean functions of different components share the same degree of smoothness because there is a parameter controlling the smoothness globally. In order to get rid of these limitations, we propose a new kind of EM algorithm for mixtures of Gaussian processes with average mean functions from time-aligned batch trajectory or temporal data. In this way, the mean functions are iteratively updated according to the distributed trajectory data of the estimated Gaussian processes at each iteration of the EM algorithm and the effectiveness of this estimation is also theoretically analyzed. It is demonstrated by the experimental results on both synthetic and real-world datasets that the proposed method performs well.

1 Introduction

Gaussian process (GP) [1] is the dominant non-parametric Bayesian model and has been applied in many research fields [2–4]. In machine learning, a Gaussian process is determined by its mean function and covariance function. Usually, Gaussian processes are used for nonlinear regression or classification, but they can also be used to process batch datasets [5].

The mean function of Gaussian processes is important for processing batch datasets. Usually, the mean function is assumed to be zero. However, the zero mean function fails to model batch datasets with a shared global trend. Shi proposed the Gaussian Process Functional Regression (GPFR) model [5,6], which provides a feasible way to learn nonlinear mean functions. In GPFR, the mean function is assumed to be a linear combination of B-spline basis functions. However, GPFR fails to model heterogeneous/multi-modal data accurately [7]. In real

© Springer Nature Switzerland AG 2021
T. Mantoro et al. (Eds.): ICONIP 2021, CCIS 1516, pp. 549–557, 2021.
https://doi.org/10.1007/978-3-030-92307-5_64

applications, the curves may be generated from different signal sources, thus a single GPFR is not flexible enough to model all the curves. Shi *et al.* suggested introducing mixture structures on GPFRs (mix-GPFR) [7] to further enhance the model flexibility. In mix-GPFR, curves generated by a common signal source are regarded as a GPFR component. This model is naturally suitable for the curve clustering task. Recently, Wu and Ma [8] further extended mix-GPFR to a Two-layer Mixture of Gaussian Process Functional Regressions (TMGPFR) for modeling general stochastic processes from different sources.

The mix-GPFR model suffers from several problems. First, the number of B-spline basis functions D is difficult to set in practice. A large D leads to overfitting, while a small D results in under-fitting, and the performances are usually frustrating in both circumstances. One can run the mix-GPFR with different D and choose the most proper D by trial and error, but this procedure is tedious and time-consuming. Second, different GPFR components in mix-GPFR share a common D. Therefore, when different components have different smoothness, it would be even more difficult to set a proper D, as illustrated in Sect. 3.1 and Fig. 1. Third, learning coefficients of B-spline basis functions in the M-step of the EM algorithm is both time-consuming and difficult since there are many local maximums and the optimization procedure often gets trapped in a local maximum as indicated [9].

To tackle these problems, we propose the mixture of Gaussian Processes with Average Mean Functions (mix-GPAVM). In the proposed method, the mean functions are estimated non-parametrically by averaging observations. Compared with mix-GPFR, this method is specifically designed for time-aligned datasets and it can adjust the smoothness in each component adaptively. Using average mean functions in the EM algorithm for learning mixtures of Gaussian processes is also more efficient than mix-GPFR. Experimental results on both synthetic and real-world datasets demonstrate the effectiveness of the proposed method.

2   Preliminaries

Suppose we are given a batch dataset $\mathcal{D} = \{\mathcal{D}_i\}_{i=1}^N$, each $\mathcal{D}_i = \{(x_{im}, y_{im})\}_{m=1}^{N_i}$ can be regarded as a sampled signal from an underlying function $y_i(x)$. Gaussian Process Functional Regression (GPFR) assumes that these functions $\{y_i(x)\}_{i=1}^N$ share a global mean function $\mu(x)$ and a structured noise $\tau(x)$. More specifically, Shi *et al.* [6] assume that $\mu(x)$ is a linear combination of D B-spline basis functions $\{\phi_j(x)\}_{j=1}^D$, and the noise term $\tau(x)$ is a Gaussian process:

$$y_i(x) = \mu(x) + \tau(x) \quad , \quad \mu(x) = \sum_{j=1}^D b_j \phi_j(x) \quad , \quad \tau(x) \sim \mathcal{GP}(0, c(x, x'; \boldsymbol{\theta})).$$

Here, $c(x, x'; \boldsymbol{\theta})$ is the covariance function of the Gaussian process and $\boldsymbol{\theta}$ is the parameter. More compactly, we can write this model as $y_i(x) \sim \mathcal{GPFR}(x; \mathbf{b}, \boldsymbol{\theta})$. Both $\boldsymbol{\theta} = [b_1, \cdots, b_D]^{\mathsf{T}}$ and the coefficients of B-spline basis functions $\mathbf{b}$ need to be learned. We apply the maximum likelihood method to learn these parameters. Let $\mathbf{y}_i = [y_{i1}, \cdots, y_{iN_i}]^\mathsf{T}$, $\mathbf{x}_i = [x_{i1}, \cdots, x_{iN_i}]^\mathsf{T}$, $\boldsymbol{\Phi}_i = [\phi_j(x_{im})]_{N_i \times D}$, $\mathbf{C}_i = [c(x_{im}, c_{in}; \boldsymbol{\theta})]_{N_i \times N_i}$, then $\mathbf{y}_i | \mathbf{x}_i \sim \mathcal{N}(\boldsymbol{\Phi}_i \mathbf{b}, \mathbf{C}_i)$. Therefore, the parameter learning boils down to maximizing

$$\sum_{i=1}^{N} \log \mathcal{N}(\mathbf{y}_i; \boldsymbol{\Phi}_i \mathbf{b}, \mathbf{C}_i) = \sum_{i=1}^{N} -\frac{1}{2} \log |\mathbf{C}_i| - \frac{1}{2}(\mathbf{y}_i - \boldsymbol{\Phi}_i \mathbf{b})^\mathsf{T} \mathbf{C}_i^{-1}(\mathbf{y}_i - \boldsymbol{\Phi}_i \mathbf{b}) + \mathrm{const}.$$

Suppose we are given an $(N+1)$-th curve $\mathcal{D}_{N+1} = \{(x_{N+1,m}, y_{N+1,m})\}_{m=1}^{N_*}$ and need to predict the response at input x_*. According to the conditional property of multivariate Gaussian distribution [1,10], we predict the response as

$$\hat{y} = \boldsymbol{\phi}_*^\mathsf{T} \mathbf{b} + \mathbf{c}_* \mathbf{C}_{N+1}^{-1}(\mathbf{y}_{N+1} - \boldsymbol{\Phi}_{N+1} \mathbf{b}),$$
$$\boldsymbol{\phi}_* = [\phi_1(x_*), \cdots, \phi_D(x_*)]^\mathsf{T}, \mathbf{c}_* = [c(x_*, x_{N+1,1}; \boldsymbol{\theta}), \cdots, c(x_*, x_{N+1,N_*}; \boldsymbol{\theta})]^\mathsf{T}$$

Furthermore, to enhance the model flexibility and deal with the heterogeneity problem, a mixture of GPFR (mix-GFPR) was proposed [7]. In mix-GPFR, we assume that there are K GPFR components $\mathcal{GPFR}(x; \mathbf{b}_k, \boldsymbol{\theta}_k)$ and each $\mathcal{D}_i$ is generated from one of them given the latent indicator variable z_i,

$$y_i(x) | z_i = k \sim \mathcal{GPFR}(x; \mathbf{b}_k, \boldsymbol{\theta}_k), i = 1, 2, \cdots, N. \tag{1}$$

The mix-GPFR model is usually learned by the EM algorithm [11]. The final prediction is given by a weighted sum of the results predicted by each component separately.

3 Proposed Approach

3.1 Time Aligned Batch Dataset and Average Mean Functions

In general, these signals may have different lengths, i.e., $N_i \neq N_j$ for $i \neq j$. GPFR enables us to deal with such variable-length signals effectively. When these signals are sampled at the same time-steps, the question can be simplified. We first define the time-aligned batch dataset.

Definition 1 (Time-aligned batch dataset). *A batch dataset* $\mathcal{D} = \{\mathcal{D}_i\}_{i=1}^{N}$ *is said to be time-aligned if* $N_i = N_j = T$ *for all* $i, j = 1, \cdots, N$ *and* $x_{it} = x_{jt} = x_t$ *for all* $i, j = 1, \cdots, N$, $t = 1 \cdots T$. *In this case, each* $\mathcal{D}_i$ *consists of* $\{(x_t, y_{it})\}_{t=1}^{T}$.

We write $\mathbf{x} = [x_1, \cdots, x_T]^\mathsf{T}, \boldsymbol{\mu} = [\mu(x_1), \cdots, \mu(x_T)]^\mathsf{T}, \mathbf{C} = [c(x_m, x_n; \boldsymbol{\theta})]_{T \times T}$, then we have $\mathbf{y}_i | \mathbf{x} \sim \mathcal{N}(\boldsymbol{\mu}, \mathbf{C})$. Since the dataset is time-aligned, different signals share the same mean $\boldsymbol{\mu}$ and covariance matrix $\mathbf{C}$. Unlike GPFR, we do not assume $\mu(x)$ is a linear combination of B-spline basis functions here. Instead, we can estimate the global mean function $\mu(x)$ non-parametrically. A naive idea is to estimate $\mu(x_t)$ by $\hat{\mu}(x_t) = \frac{1}{N} \sum_{i=1}^{N} y_{it}$ and then interpolate on general x. Theoretically, $y_{it} = y_i(x_t) = \mu(x_t) + \tau(x_t)$. Once we fix t and integrate out

y_{is} for $s \neq t$, we immediately obtain $y_{it} = \mu(x_t) + \varepsilon_i$ where ε_i is a Gaussian noise subject to $\mathcal{N}(0, \sigma^2)$ and $\sigma^2 = c(x, x; \boldsymbol{\theta})$. Therefore, $\hat{\mu}(x_t) \sim \mathcal{N}(\mu(x_t), \frac{\sigma^2}{N})$. This derivation justifies that $\hat{\mu}(x_t)$ is a good estimator of $\mu(x_t)$ as long as N is large enough. For general $x \neq x_t, \forall t = 1, \cdots, T$, we can linear interpolate on x to obtain the corresponding $\hat{\mu}(x)$ based on $\{(x_t, \hat{\mu}(x_t))\}_{t=1}^{T}$. We refer to this method as Gaussian Processes with Average Mean Functions (GPAVM).

We can extend GPAVM to mixture models and we refer to it as mix-GPAVM. In mix-GPFR, the number of B-spline basis functions D is the same among all components. Although there are K components, the smoothness of their mean functions $\{\mu_k(x)\}_{k=1}^{K}$ is globally controlled by the hyper-parameter D. Therefore, mix-GPFR cannot effectively model batch datasets with different smoothness in each component, while mix-GPAVM can adjust the smoothness within each component separately and adaptively. See Fig. 1 for a concrete example.

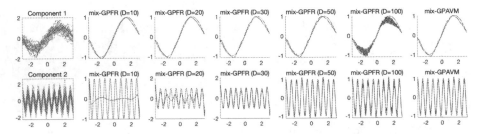

Fig. 1. The fitted results of mix-GPFR with different D on a batch dataset with two components.

3.2 Average Mean Functions Based EM Algorithm

Let $\mathbf{C}_k = [c(x_m, x_n; \boldsymbol{\theta}_k)]_{T \times T}$, $\hat{\boldsymbol{\mu}}_k$ be the mean function estimated in component k, and $\boldsymbol{\Theta} = \{\boldsymbol{\theta}_k\}_{k=1}^{K} \cup \{\pi_k\}_{k=1}^{K} \cup \{\hat{\boldsymbol{\mu}}_k\}_{k=1}^{K}$ be the parameters to be estimated. The complete data log-likelihood is given by

$$\log p(\mathcal{D}, \{z_i\}_{i=1}^{N} | \boldsymbol{\Theta}) = \sum_{i=1}^{N} \sum_{k=1}^{K} \mathbb{I}(z_i = k)(\log \pi_k + \log \mathcal{N}(\mathbf{y}_i | \hat{\boldsymbol{\mu}}_k, \mathbf{C}_k)).$$

Note that $\mathbf{C}_k$ depends on $\boldsymbol{\theta}_k$. In the E-step, we need to calculate the posterior distribution of z_i, which is $p(z_i = k | \mathcal{D}, \boldsymbol{\Theta}^{\text{old}}) \propto \pi_k \mathcal{N}(\mathbf{y}_i | \hat{\boldsymbol{\mu}}_k, \mathbf{C}_k)$. In the E-step, we update $\alpha_{ik} = p(z_i = k | \mathcal{D}, \{\boldsymbol{\theta}_k^{\text{old}}\}_{k=1}^{K})$, then the $\mathcal{Q}$-function is

$$\mathcal{Q}(\boldsymbol{\Theta} | \boldsymbol{\Theta}^{\text{old}}) = \mathbb{E}_{p(z_i = k | \mathcal{D}, \{\boldsymbol{\theta}_k^{\text{old}}\}_{k=1}^{K})}[\log p(\mathcal{D}, \{z_i\}_{i=1}^{N} | \{\boldsymbol{\theta}_k\}_{k=1}^{K})]$$

$$= \sum_{i=1}^{N} \sum_{k=1}^{K} \alpha_{ik}(\log \pi_k + \log \mathcal{N}(\mathbf{y}_i | \hat{\boldsymbol{\mu}}_k, \mathbf{C}_k)).$$

In the M-step, we need to maximize $\mathcal{Q}(\boldsymbol{\Theta} | \boldsymbol{\Theta}^{\text{old}})$ with respect to $\boldsymbol{\Theta}$. For π_k and $\hat{\boldsymbol{\mu}}_k$, we can update them explicitly via $\pi_k = \frac{1}{N} \sum_{i=1}^{N} \alpha_{ik}$, $\hat{\boldsymbol{\mu}}_k = \frac{1}{N} \sum_{i=1}^{N} \alpha_{ik} \mathbf{y}_i$.

Table 1. Mean functions and hyper-parameters of Gaussian processes of the synthetic datasets.

Mean function	Hyper-parameters of GPs		
	θ_1	θ_2	θ_3
x^2	0.500	2.000	0.150
$(-4(x+1.5)^2+9)\mathbb{I}(x<0)$ $+(4(x-1.5)^2-9)\mathbb{I}(x\geq 0)$	0.528	2.500	0.144
$8\sin(1.5x-1)$	0.556	3.333	0.139
$\sin(1.5x)+2x-5$	0.583	5.000	0.133
$-0.5x^2+\sin(4x)-2x$	0.611	10.000	0.128
$-x^2$	0.639	10.000	0.122
$(4(x+1.5)^2-9)\mathbb{I}(x<0)$ $+(-4(x-1.5)^2+9)\mathbb{I}(x\geq 0)$	0.667	5.000	0.117
$5\cos(3x+2)$	0.694	3.333	0.111
$\cos(1.5x)-2x+5$	0.722	2.500	0.106

For $\{\boldsymbol{\theta}_k\}_{k=1}^K$, we perform gradient ascent on $\mathcal{Q}(\boldsymbol{\Theta}|\boldsymbol{\Theta}^{\mathrm{old}})$. The main difference between mix-GPFR and mix-GPAVM in terms of parameter learning is that we do not need to perform gradient ascent on coefficients $\{\mathbf{b}_k\}_{k=1}^K$. Estimating $\{\hat{\boldsymbol{\mu}}_k\}_{k=1}^K$ by a weighted sum is easy and fast, while optimizing $\{\mathbf{b}_k\}_{k=1}^K$ and $\{\boldsymbol{\theta}_k\}_{k=1}^K$ simultaneously is difficult and time-consuming.

3.3   Prediction Strategy

Suppose an $(N+1)$-th curve $\mathcal{D}_{N+1} = \{x_t, y_{N+1,t}\}_{t=1}^{T_*}$ is given, where $T_* < T$ is the signal length. To estimate the response y_* of $(N+1)$-th signal at x_*, we first calculate the probability that $(N+1)$-the curve belongs to k-th component, which is given by

$$p(z_{N+1}=k|\mathcal{D},\mathcal{D}_{N+1};\boldsymbol{\Theta}) \propto \pi_k \mathcal{N}(\mathbf{y}_{N+1}; \hat{\boldsymbol{\mu}}_k(1:T_*), \mathbf{C}_k(1:T_*,1:T_*)).$$

Here, $(1:T_*)$ is the slicing syntax. In k-the component, the prediction is

$$\hat{y}_k = \hat{\mu}(x_*) + \mathbf{c}_* \mathbf{C}_k(1:T_*,1:T_*)^{-1}(\mathbf{y}_{N+1} - \hat{\boldsymbol{\mu}}_k(1:T_*)),$$

where $\mathbf{c}_* = [c(x,x_1;\boldsymbol{\theta}_k), \cdots, c(x,x_{T_*};\boldsymbol{\theta}_k)]^{\mathsf{T}}$. The final prediction is the weighted average of these predictions, *i.e.*, $\hat{y} = \sum_{k=1}^K p(z_{N+1}=k|\mathcal{D},\mathcal{D}_{N+1};\boldsymbol{\Theta})\hat{y}_k$.

4   Experimental Results

4.1   On Synthetic Datasets

Dataset Description. We use the mix-GPFR model with K components to generate the time-aligned synthetic datasets, with each component consists of 20 curves for training and 10 curves for testing. We have 100 observed samples in

Table 2. Average RMSEs, CARs and running times (in seconds) with standard deviations of the proposed and competing methods on synthetic datasets.

Method	D	$\mathcal{S}_3$			$\mathcal{S}_5$		
		RMSE	CAR	Time	RMSE	CAR	Time
GP	–	4.6923 ± 0.0000	–	0.39 ± 0.01	4.5716 ± 0.0000	–	0.56 ± 0.01
GPFR	10	4.6147 ± 0.0000	–	0.79 ± 0.01	4.4549 ± 0.0000	–	1.02 ± 0.02
	20	4.6074 ± 0.0000	–	0.77 ± 0.01	4.4560 ± 0.0000	–	1.03 ± 0.07
	30	4.6051 ± 0.0000	–	0.77 ± 0.01	4.4592 ± 0.0000	–	0.96 ± 0.01
	50	4.6150 ± 0.0000	–	0.78 ± 0.02	4.4697 ± 0.0000	–	1.10 ± 0.19
mix-GP	–	4.5834 ± 0.0055	–	3.31 ± 0.54	4.1826 ± 0.0206	–	15.35 ± 8.83
mix-GPAVM	–	0.4814 ± 0.0000	$100.00\% \pm 0.00\%$	2.00 ± 0.68	0.6845 ± 0.2736	$96.84\% \pm 8.79\%$	3.93 ± 0.73
mix-GPFR	10	0.4822 ± 0.0000	$100.00\% \pm 0.00\%$	2.45 ± 0.40	0.8484 ± 0.4201	$93.60\% \pm 10.84\%$	8.15 ± 5.46
	20	0.4882 ± 0.0000	$100.00\% \pm 0.00\%$	2.40 ± 0.30	0.9422 ± 0.4311	$91.17\% \pm 11.86\%$	9.47 ± 5.94
	30	0.5876 ± 0.0000	$100.00\% \pm 0.00\%$	2.43 ± 0.38	0.8003 ± 0.3298	$96.03\% \pm 8.86\%$	7.27 ± 5.87
	50	1.3762 ± 0.0000	$100.00\% \pm 0.00\%$	2.45 ± 0.37	1.1163 ± 0.1790	$96.17\% \pm 8.72\%$	6.95 ± 4.11
Method	D	$\mathcal{S}_7$			$\mathcal{S}_9$		
		RMSE	CAR	Time	RMSE	CAR	Time
GP	–	5.3324 ± 0.0000	–	0.78 ± 0.02	4.6994 ± 0.0000	–	1.02 ± 0.19
GPFR	10	5.2751 ± 0.0000	–	1.33 ± 0.21	4.6234 ± 0.0000	–	1.61 ± 0.24
	20	5.2786 ± 0.0000	–	1.31 ± 0.28	4.6231 ± 0.0000	–	1.62 ± 0.23
	30	5.2768 ± 0.0000	–	2.17 ± 0.94	4.6265 ± 0.0000	–	1.62 ± 0.22
	50	5.2786 ± 0.0000	–	1.28 ± 0.06	4.6266 ± 0.0000	–	1.63 ± 0.22
mix-GP	–	4.9123 ± 0.0138	–	22.47 ± 11.20	4.3753 ± 0.0087	–	27.04 ± 9.97
mix-GPAVM	–	0.7665 ± 0.3102	$97.23\% \pm 6.66\%$	6.59 ± 0.56	0.9209 ± 0.3142	$92.57\% \pm 7.36\%$	10.12 ± 1.70
mix-GPFR	10	0.8128 ± 0.3623	$96.97\% \pm 7.09\%$	14.04 ± 10.41	0.9657 ± 0.3337	$93.42\% \pm 6.56\%$	29.41 ± 16.96
	20	0.8955 ± 0.4237	$94.54\% \pm 8.83\%$	16.85 ± 12.37	0.9256 ± 0.3403	$94.27\% \pm 6.87\%$	26.91 ± 22.48
	30	1.1095 ± 0.3338	$93.29\% \pm 8.58\%$	17.14 ± 15.18	1.1776 ± 0.2280	$92.55\% \pm 7.72\%$	30.28 ± 22.98
	50	1.5697 ± 0.1396	$94.46\% \pm 7.81\%$	14.06 ± 9.13	1.2276 ± 0.2103	$92.09\% \pm 7.51\%$	33.78 ± 30.71

each curve, randomly positioned in the interval $[-3, 3]$. For a testing curve, the first half of the samples are known and the task is to predict the rest points. We vary the number of components K in $\{3, 5, 7, 9\}$, and these datasets are referred to as $\mathcal{S}_3, \mathcal{S}_5, \mathcal{S}_7, \mathcal{S}_9$, respectively. The mean functions and parameters of Gaussian processes used to generated these datasets are detailed in Table 1, and a dataset with K components involves the first K rows of Table 1.

Comparison Methods and Parameter Settings. We apply GP, GPFR and mix-GPFR methods on these synthetic datasets for comparison. For mix-GPFR and mix-GPAVM, the number of components K is set to be the ground-truth number of components. For GPFR and mix-GPFR, there is an extra parameter: the number of B-spline basis functions D. We vary D in $\{10, 20, 30, 50\}$. We run each method 10 times and report the averaged performance metrics.

Evaluation Metrics. We consider the performances of these methods from two aspects. On the one hand, we concern whether the algorithm can predict the evolving trend of testing curves, and we evaluate the prediction performances via Rooted Mean Square Errors (RMSEs). Suppose there are M testing curves in total, and for the i-th testing curve we need to estimate $y_{i,T/2+1}, y_{i,2}, \cdots, y_{i,T}$,

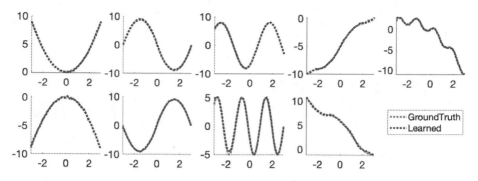

Fig. 2. Ground-truth mean functions (in red) and learned mean functions by mix-GPAVM (in blue). (Color figure online)

the RMSE is defined as RMSE $= \frac{2}{MT} \sum_{i=1}^{M} \sum_{t=T/2+1}^{T} (\hat{y}_{i,t} - y_{i,t})^2$. Here, $\{\hat{y}_{i,t}\}$ are predictions obtained by the algorithms. On the other hand, we concern whether the algorithm successfully partition the training time-series into meaningful groups and reveal the underlying cluster structure of the dataset. We use the Classification Accuracy Rate (CAR) to evaluate the performance of component identification, which is defined as CAR $= \max_{\xi \in \Pi_K} \frac{1}{N} \sum_{i=1}^{N} \mathbb{I}(z_i = \xi(\hat{z}_i))$. Here, $\{z_i\}_{i=1}^{N}$ are ground-truth labels as in Eq. 1 and $\{\hat{z}_i\}_{i=1}^{N}$ are cluster labels assigned by the algorithms. Π_K denotes the set of K-permutations, and the permutation ξ is employed to account for the label switching problem.

The results are reported in Table 2. We find that a single GP or a single GPFR is not flexible enough to model these datasets, since in each dataset the curves are generated by various signal sources. Besides, mix-GP fails to cluster synthetic datasets into meaningful groups since the global mean function is ignored. Usually, mix-GPAVM performs better than mix-GPFR in terms of RMSE and CAR, which demonstrates that mix-GPAVM is effective in curve prediction and clustering. Furthermore, mix-GPAVM is significantly faster than mix-GPFR, and it is even faster than mix-GP. The reason is introducing global mean functions in the model accelerates the convergence of the EM iteration, and the computational cost of estimating mean functions in mix-GPAVM is marginal. We also observe that the setting of D influences the results severely. On $\mathcal{S}_3$ and $\mathcal{S}_7$, mix-GPFR with $D = 10$ attains the best results, and increasing D has a negative effect on the results. However, on $\mathcal{S}_5$, the optimal D equals to 30, while $D = 20$ leads to the best performances on $\mathcal{S}_9$. Therefore, setting a proper D is very challenging in mix-GPFR, while mix-GPAVM can adjust the smoothness of mean functions adaptively.

We illustrate the mean functions estimated by mix-GPAVM on $\mathcal{S}_9$ in Fig. 2. We observe that mix-GPAVM successfully learns the mean functions without obvious over-fitting or under-fitting.

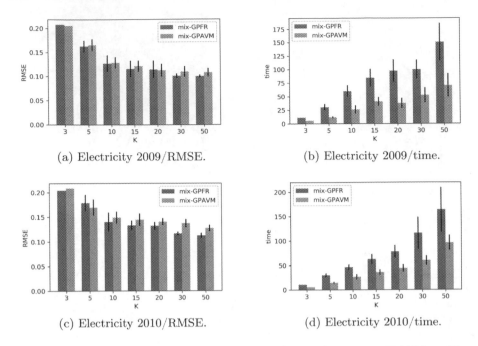

(a) Electricity 2009/RMSE.

(b) Electricity 2009/time.

(c) Electricity 2010/RMSE.

(d) Electricity 2010/time.

Fig. 3. RMSEs and running times of mix-GPFR ($D = 30$) and mix-GPAVM on Electricity 2009 and Electricity 2010.

4.2 On Real-World Datasets

We use the electricity load dataset issued by the Northwest China Grid Company in this experiment. The electricity dataset records electricity loads in 2009 and 2010 every 15 min. Therefore, daily electricity loads can be regarded as a time-series of length 96, and this dataset is naturally time-aligned since the record times keep the same everyday. We further split the dataset according to the year, and refer to them as Electricity 2009/2010, respectively. Within each sub-datasets, we randomly select 200 curves for training and the rest 165 curves for testing. Since the number of components K is unknown on real-world datasets, we vary K in $\{3, 5, 10, 15, 20, 30, 50\}$. The RMSEs and running times of mix-GPFR ($D = 30$) and mix-GPAVM are shown in Fig. 3. On these two real-world datasets, the performance of mix-GPFR ($D = 30$) is slightly better than mix-GPAVM, but mix-GPFR is 2× to 3× slower than mix-GPAVM. Therefore, mix-GPAVM is able to achieve comparable results as mix-GPFR with a significantly shorter running time.

5 Conclusion

In this paper, we utilize average mean functions in the EM algorithm and propose the mixtures of Gaussian processes with average mean functions for time-aligned batch data. In mix-GPAVM, the mean functions are estimated by sample average non-parametrically, and the effectiveness of this estimation is justified theoretically. Compared with mix-GPFR, mix-GPAVM can adaptively adjust the smoothness of mean functions. Furthermore, the proposed method is faster than mix-GPFR since estimating mean functions by sample average is computationally efficient. Experimental results validate the effectiveness and efficiency of the proposed method.

Acknowledgements. This work was supported by the National Key Research and Development Program of China under grant 2018AAA0100205.

References

1. Rasmussen, C.E.: Gaussian processes in machine learning. In: Bousquet, O., von Luxburg, U., Rätsch, G. (eds.) ML -2003. LNCS (LNAI), vol. 3176, pp. 63–71. Springer, Heidelberg (2004). https://doi.org/10.1007/978-3-540-28650-9_4
2. Zhao, J., Sun, S., Wang, H., Cao, Z.: Promoting active learning with mixtures of Gaussian processes. Knowl.-Based Syst. **188**, 105044 (2020)
3. Xu, M., Ding, W., Zhu, J., Liu, Z., Chen, B., Zhao, D.: Task-agnostic online reinforcement learning with an infinite mixture of Gaussian processes. arXiv preprint arXiv:2006.11441 (2020)
4. Velásquez, R.M.A., Lara, J.V.M.: Forecast and evaluation of COVID-19 spreading in USA with reduced-space Gaussian process regression. Chaos Solitons Fractals **136**, 109924 (2020)
5. Shi, J.Q., Choi, T.: Gaussian Process Regression Analysis for Functional Data. Chapman and Hall/CRC press (2011). https://doi.org/10.1201/b11038
6. Shi, J.Q., Wang, B., Murray-Smith, R., Titterington, D.M.: Gaussian process functional regression modeling for batch data. Biometrics **63**(3), 714–723 (2007)
7. Shi, J.Q., Wang, B.: Curve prediction and clustering with mixtures of Gaussian process functional regression models. Stat. Comput. **18**(3), 267–283 (2008)
8. Di, W., Ma, J.: A two-layer mixture model of Gaussian process functional regressions and its MCMC EM algorithm. IEEE Trans. Neural Netw. Learn. Syst. **99**, 1–11 (2018)
9. Wu, D., Ma, J.: A DAEM algorithm for mixtures of Gaussian process functional regressions. In: Huang, D.-S., Han, K., Hussain, A. (eds.) ICIC 2016. LNCS (LNAI), vol. 9773, pp. 294–303. Springer, Cham (2016). https://doi.org/10.1007/978-3-319-42297-8_28
10. Bishop, C.M.: Pattern Recognition and Machine Learning. Springer, New York (2006). 738 pages. https://link.springer.com/book/9780387310732. ISBN: 978-0-387-31073-2
11. Dempster, A.P., Laird, N.M., Rubin, D.B.: Maximum likelihood from incomplete data via the EM algorithm. J. R. Stat. Soc. Ser. B (Methodol.) **39**(1), 1–22 (1977)

Dynamic Convolution Pruning Using Pooling Characteristic in Convolution Neural Networks

Yu Zhang, Dajiang Liu$^{(\boxtimes)}$, and Yongkang Xing

College of Computer Science, Chongqing University, Chongqing, China
`liudj@cqu.edu.cn`

Abstract. Dynamic pruning is an effective technique that has been widely applied to deep neural network compression. However, many existing dynamic methods involve network modification and time-consuming retraining. In this paper, we propose a dynamic region pruning method to skip partial regions in CNNs by considering the characteristic of pooling (max- or min-pooling). Specifically, kernels in a filter are ordered according to their ℓ_1-norm so that a smaller left partial sum could be obtained, leading to more opportunities for pruning. Without fine-tuning or network retraining, scale factors approximating the left partial sum are efficiently and thoroughly explored by model inferencing on the validation dataset. The experimental results on the testing dataset show that we could achieve up to 43.6% operation reduction while keeping a negligible accuracy loss.

Keywords: Dynamic network · Network pruning · Inference acceleration

1 Introduction

Deep learning methods, especially convolutional neural networks (CNNs) have been proved to be effective in various computer vision tasks, such as image classification [6], face recognition [11] and object detection [4], etc. The credible results generated by the CNN network rely on many parameters and complicated computations, limiting their usage in devices with limited computing power and storage. Therefore, researches on effective calculation acceleration and model compression are emerging.

However, most of the methods mentioned above perform the inference phase in a static manner. Once the training phase is completed, their graphs for computation and network parameters are fixed, which may limit their efficiency, representation power, etc. [9,15]. Dynamic networks [13] can adapt their structures and parameters to the input during the inference stage, and therefore enjoy beneficial properties that are absent in static models. However, most of the existing dynamic network work requires significant modifications to the original network

© Springer Nature Switzerland AG 2021
T. Mantoro et al. (Eds.): ICONIP 2021, CCIS 1516, pp. 558–565, 2021.
https://doi.org/10.1007/978-3-030-92307-5_65

structure or the introduction of other structures that need to be trained in the training phase, increasing complexity.

In order to reduce the complexity caused by architecture modification or retraining, we try to dynamically prune region convolution operations in CNNs by considering the characteristic of pooling (max- or min-pooling). Our main contributions are summarized as follows:

1. We explored the correlation between the convolution layer's input and the pooling layer's output in the convolution-pooling structure (CPS).
2. We use ℓ_1-norm to reorder the kernels in a filter so that a smaller left partial sum could be obtained, leading to more opportunities for pruning.
3. We efficiently explored the scale factors for each CPS to achieve 26.7% to 43.6% operation reduction with s slight accuracy loss.

2   Related Works

Channel gating network (CGNet) [5] uses a subset of convolution filters in each layer and activates the remaining filters only on selected areas. Dynamic neural architecture search (S2DNAS) [16] uses neural architecture search to find the optimal architecture among multiple structures with different widths. Different from methods that rely on the previous layer's activation value, Runtime neural pruning (RNP) [7] conducts pruning according to the input image and feature maps adaptively, which models the layer-by-layer pruning as a Markov decision process and uses reinforcement learning for training. The study [3] not only introduces a new residual block that gates channels in a fine-grained way but also introduces a tool batch-shaping to force gates to be more conditional on the feature map.

Table 1. Comparison of our design with some works.

	CGNet [5]	S2DNAS [16]	RNP [7]	DCP [3]	IwS [8]	Ours
Re-design networks	Yes	Yes	Yes	Yes	No	No
Additional structure	Yes	Yes	Yes	Yes	No	No
Retraining	Yes	Yes	Yes	Yes	Yes	No
Loss of accuracy	No	No	No	Yes	No	No
ImageNet dataset	Yes	No	Yes	Yes	Yes	Yes

Unlike the previous study of skipping layer or filter, some work combines skipping layer and filter simultaneously. These works are based on the fact that computational graphs can be more flexibly adapted, and channels would be selectively activated only when a specific layer is determined to be executed [1, 12,14]. They will bring more challenges to the training and inference stage and add additional structures to the networks.

While the above works have achieved good results, they also introduce additional problems that need to be solved. We try to accelerate network inference with minimal network changes. Here, we make some qualitative comparisons between these works and ours, and the results are shown in Table 1.

3   Method

Let C_I/C_O indicate the number of input/output channels of the convolution layer, W_I/H_I is the width/height of the input feature map, W_K/H_K is the width/height of the filter kernel, and the activation map denotes the output feature map of the convolutional layer. As shown in Fig. 1, each kernel of a filter will act on a $W_K \times H_K$ sliding window in the corresponding channel of the input feature map and generate a partial sum (Psum) of the sliding window. Then, the Psums of all the input channels will be accumulated to generate an activation value in an output channel. After all the activation values in the output feature maps are calculated, max/min pooling is commonly performed on the activation map to generate the output feature map.

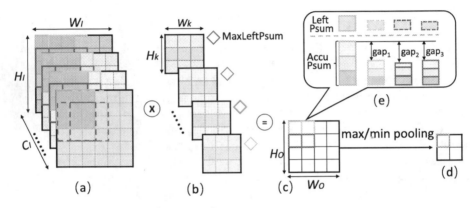

Fig. 1. A common convolution and pooling process. The subgraph (a), (b), (c), (d), and (e) indicate C_I input feature maps, 1 filter, 1 activation map, 1 output feature map, the computation process of AccumPsum and LeftPsum, respectively. Among them, AccuPsum denotes the sum of calculated Psum, and LeftPsum denotes the sum of Psum that needs to be calculated.

3.1   Core Idea

If we can predict which value in the pooling window is the maximum/minimum in advance, rather than calculating the Psums of all the input channels, it would save many computations and speed up the inference of the neural network. By separating AccuPsum of the former c input channels, the activation value could be presented as follows:

$$A_k = ReLU(\underbrace{\sum_{i=0}^{c} Psum_k^i}_{AccuPsum_k^c} + \underbrace{\sum_{i=c+1}^{C_I-1} Psum_k^i}_{LeftPsum_k^c}) \tag{1}$$

where A_k, $AccuPsum_k^{c}$, $LeftPsum_k^{c}$ indicate the kth activation value in the activation map, the kth accumulated Psums of the former c calculated input channels, the left accumulated Psums of input channels larger than c.

3.2 Determine the Maximal LeftPsum

From Eq. 1, if the LeftPsum is accurately calculated, there would be no oppor-
tunity to skip redundant multiply and accumulate (MAC) computations. Alternatively, we determine the maximal LeftPsum (MaxLeftPsum) according to the
corresponding kernel values in the filter. As the value range of each cell in input
feature maps and filters is restricted by the data/weight bit-width (N) in a quantized neural network, the MaxLeftPsum could be easily calculated. Therefore,
the MaxLeftPsum for any activation value A_k could be determined by the ℓ_1-
norm of filter kernel as follows:

$$MaxLeftPsum^c = \alpha \times \sum_{i=c}^{CI-1} L^c, \alpha \in (0, 2^N - 1] \tag{2}$$

where α and L^c indicate the scale factor, and the sum of ℓ_1-norm of kernels
from c to $C_I - 1$ channel in the filter. In most cases, the values in the input
feature map would not approach $2^N - 1$ and depend on the data distribution.

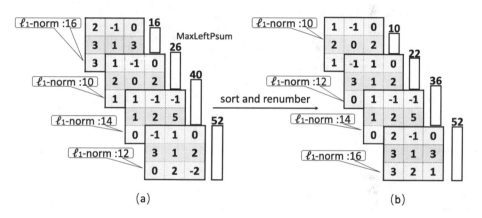

Fig. 2. Kernel sorting inside the filter according to the ℓ_1-norm. The subgraph (a) (b)
denotes the original kernels in a filter with corresponding MaxLeftPsum, the sorted
and renumbered kernels in a filter with corresponding MaxLeftPsum.

3.3 Put Them Together

If kernels with less ℓ_1-norm value are ordered with lower computing priority in a
filter, the corresponding MaxLeftPsum will be reduced. Therefore, kernels in a
filter are sorted according to their ℓ_1-norm value. As shown in Fig. 2(a), assuming
that the scale factor is 1, the MaxLeftPsum in the left filter in channel 0, 1, 2 and
3 are 52, 40, 26, and 16, respectively. After kernel reordering, the MaxLeftPsum
in channel 0, 1, 2 and 3 becomes 52, 36, 22 and 10, respectively as shown in
Fig. 2(b). Therefore, the gaps among AccuPsums are pone to be greater than
the corresponding MaxLeftPsum, and could save more MAC computations.

With the MaxLeftPsum elaborated above, we could determine whether convolution operations for an activation value should be skipped or not as follows:

$$AccuPsum_k^c - AccuPsum_j^c \geq MaxLeftPsum^c \tag{3}$$

where $AccuPsum_k^c$ and $AccuPsum_j^c$ denote the AccPsum from 0 to c channels for the ith and j^{th} activation value in a pooling window. When above condition is satisfied, the convolution operation for the jth activation value could be terminated. As shown in Fig. 3, the 3×3 convolution operations are performed in a 4×4 sliding window of the input feature map to get the four activation values for the 2×2 pooling window. Then, the 4×4 sliding window is moved from left to right and up to bottom with stride equaling the pooling window's size. After one input feature map channel is finished, the 4×4 sliding window moves to the following input feature map. Once the gaps among different AccuPsums are more extensive than the current MaxLeftPsum, the convolution operations for the fewer AccuPsums would be terminated.

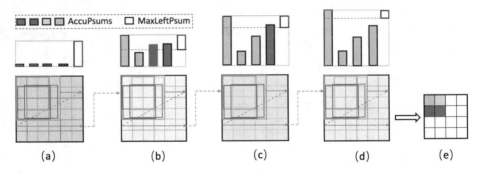

Fig. 3. Schematic diagram of the calculation process of our method. The subgraph (a), (b), (c), (d), and (e) indicate the 0th, 1st, 2nd, and third input feature maps participating in the calculation and an output activation map, respectively.

4   Experiments

Since our method targets the CPS, we choose neural network CIFAR10 [2] on CIFAR-10 dataset, VGG-13 [10] on ImageNet dataset and VGG-16 [10] on ImageNet dataset, where they have 4, 5, and 5 CPSs, respectively. We quantize the pre-trained models using int8 data type. In order to measure the computation complexity of our approach, we use the number of MAC operations (OPs) reduced as an essential metric.

4.1 Scale Factor Exploration for MaxLeftPsum

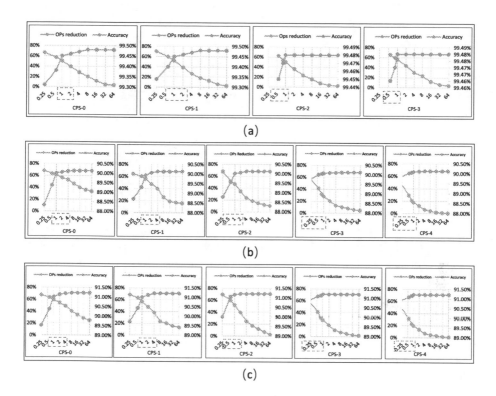

Fig. 4. Scale factor exploration on each CPS considering both OP reduction of current CPS and inference accuracy for (a) CIFAR10, (b) VGG-13, and (c) VGG-16. In each sub-figure, the ordinate on the left denotes the OPs percent of the current CPS, and the ordinate on the right denotes the value of inference accuracy.

From Fig. 4, we note that the amount of OPs reduction decreases with the increase of scale factor while inference accuracy increases with that. That is because the small scale factor will form a small MaxLeftPsum so that more filter kernels could be pruned for corresponding activation values. It is also worth noting that it will get into saturation region when the factor is greater than 2/4/8 for different CPSs, which are much less than the maximal value of a feature map in the neural network.

4.2 Parameter Exploration on Whole Networks and Overall Results

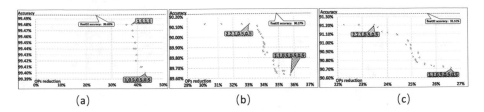

Fig. 5. Scale factor combinations results on each network considering both OP reduction of the whole network and inference accuracy for (a) CIFAR10, (b) VGG-13, and (c) VGG-16.

Based on the range of scale factors in each CPS, we further explore the factor combinations with grid search. Figure 5 depicted the 2-D Pareto points for factor combinations, OPs reduction of the whole network and inference accuracy, which are also conducted on the validation dataset. Our approach could achieve 43.6%, 35.8%, and 26.7% OPs reduction with 0.1%, 0.5%, and 0.7% accuracy loss in the testing dataset corresponding to original networks for low-energy scenarios for CIFAR10, VGG-13, and VGG-16, respectively. From Fig. 5, we also note that our approach gets less benefit in the more extensive network. That is because our approach targets to CPSs, and they take up less proportion in large networks. Our approach could achieve considerable OP reductions with only factor exploration on the validation dataset, rather than time-consuming retraining.

5 Conclusions

Network retraining involved in many existing dynamic methods needs a time-consuming and power-consuming process. To this end, this paper proposes a dynamic region pruning method by considering the computation redundancies introduced by the pooling operation. The experimental could achieve up to 43.6% OP reduction while keeping a negligible accuracy loss. Consequently, this paper introduces a new dimension to dynamic pruning and brings new opportunities to neural networks' software or hardware acceleration.

Acknowledgments. This work was supported in part by the National Natural Science Foundation of China under Grant 61804017 and in part by the National Key Research and Development Project of China (No. 2020AAA0104603).

References

1. Ehteshami Bejnordi, A., Krestel, R.: Dynamic channel and layer gating in convolutional neural networks. In: Schmid, U., Klügl, F., Wolter, D. (eds.) KI 2020. LNCS (LNAI), vol. 12325, pp. 33–45. Springer, Cham (2020). https://doi.org/10.1007/978-3-030-58285-2_3

2. Chen, A., Smith, G.: (2017). https://github.com/aaron-xichen/pytorch-playground

3. Gao, X., Zhao, Y., Dudziak, L., Mullins, R., Zhong Xu, C.: Dynamic channel pruning: feature boosting and suppression. In: International Conference on Learning Representations (2019)

4. Girshick, R., Donahue, J., Darrell, T., Malik, J.: Rich feature hierarchies for accurate object detection and semantic segmentation. In: Proceedings of the IEEE Conference on Computer Vision and Pattern Recognition, pp. 580–587 (2014)

5. Hua, W., Zhou, Y., De Sa, C., Zhang, Z., Suh, G.E.: Channel gating neural networks. In: Proceedings of the 33rd International Conference on Neural Information Processing Systems, pp. 1886–1896 (2019)

6. Krizhevsky, A., Sutskever, I., Hinton, G.E.: Imagenet classification with deep convolutional neural networks. Adv. Neural Inf. Process. Syst. **25**, 1097–1105 (2012)

7. Lin, J., Rao, Y., Lu, J., Zhou, J.: Runtime neural pruning. In: Proceedings of the 31st International Conference on Neural Information Processing Systems, pp. 2178–2188 (2017)

8. Liu, C., Wang, Y., Han, K., Xu, C., Xu, C.: Learning instance-wise sparsity for accelerating deep models. In: Proceedings of the Twenty-Eighth International Joint Conference on Artificial Intelligence, IJCAI-19, pp. 3001–3007. International Joint Conferences on Artificial Intelligence Organization (2019)

9. Sabour, S., Frosst, N., Hinton, G.E.: Dynamic routing between capsules. In: NIPS (2017)

10. Simonyan, K., Zisserman, A.: Very deep convolutional networks for large-scale image recognition. CoRR (2015)

11. Taigman, Y., Yang, M., Ranzato, M., Wolf, L.: Deepface: closing the gap to human-level performance in face verification. In: Proceedings of the IEEE Conference on Computer Vision and Pattern Recognition, pp. 1701–1708 (2014)

12. Wang, Y., et al.: Dual dynamic inference: enabling more efficient, adaptive, and controllable deep inference. IEEE J. Sel. Top. Signal Process. **14**(4), 623–633 (2020)

13. Wu, Z., et al.: Blockdrop: dynamic inference paths in residual networks. In: Proceedings of the IEEE Conference on Computer Vision and Pattern Recognition, pp. 8817–8826 (2018)

14. Xia, W., Yin, H., Dai, X., Jha, N.K.: Fully dynamic inference with deep neural networks. IEEE Trans. Emerg. Top. Comput. **01**, 1 (2021)

15. Yang, B., Bender, G., Le, Q.V., Ngiam, J.: CondConv: conditionally parameterized convolutions for efficient inference. In: Proceedings of the 33rd International Conference on Neural Information Processing Systems, pp. 1307–1318 (2019)

16. Yuan, Z., Wu, B., Sun, G., Liang, Z., Zhao, S., Bi, W.: S2DNAS: transforming static CNN model for dynamic inference via neural architecture search. In: Vedaldi, A., Bischof, H., Brox, T., Frahm, J.-M. (eds.) ECCV 2020, Part II. LNCS, vol. 12347, pp. 175–192. Springer, Cham (2020). https://doi.org/10.1007/978-3-030-58536-5_11

Adversarial Defenses via a Mixture of Generators

Maciej Żelaszczyk[(⊠)] and Jacek Mańdziuk[iD]

Faculty of Mathematics and Information Science, Warsaw University of Technology,
Koszykowa 75, 00-662 Warsaw, Poland
{m.zelaszczyk,mandziuk}@mini.pw.edu.pl

Abstract. In spite of the enormous success of neural networks, adversarial examples remain a relatively weakly understood feature of deep learning systems. There is a considerable effort in both building more powerful adversarial attacks and designing methods to counter the effects of adversarial examples. We propose a method to transform the adversarial input data through a mixture of generators in order to recover the correct class obfuscated by the adversarial attack. A canonical set of images is used to generate adversarial examples through potentially multiple attacks. Such transformed images are processed by a set of generators, which are trained adversarially as a whole to compete in inverting the initial transformations. To our knowledge, this is the first use of a mixture-based adversarially trained system as a defense mechanism. We show that it is possible to train such a system without supervision, simultaneously on multiple adversarial attacks. Our system is able to recover class information for previously-unseen examples with neither attack nor data labels on the MNIST dataset. The results demonstrate that this multi-attack approach is competitive with adversarial defenses tested in single-attack settings.

Keywords: Adversarial defense · Mixture of generators · MNIST · Classification

1 Introduction

The discovery of adversarial examples in the image domain has fueled research to better understand the nature of such examples and the extent to which neural networks can be fooled. Work on new adversarial methods has produced various approaches to the generation of adversarial images. These *adversarial attacks* can be either geared toward misclassification in general or toward inducing the classifier to assign the adversarial example to a specific class. Conversely, *adversarial defenses* are approaches designed with the goal of nullifying the effect of adversarial effects on a classifier.

In this work, we aim to show the possibility of defending against adversarial examples by utilizing a set of neural networks competing to reverse the effects of adversarial attacks.

© Springer Nature Switzerland AG 2021
T. Mantoro et al. (Eds.): ICONIP 2021, CCIS 1516, pp. 566–574, 2021.
https://doi.org/10.1007/978-3-030-92307-5_66

Main Contribution. The main contribution of this work can be summarized as follows: (1) We show that it is possible to use a GAN-inspired architecture to transform adversarial images to recover correct class labels. (2) We show that such an architecture can be extended to handle multiple adversarial attacks at once by making the generators compete to recover the original images on which the adversarial examples are based. (3) We demonstrate that such a system can be trained with no supervision, i.e. with no knowledge of: (a) the type of the adversarial attacks used, (b) the original images, (c) the class labels of the original images. (4) A system trained in this way is able to recover correct class labels on previously-unseen adversarial examples for a number of adversarial attacks. (5) The accuracy of a pretrained classifier on the images transformed by the system is meaningfully higher than that of a random classifier. For a number of our setups, including multi-attack ones, it is on par with the results of modern adversarial defenses, which are typically tested in single-attack settings. (6) For a range of adversarial attacks, the system is able to invert the adversarial attack and produce images close to the clean images that were attacked. (7) We highlight the fact that the components of such an unsupervised system specialize to some extent, revealing the distinction between attacks which produce images interpretable to humans and attacks which severely distort the visual aspects of the original images.

2   Related Work

This work is related to a number of lines of research linked to adversarial examples. Szegedy et al. [12] show that it is possible to construct adversarial images by adding perturbations to original images with the goal of the perturbation causing misclassification. Goodfellow et al. [3] show that the linear behavior of neural networks in high-dimensional spaces suffices to produce adversarial examples. They introduce the *fast gradient sign method* (FGSM) - a method of obtaining adversarial examples computationally less intensive than [12]. Ilyas et al. [4] tie the existence of adversarial examples to the presence of statistical, but not human-interpretable, features in the data. Madry et al. [6] suggest that *projected gradient descent* (PGD) can be used to generate adversarial examples and that PGD is an universal adversarial method.

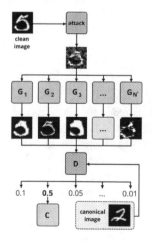

Fig. 1. Overview of the system. See description within the text.

The emergence of adversarial examples has led to research on *adversarial defenses*. Papernot et al. [9] introduce the *distillation defense* as a mechanism to counter adversarial attacks. Buckman et al. [1] present the possibility of using image discretization as an adversarial defense. Mustafa et al. [7] propose to disentangle the intermediate learned features and show that this increases the robustness of the classifiers without deteriorating the performance on unperturbed images. Pang et al. [8] posit that the robustness of neural networks to adversarial attacks can be improved by ensuring more diversity in ensemble models.

Generative adversarial networks (GANs) [2] are a network architecture directly stemming from the existence of adversarial examples. They are linked to our work not only via adversarial examples but also by the fact that we use a GAN-inspired architecture to handle image transformations. A more direct inspiration comes from the idea that it may be possible to train ensembles of conditional generators to identify and reverse transformations in the image domain - a concept proposed in [10].

3   Recovering Relevant Features Through a Set of Generators

We approach the problem of finding adversarial defenses at the data preprocessing step. We aim to link ensemble methods with GAN-based training to invert the adversarial transformations.

Adversarial Attacks as Mechanisms. Following [10], let us consider a canonical distribution P on $\mathbb{R}^d$ and N *mechanisms* $A_1, \ldots, A_N$, which are functions. These mechanisms give rise to N distributions $Q_1, \ldots, Q_N$, where $Q_j = A_j(P)$. We specifically consider a given mechanism A_j to be an adversarial attack built with respect to a classifier C on a given dataset. An important assumption is that at training time we receive two datasets: (1) a canonical, unperturbed dataset $\mathcal{D}_P$ drawn from the canonical distribution P and (2) a transformed dataset $\mathcal{D}_Q = (x_i)_{i=1}^n$ sampled independently from a mixture of $Q_1, \ldots, Q_N$.

The aim is to learn, if possible, approximate inverse mappings from the transformed examples from $\mathcal{D}_Q$ to the base unperturbed images from P. In general, the task of inverting adversarial images may be a difficult one as adversarial attacks can be complex transformations, possibly severely distorting the canonical images they are based upon. Keeping this in mind, the learned mappings may not necessarily preserve the visual features but instead preserve features necessary for a neural network classifier to recover the correct label unseen by the inverse mappings.

An important point is that $\mathcal{D}_Q$ is constructed by randomly applying one of the attacks $A_1, \ldots, A_N$ to images from P. $\mathcal{D}_P$ contains images from P, other than the ones used to construct $\mathcal{D}_Q$.

Competitive Generators. We consider a set of N' functions $G_1, \ldots, G_{N'}$, which will be referred to as *generators*, parameterized by $\theta_1, \ldots, \theta_{N'}$. In principle, we do not require $N = N'$. We additionally consider a function $D : \mathbb{R}^d \to [0, 1]$, a *discriminator*, parameterized by θ_D which is required to take values close to

0 for input outside of the support of the canonical distribution and values close to 1 for input from within this support.

The training is an adversarial procedure inspired by the training process of GANs [2]. For each input example $x' \in \mathcal{D}_Q$, each generator G_j is conditioned on this input. Based on the evaluation of the discriminator $D(G_j(x'))$, the generator with the highest score receives an update to its parameters θ_{j^*}, where $j^* = $ argmax $D(G_j(x'))$. Following that, D receives an update to its parameters θ_D based on the output of all the generators and on the samples from the canonical distribution. The optimization problem can be stated as:

$$\theta_1^*, \ldots, \theta_{N'}^* = \underset{\theta_1, \ldots, \theta_{N'}}{\operatorname{argmax}} \mathbb{E}_{x' \sim Q} \left(\max_{j \in \{1, \ldots, N'\}} D(G_{\theta_j}(x')) \right). \tag{1}$$

The discriminator is trained to maximize the objective:

$$\max_{\theta_D} \left(\mathbb{E}_{x \sim P} \log \left(D_{\theta_D} \right) + \frac{1}{N'} \sum_{j=1}^{N'} \mathbb{E}_{x' \sim Q} \left(\log \left(1 - D_{\theta_D}(G_{\theta_j}(x')) \right) \right) \right) \tag{2}$$

4   Experiments

We evaluate the potential to recover the features necessary for correctly classifying adversarial images from the MNIST dataset. The generators are chosen to be fully-convolutional networks [5] designed to preserve the size of the input data. The discriminator is a convolutional neural network with an increasing number of filters. The architectural details of the networks as well as the overall proposed algorithm are presented in the extended version of this article [13] along with additional experiments.

An overview of the system is presented in Fig. 1. A clean image is attacked and fed to the generators. The output of the generators is scored by the discriminator and the best-performing generator (G_2) is updated. The discriminator is trained on the output of all the generators and on canonical images. At test time, the output of the best-performing generator is passed to the pretrained classifier (C).

Raw 28×28 pixel MNIST images are scaled to the $(0, 1)$ range. A separate LeNet5-inspired classifier, chosen for its simplicity and relatively high accuracy, is pretrained on the MNIST train set for 100 epochs with Adam, with an initial learning rate of 10^{-3}. The network achieves a 98.7% accuracy on the MNIST test set. The MNIST train set is divided equally into two disjoint train subsets. The first one serves as the canonical train set, which is not transformed further. The images from the other one are subject to adversarial attacks and form the transformed train set. It is worth stressing that there is no overlap between the canonical and transformed datasets, i.e. no images from the canonical train set are the basis for the images in the transformed dataset. Additionally, the system is unsupervised in that it does not use labels at train or test time.

The full list of potential attacks is given in Table 1 along with ϵ hyperparameters and the success rate of an attack on a random batch of 128 clean images from the MNIST train set. The attacks employed result in distinct visual distortions to the original images, while retaining relatively high success rates. Figure 2 shows the effects of applying the attacks to a random image from the MNIST train set. While most of the images are still recognizable to a human observer, the additive uniform noise and additive Gaussian noise attacks are not. Based on this, it can be expected that any system trying to recover original images from adversarial ones would have a hard time on these two attacks.

Table 1. Types of attacks.

Attack	ϵ	Success
FGSM	0.5	89.8%
PGD	0.5	100.0%
DF	0.5	100.0%
AUN	3.5	90.6%
BIM	0.2	90.6%
AGN	100	90.6%
RAGN	15	94.5%
SAPN	10	90.6%
SLIDE	25	88.3%

Training. We train our system by first initializing the generators over 10 epochs on the transformed images to approximate the identity transformation. This *identity initialization* procedure helps to stabilize training and partially mitigates the problem of one generator dominating the other ones [10]. Once identity initialization is complete, the system is trained for 100 epochs following the procedure outlined in Sect. 3. Adversarial images are fed into all the generators, which produce new images based on the input. The output of all the generators is then scored by the discriminator. The generator which achieves the highest score is then updated accordingly, as would be the case in a standard GAN training procedure. The rest of the generators remain unchanged (1). The discriminator additionally receives canonical images and scores them. It is then updated against the output of all the generators and based on the scores of the canonical images (2). We use Adam with an initial learning rate of 10^{-3} for all networks in both identity initialization and actual training.

FGSM   PGD   DF   AUN   BIM   AGN   RAGN   SAPN   SLIDE

Fig. 2. Sample attack images

Single-Attack Settings. We train the system in single-attack settings with one generator. We repeat this for each attack separately. This means that the generator only receives images transformed by one attack in each setting. We evaluate the system on the previously-unseen MNIST test set by feeding transformed images to the generators, scoring the output of the generators by the discriminator and passing the highest-scored output on to the pretrained LeNet5 classifier. We measure the accuracy of the predictions in terms of the percentage of the correctly classified images. The results are presented in Table 2. For most attacks, the accuracy of the classification after the defense is above 90%. We also see that the success of the method seems to be related to the degree of visual distortions in the transformed images. The attacks for which our method generated less satisfactory results are also the ones which generate the most distorted images. Interestingly, for the DeepFool attack our method was able to marginally improve the original accuracy of the pretrained LeNet5 classifier on the test set. This suggests that for this particular attack our method comes close to completely removing the impact of the adversarial attack on classification.

Table 2. LeNet5 accuracy after defense in single attack/generator setting

Attack	FGSM	PGD	DF	AUN	BIM	AGN	RAGN	SAPN	SLIDE
Accuracy	97.5%	93.5%	98.9%	18.9%	97.5%	11.4%	92.9%	98.1%	95.3%

Multi-attack Settings. We evaluate our system in settings with multiple attacks and generators. The number of attacks does not necessarily need to be equal to the number of generators. In preliminary tests, we observed that limiting the number of generators can have adverse effects on the performance of the system but using a number of generators slightly lower than the number of attacks generally does not lead to a breakdown

Table 3. LeNet5 accuracy after defense with multiple attacks/generators. Additional results are presented in the preprint [13]

Number of attacks	3	5	9
Trained separately	94.9%	73.9%	73.9%
Trained jointly	84.4%	64.2%	63.3%

in performance. For simplicity, we proceed with a number of generators equal to the number of attacks.

We train and evaluate our system in three multi-attack settings: **(a)** 3 generators, 3 attacks: FGSM, PGD, DeepFool, **(b)** 5 generators, 5 attacks: FGSM, PGD, DeepFool, AUN, BIM, **(c)** 9 generators, 9 attacks: all the attacks listed in Table 1.

For each of these settings, it is possible to adopt two approaches to training the architecture. In the first one, the system is trained jointly, end-to-end. This means that at train time neither of the generators has access to the information about the type of an attack applied to the images. In the other approach, we simply reuse the generators trained in single-attack settings and the discriminator trained in the first multi-attack approach. The main difference is that in the latter setting the generators do have information about the particular attack at train time. Such an adversarial defense is inherently an easier task - a reality reflected in the results presented in Table 3. A system trained separately (first row) consistently outperforms the system trained jointly (second row) to the tune of a 10% difference in accuracy after the defense. However, our main interest is in the jointly-trained system, which does not have access to the type of attack at train time and can be trained in a fully unsupervised manner.

The results for the 3-attack version of the jointly-trained system are comparable to other adversarial defense methods [11] evaluated in single-attack settings. The advantage of our method is that it can be applied to multiple attacks at once with no supervision. Additionally, it can be used in a modular manner with pretrained classifiers. For the 5- and 9-attack versions of this system, the accuracy drops as the defense becomes increasingly difficult, but the negative impact of increasing the number of attacks from 5 to 9 is visibly less pronounced than in the case of moving from 3 to 5 attacks.

The defenses generated by our system tend to reverse the effects of the adversarial attack, at least as far as a simple eyeball test is able to determine. The attack images based on one sample from the MNIST train set are presented in Fig. 3 (first and third row) along with the images generated by our 9-attack system trained jointly (second and fourth row). Each defense is the image generated by the best-scored generator. We see that for less distorted attack images our system is generally able to recover features corresponding to the clean image. In such cases, it does seem that the system is able to approximate the inversion of a particular attack. For more distorted images, for instance those generated by the AUN and AGN attacks, the system does not seem to approximate the inversion closely.

We also consider: (1) a possibility to simplify generator initialization and (2) an approach to analyze the capacity of the system. A full discussion of these experiments is available in the extended version of this article [13].

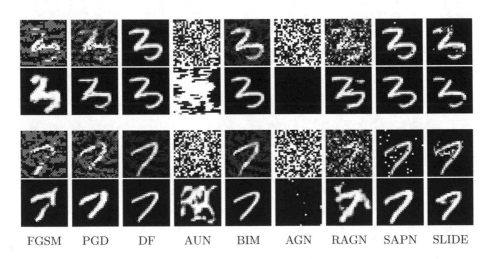

FGSM   PGD   DF   AUN   BIM   AGN   RAGN   SAPN   SLIDE

Fig. 3. Sample attacks (first and third row) with the respective defenses (second and fourth row)

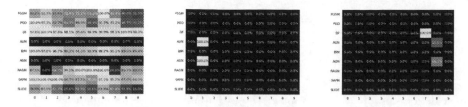

Fig. 4. Examples of generator specialization: accuracy for a given class/attack for the *generalist* (left), *specialist* (middle) and *marginalist* (right).

Generator *Expertise*. An interesting aspect of the mixture of generators is the extent to which particular generators specialize in either specific attacks or image classes. We perform a breakdown of the accuracy measure by digit class and by attack for the 9-attack jointly-trained system. In Fig. 4, we present the results for 3 out of the 9 generators to highlight the potential types of generators trained.

The first generator is a *generalist* - it wins on a large number of sample images and achieves relatively high accuracy on the majority of the attacks. Notably, the two hard attacks we have identified so far (additive uniform noise and additive Gaussian noise attacks) are precisely the attacks this generator does not cover - it does not win on a single sample image from these attacks. *Generalists* are the most ubiquitous among the 9 trained generators. The second generator only ever wins on samples from the two hard attacks. This generator is a *specialist* in that it focuses on specific kinds of attacks at the expense of other ones. The accuracy of the *specialist* is very high in only a handful of specific cases. Finally, the third generator is a *marginalist* - much like the *specialist*, it focuses on two hard attacks but fails to win on a significant number of samples and has questionable accuracy levels.

5   Conclusions

In this work we show that it is possible to train a GAN-based mixture of generators to defend against adversarial examples in a fully unsupervised manner. Trained with competing generators, this system is able to extract from adversarial images features relevant for classification in both single-attack and multi-attacks settings. For a majority of tested attacks, the system not only recovers features important for classification but the generators also approximate the inverses of the adversarial transformations, at least on a visual level. The recovered images retain internal visual coherence and are immediately interpretable by a human observer, except for those generated by two attacks which severely distort the original images (AUN, AGN).

The training process is able to produce more general generators, which mainly operate on easier attacks, and more specialized generators, which in turn tend to focus on harder attacks with different levels of success. We also show that infusing the system with knowledge as to the type of the attack by training generators separately increases the post-defense accuracy by about 10% in 3-, 5- and 9-attack settings.

Our research links adversarial defenses with ensemble methods and GAN-based training. It provides a fully-unsupervised approach to defending against adversarial examples without modifying the underlying classifier. This could provide for a practically-relevant method to approach the problem of adversarial examples in a real-life setting, particularly when the type of attack is not known beforehand and it is not feasible to modify the classifier.

Acknowledgments. This project was funded by the POB Research Centre Cybersecurity and Data Science of the Warsaw University of Technology within the Excellence Initiative Program - Research University (ID-UB).

References

1. Buckman, J., Roy, A., Raffel, C., Goodfellow, I.: Thermometer encoding: One hot way to resist adversarial examples. In: ICLR (2018)
2. Goodfellow, I., et al.: Generative adversarial nets. In: NIPS (2014)
3. Goodfellow, I., Shlens, J., Szegedy, C.: Explaining and harnessing adversarial examples. In: ICLR (2015)
4. Ilyas, A., Santurkar, S., Tsipras, D., Engstrom, L., Tran, B., Madry, A.: Adversarial examples are not bugs, they are features. In: NIPS (2019)
5. Long, J., Shelhamer, E., Darrell, T.: Fully convolutional networks for semantic segmentation. In: CVPR (2015)
6. Madry, A., Makelov, A., Schmidt, L., Tsipras, D., Vladu, A.: Towards deep learning models resistant to adversarial attacks. In: ICLR (2018)
7. Mustafa, A., Khan, S., Hayat, M., Goecke, R., Shen, J., Shao, L.: Adversarial defense by restricting the hidden space of deep neural networks. In: ICCV (2019)
8. Pang, T., Xu, K., Du, C., Chen, N., Zhu, J.: Improving adversarial robustness via promoting ensemble diversity. In: ICML (2019)
9. Papernot, N., McDaniel, P., Wu, X., Jha, S., Swami, A.: Distillation as a defense to adversarial perturbations against deep neural networks. In: 2016 IEEE Symposium on Security and Privacy (SP), pp. 582–597 (2016)
10. Parascandolo, G., Kilbertus, N., Rojas-Carulla, M., Schölkopf, B.: Learning independent causal mechanisms. In: ICML, vol. 80, pp. 4033–4041 (2018)
11. Schott, L., Rauber, J., Bethge, M., Brendel, W.: Towards the first adversarially robust neural network model on MNIST. In: ICLR (2019)
12. Szegedy, C., et al.: Intriguing properties of neural networks. In: ICLR (2014)
13. Żelaszczyk, M., Mańdziuk, J.: Adversarial defenses via a mixture of generators. arXiv:2110.02364 (2021)

Fractional Multi-view Hashing with Semantic Correlation Maximization

Ruijie Gao, Yun Li[✉], Yun-Hao Yuan, Jipeng Qiang, and Yi Zhu

School of Information Engineering, Yangzhou University, Yangzhou, China
liyun@yzu.edu.cn

Abstract. Hashing has been extensively concerned in multimedia research due to its low storage cost and high retrieval efficiency. The purpose of multi-view hashing is to project heterogeneous data from different views in high dimensional space into compact and discrete binary codes in Hamming space and meanwhile maintains the similarity of the original data. In this paper, we propose a Fractional Multi-view Hashing with Semantic Correlation Maximization (FMH-SCM), where the learning objective is to seek the maximum semantic correlation from various views. The proposed method uses labels to learn multi-view hash codes and fractional-order embedding to reduce the negative effect of noise. Moreover, a sequential optimization is used to solve the hash functions for improving the performance of this method. FMH-SCM is compared with related algorithms on two image retrieval datasets. Extensive experiments verify the effectiveness of the proposed method.

Keywords: Multi-view hashing · Correlation · Fractional-order embedding · Multimedia retrieval

1 Introduction

Approximate nearest neighbor (ANN) [1] retrieval plays a significant role in multimedia retrieval. However, with the rapid growth of multimedia data on the Internet, traditional ANN-based methods have been unable to meet the increasing practical retrieval tasks. Because of the benefits of low storage cost and highly computational efficiency of hashing learning, ANN search based on hashing becomes more and more popular in the task of multi-view retrieval. The purpose of hashing learning is to project the high dimensional space data to a low dimensional Hamming space, where the similarity of data points in the original space should be kept in the discrete Hamming space.

Supported by the National Natural Science Foundation of China under Grant Nos. 61402203 and 61703362, the Yangzhou Science Project Foundation under Grant No. YZ2020173. It is also sponsored by Excellent Young Backbone Teacher (Qing Lan) Project and Scientific Innovation Project Fund of Yangzhou University under Grant No. 2017CXJ033.

T. Mantoro et al. (Eds.): ICONIP 2021, CCIS 1516, pp. 575–582, 2021.
https://doi.org/10.1007/978-3-030-92307-5_67

Currently, most of hashing learning works make efforts on single-view scenario [2]. In daily multimedia retrieval, data are often represented by various features from different views. For instance, images can be represented by different feature descriptors such as Histogram of Oriented Gradient (HOG), Scale Invariant Feature Transform (SIFT), and Local Binary Pattern (LBP). These data are called multi-view data. It is not proper for single-view hashing methods to directly handle multi-view data. Therefore, researchers have proposed many hashing methods based on multiple views. Hashing methods for dealing with different views can be divided into two categories: cross-view hashing and multi-view hashing. Cross-view hashing mainly performs cross-view retrieval tasks [3].

In this paper, we study the second category, i.e., multi-view hashing. The goal of multi-view hashing is to fully integrate different view characteristics from the same objects into compact and similarity-preserving binary codes, which can provide complementary information and are more comprehensive than those obtained from single-view methods. On the basis of the use of label information about training data, multi-view hashing methods can be classified into unsupervised and supervised methods. Unsupervised hashing methods, such as Composite Hashing with Multiple Information Sources (CHMIS) [4] and Multiview Discrete Hashing (MVDH) [5], do not use labels that can boost the discriminant ability of binary hash codes, so the learned codes are usually limited by semantics. Supervised multi-view hashing methods that use label information have attracted more and more attention than unsupervised methods. Flexible Discrete Multi-view Hashing (FDMH) [6] is a representative method.

The performance of existing multi-view hashing methods has been significantly improved. However, existing supervised multi-view hashing methods still have some problems. First, most of them use pre-constructed graphs to maintain the similarity between data points, resulting in high time complexity and storage costs. Second, most methods do not consider the negative effect of noise of training samples. To solve these limitations, this paper proposes a Fractional Multi-view Hashing with Semantic Correlation Maximization (FMH-SCM) method. This method directly uses labels to search the maximum correlation between different views. Moreover, fractional-order embedding is used to reduce the negative effect of noise of the data. Experimental results show that our FMH-SCM is superior to existing related methods.

2   Related Work

2.1   Single-View Hashing

Spectral Hashing (SH) [2] is used to project data into a Hamming space by maintaining the similarity of the original data. In SH, the requirement that the data should be sampled from multi-dimensional uniform distribution limits its wide applications. Based on the idea of SH, Anchor Graph Hashing (AGH) [7] is proposed to learn a low-rank adjacency matrix about anchors, which allows the low-rank adjacency matrix to approximate the real adjacency matrix. Iterative Quantization (ITQ) [8] takes into account the error caused by directly relaxing the discrete constraints, so the quantization error is reduced between the learned hash codes and the mapped data through alternating iterations.

2.2 Multi-view Hashing

Single-view hashing methods only focuses on one view for learning hash functions. In real life, multimedia data are often described by multiple features and each feature describes the data from a different perspective. Multiple Feature Hashing (MFH) [9] is used to store local structure information of each feature. In addition, it is proposed to consider the structure of features globally. Discrete Multi-Graph Hashing (DMGH) [10] is based on multi-graph learning techniques to integrate multi-view features and is trained to learn the weights of each view adaptively. Supervised Discrete Multi-view Hashing (SDMH) [11] is used to learn discrete codes that are discriminant from multi-view features.

3 Proposed Approach

3.1 Notation and Problem Definition

Suppose $O = \{o_i\}_{i=1}^n$ is the training set including n training samples with M different views, that is, $\{X_m = [(x_m^{(1)})^T, (x_m^{(2)})^T, \cdots, (x_m^{(n)})^T]^T \in R^{n \times d_m}\}_{m=1}^M$ with d_m as dimension of m-th view. Different views of object o_i share the same label given as $l_i \in \{0,1\}^p$, where p is the number of classes. Let $L = [l_1^T, l_2^T, \cdots, l_n^T]^T \in R^{n \times p}$ be the label matrix and $B = [b_1^T, b_2^T, \cdots, b_n^T]^T \in \{-1,1\}^{n \times K}$ be the hash codes, where $b_i \in \{-1,1\}^K$ is the hash code associated with o_i and K is the code length. Our goal is to learn hash functions $f_m(\cdot) : R^{d_m} \to \{-1,1\}^K$, defined by $f_m(X_m) = \text{sgn}(X_m W_m)$, where $\text{sgn}(\cdot)$ denotes the element-wise sign function mapping continuous data into discrete binary codes and $W_m = [\omega_m^{(1)}, \omega_m^{(2)}, \cdots, \omega_m^{(K)}] \in R^{d_m \times K}$ is the projection matrix of m-th view.

3.2 Formulation

We calculate the pairwise semantic similarity matrix $\hat{S}$ by cosine similarity of label vectors. The similarity of i-th and j-th objects is defined as $\hat{S}_{ij} = \langle l_i, l_j \rangle / (\|l_i\|_2 \|l_j\|_2)$, where $\langle \cdot \rangle$ is an inner product operator and $\| \cdot \|_2$ is the 2-norm of a vector. Let $\hat{L}$ be a normalized label matrix with i-row as $l_i / \|l_i\|_2$. Thus, $\hat{S} = \hat{L}\hat{L}^T$. The element-wise linear transformation [12] is applied to $\hat{S}$ and thus get final semantic similarity matrix S by $S = 2\hat{S} - E = 2\hat{L}\hat{L}^T - 1_n 1_n^T$, where E is an all-one matrix and 1_n is an all-one column vector with length n.

Due to the deviation error caused by noise, Fractional-order Embedding Multiset Canonical Correlations (FEMCCs) [13] was proposed to reduce the negative effect of noise by using fractional-order embedding. Borrowing this idea, we decompose X_m by

$$X_m^{\tau_m} = U_m \Sigma_m^{\tau_m} V_m^T, \ \Sigma_m = \text{diag}(\sigma_{m,1}, \sigma_{m,2}, \ldots, \sigma_{m,r}) \tag{1}$$

where U_m and V_m are the left and right singular vector matrices of X_m, respectively, $\{\sigma_{m,i}\}_{i=1}^r$ are the singular values in descending order, τ_m is a fractional order parameter with $0 \le \tau_m \le 1$, $r = \mathrm{rank}(X_m)$, and $m = 1, 2, \cdots, M$.

Our model uses the inner product between hash codes to maintain semantic similarity and meanwhile reduces the negative effect of noise. Hence, we define the objective function for semantic consistency as below:

$$\min_{W_1,\cdots,W_M} \sum_{i=1}^M \sum_{j=1}^M \|\mathrm{sgn}(X_i^{\tau_i} W_i)\mathrm{sgn}(X_j^{\tau_j} W_j)^T - KS\|_F^2, \tag{2}$$

where $\| \cdot \|_F$ denotes the Frobenius norm of a matrix.

3.3   Model Solving

To optimize the problem in (2), we borrow the idea of solution from [12] and relax it with orthogonality constraint by the following form of

$$\min_{W_1,\cdots,W_M} \sum_{i=1}^M \sum_{j=1}^M \|(X_i^{\tau_i} W_i)(X_j^{\tau_j} W_j)^T - KS\|_F^2$$
$$\text{s.t.} \sum_{i=1}^M W_i^T X_i^{\tau_i T} X_i^{\tau_i} W_i = nI_K, \tag{3}$$

where $I_K \in R^{K \times K}$ is the identity matrix.

For the convenience of expression, let $H_i = X_i^{\tau_i}$, $i = 1, 2, \cdots, M$. With simple derivations, the objective function in (3) is written as follows:

$$\sum_{i=1}^M \sum_{j=1}^M \|(H_i W_i)(H_j W_j)^T - KS\|_F^2$$
$$= \sum_{i=1}^M \sum_{j=1}^M \mathrm{tr}[((H_i W_i)(H_j W_j)^T - KS)((H_i W_i)(H_j W_j)^T - KS)^T]$$
$$= \mathrm{tr}\left\{ \sum_{i=1}^M \sum_{j=1}^M [((H_i W_i)(H_j W_j)^T - KS)((H_i W_i)(H_j W_j)^T - KS)^T] \right\} \tag{4}$$
$$= Kn^2 - 2K\mathrm{tr}\left[\sum_{i=1}^M \sum_{j=1}^M (W_i^T H_i^T S H_j W_j) \right] + K^2 M^2 \mathrm{tr}(S^T S)$$
$$= -2K\mathrm{tr}\left[\sum_{i=1}^M \sum_{j=1}^M (W_i^T H_i^T S H_j W_j) \right] + const$$

where $\mathrm{tr}(\cdot)$ denotes the trace of a matrix and *const* denotes a constant. With (4), the problem in (3) can be reformulated equivalently as

$$\max_{W_1,\cdots,W_M} \sum_{i=1}^M \sum_{j=1}^M \mathrm{tr}(W_i^T H_i^T S H_j W_j) \quad \text{s.t.} \sum_{i=1}^M W_i^T H_i^T H_i W_i = nI_K \tag{5}$$

It is easy to know that the problem in (5) can be solved by a generalized eigenvalue problem.

Existing work [12] has shown that non-orthogonal constraint can improve the performance of hash codes. Thus, we use a sequential optimization strategy [12] to improve the orthogonal solution. Suppose that $\{\omega_m^{(1)}, \omega_m^{(2)}, \cdots, \omega_m^{(t-1)}\}_{m=1}^M$ have been obtained. Next, we need to learn the t-th set of projection vectors, i.e., $\{\omega_m^{(t)}\}_{m=1}^M$.

The residue matrix $F^{(t)}$ is denoted by

$$
\begin{aligned}
F^{(t)} &= \sum_{i=1}^M \sum_{j=1}^M (KS - \sum_{k=1}^{t-1} \mathrm{sgn}(H_i\omega_i^{(k)})\mathrm{sgn}(H_j\omega_j^{(k)})^T) \\
&= KM^2 S - \sum_{k=1}^{t-1} \left(\sum_{i=1}^M \sum_{j=1}^M \mathrm{sgn}(H_i\omega_i^{(k)})\mathrm{sgn}(H_j\omega_j^{(k)})^T \right)
\end{aligned}
\tag{6}
$$

With (6), our objective function can be written as follows:

$$
\min_{\omega_1^{(t)}, \cdots, \omega_M^{(t)}} \sum_{i=1}^M \sum_{j=1}^M \|\mathrm{sgn}(H_i\omega_i^{(t)})\mathrm{sgn}(H_j\omega_j^{(t)})^T - F^{(t)}\|_F^2
\tag{7}
$$

Using the same relaxation strategy as the above, we can get $\omega_m^{(t)}$ ($m = 1, 2, \cdots, M$) by the following generalized eigenvalue problem

$$
\begin{bmatrix}
0 & C_{12}^{(t)} & \cdots & C_{1M}^{(t)} \\
C_{21}^{(t)} & 0 & \cdots & C_{2M}^{(t)} \\
\vdots & \vdots & \ddots & \vdots \\
C_{M1}^{(t)} & C_{M2}^{(t)} & \cdots & 0
\end{bmatrix}
\begin{bmatrix}
\omega_1^{(t)} \\
\omega_2^{(t)} \\
\vdots \\
\omega_M^{(t)}
\end{bmatrix}
= \lambda
\begin{bmatrix}
H_1^T H_1 & & & \\
& H_2^T H_2 & & \\
& & \ddots & \\
& & & H_M^T H_M
\end{bmatrix}
\begin{bmatrix}
\omega_1^{(t)} \\
\omega_2^{(t)} \\
\vdots \\
\omega_M^{(t)}
\end{bmatrix}, \tag{8}
$$

where $C_{ij}^{(t)}$ is a $d_i \times d_j$ matrix computed by

$$
\begin{aligned}
C_{ij}^{(t)} &= H_i^T F^{(t)} H_j \\
&= H_i^T F^{(t-1)} H_j - H_i^T \sum_{p=1}^M \sum_{q=1}^M \mathrm{sgn}(H_p\omega_p^{(t-1)})\mathrm{sgn}(H_q\omega_q^{(t-1)})^T H_j \\
&= C_{ij}^{(t-1)} - H_i^T \sum_{p=1}^M \sum_{q=1}^M \mathrm{sgn}(H_p\omega_p^{(t-1)})\mathrm{sgn}(H_q\omega_q^{(t-1)})^T H_j.
\end{aligned}
\tag{9}
$$

4   Experiment

4.1   Dataset

The CIFAR-10 dataset[1] has $60,000$ color images with size as 32×32 in 10 classes. We extract 128-D SIFT feature, 512-D GIST feature, and 144-D HOG feature

---

[1] https://www.cs.toronto.edu/~kriz/cifar.html.

Table 1. MAP results of different methods with various codes length. The best results are shown in boldface.

Methods	CIFAR-10					NUS-WIDE				
	32bit	48bit	64bit	96bit	128bit	32bit	48bit	64bit	96bit	128bit
SH	0.152	0.147	0.143	0.139	0.136	0.129	0.128	0.126	0.125	0.125
AGH	0.156	0.153	0.152	0.151	0.150	0.131	0.131	0.128	0.127	0.126
ITQ	0.209	0.210	0.211	0.213	0.213	0.149	0.150	0.151	0.151	0.151
CHMIS	0.166	0.169	0.170	0.171	0.172	0.132	0.133	0.132	0.132	0.132
MFH	0.167	0.171	0.174	0.177	0.179	0.121	0.121	0.119	0.118	0.117
MVDH	0.207	0.209	0.210	0.211	0.212	0.144	0.145	0.147	0.147	0.148
MH-SCM	0.325	0.337	0.344	0.352	0.355	0.165	0.175	0.175	0.178	0.178
FMH-SCM	**0.342**	**0.354**	**0.360**	**0.366**	**0.373**	**0.182**	**0.188**	**0.190**	**0.193**	**0.193**

from images to form three views. To reduce the training cost, we randomly select 1000 images for training and 1000 images for testing.

The NUS-WIDE dataset[2] contains $269,648$ web images that are annotated with at least one of 81 concepts manually. This dataset has six features and has been divided into two parts in advance, i.e., $161,789$ images for training and the rest for testing. We select three features, i.e., 144-D color correlogram, 225-D block-wise color moments, and 75-D edge direction histogram to form three different views. We randomly select 1000 images for training and 500 images for testing.

4.2   Baselines and Evaluation Metrics

In this experiment, we compare our method with six multi-view hashing methods including single-view hashing methods SH [2], AGH [7], and ITQ [8], multi-view hashing methods CHMIS [4], MFH [9], and MVDH [5]. In the proposed FMH-SCM, fractional parameters on CIFAR-10 are respectively set as 0.8, 0.9, and 0.7 for three views, while on NUS-WIDE as 0.8, 0.8, and 0.7. To verify the effectiveness of fractional order parameters, we also compare the method without these parameters, denoted as MH-SCM.

The mean average precision (MAP) and precision-recall curves are adopted as evaluation metrics. Given a query q, the average precision (AP) is defined as $AP = (1/L_q) \sum_{r=1}^{|\mathcal{N}|} P_q(r)\delta_q(r)$, where L_q is the number of relevant instances in retrieved set $\mathcal{N}$, $P_q(r)$ is the precision of top r retrieved instances, and $\delta_q(r) = 1$ if the r-th instance is relevant to query q and 0 otherwise. MAP is obtained by the averaged AP of all queries.

4.3   Experimental Results

The MAP results are presented in Table 1. From Table 1, we find FMH-SCM surpasses all compared methods on different hash codes length on two datasets. This

---

[2] https://lms.comp.nus.edu.sg/wp-content/uploads/2019/research/nuswide/NUS-WIDE.html.

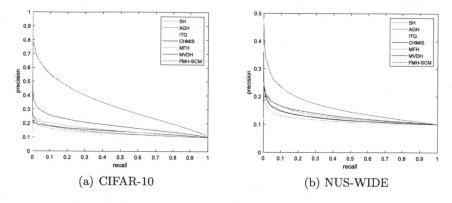

(a) CIFAR-10   (b) NUS-WIDE

Fig. 1. Precision-recall curves of different methods with 64 bits.

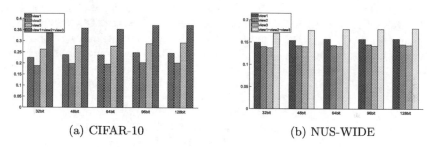

(a) CIFAR-10   (b) NUS-WIDE

Fig. 2. MAPs of FMH-SCM in multi-view and single view scenarios.

proves that our algorithm is an effective tool for learning hash codes. Moreover, FMH-SCM improves the MAP results via longer code length. Compared to MH-SCM, FMH-SCM performs better. This means that fractional-order embedding can improve the performance of hash codes.

Figure 1 shows the precision-recall curves of different methods with 64-bit hash code on two datasets. As seen, the proposed FMH-SCM is superior to other methods.

4.4   Effectiveness of Multiple Views

We compare the MAP results of FMH-SCM in single view and multi-view scenarios. Figure 2 shows the MAPs of FMH-SCM on two datasets. From Fig. 2, it can be clearly seen that the performance of FMH-SCM in multi-view scenario exceeds that in single view scenario. It means that FMH-SCM can well integrate the information of multiple views to obtain better performance.

5   Conclusion

In this paper, we propose a supervised multi-view hashing method called FMH-SCM, which uses labels to learn binary hash codes. FMH-SCM utilizes the complementarity of different views and maximizes the semantic correlation between different views. To reduce the negative effect of noise in the data, fractional order embedding is used to reconstruct the samples. Moreover, a sequential optimization is used to solve the hash functions. Experimental results on two datasets show that the proposed method is superior to other related methods.

References

1. Zhu, L., Huang, Z., Li, Z., Xie, L., Shen, H.T.: Exploring auxiliary context: discrete semantic transfer hashing for scalable image retrieval. IEEE Trans. Neural Netw. Learn. Syst. **29**(11), 5264–5276 (2018)
2. Weiss, Y., Torralba, A., Fergus, R.: Spectral hashing. Adv. Neural. Inf. Process. Syst. **282**(3), 1753–1760 (2009)
3. Fang, Y., Li, B., Li, X., Ren, Y.: Unsupervised cross-modal similarity via latent structure discrete hashing factorization. Knowl.-Based Syst. **218**, 106857 (2021)
4. Zhang, D., Wang, F., Si, L.: Composite hashing with multiple information sources. In: Proceedings of the 34th International ACM SIGIR Conference on Research and Development in Information Retrieval, pp. 225–234 (2011)
5. Shen, X., et al.: Multiview discrete hashing for scalable multimedia search. ACM Trans. Intell. Syst. Technol. **9**(5), 1–21 (2018)
6. Liu, L., Zhang, Z., Huang, Z.: Flexible discrete multi-view hashing with collective latent feature learning. Neural Process. Lett. **52**(3), 1765–1791 (2020)
7. Liu, W., Wang, J., Kumar, S., Chang, S.F.: Hashing with graphs. In: Proceedings of the 28th International Conference on Machine Learning, pp. 1–8 (2011)
8. Gong, Y., Lazebnik, S., Gordo, A., Perronnin, F.: Iterative quantization: a procrustean approach to learning binary codes for large-scale image retrieval. IEEE Trans. Pattern Anal. Mach. Intell. **35**(12), 2916–2929 (2012)
9. Song, J., Yang, Y., Huang, Z., Shen, H.T., Luo, J.: Effective multiple feature hashing for large-scale near-duplicate video retrieval. IEEE Trans. Multimedia **15**(8), 1997–2008 (2013)
10. Xiang, L., Shen, X., Qin, J., Hao, W.: Discrete multi-graph hashing for large-scale visual search. Neural Process. Lett. **49**(3), 1055–1069 (2019)
11. Lu, X., Zhu, L., Li, J., Zhang, H., Shen, H.T.: Efficient supervised discrete multiview hashing for large-scale multimedia search. IEEE Trans. Multimedia **22**(8), 2048–2060 (2019)
12. Zhang, D., Li, W.J.: Large-scale supervised multimodal hashing with semantic correlation maximization. In: Proceedings of the AAAI conference on Artificial Intelligence, pp. 2177–2183 (2014)
13. Yuan, Y.-H., Sun, Q.S.: Fractional-order embedding multiset canonical correlations with applications to multi-feature fusion and recognition. Neurocomputing **122**, 229–238 (2013)

A Supervised Learning Algorithm for Recurrent Spiking Neural Networks Based on BP-STDP

Wenjun Guo, Xianghong Lin$^{(\boxtimes)}$, and Xiaofei Yang

College of Computer Science and Engineering, Northwest Normal University,
Lanzhou 730070, China
linxh@nwnu.edu.cn

Abstract. Spiking neural network model encodes information with precisely timed spike train, it is very suitable to process complex spatiotemporal patterns. Recurrent spiking neural network has more complex dynamics characteristics because of feedback connections, which makes it difficult to design efficient learning algorithms. This paper proposes a supervised learning algorithm to train recurrent spiking neural networks. By mapping the integrate-and-fire neuron model to the rectified linear unit activation function, the learning rule is induced using error backpropagation and spike-timing dependent plasticity mechanism. The results of spike train learning task and non-linear pattern classification show that the algorithm is effective to learn spatiotemporal patterns. In addition, the influences of different parameters on learning performance are analyzed.

Keywords: Recurrent spiking neural networks · Supervised learning algorithm · Spiking-timing dependent plasticity · Backpropagation

1 Introduction

The learning algorithms for artificial neural networks (ANNs) that encode information with spike frequency is to adjust synaptic weights to minimize the error function. However, experimental evidence has confirmed that the information processing in brain is real-time and nervous system encodes information with precisely timed spike trains. As a new computational model, spiking neural networks (SNNs) consist of spiking neuron models and encode information with precisely timed spike trains and more powerful in computing capacity, it can process spatiotemporal information better. Recurrent spiking neural networks (RSNNs) introduce feedback mechanism on the basis of feedforward SNNs.

Two classic algorithms for Recurrent neural networks (RNNs) are real-time recurrent learning (RTRL) [1] and backpropagation through time (BPTT) [2]. Although RTRL updates synaptic weights online, its computational complexity is high. BPTT transforms RNN into an equivalent feedforward network and propagates the error signal backward through time, it is an offline learning algorithm while improves computational efficiency. Many gradient-based algorithms

© Springer Nature Switzerland AG 2021
T. Mantoro et al. (Eds.): ICONIP 2021, CCIS 1516, pp. 583–590, 2021.
https://doi.org/10.1007/978-3-030-92307-5_68

for RSNNs are variants of RTRL and BPTT. Tino et al. [3] extended the existing gradient-based SpikeProp algorithm into RSNNs. Diehl et al. [4] proposed a train-and-constrain methodology that maps the BPTT on a substrate of spiking neurons, it first trains RNNs using BPTT, then coverts the discretized weights to RSNNs. Another effective learning algorithm was proposed by Kuroe et al. [5] based on adjoint equation, which reduces the calculation time significantly.

In recent studies, researchers have introduced STDP learning mechanism into RSNNs. Brea et al. [6] minimized the upper bound of Kullback-Leibler (KL) divergence, and proposed a general synaptic learning rule that matches neural dynamics. Thiele et al. [7] proposed an algorithm called "wake-sleep" to solve the following problem: when training with high learning rate in RSNNs with STDP learning mechanism, recurrent connections in the network dynamics will result strong feedback loops. Gilra et al. [8] proposed a supervised learning rule called feedback-based online local learning of weights (FOLLOW). Wang et al. [9] compared the learning efficiency of FOLLOW algorithm and R-STKLR algorithm in a review paper on supervised learning algorithms for SNNs.

In this paper, we propose a supervised learning method for RSNNs based on BP-STDP [10]. On the basis of mapping Integrate-and-Fire neuron model to rectified linear unit (ReLU) activation function to solve discontinous problem in SNNs, we apply STDP and BPTT learning rules to RSNNs and propose the supervised learning algorithm. Finally, the effectiveness of the proposed algorithm is verified on spike train learning task and non-linear pattern classification experiment while the influences of different parameters on learning effect are analyzed.

2   Supervised Learning Algorithm: BP-STDP for RSNNs

2.1   Mapping the LIF Neuron Model to ReLU Activation Function

The membrane potential $U(t)$ of leaky-free LIF neuron at time t is expressed as:

$$U(t) = U(t - \Delta t) + \sum_n w_n(t) s_n(t) \tag{1}$$

where Δt is time step, $s_n(t)$ and $w_n(t)$ are spike and synaptic weight of presynaptic neuron n at time t. And the presynaptic spike train $G_n(t)$ in time interval T is given by:

$$G_n(t) = \sum_{t_n^p \in \{s_n(t)=1\}} \delta(t - t_n^p) \tag{2}$$

where $\delta(t)$ is Dirac function that $\delta(t) = 1$ if $t = 0$, otherwise $\delta(t) = 1$. In a period$(t - \alpha, t]$ of two consecutive postsynaptic spikes $r(t - \alpha)$ and $r(t)$, the membrane potential of a neuron can be expressed as:

$$U(t) = \sum_n w_n \left(\int_{t-\alpha}^t \sum_{t_n^p} \delta(t' - t_n^p) \, dt' \right) \tag{3}$$

Assuming that the LIF neuron is leaky-free, and the membrane potential is reset to 0 when a spike is fired. Thus, the accumulative membrane potential U^{sum} in time interval T is linear sum of membrane potentials in sub-interval $(t - \alpha, t]$:

$$U^{sum} = \hat{y} = \sum_{t^f \in \{r(t)=1\}} U\left(t^f\right) \tag{4}$$

Combining with ReLU activation function, the activation function for LIF neuron can be defined as follows, in which θ is threshold of ReLU, and γ is a constant.

$$f(\hat{y}) = \begin{cases} R = \gamma\hat{y}, & \gamma\hat{y} > \theta \\ 0, other \end{cases} \tag{5}$$

2.2 BP-STDP Learning Rule for RSNNs

In RNNs with M neurons in output layer, the error function is defined as:

$$E = \frac{1}{2} \sum_{o=1}^{M} (d_o - o_o)^2 \tag{6}$$

where d_o and o_o are desired and actual output. However, the input and output in RSNN are spike trains, which are shown in Fig. 1.

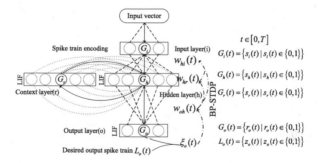

Fig. 1. Structure and parameters of recurrent spiking neural network.

Synaptic Weight Learning Rules for Output Layer. In ReLU neuron model adopting error backpropagation and gradient descent rules, the synaptic weight change Δw_{oh} between hidden layer neuron h and output layer neuron o is:

$$\Delta w_{oh} = -\eta \frac{\partial E}{\partial w_{oh}} = -\eta \frac{\partial E}{\partial o_o} \cdot \frac{\partial o_o}{\partial w_{oh}}$$

$$= -\eta \frac{\partial \left[\frac{1}{2} \sum_{o=1}^{N_o} (d_o - o_o)^2 \right]}{\partial o_o} \frac{\partial \sum_{h=1}^{N_h} \left(w_{oh} + \sum_{r=1}^{N_r} w_{hr} w_{or} \right)}{\partial w_{oh}} = \eta (d_o - o_o) o_h \tag{7}$$

where η is learning rate, o_o and o_h are outputs of neuron o in output layer and neuron h in hidden layer. We assume that the desired and actural output spike trains are $L_o(t)$ and $G_o(t)$ in output layer and the output spike trains $G_h(t)$ in hidden layer in RSNNs respectively correspond to d_o, o_o, o_h in RNNs, and $L_o(t)$, $G_o(t)$ and $G_h(t)$ can be represented as Eq. 2. Thus, in RSNNs, the change of w_{oh} during time interval T can be defined as:

$$\Delta w_{oh} = \eta \int_0^T [L_o(t) - G_o(t)]\, dt \int_0^T G_h(t)\, dt \qquad (8)$$

To enable the learning rule local in time, we divide the time interval T into several sub-intervals during which only 0 or 1 spike is fired. In the short sub-interval, the learning rule can be expressed as:

$$\Delta w_{oh}(t) = \eta \varepsilon_o(t) \sum_{t'=t-\varepsilon}^{t} s_h(t') \qquad (9)$$

where $\varepsilon_o(t)$ is a simplification of STDP learning rule that when the pre-synaptic neuron fire a spike before the post-synaptic neuron, the synaptic connection is strengthened, conversely, the synaptic connection is weakened. It is defined as:

$$\varepsilon_o(t) = z_o(t) - r_o(t) = \begin{cases} 1, z_o(t) = 1, r_o(t) = 0 \ in \ [t-\varepsilon] \\ -1, z_o(t) = 1, r_o(t) = 1 \ in \ [t-\varepsilon] \\ 0, otherwise \end{cases} \qquad (10)$$

Synaptic Weight Learning Rules for Context Layer. It is similar to the output layer that the synaptic weight change Δw_{hr} between neuron h in hidden layer and neuron r in context layer can be expressed as:

$$\Delta w_{hr} = -\eta \frac{\partial E}{\partial w_{hr}} = -\eta \sum_{o=1}^{N_o} \frac{\partial E}{\partial o_o} \cdot \frac{\partial o_o}{\partial o_h} \cdot \frac{\partial o_h}{\partial w_{hr}}$$
$$= \eta \sum_{o=1}^{N_o} (d_o - o_o) \cdot \left(w_{oh} + \sum_{r=1}^{N_r} w_{hr} w_{or} \right) \cdot o_r, \ o_h > 0 \qquad (11)$$

Combing the STDP learning rule with Eq. 11, the change of w_{hr} in RSNNs during time interval T can be defined as:

$$\Delta w_{hr} = \eta \sum_{o=1}^{N_o} \int_0^T \varepsilon_o(t) \left(w_{oh}(t) + \sum_{r=1}^{N_r} w_{hr}(t) w_{or}(t) \right) dt \int_0^T \sum_{t_h^p} \delta(t - t_h^p) dt,$$
$$\int_0^T \sum_{t_h^p} \delta(t - t_h^p) dt > 0 \qquad (12)$$

To enable the learning rule local in time, we divide the time interval T into several sub intervals during which only 0 or 1 spike is fired. In the sub-interval, the update rule of w_{hr} can be expressed as:

$$\Delta w_{hr}(t) = \begin{cases} \eta \sum_{o=1}^{N_o} \varepsilon_o(t) \left(w_{oh}(t) + \sum_{r=1}^{N_r} w_{hr}(t) w_{or}(t) \right) \sum_{t'=t-\varepsilon}^{t} s_r(t'), & s_h(t) = 1 \, in \, [t', t] \\ 0, \, otherwise \end{cases} \quad (13)$$

Synaptic Weight Learning Rules for Hidden Layer. As is in context layer, the update of w_{hi} can be expressed as:

$$\Delta w_{hi} = -\eta \frac{\partial E}{\partial w_{hi}} = -\eta \frac{\partial E}{\partial o_h} \frac{\partial o_h}{\partial w_{hi}} = \eta (d_o - o_o) \sum_{o=1}^{N_o} \left(w_{oh} + \sum_{r=1}^{N_r} w_{hr} wor \right) o_i, \quad o_h > 0 \tag{14}$$

By introducing the STDP learning rule into Eq. 14, the change of w_{hi} in RSNNs during time interval T can be defined as:

$$\Delta w_{hi} = \eta \sum_{o=1}^{N_o} \int_0^T \varepsilon(t) \left(w_{oh} + \sum_{r=1}^{N_r} w_{hr(t) w_{or}(t)} \right) dt \int_0^T \sum_{t_h^p} \delta \left(t - t_h^p \right) dt,$$

$$\int_0^T \sum_{t_h^p} \delta \left(t - t_h^p \right) dt > 0 \tag{15}$$

As is Eq. 13, to enable the learning rule local in time, the update rule of w_{hi} in sub-interval during which only 0 or 1 spike is fired can be expressed as:

$$\Delta w_{hi}(t) = \begin{cases} \eta \sum_{o=1}^{N_o} \varepsilon_o(t) \left(w_{oh}(t) + \sum_{r=1}^{N_r} w_{hr}(t) w_{or}(t) \right) \sum_{t'=t-\varepsilon}^{t} s_i(t'), & s_h(t) = 1 \, in \, [t', t] \\ 0, \, otherwise \end{cases} \quad (16)$$

3   Experiment and Result

3.1   Spike Train Learning Tasks

In this section, we evaluate our algorithm based on different parameters by comparing with the result of FOLLOW algorithm in the same conditions. All the following experimental results are the average of 5 trials. Learning epochs of the algorithm is 100 for each trial. The parameters used in experimental simulation are as follows: threshold θ_{LIF} and resting potential U_{rest} are 1 and 0 for LIF neuron model. Numbers of neurons in input layer, hidden layer, output layer are 10, 20, 1 respectively. Desired output spike frequency r_{out} 50 Hz, length of spike train Γ is 100 ms, connectivity degree C is 0.5, synaptic weights are in range of [0, 0.3], learning rate η is 0.0001.

Figure 2(a) illustrates accuracies of two algorithms are both increase first and then decrease as length of spike train increases, and they reach the maximum value when spike train length is 100 ms. Figure 2(b) shows that the average learning accuracy reaches 0.7776 when the spike firing frequency is 50 Hz.

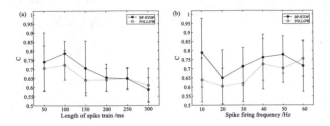

Fig. 2. (a) The accuracies for different lengths of spike train, (b) The learning results for different spike firing frequency.

It is illustrated in Fig. 3(a) that learning accuracy of BP-STDP increases as the connectivity degree increases while the running speed of program will slow down, which is set 0.5 in other experiments by a comprehensive trade off. Figure 3(b) depicts that accuracies of BP-STDP and FOLLOW increase as the hidden neurons number increases, when it is 20, the accuracy of BP-STDP is highest.

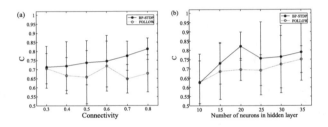

Fig. 3. (a) The accuracies for different connectivity, (b) The accuracies for different number of neurons in hidden layer.

3.2 Non-linear Pattern Classification

In this section, the ability to classify nonlinear patterns of the proposed algorithm is evaluated by comparing the classification results on WBC and Iris datasets with that of the FOLLOW algorithm.

In the experiment on WBC dataset, the 683 WBC samples are randomly divided into 350 training samples and 333 test samples. Each sample contains 9 attributes and 1 category label. The RSNN for experiment on WBC dataset contains 9 input layer neurons, 50 hidden layer neurons, and 1 output layer neuron. The synaptic weights are randomly generated in the range of [0, 0.3], the learning rates are 0.002 and 0.005 for the proposed algorithm and FOLLOW respectively. As the inputs of RSNN, 9 attributes are normalized and encoded to 9 spike trains with a frequency between 30 Hz and 50 Hz in time interval [0, 50 ms] by a linear encode method. 32 Hz and 38 Hz are used as linear encoding frequency to generate two desired spike trains representing benign and malignant tumors.

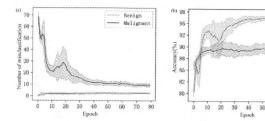

Fig. 4. (a) Average number of samples misclassified by BP-STDP on training set, (b) The trend of classification accuracy of BP-STDP and FOLLOW as epoch increases.

Figure 4(a) shows that the numbers of misclassified samples are 2.6 and 9.4 for benign and malignant tumors. Figure 4(b) illustrates that the classification accuracies of two algorithms both increase with slight fluctuation as the epoch increases. The classification accuracy of BP-STDP is finally 96.57%, higher than that of FOLLOW, 89.94%.

The Fisher Iris dataset is also a commonly used benchmark dataset in pattern classification. 150 samples are randomly divided into 75 training samples and 75 test samples in this experiment, each sample contains 4 attributes and 1 category label. The RSNN for experiment on Fisher Iris dataset contains 4 input layer neurons, 50 hidden layer neurons and 1 output layer neuron. The learning rate are 0.0005 and 0.005 for the proposed algorithm and FOLLOW respectively. The initialization of synaptic weight and encoding of input are same as experiment for WBC dataset. 32 Hz, 36 Hz and 44 Hz are used as linear encoding frequency to generate desired spike trains representing Setosa, Versicolor and Virginica, respectively.

Figure 5(a) illustrates the numbers of samples misclassified are 0.4 in Setosa, 3.8 in Versicolor, and 3.8 in Virginica. It can be seen in Fig. 5(b) that the classification accuracy of BP-STDP rises rapidly in the initial stage and finally reaches 89.33% after slight fluctuation, which is comparable with that of FOLLOW.

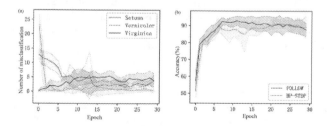

Fig. 5. (a) Average number of samples misclassified by BP-STDP on the training set, (b) Classification accuracies trend of BP-STDP and FOLLOW as the epoch increases.

4   Conclusion

Training RSNNs has been attracting an aroused research interest. Due to the recurrent connection and the use of spike time coding, learning through RSNNs is a relatively difficult task. A supervised learning algorithm to train RSNNs is proposed in this paper as an attempt to enrich the research results in this field. As the basis to apply error-backpropagation to SNNs, The LIF neuron model is mapped to the ReLU activation function. To imitate the learning process of the brain better and make the algorithm more biologically interpretable, STDP learning mechanism is combined with BPTT and formulates the learning algorithm for RSNNs proposed in this paper. It is proved through spike train learning task and nonlinear pattern classification on WBC and Fisher Iris datasets that the proposed algorithm is promising. Meanwhile, the influences of different parameters on the spike train learning effect are analyzed. All experimental results are compared with that of the FOLLOW algorithm.

Acknowledgments. This work was supported by the National Natural Science Foundation of China under grant no. 61762080, the Key Research and Development Project of Gansu Province under grant no. 20YF8GA049, the Youth Science and Technology Fund Project of Gansu Province under grant no. 20JR10RA097, the Lanzhou Municipal Science and Technology Project under grant no. 2019-1-34.

References

1. Chang, F.J., Chang, L.C., Huang, H.L.: Real-time recurrent learning neural network for stream-flow forecasting. Hydrol. Process. **16**(13), 2577–2588 (2002)
2. Werbos, P.J.: Backpropagation through time: what it does and how to do it. Proc. IEEE **78**(10), 1550–1560 (1990)
3. Bohte, S.M., Kok, J.N., La Poutre, H.: Error-backpropagation in temporally encoded net-works of spiking neurons. Neurocomputing **48**(1–4), 17–37 (2002)
4. Diehl, P.U., Zarrella, G., Cassidy, A. (eds.): Conversion of artificial recurrent neural net-works to spiking neural networks for low-power neuromorphic hardware. In: 2016 IEEE International Conference on Rebooting Computing (ICRC) (2016)
5. Kuroe, Y., Ueyama, T.: Learning methods of recurrent Spiking Neural Networks based on adjoint equations approach. In: The 2010 International Joint Conference on Neural Networks (IJCNN). IEEE (2010)
6. Brea, J., Senn, W., Pfister, J.P.: Matching recall and storage in sequence learning with spiking neural networks. J. Neurosci. **33**(23), 9565–9575 (2013)
7. Thiele, J., Diehl, P., Cook, M.: A wake-sleep algorithm for recurrent, spiking neural networks (2017)
8. Gilra, A., Gerstner, W.: Predicting non-linear dynamics by stable local learning in a recurrent spiking neural network. Elife **6**, e28295 (2017)
9. Wang, X., Lin, X., Dang, X.: Supervised learning in spiking neural networks: a review of algorithms and evaluations. Neural Netw. **125**, 258–280 (2020)
10. Tavanaei, A., Maida, A.: BP-STDP: approximating backpropagation using spike timing dependent plasticity. Neurocomputing **330**(FEB.22), 39–47 (2019)

Incorporating Neighborhood Information During NMF Learning

Michel Kaddouh[1,2], Guénaël Cabanes[1,2(✉)], and Younès Bennani[1,2]

[1] LIPN UMR 7030 CNRS, Université Sorbonne Paris Nord, Villetaneuse, France
{michel.kaddouh,guenael.cabanes,younes.bennani}@sorbonne-paris-nord.fr
[2] LaMSN, La Maison des Sciences Numériques, USPN, Villetaneuse, France

Abstract. Self-Organizing Map is an algorithm that computes a set of artificial neurons to model the distribution of a data-set. This model is composed of a graph of neurons connected by neighborhood links. The main advantage of a SOM model is the conservation of a low-dimensional topology, which allows a visual representation of the data distribution. It is a non-linear projection that preserves the neighborhood, while reducing both the dimensions and the size of the data. In this paper, we propose a modified version of the convex Non-negative Matrix Factorization to compute a similar projection. Experimental results show that the proposed algorithm significantly decreases the topological error in comparison to SOM, without loss of computational speed.

Keywords: Unsupervised learning · Artificial neural network · Self-organizing map (SOM) · Non-negative matrix factorization (NMF)

1 Introduction

Machine learning is a branch of artificial intelligence aiming at producing computer models from data. In the case of supervised learning, the obtained models are generally used to predict an unknown feature (regression) or the membership in one or more classes (classification). The learning algorithm has access to examples labeled with the values to be predicted, in order to design a model able to map the inputs data with the expected outputs prediction. On the contrary, in the unsupervised case, there is no target variable to predict and the algorithm has only access to unlabeled data. The objective is then to learn from the data-set a model of the distribution of these data.

Among the many existing approaches for unsupervised learning, those based on the learning of prototypes, i.e. objects of the representation space representing a subset of the data, are particularly studied because of their interesting scaling characteristics: very compact models and low complexity in time and memory. The best known algorithm in this category is the K-means algorithm [1] and all its derivatives. There are however other approaches to compute prototypes. One can for example mention the algorithms based on Non-negative Matrix Factorization (NMF), which decompose the data into the product of two or more

© Springer Nature Switzerland AG 2021
T. Mantoro et al. (Eds.): ICONIP 2021, CCIS 1516, pp. 591–598, 2021.
https://doi.org/10.1007/978-3-030-92307-5_69

matrices, one of which can in some cases be interpreted as a prototype matrix [2]. In addition, prototype-based unsupervised neural network approaches are fast and efficient, including the Self-Organizing Maps family [3], Neural Gas [4], and their extensions [5,6].

In this article, we focus on the Self-Organizing Map (SOM). SOM is an algorithm that computes a set of artificial neurons to model the distribution of potentially high dimensional data in the form of a low dimensional "map" (usually one or two dimensions). This map is composed of a graph of neurons connected by neighborhood links. Each neuron is associated with a prototype (the neuron's weight vector) and the graph maintains a uni or bi-dimensional topology during learning. When two neurons are connected by a neighborhood link, they should represent similar data, and vice versa. These properties are set up during the learning process by using neighborhood information as topological constraints. If a neuron is activated by a data point, its neighbors are also activated, to a lesser degree.

The main advantage of a SOM model is the conservation of a low-dimensional topology, which allows a visual representation of the data distribution projected on the map. It is a non-linear projection that preserves the neighborhood, while reducing both the dimensions and the size of the data. The Batch version of the algorithm [7] is known for its speed of execution and is the most widely used. However, during training, the deployment of the map can be hampered by the existence of local minima that can result in significant distortions when projecting the data onto the map [8,9]. The most common distortions are: the "folding" of the map on itself, resulting in similar data projected on distant neurons on the map, or a poor coverage of the peripheral areas of the representation space, less dense, resulting in dissimilar data projected on nearby neurons on the map [10].

In this paper, we propose to rewrite the SOM algorithm in the Non-negative Matrix Factorization (NMF) formalism, which is becoming increasingly popular in the field of dimension reduction and clustering because of its convergence and stability properties [11,12]. In particular, it has been shown [13] that the K-means algorithm can be rewritten as a decomposition of a matrix of prototypes representing data clusters and a matrix of membership of the data to each cluster. This decomposition presents very good results for the computation of prototypes. We show here that the NMF formalism for learning the weights of a SOM reduces the risk of distortion of the map, and thus improves the conservation of the neighborhood properties of the data projected on the map, without loss of computational speed.

In the remainder of this paper, we present the SOM algorithm in Sect. 2 and different families of NMFs in Sect. 3. The new SOM-NMF algorithm is described in Sect. 4. We detail the experimental protocol and the results in Sect. 5, before concluding in Sect. 6.

2   Self-organizing Map

A Self-Organizing Map is a two-dimensional network of r neurons connected depending on the n input data and their neighborhood relationship. The topology of the network is fixed at the beginning of the training process. The number of neurons r defines the compactness of the model and the computational load of the training. An efficient rule of thumb is to scale the number of neurons to the square root of the number of data inputs [14]. Here we use $r = 5\sqrt{n}$.

The connections network between the neurons are chosen to have a low dimensional topology, usually one or two. The network forms a 2D "map" of neurons i, each associated to a prototype vector w_i defined in the same representation space as the data. The number of neurons in the rows and columns of the map, as well as the initial values of the prototypes, can be defined from the same space spanned by the linear principal component of the data: the prototypes are initialized on the plane defined by the two first eigenvectors, the ratio of the number of neurons in the rows and columns is adjusted to correspond to the ratio of the two first eigenvalues (see [15]).

During the training of the map, each input data $\mathbf{x^i}$ is associated to its "Best Matching Unit" (BMU) $B(x^{(i)})$: i.e. the neuron having the closest weight vector according to the euclidean distance. The prototype of the BMU is updated in order to decrease this distance, and the prototypes of its neighbors are updated the same way, to a lesser degree depending on how close they are to the BMU on the map network. This neighborhood is computed with the following function:

$$K_{kl} = \exp(-\frac{d^2(k,l)}{2\sigma^2(t)}),$$
(1)

where $d^2(k,l)$ is the squared distance between neurons k and l on the map (usually the Manhattan distance) and σ is the neighborhood coefficient, decreasing over time.

The training is often carried out by the minimization of the distance between the input data $\mathbf{x^i}$ and the prototypes $\mathbf{w_j}$, weighted by the neighborhood function K. This cost function to be minimized is defined by:

$$J(W) = \sum_{i=1}^{n} \sum_{j=1}^{r} K_{jB(x^i)} ||\mathbf{x^i} - \mathbf{w_j}||^2.$$
(2)

3   Non-negative Matrix Factorization

Non-negative Matrix Factorization (NMF) aims at factorizing a matrix X into two matrices F and G, where $X \in \mathbb{R}^{m \times n}$, $F \in \mathbb{R}^{m \times r}$, $G \in \mathbb{R}^{n \times r}$ and r is a chosen value usually smaller than m and n [13].

F is the features matrix and G the coefficients matrix. F and G are non-negative, such that:

$$X \simeq F_+ G_+^T.$$
(3)

The learning of the two matrices is the minimization of a cost function:

$$J(FG) = ||X - FG^T||^2, \tag{4}$$

usually done by using Lee and Seung's multiplicative update rule [2].

Semi-NMF is useful when X contains negative values. In this case, the main difference with NMF is that F can have negative values:

$$X \simeq FG_+^T. \tag{5}$$

In Convex-NMF, we want F to be interpreted by prototypes capturing the centers of gravity of the clusters. Therefore, F is constrained to be a linear combination of the data matrix: $F = XW$ where $W \in \mathbb{R}^{n \times r}$. We obtain:

$$X \simeq XW_+ G_+^T. \tag{6}$$

Cluster-NMF is an adaptation of Convex-NMF, where the columns of F are required to be convex combinations of the input data. The inputs of G are interpreted as *a posteriori* cluster probabilities. In this case, the cluster centroids can be computed as $F = XGD_n^{-1}$, with $D_n = diag(n_1, \ldots, n_k)$ and n_k the number of inputs of cluster k. We obtain:

$$X \simeq XGD_n^{-1}G_+^T. \tag{7}$$

4   The Proposed Approach: SOM-NMF

The idea of the proposed algorithm is to compute the prototypes of a SOM using a Convex-NMF with topological constraints:

$$X \simeq FKG_+^T, \tag{8}$$

where $X \in \mathbb{R}^{m \times n}$ is the data matrix, $K \in \mathbb{R}^{r \times r}$ the matrix representing the neighborhood function (always positive), $F \in \mathbb{R}^{m \times r}$ the matrix of prototype vectors and $G \in \mathbb{R}^{r \times n}$ the partition matrix. Matrix K contains the distances between neurons on the map and encodes the information on the topological constraints.

Let $A = GK$, with $A \in \mathbb{R}^{n \times r}$, therefore:

$$X \simeq FA_+^T. \tag{9}$$

The update of F and G follows the formalism of Convex-NMF, and more precisely the one of Cluster-NMF. Therefore, we have:

$$X \simeq XAD_n^{-1}A^T. \tag{10}$$

To update G, we use the following equation:

$$G_{ij} \leftarrow A_{ij} \sqrt{\frac{(X^TF)_{ij}^+ + [A(F^TF)^-]_{ij}}{(X^TF)_{ij}^- + [A(F^TF)^+]_{ij}}}. \tag{11}$$

The update of F is straightforward:

$$F = XAD_n^{-1}. \tag{12}$$

The algorithm is detailed in Algorithm 1.

Algorithm 1: SOM-NMF

Input : matrix X of dimension $m \times n$, the input dataset with m data and n dimensions

Output: matrix F of dimension $m \times r$ (the prototype vectors) and matrix G of dimension $n \times r$ (the partition matrix).

Initialization :

$r = 5\sqrt{n}$;

Initialize the topology of the map and the prototype matrix F using a linear principal component analysis (see [15]) ;

$G[i,j] = 1$ if neuron j is the BMU of data i, else $G[i,j] = 0$;

while *F and G have not converged* **do**

  $\quad K \leftarrow$ neighborhood function, using Eq. (1) ;

  $\quad$ Update F with Eq. (12) ;

  $\quad$ Update G with Eq. (11).

end

To implement the proposed algorithm we used Python 3.7 with the packages Somperf [16] (to compute quantization and topological errors), Sompy [17] (the SOM algorithm) and PyMF [18] (the NMF algorithms).

The experimental tests were computed on a processor AMD Ryzen 5 2500U with Radeon Vega Mobile Gfx 2.00 GHz and 8 Go RAM.

5   Experimental Results

To test the validity of the SOM-NMF algorithm, we used several data-sets with different numbers of data and features. Data-sets "Iris", "Wine", "Leaf", "Breast cancer", "Bank", "Parkinson", "Air quality", "Dry bean", "Avila" and "Superconductivity" come from the UCI repository [19]. These data-sets reflect the diversity of the modeling problems that can be encountered. We chose a mix of different sizes and dimensions, from 150×4 (Iris) to 21263×82 (Superconductivity).

For the following experiments, we run for each index all the algorithms 30 times to get the mean and the standard error. In addition to the computation time, we chose two indexes of quality: the topographic error [20] and the quantization error [3]. A relative score is then computed for each algorithm and each index. This score indicates how well an algorithm performs globally on all of the data-sets in comparison to the other algorithms:

$$Sc(k) = 1 - \frac{1}{D} \sum_{d=1}^{D} \frac{d^a}{\max_i(d^i)}, \tag{13}$$

where D is the number of data-sets, d^a is the quality index for the data-set number d and algorithm a. The score depends on the quality of all of the tested algorithms. The higher the score of an algorithm, the better.

Table 1. Computation time (in seconds) for each algorithm and each data-set.

Data-sets	SOM-NMF	SOM	Semi-NMF	Convex-NMF
Iris	2.1e-3 ± 7.53e-5	3.43 ± 0.04	1e-3 ± 1.24e-18	0.03 ± 3.0e-3
Wine	5.4e-3 ± 2.87	0.24 ± 3.3e-3	2.4e-3 ± 1.0e-4	4.4e-2 ± 2.1e-3
Leaf	3.6e-3 ± 2.21	3e-3 ± 1.0e-1	2.4e-3 ± 1.0e-4	0.07 ± 0.005
Breast C	9.8e-3 ± 3.0e-4	1.78 ± 3.0e-3	8.0e-3 ± 4.0e-4	0.19 ± 1.4e-2
Bank	3.5e-2 ± 1.6e-3	1.23 ± 2.0e-3	3.4e-2 ± 2.0e-3	0.49 ± 2.3e-2
Parkinsons	0.37 ± 1.6e-2	0.65 ± 3.0e-3	0.34 ± 1.9e-2	7.72 ± 0.17
Air quality	0.77 ± 0.05	0.86 ± 4.6e-2	0.7 ± 3.6e-2	17.1 ± 0.41
Dry bean	1.70 ± 0.05	1.04 ± 4.0e-3	1.58 ± 3.4e-2	69.1 ± 1.24
Letter	2.96 ± 8.8e-2	1.61 ± 0.04	2.69 ± 0.06	507.3 ± 9.7
Avila	3.01 ± 0.1	1.64 ± 0.04	2.75 ± 5.3e-2	742.37 ± 13.12
Superconductivity	3.20 ± 0.11	2.68 ± 0.2	3.16 ± 6.2e-2	745.49 ± 9.11
Score	0.97	0.62	0.98	0.3

Table 2. Quantization error for each algorithm and each data-set.

Data-sets	SOM-NMF	SOM	Semi-NMF	Convex-NMF
Iris	0.31 ± 4.0e-17	0.31 ± 1.98e-17	6.32 ± 0.08	0.60 ± 2.0e-3
Wine	5.3e-3 ± 6.2e-19	6.7e-3 ± 6.2e-19	0.91 ± 5.3e-3	5.1e-2 ± 7.3e-5
Leaf	0.13 ± 0	9.3e-2 ± 9.93e-18	0.91 ± 1.8e-2	0.15 ± 8.0e-4
Breast cancer	1.5e-2 ± 6.2e-19	1.6e-2 ± 1.2e-18	0.96 ± 2.5e-3	2.4e-2 ± 2.0e-3
Bank	0.19 ± 1.98e-17	0.14 ± 1.99e-17	0.84 ± 3.0e-3	0.61 ± 3.0e-3
Parkinsons	4.3e-2 ± 4.97e-18	4.2e-2 ± 4.97e-18	0.98 ± 3.0e-3	0.2 ± 2.0e-3
Air quality	9.6e-2 ± 0	5.8e-2 ± 9.93e-18	0.96 ± 1.0e-3	0.64 ± 0.01
Dry bean	1.4e-4 ± 0	3.2e-4 ± 5.81e-19	0.99 ± 8.4e-5	1.8e-3 ± 5.1e-6
Letter	0.2 ± 2.3e-7	0.15 ± 7.64e-5	0.99 ± 6.6e-6	0.28 ± 7.86e-5
Avila	0.60 ± 3.97e-17	0.40 ± 3.97e-17	0.97 ± 3.0e-4	0.87 ± 6.0e-4
Superconductivity	5.5e-2 ± 9.93e-18	5.2e-2 ± 4.49e-17	0.98 ± 3.0e-4	0.31 ± 8.0e-4
Score	0.87	0.90	0.0	0.69

We compared the proposed algorithm, SOM-NMF, with the classical SOM as coded in the Python package SOMPy [17], and with the Semi-NMF and Convex-NMF algorithms as coded in the package PyMF [18]. Please note that the SOM algorithm in SOMPy have a stop constraint t_{max} equal to the minimum between t_{max} and the number of neurons divided by the size of the data-set, meaning that big data-sets require fewer iterations. This is visible in Table 1.

Table 3. Topographic error for each algorithm and each data-set.

Data-sets	SOM-NMF	SOM
Iris	0.20 ± 0	0.55 ± 0
Wine	0.045 ± 7.45e-18	0.51 ± 3.97e-17
Leaf	0.17 ± 9.93e-18	0.24 ± 7.94e-18
Brest C	0.058 ± 4.97e-18	0.46 ± 3.37e-17
Bank	0.19 ± 1.98e-17	0.11 ± 4.96e-18
Parkinsons	0.044 ± 2.48e-18	0.34 ± 1.98e-17
Air Q	0.21 ± 1.98e-17	0.41 ± 3.97e-17
Dry B	0.032 ± 2.48e-17	0.50 ± 0
Letter	0.15 ± 1.6e-5	0.18 ± 7e-4
Avila	0.16 ± 2.97e-17	0.59 ± 0
Superconductivity	0.11 ± 9.93e-18	0.20 ± 9.93e-18
Score	0.58	0.04

These results lead to several remarks. Semi-NMF is generally the fastest algorithm. However, SOM-NMF is almost equivalent to Semi-NMF and globally faster than SOM. The Quantization error is approximately equal for SOM and SOM-NMF, SOM being relatively slightly better. Both are much better than the other algorithms (see Table 2). In comparison to SOM, in SOM-NMF we observe a significant decrease of the topographic error for almost all the data-sets (Table 3). This shows that SOM-NMF avoids most of the topological distortions that can appear in the SOM model. The global topology is better preserved, at the cost of a slight decrease of the local representation.

6   Conclusion

The proposed approach is based on the principle of the Self-Organizing Map, which uses neighborhood constraints to conserve a low-dimensional topology. The approach is a version of the convex Non-negative Matrix Factorization taking into account the neighborhood constraints to compute a projection similar to the SOM. We added a new matrix in the factorization to take into account the expected topology of the projection, similarly to the neighborhood function of the SOM. The resulting prototype matrix preserves the topological relationship between the data input. Experimental results show that the proposed algorithm significantly decreases the topographic error in comparison to SOM, without notable loss of computational speed. In addition, the obtained prototype matrix is a better representation of the data than classical NMF.

References

1. MacQueen, J.B.: Some methods for classification and analysis of multivariate observations. In: Proceedings of 5th Berkeley Symposium on Mathematical Statistics and Probability, vol. 1, pp. 281–297. University of California Press (1967)
2. Lee, D., Seung, H.: Algorithms for non-negative matrix factorization. In: Advances in Neural Information Processing Systems 13: Proceedings of the 2000 Conference, pp. 556–562. MIT Press (2000)
3. Kohonen, T.: Self-organizing Maps. Springer, Heidelberg (2001)
4. Martinetz, T., Schulten, K.: A "neural gas" network learns topologies. In: Artificial Neural Networks, pp. 397–402. Elsevier (1991)
5. Cottrell, M., Barbara, H., Hasenfuß, T., Villmann, T.: Batch and median neural gas. Neural Netw. **19**(6–7), 762–771 (2006)
6. Cabanes, G., Bennani, Y., Fresneau, D.: Enriched topological learning for cluster detection and visualization. Neural Netw. **32**, 186–195 (2012)
7. Boulet, R., Jouve, B., Rossi, F., Villa, N.: Batch Kernel SOM and related Laplacian methods for social network analysis. Neurocomputing **71**(7–9), 1257–1273 (2008)
8. Rynkiewicz, J.: Self-organizing map algorithm and distortion measure. Neural Netw. **19**(6–7), 830–837 (2006)
9. Cabanes, G., Bennani, Y.: A simultaneous two-level clustering algorithm for automatic model selection. In: Sixth International Conference on Machine Learning and Applications (ICMLA), pp. 316–321 (2007)
10. Aupetit, M.: Visualizing distortions in dimension reduction techniques. In: European Symposium on Artificial Neural Networks (ESANN), pp. 465–470 (2004)
11. Wang, Y.-X., Zhang, Y.-J.: Nonnegative matrix factorization: a comprehensive review. IEEE Trans. Knowl. Data Eng. **25**(6), 1336–1353 (2013)
12. Badeau, R., Bertin, N., Vincent, E.: Stability analysis of multiplicative update algorithms and application to nonnegative matrix factorization. IEEE Trans. Neural Netw. **21**(12), 1869–1881 (2010)
13. Ding, C., Lie, D., Jordan, M.: Convex and semi-nonnegative matrix factorizations. IEEE Trans. Pattern Anal. Mach. Intell. **32**(1), 45–55 (2006)
14. Tian, J., Azarian, M., Pecht, M.: Anomaly detection using self-organizing maps-based K-nearest neighbor algorithm. PHM Soc. Eur. Conf. **2**(1) (2014). https://doi.org/10.36001/phme.2014.v2i1.1554.
15. Attik, M., Bougrain, L., Alexandre, F.: Self-organizing map initialization. In: Duch, W., Kacprzyk, J., Oja, E., Zadrożny, S. (eds.) ICANN 2005. LNCS, vol. 3696, pp. 357–362. Springer, Heidelberg (2005). https://doi.org/10.1007/11550822_56
16. Florest F.: SOMperf: self-organizing maps performance metrics and quality indices. https://github.com/FlorentF9/SOMperf
17. Moosavi, V., Packmann, S.: SOMPY: a python library for self organizing map (SOM) (2014). https://github.com/sevamoo/SOMPY
18. Thurau C.: PyMF - Python Matrix Factorization Module. https://github.com/cthurau/pymf
19. Frank, A., Asuncion, A.: UCI machine learning repository (2010). https://archive.ics.uci.edu/ml/index.php
20. Kiviluoto, K.: Topology preservation in self-organizing maps. In: Proceedings of International Conference on Neural Networks (ICNN 1996), pp. 294–299 (1996)

Efficient Two-Stage Evolutionary Search of Convolutional Neural Architectures Based on Cell Independence Analysis

Boyu Hou[1], Junwei Dong[1], Liang Feng[1(✉)], and Minghui Qiu[2]

[1] Chongqing University, Chongqing 400044, CQ, China
{byhou,jwdong,liangf}@cqu.edu.cn
[2] Alibaba Group, Hangzhou 311121, ZJ, China
minghui.qmh@alibaba-inc.com

Abstract. In the literature, cell-based neural architecture search (NAS) has achieved efficient NAS performance by decomposing the general search space and focusing the search on the micro-architecture. Recently, it has attracted much attention and achieved considerable success in the design of deep convolutional neural networks (CNNs) for vision-oriented tasks, such as image recognition, object detection, etc. However, in most heuristic cell-based NAS methods, the joint optimization of normal cells and reduction cells leads to an extremely time-consuming search. Taking this cue, in this paper, we present a preliminary study on investigating the independence between different cells towards efficient cell-based NAS design. Based on the investigation, we further propose a two-stage search paradigm for cell-based NAS, which can be easily integrated into existing heuristic search methods. To validate the efficacy of the proposed approach, an empirical study has been conducted on the CIFAR-10 dataset, using a genetic algorithm as the basic heuristic solver.

Keywords: Neural architecture search · Automated machine learning · Evolutionary algorithm

1 Introduction

Neural Architecture Search (NAS) has been proposed in anticipation of achieving a deep neural network design methodology that does not rely on expert experience and extensive knowledge, which has shown remarkable performance surpassing manual deep neural network designs in several tasks [5,8,15].

One of the fundamental tasks of NAS is to design the search space, specifically how to encode a neural architecture. A straightforward idea is encoding the entire neural network architecture [9,14], which is often difficult to explore. The researchers then further designed the cell-based search space by incorporating a priori knowledge from the manual design architecture [15], so that only micro-architectures (cells) need to be explored and then stacked in a specific way. Following the design of [15], the cell-based space contains two types of cells, i.e.,

© Springer Nature Switzerland AG 2021
T. Mantoro et al. (Eds.): ICONIP 2021, CCIS 1516, pp. 599–607, 2021.
https://doi.org/10.1007/978-3-030-92307-5_70

normal cell and reduction cell, to facilitate the architecture transfer among different tasks. Cell-based NAS approaches typically consider normal and reduction cells to be correlated, where the searches of two kinds of cells are combined to solve as a higher dimensional problem [5,8,15]. It thus can be envisaged that the search efficiency could be greatly improved if the search performs in two separate parts, i.e., normal cell and reduction cell independently. However, to the best of our knowledge, in the literature, only few works have been devoted to the relationship between the two types of cells in cell-based space, and this paper thus present an attempt to fill this gap.

Particularly, in this paper, we first analyze the relationship between these two types of cells by randomly sampling architectures in the cell-based space with complete training. Based on the analysis, we further propose a two-stage search paradigm. Moreover, to validate the speedup of the proposed approach, empirical studies have been conducted using a genetic algorithm as the basic evolutionary solver.

The rest of this paper is organized as follows. The background of the fundamentals related to the proposed method is discussed in Sect. 2. Next, the details and conclusion of the analysis are described in Sect. 3. The specifics of the proposed method are detailed in Sect. 4. The experiment settings and the numerical results are shown in Sect. 5. Finally, we summarize the conclusions and discuss the for future work in Sect. 6.

2   Related Work

2.1   Efficiency-Targeted NAS

Efficiency-targeted NAS has emerged as a focal topic of research since the excessive computing resource requirements were hindering the industrial adoption of NAS. As described in [13], there is no significant difference in the time spent on decision making among the various search strategies described above, while the heavy computational overhead of NAS comes from estimating the performance of the searched architecture. In order to speed up the performance estimation, most of the work used low-fidelity estimation methods, which includes training fewer epochs [12,15], training on a randomly sampled subset of the original data [5,11], down-sampling the data [5,11], using a reduced model [5,11,15], etc. This may introduce some bias, but the general search strategy relies only on the performance ranking between different architectures.

Another effective class of methods to estimate performance is to avoid training by sharing weights among models, namely one-shot NAS [1,5,6,11]. Such methods construct the search space as a hyper-graph, whose weights are shared among the different architectures to avoid training.

The above approaches mainly focus on how to obtain the performance evaluation of the model under the restricted computational power. In this paper, we consider how to decompose the search problem to reduce the complexity and size of the search, which is orthogonal with the efficient NAS solutions described above.

2.2 Cell-Based Search Space

As mentioned in [15], a cell can be defined as a basic building block with the same structure but different weights. The searched cells are then repeatedly stacked to form a complete network architecture. A Cell contains 2 input nodes, H hidden nodes, and one output node inside, where the nodes are specific tensors while the edges are operations. The information of the input node is derived from the output of the previous 2 cells. Each hidden node takes two inputs from either the input nodes or the hidden nodes in the previous order. Eventually, the results of all the hidden nodes are aggregated to the output node. The spatial sizes of the information are consistent throughout each cell.

Typically, to ensure portability across tasks among different sizes, two types of cells are searched, namely normal cells and reduction cells. A normal cell will keep the input and output spatial size constant, while a reduction cell will reduce the edge length of the feature map by half. In general, a reduction cell is inserted after every B normal cells. The normal cell and the reduction cell together form the complete architecture, therefore they are searched together in general. For instance, Zoph et al. [15] designs the cell architecture as a prediction sequence, which in practice predicts a sequence of twice the length to represent each of the two cells; Real et al. [8] collocates the genes of two cells as the individual encoding.

According to the usual observations, we propose a hypothesis that cells have some independence from each other, i.e. when a series of different normal cells form a model with one reduction cell respectively, there will be an obvious order in their performance. To verify the above hypothesis, we first randomly sampled the architectures in the search space and trained them from scratch to convergence, and analyzed their order correlations. Thanks to Radosavovic et al. [7] and Zheng et al. [13], who concluded that sampling about 100 architectures in a given search space is sufficient to obtain a robust estimate to verify some properties of the search space.

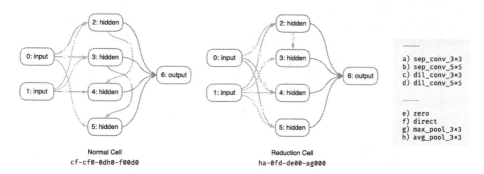

Fig. 1. The best architecture searched by TSGA-Net, including the normal cell and the reduction cell. The red edges represent the convolutional operations, while the green edges represent the parameter-free operations. (Color figure online)

3   Cell Independence Analysis

3.1   Search Space

As the basis for all subsequent processes, we need to determine the architecture search space first. Based on the design of DARTS [5], we restrict a cell architecture containing $H = 4$ hidden nodes. In addition, we surveyed some of the state-of-the-art cell-based NAS works and selected some of the popular operators to be embedded in our cell architecture, which includes: separable convolution with kernel side 3 and 5, dilation convolution with kernel side 3 and 5, zero connection, direct connection, and max pooling and average pooling with kernel side 3. For each hidden node, there are two pieces of information from the input node or the predecessor node as input, and we restrict them to pass through convolutional operations and other operations respectively, as shown in Fig. 1.

3.2   Sampling and Analysis

We reflect the independence between cells by analyzing the correlation between the two cells and the performance respectively. To explore the independence between the two cells, we randomly sampled 10 normal cells and 10 reduction cells respectively, i.e., a total of 100 combinations, following this search space. The sampled models were trained from scratch to convergence on CIFAR-10 dataset by employing the hyper-parameters mentioned in Subsect. 5.1. As shown in Fig. 2a, the rows and columns of the matrix K represent different normal cells and reduction cells, respectively, where $K(i, j)$ is the performance of the model constructed by the i-th normal cell and the j-th reduction cell.

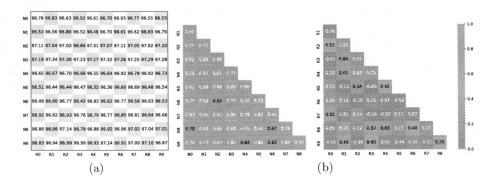

(a)   (b)

Fig. 2. Sampling results and analysis. (a): The classification performance of the model obtained from the combination of the two types of cells, which are trained from scratch to convergence on the CIFAR10 dataset, where $K(i, j)$ means the performance of the model that constructed by N^i and R^j. (b): The Spearman's rank correlation coefficients were obtained with rows and columns, respectively. Since the result is symmetric, only the lower triangle of the matrices is taken. Values in the matrices represent the correlation between the corresponding two cells.

In NAS performance estimation, only order relations are considered. Therefore we adopted Spearman's Rank Correlation as a measure, formally

$$\rho = 1 - \frac{6\sum_{i=1}^{n} d_i^2}{n\left(n^2 - 1\right)}, \tag{1}$$

where $n = 10$ is the number of candidate cells, d_i is the rank of the i-th cell architecture. Figure 2b shows the Spearman's Rank Correlation of normal cells and reduction cells, which are denoted as S_N and S_R, respectively. According to the results from the preliminary analysis, two main observations were obtained: (1) normal cell is the critical factor to determine the final performance, as most of the $s_N \in S_N$ are greater than 0.85; (2) reduction cell shows a very weak correlation, as a majority of $s_R \in S_R$ are less than 0.35, which means two "compatible" cells can achieve better performance but without an obvious pattern.

4   Proposed Method

The preceding observations guided us to design a two-stage search paradigm, i.e., to search for sufficiently high-quality normal cells first according to their strong rank correlation, and then for reduction cell compatible with the searched normal cell. We design a two-stage NAS based on a general GA solver to show how the paradigm works. An initial population of size x is generated, which is made to search for normal cells. To reflect the quality of the normal cell, it will also act as a reduction cell, to construct a model entirely by itself. After the first stage of t_n-generation evolution, we can get an optimal normal cell n^*. Next, a new population is initialized, which is aimed at searching for suitable reduction cells. In this stage, the cells in the population act as reduction cells and constitute models with n^*. After the second stage of evolution, the most compatible reduction cell with n^* can be obtained, namely r^*. We can finally find a pair of cells $\alpha^* = (n^*, r^*)$.

Encoding. To facilitate the evolutionary operations, we encode a cell structure as a fixed-length sequence of characters. The cell encoding contains H parts separated by dash where each corresponds to a hidden node. As each node can only select two of its preorder nodes as input sources, the first hidden node has only two choices, i.e., the two input nodes. Similarly, the k-th hidden node has $k + 1$ choices, which equals the length of the corresponding part. Once the search space is decided, all operations are represented as a single letter, generally in increasing order from "a". The i-th letter in j-th part represents the connection state from node i to node $j + 2$, where 0 means no connection and other operations are indicated by the corresponding letter. As an example, Fig. 1 shows a cell encoding with 4 hidden nodes. A model is encoded by two cells, as for normal cell and reduction cell respectively.

Initialization. We initialize a set of randomized cells as the population. To generate a cell, two of its preorder nodes are firstly selected as the input sources, and then they are assigned to pass through a certain type of operation, which are of the convolution (marked as 1) and other types (marked as 2), respectively. Further, for each non-zero bit, we randomly select the corresponding type of operation according to its value. For example, we first get `12-102-0102-02100` and then fill it as `ag-a0h-0c0e-0fc00`. All samples are based on a uniform distribution.

Crossover and Mutation. In order to preserve the rules of the search space, we use a part-level single-point crossover (see Fig. 3), i.e., the crossover point can only be between parts. The two segments of the code will be cut off at a randomly chosen position and then swap parts of each other. For mutation, a non-zero bit is randomly selected and modified in one of the following ways: change the operation or swap it with another bit among this part. As a rule, operations can only be modified within the same type, e.g., from separable convolution to dilation convolution.

Fig. 3. Example of a crossover between two individuals

Enviromental Selection. To maintain population elitism, we will directly retain the top ϕ proportion of individuals into the next generation of populations. To accommodate diversity, we perform binary tournament selection on the remaining individuals until the next generation of populations is filled.

5   Experiments

5.1   Experimental Settings

To demonstrate the effectiveness of the proposed method, we designed an ablation experiment with a typical GA solver. The difference lies mainly in that all evolutionary operations are performed on both cells simultaneously. In a word, considering that the problem dimension for optimizing a single cell is β, then the ablation experiment is a 2β-dimensional optimization problem.

We extensively refer to the hyper-parameters settings of our competitors to prevent unfairness [5,8]. Particularly, in the ablation experiment, the population size and maximal generation number are set to 20. The probability of crossover and mutation are set to 0.5. As for the proposed method, we designed two sets of parameters named TSGA-Net-A and TSGA-Net-B, respectively. Based on the typical GA setting, TSGA-Net makes adjustments in population size and maximal generation number as shown in Table 1, with maintaining other settings consistent. Overall, our settings reduce the number of performance estimates.

Table 1. Search parameter settings

	Typical GA	TSGA-Net-A	TSGA-Net-B
Population size	20	10	20
Max generation	20	15+5	15+5
Elite rate	0.3	0.3	0.3
Crossover probability	0.5	0.5	0.5
Mutation probability	0.5	0.5	0.5

For the search scenario, a budget model constructed by stacking 5 cells ($B = 1, N = 1$) is trained for 10 epochs with batch size 64. The base number of channels is 18. The training set of CIFAR-10 containing 50,000 images will be equally divided into two subsets, which are used as the training data and the validation data for the performance estimation without any data enhancement methods used. In practice, we train 5 budget models in parallel on a single GPU simultaneously.[1]

For evaluating the exact performance of the searched architectures, we set the hyper-parameters following DARTS [5], where the network consists of 20 cells ($B = 6, N = 2$), and the base number of channels is 36. The complete networks are trained for 600 epochs with batch size 96. As in related works, we also used path dropout with probability 0.2 and auxiliary towers with a weight of 0.4. Moreover, we used data enhancements including random flips, random crop, and cutout [3] with a length of 16. The training takes 1.4 days on a single GPU with implementation in PyTorch.

5.2 Result Analysis

The results are summarized in Table 2. In the end, TSGA-Net-A achieved a classification error rate of 2.51%, which outperformed the typical GA. As the optimal architecture searched by TSGA-Net, the architecture and encoding of the cells are shown in Fig. 1. In addition, more than $2\times$ the speedup was obtained due to reduce the number ($10 \times 20 = 200$) of performance estimations, reducing the computational overhead to within 0.33 GPU days. On the other hand, TSGA-Net-B has the same number ($20 \times 20 = 400$) of performance estimations as to the control experiment, in which case there is no significant difference in computational overhead, but better performance is obtained. At nearly half the computational expense, TSGA-Net-A achieves comparable results to typical GAs; and with the same number of performance estimates, TSGA-Net-B obtains better performance stably.

---

[1] The GPUs used throughout the experiment were NVIDIA RTX 2080Ti.

Table 2. Results of different architectures on CIFAR-10

NAS algorithm	Error rate (%)	GPU days	#Params (M)	Solver
ResNeXt [10]	3.58	–	68.1	Manual
DenseNet-BC [4]	5.19	–	15.3	Manual
NASNet-A [15]	3.41	22400	3.3	RL
ProxylessNAS [2]	2.08	1500	5.7	RL
DARTS + c/o [5]	2.67	1	3.4	GD
PC-DARTS + c/o [11]	2.50	0.1	3.6	GD
AmoebaNet-B-36 + c/o [8]	2.55	3150	2.8	EA
AE-CNN [9]	4.3	27	2.0	EA
Typical GA (ablation) + c/o	2.79	0.83	3.4	EA
TSGA-Net-A (ours) + c/o	2.51	0.33	3.5	EA
TSGA-Net-B (ours) + c/o	2.53	0.75	3.5	EA

However, there are some regrets in the experiment as well. To achieve higher search efficiency, we used a more aggressive low-fidelity performance estimation strategy, resulting in that we did not always get sufficiently good results. As a result, TSGA-Net-A beat out TSGA-Net-B, the more computationally intensive parametric setting, achieving better results. Despite this, our results remain competitive compared to competitors. In related work using EA solver, our approach has a significant advantage in terms of search time. For works at the same parametric level, our performance is close to the state-of-the-art results. In particular, we achieve comparable and efficient searches with EA compared to differential-based works.

6   Conclusions

In this paper, we have provided a preliminary analysis of the correlation between cells in cell-based architecture space. Based on this, we have designed a two-stage search paradigm to pursue higher efficiency and performance by the way of reducing the dimensionality of the optimization problem. TSGA-Net, an implementation based on an EA solver, has been proposed and empirically studied. In particular, our approach can accomplish the entire search within 0.33 GPU days on CIFAR-10, with superior and competitive accuracy against on the state-of-the-art results.

Moreover, in this paper, we have made crude use of the relationship between cells, and there is thus more to be explored. In particular, the search space used in this paper contains some limitations of a priori assumptions, and we thus would like to explore a broader space in the our future works.

Acknowledgement. This work is partially supported by the Alibaba Group through the Alibaba Innovative Research Program under Grant No. H20210412 and the *National Natural Science Foundation of China* (NSFC) under Grant No. 61876025.

References

1. Brock, A., Lim, T., Ritchie, J., Weston, N.: Smash: one-shot model architecture search through hypernetworks. In: International Conference on Learning Representations (2018)
2. Cai, H., Zhu, L., Han, S.: ProxylessNAS: direct neural architecture search on target task and hardware. In: International Conference on Learning Representations (2019). https://arxiv.org/pdf/1812.00332.pdf
3. DeVries, T., Taylor, G.W.: Improved regularization of convolutional neural networks with cutout. arXiv preprint arXiv:1708.04552 (2017)
4. Huang, G., Liu, Z., van der Maaten, L., Weinberger, K.Q.: Densely connected convolutional networks. In: Proceedings of the IEEE Conference on Computer Vision and Pattern Recognition (2017)
5. Liu, H., Simonyan, K., Yang, Y.: DARTS: differentiable architecture search. In: International Conference on Learning Representations (2019)
6. Pham, H., Guan, M.Y., Zoph, B., Le, Q.V., Dean, J.: Efficient neural architecture search via parameters sharing. In: International Conference on Machine Learning, pp. 4092–4101 (2018)
7. Radosavovic, I., Johnson, J., Xie, S., Lo, W.Y., Dollár, P.: On network design spaces for visual recognition. arXiv preprint arXiv:1905.13214 (2019)
8. Real, E., Aggarwal, A., Huang, Y., Le, Q.V.: Regularized evolution for image classifier architecture search. Proc. AAAI Conf. Artif. Intell. **33**(01), 4780–4789 (2019). https://doi.org/10.1609/aaai.v33i01.33014780
9. Sun, Y., Xue, B., Zhang, M., Yen, G.G.: Completely automated CNN architecture design based on blocks. IEEE Trans. Neural Netw. Learn. Syst. **31**(4), 1–13 (2019). https://doi.org/10.1109/TNNLS.2019.2919608
10. Xie, S., Girshick, R., Dollár, P., Tu, Z., He, K.: Aggregated residual transformations for deep neural networks. arXiv preprint arXiv:1611.05431 (2016)
11. Xu, Y., et al.: PC-DARTS: partial channel connections for memory-efficient architecture search. In: International Conference on Learning Representations (2020)
12. Zela, A., Klein, A., Falkner, S., Hutter, F.: Towards automated deep learning: efficient joint neural architecture and hyperparameter search. In: ICML 2018 AutoML Workshop, July 2018
13. Zheng, X., et al.: Rethinking performance estimation in neural architecture search. In: Proceedings of the IEEE/CVF Conference on Computer Vision and Pattern Recognition, pp. 11356–11365 (2020)
14. Zoph, B., Le, Q.V.: Neural architecture search with reinforcement learning. arXiv:1611.01578 [cs], February 2017
15. Zoph, B., Vasudevan, V., Shlens, J., Le, Q.V.: Learning transferable architectures for scalable image recognition. In: Proceedings of the IEEE Conference on Computer Vision and Pattern Recognition, pp. 8697–8710 (2018)

Enforcing Individual Fairness via Rényi Variational Inference

Vincent Grari[1,3](✉), Oualid El Hajouji[2](✉), Sylvain Lamprier[1](✉),
and Marcin Detyniecki[3](✉)

[1] Sorbonne Université LIP6/CNRS Paris, Paris, France
{vincent.grari,sylvain.lamprier}@lip6.fr
[2] Ecole polytechnique, Palaiseau, France
oualid.el-hajouji@polytechnique.edu
[3] AXA REV Research Paris, Paris, France
marcin.detyniecki@axa.com

Abstract. As opposed to group fairness algorithms which enforce equality of distributions, individual fairness aims at treating similar people similarly. In this paper, we focus on individual fairness regarding sensitive attributes that should be removed from people comparisons. In that aim, we present a new method that leverages the Variational Autoencoder (VAE) algorithm and the Hirschfeld-Gebelein-Renyi (HGR) maximal correlation coefficient for enforcing individual fairness in predictions. We also propose new metrics to assess individual fairness. We demonstrate the effectiveness of our approach in enforcing individual fairness on several machine learning tasks prone to algorithmic bias.

Keywords: Individual fairness · Neural network · Variational autoencoder

1 Introduction

Machine learning models have taken an important place in our daily lives, with some critical implications for citizens such as loan applications and credit ratings. This increasingly important role of machine learning calls for caution: the data used for training the models can reflect sensitive biases that exist in our society. To tackle this problem, the recent *fair machine learning* research field has emerged. Most of the research in fair machine learning focuses on enforcing group fairness, which involves variable independence between the sensitive attribute S and the prediction $\hat{Y}$, with possible conditioning on the true outcome Y. For example, one of the most well-known objectives *Demographic parity* ensures that the output prediction is not dependent of the sensitive feature [2,20]. However, a shortcoming of enforcing group fairness is that it may induce dramatic consequences at the individual level. For instance, a person may be refused a position by a group fairness model only because of belonging to a privileged group, since a negative impact on this person can reduce the disparity of outcomes between groups. The field of individual fairness [5] tackles this issue of group fairness,

V. Grari and O. El Hajouji—Equal contribution.

© Springer Nature Switzerland AG 2021
T. Mantoro et al. (Eds.): ICONIP 2021, CCIS 1516, pp. 608–616, 2021.
https://doi.org/10.1007/978-3-030-92307-5_71

by enforcing similarity of outcomes between similar individuals. The intuition behind individual fairness is that the treatment of individuals is fair when similar people get similar treatments. The assessment of individual fairness is therefore dependent on the choice of a similarity distance on the input space (the fair distance) that compares individuals in a fair way with respect to the sensitive attributes. A standard of fair distance is the Mahalanobis distance between embedded features, with a parameter Σ that is the projection matrix onto a subspace of relevant (non-sensitive) attributes [15]. We claim that a strong limitation of this distance relies in the linearity of the induced projection. To circumvent this limitation, we introduce a new individual fairness definition based on Variational Autoencoding [12] and the recent neural estimator of the Hirschfeld-Gebelein-Renyi (HGR) maximal correlation coefficient [8, 17], for which we provide an optimization algorithm.

2   Related Work

The idea behind individual fairness, as defined by Dwork et al. [5], is that "similar people should be treated similarly". This implies the existence of a similarity distance on the input space, referred to as $d_{\mathcal{X}}$, which generally comes from expert knowledge about the domain at hand but can also be learnt from data [10, 15] with either a human feedback or the assumption of access to embedded features satisfying a factor model. Some approaches assume access to this distance and propose to enforce individual fairness via regularization [19] or distributionally robust optimization [18]: the process involves, at each iteration, finding similar individuals with the most disparate treatments. Other methods consist in enforcing individual fairness without access to $d_{\mathcal{X}}$ [6, 11], but with access to an oracle that identifies fairness violations across pairs of individuals.

3   Problem Statement

3.1   Individual Fairness

Definition 1. *A machine learning algorithm, with an associated predictor h, achieves Individual Fairness with respect to a fair distance $d_{\mathcal{X}}$ on the input space $\mathcal{X}$ if h is K-lipschitz for a certain K:*

$$\forall\, x_1, x_2 \in \mathcal{X}, |h(x_1) - h(x_2)| \leq K d_{\mathcal{X}}(x_1, x_2)$$

Individual fairness is therefore dependent on the choice of the input space distance $d_{\mathcal{X}}$. We propose, in this work, two new individual fairness distances that are dependent on $d_{\mathcal{X}}$. For $\alpha \in [0, 1]$, we denote as q_α the quantile of level α of the set $\{d_{\mathcal{X}}(x_i, x_j), 0 \leq i < j \leq n\}$ and $\tilde{q}_\alpha$ the quantile of level α of the set $\{\|x_i - x_j\|, 0 \leq i < j \leq n\}$

Definition 2. *We define Mean Region Discrepancy of level α (MRD_α) as:*

$$MRD_\alpha = \frac{\sum_{i<j} |h(x_i) - h(x_j)| \mathbb{1}_{\{d_{\mathcal{X}}(x_i, x_j) \leq q_\alpha\}}}{\sum_{i<j} \mathbb{1}_{\{d_{\mathcal{X}}(x_i, x_j) \leq q_\alpha\}}}$$

Definition 3. *We define Mean Double Region Discrepancy of levels* α, β *(MDRD$_{\alpha,\beta}$):*

$$MDRD_{\alpha,\beta} = \frac{\sum_{i<j}|h(x_i) - h(x_j)|\mathbb{1}_{\{d_\mathcal{X}(x_i,x_j)\leq q_\alpha\}}\mathbb{1}_{\{||x_i-x_j||\geq \tilde{q}_\beta\}}}{\sum_{i<j}\mathbb{1}_{\{d_\mathcal{X}(x_i,x_j)\leq q_\alpha\}}\mathbb{1}_{\{||x_i-x_j||\geq \tilde{q}_\beta\}}}$$

Definition 2 directly encodes the idea that "similar people should be treated similarly": we select data point pairs that are similar to a predefined level α and measure the mean discrepancies of outputs for these pairs. The smaller the MRD_α, the fairer the algorithm at the individual level. Definition 3 considers an additional $\mathbb{1}_{\{||x_i-x_j||\geq \tilde{q}_\beta\}}$ factor that eliminates data point pairs that are already similar in an euclidean sense. Indeed, the predictor h, assuming an adequate choice of activation functions, can be considered as a lipschitz function with respect to euclidean distances, which guarantees closeness of outputs for close pairs (in the euclidean sense). By weeding out those pairs, we ensure that we measure discrepancies for relevant data points.

3.2 Standard Distance for Individual Fairness

The distance $d_\mathcal{X}$ can come from expert knowledge, or can be learnt from data as outlined in [15]. In particular, to compute the individual fairness metrics defined above in our experiments (Sect. 3.1), we learn the distance $d_\mathcal{X}$ with the sensitive subspace method of [18]. We define the fair distance as:

$$d_\mathcal{X}(x_1, x_2) = (x_1 - x_2)^T(I - P_{ran(A)})(x_1 - x_2) \tag{1}$$

where $P_{ran(A)}$ is the projection matrix onto the span of $A = [a_1, .., a_k]$ which is referred to as the sensitive subspace. The sensitive subspace can be learnt by fitting a model to predict S with X as a variable: either a softmax regression model for a discrete sensitive variable, or an appropriate generalized linear model for a continuous sensitive variable. The vectors $[a_1, .., a_k]$ can then be defined as the weights of the fitted model.

3.3 HGR Coefficient

The Hirschfeld-Gebelein-Renyi (HGR) maximal correlation coefficient is a measure of statistical dependence.

Definition 4. *For two jointly distributed random variables $U \in \mathcal{U}$ and $V \in \mathcal{V}$, the Hirschfeld-Gebelein-Rényi maximal correlation is defined as:*

$$HGR(U, V) = \sup_{f:\mathcal{U}\to\mathbb{R}, g:\mathcal{V}\to\mathbb{R}} \rho(f(U), g(V)) \tag{2}$$

where ρ is the Pearson linear correlation coefficient with some measurable functions f and g with positive and finite variance.

The HGR coefficient is equal to 0 if the two random variables are independent. If they are strictly dependent the value is 1. Since the spaces for f and g are infinite-dimensional, the HGR coefficient proved difficult to compute. An efficient way of estimating the HGR coefficient is by neural networks [8]: the method consists in using the empirical correlation as an objective function and maximizing it by gradient ascent, functions f and g being parametrized by neural networks. This method, referred to as HGR_NN, was proved to be consistent [7] and efficient in capturing non-linear dependencies. We will make use of this estimation method in the first step of our algorithm, Renyi variational inference.

4   Method

The method that we propose in order to enforce individual fairness is based on Variational Autoencoding methods (VAE) [12], which is the basis of the first step of our algorithm. While some recent work leverage VAE methods for counterfactual inference [4,13,14,16], which consists in learning a generator of counterfactual versions of original individuals, we make use of this technique to generate similar individuals via the encoding-decoding process. We learn an unobserved confounder U of which we mitigate the bias w.r.t the sensitive variable, and generate new individuals based on the latent variable U. Then, we make use of this learnt generator in the prediction step, by adding a regularization term representing differences of outputs between similar individuals.

4.1   Step 1: Renyi Variational Inference

The original formulation of VAE consists in optimizing the classical lower bound (ELBO) [12]:

$$\mathcal{L}_{ELBO} = -E_{u \sim q_\phi(u|x)}(\log p_\theta(x|u)) + D_{KL}(q_\phi(u|x)||p(u)) \tag{3}$$

D_{KL} is defined as the Kullback-Leibler divergence, which computes distances between distributions, and the prior $p(u)$ is typically a standard Gaussian distribution. $q_\phi(u|x)$ is represented as a neural network, referred to as the encoder, that outputs the mean μ_ϕ and variance σ_ϕ of a Gaussian distribution, which allow to generate, stochastically, the variable U. The decoding process, corresponding to $p_\theta(x|u)$ and materialized by a neural network, consists in predicting X based on U. The overall objective 3 consists in both minimizing the reconstruction error (first term) and the divergence (distance) with a standard Gaussian. We adapt the ELBO by making two changes to the global step 1 objective. If we directly learnt the VAE with 3, we would obtain a generator that does generate, for a given x, a similar individual, but not similar in an acceptable sense for individual fairness. The underlying notion of similarity would be closer to an euclidean one, and thus would not be fair. However, by debiasing the latent variable U, generated individuals could be similar to the original one (depending on the level of debiasing) in a fairer sense. The assumption is that, if U both adequately represents the input data and eliminates information about the sensitive attribute, individuals generated from U will be close to the original one in terms of debiased attributes. As shown in previous sections, a good candidate for debiasing the latent variable is the HGR, which has the ability to capture non-linear dependencies. We add the term $HGR(U, S)$ to 3, with a hyperparameter λ_{HGR} that controls the trade-off between debiasing and reconstruction, and therefore use the HGR_NN to estimate the HGR coefficient. Also, similarly to [16], we replace the KL-divergence with a Maximum Mean Discrepancy (MMD) term [9] $\mathcal{L}_{MMD}(q_\phi(u)||p(u))$. As shown in [3,22], the D_{KL} can be too restrictive (uninformative latent code problem) and tends to overfit the data.

Therefore, the final minimization objective for the VAE step is:

$$\mathcal{L}_{VAE} = -E_{u \sim q_\phi(u|x)}(\log p_\theta(x|u)) + \lambda_{MMD}\mathcal{L}_{MMD}(q_\phi(u)||p(u)) + \lambda_{HGR}HGR(U, S) \tag{4}$$

This heuristic approach does not make use of the distance $d_\mathcal{X}$, but actually learns its own notion of similarity: individuals can be considered similar if they are close, in an euclidean sense, on the latent space. Additionally, we can also note that a significant difference with counterfactual inference is that the sensitive attribute is not used as input for the VAE. In counterfactual inference, having the sensitive attribute as input allows to generate counterfactual individuals with different values of S.

4.2   Step 2: Individually Fair Prediction

Once the inference model is learnt, we can generate similar versions of each training individual, and use that to learn an individually fair predictive function h_{w_ψ}. The global objective function for step 2 is:

$$\mathcal{L}_{global} = \mathcal{L}(h_{w_\psi}(X), Y) + \lambda \mathcal{L}_{IF}(h_{w_\psi}, X, \widehat{X_1}, ... \widehat{X_m}) \tag{5}$$

where $\mathcal{L}$ is a suitable loss function for the problem at hand (regression or classification), $\widehat{X_1}, ... \widehat{X_m}$ are m individuals generated by the VAE learnt at step 1 and similar to X, and $\mathcal{L}_{IF}$, referred to as the Individual Fairness Loss, can be defined as:

$$\mathcal{L}_{IF}(h_{w_\psi}, X, \widehat{X_1}, ... \widehat{X_m}) = \frac{1}{m} \sum_{i=1}^{m} \mathcal{L}(h_{w_\psi}(\widehat{X_i}), h_{w_\psi}(X)) \tag{6}$$

$\mathcal{L}_{IF}$ is a regularization term that, if minimized, ensures that similar individuals (in the sense of the step 1 VAE) have similar outputs. The hyperparameter λ controls the trade-off individual fairness/accuracy. Therefore, for sufficiently high values of λ, the algorithm is individually fair w.r.t a distance $d_\mathcal{X}$ if the generated individuals are close to X in the sense of $d_\mathcal{X}$. Since we assume no access to $d_\mathcal{X}$, we do not directly enforce, in step 1, closeness of generated individuals in the sense of $d_\mathcal{X}$, and we therefore have to rely on experimental results to assess the individual fairness of our algorithm w.r.t to a given distance $d_\mathcal{X}$.

5   Experiments

We empirically evaluate the performance of our contribution on 3 real world data sets. For the discrete scenario and specifically in the binary case ($Y \in \{0, 1\}, S \in \{0, 1\}$), we use the popular Adult UCI data set. For the continuous setting (Y and A are continuous), we use the 2 following data sets Motor and Crime data sets.

We repeat five experiments with random 80%/20% train-test splits. We report the averages of mean squared error (MSE) or balanced accuracy (B-Acc%), the Individual Fairness Loss (IFL) defined in 6, the MRD and MDRD metrics defined in Subsect. 3.1, the demographic parity [2]) metric ΔDP for binary sensitives or the HGR for continuous sensitives. Therefore, we can assess both the individual fairness of algorithms w.r.t the distance $d_\mathcal{X}$ (MRD, MDRD) and individual fairness w.r.t the intrinsic metric of the step 1 VAE (IFL). We can also assess the group fairness with the HGR and ΔDP, as it is interesting to observe whether models trained for individual fairness perform well in terms of group fairness. Note that, for the Adult experiment, we report 2 group fairness metrics. Note that the MRD and MDRD metrics are computed as the average values of different range of α (between $e-4$ and $e-2$) and β (between $e-4$ and $e-2$), it allows to compare different level of individual fairness. The baseline we use is a classic deep neural network (Standard NN). We compare our method with state of the art algorithms, among which the SenSR [18] algorithm which enforces Individual Fairness with knowledge of the fair distance $d_\mathcal{X}$, as well as group fairness algorithms. Among the group fairness algorithms, we compare our approach to two adversarial methods [1,21] which both involve an adversary that aims at predicting the sensitive attribute (from either a representation of the input, or from the prediction outputs). We also compare our method to a Renyi minimization approach [7] that consists in mitigating bias by minimizing the HGR between a latent variable and the sensitive attribute.

Results can be found in Tables 1 and 2. For all of the fair algorithms, we attempted to obtain comparable predictive performances by giving similar balanced accuracies (B-Acc%) for classification or mean squared errors (MSE) for regression for all the algorithms, in the same settings. Each of the algorithms considered has a hyperparameter that allows to balance the relative importance of accuracy and fairness while learning. Best performances among fair algorithms are in bold.

Table 1. Experimental results for the discrete dataset

		B-Acc%	IFL	MRD	MDRD	ΔDP_G	ΔDP_R
Adult	Standard NN	82.6% $\pm$ 0.2	0.239 $\pm$ 0.028	0.031 $\pm$ 0.012	0.052 $\pm$ 0.010	0.249 $\pm$ 0.002	0.129 $\pm$ 0.001
	SenSR [18]	79.2% $\pm$ 0.7	0.327 $\pm$ 0.057	0.020 $\pm$ 0.008	0.015 $\pm$ 0.010	**0.143** $\pm$ 0.023	0.110 $\pm$ 0.016
	Zhang et al. [21]	79.1% $\pm$ 2.3	0.362 $\pm$ 0.054	0.026 $\pm$ 0.019	0.081 $\pm$ 0.029	0.264 $\pm$ 0.042	0.126 $\pm$ 0.032
	Adel et al. [1]	79.9% $\pm$ 0.6	0.348 $\pm$ 0.013	0.013 $\pm$ 0.008	0.023 $\pm$ 0.022	0.209 $\pm$ 0.016	0.110 $\pm$ 0.006
	Grari et al. [7]	80.1% $\pm$ 0.9	0.321 $\pm$ 0.011	0.022 $\pm$ 0.004	0.018 $\pm$ 0.027	0.154 $\pm$ 0.015	**0.089** $\pm$ 0.003
	Ours IF	**80.2%** $\pm$ 0.6	**0.001** $\pm$ 0.001	**0.010** $\pm$ 0.006	**0.010** $\pm$ 0.013	0.249 $\pm$ 0.040	0.113 $\pm$ 0.019

For the three data sets, our algorithm enforces individual fairness at the best level among the other algorithms, not only with respect to its inner metric (IFL), but also and most importantly with respect to the $d_\mathcal{X}$ distance as shown by the MRD and MDRD metrics. In particular, our method outperforms SenSR in individual fairness while having better accuracy, even knowing that the SenSR algorithm makes use of the fair distance $d_\mathcal{X}$. Unsurprisingly, in terms of group fairness metrics, our algorithm does not

Table 2. Experimental results for the continuous dataset

		MSE	IFL	MRD	MDRD	HGR
Motor	Standard NN	0.946 ± 0.003	0.023 ± 0.005	0.043 ± 0.004	0.118 ± 0.026	0.208 ± 0.045
	SenSR [18]	0.996 ± 0.029	0.039 ± 0.005	0.065 ± 0.003	0.209 ± 0.031	0.168 ± 0.024
	Zhang et al. [21]	0.976 ± 0.016	0.042 ± 0.020	0.116 ± 0.026	0.139 ± 0.045	0.196 ± 0.015
	Adel et al. [1]	0.981 ± 0.009	0.001 ± 0.001	0.009 ± 0.004	$\mathbf{0.028 \pm 0.012}$	0.150 ± 0.076
	Grari et al. [7]	$\mathbf{0.972 \pm 0.004}$	0.008 ± 0.003	0.019 ± 0.005	0.042 ± 0.014	$\mathbf{0.079 \pm 0.018}$
	Ours	$\mathbf{0.972 \pm 0.001}$	$\mathbf{0.001 \pm 0.000}$	$\mathbf{0.008 \pm 0.001}$	$\mathbf{0.028 \pm 0.008}$	0.169 ± 0.022
Crime	Standard NN	0.387 ± 0.008	0.448 ± 0.080	0.185 ± 0.015	0.164 ± 0.095	0.772 ± 0.022
	SenSR [18]	0.999 ± 0.084	0.379 ± 0.028	0.123 ± 0.041	0.274 ± 0.063	0.608 ± 0.061
	Zhang et al. [21]	0.990 ± 0.069	0.051 ± 0.012	0.014 ± 0.004	0.028 ± 0.020	0.496 ± 0.031
	Adel et al. [1]	0.996 ± 0.021	0.001 ± 0.000	$\mathbf{0.002 \pm 0.000}$	$\mathbf{0.002 \pm 0.001}$	0.549 ± 0.012
	Grari et al. [7]	1.001 ± 0.017	$\mathbf{0.000 \pm 0.000}$	$\mathbf{0.002 \pm 0.001}$	$\mathbf{0.002 \pm 0.002}$	$\mathbf{0.254 \pm 0.096}$
	Ours	$\mathbf{0.972 \pm 0.004}$	$\mathbf{0.000 \pm 0.000}$	$\mathbf{0.002 \pm 0.001}$	$\mathbf{0.002 \pm 0.001}$	0.531 ± 0.050

perform as well as the group fairness algorithms such as Grari et al. as shown with the ΔDP_R and the HGR for the three data sets. Our algorithm still achieves group fairness debiasing (better than baseline) except for the Gender variable in the Adult experiment.

In Fig. 1, we plot 3 Pareto fronts displaying the IFL, MRD and the MDRD against the MSE with different values of the hyperparameter λ. These plots were obtained on the Crime data set with 4 algorithms: ours, Adel et al., Grari et al. and Zhang et al. Varying the hyperparameter λ allows to control the fairness/accuracy trade-off. Here, we clearly observe for all algorithms that the MSE, or predictive performance, decreases when fairness increases. Higher values of λ produce fairer predictions w.r.t the three fairness metrics, while near 0 values of the hyperparameter λ result in the optimization of the predictor loss with no fairness consideration. We note that, for all levels of predictive performance, our method outperforms the state of the art algorithms in terms of the three fairness metrics. The gap is even higher (in our favour) on the IFL metric, since our method consists in mitigating this latter metric.

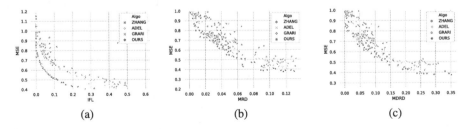

| (a) | (b) | (c) |

Fig. 1. Pareto fronts for IFL, MRD, MDRD. Higher values of λ produce fairer predictions, while λ near 0 only focuses on optimizing the predictor.

6 Conclusion

We present a new method based on variational inference and HGR neural estimation for enforcing individual fairness without access to the fair distance that assesses similarity of individuals. In a first step, entitled Renyi Variational Inference, we infer an unbiased confounder by combining ELBO optimization with HGR minimization. In a second step, we mitigate individual bias by adding a regularization term, representing output discrepancies between similar individuals, to global objective of a predictive neural network. This method proved to be very efficient on 3 real-world data sets for several individual fairness metrics that we proposed.

References

1. Adel, T., Valera, I., Ghahramani, Z., Weller, A.: One-network adversarial fairness. In: AAAI 2019, vol. 33, pp. 2412–2420 (2019)
2. Calders, T., Kamiran, F., Pechenizkiy, M.: Building classifiers with independency constraints. In: ICDM Workshops, pp. 13–18. IEEE (2009)
3. Chen, X., et al.: Variational lossy autoencoder. arXiv preprint arXiv:1611.02731 (2016)
4. Chiappa, S.: Path-specific counterfactual fairness. In: Proceedings of the AAAI Conference on Artificial Intelligence, vol. 33, pp. 7801–7808 (2019)
5. Dwork, C., Hardt, M., Pitassi, T., Reingold, O., Zemel, R.: Fairness through awareness. In: ITCS 2012, pp. 214–226 (2012)
6. Gillen, S., Jung, C., Kearns, M., Roth, A.: Online learning with an unknown fairness metric. In: Advances in Neural Information Processing Systems, pp. 2600–2609 (2018)
7. Grari, V., Hajouji, O.E., Lamprier, S., Detyniecki, M.: Learning unbiased representations via rényi minimization (2020)
8. Grari, V., Lamprier, S., Detyniecki, M.: Fairness-aware neural rényi minimization for continuous features. In: Bessiere, C. (ed.) IJCAI 2020, pp. 2262–2268. ijcai.org (2020)
9. Gretton, A., Borgwardt, K.M., Rasch, M.J., Schölkopf, B., Smola, A.: A kernel two-sample test. J. Mach. Learn. Res. **13**, 723–773 (2012)
10. Ilvento, C.: Metric learning for individual fairness. arXiv preprint arXiv:1906.00250 (2019)
11. Jung, C., Kearns, M., Neel, S., Roth, A., Stapleton, L., Wu, Z.S.: Eliciting and enforcing subjective individual fairness. arXiv preprint arXiv:1905.10660 (2019)
12. Kingma, D.P., Welling, M.: Auto-encoding variational Bayes. arXiv preprint arXiv:1312.6114 (2013)
13. Louizos, C., Swersky, K., Li, Y., Welling, M., Zemel, R.: The variational fair autoencoder. arXiv preprint arXiv:1511.00830 (2015)
14. Madras, D., Creager, E., Pitassi, T., Zemel, R.: Fairness through causal awareness: Learning causal latent-variable models for biased data. In: Proceedings of the Conference on Fairness, Accountability, and Transparency, pp. 349–358 (2019)
15. Mukherjee, D., Yurochkin, M., Banerjee, M., Sun, Y.: Two simple ways to learn individual fairness metrics from data. arXiv preprint arXiv:2006.11439 (2020)
16. Pfohl, S., Duan, T., Ding, D.Y., Shah, N.H.: Counterfactual reasoning for fair clinical risk prediction. arXiv preprint arXiv:1907.06260 (2019)
17. Rényi, A.: On measures of dependence. Acta Mathematica Hungarica **10**(3–4), 441–451 (1959)
18. Yurochkin, M., Bower, A., Sun, Y.: Training individually fair ml models with sensitive subspace robustness. In: International Conference on Learning Representations (2019)

19. Yurochkin, M., Sun, Y.: Sensei: Sensitive set invariance for enforcing individual fairness. arXiv preprint arXiv:2006.14168 (2020)
20. Zafar, M.B., Valera, I., Rogriguez, M.G., Gummadi, K.P.: Fairness constraints: mechanisms for fair classification. In: AISTATS 2017, pp. 962–970. Fort Lauderdale, FL, USA, April 2017
21. Zhang, B.H., Lemoine, B., Mitchell, M.: Mitigating unwanted biases with adversarial learning. In: AAAI 2018, pp. 335–340 (2018)
22. Zhao, S., Song, J., Ermon, S.: Infovae: Information maximizing variational autoencoders. arXiv preprint arXiv:1706.02262 (2017)

Group-Based Deep Reinforcement Learning in Multi-UAV Confrontation

Shengang Li[ORCID], Baolai Wang, and Tao Xie[✉]

College of Computer, National University of Defense Technology, Changsha, China
wangbaolai18@nudt.edu.cn, hamishxie@vip.sina.com

Abstract. The application of deep reinforcement learning (DRL) algorithms in multi-agent environments has become more and more popular. However, most DRL algorithms do not solve the problem of group cooperation. Each agent explores in a direction that is beneficial to itself, but ignores the situation of its teammates, which is easy to fall into the local optimum. This paper aims to solve this problem in a multi-UAV confrontation scenario. We try to find the optimal cooperative policy by dividing UAVs into several groups and make UAVs learn to cooperate with teammates autonomously. Specifically, we propose an algorithm called group-based actor-critic (GBAC). We group UAVs by setting the observation radius, and we use a double Q network to process rewards. We divide rewards into individual rewards and group rewards. The Q network is used to process individual rewards, and the group-Q network is used to process group rewards. As a result, UAVs can get higher rewards through group cooperation. The performance of UAVs trained by our method outperforms other DRL methods. In this paper, we use the group-based DRL method to solve the problem of group cooperation and maximize the expected return in multi-UAV confrontation.

Keywords: Deep reinforcement learning · Actor-Critic · Multi-UAV confrontation · Group cooperation

1 Introduction

With the development of UAV technology, multi-UAV confrontation has gradually become a hot spot. Multi-UAV confrontation is a conflict between two UAV teams. In a multi-UAV confrontation scenario, UAVs cooperate with teammates and confront the enemy. During the confrontation, the control methods of UAVs include rule-based methods and reinforcement learning methods, etc. Compared with rule-based methods, reinforcement learning methods are more flexible and autonomous. For some scenarios with small data dimensions, such as snake games or robotic control [1], reinforcement learning works well. As learning tasks become more and more complex, reinforcement learning does not perform well when processing high-dimensional data. Therefore, researchers use deep neural networks as function approximations and combine deep learning with reinforcement learning, called deep reinforcement learning (DRL).

© Springer Nature Switzerland AG 2021
T. Mantoro et al. (Eds.): ICONIP 2021, CCIS 1516, pp. 617–624, 2021.
https://doi.org/10.1007/978-3-030-92307-5_72

For example, the well-known Alphago Zero [2], the artificial intelligence go software developed by Google Deepmind, is realized by DRL. With the development of DRL in recent years, many advanced algorithms appeared, such as DQN [3] and DDPG [4]. Later, to deal with the relationship between agents in multi-agent environments, Lowe et al. [5] proposed MADDPG.

However, in a multi-agent environment, the current DRL algorithms can not solve the problem of group cooperation, causing agents to fall into the local optimum during learning. Each agent explores in a direction that is beneficial to itself continuously, but ignores the situation of its teammates, which makes it difficult for agents to learn cooperative policies. Tan [6] found that agents engaging in partnership can significantly outperform independent agents in joint tasks.

This paper aims to solve the problem of group cooperation in multi-UAV confrontation. We build a multi-UAV confrontation scenario, which contains a military base, a blue team, and a red team. The blue team intends to attack the military base, and the red team learns cooperative policies to confront the blue team to protect the military base. Based on the actor-critic method, we propose an algorithm called group-based actor-critic (GBAC). And we use this new actor-critic framework to train cooperative policies for the red team to confront the blue team.

Our main contributions are as follows:

- A method based on the observation radius is proposed to divide the red team into several groups, and we provide a mechanism of individual rewards and group rewards for each red UAV.
- We propose a group-based actor-critic framework to train cooperative policies, which uses the Q network to process individual rewards and uses an additional group-Q network to process group rewards.
- We solve the problem of group cooperation and maximize the expected return in multi-UAV confrontation.

2   Related Work

In this section, we introduce the development of the actor-critic method. Witten [7] first proposed a method similar to the actor-critic algorithm in 1977, and Barto et al. [8] introduced the actor-critic architecture in 1983. Later, Sutton et al. [9] discussed policy gradient methods for function approximation, which became the basic theory of actor-critic. The actor-critic method has been widely used in deterministic policy gradient algorithms, such as DPG [10] and DDPG [4]. In 2016, Mnih et al. [11] proposed the A3C algorithm, an asynchronous variant of actor-critic, which uses an asynchronous method instead of experience replay. In 2017, Lowe et al. [5] proposed the MADDPG method, which adopts the actor-critic framework for centralized training and decentralized execution. During training, the critic calculates a Q-value by inputting information from all agents to train the actor. During execution, the actor only needs to input local information to give the optimal action. In 2018, Haarnoja et al. [12] proposed an off-policy actor-critic DRL algorithm based on the maximum entropy reinforcement learning framework, called soft actor-critic (SAC). However, although these methods optimize the actor-critic method, they still can not solve the problem of group cooperation using the actor-critic framework in multi-agent environments.

3   Methods

Since the previous actor-critic algorithms can not solve the problem of group cooperation, we propose an algorithm based on actor-critic to train cooperative policies in a multi-UAV confrontation scenario. This confrontation scenario contains a military base, a red team, and a blue team. The red team uses the GBAC method as shown in Fig. 1, and the blue team uses the rule-based method as shown in Fig. 2.

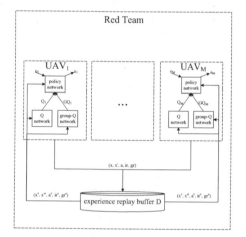
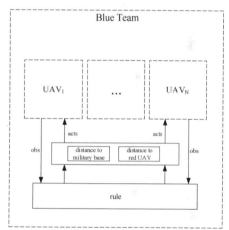

Fig. 1. The structure of GBAC.   **Fig. 2.** The rule-based method.

We suppose that this confrontation scenario contains M red UAVs and N blue UAVs. We take blue UAV j as an example to describe the rule-based method. First, the observations of blue UAV j are submitted to the rule. Then the rule finds the positions of red UAVs and the military base by analyzing the observations. Finally, the rule calculates the distances from blue UAV j to red UAVs and the military base, and selects actions for blue UAV j to attack the nearest target.

For our method GBAC, each red UAV contains a policy network, a Q network, and a group-Q network. Each network corresponds to a target network, which is proposed in DQN [3]. We omit the structure of the target network in Fig. 1. Besides, there is an experience replay buffer D, which contains observations, actions, the next observations, individual rewards, and group rewards information about all red UAVs. During training, we sample experience from D to train the policy network, the Q network, and the group-Q network.

We use deterministic policies $\mu_\theta : \mathcal{S} \to \mathcal{A}$ [10]. For red UAV i, μ_{θ_i} (abbreviated as μ_i) represents its policy. ir_i represents its individual reward. a_i represents its action, and o_i represents its observation. The observation contains the state information (e.g., position and direction information) of other UAVs. The Q function is defined as:

$$Q_i^\mu(x, a_1, a_2, ..., a_M) = \mathbb{E}[IR], \tag{1}$$

where $IR = \sum_{t=0}^{T} \gamma^t ir^t$ is the expected individual return. Red UAV i's Q network is updated by minimizing the loss$_1$:

$$\mathcal{L}_1(\theta_i) = \mathbb{E}_{x,a,ir,x'}[(Q_i^\mu(x, a_1, a_2, ..., a_M) - y_1)^2],$$
$$y_1 = ir_i + \gamma Q_i^{\mu'}(x', a_1', a_2', ..., a_M')|_{a_i' = \mu_i'(o_i)}, \tag{2}$$

where $x = (o_1, o_2, ..., o_M)$ represents all observations of the red team, and x' represents the next observations, and $ir = (ir_1, ir_2, ..., ir_M)$ represents all individual rewards of the red team. $\mu = \{\mu_{\theta_1}, \mu_{\theta_2}, ..., \mu_{\theta_M}\}$ is the set of all red UAVs' policies, and μ' is the set of target policies with delayed parameters θ_i'. $Q_i^{\mu'}$ is the target Q function. Besides, for red UAV i, it can get group rewards through cooperation with teammates. Next, we introduce the GQ function, which is approximated by the group-Q network. The GQ function has the same structure as the Q function, but the difference is that the GQ function uses group rewards. Similarly, the GQ function is defined as:

$$GQ_i^\mu(x, a_1, a_2, ..., a_M) = \mathbb{E}[GR], \tag{3}$$

where $GR = \sum_{t=0}^{T} \gamma^t gr^t$ is the expected group return. Red UAV i's group-Q network is updated by minimizing the loss$_2$:

$$\mathcal{L}_2(\theta_i) = \mathbb{E}_{x,a,gr,x'}[(GQ_i^\mu(x, a_1, a_2, ..., a_M) - y_2)^2],$$
$$y_2 = gr_i + \gamma GQ_i^{\mu'}(x', a_1', a_2', ..., a_M')|_{a_i' = \mu_i'(o_i)}, \tag{4}$$

where $gr = (gr_1, gr_2, ..., gr_M)$ represents all group rewards of the red team, and gr_i represents the group reward obtained by red UAV i. $GQ_i^{\mu'}$ is the target GQ function. In fact, the Q network and the group-Q network are updated synchronously, and they promote each other. Under the influence of this double Q network, red UAV i can learn the optimal cooperative policy μ_{θ_i}. Red UAV i's policy network is updated by the policy gradient, which can be written as:

$$\nabla_{\theta_i} J(\mu_i) = \mathbb{E}_{x,a \sim D}[\nabla_{\theta_i} \mu_i(a_i|o_i) \nabla_{a_i}(Q_i^\mu(x, a_1, a_2, ..., a_M)$$
$$+ GQ_i^\mu(x, a_1, a_2, ..., a_M))|_{a_i = \mu_i(o_i)}]. \tag{5}$$

As a result, we can see that the policy gradient is calculated by the Q network and the group-Q network together. After getting the policy gradient $\nabla_{\theta_i} J(\mu_i)$, we can update parameters θ_i of the policy network. The overall algorithm, GBAC, is summarized as Algorithm 1.

Algorithm 1. Group-Based Actor-Critic (GBAC)

1: **for** episode = 1 to K **do**
2:      Initialize a random process $\mathcal{P}$ for action exploration
3:      Initialize state information x
4:      **for** step = 1 to max-length **do**
5:          for each red UAV i, get observation o_i and select action $a_i = \boldsymbol{\mu}_{\theta_i}(o_i) + \mathcal{P}_{step}$
6:          Execute actions $a = (a_1, a_2, ..., a_M)$ and transfer state x to the next state x'
7:          Get individual rewards ir and group rewards gr from the environment
8:          Save (x, x', a, ir, gr) in buffer $\mathcal{D}$, and then make $x = x'$
9:          **for** red UAV $i = 1$ to M **do**
10:              Sample a minibatch of $\mathcal{W}$ samples $(x^e, x'^e, a^e, ir^e, gr^e)$ from $\mathcal{D}$
11:              Set $y_1^e = ir_i^e + \gamma Q_i^{\boldsymbol{\mu}'}(x'^e, a_1', a_2', ..., a_M')|_{a_i' = \boldsymbol{\mu}_i'(o_i^e)}$
12:              Set $y_2^e = gr_i^e + \gamma GQ_i^{\boldsymbol{\mu}'}(x'^e, a_1', a_2', ..., a_M')|_{a_i' = \boldsymbol{\mu}_i'(o_i^e)}$
13:              Update Q network by minimizing the $loss_1$:
14:                  $\mathcal{L}_1(\theta_i) = \frac{1}{\mathcal{W}} \sum_c (Q_i^{\boldsymbol{\mu}}(x^e, a_1^e, a_2^e, ..., a_M^e) - y_1^e)^2$
15:              Update group-Q network by minimizing the $loss_2$:
16:                  $\mathcal{L}_2(\theta_i) = \frac{1}{\mathcal{W}} \sum_e (GQ_i^{\boldsymbol{\mu}}(x^e, a_1^e, a_2^e, ..., a_M^e) - y_2^e)^2$
17:              Update policy network using the sampled policy gradient:
18:                  $\nabla_{\theta_i} J \approx \frac{1}{\mathcal{W}} \sum_e \nabla_{\theta_i} \boldsymbol{\mu}_i(o_i^e) \nabla_{a_i} (Q_i^{\boldsymbol{\mu}}(x^e, a_1^e, a_2^e, ..., a_M^e)$
19:                  $+ GQ_i^{\boldsymbol{\mu}}(x^e, a_1^e, a_2^e, ..., a_M^e))|_{a_i = \boldsymbol{\mu}_i(o_i^e)}$
20:          Update target network parameters for each red UAV i:
21:              $\theta_i' \leftarrow \tau \theta_i + (1 - \tau)\theta_i'$

---

4   Experiments

We build a multi-UAV confrontation scenario to compare our approach with three advanced deep reinforcement learning (DRL) methods. This confrontation scenario contains a military base, a red team, and a blue team. We assign 10 UAVs to both the red team and the blue team. Red UAVs are controlled by our algorithm GBAC, and blue UAVs are controlled by the rule-based method. During the confrontation, if the blue team destroys the military base then the blue team wins, otherwise the red team wins.

4.1   Experiment Setup

Network Setup. We use the same network structure to achieve four DRL methods. All networks contain 1 input layer, 2 hidden layers, and 1 output layer. Each hidden layer contains 64 units, and we set ReLU as the activation function. Besides, we set the target update rate τ to 0.01, the discount factor γ to 0.95, the learning rate to 0.01, and the batch size to 1024.

Reward Setup. We divide reward into individual reward and group reward. For red UAV i, if it kills a blue UAV, its individual reward will add 10. If it dies, its individual reward will reduce 10. If the military base is destroyed, all red UAVs' individual rewards will reduce 40. Besides, if its groupmates kill a blue UAV, its group reward will add 5. If its groupmates die, its group reward will reduce 5.

4.2 Group Based on the Observation Radius

In this section, we introduce a method, which divides the red team into several groups. We take red UAV i as an example. First, it forms a group with its nearby teammates. If there are no teammates nearby, it can only form a group by itself. Then, its groupmates continue to find other red UAVs to form a group. If there are more red UAVs in its groupmate's group, then red UAV i is merged into that group. We set an observation radius to represent the maximum distance for red UAV i to find other red UAVs.

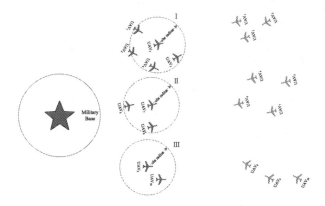

Fig. 3. Group the red team based on the observation radius.

As shown in Fig. 3, we can see that the red team is divided into three groups. $Group_1$ has 5 red UAVs, and $Group_2$ has 3 red UAVs, and $Group_3$ has 2 red UAVs. The grouping method is summarized as Algorithm 2.

Algorithm 2. Grouping Method Based on The Observation Radius

1: Start: Set $\Omega = \{red_1, red_2, ..., red_{10}\}$
2: $Step_1$: Take out a red UAV from Ω in order and calculate the number of teammates in its observation range (i.e., circular area formed by dashed lines in Fig. 3).
3: $Step_2$: If the number is the largest, then this red UAV and its teammates in the observation range are grouped together. And this group is defined as $Group_1$.
4: $Step_3$: Remove red UAVs in $Group_1$ from Ω.
5: $Step_4$: Repeat $Step_1$–$Step_3$ to get $Group_2$, $Group_3$...
6: Stop: Until Ω is empty

4.3   Experimental Results

We compare our method GBAC with three DRL methods, including MADDPG, DDPG, and SAC. In this experiment, we calculate the win rate and the reward of 10 red UAVs. After training for 120,000 episodes, the win rate and the mean reward are drawn in Fig. 4. As a result, the red UAVs trained by our method GBAC have a higher win rate and mean reward than other methods during the confrontation.

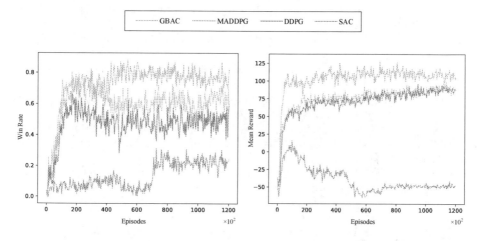

Fig. 4. Comparison of our algorithm GBAC with three DRL methods.

5   Conclusion

In this paper, we propose an algorithm, group-based actor-critic (GBAC), which solves the problem of group cooperation and maximizes the expected return in multi-UAV confrontation. We divide the red team into several groups by setting the observation radius. Besides, we set the mechanism of individual rewards and group rewards, and we adopt a double Q network to train cooperative policies. The Q network is used to process the individual rewards, and the group-Q network is used to process the group rewards. We compare our method with three advanced DRL methods, including MADDPG, DDPG, and SAC. The experiment shows that our method significantly outperforms these methods and greatly improves the performance of DRL. Our group-based DRL method provides a promising avenue to deal with multi-agent cooperative learning. In future work, we will further explore its application in more complex environments, and solve the problem of increased data dimensionality and non-stationarity due to cooperation.

Acknowledgments. This paper is supported by the World Park of Digital Economy EVONature Foundation and the national Science Foundation of China, under the project No. 61472476.

References

1. Schulman, J., Levine, S., Abbeel, P., Jordan, M., Moritz, P.: Trust region policy optimization. In: International Conference on Machine Learning. PMLR, pp. 1889–1897 (2015)
2. Silver, D., et al.: Mastering the game of go without human knowledge. Nature **550**(7676), 354–359 (2017)
3. Mnih, V., et al.: Human-level control through deep reinforcement learning. Nature **518**(7540), 529–533 (2015)
4. Lillicrap, T., et al.: Continuous control with deep reinforcement learning. CoRR abs/1509.02971 (2016)
5. Lowe, R., Wu, Y., Tamar, A., Harb, J., Abbeel, P., Mordatch, I.: Multi-agent actor-critic for mixed cooperative-competitive environments. In: NIPS (2017)
6. Tan, M., Multi-agent reinforcement learning: independent versus cooperative agents. In: ICML (1993)
7. Witten, I.H.: An adaptive optimal controller for discrete-time Markov environments. Inf. Control **34**(4), 286–295 (1977)
8. Barto, A., Sutton, R., Anderson, C.: Neuronlike adaptive elements that can solve difficult learning control problems. IEEE Trans. Syst. Man Cybern. **SMC-13**, 834–846 (1983)
9. Sutton, R., McAllester, D.A., Singh, S., Mansour, Y.: Policy gradient methods for reinforcement learning with function approximation. In: NIPS (1999)
10. Silver, D., Lever, G., Heess, N., Degris, T., Wierstra, D., Riedmiller, M.A.: Deterministic policy gradient algorithms. In: ICML (2014)
11. Mnih, V., et al.: Asynchronous methods for deep reinforcement learning. In: International Conference on Machine Learning. PMLR, pp. 1928–1937 (2016)
12. Haarnoja, T., Zhou, A., Abbeel, P., Levine, S.: Soft actor-critic: off-policy maximum entropy deep reinforcement learning with a stochastic actor. In: International Conference on Machine Learning. PMLR, pp. 1861–1870 (2018)

Fuzzy Data Augmentation for Handling Overlapped and Imbalanced Data

Rukshima Dabare, Kok Wai Wong[✉], Mohd Fairuz Shiratuddin,
and Polychronis Koutsakis

Murdoch University, Murdoch, WA, Australia
{rukshima.dabare2,K.Wong,F.Shiratuddin,
p.koutsakis}@murdoch.edu.au

Abstract. Class imbalance is a serious issue in classification as a traditional classifier is generally biased towards the majority class. The accuracy of the classifier could be further impacted in cases where additionally to the class imbalance, there are overlapped data instances. Further, data sparsity has shown to be a possible issue that may lead to non- invariance and poor generalisation. Data augmentation is a technique that can handle the generalisation issue and improve the regularisation of the Deep Neural Network (DNN). A method to handle both class overlap and class imbalance while also incorporating regularisation is proposed in this paper. In our work, the imbalanced dataset is balanced using SMOTETomek, and then the non-categorical attributes are fuzzified. The purpose of fuzzifying the attributes is to handle the overlapping in the data and provide some form of data augmentation that can be used as a regularisation technique. Therefore, in this paper, the invariance is achieved as the augmented data are generated based on the fuzzy concept. The balanced augmented dataset is then trained using a DNN classifier. The datasets used in the experiments were selected from UCI and KEEL data repositories. The experiments show that the proposed Fuzzy data augmentation for handling overlapped and imbalanced data can address the overlapped and imbalanced data issues, and provide regularisation using data augmentation for numerical data to improve the performance of a DNN classifier.

Keywords: Imbalanced and overlapped data classification · Data augmentation · Regularisation · Fuzzy

1 Introduction

Imbalanced data is a problem that occurs in classification when the data distribution is not equal in the dataset. The majority class, in an imbalanced dataset, usually is not the class of interest. The opposite applies to datasets in many classification problems [1, 2], where the interest lies in the minority class. Standard classification techniques are not able to handle this imbalance without adopting special techniques. The balancing of minority and majority classes is a meaningful way to handle this, and some techniques have commonly been used, such as random oversampling, Synthetic Minority Oversampling Techniques (SMOTE) [3], TomekLinks [4] and SMOTETomek [2].

© Springer Nature Switzerland AG 2021
T. Mantoro et al. (Eds.): ICONIP 2021, CCIS 1516, pp. 625–633, 2021.
https://doi.org/10.1007/978-3-030-92307-5_73

However, the handling of imbalanced data becomes more complicated when overlapped data instances also appear in the datasets [1, 5, 6]. The classification performance could degrade significantly depending on the degree of overlapping of the classes [5]. Thus, when designing an effective classifier in the presence of imbalanced and overlapped instances, there is a need to consider the overlapped and the imbalanced data issues concurrently. Some techniques are used to handle this case [7, 8], but they mainly concentrate on two major approaches. The first approach is to separate the overlapping data and classify each separated area. The second approach is to ignore the overlapped instances totally and simply handle the imbalanced issue only. Even though the techniques mentioned above are popular in this regard, [1] suggest that simply removing instances from an overlapped situations sometimes leads to valuable information to be removed and thus affects the classification performance. Besides, the training of many classifiers for each region is cumbersome and time-consuming. Therefore, there is a necessity to identify alternative approaches to handle overlapped data issues when the data is imbalanced. In the literature, no known work has tried to solve the issue of class overlap appears in the imbalanced dataset while improving the generalisation in a model by using an efficient regularisation technique concurrently. In developing the proposed technique that handled the imbalanced, overlapped, and generalisation issues concurrently, we have incorporated the commonly used balancing technique of SMOTETomek [2, 7, 8]. In SMOTETomek, not only instances from the majority class are removed, but instances from both classes are removed to achieve a balance between the classes while also oversample as required. Therefore, the use of SMOTETomek leads to equal data distribution and a balanced dataset. Hence, the SMOTETomek is used as a balancing technique to develop the proposed method in this paper.

Deep Neural Networks (DNNs) extend shallow ANNs with many layers between the input and the output layer [9]. Due to their abstraction quality, DNNs have been shown to work in several domains such as pharmacological science [10], medical [11], emotion predictions [12], and speech enhancement [13], where the dataset is numerical without involving any images or text data, successfully. However, the DNN classifier, like any other traditional classifier, performs poorly when overlapped data appears in an imbalanced dataset [14, 15]. Furthermore, DNNs with many learnable parameters are likely to overfit when trained on a relatively small training dataset [16]. It is because when the training dataset is small, the seen data for the model is limited. However, the main task of a classifier is to be invariant to a wide variety of transformations or patterns and generalise [16]. When DNNs are used for classification tasks, if sufficient patterns from each class cannot be identified from a small set of data, then predictions depend only on the available data. Therefore, when the training data is small in size, the pattern variations are usually limited, leading to poor classification [17]. To make the training dataset large enough so that the classifier would be invariant to many data patterns, data augmentation can be used. Furthermore, when data items are overlapped, the degree of belonging can be identified through Fuzzy C-means clustering. Therefore, when overlapped data is clustered using Fuzzy C-means, it may belong to two or more clusters. In the proposed method, we identify the features which will have an overlapping behaviour and address them separately by fuzzifying the non-categorical features. It should also be noted that, a Fuzzy number does not denote a single value but rather to an associated set of likely values, where each possible value has its own belongings to the fuzzy set [18–20]. Therefore, using fuzzy concepts it is possible to identify likely values to a crisp number which can be used to generate more data from the original crisp data. Hence, in this paper fuzzy concepts are used for handling the overlapped data and also to make the classifier more invariant to different patterns of data.

2 Proposed Fuzzy Data Augmentation Method to Handle Overlapped Data for Imbalanced Dataset

The proposed Fuzzy Data Augmentation Method to handle Overlapped data for Imbalanced dataset (FAugOImb) can handle overlapped data and improve generalisation for an imbalanced dataset. The proposed method uses the SMOTETomek resampling technique [2] to balance the training dataset before feeding it into the Fuzzy C-Means clustering algorithm. In the proposed method, the fuzzy concept is adopted to handle the overlapping issue. With the fuzzy approach, the overlapping degree of the instance to each class generated by the Fuzzy C - Means can be identified. With the use of Fuzzy C-Means, it is more likely to identify the degree of overlapping for each class. In this paper, fuzzification refers to the clustering of each non-categorical attribute and identifying the membership grade for each input attribute. The degree of overlapping, measured by the membership degree to each class, is used to build a cluster centre dataset. With a suitable α-cut, an appropriate number of data can be selected for the augmentation of the balanced dataset. Thereafter, this newly augmented dataset is used to train the classifier. The algorithm of the proposed FAugOImb method is described in detailed below.

Algorithm 3.1: Balancing the dataset, forming of the cluster centre dataset and generating the augmented dataset

Input: Number of clusters c, Original training dataset X matrix with k attributes and i records

Output: Cluster centre matrix C with k attributes and j number of generated records, new training dataset (augmented) with k attributes and j number of generated records

1. **if** X is balanced **then**
2. move to step 6
3. else
4. $X_s \leftarrow$ SMOTETomek (X)
5. **endif**
6. Initialise fuzzy membership matrix W to an empty array where $W \in \mathbb{R}^{c \times k+1}$
7. Derive the fuzzy membership degree (μ_{ic}) and cluster center (cc) by clustering each non categorical attribute (p) using Fuzzy C-Means for c number of clusters
8. **foreach** record (i) of training dataset **do**
9.   **foreach** c do
10.   **foreach** p do
11.   identify μ_{ic}
12.   **if** isnotzero(μ_{ic}) **then**
13.   W[index$_i$][index$_c$]$\leftarrow \mu_{ic}$
14.   **else**
15.   discard the record
16.   **endif**
17.   **enddo**
18. **enddo**
19. identify the best fuzzy α cut value (α-cut) for the dataset
20. **foreach** record (w) of W dataset do
21.   **if** $\mu_{ic} < \alpha$-cut then
22. discard the record
23.   **else**
24.   C[index$_j$][index$_c$]$\leftarrow cc_{jc}$
25.   **endif**
26. **end do**
27. New training dataset $\leftarrow$ Original Training dataset (X) + cluster center dataset (C)
28. Train the classifier using New training dataset (Augmented dataset) with Dropout

3   Experimental Procedure

First, the dataset is divided into 10-folds for each experiment, 80% is used for training, and 20% is used for testing. After that, attributes that need to be clustered are identified from the training data. Here, only the non-categorical or continuous attributes are identified as the attributes to be fuzzified. The attributes thus identified are fuzzified attribute-wise by using the technique proposed by the authors in [21] and explained in the previous section. The datasets used in the experiments are German, Abalone 19, and WDBC datasets obtained from the UCI and KEEL data repositories. The imbalance ratios are 2.33 for German, 129.44 for Abalone 19, and 2.68 for WDBC.

The architecture of the DNN is decided by trial and error. The average of the ten experiments conducted for the 10-folds is used for evaluation. The activation function used in the nodes of the hidden layers is the Rectified Linear Unit (relu) [16]. The nodes of the last layer use the sigmoid activation function for the datasets as they are binary classification problems. The DNN model used the loss function binary cross-entropy and a batch size of 100, 10, and 10 for German, Abalone 19, and WDBC datasets, respectively. Dropout is also used to avoid overfitting when training the proposed model. After many trial and error experiments, it is identified that the best α-cut value for the German dataset is 0.7, 0.5 for the Abalone 19 dataset, and the WDBC dataset is 0.6. The best value for the α-cut is selected by looking into how the models generalise by observing the model loss curves and the performance of the evaluation metric values achieved by each dataset. Friedman's statistical significance test [22] and a post hoc test known as Holm step-down procedure (Holm's Bonferroni method) were performed to analyse the results statistically. The total ranking, p-values and α^* of the statistical test results are reported in the next section.

4   Results and Evaluation of Results

This section presents the experiments' results to investigate the classifier's performance for imbalanced datasets when FAugOImb was used and the evaluation of the results is thus obtained. The statistical significance test results and the discussions of the experiments are also presented in this section. As there was a necessity to identify the most suitable balancing technique for the FAugOImb technique, two rebalancing techniques were used. Hence, the datasets were first balanced using different balancing techniques, namely, SMOTE and SMOTETomek. The datasets were then fuzzified, as explained in Sect. 3. Evaluation metrics used to examine the classifier's performance are AUC, G-Mean, and F-Measure, as the datasets used are imbalanced. Tables 1, 2 and 3 present the performance of the different techniques used to handle the overlapped and imbalanced nature of the datasets for German, Abalone 19, and WDBC, respectively. The techniques used are SMOTE, SMOTE-Tomek, SMOTE + FAugOImb, and SMOTETomek + FAugOImb. The classifier used in all experiments is DNNs.

When the German dataset is considered, as presented in Table 1, the proposed SMOTETomek + FAugOImb, improves the classification performance by 2.1% of AUC, 1.93% of G-Mean and 2.9% of F-Measure than the SMOTETomek, which is the second-best.

Table 1. Results for the German dataset

Balancing technique	AUC	G-mean	F-measure
SMOTE	0.6912	0.6835	0.5707
SMOTETomek	0.7003	0.7135	0.5804
SMOTE + FAugOImb	0.6999	0.6864	0.5725
SMOTETomek + FAugOImb	**0.7222**	**0.7328**	**0.6102**

Table 2 presents the results obtained for the Abalone 19 dataset. The results suggest that the technique proposed which used SMOETomek + FAugOImb gives better results for AUC, G-Mean, and F-Measure values than the other techniques compared in this paper. The AUC value is 1.82% higher than the next highest technique that provides the best results. The G-Mean of the technique proposed SMOTETomek + FAugOImb is 0.7923, which is 2.03% higher than the second-best technique. When the F-Measure is considered, the value 0.0505 shown by the proposed SMOTETomek + FAugOImb is better than the other techniques compared.

Table 2. Results for the Abalone 19 dataset

Balancing technique	AUC	G-mean	F-measure
SMOTE	0.7647	0.7527	0.0428
SMOTETomek	0.7800	0.7717	0.0482
SMOTE + FAugOImb	0.7778	0.7736	0.0485
SMOTETomek + FAugOImb	**0.7982**	**0.7923**	**0.0505**

Table 3 presents the results obtained for the WDBC dataset. From the results presented in Table 3, it is clear that the proposed SMOTETomek + FAugOImb can provide better performance in AUC, which is 0.9047, G-Mean, which is 0.9016, and F-Measure with a value of 0.8870.

Table 3. Results of the WDBC dataset

Balancing technique	AUC	G-mean	F-measure
SMOTE	0.8984	0.8946	0.8799
SMOTETomek	0.9019	0.8988	0.8829
SMOTE + FAugOImb	0.8863	0.8804	0.8656
SMOTETomek + FAugOImb	**0.9047**	**0.9016**	**0.8870**

Therefore, when the above three tables were considered, it was worth mentioning that for the balancing technique, SMOTETomek performs better for balancing the dataset, followed by the FAugOImb that can be used to handle the overlapped instances that may appear in the dataset. After considering the aforementioned, it could be implied that the proposed SMOTETomek + FAugOImb technique outperforms the other techniques for AUC, G-Mean, and F-Measure for all datasets considered in this paper. The results also indicated that the FAugOImb could generalise well to the unseen data by handling the invariance issue. Therefore, the FAugOImb with the balancing technique SMOTETomek achieved higher performance in all cases.

When the AUC is considered, the critical value was selected using Friedman's rank critical table for $k-1$ degree of freedom; Friedman's measurement is 7.8 with a confidence level of 0.05. The calculated Friedman's measurement (44.5) is greater than the value obtained from Friedman's rank critical table. Therefore, it can be concluded that there is a difference between the AUC scores of different techniques. Thereafter, Holm's Bonferroni step down procedure was carried as the post hoc test. Holm's Bonferroni method compares each p-value with modified α^*. As per the results, the modified α^* was greater than their p-values, so it can be concluded that the results of the SMOTE + FAugOImb were statistically significant. When the G-Mean is considered, the critical value was selected using Friedman's rank critical table for $k-1$ degree of freedom; Friedman's measurement is 7.8 with a confidence level of 0.05. The calculated Friedman's measurement (43) is greater than the value obtained from Friedman's rank critical table. As in the earlier case, there is a difference between the G-Mean scores of different techniques. Thereafter, Holm's Bonferroni step down procedure was carried as the post hoc test. As per the comparison between each p-value with modified α^*, the modified α^* was greater than their p-values. Therfore, it can be concluded that the results of the SMOTE + FAugOImb were statistically significant. When the F-Measure is considered, the critical value was selected using Friedman's rank critical table for $k-1$ degree of freedom; Friedman's measurement is 7.8 with a confidence level of 0.05. The calculated Friedman's measurement (43) is greater than the value obtained from Friedman's rank critical table. Therefore, it can be concluded that there is a difference between the F-Measure scores of different techniques. Thereafter, Holm's step down procedure was carried out to identify the best technique used. Holm's Bonferroni method compares each p-value with modified α^*. As per the results, the modified α^* was greater than their p-values, so it can be concluded that the results of the SMOTE + FAugOImb were statistically significant.

5   Conclusion

In this paper, the proposed FAugOImb is used to handle overlapped data in an imbalanced dataset for better generalisation with improved regularization in DNN. Here the proposed FAugOImb is developed using fuzzy concept. The datasets used in the experiments are German, Abalone 19, and WDBC datasets obtained from the UCI and KEEL data repositories. The datasets are first balanced using a balancing technique, and then the overlapped issue is handled. SMOTETomek is identified as the most suitable balancing technique to be used together with the proposed FAugOImb method. The performance of the method was assessed using three metrics, AUC, F-Measure, and G-Mean. Friedman's statistical significance test and Holm's Bonferroni method showed that the proposed FAugOImb model with SMOTETomek was statistically significant.

References

1. Krawczyk, B.: Learning from imbalanced data: open challenges and future directions. Prog. Artif. Intell. **5**(4), 221–232 (2016). https://doi.org/10.1007/s13748-016-0094-0
2. Batista, G.E., Prati, R.C., Monard, M.C.: A study of the behavior of several methods for balancing machine learning training data. ACM SIGKDD Explor. Newsl. **6**(1), 20–29 (2004)
3. Chawla, N.V., et al.: SMOTE: synthetic minority over-sampling technique. J. Artif. Intell. Res. **16**, 321–357 (2002)
4. Tomek, I.: Two modifications of CNN. IEEE Trans. Syst. Man Cybern. **6**, 769–772 (1976)
5. Prati, R.C., Batista, G.E., Monard, M.C.: Class imbalances versus class overlapping: an analysis of a learning system behavior. In: Mexican International Conference on Artificial Intelligence. Springer (2004)
6. García, V., et al.: Combined effects of class imbalance and class overlap on instance-based classification. In: International Conference on Intelligent Data Engineering and Automated Learning. Springer (2006)
7. Wang, Z., et al.: SMOTETomek-based resampling for personality recognition. IEEE Access **7**, 129678–129689 (2019)
8. Zixi, L., et al.: Nondestructive detection of apple mouldy core disease based on unbalanced dielectric data. In: 2019 Chinese Automation Congress (CAC). IEEE (2019)
9. LeCun, Y., Bengio, Y., Hinton, G.: Deep learning. Nature **521**(7553), 436–444 (2015)
10. Wang, C.-S., et al.: Detecting potential adverse drug reactions using a deep neural network model. J. Med. Internet Res. **21**(2), e11016 (2019)
11. Katzman, J.L., et al.: DeepSurv: personalized treatment recommender system using a Cox proportional hazards deep neural network. BMC Med. Res. Methodol. **18**(1), 24 (2018)
12. Kim, H.-C., Bandettini, P.A., Lee, J.-H.: Deep neural network predicts emotional responses of the human brain from functional magnetic resonance imaging. Neuroimage **186**, 607–627 (2019)
13. Saleem, N., et al.: Deep neural network for supervised single-channel speech enhancement. Arch. Acoust. **44**(1), 3–12 (2019)
14. Sumit, S.H., Akhter, S.: C-means clustering and deep-neuro-fuzzy classification for road weight measurement in traffic management system. Soft. Comput. **23**(12), 4329–4340 (2018). https://doi.org/10.1007/s00500-018-3086-0
15. Johnson, J.M., Khoshgoftaar, T.M.: Survey on deep learning with class imbalance. J. Big Data **6**(1), 1–54 (2019). https://doi.org/10.1186/s40537-019-0192-5
16. Goodfellow, I., Bengio, Y., Courville, A.: Deep Learning. MIT press, Cambridge (2016)
17. Cui, X., Goel, V., Kingsbury, B.: Data augmentation for deep neural network acoustic modeling. IEEE/ACM Trans. Audio Speech Lang. Process. (TASLP) **23**(9), 1469–1477 (2015)
18. Tomaszewska, K.: The application of horizontal membership functions to fuzzy arithmetic operations. J. Theoret. Appl. Comput. Sci. **8**(2), 3–10 (2014)
19. Zadeh, L.A.: Fuzzy sets. Inf. Control **8**(3), 338–353 (1965)
20. Pruengkarn, R., Wong, K.W., Fung, C.C.: Imbalanced data classification using complementary fuzzy support vector machine techniques and SMOTE. In: Systems, Man, and Cybernetics (SMC), 2017 IEEE International Conference on 2017. IEEE (2017)

21. Dabare, R., Wong, K.W., Shiratuddin, M.F., Koutsakis, P.: Fuzzy deep neural network for classification of overlapped data. In: Gedeon, T., Wong, K.W., Lee, M. (eds.) ICONIP 2019. LNCS, vol. 11953, pp. 633–643. Springer, Cham (2019). https://doi.org/10.1007/978-3-030-36708-4_52
22. Chen, S.-Y., Feng, Z., Yi, X.: A general introduction to adjustment for multiple comparisons. J. Thorac. Dis. **9**(6), 1725 (2017)

Malware Detection Using Rough Set Based Evolutionary Optimization

Manel Jerbi[1]([✉]) [iD], Zaineb Chelly Dagdia[2,3] [iD], Slim Bechikh[1] [iD],
and Lamjed Ben Said[1] [iD]

[1] SMART Lab, CS Department, University of Tunis, ISG, Tunis, Tunisia
[2] Université Paris-Saclay, UVSQ, DAVID, Versailles, France
[3] LARODEC, University of Tunis, ISG, Tunis, Tunisia

Abstract. Despite the existing anti-malware techniques and their interesting achieved results to "hook" attacks, the unstoppable evolution of malware makes the need for more capable malware detection systems overriding. In this paper, we propose a new malware detection technique named Bilevel-Roughset based Malware Detection (BLRDetect) that is based on, and exploits the benefits of, Bilevel optimization and Rough Set Theory. The upper-level of the Bilevel optimization component uses a Genetic Programming Algorithm in its chase of generating powerful detection rules while the lower-level leans on both a Genetic Algorithm and a Rough-Set module to produce high quality, and reliable, malware samples that escape, to their best, the upper-level's generated detection rules. Both levels interact with each other in a competitive way in order to produce populations that depend on one another. Our detection technique has proven its outperformance when tested against various state-of-the-art malware detection systems using common evaluation metrics.

Keywords: Evolutionary optimization · Rough set theory · Malware detection

1 Introduction

Malware authors tend to use obfuscation techniques to infiltrate and hack a targeted system. To counter these attacks, a "good" malware detection system has to detect every sort of attacks and neutralize them. We will focus specifically on the works that opted to generate new, and evolve, malware aiming at keeping the base of malware samples varied and rich; as a way to better detect malicious code. Among these works, we mention [6,7], where authors applied evolutionary algorithms to generate malware samples. Among the most recent and efficient ones, we mention [5], where a malware detection system (AMD) was proposed that produces patterns using a Genetic Algorithm (GA) in order to mimic real malware patterns. This is to keep the data set used in the conception of the detection system as varied as possible, which allows AMD to be resistant to obfuscated malware. Also, the work of [6], opted for a system using

© Springer Nature Switzerland AG 2021
T. Mantoro et al. (Eds.): ICONIP 2021, CCIS 1516, pp. 634–641, 2021.
https://doi.org/10.1007/978-3-030-92307-5_74

co-evolutionary algorithms where a first population generates detection rules, and a second population generates artificial malware. In this work, both populations are executed in parallel without any hierarchy. In spite of their interesting detection rates, these works suffer from many limitations: (1) they refer to a limited number of malware samples which makes the produced base of malicious malware not varied enough, (2) there is no check of the structure of the generated malicious patterns, (3) the malware generation and detection tasks are achieved separately. To overcome the above mentioned shortcomings, our BLRDetect detection technique, also, generates artificial malware – technically called "patterns" which are a set of Application Programming Interface (API) call sequences – but its main distinction and novelty rely on combining evolutionary algorithms, responsible for producing both detection rules and malware patterns, following a BiLevel OPtimization (BLOP) [3] process, and Rough Set Theory [4] to guarantee the "reliability" of the generated patterns.

2   The Bi-level Rough Set Malware Detection Technique

Figure 1 presents the overall running process of BLRDetect: (1) *Module 1* is based on a GP which aims to produce a set of efficient detection rules ($FSDR$) and (2) *Module 2* leans on a GA that produces artificial malicious patterns ($SAMP$) (step 1) and a rough set based component that keeps only the reliable set of artificial malicious patterns that does not present deficiencies concerning their structure, referred to as "High-quality" artificial patterns (FAP) (step 2).

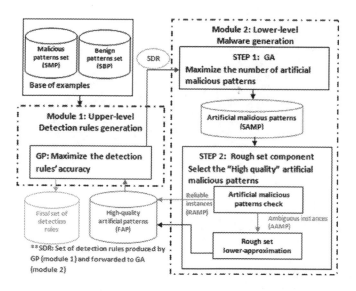

Fig. 1. BLRDetect overview.

First Module: Upper-Level. In order to produce a set of effective detection rules, and as shown in Fig. 1 and Algorithm 1, the upper-level's first step consists of generating a set of detection rules (Algorithm 1, line 1) which will go through an evaluation process (Algorithm 1, lines 2–3). This evaluation is based on the coverage of the base of examples (input) and also the coverage of the artificial malicious patterns generated by the lower-level. These two measures are used to be maximized by the population of detection rules solutions (Algorithm 1, lines 4–6). The output of this module is a set of final detection rules $(FSDR)$ that will be used by the detection task which is responsible for labelling new apps either as malicious or as benign. As the upper-level relies upon a GP process, the GP evolutionary operators require a specific formalization to deal with the manipulated solutions (i.e., the detection rules). These are the following: *(1) Solution Representation:* The solution is formalized as a set of terminals,

---

Algorithm 1: The Upper-Level Algorithm

Inputs: SMP: set of malicious patterns, SBP: set of benign patterns, FAP: set of High-quality artificial malicious patterns, NDR: number of detection rules, NAP: number of High-quality artificial malicious patterns in $SAMP$, NU: number of iterations in the upper-level, NL: number of iterations in the lower-level

Output: Final set of detection rules $FSDR$

1:   $SDR_0 \leftarrow$ Initialization($NDR,SAMP,SBP$)

2:   **For** each DR_0 in SDR_0 **do**

2.1: $SAP_0 \leftarrow$ APGeneration($DR_0,FAP,NAP,\ NL$)

2.2: $DR_0 \leftarrow$ Evaluation($DR_0,SAMP,SAP_0$)

3:   **End For**

4:   $t \leftarrow 1$

5:   **While** ($t < NU$) **do**

5.1: $Q_t \leftarrow$ Variation(SDR_{t-1})

5.2:   **For** each DR_t in Q_t **do**

5.2.1: $DR_t \leftarrow$ UpperEvaluation($DR_t,SAMP$)

5.2.2: $SAP_t \leftarrow$ APGeneration($DR_t,SAMP,NAP,NL$)

5.2.3: $DR_t \leftarrow$ EvaluationUpdate(DR_t,SAP_t)

5.3:   **End For**

5.4: $U_t \leftarrow Q_t \cup SDR_t$

5.5: $SDR_{t+1} \leftarrow$ Selection(NDR,U_t)

5.6: $t \leftarrow t+1$

6:   **End While**

7:   $FSDR \leftarrow$ FittestSelection(SDR_t)

---

referring to different patterns (API call sequences), and functions (Intersection (AND) and Union (OR)). *(2) Solution variation:* The GP *mutation operator* is applied to a function or to a terminal by randomly selecting one of them. If a terminal is selected then it is replaced by another terminal; if it is a function then it is replaced by a new function. As for the GP *crossover operator*, two parent individuals are selected, and a sub-node is picked on each selected parent. The *crossover* swaps the nodes and their related sub-node from one parent to the other. *(3) Solution evaluation:* The encoding of an individual is formalized as a mathematical function called the "fitness function" that quantifies the quality of the proposed detection rules and the artificial malicious patterns. For the GP adaptation, we used the fitness function f_{upper} defined in Eq. 1 to evaluate detection-rules solutions (DR).

$$f_{upper}(DR) = Max(\frac{\frac{Precision(DR)+Recall(DR)}{2} + \frac{\#damp}{\#amp}}{2}) \tag{1}$$

where $\#damp$ refers to the number of detected artificial malicious patterns and $\#amp$ refers to the number of artificial malicious patterns and

$$Precision(DR) = \frac{\sum_{i=1}^{p} DR_i}{t}, \ Recall(DR) = \frac{\sum_{i=1}^{p} DR_i}{p} \tag{2}$$

p is the number of detected malicious patterns after executing the solution, i.e., the detection rule, on the base of malicious patterns examples (SMP), t is the total number of malicious patterns within SMP, and DR_i is the ith component of a detection rule DR such that: $DR_i = 1$ if the ith detected malicious pattern exists in SMP ; 0 otherwise.

Second Module: Lower-Level. The generation process of "High-quality" artificial malicious patterns $(FAP,$ Algorithm 2, line 4.8) is performed as follows:

– *Step 1:* A GA is applied that (i) maximizes the distance between the generated malicious patterns $(SAMP)$ and the reference benign patterns (input, not-generated patterns (SBP)), (ii) minimizes the distance between the generated malicious patterns $(SAMP)$ and the reference malicious ones (SMP), and (iii) maximizes the number of the generated malicious patterns that are not detected by the upper-level; i.e., by the detection rules (SDR) (Algorithm 2, lines 1–4.6). To generate the patterns, the GA evolutionary operators require a specific formalization to deal with the manipulated solutions (i.e., the patterns). These are defined as follows: *(1) Solution representation:* The GA solutions are formalized as chromosomes which are composed of API call sequences. These are identified via their identifiers (IDs) and described by their class labels which indicate their nature (malicious or benign), their different calling depths, and a set of binary values indicating if an API call shows or not in the whole API call sequence. *(2) Solution variation:* For the GA, as previously explained for the GP, the crossover and the mutation operators are applied. *(3) Solution evaluation:* An artificial malicious pattern (AP) is evaluated based on the following GA fitness function:

$$f_{lower}(AP) = Max((\#gamp - \#dagmp) + \sum_{i=1}^{N} f_{Qual}(AP_i)) \tag{3}$$

where $i \in [1, n]$; n indicates the total number of artificial patterns, and $\#gamp$ refers to the number of artificial malicious patterns and $\#dagmp$ refers to the number of detected artificial malicious patterns. The function $f_{Qual}()$ defined in Eq. 4, and its components in Table 1, guarantees the diversity of the artificial malicious patterns.

$$f_{Qual}(AP_i) = \frac{Sim_1 + Sim_2 + Overlap(AP_i)}{3} \tag{4}$$

A detailed description of the similarity function $Sim()$ can be found in [5].

Table 1. The different $f_{Qual}()$ components.

Similarity used	Description
$Sim_1 = Sim(MS, AP_i)$	
$Sim(MS, AP_i) = \frac{\sum MS_{j \in MS} Sim(AP_i, MS_j)}{\|MS\|}$ (5) where $j \in [1, m]$; m indicates the total number of malicious patterns	The similarity between the generated pattern AP_i and the malicious patterns (MS). This measure of similarity needs to be maximized
$Sim_2 = Sim(BS, AP_i)$	
$Sim(BS, AP_i) = \frac{\sum BS_{k \in BS} Sim(AP_i, BS_k)}{\|BS\|}$ (6) where $k \in [1, p]$; p indicates the total number of benign patterns	The similarity between the generated pattern AP_i and the benign patterns (BS) which has to be the lowest
$Overlap(AP_i)$	
$Overlap(AP_i) = 1 - \frac{\sum AP_{l, i \neq l} Sim(AP_i, AP_l)}{\|AP\|}$ (7)	Measured as the average value of the individual $Sim(AP_i, AP_l)$ between the generated pattern AP_i and all the other generated patterns AP_l in the generated data set SAP. l refers to the total number of the generated artificial patterns

- *Step 2:* The GA above mentioned evolutionary operators may cause the manipulated solutions to be distorted, and hence ambiguous. Technically, a set of patterns is declared to be ambiguous when they share the same values of the features (API calls) but do have different label values (malicious/benign). To handle this ambiguity issue and to guarantee the reliability of the generated malicious patterns, a rough set component which uses mainly the rough set lower approximation concept is plugged to the lower-level (see Fig. 1 and Algorithm 2, lines 4.7–4.8).

Algorithm 2: The Lower-Level Algorithm

Inputs: SMP, SBP, SDR: set of detection rules, G: number of generations,
   N: population size
Output: Set of High-quality artificial malicious patterns FAP
1: $SAP_0 \leftarrow$ Initialization(SBP,SMP,N,G)
2: $SAP_0 \leftarrow$ Evaluation(SAP_0,SBP,SMP,SDR)
3: $t \leftarrow 1$
4: **While** ($t < G$) **do**
4.1: $Q_t \leftarrow$ Variation(SAP_{t-1})
4.2: $Q_t \leftarrow$ Evaluation(Q_t,SBP,SMP,SDR)
4.3: $U_t \leftarrow Q_t \cup SAP_t$
4.4: $SAP_{t+1} \leftarrow$ Selection(N,U_t)
4.5: $t \leftarrow t{+}1$
4.6: $SAMP \leftarrow$ FittestSelection(SAP_t)
4.7:   ($RAMP$, $AAMP$) $\leftarrow$ ReliabilityCheck($SAMP$)
4.8: $FAP \leftarrow$ LowerApproximation($AAMP$) $\cup$ $RAMP$
5: **End While**

Detection Task Based on Detection Rules. Each pattern is labeled as benign or as malicious by comparing it to the patterns of the SMP and SBP databases. Then, the obtained patterns are compared to the antecedent of $FSDR$.

3   Experimental Setup and Results

To evaluate the performance of BLRDetect, we have considered datasets obtained from the Android Malware Data set (AMD set) [2], and from various portable benign tools such as Google play. We have gathered 3 000 Android apps where 2 000 are malicious and 1 000 apps are benign files. The Drebin dataset [1], which contains 123 453 benign applications and 5 560 malware samples, is used for the evaluation of our approach against the new variants of malware and 0-day attacks. Different state-of-the-art methods were considered for comparisons. These are the classical classifiers named in Table 2, tested using Weka[1] with the proposed default parameters settings, the two most recent EA-based methods (AMD [5] and Sen et al. [6]) previously described in Sect. 1. To ensure the fairness of comparisons between evolutionary approaches, we set to 0.9 the crossover rate and to 0.5 the mutaion rate. All of the evolutionary approaches perform 810 000 function evaluations in each run. When running the experiments, we concluded that the fitness functions become stabilized around the 40th generation. For these reasons, the algorithms did not suffer from premature convergence. The metrics used for the evaluation are: true positives (TP), false positives (FP), true negatives (TN), false negatives (FN), recall (RC), specificity (SP), accuracy (AC), precision (PR), F1_score (FS), and the Area Under the Receiver Operating Characteristics (ROC) Curve (AUC). All of the conducted experiments,

---

[1] https://www.cs.waikato.ac.nz/ml/weka/.

based on a 10-fold cross validation, are run on an $Intel^{®}$ $Xeon^{®}$ Processor CPU E5-2620 v3, with a 16 GB RAM.

We compare the BLRDetect obatined results to a set of state-of-the-art non-EA based classifiers (Table 2) and two EA-based approaches (Sen et al. [6] and AMD [5]). Concerning the comparison with non-EA based classifiers, Table 2 shows that BLRDetect outperforms all classifiers based on all the used evaluation metrics. For instance, BLRDetect achieved a precision of 98.09%, an accuracy of 98.21%, an F1_score of 97.82%, and a specificity of 98.36% in comparison to the LDA and $J48$ classifiers, which achieved the second best results among the rest of the classifiers, with a pair of precision and accuracy of (98.36%, 97.82%) for LDA and (97.73%, 96.58%) for $J48$ and a pair of F1_score and specificity of (97.32%,97.31%) for LDA and (98.37%,97.13%) for $J48$. These interesting BLRDetect results are based on its interesting reached values of true positives (98.09%) and the low false positives (01.91%); which are, indeed, the best achieved values among the classifiers' obtained results. These satisfying results confirm that BLRDetect is powerful in performing its detection task between the two possible labels (malicious/benign).

Table 2. Comparison between BLRDetect and other detection techniques.

Classifier/ Approach	TP	FP	TN	FN	RC	SP	AC	PR	FS	AUC	FPR	FNR
BLRDetect	98.09	01.91	98.15	01.65	98.37	98.36	98.21	98.09	97.82	86.83	01.90	01.65
LR	93.81	06.19	96.75	03.25	96.65	93.98	95.28	93.17	95.60	63.69	06.01	03.34
NB	92.30	07.70	28.41	71.59	56.31	78.67	60.35	92,37	93,62	65.06	02.13	09.03
RF	97.41	02.59	95.90	04.10	96.00	98.37	97.16	97.36	97.17	73.04	02.62	04.03
J48	97.18	02.82	93.98	06.02	94.27	97.13	96.58	97.73	98.37	83.90	02.91	05.83
k-NN	89.52	10.48	95.21	04.79	94.92	90.08	92.37	85.74	90.56	57.69	09.91	05.07
LDA	97.29	02.71	98.36	01.64	98.34	97.31	97.82	98.36	97.32	75.96	02.68	01.65
BLRDetect	97.20	02.80	97.99	02.01	98.05	97.77	96.46	96.93	96.41	87.00	02.77	02.02
Sen et al.	97.10	02.80	93.25	06.75	98.24	95.37	95.15	97.13	95.88	82.10	02.91	06.49
AMD	93.80	06.19	90.90	09.10	96.20	92.70	92.28	93.60	92.37	57.69	06.37	08.84

LR: Logistic Regression; LDA: Linear Discriminant Analysis; RF: Random Forest;
J48: Decision Tree; NB: Naive Bayes; k-NN: k-Nearest Neighbours.

Furthermore, from Table 2, we can deduce that, when compared against EA-based methods using the unknown dataset [1], BLRDetect came first with particularly an accuracy = 96.46%, a specificity = 97.77%, a recall = 98.05%, a precision = 96.93%, and an AUC = 87.00%. As for Sen et al. and AMD, they achieved an accuracy of 95.15% and 92.28%, a precision of 97.13% and 93.60%, and an AUC of 82.10% 57.69%, respectively, which are lower than those obtained by our proposed technique. The results reported from Table 2 highlights the ability of BLRDetect – thanks to its set of efficient produced rules which are generated using the most reliable set of the generated artificial malicious malware; both guaranteed via the use of the BLOP architecture and the rough set component – to achieve accurate detection operations against new and unknown variants of malware. To better clarify the efficiency and benefits of relying on the bilevel architecture within BLRDetect, we analyse the results in terms of false positive and the false negative rates. The registered BLRDetect values of those two metrics (Table 2) confirm the usefulness of a bilevel architecture to detect efficiently malicious code. The continuous competition between both levels permitted good solutions generation (detection rules and artificial malicious patterns) and this had positive impact on the values of FPR (02.77%) and FNR (02.02%). In comparison to BLRDetect, the registered FPR/FNR values for both [6] and [5], which rely on a single-layer based architecture via the use of EAs, are (02.91%/06.49%) and (06.37%/08.84%), respectively. In addition, we can state that the rough-set based module succeeded to set apart 212 000 ambiguous instances among the generated artificial patterns $SAMP$ (468 000 instances) and to produce 256 000 reliables instances. This distinction brings to light the rough set component's important contribution in improving the quality of the artificial malicious patterns by the lower-level and which, consequently, positively affected the false alarms rate.

4   Conclusion

We developed a malware detection technique named BLRDetect which leans on a bilevel architecture and a rough set module. Within the bilevel architecture, the malware generation task (lower-level) and the rules generation task (detection task, upper-level) are in mutual competition. The lower-level generates "High-quality" malicious patterns which are generated by a GA and thoroughly checked by a rough set component that only keeps the most reliable ones, and which are capable to escape the set of detection rules which are produced by a GP within the upper-level. These efficient generated detection rules try their best to detect the set of artificial malicious patterns generated in the lower-level.

References

1. Arp, D., Spreitzenbarth, M., Hubner, M., Gascon, H., Rieck, K., Siemens, C.E.R.T.: Drebin: effective and explainable detection of android malware in your pocket. In: NDSS, vol. 14, pp. 23–26, February 2014
2. Wei, F., Li, Y., Roy, S., Ou, X., Zhou, W.: Deep ground truth analysis of current android malware. In: Polychronakis, M., Meier, M. (eds.) DIMVA 2017. LNCS, vol. 10327, pp. 252–276. Springer, Cham (2017). https://doi.org/10.1007/978-3-319-60876-1_12
3. Colson, B., Marcotte, P., Savard, G.: An overview of bilevel optimization. Ann. Oper. Res. **153**(1), 235–256 (2007)
4. Zhang, Q., Xie, Q., Wang, G.: A survey on rough set theory and its applications. CAAI Trans. Intell. Technol. **1**(4), 323–333 (2016)
5. Jerbi, M., Dagdia, Z.C., Bechikh, S., Said, L.B.: On the use of artificial malicious patterns for android malware detection. Comput. Secur. **92**, 101743 (2020)
6. Sen, S., Aydogan, E., Aysan, A.I.: Coevolution of mobile malware and anti-malware. IEEE Trans. Inf. Forensics Secur. **13**(10), 2563–2574 (2018)
7. Xue, Y., et al.: Auditing anti-malware tools by evolving android malware and dynamic loading technique. IEEE Trans. Inf. Forensics Secur. **12**(7), 1529–1544 (2017)

Revdbscan and Flexscan—$O(n \log n)$ Clustering Algorithms

Norbert Jankowski[✉]

Department of Informatics, Nicolaus Copernicus University, Toruń, Poland
norbert@umk.pl

Abstract. The goal of this paper is to present two new algorithms conceptually close to density-based clustering. Both algorithms deal with problems no worse than the dbscan algorithm, and additionally, flexscan deals with nonuniform distributions of data. The complexity of both algorithms is $O(n \log n)$ in contrary to the well-known dbscan algorithm which complexity is $O(n^2)$. Additionally, we show that the complexity of dbscan cannot be reduced to $O(n \log n)$ just by using locality sensitive hashing trees (or either r-trees or kd-trees).

In the final part of the paper, we present results on benchmark datasets. Results clearly show the superiority of the proposed algorithms.

Keywords: Clustering · Cluster analysis · Unsupervised learning · Machine learning · Locality sensitive hashing · dbscan algorithm

1 Introduction

The clustering algorithms play a significant role in the applications of computational intelligence algorithms. Clustering algorithms belong to unsupervised learning. The goal of clustering can be defined as the grouping of similar objects in clusters. We will assume that there is a dataset $X = \{\mathbf{x}_1, \ldots, \mathbf{x}_m\}$ and $\mathbf{x}_i \in R^n$. Finally, each data vector $\mathbf{x}_i$ is labeled by the cluster index. The grouping process can be made in several ways, and in consequence, several algorithms and their variants were proposed. Some of algorithms are concentrated around the idea which tries to minimize total sum of distances from centroids to its cluster elements [11]: $\arg \min_S \sum_{S_i} I(S_i, t_i)$, where S_i is set of i-th cluster elements, t_i is center of cluster and I was called *inertia* of S_i and t_i. The $I(S_i, t_i)$ can be defined by $\sum_{j \in S_i} ||\mathbf{x}_j - t_i||^2$. Such defined goal is the heart of k means algorithm [5,8,9]. The complexity of *k-means* is $O(mnki)$ (i is the number of iterations to converge). Another goal of clustering was defined by preservation (approximately) a similar number of vectors in clusters, typically used in vector quantization. The main problem of algorithms similar to k means is that final clusters can be of simple shapes, and the number of clusters k is selected arbitrarily by the user. Another group of clustering algorithms is *hierarchical agglomerative clustering* (or dendrograms). They are based on the idea of joining closest objects (at the beginning, the original vectors compose the tree leaves) as many times as the

© Springer Nature Switzerland AG 2021
T. Mantoro et al. (Eds.): ICONIP 2021, CCIS 1516, pp. 642–650, 2021.
https://doi.org/10.1007/978-3-030-92307-5_75

desired number of clusters remain. There are a few tuning possibilities of HAC which base on the linkage selection and the metric selection. However, HAC can deal with more sophisticated cluster shapes than k-means can, but still, some cuts of original clusters were observed (in the human meaning). In general, HAC has immense complexity $(O(m^3))$, which was reduced in some cases to $O(m^2)$. The next step was made by Ester et al. in [4] by proposing the *density-based scan* (dbscan) clustering algorithm. In contrary to previous algorithms, the dbscan can deal with a wide range of cluster shapes of (relatively) uniform density of data in clusters (as stated in the algorithm's name). If the distribution is not so uniform inside a cluster or is significantly different between clusters in the given dataset, the results may vary from expectations. The complexity of dbscan is $O(m^2n)$. Another significant step was made by authors of *Chameleon* [7] and Chameleon 2 [1] algorithms. Both algorithms were trying to build an algorithm that produces more human-like clustering comparing to dbscan. Chameleon 2 is currently the most sophisticated clustering algorithm. The only disadvantage is the complexity of algorithm: $O(m^2n + m + (m + l^2) \log l)$ (l is desired number of partitions in bisection, see [1] for details).

The above algorithms were inspirations for the construction of new algorithms. The following section presents information about the complexity of dbscan and presents new clustering revdbscan, which complexity is $O(nm \log m)$. The exact section also presents another new clustering algorithm—the flexscan—which can deal with more complex clusters than the dbscan algorithm, but its complexity is also $nm \log m$. The last section presents few examples of results calculated by dbscan, revdbscan and flexscan.

2 Analysis of Dbscan Complexity and New Revdbscan Algorithm

The starting point for further consideration is the dbscan algorithm [4] proposed by Ester et al. The meta-code of algorithm was presented in Algorithm 1 and Algorithm 2. The base idea of the algorithm is to join points in the dense region. The density is characterized by two factors: the radius ϵ and the $minPts$. A given region centered in a point $\mathbf{x}$ is dense if in hypher-sphere centered in p with radius ϵ contains at least $minPts$ points from X. All points in the dense region belong to the same cluster, and for each such point, its region is analyzed, whether it is dense or not. Moreover, in the case of the dense region of neighboring points, their neighbors extend the cluster.

In the beginning, all points of X are unvisited. The goal of regionQuery($\mathbf{x}, \epsilon$) is to extract all points from X around $\mathbf{x}$ in radius ϵ. Inside dbscan or expandCluster points of dataset, X becomes one by one visited (each only ones). This means that for each point $\mathbf{x} \in X$, the regionQuery is called to extract all points in radius ϵ around $\mathbf{x}$. In consequence, for each point $\mathbf{x}$, its region is computed. The straightforward implementation of regionQuery is $O(mn)$ (a check whether or not each point of X follows in the region). If kd-trees or vantage-points trees or r-trees are used to extract points in regionQuery then the complexity will

---

Algorithm 1: DBscan($X, \epsilon, minPts$)

Data: ϵ, $minPts$ — configuration params of DBscan

1 **foreach** *unvisited point* **x** *in* X **do**
2   mark P as visited
3   NeighborPts = regionQuery(**x**, ϵ)
4   **if** *sizeof(NeighborPts)* < *minPts* **then**
5   mark **x** as NOISE

6   **else**
7   C = new cluster
8   expandCluster(**x**, NeighborPts, C, ϵ, $MinPts$)

Algorithm 2: expandCluster($X, \epsilon, minPts$)

Data: **x**, NeighborPts, C, *epsilon*, *minPts*

1 add **x** to cluster C
2 **foreach** *point Q in NeighborPts* **do**
3   **if** *Q is not visited* **then**
4   mark Q as visited
5   NeighborPtsQ = regionQuery(Q, ϵ)
6   **if** *sizeof(NeighborPtsQ)* $\geq$ *minPts* **then**
7   NeighborPts += NeighborPtsQ

8   **if** *Q is not yet member of any cluster* **then**
9   add Q to cluster C

---

not reduce to $O(n \log m)$ and remain the same—it was presented in [10]. The reduction of complexity is observed only in (very) low dimensional spaces like $n = 2$ or $n = 3$. This means that information presented in [4] was wrong. Finally, the complexity of dbscan remains $O(nm^2)$. However, the computation of region-Query can be made with the help of locality sensitive hashing [6]. The complexity of regionQuery (at least) must be the number of points in the resulting region. In such case the average complexity of regionQuery is $O(n \log m + n * rSize)$ (where $rSize$ is the number of all points in given region).

The problem is that $rSize = O(m)$. For simpler observation assume $n = 1$ then the region around given **x** is an interval $[\mathbf{x} - \epsilon, \mathbf{x} + \epsilon]$. The length of this interval is a fraction of interval $[\min_{\mathbf{x} \in X}, \max_{\mathbf{x} \in X}]$. For example in case of uniform or Gaussian distribution of X the $rSize$ has complexity $O(m)$ because expected number of points in $[\mathbf{x} - \epsilon, \mathbf{x} + \epsilon]$ is a fraction of m.

2.1 Revdbscan Algorithm

Above considerations presents a trap in the context of complexity, which is crucial for the applicability of clustering algorithm for large datasets. However, the concept of a dense region can be defined in another way—and this is the main idea

---

Algorithm 3: Revdbscan(X, ϵ, K)

Data: ϵ, K — configuration params of RevDBscan ($K = O(1)$)
Result: sets from union-find as clusters
```
/* phase I: computation of nearest neighbours          */
```
1   construction of forests of balanced Locality-Sensitive Hashing Trees
2   **for** $i = 0$ **to** $m - 1$ **do**
3      $N_i = K$ nearest neighbours of $\mathbf{x}_i$ from forest of trees

```
/* phase II: clustering                                 */
```
4   initialize union-find: parent[i]=i; name[i]=i; root[i]=i; count[i]=1;
       $\forall_{i=0,\ldots,m-1}$
5   **for** $i = 0$ **to** $m - 1$ **do**
6      $d = \max_{\mathbf{x} \in N_i} \|\mathbf{x}_i - \mathbf{x}\|$
7   **if** $d \leq \epsilon$ **then** if dense, join all points from N_i
8   Union(N_i)

9   **for** $i = 0$ **to** $m - 1$ **do**
10     $c = $ Find(i)
11   **if** $count[root[c]] = 1$ **then**
12   mark i as noise

---

of the revdbscan algorithm proposed here. In the case of the revdbscan algorithm region centered in $\mathbf{x}$ is dense if the distance between $\mathbf{x}$ and each of K nearest neighbors is not greater than ϵ. Additionally, it is assumed that $K = O(1)$. The metacode of the algorithm is presented in Algorithm 3.

In the first phase of the algorithm, a forest of balanced locality-sensitive hashing trees is constructed. The tree forest is used to fast computation of nearest neighbors. The construction of a tree forest is $O(nm \log m)$. Finally, the sets of nearest neighbors are collected in $O(nm)$. The construction of the forest was introduced by us in [10] (see section 3.1).

The second phase of the algorithm starts the central clustering part, which begins with the initialization of structures to represents a set for classical union-find operations (as it was presented in [3]). In the beginning, each vector is a single cluster. In the main loop (line 5 of Algorithm 3), the density is checked, and if region of given point is dense, then all neighbors are joined in one cluster. All neighbors will be in one cluster, and if some of the neighbors were already assigned to clusters, those clusters would be joined with the rest of the neighbors. This joining process is done by the Union(N_i) (which joins unjoined instances from given N_i). The complexity of main loop is $O(nm + m \log^* m)$ because computation of maximal distance is $O(n)$ and m iterations of Union(N_i) has complexity $O(m \log^* m)$[1]. The last loop executes the Find m times—the cost is $O(m \log^* m)$. Finally, the complexity of revdbscan is $O(nm \log m)$.

The additional advantage of the revdbscan algorithm is that it is composed of two separate phases. The first phase can be computed ones and following the

---

[1] The $\log^*$ denotes iterative logarithm.

second phase may be computed several times with different configurations of K and ϵ (if only appropriate K were used in the first phase, and nearest neighbors were sorted (cost of sorts is just $O(m)$)).

2.2   Flexscan

The flexscan algorithm is another fast clustering algorithm but with higher flexibility in the context of distribution. The primary goal was to enable continuous changes in data density inside a cluster. The meta-code of flexscan was presented in Algorithm 4 and in Algorithm 5. The first phase of the flexscan algorithm is the same as in revdbscan. The second phase starts the central part of clustering, and it differs strongly from the revdbscan algorithm. The dataset points are sorted according to ascending order of the distance between the given point and its furthest (of K) neighbor. This order is used in the following vector analysis.

Algorithm 4: Flexscan$(X, K, \epsilon, \beta, \rho)$

Data: K — number of neighbours for density check, ϵ — density radius, β — flexibility scale (default value 1.05), ρ — flexibility path length

Result: sets from union-find as clusters

1 initialize union-find: parent[i]=i; name[i]=i; root[i]=i; count[i]=1; $\forall_{i=0,\ldots,m-1}$

   /* phase I: computation of nearest neighbours   */
2 construction of forests of balanced Locality-Sensitive Hashing Trees
3 **for** $i = 0$ **to** $m - 1$ **do**
4 $\quad$ $N_i = K$ nearest neighbours of $\mathbf{x}_i$ from forest of trees;

   /* phase II: clustering   */
5 **for** $i = 0$ **to** $m - 1$ **do**
6 $\quad$ $d_{ij} = \|\mathbf{x}_i - \mathbf{x}_j\|$ $\forall_{j \in N_i}$;
7 $\quad$ $d_i = \max_{\mathbf{x}' \in N_i} \|\mathbf{x}_i - \mathbf{x}'\|$;
8 $\quad$ $\epsilon_i = \epsilon/\beta$;
9 $\quad$ $visited_i = false$;
10 $\quad$ $p_i = -1$;
11 sort points in X according to ascending values of d_i
12 **for** $i = 0$ **to** $m - 1$ **do**
13 $\quad$ **if** $IsDense(i)$ **then**
14 $\quad\quad$ Union(N_i)
15 $\quad\quad$ **foreach** $q \in N_i$ **do**
16 $\quad\quad\quad$ **if** $\neg visited_q$ **then**
17 $\quad\quad\quad\quad$ $visited_q = true$;
18 $\quad\quad\quad\quad$ $p_q = i$;
19 $\quad\quad\quad\quad$ $\epsilon_q = \max\{\epsilon_i, d_{iq}\}$;

20 **for** $i = 0$ **to** $m - 1$ **do**
21 $\quad$ $c = Find(i)$;
22 $\quad$ **if** $count[root[c]] = 1$ **then**
23 $\quad\quad$ mark i as noise

Algorithm 5: IsDense(i)

    Result: q
1 $k = 1; q = false; \gamma = \beta; e = d_i/\epsilon_i;$
2 **while** $k \leq \rho \wedge \neg q$ **do**
3   **if** $e > \gamma$ **then**
4         $i = p_i; \gamma = \gamma * \beta; k = k + 1;$
5   **if** $i = -1$ **then**
6            $k = \rho + 1$
7   **else**
8            $e = e * d_i/\epsilon_i;$
9   **else**
10        $q = true;$

If it was check that region around vector i is dense according to the below description, then

- (as in revdbscan too) all K neighbors are joined in the cluster, and if some of those neighbors were already assigned to some clusters, those clusters become joined together (by the Union(N_i)).
- For each unvisited neighbor q, we set up its parent (i), and the radius ϵ_q is corrected if necessary.

The parent relation plays an essential role in the density checking process. Contrary to dbscan and revdbscan, the flexscan do not use fixed radius ϵ everywhere, but the radius is a subject of continuous changes. Every point i has its own ϵ_i radius. The child vectors may have a bigger radius to enable continuous density reduction if necessary.

The density checking in point i is defined by

$$Q_i = \exists_{j \leq \rho} \; q_i^j \leq \beta^j \tag{1}$$

where q_i^j is defined by

$$q_i^j = \begin{cases} \frac{d_i}{\epsilon_i}, & \text{if } j = 1 \vee p_i = -1 \\ \frac{d_i}{\epsilon_i} \cdot q_{p_i}^{j-1}, & \neg \end{cases} \tag{2}$$

Positive Q_i means that the region around point i is dense. The β regulates the ability of radius extension. ρ defines the maximal length of the path in the density check.

At the beginning each point has assigned initially $\epsilon_i = \epsilon/\beta$ (see line 8). The ϵ_q is corrected in the line 19 according to the density of its parent—if it is possible, then it remains equal to parent ϵ_i; if not, it is set to d_{iq}. The second option is directly connected with the continuous growth of radius.

The complexity of the first phase of the flexscan algorithm is the same as in revdbscan: $O(nm \log m)$. The first loop in the second phase has complexity

$O(nm)$. The followed sorting costs are $O(m \log m)$. And last two loops, similarly to revdbscan has costs $O(m \log^* m)$. Finally, the complexity of flexscan is $O(nm \log m)$.

3   Results

We have selected six datasets to prepare an influent and trustworthy comparison of revdbscan and flexscan with dbscan. The selected benchmarks are: 2sp2glob (2000 instances), impossible (3673 instances), cluto-t7-10k (10000 instances), ds2c2sc13 (588 instances), compound (399 instances), wingnut (1016 instances). All benchmark are 2D and can be found in [2]. Visual results of clustering algorithms can be seen in Fig. 1.

All configuration parameters are placed in titles of subfigures. Additionally, in the subfigure's titles is presented the ARI and the number of noise instances. The ARI was computed between the original benchmark and the results of a clustering algorithm. The ARI was computed between instances of clusters against original classes (except the noise vectors). Information about noise for a given clustering algorithm is separated.

It can be seen that **2sp2glob** benchmark is relatively easy for all algorithms. The ARI is 1, and the amount of noise is tiny. The **impossible** benchmark is not so easy for clustering. However, the ARI is relatively high even for dbscan, especially the dbscan results with huge noise: 235 instances. Best results were obtained by flexscan with ARI = 0.998 and with 105 noise vectors. Although, please note that in the original *impossible* benchmark last class (brawn dots) looks like noise (73 instances), and flexscan algorithm add those instances to noise (dark blue dots). The **cluto-t7-10k** benchmark was the most difficult. The ARI, especially for revdbscan and flexscan, are pretty high, but all algorithms finished with 800–1100 noise vectors. However, in the original dataset, the brawn dots represent a class with 792 instances. This means that 893 noise instances (for flexscan) are indeed equal to (approximately) 893–792. Benchmark named **ds2c2sc13** was also not easy for clustering because some of the original classes are very close, while others are of (slight) different densities. This benchmark shows that revdbscan and flexscan separate easier the close classes. According to the difference in definitions of density checking, the role of K is different between dbscan and proposed algorithms. In the case of the **compound** benchmark, the configuration parameters of all algorithms were selected to separate original classes, even if it has mean growth of the number of noisy instances. Finally, all three algorithms finished with comparable results. The **wingnut** benchmark is an example of clusters with changing density of distribution. As it is easy to guess, the winner can be the only one in such a case: the flexscan. The flexscan finished with ARI = 1 and with 24 noisy instances. Such a result is incomparable with dbscan and revdbscan as well.

The selection of configuration parameters of new algorithms remains on the similar level of difficulty as for the dbscan algorithm. The most important is to select ϵ, which is responsible for *resolution*. However, it is a bit simpler in case of new algorithms if it is selected consciously.

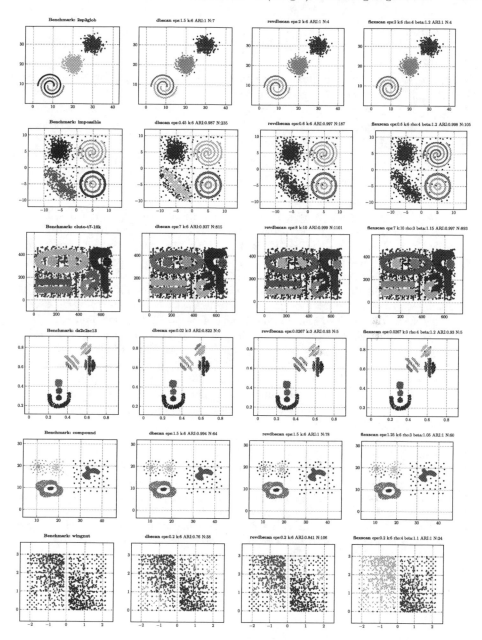

Fig. 1. Clustering results for dbscan, revdbscan and flexscan algorithms.

Of course, those problems can be solved so well with the Chameleon algorithm, but proposed algorithms have better complexity ($O(nm \log m)$) which was confirmed by real time execution by appropriate algorithms.

4   Summary

This paper has presented two new clustering algorithms: revdbscan and flexscan. Both algorithms have complexity $O(nm \log m)$, while dbscan has complexity $O(nm^2)$ and Chameleon 2 has complexity $O(mn^2 + m + (m + l^2) \log l)$. It was shown that revdbscan is similar or slightly better in clustering comparing to dbscan. The flexscan algorithm works in more complex cases than dbscan— flexscan can deal with clusters with continuous density changes.

References

1. Barton, T., Bruna, T., Kordik, P.: Chameleon 2: an improved graph-based clustering algorithm. ACM Trans. Knowl. Discov. Data **13**(1), 10:2–10:27 (2019)
2. Barton, T., Bruna, T., Kordik, P.: Web page (2021). https://github.com/deric/clustering-benchmark
3. Cormen, T.H., Leiserson, C.E., Rivest, R.L., Stein, C.: Data structures for disjoint sets. In: Introduction to Algorithms, pp. 571–572. MIT Press, Cambridge (2009)
4. Ester, M., Kriegel, H.P., Sander, J., Xu, X.: A density-based algorithm for discovering clusters in large spatial databases with noise. In: Evangelos Simoudis, J.H., Fayyad, U.M. (eds.) Proceedings of the 2nd International Conference on Knowledge Discovery and Data Mining (KDD), pp. 226–231. AAAI Press (1996)
5. Forgy, E.W.: Cluster analysis of multivariate data: efficiency versus interpretability of classifications. Biometrics **21**(3), 768–769 (1965)
6. Indyk, P., Motwani, R.: Approximate nearest neighbor–towards removing the curse of dimensionality. In: The Thirtieth Annual ACM Symposium on Theory of Computing, pp. 604–613 (1998)
7. Karypis, G., Han, E.H.S., Kumar, V.: Chameleon: hierarchical clustering using dynamic modeling. Computer **32**(8), 68–75 (1999)
8. Lloyd, S.P.: Least square quantization in PCM. Technical Report, Bell Telephone Laboratories Paper (1957)
9. Lloyd, S.P.: Least squares quantization in PCM. IEEE Trans. Inf. Theor. **28**(2), 129–137 (1982). https://doi.org/10.1109/TIT.1982.1056489
10. Orliński, M., Jankowski, N.: Fast t-SNE algorithm with forest of balanced LSH trees and hybrid computation of repulsive forces. Knowl. Based Syst. **206**, 1–16 (2020). https://doi.org/10.1016/j.knosys.2020.106318
11. Steinhaus, H.: Sur la division des corps matériels en parties. Bull. Acad. Polon. Sci. Cl. III. **4**(1956), 801–804 (1957)

TRGAN: Text to Image Generation Through Optimizing Initial Image

Liang Zhao[✉], Xinwei Li, Pingda Huang, Zhikui Chen, Yanqi Dai, and Tianyu Li

School of Software Technology, Dalian University of Technology, Dalian, China
liangzhao@dlut.edu.cn

Abstract. Generative Adversarial Networks (GANs) have shown success in text-to-image generation tasks. Most of the current methods use multi-stages to generate images, but the quality of the final images is largely dependent on the quality of the initial generated images, thus it is difficult to generate high-quality images in the end if the initial images in the first stage are of low quality, low resolution, irregular shape, strange color, and unrealistic entity relations. Therefore, in this paper, we propose to design a multi-stage generation model, and we address this problem by developing a novel generation model called Text-representation Generative Adversarial Network (TRGAN). TRGAN contains two modules: Joint attention stacked generation module (JASGM) and Text generation in the opposite direction and correction module (TGOCM). In the JASGM module, the detailed feature is extracted from word-level information and the images are generated based on the global sentence attention. In the TGOCM module, the text descriptions are generated reversely, which can improve the quality of the initial images by matching the word-level feature vector. Experimental results present that our proposed model TRGAN outperforms the compared state-of-the-art text-to-image generation methods on CUB and COCO datasets.

Keywords: Text-to-image synthesis · Generative Adversarial Network · Text-image semantic understanding · Text generation reversely

1 Introduction

Nowadays, text-to-image synthesis [1–3] is one of the important applications of GANs, which is one of the most active research areas in recent years. Most early proposed methods of text-to-image using one-step to directly generate final results. However, with the development of text-to-image synthesis methods, the more recent approaches explore multi-stages to generate images from text descriptions, such as AttnGAN [4], StackGAN [5] and MirrorGAN [6]. Some researchers [4–7] take the entire sentence encoding as the basis, and then change the corresponding attribute for each word vector [8]. However, if the initial

© Springer Nature Switzerland AG 2021
T. Mantoro et al. (Eds.): ICONIP 2021, CCIS 1516, pp. 651–658, 2021.
https://doi.org/10.1007/978-3-030-92307-5_76

images are not real (that is, lacks substance, loses form, and is far from the real image), the quality of the image in the next stage will not improve promisingly. Therefore, the text-to-image generation not only needs multi-stage generation, but also needs to achieve different functions in different stages to generate more realistic images.

To tackle it, in this paper a text-to-image model is proposed for synthesizing images from text descriptions by multi-stages, called Text-representation Generative Adversarial Network (TRGAN). And its main contributions are as follows: Firstly, each stage performs different generation tasks for different functions in TRGAN. Secondly, in order to improve the quality of low-quality generated images in the initial stage, a layer of processing is designed in the second stage of generation, in which the generated image is encoded into the image vector as the condition for text vector generation. After that the method utilizes a discriminator to distinguish between the ground truth text vector and generated text vector (see Fig. 1).

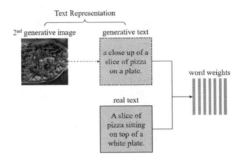

Fig. 1. A discriminator to distinguish between the ground truth text vector and generated text vector.

2   Text-Representation Generative Adversarial Network

In order to favorably generate images from the text description, we proposed the Text-representation Generative Adversarial Network (TRGAN) model. TRGAN is a complex structure with three stages. As shown in Fig. 2, the proposed TRGAN also contains two modules: JASGM and TROGM. The first two stages belong to module JASGM and the last stage belongs to module TROGM. In the JASGM module, the detailed feature information is captured from word-level information and the images are generated based on global sentence attention. In the TGOCM module, the text description is generated reversely from generated images to improve the quality of the initial images by matching the word-level feature vector. Details of the model will be introduced in the subsections.

2.1   JASGM: Joint Attention Stacked Generation Module

In this section, we mainly focus on the properties of detail and embed the given text description into local word-level features. Specifically, we need to process

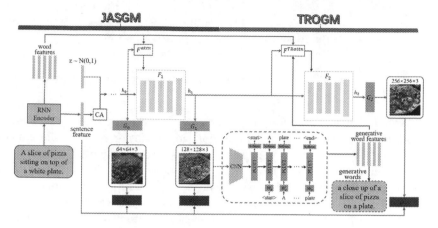

Fig. 2. The architecture of the proposed TRGAN, including JASGM and TROGM modules, which realize different functions, respectively.

word by word in the sentence, so we choose RNN, the recurrent neural network (RNN) [9], to extract word embedding (w_0, w_1, w_{t-1}) from the given text description T.

$$f_t = g_1 \left(v_{w_t} + w_{s_{t-1}} \right);$$
$$W_t = g_2 \left(v_{h_t} \right), \tag{1}$$

where $w = \{ w^l \mid l = 0, \ldots, L-1 \}$, f represents the output of hidden layer.

In our module, an attention word-level feature context matrix Att_{i-1}^w is generated. After that, the word-level weight matrix Att_{i-1}^w and visual feature f_i are as inputs to the perceptron, and then the perceptual layer transforms word-level features into the common semantic space of visual features. Finally, the visual feature f_i of the next stage is further generated through the computation of word-level weight matrix Att_{i-1}^w and visual feature f_{i-1}.

As shown in Fig. 2, the proposed TRGAN has three generators (G0, G1, G2), which take the hidden states (h0, h1, h2) as input, and three discriminators (D1, D2, D3). The images (X1, X2, X3) are generated from low-resolution to high-resolution by generators. First, the feature is extracted from a global sentence vector using a random noise vector, and then the visual feature vector extracted from the perceptron is combined to generate the image of the initial stage.

$$f_0 = F_0 \left(z, F^{ca}(s) \right);$$
$$f_i = F_i \left(f_{i-1}, F_{att_i} \left(f_{i-1}, w \right) \right), i \in \{1, 2\}; \tag{2}$$
$$\hat{I}_i = G_i \left(f_i \right).$$

Herein, z is a noise vector usually sampled from a standard normal distribution, $f_i \in \mathbb{R}^{M_i \times N_i}$, $I_i \in \mathbb{R}^{q_i \times q_i}$, and $z \sim N(0, 1)$. F_{att_i} is the proposed word level attention model. Then, each word vector is computed for each region of the image based on its hidden features h (query). Each part of the initial image is plotted according to the weight of each word for each region.

2.2   TGOCM: Text Generation in the Opposite Direction and Correction Module

The TGOCM is divided into four parts, which are generating text in the opposite direction, matching word-level attention, jointing attention mechanism and correcting image. The following is a detailed description of each part. We employ the widely used encoder-decoder architecture, which needs to be implemented using CNN [10] and RNN [11] models, respectively. The structure of the model mainly includes three parts: a) Feature Extractor, the size of the extracted image features is 2048, with dense layers, and we reduce the size to 256 nodes. b) Sequence Processor, the embedding layer handles the text input, followed by the LSTM layer [12]. c) Decoder, combining the outputs of the above two layers, we process them as dense layers to make the final prediction.

$$
\begin{aligned}
x_2 &= CNN\left(I_2\right); \\
x_t &= W_e T_t, t \in \{0, \ldots L-1\}; \\
p_{t+1} &= LSTM\left(x_t\right), t \in \{0, \ldots L-1\},
\end{aligned}
\tag{3}
$$

in which $x_2 \in \mathbb{R}^{M_{m-1}}$ is the visual feature used as the input to inform the LSTM for the image content. $W_e \in \mathbb{R}^{M_{m-1} \times D}$ represents a word embedding matrix, which maps word features to the visual feature space. p_{t+1} is a predicted probability distribution over the words.

Here, we can compare the real semantics with the generated semantics. By calculating the similarity [13] between the two semantics, and according to the similarity of the word, it gives the corresponding weight to each word.

$$
\cos(\theta) = \frac{\sum_{i=1}^{n}\left(x_i \times y_i\right)}{\sqrt{\sum_{i=1}^{n}\left(x_i\right)^2} \times \sqrt{\sum_{i=1}^{D}\left(y_i\right)^2}}
\tag{4}
$$

where x_i represents the actual text, y_i represents the generated text, if the cosine is closer to 1, it means that the angle between them is closer to $0°$, which means that the two vectors are more similar, and the angle between them is equal to 0, which means that the two vectors are equal.

Meanwhile, each column of h is a feature vector of a sub-region of the image. For the jth sub-region, its word-context vector is a dynamic representation of word vectors relevant to h_j, which is calculated by

$$
c_j = \sum_{i=0}^{T-1} \beta_{j,i} e_i', \text{ where } \beta_{j,i} = \frac{\exp\left(s_{j,i}'\right)}{\sum_{k=0}^{T-1}\exp\left(s_{j,k}'\right)},
\tag{5}
$$

where $s_{j,i}' = h_j^T e_i'$, and $\beta_{j,i}$ indicates the weight that the model attends to the ith word when generating the jth sub-region of the image.

Each word is given the corresponding weight from the matching and word-level attention module. In this way, we can not only locate the specific region, but also focus on the word vector with great loss. Based on the above work, we multiply two matrices. This points the way for the final phase of the generation. The final stage has the function of correcting and optimizing the generated image according to the attention mechanism. Such targeted optimization generation will make the generated image quality promisingly.

2.3   Objective Function

The whole model is divided into three generation stages, so we will describe the objective function in three stages. The generator losses can be defined as:

$$L_G = \sum_{i=0}^{2} \mathcal{L}_{G_i} + \alpha L_{G1} + \beta L_{cap} + \lambda L_{ws}, \tag{6}$$

Herein, L_{G1}, L_{cap} and L_{ws} represent three stages of the loss, respectively. The discriminator works against the generator to determine whether the generated image is true, the calculation method is a conventional algorithm.

The adversarial loss for D_i [4] is defined as:

$$\begin{aligned}
\mathcal{L}_{D_i} = &-\frac{1}{2}\mathbb{E}_{x_i \sim p_{\text{data } i}} \left[\log D_i \left(x_i\right)\right] \\
&-\frac{1}{2}\mathbb{E}_{\hat{x}_i \sim p_{G_i}} \left[\log \left(1 - D_i \left(\hat{x}_i\right)\right)\right] \\
&-\frac{1}{2}\mathbb{E}_{x_i \sim p_{\text{data}_i}} \left[\log D_i \left(x_i, \bar{e}\right)\right] \\
&-\frac{1}{2}\mathbb{E}_{\hat{x}_i \sim p_{G_i}} \left[\log \left(1 - D_i \left(\hat{x}_i, \bar{e}\right)\right)\right].
\end{aligned} \tag{7}$$

3   Experiments

In this section, we first introduce the datasets, training details, and evaluation metrics used in our experiments. In addition, we carried out extensive experiments that evaluate the proposed model, which is compared with some state-of-the-art models (i.e., StackGAN [14], StackGAN++ [5], AttnGAN [4] and MirrorGAN [6]) by some basic evaluation indicators.

3.1   Datasets

Most of the studies on text-to-image are based on CUB and complex integrated COCO datasets. Each image has 10 text descriptions in the CUB dataset and each image has 5 text descriptions in the COCO dataset.

3.2 Training Details

Firstly, we pre-train the three models of text encoding, image encoding and text reproduction. To simplify the training process, we directly load the pre-trained model and parameters into our overall model. We preprocess the COCO dataset and randomly select a quarter of the original training sets and test sets for training and testing. The training process is performed for 300 epochs on the CUB birds dataset and 300 epochs on the COCO dataset.

Fig. 3. Examples of images generated by AttnGAN, MirrorGAN and TRGAN conditioned on text descriptions from CUB and COCO test datasets and the corresponding ground truth.

3.3 Results

Quantitative Results: The TRGAN we proposed is based on a multi-stage structure generated from low resolution to high resolution. GAN-INT-CLS [15], GAWWN [16], AttnGAN, StackGAN++ and MirrorGAN proposed in previous studies are also based on a multi-stage structure generated from low resolution to high resolution. So we compared the TRGAN with the previous models (AttnGAN, StackGAN++ and MirrorGAN). As shown in Table 1, compared with MirrorGAN which employs Siamese Network to ensure text-image semantic consistency on a simple dataset CUB, our TRGAN improves the IS from 4.56 to 4.66 and the R-Precision from 60.42 to 69.05. This is because our TRGAN can generate a better initial image and optimizing it in the subsequent generation process. It proved that our model has a higher resolution on images of a single entity and multiple entities.

Qualitative Results: For qualitative evaluation, Fig. 3 shows text-to-image synthesis examples generated by our TRGAN and the state-of-the-art models. In general, our TRGAN approach generates images with more vivid details as well as more clear backgrounds in most cases, comparing to the AttnGAN, Mirror-GAN and ground truth. In conclusion, the reason is that although StackGAN, AttnGAN, MirrorGAN used their stacked architecture or cross-modal spatial attention, it is not completely solved. However, our model aims at improving

Table 1. IS scores and R-Precision of the six models on the CUB dataset.

Dataset	Method	IS	R-Precision	Dataset	IS	R-Precision
CUB	GAN-INT-CLS [15]	2.88 ± 0.04	/	COCO		
CUB	GAWWN [16]	3.62 ± .07	/	COCO		
CUB	StackGAN++ [5]	4.04 ± 0.06	/	COCO	1.09 ± 0.12	/
CUB	AttnGAN [4]	4.36 ± 0.03	67.82 ± 4.43	COCO	1.69 ± 0.09	56.95 ± 0.45
CUB	MirrorGAN [6]	4.56 ± 0.05	60.42 ± 2.75	COCO	4.46 ± 0.20	60.78 ± 0.41
CUB	**TRGAN**	**4.66 ± 0.13**	**69.05 ± 2.25**	**COCO**	**4.52 ± 0.11**	**62.3 ± 0.33**

the quality of the initial image first, and targeted optimization aims at generating regions.

Ablation Study: We next conduct ablation studies on the proposed model and its variants. To validate the effectiveness of generating the text module in reverse, we conduct several comparative experiments by excluding/including these components in TRGAN. We compare the baseline model and reverse generated text module in the second and last stage, respectively. The IS score increases from 4.33 to 4.49 by adding a reverse-generated text module, then the IS score increases from 4.49 to 4.69 by adding the model on different stages (stage 2 and stage 3), as shown in Fig. 4. That's why we can change the quality of the initial image to ensure the quality of the result.

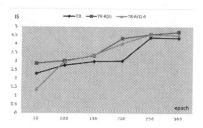

Fig. 4. The results of baseline model, adding reverse generated text model comparison.

4   Conclusions

In this paper, we have proposed a new framework called Text-representation Generative Adversarial Network (TRGAN). The whole framework consists of two modules, namely JASGM and TROGM. The first modules focus on the generation of fine-grained features. In the second module, the image of the previous stage is repaired and corrected based on the attention mechanism. Extensive experiment results show that our proposed TRGAN significantly outperforms state-of-the-art models on the CUB and COCO datasets.

Acknowledgement. This work is supported by the National Natural Science Foundation of China (61906030), the Fundamental Research Funds for the Central Universities (DUT20RC(4)009), Natural Science Foundation of Liaoning Province (2020-BS-063), and the Equipment Advance Research Fund (80904010301).

References

1. Zhe, G., Gan, C., He, X., Pu, Y., Li, D.: Semantic compositional networks for visual captioning. In: 2017 IEEE Conference on Computer Vision and Pattern Recognition (CVPR) (2017)
2. Nam, S., Kim, Y., Kim, S.J.: Text-adaptive generative adversarial networks: manipulating images with natural language (2018)
3. Li, B., Qi, X., Lukasiewicz, T., Torr, P.: Text-guided image manipulation, Manigan (2019)
4. Tao, X., Zhang, P., Huang, Q., Han, Z., He, X.: AttnGAN: fine-grained text to image generation with attentional generative adversarial networks (2017)
5. Han, Z., et al.: StackGAN++: realistic image synthesis with stacked generative adversarial networks. IEEE Trans. Pattern Anal. Mach. Intell. **99**, 1 (2017)
6. Qiao, T., Zhang, J., Xu, D., Tao, D.: MirrorGAN: learning text-to-image generation by redescription. IEEE (2019)
7. Banerjee, S., Das, S.: SD-GAN: structural and denoising GAN reveals facial parts under occlusion (2020)
8. Baraheem, S.S., Nguyen, T.V.: Text-to-image via mask anchor points. Pattern Recogn. Lett. **133**, 25–32 (2020)
9. Cho, K., et al.: Learning phrase representations using RNN encoder-decoder for statistical machine translation, Computer Science (2014)
10. Wu, S., Zhong, S., Liu, Y.: Deep residual learning for image steganalysis. Multimedia Tools Appl. **77**(9), 10437–10453 (2017). https://doi.org/10.1007/s11042-017-4440-4
11. Hochreiter, S., Schmidhuber, J.: Long short-term memory. Neural Comput. **9**(8), 1735–1780 (1997)
12. Sundermeyer, M., Schlüter, R., Ney, H.: LSTM neural networks for language modeling. In: Interspeech (2012)
13. Nguyen, H.V., Bai, L.: Cosine similarity metric learning for face verification. In: Kimmel, R., Klette, R., Sugimoto, A. (eds.) ACCV 2010. LNCS, vol. 6493, pp. 709–720. Springer, Heidelberg (2011). https://doi.org/10.1007/978-3-642-19309-5_55
14. Zhang, H., et al.: StackGAN: text to photo-realistic image synthesis with stacked generative adversarial networks. IEEE (2017)
15. Reed, S., Akata, Z., Yan, X., Logeswaran, L., Schiele, B., Lee, H.: Generative adversarial text to image synthesis. JMLR.org (2016)
16. Reed, S., Akata, Z., Lee, H., Schiele, B.: Learning deep representations of fine-grained visual descriptions. In: 2016 IEEE Conference on Computer Vision and Pattern Recognition (CVPR) (2016)

Integrating Policy Reuse with Learning from Demonstrations for Knowledge Transfer in Deep Reinforcement Learning

Pei Yao and Liang Feng[✉]

College of Computer Science, Chongqing University, Chongqing, China
{peiyao1207,liangf}@cqu.edu.cn

Abstract. Transfer learning (TL) assisted deep reinforcement learning (DRL) has attracted much attention in recent years, which aims to enhance reinforcement learning performance by leveraging prior knowledge from past learned tasks. However, it still remains challenging to conduct positive knowledge transfer when the target tasks are dissimilar to the source tasks, e.g., the source and target tasks possess diverse environmental dynamics. Taking this cue, this paper presents an attempt to explore TL in DRL across tasks with heterogeneous dynamics towards enhanced reinforcement learning performance. In particular, we propose to combine policy reuse and learning from demonstrations for knowledge transfer in DRL. It allows multiple learned policies in separate source tasks to adaptively fuse to generate a teacher policy for the target task, which will be further used for knowledge transfer via learning from demonstrations to boost the learning process of the target DRL agent. To evaluate the performance of our proposed method, comprehensive empirical studies have been conducted on continuous control tasks, i.e., Reacher and HalfCheetah. The obtained results show that the proposed method is superior in contrast to recently proposed algorithms in terms of both accumulated reward and training computational cost.

Keywords: Deep reinforcement learning · Policy reuse · Learning from demonstrations · Knowledge transfer

1 Introduction

Over the years, deep reinforcement learning (DRL) has been proposed to enable an agent to perform well in sequential decision-making tasks for many real applications, such as game playing [1], robotics control [2] and autonomous driving [3]. Despite the success enjoyed by DRL, it is worth noting that the training of a DRL agent often requires huge number of samples, which could be impractical in real-world applications where only limited computational budgets are given. It is thus a non-trivial task to speed up the learning process of DRL by reducing the number of samples.

© Springer Nature Switzerland AG 2021
T. Mantoro et al. (Eds.): ICONIP 2021, CCIS 1516, pp. 659–667, 2021.
https://doi.org/10.1007/978-3-030-92307-5_77

To this end, transfer learning assisted DRL has been proposed and has attracted much attention in recent years [4,5]. TL allows to accelerate the learning of a DRL agent in new target domains by reusing knowledge from well-learned source domains. For instance, by measuring the similarity between the source and target tasks, Lazaric *et al.* [6] selected similar source samples to transfer for target task. Fernández *et al.* [7] reused expert policies from various source tasks based on a designed probability distribution across the source and target tasks. Barreto *et al.* [8] proposed a transfer framework in RL, in which the value function is formulated as a linear combination of the successor features for knowledge transfer. Due to the simple linear combination, TL could lead to poor RL performance in cases the source and target tasks having different environmental dynamics. Moreover, Laroche *et al.* [9] re-estimated the reward function of the target task by reusing transition samples with the assumption that all tasks share the same dynamics and only differ in the reward function. Rajendran *et al.* [10] proposed "attend, adapt and transfer" (A2T) framework that learns from an attention network to combine multiple source policies which will be directly reused in the target task with discrete action space. However, although TL has been successfully be developed to improve the DRL performance, we note that existing works mainly focused on the knowledge transfer across similar source and target RL tasks. They may fail in the situations where the target tasks are dissimilar to the source tasks, e.g., target and source tasks have diverse environmental dynamics. To leverage knowledge from dissimilar source tasks to enhance the DRL in target task, a major challenge is how to adapt the transferred knowledge in the target task so as to avoid negative transfer.

In this paper, we propose a knowledge transfer method for DRL which combines policy reuse and learning from demonstrations. The proposed method allows multiple learned policies in separate and diverse source tasks to adaptively fuse to generate a teacher policy for the target task. The teacher policy will then be used to transfer knowledge via learning from demonstrations to enhance the learning process of a DRL agent in the target domain. In this way, the proposed method can not only effectively use the knowledge from source policies of multiple dissimilar source tasks, but also transfer the learned knowledge to guide the DRL agent to explore the target environment instead of random exploration. To assess the efficacy of our proposed method, comprehensive empirical studies are conducted based on continuous control tasks, i.e., Reacher and HalfCheetah, over recently proposed TL methods for DRL. The obtained results confirmed the effectiveness and efficiency of the proposed approach of TL for DRL across tasks possessing diverse dynamics.

2 Preliminaries

2.1 Deep Reinforcement Learning

A general RL task can be described as an Markov Decision Process (MDP) [11]. An MDP is a tuple $\langle \mathcal{S}, \mathcal{A}, \mathcal{P}, \mathcal{R}, \gamma \rangle$, and its components are introduced as follows. The sets $\mathcal{S}$ and $\mathcal{A}$ are the state and action spaces respectively. The function $\mathcal{P}$

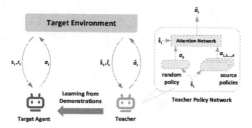

Fig. 1. Overview of the proposed integrating policy reuse with learning from demonstrations for knowledge transfer.

is the dynamics of MDP, which gives the next-state distribution under a specific state $s \in \mathcal{S}$ and a corresponding action $a \in \mathcal{A}$. The reward function $\mathcal{R}$ determines the received reward r after taking an action. Finally, the discount factor $\gamma \in [0, 1]$ implies the influence of future rewards. Specifically, the RL agent aims to learn a policy $\pi(a|s)$ that maps a state s to a probability distribution over actions a by interacting with the environment so as to maximize the expected discounted total reward $G_t = \sum_{i=0}^{\infty} \gamma^i r_{t+1+i}$.

Deep reinforcement learning (DRL) combines deep neural networks with the framework of RL. Most of existing studies in deep reinforcement learning concentrated on the actor-critic architecture, where the critic estimates the value function and the actor learns the policy with the assistance of the critic. In this paper, we focus on proximal policy optimization (PPO) [12]. The policy's objective function is then given by:

$$\mathcal{L}^{clip}(\theta) = \hat{\mathbb{E}}_t[\min(r_t(\theta)\hat{A}_\pi^t, clip(r_t(\theta), 1 - \varepsilon, 1 + \varepsilon)\hat{A}_\pi^t)] \tag{1}$$

where $r_t(\theta)$ is the likelihood ratio that $r_t(\theta) = \frac{\pi_\theta(a_t|s_t)}{\pi_{\theta_{old}}(a_t|s_t)}$. Additionally, the operation $clip$ truncates $r_t(\theta)$ to the range of $(1 - \varepsilon, 1 + \varepsilon)$. $\hat{A}_\pi^t$ is n-step advantage estimation. Interested readers may refer to [12] for more detailed discussions of PPO algorithm.

3   Proposed Approach

In this section, we describe the details of the proposed knowledge transfer method, which is illustrated in Fig. 1. During the training process, the teacher policy and the target agent learn in the same target environment with different initialization. The teacher policy combines the policies from all source tasks to generate a teacher policy for the target task, while the DRL agent learns the target task by self-learning and knowledge transfer via learning from demonstrations through selecting samples from the teacher policy. In what follows, the details of the two main components, i.e., learning of teacher policy from multiple source policies, and knowledge transfer via learning from demonstrations, are introduced.

3.1   Learning of Teacher Policy from Multiple Source Policies

In order to learn teacher policy, besides available optimal or sub-optimal source policies, we add an additional random policy to facilitate exploration in the target task, which is inspired by "attend, adapt and transfer" (A2T) method [10]. Moreover, suppose each source policy outputs the deterministic action $\pi_k(\cdot)$: $s \to a$, where $a \in \mathbb{R}^D$ is a D-dimensional real-value vector for the continuous action space. Considering diverse dynamics may exist in the source policies, first of all, we propose to aggregates the source policies adaptively via:

$$\mu(s_t) = \sum_{k=1}^{N} \omega_k \pi_k(s_t) \tag{2}$$

where N denotes the number of policies including the source policies and a random policy, and $\pi_k(\cdot)$ represents a policy. ω_k represents the weight of each policy and $\sum_{k=1}^{N} \omega_k = 1$. To adaptively learn the weight of each policy for the target task, an attention network is developed to update the weight according to the input state. We use a soft-attention mechanism, in which more than one weight can be non-zero values [13]. When the attention network and random policy are trained in the target task, the source policy networks do not participate in parameter updates, and the teacher policy automatically adjust the usage of each source policies through feedback from the target environment. Furthermore, unlike A2T, as can be observed in Eq. (2), we directly use weighted sum of the deterministic actions as the output of the source policies, it thus do not have to access the probability distribution of potential actions, which is often hard to estimate, especially in the continuous action space. Last but not the least, the teacher policy $\hat{\pi}(s_t)$ can be model as Gaussian distribution, which is given by $\hat{\pi}(s_t) = \mathcal{N}(\mu(s_t), \Sigma)$, where $\mu(s_t)$ is regarded as mean action, which is given by Eq. (2), and Σ represents a covariance matrix which is estimated based on the adopted DRL algorithm.

3.2   Knowledge Transfer via Learning from Demonstrations

In this section, the details of knowledge transfer via learning from demonstrations are presented. First of all, the actor-critic DRL is considered as the agent in the target task, which performs self-learning in the target environment and learning from demonstrations transferred by the generated teacher policy simultaneously. In particular, we tend to store teacher policy's useful samples $(\hat{s}_t, \hat{a}_t, \hat{R}_t)$ in a replay buffer $\hat{\mathcal{D}} = \left\{ (\hat{s}_t, \hat{a}_t, \hat{R}_t) \right\}$, where $(\hat{s}_t, \hat{a}_t)$ is a state and action at timestep t, and $\hat{R}_t = \sum_{i=t}^{\infty} \gamma^{i-t} \hat{r}_i$ is the Monte-Carlo return, which is the discounted sum of rewards with a discount factor γ in one episode. Intuitively, to obtain teacher policy's samples to encourage the agent to explore in the target task, we propose to utilize useful samples which have return $\hat{R}_t$ in $(\hat{s}_t, \hat{a}_t)$ that is greater than the agent's state value estimation $V_\theta(\hat{s}_t)$. Afterward, we leverage the positive samples to update the agent's actor-critic network. The objective function is given by:

$$\mathcal{L}_{LfD} = \mathbb{E}_{(\hat{s}_t, \hat{a}_t, \hat{R}_t) \sim \hat{\mathcal{D}}} [\mathcal{L}_{LfD_{policy}} + \beta^{LfD} \mathcal{L}_{LfD_{value}}] \tag{3}$$

Algorithm 1. Integrating Policy Reuse with Learning from Demonstrations for Knowledge Transfer

---

Input: teacher policy $\hat{\pi}_{\hat{\theta}}$ with an attention network, a random policy and learned source policies; the agent's policy π_θ

Output: the learned policy π_θ

Initialize θ and $\hat{\theta}$; replay buffer $\mathcal{D} \leftarrow \emptyset$, $\hat{\mathcal{D}} \leftarrow \emptyset$; trajectory buffer $\mathcal{E} \leftarrow \emptyset$, $\hat{\mathcal{E}} \leftarrow \emptyset$

for iteration k = 1, ... , T do

    The teacher policy $\hat{\pi}_{\hat{\theta}}$ generates trajectories $\{(\hat{s}_t, \hat{a}_t, \hat{r}_t)\}$ and save them into $\hat{\mathcal{E}}$

    The agent executes π_θ to generate trajectories $\{(s_t, a_t, r_t)\}$ and save them into $\mathcal{E}$

    Compute returns $\hat{\mathcal{R}}_t = \sum_{i=t}^{\infty} \gamma^{i-t}\hat{r}_i$ for all t in $\hat{\mathcal{E}}$

    $\hat{\mathcal{D}} \leftarrow \hat{\mathcal{D}} \cup (\hat{s}_t, \hat{a}_t, \hat{\mathcal{R}}_t)$ for all t in $\hat{\mathcal{E}}$

    Compute returns $\mathcal{R}_t = \sum_{i=t}^{\infty} \gamma^{i-t} r_i$ for all t in $\mathcal{E}$

    $\mathcal{D} \leftarrow \mathcal{D} \cup (s_t, a_t, \mathcal{R}_t)$ for all t in $\mathcal{E}$

    Update teacher policy $\hat{\pi}_{\hat{\theta}}$ and the agent's policy π_θ via RL objective

    Update the agent's policy π_θ via learning from demonstrations based on Eq. (4)

    Empty replay buffer $\mathcal{D} \leftarrow \emptyset$, $\hat{\mathcal{D}} \leftarrow \emptyset$; trajectory buffer $\mathcal{E} \leftarrow \emptyset$, $\hat{\mathcal{E}} \leftarrow \emptyset$

end for

$$\mathcal{L}^{LfD_{policy}} = -\min(r_t(\theta)\mathcal{Q}_t, clip(r_t(\theta), 1 - \varepsilon, 1 + \varepsilon)\mathcal{Q}_t) \qquad (4)$$

$$\mathcal{L}_{LfD_{value}} = (\hat{R}_t - V_\theta(\hat{s}_t))^2 \qquad (5)$$

where $\beta^{LfD} \in \mathcal{R}^+$ is a hyperparameter for Eq. (3), and ε is a hyperparameter which describes how far away the new policy is allowed to go from the old one. $\pi_\theta(\cdot), V_\theta(\cdot)$ are the agent's policy and value function parameterized by θ. The role of $r_t(\theta) = \frac{\pi_\theta(a_t|s_t)}{\pi_{\theta_{old}}(a_t|s_t)}$ is the same as that in the PPO algorithm. $\mathcal{Q}_t = \max(0, \hat{R} - V_\theta(\hat{s}_t))$ is used to select useful samples to update the policy network and the value network.

In summary, the agent in the target task performs reinforcement learning with environmental feedback and learning from demonstrations in the form of useful samples generated by the teacher policy. The pseudo code of our proposed algorithm is summarized in Algorithm 1.

4   Experimental Evaluation

To assess the performance of our proposed method, the Reacher and HalfCheetah continuous control tasks [14], are considered in this experimental study. The PPO [12] and A2T [10] algorithms are considered as the baseline algorithms. More detailed empirical configurations and results discussions are given in the following subsections.

4.1   Experimental Setup

To ensure a fair comparison, the shared hyper-parameters of all the studied three methods are kept the same [12]. The averaged episode reward over training samples is used as the evaluation metric, and the results of each algorithm

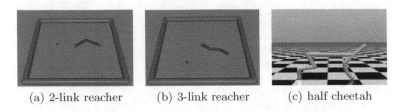

(a) 2-link reacher   (b) 3-link reacher   (c) half cheetah

Fig. 2. Renderings of the reinforcement learning tasks

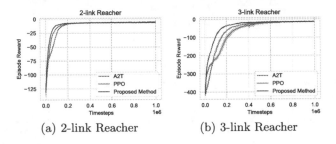

(a) 2-link Reacher   (b) 3-link Reacher

Fig. 3. Results obtained on Reacher. X-axis and Y-axis represent timesteps and averaged episode reward, respectively. The learning curves are averaged over 3 independent runs using different random seeds.

are averaged over three different random seeds. We normalize neither observations nor rewards during the training process. The RL agents in our proposed method and PPO algorithm have the same actor-critic architecture. The teacher policy network contains several pre-trained source policies networks with fixed parameters, a random network and an attention network. In order to allow the A2T algorithm to be used for tasks in the continuous action space, we modified the last layer of the network to make the network structure as the same as that of the teacher policy network.

4.2   Reacher

Reacher consists of an arm simulator and a target position which requires the agent to move the arm's end-effector to the randomly target point, which is depicted in Fig. 2(a) and 2(b). Moreover, each episode begins with a random initial state and ends when the arm interacts with the environment for more than 50 steps. Here we consider two sets of experiments, i.e., 2-link reacher and 3-link reacher. In each experiment, the link lengths of the robotic arms in the source tasks and the target task are different, which thus creates diverse environmental dynamics between tasks. Therefore, the directly reuse policies may lead to negative transfer in these scenarios.

Next, we provide two pre-trained source policies for learning teacher policy. The results on the reacher are presented in Fig. 3. In the 2-link reacher, it can be observed that our method obtained faster learning speed than the other two baseline methods. In the 3-link reacher, we observe that our method outperforms other methods regarding to the improvement of learning speed. The final converged performance obtained by the algorithms are competitive. This is because our experimental design allows them to reach the target point at the end. Meanwhile, it can be observed that the learning speed of A2T is slower than the other two methods. The reason could be that the attention network only relies on the data generated by the interactions with the environment, which thus ignored the relatedness between source and target tasks. The decline of the attention network's quality may result in poor performance. However, in our proposed method, the design of learning from demonstration can effectively address this issue of the attention network. Because useless experiences from the teacher policy will be discarded by comparing the corresponding return with the agent's state value in the target task.

4.3   HalfCheetah

In HalfCheetah, as illustrated in Fig. 2(c), the agent is trained to run forward as balanced as possible. The target task is HalfCheetah-v2 in OpenAI Gym [14]. HalfCheetah task group in [15] is considered as source task set where the mass and width of "Big" body parts are scaled by 1.25 and "Small" body parts are scaled by 0.75. As the above tasks vary in the morphology of a specific body part of the agent, they possess diverse environmental dynamics. We thus assemble the source tasks into 9 groups: {HCSmallTorso, HCSmallThigh}, {HCBigTorso, HCBigThigh}, {HCSmallFoot, HCBigFoot}, {HCBigFoot, HCBigThigh}, {HCBig-Foot, HCBigTorso}, {HCSmallLeg, HCBigLeg}, {HCBigTorso, HCBigLeg}, {HC-SmallTorso, HCSmallFoot} and {HCSmallFoot, HCmallThigh}. The naming rules of each of the above task and how to generate the tasks can be referred to [15].

The results obtained in our experiments are shown in Fig. 4. As can be observed, our proposed method outperforms other methods in most cases. Figures 4(a), 4(b) and 4(e) demonstrate that our method can improve target policy's learning speed compared to A2T and PPO. It can also infer that the learning from demonstrations process may eliminate bad experiences transferred from the teacher policy. In Figs. 4(c), 4(g) and 4(i), although the total accumulated reward among three algorithms are similar, our proposed method reduced training time while achieving the same performance at early stages. In Figs. 4(d) and 4(h), each method has the similar initial performance, but our method improves the total accumulated reward and reduces training time while achieving the same performance. Furthermore, it can be observed that the proposed method has achieved the different improvements of total accumulated reward and learning speed by selecting various source tasks to complete the knowledge transfer on the same target task. We thus can infer that the selected source task will affect the learning on the target task because the similarities between tasks are different. Overall, the experimental results show that our method improved the total accumulated reward and reduced training time while achieving the same performance.

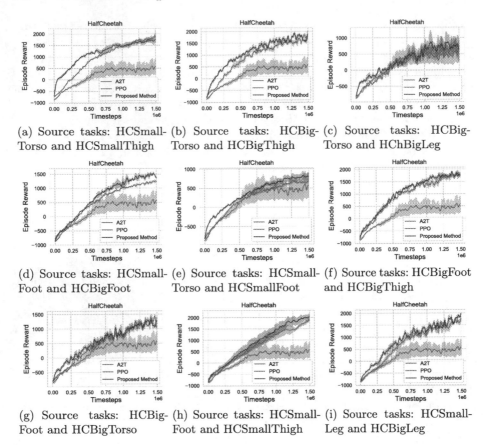

(a) Source tasks: HCSmall-Torso and HCSmallThigh

(b) Source tasks: HCBig-Torso and HCBigThigh

(c) Source tasks: HCBig-Torso and HChBigLeg

(d) Source tasks: HCSmall-Foot and HCBigFoot

(e) Source tasks: HCSmall-Torso and HCSmallFoot

(f) Source tasks: HCBigFoot and HCBigThigh

(g) Source tasks: HCBig-Foot and HCBigTorso

(h) Source tasks: HCSmall-Foot and HCSmallThigh

(i) Source tasks: HCSmall-Leg and HCBigLeg

Fig. 4. Results obtained on HalfCheetah. X-axis and Y-axis represent timesteps and averaged episode reward respectively. The learning curves are averaged over 3 random seeds. The shaded area shows mean ± standard deviation.

5   Conclusion

In this paper, we have proposed a knowledge transfer method for DRL by considering the diverse dynamics existed in the source policies. The proposed method combines policy reuse and learning from demonstrations for knowledge transfer across RL tasks. In particular, a teacher policy network has been presented to learn an aggregation policy adaptively using the learned source policies. The agent in the target tasks selects positive samples generated by teacher policy for learning from demonstrations to improve the learning performance. Comprehensive empirical studies have been conducted to evaluate the efficacy of the proposed method. The empirical results on the commonly used Reacher and HalfCheetah show that our proposed approach outperforms the baseline methods in terms of total accumulated reward and training time while achieving the same performance level.

Acknowledgement. This work is partially supported by the *National Natural Science Foundation of China* (NSFC) under Grant No. 61876025.

References

1. Mnih, V., et al.: Human-level control through deep reinforcement learning. Nature **518**(7540), 529–533 (2015)
2. Levine, S., Finn, C., Darrell, T., Abbeel, P.: End-to-end training of deep visuomotor policies. J. Mach. Learn. Res. **17**(1), 1334–1373 (2016)
3. Kiran, B.R.: Deep reinforcement learning for autonomous driving: a survey. IEEE Trans. Intell. Transp. Syst., 1–18 (2021)
4. Taylor, M.E., Stone, P.: Transfer learning for reinforcement learning domains: a survey. J. Mach. Learn. Res., **10**(7) (2009)
5. Lazaric, A.: Transfer in reinforcement learning: a framework and a survey. In: Wiering, M., van Otterlo, M. (eds.) Reinforcement Learning. Adaptation, Learning, and Optimization, vol 12. Springer, Berlin (2012)
6. Lazaric, A., Restelli, M., Bonarini, A.: Transfer of samples in batch reinforcement learning. In: Proceedings of the 25th international conference on Machine learning, pp. 544–551 (2008)
7. Fernández, F., Veloso, M.: Probabilistic policy reuse in a reinforcement learning agent. In: Proceedings of the fifth international joint conference on Autonomous agents and multiagent systems, pp. 720–727 (2006)
8. Barreto, A.: Successor features for transfer in reinforcement learning. arXiv preprint arXiv:1606.05312 (2016)
9. Laroche, R., Barlier, M.: Transfer reinforcement learning with shared dynamics. In: Proceedings of the AAAI Conference on Artificial Intelligence, vol. 31 (2017)
10. Rajendran, J., Srinivas, A., Khapra, M.M., Prasanna, P., Ravindran, B.: Attend, adapt and transfer: attentive deep architecture for adaptive transfer from multiple sources in the same domain. In: 5th International Conference on Learning Representations, ICLR 2017, Toulon, France, April 24–26, 2017, Conference Track Proceedings. OpenReview.net (2017)
11. Sutton, R.S., Barto, A.G.: Reinforcement Learning: An Introduction. MIT press, London (2018)
12. Schulman, J., Wolski, F., Dhariwal, P., Radford, A., Klimov, O.: Proximal policy optimization algorithms. arXiv preprint arXiv:1707.06347 (2017)
13. Bahdanau, D., Cho, K., Bengio, Y.: Neural machine translation by jointly learning to align and translate. arXiv preprint arXiv:1409.0473 (2014)
14. Brockman, G., et al.: Openai gym. arXiv preprint arXiv:1606.01540 (2016)
15. Henderson, P., Chang, W.D., Shkurti, F., Hansen, J., Meger, D., Dudek, G.: Benchmark environments for multitask learning in continuous domains. arXiv preprint arXiv:1708.04352 (2017)

Inductive Semi-supervised Learning Through Optimal Transport

Mourad El Hamri[1,2($\boxtimes$)], Younès Bennani[1,2], and Issam Falih[2,3]

[1] LIPN - CNRS UMR 7030, Université Sorbonne Paris Nord, Villetaneuse, France
{mourad.elhamri,younes.bennani}@sorbonne-paris-nord.fr
[2] LaMSN - La Maison des Sciences Numériques, Saint-Denis, France
[3] LIMOS - CNRS UMR 6158, Université Clermont Auvergne,
Clermont-Ferrand, France
issam.falih@uca.fr

Abstract. In this paper, we tackle the inductive semi-supervised learning problem that aims to obtain label predictions for out-of-sample data. The proposed approach, called Optimal Transport Induction (OTI), extends efficiently an optimal transport based transductive algorithm (OTP) to inductive tasks for both binary and multi-class settings. A series of experiments are conducted on several datasets in order to compare the proposed approach with state-of-the-art methods. Experiments demonstrate the effectiveness of our approach. We make our code publicly available (Code is available at: https://github.com/MouradElHamri/OTI).

Keywords: Optimal transport · Semi-supervised learning · Label propagation

1 Introduction

Supervised learning models, especially deep neural networks can achieve human or superhuman level performances on a broad spectrum of learning tasks. This big achievement, however, heavily relies on the availability of large-scale labeled datasets, which usually come at a significant cost, since labeling data often requires an extensive human labor. For instance, the work needed for labeling manually sequential data (e.g. speech or video) is proportional to their lengths. Moreover, some specific domain knowledge (e.g. medicine) is often critical for labeling and requires an involvement of experts. This lack of labeled data is often accompanied by an abundance of unlabeled instances, which raises the question of how to take advantage of the big amount of unlabeled samples to alleviate the need for large high quality labeled datasets.

Semi-supervised learning (SSL) [2] has emerged as one of the most promising paradigms to achieve this goal by leveraging both labeled and unlabeled data. There are two categories of semi-supervised learning models [13]: inductive learning models and transductive learning models. Inductive semi-supervised learning aims to learn using both labeled and unlabeled data a predictive model capable of

© Springer Nature Switzerland AG 2021
T. Mantoro et al. (Eds.): ICONIP 2021, CCIS 1516, pp. 668–675, 2021.
https://doi.org/10.1007/978-3-030-92307-5_78

making predictions both for unlabeled data already encountered in the training phase and for out-of-sample data, i.e. previously unseen instances. While transductive semi-supervised learning methods are only concerned with predicted the labels of unlabeled data already presented during the training.

Most of transductive learning models are graph-based approaches [12] (e.g. label propagation methods), that aim to present each data, labeled or not by a vertex in the graph, then, similarities between vertices are evaluated to determine whether or not there should be an edge between each pair of vertices, finally, edges are weighted to reflect the similarity degree between vertices. After the graph construction, labels are inferred in several ways (e.g. in the case of label propagation, labels are diffused from labeled to unlabeled data through the graph edges). The common major inconvenience of transductive methods is their inability to predict labels for out-of-sample data, so when some previously unseen test data arrive, transductive learning methods need to fusion these new samples into the previous data in our disposal to reconstruct a new augmented graph based on merged data, and then perform label propagation from scratch. This process is too costly, since the presentation of even, a single new point require to rerun all the process already done in their entirety, which is distasteful in many real-world applications, where on-the-fly prediction for previously unseen instances is highly requested.

Several works have attempted to bridge the gap between transductive and inductive semi-supervised learning, by proposing to derive an inductive function for out-of-sample data from the transductive predictions [1,4]. However, these approaches cannot be generalized to all the transductive methods, such as, Optimal Transport Propagation (OTP) [6]. This inability to generalize is mainly due to the difference of this approach from the state-of-the-art methods, since instead of a complete graph, OTP relies on a bipartite graph, which modifies its objective function, that does not follow the standard form of objective functions composed usually of two terms, a first term to penalize predicted labels that do not match the true labels and another term to penalize the difference in labels between similar samples. Such a setting motivated the development of a simple way to extend OTP (and other transductive semi-supervised approaches based on bipartite graphs) to the inductive framework.

In this paper, we derive an inductive approach called Optimal Transport Induction (OTI) from the modified objective function of OTP. In addition to being applicable in the case of binary classification, OTI can be efficiently extended to multi-class settings.

The rest of this paper is organized as follows: in Sect. 2, we present an overview of optimal transport [11,14]. Section 3 details the proposed optimal transport induction method (OTI) and in Sect. 4, we provide comparisons to state-of-the-art methods on several benchmark datasets.

2   Optimal Transport

The birth of optimal transport is dated back to 1781, with the following problem introduced by Gaspard Monge [9]: Let $(\mathcal{X}, \mu)$ and $(\mathcal{Y}, \nu)$ be two probability spaces and $c : \mathcal{X} \times \mathcal{Y} \to \mathbb{R}^+$ a measurable cost function, the problem of Monge aims at finding the transport map $\mathcal{T} : \mathcal{X} \to \mathcal{Y}$, that transport the mass represented by the measure μ to the mass represented by the measure ν and which minimizes the total cost of this transportation, more formally:

$$\inf_{\mathcal{T}} \{ \int_{\mathcal{X}} c(x, \mathcal{T}(x)) d\mu(x) | \mathcal{T} \# \mu = \nu \}, \tag{1}$$

where $\mathcal{T} \# \mu$ denotes the push-forward operator of μ through the map $\mathcal{T}$.

A long period of sleep followed Monge's formulation until the relaxation of Leonid Kantorovitch in 1942 [8]. The relaxed formulation of kantorovich, known as the Monge-Kantorovich problem, can be formulated in the following way:

$$\inf_{\gamma} \{ \int_{\mathcal{X} \times \mathcal{Y}} c(x, y) \, d\gamma(x, y) \, | \, \gamma \in \varPi(\mu, \nu) \}, \tag{2}$$

where $\varPi(\mu, \nu)$ is the set of probability measures over the product space $\mathcal{X} \times \mathcal{Y}$ such that both marginals of γ are μ and ν.

In several real world application, the access to the measures μ and ν is only available through finite samples $X = (x_1, ..., x_n) \subset \mathcal{X}$ and $Y = (y_1, ..., y_m) \subset \mathcal{Y}$, then, the measures μ and ν can be casted as the following discrete measures, $\mu = \sum_{i=1}^{n} a_i \delta_{x_i}$ and $\nu = \sum_{j=1}^{m} b_j \delta_{y_j}$, where $a \in \sum_n$ and $b \in \sum_m$ are probability vectors of size n and m respectively. The relaxation of Kantorovich becomes then the following linear program [10]:

$$\min_{T \in U(a,b)} \langle T, C_{XY} \rangle_F \tag{3}$$

where $U(a, b) = \{ T \in \mathcal{M}_{n \times m}(\mathbb{R}^+) \, | \, T1_m = a \text{ and } T^{\mathbf{T}} 1_n = b \}$ is the transportation polytope which acts as a feasible set, C_{XY} is the cost matrix and $\langle T, C_{XY} \rangle_F = trace(T^{\mathbf{T}} C_{XY})$ is the Frobenius dot-product of matrices.

This linear program, can be solved with the simplex algorithm or interior point methods. However, optimal transport problem scales cubically on the sample size, which is often too costly in practice, especially for machine learning applications that involve massive datasets. Entropy-regularization [3] has emerged as a solution to the computational burden of optimal transport. The entropy-regularized discrete optimal transport problem reads:

$$\min_{T \in U(a,b)} \langle T, C_{XY} \rangle_F - \varepsilon \mathcal{H}(T) \tag{4}$$

where $\mathcal{H}(T) = - \sum_{i=1}^{n} \sum_{j=1}^{m} t_{ij}(\log(t_{ij}) - 1)$ is the entropy of T. This regularized problem can be solved efficiently via an iterative procedure: Sinkhorn-Knopp algorithm.

3   Optimal Transport Induction

In this section, we propose an efficient way to extend OTP [1] for out-of-sample data. The main underlying idea behind this extension is the modification of

---

[1] Which would be too lengthy to detail here, please refer directly to this approach in the following paper [6].

the objective function of OTP, from which we derive a novel algorithm called Optimal Transport Induction (OTI) able to predict labels for previously unseen data.

The transductive method OTP can be casted as the minimization of the following objective function $\mathcal{C}_{\mathcal{W},l_u}^{transduction}$ in terms of the label function values at unlabeled samples $x_j \in X_U$:

$$\mathcal{C}_{\mathcal{W},l_u}^{transduction}(f) = \sum_{x_i \in X_L} \sum_{x_j \in X_U} w_{x_i,x_j} l_u(y_i, f(x_j)) \tag{5}$$

where l_u is an unsupervised loss function (e.g. a lower-bounded dissimilarity function applied on a pair of output values y_i and $f(x_j)$), and $\mathcal{W} = (w_{x_i,x_j})_{i,j}$ is the affinity matrix derived from the optimal transport plan between labeled and unlabeled data. The objective function in Eq. (5) is a smoothness criterion that seeks to penalize differences in the label predictions for similar data points in the graph, which means that a good classifier should not change too much between similar samples. The main difference between the objective function of OTP and traditional transductive approaches is the absence of a second term to penalize labels that do not match the correct ones, because OTP relies on a bipartite edge weighted graph instead of a fully connected graph to leave the labels Y_L unchanged during the training. The absence of this term in the objective function of OTP, makes the use of state-of-the-art induction formulas unfeasible. which is the main motivation behind the conception of OTI.

3.1 Problem Setup

Let $X = \{x_1, ..., x_{l+u}\}$ be a set of $l + u$ data points in $\mathbb{R}^d$ and $\mathcal{C} = \{c_1, ..., c_K\}$ a discrete label set consisting of K classes. The first l points denoted by $X_L = \{x_1, ..., x_l\}$ are labeled according to $Y_L = \{y_1, ..., y_l\}$, where $y_i \in \mathcal{C}$ for every $i \in \{1, ..., l\}$, and the remaining data points denoted by $X_U = \{x_{l+1}, ..., x_{l+u}\}$ are labeled using OTP according to $Y_U = \{y_{l+1}, ..., y_{l+u}\}$. For inductive classification, unseen data in the training phase are denoted by X_{new}. The aim of OTI is to predict labels of X_{new} using $X = X_L \cup X_U$ and $Y = Y_L \cup Y_U$, without being obliged to perform OTP from scratch.

3.2 Induction Formula: OTI

In order to extend the transductive algorithm OTP into function induction for out-of-sample data points, the same smoothness criterion as in Eq. (5) will be used for new test instances $x_{new} \in X_{new}$ [1], and then we can minimize the modified objective function with respect to only the predicted labels $\tilde{f}(x_{new})$. The novel smoothness criterion for new test samples x_{new} becomes then:

$$\mathcal{C}_{\mathcal{W},l_u}^{induction}(\tilde{f}(x_{new})) = \sum_{x_i \in X_L \cup X_U} w_{x_i,x_{new}} l_u(y_i, \tilde{f}(x_{new})) \tag{6}$$

If the loss function l_u is convex, e.g., $l_u = (y_i - \tilde{f}(x_{new}))^2$, then the cost function $\mathcal{C}^{induction}_{\mathcal{W},l_u}$ is also convex in $\tilde{f}(x_{new})$. Thus the label assignment $\tilde{f}(x_{new})$ minimizing $\mathcal{C}^{induction}_{\mathcal{W},l_u}$ is given by:

$$\tilde{f}(x_{new}) = \frac{\sum_{x_i \in X_L \cup X_U} w_{x_i,x_{new}} y_i}{\sum_{x_i \in X_L \cup X_U} w_{x_i,x_{new}}} \qquad (7)$$

The similarities $w_{x_i,x_{new}}$ are directly inferred using optimal transport as follows:

$$w_{x_i,x_{new}} = \frac{\gamma^*_{\varepsilon_{x_i,x_{new}}}}{\sum_i \gamma^*_{\varepsilon_{x_i,x_{new}}}} \quad \forall x_i \in X = X_L \cup X_U, \qquad (8)$$

where γ^*_ε is the new optimal transport plan between the empirical distributions of $X = X_L \cup X_U$ and X_{new} defined by:

$$\gamma^*_\varepsilon = \operatorname*{argmin}_{\gamma \in U(a,b)} \langle \gamma, C \rangle_F - \varepsilon \mathcal{H}(\gamma),$$

and C is the cost matrix between $X = X_L \cup X_U$ and X_{new}:

$$C = [c_{x_i,x_{new}}] \text{ defined by } c_{x_i,x_{new}} = \|x_i - x_{new}\|^2, \forall (x_i, x_{new}) \in X \times X_{new}$$

3.3   Binary Classification and Multi-class Settings

In binary classification, where $\mathcal{C} = \{+1, -1\}$, the classification problem in Eq. (7) can be casted as a regression problem, in the following way:

$$\begin{cases} y_{new} = +1 \text{ if } sign(\tilde{f}(x_{new})) \geq 0 \\ y_{new} = -1 \text{ otherwise} \end{cases}, \qquad (9)$$

Most of transductive approaches possess the ability to handle multiple classes, while the inductive methods are usually limited to the binary classification framework, where $\mathcal{C} = \{+1, -1\}$ as in Eq. (9). However, our proposed approach OTI can be adapted accurately for multi-class settings, as follows: the label $\tilde{f}(x_{new})$ is given by a weighted majority vote of the training samples in $X = X_L \cup X_U$:

$$\tilde{f}(x_{new}) = \operatorname*{argmax}_{c_k \in \mathcal{C}} \sum_{x_i \in X_L \cup X_U / y_i = c_k} w_{x_i,x_{new}} \qquad (10)$$

The predicted class of x_{new} is then the class whose representatives have the highest similarity with x_{new}.

Eq. (9) can be seen as a special case of Eq. (10) in the binary classification settings, in fact, if $\mathcal{C} = \{+1, -1\}$, then choosing between the class that maximizes $\sum_{x_i \in X_L \cup X_U / y_i = c_k} w_{x_i,x_{new}}$ is equivalent to choosing according to the sign of $\tilde{f}(x_{new})$, since the term $\sum_{x_i \in X_L \cup X_U} w_{x_i,x_{new}}$ in $\tilde{f}(x_{new})$ is always positive.

The proposed algorithm OTI, is formally summarized in Algorithm 1, where we use the algorithm OTP for training and the induction formula for testing.

Algorithm 1: OTI

Input   : X_{new}, X_L, X_U, Y_L
Parameters: ε
(1) Training phase
Compute Y_U by OTP
(2) Testing phase
for *a new test point* $x_{new} \in X_{new}$ **do**
$\quad|\quad$ Compute $w_{x_i, x_{new}} \; \forall x_i \in X = X_L \cup X_U$ by Eq(8)
$\quad|\quad$ Compute the label $\tilde{f}(x_{new})$ by Eq(9) or Eq(10)
end
return $\tilde{f}(x_{new})$

---

4 Experiments

4.1 Experimental Protocol

In this section, we provide empirical experimentation for the proposed algorithm OTI. To thoroughly evaluate the performance of the proposed approach, a total of five benchmark datasets **(Iris, Ionosphere, Dermatology, Digits, MNIST)** have been employed for experimental studies[2]. The performance of **OTI** is compared with four state-of-the-art methods, including three transductive and one inductive semi-supervised learning approaches: **LP** [16], **LNP** [15], **OTP** [6] and **SSI** [4]. To evaluate the performance of our approach, two widely-used evaluation measures were employed: the normalized mutual information **(NMI)** [5], and the adjusted rand index **(ARI)** [7]. For each dataset, we randomly sample $\zeta \times 100\%$ instances to form the labeled set X_L. For the remaining examples, 40% of them are randomly sampled to form the unlabeled set X_U and 60% of them are randomly sampled to form the out-of-sample data X_{new}. In the experiments, the training and testing procedures are conducted for the compared algorithms as follows: for the inductive semi-supervised learning methods OTI and SSI, both of them are trained on $X = X_L \cup X_U$ and tested on X_{new}. The three transductive semi-supervised learning methods LP, LNP and OTP can only make predictions on unlabeled samples already encountered in the training, so, to ensure that all the comparing algorithms are evaluated on the same out-of-sample set, the three algorithms are trained on $\tilde{X} = X_L \cup X_U \cup X_{new}$ and the evaluation is restricted to X_{new}. The sampling rate ζ for labeled data is varied from 5% to 25% with a step-size of 10%. Under each sampling rate, all the four compared algorithms were run with ten different random sampling, the mean performance out of the ten runs is recorded for the four algorithms.

4.2 Results

Table 1 reports the detailed experimental results of each algorithm on all the datasets in terms of ARI and NMI.

---

[2] The datasets are publicly available at: https://archive.ics.uci.edu/ml/datasets.php.

Table 1. Inductive performances in terms of ARI and NMI

Datasets	ζ	ARI					NMI				
		LP	LNP	OTP	SSI	OTI	LP	LNP	OTP	SSI	OTI
Iris	5	0.767	0.728	0.772	0.720	0.753	0.743	0.682	0.749	0.691	0.723
	15	0.860	0.804	0.889	0.796	0.862	0.863	0.774	0.863	0.772	0.818
	25	0.880	0.857	0.917	0.845	0.897	0.874	0.849	0.882	0.847	0.869
Ionosphere	5	0.328	0.307	0.527	0.298	0.502	0.293	0.262	0.383	0.263	0.326
	15	0.449	0.419	0.595	0.408	0.572	0.373	0.347	0.483	0.342	0.424
	25	0.483	0.462	0.618	0.460	0.591	0.404	0.375	0.530	0.362	0.445
Dermatology	5	0.806	0.799	0.850	0.789	0.837	0.814	0.795	0.835	0.783	0.819
	15	0.902	0.869	0.922	0.862	0.901	0.893	0.854	0.914	0.853	0.889
	25	0.918	0.894	0.945	0.892	0.919	0.918	0.882	0.921	0.869	0.908
Digits	5	0.842	0.820	0.887	0.827	0.868	0.851	0.803	0.872	0.809	0.853
	15	0.931	0.915	0.952	0.925	0.930	0.937	0.901	0.950	0.892	0.930
	25	0.969	0.958	0.980	0.960	0.968	0.962	0.949	0.968	0.928	0.947
MNIST	5	0.774	0.737	0.795	0.730	0.772	0.761	0.726	0.777	0.719	0.759
	15	0.811	0.784	0.855	0.783	0.836	0.826	0.793	0.830	0.782	0.812
	25	0.863	0.839	0.884	0.841	0.859	0.850	0.814	0.861	0.810	0.849
Average		0.772	0.746	0.826	0.748	0.804	0.758	0.720	0.788	0.715	0.758

The first remark that can be made from this table is that the performance of each algorithm on all the datasets grows in parallel with the growth of the sampling rate ζ, which is quite normal, because the amount of the available labeled data is an important factor to improve the performance of semi-supervised models, the more labeled data is available, the better the model is performing. The table also shows that our method outperforms the other inductive model SSI, in all the datasets and for all the sampling rates ζ, this achievement can be explained by the same reason why OTP outperforms LP, i.e. the use of optimal transport to calculate similarities between the data instead of the pairwise distances which only capture information on a bilateral level. However, the performance of OTI is inferior to that of OTP, which is reasonable because, on the one hand, in order to allow to OTP to perform inductive tasks, the out-of-sample set X_{new} was merged with the sets X_L and X_U in the training, while only predictions on X_{new} were retained to evaluate its performance, and on the other hand, OTI relies on OTP in the training, so if OTP makes errors in its predictions on Y_U, this will directly affect the performance of OTI on X_{new}. The same analysis can be extended to the case of SSI, that uses LP in its training, which explains the better performance of the latter. The difference in the average performances for both NMI and ARI, between OTP and OTI, is less than the difference between LP and SSI, demonstrating that using optimal transport to extend the label function to out-of-sample data can significantly improve the accuracy of the predictions.

5   Conclusion

In this paper, the problem of inductive semi-supervised learning is addressed. A new approach, named Optimal Transport Induction, is proposed to extend OTP from transductive parameters to inductive ones. A modification in the objective function of OTP was considered, from which an efficient algorithm OTI was derived to allow us to extend predictions to previously unseen data, by relying on optimal transport to compute the similarity between the out-of-sample data and the data already encountered in the training phase. Experimental studies have been conducted to show the effectiveness of our approach.

References

1. Bengio, Y., Delalleau, O., Le Roux, N.: Label propagation and quadratic criterion (2006)
2. Chapelle, O., Scholkopf, B., Zien, A.: Semi-supervised learning (chapelle, o. et al., eds.; 2006). IEEE Trans. Neural Netw. **20**(3), 542–542 (2009)
3. Cuturi, M.: Sinkhorn distances: Lightspeed computation of optimal transport. In: Advances in neural information processing systems, pp. 2292–2300 (2013)
4. Delalleau, O., Bengio, Y., Le Roux, N.: Efficient non-parametric function induction in semi-supervised learning. In: PMLR (2005)
5. Dom, B.E.: An information-theoretic external cluster-validity measure (2012)
6. El Hamri, M., Bennani, Y., Falih, I.: Label propagation through optimal transport. In: 2021 International Joint Conference on Neural Networks (2021)
7. Hubert, L., Arabie, P.: Comparing partitions. J. Classif. **2**(1), 193–218 (1985)
8. Leonid Vitalievich Kantorovich: On the translocation of masses. In Dokl. Akad. Nauk. USSR (NS) **37**, 199–201 (1942)
9. Monge, G.: Mémoire sur la théorie des déblais et des remblais. Histoire de l'Académie Royale des Sciences de Paris (1781)
10. Peyré, G., Cuturi, M.: Computational optimal transport: with applications to data science. Found. Trends® Mach. Learn., **11**(5-6), 355-607 (2019)
11. Santambrogio, F.: Optimal Transport for Applied Mathematicians. PNDETA, vol. 87. Springer, Cham (2015). https://doi.org/10.1007/978-3-319-20828-2
12. Subramanya, A., Talukdar, P.P.: Graph-based semi-supervised learning. Synth. Lect. Artif. Intell. Mach. Learn. **8**(4), 1–125 (2014)
13. van Engelen, J.E., Hoos, H.H.: A survey on semi-supervised learning. Mach. Learn. **109**(2), 373–440 (2019). https://doi.org/10.1007/s10994-019-05855-6
14. Villani, C.: Optimal Transport: Old and New. vol. 338. Springer, Cham (2008)
15. Wang, F., Zhang, C.: Label propagation through linear neighborhoods. IEEE Trans. Knowl. Data Eng. **20**(1), 55–67 (2007)
16. Zhu, X., Ghahramani, Z.: Learning from labeled and unlabeled data with label propagation (2002)

Random Sampling Weights Allocation Update for Deep Reinforcement Learning

Mengzhang Cai[1(✉)], Wengang Zhou[1,2], Qing Li[1], and Houqiang Li[1,2]

[1] CAS Key Laboratory of GIPAS, EEIS Department, University of Science
and Technology of China (USTC), Hefei, China
{caimz,liqingya}@mail.ustc.edu.cn
[2] Institute of Artificial Intelligence, Hefei Comprehensive National Science Center,
Hefei, China
{zhwg,lihq}@ustc.edu.cn

Abstract. Deep Reinforcement Learning (RL) has achieved great success in many tasks, and the key challenge of Reinforcement Learning now is the inefficient exploration and the unstable training problems brought by high-dimensional input state. Recently, some ensemble works have utilized multiple critics to provide a more specific Q-value and explore more by increasing the diversity of critics. However, these works can not ensure both robust training with effective exploration and thus get limited performance on high-dimensional continuous control tasks. To address this challenge, in this work, we propose Random Sampling Weights Allocation (RSWA), a new critic ensemble framework. Our method introduces the random sampling weights mechanism to increase training robustness and re-allocate the weights according to the Temporal-Difference in every training step to encourage efficient exploration. Our method is compatible with various actor-critic algorithms and can effectively improve the performance of them. We conduct experiments that couple RSWA with various current actor-critic RL algorithms on different OpenAI Gym and DM-Control tasks to verify the effectiveness of this method.

Keywords: Reinforcement learning · Ensemble · Temporal-difference

1 Introduction

With the integration of deep learning, we have witnessed the great success of reinforcement learning (RL) in many complex tasks [7,14] recent years. In RL, an agent is learned to maximize the cumulative rewards through a series of interactions with a dynamic environment. Deep Q-Network algorithm [11] is the first to combine non-linear function approximation with the Q-learning algorithm and introduce experience replay buffer to increase the training stability. In continuous

This work was supported in part by the National Natural Science Foundation of China under Contract 61836011 and U20A20183, and in part by the Youth Innovation Promotion Association CAS under Grant 2018497.

T. Mantoro et al. (Eds.): ICONIP 2021, CCIS 1516, pp. 676–684, 2021.
https://doi.org/10.1007/978-3-030-92307-5_79

control tasks, actor-critic algorithms [4,5,9,10], which combine policy iteration and value iteration, have achieved promising performance. Although these algorithms have been successful applied in many problems, they are still poor in some tasks for two main reasons: one is unstable training leads to serious shock, and the other is inefficient exploration. Recently, ensemble works like Averaged-DQN [2], Bootstrapped DQN [12], Random ensemble mixture (REM) [1] have been proved to be beneficial and efficient to solve these problems for RL. Averaged-DQN utilize averaging previously learned Q-value estimates to reduce the target approximation error variance that leads to stable training and improved performance. In offline RL task, REM uses a random convex combination of multiple Q-value estimation, which improves the stability during RL training. These works indicate that using ensemble techniques can effectively improve performance and stability of deep RL. However, these ensemble works can not ensure robust training with effective exploration and thus get limited improvement in RL algorithms on high-dimensional continuous control tasks.

To solve this problem, in this work, we propose **R**andom **S**ampling **W**eights **A**llocation Update (**RSWA**), a new multi-critic ensemble framework that updates critic Q-value by re-allocating random sampling weights to multiple critics according to Temporal-Difference (TD) [16] calculated on each head in every time step. RSWA introduces a new policy improvement strategy that use randomly parameterized critic to update the actor to ensure robust training, analogous to dropout. Besides, by giving larger weights to critics with bigger TD errors, the critics that can not estimate current state and action well will be more weighted. It means the sensitivity of each critic to different samples are diverse and the diversity of critics will encourage more effective exploration further, like Bootstrapped DQN [12]. Since RSWA allocates random weights to multiple critics, it can both improve the robustness of the updates and the efficiency of exploration.

To verify the effectiveness of our method, we couple RSWA with three state-of-the-art actor-critic algorithms: Twin Delayed Deep Deterministic policy gradient algorithm (TD3) [5], Soft Actor-Critic (SAC) [6], and Proximal Policy Optimization algorithm (PPO) [13]. We conduct experiments of these algorithms on multiple OpenAI Gym tasks (Mujoco) [3] and DeepMind Infrastructure for Physics-Based Simulation tasks (DM-Control) [15]. The experimental results show that our RSWA not only improves the performance of these actor-critic algorithms but also surpasses previous ensemble works.

2   Related Work

2.1   Actor-Critic Reinforcement Learning

Actor-critic method combines both policy gradient and Temporal-Difference learning. It consists of two models: Critic and Actor. Critic updates the value function parameters θ. Value function can be action-value $Q_\theta(s, a)$ or state-value $V_\theta(s)$ depending on the algorithm. And actor updates the policy parameters ϕ for $\pi_\phi(a \mid s)$ in the direction suggested by the critic.

2.2 Ensemble in RL

Averaged-DQN [2] is a simple extension to the DQN algorithm, based on averaging previously learned Q-value estimates, which leads to a more stable training procedure and better performance by reducing approximation error variance in the target values. Bootstrapped DQN [12] use multiple Q-functions updated with different sets of training samples to encourage deep exploration. AUMC [8] initialize critics with random parameters independently to increase the diversity of critics. In offline RL tasks, REM [1] obtains a robust Q-learning by enforcing optimal Bellman consistency on a random convex combination of multiple Q-value estimates. These ensemble works all improve the stability or performance of RL algorithm. However, they do not notice the balance between exploration and robust training. In RSWA, we update critic Q-value by matching different random weights to multiple Q-value estimates according to TD-error calculated in each head that both can ensure efficient exploration and the robustness of training.

3 Method

In this section, we introduce our proposed method: Random Sampling Weights Allocation (RSWA), a critic ensemble framework that achieves both effective exploration and robust training in RL. In RSWA, we use multiple parameterized Q-functions to estimate the Q-value, similar to Average-DQN [2]. Different from previous ensemble works, we randomly generate Q-value weights for multiple critics that the convex combination of multiple Q-value estimates leads to more robust training and stable updates. Besides, RSWA introduces TD-error, to allocate random generated weights to multiple critics. And the diversity of multiple critics brought by TD allocation will encourage deep exploration.

3.1 Random Sampling Weights Allocation

In actor-critic RL algorithm, we get the action tuple (s, a, r, s') at each time step. We then compute the absolute value of TD-error for all critics:

$$\boldsymbol{\delta} = \left\{|\delta_k|\right\}_{k=1}^{K} = \left\{\left|r + \gamma Q_{\bar{\theta}}^k\left(s', \tilde{a}'\right) - Q_{\theta}^k(s, a)\right|\right\}_{k=1}^{K}, \tilde{a}' \sim \pi_{\bar{\phi}}\left(s'\right), \qquad (1)$$

where i represents the index of the critic, $\bar{\phi}$ and $\bar{\theta}$ are the delayed parameters of the actor and the critic, respectively. Since SAC add the entropy bonus to value function, when coupling RSWA with SAC, Eq. (1) is defined as follows:

$$|\delta_k| = \left|r + \gamma \left(Q_{\bar{\theta}}^k\left(s', \tilde{a}'\right) + \alpha \mathcal{H}\left(\pi_{\phi}\left(\cdot \mid s'\right)\right)\right) - Q_{\theta}^k(s, a)\right|, \quad \tilde{a}' \sim \pi_{\phi}\left(s'\right). \qquad (2)$$

We draw K dimensional weights for the critics from the $Uniform(0, 1)$ and normalize them to get a valid categorical distribution at each time step as follows:

$$\bar{\boldsymbol{w}} = \left\{\bar{w}_k = w_k' / \sum w_i'\right\}_{k=1}^{K}, \boldsymbol{w}' = \left\{w_k' \sim \mathrm{U}(0, 1)\right\}_{i=1}^{K}. \qquad (3)$$

Then we resort $\boldsymbol{w}$ according to current TD-errors $\boldsymbol{\delta}$ in non-increasing order and get the re-allocated weights $\boldsymbol{w}$. And $w_1, \cdots, w_K \in (0,1)$ indicate the sensitivity of each citric to current samples. We make the citric be more sensitive to the unfamiliar tuples, which improve the diversity of critics that encourage more effective exploration.

3.2 Policy Evaluation

In RSWA, we use K critics $Q_1, Q_2, ..., Q_K$ to estimate Q-values and minimize the loss of critics:

$$y_k \leftarrow r + \gamma Q_{\bar{\theta}}^k \left(s', \pi_{\bar{\phi}} (s') \right),$$

$$J_Q(\theta) = \sum_{k=1}^{K} J_{Q^k}(\theta) = \sum_{k=1}^{K} w_k \left(y_k - Q_{\theta}^k(s, a) \right)^2. \tag{4}$$

The target Q-value of critic k is y_k, and RSWA tries to minimize the loss remixed by the weights w_k. Since SAC and TD3 both use clipped double Q-learning mechanism, when coupling RSWA with them, the target Q-value is formulated as:

$$y = r + \gamma \min_{i=1,2} \sum_{k=1}^{K} w_k Q_{\bar{\theta}_i}^k \left(s', \pi_{\bar{\phi}} (s') \right). \tag{5}$$

In SAC, the target Q-value function includes entropy regularization item:

$$y = r + \gamma \min_{i=1,2} \left(\sum_{k=1}^{K} Q_{\bar{\theta}_i}^k \left(s', \tilde{a}' \right) + \alpha \mathcal{H} \left(\pi_\phi (\cdot \mid s') \right) \right), \tag{6}$$

where actions $\tilde{a}$ are stochastically sampled from the current policy π_ϕ.

PPO is an on-policy algorithm and use advantage function to measure the relative advantage of action a in state s. When coupling RSWA with PPO, we change the computation of value function as:

$$V_{\bar{\theta}}(s) = \sum_{k=1}^{K} w_k V_{\bar{\theta}}^k(s). \tag{7}$$

3.3 Policy Improvement

RSWA mixes multiple critics to evaluate the policy and increase the diversity by allocating random sampling weights to different critics according to TD-error. In this way, the algorithm can both maintain the robust training and more efficient exploration. The gradient of the deterministic policy (TD3) is:

$$\nabla_\phi J_\pi(\phi) = \nabla_a Q_\theta(s, a)|_{a=\pi_\phi(s)} \nabla_\phi \pi_\phi(s). \tag{8}$$

and the gradient of the stochastic policy (SAC) is:

$$\nabla_\phi J_\pi(\phi) = \nabla_\phi \left[(Q_\theta(s, a) - \alpha \log \pi_\phi(a \mid s))|_{a \sim \pi_\phi(s)} \right], \tag{9}$$

where the critic Q_θ is random sampling weights mixed critics at each training step. The the gradient of Proximal Policy Optimization (PPO) in RSWA is formulated as:

$$\nabla_\phi J_\pi(\phi) = \nabla_\phi \left[(\frac{\pi_\phi(a \mid s)}{\pi_{\bar\phi}(a \mid s)} A_{\pi_{\bar\phi}}(s,a)) \mid_{a \sim \pi_{\bar\phi}} \right], \tag{10}$$

where the advantage function $A_{\pi_{\bar\phi}}$ is based on the current mixed value function $V_{\bar\theta}$.

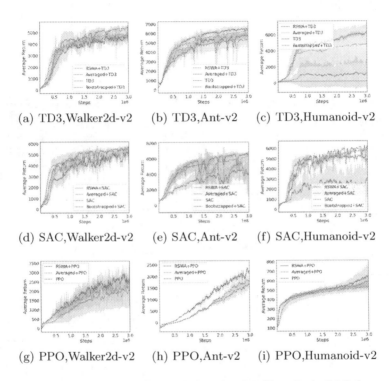

(a) TD3,Walker2d-v2   (b) TD3,Ant-v2   (c) TD3,Humanoid-v2

(d) SAC,Walker2d-v2   (e) SAC,Ant-v2   (f) SAC,Humanoid-v2

(g) PPO,Walker2d-v2   (h) PPO,Ant-v2   (i) PPO,Humanoid-v2

Fig. 1. Learning curves of RSWA coupled with TD3 (first line), SAC (second line), and PPO (third line) compared to Bootstrapped(PPO is not compatible with Bootstrapped), Averaged ensemble method and original algorithms separately.

4   Experiments

In this section, we couple our method RSWA with state-of-the-art actor-critic RL algorithms, like TD3 [5], SAC [6], and PPO [13], to verify the effectiveness of RSWA. We also compare our method with previous ensemble works, such as the Bootstrapped [12] and Averaged ensemble method [2]. Moreover, we further make ablation study to verify the effectiveness of random weights allocation.

4.1   Benchmarks

We separately couple RSWA, Bootstrapped method and Averaged Ensemble method with three state-of-the-art RL algorithms and evaluate these methods on 3 MuJoCo continuous tasks (Walker2d-v2, Ant-v2, and Humanoid-v2) in OpenAI Gym [3]. Besides, we further implement our method on 12 DM-Control tasks [15] to verify the improvement to original RL algorithms. The performance of algorithms on each environment is demonstrated by plotting the mean cumulative reward. For results plots, the solid lines represent the mean cumulative rewards and the shaded regions represent the standard deviation of the average evaluation over 4 different random seeds.

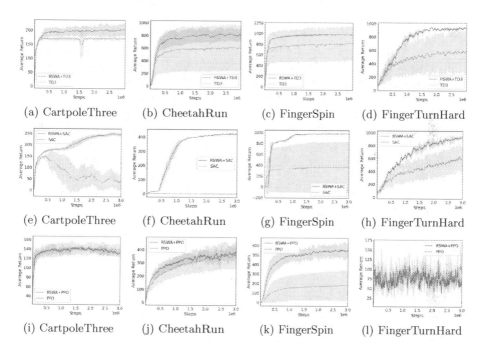

Fig. 2. Learning curves of TD3, SAC, and PPO with and without RSWA on four DM-Control (CartpoleThree, CheetahRun, FingerSpin and FingerTurnHard) tasks over 3 million time steps. Other tasks in DM-control are in appendix.

4.2   Implementation Details

For existing RL algorithms (TD3, SAC, and PPO), value-network and policy-network are implemented with MLP consist of two hidden layers and learning rate is $3e^{-4}$. The batch size is 256, the replay buffer size is 1×10^6, and the discount factor is 0.99 during training process. For Random Sampling Weights Allocation, we sample the weights from the $Uniform\ (0, 1)$ and the number of critics is set to 100 ($K = 100$). While in Bootstrapped Method and averaged ensemble method the number of critics is set to 10 ($K = 10$). For Bootstrapped Method, we sample K-dimensional binary masks from Bernoulli distribution with fixed parameter that denotes the probability of allocating the samples to the critics for Bootstrapped Method. And in Bernoulli distribution, we set $p =$ 0.5. For fair comparison, other hyper-parameters in Bootstrapped and Averaged method is the same with our RSWA.

4.3   Results

The results of total average return during training for RSWA, Bootstrapped and Averaged ensemble method on PPO, TD3 and SAC in Mujoco environments are shown in Fig. 1. For all Mujoco tasks, our method RSWA consistently improves the performance of three algorithms. And the improvement in PPO and TD3 is larger than in SAC. It should be noting that the performance of Bootstrapped method in SAC is also worse. In SAC, the introducing of entropy regularization playing the same role as diverse multiple critics limits the performance of method that encourage to explore more. However, our method in Mujoco tasks still perform better than original SAC algorithm, which verify performance improvement in RSWA not only from the effective exploration but also from the robustness brought by random sampling weights in each time step. Besides, Fig. 2 shows the performance of RSWA on 12 different DM-Control tasks. RSWA improve the performance of three actor-critic RL algorithms on almost all tasks. These results demonstrate that RSWA can improve current state-of-the-art actor-critic RL algorithms and work better than other existing ensemble methods. It verifies that our method can achieve both exploration and robust update efficient by reasonably allocating random sampling weights.

4.4   Ablation Study

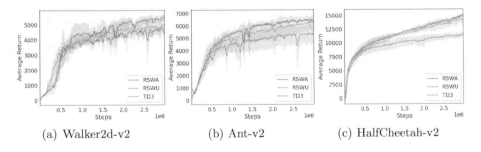

(a) Walker2d-v2   (b) Ant-v2   (c) HalfCheetah-v2

Fig. 3. Performance comparison of RSWA, RSWU and TD3 on Walker2d-v2, HalfCheetah-v2 and Ant-v2 to verify effectiveness of random sampling weights and TD allocation.

We conduct ablation study to further examine which particular component of RSWA is essential for the performance. We set TD3 as the baseline algorithm to conduct the following experiments.

As discussed in the previous section, the improvement of performance in RSWA is mainly contributed by robust training and effective exploration, which is separately brought by random weighs sampling and the allocation according to TD-error. We therefore run the experiments that remove the TD allocation from RSWA called Random sampling weights Update (RSWU). The learning curve compared to RSWA and baseline TD3 are shown in Fig. 3. On Ant-v2 and HalfCheetah-v2, RSWU is better than baseline TD3 while it is worse than RSWA. The results verify our ideas that the random weighs sampling and the TD allocation are complementary to each other and can both improve the performance of actor-critic RL algorithms.

5 Conclusion

In this work, we propose the RSWA framework, a multi-critic ensemble mechanism that is compatible with various current state-of-the-art actor-critic RL algorithms. RSWA achieves robust training with effective exploration through the allocation of random sampling weights according to TD-errors. The experiments on the OpenAI Gym and DM-Control benchmarks demonstrate that our method can significantly improve the performance of RL algorithms, such as TD3, SAC, and PPO. And we further conduct ablation study to verify that the random weighs sampling and TD allocation are Complementary. Moreover, our method is time efficient and compatible to various actor-critic RL algorithms.

References

1. Agarwal, R., Schuurmans, D., Norouzi, M.: An optimistic perspective on offline reinforcement learning. In: IMCL, pp. 104–114. PMLR (2020)
2. Anschel, O., Baram, N., Shimkin, N.: Averaged-DQN: Variance reduction and stabilization for deep reinforcement learning. In: ICML, pp. 176–185. PMLR (2017)
3. Brockman, G., Cheung, V., Pettersson, L., Schneider, J., Schulman, J., Tang, J., Zaremba, W.: Openai gym. arXiv preprint arXiv:1606.01540 (2016)
4. Ciosek, K., Vuong, Q., Loftin, R., Hofmann, K.: Better exploration with optimistic actor-critic. arXiv preprint arXiv:1910.12807 (2019)
5. Fujimoto, S., Hoof, H., Meger, D.: Addressing function approximation error in actor-critic methods. In: ICML, pp. 1587–1596. PMLR (2018)
6. Haarnoja, T., Zhou, A., Abbeel, P., Levine, S.: Soft actor-critic: Off-policy maximum entropy deep reinforcement learning with a stochastic actor. In: ICML, pp. 1861–1870. PMLR (2018)
7. Li, J., Koyamada, S., et al.: Suphx: Mastering mahjong with deep reinforcement learning. arXiv preprint arXiv:2003.13590 (2020)
8. Li, Q., Zhou, W., Zhou, Y., Li, H.: Attentive update of multi-critic for deep reinforcement learning. In: ICME, pp. 1–6. IEEE (2021)
9. Lillicrap, T.P., Hunt, J.J., et al.: Continuous control with deep reinforcement learning. arXiv preprint arXiv:1509.02971 (2015)
10. Mnih, V., et al.: Asynchronous methods for deep reinforcement learning. In: ICML, pp. 1928–1937. PMLR (2016)

11. Mnih, V., Kavukcuoglu, K., et al.: Playing atari with deep reinforcement learning. arXiv preprint arXiv:1312.5602 (2013)
12. Osband, I., Blundell, C., Pritzel, A., Van Roy, B.: Deep exploration via bootstrapped DQN. arXiv preprint arXiv:1602.04621 (2016)
13. Schulman, J., Wolski, F., Dhariwal, P., Radford, A., Klimov, O.: Proximal policy optimization algorithms. arXiv preprint arXiv:1707.06347 (2017)
14. Silver, D., Huang, A., et al.: Mastering the game of go with deep neural networks and tree search. Nature **529**(7587), 484–489 (2016)
15. Tassa, Y., Tunyasuvunakool, S., et al.: dm_control: software and tasks for continuous control. arXiv preprint arXiv:2006.12983 (2020)
16. Tesauro, G., et al.: Temporal difference learning and TD-Gammon. Commun. ACM **38**(3), 58–68 (1995)

Domain Adaptation with Stacked Convolutional Sparse Autoencoder

Yi Zhu[1,2,3]($\boxtimes$), Xinke Zhou[1], Yun Li[1]($\boxtimes$), Jipeng Qiang[1], and Yunhao Yuan[1]

[1] School of Information Engineering, Yangzhou University, Yangzhou, China
{zhuyi,liyun}@yzu.edu.cn
[2] School of Computer Science and Information Engineering,
Hefei University of Technology, Hefei, China
[3] Key Laboratory of Knowledge Engineering with Big Data (Hefei University of Technology), Ministry of Education, Hefei, China

Abstract. Domain adaptation aims to transfer knowledge from source domain to promote the learning task in target domain. The key problem of domain adaptation is how to learn more abstract and discriminative features for across domains. Recently, autoencoder based methods have achieved substantial performance in domain adaptation for the advantages of no label requirement and fast convergence speed. However, most of existing methods rely on the classical structure of autoencoder or integrate the regularization item into the objective function, which poses challenges for more abstract feature representation learning. To address this problem, we propose a domain adaptation method with Stacked Convolutional Sparse Autoencoder (short for SCSA). More specifically, more discriminative features are learned by convolutional lower layers with kernels learned by a sparse autoencoder. Meanwhile, the Reconstruction Independent Component Analysis (RICA) is introduced for independent component analysis of the input data. Extensive experimental results demonstrate the effectiveness of our proposed methods compared to several state-of-the-art domain adaptation methods.

Keywords: Domain adaptation · Representation learning · Convolutional autoencoder · Sparse autoencoder

1 Introduction

In recent decades, domain adaptation methods have been proposed to break the limitations of traditional machine learning: training and test data are independent and identically distributed [1,2]. The key problem of domain adaptation is how to learn more abstract features for alleviating the discrepancy of domain distribution [3–5].

Recent studies have shown that deep networks can learn higher-level and more abstract features for domain adaptation [3,4]. Lots of deep domain adaptation methods based on autoencoder have achieved substantial performance for

© Springer Nature Switzerland AG 2021
T. Mantoro et al. (Eds.): ICONIP 2021, CCIS 1516, pp. 685–692, 2021.
https://doi.org/10.1007/978-3-030-92307-5_80

reducing the domain divergence [5–7]. For example, Stacked Denoising Autoencoder (SDA) [8] exacted higher-level features from all available domains and a classifier is trained on the new representations for classification in target domain. Along this line, Marginalized Stacked Denoising Autoencoders (mSDA) [9] is proposed to address two crucial problems of SDA: high computational cost and lack of scalability to high-dimensional features. The representation learning of mSDA is as effective as that of SDA, but it has been proved to be more effective.

Though the autoencoder-based domain adaptation methods can learn the robust representations across different domains, most of existing methods rely on the classical structure of autoencoder or integrate the regularization item into the objective function [10–12]. To further explore the ability of feature representation learning, we propose a representation learning method via Stacked Convolutional Sparse Autoencoder (SCSA), in which we can learn more abstract features by layers mapping from original data for domain adaptation. More specifically, firstly, a stacked sparse autoencoder is introduced to exact features from the original data, and RICA with whitening is used for the model training. Secondly, the convolutional kernels are used to reserve the local relevance and learn more abstract representations. Finally, several layers of convolutional sparse autoencoder are stacked to learn more abstract representations for domain adaptation. Extensive experimental results demonstrate the effectiveness of our proposed methods compared to several domain adaptation methods.

In summary, the main contributions of our proposed SCSA are listed as follows:

- Different from the existing works, which focus on learning representations with classical structure of autoencoders or integrate the regularization item into the objective function, we propose a domain adaptation method via stacked convolutional sparse autoencoder (SCSA).
- There are two main components in each layer of our proposed SCSA. Firstly, the stacked sparse autoencoder with RICA is introduced for discriminative features learning. Secondly, the convolutional kernels are utilized to reserve the local relevance for improving domain adaptation performance.

2   Related Work

In domain adaptation methods, the feature-based methods have been applied to a broader set of scenarios due to the loose restrictions on the source data. Existing methods can roughly be categorized into two classes according to the used technology: shallow learning and deep learning methods.

Transfer component analysis (TCA) [13] is a typical shallow learning method for domain adaptation, which tries to minimize the distance between different domains in a new features space with Maximum Mean Discrepancy (MMD). In light of TCA, Chen et al. proposed a unsupervised Domain Space Transfer Extreme Learning Machine (DST-ELM) method [14], the MMD distance was introduced to measure difference and minimize the distance between different domains in the latent space. Luo et al. proposed a general flexible Heterogeneous

Transfer Distance Metric Learning (HTDML) method [15], which leveraged the knowledge fragments of source domain to assist the metric learning in target domain.

Recently, deep learning methods have attained much attention in domain adaptation for the powerful ability of feature representations learning. For example, Glorot et al. introduced Stacked Denoising Autoencoder (SDA) for domain adaptation on a large-scale data set [16]. Zhu et al. proposed Transfer Learning with Manifold Regularized Autoencoders (TLMRA) [17], the model of SDA with Softmax Regression is integrated to learn more discriminative features, and the manifold regularization is introduced to optimize parameters of this method.

3   Proposed Algorithm

The proposed Stacked Convolutional Sparse Autoencoder (SCSA) for domain adaptation is illustrated as Fig. 1.

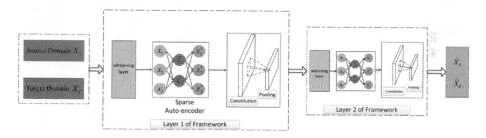

Fig. 1. The whole framework of the proposed SCSA.

3.1   Stacked Sparse Autoencoder

The stacked sparse autoencoder with whiting layer is combined with label information in source domain and extracts higher-level features from different domains.

The RICA with the whitening layer is introduced for independent component analysis of the input data. The objective function of RICA is defined as (1):

$$L(W) = \lambda \sum (\sqrt{(Wx_i)^2 + \varepsilon}) + \frac{1}{2n} \sum_{i=1}^{n} (\frac{1}{m} \|W^T W x_i - x_i\|_2^2) \qquad (1)$$

where x_i is the ith output of input x, and $\varepsilon = 0.1$ is a small constant value to avoid the first item $(\sqrt{(Wx_i)^2 + \varepsilon})$ in (1) be numerically close to zero. The partial derivatives of $L(W)$ in (1) with respect to W and W^T can be shown as (2):

$$\nabla_W L(W) = \frac{2}{m}(W(W^T W X - X)X^T + (WX)(W^T W X - X)^T) + \lambda((WX)^2 + \varepsilon)^{-1/2}(WX)X^T \qquad (2)$$

Based on the partial derivatives in (1), the output $W^T W X$ of RICA with the whitening layer is utilized as the input of the next stacked sparse autoencoder.

The stacked sparse autoencoder with Softmax Regression which incorporates the labeled information in source domain has been used for representation learning, the whole objective function of sparse autoencoder with Softmax Regression can be formalized as (3):

$$J = J_1(x, \hat{x}) + \alpha J_2(\xi, \theta) + \beta J_3(W_1, W_2, b_1, b_2) \tag{3}$$

where α and β are the trade-off parameters to balance different items in (3).

The first term $J_1(x, \hat{x})$ in (3) is the reconstruction error, which can be defined as (4):

$$J_1(x, \hat{x}) = \sum_{i=1}^{n} \left\| x^{(i)} - \hat{x}^{(i)} \right\|^2 \tag{4}$$

The second term $J_2(\xi, \theta)$ in (3) is the cost function of Softmax Regression to incorporate the labeled data information, which can be written as (5):

$$J_2(\xi, \theta) = -\frac{1}{n} \sum_{i=1}^{n} \sum_{j=1}^{c} 1\{y_i^{(s)} = j\} \log \frac{e^{\theta_j^T \xi_i^{(s)}}}{\sum_{l=1}^{c} e^{\theta_l^T \xi_i^{(s)}}} \tag{5}$$

where θ_j^T is the j-th row of W_2.

The last term $J_3(W_1, W_2)$ in (3) is a regularization of the model weight, which can be defined as (6):

$$J_3(W_1, W_2) = \|W_1\|^2 + \|W_2\|^2 + \|b_1\|^2 + \|b_2\|^2 \tag{6}$$

The minimization of J is a function with respect to W_1, W_2, b_1, b_2 and θ_j, and the l-bfgs method is adopted.

3.2   Convolution and Pool Layer

The second component is the convolutional and pool layer. After obtaining convolved features, the input features are divided into disjoint $n_1 \times n_2$ regions and the mean (or maximum) feature activation over these regions is used to obtain the pooled convolved features, where n_1 and n_2 represent the size of patches. The stochastic gradient descent method is introduced for the parameters optimization in our experiments, and the parameter θ in the objective function $J(\theta)$ is updated as (7):

$$\vartheta = \vartheta - \gamma \nabla_\vartheta J\left(\vartheta; x^{(i)}\right) \tag{7}$$

where $x_i \in (n_1 \times n_2 \times d) \times 1$ is the input vector, and d is the number of channels. γ denotes the learning rate, which is typically much smaller than a corresponding learning rate in batch gradient descent due to there is much more variance in the update. The Momentum method is used for pushing the objective more quickly along the shallow ravine in our experiments, which can be shown as (8):

$$v = \phi v + \gamma \nabla_\vartheta J\left(\vartheta; x^{(i)}\right)$$
$$\vartheta = \vartheta - v \tag{8}$$

where v represents the current velocity vector with the same dimension as the parameter vector ϑ. $\phi \in (0, 1]$ determines for how many iterations the previous gradients are incorporated into the current update.

4 Experiments

4.1 Datasets

Corel Data Set[1] Two different top categories (flower and traffic) in Corel dataset are selected, the category of flower and traffic is used as positive and negative instances respectively. In the experiments, one subcategory from flower and one from traffic are randomly selected as the source domain, another subcategory from the remaining subcategories of flower and another one from traffic are selected to construct the target domain.

ImageNet Data Set[2] We choose five domains in ImageNet dataset [18] to construct domain adaptation tasks, including ambulance, taxi, jeep, minivan and scooter. The domain scooter is divided into other four domains randomly as negative instances. In our experiments, two of these new four domains are selected randomly, one is considered as the source domain and the other one is considered as target domain.

4.2 Compared Methods

We compare our proposed SCSA with the following baseline methods:

- The standard Support Vector Machine (SVM) [19] without domain adaptation technique.
- Transfer Component Analysis (TCA) [13], which tries to reduce dimensionality in latent feature space for domain adaptation.
- Marginalized Stacked Denoising Autoencoders (mSDA) [9], which has been proven to be an effective way to learn more abstract and discriminative feature representations for domain adaptation.
- Transfer Learning with Deep Autoencoders (TLDA) [20], which is a semi-supervised domain adaptation method based on stacked autoencoders. The distribution of both source and target domains are explicitly enforced to be similar in this method.
- Transfer Learning with Manifold Regularized Auto-encoders (TLMRA) [17]. It is a domain adaptation framework which integrated manifold regularization and softmax regression to learn more abstract feature representations.

---

[1] http://archive.ics.uci.edu/ml/datasets/Corel+Image+Features.
[2] http://www.image-net.org/.

4.3   Experiment Settings

In the experiments, $\alpha = 0.01$, $\beta = 0.005$ and $\lambda = 0.01$ are set for all the datasets. Moreover, the hyper-parameters in convolution layer such as the depth of the whole framework, the number of maps on each layer, the convolutional kernel size and the pool size are all listed in Table 2. In the method of mSDA[3], the best parameters will be calculated in the experiment. For TCA, the number of latent subspace dimension is carefully fixed, and its best result is reported. For TLDA, we use the default parameters as reported in [20] (Table 1).

Table 1. Main configurations of CAE in IATL on data sets

Data sets	Configurations	
Corel data set	Kernel size	$11 \times 11 \times 3$
	Maps number	1000
	Pool type	Max
	Pool size	12×12
ImageNet dataset	Kernel size	$10 \times 10 \times 3$
	Maps number	500
	Pool type	Max
	Pool size	24×24

4.4   Experimental Results

All the experimental results on two data sets are listed in Table 3, we have the following observations from experimental results:

- mSDA and TLDA deliver a relatively good result in most cases, which reveals the superiority of deep-based domain adaptation methods.
- Our SCSA significantly outperforms SVM, which shows the efficiency of the proposed method in domain adaptation.
- Our method achieves a more desirable performance than TCA, which indicates the advantages of deep model in higher-level feature representations learning for domain adaptation.
- Among the deep learning methods, our SCSA performs better than TLDA and TLMRA, which shows that the proposed Stacked Convolutional Sparse Autoencoder successfully guide the training process to learn better representations.
- Overall, our SCSA performs best on all groups, which demonstrate the effectiveness of our proposed methods.

---

[3] http://multitask.cs.berkeley.edu.

Table 2. Average accuracies on three data sets (%)

SVM	TCA	mSDA	TLDA	TLMRA	SCSA
ImageNet Data Set					
62.6±0.9	75.6±1.1	77.6±1.2	83.6±1.1	88.9±1.1	**89.3±0.9**
Corel Data Set					
52.9±0.8	76.5±0.7	73.4±0.6	80.2±0.6	84.5±0.5	**85.1±0.4**

5   Conclusion

In this paper, we proposed a deep method to learn feature representations with Stacked Convolutional Sparse Autoencoder for domain adaptation, called SCSA. SCSA is constructed by stacking sparse autoencoder which is optimized through patch-wise training in a convolution way. The deep model can learn more abstract and discriminative features for domain adaptation, and the label information in source domain is encoded by Softmax Regression in the training stage for improving domain adaptation performance. The network is trained with layer-wise RICA method with whitening, which proves to be an effective regularization method by the classification performance on the benchmarks. Extensive experiments demonstrate the proposed method outperforms other compared methods in the effectiveness.

Acknowledgments. This work is supported by the National Natural Science Foundation of China under grant 61906060.

References

1. Wilson, G., Cook, D.J.: A survey of unsupervised deep domain adaptation. ACM Trans. Intell. Syst. Technol. (TIST) **11**(5), 1–46 (2020)
2. Yang, S., Wang, H., Zhang, Y., Li, P., Zhu, Y., Hu, X.: Semi-supervised representation learning via dual autoencoders for domain adaptation. Knowl.-Based Syst. **190**, 105161 (2020)
3. Pan, S.J., Yang, Q.: A survey on transfer learning. IEEE Trans. Knowl. Data Eng. **22**(10), 1345–1359 (2009)
4. Tzeng, E., Hoffman, J., Saenko, K., Darrell, T.: Adversarial discriminative domain adaptation. In: Proceedings of the IEEE Conference on Computer Vision and Pattern Recognition, pp. 7167–7176 (2017)
5. Yi, Z., Hu, X., Zhang, Y., Li, P.: Transfer learning with stacked reconstruction independent component analysis. Knowl.-Based Syst. **152**, 100–106 (2018)
6. Wang, X., Ma, Y., Cheng, Y.: Domain adaptation network based on hypergraph regularized denoising autoencoder. Artif. Intell. Rev. **52**(3), 2061–2079 (2017). https://doi.org/10.1007/s10462-017-9576-0
7. Yang, S., Zhang, Y., Wang, H., Li, P., Hu, X.: Representation learning via serial robust autoencoder for domain adaptation. Expert Syst. Appl. **160**, 113635 (2020)

8. Vincent, P., Larochelle, H., Lajoie, I., Bengio, Y., Manzagol, P.-A.: Stacked denoising autoencoders: learning useful representations in a deep network with a local denoising criterion. J. Mach. Learn. Res. **11**(12), 3371–3408 (2010)

9. Chen, M., Xu, Z., Weinberger, K., Fei, S.: Marginalized denoising autoencoders for domain adaptation. In: Proceedings of the 29th International Conference on Machine Learning, pp. 767–774 (2012)

10. Zhuang, F., Cheng, X., Luo, P., Pan, S.J., He, Q.: Supervised representation learning with double encoding-layer autoencoder for transfer learning. ACM Trans. Intell. Syst. Technol. (TIST) **9**(2), 1–17 (2017)

11. Clinchant, S., Csurka, G., Chidlovskii, B.: A domain adaptation regularization for denoising autoencoders. In: Proceedings of the 54th Annual Meeting of the Association for Computational Linguistics (Volume 2: Short Papers), pp. 26–31 (2016)

12. Yang, S., Zhang, Y., Zhu, Y., Li, P., Hu, X.: Representation learning via serial autoencoders for domain adaptation. Neurocomputing **351**, 1–9 (2019)

13. Pan, S.J., Tsang, I.W., Kwok, J.T., Yang, Q.: Domain adaptation via transfer component analysis. IEEE Trans. Neural Networks **22**(2), 199–210 (2011)

14. Chen, Y., Song, S., Li, S., Yang, L., Wu, C.: Domain space transfer extreme learning machine for domain adaptation. IEEE Trans. Cybern. **49**(5), 1909–1922 (2019)

15. Luo, Y., Wen, Y., Liu, T., Tao, D.: Transferring knowledge fragments for learning distance metric from a heterogeneous domain. IEEE Trans. Pattern Anal. Mach. Intell. **41**(4), 1013–1026 (2019)

16. Glorot, X., Bordes, A., Bengio, Y.: Domain adaptation for large-scale sentiment classification: a deep learning approach. In: International Conference on Machine Learning, pp. 513–520 (2011)

17. Zhu, Y., Xindong, W., Li, P., Zhang, Y., Hu, X.: Transfer learning with deep manifold regularized auto-encoders. Neurocomputing **369**, 145–154 (2019)

18. Krizhevsky, A., Sutskever, I., Hinton, G.E.: ImageNet classification with deep convolutional neural networks. In: International Conference on Neural Information Processing Systems, pp. 1097–1105 (2012)

19. Matasci, G., Tuia, D., Kanevski, M.: SVM-based boosting of active learning strategies for efficient domain adaptation. IEEE J. Sel. Top. Appl. Earth Obs. Remote Sens. **5**(5), 1335–1343 (2012)

20. Zhuang, F., Cheng, X., Luo, P., Pan, S.J., He, Q.: Supervised representation learning: transfer learning with deep autoencoders. In: International Conference on Artificial Intelligence, pp. 4119–4125 (2015)

Link-Based Consensus Clustering
with Random Walk Propagation

Xiaosha Cai[1,2] and Dong Huang[1,2(✉)]

[1] College of Mathematics and Informatics, South China Agricultural University,
Guangzhou, China
[2] Guangzhou Key Laboratory of Intelligent Agriculture, Guangzhou, China

Abstract. In the paper, we propose a link-based consensus clustering approach with random walk propagation (LCC-RW), which is able
to incorporate common neighborhood information as well as multi-
scale indirect relationships. Specifically, the microcluster representation
is adopted to facilitate the computation. With the ensemble of base
clusterings represented by the microclusters, a microcluster-based co-
association matrix is built, which is then refined by weighted connected
triple. The refined matrix is further sparsified by preserving a small proportion of reliable entries. Then random walks are conducted on the
sparsified matrix to obtain a new dense similarity measure, which will
be used to build a weighted bipartite graph for obtaining the final clustering result. Experimental results demonstrate the superior performance
of our approach.

Keywords: Consensus clustering · Ensemble clustering ·
Microcluster · Connected-triple · Random walk

1 Introduction

Consensus clustering, which is also known as ensemble clustering, has been a
hot research topic in recent years [1–10,13,17,18]. As one of the earliest consensus clustering algorithms, Fred and Jain [3] proposed the evidence accumulation clustering (EAC) method, which first constructs a co-association matrix
between objects by considering the pair-wise co-occurrence relationship and then
perform hierarchical agglomerative clustering on the co-association matrix to
obtain the final clustering result. But the EAC method [3] only considers the
direct co-occurrence relationship between objects and cannot take the indirect
relationship into account. To incorporate the indirect relationship, Iam-On et al.
[11] proposed the link-based consensus clustering approach, where the weighted
connected-triple (WCT) method is presented to refine the co-association matrix
by considering common neighbors. However, there are still two limitations to the
WCT method. First, it works at the object-level, whose computational burden
may increase drastically as the number of objects grows. Second, it only considers
the common neighborhood yet neglects the multi-scale indirect relationships.

© Springer Nature Switzerland AG 2021
T. Mantoro et al. (Eds.): ICONIP 2021, CCIS 1516, pp. 693–700, 2021.
https://doi.org/10.1007/978-3-030-92307-5_81

To address the above-mentioned problem, in the paper, we propose a link-based consensus clustering approach with random walk propagation (LCC-RW). The multiple base clusterings are first represented through the microclusters, based on which the microcluster-based co-association matrix is built and then refined by weighted connected triple. The refined matrix is further sparsified, which preserves a small proportion of reliable entries. Thereafter, random walks are performed on the sparsified matrix to obtain a new dense similarity measure, which will be used to build the weighted bipartite graph for obtaining the final clustering result. Experiments on four benchmark datasets demonstrate the superior performance of the proposed approach.

The rest of the paper is organized as follows. Section 2 describes the overall algorithm of LCC-RW. Experimental results are reported in Sect. 3. Finally, in Sect. 4, we conclude the paper.

2   Proposed Algorithm

2.1   Problem Formulation

Given a dataset $\mathcal{X} = \{x_1, x_2, \cdots, x_N\}$ with N objects and d features. Let $\mathcal{P} = \{P^1, \cdots, P^M\}$ be the ensemble of M base clusterings, where $P^i = \{C_1^i, \cdots, C_{n^i}^i\}$ is the i-th base clustering, C_j^i is the jth cluster, and n^i is the number of clusters in P^i. Each base clustering consists of multiple clusters. The set of clusters in the entire ensemble can be represented as $\mathcal{C} = \{C_1, \cdots, C_{N_c}\}$, where N_c is the total number of clusters. The purpose of consensus clustering is to fuse the information of the M base clusterings to obtain a better clustering result P^*.

2.2   Weighted Co-association Matrix Based on Microclusters

To facilitate the computation, in this paper, the microcluster presentation [7] is adopted. Specifically, given the ensemble $\mathcal{P}$, the set of microclusters can be denoted as $\mathcal{MC} = \{mc_1, mc_2, \cdots, mc_{\hat{N}}\}$, where mc_i is the ith microcluster, and $\hat{N}$ is the number of microclusters. If x_i and x_j belong to the same cluster in all base clusterings, then they will be placed in the same microcluster.

To explore indirect structure information, we exploit the WCT [11] to refine the microcluster-based co-association matrix. The similarity between clusters C_i and C_j can be defined as

$$w_{ij} = \frac{|C_i \bigcap C_j|}{|C_i| \bigcup |C_j|}, \tag{1}$$

where $|\cdot|$ denotes the number of objects in a set (or cluster). Given a graph $G = (V, E)$, where $V = \mathcal{C}$ is the vertex set, and E is the edge set. Inspired by the concept of connected-triple [14], with vertices $V_{sub} = \{v_x, v_y, v_z\} \subset V$, edges $E_{sub} = \{e_{xz}, e_{yz}\} \subset E$, and $e_{xy} \notin E$, a subgraph $G_{sub} = (V_{sub}, E_{sub})$ can be constructed. With respect to each center of a triple $v_z \in V$, the WCT measure between v_x and v_y is computed as $WCT(v_x, v_y)^{v_z} = min(|w_{xz}|, |w_{yz}|)$, where $|w_{xz}|$ and $|w_{yz}|$ are the weights of the edges e_{xz} and e_{yz}, respectively. For all triples $(1 \cdots \gamma)$, the WCT measure between v_x and v_y can be computed by

$$WCT(v_x, v_y) = \sum_{z=1}^{\gamma} WCT(v_x, v_y)^{v_z} \tag{2}$$

Then the similarity between v_x and v_y can be defined as

$$Sim(v_x, v_y) = \frac{WCT(v_x, v_y)}{WCT_{max}} \times DC \tag{3}$$

where $DC \in [0, 1]$ is a constant decay factor. For each base clustering $P^k, \forall k = 1, \cdots, M$, the similarity between microcluster mc_i and mc_j is computed as

$$w_{ij}^k = \begin{cases} 1, & \text{if } C_*^k(mc_i) = C_*^k(mc_j), \\ Sim(C_*^k(mc_i), C_*^k(mc_j)), & \text{otherwise}, \end{cases} \tag{4}$$

where $C_*^k(mc_i)$ denotes the cluster in P^k that contains mc_i. Following that, the weighted microcluster based co-association (WMCA) matrix is defined as

$$S = \{s_{ij}\}_{\hat{N} \times \hat{N}}, \tag{5}$$

$$s_{ij} = \frac{\sum_{k=1}^{M} w_{ij}^k}{M} \tag{6}$$

Then the weighted microcluster based similarity graph (WMSG) can be denoted as $\widetilde{G} = (\widetilde{V}, \widetilde{W})$, where $\widetilde{V} = \mathcal{MC}$ is the vertex set and $\widetilde{W}$ is the set of weighted edges between microclusters with $\widetilde{w}_{ij} = s_{ij}$.

2.3 Random Walk on Graphs

In the section, we first sparsify the WMSG by preserving the K-elite neighbors (K-EN) [7], and denote the K-EN graph as $\bar{G} = (\bar{V}, \bar{W})$, where $\bar{V} = \mathcal{MC}$ is the vertex set and $\bar{W}$ is the edge set, with the edge weight defined as

$$\bar{w}_{ij} = \begin{cases} \widetilde{w}_{ij}, & \text{if } mc_i \in K - EN(mc_j), \\ 0, & \text{otherwise} \end{cases} \tag{7}$$

Then, we proceed to exploit the random walks to achieve a new dense similarity matrix from the sparsified graph. Let $\hat{n}_j$ denote the size of mc_j. The transition probability matrix $Q = \{q_{ij}\}_{\hat{N} \times \hat{N}}$ can be defined as [7]

$$q_{ij} = \frac{\hat{n}_j \cdot \widetilde{w}_{ij}}{\sum_{k \neq i} \hat{n}_k \cdot \widetilde{w}_{ik}} \tag{8}$$

where q_{ij} is the transition probability from mc_i to mc_j. Let Q^T denote the transition probability matrix of T steps. We have

$$
Q^T = \begin{cases} Q \cdot Q^{T-1}, & \text{if } T \geq 2, \\ Q, & \text{otherwise} \end{cases} \tag{9}
$$

The i-th row of Q^T, represented as $q_{i:}^T = \{q_{i1}^T, \cdots, q_{i\tilde{N}}^T\}$, is the probability of going from mc_i to other microclusters after T steps. To make better use of the multi-scale information, we integrate the transition probability information from step 1 to step T. Thus the probability trajectory of mc_i from step 1 to step T can be represented as $QT_i^T = \{q_i^1, \cdots, q_i^T\}$. The probability trajectory vector QT_i^T can be regarded as a new feature vector of mc_i with high-order relationship considered. The PTS similarity [7] between microclusters is computed as

$$
pts_{ij} = \frac{< QT_i^T, QT_j^T >}{\sqrt{< QT_i^T, QT_i^T > \cdot < QT_j^T, QT_j^T >}} \tag{10}
$$

where $<,>$ denotes the inner product of two vectors.

2.4 Clustering via Weighted Bipartite Graph Formulation

With the new similarity based on random walk propagation obtained, a weighted microcluster-cluster bipartite graph (WMCBG) can be constructed, denoted as $\ddot{G} = (\ddot{V}, \ddot{W})$, where $\ddot{V} = \mathcal{MC} \bigcup \mathcal{C}$ is the vertex set and $\ddot{W}$ is the set of weighted edges between a microclusters and the cluster that contains it. The $\ddot{w}_{ij}$ indicates the reliability that the microcluster belongs to the cluster, which is defined as

$$
\ddot{w}_{ij} = \begin{cases} \frac{1}{|C_j|} \sum_{mc_k \in C_j} pts_{ik}, & \text{if } mc_i \in \mathcal{MC}, C_j \in \mathcal{C}, \\ \frac{1}{|C_i|} \sum_{mc_k \in C_i} pts_{jk}, & \text{if } C_i \in \mathcal{C}, mc_j \in \mathcal{MC}, \\ 0, & \text{otherwise} \end{cases} \tag{11}
$$

where $|C_i|$ is the number of microclusters in C_i. Upon this graph, the Tcut algorithm [12] is then performed to efficiently obtain the clustering at the microcluster-level. By mapping the clustering result from the microcluster-level to the object-level, the final consensus clustering is obtained.

3   Experiments

In this section, we conduct experiments on several real-world datasets to compare LCC-RW against several baseline methods.

3.1   Datasets and Setup

In our experiments, we compare the proposed LCC-RW algorithm with the state-of-the-art consensus clustering algorithms, including EAC [3], Probability

Table 1. Dataset description

Dataset	Abbr.	#Instance	Dimension	#Class
Vertebral column	*DS-1*	310	6	3
Vehicle silhouette	*DS-2*	846	18	4
Image segmentation	*DS-3*	2310	19	7
Gisette	*DS-4*	7000	5000	2
MNIST	*DS-5*	5000	784	10
Flowers17	*DS-6*	1360	30000	17

Table 2. Average NMI (%) over 20 runs by different ensemble clustering methods on the benchmark datasets. The best score in each row is in bold.

Dataset	EAC	WCT	PTA	PTGP	ECPCS-HC	ECPCS-MC	LCC-RW
DS-1	$42.59_{\pm15.35}$	$34.60_{\pm16.21}$	$31.72_{\pm20.24}$	$42.88_{\pm8.29}$	$21.94_{\pm12.11}$	$20.51_{\pm7.24}$	$\mathbf{43.27}_{\pm9.17}$
DS-2	$\mathbf{19.14}_{\pm1.16}$	$18.97_{\pm1.87}$	$16.39_{\pm3.38}$	$17.94_{\pm2.10}$	$16.86_{\pm2.66}$	$17.84_{\pm2.17}$	$18.87_{\pm1.94}$
DS-3	$59.88_{\pm1.85}$	$60.37_{\pm1.80}$	$51.77_{\pm8.18}$	$61.79_{\pm2.47}$	$61.54_{\pm0.93}$	$62.37_{\pm1.50}$	$\mathbf{62.94}_{\pm2.21}$
DS-4	$28.17_{\pm10.74}$	$37.69_{\pm11.13}$	$41.71_{\pm7.81}$	$44.90_{\pm3.49}$	$38.29_{\pm11.85}$	$46.59_{\pm2.03}$	$\mathbf{47.84}_{\pm2.15}$
DS-5	$61.88_{\pm1.96}$	$62.28_{\pm1.49}$	$60.84_{\pm3.59}$	$61.31_{\pm2.38}$	$60.28_{\pm1.28}$	$\mathbf{63.86}_{\pm1.92}$	$62.81_{\pm2.48}$
DS-6	$25.21_{\pm0.57}$	$24.73_{\pm0.86}$	$\mathbf{25.39}_{\pm0.57}$	$25.08_{\pm0.63}$	$23.17_{\pm0.69}$	$21.84_{\pm1.09}$	$25.29_{\pm0.69}$
Avg. score	39.48	39.77	37.97	42.32	37.01	38.84	43.50
Avg. rank	4.00	4.17	5.00	3.50	5.67	4.00	1.67

Table 3. Average ARI (%) over 20 runs by different ensemble clustering methods on the benchmark datasets. The best score in each row is in bold.

Dataset	EAC	WCT	PTA	PTGP	ECPCS-HC	ECPCS-MC	LCC-RW
DS-1	$\mathbf{34.44}_{\pm21.10}$	$32.82_{\pm28.20}$	$20.19_{\pm20.70}$	$32.89_{\pm6.11}$	$10.72_{\pm20.63}$	$8.16_{\pm12.96}$	$32.74_{\pm9.53}$
DS-2	$12.67_{\pm1.30}$	$13.03_{\pm2.11}$	$11.21_{\pm3.31}$	$12.47_{\pm1.53}$	$11.63_{\pm2.59}$	$12.65_{\pm1.73}$	$\mathbf{13.51}_{\pm1.84}$
DS-3	$49.35_{\pm3.31}$	$51.68_{\pm3.19}$	$34.97_{\pm11.08}$	$50.83_{\pm3.77}$	$52.85_{\pm1.48}$	$\mathbf{53.10}_{\pm2.59}$	$51.91_{\pm3.75}$
DS-4	$27.78_{\pm15.22}$	$44.17_{\pm13.54}$	$49.18_{\pm10.92}$	$54.77_{\pm4.14}$	$45.14_{\pm14.24}$	$57.12_{\pm2.19}$	$\mathbf{58.09}_{\pm2.40}$
DS-5	$49.94_{\pm2.94}$	$51.38_{\pm1.77}$	$48.15_{\pm4.82}$	$49.28_{\pm3.59}$	$49.74_{\pm1.26}$	$\mathbf{53.36}_{\pm3.08}$	$51.39_{\pm4.40}$
DS-6	$9.39_{\pm0.38}$	$9.28_{\pm0.76}$	$9.53_{\pm0.47}$	$9.60_{\pm0.42}$	$8.43_{\pm1.01}$	$9.43_{\pm0.66}$	$\mathbf{9.71}_{\pm0.50}$
Avg. score	30.59	33.73	28.87	34.97	29.75	32.30	36.23
Avg. rank	4.33	4.00	5.50	3.83	5.17	3.17	2.00

Trajectory Accumulation (PTA) [7], PTGP [7], ensemble clustering by propagating cluster-wise similarities with hierarchical consensus function (ECPCS-HC) [10], and ensemble clustering by propagating cluster-wise similarities with meta-cluster-based consensus function (ECPCS-MC) [10].

Six datasets are used in our experiments, whose statistics are provided in Table 1. For clarity, we denote the six datasets as *DS-1* to *DS-6*, respectively. On each dataset, we perform the K-means algorithm repeatedly to obtain an ensemble of base clusterings, with the number of clusters in each base clustering randomly chosen in the interval of $[k', \sqrt{N}]$, where k' is the number of classes in the dataset and N is the number of objects.

Two widely-used evaluation measure, i.e., the normalized mutual information (NMI) [15] and the adjusted Rand index (ARI) [16] are used for evaluation.

3.2   Comparison with Other Consensus Clustering Methods

In this section, we compare the proposed LCC-RW algorithm against the baseline consensus clustering algorithms. In the experiment, the ensemble size $M = 20$,

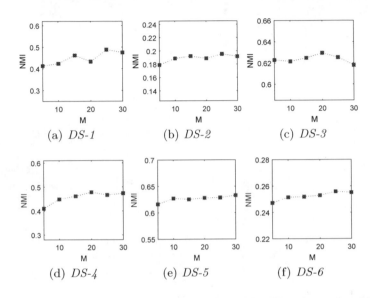

Fig. 1. Average NMI (%) over 20 runs by LCC-RW with varying M.

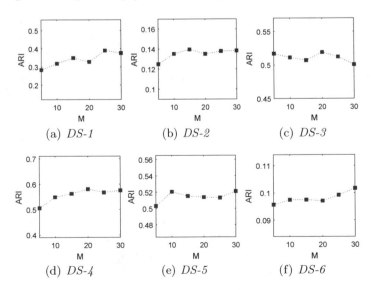

Fig. 2. Average ARI (%) over 20 runs by LCC-RW with varying M.

the number of elite neighbors $K = 5$, and the number of steps of the random walk $T = 5$ are used. Tables 2 and 3 respectively report the NMI and ARI scores of different consensus clustering algorithms. As shown in Tables 2 and 3, the proposed algorithm achieves the best or almost the best scores w.r.t. NMI and ARI on most of the datasets. In terms of average score and average rank, the proposed algorithm also obtains the best result on the benchmark datasets, which show the effectiveness of the proposed LCC-RW algorithm.

3.3   Robustness to Ensemble Sizes

In this section, we test the influence of the ensemble size M, i.e., the number of base clusterings, upon the consensus clustering performance. In the experiments, we vary the ensemble size M in the interval [5,30]. By performing the LCC-RW algorithm 20 times on the benchmark datasets, we obtain the average NMI and ARI scores as shown in Figs. 1 and 2, respectively. As can be seen in Figs. 1 and 2, when the ensemble size varies, the clustering performance of LCC-RW is quite stable. And a relatively larger value of M can be beneficial. In this paper, $M = 20$ is used on all benchmark datasets.

4   Conclusion

In the paper, we have designed a link-based consensus clustering approach with random walk propagation (LCC-RW). We take advantage of the microcluster representation to reduce the problem size and facilitate the computation. Based on the microcluster representation, we construct a microcluster-based co-association matrix, and then refine it by weighted connected triple, which is further sparsified by preserving a small proportion of reliable entries. To obtain a new dense similarity measure, the random walks are conducted on the sparsified matrix (corresponding to a sparsified graph). Finally, a weighted bipartite graph is constructed using the new similarity measure, and the final clustering result can be obtained by efficiently partitioning this graph. Experimental results on multiple datasets have shown the superiority of the proposed approach.

Acknowledgement. This work was supported by the NSFC (61976097), the Natural Science Foundation of Guangdong Province (2021A1515012203), and the Project of Guangzhou Key Laboratory of Intelligent Agriculture (201902010081).

References

1. Bai, L., Liang, J., Du, H., Guo, Y.: An information-theoretical framework for cluster ensemble. IEEE Trans. Knowl. Data Eng. (TKDE) **31**(8), 1464–1477 (2018)
2. Carpineto, C., Romano, G.: Consensus clustering based on a new probabilistic rand index with application to subtopic retrieval. IEEE Trans. Pattern Anal. Mach. Intell. (TPAMI) **34**(12), 2315–2326 (2012)
3. Fred, A.L.N., Jain, A.K.: Combining multiple clusterings using evidence accumulation. IEEE Trans. Pattern Anal. Mach. Intell. (TPAMI) **27**(6), 835–850 (2005)

4. Huang, D., Wang, C.D., Lai, J.H.: Locally weighted ensemble clustering. IEEE Trans. Cybern. (TCYB) **48**(5), 1460–1473 (2018)
5. Huang, D., Wang, C.D., Wu, J.S., Lai, J.H., Kwoh, C.K.: Ultra-scalable spectral clustering and ensemble clustering. IEEE Trans. Knowl. Data Eng. (TKDE) **32**(6), 1212–1226 (2020)
6. Huang, D., Lai, J.H., Wang, C.D.: Combining multiple clusterings via crowd agreement estimation and multi-granularity link analysis. Neurocomputing **170**, 240–250 (2015)
7. Huang, D., Lai, J.H., Wang, C.D.: Robust ensemble clustering using probability trajectories. IEEE Trans. Knowl. Data Eng. (TKDE) **28**(5), 1312–1326 (2016)
8. Huang, D., Lai, J., Wang, C.D.: Ensemble clustering using factor graph. Pattern Recogn. **50**, 131–142 (2016)
9. Huang, D., Wang, C.D., Lai, J.H., Kwoh, C.K.: Toward multidiversified ensemble clustering of high-dimensional data: from subspaces to metrics and beyond. IEEE Trans. Cybern. (TCYB) (2021, in press)
10. Huang, D., Wang, C.D., Peng, H., Lai, J., Kwoh, C.K.: Enhanced ensemble clustering via fast propagation of cluster-wise similarities. IEEE Trans. Syst. Man Cybern. Syst. (TSMC-S) **51**(1), 508–520 (2021)
11. Iam-On, N., Boongoen, T., Garrett, S., Price, C.: A link-based approach to the cluster ensemble problem. IEEE Trans. Pattern Anal. Mach. Intell. (TPAMI) **33**(12), 2396–2409 (2011)
12. Li, Z., Wu, X.M., Chang, S.F.: Segmentation using superpixels: a bipartite graph partitioning approach. In: Proceedings of IEEE Conference on Computer Vision and Pattern Recognition (CVPR) (2012)
13. Nguyen, N., Caruana, R.: Consensus clusterings. In: Prof. of IEEE International Conference on Data Mining (ICDM), pp. 607–612 (2007)
14. Reuther, P., Walter, B.: Survey on test collections and techniques for personal name matching. Int. J. Metadata Semant. Ontol. **1**(2), 89–99 (2006)
15. Strehl, A., Ghosh, J.: Cluster ensembles: a knowledge reuse framework for combining multiple partitions. J. Mach. Learn. Res. (JMLR) **3**, 583–617 (2003)
16. Vinh, N.X., Epps, J., Bailey, J.: Information theoretic measures for clusterings comparison: variants, properties, normalization and correction for chance. J. Mach. Learn. Res. (JMLR) **11**(11), 2837–2854 (2010)
17. Wang, T.: CA-Tree: a hierarchical structure for efficient and scalable coassociation-based cluster ensembles. IEEE Trans. Syst. Man Cybern. Part B Cybern. (TSMC Part B) **41**(3), 686–698 (2011)
18. Yu, Z., et al.: Incremental semi-supervised clustering ensemble for high dimensional data clustering. IEEE Trans. Knowl. Data Eng. (TKDE) **28**(3), 701–714 (2016)

A Particle Swarm Optimization Based Feature Selection Approach for Multi-source Visual Domain Adaptation

Mrinalini Tiwari[1]([envelope]), Rakesh Kumar Sanodiya[2], Jimson Mathew[1], and Sriparna Saha[1]

[1] Indian Institute of Technology Patna, Patna, India
mrinalini_1921cs02@iitp.ac.in
[2] Indian Institute of Information Technology Sri City, Sri City, India

Abstract. Labeled data plays a pivotal role in training primitive machine learning models to classify the target domain information. But acquiring the necessary amount of labeled data is not always possible. Hence Domain adaptation utilizes the existing knowledge from a related source domain for training the target domain classifier. It can be possible that one or more related source domains can even be deployed for training the model. By taking multiple sources into account, we can have a massive database for the training purpose. The concept of multi-source domain adaptation makes use of related multiple source domains. Existing multi-source methods do not consider the problem of distorted features, which can lead to a decline in the overall accuracy of the model. To overcome this issue, we have proposed a novel Particle Swarm Optimization based Feature selection approach for multi-source domain adaptation (PSO-MDA) which provides an optimal set of features that ultimately enhances the performance of the target domain classifier. PSO-MDA utilizes the fitness function that consists of different relevant objectives for minimization of distribution differences between multiple source domains and the target domain. We have considered several multi-source scenarios like double-source, triple-source, and quadruple-source domain adaptation scenarios for two publicly available real-world datasets. Comprehensive experiments on different multi-source scenarios have proved the efficacy of our proposed PSO-MDA over existing approaches.

Keywords: Feature selection · Domain adaptation · Particle Swarm Optimization · Multi-source domain adaptation · Transfer learning

1 Introduction

Machine learning (ML) has emerged as a powerful field that effectively handles various real-world problems, and it has applications in enormous areas like medical data analysis, imaging, etc. These traditional techniques, however, assume

T. Mantoro et al. (Eds.): ICONIP 2021, CCIS 1516, pp. 701–709, 2021.
https://doi.org/10.1007/978-3-030-92307-5_82

that the data that is used for training purpose and the data used for testing purpose follows a common set of distributions. But, practically due to different varying conditions, the distribution of testing and training data is quite different. Also, it is very time-consuming to gather the labeled dataset for every domain as the labeled data is not always readily available. So, to handle these issues related to traditional ML techniques, Transfer Learning (TL)/Domain Adaptation (DA) came into existence. The main focus of TL/DA approaches is to use the labeled information that is readily available in the source domain for classifying the unlabelled information in the target domain. Existing DA Approaches can be classified as i) Semi-Supervised DA, which has very few labeled target domain data, and ii) Unsupervised DA, which doesn't have any available labeled target domain data. Instance re-weighting [1] and feature matching [2,3] are two popular approaches to domain adaptation. Some of the existing approaches [4] take advantage of both approaches to get better classifier performance. Also, these approaches have been utilized for single-source as well as multi-source domain adaptation. In this paper, we have introduced a novel particle swarm optimization-based feature selection approach for multi-source visual domain adaptation (PSO-MDA) in which the PSO technique has been utilized to obtain an optimum set of features for getting maximum accuracy. The fitness function incorporated with PSO determines both projection as well as classification in order to bridge the distribution gap between the domains.

2 Related Works

2.1 Existing Work on Primitive and DA Approaches

Domain adaptation (DA) approaches are majorly classified into three types a) feature-based DA [2] b) instance-based DA [1], and c) model-based DA [5].

Transfer Component Analysis (TCA) [3] is one of the feature-based DA approaches that aim at reducing the marginal distribution discrepancy between the source and the target domains. Geodesic flow kernel (GFK) [6] is another method where both domain data are projected into a Grassmann manifold. TCA concept is extended in the form of Joint Distribution Adaptation (JDA) [2] that aims at reducing both the marginal and conditional distribution gap across domains. For preserving the discriminative information of classes, one more approach, visual domain adaptation (VDA) [7] makes use of various domain-invariant clusters. A model-based approach, i.e., Adaptive regularization-based transfer learning (ARTL) [5] focus on making the manifold consistency better and also reducing the structural risk to reduce the distribution gap. The single-source domain adaptation utilizes the data from a single domain for training the target domain classifier while the multi-source domain adaptation utilizes the data from related multiple source domains for classifying the target domain data. One framework, BLRT, which is an iterative approach, takes into account multiple incomplete sources. MSDA [8] approach focuses on preserving the structure of data while transferring the knowledge from numerous source domains to the target domain. MDA approach [9] takes into account several objectives for multi-source domain adaptation. Still, it suffers from the issue of degenerated feature transformation because some of the features may be distorted due to several conditions like noise. Nguyen first utilized the PSO [10] approach for feature selection in domain adaptation. Later on, the FSUTL-PSO approach proposed by Sanodiya et al. [11] enhances the previous approach by taking into account all the relevant objectives needed to reduce the distribution gap between domains. Previous works was done on single-source setting. In this work, we have taken multi-source domain scenarios into account for visual domain adaptation.

3   PSO Based Feature Selection Approach for Multi-source Visual Domain Adaptation

3.1   Particle Swarm Optimization (PSO)

PSO is an efficient evolutionary approach which had produced enormous results. This paper has utilized PSO as the optimization technique for gathering the optimum feature set across multiple source domains and the target domain. Two fields are incorporated within every particle i.e. Position(P) and Value(v). Position field corresponds to different position values of common feature subsets across multiple source domains and the target domain. For a particular iteration, the best particle information out of all the particles, i.e., having the highest value (v), is stored in P_{best} while G_{best} holds the information of the best particle obtained so far till the current iteration. PSO is initialized with a random subset of features, then depending on the values of P_{best} and G_{best}, it tries to optimize the solution in an iterative manner. The following formula can calculate the velocity and position values for the next iteration:

$$V_{t+1} = w * V_t + f_1 * r_1 * (P_{best} - P_t) + f_2 * r_2 * (G_{best} - P_t) \qquad (1)$$

$$P_{t+1} = P_t + V_{t+1} \qquad (2)$$

where V_{t+1} and P_{t+1} are the particle velocity and position values at time t+1, w is the initial weight, $r_1, r_2 \in (0,1)$ are the random numbers and $f_1, f_2 \in (0,2)$ are the learning factors.

3.2   Proposed PSO-MDA Description

In this section, our proposed method PSO-MDA is described in detail. PSO-MDA utilizes the PSO optimization technique to capture the best set of features that are providing maximum accuracy. To guide PSO, we have employed the fitness function consists of several objectives that ultimately reduce the distribution gap between multiple source domains and the target domain.

I. Fitness Function Description: With the PSO-MDA fitness function, to minimize the distribution mismatch between multiple source domains and the target domain, we aim to figure out an adept projection and classification for the domains. Firstly the projected subspace will be determined where the data from multiple source domains as well as the target domain are projected. Then on that subspace, an adaptive classifier will be designed. After completing both the steps, we have calculated the accuracy of the classifier. The description of both the steps is provided in the upcoming subsections.

STEP I: Determining Projected Subspace: For determining the projected subspace, we need to consider various components which are described as follows:

– **Maximizing the covariance between subspaces:** For preventing the data features from being projected into incorrect spaces, the data variance needs to be maximized w.r.t the projection matrix Z as follows:

$$\arg \max_Z Z^T X H X^T Z, \tag{3}$$

where H is the centering matrix and XHX^T is the covariance matrix. Here multiple sources are denoted as $X_s = \{X^1, X^2 ...... X^N\}$ where N is the total number of source domain datasets and target domain is denoted as X_t. X is the combined data matrix that consists of all the data points ($[X_s\ X_t]$).

– **Marginal and Conditional Distribution Alignment:** With the help of Maximum Mean Discrepancy (MMD), the distribution differences (conditional and marginal) between multiple source domains and the target domain can be reduced by the following equation:

$$tr\left(\begin{bmatrix} Z_s \\ Z_t \end{bmatrix}^T \sum_{u=1}^{N} \left(\begin{bmatrix} X^u_s \\ X_t \end{bmatrix} \begin{bmatrix} Mc_{s^u,s^u} & Mc_{s^u,t} \\ Mc_{t,s^u} & Mc_{t,t} \end{bmatrix} \begin{bmatrix} X^u_s \\ X_t \end{bmatrix}^T \right) \begin{bmatrix} Z_s \\ Z_t \end{bmatrix} \right) \tag{4}$$

For each $X^u \in X_s$ and X_t, MMD coefficient matrix (M_c) that includes class labels as well, is determined as follows:

$$(M_c)_{ij} = \begin{cases} \frac{1}{n_{s_c}^u n_{s_c}^u} & x_i, x_j \in X^u_{s\,c} \\ \frac{1}{n_{t_c} n_{t_c}} & x_i, x_j \in X_{tc} \\ \frac{-1}{n_{s_c}^u n_{t_c}} & \begin{cases} x_i \in X^u_{s\,c}\ x_j \in X_{tc} \\ x_j \in X^u_{s\,c}\ x_i \in X_{tc} \end{cases} \\ 0 & \text{otherwise} \end{cases} \tag{5}$$

– **Preserving class discriminative information:** We have calculated the within-class variance that ultimately reduces the distance of the projected samples from their means in order to preserve the class-wise discriminative information. Domain invariant clusters are constructed for each $X^u \in X_s$ as follows:

$$\min.tr\left(\begin{bmatrix} Z_s \\ Z_t \end{bmatrix}^T S \begin{bmatrix} Z_s \\ Z_t \end{bmatrix} \right) \tag{6}$$

$$S = \sum_{u=1}^{N} \sum_{c=1}^{C} n_{s\,c}^u (m_{s\,c}^u - \bar{m}_s^u)(m_{s\,c}^u - \bar{m}_s^u)^T \tag{7}$$

Here $m^u_{s\,c}$ is the mean of uth source domain data samples and $n^u_{s\,c}$ is the number of uth source domain data points belonging to c^{th} class, and $\bar{m}^u_s$ is the total mean of uth source domain data samples.

- **Instance reweighting:** The $l_{2,1}$ norm term is incorporated in the objective function so that the least priority is given to unnecessary data samples. It is applied to Z_s, which is sparse in rows. The instance reweighting term is shown as:

$$Z_i = ||Z_s||_{2,1} + ||Z_t||^2_F \tag{8}$$

where $||.||_F$ is the Frobenius norm.

- **Overall Objective Function:** To determine the projection vector matrix Z, we need to optimize the objectives mentioned in the upper subsections by utilizing PCA as the principled dimensionality reduction procedure as:

$$\min_{Z^T X H X^T Z = I} \mathrm{tr}(Z^T X M_c X^T Z) + Z^T S Z + \lambda(Z_i) \tag{9}$$

where $Z = \begin{bmatrix} Z_s \\ Z_t \end{bmatrix}$, $X = \begin{bmatrix} X_s \\ X_t \end{bmatrix}$, M_c is the MMD coefficient matrix and λ is the instance reweighting parameter. The above equation can be solved using kernel trick where Z is considered as the kernel. The generalized eigen decomposition of MDA-PSO is as follows:

$$(X M_c X^T + S + \lambda G)Z = X H X^T Z \phi \tag{10}$$

After solving this eigen decomposition problem, the leading eigen values and eigen vectors will be further used to compute the projection matrix Z.

STEP II: Determining Adaptive Classifier: After determining the projected space Z, the adaptive classifier will be designed by taking some more objectives into account. We will determine the robust adaptive classifier by using same procedure as in MDA [9] work.

II. Steps Involved in Proposed PSO-MDA: Initialize the parameter values needed for the PSO algorithm: no. of maximum available features (F_m), no of selected features (F_s), max. iterations (I_m), population size (S), constant values (f_1, f_2, w) etc. Two field values are associated with each particle i.e. a) Position(P) which consists of positions of various features, and Value(v) which holds the accuracy that is computed from the defined fitness function. These two fields are also incorporated in P_{best} and G_{best} particles. Two different matrices are also utilized for the particle set i.e. the velocity matrix V and the position matrix P which comprises of all particle velocities and position values respectively. Initialize value v field of V matrix to 0. P matrix is initialized with random numbers between $(1, F_m)$ in order to select random feature subset. Then the feature subset is selected from the Position Matrix (P) and corresponding fitness value v is calculated. After that,

Table 1. Accuracy of PSO-MDA for PIE face dataset: triple domain scenario.

Tasks	Non-DA algorithms		DA algorithms								
	NN	PCA	TCA	GFK	TSL	JDA	TJM	FIDOS	VDA	MDA	Proposed
Pie1, Pie2, Pie3→Pie5	37	27.5	20.1	32.5	30.6	44.7	13.3	30.7	50.4	71.2	**78.3**
Pie1, Pie2, Pie3→Pie4	43.6	59.6	60.6	63.8	43.3	89.5	36.4	54.3	90.3	93.6	**96.7**
Pie1, Pie2, Pie4→Pie3	44.1	56.7	63.3	57.5	41.8	84.4	35.6	52	84.8	95.5	**96.4**
Pie1, Pie2, Pie4→Pie5	33.8	28.3	22.8	34.2	30.6	55.5	12.1	31.7	54.1	77.9	**84.3**
Pie1, Pie2, Pie5→Pie3	50.7	41.9	33.3	43.5	41.9	54.3	20.2	39.5	64.4	80	**84.7**
Pie1, Pie2, Pie5→Pie4	41.9	50.2	48.2	54.3	43.7	54.3	31.8	47.8	84.4	93.5	**95.1**
Pie1, Pie3, Pie4→Pie2	45.4	46.2	52.6	48.2	41.7	79.3	33.6	38.6	83.8	89.1	**91.6**
Pie1, Pie3, Pie4→Pie5	31.4	28	22.8	34.6	30.7	57.8	11.7	34.3	58.2	80.1	**83.4**
Pie1, Pie3, Pie5→Pie2	51.4	39.2	34.5	41	41.8	57.7	21.2	35.1	62.9	82.4	**85.9**
Pie1, Pie3, Pie5→Pie4	41.7	56.3	53	58.5	43.3	83.2	30.6	52.2	86.1	92.8	**92.9**
Pie1, Pie4, Pie5→Pie2	34.6	41.7	53.2	44.5	41.3	83.5	31.2	36.9	85	**94.5**	92.4
Pie1, Pie4, Pie5→Pie3	31.4	53.6	64.7	53.6	41.7	80.4	33.7	50.3	83.2	93.8	**96.5**
Pie2, Pie3, Pie4→Pie1	48.8	41	32.1	46.9	42.7	79.1	18.5	42.3	81.5	90	87.6
Pie2, Pie3, Pie4→Pie5	35.2	31.3	22.3	36.8	32.8	51	11.1	36.2	48.1	79.5	**81.2**
Pie2, Pie3, Pie5→Pie1	11	30.3	25.1	36.7	43.2	53.9	13.6	29.7	53.3	82.7	**83.4**
Pie2, Pie3, Pie5→Pie4	17.2	59.9	57.6	61.9	54.8	80.4	31.8	51.2	81	**91.4**	86.5
Pie2, Pie4, Pie5→Pie1	49	40.9	32.7	46.3	42.4	75.5	18.8	43.4	78.5	90.4	**92.0**
Pie2, Pie4, Pie5→Pie3	46.6	57.8	63.2	58.9	42.4	85.9	35.9	53.3	86.3	**90.8**	89.5
Pie3, Pie4, Pie5→Pie1	49.7	40.1	31.6	46.1	41.4	73.5	17.4	42.3	73.2	89.6	**95.2**
Pie3, Pie4, Pie5→Pie2	49.7	47.9	51.4	50.5	39.7	81.9	33.6	40.2	83.9	**95.5**	96.7
Average	39.7	43.9	42.3	47.5	40.6	71.7	24.6	42.1	73.7	87.7	**89.5**

Table 2. Accuracy of PSO-MDA for PIE face dataset: quadruple domain scenario.

Tasks	Non-DA algorithms		DA algorithms								
	NN	PCA	TCA	TSL	TJM	GFK	JDA	FIDOS	VDA	MDA	Proposed
Pie1, Pie2, Pie3, Pie4→Pie5	35.9	28.4	23.4	31.3	13.8	36.3	57.9	31.3	63.7	**75.2**	85.6
Pie1, Pie2, Pie3, Pie5→Pie4	41.6	59.5	60.4	45.4	35.8	63.1	86.4	52.5	87.5	93.1	**96.3**
Pie1, Pie2, Pie4, Pie5→Pie3	46.3	55.4	63.2	42.3	34.8	57.6	85.1	49.8	84.7	90.6	**96**
Pie1, Pie3, Pie4, Pie5→Pie2	46.9	49.7	52.1	42.1	31.8	47.9	79.4	38.3	84.8	94.6	**95.6**
Pie2, Pie3, Pie4, Pie5→Pie1	40.2	48.8	32.6	42.5	18.4	47.3	72.9	39.8	80.8	**89.4**	87.9
Average	44.5	46.1	46.4	40.7	26.9	50.4	76.3	42.3	80.3	88.6	**92.3**

P_{best} is chosen as the particle with maximum fitness value from P. Now, If $P_{best}.v$ value is higher than $G_{best}.v$ then G_{best} is assigned with the P_{best} particle details. According to the calculated values, update each particle velocity according to Eq. (1) and update the V matrix. Also, update each particle position according to Eq. (2) and update the P matrix. Repeat the above steps until the number of iterations is less than or equal to I_m.

4   Experimental Evaluations

4.1   Benchmark Data Sets

For experimentation purpose, we have utilized two benchmark datasets, namely PIE face and Office-Caltech. PIE Face dataset comprises images of

68 subjects with different poses, illumination conditions, and expressions. It consists of five groups (Pie1(left), Pie2(up), Pie3(bottom), Pie4(face), Pie5(right)) based on different poses. Caltech-Office dataset contains four domains of images, i.e., DSLR(D), Caltech(C), Webcam(W) and Amazon(A).

4.2   Parameter Values Description

Four parameters were utilized for the fitness function of the proposed PSO-MDA, i.e., k for subspace bases, λ as the instance reweighting parameter, α and γ as the regularization parameters. The optimal values of k, λ, α, and γ are taken from the MDA [9] work. For the PSO algorithm, we are getting better performance when the value of $S = 50$, $I_m = 10$, $f_1 = f_2 = 2$, and $w = 0.5$ for both the datasets. However, the value of $F_m = 950$ for PIE Face dataset and $F_m = 750$ is chosen for the Office-Caltech dataset.

Table 3. Accuracy of PSO-MDA for Office-Caltech dataset: double domain scenario.

Tasks	Non-DA algorithms		DA algorithms									
	NN	PCA	TCA	TSL	TJM	GFK	JDA	FIDOS	MSDA	VDA	MDA	Proposed
A,C→D	27.4	37.6	51.6	28	52.2	39.5	46.5	43.3	51	45.2	54.8	**59.9**
A,C→W	27.5	32.5	38.3	40	39.3	38.4	46.1	41.7	52.5	44.8	49.8	**57.3**
A,D→C	26.4	35.8	40.7	20.7	40.5	37.8	41.1	41.1	43.5	42.8	46.1	**49.6**
A,D→W	41	64.1	69.2	37	75.3	54.8	75.9	53.6	76.3	**81.4**	70.5	79.7
A,W→C	26.6	36.2	39.3	22.7	39.5	38.1	41.1	39.9	40.8	41.9	45.8	**49.7**
A,W→D	49.7	66.9	72	38.2	82.8	66.6	84.7	73.3	73.9	**87.9**	70.2	87.3
C,D→W	24	36.5	43.1	29.8	45.1	38	44.9	45.3	80	51.4	53.4	**82.7**
C,D→A	32.2	59.3	68.1	48.1	73.9	55.9	71.9	48.5	54.4	**78.3**	74.6	56.8
C,W→A	24.8	37.7	44.6	31.8	45.4	38.5	44.8	46	54.8	49.9	52.4	**55.0**
C,W→D	45.2	72.6	75.2	49.7	80.3	66.6	79.6	65.6	80.3	79.6	79.6	**86.6**
D,W→A	29	36.4	34.3	21.7	35.3	35.1	35.2	35.4	43.8	37.1	39.4	**46.5**
D,W→C	24.5	30.9	33.5	19	34	31.6	35.4	30.1	35.1	36.7	37.6	**41.4**
Average	31.5	45.5	50.8	32.2	53.6	45.1	53.9	47	57.2	56.4	56.2	**62.7**

Table 4. Accuracy of PSO-MDA for Office-Caltech dataset: triple domain scenario.

Tasks	Non-DA algorithms		DA algorithms								
	NN	PCA	TCA	TSL	TJM	JDA	GFK	FIDOS	VDA	MDA	Proposed
A,W,D→C	26.7	37.7	39.3	20.3	40.3	41.7	37.4	41.6	50.1	50.1	49.2
C,W,D→A	25	38.1	44.1	28	44.2	45.7	40.2	46	48.4	52.3	**54.6**
C,A,D→W	33.2	57.3	60	43.1	72.9	69.8	39	46.4	71.5	71.2	**78.3**
C,A,W→D	45.2	68.8	71.3	51.6	80.9	77.1	39.4	63.1	**77.7**	79.7	**84.7**
Average	32.5	50.5	53.7	35.7	59.5	58.6	39	49.3	61.9	63.3	**66.7**

4.3   Analysis of Experimental Results

We have compared the accuracy of the proposed PSO-MDA with other existing approaches for different multiple-domain scenarios. Our proposed PSO-MDA attains an average accuracy of 89.5% for triple-domain scenario and 92.3% for quadruple-domain scenario, which is better than the accuracies of the existing approaches for PIE Face dataset as shown in Table 1 and Table 2 respectively. For Office-Caltech dataset, as can be seen from Table 3, for the double domain scenario, the average accuracy of PSO-MDA is 62.7% that shows our proposed approach achieves an improvement over already existing methods. Also, it attains an average accuracy value of 66.7%, which is better than the MDA approach that is having the next higher accuracy value for the triple-domain scenario as shown in Table 4.

5   Conclusion

In this work, we have proposed a novel Particle Swarm Optimization based Feature selection approach for multi-source domain adaptation (PSO-MDA) in which the PSO technique is used to select the best set of features that enhances the performance of target domain classifier. PSO utilizes the fitness function that is designed to reduce the distribution difference between multiple source domains and the target domain. The results have proved the efficacy of our proposed method over other existing techniques. In future, we employ the PSO technique for both feature and parameter selection for multi-source domain adaptation.

Acknowledgement. Mrinalini Tiwari, UGC NET JRF (ID-3610/(NET - JULY 2018)) acknowledges the support of University Grants Commission, Govt. of India for carrying out this research. Dr. Sriparna Saha gratefully acknowledges the Young Faculty Research Fellowship (YFRF) Award, supported by Visvesvaraya Ph.D. Scheme for Electronics and IT, Ministry of Electronics and Information Technology (MeitY), Government of India, being implemented by Digital India Corporation (formerly Media Lab Asia) for carrying out this research.

References

1. Xu, Y., et al.: A unified framework for metric transfer learning. IEEE Trans. Knowl. Data Eng. **29**(6), 1158–1171 (2017)
2. Long, M., Wang, J., Ding, G., Sun, J., Yu, P.S.: Transfer feature learning with joint distribution adaptation. In: Proceedings of the IEEE International Conference on Computer Vision, pp. 2200–2207 (2013)
3. Pan, S.J., Tsang, I.W., Kwok, J.T., Yang, Q.: Domain adaptation via transfer component analysis. IEEE Trans. Neural Netw. **22**(2), 199–210 (2011)
4. Long, M., Wang, J., Ding, G., Sun, J., Yu, P.S.: Transfer joint matching for unsupervised domain adaptation. In: Proceedings of the IEEE Conference on Computer Vision and Pattern Recognition, pp. 1410–1417 (2014)

5. Long, M., Wang, J., Ding, G., Pan, S.J., Philip, S.Y.: Adaptation regularization: a general framework for transfer learning. IEEE Trans. Knowl. Data Eng. **26**(5), 1076–1089 (2014)

6. Gong, B., Shi, Y., Sha, F., Grauman, K.: Geodesic flow kernel for unsupervised domain adaptation. In: 2012 IEEE Conference on Computer Vision and Pattern Recognition (CVPR), pp. 2066–2073. IEEE (2012)

7. Tahmoresnezhad, J., Hashemi, S.: Visual domain adaptation via transfer feature learning. Knowl. Inf. Syst. **50**(2), 585–605 (2016). https://doi.org/10.1007/s10115-016-0944-x

8. Liu, H., Shao, M., Fu, Y.: Structure-preserved multi-source domain adaptation. In: 2016 IEEE 16th International Conference on Data Mining (ICDM), pp. 1059–1064 (2016)

9. Karimpour, M., Noori Saray, S., Tahmoresnezhad, J., Pourmahmood Aghababa, M.: Multi-source domain adaptation for image classification. Mach. Vis. Appl. **31**(6), 1–19 (2020). https://doi.org/10.1007/s00138-020-01093-2

10. Nguyen, B.H., Xue, B., Andreae, P.: A particle swarm optimization based feature selection approach to transfer learning in classification (2018)

11. Sanodiya, R.K., Tiwari, M., Mathew, J., Saha, S., Saha, S.: A particle swarm optimization-based feature selection for unsupervised transfer learning. Soft Comput. **24**(24), 18 713–18 731 (2020)

Discovering Periodic-Frequent Patterns in Uncertain Temporal Databases

R. Uday Kiran[1,2($\boxtimes$)], P. Likhitha[3], Minh-Son Dao[2], Koji Zettsu[2],
and Ji Zhang[4]

[1] The University of Aizu, Aizu-Wakamatsu, Fukushima, Japan
udayrage@u-aizu.ac.jp
[2] NICT, Tokyo, Japan
dao@nict.go.jp, zettsu@nict.gov.jp
[3] IIIT-Idupulapaya, Vempalli, Andhra Pradesh, India
[4] University of Southern Queensland, Toowoomba, Australia
Ji.Zhang@usq.edu.au

Abstract. Periodic-frequent pattern mining aims to discover all periodically occurring frequent patterns in a temporal database. Most previous studies focused on finding these patterns by disregarding the items' uncertainty nature in the data. This paper proposes a novel model of periodic-frequent patterns that exist in an uncertain temporal database. We introduce a new tree-structure and an algorithm to find all desired patterns in the database effectively. We have also presented two tighter upper bound measures to reduce the computational cost effectively. Experimental results on various databases demonstrate that our algorithm is memory and runtime efficient.

Keywords: Periodic patterns · Pattern mining · Uncertain data

1 Introduction

Many big data applications naturally produce uncertain data due to veracity. Useful information that can empower the end-users with competitive knowledge lies in this uncertain data. Most previous studies [1,8,9] focused on finding frequent patterns that exist in an uncertain transactional database. Unfortunately, these studies are inadequate to find periodically occurring frequent patterns in a temporal database as they ignore the temporal occurrence information of the items in an uncertain temporal database. This paper aims to discover periodic-frequent patterns that may exist in an uncertain temporal database.

Finding periodic-frequent patterns in an uncertain database is a challenging task due to the following two reasons:

1. Mining periodic-frequent patterns in a precise (or binary) temporal database has been widely studied in the literature [4,6,11]. Since these studies disregard the items' existential probabilities in the data, they cannot be employed to mine the desired patterns in an uncertain temporal database.

T. Mantoro et al. (Eds.): ICONIP 2021, CCIS 1516, pp. 710–718, 2021.
https://doi.org/10.1007/978-3-030-92307-5_83

2. Several algorithms [1,8,9] exist to find the frequent patterns in an uncertain transactional database. As they consider only the occurrence *frequency* and completely disregard the temporal occurrence information of an item in the database, they cannot be utilized to mine the periodic-frequent patterns in an uncertain database.

This paper addresses the above two challenges by proposing a novel model and an algorithm to find the patterns in an uncertain temporal database.

This paper's contributions are as follows: (*i*) We propose a novel model of periodic-frequent patterns that may exist in an uncertain temporal database. Two constraints, *minimum support* and *maximum periodicity* were utilized to determine a pattern's interestingness in the database. The former measure controls the minimum probabilistic support a pattern must maintain in the database. The latter measure controls the maximum time interval in which a pattern must reappear in the database. (*ii*) We also introduced two tighter upper-bound measures to effectively reduce the search space and the computational cost of finding the desired patterns. (*iii*) We introduce a new data structure, called Uncertain Periodic Frequent Pattern-Tree (UPFP-tree), to capture the items' temporal occurrence information and their existential probability information in the database. (*iv*) We propose a pattern-growth algorithm, called Uncertain Periodic Frequent Pattern-Growth (UPFP-growth), to find all desired patterns from UPFP-tree. (*v*) Experimental results on both synthetic and real-world databases demonstrate that our algorithm is memory and runtime efficient.

The rest of the paper is organized as follows. Section 2 describes the related work. Section 3 describes the proposed model of a periodic-frequent pattern. Section 4 introduces the UPFP-growth algorithm. Section 5 reports on experimental results. Finally, Sect. 6 concludes the paper with future research directions.

2 Related Work

Chui et al. [3] introduced the model of frequent pattern that may exist in an uncertain transactional database. Since then, mining frequent patterns in an uncertain transactional database has received a great deal of attention. An in-depth survey on frequent pattern mining algorithms may be found at [1,10]. Since the existing frequent pattern mining algorithms do not take into account the temporal occurrence information of an item in the database, they cannot be utilized to mine the periodic-frequent patterns in an uncertain temporal database.

Tanbeer et al. [11] introduced periodic-frequent pattern model to discover all periodically occurring frequent patterns in a binary (or precise) temporal database. Several fast algorithms [2,4–7] were explored in the literature to find different types of periodic-frequent patterns in a binary temporal database effectively. Unfortunately, these algorithms cannot be extended to handle uncertain temporal database as they disregard the items' existential probabilities in the data.

3   Proposed Model

Let $I = \{i_1, i_2, \cdots, i_n\}$, $n \geq 1$, be the set of items. Let $X \subseteq I$ be an itemset (or a pattern). A pattern containing k number of items is called a k-pattern. A uncertain transaction, t_{tid}, is a triplet consisting of a transaction identifier (tid), a timestamp (ts) and a pattern Y. That is, $t_{tid} = (tid, ts, Y)$. More important, each item $i_k \in Y$ is also associated with an existential probability value $P(i_k, t_{tid}) \in (0, 1)$, which represents the likelihood of the presence of i_k in t_{tid}. A non-uniform uncertain temporal database, $UTDB = \{t_1, t_2, \cdots, t_m\}$, $m \geq 1$. This definition of an uncertain temporal database is generic as it allows non-uniform gaps between the transactions and allows multiple transactions to share a common timestamp. These features are crucial for some of the real-world applications (e.g., social network applications, eCommerce applications, and IoT applications) that produce data at a very rapid pace.

Example 1. Let $I = \{a, b, c, d, e, f, g, h\}$ be the set of items. The set of items a, b and c, i.e., $\{a, b, c\}$ (or abc, in short) is a pattern. This pattern contains three items. Therefore, it is a 3-pattern. A hypothetical uncertain temporal database generated by the items in I is shown in Table 1. It can be observed that this database allows not only multiple transactions to share a common timestamp but also irregular gaps between the transactions. Thus, generalizing the basic model of an uncertain transactional database. The first transaction in this database indicates that the likelihood of a, b, and c occurring at the timestamp of 1 is 0.8, 0.3, and 0.1, respectively.

Table 1. Uncertain temporal database

tid	ts	transactions	tid	ts	transactions
1	1	$a(0.8), b(0.3), c(0.1)$	7	7	$a(0.5), b(0.5), c(0.3), d(0.8)$
2	2	$b(0.9), e(0.03), f(0.7)$	8	8	$c(0.01), d(0.4), e(0.6), f(0.9)$
3	2	$g(0.6), h(0.2)$	9	9	$a(0.6), b(0.8), c(0.4)$
4	3	$b(0.6), c(0.4), d(0.7), e(0.8)$	10	10	$a(0.6), b(0.2), c(0.9), d(0.1)$
5	4	$a(0.3), b(0.7), c(0.9), d(0.4)$	11	10	$g(0.6), h(0.2)$
6	5	$d(0.3), f(0.9), h(0.2)$	12	11	$a(0.6), e(0.9), f(0.3)$

Definition 1 *(Expected support of pattern X in a transaction)*. *The existential probability of X in t_{tid}, denoted as $P(X, t_{tid})$, represents the product of corresponding existential probability values of all items in X when these items are independent. That is, $P(X, t_{tid}) = \prod\limits_{\forall i_j \in X} P(i_j, t_{tid})$. The expected support of X in $UTDB$, denoted as $expSup(X) = \sum\limits_{tid=1}^{m} P(X, t_{tid})$.*

Example 2 Continuing with the previous example, the pattern abc occurs in the tids of 1, 5, 7, 9 and 10. The existential probability of abc in the first transaction, i.e., $P(abc, t_1) = P(a, t_1) \times P(b, t_1) \times P(c, t_1) = 0.8 \times 0.3 \times 0.1 = 0.024$. Similarly, $P(abc, t_5) = 0.189$, $P(abc, t_7) = 0.075$, $P(abc, t_9) = 0.192$ and $P(abc, t_{10}) = 0.108$. The expected support of abc, i.e., $expSup(abc) = 0.024 + 0.189 + 0.075 + 0.192 + 0.108 = 0.588$.

Definition 2. *A pattern X is a frequent pattern if $expSup(X) \geq minSup$. The $minSup$ represents the minimum support value specified by the user.*

Example 3. If the user-specified $minSup = 0.5$, we consider abc as a frequent pattern. It is because $expSup(abc)$ is greater than or equal to $minSup$.

Definition 3 (A period of X in a database). *If $X \subseteq Y$, it is said that X occurs in Y (or Y contains X). Let ts_i^X denote the timestamp of a transaction containing X. Let $TS^X = \{ts_a^X, ts_b^X, \cdots, ts_c^X\}$, $ts_a^X \leq ts_b^X \leq \cdots \leq ts_c^X$, be the set of all timestamps at which X has occurred in UTDB. A period of X in UTDB is calculated using the following three ways: (i) $p_1^X = ts_a^X - ts_{min}$, (ii) $p_i^X = ts_q^X - ts_p^X$, where $2 \leq i \leq |TS^X|$ and $a \leq p \leq q \leq c$ represent the periods (or inter-arrivals) of X in the database, and (iii) $p_{|TS^X|+1}^X = ts_{max} - ts_c^X$. The ts_{min} and ts_{max} represent the minimal and maximal timestamps of all transactions in the database. The first and last periods of a pattern are crucial to determine the periodic interestingness of a pattern in the entire database.*

Example 4. The pattern abc occurs in the transactions whose timestamps are 1, 4, 7, 9 and 10. Thus, $TS^{abc} = \{1, 4, 7, 9, 10\}$. In this database, $ts_{min} = 1$ and $ts_{max} = 11$. The *periods* of abc in this table are: $p_1^{abc} = (ts_{min} - 1) = 0$, $p_2^{abc} = (4 - 1) = 3$, $p_3^{abc} = (7 - 4) = 3$, $p_4^{abc} = (9 - 7) = 2$, $p_5^{abc} = (10 - 9) = 1$ and $p_6^{abc} = (ts_{max} - 10) = 1$.

Definition 4 (Periodicity of X [11]). *Let $P^X = \{p_1^X, p_2^X, \cdots, p_k^X\}, k = |TS^X| + 1$, be the set of all periods of X in UTDB. The periodicity of X, denoted as $per(X) = max(p_1^X, p_2^X, \cdots, p_k^X)$.*

Example 5. All *periods* of abc in Table 1, i.e., $P^{abc} = \{0, 3, 3, 2, 1, 1\}$. Thus, the periodicity of abc, i.e., $per(abc) = max(0, 3, 3, 2, 1, 1) = 3$.

Definition 5 (Periodic-frequent pattern X). *The frequent pattern X is a periodic-frequent pattern if $per(X) \leq maxPer$, where $maxPer$ represents the maximum periodicity threshold value specified by the user. In other words, X is a periodic-frequent pattern if $expSup(X) \geq minSup$ and $per(X) \leq maxPer$.*

Example 6. If the user-specified $maxPer = 3$, then the frequent pattern abc is said to be a periodic-frequent pattern because $per(abc) \leq maxPer$.

The periodic-frequent patterns satisfy the *anti-monotonic property*.

Definition 6 (Problem definition). *Given an uncertain temporal database (UTDB) and the user-specified maximum periodicity (maxPer) and minimum support (minSup) constraints, find all desired patterns that satisfy the maxPer and minSup constraints.*

4 Proposed Algorithm

4.1 Potential Periodic-Frequent Patterns

Storing the existential probability values of every occurrence of an item in the *tree* significantly increases the *tree* size. Thus, increasing the overall memory and runtime requirements of a mining algorithm. In this context, we introduce two upper-bound measures, called *prefixed item cap* (see Definition 7) and *cap of expected support* (see Definition 8), to identify potential periodic-frequent patterns from which all periodic-frequent patterns can be later discovered by performing another scan on the database. We now define these upper-bound measures.

Definition 7 (Prefixed item cap). *Let $PI \subseteq I$ denote the complete set of periodic-frequent items in $UTDB$. The (prefixed) item cap of a periodic-frequent item $i_k \in PI$ in a transaction $t_{tid}.Y = \{i_1, i_2, \cdots, i_k, \cdots, i_l\}$, $1 \leq k \leq l \leq n$, denoted as $PI^{cap}(i_k, t_{tid})$ is defined as the product of $P(i_k, t_{tid})$ and the highest existential probability value among all periodic-frequent items from i_1 to i_{k-1} in t_{tid}. That is, $PI^{cap}(i_k, t_{tid}) = P(i_k, t_{tid}) \times max(P(i_1, t_{tid}), - P(i_2, t_{tid}), \cdots, P(i_{k-1}, t_{tid}))$, where $i_j \in PI, k \geq j \geq 1$.*

Example 7. Consider the first transaction in Table 1. The item cap of the first item a in this transaction, i.e., $I^{cap}(a, t_1) = 0.8$. Similarly, $PI^{cap}(b, t_1) = P(b, t_1) \times max(P(a, t_1)) = 0.3 \times 0.8 = 0.24$ and $PI^{cap}(c, t_1) = P(c, t_1) \times max(P(a, t_1), P(b, t_1)) = 0.1 \times max(0.8, 0.3) = 0.1 \times 0.8 = 0.08$.

Definition 8 (The cap of expected support of a k-pattern). *The cap of expected support of a k-pattern X, denoted as $expSup^{cap}(X)$, is defined as the sum of all prefixed item caps of i_k in all the transactions that contain X. That is, $expSup^{cap}(X) = \sum_{j=1}^{m} \{PI^{cap}(i_k, t_j) | X \subseteq t_j\}$.*

Example 8. In the pattern abc, c is the last (or k^{th}) item. This pattern appears in the transactions whose *tids* are 1, 5, 7, 9 and 10. The item cap of c in t_1, i.e., $PI^{cap}(c, t_1) = 0.08$ (see Example 7). Similarly, $PI^{cap}(c, t_5) = 0.63$, $PI^{cap}(c, t_7) = 0.15$, $PI^{cap}(c, t_9) = 0.32$ and $PI^{cap}(c, t_{10}) = 0.54$. The cap of expected support of abc, i.e., $expSup^{cap}(abc) = 0.08 + 0.63 + 0.15 + 0.32 + 0.54 = 1.72$.

Definition 9 (Potential periodic-frequent pattern X). *The pattern X is said to be a potential periodic-frequent pattern if $expSup^{cap}(X) \geq minSup$ and $per(X) \leq maxPer$.*

Example 9. Continuing with the previous example, abc is a potential periodic-frequent pattern because $expSup^{cap}(abc) \geq minSup$ and $per(abc) \leq maxPer$.

Algorithm 1. UPFP-list ($UTDB$: uncertain temporal database, $minSup$: Minimum Support and per: period)

1: Let TS_l be a temporary array that records the last occurrences of all items in the UPFP-list. Let ts_{min} and ts_{max} denote the minimum and maximum timestamps of all transactions in $UTDB$.
2: **for** each transaction $t \in UTDB$ **do**
3:     **if** ts_{cur} is i's first occurrence **then**
4:         Set $es[i] = i.probability$, $p[i] = (ts_{cur} - ts_{min})$ and $TS_l[i] = ts_{cur}$.
5:     **else**
6:         Set $es[i]+ = i.probability$, $p[i] = max(p[i], (ts_{cur} - TS_l[i]))$ and $TS_l[i] = ts_{cur}$.
7: **for** each item i in UPFP-list **do**
8:     **if** $es^i \leq minSup$ **then**
9:         Prune i from the PFP-list;
10:     **else**
11:         Calculate $p[i] = max(p[i], (ts_{max} - TS_l[i]))$. If $p[i] > maxPer$, then prune i from the PFP-list.
12: Let us consider the remaining items in the UPFP-list as periodic-frequent items. Sort these items in $expSup$ descending order, and be denoted as L.

Algorithm 2. UPFP-Tree ($UTDB$, UPFP-list)

1: Generate a *root* node in UPFP-tree, *Tree*, and label it as "*null*".
2: **for** each $t \in UTDB$ **do**
3:     Sort the periodic-frequent items in t in L order. Let $[e|E]$ denote this sorted list of items, where e is the first item with its existential probability value and E is the remaining list. Call $insert\_tree([e|E], ts_{cur}, Tree)$.
4: call UPFP-growth ($Tree, null$);

4.2 UPFP-Growth

The UPFP-growth algorithm compress the uncertain temporal database into an uncertain periodic-frequent pattern tree (UPFP-tree) and mines it recursively to find the desired patterns. The structure of UPFP-tree contains UPFP-list and prefix-tree. The UPFP-list consists of three fields: *item name* (i), *expected support* (es) and *periodicity* (p). Two types of nodes are maintained in the prefix-tree of UPFP-tree: *ordinary node* and *tail-node*. The ordinary node records the *item name* and *prefixed item cap* information of a transaction. The tail-node represents the last item of any sorted transaction. The tail-node records the *item name*, *prefixed item cap* and the *timestamp* of a transaction. The structure of ordinary node is $\langle i_j : prefixed\ item\ cap\ of\ i_j \rangle$. The structure of tail-node is $\langle i_j : prefixed\ item\ cap\ of\ i_j : \{t_a, t_b, \cdots, t_c\} \rangle$, where $1 \leq a \leq b \leq c \leq m$. The construction and mining process of UPFP-tree is presented in the Algorithms 1, 2, 3 and 4.

Algorithm 3. insert_tree($[e|E]$, ts_{cur}, T)
___
1: **while** E is non-empty **do**
2:    **if** T has a child N such that $e.itemName \neq N.itemName$ **then**
3:        Create a new node N. Set $N.itemName = e.itemName$ and $N.expSup^{cap} = PI^{cap}(e.itemName, ts_{cur})$. Let its parent link be linked to T. Let its node-link be linked to nodes with the same $itemName$ via the node-link structure. Remove e from E.
4:    **else**
5:        update $N.expSup^{cap} += PI^{cap}(e.itemName, ts_{cur})$;
6: Add ts_{cur} to the leaf node.

Algorithm 4. UPFP-growth ($Tree$, α)
___
1: **while** item i_j in the header of $Tree$ **do**
2:    Create pattern $\beta = i_j \cup \alpha$. Construct TS^β by traversing $Tree$ using the node-links of β. TS^β represents the timestamp list in which β has appeared periodically in $UTDB$. Generate β's conditional pattern base and β's conditional UPFP-tree $Tree_\beta$ if $expSup$ is greater than or equal to the user-specified $minSup$ and the $periodicity$ is no more than $maxPer$.
3:    **if** $Tree_\beta \neq \emptyset$ **then**
4:        call UPFP-growth ($Tree_\beta$, β);
5:    Remove i_j from the $Tree$ and push the i_j's ts-list to its parent nodes.

---

5   Experimental Results

Since there exists no algorithm to find periodic-frequent patterns in an uncertain temporal database, we compare UPFP-growth against a naïve algorithm and show that UPFP-growth is efficient. The naïve algorithm involves the following two steps: (i) finding all frequent patterns in an uncertain temporal database using PUF algorithm [9] and (ii) generating periodic-frequent patterns from frequent patterns by performing additional scan on the database.

Both UPFP-growth and naïve algorithms were written in Python 3.8 and executed on an Intel I7 2.6 GHz machine running Ubuntu 20.04 operating system. The experiments have been conducted on both synthetic (**T10I10D200K**) and real-world (**Retail** and **Congestion**) databases. The T10I10D200K database is a synthetic database containing 870 items and 200,000 transactions. The *minimum*, *average*, and *maximum* transaction lengths of this database are 2, 11, and 29, respectively. The Retail database is a real-world database containing 28,549 items and 88,162 transactions. The *minimum*, *average*, and *maximum* transaction lengths of this database are 1, 10, and 75, respectively. Both of these databases were widely employed in the literature to evaluate pattern mining algorithms. In all of the above databases, uncertainty values were randomly set between 0 to 1. The code and the datasets were provided in [12] to verify the correctness of our experiments.

Figures 1a, 1b and 1c show the runtime consumption of UPFP-growth and naïve algorithms at various $minSup$ values in T10I10D200K, Congestion and

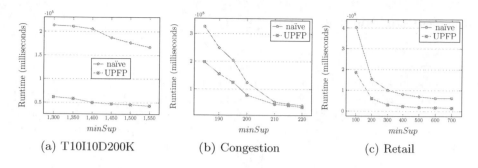

Fig. 1. Runtime requirements of naïve and UPFP-growth algorithms

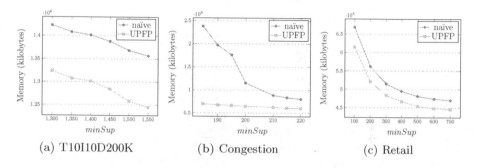

Fig. 2. Memory consumption of naïve and UPFP-growth algorithms

Retail databases, respectively. The following two observations can be drawn from these figures: (i) increase in $minSup$ decreases the runtime requirements of both the algorithms. It is because both algorithms have to discover fewer periodic-frequent patterns. (ii) UPFP-growth outperforms naïve algorithm on every database at any given $minSup$ value. The runtime gap between both the algorithms increases with the decrease in $minSup$ value.

Figures 2a, 2b and 2c show the memory consumption of UPFP-growth and naïve algorithms at various $minSup$ in T10I10D200K, Congestion and Retail databases, respectively. One can draw similar statements as stated above regarding the memory consumption of both algorithms. More important, it can be observed that memory requirements of UPFP-growth were order of magnitude times lower than the naïve algorithm on real-world databases.

In the above experiments, at a fixed the $maxPer$, we have shown that UPFP-growth outperforms naïve algorithm by a vary large margin. Similar observations were made on these datasets when we have fixed $minSup$ and varied $maxPer$ value. Due to page limitation, we were unable to present these results in this paper.

6   Conclusions and Future Work

This paper has proposed a new periodic-frequent pattern model to discover interesting regularities in an uncertain temporal database. Two new upper-bound measures, *prefixed item cap* and *cap of expected support*, have been introduced to effectively reduce the search space and the computational cost of the desired patterns. A new data structure and an efficient pattern-growth algorithm were also described to find desired patterns in the database. Experimental results on synthetic and real-world databases demonstrated that our algorithm is memory and runtime efficient as compared against the naïve solution.

As a part of future work, we would like to extend our model to data streams and non-binary uncertain temporal databases. In this paper, we have considered database remains unchanged over the time. However, in reality, the databases can get updated over time. As a part of future work, we would like to extend our work to mine periodic-frequent patterns in uncertain temporal incremental databases.

References

1. Aggarwal, C.C., Yu, P.S.: A survey of uncertain data algorithms and applications. IEEE Trans. Knowl. Data Eng. **21**(5), 609–623 (2009)
2. Anirudh, A., Kiran, R.U., Reddy, P.K., Kitsuregawa, M.: Memory efficient mining of periodic-frequent patterns in transactional databases. In: 2016 IEEE Symposium Series on Computational Intelligence, pp. 1–8 (2016)
3. Chui, C.-K., Kao, B., Hung, E.: Mining frequent itemsets from uncertain data. In: Zhou, Z.-H., Li, H., Yang, Q. (eds.) PAKDD 2007. LNCS (LNAI), vol. 4426, pp. 47–58. Springer, Heidelberg (2007). https://doi.org/10.1007/978-3-540-71701-0_8
4. Kiran, R.U., Kitsuregawa, M., Reddy, P.K.: Efficient discovery of periodic-frequent patterns in very large databases. JSS **112**, 110–121 (2016)
5. Kiran, R.U., et al.: Discovering fuzzy periodic-frequent patterns in quantitative temporal databases. In: FUZZ-IEEE, pp. 1–8 (2020)
6. Kiran, R.U., Shang, H., Toyoda, M., Kitsuregawa, M.: Discovering partial periodic itemsets in temporal databases. In: SSDBM, pp. 30:1–30:6 (2017)
7. Kiran, R.U., Watanobe, Y., Chaudhury, B., Zettsu, K., Toyoda, M., Kitsuregawa, M.: Discovering maximal periodic-frequent patterns in very large temporal databases. In: DSAA, pp. 11–20 (2020)
8. Leung, C.K., MacKinnon, R.K., Tanbeer, S.K.: Fast algorithms for frequent itemset mining from uncertain data. In: ICDM, pp. 893–898 (2014)
9. Leung, C.K.-S., Tanbeer, S.K.: PUF-Tree: a compact tree structure for frequent pattern mining of uncertain data. In: Pei, J., Tseng, V.S., Cao, L., Motoda, H., Xu, G. (eds.) PAKDD 2013. LNCS (LNAI), vol. 7818, pp. 13–25. Springer, Heidelberg (2013). https://doi.org/10.1007/978-3-642-37453-1_2
10. Luna, J.M., Fournier-Viger, P., Ventura, S.: Frequent itemset mining: a 25 years review. Wiley Interdiscip. Rev. Data Min. Knowl. Discov. **9**(6), e1329 (2019)
11. Tanbeer, S.K., Ahmed, C.F., Jeong, B.-S., Lee, Y.-K.: Discovering periodic-frequent patterns in transactional databases. In: Theeramunkong, T., Kijsirikul, B., Cercone, N., Ho, T.-B. (eds.) PAKDD 2009. LNCS (LNAI), vol. 5476, pp. 242–253. Springer, Heidelberg (2009). https://doi.org/10.1007/978-3-642-01307-2_24
12. UPFP: Uncertain Periodic Frequent Patterns (UPFP) (2020). https://github.com/Likhitha-palla/UPFP. Accessed 4 June 2020

Measuring Shift-Invariance
of Convolutional Neural Network
with a Probability-Incorporated Metric

Hikaru Higuchi[1], Satoshi Suzuki[1,2], and Hayaru Shouno[1(✉)]

[1] The University of Electro-Communications, Chofu, Tokyo, Japan
{h.higuchi,shouno}@uec.ac.jp
[2] NTT Computer and Data Science Laboratories, Yokosuka, Kanagawa, Japan
satoshi.suzuki.xv@hco.ntt.co.jp

Abstract. In image classification tasks, convolutional neural networks (CNNs) have exhibited higher performance than many other methods. However, some recent studies have shown that CNNs are not shift-invariant, that is, even small spatial shifts in the image can drastically change the output distribution. This finding is non-intuitive because CNNs have long been believed to be shift-invariant. Therefore, we need to measure the shift-invariance of CNNs to better understand the performance of CNNs with respect to image classification. Previous research proposed the utilization of consistency as a metric for measuring shift-invariance. The consistency metric measures how often a CNN classifies the same top-1 class, given two different shifts on the same image. Herein, we identify two shortcomings of the consistency-based approach. First, consistency cannot perfectly capture the change in the output distribution of the CNN because it only considers the top-1 class from the distribution; therefore, other relevant information is lost. Second, the consistency metric is biased by the classification accuracy because the consistency value increases when the images are classified correctly; otherwise, it decreases. To overcome these shortcomings, this paper proposes the correctness-aware distribution distance (CADD). In CADD, we use the Jensen-Shannon (JS) divergence to measure the difference among the entire output distributions. Furthermore, the JS divergence on the correct and incorrect subsets that are split by the classification correctness is separately calculated and averaged. The experimental results demonstrate that the CADD is more stable and interpretable than the consistency-based approach.

Keywords: Shift-invariance · Consistency · Convolutional neural network · Jensen-Shannon divergence

1 Introduction

Convolutional neural networks (CNNs) [4,8] play a central role in computer vision tasks such as an image classification [5,7,11]. In many cases, CNNs

© Springer Nature Switzerland AG 2021
T. Mantoro et al. (Eds.): ICONIP 2021, CCIS 1516, pp. 719–728, 2021.
https://doi.org/10.1007/978-3-030-92307-5_84

perform well in practice to solve such tasks; however, the precise reasons or mechanism why these applied CNNs exhibit high performance is not well known. To better understand the performance of CNNs, many researchers have evaluated them from several perspectives to elucidate their internal mechanisms.

In this study, we analyze CNN performance by focusing on a basic property called the "shift-invariance". Shift-invariance refers to the differences in the outputs between an original image and other spatially shifted images resulting from a single CNN. Usually, the CNN adopts a convolution operation in the inter-layer connections; thus, we assumed that a CNN naturally exhibits "shift-invariance". However, recent studies [1,3] have demonstrated that even small spatial shifts in the image can drastically change the output distribution of the CNN, that is, CNNs cannot be considered sufficiently shift-invariant. This differs from our intuition because human beings have a shift-invariant visual system. Therefore, measurement of the shift-invariance of CNNs will help us better understand the mechanisms governing CNN operation. To measure shift-invariance accurately, we require an objective and fair metric. Such a metric should capture the changes in the output distribution based on the image shift. In addition, a fair metric should not be biased by factors other than shift-invariance, such as classification accuracy.

Recently, Zhang [13] proposed a metric for measuring shift-invariance, called "consistency". Consistency measures how often a CNN classifies the two shifted images considered to belong to the same class. In other words, consistency measures the average coincidence of the classification results between the output distributions for two shifted images. This metric enables us to quantitatively evaluate the shift-invariance of CNNs [13,14]. However, the consistency measure has the following shortcomings. First, it cannot perfectly capture the changes in the output distribution of the CNN, because it uses the argmax operation, which selects only one winner with the maximum output. This indicates that other detailed information from the output distribution might be lost in the evaluation. Furthermore, we argue that the consistency metric is biased by classification accuracy and is thus not a fair metric. We found that consistency values are higher when the images are classified correctly, and lower when the images are classified incorrectly. Therefore, in a CNN that performs with high accuracy, a greater number of images are correctly classified, and the consistency metric becomes deceptively higher. Due to these shortcomings, consistency does not accurately measure shift-invariance.

To overcome the shortcomings of the consistency metric, this paper proposes a new metric to measure the shift-invariance—it is called the correctness-aware distribution distance (CADD). In the CADD, we use Jensen-Shannon (JS) divergence for measuring the difference of the output distributions, instead of argmax used in the consistency metric. The CADD can capture changes in the entire output distribution of the CNN because the JS divergence measures the difference between two probability distributions. Furthermore, to eliminate the bias associated with accuracy, herein, the JS divergence for the correct and incorrect subsets that are split by the classification correctness is separately calculated and these scores are averaged. The main differences between the consistency metric and the CADD are shown in Fig. 1. With these modifications, the CADD

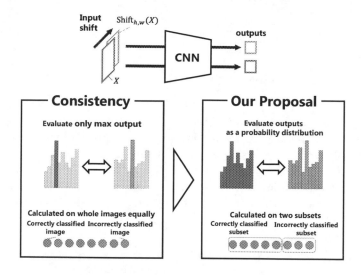

Fig. 1. Advantages of our proposal over consistency

overcomes the shortcomings of consistency; therefore, it can be considered as an proper and fair metric for measuring shift-invariance. Our experiments using the CIFAR-10 dataset demonstrate that the results of CADD are more reliable than those of the consistency metric and show interpretable results in light of previous work. Furthermore, according to experiments conducted on ImageNet 2012, by using the CADD, we found that VGG-based CNNs [11] may have higher shift-invariance than ResNet-based CNNs [5]. This finding was not observed in the evaluation using the consistency metric.

The contributions of this study can be summarized as follows:

- We propose a metric called the correctness-aware distribution distance (CADD) for measuring the shift-invariance of CNNs.
- The CADD metric shows higher performance than the existing "consistency" measure.
- We analyze why the "consistency" is biased by classification accuracy.

The remainder of this paper is organized as follows. Section 2 experimentally reviews the existing consistency metric. Section 3 describes our proposed method. Section 4 describes the experiments we performed in detail and presents the results. We conclude the paper with a summary and discuss future work in Sect. 5.

2 Experimental Review of an Existing Metric

In this section, we experimentally review an existing metric called "consistency", which was proposed by Zhang [13]. We first provide the definition of the metric. Consistency is defined as follows:

$$\text{Consistency} = \frac{1}{\sum_X |\Lambda_X^1| \, |\Lambda_X^2|} \sum_{X \in \mathcal{D}} \sum_{(h_1, w_1) \in \Lambda_X^1} \sum_{(h_2, w_2) \in \Lambda_X^2} \text{Agreement}_{X, h_1, w_1, h_2, w_2}, \tag{1}$$

$$\text{Agreement}_{X, h_1, w_1, h_2, w_2} = \mathbb{1}(\arg\max P(\text{Shift}_{h_1, w_1}(X)) = \arg\max P(\text{Shift}_{h_2, w_2}(X))) \tag{2}$$

Here, Λ_X^1, Λ_X^2 are the subsets of $\Lambda\{(h, w) \mid h = 1, \ldots, H, \; w = 1, \ldots, W\}$. $\text{Shift}_{h,w}(X)$ is an operator that shifts image X by w pixels vertically and h pixels horizontally. $P(X)$ is the output distribution of the CNN when image X is given. Notation $\mathbb{1}(condition)$ denotes the indicator function, which takes 1 when $condition$ is true and 0 in other cases. In other words, consistency measures the average coincidence of the argmaxes of the output distributions between two shifted images.

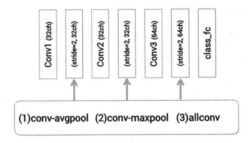

Fig. 2. Overviews of the architectures to evaluate the metrics

In this study, we measure the shift-invariance of CNNs. Although consistency appears to be a good measure to evaluate shift-invariance, it is inappropriate because it counts the coincidence of argmaxes, which might not capture the change in the entire output distribution. Thus, we first evaluated the effectiveness of the consistency metric in several CNNs. To evaluate consistency as a measure of shift-invariance, we calculated the consistency of three architectures: conv-avgpool, conv-maxpool, and allconv. The overview of these architectures is shown in Fig. 2. Each architecture consists of three units that have a convolution layer with the same configuration, followed by a different layer with strides. The layers with strides have the following differences in each architecture:

- conv-avgpool: Average pooling that outputs the average of the values input to the fixed size kernel [9].
- conv-maxpool: Max pooling that outputs the maximum of the values input to the fixed size kernel [7].
- allconv: Convolution with the stride, wherein the weights are determined by training in contrast to the above two architectures [12].

To assess the variance caused by initial weights, which are determined by random numbers, we trained each model with four different initial weights. As a training and validation dataset, we used the CIFAR-10 dataset [6], which is one of the most widely used datasets for image classification tasks.

The mean and variance values of the consistency metric of each architecture are presented in Fig. 3. There is a slight difference in the mean consistency values between the three architectures, which are shown with different colors in Fig. 3. Additionally, the variances (shown as the length of the error bars) are much larger than the differences. This result indicates that consistency is unstable with a large variance as a result of the initial weights. In Sect. 1, we described that consistency is not an "appropriate" metric that can capture the change in the entire output distribution of the CNN. This shortcoming makes consistency unstable because it cannot capture the continuous change in the output distributions.

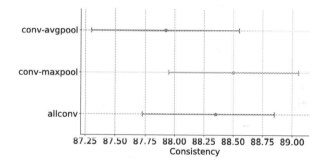

Fig. 3. Mean and variance values of the consistency measure for each architecture trained by CIFAR-10

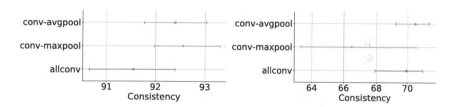

Fig. 4. Means and variances of consistency for correctly (left) and incorrectly (right) predicted images

Next, we experimentally demonstrated that consistency is biased by classification accuracy and is thus not a "fair" metric. Here, we calculated consistency by splitting the images by the correctness (correct or incorrect) of the prediction for each architecture. The means and variances of consistency for correctly predicted and incorrectly predicted images are shown in Fig. 4 (left) and Fig. 4 (right), respectively. These figures show that consistency decreases drastically for incorrectly predicted images. Therefore, because consistency for correctly predicted images is higher than that for incorrectly predicted ones, the

CNNs with higher accuracy also tend to have higher consistency. This indicates that consistency is biased by the classification accuracy. Therefore, consistency is not a "fair" metric.

3 Proposal Metric: Correctness-Aware Distribution Distance

To overcome the shortcomings of the consistency metric, we propose a new metric to measure shift-invariance—it is called the correctness-aware distribution distance (CADD). First, we focus on using the Jensen–Shannon (JS) divergence, which calculates the difference between the probability distributions, P, Q. The JS divergence is a symmetrized and smoothed version of the Kullback–Leibler divergence D_{KL} and is defined as:

$$D_{JS}(P \parallel Q) = \frac{1}{2} D_{KL}(P \parallel M) + \frac{1}{2} D_{KL}(Q \parallel M). \tag{3}$$

Here, $M = \frac{1}{2}(P + Q)$, and D_{KL} is defined as

$$D_{KL}(P \parallel Q) = \sum_i P_i \log \frac{P_i}{Q_i}. \tag{4}$$

By using the JS divergence, the CADD can capture changes in the entire output distributions of the CNN, which is different from the argmax operation used for consistency.

Second, we attempt to eliminate the biases caused by the accuracy that was experimentally demonstrated in Sect. 2. The results shown in Sect. 2 indicate that the shift-invariance considerably varies depending on the classification correctness of the image. In the CADD, we split the images into two subsets in accordance with their correctness (classified correctly or incorrectly). Then, we separately calculate the JS Divergence for each subset and average them. This enabled the CADD to eliminate the bias caused by accuracy because the two subsets that have different shift-invariance are evenly evaluated, that is, through 1:1 averaging and not weighted averaging, as is done for consistency.

Consequently, we define the CADD as follow:

$$\text{CADD} = \frac{1}{2} \left(\frac{1}{|\mathcal{D}_{\text{correct}}|} \sum_{X \in \mathcal{D}_{\text{correct}}} \text{DD}(X) + \frac{1}{|\mathcal{D}_{\text{incorrect}}|} \sum_{X \in \mathcal{D}_{\text{incorrect}}} \text{DD}(X) \right) \tag{5}$$

$$\text{DD}(X) = \frac{1}{|\Lambda_X^1| \, |\Lambda_X^2|} \sum_{(h_1,w_1) \in \Lambda_X^1} \sum_{(h_2,w_2) \in \Lambda_X^2} D_{JS}(P(\text{Shift}_{h_1,w_1}(X)) \parallel P(\text{Shift}_{h_2,w_2}(X))) \tag{6}$$

where $\mathcal{D}_{\text{correct}}$ is the subset in which the images are recognized correctly, and $\mathcal{D}_{\text{incorrect}}$ is another subset in which the images are recognized incorrectly. With these modifications, the CADD overcomes the shortcomings of consistency and is expected to become an proper and fair metric for measuring shift-invariance. In the CADD, a lower value indicates that the two output distributions of the CNN are more similar. Therefore, the smaller the CADD, the higher the shift-invariance.

4   Experiments

In this section, we describe the experiments we conducted to evaluate the CADD. First, we calculated the CADD for the three architectures trained by the CIFAR-10 dataset under the same conditions as those described in Sect. 2, and compared the results to those of the consistency metric. The results are shown in Fig. 5. Figure 5 shows that the variances of the CADD resulting from the initial weights (shown as the length of the error bars) were much smaller than those of the consistency shown metric, in Fig. 3. In addition, the evaluation using the CADD showed differences between the three architectures, conv-avgpool, conv-maxpool, and allconv, with respect to shift-invariance. These differences were not observed during the consistency evaluation, as shown in Fig. 6 (left).

Next, we analyzed larger-scale CNNs from the shift-invariance perspective using the CADD. We used two types of architectures, namely, VGG-based CNNs (VGG11, VGG13 and VGG16) and ResNet-based CNNs (ResNet18, ResNet34 and ResNet50). All these CNNs were trained using the ImageNet 2012 dataset [2], which is one of the most widely used datasets for large-scale image classification tasks. Note that we used the pre-trained weights provided by PyTorch [10].

Following previous research [13], we present the results of the shift-invariance (CADD) on the x-axis and accuracy on the y-axis. Figure 6 (right) shows that the VGG-based CNNs have higher shift-invariance in the CADD than the ResNet-based ones.

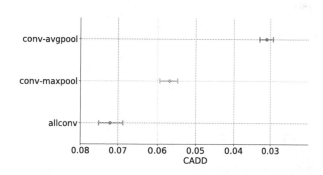

Fig. 5. Mean and variance values of the CADD for each architecture trained by CIFAR-10. As with consistency graphs shown above, the model on the right has higher shift-invariance.

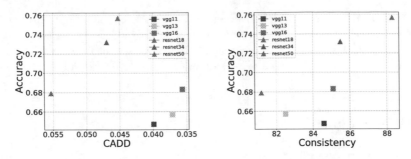

Fig. 6. Relationship between the CADD and accuracy (left) and relationship between consistency and accuracy (right) for each architecture trained by ImageNet 2012. The squares represent the VGG-based CNNs, and the triangles represent the ResNet-based CNNs.

Furthermore, we introduced and compared the blur layer, which was proposed by Zhang [13], and we improved the shift-invariance from the perspective of consistency in each of the above architectures. The results of the VGG-based CNNs and the results of the ResNet-based CNNs are shown in Fig. 7 (left) and Fig. 7 (right), respectively. These figures show that the introduction of the blur layer improves the shift-invariance with respect to the CADD for any architecture.

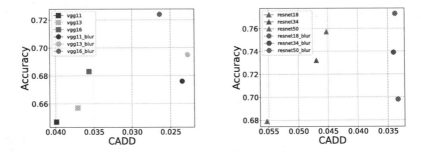

Fig. 7. Changes in the CADD and accuracy of the VGG-based CNNs (left) and ResNet-based CNNs (right) before and after introducing the blur layer. Circles in each figure represent the architectures with a blur layer.

5   Conclusion and Discussion

In this paper, we proposed a new metric to measure shift-invariance, which we refer to as the correctness-aware distribution distance (CADD), to overcome the shortcomings of the existing consistency metric [13]. In the CADD, we used the JS divergence to calculate the difference between the two output distributions of the CNN given two different shifts on the same image. In addition, we separately calculated the JS divergence for the correct and incorrect subsets that were split by the classification correctness and averaged them. As a result, the CADD shows a smaller variance than consistency. This characteristic of the CADD enables a more stable and objective evaluation independent of the initialization of CNNs.

In demonstrating the CIFAR-10 dataset, we found that conv-avgpool shows a higher CADD value than other architectures (conv-maxpool and allconv), which was not observed with consistency. This is an interpretable result in light of the previous work by Zhang [13]. Furthermore, with the ImageNet 2012 dataset, we found that the VGG-based CNNs had a higher CADD value than the ResNet-based CNNs. The VGG-based CNNs consist of a conv-maxpool architecture, whereas the ResNet-based CNNs consist of an allconv architecture. Therefore, our results suggest that the conv-maxpool architecture may exhibit higher shift-invariance than the allconv architecture. This consideration is consistent with results from the CIFAR-10 dataset, in which conv-maxpool shows a higher CADD value than allconv.

In future work, we plan to further analyze CNNs with the CADD. We also plan to use the CADD as a loss function for training shift-invariant CNNs. The CADD does not have non-differentiable operations in contrast to consistency; thus, it can be used as the loss function.

Acknowledgement. This study was partly supported with MEXT KAKENHI, Grant-in-Aid for Scientific Research on Innovative Areas, 19H04982, Grant-in-Aid for Scientific Research (A) 18H04106.

References

1. Azulay, A., Weiss, Y.: Why do deep convolutional networks generalize so poorly to small image transformations? ArXiv abs/1805.12177 (2018)
2. Deng, J., Dong, W., Socher, R., Li, L.J., Li, K., Fei-Fei, L.: ImageNet: a large-scale hierarchical image database. In: 2009 IEEE Conference on Computer Vision and Pattern Recognition, pp. 248–255. IEEE (2009)
3. Engstrom, L., Tran, B., Tsipras, D., Schmidt, L., Madry, A.: Exploring the landscape of spatial robustness. In: International Conference on Machine Learning (ICML) (2019)
4. Fukushima, K.: Neocognitron: a self-organizing neural network model for a mechanism of pattern recognition unaffected by shift in position. Biol. Cybern. **36**(4), 193–202 (1980). https://doi.org/10.1007/BF00344251
5. He, K., Zhang, X., Ren, S., Sun, J.: Deep residual learning for image recognition. In: IEEE Conference on Computer Vision and Pattern Recognition (CVPR) (2016)
6. Krizhevsky, A.: Learning multiple layers of features from tiny images. Technical report (2009)
7. Krizhevsky, A., Sutskever, I., Hinton, G.E.: ImageNet classification with deep convolutional neural networks. In: Advances in Neural Information Processing Systems (NeurIPS) (2012)
8. LeCun, Y., et al.: Backpropagation applied to handwritten zip code recognition. Neural Comput. **1**(4), 541–551 (1989)

9. LeCun, Y., Haffner, P., Bottou, L., Bengio, Y.: Object recognition with gradient-based learning. In: Shape, Contour and Grouping in Computer Vision. LNCS, vol. 1681, pp. 319–345. Springer, Heidelberg (1999). https://doi.org/10.1007/3-540-46805-6_19

10. Paszke, A., et al.: PyTorch: an imperative style, high-performance deep learning library. In: Advances in Neural Information Processing Systems (NeurIPS) (2019)

11. Simonyan, K., Zisserman, A.: Very deep convolutional networks for large-scale image recognition. In: International Conference on Learning and Representations (ICLR) (2015)

12. Springenberg, J., Dosovitskiy, A., Brox, T., Riedmiller, M.: Striving for simplicity: the all convolutional net. In: ICLR (Workshop Track) (2015)

13. Zhang, R.: Making convolutional networks shift-invariant again. In: International Conference on Machine Learning (ICML) (2019)

14. Zou, X., Xiao, F., Yu, Z., Lee, Y.J.: Delving deeper into anti-aliasing in convnets. In: British Machine Vision Conference (BMVC) (2020)

AI and Cybersecurity

Retinal Vessel Segmentation Based on Gated Skip-Connection Network

Huixia Yao, Yun Jiang$^{(\boxtimes)}$, Tongtong Cheng, and Jing Gao

College of Computer Science and Engineering, Northwest Normal University,
Lanzhou 730070, China
jiangyun@nwnu.edu.cn

Abstract. Semantic segmentation of the retinal vessels is a pivotal stage in the treatment of certain eye disorders. Efficient and accurate segmentation is a challenge for retinal vessel segmentation. In this article, we presented a technique which is based on a Gated Skip-connection Network (GS-CNN), which implements the simultaneous segmentation of retinal vessel. In GS-CNN, a novel skip-connection with gating is first used in extension path, which facilitates flow of information from down-sampling to up-sampling. Specifically, we use gated skip-connection between encoder and decoder to gate the lower-level information from the encoder. This can effectively remove noise and help the decoder to focus on processing the relevant boundary related information. Secondly, multi-scale input images are constructed in UNet. Finally, we verified the GS-CNN on DRIVE, CHASE datasets. The experimental results proved the effectiveness of the GS-CNN.

Keywords: Deep convolutional neural work · Retinal vessel segmentation · Skip connection · Gating mechanism

1 Introduction

Many chronic fundus diseases can lead to blindness in severe cases [1]. Segmentation of retinal vessels is a critical step in screening and diagnosis of fundus diseases [2]. Therefore, it is extremely important to segment retinal vessels accurately and automatically from fundus images. However, extensive screening or diagnosis is time-consuming and laborious. The automatic segmentation method is particularly important for doctors to diagnose and predict related diseases. This can further assist doctors to diagnose and analyze patients'conditions, make early prevention, diagnosis and treatment of fundus diseases, and avoid eyesight loss to a certain extent resulting from chronic fundus diseases [2].

In these recent years, many national and international fellows have used deep learning methods to assist the physician in segmenting retinal vessel images. The method based on deep learning has also made many achievements. In deep learning methods, most of them are based on convolution neural network (CNN). A typical example based on CNNs is the retinal vessel segmentation method

© Springer Nature Switzerland AG 2021
T. Mantoro et al. (Eds.): ICONIP 2021, CCIS 1516, pp. 731–738, 2021.
https://doi.org/10.1007/978-3-030-92307-5_85

proposed by Khalaf et al. [3]. In the same year, Liskowski et al. [4] also used CNN for blood vessel segmentation. Yu et al. [5] also used CNN for blood vessel segmentation. Encoder and decoder structures are widely used in fundus image segmentation due to their excellent feature extraction capability, especially UNet [6]. Zhang et al. [7] proposed a multi-label architecture. Their proposed base model uses U-Net with skip connections as the baseline network. A lateral output layer is also used to acquire multi-scale signatures. On the basis of encoder and decoder, in order to improve the segmentation ability of the network, attention mechanism is gradually applied to retinal vessel segmentation. Zhang et al. [8] proposed an attention guiding network (AG-Net) for blood vessel segmentation.

However, the accuracy of most segmentation results also has space for improvement. Aiming at the problems of insufficient segmentation of retinal blood vessels by existing methods, low accuracy, sensitivity to noise and lesions. The gated skip-connection idea is used to segment high-precision and high-accuracy retinal blood vessel images. The main work of this paper includes:

1. After a detailed analysis of the limitations of the previously proposed methods, aiming at the problem that the previous methods are not ideal for retinal blood vessel segmentation, this paper uses a improved UNet framework to segment retinal vessels. The framework is called Gated Skip-connection Network (GS-CNN), which realizes the simultaneous segmentation of retinal vessels.
2. A gating is introduced to skip connection between encoder and decoder. A gated skip connection is designed to facilitate flow of information, which can effectively remove noise and help the decoder to focus on processing the relevant boundary-related information.
3. Finally, We verified the GS-CNN on two retinal image datasets(DRIVE [9], CHASE [10]), showing its effectiveness.

2   GS-CNN Network Structure

In this section, we present our GS-CNN architecture for semantic segmentation. As depicted in Fig. 1, our network consists of decoder and encoder. In the encoder, multi-scale inputs can ensure the network to learning characteristics at a wide range of levels of scale, which can improve the reliability of the GS-CNN. The encoder contains four down-sampled convolution blocks. In the down-sampling of GS-CNN, the small information of retinal vessels is weakened and blurred. In the traditional U-Net, the encoder transmits information directly to the decoder by skipping the connection, and noise is also transmitted to the decoder in this process. Then we introduce gated skip-connect to reduce noise.

2.1   Gated Skip-Connection (GS)

GS modified the original skip connection to serve as a bridge between the encoder and the decoder to transmit information. The organization of GS is demonstrated

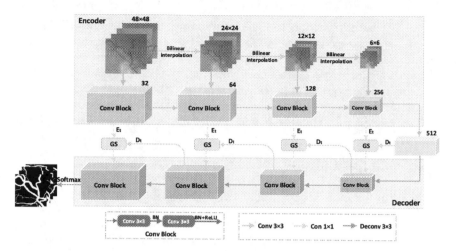

Fig. 1. Network structure of GS-CNN

in the Fig. 2. The structure of GS is shown in Fig. 2. In GS-CNN, we use GS to transmit the edge information of the encoder to the decoder. The output of the four convolution blocks in the encoder and the output of the upper layer of the upsampling block in the decoder can also be transitioned through GS.

We use GS in multiple locations between encoder and decoder. Let t denote the number of locations. $t \in 0, 1, 2, 3$. E_t is the boundary semantic information transmitted from the encoder, and D_t is the information sampled by the decoder. To apply GS, we first obtain an attention feature map α_t by concatenating E_t and D_t followed by a 1×1 convolution layer($Conv_{1\times1}$). This convolution layer is followed by a sigmoid function σ in turn:

$$\alpha_t = \sigma \left(\mathrm{Conv}_{1\times1} \left(E_t \oplus D_t \right) \right) \tag{1}$$

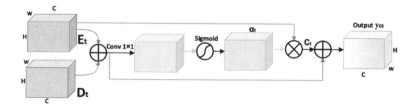

Fig. 2. Structure of gated skip connection

$$
\begin{aligned}
Y_{GS} &= C_t + (E_t \oplus D_t) \\
&= (E_t \odot \alpha_t) + (E_t \oplus D_t)
\end{aligned}
\tag{2}
$$

where $\oplus$ denotes concatenation of feature maps. Given the attention map α_t, GS is applied on E_t as an element-wise product $\odot$ with t followed by a skip connection. C_t is obtained by this operation. Then the result of the aggregation of E_t and D_t and C_t is processed by channel-wise concatenation. At each pixel, Output Y_{GS} of GS is computed as important information about the boundary region in the fundus image, which is obtained by the Gated Skip connection processing of E_t and D_t. That is the attention weight feature maps about the boundary region.

3   Experiments and Analysis

3.1   Training Parameter Settings and Dataset

The training method of the model and the partitioning method of the data set are the same as the previous work [11]. The loss function is the same as that of the literature [11].

The proposed method was validated on DRIVE [9] and CHASE [10] datasets. We use the same evaluation metrics as in the literature [11].

3.2   Analysis of Experimental Results

To further validate the effectiveness of the proposed algorithm, the proposed method is compared with some methods. The bold values in the table are the highest among each evaluation index. Tables 1 and 2 show the experimental results of different methods on DRIVE and CHASE data sets, respectively.

Table 1. Experimental results of our method and existing methods on the DRIVE

Methods	Year	Accuracy	Sensitivity	Specificity	F-measure	AUC$_{ROC}$
Cheng [12]	2014	0.9474	0.7252	0.9798	-	0.9648
Aslani [13]	2016	0.9513	0.7545	0.9801	-	0.9682
Mo [14]	2017	0.9521	0.7779	0.9780	-	0.9782
U-Net [15]	2018	0.9531	0.7537	0.9820	0.8149	0.9755
Residual U-Net [15]	2018	0.9553	0.7726	0.9820	0.8149	0.9779
Samuel [16]	2019	0.9609	0.8282	0.9738	-	0.9786
AG-Net [8]	2019	0.9692	0.8100	**0.9848**	-	0.9856
Lv [17]	2020	0.9558	0.7854	0.9810	0.8216	0.9682
SA-Net [19]	2021	0.9569	0.8252	0.9764	0.8289	0.9822
Ours	2021	**0.9701**	**0.8299**	0.9836	**0.8294**	**0.9872**

For DRIVE data set, the F-measure of retinal vessel segmentation in this method reaches 82.94%, which is 0.05% higher than SA-Net [19], and the sensitivity is 0.17% higher than that in [16].

From Tables 1 and 2, it can be seen that the specificity, accuracy and F-measure of our method on different data sets are the highest in the table.

Table 2. Comparison of proposed methods with other methods on the CHASE.

Methods	Year	Accuracy	Sensitivity	Specificity	F-measure	AUC$_{ROC}$
Azzopardi [18]	2015	0.9442	0.7655	0.9704	-	-
Jiang [20]	2018	0.9668	**0.8640**	0.9745	-	0.9810
U-Net [15]	2018	0.9578	0.8288	0.9701	0.7783	0.9772
Recurrent U-Net [15]	2018	0.9622	0.7459	0.9836	0.7810	0.9803
R2U-Net [15]	2018	0.9634	0.7756	0.9820	0.7928	0.9815
AG-Net [8]	2019	0.9743	0.8186	0.9848	-	**0.9863**
Sine-Net [21]	2020	0.9676	0.7856	0.9845	-	0.9828
Ours	2021	**0.9757**	0.8191	**0.9862**	**0.8092**	0.9830

Although the sensitivity of [20] on CHASE data set is higher than that of our method, the segmentation effect on small blood vessels is not very good, and sometimes fracture occurs. Moreover, the specificity of our method remains relatively stable, and the noise contained in the segmented image is relatively small.

4   Ablation Study

GS module is instrumental in filtering background noise in fundus images. This module combines gating and skip connection to generate GS to improve experimental results. To test the validity of our suggested GS, two attention modules are also added to the baseline network—Multi-scale Uet (MUet) for comparison with the GS module. The MUet is a baseline. Two attenuation techniques are applied to MUet.

The first tested attention module is the Efficient Channel Attention (ECA) module of ECA-Net [22]. It is employed for object detection and instance segmentation tasks. ECA is improved from the SE module [23]. Experience has shown that avoiding drop-offs and adequate cross-channel engagement are important for learning effective attendance. Another attention module is the Dense Atrous Convolution module (DAC) of CE-Net [24], which used inception structure and atrous convolution to capture more information from the deep network and retain the individual pixel location information of 2D medical images.

Table 3. Using MUet as the baseline model, performance comparison between different attention modules and GS modules on the DRIVE.

Methods	Accuracy	Sensitivity	Specificity	F-measure	AUC$_{ROC}$
MUet	0.9686	0.7345	**0.9911**	0.8040	0.9654
MUet+ECA	0.9700	0.8116	0.9852	0.8258	0.9804
MUet+DAC	0.9700	0.7770	0.9885	0.8195	0.9861
MUet+GS	**0.9701**	**0.8299**	0.9836	**0.8294**	**0.9872**

Table 3 shows the experimental results of the GS module with the ECA module and DAC module added into the baseline network—MUet respectively. ECA and DAC improve the accuracy and F-measure of the model, the overall segmentation results of GS are higher than ECA and DAC.

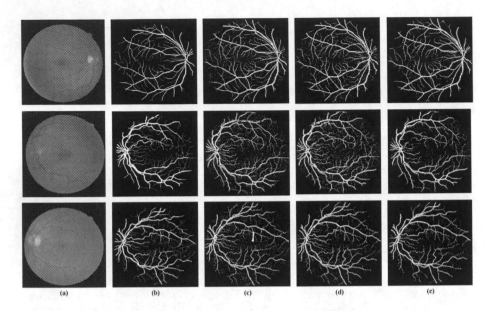

Fig. 3. Attention module comparison visualization results on DRIVE dataset. (a) image; (b) groundtruth; (c) ECA-Net [22]; (d) CE-Net [24]; (e) our method

We compare the proposed method with other methods, ECA-Net [22] and CE-Net [24]. Figure 3 is the visualization results of DRIVE data set. Experimental results of CE-Net [24] contained more noise, the background is mistakenly segmented into blood vessels. There are some marginal vessels that are incorrectly segmented. Although Experimental results of ECA-Net [22] contained less noise, there are still some problems such as fuzzy boundary. The background region noise of the fundus image segmented by our model GS-CNN is the least. This also demonstrates the relevance and effectiveness of the GS module in background denoising.

5   Conclusions

Segmentation of the retinal vasculature is a major component of procedures to detect ocular disease. In this paper, we proposed a model based on a Gated Skip-connection Network (GS-CNN) to segment retinal vessel images. The skip connection with gating is used between the encoder and decoder, which facilitates the exchange of information between the encoder and decoder and filters background noise to help the decoder obtain more semantic information.

The multi-scale input allows the model to capture feature information at different scales, thus making the model more robust. We validated the GS-CNN on DRIVE and CHASE data sets, and results show that our approaches in this paper have superior properties in retinal vessel segmentation than some existing algorithms. (such as AG-Net [8] and Sine-Net [21]).

Acknowledgments. This work was supported in part by the National Natural Science Foundation of China (61962054), in part by the National Natural Science Foundation of China (61163036), in part by the Northwest Normal University Major Research Project Incubation Program (nwnu-LKZD2021_06), and in part by the Northwest Normal University's Third Phase of Knowledge and Innovation Engineering Research Backbone Project (nwnu-kjcxgc-03-67).

References

1. Abràmoff, M.D., Folk, J.C., Han, D.P., et al.: Automated analysis of retinal images for detection of referable diabetic retinopathy. JAMA Ophthalmol. **131**(3), 351–357 (2013)
2. Fraz, M.M., Remagnino, P., Hoppe, A., et al.: Blood vessel segmentation methodologies in retinal images-a survey. Comput. Methods Prog. Biomed. **108**(1), 407–433 (2012)
3. Khalaf, A.F., Yassine, I.A., Fahmy, A.S.: Convolutional neural networks for deep feature learning in retinal vessel segmentation. In: 2016 IEEE International Conference on Image Processing (ICIP), pp. 385–388. IEEE (2016)
4. Liskowski, P., Krawiec, K.: Segmenting retinal blood vessels with deep neural networks. IEEE Trans. Med. Imag. **35**(11), 2369–2380 (2016)
5. Yu, L., Qin, Z., Zhuang, T., et al.: A framework for hierarchical division of retinal vascular networks. Neurocomputing **392**, 221–232 (2020)
6. Ronneberger, O., Fischer, P., Brox, T.: U-Net: convolutional networks for biomedical image segmentation. In: Navab, N., Hornegger, J., Wells, W.M., Frangi, A.F. (eds.) MICCAI 2015. LNCS, vol. 9351, pp. 234–241. Springer, Cham (2015). https://doi.org/10.1007/978-3-319-24574-4_28
7. Zhang, Y., Chung, A.C.S.: Deep supervision with additional labels for retinal vessel segmentation task. In: Frangi, A.F., Schnabel, J.A., Davatzikos, C., Alberola-López, C., Fichtinger, G. (eds.) MICCAI 2018. LNCS, vol. 11071, pp. 83–91. Springer, Cham (2018). https://doi.org/10.1007/978-3-030-00934-2_10
8. Zhang, S., Fu, H., Yan, Y., et al.: Attention guided network for retinal image segmentation. International Conference on Medical Image Computing and Computer-Assisted Intervention, pp. 797–805.Springer, Cham (2019). https://doi.org/10.1007/10704282
9. Staal, J., Abràmoff, M.D., Niemeijer, M., et al.: Ridge-based vessel segmentation in color images of the retina. IEEE Trans. Med. Imag. **23**(4), 501–509 (2004)
10. Owen, C.G., Rudnicka, A.R., Mullen, R., et al.: Measuring retinal vessel tortuosity in 10-year-old children: validation of the computer-assisted image analysis of the retina (CAIAR) program[J]. Invest. Ophthalmol. Visual Sci. **50**(5), 2004–2010 (2009)
11. Jiang, Y., Yao, H., Wu, C., et al.: A multi-scale residual attention network for retinal vessel segmentation. Symmetry **13**(1), 24 (2021)

12. Cheng, E., Du, L., Wu, Y., et al.: Discriminative vessel segmentation in retinal images by fusing context-aware hybrid features. Mach. Vis. Appl. **25**(7), 1779–1792 (2014)
13. Aslani, S., Sarnel, H.: A new supervised retinal vessel segmentation method based on robust hybrid features. Biomed. Sig. Proces. Control **30**, 1–12 (2016)
14. Mo, J., Zhang, L.: Multi-level deep supervised networks for retinal vessel segmentation. Int. J. Comput. Assist. Radiol. Surg. **12**(12), 2181–2193 (2017)
15. Alom, M.Z., Hasan, M., Yakopcic, C., et al.: Recurrent residual convolutional neural network based on U-Net (R2U-Net) for medical image segmentation (2018)
16. Samuel, P.M., Veeramalai, T.: Multilevel and multiscale deep neural network for retinal blood vessel segmentation. Symmetry **11**(7), 946 (2019)
17. Lv, Y., Ma, H., Li, J., et al.: Attention guided u-net with atrous convolution for accurate retinal vessels segmentation. IEEE Access **8**, 32826–32839 (2020)
18. Azzopardi, G., Strisciuglio, N., Vento, M., et al.: Trainable COSFIRE filters for vessel delineation with application to retinal images. Med. Image Anal. **19**(1), 46–57 (2015)
19. Hu, J., Wang, H., Wang, J., et al.: SA-Net: A scale-attention network for medical image segmentation. PLoS ONE **16**(4), e0247388 (2021)
20. Jiang, Z., Zhang, H., Wang, Y., et al.: Retinal blood vessel segmentation using fully convolutional network with transfer learning. Comput. Med. Imag. Graph. **68**, 1–15 (2018)
21. Atli, İ, Gedik, O.S.: Sine-Net: a fully convolutional deep learning architecture for retinal blood vessel segmentation. Eng. Sci. Technol. **24**(2), 271–283 (2021)
22. Wang, Q., Wu, B., Zhu, P., et al.: ECA-Net: efficient channel attention for deep convolutional neural networks, 2020 IEEE. In: CVF Conference on Computer Vision and Pattern Recognition (CVPR). IEEE (2020)
23. Hu, J., Shen, L., Sun, G.: Squeeze-and-excitation networks. In: Proceedings of the IEEE Conference on Computer Vision and Pattern Recognition, pp. 7132–7141 (2018)
24. Gu, Z., Cheng, J., Fu, H., et al.: Ce-net: context encoder network for 2d medical image segmentation. IEEE Trans. Medi. Imag. **38**(10), 2281–2292 (2019)

Combining Wikipedia to Identify Prerequisite Relations of Concepts in MOOCs

Haoyu Wen, Xinning Zhu$^{(\boxtimes)}$, Moyu Zhang, Chunhong Zhang, and Changchuan Yin

School of Posts and Telecommunications, Beijing University, Beijing, China
{wenhaoyu,zhuxn,zhangmoyu,zhangch,ccyin}@bupt.edu.cn

Abstract. Many applications like the personalization recommendation system of online learning are based on prerequisite relations of concepts, which prompted us to automatically infer the prerequisite relations between the concepts in Massive Open Online Courses (MOOCs). The previous methods mostly use artificial features to identify the prerequisite relations from learning materials and Wikipedia. However, artificial features are complicated to deeply mine prerequisite information in MOOC videos and the Wikipedia-directed graph, resulting in poor performance. We propose a new and more effective method to identify prerequisite relations from the above two data resources. We first use a graph embedding algorithm to learn the vector representations of concepts from the created Wikipedia-directed graph and use the cosine similarity between the vectors to represent the semantic and structural relevance between the concepts. Second, we pre-train a Siamese network whose inputs are representations of course concepts learned by a variation of the LDA model to find more practical information of prerequisite relations from MOOC subtitles. Then, the concept similarities related to topic distribution can be represented by the pre-trained Siamese network's outputs. Finally, we add some excellent artificial features to expand the information of the prerequisite relations and input them together into a binary classifier to identify the prerequisite relations of the concepts in MOOCs. Our experiments on two MOOC datasets indicate that the proposed method achieves significant improvements comparing with existing methods.

Keywords: Prerequisite relation · Graph embedding · Siamese network

1 Introduction

Recently, the growth of available educational data has made a variety of emerging educational applications possible [1]. And prerequisite relations are important for describing the fundamental directed relations among concepts in knowledge structures. This paper focuses on the concept prerequisite learning problem in MOOCs, whose purpose is to predict whether a concept A is a prerequisite of a concept B given the pair (A, B) by considering different data sources comprehensively.

The data sources for discovering prerequisite relations can be divided into two categories: Wikipedia [2, 4, 5] and learning materials such as MOOCs or textbooks

© Springer Nature Switzerland AG 2021
T. Mantoro et al. (Eds.): ICONIP 2021, CCIS 1516, pp. 739–747, 2021.
https://doi.org/10.1007/978-3-030-92307-5_86

[3, 6, 7, 9]. A Wikipedia article, usually identifying a notable topic or concept with varying granularity levels, contains many hyperlinks which imply various relations between concepts, are exploited by many previous methods to detect prerequisite relations of concepts. However, most of these methods, only based on some handcrafted graph features, do not fully explore concepts with their relations in hyperlinks. On the other hand, students usually gain knowledge by watching instructional videos in MOOCs, so the order in which students acquire new concepts is highly consistent with the video playback sequence. When using MOOC videos as data sources to detect prerequisite relations, it is common to construct various manually defined features to excavate the information in educational materials and model it as a binary classification problem [10, 12]. However, due to the complexity of online resources, it is hard to achieve high performance with purely handcrafted features.

Based on the challenges raised above, we put forward a new model that fully excavates the information from Wikipedia and MOOC data. For Wikipedia data sources, we first construct a directed graph of concepts based on hyperlinks between Wikipedia articles. Then, use the node2vec [14] graph embedding algorithm to learn low-dimensional representations for concepts, capturing the diversity of connectivity patterns in the constructed concept graphs. For MOOC data, we make use of the Pairwise-Link-LDA [13] and Siamese network as a pre-training model to obtain the topic distribution of concepts. Instead of predicting the prerequisite relations directly as in [12], the pre-trained topic distribution of concepts is aggregated into the final classification model, with concept embeddings obtained from Wikipedia and some other important manually extracted features, further to improve the performance of identification of prerequisite relations. To evaluate the proposed method, we compare our method with the representative works of prerequisite learning on two MOOC datasets [6,12] and the experimental results show that our method achieves state-of-the-art results in the prerequisite relations discovery in MOOCs.

2 Problem Statement

In this section, we first give some definitions and then formulate the prerequisite identification problem.

Generally, there will be multiple courses in MOOC related to one subject area. Let $V = \{V_1 \ldots V_k\}$ denotes the corpus of k courses, and $V_k = \{v_{k1} \ldots v_{km}\}$ denotes a video sequence of kth course, where v_{ki} is composed of concepts in the video subtitle text of the ith video of the kth course. According to the order of video playlists, a directed graph $G_V(V, E_V)$ can be constructed, in which nodes represent MOOC videos, and edges indicate the order of videos, i.e., E_V contains a directed edge $e_{v_k}(i, j)$ if and only if MOOC video v_{ki} plays before video v_{kj}. Let C be the set of all concepts of interest in one subject area that is assumed to be known in advance in this study. For the ith video of the kth course, $v_{ki} = \{C \cap W_{ki}\}$, where W_{ki} is the set of n-grams in v_{ki}, $n \in \{1, 2, 3\}$. As for Wikipedia, many concepts have their corresponding Wikipedia articles, which contain hyperlinks to related articles. We build a directed graph based on the linked information in Wikipedia, expressed as $G_W(C_W, E_W)$, where nodes set C_W is a subset of C, that includes only the concepts having corresponding articles in Wikipedia. Edges set E_W

represent hyperlinks between Wikipedia articles, i.e., the directed edge $e_w(i, j)$ exists in E_W if and only if the concept c_j's wiki article contains a hyperlink to the concept c_i. Let $G_C(C, E_C)$ be a directed graph, called concept graph, where nodes represent concepts and edges represent prerequisite dependency, i.e., E_C contains the directed edge $e_c(i, j)$ if and only if the concept c_i is a prerequisite of concept c_j. For a given set of concepts C, we want to infer concept prerequisites E_C from the set of MOOC videos V, the known video directed graph G_V and the directed graph $G_W(C_W, E_W)$ created from Wikipedia.

3 Prerequisite Relations Extraction

3.1 An Overview of the Proposed Method

This paper proposes a novel prerequisite relation identification method that can make full use of Wikipedia and MOOC data. A framework of our proposed prerequisite identification model, called GESN, is shown in Fig. 1. For Wikipedia data, we first construct a directed graph represented as $G_W(C_W, E_W)$, and then use node2vec to obtain the vector representations of the concepts. The features about Semantic and Structural Relevance (SSR) between two concepts can be defined and used as an essential feature in the final prerequisite classifier. For MOOC data, the set of MOOC videos V and the directed graph $G_V(V, E_V)$ are used to pre-train the Pairwise-Link-LDA model. The topic distribution of the concepts obtained from this model is used to pre-train a Siamese network with the known prerequisites' labels to get the features of the concepts' Similarities related to Topic Distribution (STD). Finally, the SSR, STD, and some other excellent handcrafted are used as the input of a binary classifier.

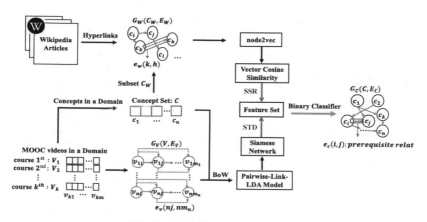

Fig. 1. Overall process of GESN.

3.2 Graph Embedding Based Wiki Information Extraction

Hypertexts in a Wikipedia article could help understand that article, reflecting the information about the prerequisite relations of concepts. It is worth noting that there may be some concepts that do not have related Wikipedia articles. We first need to find a set of concepts C_W from C that have related Wikipedia articles. Then the directed graph $G_W(C_W, E_W)$ can be built based on the hyperlinks between Wikipedia articles of the concepts in C_W. The direction of the edge is similar to the direction of the prerequisite relations between concepts.

We thought of using a practical and scalable representation learning algorithm that can reflect network and node neighbors' characteristics to comprehensively consider the relations between all nodes in the whole digraph. The node2vec algorithm is a good choice. Node2vec improves the random walk method in DeepWalk [8], comprehensively considering the characteristics of Breadth-First Search (BFS) and Depth-First Search (DFS) due to the return parameter p and in-out parameter q.

After obtaining the vector representation of each concept, the information of the prerequisite relations between two concepts can be represented by the cosine similarity of two vectors, and its essence is also a measure of the distance between the vectors. We define this distance as the Semantic and Structural Relevance (SSR) between two concepts.

3.3   Information of Topic Distribution from a Pre-trained Siamese Network

Recently, many handcrafted features have been proposed to mine the information about the prerequisite relations in MOOCs, but the complexity and scale of learning resources make it hard to improve the performance further.

Inspired by the method in [12], we use the combination of the Pairwise-Link-LDA model and a Siamese network to learn the topic distribution of concepts and get the similarities of the concepts related to the topic distribution by pre-training the Siamese network. The whole process is shown in Fig. 2. The Bag-of-Words (BoW) model is used to represent the subtitles of each video. After that, the MOOC video graph G_V and the BoW vectors of MOOC videos V are input into the Pairwise-Link-LDA model. Explicit modeling of directed links between ordered pairs of MOOC videos E_V can better capture the MOOC videos' topics and the distribution of words over topics to capture the prerequisite relations between the words themselves. Each MOOC video generation process is the same as LDA. The topic-word distribution β describes the topic distribution of each word. Based on the Pairwise-Link-LDA model, the word distribution over topics $\beta_{K \times |V|}$ can be obtained, where V is the number of n-grams, and K is the chosen number of topics. Please refer to [12] for more details of the Pairwise-Link-LDA model. The learned β will be used as the input of a pre-training Siamese Network whose weights of the sub-networks are tied. Each concept is represented as a vector of dimension K. The input of the Siamese Network is the obtained vector representation of each pair of concepts symbolized as (x_i, x_j). The pair (x_i, x_j) is passed through the corresponding sub-network $G_w(.)$ which include fully connected neural network layers and a rectified linear unit, yielding two corresponding outputs (o_i, o_j).

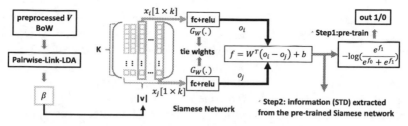

Fig. 2. Overall process of obtaining STD.

As we can see in Fig. 2, the whole process is divided into two steps. First, in the pre-training phase of the Siamese network, labeled pairs of such vectors from our training set are used to pre-train the Siamese network. These vectors are passed through the sub-networks $G_w(.)$. We denote f as the sum of the weighted element-wise differences between the two feature vectors o_i and o_j, and then obtain the probability P_{x_1, x_2} of the first input vector x_1 is a prerequisite to the second vector x_2:

$$P_{x_1, x_2} = log\left(\frac{e^{f_1}}{e^{f_0} + e^{f_1}}\right) \tag{1}$$

where $f = W^T\left(G_w\left(\beta_{x_1}^T\right) - G_w\left(\beta_{x_2}^T\right)\right) + b$ is a two-dimensional vector and f_n is the nth element in it. Finally, the cross-entropy loss function is optimized concerning the parameter vectors controlling both the subnets through the stochastic gradient descent method using the Adam optimizer.

In step 2, for each pair of concepts, we obtain $\frac{e^{f_1}}{e^{f_0} + e^{f_1}}$ from the pre-trained Siamese network and use it as the feature of the concepts, defined as Similarities related to Topic Distribution (STD), for the final classification.

3.4 Classification for Prerequisite Relations

Some essential existing manually defined features include some information that cannot be obtained through SSR (#1) and STD (#2) at the same time, so we add them to the final binary classifier. First, some of these features are from [6], including Structural Features (#3) and Contextual Features that are variants of RefD (#4) and semantic similarity (#5). For more details of these features, please refer to [6]. Second, From many Wikipedia-based features proposed by [5], we use the Wikipedia-directed graph we constructed to calculate the PageRank difference of each pair of concepts (#6). Finally, all these six parts are combined as a binary classifier's input to capture the prerequisite information as much as possible.

4 Experiment

4.1 Data

We conducted related experiments on two datasets from different domains. First, we use a published MOOC dataset, named NPTEL, which belongs to the domain of computer science. This dataset, from [12], is based on video playlists from a MOOC corpus. There are 382 videos from 38 different courses, and from 345 concepts, 1008 pairs of concept pairs with prerequisite relation were manually labeled. Out of 345 concepts, two concepts do not have related Wikipedia articles.

Second, we use a MOOC dataset in the domain of machine learning proposed by Pan et al. in 2017, named W-ML [6]. Then the W-ML dataset extracts 120 concepts from 244 concepts in the ML dataset and contains 486 pairs of annotated concept pairs with prerequisite relations. Besides, a total of 548 videos are included in the five courses. We regard the video under each main course's first-level heading as a short course, dividing the five main courses into 49 miniature courses.

Dataset statistics are detailed in Table 1.

Table 1. Dataset statistics.

Dataset	| |	| |	| |	*Pairs +*	| |	| |
NPTEL	382	38	1445	1008	345	343
W-ML	548	49	1171	486	120	120

4.2 Parameter Settings

First, for the Pairwise-Link-LDA model, the parameters we chose are the same as those used in [12]. In particular, we choose the number of topics $K = 100$ and a fixed Dirichlet parameter $\alpha = 0.01$. The Siamese network is pre-trained with a learning rate of 0.0001 and a batch size of 128. For the parameters in node2vec, we have done the same experiment as in [14] to analyze the parameter sensitivity. Except for the parameter being tested, all other parameters assume default values. The best in-out and return hyperparameters were learned using 10-fold cross-validation on 10% labeled data with a grid search over $p, q \in \{0.25, 0.50, 1, 2, 4\}$. Finally, we set dimensions $d = 128$, return parameter $p = 0.25$, in-out parameter $q = 4$, walk length $l = 80$, walks per node $r = 10$ and context size $k = 10$. For the NPTEL dataset, it is worth noting that two concepts do not have related wiki pages, and the calculation result of the cosine similarity of the above two concepts involved is set to 0.

Finally, we choose Random Forest (RF) as the binary classifier.

4.3 Results

The baselines we use are: RefD [2], iPRL [11], PREREQ [12], and MOOC-RF [6]. We compare our method with these baselines using precision (P), recall (R), and F1-score (F1). We summarize the comparing results of different methods across the two datasets in Table 2. We find that our method outperforms baseline methods across both two datasets. For example, the F1-score of our method on NPTEL outperforms PREREQ and MOOC-RF by 18.7% and 8.5%, respectively. Specifically, we have the following observations.

First, RefD achieves relatively high precision but the lowest recall. The reason may be that the interpretation of Wikipedia concepts is different from the teacher's interpretation of knowledge points. Second, the features extracted by MOOC-RF do not fully reflect the information about the prerequisite relations of concepts. Third, PREREQ achieves relatively high recall but with the lowest precision, which tends to identify more concept pairs that have prerequisite relations and will identify more negative samples as positive samples. Finally, even if iPRL considers the information in Wikipedia, its performance is not good due to the incomplete mining of prerequisite relation information and lack of annotated data.

Table 2. Comparison with baselines.

Methods	NPTEL			W-ML		
	P	R	F1	P	R	F1
RefD	68.3	34.7	46.0	72.6	36.4	48.4
iPRL	65.7	46.5	54.4	64.6	46.0	53.7
PREREQ	53.2	70.7	60.7	56.3	71.6	63.0
MOOC-RF	67.9	74.2	70.9	71.7	70.1	70.9
GESN	**76.5**	**82.6**	**79.4**	**75.2**	**83.3**	**79.0**

To get an insight into the importance of different six parts in our method, we perform a contribution analysis. Here, we run our approach seven times on the NPTEL MOOC Dataset. In each of the seven times, one or two parts are removed. We focus on the decrease of the F1-score for each setting. Table 3 lists the evaluation results after ignoring different parts. According to the decrement of F1 scores, we find that all the proposed parts help predict prerequisite relations. Primarily, we observe that SSR, decreasing our best F1-score by 4.5%, plays the most crucial role. On the contrary, with a 1.8% decrease, variants of RefD and the structural features are relatively less important, the cause might be that STD can capture structural information better, and the variants of RefD are sensitive to the length and number of the MOOC videos. We experience a decrease of 2.4% when we do not consider STD, which can more effectively dig out the prerequisite information hidden in MOOCs than the above artificial features. Semantic similarity can also help identify the prerequisite relations between concepts because it provides semantic information not contained in other parts. As for the PageRank difference, with a decrease of 3.7%, it is the same as mentioned in [5] that PageRank difference is an excellent feature. Finally, if we ignore SSR and STD simultaneously, the performance will be significantly affected, reflecting the importance of the proposed two parts.

Table 3. Contribution analysis

Ignored part	Precision	Recall	F1 score
SSR	72.7	77.1	74.9 (-4.5)
STD	73.8	80.7	77.0 (-2.4)
SSR+STD	**72.6**	**75.0**	**73.8 (-5.6)**
Semantic Similarity	74.2	79.8	77.0 (-2.4)
PageRank Difference	72.7	79.0	75.7 (-3.7)
Variants of RefD	74.7	80.8	77.6 (-1.8)
Structural Features	75.3	80.0	77.6 (-1.8)

5 Conclusion

We develop GESN, a supervised learning method, to learn concept prerequisites from MOOCs and Wikipedia. GESN first uses node2vec to capture the semantic and structural relevance between concepts from the Wikipedia-directed graph we built. Second, GESN obtains latent representations of concepts through the Pairwise-Link-LDA model, which are then used to pre-train a Siamese network. The pre-trained Siamese network can output the similarities between the concepts related to topic distribution. Finally, we combine some excellent features and input them together into a binary classifier to identify the prerequisite relations. GESN outperforms state-of-the-art methods on the dataset NPTEL and W-ML in two different domains.

References

1. Hu, C., Xiao, K., Wang, Z., Wang, S., Li, Q.: Extracting prerequisite relations among wikipedia concepts using the clickstream data. In: Qiu, H., Zhang, C., Fei, Z., Qiu, M., Kung, S.-Y. (eds.) KSEM 2021. LNCS (LNAI), vol. 12815, pp. 13–26. Springer, Cham (2021). https://doi.org/10.1007/978-3-030-82136-4_2
2. Liang, C., Wu, Z., Huang, W., Giles, C.L.: Measuring prerequisite relations among concepts. In: EMNLP, pp. 1668–1674 (2015)
3. Gasparetti, F.: Discovering prerequisite relations from educational documents through word embeddings. Futur. Gener. Comput. Syst. **127**, 31–41 (2021)
4. Zhou, Y., Xiao, K., Zhang, Y.: An ensemble learning approach for extracting concept prerequisite relations from Wikipedia. In:International Conference on Mobility, Sensing and Networking (2020)
5. Liang, C., Ye, J., Wang, S., Pursel, B., Lee Giles, C.: Investigating active learning for concept prerequisite learning. In: AAAI (2018)
6. Pan, L., Li, C., Li, J., Tang, J.: Prerequisite relation learning for concepts in MOOCs. In: Proceedings of the 55th Annual Meeting of the Association for Computational Linguistics, vol. 1, pp. 1447–1456 (2017)
7. Adorni, G., Alzetta, C., Koceva, F., Passalacqua, S., Torre, I.: Towards the identification of propaedeutic relations in textbooks. In: Isotani, S., Millán, E., Ogan, A., Hastings, P., McLaren, B., Luckin, R. (eds.) AIED 2019. LNCS (LNAI), vol. 11625, pp. 1–13. Springer, Cham (2019). https://doi.org/10.1007/978-3-030-23204-7_1

8. Perozzi, B., Al-Rfou, R., Skiena, S.: DeepWalk: online learning of social representations. In: KDD, pp. 701–710 (2014)

9. Alzetta, C., Miaschi, A., Adorni, G., Dell'Orletta, F., Koceva, F., Torre, I.: Prerequisite or not prerequisite? That's the problem! an NLP-based approach for concept prerequisite learning. In: CLiC-it (2019)

10. Liang, C., Ye, J., Wu, Z., Pursel, B., Giles, C.: Recovering concept prerequisite relations from university course dependencies. In: AAAI (2017)

11. Lu, W., Zhou, Y., Yu, J., Jia, C.: Concept extraction and prerequisite relation learning from educational data. In: AAAI (2019)

12. Roy, S., Madhyastha, M., Lawrence, S., Rajan, V.: Inferring concept prerequisite relations from online educational resources. In: AAAI (2019)

13. Nallapati, R.M., Ahmed, A., Xing, E P., Cohen, W W.: Joint latent topic models for text and citations. In: KDD, pp. 542–550 (2008)

14. Grover, A., Leskovec, J.: Node2vec: scalable feature learning for networks. In: KDD, pp. 855–864 (2016)

A Comparative Study of Transformers on Word Sense Disambiguation

Avi Chawla[1](✉), Nidhi Mulay[1](✉), Vikas Bishnoi[1](✉), Gaurav Dhama[1](✉), and Anil Kumar Singh[2](✉)

[1] Mastercard AI, Gurgaon, India
{avi.chawla,nidhi.mulay,vikas.bishnoi,gaurav.dhama}@mastercard.com
[2] Indian Institute of Technology (BHU), Varanasi, India
aksingh.cse@iitbhu.ac.in

Abstract. Recent years of research in Natural Language Processing (NLP) have witnessed dramatic growth in training large models for generating context-aware language representations. In this regard, numerous NLP systems have leveraged the power of neural network-based architectures to incorporate sense information in embeddings, resulting in Contextualized Word Embeddings (CWEs). Despite this progress, the NLP community has not witnessed any significant work performing a comparative study on the contextualization power of such architectures. This paper presents a comparative study and an extensive analysis of nine widely adopted Transformer models. These models are BERT, CTRL, DistilBERT, OpenAI-GPT, OpenAI-GPT2, Transformer-XL, XLNet, ELECTRA, and ALBERT. We evaluate their contextualization power using two lexical sample Word Sense Disambiguation (WSD) tasks, SensEval-2 and SensEval-3. We adopt a simple yet effective approach to WSD that uses a k-Nearest Neighbor (kNN) classification on CWEs. Experimental results show that the proposed techniques also achieve superior results over the current state-of-the-art on both the WSD tasks.

Keywords: Word sense disambiguation · Transformers

1 Introduction

Developing powerful language representations technique has been a key area of research in Natural Language Processing (NLP). The employment of effective representational models has also been an essential contributor in improving the performance of many NLP systems. Word vectors or embeddings are fixed-length vectors that are proficient in capturing the semantic properties of words. Emerging from a simple Neural Network-based Word2Vec model and recently transitioning to Contextualised Word Embeddings (CWEs), the advancements have consistently brought a revolution to every NLP sub-domain. The introduction of naive Word2Vec model not only brought an unprecedented increase in the performance of a wide variety of downstream tasks such as Machine Translation, Sentiment

© Springer Nature Switzerland AG 2021
T. Mantoro et al. (Eds.): ICONIP 2021, CCIS 1516, pp. 748–756, 2021.
https://doi.org/10.1007/978-3-030-92307-5_87

Analysis, and Question Answering, but it also laid the foundation for a majority of Natural Language Understanding (NLU) architectures that we use today.

Recent attempts in NLU research have fundamentally focused on generating context-aware word representations, i.e., embeddings that take into account the polysemous nature of words. Polysemy refers to the changes in the meaning of a word when the context around it changes. One related task in NLP is Word Sense Disambiguation (WSD) which deals with the automatic recognition of the correct sense of a word appearing in a specific context. WSD is an essential component of any NLP system as it helps in generating better semantic representations of words.

Contribution: The Transformer architectures implemented in the HuggingFace framework [19] implicitly provide a model for WSD. We test the performance of nine such pre-trained models on WSD and extensively analyse each one of them. These models are BERT [8], OpenAI-GPT [1], OpenAI-GPT2 [13], CTRL [9], DistilBERT [15], Transformer-XL [7], XLNet [20], ELECTRA [5] and ALBERT [10]. This comprehensive study helps us in comparing the ability of different transformer models in incorporating polysemy in embeddings, i.e., their power of segregating various senses of a word in the word-vector space. Through our experiments, we also report a new state-of-the-art on both the lexical sample WSD datasets we experimented on, i.e., SensEval-2 and SensEval-3.

Note: Although the prime use of the CTRL, OpenAI-GPT, and OpenAI-GPT2 model is Natural Language Generation (NLG), we still include them in our comparative study. We do this to determine the extent to which these models consider polysemy while carrying out NLG as their primary objective.

2 Related Work

Word Sense Disambiguation (WSD) is an old and common problem in NLP. In the early days of Artificial Intelligence, WSD was conceived as a fundamental task of Machine Translation [17]. Since then, advancements in NLP have led to the development of a variety of WSD systems. Recent attempts in this respect have tried to tackle the problem by introducing the concept of sense embeddings. For instance, [2] induced sense embeddings using a pre-training based approach. [11] proposed methods that focus on generating sense embeddings using pre-trained word embeddings such as Glove vectors [12]. [16] proposed 'Sense2Vec', which utilized the part-of-speech and named entity tag information to distinguish between different meanings of a word. An extensive survey on further ideas and research on sense representations of words is given by [4].

Most of the recent approaches have leveraged the power of Deep Learning to build WSD systems. [3] proposed an auto-encoder-based approach that goes from the target word embedding back to the word definition. The method proposed by [21] revolved around the computation of sentence context vector for ambiguous words. They adopted a k-Nearest Neighbor (kNN) [6] based approach for classification of ambiguous words. In contrast to all the approaches described above,

Table 1. An overview of the datasets used for the study of nine Transformer Models. Average Sentence Length has been rounded off to the nearest integer.

Dataset	No. of sentences	Avg. sentence length	No. of distinct sense identifiers	No. of sense embeddings	Distinct words	Nouns	Adjectives	Verbs
SensEval-3 Train	7860	30	285	9280	172	3632	308	3879
SensEval-3 Test	3944	30	260	4520	168	1777	153	1999
SensEval-2 Train	8611	29	783	8742	187	3492	1400	2559
SensEval-2 Test	4328	29	620	4385	184	1737	702	1800

[18] proposed a simple yet effective approach for the classification of ambiguous words. Instead of using any pre-trained embeddings like the glove embeddings, they used the BERT [8] to obtain Contextualised Word Embeddings (CWEs). For prediction, they used a kNN based approach. The use of BERT also achieved new state-of-the-art results over previously proposed approaches.

3   Datasets

In our experiments, we use two widely-adopted lexical sample corpora available for WSD, SensEval-2 and SensEval-3. Both come with a train and test set to train and evaluate a WSD model. The words in these datasets are annotated with the sense identifiers defined in WordNet 3.0. A brief overview of both datasets is shown in Table 1. To evaluate the performance of a WSD model, we refer to the testing scripts from the comprehensive framework of [14][1].

4   Experiments

For our experimentation, we take inspiration from a simple yet effective kNN based approach on CWEs to WSD proposed by [18]. This approach uses a cosine similarity-based distance metric for the classification of ambiguous words in the test data. In a nutshell, we obtain the CWEs of all the ambiguous words in the training data by providing their respective contexts to one of the nine contextualization approaches. While classifying an ambiguous word in a test sentence, a kNN classification approach is used, with cosine similarity between the CWE of the ambiguous word and all its instances observed during training as the similarity metric. Such an experiment is carried out for six different values of the hyper-parameter $k \in \{1, 3, 5, 7, 10, 11\}$ in the kNN classifier. An ambiguous word is classified to the sense with the maximum number of nearest neighbors in the "k" nearest neighbors.

We propose few additions to existing approach to improve the overall performance. The first improvement lies in the way data is collected. [18] used the lemma of every word in a sentence to obtain sentences from the dataset. This, in some cases, generated inappropriate sentences such as: *"Nor be this feeling only*

---

[1] https://github.com/getalp/UFSAC.

provoked by the sight or the thought of art, he write. " instead of *"Nor is this feeling only provoked by the sight or the thought of art, he wrote.".* Another sentence collected by their method and our method is *"The art_critic critic be thus bind to consider with care what standard of comparison should be use."* and *"The art critic is thus bound to consider with care what standards of comparison should be used."* respectively. The sentences collected by their method lack a proper grammatical sense and structure. We improve this by collecting the lemma only for ambiguous words and surface form for every other word in the sentence.

Our second improvement is an empirical finding. While obtaining the CWEs from BERT, they treated the concatenation of the output of the last four layers of BERT as the word embeddings. Instead, we used only the final layer of BERT to obtain the embedding of a word.

5   Experimental Results

To study and analyze each of the transformer models in detail, we conduct three rounds of experiments. In the first round, we carry out the task of WSD on nine pre-trained Transformer architectures using the kNN approach described above and compare their performance on two WSD Lexical Sample tasks. Further, to visualize each model's power to separate different senses of a word in their embedding space, we draw the t-SNE plots for the CWEs generated by the transformer models. Lastly, we provide a qualitative analysis by examining the correct predictions and the wrong predictions made by each of our WSD models.

5.1   Contextualized Embeddings

To compare the models based on their contextualization power, we perform the task of WSD using the language representation provided by them. Table 2 lists the results obtained by each of these models for $k \in \{1, 3, 5, 7, 10, 11\}$. The BERT model achieved a new state-of-the-art on the SensEval-2 and SensEval-3 tasks [18]. The modification also facilitates the DistilBERT model in beating the current state-of-the-art on SensEval-3 dataset. Also, it becomes evident from the results obtained by the ALBERT and the DistilBERT model that they highly resemble BERT's architecture. Through our observations, we also state that the employment of DistilBERT and ALBERT in place of BERT could take off a major overhead of the training time without incurring a significant loss in the performance.

An unexpected drop in performance is observed for the XLNet and Transformer-XL model compared to the other well-performing models. Though both the models are effective on various NLP tasks using their powerful recurrence-based Transformer architectures, we notice that the model still underperforms.

Coming towards the end, the three NLG models—OpenAI-GPT, OpenAI-GPT2, and CTRL also performed poorly. CTRL and OpenAI-GPT2 performed slightly better than the Most Frequent Sense (MFS) baseline on SensEval-3 dataset. In addition to this, they even failed to beat the MFS baseline on the SensEval-2 dataset, demonstrating that they are ineffective in capturing polysemy.

Table 2. Results (F1%) of all the Transformer models for different values of k on the k-Nearest Neighbor classification approach vs. the Most Frequent Sense (MFS) baseline and current state-of-the-art results. The Best results for each model are underlined, and the best result on a particular dataset is bold. The previous state-of-the-art is in italics.

Model	SensEval-2						SensEval-3					
	$k=1$	$k=3$	$k=5$	$k=7$	$k=10$	$k=11$	$k=1$	$k=3$	$k=5$	$k=7$	$k=10$	$k=11$
BERT	76.02	76.78	76.62	76.62	76.76	**76.81**	79.40	80.31	80.49	**80.96**	80.75	80.72
DistilBERT	74.81	75.64	75.36	75.43	75.41	75.43	78.62	79.71	80.05	80.15	80.23	80.07
ALBERT	74.84	75.33	75.43	74.98	75.07	75.07	77.94	78.93	79.44	79.60	79.71	79.57
XLNet	64.74	66.24	66.48	66.45	66.38	66.45	69.97	70.64	71.50	71.78	71.42	71.42
ELECTRA	65.98	65.88	65.98	66.10	66.07	65.95	69.45	70.10	70.82	71.14	71.11	71.01
GPT	59.80	60.84	61.29	61.24	61.15	61.54	65.63	67.65	68.51	69.29	69.58	69.60
Trans-XL	53.36	54.35	55.01	55.18	55.01	54.45	62.07	62.82	63.32	63.99	63.50	63.50
CTRL	52.39	53.64	54.28	54.45	54.49	54.82	58.09	60.38	60.92	61.50	61.78	61.63
GPT2	50.96	53.57	53.88	53.88	53.86	53.80	57.03	59.83	60.92	61.21	61.29	61.19
MFS	54.79						58.95					
kNN [18]	*76.52*						*80.12*					

5.2 Sense-Space Analysis Using t-SNE Plots

To understand and interpret a model's power to segregate different senses of a word in the embedding space, we draw the t-SNE plots of the embeddings obtained for the word 'bank' from the training data of SensEval-3 for each of the nine models. Figure 1 represents the t-SNE plots thus obtained. Sub-figure 1.(j) represents the interpretable meanings of the senses represented in the t-SNE plots along with their respective frequencies in the SensEval-3 training corpus. We exclude any sense with a frequency of less than three from the t-SNE plot for clarity. It is evident from the t-SNE plot of OpenAI-GPT2 that it hardly distinguishes between different senses, and we see this as a possible reason why its accuracy is very close to the MFS baseline. As all the sense embeddings are in the vicinity of each other, the model hardly learns any decision boundary for sense classification. Therefore, the approach performs slightly better than the MFS baseline. We can draw a similar conclusion by observing the t-SNE plots of CTRL and Transformer-XL, implying that the NLG objective of OpenAI-GPT2 and CTRL hardly takes polysemy into account.

On the other hand, plots obtained for the OpenAI-GPT, ELECTRA, and XLNet models depict that these models capture polysemy relatively better than the NLG models. They do stress a little on making a distinction between different senses of a word. Lastly, models that performed the best among the nine models we experimented on are BERT, DistilBERT, and ALBERT. These models possess exceptional proficiency in identifying polysemy, which is evident from their t-SNE plots as well as their accuracy on both the datasets.

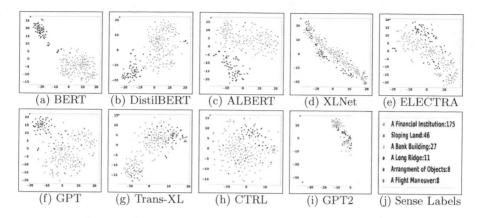

Fig. 1. t-SNE plots of different senses of 'bank' and their contextualized embeddings. The legend(shown separately in Sub-figure (j)) shows a short description of the respective WordNet sense and the frequency of occurrence in the training data. We used the SensEval-3 training dataset for obtaining these plots.

5.3   Additional Experiments

Part-of-Speech information of a word has been regarded as a crucial influencer in determining its possible sense. [18] proposed a POS-sensitive approach to WSD for the determination of the sense of an ambiguous word. Their experiments resulted in an accuracy lift of approximately 2–3 F1 on the SemEval datasets. Still, this approach did not prove to be beneficial for models trained on SensEval-2 and SensEval-3 datasets. This was because each word in these datasets is annotated with only one POS. Aligning our analysis on similar lines, as a final set of error analyses in our comparative study, we attempt to understand each model's behavior to different POS tags. We estimate the percentage of correct classifications made by each model for Nouns, Verbs, and Adjectives in the two datasets. This is presented in Table 3 for $k = 1$.

For SensEval-2 dataset, we observe that each model was able to classify both Nouns and Adjectives correctly to a considerable extent. But, for Verbs, a difference of approximately 15–20% was observed from that of Nouns and Adjectives. A similar drop in classification accuracy was observed in SensEval-3 for Adjectives. Each model classified Nouns and Verbs in this dataset to a reasonable extent but underperformed during the classification of Adjectives.

Table 3. The percentage of correct classifications made by the models for Nouns, Verbs and Adjectives on SensEval-2 Test and SensEval-3 Test data. The values are for $k = 1$. The best results on a particular POS tag have been marked in bold.

Model	SensEval-2			SensEval-3		
	Nouns	Verbs	Adj	Nouns	Verbs	Adj
BERT	**81.64**	**67.22**	**81.62**	**78.17**	82.33	**56.86**
DistilBERT	81.00	65.61	80.06	76.14	**82.86**	54.25
ALBERT	82.38	64.33	80.06	75.63	81.87	55.56
XLNet	71.50	56.39	66.81	67.92	73.58	48.37
ELECTRA	75.30	54.83	68.80	67.02	73.16	50.98
OpenAI-GPT	70.87	47.44	64.10	64.15	68.06	52.29
Tranformer-XL	61.95	42.67	59.54	60.89	64.36	47.06
CTRL	62.29	41.11	56.84	57.01	60.55	39.87
OpenAI-GPT2	55.79	42.72	60.11	51.55	63.42	40.52

6   Conclusion

In this paper, we evaluated the contextualisation power of nine pre-trained Transformer Models on a WSD task. We presented a comparative study on each model's power to capture polysemy in the embeddings they generate. To accomplish this, we used a kNN based approach to WSD proposed by [18] and proposed two improvements in their method that also accompanied us in establishing a new state-of-the-art on WSD Lexical Sample Task of SensEval-2 and SensEval-3. We concluded our study by stating that BERT, DistilBERT, and ALBERT models prove out to be most effective on the WSD task solely based on text encodings they provide. We found these models to possess an extraordinary potential to identify a word's different senses compared to all the other models.

As future work, we plan to make use of POS information as well to classify an ambiguous word. We firmly believe that incorporating POS information in WSD could be very useful and further increase the performance of these models. In addition to this, we also believe that fine-tuning these models could be a potential area of focus. In our experiments, we leveraged the pre-trained models as provided by the authors, and a bit of fine-tuning could be beneficial.

References

1. Radford, A., Narasimhan, K., Salimans, T., Sutskever., I.: Improving language understanding by generative pre-training (2018)
2. Bartunov, S., Kondrashkin, D., Osokin, A., Vetrov, D.: Breaking sticks and ambiguities with adaptive skip-gram. In: Proceedings of the International Conference on Artificial Intelligence and Statistics (AISTATS), Cadiz, Spain, pp. 130–138 (2016)

3. Bosc, T., Vincent, P.: Auto-encoding dictionary definitions into consistent word embeddings. In: Proceedings of the 2018 Conference on Empirical Methods in Natural Language Processing, pp. 1522–1532. Association for Computational Linguistics, Brussels (2018). https://doi.org/10.18653/v1/D18-1181, https://www.aclweb.org/anthology/D18-1181

4. Camacho-Collados, J., Pilehvar, M.T.: From word to sense embeddings: a survey on vector representations of meaning (2018). CoRR abs/1805.04032, http://arxiv.org/abs/1805.04032

5. Clark, K., Luong, M.T., Le, Q.V., Manning, C.D.: ELECTRA: pre-training text encoders as discriminators rather than generators. In: ICLR (2020). https://openreview.net/pdf?id=r1xMH1BtvB

6. Cover, T., Hart, P.: Nearest neighbor pattern classification. IEEE Trans. Inf. Theory **13**(1), 21–27 (1967)

7. Dai, Z., Yang, Z., Yang, Y., Carbonell, J.G., Le, Q.V., Salakhutdinov, R.: Transformer-xl: attentive language models beyond a fixed-length context (2019). CoRR abs/1901.02860, http://arxiv.org/abs/1901.02860

8. Devlin, J., Chang, M.W., Lee, K., Toutanova, K.: BERT: pre-training of deep bidirectional transformers for language understanding (2018). arXiv preprint arXiv:1810.04805

9. Keskar, N.S., McCann, B., Varshney, L., Xiong, C., Socher, R.: CTRL - a conditional transformer language model for controllable generation (2019). arXiv preprint arXiv:1909.05858

10. Lan, Z., Chen, M., Goodman, S., Gimpel, K., Sharma, P., Soricut, R.: Albert: a lite bert for self-supervised learning of language representations (2019)

11. Pelevina, M., Arefiev, N., Biemann, C., Panchenko, A.: Making sense of word embeddings. In: Proceedings of the 1st Workshop on Representation Learning for NLP, Berlin, Germany, pp. 174–183 (2016)

12. Pennington, J., Socher, R., Manning, C.D.: Glove: global vectors for word representation. In: Empirical Methods in Natural Language Processing (EMNLP), pp. 1532–1543 (2014). http://www.aclweb.org/anthology/D14-1162

13. Radford, A., Wu, J., Child, R., Luan, D., Amodei, D., Sutskever, I.: Language models are unsupervised multitask learners (2019)

14. Raganato, A., Camacho-Collados, J., Navigli, R.: Word sense disambiguation: a unified evaluation framework and empirical comparison. In: Proceedings of the 15th Conference of the European Chapter of the Association for Computational Linguistics, vol. 1, Long Papers, Valencia, Spain, pp. 99–110 (2017)

15. Sanh, V., Debut, L., Chaumond, J., Wolf, T.: Distilbert, a distilled version of bert: smaller, faster, cheaper and lighter (2019)

16. Trask, A., Michalak, P., Liu, J.: sense2vec - a fast and accurate method for word sense disambiguation in neural word embeddings (2015). CoRR abs/1511.06388, http://arxiv.org/abs/1511.06388

17. Weaver, W.: Machine Translation of Languages: Fourteen Essays. Technology Press of M.I.T, Cambridge (1955)

18. Wiedemann, G., Remus, S., Chawla, A., Biemann, C.: Does bert make any sense? interpretable word sense disambiguation with contextualized embeddings (2019). ArXiv abs/1909.10430

19. Wolf, T., et al.: Huggingface's transformers: state-of-the-art natural language processing (2019). ArXiv abs/1910.03771

20. Yang, Z., Dai, Z., Yang, Y., Carbonell, J.G., Salakhutdinov, R., Le, Q.V.: Xlnet: generalized autoregressive pretraining for language understanding (2019). CoRR abs/1906.08237, http://arxiv.org/abs/1906.08237
21. Yuan, D., Richardson, J., Doherty, R., Evans, C., Altendorf, E.: Semi-supervised word sense disambiguation with neural models. In: Proceedings of COLING 2016, the 26th International Conference on Computational Linguistics: Technical Papers, Osaka, Japan, pp. 1374–1385 (2016)

A Segment-Based Layout Aware Model for Information Extraction on Document Images

Maizhen Ning[1], Qiu-Feng Wang[1(✉)], Kaizhu Huang[1], and Xiaowei Huang[2]

[1] School of Advanced Technology, Xi'an Jiaotong-Liverpool University,
Suzhou, China
Maizhen.Ning16@student.xjtlu.edu.cn,
{Qiufeng.Wang,Kaizhu.Huang}@xjtlu.edu.cn
[2] Department of Computer Science, University of Liverpool, Liverpool, UK
Xiaowei.Huang@liverpool.ac.uk

Abstract. Information extraction (IE) on document images has attracted considerable attention recently due to its great potentials for intelligent document analysis, where visual layout information is vital. However, most existing works mainly consider visual layout information at the token level, which unfortunately ignore long contexts and require time-consuming annotation. In this paper, we propose to model document visual layout information at the segment level. First, we obtain segment representation by integrating the segment-level layout information and text embedding. Since only segment-level layout annotation is needed, our model enjoys a low cost in comparison with the full annotation as needed at the token level. Then, word vectors are also extracted from each text segment to get the fine-grained representation. Finally, both segment and word vectors are fused for obtaining prediction results. Extensive experiments on the benchmark datasets are conducted to demonstrate the effectiveness of our novel method.

Keywords: Document intelligence · Information extraction · Visual layout information · Segment representation · Weak annotation

1 Introduction

Recently, information extraction (IE) on document images (e.g., receipts and form documents) has attracted much interest and widely studied in document analysis [1,2]. Over the years, researchers have attempted to consider IE as a sequence tagging task (e.g., Named Entity Recognition) with deep neural networks [3] and obtained great success in textual IE [4,5]. Nevertheless, visual information is seldom considered in these methods. As indicated on form understanding in noisy scanned documents [6], the visual information such as document layout plays a vital role for document understanding. To this end, some works pre-determine rules and exploit template/regex matching on simple visual

© Springer Nature Switzerland AG 2021
T. Mantoro et al. (Eds.): ICONIP 2021, CCIS 1516, pp. 757–765, 2021.
https://doi.org/10.1007/978-3-030-92307-5_88

information [7], which proves difficult to design and re-use. To fully utilize visual layout information, Katti et al. proposed to map document images to the character level with visual information [8]. However, the annotation at the character level is time-consuming and defective to process long texts.

In recent years, pre-training method have been demonstrated successfully in numerous NLP tasks [9,10], however, most of these models only focus on texts ignoring valuable visual features. To tackle this drawback in document IE, Xu et al. [11] proposed LayoutLM to fuse text and 2-D spatial layout information in documents. Although LayoutLM has achieved great success in various document understanding tasks, this model is limited to token-level architecture. On one hand, LayoutLM is incapable of modeling long texts due to its quadratically increasing memory and time consumption [12]; on the other hand, the token-level annotation is very time-consuming.

Fig. 1. Examples of different input levels to the IE model. (a) Word-level tokens, (b) Segment level. Each color represents one word or segment.

To alleviate these issues, we propose a segment-based layout aware model for information extraction on document images. In this model, only segment-level layout information is considered, enabling a much easier annotation. In addition, the segment-based model can capture longer contexts since each segment has multiple words. As shown in Fig. 1, there are eighteen words in the existing LayoutLM (Fig. 1(a)), while ours (Fig. 1(b)) only contains nine segments in the sequence. We evaluate our model on three benchmark datasets, i.e., CORD [13], SROIE [1], and FUNSD [6], and extensive experimental results show its effectiveness. The main contributions of this paper can be summarised as: **(1)** We propose a segment-based layout aware model for IE task on document images, which can capture long contexts. In addition, our model requires layout position only at segment-level annotation, which enjoys a lower cost in comparison with the full annotation at the token level. **(2)** We conduct a series of experiments on benchmark datasets, which validate the effectiveness of our model. Specifically, on benchmark datasets of FUNSD and CORD, we attain higher accuracy than that of the LayoutLM model with full annotation.

2   Related Work

In past decades, numerous rule-based and learning-based studies on information extraction were conducted [14], however, these rules are hard to extend in various documents. Recently, numerous deep learning methods showed powerful modeling ability on a variety of tasks [3]. To represent natural text order and context information, recurrent neural networks (RNNs) have been utilized in various sequence labeling tasks [5,15]. In contrast with textual IE, the visual layout information plays an important role in the document IE task. Yang et al. [16] integrated pixel-level visual information with the document textual information under the heuristic framework. To model the relationship of visual layout information, graph convolutional networks (GCN) [17] have been applied in the document understanding [18]. However, it is challenged to construct suitable graphs.

Recently, the pre-training techniques and attention mechanism [19] have been widely used in NLP and CV tasks, where BERT [9] is the representative work. Specifically, BERT utilize tokenized and embedded text with token's corresponding order position as inputs of the multi-layer Transformers. Through the segment prediction and masked language modeling pre-training tasks, BERT is able to obtain contextualized representations of texts. However, BERT-like models [10] usually only focus on textual information without spatial layout information of texts in documents. To overcome this issue, Xu et al. [11] proposed the LayoutLM model to fuse layout information with texts. In the LayoutLM, document visually 2-D layout information is aligned with embedded texts and 1-D token order as the input of multi-layer Transformers (i.e., BERT). Nevertheless, it focuses on the token-level features, which is difficult to capture long contexts in the document due to its quadratically increasing model complexity [12].

3   Methodology

In this paper, we propose to integrate the segment-level layout information in the IE framework, which is shown in Fig. 2 including three parts: input, segment modeling and information extraction. In the input block, we require the segment-level annotation on the document image, including text segments (S_i) and their layout spatial information (B_i, e.g., 2-D box). The block of segment modeling

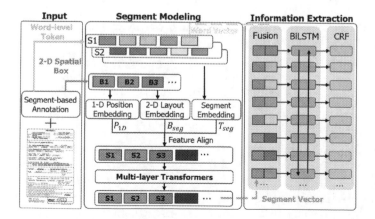

Fig. 2. The system framework including Input, Segment modeling and IE.

is the core part of the proposed method, where we aim to obtain each segment representation. In the IE block, we adopt a general IE framework by BiLSTM and CRF. More details will be given in the following parts.

3.1 Segment Modeling

In the segment modeling, we intend to learn segment-level context semantic information, which is obtained by the combination of three sources: text segment embedding, 2-D layout embedding, and 1-D position embedding.

Text Segment Embedding. We obtain text segment embedding (t_{seg}) from the sequence of word vectors, which are output by a pre-trained BERT model. Based on the work [20], we discussed four methods to get the segment embedding from the BERT model in our experiments: (1) **SE1**: simply using the representation of $[CLS]$ of the last layer; (2) **SE2**: mean value of all tokens from the last layer; (3) **SE3**: mean value of all tokens from the second last layer; (4) **SE4**: mean value of all tokens from the last two layers. Hence, all segment-level text embedding can be represented $T_{seg} = (t_{seg_1}, t_{seg_2}, \ldots, t_{seg_n})$, where n means the number of segments in this document.

Layout Position Embedding. In the annotation, we have one 2-D spatial position box $b = (x_1, y_1, x_2, y_2)$ for each segment representing top-left and bottom-right corner, with the coordinate origin at the document top-left corner. In addition, the height (h) and width (w) of each box are considered. We first encode all of these layout information to vector representation by separate trainable layers E_x, E_y, E_h, E_w for x and y coordinates, height and width, respectively [11], then these vectors are added to get the segment layout embedding $b_{seg} = (E_x(x_1) + E_x(x_2) + E_y(y_1) + E_y(y_2) + E_h(h) + E_w(w))$, finally, all segments layout embedding can be represented by $B_{seg} = (b_{seg_1}, b_{seg_2}, \ldots, b_{seg_n})$.

1-D Position Embedding. To keep the order information of each segment in the whole document, we put the 1-D position embedding in our model. According to the annotation, we can get the index for each segment in the document. Then, the 1-D position (index) is mapped to the vector representation by a trainable layer E_p. Finally, all 1-D position embedding in the document can be represented by $P_{1D} = (p_{seg_1}, p_{seg_2}, \ldots, p_{seg_n})$.

Feature Align. All the embedded features in one document are aligned based on their indices and added together by: $s_k = t_{seg_k} + b_{seg_k} + p_{seg_k}$, then the aligned features $S = (s_1, s_2, \ldots, s_n)$ are transformed by the multi-layer transformers (e.g., LayoutLM [11]) to obtain the final segment vectors for the document $\widehat{S} = (\widehat{s}_1, \widehat{s}_2, \ldots, \widehat{s}_n)$, which will be input to the next IE block.

Training. The segment modeling is optimized to correctly predict the segment class, which is defined by its entity class[1]. We use the cross entropy loss in Eq. (1) as the training loss:

$$\mathcal{L}_{SegModel} = -\frac{1}{N} \sum_{i=1}^{N} \sum_{j=1}^{C} p_{i,j} \log(q_{i,j}) \tag{1}$$

where $p_{i,j} = 1$ if the label of the segment i is the class j, otherwise $p_{i,j} = 0$; the probability $q_{i,j}$ denotes the prediction probability of segment i belonging to class j, N is the number of segments and C is the number of classes.

3.2 Information Extraction

Once we obtain all segment representation in the document, we can adopt the popular IE framework to predict the final result, which contains three steps as shown in Fig. 2: Fusion, BiLSTM and CRF. We firstly fuse word-level features with corresponding segment-level features to get input sequence features F_{IE_k} of the kth segment: $F_{IE_k} = [(T_{k_1} \oplus \widehat{s_k}), (T_{k_2} \oplus \widehat{s_k}), \dots, (T_{k_N} \oplus \widehat{s_k})]$, where $\widehat{s_k}$ is the final segment vector for the kth segment, T_{k_n} is the word-embedding vector from the embedding layer of the pre-trained BERT for the nth token in the kth segment, symbol $\oplus$ denotes concatenation operation. In this fusion, the word-level features are used to represent the local detailed information, while the segment-level features can capture long contexts in the whole document. Then, this sequence is input to the BiLSTM to model the context information, which can learn both forward and backward direction contexts to better understand semantics. Finally, CRF layer can help to capture the relationship between output labels in the sequence, and output the prediction results. To train this module, we minimize the negative log-likelihood loss between the prediction entity sequence and the ground truth.

4 Experiments

In this section, we will verify the proposed method on three benchmark datasets, including a dataset of noisy scanned form documents **FUNSD** [6], and two scanned receipt datasets **CORD** [13] and **SROIE** [1]. In our system, the training of segment modelling and IE framework is separated. The segment modelling is trained by the segment classification task, and the class numbers are 5, 4 and 30 for the dataset of SROIE, FUNSD and CORD, respectively. All experiments were conducted by PyTorch framework on 4 NVIDIA GTX-1080Ti GPUs.

4.1 Segment Modeling

In this section, we conducted experiments on the dataset of FUNSD for the segment modeling as shown in the Subsect. 3.1, including layout position

---

[1] We assume each segment only contains one entity class.

embedding, 1-D position embedding and text segment embedding, and we use the accuracy of segment classification as the evaluation metric.

To verify the effectiveness of 2-D layout position embedding, we remove it from the feature alignment model (i.e., removing b_{seg}), and the results can be found in Table 1. We can see that the performance is decreased significantly from 82.63% to 81.13%, which demonstrates the effectiveness of the spatial layout information. Hence, the 2-D layout information is integrated by default.

Similarly, we evaluate the effectiveness of the 1-D position embedding (p_{seg}) by removing it in the feature alignment model, and the results are reported in Table 2. We can see that the accuracy is decreased significantly from 95.41% to 92.98% on the dataset CORD, which demonstrates the effectiveness of the 1-D position embedding. This is because the 1-D position embedding can capture semantic order in the text sequence [9]. However, the accuracy is increased instead on the dataset FUNSD. This is because the 1-D position in the FUNSD is not correct, which is from OCR output ignoring the segment index. Hence, we remove the 1-D position embedding on the FUNSD in the following experiments.

We evaluate the four methods to obtain the text segment embedding, namely **SE1**, **SE2**, **SE3**, **SE4** as shown in the Subect. 3.1, and the results are shown in Table 3. We can see that accuracy of the method **SE2** (i.e., the mean of the last layer) is the lowest, and the reason is that this layer is usually over-fitted to the pre-training tasks. Similarly, the accuracy of the method **SE1** ([CLS] representation) is not high. Among this four methods, we can see the method **SE4** (combination of last two layers) obtains the best performance. Hence, we adopt this method to obtain the text segment embedding in the following experiments.

Table 1. Performance (%) of 2-D spatial layout embedding on FUNSD

	Accuracy
Without 2-D Spatial Box	81.13
With 2-D Spatial Box	**82.63**

Table 2. Accuracy (%) of 1-D position embedding

	FUNSD	CORD
Without 1-D Position	**84.21**	92.98
With 1-D Position	82.63	**95.41**

Table 3. Performance (%) of different **SE** methods on FUNSD

Segment embedding method	SE1	SE2	SE3	SE4
Accuracy	82.55	81.60	82.89	**84.21**

Table 4. Performance (%) of information extraction. The work [11] is trained on the full annotation dataset, while ours is only on the partial annotation dataset.

Dataset	FUNSD			CORD			SROIE		
Performance	Precision	Recall	F1	Precision	Recall	F1	Precision	Recall	F1
BERT [9]	54.69	67.10	60.26	88.33	91.07	89.86	90.99	90.99	90.99
LayoutLM [11]	75.97	81.55	78.66	94.36	95.08	94.72	**94.38**	**94.38**	**94.38**
Ours	**78.42**	**83.93**	**81.09**	94.40	**95.14**	**94.77**	93.03	93.03	93.03

4.2   Performance of Information Extraction

In this section, we verify the effectiveness of our method on the IE task. We compare two representative approaches, i.e., BERT [9] and LayoutLM [11]. In BERT, there is not any spatial layout information. Table 4 reports the experimental results, and we can see that our proposed model obtains better performance than BERT in all datasets, which demonstrates the benefit of the layout spatial information. Compared to the LayoutLM, our model gets better performance on FUNSD, competitive performance on CORD, and lower performance on SORIE.

On the dataset of FUNSD, our proposed method can extract latent relationship over segments, and capture segment-level information with box position to better understand form documents, Hence, the proposed method increases the F1 value from 78.66% to 81.09% with the comparison to LayoutLM. On receipt documents, our method achieved competitive performance with reasonable OCR segment orders, although we only utilize the weak annotation on the segment-level. We increased CORD recall from 95.08% to 95.14% with ordered segment sequence, which shows that our method effectively obtains additional segment-level information to extract target information. On the dataset of SROIE, the LayoutLM obtains better performance due to the relatively fixed formats and the normal reading order, and another reason is that the LayoutLM is trained on the full annotation dataset (i.e., token-level) while our model is only on the partially annotated dataset (i.e., segment-level).

5   Conclusion

In this paper, we proposed a layout aware model for IE on document images, which integrates both segment-level and word-level features. We fuse the segment-level layout, text and order information then concatenated with word-level text features as the input of a general IE framework. Compared to the existing models, our model can capture long contexts including both layout and text contexts in the document, which are beneficial to the IE performance. In addition, our model only requires the weak annotation at the segment level, which is of lower cost in comparison with the full annotation at the word level. The evaluation on three benchmark datasets demonstrated its effectiveness. Specifically, we obtain even higher accuracy than that of the fully annotated LayoutLM on the datasets of FUNSD and CORD. In future, we will focus on the unsupervised learning in the document IE task, to reduce the annotation cost further.

Acknowledgments. The work was partially supported by the following: National Natural Science Foundation of China under no. 61876154 and no. 61876155; Jiangsu Science and Technology Programme (Natural Science Foundation of Jiangsu Province) under no. BE2020006-4 and BK20181190; Key Program Special Fund in XJTLU under no. KSF-T-06, KSF-E-26, and KSF-A-10, and XJTLU Research Development Fund RDF-16-02-49.

References

1. Huang, Z., Chen, K., He, J., et al.: ICDAR2019 competition on scanned receipt OCR and information extraction. In: 2019 International Conference on Document Analysis and Recognition (ICDAR), pp. 1516–1520 (2019)
2. Wang, J., Liu, C., Jin, L., et al.: Towards robust visual information extraction in real world: new dataset and novel solution. In: The Thirty-Fifth AAAI Conference on Artificial Intelligence (AAAI), pp. 2738–2745 (2021)
3. Huang, K., Hussain, A., Wang, Q., Zhang, R. (eds.): Deep Learning: Fundamentals, Theory and Applications. Cognitive Computation Trends, vol. 2. Springer, Cham (2019). https://doi.org/10.1007/978-3-030-06073-2
4. Shaalan, K.: A survey of Arabic named entity recognition and classification. Comput. Linguist. **10**(2), 469–510 (2014)
5. Ma, X., Hovy, E.: End-to-end sequence labeling via bi-directional LSTM-CNNs-CRF. In: Proceedings of the 54th Annual Meeting of the Association for Computational Linguistics, pp. 1064–1074 (2016)
6. Jaume, G., Ekenel, H.K., Thiran, J.: FUNSD: a dataset for form understanding in noisy scanned documents. In: Accepted to ICDAR-OST (2019)
7. Schuster, D., Muthmann, K., Esser, D., et al.: Intellix-end-user trained information extraction for document archiving. In: 2013 12th International Conference on Document Analysis and Recognition, pp. 101–105 (2013)
8. Katti, A.R., Reisswig, C., Guder, C., et al.: Chargrid: towards understanding 2D documents. In: Proceedings of the 2018 Conference on Empirical Methods in Natural Language Processing, pp. 4459–4469 (2018)
9. Devlin, J., Chang, M., Lee, K., et al.: BERT: pre-training of deep bidirectional transformers for language understanding. In: Proceedings of the 2019 Conference of the North American Chapter of the Association for Computational Linguistics: Human Language Technologies, pp. 4171–4186 (2019)
10. Liu, Y., Ott, M., Goyal, N., et al.: RoBERTa: a robustly optimized BERT pre-training approach (2019). arXiv preprint arXiv:1907.11692
11. Xu, Y., Li, M., Cui, L., et al.: LayoutLM: pre-training of text and layout for document image understanding. In: 26th ACM SIGKDD International Conference on Knowledge Discovery & Data Mining, pp. 1192–1200 (2020)
12. Ding, M., Zhou, C., Yang, H., et al.: CogLTX: applying BERT to long texts. In: 34th Conference on Neural Information Processing Systems (NeurIPS 2020) (2020)
13. Park, S., Shin, S., Lee, B., et al.: CORD: a consolidated receipt dataset for post-OCR parsing. In: Document Intelligence Workshop at NeurIPS 2019 (2019)
14. Schuster, D., Muthmann, K., Esser, D., et al.: Intellix - end-user trained information extraction for document archiving. In: 2013 International Conference on Document Analysis and Recognition, pp. 101–105 (2013)
15. Sage, C., Aussem, A., Elghazel, H., et al.: Recurrent neural network approach for table field extraction in business documents. In: 2019 International Conference on Document Analysis and Recognition, pp. 1308–1313 (2019)
16. Yang, X., Yumer, E., Asente, P., et al.: Learning to extract semantic structure from documents using multimodal fully convolutional neural network. In: 2017 IEEE Conference on Computer Vision and Pattern Recognition (CVPR), pp. 4342–4351 (2017)
17. Kipf, T., Welling, M.: Semi-supervised classification with graph convolutional networks. In: 5th International Conference on Learning Representations (2017)

18. Wang, S., Zhang, Y., Che, W., et al.: Joint extraction of entities and relations based on a novel graph scheme. In: Proceedings of the Twenty-Seventh International Joint Conference on Artificial Intelligence (IJCAI-18), pp. 4461–4467 (2018)
19. Vaswani, A., Shazeer, N., Parmar, N., et al.: Attention is all you need. In: Proceedings of the 31st International Conference on Neural Information Processing Systems, pp. 6000–6010 (2017)
20. Reimers, N., Gurevych, I.: Sentence-BERT: sentence embeddings using siamese BERT-networks. In: Proceedings of the 2019 Conference on Empirical Methods in Natural Language Processing and the 9th International Joint Conference on Natural Language Processing (EMNLP-IJCNLP), pp. 3982–3992 (2019)

Question Answering over Knowledge Base Embeddings with Triples Representation Learning

Zicheng Zuo[1] , Zhenfang Zhu[1](✉) , Wenqing Wu[1], Qiang Lu[1] ,
Dianyuan Zhang[1], Wenling Wang[2](✉), and Guangyuan Zhang[1](✉)

[1] School of Information Science and Electrical Engineering,
Shandong Jiaotong University, Jinan 250357, China
zhuzf@sdjtu.edu.cn
[2] Ludong University, Yantai 264010, China

Abstract. Question answering based on knowledge graph aims to help users answer natural language questions through the facts in the knowledge graph without the user needing to understand its data structure. This is a challenging task because it is difficult for machines to correctly understand the semantics of the question. For machines to understand semantics correctly, we need to face two challenges. One is that different entities connected by the same predicate. The other one is entity ambiguity. The entity usually has different expressions which makes the number of candidate answers become huge. To solve these problems, we propose an elegant method named TRL-KEQA. It doesn't directly infer its subject and predicate, but restores the vector representation of the subject and predicate of the problem in KG embedding space. And syntactic analysis is used to construct the connection between the predicate and the entity. This connection is aggregated into the vector representation of the predicate. According to a well-designed joint distance metric, the fact which has learned vector is closest in KG will be returned as the answer. Experiments conducted on widely adopted benchmarks show that the proposed model is superior to the latest KBQA method.

Keywords: Question answering · Knowledge graph embedding · Triples representation

1 Introduction

With the rise of large-scale knowledge graphs such as Wikidata, DBPedia, Yago and NELL, question answering based on knowledge base or knowledge graph (hereinafter referred to as KBQA or KGQA) has become a crucial task. It gives a natural language question by a user, the machine converts it into a structured query (such as SPARQL) and returns an entity in knowledge graphs as the result. In KGQA, how to correctly understand the semantic information of a question is the key to answering question. At present, commonly used methods are based on semantic parsing and information retrieval.

© Springer Nature Switzerland AG 2021
T. Mantoro et al. (Eds.): ICONIP 2021, CCIS 1516, pp. 766–773, 2021.
https://doi.org/10.1007/978-3-030-92307-5_89

The main idea of semantic parsing is to transform natural language into a series of formal logical forms [1, 2]. The method based on information retrieval is to extract the entity from the question. Then search the subgraph connected with the entity according to the rules. Finally, select the answer according to scoring function [3]. However, the disadvantages of the above two methods are that the training data is difficult to annotation and the complexity of the algorithm increases exponentially when the question is complex. Owing to entity ambiguity and omission, it is hardly to accurately find the correct meaning of the question. In order to solve the above problem, we make the following contributions in this paper:

1. Based on the difference between predicate representation and entity representation, we use different modules to perform predicate learning and entity learning.
2. For the first time, dependency parsing is applied to question answering tasks based on information retrieval. We use dependency parsing to build the connection between the predicate and the entity, and integrate the representation information of the entity into the vector representation of the predicate.
3. Through experiments on real world datasets, we have proved the effectiveness of TRL-KEQA on the most advanced baseline.

2   Related Work

In previous work [4], it was proposed to extract specific subgraphs to answer questions. Recently, there is a method [5] to project the subgraph generated by the tail entity into a high-dimensional space for question answering. Method like [2] used high-dimensional embedding of learning knowledge through a memory network to complete the QA task. The method proposed by Bordes et al. [6] learns the similarity function, scores the question and corresponding triples during training, uses all candidate triples to score the question during testing, and selects the entity with the highest score as the answer. Method like [7] learns a scoring function to rank candidate triples. Recently there exists a work [8] which introduce the text corpus as external knowledge into the knowledge graph to handle the question answering. This method is effective when the KG is incomplete, but external knowledge is not always available. Recently, people use KG embedding to complete question answering [9]. KG embedding can handle the incompleteness of KG and retain the potential semantic information.

The most commonly used method of knowledge graph embedding in question answering task is TransE [10]. This method represents the entity and the relationship in the same space, and regards the relationship vector $\mathbf{r}$ as the translation between the head entity vector $\mathbf{h}$ and the tail entity vector $\mathbf{t}$, that is $h + r \approx t$. A previous method like [11] shows that TransE has better performance on the SimpleQuestion dataset.

Recently, some work combined GCN and KG for recommendation system [11] proposed to combine neighbor information and bias when calculating a given entity representation in KG. We use the syntax analysis package

'StanfordCoreNLP' released by Stanford University to analyze sentence structure. Then an improved dependency matrix as the input of GCN to make it more suitable for shorter and fixed-format interrogative sentences.

3   Proposed Method

3.1   TRL-KEQA Overview

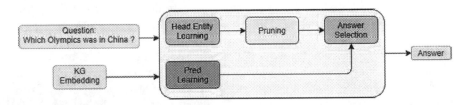

Fig. 1. First given a question, we assume that there is only one entity in the question. It learns the vector representation of the entities and predicates of the problem in the embedding space. Then the search space is reduced by pruning operation, and a well-designed joint distance metric is used to find the tail entity in the triple according to $h + r \approx t$ and return it as the answer.

TRL-KEQA model uses knowledge graph embedding to answer simple questions in natural language. The main idea is shown in Fig. 1. In the following sections, we introduce the TRL-KEQA model. It consists of four main modules:

1. Head Entity Learning Module learns the vector representation of the head entities in KG.
2. Pred Learning Module learns the vector representation of the predicates in KG.
3. Pruning Moudule identify the entities in the question, and reduce the search space according to the learned head entity representation.
4. Answer Selection Module according to the learned predicate and entity representation, the answer to the question is retrieved based on the knowledge graph.

3.2   Pred Learning Module

We use the global information of entities and predicates in the embedding space to potentially improve the accuracy of question answering. So we adopt a constrained neural network architecture. It is mainly composed of a bidirectional recurrent neural network layer, a graph convolutional layer and an attention layer. The core idea is to consider the importance of the word order. Establish dependencies between predicates and entities through syntactic analysis. This relationship is aggregated into the vector representation of the predicate through the graph convolutional layer. Use the attention mechanism to eliminate the interference of questions and conjunction. Through this constraint, it can be solved that the same predicate generates different vector representations when connecting different entities. On the right of Fig. 2 shows the architecture of our proposed solution.

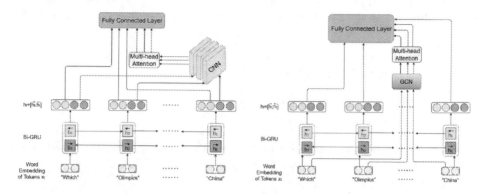

Fig. 2. The left picture is the head entity learning model and the right picture is the predicate learning model

Given a question, we map its tokens to the sequence of word embedding vectors x_t. Taking the forward direction as an example, calculate h_t by the following equation.

$$r_t = \sigma \left(W_r x_t + U_r \overrightarrow{h}_{t-1} + b_r \right) \tag{1}$$

$$z_t = \sigma \left(W_z x_t + U_z \overrightarrow{h}_{t-1} + b_z \right) \tag{2}$$

$$h'_t = tanh \left(W_h x_t + U_h \left(r_t \times \overrightarrow{h}_{t-1} \right) + b_h \right) \tag{3}$$

$$h_t = z_t \times \overrightarrow{h}_{t-1} + (1 - z_t) \times h'_t \tag{4}$$

r_t, z_t and h_t are the activation vectors of forget, input and output gates, h'_t is the unit state vector, σ and $tanh$ are sigmoid and Hyperbolic tangent functions. '×' represents the Hadamard product. We connect the forward and backward hidden state vectors to obtain $h_t = \left[\overrightarrow{h_t}; \overleftarrow{h_t} \right]$.

$$\frac{1}{c_{ij}} = \hat{D}^{-\frac{1}{2}} \hat{A} \hat{D}^{-\frac{1}{2}} \tag{5}$$

$$x_i^{(l+1)} = \sigma \left(\sum_{j \in N_i} \frac{1}{c_{ij}} x_t^{(l)} w^{(l)} + b^{(l)} \right) \tag{6}$$

$$\partial_t = softmax \left(\frac{x_i x_i^T}{\sqrt{d_k}} \right) x_i \tag{7}$$

$$y = \frac{1}{L} \sum_{t=1}^{L} (h_t + \partial_t) \tag{8}$$

$\hat{A}$ represents the sum of the adjacency matrix and the identity matrix corresponding to node **i**, $\hat{D}$ represents the degree matrix corresponding to $\hat{A}$, $x_i^{(l)}$ represents the feature of node **i** in the lth layer. $w^{(l)}$ and $b^{(l)}$ represent the weight and bias of the lth layer. N_i means all neighbors of node **i** include node **i** itself. d_k represents the dimension of the word.

3.3   Head Entity Learning Module

Similar to predicate learning module, we use the Bi-GRU to reserve the global information of question, CNN captures local information that close to the entity, and the multi-head attention mechanism eliminates interference information. Let the size of a single convolution kernel be $p \times q$. The bias of the model is **b**. The calculation process of each convolution kernel is the following process.

$$c = \sigma \left(\sum_t^{p \times q} w_t h_t + b \right) \tag{9}$$

$$\partial_t = softmax \left(\frac{cc^T}{\sqrt{d_k}} \right) c \tag{10}$$

$$y = \frac{1}{L} \sum_{t=1}^{L} (h_t + \partial_t) \tag{11}$$

w_t is the weight value assigned to the input word vector in the convolution kernel. On the left of Fig. 2 shows the head entity learning model of TRL-KEQA.

3.4   Pruning Module

In this module, our goal is to mark one or several consecutive words in question as an entity in order to set the entire search space to a plurality of entities having the same or similar name. In order to simplify the module, we only use "Bi-LSTM+softmax" for head entity recognition. We use the question and its main entity name as training data to train the pruning model. Because the subject entities in the question are continuous, the model will return consecutive words in the test set as entities or part of the correct subject entities. Therefore, all words that are the same as the subject entity or contain the subject entity will be regarded as candidate entities. This can solve the problems caused by the user's habit of abbreviation.

3.5   Answer Selection

We use the joint distance metric proposed in [9] to achieve the above process. If the head entity of a fact belongs to the candidate head entity, then we call it a candidate fact.

Let $\mathbf{C}$ be a set of all candidate facts, (h,l,t) is a fact. p_l and e_h are embedding representations of predicates and entities respectively. $\hat{p}_l$ and $\hat{e}_h$ are the predicted representations of the predicate and entity respectively. HED_{entity} and HED_{non} is the entity and non-entity tokens returned by the head entity prediction model. f is a relational function. $sim\,[,]$ measures the similarity of two strings. $\beta_1, \beta_2, \beta_3, \beta_4$ are predefined weights, used to balance the contribution of each term.

$$
\begin{aligned}
minimize_{h,l,t \in C}\, & \|p_l - \hat{p}_l\|_2 + \beta_1 \|e_h - \hat{e}_h\|_2 + \beta_2 \|f(e_h, p_l) - \hat{e}_t\|_2 \\
& - \beta_3 sim\,[n(h), HED_{entity}] - \beta_4 sim\,[n(l), HED_{non}]
\end{aligned}
\tag{12}
$$

4   Experiments and Results

In this section, we describe the datasets that we evaluated our method on, then explain the experimental setup and the results.

4.1   Datasets

Freebase is generally regarded as a reliable KG because it is mainly collected and organized by community members. This article uses one of the larger Freebase subsets namely FB5M. SimpleQuestions [2] contains more than 10,000 simple questions related to related facts. All questions are expressed by English speakers based on facts and context. It has been used as a benchmark for the recent KGQA method [2,7,12]. We use FB5M as a knowledge graph and SimpleQuestion as a query. The performance of the model is evaluated using 'Precision' in the field of information retrieval.

4.2   Baseline

Now we will discuss the precision of TRL-KEQA. We use the latest KGQA models as benchmarks. Bordes et al. [2]: It learns the representation of entities and predicates according to the training problem, so that the entities and predicates in the new problem can be projected into the same space for comparison. Dai et al. [7]: It uses a two-way gated recurrent unit to rank candidate predicates. Yin et al. [13]: It uses character-level convolutional neural networks to match questions and predicates. Golub and He [12]: It designs a character-level and attention-based LSTM to encode and decode problems. Huang et al. [9]: It uses KG embedding to learn the entity and predicate expression of the problem. We compare the results in the above papers, Table 1 lists the performance of different methods on SimpleQuestion [2].

Table 1. Performance of all methods on SimpleQuestions

	FB5M
Dai et al. [7]	0.626
Bordes et al. [2]	0.639
Yin et al. [13]	0.672
Golub and He [12]	0.703
Huang et al. [9]	0.749
TRL-KEQA (our method)	**0.752+(12.6%)**

4.3   Result Analysis

The Fig. 3 shows the embedding vectors obtained by different models of the same sentence. The pink dots represent the sentence vector representation of the improved predicate learning model, and the blue dots represent the sentence vector from [9]. By observing the scatter plot, we can find that the improved model can distinguish different words to give different weights. This proves the effectiveness of introducing syntactic analysis to the QA task.

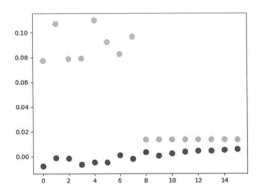

Fig. 3. Result analysis of different model

5   Conclusion

In this paper, we propose a KG embedding question answering based on triple representation learning. It solves the difficulty of the machine in understanding the semantics of the question. Model learns the vector representation of the entities and predicates of the question. Similar entities have the same embedded expression to solve the problem of not being able to find the corresponding triples due to short-hands. Use different submodules to complete different types of word embedding learning. The characteristics of entities are transferred to predicates through graph convolutional neural network, so that the same predicate can obtain more accurate embedding expression when connecting different entities. Experiments show that our model is better than previous methods. In the future work, we will start to solve the problem of low accuracy of the head entity learning model. In reality, KG is usually updated dynamically, we will extend the framework to solve this problem.

References

1. Berant, J., Chou, A., Frostig, R., Liang, P.: Semantic parsing on freebase from question-answer pairs (2012)
2. Bordes, A., Usunier, N., Chopra, S., Weston, J.: Large-scale simple question answering with memory networks. ArXiv150602075 Cs. (2015)
3. Yao, X., Van Durme, B.: Information extraction over structured data: question answering with freebase. In: Proceedings of the 52nd Annual Meeting of the Association for Computational Linguistics, vol. 1: Long Papers, pp. 956–966. Association for Computational Linguistics, Baltimore (2014). https://doi.org/10.3115/v1/P14-1090
4. Yang, B., Yih, W., He, X., Gao, J., Deng, L.: Embedding entities and relations for learning and inference in knowledge bases. ArXiv14126575 Cs. (2015)
5. Bordes, A., Chopra, S., Weston, J.: Question answering with subgraph embeddings. ArXiv14063676 Cs. (2014)
6. Bordes, A., Weston, J., Usunier, N.: Open question answering with weakly supervised embedding models. ArXiv14044326 Cs. (2014)
7. Dai, Z., Li, L., Xu, W.: CFO: conditional focused neural question answering with large-scale knowledge bases. In: Proceedings of the 54th Annual Meeting of the Association for Computational Linguistics, vol. 1: Long Papers, pp. 800–810. Association for Computational Linguistics, Berlin (2016). https://doi.org/10.18653/v1/P16-1076
8. Sun, H., Dhingra, B., Zaheer, M., Mazaitis, K., Salakhutdinov, R., Cohen, W.: Open domain question answering using early fusion of knowledge bases and text. In: Proceedings of the 2018 Conference on Empirical Methods in Natural Language Processing, pp. 4231–4242. Association for Computational Linguistics, Brussels (2018). https://doi.org/10.18653/v1/D18-1455
9. Huang, X., Zhang, J., Li, D., Li, P.: Knowledge graph embedding based question answering. In: Proceedings of the Twelfth ACM International Conference on Web Search and Data Mining, pp. 105–113. ACM, Melbourne (2019). https://doi.org/10.1145/3289600.3290956
10. Bordes, A., Usunier, N., Garcia-Duran, A., Weston, J., Yakhnenko, O.: Translating embeddings for modeling multi-relational data (2019)
11. Wang, H., Zhao, M., Xie, X., Li, W., Guo, M.: Knowledge graph convolutional networks for recommender systems. In: World Wide Web Conference - WWW, vol. 19, pp. 3307–3313 (2019). https://doi.org/10.1145/3308558.3313417
12. Golub, D., He, X.: Character-level question answering with attention. ArXiv160400727 Cs. (2016)
13. Yin, W., Yu, M., Xiang, B., Zhou, B., Schütze, H.: Simple question answering by attentive convolutional neural network. ArXiv160603391 Cs. (2016)

Author Index